Marriages & Families

Changes, Choices, and Constraints

SIXTH EDITION

Nijole V. Benokraitis
University of Baltimore

PEARSON
Prentice Hall

Upper Saddle River, New Jersey 07458

Library of Congress Cataloging-in-Publication Data

Benokraitis, Nijole V. (Nijole Vaicaitis)
  Marriages and families : changes, choices, and constraints / Nijole V.
Benokraitis.—6th ed.
    p. cm.
  ISBN 0-13-243173-4
  1. Family—United States. 2. Marriage—United States. I. Title.
  HQ536.B45 2007
  306.850973—dc22

                                          2006102009

Editorial Director: Leah Jewell
Executive Editor: Jennifer Gilliland
Editorial Assistant: Lee Peterson
Developmental Editor: Carolyn Smith
Marketing Manager: Lindsey Prudhomme
Production Liaison: Marianne Peters-Riordan
Permissions Supervisor: Kathleen Karcher
Manufacturing Buyer: Brian Mackey
Creative Design Director: Leslie Osher
Art Director: Nancy Wells
Interior Design: GGS Book Services
Cover Design: Nancy Wells

Cover Illustration: Kaáda/Veer
Director, Image Resource Center: Melinda Patelli
Manager, Rights and Permissions: Zina Arabia
Manager, Visual Research: Beth Brenzel
Manager, Cover Visual Research & Permissions: Karen
  Sanatar
Image Permission Coordinator: Angelique Sharps
Photo Researcher: Rachel Lucas
Composition/Full-Service Project Management: Patty
  Donovan/Pine Tree Composition
Printer/Binder: Quebecor Printing
Cover Printer: Phoenix Color Corp.

Credits and acknowledgments borrowed from other sources and reproduced, with permission, in this textbook appear on appropriate page within text or on page 621.

Pearson Education LTD.
Pearson Education Singapore, Pte. Ltd
Pearson Education, Canada, Ltd
Pearson Education-Japan
Pearson Education Australia PTY, Limited

Pearson Education North Asia Ltd
Pearson Educación de Mexico, S.A. de C.V
Pearson Education Malaysia, Pte. Ltd
Pearson Education, Upper Saddle River, New Jersey

10 9 8 7 6 5 4 3 2 1
ISBN 13:978-0-20-565650-9
ISBN 10: 0-20-565650-1

10 9 8 7 6 5 4 3
ISBN 13:978-0-13-243173-6
ISBN 10: 0-13-243173-4

To Andrius and Gema

Brief Contents

Contents

Chapter 18
The Family in the Twenty-First Century   545

Appendices

Boxed Features

Changes

Choices

Constraints

Crosscultural and Multicultural Families

Applying What You've Learned

Ask Yourself

A Few Words to Students

In the last few years, I've started asking my students how many read the Preface, in this textbook or others. About one out of fifty raises her or his hand.

You're welcome to read the Preface, of course, because I write it with the student in mind. If you're like many of my students and will skip the Preface, however, I wanted to say a few things to all of you before you plunge into the assigned readings.

You're going to enjoy your marriage and family course. Because the family is something *all* of us have in common, it's always one of the liveliest courses I teach. In fact, you'll probably remember this course as one of the most important and interesting that you've taken in college.

I hope that this textbook will be one of the reasons that your marriage and family course will be informative and memorable. Here are a few comments I've received from my own students and others outside our university:

"Frankly, I was surprised that I could apply a lot of the information to my family and relationships. I've learned a lot about do's and don'ts in marriage."

"You not only present the material in a clear way but also do it humorously."

"I especially appreciate the in-depth coverage of ethnic issues and the tremendous diversity of family styles and patterns in America, past and present."

"I looked forward to reading the chapters each week. I enjoyed reading the book and have recommended it to many of my friends—to help give them a dose of reality and the facts concerning the stages of dating, mating, marriage, separation, divorce, remarriage and aging."

"I found the online tests very helpful. It was a good way to review the material in each chapter. Professor (X) used similar essay questions for exams, so I was really ready!"

"I liked the Web links a lot. I used some of them for research projects in other classes."

"I know more about families and culture and how to deal better with relationships. This book gave me a positive outlook on family life."

"I have a better knowledge of my family. I now understand why we have some of the problems we do."

"When we were driving to Florida during Spring break, I brought this book along to study for an exam. I read some of the passages to my husband to keep him awake because it was a 12-hour drive. We started discussing some issues about our marriage for the first time. It was great!"

"I talked about some of the stuff in the textbook with my teenage son when I was studying. We had some interesting conversations. Believe it or not, he read several of the chapters, and on his own!"

"This is the most interesting book I've had so far in college. It's not as good as a mystery novel :-), but I never dozed off in the middle of a chapter."

"I'm not afraid of figures and tables any more."

Even if you shudder every time you see figures and tables, you'll enjoy this textbook. You may not agree with everything (and neither do I as I summarize the most recent research), but the material will help you think about your own family or marriage, reflect on ways to improve your current relationships, get out of bad relationships, make better decisions in the future, and understand the diversity of families in the United States and other countries.

I hope all of you enjoy your course and this textbook. The "About the Author" page provides my e-mail address if you'd like to contact me. I'm *always* happy to hear from students.

Have a good semester. And for those of you who are graduating this year, congratulations!

Dr. B (as my students call me)

Preface

Welcome to the sixth edition of *Marriages and Families: Changes, Choices, and Constraints*. In 2007, the U.S. population climbed to more than 300 million people. There have been several other notable family-related changes since the last edition. Americans struggled with (but didn't resolve) the issue of extending more rights to undocumented immigrants. The oldest baby boomers turned age 60 in 2006, generating considerable discussion and research on our nation's ability to provide medical care and retirement benefits for older people in the coming years. Massachusetts was the first state to legalize same-sex marriage but its citizens will vote on a constitutional amendment to permit or ban same-sex marriages after this book goes to press.

The economy recovered after the dot.com crash of the early 2000s, but most of the new jobs are largely in lower paying industries such as service (retail and restaurants) or require workers to have relatively sophisticated high-tech skills. And tougher welfare legislation increased the number of families living at or just above the poverty level. Thus, macro-level constraints continue to shape and limit many of our individual choices.

Scholarly Work, Comprehensiveness, and Readability

This revision incorporates almost 1,000 new books, scholarly articles, and reports that have been published since the last edition. Whenever possible, I provide Web links, rather than hard copy citations, for faculty and students who want to access the material quickly and avoid traveling to a library.

Marriages and Families offers students a comprehensive introduction to many issues facing families in the twenty-first century. Although written from a sociological perspective, the book incorporates material from other disciplines: history, economics, social work, psychology, law, biology, medicine, and anthropology. The material also encompasses family studies, women's studies, and gay and lesbian studies, as well as both quantitative and qualitative studies. Nationally representative and longitudinal data are supplemented by insights from clinical, case, and observational studies.

Readability continues to be one of this textbook's most attractive features. A major reason why this book has been successful is that it discusses theories and recent studies that students find interesting. As one of my students once said, "This is the first textbook I've had where I don't count how many more pages I have to read while I'm still on the first page."

In addition, reviewers have consistently described the writing as "very clear" and "excellent." According to one reviewer, for example, "The interesting anecdotes and quotes help to maintain the student's interest while also providing examples of the subject under discussion."

Continuity of Major Themes on the Contemporary Family

Marriages and Families continues to be distinguished from other textbooks in several important ways. It offers comprehensive coverage of the field, allowing instructors to select chapters that best suit their needs. It balances theoretical and empirical discussions with practical examples and applications.

It highlights important contemporary *changes* in society and the family. It explores the *choices* that are available to family members and the *constraints* that often limit our choices. It examines the diversity of U.S. families, using *cross-cultural and multicultural* material to encourage students to think about the many critical issues that confront the family of the twenty-first century.

More Changes

Changes that affect the structure and functioning of today's families inform the pages of every chapter of this book. In addition, several chapters focus on some major transformations in American society. Chapter 4, for example, examines the growing cultural diversity of the United States, focusing on African American, American Indian, Latino, Asian American, Middle Eastern, and interracial marriages and families.

Chapter 17 discusses the ways in which the rapid "graying of America" has affected adult children, grandchildren, and even great-grandchildren, family members' roles as caregivers, and family relations in general. Chapter 18 analyzes some of the social policy changes that affect the family.

More Choices

On the individual level, family members have many more choices today than ever before. People feel freer to postpone marriage, to cohabit, or to raise children as single parents. As a result, household forms vary greatly, ranging from commuter marriages to those in which several generations live together under the same roof.

As reproductive technology becomes increasingly sophisticated, many infertile couples can now have children. With the growing acceptance of civil unions, many agencies, colleges, businesses, and state governments now offer same-sex couples more health, retirement, and other benefits. And as the U.S. population continues to age, many elderly family members are participating in innovative housing arrangements (such as senior communes), and they are demanding legislation that allows them to die with dignity. Although some of these issues are controversial, they increase the options that family members have now and will experience in the future.

More Constraints

Although family members' choices are more varied today, we also face greater macro-level constraints. Our options are increasingly limited, for example, by government policies that ignore the need for national health insurance coverage for families and child care resources for middle class and lower class households.

Economic changes often shape family life and not vice versa. Political and legal institutions also have a major impact on most families in tax laws, welfare reform, and even in defining what a family is. Because laws, public policies, and religious groups affect our everyday lives, I have framed many discussions of individual choices within the larger picture of the institutional constraints that limit our choices.

Cross-Cultural and Multicultural Diversity in the United States

Contemporary American marriages and families vary greatly in structure, dynamics, and cultural heritage. Thus, discussions of gender roles, social class, race, ethnicity, age, and sexual orientation are integrated throughout this book. To further strengthen students' understanding of the growing diversity among today's families, I have also included a series of boxes that focus on families from many cultures. Both text and boxed materials should encourage students to think about the many forms families may take and the different ways in which family members interact.

Encouraging Students to Think More Critically

All editions of this textbook have prodded students to think about themselves and their families in the "Ask Yourself" boxes. Because of their popularity, especially in sparking lively class discussions, I've expanded two features, ("Making Connections" and "Stop and Think") that were introduced in the last edition:

- **Making Connections:** At several points in each chapter, these questions ask students to link the material to their own lives by relating it to a personal experience, by integrating it with scholarly studies discussed in the chapter, or by "connecting" with classmates who might be sitting next to them in a class.

- **Stop and Think:** These critical thinking questions follow important issues in boxes throughout the textbook. These items encourage reflective thought about current topics, both personally and across other cultures.

According to most professors, the more critical thinking material there is, the better. I agree and, as a result, have added **two new features:**

- **Since You Asked:** Each chapter has between eight to ten questions that introduce an important idea or concept or preview a controversial issue about families and marriages. Many of these questions are similar to those that my students have raised in the courses that I teach.

- **Applying What You've Learned:** This is a new series of boxes that emphasizes the connection between research findings and students' own feelings and experiences. The material, both new and revised, asks students to apply what they're reading to their own personal situations and to consider how to improve their decisions and current relationships.

New and Expanded Topics

As past users know, a top priority of each new edition of this textbook is to thoroughly update national data and to provide the results of groundbreaking research that addresses the diversity of marriages and families. In most chapters, a global view adds new material to the *Data Digest* or text. In addition, many chapters include more examples from popular culture (television, videos, movies) to which students relate. Specifically, new, updated, and expanded coverage includes the following:

- **Chapter 1, The Changing Family,** updates the demographic changes that characterize U.S. families, the promarriage movement, and the growing importance of understanding families and marriages from cross-cultural perspectives. There is new material on polygamy in the United States, Europe, and some developing countries.

- **Chapter 2, Studying Marriage and the Family,** updates recent studies on family self-help books, focus groups, and evaluation research. There is new material on random sampling and the politics of sex research.

- **Chapter 3, The Family in Historical Perspective,** expands the section on "The Family Since the 1960s," updates information on common misconceptions about the "modern family," and offers a **new box** ("How Colonial Is Your Family?").

- **Chapter 4, Racial and Ethnic Families: Strengths and Stresses,** updates material on family income and recent research on Mexican day laborers. There is new material on undocumented immigrants, infant deaths among minority families, the effect of bilingualism on children's academic performance, and **three new boxes** ("Somalis in Maine," "Is Bill Cosby Right about Black Families?" and "Am I Privileged?").

- **Chapter 5, Socialization and Gender Roles,** updates the discussion of the effect of nature and nurture on gender roles, the racial diversity of prime-time characters on television, and the recent backlash against women's progress, especially in higher education. There is new material on people who are transgendered, reality TV and family processes, how religion affects gender role socialization, and a **new box** ("Are Children's Toys Becoming More Sexist?").

- **Chapter 6, Love and Loving Relationships,** updates the material on love, jealousy, stalking, cyberstalking, long-term love, and biological perspectives on love. There is new material on passionate love and a **new box** ("What do *you* expect from love?").

- **Chapter 7, Sexuality and Sexual Expression Throughout Life,** updates material on a number of topics: homosexuals in non-Western cultures, sexual scripts, female genital mutilation/cutting, sexual activity of adolescents, sex content of television and movies, effectiveness of abstinence-only sex education programs, virginity pledges, forced sexual intercourse, and sexually transmitted infections. Some of the new material examines asexuals, being "on the down low," sexual activity of college students, myths about sex, cheating in close relationships, and hate crimes. There is also a **new box** ("If She Says 'No,' Just Kidnap Her").

- **Chapter 8, Choosing Others: Dating and Mate Selection,** updates material on the *quinceañera*, "hookin' up," cyberdating, interdating, same-sex dating, mate selection in other countries, mail-order brides, professional matchmakers, and dating violence. There is new material on speed dating among American Muslims, online dating, and mate selection across cultures.

- **Chapter 9, Singlehood, Cohabitation, Civil Unions, and Other Options,** updates material on singlehood, living alone, postponing marriage, the marriage squeeze in other countries, racial-ethnic singles, cohabitation, the benefits and costs of cohabitation, and the effect of cohabitation on children. New material includes *inertia theory* in cohabitation, recent state laws on same-sex marriage in the United States and globally, and a **new box** ("Does Living Together Make More Sense Than Marriage?").

- **Chapter 10, Marriage and Communication in Committed Relationships,** updates material on happily married couples; how marriage affects health, domestic work and gender roles; what couples fight about; and marriage and relationship education. There is new material on living apart together (LAT) marriages, men's "emotional work" in marriage, and a **new box** ("Forced to Marry Before Puberty").

- **Chapter 11, To Be or Not to Be a Parent: More Choices, More Constraints,** updates information on U.S. fertility patterns, the characteristics of older parents, domestic international adoptions, artificial insemination, nonmarital childbearing, and recent laws and policies on abortion. There is new material on spacing pregnancies; education, ethnicity, and birth rates; family sizes worldwide; infant mortality rates and causes in the United States and globally; using overseas surrogates; how never-married teens feel about getting pregnant; and contraception and abortion in other countries.

■ **Chapter 12, Raising Children: Promises and Pitfalls,** updates material on egalitarian parenting, corporal punishment (including other countries), birth order of siblings, parents not talking to their teens about drugs, young adults who move back with their parents, parenting in gay and lesbian families, teens and using new drugs (such as painkillers), latchkey kids, child care arrangements, watching TV and lower academic achievement, and foster care. There is new material on the "new momism," mommy myths and idealized motherhood roles, uninvolved parenting, overweight adolescents, the impact of electronic media on child rearing, and a **new box** ("Should Parents Track Their Teens?").

■ **Chapter 13, Balancing Work and Family Life,** updates the discussion of why middle classes are shrinking, the working poor, why families are homeless, who works shifts and why, unemployment, stay-at-home dads, two-income couples, trailing spouses, wives who earn more than their husbands, the division of household labor, sexual harassment, and family and work policies. There is new material on the concepts of *wealth* versus *income,* corporate welfare, offshoring/outsourcing, whether it pays for women to work outside the home, the two person single career, family and stress, comparable worth, the gender wage gap, and a **new box** ("How Much Do You Know about Poverty?").

■ **Chapter 14, Family Violence and Other Health Issues,** updates the statistics on intimate partner violence, marital rape, child maltreatment, sibling and adolescent abuse, elder abuse and neglect, violence in cross-cultural families globally, drug abuse, and combating domestic violence. There is new material on the concept of learned helplessness in intimate partner violence, status compatibility and intimate partner violence, immigrants and domestic violence, ecological system theory in explaining domestic violence, symptoms of depression, and the relationship among eating disorders, genes, and brain chemistry.

■ **Chapter 15, Separation and Divorce,** updates the statistics on U.S. divorce trends, divorce around the world (especially in developing countries),

how divorce affects adults and children, custody between gay parents, child support, what hurts children after a divorce, the positive outcomes of separation and divorce, and effectiveness of counseling and marital therapy. This chapter introduces two new concepts—*intergenerational transmission of divorce* and *co-custody*—and provides new material on divorce among midlife and older couples, why many women's attitudes about divorce are becoming more conservative, why divorce depletes family wealth, how people adjust to divorce, and a **new box** ("Why Are African American Divorce Rates High?").

■ **Chapter 16, Remarriages and Stepfamilies,** updates the material on forming stepfamilies through cohabitation, remarriage rates, redivorce, the "evil stepmother" myth, naming in stepfamilies, having a baby to "cement" a stepfamily, and the effects of stepfamily living on children. This chapter introduces the concept of *de facto* stepfamilies and provides new information on the percentage of remarriage, how the presence of children affects remarriages rates, and the relationship between marital roles and power in stepfamilies.

■ **Chapter 17, Families in Later Life,** updates statistics on life expectancy, depression and dementia (including Alzheimer's), retirement, grandparenting, death and grief, being widowed, caregiving, and support systems outside of the family. This chapter introduces the concept of *intergenerational ambivalence* and offers new material on the sex ratio of older women and men, the growing racial and ethnic diversity of our older population, how to live longer, suicide and elderly people, variations in retirement income, sibling relationships and being single in later life, family caregiving by children, recent data on the characteristics of caregiving recipients, and **two new boxes** ("The Retired Husband Syndrome in Japan" and "Death and Funeral Traditions among Racial-Ethnic Families").

■ **Chapter 18, The Family in the Twenty-First Century,** updates material on the world's aging population, racial-ethnic diversity, child poverty, parental leave in the United States compared with other Western countries, Canada's health care system, global aging, and the right-to-die Supreme Court decision in 2006. This chapter introduces the concept of the *older support ratio,* and offers new material on the major reasons for death since 1950, unequal health care, health differences between native-born and immigrant blacks, the new welfare rules implemented in 2006, how welfare reform has worked, and Americans' reactions to physician-assisted suicide.

Features in the Sixth Edition

I have maintained several popular features such as the *Data Digest* and the "author's files" quotations based on my students' reactions and class discussion. In response to student and reviewer comments, I have revised some figures and the end-of-chapter materials, including the *Taking It Further* sections.

Data Digest

I introduced the Data Digest in the second edition because "all those numbers" from the Census Bureau, empirical studies, and demographic trends often overwhelmed students (both mine and others'). Because this has been a popular feature, I've updated the U.S. statistics and have included information from other countries. The Data Digest that introduces each chapter not only provides students with a thought-provoking overview of current statistics and trends but makes "all those numbers" more interesting and digestible.

The first question from my students is usually "Will this material be on the exam?" Not in my classes. I see the Data Digest as piquing student curiosity about the chapter rather than providing a lot of numbers to memorize. Some instructors tell me that their students have used the Data Digest to develop class presentations or course papers.

Material from the Author's Files

Faculty who reviewed previous editions of *Marriages and Families,* and many students as well, liked the anecdotes and personal experiences with which I illustrate sometimes "dry" theories and abstract concepts. In this new edition I weave more of this material into the text. Thus, I include many examples from discussions in my own classes (cited as "author's files") to enliven theoretical perspectives and abstract concepts.

Figures

Many students tend to skip over figures and tables because they're afraid of numbers, they don't trust statistics (see Chapter 2), or the material seems boring or complicated. Regardless of what textbooks I use and in *all* the courses I teach, I routinely highlight some of the figures in class. As I tell my students, a good figure or table may be more important (or at least more memorable) than the author's explanation. To encourage students to look at data, I have streamlined many figures and often provide brief summaries to accompany the figures.

Taking It Further

A common question from my own students is "Can't we do something about [issue X]?" And sometimes students have asked me for practical information: "How can I find a good child care center?" or "Can anyone help my sister get out of an abusive marriage?"

The "Taking It Further" section addresses such questions and concerns. It tells students how to get information on particular topics, how to get personal assistance such as counseling or legal advice for themselves or others, how to contact organizations that deal with specific problems, and provides URLs for a wealth of Internet sites that delve deeper into topics discussed in each chapter. Some of the Web sites are fun (such as those on love and dating), some provide up-to-date information (especially many of the U.S. Census Bureau and Centers for Disease Control sites), and others offer practical advice and community resources on the workplace, family research, aging, sex and sexually transmitted infections, gender roles, sexual orientation, and many other family-related topics.

What is on the Internet, today may be gone tomorrow. I have tried to include only the Web sites that have been around for a while and won't vanish overnight.

Pedagogical Features

The pedagogical features in *Marriages and Families* have been designed specifically to capture students' attention and to help them understand and recall the material. Some of these features are familiar from the earlier editions, but some are new. Each has been carefully crafted to ensure that it ties in clearly to the text material, enhancing its meaning and applicability.

Informative and Engaging Illustration Program

Many chapters contain figures that, in bold and original artistic designs, demonstrate such concepts as the exchange theory of dating, romantic versus lasting love, and theories of mating, as well as presenting simple statistics in innovative and visually appealing ways. Many of the photographs are new. We have taken great care to select substantive photographs (rather than what I call "pretty postcards") that illustrate the material.

Thought-Provoking Box Series

Reflecting and reinforcing the book's primary themes, three groups of boxes focus on the changes, choices, and constraints that confront today's families. A fourth category discusses cultural differences. The other two series of boxes are applied to help students evaluate their own knowledge and acquire insights about family life.

C h a n g e s
Variations in the Working Mother Role

Employed mothers reflect a variety of motivations. Here are four general categories (Moen, 1992: 42–44):

■ *Captives* would prefer to be full-time homemakers. These mothers may be single parents who are sole breadwinners, wives of blue-collar workers whose incomes are insufficient to support the family, or middle-class wives who find two salaries necessary to maintain a desired standard of living. Captives find their multiple responsibilities overwhelming and remain in the labor force reluctantly.

C h a n g e s boxes illustrate some historical, some anecdotal, and some empirically based-show how marriages and families have been changing or are expected to change in the future. For example, a box in Chapter 13 describes how the role of the working mother has evolved over the years.

C h o i c e s boxes illustrate the kinds of decisions families can make to improve their well-being, often highlighting options of which family members may be unaware. In Chapter 12, for instance, a box shows that parents have more options than spanking to discipline their children.

C h o i c e s
Is Spanking Effective or Harmful?

Fifteen nations—including Austria, Croatia, Cyprus, Denmark, Germany, Hungary, Israel, Italy, Latvia, and the Scandinavian countries—have made it illegal for parents to spank their children. In contrast, many adults in the United States support spanking (see "Data Digest").

Advocates feel that spanking is effective, prepares children for life's hardships, and prevents misbehavior. They feel that spanking is acceptable if it is age-appropriate, used selectively, and to teach and correct rather

C o n s t r a i n t s
Does Living Together Make More Sense Than Marriage?

Many people, especially young adults, say that they cohabit to save money—for example, by pooling the costs of housing, electric bills, and cable. People who are older and have accumulated possessions might be better off cohabiting rather than marrying for several reasons:

■ *Liability:* If you get married, you've also married your partner's debts. In contrast, unmarried people can keep their finances separate, can maintain their individual credit ratings, and don't risk losing everything if a cohabiting partner is sued.

C o n s t r a i n t s boxes illustrate some of the obstacles that limit our options. They highlight the fact that although most of us are raised to believe that we can do whatever we want, we are often constrained by macro-level socioeconomic, demographic, and cultural factors. For example, a box in Chapter 4 on the myths about the African American family examines some of the stereotypes that black families confront on a daily basis.

Cross Cultural Families

If She Says "No," Just Kidnap Her

In some parts of Turkey, males abduct women for a number of reasons: to get a bride even though her family disapproves, to avoid dowries that the bride's family can't afford, or when both sides of the family have other mates in mind.

In some other societies, men simply kidnap women who refuse to marry them. One example is Kyrgyzstan,

a country to the west of China that broke away from the Soviet Union in 1991. Even though the practice has been illegal for many years, more than half of Kyrgyzstan's married women were snatched from the street by their husbands. This custom, ala kachun, translates roughly into "grab and run."

Some women don't mind ala kachun because it's a form of elopement, but many see it as a violent act because they are taken against their will. Once a kidnapped girl or woman has been kept in the abductor's home overnight, her virginity is suspect, her reputation is disgraced, and she will find it difficult to attract a husband of her choice.

Cross Cultural Families boxes illustrate the richness of varying family structures and dynamics, both in the United States and in other countries. For example, a box in Chapter 6 contrasts the American style of dating with arranged courtship and marriage in India.

Applying What You've Learned boxes ask students to think critically about important research on a personal level. Such reflections should stimulate students to challenge common misconceptions about family life and to improve their own decision making and relationships. For example, a box in Chapter 14 provides early warning signs of intimate partner violence and asks readers to consider whether they or other family members are at risk.

Applying What You've Learned

Some Warning Signs of Domestic Violence

There are numerous clues to the potential for violence before it actually occurs. How many of these "red flags" do you recognize in your or your friends' relationships?

- Verbal abuse: Constant criticism, ignoring what you are saying, mocking, name-calling, yelling, and swearing.
- Sexual abuse: Forcing or demanding sexual acts that you don't want to perform.
- Disrespect: Interrupting, telling you what you should think and how you should feel, putting you down in

Ask Yourself

If This Is Love, Why Do I Feel So Bad?

If you feel bad, what you're experiencing may be *control*, not love. Controllers use whatever tactics are necessary to maintain power over another person: nagging, cajoling, coaxing, flattery, charm, threats, self-pity, blame, insults, or humiliation.

In the worst cases, controllers may physically injure and even murder people who refuse to be controlled. As you read this list, check any items that seem familiar to you. Individually, the items may seem unimportant, but if you check off more than two or three, you may be dealing with a controller instead of forging your own choices in life.

Ask Yourself self-assessment quiz boxes not only encourage students to think about and to evaluate their knowledge about marriage and the family, but they also help students to develop guidelines for action, both on their own or on another's behalf. For example, the "If This Is Love, Why Do I Feel So Bad?" box in Chapter 6 helps the reader evaluate and make the decision to leave an abusive relationship.

Outlines

Each chapter contains an opening outline. The outlines help students organize their learning by focusing on the main topics of each chapter.

Key Terms and Glossary

Important terms and concepts are boldfaced and defined in the text and listed at the end of each chapter. All key terms and their definitions are repeated in the Glossary at the end of the book.

Supplements

The supplement package for this textbook is exceptional. Each component has been meticulously crafted to amplify and illuminate materials in the text.

Print and Media Supplements for Instructors

myfamilylab **NEW MYFAMILYLAB** MyFamilyLab is an easy-to-use online resource that allows instructors to assess student progress and adapt course material to meet the specific needs of the class.

MyFamilyLab enables students to diagnose their progress by completing an online self-assessment test. Based on the results of this test, each student is provided with a customized study plan, including a variety of tools to help them fully master the material.

MyFamilyLab then reports the self-assessment results to the instructor, as individual student grades as well as an aggregate report of class progress. Based on these reports, the instructor can adapt course material to suit the needs of individual students or the class as a whole.

Additionally, MyFamilyLab offers the major resources for *Marriages and Families, Sixth Edition* including the *Instructor's Resource Manual with Tests, PowerPoint Slides and Overhead Transparencies,* and the ABCNews Videos in one convenient location. Contact your local Prentice Hall representative for ordering information or visit www.myfamilylab.com.

INSTRUCTOR'S RESOURCE MANUAL WITH TESTS ISBN 0-13-232048-7 Created by Xuanning Fu at California State University, Fresno and Ann Marie Kinnell at University of Southern Mississippi, each chapter in the manual includes the following resources: chapter learning objectives; chapter overview; lecture suggestions and classroom discussions; activities, handouts, demonstrations; student assignments and projects; and multimedia resources. Designed to make your lectures more effective and to save you preparation time, this extensive resource gathers together the most effective activities and strategies for teaching your Marriage and Family course.

Also included in this manual is a test bank of approximately 2,000 multiple-choice, short-answer, and essay questions. Each chapter's question types are organized into a test planner called the Total Assessment Guide designed to make creating tests easier by listing all of the test items on an easy-to-reference grid. The Total Assessment Guide organizes all of the test items by text section, question type, and level of difficulty. Additionally, each chapter of the test bank includes a ready-made ten-item quiz with an answer key for immediate use in class.

PRENTICE HALL'S *TESTGEN* ISBN 0-13-157700-X Available on one dual platform CD-ROM, this test generator program provides instructors "best in class" features in an easy-to-use program. Create tests using the TestGen Wizard and easily select questions with drag-and-drop or point-and-click functionality. Add or modify text questions using the built-in Question Editor. TestGen also offers algorithmic functionality, which allows for the creation of unlimited versions of a single text. The Quiz Master features allow for online test delivery. Complete with an instructor gradebook and full technical support.

***NEW* PRENTICE HALL'S MYTEST POWERPOINT SLIDES WITH *NEW* CLASSROOM RESPONSE SYSTEM QUESTIONS AVAILABLE ONLINE AND ON THE INSTRUCTOR'S RESOURCE CD-ROM** Created by Larry Rosenberg at Millersville University, each chapter's presentation highlights the key points covered in the text and include ten to fifteen questions to incorporate into your course using a Classroom Response System. Available on the Instructor's Resource CD-ROM or online at www.prenhall.com.

INSTRUCTOR'S RESOURCE CD-ROM ISBN 0-13-613192-1 Pulling together all of the media assets available to instructors, this CD-ROM allows instructors to insert media video, PointPoint, and line art into their classroom presentations. This CD-ROM also includes an electronic version of the Instructor's Manual with Tests.

MARRIAGE AND FAMILY OVERHEAD TRANSPARENCIES ISBN 0-13-144384-4 Taken from graphs, diagrams, and tables in this text and other sources, more than 50 full color transparencies offer an effective way to illustrate lecture topics.

ABCNEWS PRENTICE HALL VIDEO LIBRARY: MARRIAGE AND FAMILY DVD ISBN 0-13-157702-6 This video library consists of brief segments from award-winning news programs such as *Good Morning America, Nightline, 20/20,* and *World News Tonight.* These brief segments provide current issues, lecture-launcher videos, and demonstrate the applicability of what students are learning in class to everyday situations.

FILMS FOR HUMANITIES AND SCIENCES VIDEO LIBRARY Qualified adopters can select full length feature videos on various topics in sociology from the extensive library of Films for the Humanities and Sciences. Contact your Prentice Hall representative for a list of videos.

Print and Media Supplements for Students

STUDY GUIDE ISBN 0-13-224883-2 Created by Naima Prince at Santa Fe Community College, this guide includes Chapter Objectives and a Chapter Overview; Practice Tests; Applications, Exercises and Activities; and a Crossword Puzzle to help students master the core concepts presented in each chapter.

 *NEW* **MYFAMILYLAB** MyFamily-Lab is an easy-to-use online resource that enables students to diagnose their progress by completing an online self-assessment test. Based on the results of this test, each student is provided with a customized study plan, including a variety of tools to help them fully master the material.

SAFARIX WEBBOOKS This Pearson Choice offers students an online subscription to *Marriages and Families, Sixth Edition* online at a 50% savings. With the SafariX WebBook, students can search the text, make notes online, print out reading assignments, and book mark important passages. Visit www.safarix.com for details.

THE PRENTICE HALL GUIDE TO RESEARCH NAVIATOR The easiest way to do research! This guide focuses on using **Research Navigator**™—Prentice Hall's own gateway to databases including *The New York Times* Search-by-Subject Archive, *Content-Select*™ Academic Journal Database powered by EBSCO, *The Financial Times,* and the *Best of the Web* Link Library. It also includes extensive appendices on documenting online sources and on avoiding plagiarism. This supplement—which includes an access code to the Research Navigator™ Web site—is available at no charge for college adoptions when packaged with a new text.

Acknowledgments

A number of people have contributed to this edition of *Marriages and Families: Changes, Choices, and Constraints.* First, I would like to thank my students. Their lively and passionate exchanges during class and in online discussions always help me refocus some of my research and writing.

Linda Fair, our division's administrative wizard, is always good-natured and responsive in solving everyday office-related glitches and making sure that our computer equipment is serviced quickly. Her sense of humor and aplomb have made a sometimes frenzied academic schedule more manageable. I am also grateful to Karen Colvin, one of our stellar alums in sociology, for teaching the family/marriage course while I was on sabbatical leave a few years ago and for passing on her students' comments on the *Marriages and Families* textbook.

Many thanks to the reference and circulation staff at the University of Baltimore's Langsdale Library for their continuous support. Tammy Taylor is amazingly adept in anticipating and solving loan problems. Tim Balcer, Rodney Brown, Brian Chetelet, Carole Mason, Laura Melamed, Delores Redman, and Steven Thorpe kept track of hundreds of books checked out from a dozen Maryland system libraries. They facilitated my research and resolved all problems patiently and graciously. "You can't" and "I don't know" aren't part of their vocabulary.

Carol Vaeth is extraordinary in accessing materials from a variety of academic and public libraries. Carol's amazing interlibrary skills have provided me with all of the articles and books I've needed to research and revise this edition of *Marriages and Families.*

Our reference librarians—Thomas Arendall-Salvetti, Lucy Holman, Jeffrey Hutson, Michael Shochet, Tami Smith, and Susan Wheeler—always respond very quickly. They have trained my students on the Internet and article databases, have spent hours helping me track down elusive information, and have *always* willingly provided personal instruction when I ran into Internet or online problems. Their average turn-around time in helping me locate materials online is about 10 minutes. I've worked at a dozen academic libraries and consider our reference librarians among the most helpful I've ever met.

Colleagues play a critical role in revisions. For this edition, I received valuable input from:

Robert R. Cordell, West Virginia University at Parkersburg

Cynthia J. Crivaro, Northern Essex Community College

Denise Dalaimo, Mt. San Jacinto College

Theresa Fish, Lake Superior College

Rebecca Ford, Florida Community College at Jacksonville

Cynthia Riffe Hancock, University of North Carolina at Charlotte

Chad Hanson, Casper College

Deborah Helsel, California State University at Fresno

Kathleen M. McKinley, Cabrini College

James P. Marshall, Utah State University

Patricia H. O'Brien, Elgin Community College

Amy J. Orr, Linfield College

Vânia Penha-Lopes, Bloomfield College

I want to express my sincere gratitude to a dedicated and extremely talented team at Pearson Prentice Hall. Leah Jewell, Editorial Director, Rochelle Diogenes, Editor in Chief, Development, and Nancy Roberts, Publisher offered wonderful suggestions and were enthusiastic about this edition's revisions and new features. Jennifer Gilliland, Executive Editor, has been committed to producing an excellent textbook. She is responsible for a number of books but always made me feel that *Marriages and Families* was a top priority.

Editorial assistants Kristin Haegele, Lee Peterson, and Valle Hansen have been godsends. I can't imagine a book's publication without all of their nitty-gritty and behind-the-scenes work that includes obtaining reviewer's comments, responding to an author's questions, and responding to "I need this right now" requests quickly and efficiently.

I also want to thank others at Prentice Hall for their high-quality contributions to this edition of *Marriages and Families*. Brandy Dawson, Director of Markeing and Lindsey Prudhomme, Marketing Manager, are a very talented marketing team. Carolyn Smith, my development editor, provided invaluable input and feedback. Carolyn suggested a number of changes that made this edition even more readable and student-friendly. She raised important questions from beginning to end (for example, "Is this *really* what you meant to say here?").

I am especially grateful to the Prentice Hall sales representatives who have supported this textbook and ensured that instructors receive the examination copies and supplements.

Tally Morgan, my excellent copy editor, caught a number of errors, corrected awkward phrases, noted non sequiturs, and "flagged" some missing references. Rachel Lucas, a superb photo researcher, persevered in finding exactly the photos that I wanted and offered suggestions on new photos.

Patty Donovan, my production editor at Pine Tree Composition, has been a marvel. She has been meticulous in orchestrating myriad tasks such as copyediting, preparing the illustrations, and keeping track of several last-minute changes. When I thought that I was the only one working on *Marriages and Families* on early Saturday mornings, I'd get an email from Patty about photo captions or "alerts" that a new batch of chapter proofs would arrive on Monday. Patty worried about the book's details as much as I did, even over the weekend. Katie Boilard, Patty's assistant project manager, has been terrific. She always had a "can do" attitude in addressing many of my questions and concerns.

I thank my family for their unfaltering patience and sense of humor throughout life's little stresses, especially my research and writing. Throughout our 40 years of marriage, Vitalius, my husband, has always been my greatest supporter, a sympathetic and intelligent sounding board, and an incredibly patient high-tech consultant. When I've been especially grumpy about revisions and snapped at Vitalius over "stuff" that had nothing to do with the textbook, he listened quietly. He'd then make a joke (usually a pun), I'd burst into laughter, and I'd continue my research and writing with a lighter heart.

Andrius, our son, helps me maintain my sanity by keeping my computer humming. About twice a year, he updates my hardware and software and makes sure that my backup tapes are working. He also cheers me up in the middle of the night with humorous Instant Messenger quips and conversations. Gema, our daughter, manages to drag me away from the monitor and into the sunshine despite my "But I have so much to do!" protests. My body ached for two days after she enrolled me in a Pilates class as a birthday present, but the yoga classes, a Christmas present, have been less painful and more enjoyable.

Last, but not least, I have benefited greatly from the suggestions of faculty and students who have contacted me during the last few years. I have incorporated many of their reactions in the sixth edition and look forward to future comments.

Thank you, one and all.

About the Author

Nijole V. Benokraitis, professor of sociology at the University of Baltimore, has taught the marriage and family course for almost 25 years. It's her favorite class but her courses in racial and ethnic relations and gender roles run a close second. Professor Benokraitis received a B.A. in sociology and English from Emmanuel College, an M.A. in sociology from the University of Illinois at Urbana, and a doctorate in sociology from the University of Texas at Austin.

She is a strong proponent of applied sociology and requires her students to enhance their study through interviews, direct observation, and other hands-on learning methods. She also enlists her students in community service activities such as tutoring and mentoring inner-city high school students, writing to government officials and other decision makers about specific social problems, and volunteering research services to nonprofit organizations.

Professor Benokraitis, who immigrated to the United States from Lithuania with her family when she was 6 years old, is bilingual and bicultural and is very empathetic of students who try to balance several cultural worlds. She has authored, co-authored, edited, or co-edited eight books, including *Contemporary Ethnic Families in the United States: Characteristics, Variations, and Dynamics; Feuds about Families: Conservative, Centrist, Liberal, and Feminist Perspectives; Modern Sexism: Blatant, Subtle, and Covert Discrimination;* and *Seeing Ourselves: Classic, Contemporary, and Cross-Cultural Readings in Sociology.*

Dr. Benokraitis has published numerous articles and book chapters on such topics as institutional racism, discrimination against women in government and higher education, fathers in two-earner families, displaced homemakers, and family policy. She has served as both chair and graduate program director of the University of Baltimore's Department of Sociology and has chaired numerous university committees.

She has received grants and fellowships from many institutions, including the National Institute of Mental Health, the Ford Foundation, the American Educational Research Association, the Administration on Aging, and the National Endowment for the Humanities. She has for some time served as a consultant in the areas of sex and race discrimination to women's commissions, business groups, colleges and universities, and federal government programs. She has also made several appearances on radio and television on gender communication differences and single-sex educational institutions. She currently serves on the editorial board of *Women & Criminal Justice* and reviews manuscripts for several academic journals.

Professor Benokraitis lives in Maryland with her husband, Dr. Vitalius Benokraitis, associate chair and director of graduate studies in computer science, Loyola College in Maryland. They have two adult children, Gema and Andrius.

The author looks forward (and always responds) to comments on the 6th edition of *Marriages and Families: Changes, Choices, and Constraints.* She can be contacted at

University of Baltimore
Division of Criminology, Criminal Justice
and Social Policy
1420 North Charles Street
Baltimore, MD 21201

E-mail: nbenokraitis@ubalt.edu

Outline

1

The Changing Family

Data Digest

- The **"traditional" family** (in which the husband is the breadwinner and the wife is a full-time homemaker) has declined from 60 percent of all U.S. families in 1972 to 30 percent.

- Almost 15 million people aged 25 to 34 years **have never been married,** representing 37 percent of all people in that age group.

- Today, the **median age at first marriage** is higher than at any time in the twentieth century: 27.4 years for men and 25.8 years for women.

- On average, **first marriages that end in divorce** last about 8 years.

- **Single-parent households** increased from 11 percent of all U.S. households in 1970 to 28 percent in 2005.

Sources: Smith, 2001; Fields, 2004; U.S. Census Bureau, 2006; U.S. Census Bureau News, 2006.

Two generations ago, the typical American family consisted of a father, a mother, and three or four children. In contrast, in a recent survey that asked respondents what constitutes a family, a woman in her 60s wrote the following:

My boyfriend and I have lived together with my youngest son for several years. However, our family (with whom we spend holidays and special events) also includes my ex-husband and his wife and child; my boyfriend's ex-mother-in-law and her sister; his ex-wife and her boyfriend; my oldest son who lives on his own; my mom and stepfather; and my stepbrother and his wife, their biological child, adopted child, and "Big Sister" child. Needless to say, introductions to outsiders are confusing (Cole, 1996: 12, 14).

Clearly, contemporary family arrangements are more fluid than in the past. Does this shift reflect changes in individual preferences, as people often assume? Or are other forces at work? As you will see in this chapter, although individual choices have altered some family structures, many of these changes reflect adaptations to larger societal transformations.

Ask Yourself

How Much Do You Know about Contemporary Marriage and Family Life?

True False

☐ ☐ 1. Teenage out-of-wedlock births have increased dramatically over the past 20 years.

☐ ☐ 2. Cohabitation (living together) promotes a happy and lasting marriage.

☐ ☐ 3. Singles have better sex lives than married people.

☐ ☐ 4. The more educated a woman is, the less likely she is to marry.

☐ ☐ 5. People get married because they love each other.

☐ ☐ 6. Romance is a key to marital success.

☐ ☐ 7. Having children increases marital satisfaction.

☐ ☐ 8. Married couples have healthier babies than unmarried couples.

☐ ☐ 9. Most black and Latino families are poor and on welfare.

☐ ☐ 10. Family relationships that span several generations are less common now than they were in the past.

(The answers to these questions are on page 6.)

You will also see that, despite both historical and recent evidence to the contrary, we continue to cling to a number of myths about the family. But before we examine these and other issues, we need to define what we mean by *marriage* and *family*. First, test your knowledge about current trends in U.S. families by taking the quiz above.

What is Marriage?

Defined broadly, **marriage** is a socially approved mating relationship that is expected to be stable and enduring. Marriage forms vary from one society to another because the members of each society construct **norms,** or culturally defined rules for behavior. Norms that define marriage include formal laws and religious doctrines. In the United States, to be legally married we must meet specific requirements, such as a minimum age, which may differ from one state to another. Kansas, for example, is one of the few states that allow children as young as 12 to marry if they have parental permission (Wilgoren, 2005).

Although the laws are rarely enforced, 24 states prohibit marriage between first cousins. And because the Catholic Church forbids the dissolution of what it considers the holy sacrament of marriage, devout Catholics may seek annulments but not divorces.

How Are Marriages Similar?

Despite numerous societal and cultural variations, marriages in most Western industrialized countries have some characteristics in common. In general, married couples are expected to share economic responsibilities, to engage in sexual activity only with their spouse, and to bear and raise children.

In the United States, laws governing marriage have changed more rapidly than social customs or regional practices. In 1967, for example, the U.S. Supreme Court ruled that *miscegenation laws,* which prohibit interracial marriages, are unconstitutional. However, local customs and attitudes among many groups still discourage interracial marriages (see Chapter 4). And as recent violent outbursts in white neighborhoods in Massachusetts, New York, and New Jersey have shown, intolerance of interracial dating is not limited to the South or to rural areas (see Chapter 8).

How Do Marriages Differ?

Marriages in the United States are legally defined as either ceremonial or nonceremonial. A *ceremonial* marriage is one in which the couple must follow procedures specified by the state or other jurisdiction, such as buying a license, getting blood tests, and being married by an authorized official.

since you asked

Are common-law marriages legal in the United States?

Some states also recognize **common-law marriage,** a *nonceremonial* form of marriage that people establish through cohabitation (living together) or evidence of *consummation* (sexual intercourse). Common-law marriages are recognized as legal in 14 states and the District of Columbia. In both kinds of marriage, the parties must meet minimum age requirements, and they cannot engage in **bigamy,** or marrying a second person while a first marriage is still legal.

When common-law relationships break up, the legal problems can be complex. These problems may include the child's inheritance rights and the father's responsibility to pay child support. Even when common-law marriage is considered legal, ceremonial marriage provides more advantages (such as health benefits and social approval).

What is a Family?

Although it may seem unnecessary to define familiar terms such as *family,* the meanings of many such terms differ from one group of people to another; they may also change over time. The definitions also have important consequences for policy decisions, often determining family members' rights and obligations. Under Social Security laws, for example, only a worker's spouse, dependent parents, and children can claim benefits based on the worker's record. And in most adoptions, a child is not legally a member of an adopting family until social service agencies and the courts have approved the adoption. Thus, definitions of family affect people's lives by limiting their options.

Definitions of the family can be placed at different points on a continuum that extend from those that are biological on one end to those that are social on the other end. Definitions that fall somewhere in the middle of the continuum incorporate both biological and social conceptions (Holtzman, 2005). For the most part,

both traditional and more current definitions of the family are somewhere in the middle.

Some Traditional Definitions of the Family

There is no universal definition of the family because contemporary household arrangements are very complex. Traditionally, however, *family* has been defined as a unit made up of two or more people who are related by blood, marriage, or adoption and who live together, form an economic unit, and bear and raise children. The U.S. Census Bureau defines the family simply as two or more people living together who are related by birth, marriage, or adoption.

since you asked

Are people living in the same household a family if they don't have children?

Many social scientists have challenged such traditional definitions because they exclude a number of diverse groups that also consider themselves families. Social scientists have asked: Are childfree couples families? What about cohabiting couples? Foster parents and their charges? Elderly sisters living together? Gay and lesbian couples, with or without children? Grandparents raising grandchildren?

Some Current Definitions of the Family

For our purposes, a **family** is an intimate environment in which two or more people: (1) live together in a committed relationship, (2) see their identity as attached to that of the group in important ways, and (3) share functions and close emotional ties. However, not all social scientists will agree with this definition because it does not explicitly include legal marriage, procreation, or child rearing.

Definitions of the family may become even more complicated—and more controversial—in the future. As reproductive technology advances, a baby might have several "parents": an egg donor, a sperm donor, a woman who carries the baby during a pregnancy, and the couple who intends to raise the child. If that's not confusing enough, the biological father may be dead for years by the time the child is actually conceived because his sperm can be frozen and stored (see Chapter 11).

Fictive Kin and Families

Some researchers believe that definitions of the family should emphasize affection and mutual cooperation among people who are living together. Particularly in

Gilmore Girls, a popular TV show, portrays an unmarried mother and her daughter, a nontraditional family.

African American and Latino communities, ties with **fictive kin,** or nonrelatives who are accepted as part of the family, may be stronger and more lasting than the ties established by blood or marriage (Dilworth-Anderson et al., 1993). James, one of my black students, who is now in his forties, still fondly recalls Mike, a boarder in his home. His description provides a good illustration of fictive kinship:

Mike was an older gentleman who lived with us from my childhood to my teenage years. He was like a grandfather to me. He taught me how to ride a bike, took me fishing, and always told me stories. He was very close to me and my family until he died. When the family gets together, we still talk about old Mike because he was just like family and we still miss him dearly (Author's files).

A recent variation on fictive kinship found among Unitarian congregations is "intentional families," which

Answers to How Much Do You Know about Contemporary Marriage and Family Life?

All the answers are **false:**

1. Teenage out-of-wedlock births have decreased over the past 20 years, especially in the early 2000s (see Chapters 10 and 11).

2. Couples who are living together and plan to marry each other *soon* have a good chance of staying together after a marriage. In most cases, however, "shacking up" decreases the likelihood of marriage (see Chapter 9).

3. Compared with singles, married people have more and better sex and enjoy it more, both physically and emotionally (see Chapter 7).

4. College-educated women tend to postpone marriage but are more likely to marry, over a lifetime, than their non–college-educated peers (see Chapters 9 and 10).

5. Love is not the major or even the only reason for getting married. Other reasons include societal expectations, economic insecurity, or fear of loneliness (see Chapters 6, 10, 16, and 17).

6. The best indicators of long-term marital success include hard work, sharing compatible values and interests, and resolving conflicts in a "civilized" manner (see Chapters 10, 14, and 15).

7. The arrival of a first baby typically pushes mothers and fathers apart. Generally, child rearing lowers marital satisfaction for both partners (see Chapters 11, 12, and 16).

8. Social class is a more important factor than marital status in a baby's health. Low-income mothers are less likely to have healthy babies than are high-in-

come mothers, whether they are married or not (see Chapters 11–14).

9. Although many black and Latino families live below the poverty level, in 2001 almost 28 percent of African American families and 31 percent of Latino families had annual incomes of $50,000 or more (see Chapters 4, 12, and 13).

10. Family relationships across several generations are more common and more important now than they were in the past. People live longer and get to know their kin, aging parents and grandparents often provide financial support and child care, and many relatives maintain ties with one another after a divorce or remarriage (see Chapters 3, 4, 12, 16, and 17).

are made up primarily of white, professional people. Their members are separated from their own relatives by distance or estrangement but yearn for a feeling of familial closeness. Members of intentional families live apart but meet regularly for meals, holidays, and milestones in the life course, such as weddings and funerals. They also plan outings together, help each other during crises, and sometimes have older people "stand in" for a child's deceased grandparents during community activities (E. Graham, 1996).

Making Connections

- Ask three of your friends to define *family*. Are their definitions the same as yours? Or are they different?

- According to one of my students, "I never view my biological family as 'my family' because my parents were abusive and didn't love me." Do you agree that people should be able to choose whomever they want to be their family?

Family Structure and Social Change

For nearly a century, the nation's family structure remained remarkably stable. Between 1880 and 1970, about 85 percent of all children lived in two-parent households. Then, in the next three decades, the numbers of divorces and single-parent families skyrocketed. By 2003, almost one in four children was living in a mother-only home (see *Figure 1.1*).

Some people are concerned that the **nuclear family**—made up of a husband, a wife, and their biological or adopted children—has dwindled. Many social scientists contend, however, that viewing the nuclear family as the only "normal" or "natural" type of family ignores many other prevalent household forms. One researcher, for example, has identified 23 types of family structures, some of which include only friends or group-home members (Wu, 1996). Family structures have varied not only across cultures and eras but also within any particular culture or historical period (see Chapter 3).

As reflected in many television shows, diverse family structures are more acceptable today than ever before (see *Table 1.1*). At the same time, the lineup of shows is rarely representative of "real" families. For example, at least 12 shows have focused on single-father households, but only four have portrayed single-mother families. In real life, only 5 percent of all children live in father-only families, compared with 23 percent in mother-only families (see *Figure 1.1*). And although the number of traditional families has decreased since the 1970s (see "Data Digest"), the number of prime-time programs featuring such families increased in the early 2000s (for example, *The Hughleys, 7th Heaven, Everybody Loves Raymond, American Dreams,* and *Yes, Dear*).

since you asked

Do TV shows accurately reflect family structure?

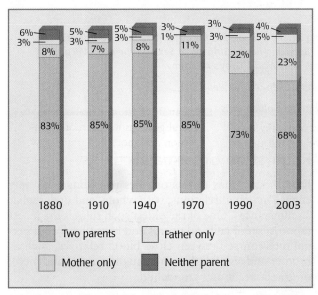

FIGURE 1.1   Where Children Live: Selected Years, 1880–2003

SOURCE: Based on Fields, 2001, Figure 7, and Fields, 2004, Table C2.

Making Connections

You may not even remember some of the television shows that came and went in the 1990s. Some, such as *Married . . . with Children, Mad about You, Home Improvement,* and *The Bill Cosby Show,* are now syndicated. Television shows have portrayed a wide variety of family structures.

- How many of these programs are *really* representative of most U.S. families today? Or of your own family?

- How do these shows shape our ideas about how family members should relate to one another?

TABLE 1.1

Family Structure According to 1990s and Early 2000s Television

Family Structure	Television Show
Married couple with children; father as breadwinner	*Married . . . with Children, The Simpsons, Family Ties, Dave's World, Everybody Loves Raymond, 7th Heaven, The Hughleys, The PJs, Family Guy, That '70s Show, American Dreams, Desperate Housewives, The Sopranos, Yes, Dear*
Married couple with children; two earners	*The Cosby Show, Roseanne, Home Improvement, Mad about You, Malcolm in the Middle, My Wife and Kids, George Lopez, Still Standing, Life with Bonnie*
Married couple with no children	*Dharma and Greg, My Big Fat Greek Life, King of Queens, Curb Your Enthusiasm*
Married couple with children and related adults	*Under One Roof, All-American Girl, Family Matters*
Male householder with children	*Soul Man, Smart Guy, Blossom, One on One*
Male householder with children and unrelated adults	*Full House, The Nanny*
Male householder with children and related adults	*Me and the Boys, The Gregory Hines Show, Two and a Half Men*
Male householder with children and grandchildren	*Thunder Alley*
Male householder with unmarried adult children	*Empty Nest, Providence*
Female householder with children	*Grace under Fire, Cybill, Gilmore Girls, The Parkers*
Married couple with stepchildren	*True Colors, Major Dad*
Married couple with biological or nonbiological children	*Fresh Prince of Bel Air, Step by Step, The Bernie Mac Show, One World, Moesha*
Children, no adults present	*On Our Own, Party of Five, The OC*
Unmarried mother	*Murphy Brown*
Related adults	*Head over Heels, Between Brothers, Charmed*
Related and unrelated adults	*Frasier*
Unrelated adults	*Living Single, Friends, 3rd Rock from the Sun, George and Leo, Men Behaving Badly, Girlfriends, Sex and the City, Will and Grace, Real World, Grey's Anatomy*
Single-person households	*Seinfeld, Ellen, Ally McBeal*
Retired couple or roommates	*Cosby, The Golden Girls*

Functions of the Family

Although family structures differ, most contemporary families fulfill five important functions. They legitimize sexual activity, bear and raise children, provide economic security, offer emotional support, and establish family members' places in society. As you read this section, think about your own family. How does its structure—whether nuclear, divorced, stepfamily, or another form—fulfill these functions?

since you asked

Why do we need families?

Regulation of Sexual Activity

Every society has norms or rules regarding who may engage in sexual relations, with whom, and under what circumstances. One of the oldest such rules is the **incest taboo,** a set of cultural norms and laws that forbid sexual intercourse between close blood relatives, such as brother and sister, father and daughter, uncle and niece, or grandparent and grandchild.

INCEST TABOOS Sexual relations between close relatives can increase the incidence of inherited genetic diseases and abnormalities by about 3 percent (Bennett et al., 2002). Incest taboos are based primarily on social conditions, however, and probably arose to maintain the family. They do this in several ways:

- Incest taboos minimize jealousy and destructive sexual competition that might interfere with the functioning of the family.

- Incest taboos ensure a group's survival. If family members who are sexual partners lose interest in each other, for example, they may avoid mating.

- Because incest taboos ensure that mating will take place outside the family, a wider circle of people can band together in cooperative efforts (such as hunting), in the face of danger, or in war (Ellis, 1963).

- By controlling the mother's sexuality, incest taboos prevent doubts from arising about the legitimacy of her offspring and the children's property rights, titles, or inheritance.

Most social scientists believe that incest taboos are universal. There have been exceptions, however. The rulers of the Incan empire, Hawaii, ancient Persia, and the Ptolemaic dynasty in Egypt practiced incest, which was forbidden to commoners. Cleopatra is said to have been the issue of at least 11 generations of incest; she in turn married her younger brother. Some anthropologists speculate that wealthy Egyptian families practiced sibling marriage to prevent losing or fragmenting their land. If a sister married her brother, the property would remain in the family in the event of divorce or death (Parker, 1996).

ENDOGAMY AND EXOGAMY   Two other cultural rules specify the "right" marriage partner. The principle of **endogamy** requires that people marry or have sexual relations within a certain group. These groups might include those that are similar in religion (such as Jews marrying Jews), race or ethnicity (such as Latinos marrying Latinos), social class, or age (such as young people marrying young people).

Exogamy requires marriage outside the group, such as not marrying one's relatives. In some states, as you saw earlier, U.S. laws prohibit marriage between first cousins. Even when there are no such laws, cultural traditions and practices, as well as social pressure, usually govern our choice of sexual and marital partners. According to some of my students, for instance, "It's disgusting to even think about marrying a cousin or a stepsister." (We will discuss two related terms— *homogamy* and *heterogamy*—in several later chapters.)

Procreation and Socialization of Children

Procreation is an essential function of the family. Although some married couples choose to remain child-free, most plan to raise families. Some go to great lengths to conceive the children they want through reproductive technologies (see Chapter 11). Once a couple becomes parents, the family embarks on socialization, another critical function.

Through **socialization**, children acquire language; absorb the accumulated knowledge, attitudes, beliefs, and values of their culture; and learn the social and interpersonal skills they need if they are to function effectively in society. Some socialization is unconscious and may be unintentional, such as teaching culturally accepted stereotypical gender traits (see Chapter 5). Much socialization, however, is both conscious and deliberate, such as carefully selecting preschoolers' playmates or raising children in a specific religion.

We are socialized through **roles**, the obligations and expectations attached to a particular situation or position. Families are important role-teaching agents because they delineate relationships between mothers and fathers, siblings, parents and children, and other relatives and non-family members.

Some of the rights and responsibilities associated with our roles are not always clear because family structures shift and change. If you or your parents have experienced divorce or remarriage, have some of the new role expectations been fuzzy or even contradictory? For example, children may be torn between loyalty to a biological parent and to a stepparent if the adults compete for their affection (see Chapter 16).

Economic Security

The family is also an important economic unit that provides financial security and stability. Families supply food, shelter, clothing, and other material resources for their members. These ensure the family's physical survival. In contrast, homeless families often wind up on the streets or in shelters, not because the parents are mentally ill or drug users but simply because they can't purchase some of life's basic necessities, such as housing and food.

In traditional families, the husband is the breadwinner and the wife does the housework and cares for the children. Increasingly, however, many mothers are entering the labor force. The traditional family, in which Mom stays home to raise the kids, is a luxury that most families today simply can't afford. Because of high unemployment rates, depressed wages and salaries, and job insecurity, many mothers must work outside the home whether they want to or not (see Chapter 13).

Emotional Support

A fourth function of the family is providing emotional support for its members, who are a close-knit group. The American sociologist Charles Horton Cooley (1864–1929) proposed the concept of **primary groups,** those characterized by close, long-lasting, intimate, and face-to-face interaction. The family is a critical primary group because it provides the nurturance, love, and emotional sustenance that its members need if they are to be happy, healthy, and secure.

Later writers introduced the notion of **secondary groups,** those characterized by impersonal and short-term relationships in which people work together on common tasks or activities. Members of secondary groups have few emotional ties to one another, and they typically leave the group after attaining a specific goal. While you're taking this course, for example, you, most of your classmates (except, perhaps, for a few close friends), and your instructor make up a secondary group. You've all come together for a quarter or a semester to study marriage and the family. Once the course is over, most of you may never see one another again.

You might discuss your course with people in other secondary groups, such as co-workers. They will probably listen politely, but they usually don't really care how you feel about a class or an instructor. Primary groups such as your family and close friends, in contrast, usually sympathize, drive you to class or your job when your car breaks down, offer to do your laundry during exams, and console you if you don't get that much-deserved "A" in a course or a promotion at work.

I use a simple test to distinguish between my primary and secondary groups: I don't hesitate to call the former at 3:00 A.M. to pick me up at the airport because I know they'll be happy (or at least willing) to do so.

Social Class Placement

A **social class** is a category of people who have a similar standing or rank in society based on their wealth, education, power, prestige, and other valued resources. People in the same social class tend to have similar attitudes, values, and leisure interests.

Social class affects many aspects of family life. There are class variations in terms of when people marry, how many children they have, how parents socialize their children, and even how partners and spouses relate to each other. Middle-class couples are more likely than

The family provides the love, comfort, and emotional support that children need if they are to develop into happy, healthy, and secure adults.

their working-class counterparts to share housework and child rearing, for example. And as you will see in later chapters, families on the lower rungs of the socioeconomic ladder face greater risks than their middle-class counterparts of adolescent nonmarital childbearing, dropping out of high school, committing street crimes, neglecting their children, and engaging in domestic violence (see Chapters 10, 12, and 13).

Diversity in Marriages, Families, and Kinship Systems

Although the basic family functions you have just read about are common to most cultures, each society has its own norms that specify acceptable marriage and family forms. Thus, there is much diversity among families both across and within cultures. Let's begin with a few basic concepts.

Basic Family Structures

Most people are born into a biological family, or *family of origin*. If the person is adopted or raised in this family, it is her or his **family of orientation.** By leaving this family to marry or cohabit, the individual becomes part of a **family of procreation,** the family a person forms by marrying and having or adopting children. This term is somewhat dated, however, because in several types of households—such as childfree or gay and lesbian families—procreation may not be part of the relationship.

Each type of family is part of a larger **kinship system,** a network of people who are related by blood, marriage, or adoption. In much of the preindustrial world, which contains most of the earth's population, the most common family form is the **extended family,** in which two or more generations (such as the family of orientation and the family of procreation) live together or in adjacent dwellings.

In industrialized societies where the numbers of single-parent families are increasing, extended families living together or nearby are becoming more common. Such families can make it much easier for a single parent to work outside the home, raise children, and perform household tasks. Because remarriage rates are high, however, it remains to be seen whether extended families will become widespread.

A variety of formal laws and informal norms regulate inheritance rights, define whom one may marry, and determine whether children will take the surname of the father, the mother, or both. There are also worldwide variations in the types of marriages and residential patterns that characterize families and kinship systems.

Types of Marriage

Several types of marriage—including monogamy, polygamy, or a combination of these types—are common in most societies. One anthropologist concluded that only about 20 percent of societies are strictly monogamous. Others permit either polygamy or combinations of polygamy and monogamy (Murdock, 1967).

MONOGAMY In **monogamy,** one person is married exclusively to another person. Because divorce and remarriage rates are high in the United States and in many European countries, many residents of these countries are said to practice **serial monogamy.** That is, they marry several people, but one at a time—they marry, divorce, remarry, redivorce, and so on.

POLYGAMY Polygamy, in which a man or woman has two or more spouses, is subdivided into *polygyny* (one man married to two or more women) and *polyandry* (one woman married to two or more men). In group marriage, two or more men and two or more women live together and have sexual

since you asked

Are there any societies in which a woman may marry more than one man?

relations with one another. Polygyny is common in many societies, especially in Africa, South America, and the Middle East. In Saudi Arabia, for example, some wealthy men have as many as 11 wives and 54 children (Dickey and McGinn, 2001). No one knows the actual figures for polygamy worldwide, however, because "accurate censuses of polygyny are generally unavailable" (Hern, 1992: 504).

Although industrial societies forbid polygamy, small polygynous groups exist in those societies. The Church of Jesus Christ of Latter-day Saints (Mormons) banned polygamy in 1890 and excommunicates members who follow such beliefs. Still, an estimated 300,000 families are headed by fundamentalist men in Texas, Arizona, Utah, and Canada. These dissident leaders maintain that they practice polygamy according to nineteenth-century Mormon religious beliefs. The leaders perform secret marriage ceremonies and marry off girls—as young as 11—to older men (who are sometimes in their 50s and 60s) at the first sign of menstruation (Divoky, 2002; Madigan, 2003).

Wives who have escaped from these plural families report forced marriage, sexual abuse, child rape, and incest. Why don't these girls refuse to marry or try to escape? They can't. Among other things, they're typically isolated from outsiders: They live in remote rural areas and their education is cut off when they're about 10 years old. Their parents support the marriages because elderly men, the patriarchs, have brainwashed them to believe that "This is what the heavenly father wants" (Egan, 2005).

Sexual abusers are rarely prosecuted and, even then, receive remarkable leniency. A father who was convicted of regularly molesting his five daughters spent only 13 days in jail. The presiding judge said that the abuse was really just "a little bit of breast touching" (Kelly and Cohn, 2006).

Some church elders have banished hundreds of teenage boys—some as young as 13—to reduce the competition for young wives. Gideon, 17, is one of these boys. He is one of 71 children born to his 73-year-old father, who has eight wives. Because most of the boys don't attend school past the eighth grade, they have few skills with which to fend for themselves after being expelled from the community (Kelly, 2005; Knickerbocker, 2006).

Polygynous marriages can be either formal or informal. In a study of marriage forms in Nigeria, Karanja (1987) differentiates between an inside wife and an outside wife. An "inside wife," who marries in a church or civil ceremony, typically subscribes to the Christian ideal of monogamy in marriage. Under native law and custom, however, her husband may also "marry" (there is no official ceremony) an "outside wife."

As the box "The Outside Wife" shows, the unofficial wife has regular sexual relations with her "husband," establishes a separate residence that the husband pays for, and has children that the man acknowledges

Tom Green from Snake Valley, Utah, is shown here with his 5 wives and some of their 29 children. In 2002 Green was found guilty of polygamy, having sex with one of his wives when she was just 13 years old, and welfare fraud.

as his. Outside wives, however, have limited social status and little legal recognition. When a well-known Nigerian businessman and politician died at age 60, he had four official wives (because "under Muslim law, a man may have four wives") and more than 40 outside (Vick, 1998: A9).

Some African and Middle Eastern families that immigrate to other countries continue to live in polygamous families but often run into problems. The French government, which declared polygamy illegal in 1993, estimates that there are about 15,000 polygamous families within the nation's borders. Because second wives are not legal residents, they are not allowed to work and are not entitled to any form of social welfare, such as public housing. The families end up living in crowded and impoverished conditions. Also, "tensions arise with French neighbors who tend to be flabbergasted when confronted with families consisting of a husband, two or more wives, and as many as 20 children" (Renout, 2005: 17).

Why is polygyny widespread in some countries? A study of marriage patterns in South Africa concluded that there is often a shortage of men (usually because of war), that poor women would rather marry a rich polygamist than a poor monogamist, that wives often pool income and cooperative child care, and that rural wives often contact urban wives when they're looking for jobs. Thus, polygyny is functional because it meets many women's needs (Anderson, 2002).

The very rare practice of polyandry is illustrated by the Todas, a small pastoral tribe that flourished in southern India until the late nineteenth century. A Toda woman who married one man became the wife of his brothers—including brothers born after the marriage—and they all lived in the same household. When one of the brothers was with the wife, "he placed his cloak and staff outside the hut as a warning to the rest not to disturb him" (Queen et al., 1985: 19). Marital privileges rotated among the brothers; there was no evidence of sexual jealousy; and one of the brothers, usually the oldest, was the legal father of the first two or three children. Another brother could become the legal father of children born later.

According to some anthropologists, polyandry might have existed in societies where property was difficult to accumulate. Because there was a limited amount of available land, the kinship group was more likely to survive in harsh environments if there was more than one husband to provide food (Cassidy and Lee, 1989).

Residential Patterns

Families also vary in terms of where they live. In a *patrilocal* residential pattern, newly married couples live with the husband's family. In a *matrilocal* pattern, newly married couples live with the wife's family. A *neolocal* residential pattern is one in which a newly married couple sets up its own residence. Around the world families tend to be extended rather than nuclear, and the most common pattern is residence with the husband's family.

In modern industrial societies, married couples typically establish their own residences. Since the early 1990s, however, the tendency for young married adults to live with the parents of either the wife or the husband—or sometimes with the grandparents of one of the partners—has increased. At least half of all families starting out cannot afford a medium-priced house because they don't have the cash for a down payment and closing costs. Divorced mothers and their children often live with parents or grandparents for economic reasons (see Chapters 12, 13, and 15).

Cross-Cultural Families

The Outside Wife

Temi, 38 years old, is a British-trained doctor in private practice in Lagos, Nigeria. Her father (now retired) was a university professor, and her mother was a high school teacher. Temi's first church marriage, in which she had two children, ended in divorce. She is now an outside wife of an eminent businessman, with whom she has a child. She lives in an apartment rented by her husband on Victoria Island, said to be where the who's-who of Nigeria live.

Temi sees no contradiction in her way of life:

Look, I lived in England for years and I know there you are expected to be monogamously married. Well, I am not in England now, am I? (She laughs.) My first husband was a fine gentleman, but, let's face it, he had no money. Most of our spare time was spent bickering over who was going to pay the bills. It was intolerable. In the end I decided to quit. Financial straits for me are history. My children are in school abroad. My husband recently bought me a Mercedes Benz, and I am building a house here in Lagos with his help. We also plan to buy a home in the U.S.

Temi's "husband" has two other wives. The church wife, or inside wife, is also a doctor; the other outside wife is an attorney who practices and lives in Lagos (Karanja, 1987: 255–56).

Clearly, there is much diversity in family arrangements both in the United States and around the world. As families change, however, we sometimes get bogged down by idealized images of what a "good" family looks like. Our unrealistic expectations can result in dissatisfaction and anger. Instead of enjoying our families as they are, we may waste a lot of time and energy searching for family relationships that exist only in fairy tales and TV sitcoms.

Myths about Marriage and the Family

Ask yourself the following questions:

- Were families happier in the past than they are now?
- Is marrying and having children the "natural" thing to do?
- Are "good" families self-sufficient, whereas "bad" families depend on welfare?
- Is the family a bastion of love and support?
- Should all of us strive to be as perfect as possible in our families?

If you answered "yes" to any of these questions, you—like most people in the United States—believe several myths about marriage and the family. Although most of these myths are dysfunctional, some can be functional.

Myths Can Be Dysfunctional

Myths can be *dysfunctional* when they result in negative (though often unintended) consequences that disrupt a family. The myth of the perfect family can make us miserable. We may feel that there is something wrong with *us* if we do not live up to some idealized image. Instead of accepting our current families, we may pressure our children to become what we want them to be or spend a lifetime waiting for our parents or in-laws to accept us. We may become very critical of family members or withdraw emotionally because they don't fit into a mythical mold.

since you asked

Do myths *really* affect me and my family?

Myths can also divert our attention from widespread social problems that lead to family crises. If people blame themselves for the gap they perceive between image and reality, they may not recognize the external forces, such as social policies, that create difficulties on the individual level. For example, if we believe that only bad, sick, or maladjusted people beat their children, we will search for solutions at the individual level, such as counseling, support groups, and therapy. As we will see in later chapters, however, many family crises result from large-scale problems such as racism, poverty, and unemployment.

Like these Nebraska homesteaders, many families in the so-called "good old days" lived in dugouts like this one, made from sod cut from the prairie.

Myths Can Be Functional

Not all myths are harmful. Some are *functional* because they bring people together and promote social solidarity (Guest, 1988). If myths give us hope that we can have a good marriage and family life, for example, we won't give up at the first sign of problems. In this sense, myths can help us maintain emotional balance during crises.

Myths can also free us from guilt or shame. For instance, "We fell out of love" is a more face-saving explanation for getting a divorce than "I made a stupid mistake" or "I married an alcoholic."

The same myth may be both functional and dysfunctional. Belief in the decline of the family has been functional in generating social policies (such as child-support legislation) that try to keep children of divorced families from sinking into poverty. But this same myth is dysfunctional if people become unrealistically preoccupied with finding self-fulfillment and happiness.

Myths about the Past

We often hear that in "the good old days" there were fewer problems, people were happier, and families were stronger. Because of the widespread influence of movies and television, many of us cherish romantic notions of life in earlier times. These highly unrealistic images of the family have been portrayed in John Wayne films,

the antebellum South of *Gone with the Wind,* and the strong, poor, but loving rural family presented in such television shows as *The Waltons* and *Little House on the Prairie* in the 1970s, *Dr. Quinn, Medicine Woman* in the late 1990s, and *7th Heaven* most recently.

Many historians maintain that such golden ages never existed. We glorify them only because we know so little about the past. Even in the 1800s, many families experienced out-of-wedlock births or desertion by a parent (Demos, 1986; Coontz, 1992).

Family life in "the good old days" was filled with deprivation, loneliness, and dangers, as the "Diary of a Pioneer Daughter" box illustrates. Families worked very hard and often were crushed by accidents, illness, and disease. Until the mid-1940s, a much shorter life expectancy meant that parental death often led to the placement of children in extended families, foster care, or orphanages. Thus, the chances of not growing up in a nuclear family were actually greater in the past than they are now (Walsh, 1993).

People who have the "nostalgia bug" aren't aware of several facts. For example, teenage pregnancy rates were higher in the 1950s than they are today, even though a higher proportion of teen mothers were married (many because of "shotgun marriages"). Until the 1970s, few people ever talked or wrote about child abuse, incest, domestic violence, marital unhappiness, sexual harassment, or gay bashing. Many families lived in silent misery and quiet desperation because these issues were largely invisible. In addition, parents spend more time with their children today than they did in "the good old days" (see Chapter 12).

Myths about What Is Natural

Many people have strong opinions about what is "natural" or "unnatural" in marriages and families. Although remaining single is more acceptable today than it was in the past, there is still a lingering suspicion that there's something wrong with a person who doesn't marry (see Chapter 9).

Constraints

Diary of a Pioneer Daughter

Many scholars point out that frontier life was anything but romantic. Malaria and cholera were widespread. Because of their darkness, humidity, and warmth, as well as their gaping windows and doors, pioneers' cabins were ideal environments for mosquitoes. Women and children have been described as doing household tasks with "their hands and arms flailing the air" against hordes of attacking mosquitoes (Faragher, 1986: 90).

Historian Joanna Stratton examined the letters, diaries, and other documents of pioneer women living on the Kansas prairie between 1854 and 1890. The following selection is from the diary of a 15-year-old girl:

A man by the name of Johnson had filed on a claim just west of us and had built a sod house. He and his wife lived there 2 years, when he went to Salina to secure work. He was gone 2 or 3 months and wrote home once or twice, but his wife grew very homesick for her folks in the east and would come over to our house to visit Mother.

Mother tried to cheer her up, but she continued to worry until she got bedfast with the fever. At night she was frightened because the wolves would scratch on the door, on the sod, and on the windows, so my mother and I started to sit up nights with her. I would bring my revolver and ammunition and ax and some good-sized clubs.

The odor from the sick woman seemed to attract the wolves, and they grew bolder and bolder. I would step

out, fire off the revolver, and they would settle back for a while when they would start a new attack.

Finally the woman died and mother laid her out. Father took some wide boards that we had in our loft and made a coffin for her. Mother made a pillow and trimmed it with black cloth, and we also painted the coffin black.

After that the wolves were more determined than ever to get in. One got his head in between the door casing, and as he was trying to wriggle through, mother struck him in the head with an ax and killed him. I shot one coming through the window. After that they quieted down for about half an hour, when they came back again. Their howling was awful. We fought these wolves five nights in succession. . . .

When Mr. Johnson arrived home and found his wife dead and his house badly torn down by wolves he fainted away. After the funeral he sold out and moved away (Stratton, 1981: 81).

Rebecca Bryan Boone, wife of the legendary pioneer Daniel Boone, endured months and sometimes even years of solitude when Boone hunted in the woods or went on trading trips.

Besides doing household chores, she chopped wood, cultivated the fields, harvested the crops, and hunted for small game in the woods near her cabin. Although Rebecca was a strong and resourceful woman, she told a traveling preacher that she felt "frequent distress and fear in her heart" (Peavy and Smith, 1994: xi).

We sometimes have misgivings about childfree marriages or other committed relationships. We often hear, for instance, that "It's only natural to want to get married and have children" or that "Gays are violating human nature." Other beliefs, also surviving from so-called simpler times, claim that family life is "natural" and that women are "natural" mothers (see Chapter 5).

The problem with such thinking is that if motherhood is natural, why do many women choose not to have children? If homosexuality is unnatural, how do we explain its existence since time immemorial? If getting married and creating a family are natural, why do millions of men abandon their children or refuse to marry their pregnant partners?

Myths about the Self-Sufficient Family

Among our most cherished values are individual achievement, self-reliance, and self-sufficiency. The numerous best-selling self-help books on such topics as parenting, combining work and marriage, and having "good sex" also reflect our belief that we should improve ourselves, that we can pull ourselves up by our bootstraps.

Although we have many choices in our personal lives, few families—past or present—have been entirely self-sufficient. Most of us need some kind of help at one time or another. Because of unemployment, underemployment, and recessions, the poverty rate has increased by 40 percent since 1970, and many of the working poor are two-parent families (see Chapter 13). From time to time, these families need assistance to survive.

The middle class isn't self-sufficient, either. In the 1950s and 1960s, for example, many middle-class families were able to prosper not because of family savings or individual enterprise but as a result of federal housing loans, education payments, and publicly-financed roads linking homes in the suburbs to jobs in the cities (Coontz, 1992).

Currently, all older people, whether poor or rich, are eligible for Medicare, and the government provides numerous tax cuts for middle-income and affluent families (see Chapters 13 and 18). Even if you're middle class, you or other family members have probably collected unemployment payments after being laid off from a job. In addition, state-based merit scholarships are more likely to subsidize the college costs of students from rich families than those of students from poor and minority families (Hong, 2005).

The Myth of the Family as a Loving Refuge

One sociologist has described the family as a "haven in a heartless world" (Lasch, 1977: 8). That is, one of the major functions of the family is to provide love, nurturance, and emotional support. The home can also be one of the most physically and psychologically brutal settings in society. An alarming number of children suffer from physical and sexual abuse by family members, and rates of violence between married and cohabiting partners are high (see Chapter 14).

Many parents experience stress while balancing the demands of work and family responsibilities. Furthermore, concern about crime, drugs, and unemployment has made many parents pessimistic about their children's future. In a recent national poll, for example, 27 percent of white, 38 percent of Latino, and 42 percent of African American adults said that they worry "all or most of the time" that the family's total income will not be enough to pay for their family's expenses and bills (Carroll, 2006). The anxiety underlying such fears is bound to affect family dynamics.

Sometimes family members are unrealistic about the daily strains they encounter. For example, if people expect family interactions to always be cheery and pleasant, the level of tension may surge even when routine problems arise. And especially for families with health or economic problems, the home may be loving, but it's hardly a "haven in a heartless world."

Myths about the Perfect Marriage, the Perfect Family

Here's how one woman described the clash between marital expectations and reality:

> *Marriage is not what I had assumed it would be. One premarital assumption after another has crashed down on my head. . . . Marriage is like taking an airplane to Florida for a relaxing vacation in January, and when you get off the plane you find you're in the Swiss Alps. There is cold and snow instead of swimming and sunshine. Well, after you buy winter clothes and learn how to ski and learn how to talk a new foreign language, I guess you can have just as good a vacation in the Swiss Alps as you can in Florida. But I can tell you . . . it's one hell of a surprise when you get off that marital airplane and find that everything is far different from what one had assumed (Lederer and Jackson, 1968: 39).*

Even if partners live together and feel that they know each other well, many couples may find themselves in the Swiss Alps instead of Florida after tying the knot. Numerous marriages dissolve because the partners cling to myths about conjugal life. After the perfect wedding, the perfect couple must be everything to each other: good providers, fantastic sexual partners, best friends, sympathetic confidantes, stimulating companions, and spiritual soul mates (Rubin, 1985). Are such expectations realistic?

Myths about the perfect family are just as pervasive as those about the perfect marriage. According to historian John Gillis (1996, 2004), we all have two families: one that we live *with* (the way families really are) and another that we live *by* (the way we would like families to be). Gillis maintains that people have been imagining and reimagining the family since at least the late Middle Ages because the families we are born and marry into seldom satisfy most people's need for a sense of continuity, belonging, unity, and rootedness.

Family Values: Three Perspectives on the Changing Family

We began this chapter with several definitions of the family. Then we examined the functions of the family, the ways families vary, and some myths about family

Making Connections

- Do media images of the family affect your perceptions? When you watch some TV shows, for example, do you feel disappointed in your own family?

- Do you believe any (or all) of the myths about marriage and the family that you have just read about? If so, are these beliefs functional or dysfunctional in your life?

life. Now we are ready to look at the major theme of this chapter: how the family is changing.

Several national surveys show that we place a high value on marriage and family. For example,

- Americans rank their family as the most important aspect of life, above health, work, money, and even religion (see *Figure 1.2*).

- Only 3 percent of Americans feel that morality and family values are problematic (Walczak et al., 2000).

- People cite traffic, urban sprawl, and crime as the biggest problems in their lives. Only 6 percent feel

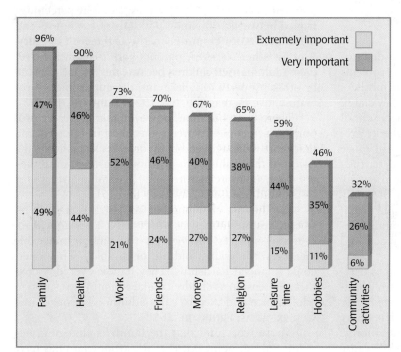

FIGURE 1.2   How Important Is Family Life?

Note: Results of Gallup Poll conducted December 5–8, 2002.

Source: David W. Moore, 2003, Gallup Poll Analysis.

that child and teen issues are a major concern (Knickerbocker, 2000).

- Nine in ten "millennial" teens (those born after 1982) say they trust and feel close to their parents and describe themselves as happy, confident, and positive (Howe et al., 2000).

Despite such upbeat findings, many people worry that the family is falling apart. Some journalists and scholars refer to the "vanishing" family, "troubled" marriages, and "appalling" divorce statistics as sure signs that the family is disintegrating. Others contend that such hand-wringing is unwarranted.

Who's right? There are three schools of thought. One group contends that the family is deteriorating, a second group argues that the family is changing but not deteriorating, and a third, smaller group maintains that the family is stronger than ever (see Benokraitis, 2000, for a discussion of these perspectives).

The Family Is Deteriorating

More than 100 years ago, the *Boston Quarterly Review* issued a dire warning: "The family, in its old sense, is disappearing from our land, and not only are our institutions threatened, but the very existence of our society is endangered" (cited in Rosen, 1982: 299). In the late 1920s, E. R. Groves (1928), a well-known social scientist, warned that marriages were in a state of "extreme collapse." Some of his explanations for what he called the "marriage crisis" and high divorce rates have a surprisingly modern ring: self-indulgence, too much luxury, extreme independence, financial strain, and incompatible personalities.

Even those who were optimistic a decade ago have become more pessimistic because of recent data on family "decay." Some of these data include high rates of divorce and children born out of wedlock, millions of "latchkey children," an increase in the number of people deciding not to get married, unprecedented numbers of single-parent families, and a decline of parental authority in the home.

Why have these changes occurred? Those who feel that the family is in trouble echo Groves, citing such reasons as lack of individual responsibility, lack of commitment to the family, and just plain selfishness. Many conservative politicians and

since you asked

"Most of the families I know are loving and close-knit. So why do many people think the family is in trouble?"

influential academics argue that the family is deteriorating because most people put their own needs above family duties. This school of thought claims that many adults are unwilling to invest their psychological and financial resources in their children or that they give up on their marriages too quickly when they encounter problems (Popenoe, 1996; Wilson, 2002).

Adherents of the family-decline school of thought point out that marriage should exist for the sake of children and not just for adults. Simply telling children we love them is not enough. Instead of wasting our money on divorce, the argument goes, we should be investing in children by maintaining a stable marriage. According to one observer:

A large divorce industry made up of lawyers, investigative accountants; real estate appraisers and salespeople; pension specialists; therapists and psychologists; expert witnesses; and private collectors of child support has sprung up to harvest the fruits of family discord. However necessary their services, these professionals are the recipients of family income that might, in happier circumstances . . . [be] invested in children (Whitehead, 1996: 11).

Many of those who endorse the "family is deteriorating" perspective blame most of the family's problems on mothers who work outside the home. If mothers stayed home and took care of their children, they claim, we would have less delinquency, fewer high school dropouts, and better-behaved children. Gallagher (1996: 184) argues, for example, that if women spent more time finding husbands who are good providers, they could "devote their talents and education and energy to the rearing of their children, the nurturing of family relationships, and the building of community and neighborhood." The implication is that the deteriorating family could be shored up if fathers were breadwinners and mothers were homemakers.

Many of those who believe that the family is deteriorating are communitarians, people who are politically more moderate than conservatives on some family issues. For example, they accept the idea that many mothers have to work outside the home for economic reasons. Communitarians claim, however, that because many adults focus almost exclusively on personal gratification, traditional family functions such as the care and socialization of young children have become a low priority (Glenn, 1996). They contend that there has been a general increase in a sense of entitlement (what people believe they should receive from others) and a decline in a sense of duty (what people believe they should give to others).

The Family Is Changing, Not Deteriorating

Other scholars argue that the family has not deteriorated as much as some people think. Instead, they say, the changes we are experiencing are extensions of long-standing family patterns.

Although more women have entered the labor force since 1970, the mother who works outside the home is not a new phenomenon. Mothers sold dairy products and woven goods during colonial times, took in boarders around the turn of the twentieth century, and held industrial jobs during World War II (see Chapter 3).

Many analysts contend that family problems such as desertion, out-of-wedlock birth, and child abuse have *always* existed. Family literature published in the 1930s, for example, included studies that dealt with issues such as divorce, desertion, and family crises due to discord, delinquency, and depression (Broderick, 1988).

Similarly, there have always been single-parent families. The percentage of single-parent households has doubled in the last three decades, but that percentage tripled between 1900 and 1950. Divorce is not recent; it became more common in the eighteenth century. Among other changes, parents had less control over their adult married children because there was little land or other property to inherit and the importance of romantic love increased (Cott, 1976; Stannard, 1979).

There is no question, however, that a greater proportion of people divorce today than in the past and that more marriages end in divorce. As a result, the decision of many singles to postpone marriage until they are older, are more mature, and have stable careers may be a sound one (see Chapters 9 and 15).

Families are changing but are also remarkably resilient, despite numerous adversities. They cope with everyday stresses and protect their most vulnerable members: the young, old, ill, or disabled. They overcome financial hardships. They handle everyday conflict and tension as children make a bumpy transition to adolescence and then to early adulthood (Conger and Conger, 2002; Patterson, 2002).

Those who hold that the family is changing, not deteriorating, point out that most poor families have stable and loving relationships despite constant worries and harsh economic environments. And many gay and lesbian families, despite rejection by much of "mainstream" society, are resilient and resourceful in developing successful family relationships (Oswald, 2002; Seccombe, 2002).

According to many researchers, there is little empirical evidence that family change is synonymous with family decline. Instead, there are data that support both perspectives—the belief that the family is in trouble as well as the notion that most families are resilient despite ongoing changes in gender roles, divorce rates, and alternatives to marriage such as living together (Amato, 2004).

The Family Is Stronger than Ever

Do our nostalgic myths about the past misinterpret the contemporary family as weak and on the decline? Yes, according to a third school of thought. These writers assert that family life is much more loving today than it was in the past. Consider the treatment of women and children in colonial days: If they disobeyed strict male authority, they were often severely punished. And, in contrast to some of our sentimental notions about "the good old days," only a small number of white, middle-class families enjoyed a life that was both gentle and genteel:

> *For every nineteenth-century middle-class family that protected its wife and child within the family circle . . . there was an Irish or a German girl scrub-*

bing floors in that middle-class home, a Welsh boy mining coal to keep the home-baked goodies warm, a black girl doing the family laundry, a black mother and child picking cotton to be made into clothes for the family, and a Jewish or an Italian daughter in a sweatshop making "ladies" dresses or artificial flowers for the family to purchase (Coontz, 1992: 11–12).

Some social scientists argue that despite myriad problems, families are happier today than in the past because of the increase in multigenerational relationships. Many people have living grandparents, feel closer to them, and often receive both emotional and economic support from these family members. The recent growth of the older segment of the population has produced four-generation families. More adults in their 60s may be stressed out because they are caring for 80- to 100-year-old parents. On the other hand, more children and grandchildren grow up knowing and enjoying their older relatives (see Chapter 17).

Some claim that families are stronger now than they were in the past because family members have more equitable roles at home and are more accepting of diverse family forms (such as single-parent homes, unmarried couple homes, and families with adopted children). And most Americans believe that marriage is a lifetime commitment that should end only under extreme circumstances, such as domestic violence (Thornton and Young-DeMarco, 2001).

Despite a sharp increase in the number of two-income families, in 1997 children between the ages of 3 and 12 spent, on average, about three to five more hours a week with their parents than comparable children did in 1981. The time spent together included activities such as reading, playing, conversing, and being in the same room while a parent did household tasks. Thus, contrary to popular belief, children spend more time with parents today than was the case several decades ago, and despite women's greater participation in the labor force (Sandberg and Hofferth, 2001).

Each of the three schools of thought provides evidence for its position. How, then, can we decide which perspective to believe? Is the family weak, or is it strong? The answer depends

Some cities and towns have refused to give unmarried partners, like the ones pictured here, a "permit of occupancy" because they and their children are not "a family." City officials say that the laws prevent "overcrowding." Others argue that such laws are "legislating morality" by defining the family as a married couple and their children.

largely on how we define, measure, and interpret family "weakness" and "strength," issues we address in Chapter 2. For better or worse, the family has never been static and continues to change.

Making Connections

- Which of the three perspectives on the family is closest to your own views? Why?

- Some of my students refuse to believe the data showing that many parents spend more time with their children than did earlier generations. Others agree with the studies because they feel that today's parents spend more "quality time" with their children, including school and community activities. What do you think?

Trends in Changing Families

The family is clearly changing. But how? And why? Demographic transitions, shifts in the racial and ethnic composition of families, and economic transformations all play a role in these changes.

Demographic Changes

Two demographic changes have had especially far-reaching consequences for family life. First, U.S. birth rates have declined. Since the end of the eighteenth century, most American women have been bearing fewer children, having them closer together, and finishing child rearing at an earlier age. Second, the average age of the population has risen from 17 in the mid-1800s to nearly 36 in 2004. Both of these shifts mean that a large proportion of the U.S. population now experiences the "empty-nest syndrome"—the departure of grown children from the home—at an earlier age, as well as earlier grandparenthood and prolonged widowhood (see Chapters 11, 17, and 18).

We see other changes in the composition of households as well: large numbers of cohabiting couples, higher divorce rates, and more one-parent families and working mothers (see *Figure 1.3*). We'll look at these changes briefly now and examine them more closely in later chapters.

CHANGES IN FAMILY AND NONFAMILY HOUSEHOLDS
The Census Bureau divides households into two categories: family and nonfamily. A *family household* con-

sists of two or more people living together who are related through marriage, birth, or adoption. *Nonfamily households* include people who live alone or with non-relatives (roommates, boarders, or cohabiting couples). In 2003, 32 percent of all households were nonfamily households, a substantial increase from 19 percent in 1970 (Fields, 2004).

The number of married-couple households with children under age 18 declined from 40 percent in 1970 to 23 percent in 2003 (see *Figure 1.3a*). The percentage of children under age 18 living in one-parent families more than doubled during this same period (see "Data Digest"). Part of the increase in one-parent families is due to the surge of births to unmarried women (see *Figure 1.3b*).

SINGLES AND COHABITING COUPLES
Singles make up one of the fastest-growing groups for three reasons. Many young adults are postponing marriage. At the other end of the age continuum, because people live longer, they are more likely than in the past to outlive a partner. In addition, older women who are divorced or widowed remarry at much lower rates than do older men (see Chapters 16 and 17).

The percentage of cohabiting couples has also climbed since 1970 (see *Figure 1.3c*). This number will probably grow because there is greater societal acceptance of unmarried couples living together (see Chapters 8 and 9).

MARRIAGE–DIVORCE–REMARRIAGE
The number of divorces rose between 1970 and 2004 (see *Figure 1.3d*). Even though divorce rates have decreased since 2000, almost one out of every two first marriages is expected to end in divorce. Teen marriages and marriages entered into because the woman became pregnant are especially likely to unravel (see Chapter 15).

Stepfamilies are also becoming much more common. About 12 percent of Americans are currently in their second, third, or fourth marriage. One of three Americans is now a stepparent, a stepchild, a stepsibling, or some other member of a stepfamily. We'll examine marriage, divorce, and remarriage more extensively in Chapters 10, 15, and 16.

ONE-PARENT FAMILIES
As more adults remain single into their 30s and because divorce rates are high, the number of children living with one parent has also increased (see "Data Digest"). The proportion of children living with a never-married parent has also grown, from 4 percent in 1960 to 42 percent in 2000.

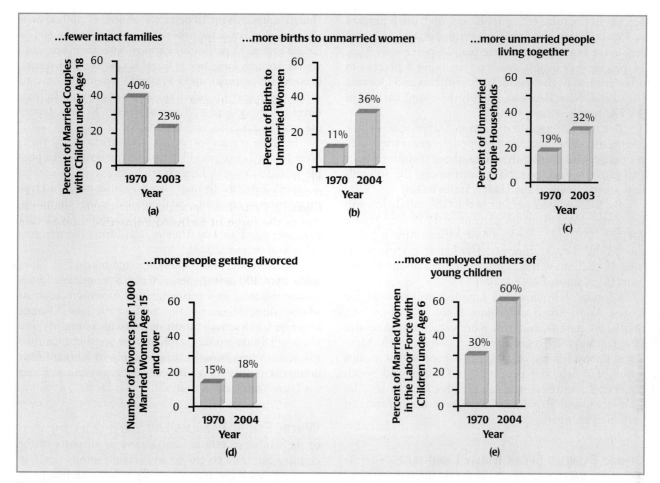

FIGURE 1.3   An Overview of Changes in U.S. Households since 1970

SOURCES: Fields, 2004; Popenoe and Whitehead, 2006; U.S. Census Bureau, 2006, Table 586.

Of all one-parent families, 83 percent are mother–child families (Hobbs and Stoops, 2002). We'll look at one-parent households more closely in several later chapters.

EMPLOYED MOTHERS The higher participation of mothers in the labor force is one of the most striking changes in American families. The percentage of two-earner married couples with children under age 18 rose from 31 percent in 1976 to 65 percent in 2004 (U.S. Census Bureau, 2002, 2006).

In addition, six out of every ten married women with children under 6 years old are in the labor force (see *Figure 1.3e*). This means that many couples are now coping with domestic and employment responsibilities while raising young children. We'll examine the characteristics and constraints of working mothers and two-earner couples in Chapter 13.

Racial and Ethnic Changes

What do you call a person who speaks three languages? Multilingual.

What do you call a person who speaks two languages? Bilingual.

What do you call a person who speaks one language? American.

As this joke suggests, many people stereotype (and ridicule) the United States as a single-language and a single-culture society. In reality, it's the most multicultural country in the world: Diversity is booming, ethnic groups speak many languages, and foreign-born families live in all the states.

ETHNIC FAMILIES ARE BOOMING The nation's foreign-born population, 34.2 million people, accounts for 12 percent of the total U.S. population, up from 8 percent in 1990. Within the foreign-born population, 53 percent were born in Latin America, 25 percent in Asia, 14 percent in Europe, and the remaining 8 percent in other regions of the world, such as Africa and Oceania (Australia, New Zealand, and all the island nations in the Pacific) (Bernstein, 2005).

Because of huge immigration waves, one in five people are either foreign-born or first-generation U.S. residents. Our multicultural rainbow includes about 150 distinct ethnic or racial groups among the 300 million people living in the United States today.

By 2025 only 62 percent of the U.S. population will be white, down from 86 percent in 1950 (see *Figure 1.4*). In 2003 Latinos edged past African Americans as the nation's largest minority. The Latino population is now 42 million, whereas blacks number about 35 million (U.S. Census Bureau, 2006).

Chinese, Filipinos, and Japanese still rank as the largest Asian American groups. Since 1990, however, Southeast Asians, Indians, Koreans, Pakistanis, and Bangladeshis have registered much faster growth. Mexicans, Puerto Ricans, and Cubans are the largest groups among Latinos, but people from Central and South American countries—such as El Salvador, Guatemala, Colombia, and Honduras—have been immigrating in very high numbers.

ETHNIC FAMILIES SPEAK MANY LANGUAGES Despite the earlier joke about Americans speaking only one language, approximately 336 languages are spoken in the United States. About 18 percent—almost 47 million people—speak a language other than English at home. The largest group, 11 percent, is Latinos. After them are those whose primary language at home is Chinese (2 percent), French (1.6 percent), and German (1.4 percent). Myriad other languages include Tagalog, Vietnamese, Italian, Greek, Hebrew, Arabic, Russian, Navajo, Korean, Japanese, and Hindi (Shin and Bruno, 2003).

In some states—especially California, New York, New Jersey, Texas, and Florida—the percentages of people who *don't* speak English are higher than those who *do* speak English. In many areas, for instance, a large proportion of residents speak Spanish rather than English: Hialeah, Florida (92 percent); Laredo, Texas (91 percent); and East Los Angeles, California (86 percent) (Shin and Bruno, 2003).

Nationwide, the Asian-language market includes more than 300 newspapers, 50 radio programs, 75 television shows, and miscellaneous products such as phone directories. By the mid-1990s one Orange County, California, station was broadcasting in Vietnamese 18 hours a day, and another southern California station was broadcasting entirely in Korean. One company publishes a Chinese-language Yellow Pages for New York City (Trumbull, 1995; Dortch, 1997).

WHERE ETHNIC FAMILIES LIVE Except for some areas of the Midwest, ethnic families live in all parts of the country but tend to cluster in certain regions (see *Figure 1.5*). Such clustering usually reflects employment opportunities and established immigrant communities

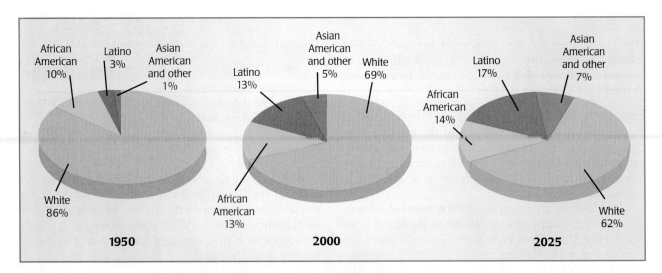

FIGURE 1.4 Racial and Ethnic Composition of the U.S. Population, 1950–2025

SOURCES: U.S. Census Bureau, www.census.gov/population/www.pop-profile/nat-proj.html and www.census.gov/population/cen2000/phc-t08/phc-t-08.pdf (accessed March 4, 2003).

that can help newcomers find housing and jobs. In some cases, however, past federal government policies have encouraged some communities to accept refugees from Southeast Asia, forced many American Indians to live on reservations, and implemented a variety of exclusionary immigration laws that limited certain Asian groups to specific geographic areas (see, for example, Kivisto and Ng, 2004).

This brief overview shows that ethnic families are numerous and increasing, speak many languages (though primarily Spanish), and live in practically every state. We'll examine ethnic families in every chapter, especially Chapter 4.

Why are Families Changing?

Clearly, families are changing. These changes reflect both the choices people make (such as deciding to marry later or to divorce) and the constraints that limit those choices (such as economic problems or caring for elderly parents).

To study people's choices, social scientists often take a **micro-level perspective,** focusing on individuals' social interactions in specific settings. To understand the constraints that limit people's options, they use a **macro-level perspective,** focusing on large-scale patterns that characterize society as a whole. Both perspectives, and

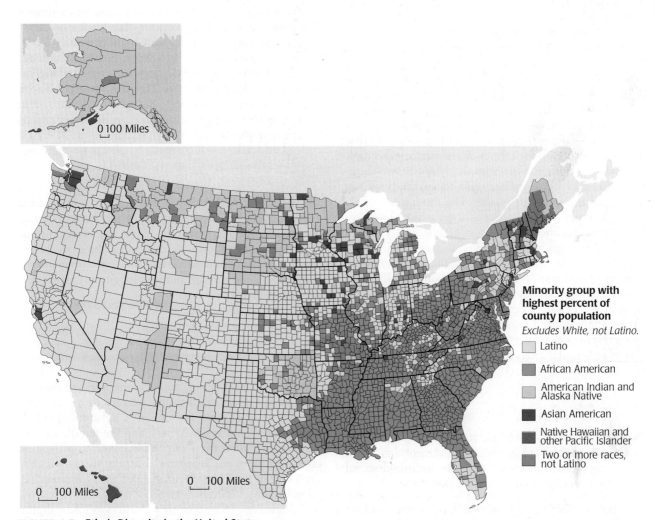

Minority group with highest percent of county population

Excludes White, not Latino.

- Latino
- African American
- American Indian and Alaska Native
- Asian American
- Native Hawaiian and other Pacific Islander
- Two or more races, not Latino

FIGURE 1.5   Ethnic Diversity in the United States

Look at where minority groups live. Do you see any patterns? Why do you think most blacks live in the East and Southeast? Why do so many Latinos live in the Midwest and Northwest?

Source: Brewer and Suchen, 2001, http://www.census.gov/population/cen2000/atlas/censr01-1.pdf (accessed February 26, 2003).

the ways in which they are interrelated, are crucial in understanding the family.

Micro-Level Influences on the Family

Consider the following scenario: Two students meet in college, fall in love, marry after graduation, find well-paying jobs, and live the good life, feasting on lobster, driving a Corvette, and the like. Then they have an unplanned child. The wife quits her job to take care of the baby, the husband loses his job, and the wife goes to work part time. She has difficulty balancing her multiple roles of mother, wife, and employee. The stress and arguments between the partners increase, and the marriage ends.

When I ask my students what went wrong, most of them take a micro viewpoint and criticize the couple: "They should have saved some money," "They didn't need a Corvette," "Haven't they heard about contraceptives?" and so on. Almost all the students blame the divorce on the two people involved because they were unrealistic or immature or made "lousy" decisions.

On the one hand, there's much to be said for micro-level explanations. As you will see throughout this book, some of the biggest societal changes affecting families began with the efforts of one person who took a stand on an issue. For example, Mary Beth Whitehead refused to give up her right to see the baby she had borne as a surrogate mother. The ensuing court battles created national debates about the ethics of new reproductive technologies. As a result, many states instituted surrogacy legislation (see Chapter 11).

On the other hand, micro explanations should be kept in perspective. Many marriage and family textbooks and pop psychology books stress the importance of individual choices but ignore macro-level variables. Micro analyses are limited. They cannot explain some of the things over which families have very little control. For these broader analyses, we must turn to macro explanations.

Macro-Level Influences on the Family

Constraints such as economic forces, technological innovations, popular culture, social movements, and family policies limit our choices. These are broad social issues that require macro-level explanations.

ECONOMIC FORCES The Industrial Revolution and urbanization sparked widespread changes that had major impacts on the family (see Chapter 3). By the late eighteenth century, factories had replaced the local industries that employed large numbers of women and children. As families became less self-sufficient and fam-

ily members increasingly worked outside the home, parents' control over their children diminished.

In the latter half of the twentieth century, many corporations moved their companies to developing countries to increase their profits. Such moves resulted in relocations and unemployment for many U.S. workers. These changes created job dissatisfaction, unemployment, and financial distress, all of which disrupted marital relationships and families.

Many African Americans have been concerned that immigration, another macro factor, is cutting into their job opportunities. As you've just read, Latinos and Asians constitute the fastest-growing groups in the United States. A large proportion of African Americans are employed in skilled and semiskilled blue-collar jobs. The influx of new immigrants, who compete with native-born workers for such jobs, constitutes a serious economic threat to many working-class blacks and, consequently, to their families (see Chapters 4 and 13).

As the nature of the U.S. economy has changed, millions of low-paying service jobs have replaced higher-paying manufacturing jobs. This has wrought havoc with many families' finances, contributing to the rise in the number of employed mothers. At the other end of the continuum, the higher-paying jobs require at least a college education, which tends to postpone marriage and parenthood (see Chapters 9 and 11).

TECHNOLOGICAL INNOVATIONS Advances in medical and other health-related technologies have led to a decline in birth rates and to longer life spans. The invention and availability of the birth-control pill in the early 1960s meant that women could prevent unwanted pregnancies, pursue higher education, and seek long-term careers. Improved prenatal and postnatal care has also released women from the need to bear six or seven children so that one or two will survive to adulthood.

since you asked

Has technology decreased the quality of our family relationships?

On the other hand, because the average man or woman can now expect to live into his or her 80s and beyond, poverty after retirement is more likely. Medical services can eat up savings, and the middle-aged—sometimes called the "sandwich generation"—must cope both with the demands of raising their own children and helping their aged parents (see Chapters 12, 17, and 18).

Television, videocassette recorders (VCRs), digital video discs (DVDs), microwave ovens, and personal computers (PCs) have also affected families. On the negative side, for example, multiple television sets in a home often dilute parental control over the programs that young children watch.

On the positive side, television can enhance children's intellectual development. According to a recent study, for example, children aged 2 to 7 who spent a few hours a week watching educational programs such as *Sesame Street, Reading Rainbow, Mr. Wizard's World,* and *3-2-1 Contact* had higher academic test scores three years later than those who didn't watch such programs. Children who viewed many hours of sitcoms and cartoons had lower test scores than those who rarely watched such programs (Wright et al., 2001).

Some people feel that electronic mail (e-mail), instant messaging (IM), and discussion lists are intrusive because some users of these technologies replace close personal relationships with superficial but time-consuming online interactions. College students who spend four to seven hours a day online for nonacademic reasons may earn low grades and experience the risk of dismissal, poorer health because of sleep loss, and greater social isolation. Among other problems, frequent Internet usage decreases participation in extracurricular activities and opportunities to meet new people. In the general population, people who spend more than ten hours a week on the Internet report a decrease in social activities and less time spent talking on the phone with friends and family (Nie and Erbring, 2000; Reisberg, 2000).

On the other hand, e-mail has encouraged long-distance conversations between parents, children, and relatives that might otherwise not occur because of busy schedules or high telephone costs. Family members who are scattered coast to coast can become more connected by exchanging photos on their own Web pages (including background music and voice commentary), organizing family reunions, tracking down distant relatives, or tracing their ancestral roots (Kanaley, 2000).

POPULAR CULTURE Popular culture—which includes television, pop music, magazines, radio, advertising, sports, hobbies, fads, fashions, and movies—is one of our major sources of information *and* misinformation about our values, roles, and family life. Television is especially influential in transmitting both fact and fiction because in a 65-year lifetime, the average American spends nine years in front of a TV set (*www.tvturnoff.org*) (see Chapter 5).

Compared with even five years ago, today there are many programs on black families (see *Table 1.1*). But even though Asian and Latino families are huge consumers of prime-time television, they're almost invisible, except for an occasional show such as *George Lopez*. And, to my knowledge, there isn't a single family program that features Asian or Middle Eastern families. We'll examine the effects of popular culture on families in Chapter 5.

In 2005, tens of thousands of men converged on Washington, D.C. for the second Million Man March. The purpose of the march was to demand social and economic equality for African American and low-income families and to inspire young men, especially, to be more responsible for their children.

SOCIAL MOVEMENTS Over the years, a number of social movements have changed family life. These macro-level movements include the civil rights movement, the women's movement, the gay rights movement, and most recently, a marriage movement.

The *civil rights movement* of the 1960s had a great impact on most U.S. families. Because of affirmative action legislation, many African Americans and Latinos were able to take advantage of educational and economic opportunities that improved their families' socioeconomic status. Many black and Latino students were accepted at privileged colleges and universities, families received money to start small businesses, and a number of productive employees were promoted (see Chapters 4 and 13).

The *women's movements*—in the late 1800s and especially in the 1970s—transformed many women's roles and, consequently, family life. As women gained more rights in law, education, and employment, many became less financially dependent on men and started questioning traditional assumptions about gender roles.

The *gay rights movement* that began in the 1970s challenged discriminatory laws in such areas as housing, adoption, and employment. Many lesbian women and gay men (as well as sympathetic heterosexuals) feel that those challenges have resulted in very modest changes so far. There has been progress, however. Children with gay or lesbian parents, for example, are likely to be less stigmatized than they were a decade ago. Numerous companies now provide benefits to their employees' gay or lesbian partners; a number of adoption agencies assist lesbians and gays who want to become parents; and numerous municipalities and states recognize civil unions (see Chapters 8–12).

People who are alarmed by high divorce rates and the increase in cohabitation are joining a burgeoning *marriage movement*. Among other things, the marriage movement seeks to repeal no-fault divorce laws and wants to reduce out-of-wedlock births and state benefits for children born to unmarried low-income mothers. It also promotes abstinence among young people, lobbies for funding for programs that promote marriage, and embraces women's homemaker roles.

In addition, the marriage movement encourages proponents to lobby lawmakers to pass state "covenant marriage" laws that require couples to take premarital counseling classes and "marital skills" programs (see Chapter 9). As the box titled "Should Uncle Sam Be a

---

Ask Yourself

Should Uncle Sam Be a Matchmaker?

In 2003, Congress passed a bill that allotted $1.5 billion over five years to promote marriage as part of welfare reform. The money would be used for a variety of promarriage initiatives, including the following:

- Encouraging caseworkers to counsel pregnant women to marry the father of the child
- Reducing the rate of out-of-wedlock births
- Teaching about the value of marriage in high schools
- Providing divorce counseling for the poor
- Sponsoring programs that might produce more marriages

A very vocal marriage movement enthusiastically endorses such initiatives. According to many of its members, government programs should encourage cohabiting parents to marry and discourage married parents from divorcing (Lichter and Crowley, 2002).

Some of the movement's members justify marriage initiatives by pointing to the economic costs—from welfare to child support enforcement—that states incur because of high divorce rates and out-of-wedlock birth rates.

Others, such as conservative religious groups, also endorse promarriage legislation. They maintain that the government should pass policies to support and strengthen marriage because "marriage and family are institutions ordained by God" (Wilcox, 2002).

Promoting matrimony is not a novel idea. For several years a number of states have been using federal welfare money to foster marriage. West Virginia, for example, gives couples on public assistance an additional $100 a month if they marry or stay married. Some states provide premarital classes. And Oklahoma paid $250,000 to "a couple of gurus to hold 'relationship rallies' on campuses around the state" (Goodman, 2003).

Compared with children raised in two-parent homes, those raised in single-parent homes are at greater risk of poverty, school dropouts, delinquency, teen pregnancy, and adult joblessness (see Chapters 11–13). Researchers don't know, however, how many people are poor because they are unmarried and how many are unmarried because they are poor.

Some scholars point out that a husband's income is often too low to lift a family out of poverty (Ooms et al., 2004). In addition, critics charge that promoting marriage for low-income women stigmatizes them (but not high-income unmarried mothers) and compels them to stay in abusive or unhappy relationships.

Some directors of fatherhood programs are also opposed to promarriage legislation. They believe that marriage is not a "quick fix" because many poor men have a lot of problems. As Robert Brady of the Young Fathers Program in Denver observed, "I wonder if these conservatives would be so dedicated to marriage promotion if it was their daughters they were trying to marry these guys off to" (Starr, 2001: 68).

Stop and Think . . .

- Should the government pressure low-income mothers to marry? Do you think that such strategies will reduce poverty?
- Is the government "meddling" in people's private affairs? Or doing "what's good for us"?

Matchmaker?" shows, however, many people feel that the government should stay out of people's private lives.

FAMILY POLICIES Government policies affect practically every aspect of family life. Thousands of rules and regulations, both civil and criminal—at the local, state, and federal levels—govern domestic matters: Laws about when and whom we can marry, how to dissolve a marriage, how to treat one another in the home, and even how to dispose of our dead. And, increasingly, there has been a "substantial" effort by the government to encourage people to form and maintain marital relationships (Brotherson and Duncan, 2004).

Families do not just passively accept policy changes, however. Parents have played critical roles in major social policy changes such as those dealing with the education of disabled children and joint custody of children after divorce. Chapter 18 and sections of several other chapters examine the effects of government policy on families in greater detail.

A Cross-Cultural and Global Perspective

Why does this textbook include material on subcultures within the United States (American Indians, African Americans, Asian Americans, Middle Eastern Americans, and Latinos) and cultures in other countries? First, unless you are a full-blooded American Indian, your kin were slaves or immigrants to this country. They contributed their cultural beliefs, and their beliefs and practices shaped current family institutions. The U.S. population today is a mosaic of many cultural, religious, ethnic, racial, and socioeconomic groups. Thus, a traditional white, middle-class model is not adequate for understanding our marriages and families.

A second reason for this multicultural and cross-cultural approach is that the world is shrinking. Compared with even ten years ago, more people are traveling outside the United States, more students from abroad attend North American colleges and universities, and more exchange programs for students and scholars are offered at all educational levels.

Students value their study-abroad experiences. In a study of students at Northern Arizona University, for example, those who had participated in international-study programs described their experiences as eye-opening and memorable in understanding other cultures. Consider, for example, a third-year hospitality

since you asked

Why does this text discuss family practices and customs in other cultures besides ours?

management student who went to Italy for a year of studies:

> When she sat down for dinner with her host family on her very first night, she asked for some water with her meal, a common request in the United States. Yet, the response she got from a 75-year-old Italian was not what she had expected: "Wine is for drinking, water is for washing," he said. With this, she was welcomed to the world of living and studying abroad (Van Hoof and Verbeeten, 2005: 42).

In the late twentieth century, the Internet changed our communication processes significantly, effectively "shrinking" the modern world. As members of the global community, we should be aware of family practices and customs in other cultures.

A third reason for this text's cross-cultural emphasis is that U.S. businesses recognize the importance of understanding other societies. Since the late 1980s, more companies have been requiring their employees to take courses about other cultures before going abroad. For example, one of my students, who won a job with a Fortune 500 company, felt that she had an edge over some very tough competitors because of her knowledge of Portuguese and of Brazilian culture.

Fourth, understanding the customs of other countries challenges our notion that U.S. family forms are the norm. According to Hutter (1998: 12), "Americans have been notorious for their lack of understanding and ignorance of other cultures. This is compounded by their gullible ethnocentric belief in the superiority of all things American and not only has made them unaware of how others live and think but also has given them a distorted picture of their own life." Hutter's perspective—and that of this book—is that understanding other people helps us understand ourselves.

Finally, families are changing around the world. Instead of clinging to stereotypes about other countries, cross-cultural knowledge and information "may result in understanding instead of conflict" (Adams, 2004: 1076).

Conclusion

Families are transforming, not destroying, themselves. Although there have been *changes* in family structures, families of all kinds seek caring, supportive, comforting, and enduring relationships. There is nothing inherently better about one type of family form than another. Moreover, family structures don't appear by themselves.

People create families that can meet their needs for love and security.

These greatly expanded *choices* in family structure and function mean that the definition of family no longer reflects the interests of any one social class, gender, or ethnic group. This fluidity generates new questions. Who, for example, will ensure that children will grow up to be healthy and responsible adults if both parents must work outside the home? Is it possible to pursue personal happiness without sacrificing obligations to other family members?

Our choices often are limited by *constraints,* especially at the macro level, because of economic conditions and government policies. To deal with changes, choices, and constraints, we need as much information as possible about the family. In the next chapter we will see how scientists conduct research on families, gathering data that make it possible for us to track the trends described in this and other chapters and to make informed decisions about our choices.

Summary

1.   Although the nuclear family—composed of husband, wife, and children—is still predominant in U.S. society, this definition of *family* has been challenged by those who believe it should include less traditional arrangements such as single parents, childfree couples, foster parents, and siblings sharing a home. Advances in reproductive technology have opened up the possibility of still more varied definitions of the family.

2.   The family continues to fulfill basic functions such as producing and socializing children, providing family members with emotional support, legitimizing and regulating sexual activity, and placing family members in society.

3.   Marriages, families, and kinship systems vary in terms of whether marriages are monogamous or polygamous, whether familial authority is vested in the man or the woman or both share power, and whether a new family resides with the family of the man or the woman or creates its own home.

4.   Myths about the family include erroneous beliefs about the nature of the family in "the good old days," the "naturalness" of marriage and family as human interpersonal and social arrangements, the self-sufficiency of the family, the family as a refuge from outside pressures, and the "perfect family."

5.   Social scientists generally agree that the family is changing. They disagree, however, as to whether it is changing in drastic and essentially unhealthy ways, whether it is simply continuing to adapt and adjust to changing circumstances, or whether it is changing in ways that will ultimately make it stronger.

6.   Many changes are occurring in U.S. families: There is more racial and ethnic diversity, family forms are more varied, and there are more single-parent families, stepfamilies, and families in which the mother works outside the home.

7.   The reasons for changes in the family can be analyzed on two levels. Micro-level explanations emphasize individual behavior: the choices that people make and the personal and interpersonal factors that influence these choices. Macro-level explanations focus on large-scale patterns that characterize society as a whole and often constrain individual options. Some constraints arise from economic factors, technological advances, popular culture, social movements, and government policies that affect families.

8.   Understanding the family requires an appreciation of racial, gender, ethnic, religious, and cultural diversity, both at home and around the world.

Key Terms

marriage   *4*
norm   *4*
common-law marriage   *5*
bigamy   *5*
family   *5*
fictive kin   *6*
nuclear family   *7*
incest taboo   *9*

endogamy   *9*
exogamy   *9*
socialization   *9*
roles   *9*
primary groups   *10*
secondary groups   *10*
social class   *10*
family of orientation   *11*

family of procreation   *11*
kinship system   *11*
extended family   *11*
monogamy   *11*
serial monogamy   *11*
polygamy   *11*
micro-level perspective   *24*
macro-level perspective   *24*

Taking It Further

Examine U.S. and Global Family Trends

Does your instructor want you to compare family trends and patterns in the United States and worldwide? Here are a few sites to get you started:

The **United Nations Statistics Division** maintains a list of statistical bureaus of nations to help you find family and household information for other countries.

unstats.un.org

The **U.S. Census Bureau,** an invaluable resource, contains current and historical material on many characteristics of marriages and families.

www.census.gov

The **International Data Base** at the U.S. Census Bureau offers a variety of country-level data, including marital status, family planning, ethnicity, religion, labor force, and employment.

www.census.gov/ipc/www/idbnew.html

Statistical Abstract of the United States, also from the U.S. Census Bureau, provides a wealth of information about marriage, remarriage, family characteristics, living arrangements, divorce, and hundreds of other variables.

www.census.gov/compendia/statab

The **Population Reference Bureau** maintains numerous sites that may be valuable in your research. The links include maps and reports on marriages and families in the United States and many other countries.

www.prb.org

And more: If your instructor assigns a "do-whatever-interests-you" project, look at www.prenhall.com/benokraitis for Websites that include information about ethnic families, black communities, social movements, global statistics, liberal and conservative think tanks about the family, the social and economic implications of information technologies, groups that endorse and denounce polygamy, and an online comic strip about a middle-class Latino family.

Investigate with Research Navigator

Welcome to the Research Navigator™ feature that will end each chapter of this textbook. To access the Research Navigator™ Website, find the access code on the inside front cover of your *Evaluating Online Resources Guide.* (If your textbook was not packaged with an *Evaluating Online Resources Guide,* you can purchase an access code at the Research Navigator™ site.) Visit the Research Navigator™ site at http://www.researchnavigator.com and click on REGISTER under the New Users tab. Enter your access code and relevant information to create your own LOGIN NAME and PASSWORD. After registering, you can return to this site and fill in the LOGIN NAME and PASSWORD on the initial page.

On the opening page, you have three relevant search engines to begin your research. They include:

(1) ContentSelect™—a collection of peer-reviewed academic journals organized by discipline; (2) the *New York Times* Search-by-Subject archive, which includes an 18-month database of articles from *The New York Times;* and (3) the *Best of the Web* Link Library—a wealth of links, divided by topic. At the end of each chapter you will find key words to use as a starting point for your research. Enter these words into the various search fields while selecting the appropriate databases.

Search the Research Navigator™ site using the following key search terms:

monogamy
kinship
patriarchy

Outline

Studying Marriage and the Family

Data Digest

■ **A typical interview can cost about $75 an hour,** including training, pretesting, transportation, wages, and follow-up interviews.

■ **The return rate for census questionnaires has decreased** over the years: 78 percent in 1970, 75 percent in 1980, and 65 percent in 1990 and 2000.

■ During the 2000 census, **the cost per individual mailing** was $2, compared with $36 every time a census worker visited a nonrespondent's home as part of a follow-up when the questionnaire wasn't filled out.

■ **People are less trusting of some types of surveys than others.** In a recent study, 81 percent of respondents were willing to rely on scientific studies that describe the causes of disease, 63 percent believed consumer survey reports of how many people like a particular product, but only 54 percent said they trusted the results of general public opinion polls.

■ From 2000 to 2001, businesses increased their spending on **online survey research** by 53 percent, to $400 million.

Sources: Crossen, 1994; Edmonston, 1999; Libbon, 2000; Wellner, 2003.

When my mother died a few years ago, the funeral director called *twice* to confirm the information about her death before submitting it to Maryland's Division of Vital Statistics. Even though I provided the same, accurate, data both times, the death certificate contained three errors. First, my mother died at age 87, *not* 88. Second, she had completed ten years of education, *not* eight. Third, because my mother never smoked, tobacco did *not* contribute to her death.

When I see such mistakes, I wince. Here's a good example, I thought, of why many people—including my students—often distrust statistics. "Statistics mean never having to say you're certain," some quip. Others firmly believe the well-known quote, "There are three kinds of lies: lies, damned lies, and statistics."

Data collection isn't perfect. Even so, it's a far better source of information about families and other topics than personal opinions, experiential anecdotes, or other nonscientific ways of understanding our world.

This chapter will help you evaluate the enormous amount of information we encounter on a daily basis. It will also help you understand how the researchers cited in this text collected their data. Let's begin with a discussion of why a basic understanding of family theory and research is important.

Why are Theories and Research Important in Our Everyday Lives?

The very words *theory* and *research* are often intimidating. Many of us may distrust statistics because they typically challenge generally accepted beliefs. Most of my students, for example, believe that cohabitation decreases the chance of divorce. They are surprised when research shows that this is not the case (see Chapter 9).

since you asked

Because I don't plan to do research, why should I read this chapter?

There are three very practical reasons why theory and research are important to us: (1) what we don't know can hurt us, (2) theories and research help us understand ourselves and our families, and (3) they improve our ability to think more critically and make informed decisions in our own marriages and families.

What We Don't Know Can Hurt Us

Millions of people use the Internet to buy products, do research related to their jobs, and get information about family issues. When people are perplexed by problems involving divorce and stepfamilies, for example, they often seek help both online and offline.

Many Websites are maintained by people who know next to nothing about family issues but are looking to make a profit. Some of these sites charge consumers up to $5,000 to become "certified stepfamily counselors," even though there is no such certification requirement in the United States. Other sites charge people $500 for eight hours of audiotapes on how to lead marriage workshops (Siwolop, 2002). Needless to say, no one can become knowledgeable about leading such workshops after listening to only a few hours of audiotapes.

An estimated 100 million Americans go online every month to search for health information. About 75 percent say that what they find influences their decisions about treatment (Baker et al., 2003). How accurate is the health information on the Web? As the box "Should I Consult Dr. Web?" shows, fewer than half the sites offer both complete and accurate information on problems such as depression and childhood obesity; this is especially true of Spanish-language sites. As a result, we are likely to obtain incorrect information, and the misinformation we get could actually shorten our lives.

Theories and Research Help Us Understand Our Family Life

Theoretical perspectives and research can illuminate many aspects of our family life. For example, does spanking correct a child's misbehavior? Suppose a 2-year-old throws a temper tantrum at a family barbecue. One adult comments, "What that kid needs is a good smack on the behind." Another person immediately disagrees: "All kids go through this stage. Just ignore it." Who's right? In fact, empirical studies show that neither ignoring a problem nor inflicting physical punishment stops bad behavior (see Chapter 12).

Theories and Research Help Us Make Informed Decisions

We rarely pick up a magazine or newspaper without coming across statistics that affect some aspect of our lives. We listen numbly to the probabilities of dying earlier than expected because of our genetic inheritance, lifestyle, or environment. We are inundated with information on the importance of exercising, losing weight, lowering cholesterol levels, and not smoking.

Some of the information is sound, but much is biased, inaccurate, or generated by unlicensed, self-proclaimed "experts." They whip up anxieties and then sell solutions that include their own books and "consulting" services. As the box "Popular Magazines and Self-Help Books: Let the Reader Beware" shows, one of the best ways to protect yourself against quacks and con artists is to be informed.

Students in family courses that include discussions of scientific studies often feel that they and their instructor are on different planets. At the beginning of a semester, for example, I've heard my students grumble, "I took this course to find out how to avoid a divorce after I get married. Who cares about divorce research!"

In fact, by learning something about scientific evidence, you will be able to make more informed decisions about finding a suitable mate and, quite possibly,

Ask Yourself

Should I Consult Dr. Web?

About 63 million Americans—37 percent of those who use the Internet—search for health information. Visits to medical sites grow by about 23 percent a year, but is the information always reliable?

A team of 34 physician-reviewers evaluated almost 20,000 printed pages in English-language sites and more than 2,000 pages from Span-

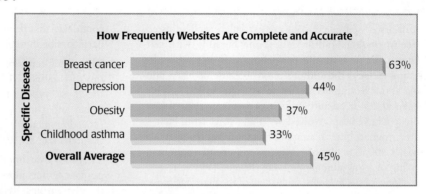

ish-language sites on four medical conditions on the Web. All the reviewers were board-certified in family medicine, pediatrics, internal medicine, and other specializations.

The researchers concluded that

- Many sites contain contradictory information. In the case of depression, for example, some sites recommend St. John's wort, whereas others state that St. John's wort is ineffective. In fact, St. John's wort, if consumed with other medications such as Prozac, can sometimes be fatal.
- Some sites recommend investigating a breast lump only if it doesn't change over time. Others urge people to consult a physician as soon as they notice a lump. Waiting for a lump to change instead of immediately seeking medical advice can cause a delay in discovering breast cancer, which might be inoperable by the time it's diagnosed.
- Many online users may not understand the information. Nearly half of all adults in the United States can't read material above the eighth-grade level. But all English-language sites and 86 percent of Spanish-language sites require that a person be able to read material at the high school level or above.

Sources: Berland et al., 2001a, 2001b; Foreman, 2005 (see the *Taking It Further* section at the end of this chapter for reliable information on health).

avoid a divorce. In addition, knowing something about *how* social scientists study families will enhance your ability to think critically and vote intelligently on family policy issues (see Chapter 18).

In scholarly journals, peers (other scholars) review research before it is published. In contrast, the mass media are largely immune to criticism, even when their reports are biased, simplistic, or wrong (Gans, 1979). As a result, many people who rely exclusively on the media for information often get a very skewed picture of marriages, families, and other aspects of life.

This chapter will not transform you into a researcher, but it will help you ask some of the right questions when you are deluged with popular nonsense. Let's begin with the most influential theories of marriage and the family that guide social-scientific investigations.

Theoretical Frameworks for Understanding Families

Someone once observed, "I used to have six theories about parenting and no children. Now I have six children and no theories." This quip suggests that there is no relationship between theory and practice. As you saw in Chapter 1, however, theories about families are often translated into policies and laws that affect all of us.

Ideas have consequences. For example, people who theorize that the family is disintegrating might propose micro-level solutions such as cutting

since you asked

Why isn't there one nice, simple theory about the family?

Choices

Popular Magazines and Self-Help Books: Let the Reader Beware

Authors of self-help books are extremely well-adjusted, free of phobias and anxieties, and bursting with self-esteem. Right? Wrong. A best-selling book on phobias, for example, lacks the author's photo because he has a phobia about having his picture taken (Quick, 1992). Husband and wife co-authors of a two-volume textbook on divorce have been involved in "'the divorce from Hell'— a very public, bitter blizzard of litigation that has spawned nearly 400 legal filings," including arguments about ownership of a low-number auto tag (Ringle, 1999: C1).

Some of the most ardent leaders of the marriage movement (see Chapter 1) have been divorced at least once. And just before he died at age 94, Dr. Benjamin Spock, a family expert and author of best-selling books on childrearing for over 50 years, agreed with his estranged sons that he had been too career-driven to spend much time with his family (Maier, 1998).

Many self-help books and articles in popular magazines are bogus because they are based on personal opinion and experience rather than on scholarly research. Perhaps the single best thing about some magazine articles is that they encourage people to try to change their lives. But they also "violate commonly accepted standards of scholarship" (Rosenblatt and Phillips, 1975). As a result, self-help books and articles can create four serious problems:

1. **They can threaten relationships.** Many articles encourage the reader to make new demands on a spouse or children. Such one-sided commands can increase conflict to levels that the family may not be able to handle.

2. **They can make partners feel inadequate.** Many popular writers tie a person's feelings of adequacy to family relationships. This ignores the satisfaction and self-confidence that people can get from work, friendships, participation in organizations, and solitary pursuits.

3. **They often reinforce gender stereotypes.** Several of the best-selling self-help parenting books insist that the "best" type of family is one with a breadwinner father and a stay-at-home mother and that employed women are selfish and terrible mothers (Kratchick et al., 2005).

4. **They may oversimplify complex problems.** Many popular writers gloss over complicated factors in family relationships. Reduced frequency of sexual intercourse can lead to depression, some "experts" claim. In fact, many factors may trigger depression, and sex isn't at the top of the list (see Chapters 7 and 10).

Stop and Think . . .

As you read articles and books about the family, ask yourself the following questions:

- Does the writer cite research or clinical experience or only anecdotal material as sources? If the writer cites himself or herself, are the references scholarly or only personal stories? According to one scholar, "If modern science has learned anything in the past century, it is to distrust anecdotal evidence" (Park, 2003: B20).

- Does the author describe only a few families with problems but generalize the "findings" to all families?

- Does the writer make it sound as though life is exceedingly simple and easy to understand, such as following ten steps for marital happiness? Family interaction and behavior are much more complex than throwing a few ingredients into the pot and stirring.

off welfare benefits for unmarried mothers. In contrast, those who theorize that the family is changing might propose macro-level remedies such as providing girls and young women with good schooling and jobs that discourage early sexual involvement and pregnancy (see Chapter 11).

As people struggle to understand family-related processes, they develop theories. A **theory** is a set of statements that explains why a particular phenomenon occurs. Theories drive research, help us to analyze our findings, and ideally, offer solutions for family problems.

One family sociologist compares theories to the fable of the six blind men who felt different parts of an elephant and arrived at different explanations of what elephants were like. The man who felt the side of the elephant compared it to a massive, immovable wall. The man who felt the trunk thought the elephant was like a rope that could move large objects. Similarly, different theories explain different aspects of the elephant—in this case, marriages and families (Burr, 1995).

There are eight influential theories about marriages and families: four macro-level theories (ecological, structural-functional, conflict, and feminist perspectives) and four micro-level theories (symbolic interaction, social exchange, family life course development, and family systems perspectives) (see *Figure 2.1*). Researchers typically use more than one theory in examining any given topic, and the theories often overlap. For greater clarity, let's look at each perspective separately. (Don't worry about concepts such as *theoretical frameworks, theories, approaches,* and *perspectives.* Many social scientists use these terms interchangeably.)

The Ecological Perspective

Ecological theory stresses the importance of understanding the relationships between individuals and the social environments that shape human development.

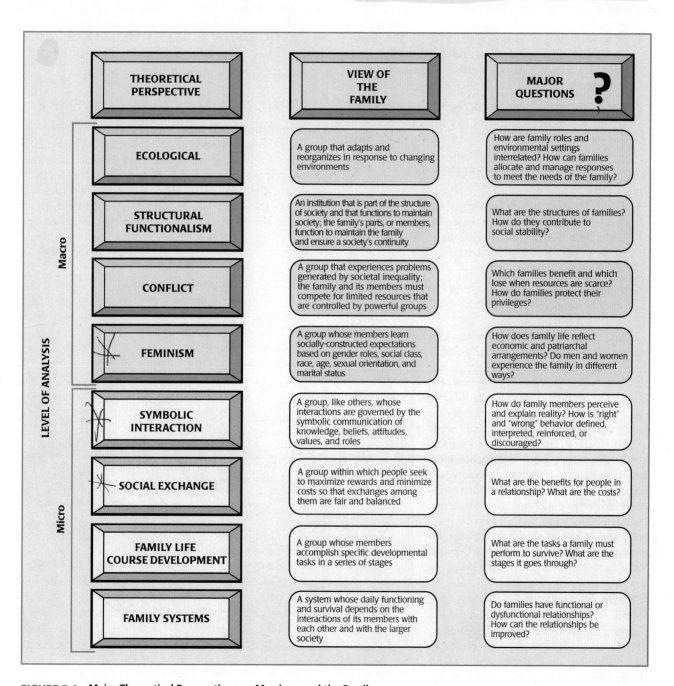

FIGURE 2.1   Major Theoretical Perspectives on Marriage and the Family

Urie Bronfenbrenner (1979, 1986), a major advocate of ecological theory, proposed that four interlocking systems mold our developmental growth.

INTERLOCKING SYSTEMS These systems range from the most "immediate" settings, such as the family and peer group, to more "remote" contexts in which the child is not involved directly, such as technological changes and ideological beliefs (see *Figure 2.2*). The four systems are the following:

1. The *microsystem,* which is made up of the interconnected behaviors, roles, and relationships that influence a child's daily life (such as parents toilet-training their child).

2. The *mesosystem,* which comprises the relationships among different settings (for example, the home, a day-care center, and schools). Parents interact with teachers and religious groups; children interact with peers; health-care providers interact with both children and parents.

3. The *exosystem,* which consists of settings or events that a child does not experience directly but that can affect her or his development (such as parents' employment).

4. The *macrosystem,* the wider society and culture that encompasses all the other systems.

All four of these embedded systems, or environments, can help or hinder a child's development and a family's functioning. Successful drug-prevention programs, for example, should be multifaceted: They must understand the teenager's specific family dynamics, address the unique needs of a particular neighborhood, and involve local organizations (such as churches, businesses, and colleges) to offer alternatives to high-risk behavior. Such alternatives include not selling alcohol to adolescents, providing education and support for parents, and involving youth in meaningful community projects (Bogenschneider, 1996).

CRITICAL EVALUATION Researchers have found ecological theory useful in explaining family dynamics and proposing programs to deal with such issues as youth violence and special needs adoptions. Critics note several weaknesses, however. Ecological theories try to ex-plain growth because of changes in the environment, but explanations of disintegration (such as aging) are "notably absent." In addition, it is not always apparent exactly how and when environments produce changes in individuals and families. Finally, it's unclear how the interactions among the four systems affect nontraditional families such as stepfamilies, gay and lesbian households, and intergenerational families living under one roof. Because the ecological perspective describes primarily nuclear, heterosexual, and white families, some critics have wondered how "nontraditional" families fit in (Ganong et al., 1995; White and Klein, 2002; Telleen et al., 2003; Schweiger and O'Brien, 2005).

The Structural-Functional Perspective

Structural-functional theory examines the relationship between the family and the larger society. When social scientists study family structure, they examine how the parts work together to fulfill the functions or tasks necessary for the family's survival. Adult family tasks are best accomplished when spouses carry out two distinct and specialized types of roles. One type is called *in-*

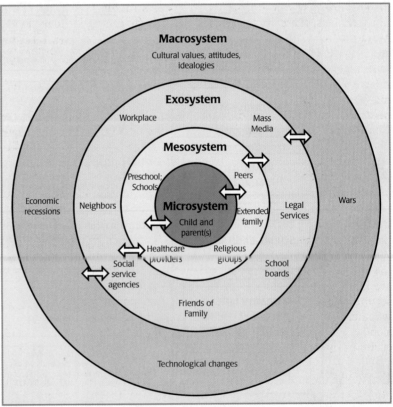

FIGURE 2.2 An Ecological Model of Development

SOURCE: Based on Bronfenbrenner, 1979.

strumental, the other *expressive* (Parsons and Bales, 1955).

FAMILY ROLES The husband or father, the "breadwinner," performs **instrumental roles**: providing food and shelter for the family and, at least theoretically, being hardworking, tough, and competitive. The wife or mother plays the **expressive roles** of the "homemaker": providing the emotional support and nurturing qualities that sustain the family unit and support the husband or father. These family roles characterize what social scientists call the *traditional family,* a family form that many conservative groups would like to preserve (see Chapter 1).

These and other roles that family members play are *functional.* That is, they preserve order, stability, and equilibrium. They also provide the physical shelter and emotional support that ensure a family's health and survival. Anything that interferes with these tasks is seen as *dysfunctional* because it jeopardizes the family's smooth functioning. For example, abuse of one family member by another is dysfunctional because its negative physical and emotional consequences threaten the family's continuity.

FAMILY FUNCTIONS According to many structural-functionalists, there are two kinds of family functions. **Manifest functions** are intended and recognized; they are clearly evident. **Latent functions** are unintended and unrecognized; they are not immediately obvious. Consider weddings. The primary manifest function of the marriage ceremony is to publicize the formation of a new family unit and to legitimize sexual intercourse (see Chapter 1). Its latent functions are to communicate a "hands-off" message to past or prospective sweethearts, outfit the new couple with household goods and products, and redefine family boundaries to include in-laws or stepfamily members.

INSTITUTIONAL CONNECTIONS Finally, structural functionalists note that the family affects and is affected by other interrelated institutions, such as law, politics, and the economy. For example, politicians (many of whom are lawyers and businesspeople) play a major role in setting policies that determine, among other things, whether a marriage is legal, who can and cannot adopt a child, and which family members can claim Social Security payments (see Chapter 1).

CRITICAL EVALUATION Structural functionalism was a dominant perspective in the 1950s and 1960s, but later it came under attack for being so conservative in its emphasis on order and stability that it ignored social change. For example, this perspective typically sees divorce as dysfunctional and as signaling the disintegration of the family rather than as indicating positive change (as when individuals end an unhappy relationship).

Nor does this perspective show how families interact on a daily basis. Structural functionalism has also been criticized for seeing the family narrowly, through a white, male, middle-class lens.

The Conflict Perspective

A third macro theory, the conflict perspective, has a long history. It became popular in the late 1960s, when African Americans and feminists started to challenge structural functionalism as the dominant explanation of marriages and families.

Conflict theory examines the ways in which groups disagree, struggle for power, and compete for scarce resources (such as wealth and prestige). In contrast to structural functionalists, conflict theorists see conflict and the resulting changes in traditional roles as natural, inevitable, and often desirable.

FAMILY PROBLEMS According to conflict theory, many family difficulties result from widespread societal problems. For example, shifts in the U.S. economy have led to a decline in manufacturing and the loss of many well-paying blue-collar jobs. This has had a profound influence on many families, sending some into a spiral of downward mobility. Racial discrimination also has a negative impact on many families, often blocking their access to health services, education, and employment (see Chapters 4, 13, and 18).

Unlike structural-functionalists, conflict theorists see society not as cooperative and stable but as a system of widespread inequality. There is continuous tension between the "haves" and the "have-nots." The latter are mainly children, women, minorities, and the poor. Much research based on conflict theory focuses on how those in power—typically white, middle-aged, wealthy, Protestant, Anglo-Saxon males—dominate political and economic decision making in American society.

CRITICAL EVALUATION Some social scientists criticize conflict theory for stressing clashes and coercion at the expense of order and stability. They believe that conflict theory presents a negative view of human nature while neglecting the importance of love and self-sacrifice, which are essential to family relationships. Some critics also feel that the conflict perspective is less useful than other approaches because it emphasizes institutional processes rather than personal choices and constraints in everyday family life.

Feminist Perspectives

Conflict theories provided a springboard for feminist theories, the fourth macro approach. **Feminist theories** include a wide range of perspectives and research procedures. These theories examine, for example, how gender roles (expectations about how men and women should behave) shape relations between the sexes in institutions such as politics, the economy, religion, education, and the family.

ARE YOU A FEMINIST? At the beginning of some classes, I ask my students how many of them are feminists. Out of about 35 students, one or two (usually women) raise their hands, but nervously and looking over their shoulders. By the end of our class, about 33 students say that they are feminists, and they aren't embarrassed to do so. Why such a big difference after only an hour's discussion?

Despite some widespread misconceptions, feminists aren't always women or lesbians. *Any* person—male or female, straight or gay—who believes that *both* sexes should have equal political, educational, economic, and other rights is a feminist, even if he or she refuses to identify with this "label." According to Rebecca West, an English journalist and novelist who died in 1983, "I myself have never been able to find out precisely what feminism is; I only know that people call me a feminist whenever I express sentiments that differentiate me from a doormat."

A second misconception is that feminists hate men. According to one of my lesbian students, "I don't know any straight or gay feminists who hate men. They like men. Lesbians just choose not to sleep with men." What *is* true is that many feminists are angry about the injustices perpetrated against women in the workplace and the family and have proposed such "radical" changes as equal pay for equal work and greater participation by fathers in raising their children.

There are many types of feminism (see, for example, Lindsey, 1997, and Lorber, 2005). *Liberal feminism,* for instance, emphasizes social and legal reforms designed to create equal opportunities for women and men. *Radical feminism* considers male domination a major cause of inequality between men and women. *Global feminism* focuses on how the intersection of gender with race, social class, and colonization has exploited women in the developing world.

Feminist theory has had a significant impact on our understanding of family life. Since the early 1980s, feminist scholars (both women and men) have contributed to family theory and social change in several ways:

- They have pointed out that family life is diverse and that perspectives should include families from many cultures and ethnic groups as well as single-parent families, lesbian and gay families, stepfamilies, and grandparent–grandchild households.

- They have initiated legislation to deal with family violence. They have also supported stiffer penalties for men who assault children and women.

- They have endorsed greater equality between husbands and wives. They have also worked for legislation that provides employed women and men with parental leave rights (see Chapters 5 and 13).

- They have refocused much of the research to include fathers as involved, responsible, and nurturing family members who have a profound effect on children and the family (see Chapters 4 and 12).

CRITICAL EVALUATION Feminists have challenged discriminatory peer review processes that routinely exclude women from the "old boy network." According to some critics, however, many feminists are part of an "old girl network." This network has not always welcomed conflicting points of view from African American, Latina, Asian American, American Indian, Muslim, lesbian, working-class, and disabled women in both research and therapeutic settings (Almeida, 1994; Lynn and Todoroff, 1995; S. A. Jackson, 1998).

Another criticism is that much feminist research uses qualitative methods to the exclusion of quantitative methods. In **quantitative research,** researchers assign numbers to qualitative (i.e., nonnumeric) observations by counting and measuring attitudes or behavior. In Chapter 1, for example, all the figures are based on quantitative research. In **qualitative research,** in contrast, researchers rely on observation and interviews and report their data from the respondents' point of view.

Many feminists maintain that quantitative methods, which emphasize detachment and "objectivity," fail to convey the respondents' experiences in such areas as everyday communication and gender power differences (see Adams and Sydie, 2002, for an analysis of some of this literature). Some critics argue, however, that findings based on quantitative methods have important political implications (Maynard, 1994). For example, policy makers are more likely to take feminist research seriously if the studies show the widespread prevalence—rather than just the respondents' personal feelings—of problems such as wife abuse, children's poverty, and gender discrimination in the workplace.

The Symbolic Interaction Perspective

In contrast to the macro-level structural-functionalist, ecological, conflict, and feminist theories, **symbolic interaction theory** is a micro-level theory that looks at the everyday behavior of individuals. Symbolic interactionists examine how our ideas, beliefs, and attitudes shape our daily lives. To a symbolic interactionist, a father's batting practice with his daughter is not simply batting practice. It's an interaction that conveys such messages as "I enjoy spending time with you" or "Girls can be good baseball players."

SYMBOLS The symbolic interaction perspective looks at subjective, interpersonal meanings and how we communicate them using *symbols:* words, gestures, or pictures that stand for something. If we are to interact effectively, our symbols must have *shared meanings,* or agreed-upon definitions. Such shared meanings are illustrated by the wristbands many people are wearing these days, which communicate a variety of messages about their attitudes and opinions on social issues. Some shelters for abused women, for example, sell wristbands with messages like "Hope, Faith, Courage, Strength" or "Stop Domestic Violence!" These wristbands are symbols of the widely shared attitude that society must

According to the symbolic interaction perspective, we interact verbally and through gestures and body language. Besides using facial expressions, signing is a "visual language" that helps people who can't hear to communicate.

make an effort to protect women against domestic violence.

SIGNIFICANT OTHERS One of the most important shared meanings is known as the *definition of the situation,* that is, the way we perceive reality and react to it. Relationships often break up, for example, because partners have different perceptions of the meaning of dating, love, communication, and sex (see Chapters 6–9). As one of my students observed, "We broke up because Dave wanted sex. I wanted intimacy and conversation." We typically learn our definitions of the situation through interaction with **significant others**—people in our primary groups, such as parents, friends, relatives, and teachers—who play an important role in our socialization (see Chapters 1 and 5).

FAMILY ROLES According to symbolic interaction theory, each family member plays more than one role. A man, for example, may be a husband, father, grandfather, brother, son, uncle, and so on. Roles are also *reciprocal.* Even before a baby is born, the prospective parents begin to take on parenting roles (see Chapters 11 and 12).

Roles require different behaviors both within and outside the family, and people modify and adjust their roles as they interact with other role players. For example, you probably interact differently with Mom, Grandma, and Uncle Ned than you do with your brothers and sisters. And you probably interact still differently when you're talking to a classmate, a professor, or an employer.

CRITICAL EVALUATION One of the most common criticisms of symbolic interaction theory is that it ignores macro-level factors that affect family relationships. As conflict theorists point out, much of our individual behavior and decision making is limited by structural or demographic factors such as ethnicity, social class, gender, age, and numerous laws (see Chapters 1, 4, 5, 13, and 17).

Some also believe that symbolic interaction theory overlooks the irrational and unconscious aspects of human behavior (LaRossa and Reitzes, 1993). That is, people don't always behave as reflectively as symbolic interactionists assume. We often act impulsively or make hurtful comments, for instance, without weighing the consequences of our actions or words.

And because symbolic interactionists often study only white, middle-class families—those that are most likely to cooperate in research—the findings are rarely representative of a wide range of racial, ethnic, and socioeconomic groups (Winton, 1995). As a result,

Rod Stewart is 26 years older than his fiancée, Penny. Would this model marry Stewart if he were a sales clerk, for example, instead of a rock star? How do such marriages illustrate social exchange theory?

according to some critics, symbolic interactionists often have an unrealistic view of everyday family life.

The Social Exchange Perspective

since you asked

Why is it so unusual for an attractive person to marry someone who is unattractive?

The fundamental premise of **social exchange theory**, another micro theory, is that people seek through their interactions with others to maximize their rewards and to minimize their costs. As a result, most people will continue in a relationship as long as there are more benefits than losses. The union often ends if another relationship seems to offer greater promise of increasing our rewards and lowering our costs.

WHAT RESOURCES DO WE EXCHANGE? We bring to our relationships a variety of resources—some tangible, some intangible—such as energy, money, material goods, status, intelligence, control, good looks, youth, power, talent, fame, or affection. People "trade" these resources for more, better, or different assets that another person possesses. And as long as the costs are equal to or lower than the benefits, the exchanges will seem fair or balanced (see Chapters 8, 10, and 14).

From a social exchange perspective, when the costs of a marriage outweigh the rewards, the people may separate or divorce. On the other hand, many people stay in unhappy marriages or unions because the rewards seem equal to the costs: "It's better than being alone," "I don't want to hurt the kids," or "It could be worse."

ARE OUR EXCHANGES CONSCIOUS? Although some of our cost–reward decisions are conscious, most are not. Much of the research on wife abuse, for example, shows that women stay in abusive relationships because their self-esteem has eroded after years of criticism, put-downs, and ridicule by their parents, spouses, or partners ("You'll be lucky if anyone marries you," "You're dumb," "You're ugly," and so on). As a result, abused girls and women rarely recognize that they have the right to expect affectionate relationships with decent and loving men.

CRITICAL EVALUATION Some critics have accused exchange theorists of putting too much weight on rational behavior. People don't always calculate the potential costs and rewards of every decision. For example, Linda, one of my students, spent every Saturday (the only day she wasn't working or in class) driving from Baltimore to Philadelphia to visit a grandmother who was showing early symptoms of Alzheimer's disease (see Chapter 17). Linda's mother and several nurses' aides were providing good care for the grandmother, who often didn't recognize her. Nevertheless, Linda gave up her "dating evening" because "I just want to make sure Grandma is OK." In this and other cases, genuine love and concern for others can override "sensible" cost–benefit decisions.

Exchange theory is also limited to explaining behavior that is motivated by immediate costs or rewards. In many ethnic groups, family duties take precedence over individual rights. Traditional Asian cultures stress filial responsibility, which requires children, especially sons, to make sacrifices for the well-being of their parents and siblings (Hurh, 1998; Do, 1999). Similarly, many Middle Eastern families teach children to value family harmony rather than "me first" benefits (see Chapters 4, 5, and 12).

The Family Life Course Development Perspective

A third micro-level perspective, **family life course development theory,** examines the changes that families experience over their lifespan. This is the only theoretical perspective that emerged out of a specific interest in families. Other theories, such as exchange theory and conflict theory, can be applied to a variety of situations, such as labor–management relations and relations between husbands and wives. The family life course development framework, in contrast, focuses exclusively on the family (White and Klein, 2002).

THE CLASSIC FAMILY LIFE CYCLE Family life course development theory evolved over many decades (see White and Klein, 2002, for a description of this evolution). One of the earliest variations, still popular among many practitioners, is Duvall's (1957) model of the family life cycle.

The **family life cycle** consists of the transitions that a family makes as it moves through a series of stages and events. According to this classic model and others like it, the family life cycle begins with marriage and continues through child rearing, seeing the children leave home, retirement, and the death of one or both spouses (see *Table 2.1*).

DEVELOPMENTAL TASKS CHANGE OVER TIME As people progress through various stages and events of the family life cycle, they accomplish **developmental tasks.** That is, they learn to fulfill various role expectations and responsibilities, such as showing affection and support for family members and socializing with people outside the family.

Many developmental tasks are important in keeping the family going. Depending on our development stage, we learn to interact and handle different "hassles" as we grow older. For example, young children must deal with teasing, children aged 6 to 10 must cope with getting bad grades and bullying at school, older children face pressure to use drugs, and 16- to 22-year-olds report that their biggest hassles are trouble at work and school. For adults, the greatest source of stress is

family conflict. For the elderly, the biggest problems include paying for prescriptions and other living expenses (Ellis et al., 2001; see, also, Chapters 17 and 18).

We also learn many developmental tasks in response to a community's pressures for conformity. For example, teachers expect even very young children to accomplish developmental tasks such as paying attention and obeying the teacher. As a child grows older, failure to comply with school standards, such as by skipping classes or being disruptive, can give the child's parents a bad reputation and lead to intervention by public authorities such as the police (Aldous, 1996).

DEVELOPMENTAL TASKS ARE MULTIFACETED Developmental stages and tasks vary in different kinds of families, such as single-parent families, childless couples, stepfamilies, and grandparent–grandchild families. Also, the complex situations and problems that confront families in an aging society are multigenerational. If a couple divorces, for instance, the ex-spouses aren't the only ones who must learn new developmental tasks in relating to their children and each other. Grandparents and even great-grandparents may also have to forge different ties with their grandchildren, an ex-son-in-law or ex-daughter-in-law, and step-grandchildren if either of the parents remarries (see Chapters 15-17).

Finally, the nature of the family life course may differ greatly between poor, minority families and white, middle-class families. As the "Kinscripts: Ensuring Family Survival in Tough Situations" box shows, poor families must be especially creative and resilient to keep their members together throughout the life course.

CRITICAL EVALUATION Family life course development theories have generated a great deal of research, especially on the internal dynamics of marital and family interaction. Although almost all the studies are micro-level, a few scholars have used the developmental approach to examine patterns of family change cross-culturally and historically (see Thornton, 2001). The family life course development perspective is especially useful for therapists and practitioners who counsel families that are experiencing problems such as constant arguments and infidelity.

Critics point out several limitations of these theories. First, some believe that the stages are artificial because "the processes of life are not always so neatly and cleanly segmented" (Winton, 1995: 39).

Second, and despite the recent work on kinscripts and extended families, most developmental theories are limited to examining nuclear, heterosexual, and nondivorced families. For example, gay and lesbian households generally are excluded from family life course analyses (Laird, 1993).

TABLE 2.1

The Classic Portrayal of the Family Life Cycle

Stage 1 Couple without children

Stage 2 Oldest child younger than 30 months old

Stage 3 Oldest child between 2½ and 6 years old

Stage 4 Oldest child between 6 and 13 years old

Stage 5 Oldest child between 13 and 20 years old

Stage 6 Period starting when first child leaves family until the youngest leaves

Stage 7 Empty nest to retirement

Stage 8 Retirement to death of one or both spouses

Choices

Kinscripts: Ensuring Family Survival in Tough Situations

Family life cycle patterns differ markedly in terms of needs, resources, gender roles, migration patterns, education, and attitudes toward family and aging. Studying low-income African American families, Burton and Stack (1993) proposed the concept of *kinscript* to explain the life courses of many multigenerational families. The kinscript arises in response to both extreme economic need and intense commitment by family members to the survival of future generations, and it requires family interaction in three domains: kin-work, kin-time, and kin-scription.

Kin-work is the collective labor that families share to endure over time. It includes providing help during childbirth, intergenerational care of children or dependents, and support for other relatives. For example, a 76-year old widower parented three preschool children after their mother started "running the streets":

There ain't no other way. I have to raise these babies, else the service people will take 'em away. This is my family. Family has to take care of family else we won't be no more (Burton and Stack, 1993: 105).

Kin-time is the shared understanding among family members of when and in what sequence kin-work should be performed. Kin-time provides for learning developmental tasks during such transitions as marriage, childbearing, and grandparenthood and includes guidelines for assuming family leadership roles and caregiving responsibilities. A woman receiving assistance from her mother and other female kin describes the complex but cooperative pattern that characterizes the care of her child:

On the days Damen has school, my mother picks him up at night and keeps him at her home. And then when she goes to work in the morning, she takes him to my grandmother's house. And when my little sister gets out of school, she picks him up and takes him back to my mother's house. And then I go and pick him up (Jarrett, 1994: 41–42).

Kin-scription is the process by which kin-work is assigned to specific family members, most often women and children. Women often find it difficult to refuse the demands of kin. One woman, who had lost her first love 14 years earlier at the age of 21, provides an example of the interplay of family power, kin-scription, and the role of women:

When Charlie died, it seemed like everyone said, since she's not getting married, we have to keep her busy. Before I knew it, I was raising kids, giving home to long-lost kin, and even helping the friends of my mother. Between doing all of this, I didn't have time to find another man (Burton and Stack, 1993: 107).

Many people believe that poor families or those on welfare are doomed to pass dependency down from one generation to the next (Hill et al., 1993). As the kinscript framework suggests, however, many low-income, multigenerational families have well-defined family scripts that enable family members to survive by depending on kin rather than on public assistance.

Rebecca Anderson, 54 years old and battling lupus, became a mother again when she took in five nieces and nephews, whose three sets of parents could not care for them. Anderson's husband, Alton, who does not live with Rebecca, helps with the children occasionally, but provides no financial support.

Third, some critics question why developmental theories ignore sibling relationships, which are among the most important emotional resources we have throughout life and especially after the last parent dies (McGoldrick et al., 1993). Thus, family life course development theory still "deals with a fairly small part of the elephant" (Burr, 1995: 81).

The Family Systems Perspective

Family systems theory, the final micro perspective we consider, views the family as a functioning unit that solves problems, makes decisions, and achieves collective goals. The emphasis is not on individual family members but on how the members interact within the family system, how they communicate, how family patterns evolve, and how individual personalities affect family members (Rosenblatt, 1994; Day, 1995).

WHAT HOLDS FAMILIES TOGETHER? Family systems analysts are interested in the implicit or explicit rules that hold families together. For example, how do family members influence each other during stressful times such as illness, unemployment, or the death of a loved one? As the boundaries of the family change—through birth, divorce, or remarriage, for example—the focus of the analysis may shift from family members to their relationships with outside groups (Broderick, 1993).

COMBINING THEORIES Family systems theorists sometimes combine their approaches with the family life course development perspective. In her systemic family development model, for example, Tracey Laszloffy (2002) uses the metaphor of a cake to illustrate the complexity and richness of most families. Once the ingredients of the cake (for example, butter, milk, flour, and eggs) are mixed and baked, the final product is different from any of the ingredients. The same is true of families. If we stir together all the ingredients (family members), we get an entirely different and unique entity.

To continue with the metaphor, if we slice a piece of the cake (which is similar to freezing a family at a particular moment in its life course), we see the various multigenerational layers, with each layer made up of one or more individuals. The individuals within each generation are experiencing different developmental tasks (such as leaving home for college) and coping with different stressors and crises (such as divorce or retirement).

CRITICAL EVALUATION Some critics maintain that family systems theory has generated a lot of terminology but little insight into how the family really functions. Because the perspective originated in the study of dysfunctional families in clinical settings, some question whether the theory can be applied to healthy families. Finally, because much of research is based on case studies, the results are limited because they can't be generalized to larger groups (Holman and Burr, 1980; Nye and Berardo, 1981; Day, 1995).

Conclusion

Although we've looked at the eight major theories of marriage and the family separately, researchers and clinicians often combine several of these perspectives to interpret data or choose intervention strategies. For example, a counselor who is helping a couple that is experiencing marital problems might draw on social exchange, symbolic interaction, life course developmental, and systems theories to shed light on the couple's situation.

Counselors who work with children with attention deficit hyperactivity disorders (ADHD) typically combine ecological and family systems perspectives in conducting assessments and developing interventions (Bernier and Siegel, 1994). Instead of simply focusing on the child or the family, clinicians usually observe the child in his or her natural environment, involve the child's teacher, and educate grandparents about ADHD. Thus, both researchers and practitioners often rely on several theories to explain or respond to family-related issues.

We've examined some of the most influential theoretical perspectives that guide researchers and practitioners in their work. We turn next to the ways that

researchers design studies and collect information about marriages and families.

Making Connections

- Return to Table 2.1 for a moment. Does this model illustrate your family of orientation? What about your family of procreation? If not, how have the stages you've experienced been different from those listed here?

- Consider the cake metaphor that describes family life course development. Does your family resemble a piece of cake? Has it shed old layers or added new ones recently?

Methods Used in Family Research

Why are we attracted to some people and not to others? Why are young adults postponing marriage these days? Why have divorce rates declined recently? To answer these and other questions about the family, social scientists use six major research methods: surveys, clinical research, field research, secondary analysis, experiments, and evaluation research.

Surveys

Researchers use **surveys** to systematically collect data from respondents through questionnaires or interviews. In social science research, a *population* is any well-defined group of people about whom we want to know something specific (like all women who use contraceptives).

For various reasons, obtaining information from populations is problematic. The population being studied may be so large that it would be too expensive and time-consuming to interview every person. For example, it would be impossible to interview every woman of childbearing age to find out what percentage use birth control. In other cases—such as obtaining the membership lists of religious groups or social clubs—it may be impossible even to identify the population we would like to study.

since you asked

Because they've never contacted me about my opinion, why do pollsters draw conclusions about what people think?

To avoid these problems, researchers typically select a *sample*, a group of people (or things) that are representative of the population they want to study. In a *probability sample*, each person (or thing) has an equal chance of being chosen because the selection is random. For example, researchers often obtain probability samples through *random-digit dialing*, which involves selecting area codes and exchanges followed by four random digits. In a procedure called *computer-assisted telephone interviewing (CATI)*, the interviewer uses a computer to select random telephone numbers and then keys the replies into the computer. Because the selection is random, the findings can be generalized to the whole population.

In a *nonprobability sample*, researchers use other criteria, such as convenience or the availability of participants. The findings can't be generalized to *any* group because the people (or things) have not had an equal chance of being selected for the study.

Television stations, newsmagazines, and entertainment shows often provide a toll-free number or an Internet site and encourage viewers to "vote" on an issue or a person (like the popular *American Idol* television contest). How representative are these voters of the general population? And how many enthusiasts "stuff the ballot box" by voting more than once? According to one observer, most Internet polls are "good for a few laughs" but are little more than "the latest in a long series of junk masquerading as indicators of public opin-

Millions of viewers choose a winner by "voting" for their favorite American Idol singer. Does the voting represent all American Idol fans? Or are such surveys a SLOP (see text)?

Changes

The Prospects and Pitfalls of Internet Surveys

One of the greatest benefits of the Internet is the ability to reach large numbers of people at a very low cost. Hundreds of Websites invite visitors to participate in a variety of studies that resemble scientific research, including personality tests and opinion surveys.

How scientific are the studies? And should you or your family members—especially children under age 18—participate?

A nationally representative study of parents and their children (aged 10 to 17) found that almost two out of three children are willing to divulge private information to online marketers in exchange for a free gift (such as a sweepstakes prize). Some of this information includes the names of parents' favorite stores, parents' weekend activities, the number of parent absences from work, and whether or not the family drinks beer or wine with dinner (Turow and Nir, 2000).

The Children's Online Privacy Protection Act now bars sites from collecting information from users under age 13 without their parents' consent. Enforcement is practically nonexistent, however. In addition, many preteens can figure out ways to get around such precautions or even forge their parents' permission electronically.

What about legitimate academic Internet surveys: Should you or your family members participate? Empir-

ical studies conducted on the Internet, though scientific, reflect a variety of problems.

In face-to-face or telephone interviews, researchers can see or sense whether respondents react negatively to an item. The researcher can stop the interview or answer a respondent's questions. Internet surveys can't provide such safeguards, even if they include "warnings" that some of the questions may be sensitive or intrusive.

Institutional review boards try to ensure that paper-and-pencil studies comply with legal and ethical standards (a topic we address later in this chapter). So far, however, there are no established guidelines for online research. Therefore, Internet users should investigate a site before participating, even in scientific studies.

Stop and Think . . .

- Have you ever participated in an online survey? Why or why not?
- Should parents block teenagers' access to Internet surveys? Or should teenagers be trusted to make their own decisions?

ion because the participants aren't representative of everyone's opinion" (Witt, 1998: 23).

But what if a million people cast a vote? Don't such large numbers reflect how most people think? No. Because the respondents are self-selected, the pollster simply has "junk" from a very large number of people.

Since the mid-1990s, the amount of social science research, including polls, has boomed. Are the results valid? The "The Prospects and Pitfalls of Internet Surveys" box examines some of the benefits and costs of online research that relies on surveys to collect data.

QUESTIONNAIRES AND INTERVIEWS Researchers collect survey data using questionnaires, face-to-face or telephone interviews, or a combination of these techniques. Questionnaires can be mailed, used during an interview, or self-administered to large groups of respondents. Student course evaluations are good examples of self-administered questionnaires.

In interviews, the researcher and the respondent interact directly, either face to face or by telephone. The latter approach is very popular because it is an inexpensive way to collect data. As you just saw, for example, *CATI* generates a probability sample and provides interviewers with a consistent set of questions.

FOCUS GROUPS Marketing companies have traditionally used *focus groups*—group interviews focusing on a specific topic—to gauge people's reactions to a new or "new and improved" product. Family researchers also use focus groups to explore issues before launching a large survey project. Usually, 6 to 12 members of a focus group participate in a guided discussion of a particular topic (Morgan, 1993; Krueger, 1994).

Focus groups can be invaluable in obtaining honest information that has not been tapped by previous studies. For example, low-income mothers are more willing to discuss childcare problems that they might otherwise lie about because they fear that child protective services will remove children from their care (Dodson and Schmalzbauer, 2005).

Focus groups are especially useful for obtaining in-depth data in relatively new areas or understudied populations. In the case of Latino families, for instance, researchers can obtain rich information from focus groups if they consider a number of factors—that participants from Mexico, Puerto Rico, and Central and Latin America are very diverse in their cultural experiences; that separating women and men will encourage women to "open up;" that some participants will be more fluent in English than in Spanish; and that ensuring confidentiality and providing monetary incentives may be critical, especially in recruiting undocumented immigrants to participate in focus groups (Umaña-Taylor and Bámaca, 2004).

STRENGTHS Surveys are usually inexpensive, easy to administer, and have a fast turnaround rate. When assured that their answers will remain anonymous, respondents are generally willing to answer questions on sensitive topics such as income, sexual behavior, and drug use.

Face-to-face interviews have high response rates (up to 99 percent) compared with other data collection techniques. Interviewers can also record the respondent's body language, facial expressions, and intonations that are often as useful as verbal responses.

If a respondent does not understand a question or is reluctant to answer, the interviewer can clarify, probe, or keep the respondent from digressing. An astute interviewer can also gather information on variables such as social class by observing the respondent's home and neighborhood.

Like questionnaires, telephone surveys are relatively inexpensive and a quick way to collect data. Telephone interviews provide a nearly unlimited pool of respondents because more than 98 percent of all homes have at least one telephone. These interviews often elicit more honest responses on controversial issues than do face-to-face interviews. In addition, researchers have more control over the procedures used by interviewers (such as probing a respondent's vague answers).

WEAKNESSES One of the major limitations of surveys that use mailed questionnaires is a low response rate, often well under 50 percent. If the questions are unclear, complicated, or offensive, a respondent may simply throw the questionnaire away. A number of studies have also found that anywhere from a third to half of respondents offer opinions on subjects they know nothing about, such as fictitious legislation or nonexistent political figures (see Bishop et al., 1980).

Moreover, those who respond to questionnaires may be very different from those who do not. Some of the least representative surveys tap self-selected respondents such as readers of particular magazines. How many times have *you* taken the time to complete and return such questionnaires? Norman Bradburn of the National Opinion Research Center calls these surveys SLOPS, for "Self-Selected Opinion Polls" (cited in Tanur, 1994).

Another problem is that people may skip or lie about questions that they consider "too nosy." In the 2000 census, for example, a third of the people who received the 53-question long form felt that none of the questions was too personal. However, 53 percent viewed questions about income as intrusive, and 32 percent felt the same way about questions on physical or mental disabilities (Cohn, 2000). If respondents lie or

Applying What You've Learned

Can I Trust This Survey?

Surveys are often used in public opinion polls and are reported on television and in newspapers. Asking a few basic questions about a survey will help you evaluate its credibility:

■ *Who sponsored the survey?* A government agency, a nonprofit partisan organization, a business, or a group that's lobbying for change?

■ *What is the purpose of the survey?* To provide objective information, to promote an idea or a political candidate, or to get attention through sensationalism?

■ *How was the sample drawn?* Randomly? Or was it a SLOP (see text)?

■ *How were the questions worded?* Were they clear, objective, loaded, or biased? If the survey questions are not provided, why not?

■ *How did the researchers report their findings?* Were they objective, or did they make value judgments?

omit items about their income or other family characteristics, the data will be invalid, or the researcher may have to scrap a key variable (such as income).

Unlike questionnaires and telephone surveys, face-to-face interviews can be very expensive (see "Data Digest"). And because people have become oversaturated with marketing research, many use caller I.D. or answering machines to avoid telephone surveys.

Because the survey is the research approach you will encounter most often, it's important to be an informed consumer. As the "Can I Trust This Survey?" box shows, you can't simply assume that the survey is accurate or representative of a larger population.

Clinical Research

Unlike survey research, which explores large-scale social processes and changes, **clinical research** studies individuals or small groups of people who seek help from mental health professionals and other scientists (Miller and Crabtree, 1994). Many clinical researchers focus on family conflict and intervene in traumatic situations such as marital rape and incest. They try to change negative interactions such as hostile communication patterns between partners or aspects of the family environment that might lead to eating disorders, drug use, and other problems.

Clinical research often relies on the *case study method,* a traditional approach used by social workers, psychologists, clinical sociologists, and marriage counselors. A case study provides in-depth information and detailed and vivid descriptions of family life (see LaRossa, 1984, for good examples of case studies across the life course). Clinical practitioners work with families or individuals on a one-to-one basis, but they often use several techniques, including interviews, record analysis, and direct observation.

STRENGTHS Case studies are typically linked with long-term counseling, which is beneficial for many individuals and families. Useful intervention strategies can be disseminated fairly quickly to thousands of other practitioners. Clinicians may also offer insights about family dynamics that can enrich theories such as symbolic interaction or general systems perspectives.

Researchers can then incorporate these insights into larger or more representative studies that use surveys or other data collection methods.

WEAKNESSES Clinical research and case studies are usually time-consuming and expensive. Clinicians typically see only people with severe problems or those who are willing and financially able to seek help. Therefore, the results are not representative of average families or even of troubled families.

Another problem is that clinical studies are subjective and rarely ask "Where's the evidence?" If a client complains that he has a terrible mother, for example, clinicians try to make the patient feel better instead of meeting the mother.

As a result, some critics contend, clinical "opinions" are widespread despite empirical evidence to the contrary. It is *not* true, for instance, that low self-esteem causes aggression, drug use, and low achievement. How parents treat a child in the first years of life does *not* determine a child's later intellectual and emotional success (see Chapter 12). Nor do abused children inevitably become abusive parents, causing a "cycle of abuse" (Tavris, 2003).

Field Research

In **field research,** researchers collect data by systematically observing people in their natural surroundings. Field research usually is highly structured. It typically

Researchers often study interaction by observing people in natural settings. What are the advantages and disadvantages of experimental designs such as this one of a classroom?

involves carefully designed projects in which the data are recorded and then converted into quantitative summaries. The studies examine complex communication patterns, measure the frequency of specific acts (such as the number of nods or domineering statements), and note the duration of a particular behavior (such as length of eye contact) (Stillars, 1991). Thus, field research is much more elaborate and sophisticated than it appears to be to the general public or to an inexperienced researcher.

Field research includes several types of observation. In *participant observation,* researchers interact naturally with the people they are studying but do not reveal their identities as researchers. For example, if you quietly note interaction patterns between the "stars" and the "black sheep" during a Thanksgiving dinner, you are engaging in participant observation.

In *nonparticipant observation,* researchers study phenomena without being part of the situation. For example, a team of Canadian researchers followed more than 400 parents and their 2-to-5-year-old children around grocery stores, noting parents' interaction with their kids. The researchers found that good-looking children, especially boys, get more attention from their parents. The "pretty" kids were more likely than the unattractive ones to be buckled into the shopping cart instead of allowed to stand up in the cart and to be held by the hand instead of being permitted to wander away (Harrell, 2005, 2006).

In many studies, researchers combine both participant and nonparticipant observation. For example, sociologist Elijah Anderson (1999) has devoted much of his research to examining households in West Philadelphia, an inner-city black community with high crime rates. Although Anderson teaches at the University of Pennsylvania, he "hung out" in West Philadelphia to learn why some poor residents take extraordinary measures to conform to mainstream values (such as maintaining a strong family life) whereas others engage in crime and violence.

STRENGTHS Field research provides an in-depth understanding of behavior that other approaches often cannot offer. In her study of families in Saudi Arabia, for example, anthropologist Soraya Altorki (1988) established rapport with the women in the community. They invited her to their homes, where Altorki could observe everyday interactions, behavior, and activities.

Field research is more flexible than some other methods. For instance, the researcher can decide to interview (rather than just observe) key people after beginning to collect data. Most importantly, field research does not disrupt a "natural" setting. Therefore, the people being studied aren't influenced by the researcher's

presence. For example, Phillip Davis (1996) and some of his research assistants have observed adults' verbal aggression and corporal punishment of children in public settings such as indoor shopping malls, zoos, amusement parks, flea markets, city streets, rapid transit stations, bus depots, and toy stores.

WEAKNESSES If a researcher needs elaborate recording equipment, must travel far or often, or lives in a different society or community for a long time, field research can be very expensive. Researchers who study other cultures often spend several years learning a new language or adjusting to different cultural norms. A researcher doing fieldwork in a country that is experiencing a civil war may be abducted or even killed (Garland, 1999).

It may also be very difficult to balance the role of participant and observer. In Anderson's studies in West Philadelphia cited earlier, he became personally involved with some of his research participants. Instead of being a detached observer, Anderson hired an ex-drug dealer as a part-time research assistant, found lawyers or jobs for community members, encouraged his respondents to avoid committing crimes, and even lent them money. In these and other ways, the researcher may bias the research by succumbing to the impulse to fix a problem and to protect the people being studied from harm (Fine, 1993; Cose, 1999).

A final problem with field research is the observer's ability (or lack of it) to recognize and address her or his biases. Because observation is very personal and subjective, it is often difficult to maintain one's objectivity while collecting and interpreting the data.

Secondary Analysis

Family researchers also rely heavily on **secondary analysis,** in which a researcher analyzes data that were collected by someone else. The data may be historical materials (such as court proceedings), personal documents (such as letters and diaries), public records (such as federal information on immigration or state or county archives on births, marriages, and deaths), and official statistics (such as Census Bureau publications).

The availability and usage of large-scale data sets have grown dramatically in the past two decades. The *Journal of Marriage and Family,* the major periodical in the field of family studies, reflects the growing reliance on secondary data sources. In 2003, 75 percent of the studies published in this journal used secondary data analysis, compared with only 33 percent in 1983 (Hofferth, 2005).

Many of the statistics in this textbook come from secondary analysis. The information sources include the U.S. Census Bureau and other government agencies, reputable nonprofit organizations, and university research centers (see Greenstein, 2006, for a good summary of the major sources of secondary analysis in family research).

STRENGTHS Secondary analysis is usually accessible, convenient, and inexpensive. Census Bureau information on topics such as household income, the number of children in single-parent families, and immigration is readily available at college and university libraries and, most recently, on the Internet (see the "Taking It Further" section in Chapter 1).

Because secondary data often are *longitudinal* (collected at two or more points in time) rather than *cross-sectional* (collected at one point in time), they offer the added advantage of allowing the researcher to examine trends (such as age at first marriage) over time. And increasingly, both longitudinal and cross-sectional publications provide the reader with colorful pie charts and other figures that are easy to read, understand, and incorporate into Power Point presentations.

Another advantage of secondary analysis is the high quality of the data. Nationally known survey organizations have large budgets and well-trained staff who can quickly handle any data-collection problems. Because the samples are representative of national populations, you can be more confident about generalizing the findings.

WEAKNESSES Secondary analysis has several drawbacks. First, secondary data may not provide all the information needed. For example, some of the statistics on remarriages and redivorces have been collected only since the early 1990s. Therefore, it is impossible for a researcher to use them to make comparisons over time.

Second, secondary analysis may be challenging because the documents may be fragile, housed in only a few libraries in the country, or part of private collections. Determining the accuracy and authenticity of historical materials also may be difficult.

A third limitation of secondary analysis is that the data may not include information the researcher is looking for. If you wanted to examine some of the characteristics of couples who are separated but not divorced, for example, you'd find little national data. Consequently, you'd have to rely on studies with small and nonrepresentative samples or collect such information yourself (see Chapter 15).

In some isolated locations, census takers must often travel to places that are inaccessible by road or without conventional postal addresses. In the 2000 census, for example, Harold Johnson transported Census Director Kenneth Prewitt into town by dog sled. Unalakdeet, a village of about 800, is on the Bering Sea 400 miles northwest of Anchorage.

Experiments

Unlike surveys, clinical research, field research, and secondary analysis, an **experiment** investigates cause-and-effect relationships under strictly controlled conditions. A researcher tests a prediction, or *hypothesis,* stating that one specified variable "causes" another specified variable.

According to many of my students, for example, heavy course assignments "cause" cheating because students don't have enough time to prepare for exams, many work part-time (or full time), and most have other interests. To test this hypothesis, a researcher would compare the cheating rates of students with heavy and light course loads, along with factors such as employment, class attendance, and the amount of time devoted to studying.

Experimental family research is rare: "Children or adults cannot be assigned at random to different family types, to different partners, to different income groups" (Hofferth, 2005: 903-4). In contrast, experimental designs are a powerful tool of medical and psychological research. In medicine, researchers routinely try to establish cause–effect relationships between many variables, such as diet and blood pressure or stress and physical illness (see Chapter 6).

Using specially designed laboratories, psychologists investigate family-related issues such as infants' attention spans, children's problem-solving techniques, and adults' interactions. In a recent study, psychologists Rachel Ebling and Robert Levenson (2003) recruited 177 participants, who viewed short videotapes of the marital interaction of ten couples. The participants then rated the couples on their level of marital satisfaction and likelihood of divorce.

The researchers found that people who were happily married or recently divorced were more accurate in their ratings than those with professional training, such as marital therapists and marital researchers, in judging marital satisfaction. This suggests that the "experts" aren't as savvy about interpersonal relationships as they or we expect them to be.

STRENGTHS The major advantage of the controlled (laboratory) experiment lies in its isolation of the "causal" variable. For example, if students who get information in sex education classes show changes in their attitude toward casual sex, a school might decide to provide such information for all of its students.

Another strength of experimental designs is their low cost. Usually, there's no need to purchase special equipment and most participants expect little or no compensation. Also, experiments often are less time-consuming than data collection methods such as field research.

A third advantage of experiments is that they can be replicated over many years and with different participants. Such replication strengthens the researchers' confidence in the *validity,* or accuracy, and *reliability,* or consistency, of the research findings.

WEAKNESSES One major disadvantage of experimental designs is their reliance on student volunteers or paid respondents. Students often feel obligated to participate as part of a grade, or they may fear antagonizing an instructor who's conducting a study. Students might also give "acceptable" answers that they think the instructor expects. In the case of paid participants, often only people with serious financial problems will participate in experiments.

A second and related disadvantage is that the results of experimental studies can't be generalized to a larger population because they come from small or self-selected samples. For example, college students who participate in experiments aren't necessarily representative of other college students, much less of people who aren't in college.

A third limitation is that experiments, especially those conducted in laboratories, are artificial. People

www.benitaepstein.com

"I already wrote the paper. That's why it's so hard to get the right data."

© Benita Epstein 1996

know that they're being observed and may behave very differently than they would in a natural setting. Finally, many experiments gauge attitudes rather than behavior. Like surveys, some experiments tell researchers only what the participants say they'll do rather than how they *really* behave.

Medical experiments probably are more accurate because they measure physiological variables (weight, blood pressure, medications). Even here, however, participants can lie about their medical history or lifestyle ("I exercise at least three times a week").

In addition, there are many variables that medical researchers don't or can't take into account. For example, in 2002, a large-scale study reported that five or more years of hormone replacement therapy (HRT) could increase women's rates of heart attack, stroke, breast cancer, and dementia for women over age 65. But a study published several years later concluded that although some short-term HRT users had a decreased risk of colorectal cancer, this form of cancer was more serious and spread more rapidly among HRT users than among non-HRT users (Chlebowski et al., 2004).

So, what's a woman to do? In the future, "we may gain clearer insights into the complex interactions of genetics, hormones, and factors like obesity and diet" (Healy, 2004: 68). Until then, women may continue to get different and even conflicting advice from their physicians.

Evaluation Research

In **evaluation research,** which relies on all the standard methodological techniques described in this section, researchers assess the efficiency and effectiveness of social programs in both the public and private sectors.

Many government and nonprofit agencies provide services that affect the family both directly and indirectly. Work-training programs, drug rehabilitation programs, and programs to prevent or deal with teenage pregnancy are examples.

Because local, state, and national governments have cut their social service budgets since the early 1980s, service delivery groups have become increasingly concerned about doing more with less. As you saw in the "Should Uncle Sam Be a Matchmaker?" box in Chapter 1, caseworkers are now required to provide counseling for which they have no training. Nevertheless, there is increasing emphasis on evaluations to help agencies determine how to achieve the best results at the lowest possible cost (Kettner et al., 1999).

Like clinical research, evaluation research is *applied*. It assesses a specific social program for a specific agency or organization, evaluating that program's achievements in terms of its original goals (Weiss, 1998). Administrators often use the final reports to improve a program or to initiate a new service such as an after-school program.

STRENGTHS Evaluation research is one of the most valuable research approaches because it examines actual efforts to deal with problems that confront many families. And if researchers use secondary analysis rather than collect new data, the expenses can be modest.

In addition, the research findings can be very valuable to program directors or agency heads. Managers are able to keep a program on course because the findings highlight discrepancies between the original objectives and the way the program is actually working (Peterson et al., 1994).

WEAKNESSES Evaluation research can be frustrating. Politics often play an important role in what is evaluated and for whom the research is done. Even though agency heads typically solicit the research, they may ignore the results if the study shows that the program isn't tapping the neediest groups, the administrators are wasting money, or caseworkers are making serious mistakes.

Finally, some evaluations are inadequate because they are poorly designed. Marriage enrichment and preparation programs have mushroomed since the early 1990s. Are they effective? The results are mixed.

An evaluation of 13 programs found that only four were useful in increasing a couple's level of communication, improving problem-solving skills, or strengthening a relationship, for example. The other nine programs claimed success but never examined any outcomes or the outcome measures were seriously flawed (Jakubowski et al., 2004).

A systematic review of 39 evaluations of marriage and relationship programs found that even the best eval-uations were seriously flawed: The sample sizes were very small; practically all the participants were middle-class whites; there were no measures of couples' outcomes over time; the evaluators studied programs that they themselves had created (a clear conflict of interest); and the authors sometimes presented only positive results (Reardon-Anderson et al., 2005; see, also, Silliman and Schumm, 2000).

What can we conclude from these and similar studies? Before investing your time and money in a particular marital enrichment or preparation program, look for evaluations of that program. Beware, however, if the evaluation research reflects a conflict of interest or is unscientific in other ways, such as relying on unrepresentative samples.

Conclusion

Researchers have to weigh the benefits and limitations of each research approach in designing their studies (see *Table 2.2*). Often, they use a combination of strategies to achieve their research objectives. Despite the researcher's commitment to objectivity, ethical debates and politically charged disagreements can influence much family research.

Making Connections

- If you get information from the Internet, how do you determine whether the material is accurate? (See, also, the "Taking It Further" section at the end of this chapter.)

- When you receive questionnaires in the mail, do you answer them? If you respond, do you ignore some questions? If so, which ones?

The Ethics and Politics of Family Research

Researchers don't work in a vacuum. Many people have very strong opinions about family issues (see Chapter 1). There is also pressure in universities to supplement shrinking budgets with outside funding sources. It is not surprising, then, that researchers sometimes encounter ethical and political dilemmas.

since you asked

If I participate in a social science research project, how can I be sure that any information about me will be kept confidential?

TABLE 2.2

Six Common Data Collection Methods in Family Research

Method	Strengths	Weaknesses
Surveys	Fairly inexpensive and simple to administer; interviews have high response rates; findings often can be generalized to the whole population.	Mailed questionnaires may have low response rates; respondents may be self-selected; interviews usually are expensive.
Clinical research	Helps people who are experiencing family problems; offers insights for theory development.	Usually time-consuming and expensive; findings can't be generalized.
Field research	Flexible; offers deeper understanding of family behavior; usually inexpensive.	Difficult to quantify and to maintain observer–participant boundaries; the observer may be biased or judgmental; findings can't be generalized.
Secondary analysis	Usually accessible, convenient, and inexpensive; often longitudinal and historical.	Information may be incomplete; some documents may be inaccessible; some data cannot be collected over time.
Experiment	Attempts to demonstrate cause and effect; usually inexpensive; many available participants; can be replicated.	Volunteers and paid participants aren't representative of larger populations; artificial laboratory setting; often measures attitudes rather than behavior.
Evaluation research	Usually inexpensive; valuable in real-life applications.	Often political; may entail training many staff members.

Ethical Issues

In a recent experiment, researchers found that an AIDS vaccine worked especially well for African Americans who volunteered to participate. Yet the researchers are having problems recruiting black volunteers for further studies. Why?

UNETHICAL RESEARCH In the Tuskegee Syphilis Study, conducted by the federal government between 1932 and 1972, researchers withheld medical treatment from poor black men in Macon County, Alabama. The men were not told they had syphilis and were not treated, even after penicillin became available, because the researchers wanted to study the progression of the disease. By the time the study was exposed in the early 1990s, 128 men had died of syphilis or complications of the disease.

For decades, scientists assumed that African Americans are underrepresented in medical research because, after the Tuskegee incident, many didn't trust medical institutions. A team of researchers who examined published health studies dating back more than 20 years found that blacks are as likely as other groups to volunteer in medical research, including surgery and test-ing new medicine. They are underrepresented primarily because scientists and research institutions don't ask African Americans to participate (Wendler et al., 2006).

ETHICS CODES AND OUTSIDE PRESSURE Because so much research relies on human subjects, the federal government and many professional organizations have devised ethics codes to protect research participants. Among other professional organizations, the National Council on Family Relations and the American Sociological Association publish codes of ethics to guide researchers. *Table 2.3* summarizes the key elements of these codes, regardless of the discipline or research design.

Ethical violations affect all families. For example, businesses sometimes pressure scientists to withhold negative findings. Recently, for instance, in the *Journal of the American Medical Association*, one of the world's most highly respected medical journals, University of California researchers reported that in clinical trials, an anti-HIV drug, Remune, was no more effective than a placebo (sugar pill). The pharmaceutical company sued

TABLE 2.3

Some Basic Principles of Ethical Family Research

- Obtain all participants' consent to participate and their permission to quote from their responses, particularly if the research concerns sensitive issues or if participants' comments will be quoted extensively.

- Do not exploit participants or research assistants involved in the research for personal gain.

- Never harm, humiliate, abuse, or coerce participants, either physically or psychologically. This includes the withholding of medications or other services or programs that might benefit participants.

- Honor all guarantees to participants of privacy, anonymity, and confidentiality.

- Use the highest methodological standards and be as accurate as possible.

- Describe the limitations and shortcomings of the research in published reports.

the university, demanding that it pay $7–10 million in damages, but later dropped the suit (Van Der Werf, 2001).

Ethically, it is essential for researchers to state whether a procedure or drug is effective. However, businesses that pay for research would rather not reveal findings that could cut into their profits or decrease the value of their stock. As a result, ethical guidelines may sometimes buckle under the weight of academic pressure to avoid discussing topics that challenge the status quo, to bring in as many grants as possible, or to please corporations that sponsor the research.

To please corporations, some researchers violate conflict-of-interest policies. A few years ago, for example, the prestigious *New England Journal of Medicine* admitted that between 1997 and 1999 its editors had published 18 articles on which the researchers also served as consultants or received "major research support" from pharmaceutical companies (Angell et al., 2000).

As these examples illustrate, some researchers engage in unethical behavior. For the most part, however, research errors are unintentional. They result from ignorance of statistical procedures, simple arithmetic mistakes, or inadequate supervision. Of the thousands of studies published every year, peers have typically reviewed the material and scholars have evaluated the funding requests.

Political Pressures

Former Senator William Proxmire became famous (or infamous, some feel) for his "Golden Fleece" awards to social research projects that he ridiculed as a waste of taxpayers' money. Some of the most recent examples include studies of stress and why people fall in love. The legitimacy of social science research becomes especially suspect in the eyes of political and religious groups when the studies focus on sensitive social, moral, or political issues.

One of the most controversial research topics is human sexuality. Alfred Kinsey and his colleagues carried out the first widely publicized research on sexuality in the late 1940s and early 1950s. Although the studies had some methodological limitations (see Chapter 7), many social scientists consider Kinsey's research to be the major springboard that launched scientific investigations of human sexuality in subsequent decades.

SUPPRESSING RESEARCH ON SEXUAL BEHAVIOR
Many people are still suspicious of research on sex. In 1992, for example, Congress withdrew the funding for two projects on adolescent and adult sexual behavior that had already been peer-reviewed, approved, and funded by the National Institutes of Health (NIH) and the Centers for Disease Control and Prevention (CDC). Congress dumped the projects because a number of conservative Christian groups complained that the research would "liberalize" opinions and laws regarding homosexuality, pedophilia, anal and oral sex, sex education, and teenage pregnancy and undermine "traditional family values" (Fiester, 1993; Udry, 1993).

More recently, the Bush administration has purged material from federal Internet sites that violate the administration's ideological stance on sexual abstinence. As "The Politics of Sex Research" box shows, government officials have the power to revise or delete information about sexual behavior on Websites, regardless of what scientific studies show (see, also, Chapter 7).

SUPPRESSING OTHER RESEARCH
Politicians tinker with other data—not just information about sexuality—that might increase their chances of being elected or reelected. During the 2002 recession, for example, President Bush's Council of Economic Advisers yanked off its Website a study that predicted mediocre job growth after Bush's proposed $674-billion economic stimulus plan. In addition, the Bureau of Labor Statistics quietly announced that it would no longer publish the mass-layoff statistics it had been putting out since 1994 (Coy and Cohn, 2003). Without such information, states find it much harder to plan for job-training and other programs.

Constraints

The Politics of Sex Research

Is the government an unbiased source of scientific health information? No. Let's consider a few recent examples dealing with sexual behavior.

Abortion and Breast Cancer

In 2002, the Bush administration quietly removed the National Cancer Institute's reports of findings that abortion does not increase a woman's risk of developing breast cancer. Instead, the NIH Website stated that the relationship between abortions and breast cancer was "inconclusive."

The administration withdrew its misinformation only several years later and after numerous protests by medical experts, scientists, and educators. All of these groups worried that instead of getting legal abortions, many women (including unmarried teens) would bear unwanted children because they feared that abortion "causes" breast cancer.

Since 2002, the Bush administration has funded 2,000 "pregnancy resource centers" which are often affiliated with religious antiabortion groups. Counselors at some of these centers are still telling women with unintended pregnancies that abortion results in an increased risk of breast cancer, infertility, and long-lasting psychological trauma.

Sex Education

In another case, the NIH and the CDC removed information about the effectiveness of condoms in decreasing unwanted pregnancies. Because the Bush administration sees abstinence as the only "acceptable" sex education program, it expunged material on using condoms to protect against HIV and other sexually transmitted diseases (STDs, but being referred to most recently as sexually transmitted infections, or STIs).

The Bush administration also deleted CDC materials showing that education about condom use does not lead to earlier or increased sexual activity, especially among teens. The new CDC version, in boldface, still advocates abstinence instead of condom use:

The surest way to avoid transmission of sexually transmitted diseases is to abstain from sexual intercourse, or to be in a long-term mutually monogamous relationship with a partner who has been tested and you know is uninfected. . . . Correct and consistent use of the male latex condom can reduce the risk of STD transmission. However, no protective method is 100 percent effective, and condom use cannot guarantee absolute protection against any STD.

Sexual Activity and Health

A federal government Website intended to help parents and teens make "smart choices about their health and future" omits important information. The parents' guide emphasizes only abstinence and warns teenagers, at length, about STDs. The few paragraphs on condoms are entirely negative: They claim that teens use condoms incorrectly or haphazardly and that condoms offer little protection against pregnancy or STDs. There isn't a single word about abortion or homosexuality.

In the ten-page "Teen Chat" guide, four pages warn of the dangers of STDs, especially sterility, and several pages imply that waiting until marriage to have sex practically guarantees a permanent and happy relationship. There isn't a single reference to condoms, abortion, or sexual orientation.

SOURCES: "Daily Reproductive Health Report," 2002; "Male latex condoms . . ," 2002; "National Cancer Institute . . . ," 2003; U.S. Department of Health and Human Services, 2006; Kaufman, 2006.

Stop and Think . . .

- Should the government endorse sexual abstinence—especially for teens—to prevent out-of-wedlock pregnancies, HIV, and other STDs?

- Or should the government provide the results of scientific studies and let people decide how to behave sexually, whether they act responsibly or not?

Making Connections

- Some researchers violate ethical guidelines to bring in more money for their institutions. Is this acceptable, especially if the grants provide funds that can be used to reduce class sizes, pay for much-needed computer labs, and increase library staff and student services?

- On a number of sites (such as www.pickaprof.com and www.ratemyprofessors.com), students can say anything they want about faculty. Should students identify themselves instead of submitting the "evaluations" anonymously? Are the comments representative of all the students in a course? Should faculty set up similar public sites and evaluate students by name?

In its most extreme form, doing research on topics that politicians don't like may jeopardize a scholar's current or future employment. For example, even a tenured professor at a large research university can come close to being fired by a Republican governor who disapproves of the research on abstinence education (Bailey et al., 2002).

Conclusion

As this chapter shows, understanding marriage and the family is *not* an armchair activity dominated by scholars and philosophers. On the contrary, like the family itself, the study of marriage and the family reflects *changes* in the evolution of theories and *constraints* due to the limitations of research designs. There has been much progress in family research, and researchers have more *choices* in the methods available to them. At the same time, "there is plenty of reason for marriage and family scholars to be modest about what they know and humble about what they do not" (Miller, 1986: 110).

Research explanations sometimes are inadequate because social scientists ignore the historical context that has shaped the contemporary family. We look at some of these historical processes in the next chapter.

Summary

1. Although many people are suspicious of statistics, data of all kinds are becoming increasingly important in our daily lives. Information derived from social science research affects much of our everyday behavior, shapes family policies, and provides explanations for social change.

2. Both theory and research are essential to understanding marriages and families.

3. The most influential theories of marriage and the family include four macro-level perspectives (ecological, structural-functional, conflict, and feminist theories) and four micro-level theories (symbolic interaction, social exchange, family life course and development, and family systems). Researchers and clinicians often use several theoretical perspectives in interpreting data or choosing intervention strategies.

4. The survey is one of the most common data-collection methods in family research. Surveys rely on questionnaires, interviews, or a combination of these techniques. Both questionnaires and interviews have advantages and limitations that researchers consider in designing their studies.

5. Clinical research and case studies provide a deeper understanding of behavior because they enable researchers to study attitudes and behavior intensively and over time. Such research, however, is also time-consuming and limited to small groups of people.

6. Field research offers a deeper understanding of behavior and is usually inexpensive. The results of this type of research are difficult to quantify, however, and the researcher may experience difficulty in maintaining a balance between observation and participation.

7. Experiments try to establish cause–effect explanations. It is impossible to "prove" such associations, however, because experiments are usually conducted in artificial settings that don't represent people's behavior in natural environments.

8. Secondary analysis uses data collected by other researchers (such as historical documents and official

government statistics). It is usually an accessible, convenient, and inexpensive source of data but may not provide information about the variables that a researcher wants to examine.

9. Evaluation research, an applied research technique, often assesses the effectiveness and efficiency of social programs that offer services to families and other groups. If the results are unflattering, however, politi-cians and administrators may ignore the findings and never publish the reports.

10. Social scientists must adhere to professional ethi-cal standards, both in conducting research and in re-porting the results. Because political issues often affect research, however, collecting data is not as simple as it seems.

Key Terms

theory *34*
ecological theory *35*
structural-functional theory *36*
instrumental role *37*
expressive role *37*
manifest functions *37*
latent functions *37*
conflict theory *37*
feminist theories *38*

quantitative research *39*
qualitative research *39*
symbolic interaction theory *39*
significant others *39*
social exchange theory *40*
family life course development
   theory *40*
family life cycle *41*
developmental tasks *41*

family systems theory *42*
surveys *44*
clinical research *47*
field research *47*
secondary analysis *48*
experiment *49*
evaluation research *50*

Taking It Further

Do Your Research Online

Here are some Internet sites that are especially germane to this chapter:

WWW Virtual Library: Sociology is a comprehensive site that offers a good overview of many sociology resources, including chat rooms that discuss family issues.
http://socserv2.mcmaster.ca/w3virtsoclib/

Social Science Information Gateway offers thousands of online resources, searchable by subject topics such as *family, theory,* and *research methods.*
www.sosig.ac.uk

The **Inter-University Consortium for Political and Social Research** (ICPSR) is the largest data warehouse in the world that holds secondary data on social issues.
www.icpsr.umich.edu

FedStats provides statistics from over 1,000 U.S. federal agencies. Among other features, you can access data on your state, county, city, and Congressional district. www.fedstats.gov

Health News Review uses a team of 20 reviewers from universities and health clinics nationwide to write articles in major newspapers, magazines, and other media outlets. (If you want information on specific diseases, start with the National Institutes of Health, www.nih .gov.)

http://www.healthnewsreview.org

And more: www.prenhall.com/benokraitis provides URLs for theory sites, practical tips for evaluating a variety of online resources, sites of major research institutions, audio clips of Studs Terkel's interviews, studies of human development across the lifespan, the rejuvenated "Golden Fleece" award sites, online journals on qualitative research, cybersociology, "mundane" behavior, and more.

Investigate with Research Navigator

Go to www.researchnavigator.com and enter your LOGIN NAME and PASSWORD. For instructions on registering for the first time, view the detailed instructions at the end of the Chapter 1. Search the Research Navigator[[TM]] site using the following key terms:

feminism or feminist theory
social exchange theory
family systems theory

Outline

The Family in Historical Perspective

In 1890, Joel Coleman, a recent Jewish immigrant to New York City, wrote home:

Dear Father, I can tell You very little about my great achievements. I am not yet a wealthy man, but for sure not a beggar either. . . . Right now, during the winter, work is very slow. It happens every winter; therefore, we see to it that we have put something aside for those winter months. On the whole my life here is not bad and I cannot complain about

America, except for one thing—my health was better at home, in Poland, where the air was better. Here I often get sick, but I prefer not to write about it (Wtulich, 1986: 218).

Immigrants' letters, like Coleman's, often spoke of loneliness, low wages, hard and intermittent work, language barriers, poverty, and numerous hardships. Life was difficult and unpredictable in the "land of plenty."

When social scientists examine the past, they find that "the good old days" never existed for most people. Historians, especially, have raised some interesting questions: Were the colonists as virtuous as they were portrayed when we were in grade school? Did people really pull together to help each other during the Depression? Were the 1950s as fabulous as many people insist they were? This chapter addresses these and similar questions.

The Colonial Family

Although colonial families differed from modern ones in social class, religious practices, and geographic dispersion, factors such as family roles and family structure were very similar. The diversity that characterizes modern families also existed in colonial times.

Family Structure

The nuclear family was the most prevalent family form both in England and in the first settlements in the United States. An elderly grandparent or an apprentice sometimes lived with or near his or her family, but few households were made up of extended families for long periods (Goode, 1963; Laslett, 1971). Although families typically started out with six or seven children, high infant death rates resulted in small households, with large age differences between the children.

The Puritans—Protestant colonists who adhered to strict moral and religious values—believed that the community had a right to intervene in families that did not perform their duties properly. In the 1670s, for example, the Massachusetts General Court directed towns to appoint "tithingmen" to ensure that marital relations were harmonious and that parents disciplined unruly children (Mintz and Kellogg, 1988).

Few people survived outside families during the colonial period. Most settlements were small (fewer than 100 families), and each family was considered a "little commonwealth" that performed a variety of functions. The family was

- a self-sufficient *business* that produced and exchanged goods, in which all family members worked together
- a *school* that taught children to read
- a *vocational institute* that instructed children and prepared them for jobs through apprenticeships
- a miniature *church* that guided its members in daily prayers, personal meditation, and formal worship in the community

- a *house of correction* to which the courts sentenced idle people and non-violent offenders to be servants
- a *welfare institution* that gave its members medical and other care and provided a home for relatives who were orphaned, aging, sick, or homeless (Demos, 1970).

As you'll see later in this chapter, all these functions changed considerably with the onset of industrialization.

Sexual Relations

The Puritans tried to prevent premarital intercourse in several ways. One was **bundling,** a New England custom in which a fully dressed young man and woman spent the night in a bed together, separated by a wooden board.

The custom was adopted because it was difficult for the young suitor, who had traveled many miles, to

Illustrated Edition **25c**

LITTLE KNOWN FACTS ABOUT

BUNDLING

IN THE NEW WORLD

•

By A. MONROE AURAND, Jr.
Member:
Pennsylvania German Folklore Society, &c.

THE OLD-FASHIONED CENTER-BOARD
The Pennsylvania Germans invented all kinds of ways and means to get the courting couples together — and all kinds of knick-knacks to keep them apart when they got together! Girls were safer in the old days, in bed with their beaux, than they are today roaming the world over in search of adventure!

The Pennsylvania Germans invented various ways of keeping courting couples apart when they were together. What do you suppose might have happened to the "centerboard" shown in this sketch after the young woman's parents went to bed? The couple could hope that other members of the family—who typically slept in the same room—were sound sleepers.

return home the same night, especially during harsh winters. Because the rest of the family shared the room, it was considered quite proper for the bundled young man and woman to continue their conversation after the fire was out (McPharlin, 1946).

Despite such safeguards as bundling, premarital and extramarital sex were common. According to some historians, between 20 and 33 percent of colonial women were pregnant at the time of marriage (Hawke, 1988; Demos, 1970). Keep in mind, however, that sexual activity was generally confined to engaged couples. The idea of a casual meeting that included sexual intercourse would have been utterly foreign to the Puritans.

Out-of-wedlock births were fairly common among young women who immigrated to the southern colonies as indentured (contracted) servants. They typically came to the United States alone because they were from poor families that could not afford to migrate together. Because these very young (under age 15) women were alone and vastly outnumbered by men, they were vulnerable to sexual attacks, especially by employers (Harari and Vinovskis, 1993).

The Puritan community condemned adultery and illegitimacy because they threatened the family structure. Sometimes local newspapers denounced a straying spouse publicly:

Catherine Treen, the wife of the subscriber, behaved in the most disgraceful manner, by leaving her own place of abode, and living in a criminal state with a certain William Collins, a plaisterer, under whose bed she was last night, discovered, endeavoring to conceal herself. Her much injured husband thinks it absolutely necessary to forewarn all persons from trusting after such flagrant proof of her prostitution . . . (cited in Lantz, 1976: 14).

Few records, however, documented men's extramarital affairs. Though frowned upon, a husband's infidelity was considered "normal." And because the courts did not enforce a father's economic obligation, it was women who paid the costs of bearing and raising out-of-wedlock children (Ryan, 1983). As you can see, the double standard (which we discuss later) is not a modern invention.

Husbands and Wives

Husbands and wives worked together to make sure that the family survived. Like modern society, colonists expected spouses to have strong relationships. Inequalities, however, were very much a part of early American family life.

PERSONAL RELATIONSHIPS In general, women were subordinate to men; the wife's chief duty was to obey her husband. New England clergymen often referred to male authority as a "government" that women must accept as "law." In the southern colonies, husbands often denounced assertive wives as "impertinent" (Ryan, 1983). A woman's social status and her power and prestige in the community came from the patriarchal head of the household: her husband or her father (see Chapter 1).

At the same time, the "well-ordered" family was based on a number of mutual responsibilities. Husbands and wives were expected to show each other "a very great affection." They should be faithful to each other, and they were instructed to be patient and to help each other: "If the one is sick, pained, troubled, distressed, the other should manifest care, tenderness, pity, compassion, and afford all possible relief and succour" (Scott and Wishy, 1982: 86).

In Plymouth, women had the right to transfer property. In 1646, for example, when one man wanted to sell his family's land, the court called in his wife to make sure that she approved of the sale. The courts also granted liquor and other business licenses to women. And they sometimes offered a woman protection from a violent husband. The Plymouth court ordered a whipping for a man who kicked his wife off a stool and into a blazing fireplace (Demos, 1970; Mintz and Kellogg, 1988). Such protections were not typical in the colonies outside Plymouth, however.

In a few cases, the local courts permitted divorce. The acceptable grounds were limited to desertion, adultery, bigamy, and impotence. Incompatibility was recognized as a problem but not serious enough to warrant divorce. It was not until about 1765, when romantic love emerged as a basis for marriage, that "loss of affection" was mentioned as a reason for divorce (Cott and Pleck, 1979).

WORK AND THE ECONOMY Men were expected to be industrious, hardworking, and ambitious, and were responsible for the family's economic survival. Husbands and wives often worked side by side. Men, women, and children all produced, cultivated, and processed goods for the family's consumption. When necessary, men cared for and disciplined the children while women worked in the fields.

Much of women's work was directed toward meeting the needs of others. In his 1793 *Female Guide*, a New Hampshire pastor defined women's role as "piety to God—reverence to parents—love and obedience to their husbands—tenderness and watchfulness over their children—justice and humanity to their dependents" (quoted in Cott, 1977: 22–23).

Although both sexes were praised for being wealthy and industrious, men were expected to initiate economic activity and women were expected to support men and to be frugal. In 1692, Cotton Mather, an influential minister and author, described women's economic role as being only "to spend (or save) what others get" (Cott, 1977).

In some cases, unmarried women, widows, and those who had been deserted by their husbands turned their homemaking activities into self-supporting businesses. Some used their homes as inns, restaurants, or schools and sold homemade foods. Others made a living by washing, mending, nursing, serving as midwives, or producing cure-all and beauty potions.

Some widows continued their husbands' businesses in such "masculine" areas as chocolate and mustard production, soap making, cutlery, coach making, rope making, publishing, printing, horseshoeing, net making, whaling, and running grocery stores, bookstores, drugstores, and hardware stores. And some of these businesswomen advertised regularly in the local newspapers (Matthaei, 1982).

In general, however, the economic roles of women, especially wives, were severely limited. Women had little access to credit, could not sue to collect debts, were not allowed to own property, and were rarely chosen as executors of wills (Ryan, 1983).

Children's Lives

Poor sanitation, crude housing, limited hygiene, and dangerous physical environments characterized colonial America. Between 10 and 30 percent of all children died before their first birthday, and fewer than two out of three children lived to see their tenth birthday. Cotton Mather fathered 14 children, but only one outlived his father: seven died shortly after birth, one died at age 2 and five died in their early 20s (Stannard, 1979).

since you asked

Why were colonial families so large?

Children's lives were dominated by the concepts of repression, religion, and respect (Adams, 1980). The Puritans believed that children were born with original sin and were inherently stubborn, willful, selfish, and corrupt. The entire community—parents, school, church, and neighbors—worked together to keep children "in their place."

Compared with contemporary children, colonial children were expected to be extraordinarily well behaved, obedient, and docile (*Figure 3.1*). Within 40 years of their arrival in Plymouth, however, many colonists worried that their families were disintegrat-ing, that parents were becoming less responsible, and that children were becoming less respectful of authority. Ministers repeatedly warned parents that their children were frequenting taverns, keeping "vicious company," and "tending to dissoluteness (unrestrained and immoral behavior)" (Mintz and Kellogg, 1988: 17). These concerns sound pretty modern, don't they?

Wealthy southern families were more indulgent with their children than were well-to-do families in the northern colonies, but in less affluent families child labor was nearly universal throughout the colonies. Even very young children worked hard, either in their own homes, as indentured servants, or as slaves. For example, several shiploads of "friendless boys and girls," who had been kidnapped in England, were sent to the Virginia colony to provide cheap and submissive labor for American planters (Queen et al., 1985).

Because girls were expected to be homemakers, they received little formal education. The New England colonies educated boys, but girls were generally barred from schooling. They were commonly admitted to public schools only during the hours and seasons when boys were occupied with other affairs or were needed in the fields. As one farmer stated, "In winter it's too far for girls to walk; in summer they ought to stay at home to help in the kitchen" (quoted in Earle, 1899: 96). Women who succeeded in getting an education were often ridiculed:

> *John Winthrop—the first governor of the Massachusetts Bay Colony—maintained that such intellectual exertion [as education and writing books] could rot the female mind. He attributed the madness of Ann Hopkins, wife of the Connecticut governor, to her intellectual curiosity: "If she had attended her household affairs . . . and not gone out of her way to meddle in the affairs of men whose minds are stronger, she'd have kept her wits and might have improved them usefully" (Ryan, 1983: 57).*

Social Class and Regional Differences

The experiences of colonial families differed because of a number of regional and social class variations. In a study of Salem families between 1790 and 1810, sociologist Bernard Farber (1972) identified three social classes with very different socialization patterns that supported the economic structure.

In the *merchant class,* or upper class, the patriarchs typically were shipping and commercial entrepreneurs. Family businesses were inherited, and partnerships were expanded through first-cousin marriages.

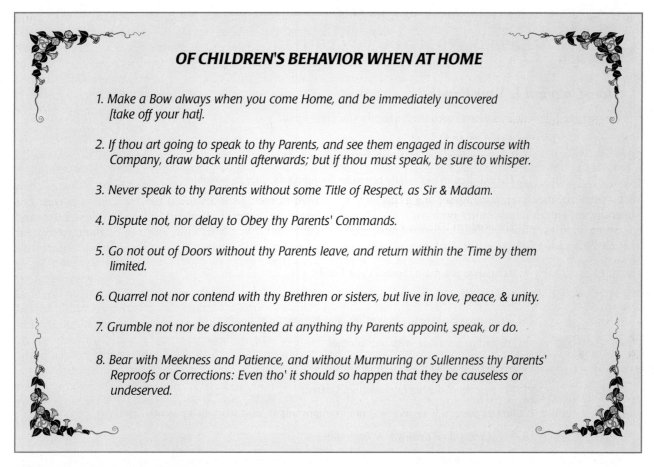

OF CHILDREN'S BEHAVIOR WHEN AT HOME

1. *Make a Bow always when you come Home, and be immediately uncovered [take off your hat].*

2. *If thou art going to speak to thy Parents, and see them engaged in discourse with Company, draw back until afterwards; but if thou must speak, be sure to whisper.*

3. *Never speak to thy Parents without some Title of Respect, as Sir & Madam.*

4. *Dispute not, nor delay to Obey thy Parents' Commands.*

5. *Go not out of Doors without thy Parents leave, and return within the Time by them limited.*

6. *Quarrel not nor contend with thy Brethren or sisters, but live in love, peace, & unity.*

7. *Grumble not nor be discontented at anything thy Parents appoint, speak, or do.*

8. *Bear with Meekness and Patience, and without Murmuring or Sullenness thy Parents' Reproofs or Corrections: Even tho' it should so happen that they be causeless or undeserved.*

FIGURE 3.1   Rules for Colonial Children

Source: Adapted from Wadsworth, 1712, in Scott and Wishy, 1982.

Highly skilled occupations, apprenticeship systems, and cooperation among relatives characterized the *artisan class,* or middle class. Children were encouraged to be upwardly mobile and to find secure jobs.

The *laboring class,* or working class, was made up mainly of migrants to the community. These people, who had no voting privileges and little education, provided much of the unskilled labor needed by the merchant class.

Colonial families also differed from one region to another. In the northern colonies, people settled in villages; in the southern colonies, they settled on isolated plantations and farms. There was an especially rigid stratification system among wealthy families, poor whites, indentured servants, and black slaves in the southern colonies.

After reading this section, some of my students dismiss the colonial family as a relic of the past. Others feel that their families of orientation reflect some similar characteristics. Take the quiz "How Colonial Is Your Family?" to decide for yourself.

Early American Families from Non-European Cultures

European explorers and settlers who invaded North America in the sixteenth and seventeenth centuries pushed the original inhabitants, American Indians and Mexicans, out of their territories. Except for people who arrived in the colonies as servants—and in general they *chose* to indenture themselves—African Americans are the only people who did not come to America voluntarily.

Applying What You've Learned

How Colonial Is Your Family?

Answer the following questions based on the family you grew up in.

Yes	No	
☐	☐	1. The main focus of my family was making ends meet.
☐	☐	2. The children in our family began to do chores as early as possible.
☐	☐	3. Discipline was harsh at times.
☐	☐	4. The needs of the family were more important than individual needs.
☐	☐	5. Our family was the center of our everyday lives.
☐	☐	6. Religion was a main theme in our family.
☐	☐	7. Father's rule was most important in our family.
☐	☐	8. We learned basic reading, writing, and arithmetic at home.
☐	☐	9. We had to get along with one another.
☐	☐	10. My parents often ignored my feelings.
☐	☐	11. My parents had a big say in whom I dated.
☐	☐	12. For my parents, romance was not as important as hard work in a potential mate.
☐	☐	13. My parents didn't really love each other.
☐	☐	14. One of my parents was subordinate to the other most of the time.
☐	☐	15. My parents still have strong control over my life.

SOURCE: Based on Hammond and Bearnson, 2003: 24.

Key to "How Colonial Is Your Family?"

Add up all the "yes" answers. A score of 15 represents high colonial family traits. A score of 0 signifies low traits. If you received a high score, does this surprise you? Do high scores suggest that many modern families have traces of the colonial family? Or not?

The experiences of these three groups were quite different. Some families and tribes fared better than others, and there was considerable diversity within each group.

American Indians

Many anthropologists believe that American Indians migrated to North America from northeastern Asia over a period of 30,000 years. By the time European settlers arrived, there were almost 18 million Indians living in North America, speaking approximately 300 languages. About 175 distinct languages are still spoken in the United States (Greenberg and Ruhlen, 1992; Trimble and Medicine, 1993; Pierre, 2003).

American Indians were enormously diverse racially, culturally, and linguistically. This variation was reflected in kinship and family systems as well as in interpersonal relations.

FAMILY STRUCTURE Family structures and customs varied from one Indian society to another. For example, polygyny was common in more than 20 percent of mar-

since you asked

Is it true that American Indian women were dominated by the men?

riages among Indians of the Great Plains and the northwest coast. In contrast, monogamy was the norm among agricultural groups such as the Hopi, Iroquois, and Huron. Some groups, such as the Creek society, allowed polygyny. Few men took more than one wife, however, because only the best hunters could support more than one wife and her children (Price, 1981; Braund, 1990).

Approximately 25 percent of North American Indian tribes were **matrilineal,** which means that children traced their family descent through the mother's line rather than through that of the father (**patrilineal**). The women owned the houses, the household furnishings, the fields and gardens, the work tools, and the livestock, and all this property was passed on to their female heirs (Mathes, 1981).

Historians say that Indian women were often better off than their white counterparts. In contrast to filmmakers' stereotypes of the docile "squaw," Indian women actually wielded considerable power and commanded respect in many bands and tribes. The box "American Indian Women: Chiefs, Physicians, Politicians, and Warriors" describes some of the societal roles of Indian women in colonial times.

MARRIAGE AND DIVORCE Most American Indian women typically married between ages 12 and 15, after reaching puberty. Men married at slightly older ages, between 15 and 20, usually after they had proven their ability to hunt and to provide for a family. Some parents arranged their children's marriages; others allowed young men and women to choose their own spouses.

Family structures and customs also varied. Among the Shoshone there were no formal marriage ceremonies; the families simply exchanged gifts. Also, there were no formal rules of residence. The newly married couple could live with the family of either the groom or the bride or establish their own independent home.

Among the Zuñi of the Southwest, marriages were arranged casually, and the groom moved into the bride's household. Divorce was easy among the Zuñi, as well as other groups. If a wife was fed up with a demanding husband, she would simply put his belongings outside their home, and they were no longer married. The man accepted the dismissal and returned to his mother's household. If a husband sought a divorce, he would tell his wife he was going hunting and then not return home (Stockel, 1991).

In the Great Plains, most Teton parents arranged marriages, but some unions were based on romantic love. Marriages were often lifetime associations, but divorce was easy and fairly common. A man could divorce a wife for adultery, laziness, or even excessive nagging. Both parties usually agreed to divorce, but a man could humiliate a wife by casting her off publicly at a dance or other ceremony.

CHILDREN Most Indian families were small because of high infant and child death rates. In addition, mothers nursed their children for several years, often abstaining from sexual relations until the child was weaned.

Throughout most American Indian groups, childhood was a happy time and parents were generally kind and loving. Mohave and Zuñi parents, for example, were indulgent; children were carefree, and discipline was rare and mild. Children were taught to be polite and gentle. Unruly children were frightened into conformity by stories of religious bogeymen rather than by physical punishment. Grandparents on both sides of the family played an active role in educating children and telling stories that exemplified the tribe's values.

PUBERTY In most Indian societies, puberty rites were more elaborate for girls than for boys. Among the Alaskan Nabesna, for example, a menstruating girl was secluded, observed strict food taboos, was forbidden to touch her own body with her hands (lest sores break out), and was forbidden to travel with the tribe. In contrast, among the Mohave, the observance of a girl's puberty was a private family matter that did not include any community rituals.

Among the Teton, a boy's puberty was marked by a series of events, such as his first successful bison hunt, his first war party, his first capture of enemy horses, and other deeds, all of which his father commemorated with feasts and gifts to other members of the tribe.

Some tribes also emphasized the *vision quest,* a supernatural experience. After fasting and taking ritual purifying baths in a small, dome-shaped sweat lodge, a young

Cross-Cultural Families

American Indian Women: Chiefs, Physicians, Politicians, and Warriors

Many American Indian women and men had egalitarian relationships. Besides being wives and mothers, many Indian women were also chiefs, physicians, politicians, and warriors.

Chiefs: In some cases, women became chiefs because of their achievements in battle. In other cases, they replaced husbands who died. Like men, female chiefs could declare war, resolve disputes in the community, and punish offenders.

Physicians: Women could be medicine women, or shamans, the Indian equivalent of doctors. In many Indian cultures, women played crucial roles as spiritual leaders.

Politicians: Because a number of tribes were matrilineal and matrilocal, many women had political power. Among the Lakota, for example, a man owned only his clothing, a horse for hunting, weapons, and spiritual items. Homes, furnishings, and other property belonged to women. In many tribes, women were influential decision makers.

Warriors: Among the Apache, some women warriors were as courageous as the men, and Cheyenne women distinguished themselves in war. Lakota women maintained warrior societies, and among the Cherokee, one of the fiercest warriors was a woman who also headed a women's military society.

Women could stop war parties by refusing to supply the food needed for the journey. An Iroquois woman could initiate a war party by demanding that a captive be obtained to replace a murdered member of her clan. Creek women often were responsible for raising "war fervor" against enemies (Mathes, 1981; Braund, 1990; Stockel, 1991; Jaimes and Halsey, 1992).

Delaware nation council chief and educator Linda Poolaw was asked to choose works for an exhibition for the Smithsonian's National Museum of the American Indian. Poolaw's ancestors once lived on Manhattan Island in New York.

boy left the camp and found an isolated place, often the top of a butte or other elevated spot. He then waited for a vision in which a supernatural being instructed him on his responsibilities as an adult (Spencer and Jennings, 1977).

THE IMPACT OF EUROPEAN CULTURES The French, Spanish, Portuguese, and British played a major role in destroying much of American Indian culture. Europeans exploited the abundant North American resources of gold, land, and fur. Missionaries, determined to convert the "savages" to Christianity, were responsible for some of the cultural destruction. Disregarding important cultural values and beliefs, missionaries tried to eliminate religious ceremonies and practices such as polygyny and matrilineal inheritance (Price, 1981).

Indian tribes coped with military slaughter, enslavement, forced labor, land confiscation, coerced mass migration, and involuntary religious conversions (Collier, 1947). By the end of the seventeenth century, staggering numbers of American Indians in the East had died from diseases for which they lacked immunity, such as influenza, measles, smallpox, and typhus. The Plymouth colony was located in a deserted Indian village whose inhabitants had been devastated by epidemics carried by European settlers.

By the 1670s, only 10 percent of the original American Indian population of New England survived. At least 50 tribes became extinct as a result of disease and massacre. In the eighteenth and nineteenth centuries, the diversity of American Indian family practices was reduced even further through ongoing missionary activities, intrusive federal land policies, and intermarriage with outside groups (John, 1988).

African Americans

One colonist wrote in his journal that on August 20, 1619, at the Jamestown settlement in Virginia, "there came . . . a Dutch man-of-warre that sold us 20 negars."

These first African Americans were brought over as indentured servants. After their terms of service, they were free to buy land, marry, and hire their own labor.

These rights were short-lived, however. By the mid-1660s, the southern colonies had passed laws prohibiting blacks from testifying in court, owning property, making contracts, traveling without permission, and congregating in public places. The slave trade grew in both the northern and southern colonies over several decades.

Some early statesmen, like President Thomas Jefferson, publicly denounced slavery but supported it privately. In 1809, for example, Jefferson maintained that "the Negro slave in America must be removed beyond the reach of mixture" for the preservation of the "dignity" and "beauty" of the white race. At the same time, Jefferson had a slave mistress, Sally Hemmings, and fathered children with her. Inconsistent to the end, he freed five of his slaves in his will but left the other 182 slaves to his heirs (Bergman, 1969).

since you asked

Did slavery destroy the black family?

FAMILY STRUCTURE Until the 1970s, sociologists and historians maintained that slavery had emasculated black fathers, forced black mothers to become the matriarchs of their families, and destroyed the African American family. Historian Herbert Gutman (1983) dispelled many of these beliefs with his study of 21 urban and rural communities in the South between 1855 and 1880. Gutman found that 70 to 90 percent of African American households were made up of a husband and wife or a single parent and their children.

Most women were heads of households because their husbands had died, not because they had never married. They usually had only one or two children. Thus, according to Gutman, in the nineteenth century black families were stable, intact, and resilient.

MARRIAGE Throughout the colonies, it was difficult for a slave to find a spouse. In northern cities, most slaves lived with their masters and were not allowed to associate with other slaves. In the southern colonies, most slaves lived on plantations that had fewer than ten slaves. Because the plantations were far apart, it was difficult for slave men and women to find a mate of roughly the same age. In addition, overwork and high death rates due to disease meant that marriages did not last very long (Mintz and Kellogg, 1988).

To ensure that slaves would remain on the plantations and bear future slaves, many owners encouraged them to marry and to have large families. Yet marriages were fragile. As the box "A Slave Auction" shows, owners often separated family members. Studies of slave families in Mississippi, Tennessee, and Louisiana show that such auctions ended 35 to 40 percent of marriages (Gutman, 1976; Matthaei, 1982).

HUSBANDS AND FATHERS Several black scholars have noted that white, male, middle-class historians and sociologists have misrepresented the slave family (McAdoo, 1986; Staples, 1988). One example is the portrayal of husbands and fathers. In contrast to popular conceptions of the African American male as powerless, adult male slaves provided important role models for boys:

> Trapping wild turkeys required considerable skill; not everyone could construct a "rabbit gum" equal to the guile of the rabbits; and running down the quick, battling raccoon took pluck. For a boy growing up, the moment when his father thought him ready to join in the hunting and to learn to trap was a much-sought recognition of his own manhood (Genovese, 1981: 239–40).

These activities increased families' nutritional intake and supplemented monotonous and inadequate diets.

African male slaves often served as surrogate fathers to many children, both blood relatives and others. Black preachers, whose eloquence and morality commanded the respect of the entire community, were also influential role models. Men made shoes, wove baskets, constructed furniture, and cultivated the tiny garden plots allotted to their families by the master (Jones, 1985).

WIVES AND MOTHERS Many historians describe African American women as survivors who resisted the slave system. Mothers raised their children, cooked, made clothes for their families, maintained the slave cabin, and toiled in the fields. Because the African American woman was often both a "mammy" to the plantation owner's children and a mother to her own, she experienced the exhausting *double day*—a full day of domestic chores plus a full day of work outside the home—at least a century before middle-class white women coined the term and later substituted *second shift* for *double day* (see Chapters 5 and 13).

Black women got little recognition for such grueling schedules and were often subjected to physical punishment. Pregnant slaves were sometimes forced to lie face down in a specially dug depression in the ground, which protected the fetus while the mother was beaten, and some nursing mothers were whipped until "blood and milk flew mingled from their breasts" (Jones, 1985: 20).

In the South, children as young as 2 or 3 were put to work. They fetched things or carried the train of a

Constraints

A Slave Auction

In the mid-1970s, Alex Haley, a journalist who had taught himself to read and write during a 20-year career in the U.S. Coast Guard, was catapulted to fame when his book *Roots: The Saga of an American Family* (1976) became a best-seller and was made into one of the first miniseries on television. In the book, Haley traced six generations of his ancestors, the first of whom was abducted at age 16 from Gambia, West Africa, in 1767. The following excerpt is a powerful description of how African families were destroyed by slavery:

During the day a number of sales were made. David and Caroline were purchased together by a Natchez planter. They left us, grinning broadly, and in a most happy state of mind, caused by the fact of their not being separated. Sethe was sold to a planter of Baton Rouge, her eyes flashing with anger as she was led away.

The same man also purchased Randall. The little fellow was made to jump, and run across the floor, and perform many other feats, exhibiting his activity and condition. All the time the trade was going on, Eliza was crying aloud and wringing her hands. She besought the man not to buy him, unless he also bought herself and Emily. She promised, in that case, to be the most faithful slave that ever lived.

The man answered that he could not afford it, and then Eliza burst into a paroxysm of grief, weeping plaintively. Freeman turned round to her, savagely, with his whip in his uplifted hand, ordering her to stop her noise, or he would flog her. Unless she ceased that minute, he would take her to the yard and give her a hundred lashes.

. . . Eliza shrunk before him and tried to wipe away her tears, but it was all in vain. She wanted to be with her children, she said, the little time she had to live.

All the frowns and threats of Freeman could not wholly silence the afflicted mother. She kept on begging and beseeching them, most piteously, not to separate the three. Over and over again she told them how she loved her boy. A great many times she repeated her former promises—how very faithful and obedient she would be, how hard she would labor day and night, to the last moment of her life, if he would only buy them all together.

But it was of no avail; the man could not afford it. The bargain was agreed upon, and Randall must go alone. Then Eliza ran to him, embraced him passionately, kissed him again and again, and told him to remember her—all the while her tears falling in the boy's face like rain.

Freeman damned her, calling her a blubbering, bawling wench, and ordered her to go to her place, and behave herself, and be somebody. . . . He would soon give her something to cry about, if she was not mighty careful, and that she might depend on.

The planter from Baton Rouge, with his new purchase, was ready to depart. "Don't cry, mama. I will be a good boy. Don't cry," said Randall, looking back, as they passed out of the door.

What has become of the lad, God knows. It was a mournful scene indeed. I would have cried myself if I had dared.

SOURCE: Adapted from Solomon Northrup, cited in Meltzer (1964: 87–89).

mistress's dress. Masters often "gave" slave children to their own offspring as gifts (Schwartz, 2000).

Only a few female slaves worked in the master's home, known as "the big house." Most females over 10 years of age worked in the field, sunup to sundown, six days a week, and as a result mothers had to struggle to maintain a semblance of family life:

Occasionally, women were permitted to leave the fields early on Saturday to perform some chores around the slave quarters. Their homes were small cabins of one or two rooms, which they usually shared with their mate and their children, and perhaps another family secluded behind a crude partition (Ryan, 1983: 159).

Popular films like *Gone with the Wind* often portray house slaves as doing little more than adjusting Miss Scarlett's petticoats and announcing male suitors. In reality, domestic work was as hard as fieldwork. Fetching wood and water, preparing three meals a day over a smoky fireplace, and pressing clothes for an entire family was backbreaking labor.

Female servants sometimes had to sleep on the floor at the foot of the mistress's bed. They were often forced into sexual relations with the master. Injuries were common, minor infractions met with swift and severe punishment, and servants suffered abuse ranging from jabs with pins to beatings that left them disfigured for life (Jones, 1985).

ECONOMIC SURVIVAL *Ethnic Notions,* a memorable documentary, shows that many Hollywood movies, books, and newspapers have portrayed slaves as helpless, passive, and dependent people who couldn't care for themselves. Recent evidence has shattered such stereotypes. An archaeological team that excavated Virginia plantations, for example, found evidence that some enslaved Africans were "entrepreneurs": They traded fish and game for children's toys, dishes, and other household items.

Also, many slaves hid important personal possessions and items stolen from plantation owners in underground storage areas. Slaves were hardly meek or submissive. Instead, they used effective tactics such as negotiating with their masters over assigned tasks and breaking tools to slow the pace of their work (Berlin, 1998; Morgan, 1998; Wheeler, 1998).

AFTER EMANCIPATION After slavery was abolished in 1863, many mothers set out to find children from whom they had been separated many years earlier. Numerous slaves formalized their marriages, even though the one-dollar fee for the marriage license cost about two weeks' pay for most. A legal marriage was an important status symbol, and a wedding was a festive event (Degler, 1981; Staples, 1988; King, 1996).

Some writers have claimed that the African American family, already disrupted by slavery, was further weakened by migration to cities in the North in the late 1800s (Frazier, 1939; Moynihan, 1970). However, many black migrants tried to maintain contact with their kin and families in the South. When black men

migrated alone, "a constant flow of letters containing cash and advice between North and South facilitated the gradual migration of whole clans and even villages" (Jones, 1985: 159). Others returned home frequently to join in community celebrations or to help with planting and harvesting on the family farm. Thus, many African American families remained resilient despite difficult conditions.

Mexican Americans

After 30 years of war and conflict, in 1848 the United States annexed territory that was originally Mexican. Despite the provisions of the Treaty of Guadalupe Hidalgo, which guaranteed security of their property, the federal government confiscated the land of most Mexican families. Land speculators defrauded countless other landowners. Most of the Mexicans, and their descendants, became laborers. The loss of land, an important economic base, had long-term negative effects on Mexican American families (see Chapter 4).

WORK AND GENDER Whether they lived and grew up in the United States or migrated from Mexico, Mexican laborers were essential to the prosperity of southwestern businesses. Employers purposely avoided hiring Mexicans for skilled jobs because "they are available in such [great] numbers and . . . they [would] do the most disagreeable work at the lowest wages" (Feldman, 1931: 115).

During the 1800s, men typically worked on the railroads or in mining, agriculture, ranching, or low-level urban occupations (such as dishwasher). Women worked as domestics, cooks, live-in house servants, or laundresses, in canning and packing houses, and in agriculture (Camarillo, 1979).

By the 1930s, Mexican women made up a major portion of the workers in the garment manufacturing

By permission of John L. Hart FLP, and Creators Syndicate, Inc.

sweatshops in the Southwest. Even though American labor codes stipulated a pay rate of $15 a week, Mexican women were paid less than $5, and some earned as little as 50 cents a week. If the women protested, they lost their jobs. Illegal migrants were especially vulnerable because they were intimidated by threats of deportation (Acuna, 1988). Despite the economic exploitation they faced, many Mexican families preserved traditional family structure, family roles, and child rearing.

FAMILY STRUCTURE Mexican society was characterized by **familism**; that is, family relationships took precedence over individual well-being. (You will see in Chapter 4 that familism still characterizes much of contemporary Latino culture, including Mexican Americans.) The nuclear family often embraced an extended family of several generations, including cousins, in which kin provided emotional and financial support.

since you asked

Why were Mexican families so tightly knit?

A key factor in conserving Mexican culture was the practice of **compadrazgo**, in which parents, children, and the children's godparents maintained close relationships. The *compadres*, or co-parents, were godparents who enlarged family ties, similar to the fictive kin described in Chapter 1. Godparents were close family friends who had strong ties with their godchildren throughout life and participated in rites of passage such as baptism, confirmation, first communion, and marriage.

The godparents in the *compadrazgo* network provided both discipline and support. They expected obedience, respect, and love from their godchildren. They were also warm and affectionate and helped the children financially whenever possible. For girls, who led cloistered and protected lives, visiting their godparents' families was a major form of recreation (Williams, 1990).

FAMILY ROLES Women were the guardians of family traditions, even though many mothers worked outside the home because of economic necessity. Despite the disruptions caused by migratory work, women nurtured Mexican culture through folklore, songs, baptisms, weddings, and celebrations of birthdays and saints' days (Garcia, 1980). In the traditional family, women defined their roles primarily as homemakers and mothers.

In the Mexican American family, the male head of the family had all the authority. Masculinity was expressed in the concept of **machismo**, which stresses male attributes such as dominance, assertiveness, pride, and sexual prowess. (Chapter 4 discusses the controversy surrounding the interpretation of *machismo*.)

This notion of male preeminence carried with it the clear implication of a double standard. Men could engage in premarital and extramarital sex, for example, but women were expected to remain virgins, to be faithful to their husbands, and to limit their social relationships, even after marriage, to family and female friends (Mirande, 1985; Moore and Pachon, 1985).

CHILDREN The handful of diaries, letters, and other writings available to us today suggests that, at least in middle- and upper-class families, children were socialized according to gender. Although boys did some of the same domestic chores as their sisters, they had much more freedom than girls did. Young girls were severely restricted in their social relationships outside the home. A girl was expected to learn how to be a good mother and wife—a virtuous example for her children and the "soul of society" (del Castillo, 1984: 81).

According to the diary of a teenage girl who lived on the outskirts of San Antonio from 1889 to 1892, her brother was responsible for helping with such tasks as laundry and chopping wood. He was allowed to go into town on errands and to travel around the countryside on his horse. In contrast, she was not allowed to go into town with her father and brother or to attend chaperoned dances in the town. She could not visit neighbors, and she attended only one social event in a six-month period, when her family traveled into town to visit her aunt during Christmas (del Castillo, 1984).

THE EUROPEAN INFLUENCE Although they suffered less physical and cultural destruction than American Indians did, Mexican Americans endured a great deal at the hands of European frontiersmen, land speculators, and politicians. By the mid-1800s, when most Mexican Americans were beginning to experience widespread exploitation, new waves of European immigrant families were also harnessed under the yoke of industrialization.

Making Connections

- Look at Figure 3.1 again. Some of my students feel that such rules for colonial children were ridiculous. Others think that we should resurrect some of these practices because many parents are too permissive. What do you think?

- Regardless of your cultural heritage, did your ancestors' experiences affect your family's values and behavior?

Industrialization, Urbanization, and European Immigration: 1820 to 1930

The lives of many U.S. families changed dramatically from about 1820 to 1930 as a result of two massive waves of immigration from Europe. More than 10 million immigrants—mostly English, Irish, Scandinavian, and German—arrived during the first wave, from 1830 to 1882. During the second wave, from 1882 to 1930, immigrants were predominantly Russian, Greek, Polish, Italian, Austrian, Hungarian, and Slavic.

The Industrial Revolution led to extensive mechanization, which shifted home manufacturing to large-scale factory production. As the economic structure changed, a small group of white, Anglo-Saxon, Protestant (often referred to as WASP), upper-class families prospered from the backbreaking labor of Mexicans, Asians, European immigrants, and many American-born whites. European immigrants endured some of the most severe pressures on family life.

Family Life

As farming became large scale and commercial and factories developed, families lost many of their production functions. Most family members had to work outside the home to earn enough to purchase goods and services. Although it is not clear exactly how it happened, family life changed.

since you asked

Why did industrialization weaken family bonds?

In the middle classes, husbands and wives developed separate spheres of activity. The husband went out to work (the "breadwinner"), and the wife stayed home to care for the children (the "housewife") (see Chapters 2 and 5). As romantic love became the basis for marriage,

Changes

Characteristics of "True Womanhood"

One author describes nineteenth-century working-class women as "without corsets, matrons with their breasts unrestrained, their armpits damp with sweat, with their hair all over the place, blouses dirty or torn, and stained skirts" (Barret-Ducrocq, 1991: 11). Expectations for upper-class women (whom middle-class women tried to emulate) were quite different.

For "true women," loss of virginity was worse than death. In *The Young Lady's Friend* (1837), Mrs. John Farrar gave practical advice about staying out of trouble: "Sit not with another in a place that is too narrow; read not out of the same book; let not your eagerness to see anything induce you to place your head close to another person's."

"True women" were expected to be gentle, passive, submissive, childlike, weak, dependent, and protected. Unlike men, they should work silently, unseen, and only for affection, not for money or ambition.

Women should marry, but not for money. They should choose "only the high road of true love and not truckle to the values of a materialistic society." A woman should stifle her own talents and devote herself "to sustain her husband's genius and aid him in his arduous career."

Domesticity was a woman's most prized virtue. Home was supposed to be a cheerful place, so that brothers, husbands, and sons would not go elsewhere to have a good time.

Women were the "highest adornment of civilization" and should keep busy at "morally uplifting tasks." Housework was seen as uplifting. For example, the repetitiveness of routine tasks (such as making beds) inculcated patience and perseverance, and proper management of the home was considered a complex art: "There is more to be learned about pouring out tea and coffee than most young ladies are willing to believe."

The true woman was expected to love flowers, to write letters ("an activity particularly feminine since it had to do with the outpourings of the heart"), and to practice singing and playing a musical instrument. If a woman had to read, she should choose spiritually uplifting books from a list of "morally acceptable authors," preferably religious biographies.

SOURCE: Welter, 1966: 151–74.

couples had more freedom in choosing their partners based on compatibility and personal attraction. As households became more private, ties with the larger community became more fragile, and spouses turned to each other for affection and happiness much more than was typical in the past (Skolnick, 1991).

New attitudes about the "true woman" became paramount in redefining the role of the wife as nurturer and caregiver rather than as workmate. In lower socioeconomic classes, many mothers worked outside the home in low-paying jobs. Children often dropped out of school to work and to help support their families. Most spouses had little time to show love and affection to their children or to each other.

THE DEBUT OF "TRUE WOMANHOOD" By the late eighteenth century, a small group of northern merchants had monopolized the import business, and wealthy southern planters had greatly expanded their landholdings and crop production. The wives and daughters of these elite business leaders devoted much of their energy to "a conspicuous display of personal adornment and social graces" (Ryan, 1983: 85).

The women spent much of their time socializing, throwing lavish parties, and adorning their homes and themselves. "The upkeep of her appearance might involve preparation of the cosmetic base, aqua vitae, a potion requiring 30 ingredients, 2 months' cultivation, and an impossible final step: 'shake the bottle incessantly for 10 to 12 hours' " (quoted in Ryan, 1983: 85–86).

By the early 1800s, most men's work was totally separated from the household, and family life revolved around the man's struggle to make a living. The "good" wife turned the home into a comfortable retreat from the pressures that the man faced in the workplace.

Between 1820 and 1860, women's magazines and religious literature defined and applauded the attributes of "true womanhood." Women were judged as "good" if they displayed four cardinal virtues: piety, purity, submissiveness, and domesticity (Welter, 1966). As the box "Characteristics of 'True Womanhood' " shows, working-class women were not "true women" because, like men, most worked outside the home.

CHILDREN AND ADOLESCENTS Fathers' control over their children began to erode. By the end of the seventeenth century, fathers had less land to divide among their sons. This meant that they had less authority over their children's sexual behavior and choice of a marriage partner. The percentage of women who were pregnant at the time of their marriage shot up to more than 40 percent by the mid-eighteenth century, suggesting that parents had become less effective in preventing premarital intercourse (Mintz and Kellogg, 1988).

Because a marriage was less likely to involve a distribution of the family's land and property, children were less dependent on their fathers for economic support. Moreover, new opportunities for nonagricultural work, along with labor shortages in cities, prompted many children to leave home and thus escape from the authority of strict fathers.

Perhaps the biggest change was that, largely in the middle class, adults began to view and treat children as more than "miniature adults." Children began to spend more time playing than working, and adolescence became a stage of life that did not involve adult responsibilities.

People published more books for and about children. Adults began to recognize children's individuality by giving them names that were different from their father's or mother's. They also began, for the first time, to celebrate birthdays, especially those of children. There was also a decline in physical punishment, and physicians and others now recognized the early onset of sexual feelings in children (Ariès, 1962; Degler, 1981; Demos, 1986).

Among the working classes and the poor, however, child labor was widespread, and children were a critical resource in their families' survival. In a survey of Massachusetts working-class families in 1875, for example, children under age 15 contributed nearly 20 percent of their families' income (Mintz and Kellogg, 1988).

These Pennsylvania miners and "breaker boys"—youngsters who sorted the mined coal into traded categories—worked as many as fourteen hours a day for very low pay. Like most miners of this period, they were immigrants who performed backbreaking labor during the U.S. Industrial Revolution.

The Impact of Immigration and Urbanization

Immigration played a key role in the Industrial Revolution in the United States. Immigrants provided a large pool of unskilled and semi-skilled labor that fueled emerging industries and gave investors huge profits.

In the first large waves of immigration in the late 1800s, paid middlemen arranged for the shipment of immigrants to waiting industries. For example, Asians were channeled into the western railroads, Italians were funneled into public works projects and used as strikebreakers, and Hungarians were directed toward the Pennsylvania coal mines. Later immigrants followed these established paths into industrial America (Bodnar, 1985).

Very few immigrant families escaped dire poverty. Because men's wages were low, most married women were also in the labor force. Some worked at home making artificial flowers, threading wires through tags, or crocheting over curtain rings. Some were cleaning women or seamstresses, did laundry, or sold cakes. Others took in boarders and lodgers, especially after their children left home (Hareven, 1984; Weatherford, 1986).

Like the men, women of different ethnic groups tended to move into specific jobs. For example, Italian women were more likely than Polish or Greek women to reject domestic labor, which would take them out of the Italian community and into other people's homes. Instead, they were more likely to work as seasonal laborers for fruit and vegetable processing companies (Squier and Quadagno, 1988). By the turn of the nineteenth century, a woman's occupation was usually tied to her race and ethnicity (see *Figure 3.2*).

Women and Work in Nineteenth-Century America

By 1890, all but 9 of the 369 industries listed by the U.S. Census Bureau employed women. Many of these industries were especially eager to hire "greenhorns" and women "just off the boat," who would work for low wages. Greenhorns were often underpaid or not paid

at all. In some cases, employers delayed wage payments for several months and then closed their shops, disappearing overnight (Manning, 1970).

By the late 1800s, Irish girls as young as 11 were leaving home to work as servants; 75 percent of all Irish teenage girls were domestic servants. Even though they were hired only for housekeeping, many had to care for children, were sexually assaulted by their male employers, and were not paid their full wages (Ryan, 1983).

Most manufacturing jobs were segregated by sex. In the tobacco industry, for example, even though cigar rolling traditionally had been a woman's task in Slavic

since you asked

Are "working women" a modern phenomenon?

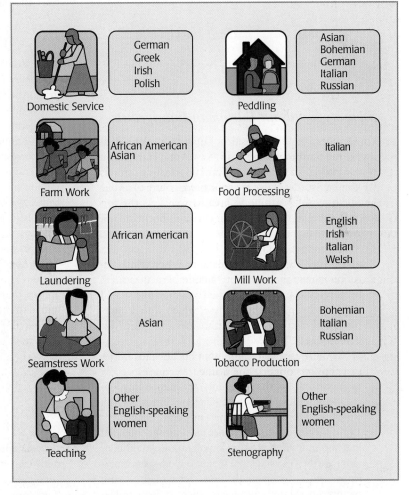

FIGURE 3.2 Women and Work in Nineteenth-Century America
As you can see, women who worked outside the home in the 1800s tended to cluster in certain low-paying jobs. Only those who spoke English well were hired as office workers or teachers.

countries, men obtained these well-paying jobs. Immigrant women were relegated to damp and smelly basements, where they stripped the tobacco, which was then rolled by men who worked "upstairs" under better conditions and for much higher wages (Ryan, 1983).

HOUSING One of the biggest problems for immigrant families was the lack of decent housing in densely populated cities. One Philadelphia tenement house, for example, housed 30 families in 34 rooms. A Lithuanian couple and their five children lived in a tiny closet of a home that contained only slightly more air space than the law required for one adult. The buildings were jammed together so tightly that the immigrant population of one block in New York City was equal to that of an entire town. Women increased their kitchen wall space by reaching out the window and hanging utensils on the outside wall of the house next door (Weatherford, 1986).

HEALTH Epidemics and disease were rampant among immigrant families. A cholera epidemic that barely touched the rest of New York City's population killed nearly 20 percent of the residents of a crowded immigrant neighborhood. Because a third of tenement rooms had no windows or ventilation, many immigrants contracted tuberculosis.

In Lawrence, Massachusetts, where 90 percent of the population consisted of immigrants, a third of the spinners in the textile mills died of respiratory diseases, such as pneumonia and tuberculosis, before they had worked there for ten years. These diseases were triggered by the lint, dust, and machine fumes of the unventilated mills. Moreover, the excruciating noise of the mills often resulted in deafness, and many workers were injured by faulty machines (Weatherford, 1986).

FAMILY CONFLICT Epidemics and dilapidated housing weren't the only problems the immigrant families faced.

 Cross-Cultural Families

Stereotypes about European Immigrants

On October 28, 1886, President Grover Cleveland dedicated the Statue of Liberty in New York Harbor, on whose pedestal are inscribed Emma Lazarus's famous welcoming words: "Give me your tired, your poor, your huddled masses yearning to breathe free." As the following examples show, however, Lazarus's poem did not reflect the reality:

> 1886: The U.S. consul in Budapest advised that Hungarian immigrants were not "a desirable acquisition" because, he claimed, they lacked ambition and would work as cheaply as the Chinese, which would interfere "with a civilized laborer's earning a 'white' laborer's wages."
>
> 1891: Congressman Henry Cabot Lodge called for restrictions on immigration because (referring especially to Jewish and Polish immigrants) the immigrants represented the "lowest and most illiterate classes," which were "alien to the body of the American people."
>
> 1910: Members of the eugenics movement contended that through intermarriage, immigration would contaminate the "old stock" of white Anglo-Saxon Americans with feeblemindedness, criminality, and pauperism. Many eugenicists, such as Robert De-Councey Ward of Harvard, were faculty members at prestigious eastern universities.
>
> 1914: Edward A. Ross, a prominent sociologist at the University of Wisconsin and a self-proclaimed immigration watchdog, wrote: "That the Mediterranean people are morally below the races of northern Europe is as certain as any social fact."
>
> 1922: Kenneth L. Roberts, a Cornell graduate, served as a correspondent for the *Saturday Evening Post* on immigration questions. He warned that "if a few more million members of the Alpine, Mediterranean, and Semitic races are poured among us, the result must inevitably be a hybrid race of people as worthless and futile as the good-for-nothing mongrels of Central America and Southeastern Europe."
>
> 1946: After World War II, the immigration of displaced persons revived old fears. Several influential senators argued that political immigrants should not be permitted to enter the United States because of their "alien philosophies" and "biological incompatibility with Americans' parent stocks."

SOURCE: Carlson and Colburn, 1972: 311–50.

Stop and Think . . .

- Did your ancestors experience prejudice and discrimination? Did their past shape how you and your parents were raised?
- If you're a recent immigrant, what kinds of prejudice and discrimination have you and your family encountered?

Most suffered many of the ills that come with poverty and isolation in a strange and often hostile new environment: crime, delinquency, a breakdown of marital and family relations, and general demoralization. Living quarters shared with relatives put additional pressures on already strained marital ties (Thomas and Znaniecki, 1927).

PREJUDICE AND DISCRIMINATION Like the American Indians, Mexicans, and blacks before them, most European immigrants met with enormous prejudice, discrimination, and economic exploitation. Much inequality was created and reinforced by high-ranking, highly respected, and influential people who had been educated in the most prestigious colleges and universities in the United States (see the box "Stereotypes about European Immigrants").

Despite the stereotypes and discrimination they encountered, most immigrant families overcame enormous obstacles. Rarely complaining, they worked at low-status jobs with low wages and encouraged their children to achieve and move up the social class ladder.

The "Modern" Family Emerges

The Great Depression of the 1930s, World War II, the baby boom of the 1950s, and the increasing economic and political unrest of the decades since the 1960s have all influenced the American family—sometimes for better, sometimes for worse. Some social scientists maintain that the "modern" family emerged around 1830: Courtship became more open, marriages were often based on affection rather than on financial considerations, and parents centered more of their attention on children. Others believe that the modern family emerged at the beginning of the twentieth century, especially with the rise of the "companionate family" (Burgess et al., 1963; Degler, 1983).

The Rise of the Companionate Family (1900–1930)

At the turn of the twentieth century, married couples increasingly emphasized the importance of sexual attraction and compatibility in their relationships. Particularly in the middle classes, the notion of companionship, or the *companionate family,* also included a couple's children. Affection between parents and children was more intimate and more open, and adolescents enjoyed greater freedom from parental supervision.

This new independence generated criticism, however. Many popular magazines, such as *The Atlantic Monthly, The Ladies' Home Journal,* and the *New Republic,* wor-

ried about "young people's rejection of genteel manners, their defiant clothing and hairstyles, their slang-filled language, and their 'lewd' pastimes . . . (such as smoking, attending petting parties, and going out on school nights). Public condemnation and moral outrage were widespread" (Mintz and Kellogg, 1988: 119). Do any of these complaints about young people sound familiar?

The Great Depression (1929–1939)

There was nothing great about the Great Depression. Still, families had a wide variety of experiences, due to factors such as residence, social class, gender, race, and ethnicity.

During the Great Depression, millions of families experienced dire poverty. Many families lived on farms, such as Alabama (above); others rummaged through garbage piles in large urban centers such as New York City.

URBAN AND RURAL RESIDENCE Many people who farmed land owned by others could not pay their rent either in cash or in a share of the crops. Husbands sometimes left their families to search for jobs. Some women who could not cope with such desertion took drastic steps to end their misery. In 1938, for example, in Nebraska a mother of 13 children committed suicide by walking into the side of a train because "she had had enough" (Fink, 1992: 172).

since you asked

Did the Depression have a devastating impact on *all* Americans?

Even when husbands remained at home, some families lost their land and personal possessions. Parents made enormous sacrifices to feed their children. As one jobless father stated, "We do not dare to use even a little soap when it will pay for an extra egg or a few more carrots for our children" (McElvaine, 1993: 172).

To help support their families, many young men and women who had been raised on farms moved to cities seeking jobs. Young women were more likely to find jobs because there was a demand for low-paying domestic help. The money they sent home from their wages of $10 or so a week helped their families buy clothes and other necessities.

SOCIAL CLASS The most devastating impact of the Great Depression was felt by working-class and poor families. More than half of all married women—especially those in poor southern states such as South Carolina, Mississippi, Louisiana, Georgia, and Alabama—were employed in low-paying domestic service or factory jobs (Cavan and Ranck, 1938; Chafe, 1972).

In contrast to middle-class children, children from working-class families did not enjoy carefree teenage years. Boys, especially, were expected to work after school or drop out of school to supplement their family's meager income. When mothers found jobs, older children, especially girls, looked after their younger brothers and sisters and often had to drop out of school to do so (McElvaine, 1993).

Some working-class children became part of the "transient army" that drifted from town to town looking for work. Most slept in lice-ridden and rat-infested housing when they could afford to pay 10 or 15 cents for a urine-stained mattress on the floor. Others slept on park benches, under shrubbery and bridges, in doorways, in packing crates, or in abandoned automobiles (Watkins, 1993).

As blue-collar employment in the male-dominated industrial sectors decreased, white-collar clerical and government jobs increased. Women took many of these jobs. The wages of white, middle-class women enabled their families, even during the Depression, to maintain the standard of living and consumer habits that they had enjoyed during the affluent 1920s.

Upper-middle-class families fared even better. Fairly affluent families made only minor sacrifices. Some families cut down on entertainment, did not renew country club memberships, and decreased services such as domestic help. Few reported cutbacks in their food budgets, however, and many of these families continued to take summer vacations and buy new cars (Morgan, 1939).

RACE Although the Depression was an economic disaster for many people, African Americans suffered even more. Unemployment was much higher among blacks than among whites. As layoffs began in 1929 and accelerated in the following years, blacks were often the first to be fired. By 1932, black unemployment had reached approximately 50 percent nationwide. As the economic situation deteriorated, many whites demanded that employers replace blacks with whites in unskilled occupations such as garbage collector, elevator operator, waiter, bellhop, and street cleaner.

In some government jobs, employers set an unofficial quota of 10 percent black, on the theory that this represented, roughly, the percentage of African Americans in the general population. In fact, though, the percentage of government employees who were black was only about 6 percent. Even those who were able to keep their jobs faced great hardship. A study conducted in Harlem in 1935, for instance, found that the wages of skilled black workers who could find work dropped nearly 50 percent during the Depression (McElvaine, 1993; Watkins, 1993).

GENDER ROLES In many families, unemployment wreaked havoc on gender roles. The authority of the husband and father was based on his occupation and his role as provider. If he lost his job, he often suffered a decline in status within the family. Understandably, men were despondent: "Sometimes the father did not go to bed but moved from chair to chair all night long" (Cavan and Ranck, cited in Griswold, 1993: 148).

Men who could not provide for their families became depressed, preoccupied, abusive, drank more, or spent much of their time searching for jobs. As fathers became physically and emotionally distant, their power in the family and their children's respect for them often decreased. Adolescents became more independent and rebellious (Griswold, 1993).

In 1932, a federal executive order decreed that only one spouse could work for the federal government. The widespread unemployment of men therefore put pressure on women, especially married women, to resign from some occupations. In addition, school boards fired married female teachers, and some companies dismissed married women. More than 77 percent of the school districts in the United States would not hire married women, and 50 percent had a policy of firing women who got married (Milkman, 1976; McElvaine, 1993).

When women did work, the federal government endorsed lower pay rates for women. For example, the federal Works Progress Administration (WPA) paid men $5 per day, compared with only $3 for women.

World War II (1939–1945)

World War II triggered even greater changes in work roles and family life. Families began to experience these changes after the United States entered the war in 1941.

WORK ROLES Workers were scarce, especially in the defense and manufacturing industries, because many able-bodied men had been drafted. Initially, employers were unwilling to recruit women for traditionally male jobs. And many women, especially white middle-class women, were reluctant to violate traditional gender roles.

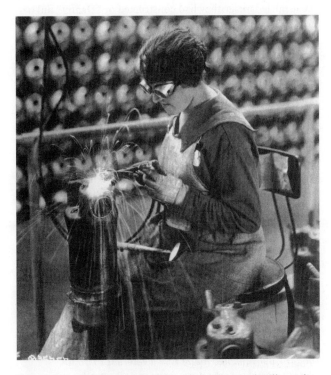

Many women worked in American factories, steel mills, and shipyards during World War II. Although many women found it hard to give up their new-found jobs and financial independence, most were replaced by men who returned from the war in 1945.

In 1942, however, prompted by both the Women's Bureau of the U.S. Department of Labor and organized women's groups, employers began to fill many jobs, especially those in nontraditional positions, with women. The government, supported by the mass media, was enormously successful in convincing both men and women that a "woman's place is in the workplace" and not the home:

> *In all the media, women at work were pictured and praised, and the woman who did not at least work as a volunteer for the Red Cross was made to feel guilty. . . . Even the movies joined in. The wife or sweetheart who stayed behind and went to work became as familiar a figure as the valiant soldier-lover for whom she waited (Banner, 1984: 219).*

Millions of women, including mothers and even grandmothers, worked in shipyards, steel mills, and ammunition factories (see "Data Digest"). They welded, dug ditches, and operated forklifts. For the first time, black women were recruited into high-paying jobs, making some of the greatest economic gains of all women during that period.

Hundreds of thousands of domestic servants and farm workers left their jobs for much better-paying positions in the defense and other industries. In the superb documentary film, *The Life and Times of Rosie the Riveter,* black women describe the pride and exhilaration they felt at having well-paying jobs that they genuinely enjoyed.

Because of the labor shortage, this was the only time when even working-class women were praised for working outside the home. Two of the best-selling magazines during that time, the *Saturday Evening Post* and *True Story,* supported the government's propaganda efforts by portraying working-class women in very positive roles:

> *Stories and advertisements glorified factory work as psychologically rewarding, as emotionally exciting, and as leading to success in love. Both magazines combated class prejudice against factory work by portraying working-class men and women as diligent, patriotic, wholesome people. . . . Working-class women were resourceful, respectable, warmhearted, and resilient (Honey, 1984: 186–87).*

FAMILY LIFE Although divorce rates had been increasing slowly since the turn of the century, they reached a new high in 1946, a year after the end of World War II. Some wives and mothers who had worked during the war enjoyed their newfound economic independence and decided to end unhappy marriages.

In other cases, families disintegrated because of the strains of living with a man who returned partially or completely incapacitated. Alcoholism, which was rampant among veterans, was believed to be the major cause of the increase in divorces after the war (Tuttle, 1993).

For some people, the war deferred rather than caused divorce. Some couples, caught up in war hysteria, courted briefly and married impulsively. In many cases, both the bride and the young soldier matured during the husband's prolonged absence and had little in common when they were reunited (Mowrer, 1972).

Perhaps one of the greatest difficulties that many families faced was the children's reaction to fathers whom they barely knew or had never even seen. As the box "Daddy's Coming Home!" shows, despite widespread rejoicing over the end of the war, a father's return was unsettling for many children.

The "Golden" Fifties

After World War II, when women were no longer welcome in the workplace because returning veterans needed jobs, propaganda about family roles changed almost overnight. Ads now depicted happy housewives engrossed in using household appliances and the latest

---

Changes

Daddy's Coming Home!

Soldiers returning from World War II encountered numerous problems, including unemployment and high divorce rates. Historian William M. Tuttle, Jr. (1993) solicited 2,500 letters from men and women, then in their 50s and 60s, who had been children during World War II. What most of these people had in common were the difficulties they and their families experienced in adjusting to the return of their fathers from military service.

Some children feared that their fathers would not stay and therefore avoided becoming too attached. Some were bitter that their fathers had left in the first place.

One "war baby" was 18 months old when her father returned from the war. When her mother told her to hug her Daddy, she ran to a large framed photo of him and took it in her arms.

Some children, especially those who were preschoolers at the time, were frightened of the strange men who suddenly moved into their homes. One woman remembered watching "the stranger with the big white teeth" come toward her. As he did, the 4-year-old ran upstairs in terror and hid under a bed.

Some recalled feeling angry because their fathers' return disrupted their lives. Grandparents had often pampered children whom they helped to raise. In contrast, the returning father, fresh from military experience, was often a strict disciplinarian and saw the child as "a brat."

If the children had been very close to their mothers, they became resentful of their fathers for displacing them in the mother's affections. Others were disappointed when the idealized image they had constructed of "Daddy" did not match reality or when a father who had been described as kind, sensitive, and gentle returned from the war troubled or violent.

Readjustment was difficult for both children and fathers. Although some households adjusted to the changes, in many families the returning fathers and their children never developed a close relationship.

The "G.I. Bill" enabled many WW II veterans to go to school and improve their job opportunities. But for many vets with families, like William Oskay, Jr., and his wife and daughter, daily life required many sacrifices and hardships.

consumer products. The women portrayed in short stories and in articles in women's magazines were no longer nurses saving soldiers' lives but mothers cooking, caring for their children, and pleasing their husbands. In the 1950s, middle-class people, especially, became absorbed in their families.

Gender Roles

Movies and television shows featured two stereotypical portrayals of women: innocent virgins such as Doris Day and Debbie Reynolds, or sexy bombshells such as Marilyn Monroe and Jayne Mansfield. Television applauded domesticity on such popular shows as *I Love Lucy, Ozzie and Harriet, Leave It to Beaver,* and *Father Knows Best.*

Marriage manuals and child-care experts like Dr. Benjamin Spock advised women to please their husbands and to be full-time homemakers. By the mid-1950s, 60 percent of female undergraduates were dropping out of college to marry (Banner, 1984).

The post–World War II period produced a generation of **baby boomers,** people born between 1946 and 1964. Family plans that had been disrupted by the war were renewed. Although women continued to enter the job market, many middle-class families, spurred by the mass media, sought a traditional family life in which the husband worked and the wife devoted herself to the home and the children.

The editor of *Mademoiselle* echoed a widespread belief that women in their teens and twenties should avoid careers and instead raise as many children as the "good Lord gave them." Many magazine and newspaper articles encouraged families to participate in "creative" activities such as outdoor barbecues and cross-country camping trips (Chafe, 1972).

Moving to the Suburbs

Suburbs mushroomed, attracting nearly two-thirds of those who had lived in cities. The interest in moving to the suburbs reflected a number of structural and attitudinal changes in American society.

The federal government, fearful of a return to economic depression, underwrote the construction of homes in the suburbs

(Rothman, 1978). The general public obtained low-interest mortgages, and veterans were offered the added incentive of purchasing a home with a $1 down-payment.

since you asked

How did suburban living change family life?

Massive highway construction programs enabled people to commute from the city to the suburbs. Families wanted more room and an escape from city noise, dirt, and crowding. One woman still recollects moving to the suburbs as "the ideal life": "We knew little about the outside world of poverty, culture, crime, and ethnic variety" (Coontz, 2005: 240).

The greater space offered more privacy for both children and parents: "The spacious master bedroom, generally set apart from the rooms of the children, was well-suited to a highly sexual relationship. And wives anticipated spending many evenings alone with their

When suburbs mushroomed during the 1950s, many critics mocked the small, detached, single-family homes as "cookie cutters" (above). Are houses practically stacked on top of each in some recently-developed suburbs—such as the one south of Denver, Colorado (below)—more original and not cookie cutters?

husbands, not with family or friends" (Rothman, 1978: 225–26).

The suburban way of life added a new dimension to the traditional role of women:

> *The duties of child-rearing underwent expansion. Suburban mothers volunteered for library work in the school, took part in PTA activities, and chauffeured their children from music lessons to scout meetings. Perhaps most important, the suburban wife was expected to make the home an oasis of comfort and serenity for her harried husband (Chafe, 1972: 217–18).*

The Blissful 1950s?

Were the fifties as idyllic as earlier generations fondly recall? Some writers argue that many of these nostalgic memories are actually myths. "Contrary to popular opinion," notes historian Stephanie Coontz (1992: 29) "*Leave It to Beaver* was not a documentary." In fact, the "golden fifties" were riddled with many family problems, and people had fewer choices than they do today. For example,

- *Consumerism* was limited primarily to middle- and upper-class families. In 1950, a supermarket stocked an average of 3,750 items; in the 1990s, most markets carried more than 17,000 items. Until the 1990s, *many prepared foods were loaded with lard, salt, sugar, and harmful preservatives.*

- Black and other ethnic families faced *severe discrimination* in employment, education, housing, and access to recreational activities.

- *Domestic violence and child abuse,* though widespread, were invisible (see Chapter 14).

- Many young people were forced into *"shotgun" marriages* because of premarital pregnancy; young women—especially if they were white—were pressured to give up their babies for adoption.

- About 20 percent of mothers had *paying jobs.* Although child-care services are still inadequate today, they were practically nonexistent in the 1950s.

- Many people, including housewives, tried to escape from their unhappy lives through *alcohol or drugs.* The consumption of tranquilizers, largely unheard of in 1955, soared to almost 1.2 million pounds in 1959 (Coontz, 1992; Crispell, 1992; Reid, 1993).

Making Connections

- Many of your grandparents or parents probably lived through the Great Depression and World War II. How did they survive these turbulent periods? If your kin were poor, how did these eras shape their attitudes and values about jobs, money, food, and other issues?

- Many people are nostalgic about the "golden fifties." Were these years really "golden" for you, your parents, or your grandparents? Or did your family experience prejudice and discrimination because of race, ethnicity, social class, gender, or sexual orientation?

The Family since the 1960s

When I was in graduate school during the early 1970s, our family textbooks typically covered three "major" topics—courtship, marriage, and having children—and in that order. The authors sometimes devoted a chapter to premarital sex and one to black families, but they often described divorce, interfaith marriage, premarital pregnancy, and homosexuality as "deviant" or as "problem areas" (see, for example, Reiss, 1971).

I gave up the idea of focusing stepfamilies for my Ph.D. dissertation because the faculty dismissed the topic as "unimportant" or "frivolous." We never read (or heard) about family violence and almost nothing about singlehood, cohabitation, or one-parent families.

Families, and the textbooks that describe them, have changed considerably since the 1970s. Although domestic violence and out-of-wedlock births have always existed, three of the major shifts during the last 30 years or so have occurred in family structure, gender roles, and economic concerns.

Family Structure

In the 1970s, families had lower birth rates and higher divorce rates compared with the 1950s and 1960s, and larger numbers of women entered colleges and graduate programs. In the 1980s, more people over age 25 postponed marriage. Many who were already married delayed having children.

Out-of-wedlock births, especially among teenage girls, declined in the late 1990s, but the number of one-parent households increased dramatically (see Chapters 7 and 9). The number of two-income families burgeoned, along with the number of adult children who continued to live at home with their parents because of financial difficulties (see Chapter 12).

Gender Roles

When we bought our first house in 1975, the mortgage payments were always addressed to my husband "and wife." Even though I worked full time as a college professor, I couldn't take out a credit card in my own name and needed my husband's signed permission to get a credit card even in his name. These were common practices because married women had little recognition in "serious" financial transactions.

By the early 1980s, women's employment was becoming central to a family's economic advancement (see Chapters 1 and 13). Two-income marriages faced the stressful task of juggling work and negotiating work and family life.

On the positive side, women felt that employment brought them more respect from society and their partners and greater decision-making power in their marriages. The percentage of stay-at-home dads is still tiny, but social acceptance of such family arrangements accelerated. Perhaps most important, men experienced less pressure to be the sole breadwinner (see Chapters 12 and 13).

Economic Concerns

The twenty-first century began with numerous problems that affected families. The stock market plunged. Many older people had to go back to work because their retirement portfolios shrank by at least 50 per-cent. Many young adults were laid off from promising high-tech jobs and scurried to find *any* employment that paid more than a minimum wage (see Chapters 13, 17, and 18).

Health-care costs skyrocketed. And because of the terrorist attacks on September 11, 2001, federal and state governments funneled billions of dollars into homeland security and the war in Iraq. As a result, agencies gutted many family programs and services, especially for poor and working-class families.

Conclusion

If we examine the family in a historical context, we see that *change*, rather than stability, has been the norm. Moreover, families differed by region and social class even during colonial times.

We also see that the experiences and *choices* open to American Indians, African Americans, Mexican Americans, and many European immigrants were very different from those available to "middle America," experiences that were romanticized by many television programs in the 1950s.

Such macro-level constraints as wars and shifting demographic characteristics have also influenced families. Many families survived despite enormous hardships, disruptions, and dislocations.

They are still coping with macro-level constraints such as an unpredictable economy as well as with micro-level variables such as greater *choices* in family roles. The next chapter, on racial and ethnic families, examines some of the ongoing changes, choices, and constraints.

Summary

1.   Historical factors have played an important role in shaping the contemporary family. The early exploitation of American Indian, African American, and Mexican families has had long-term economic effects on these families.

2.   The colonial family was a self-sufficient unit that performed a wide variety of functions. Children were part of the family work force and were expected to be docile and well behaved. Wives' work was subordinate to that of husbands, and family practices varied in different social classes and geographic regions.

3.   American Indian families were extremely diverse in function, structure, puberty rites, and child-rearing pat-terns. European armies, adventurers, and missionaries played major roles in destroying many tribes and much of American Indian culture.

4.   Contrary to popular belief, many slave households had two parents, men played important roles as fathers or surrogate fathers, and most women worked as hard in the fields as the men. Instead of succumbing to subordination, many slaves were resourceful and resilient in maintaining their families.

5.   Most Mexican American families lost their lands to European American settlers. Despite severe economic exploitation, many families survived because of cohesive family networks and strong family bonds.

6. By the nineteenth century, industrialization had changed some aspects of the family. Marriages were based more on love and choice than on economic considerations, and parental roles became more sex segregated. In the upper and middle classes, the notion of the "true woman," who devoted most of her time to looking beautiful and pleasing her husband, emerged.

7. Millions of European immigrants who worked in labor-intensive jobs at very low wages fueled the rapid advance of industrialization. Many immigrants, including women and children, endured severe social and economic discrimination, dilapidated housing conditions, and chronic health problems.

8. Working-class families felt the most devastating effects of the Great Depression. Whereas middle-class families merely cut back on some luxuries, working-class men experienced widespread unemployment and their wives worked in menial and low-paying jobs.

9. World War II had a mixed effect on families. For the first time, many women, especially black mothers, found jobs that paid a decent salary. However, death and divorce disrupted many families.

10. After the war, suburbs boomed and birth rates surged. The family roles of white middle-class women expanded to include full-time nurturance of children and husbands. Husbands' roles were largely limited to work. The "golden fifties" reflects a mythical portrayal of the family in that decade.

Key Terms

bundling 60	familism 70	baby boomers 79
matrilineal 65	compadrazgo 70	
patrilineal 65	machismo 70	

Taking it Further

Research Your Family Tree and Other Families

The **Gilder Lehrman Institute of American History** offers excellent information about families from the colonial period to the present. Some of the most delightful links include love letters written by young couples and fathers' attempts to dampen their daughters' romances. http://www.gilderlehrman.org

Thanksgiving: Memory, Myth, and Meaning dispel many common myths about this holiday. If you want to duplicate the "first" Thanksgiving, you'll enjoy the recipes for roast fowl (not turkey), seethed cod, and hominy pudding.
www.plimoth.org/visit/what/exhibits/thanksgiving.asp

Documenting the American South: North American Slave Narratives offers a collection of eighteenth-, nineteenth-, and early-twentieth-century slave narratives and an extensive bibliography.
http://docsouth.unc.edu/neh/index.html

Westward by Sea: A Maritime Perspective on American Expansion, 1820–1890 presents pictorial and textual material about the California Gold Rush, the roles of women, the immigrant experience, whaling life, and native populations. It includes materials about California, Texas, Hawaii, and the Pacific Northwest.

http://memory.loc.gov:8081/ammem/award99/mymhihtml/mymhihome.html

I think you'll enjoy exploring two excellent sites on Levittown, the "suburban legend" of the 1950s:

Levittown: Documents of an Ideal American Suburb provides a social, cultural, and visual history of the epitome of suburban living after World War II and the town's evolution over the past 50 years.

http://tigger.uic.edu/%7Epbhales/Levittown.html

Levittown, Pa: Building the Suburban Dream presents editorial cartoons and an in-depth look at a typical kitchen with modern time-saving devices such as a self-cleaning oven and a built-in blender.

http://server1.fandm.edu/levittown

And more: www.prenhall.com/benokraitis provides a wide variety of sites, including a bibliography of writings about North American Indians, interviews with former slaves, a Women of the West museum, documentary materials from the original Plymouth Colony, photographs and oral histories of American Indian traders in the Southwest, key events in the history of slavery, World War II posters featuring women, descriptions of World War II "victory gardens," an immigrant tenement museum in New York City, and much more.

Investigate with Research Navigator

Go to www.researchnavigator.com and enter your LOGIN NAME and PASSWORD. For instructions on registering for the first time, view the detailed instructions at the end of the Chapter 1. Search the Research Navigator™ site using the following key terms:

family structure
matrilineal
machismo

Outline

Racial and Ethnic Families: Strengths and Stresses

Data Digest

- Most of the world's immigrants live in Europe (56 million), Asia (50 million), and the United States and Canada (41 million). Almost **one person in every ten living in affluent nations is an immigrant.**

- About 34 percent of whites, 26 percent of Asian Americans, and 15 percent of Latinos, but only 9 percent of blacks, feel that **we have overcome the major problems facing racial minorities in the country.**

- In 2004, **married-couple households across racial and ethnic groups** were as follows: 80 percent each for whites and Asian Americans, 71 percent for Native Hawaiians and other Pacific Islanders, 55 percent for Latinos, and 47 percent for African Americans.

- In 2005, the largest number of **people with Middle Eastern roots who immigrated to the United States** came from Pakistan (14,926), Iran (13,887), Egypt (7,905), Israel (5,755), and Turkey (4,614).

- Of the 281.4 million people counted in the 2000 census, about 6.8 million (2.4 percent) **identified with two or more races.**

Sources: *Race and Ethnicity* . . . , 2001; United Nations, 2002; U.S. Department of Homeland Security, 2005; U.S. Census Bureau, 2006.

In 1990 Yolanda Zambrano married her Colombian sweetheart, who was already living in the United States. After she arrived at their new home in Worcester, Massachusetts, Yolanda volunteered in the community, including working in a travel agency, to learn English and as much as possible about her new country. The owner of the travel agency, tired of the business, suggested that Yolanda might like to buy it.

Although she had only $2,000 in savings at the time, Yolanda maxed out her credit cards and secured a small loan plus the $20,000 needed for her license. She hired and trained a bilingual staff and focused on providing top-quality, personalized service for people traveling to Latin America for business or recreation. By 2001, her company had grown to $7 million in annual sales, and she won an award from the Small Business Administration as the Minority Small Business Person of the Year for New England (Lampman, 2001: 15).

Yolanda is typical of many immigrants who arrive on American soil and work hard to turn opportunities into successes. Not all immigrants have been as successful, of course, but millions of non-European immigrants have made significant contributions to U.S. society.

Chapter 3 discussed some of the history of white immigrants and those from several minority groups. In this chapter we focus on contemporary African American, American Indian, Latino, Asian American, and Middle Eastern families. We'll also examine marriage and dating relationships across racial and ethnic lines. Let's begin with an overview of the growing diversity of American families.

The Increasing Diversity of U.S. Families

As you saw in Chapter 1, U.S. households are becoming more diverse in racial and ethnic composition. As the number and variety of immigrants increase, the ways in which we relate to each other become more complex.

To understand some of this complexity, think of a continuum. At one end of the continuum is **assimilation,** or conformity of ethnic group members to the culture of the dominant group, including intermarriage. At the other end of the continuum is **cultural pluralism,** or maintaining many aspects of one's original culture—including using one's own language and marrying within one's own ethnic group—while living peacefully with the host culture.

Still others—those in the middle of the continuum—blend into U.S. society through acculturation. **Acculturation** is the process of adopting the language, values, beliefs, roles, and other characteristics of a host culture (such as attaining high educational levels and securing good jobs). Like cultural pluralism, acculturation does not include intermarriage, but the newcomers merge into the host culture in most other ways.

Changes in the Immigration Mosaic

The current proportion of foreign-born U.S. residents is small by historical standards. In 1900, about 15 percent of the total U.S. population was foreign-born, compared with 11 percent in 2000.

There has also been a significant shift in many immigrants' country of origin.

since you asked

How has U.S. immigration changed over the last century?

In 1900, almost 85 percent of immigrants came from Europe. In 2004, in contrast, Europeans made up only 14 percent of all new immigrants. Today, immigrants come primarily from Asia (mainly China and the Philippines) and Latin America (mainly Mexico) (see *Figure 4.1*).

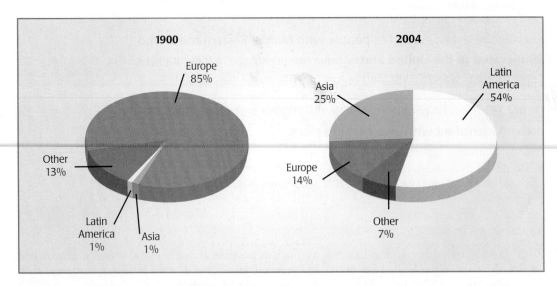

FIGURE 4.1   Origins of U.S. Immigrants: 1900 and 2004

Note: Latin America includes the Caribbean, Central America (including Mexico), and South America.
Sources: Based on data in U.S. Department of Commerce, 1993, and U.S. Census Bureau, 2006, Table 8.

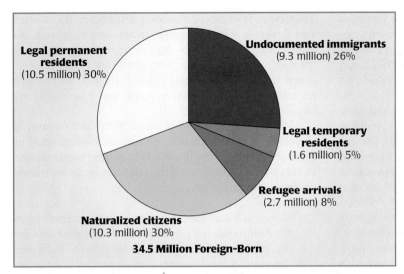

FIGURE 4.2 Legal Status of the U.S. Foreign-Born Population, 2002

SOURCE: Passel et al., 2004, Figure 1.

UNDOCUMENTED IMMIGRANTS The United States admits about one million immigrants every year—more than any other nation. Another 9.3 million immigrants, more than half from Mexico, are undocumented (illegal). Undocumented immigrants represent 26 percent of the foreign-born population (see *Figure 4.2*). Many Americans feel that undocumented immigrants are "moochers." In fact, however:

- Over 90 percent of the men work, and most pay payroll and sales taxes.

- Undocumented immigrants aren't eligible for welfare, food stamps, Medicaid, and most other public benefits.

- About 75 percent contribute a total of $6–7 billion annually in Social Security funds, which they will be unable to claim because they're not citizens (Passel et al., 2004; Capps and Fix, 2005).

An additional 4 million or so are "visa overstayers"—people who arrive on a visitor's visa (from Canada, Europe, and other countries) and decide to remain in the United States. These undocumented immigrants skip over millions of others who sometimes wait years to immigrate here legally. Once foreigners are in this country, the U.S. Immigration and Naturalization Service has no way to track where they are or whether they leave when they are supposed to (Lipton, 2005).

ATTITUDES ABOUT IMMIGRATION How do Americans feel about immigration? Many are uneasy. According to a recent poll, for example, 39 percent said that they'd like to reduce immigration rates, 42 percent want to keep rates at the same level, and only 17 percent favor increasing current immigration ("Immigration," 2006).

Compared with most other countries, the United States welcomes immigrants. Japan, for instance, historically has had very low immigration rates simply because it doesn't want to become "an immigrant country." And since 2001 almost every nation in Europe, from the Scandinavian countries to Spain, has passed laws to decrease the number of immigrants crossing its borders. Even Mexico has deported 160,000 undocumented migrants from Guatemala (MacKenzie, 2002; Francis, 2003).

THE COSTS OF IMMIGRATION Many countries are curtailing immigration for a number of reasons: fears about security, concerns about diluting national identity, and worries about displacing native-born employees. Some American critics point out that low-skilled immigrant workers depress wages, reduce the standard of living, and overload schools and welfare systems.

Every year, millions of immigrants become U.S. citizens. Here, a Vietnamese man and some members of his family participate in a naturalization ceremony.

Others note that because immigrants are younger, poorer, and less well-educated than the native-born population, they use more government services and pay less in taxes. By some estimates, hospitals spend $2 billion a year to treat illegal immigrants who are not eligible for Medicaid (Canedy, 2002; Martin and Midgley, 2003).

Immigrants themselves, both legal and illegal, also endure costs. At the low end of the pay scale, recruiters promise people good jobs and training. Instead, the immigrants often find themselves living in abject poverty. For example, the federal government has prosecuted Tyson Foods, the nation's largest meat producer and processor, for helping illegal immigrants from Mexico and Central America obtain false documents such as Social Security cards, for cheating workers out of wages, and for violating child labor laws—violations that have resulted in serious injuries and deaths of children under 16 (Reardon-Anderson et al., 2002; Day, 2003).

THE BENEFITS OF IMMIGRATION Despite the costs, immigrants provide many benefits for their host countries. They clean homes and business offices, toil as nannies and busboys, serve as nurses' aides, and pick fruit, all at low wages and in jobs that most native-born workers don't want to do. Recent immigrants have also rejuvenated many other employment sectors, working in professional, administrative, sales, and blue-collar occupations (Sum et al., 2002).

Without immigrants, many rural towns would shrivel or experience a severe shortage of workers. For example, Mason City, Iowa, has imported workers who are taxpaying members of the community at both ends of the employment spectrum:

> *Mercy Medical has brought in a pediatrician from the Philippines to complement a staff that also includes doctors from India, South Africa, and Latin America. A local cement factory has brought in engineers from Argentina and elsewhere. A local meat-processing facility employs a number of Bosnians who have moved to Mason City (Belsie, 2001: 4).*

Choices

Somalis in Maine

During the 1980s, many citizens of Somalia (a country in East Africa) became refugees after fleeing famine, torture, and violence during civil wars. U.S. social service groups resettled many of the Somalis in urban centers such as Columbus, Ohio; Atlanta, Georgia; and Memphis, Tennessee. Most of the resettled parents became unhappy with their children's adaptations to American culture—dressing differently, listening to rap music, and speaking English rather than Somali at home. In addition, some of the adults were robbed or shot.

As a result, the Somali elders sent younger men to search for new settlements. After considerable research and discussion, the Somalis targeted Lewiston, Maine, as a good place to live. Lewiston had a dwindling population, dilapidated housing, and few employment opportunities. Still, the elders felt that Lewiston was a safe town and had good schools.

Some Lewiston residents complained about the city's giving each of the 1,200 Somali families $10,000 in cash when they arrived. Others worried that the town's scarce resources were being allocated to English classes and that the town was feeding foreigners at the expense of local citizens.

On the other hand, the Somalis have revitalized this dying community. They "are shopping, paying taxes, and buying property." In addition, the Somalis have opened a new restaurant, a clothing store that features head scarves and long dresses, a National Basketball Association (NBA) jersey store, and a convenience store (Jones, 2004: 69).

Stop and Think . . .

- Violence and premarital sex seem to permeate U.S. culture (see Chapters 7 and 14). Is it realistic, then, for recent immigrants to try to escape these undesirable influences by relocating to rural towns?

- How would you feel if about 5 to 10 percent of your town was settled by immigrants like the Somalis? Would you welcome their arrival? Or would you argue that the immigrants would deplete the town's resources?

Such contributions aren't surprising. Many U.S.-born Americans often forget that their ancestors—from Italy, Ireland, Poland, or other countries—worked very hard and succeeded despite low educational levels, few skills, and not speaking English (see Chapter 3). The immigrants' countries of origin have changed (see *Figure 4.1*). However, as the box "Somalis in Maine" shows, the most recent immigrants have the same goals as your great-great grandparents: They are seeking a better life for their families.

Many demographers predict that countries with low immigration rates will experience severe problems in the future. As the populations of industrialized countries age and birth rates plunge, there will be fewer workers to keep those countries' economies from shrinking (see Chapter 18). Even if current immigration rates remain the same, the United States is likely to face labor shortages by 2010. To avoid requiring people to work well into their 70s, Germany would have to boost its immigration twentyfold and Japan fiftyfold (Baker, 2002).

Race and Ethnicity Still Matter

Social scientists routinely describe Latino, African American, Asian American, Middle Eastern, and American Indian families as minority groups. A **minority group** is a group of people who may be treated differently than the dominant group because of their physical or cultural characteristics, such as gender, sexual orientation, religion, or skin color.

Even though minority groups may outnumber whites, they typically have less power, privilege, and social status. Most whites, in contrast, are privileged because of their skin color. Feminist educator Peggy McIntosh (1995: 76–77) describes white privilege as "an invisible package of unearned assets that I can count on cashing in each day." The box "Am I Privileged?" provides some examples of "cashing in" if you're white.

since you asked

Do we live in a color-blind society?

Ask Yourself

Am I Privileged?

Do we live in a color-blind society? No, according to most social scientists. White people are rarely conscious of the advantages and disadvantages associated with skin color. Instead, they enjoy a variety of everyday benefits that they take for granted. Here are a few of the 46 privileges that McIntosh (1995: 79–81) lists:

1. I can go shopping alone most of the time, fairly well assured that I will not be followed or harassed by store detectives.
2. I can turn on the television or open to the front page of the paper and see people of my race widely and positively represented.
3. I can be sure that my children will be given curricular materials that reflect their race.
4. Whether I use checks, credit cards, or cash, I can count on my skin color to send the message that I am financially reliable.
5. If a traffic cop pulls me over, I can be sure that I haven't been singled out because of my race.
6. I can be late to a meeting without having the lateness reflect on my race.
7. I can easily buy posters, postcards, greeting cards, dolls, toys, and children's magazines featuring people of my race.
8. I can do well in a difficult situation without being called a credit to my race.

Stop and Think . . .

- What other benefits would you add to this list of white privileges?
- How do such privileges affect most racial and ethnic groups who don't have them, both individually and society-wide?

What kinds of physical and cultural characteristics differentiate minority groups from a dominant group? Two of the most important are race and ethnicity.

Race

A **racial group** is a category of people who share physical characteristics, such as skin color, that members of a society consider socially important. Both sociologists and anthropologists see race as a social label rather than a biological trait. Many biologists, similarly, view race as a social rather than a biological or scientific concept because there is very little genetic difference among members of different races: As few as 6 of the body's estimated 35,000 genes determine the color of a person's skin (Graves, 2001).

If race is a meaningless concept, why are we so obsessed with it? From a social standpoint, physical characteristics such as skin color and eye shape are easily observed and mark particular groups for unequal treatment. As you'll see in this and other chapters, as long as we sort ourselves into racial categories and act on the basis of these characteristics, our life experiences will differ in terms of access to jobs and other resources and how people treat us.

Ethnicity

An **ethnic group** (from the Greek word *ethnos*, meaning "nation") is a set of people who identify with a particular national origin or cultural heritage. Cultural heritage includes language, geographic roots, customs, traditions, and religion. Ethnic groups in the United States include Puerto Ricans, Chinese, blacks, and a variety of white ethnic groups such as Italians, Swedes, Hungarians, Jews, and many others.

Even though the U.S. government acknowledges that race is a social rather than a biological concept, it considers race and ethnicity to be two separate categories in people's self-identification. Thus, in the 2000 Census response form, the question on race included 15 separate response categories, three areas in which respondents could write in a more specific racial group, and a question on "ancestry or ethnic origin." Someone who's Latino, for example, could answer questions on both ethnicity and race.

Like race, ethnicity—an individual or group's cultural or national identity—can be a basis for unequal treatment. As you saw in Chapter 3, many white European immigrants experienced discrimination because of their ethnic roots.

Racial-Ethnic Group

Sociologists often refer to a set of people who have distinctive physical and cultural characteristics as a **racial-ethnic group**. All the families we examine in this chapter are examples of racial-ethnic groups because both physical and cultural attributes are central features of their heritage.

Although some people use the terms interchangeably, remember that *race* is a social concept that refers to physical characteristics, whereas *ethnicity* describes cultural characteristics. The term *racial-ethnic* incorporates both physical and cultural traits (Murry et al., 2001b). These distinctions can become complicated because people tend to prefer some "labels" to others, and these labels change over time.

The Naming Issue

Although *Hispanic* and *Latino* are often used interchangeably, the labels reflect regional usage and cultural background. *Hispanic* is preferred in New York and Florida, whereas *Latino* is most popular in California and Texas. *Chicano* (*Chicana* for women) arose in the 1970s and is still used to refer to people of Mexican origin who were born in the United States. *Hispano* is favored to emphasize unity with Spain rather than Mexico. And a small group in southern California prefers *Mexica* to stress its indigenous Indian roots in Mexico.

Labels for blacks have also changed over time, from hurtful racial epithets to *colored, Negro,* and *Afro-American* (Kennedy, 2002). Currently, most people, including African American scholars, use *black* and *African American* interchangeably. I find the same results when I poll my black students informally. Some are vehement about using *African American* to emphasize their African ancestry; others prefer *black* (with or without a capital B) because "black is beautiful."

We see similar variations in the usage of *Native Americans* and *American Indians*. Although these groups prefer their tribal identities (such as Cherokee, Apache, and Lumbi) to being lumped together with a single term, people often dispute whether an American Indian is full-blooded or mixed blood, belongs to a tribe or not, or is simply a "wannabe" rather than a "real" Indian after several centuries of intermarriage (Snipp, 2002).

Prejudice and Discrimination

Race and ethnicity affect whether we and members of our families will experience prejudice and discrimination. Generally, prejudice is less harmful than discrimination because it's in our thoughts rather than our

Applying What You've Learned

Am I Prejudiced?

All of us, whether we realize it or not, sometimes have strong feelings about other racial-ethnic groups. Answer the questions in this quiz as honestly as possible. After you finish, look at the key.

Usually True	Usually False	
☐	☐	**1.** Latino men have a more macho attitude than other men.
☐	☐	**2.** African Americans, both women and men, are more likely to commit a crime than members of other racial-ethnic groups, including whites.
☐	☐	**3.** Don't trust Arab-Americans. Some are decent, but most want to overthrow the United States, especially through terrorist tactics.
☐	☐	**4.** Asian American business owners are greedier than other business owners.
☐	☐	**5.** Although there are some exceptions, most Latinos don't succeed because they're lazy.
☐	☐	**6.** The majority of Asian Americans tend to be shy and quiet.
☐	☐	**7.** Most Asian Americans are not as sociable as other groups of people.
☐	☐	**8.** Most whites are simply more capable than other groups—especially African Americans and Latinos—in doing their jobs.
☐	☐	**9.** I feel that less qualified minorities are taking away my livelihood.
☐	☐	**10.** When I was growing up, my parents said negative things about African Americans, whites, Latinos, Asian-Americans, and other groups. Because of my upbringing, I feel that people outside my group are inferior.

Key to "Am I Prejudiced?"

Of these ten items, the higher your score for "usually true," the more likely it is that you have feelings and stereotypes about many racial/ethnic groups. The purpose of this quiz is simply to get you to think about how you feel about people outside your immediate circle.

Sources: Based on material in Godfrey et al., 2000, and Lin et al., 2005.

actions. Nevertheless, prejudice may lead to discrimination. Before you read any further, take the short quiz on "Am I Prejudiced?" and think about some of your feelings about racial-ethnic groups.

PREJUDICE Prejudice is an *attitude* that prejudges people, usually in a negative way, who are different from "us" in race, ethnicity, or religion. If an employer assumes, for example, that white workers will be more productive than black or Latino workers, she or he is prejudiced. *All* of us can be prejudiced. However, minorities, rather than whites, are typically the targets of discrimination.

DISCRIMINATION Discrimination is behavior that treats people unequally or unfairly. It encompasses all sorts of actions, ranging from social slights (such as inviting only the white kids in a child's class to a birthday party) to rejection of job applications, and even hate crimes.

Discrimination also occurs *within* racial-ethnic groups. In a recent national poll, for example, 83 percent of Latinos said that they had experienced discrimination by other Latinos. The most recent immigrants, especially Colombians and Dominicans, said that they had encountered unequal treatment in employment and income from U.S.-born Latinos (Brodie et al., 2002).

Although education and employment opportunities have improved since the mid-1960s, racial-ethnic families have to deal with prejudice and discrimination, often on a daily basis. Despite ongoing inequality, however, African American, American Indian, Latino, Asian American, and Middle Eastern families have numerous strengths. We now turn to a closer examination of each of these five groups.

![Making Connections]

Making Connections

■ Do you think the United States should change its immigration levels? What do you think would be the costs and benefits of increasing or decreasing current immigration rates?

■ Have you, members of your family, or friends ever experienced racial-ethnic discrimination? Also, list examples of situations in which a person who is prejudiced might not discriminate and in which a person who discriminates might not necessarily be prejudiced.

African American Families

There is no such thing as "the" African American family. Like other American families, black families vary in kinship structure, values, lifestyle, and social class. Yet profound stereotypes still exist (see the box on "The Ten Biggest Myths about the African American Family").

Family Structure

E. Franklin Frazier (1937), an African American, was one of the first sociologists to point out that there are several types of black family structures: families with matriarchal patterns, traditional families similar to those of middle-class whites, and families, usually of mixed racial origins, that have been relatively isolated from the main currents of African American life. Over time, black family structures have changed, adapting to the pressures of society as a whole. When men lose their jobs, for example, some nuclear families expand to become extended families. Others welcome nonrelatives, such as fictive kin, as members of the household (see Chapter 1).

Until 1980, married-couple families were the norm. Since then, black children have been more likely to grow up with only one parent, usually a mother, than has been the case for children in other racial-ethnic groups (see *Figure 4.3*). This shift reflects a number of social

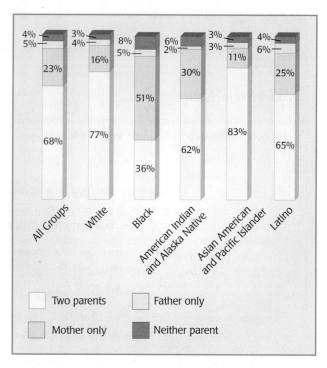

FIGURE 4.3 **Where Children Live**

SOURCES: Based on Fields, 2004, Table C2.

and economic developments: postponement of marriage, high divorce and separation rates, low remarriage rates, male unemployment, and out-of-wedlock births (see Chapters 9–13, 15, and 16).

Gender Roles

Although African American families are often stereotyped as matriarchal, the egalitarian family pattern, in which both men and women share equal authority, is a more common arrangement. Black husbands are more likely than their white counterparts to share household chores (John and Shelton, 1997; Xu et al., 1997).

The more equal sharing of housework and child care probably reflects black husbands' willingness to "pitch in" because their wives are employed. Also, many grew up in families in which the mother worked outside the home and black men were "active participants" in domestic labor (Penha-Lopes, 1995).

The division of domestic work is not equal, however. Black married women are still more likely than men to do most of the traditional chores, such as cooking, cleaning, and laundry, and to be overworked. Some of the instability in black marriages, as in white marriages, is a result of conflicts that occur when wives demand that men do more of the "traditionally female" domestic tasks (Hatchett et al., 1995).

Constraints

The Ten Biggest Myths about the African American Family

There are many misconceptions about the African American family, most of which can be reduced to the following ten myths (see also Chapter 3):

Myth 1. Black family bonds were destroyed during slavery. Historical studies show that most slaves lived in families headed by a father and a mother. Many slave couples lived in long marriages, some for 30 years or more (Bennett, 1989).

Myth 2. The black family collapsed after emancipation. In 1865, roads in the South were clogged with black men and women searching for long-lost family members. Most freed slaves, some of them elderly, remained with their mates. Few renounced their vows or sought new partners.

Myth 3. The black family has always been a matriarchy characterized by domineering women and weak or absent men. Black America has produced a long line of extraordinary fathers and many mothers and fathers working, loving, and living together (Billingsley, 1992).

Myth 4. Most black families are poor and on welfare. Although 22 percent of African Americans live below the poverty level, in 2004 almost 34 percent of black families had annual incomes of $50,000 or more (U.S. Census Bureau, 2006).

Myth 5. The major problem of black families is loose morals. In reality, black America has always condemned unrestrained sexual expression and insisted on stable mating patterns. Children are valued, whether born in or out of wedlock (Allen and James, 1998).

Myth 6. Most black single-parent families are dysfunctional. Given the obstacles they face, many single-parent families are remarkably resilient. They are raising highly motivated children who graduate from college and become quite successful (Toliver, 1998).

Although films like *Boyz'n the Hood* offer a realistic portrayal of some working-class black neighborhoods, these negative images should not be generalized to all black communities (Gaiter, 1994).

Myth 7. Black parents avoid work, fail to motivate their children, and teach them to rely on handouts. For most of the twentieth century, blacks were more likely to work than whites. Until the mid-1990s, for instance, proportionally more black mothers than white mothers were in the work force. At many Fortune 1000 companies, blacks make up 2 to 26 percent of the managers and board members (Hickman, 2002).

Myth 8. Black men can't sustain stable relationships. Many unmarried African American fathers maintain ties with their children and the mothers of their children. Middle-class black fathers are often more family-oriented than middle-class white fathers (Taylor, 2002; see, also, Chapter 12).

Myth 9. Black families no longer face widespread job and housing discrimination. In a recent poll, 34 percent of white respondents, compared with only 6 percent of black respondents, said that "blacks have achieved racial equality" (Bobo et al., 2001).

In fact, blacks report discrimination in a variety of settings, from dealings with the police to relations with local shop owners. And although high-interest mortgage loans are illegal, they are five times more prevalent in black neighborhoods than in white ones (Barnes, 2000; Hoerlyck, 2003).

Myth 10. The African American family owes its survival to white generosity and government welfare. Most blacks have survived because of support from the extended family, house rent parties, church suppers, and black schools and churches, not handouts or welfare. In fact, African Americans have made enormous contributions in education, music, business, and other areas (Kunjufu, 1987).

Stop and Think . . .

- In Chapter 1, you recall, we considered how myths can be both functional and dysfunctional. How are myths about African American families functional? How are they dysfunctional?

- What other myths might you add to the ones in this box?

Parents and Children

Most African American parents play important roles in their children's development. Many black fathers make a conscious effort to be involved in their children's lives because their own fathers were aloof. Others emulate fathers who participated actively in father–child activities. Still others are simply devoted to their kids:

Why is it difficult for many African American parents to raise their children in U.S. society today?

> [My older son and I] do everything together. I learned to roller-skate so that I could teach him and then go skating together. I'm the one who picks him up from school. I'm one of his Sunday school teachers, so he spends Sundays with me at church while my wife stays at home with our two-month-old son (Penha-Lopes, 1995: 187–88).

Black, Latino, and Asian American parents are more likely than white parents to encourage their children to exercise self-control and succeed in school. This may reflect ethnic parents' concern that their children will have to work harder to overcome prejudice and discrimination (Thomas and Speight, 1999; Toth and Xu, 1999).

The close relationship between African American parents and their children produces numerous advantages for the children. In a study of the intelligence scores of black and white 5-year-olds, for example, the researchers found that the home environment was critical in fostering a child's development. Even if the family was poor, when parents provided warmth (caressing, kissing, or cuddling the child) and stimulated the child's learning (reading to the child at least three times a week), there were no differences between white and black children in intelligence scores (Brooks-Gunn et al., 1996).

Despite such positive outcomes, parents must deal with a variety of obstacles. Three of the most important are racism, neighborhood violence, and absent fathers.

RACISM Most black children first learn to cope with **racism,** a belief that people of one race are superior or inferior to people of other races, in the family. Daniel and Daniel (1999) compare teaching children about racism to exclaiming "No!" when toddlers inch toward a hot stove.

Race awareness occurs at about 2 to 3 years of age. Some African American parents talk about race with their children, but others feel that such discussions will make the child feel inferior. Because blacks, more than any other group, experience racism on an everyday basis, many parents engage in **racial socialization,** a process in which parents teach their children to overcome race-related barriers and experiences and to take pride in their ancestry (Phinney, 1996; Van Ausdale and Feagin, 2001; McAdoo, 2002).

NEIGHBORHOOD VIOLENCE African American families—especially those in inner-city neighborhoods—are more likely than those of other racial-ethnic groups to face violence or the threat of violence on an almost daily basis. According to a study of fourth- and fifth-grade children living in inner cities, 89 percent reported that they regularly heard the sound of gunfire, and more than 25 percent said that they had seen someone stabbed or shot.

Many of the mothers weren't aware that their children had been victimized (beaten up, punched, or chased by gangs) or witnessed violence. The researchers found that exposure to violence was associated with psychological distress: stomachaches or headaches, bad dreams, troubled sleep, difficulty paying attention in school, and feeling "jumpy" (Ceballo et al., 2001).

Family reunions like this birthday celebration for John Garrett (seated, wearing white cap) of New Jersey not only bring extended families together but also remind family members of closeness and shared family history.

ABSENT FATHERS According to one black journalist, "America makes shirking daddy duty easy" (Dawsey, 1996: 112). Some black men simply dump girlfriends who become pregnant. The men don't want a long-term commitment or don't have the money to support a child. Others die young, are in jail, or are involved in crime and drugs. Some out-of-wedlock fathers visit their children, play with them, and care for them while the mothers are working. Although the number of such fathers is increasing, it's still low (see Chapters 9 and 12).

Health and Economic Well-Being

According to one of my students, hard-working African American fathers often ignore their health:

> I know many black fathers who died before reaching the age of 60. My dad was one of those men. He was a hard worker and stable provider for his family, but he died at the age of 53 due to diabetes and high blood pressure. In general, I think that black men's health often goes unnoticed (Author's files).

Numerous studies have found a strong relationship between work-related stress, financial problems, and poor physical health (see Chapter 13). And as you saw earlier, minorities typically receive lower-quality health care than do whites.

INFANT DEATHS Although there is a strong relationship between health and social class, poverty alone does not "cause" early death. The United States' **infant mortality rate,** the number of deaths of babies under 1 year of age per 1,000 live births, ranks 28th in the world. Our infant mortality rate of 7.0 is much higher than those for other industrialized nations, such as Sweden, France, Japan, and Germany, as well as the rates for some much poorer countries, such as Cuba and the Czech Republic (Health. . . , 2004).

The infant mortality rate for African Americans is nearly double that of the general population: 13.9 versus 7.0. It is also much higher than those for among some other ethnic groups. Why? Poverty isn't the major reason: Other low-income groups, such as Central and South American immigrants, have much lower infant mortality rates (see Figure 4.4).

Black infants experience high mortality rates primarily because of low birthweight (weighing less than 5 pounds, 8 ounces), followed by sudden infant death syndrome (SIDS) (Mathews et al., 2004). These and other problems reflect a number of other variables be- sides social class, such as not seeking prenatal care and making poor lifestyle choices, including drug use, smoking, poor diet, and lack of exercise.

FAMILY INCOME The percentage of black families with annual incomes of $50,000 or more has increased. Still, the median family income of African Americans is the lowest of all racial-ethnic groups (see Figure 4.5). As Congress continues to cut health services for the poor, black families—especially those headed by mothers—will be the ones most likely to experience health problems. Kin provide important emotional and financial support during hard times, but they may feel overburdened when economic difficulties are chronic (Lincoln et al., 2005).

More than two-thirds of African Americans (compared with less than one-third of whites) have no financial assets such as stocks and bonds. Black families inherit less wealth than do white families. This means that parents often cannot afford to give young adults money for college, large cash gifts for weddings, and downpayments for their first homes (Oliver and Shapiro, 2001).

Despite these and other health and economic problems, many African Americans are optimistic about the future. For example, more than 61 percent of blacks (compared with 46 percent of whites) feel that their children will enjoy a higher standard of living (Race and Ethnicity . . . , 2001).

Strengths of the African American Family

Black families have numerous strengths: strong kinship bonds, an ability to adapt family roles to outside pressures, a strong work ethic despite recessions and unemployment, determination to succeed in education, and an unwavering spirituality that helps them cope with adversity (McAdoo, 2002).

Bill Cosby, an African American actor and author, sparked an uproar when he criticized poor black parents for raising irresponsible children (see the box "Is Bill Cosby Right about Black Families?"). Although the comments stirred up considerable debate, many low-income black families, especially those headed by mothers, show enormous fortitude and coping skills (Edin and Lein, 1997).

Numerous self-help institutions (churches, voluntary associations, neighborhood groups, and extended family networks) enhance the resilience of black families, even in the poorest communities. In the last decade, for example, many black men across the country have

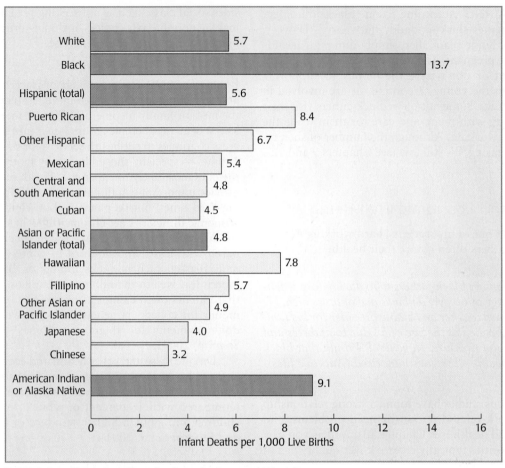

FIGURE 4.4 **U.S. Infant Mortality Rates by Race and Ethnicity**

Source: *Health . . .* , 2004, Figure 24.

organized mentoring and self-help groups for adolescents and young fathers.

Despite much economic adversity, many African Americans see their families as cohesive, love their children, provide a strong religious foundation, and teach their children to be proud of their cultural heritage and to contribute to their community. Other strengths include imbuing children with self-respect, teaching them how to be happy, and stressing cooperation in the family (St. Jean and Feagin, 1998; Hill, 2003).

American Indian Families

American Indians used to be called "the vanishing Americans." Since the 1980s, however, this population has "staged a surprising comeback" because of higher birth rates, longer life expectancy, and better health services. Although American Indians and Alaska Na-

tives make up only 1.5 percent of the U.S. population, 0.6 percent report being multiracial (Ogunwole, 2006).

American Indian families are heterogeneous. A Comanche–Kiowa educator cautions that "lumping all Indians together is a mistake. Tribes . . . are sovereign nations and are as different from another tribe as Italians are from Swedes" (Pewewardy, 1998: 71).

Of about 175 native American Indian languages still spoken in the United States, only about 20 are being passed on to the next generation. Linguists are working with tribes to preserve their languages because some of the last speakers, now elderly, are dying (Pierre, 2003).

Family Structure

About 62 percent of the nation's American Indian and Alaska Native children live with both parents (see *Figure 4.3*). Like black, Asian American, and Pacific Is-

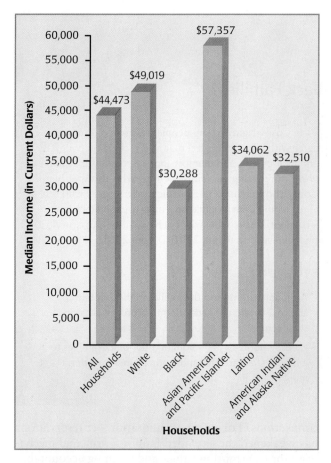

FIGURE 4.5   Median Household Incomes by Race and Ethnicity, 2003–2004

SOURCE: Based on DeNavas-Walt et al., 2005, Table 2.

lander children, almost 24 percent of American Indian children live in extended families (Fields, 2001).

Extended families are especially common among American Indians who live on reservations. Frequent contact with family members provides a buffer against stressful emotional and economic circumstances. Supportive family networks are also important if families are isolated geographically because they have migrated to urban areas to find jobs (MacPhee et al., 1996).

In many American Indian languages, there is no distinction between blood relatives and relatives by marriage. Among some groups, aunts and uncles are considered intimate family members. Sometimes the father's brothers are called "father," uncles and aunts refer to nieces and nephews as "son" or "daughter," and a great-uncle may be referred to as "grandfather" (Sutton and Broken Nose, 1996).

Gender Roles

Studies of contemporary American Indian families, husbands and wives, and gender roles are virtually nonexistent (Kawamoto, 2001). One exception is a study of 28 off-reservation Navajo families. Here, Hossain (2001) found that mothers spent significantly more time than did fathers in cleaning, food-related work, and child-care responsibilities.

Compared with fathers in other cultural groups, the Navajo fathers' involvement in household labor and child-related tasks was high—between 2 and 3 hours per day. The wives reported higher levels of commitment (always pitching in), cohesion (making sacrifices for others), and communication (expressing concerns and feelings). Both husbands and wives, however, felt equally competent in solving family problems and coping with everyday issues.

Parents and Children

Children are important members of American Indian families. Parents spend considerable time and effort in making items for children to play with or use in activities and ceremonies (such as costumes for special dances, looms for weaving, and tools for gardening, hunting, and fishing). Many tribes teach spiritual values and emphasize special rituals and ceremonies (Yellowbird and Snipp, 2002).

Most adults teach children to show respect for authority figures by listening and not interrupting. As one tribal leader noted, "You have two ears and one mouth for a reason." Mothers, especially, strive to transmit their cultural heritage to their children. They emphasize the importance of listening to and observing adults to learn about their identity (Gose, 1994; Dalla and Gamble, 1997; Cheshire, 2001).

American Indian families emphasize such values as cooperation, sharing, personal integrity, generosity, harmony with nature, and spirituality—values that are quite different from the individual achievement, competitiveness, and drive toward accumulation emphasized by many in the white community. Families teach children that men and women may have different roles but that both should be respected for their contributions to the family (Stauss, 1995; MacPhee et al., 1996; Kawamoto and Cheshire, 1997).

Sometimes American Indian parents feel that they are losing control over their children's behavior, especially hanging around with friends and drinking. Some researchers see a relationship between American Indian adolescents' risk-taking behavior (such as using drugs and dropping out of school) and fragile family

Choices

Is Bill Cosby Right about Black Families?

On several occasions, Bill Cosby has scolded "lower-economic and lower-middle-economic" black parents and their kids for foolish behavior and decisions:

"It is not all right for your 15-year-old daughter to have a child," he told 2,400 fans in a high school in Milwaukee. He lambasted young men in Baltimore for knocking up "five, six girls." He tongue-lashed single mothers in Atlanta for having sex within their children's hearing "and then four days later, you bring another man into the house" (Cose, 2005: 66).

According to Cosby, many poor blacks are bad parents because they waste what little money they have buying their kids $500 sneakers instead of "Hooked on Phonics." He also said that he was fed up with "knuckleheads" who don't speak proper English.

Is Cosby right? Many people, regardless of ethnicity, agree with him. Others feel that he is picking on poor kids and their parents and that low-income youth usually make good purchasing decisions. Those who disagree with Cosby also feel that upper-middle-income blacks who benefited from the civil rights movement are too quick to criticize poor blacks who aren't achieving the same level of financial success (Chin, 2001; Dyson, 2005).

Stop and Think. . .

- Are poor parents and their children making bad choices? Or are they adapting to problems beyond their control?
- Is Cosby right? Or is he holding poor black families to a higher standard that most other Americans don't meet?

Among many American Indian tribes, some people preserve traditional ways while others adopt the practices and products of the majority culture. These differences can be seen even within extended families.

connections. For instance, migration off reservations has weakened the extended family, a principal mechanism for transmitting values and teaching accountability (Machamer and Gruber, 1998).

Elders and Grandparents

Children are taught to respect their elders. Old age is viewed as a "badge of honor"—a sign that one has done the right things and has pleased the creator. As a result, elders have traditionally played a central role in a family's decision making.

Because of the emphasis on family unity and cooperation, family members and tribal officials often offer elders assistance without their having to ask for it (Kawamoto and Cheshire, 1997). According to the Navajo, for example, the life cycle consists of three stages: "being cared for," "preparing to care for," and "assuming care of" (Bahr and Bahr, 1995). Thus, caring for each other and for elderly family members is a cultural value that is passed on to children.

In their research on Navajo and Apache reservations, Bahr and Bahr (1995: 248) found that many grandmothers and grandchildren rely on each other:

Grandchildren may help their grandmothers gather cattails to harvest yellow pollen, "pick" worms to sell to fishermen, catch fish to help supplement the family diet, or make tortillas. The grandmothers encourage the children in their schoolwork, and many of the grandchildren help with household chores, chopping wood, sweeping floors and washing dishes.

As families move off reservations in search of decent housing and better employment and educational opportunities, some grandparents play the role of "cultural conservators." By taking their grandchildren to church meetings, tribal hearings, powwows, and other reservation activities, these conservator grandparents hope to familiarize their grandchildren with native history and wisdom (Weibel-Orlando, 1990).

As more women work outside the home, they are especially likely to turn their children over to their grandmother for care. Today many American Indian college students return to work or teach on reservations or in other American Indian communities because "they long for mothers, fathers, sisters, brothers, and perhaps most of all, their grandparents" (Garrod and Larimore, 1997: xi; Schweitzer, 1999).

Health and Economic Well-Being

Two significant issues that tribal leaders have begun to address are mental health problems (especially depression) and the physical and sexual abuse of children. Suicide rates are high among American Indians, especially among teenagers and men under age 40. Alcohol-related violence is another problem and is related to depression, high suicide rates, and crime (see the box "American Indians and Alcohol Use: Facts and Fictions").

since you asked

Why is alcohol abuse a serious problem among many American Indians?

Many American Indians believe that one of the reasons for the high alcoholism rate, especially among youth, is the gradual erosion of American Indian culture. American Indian children living in urban neighborhoods have a particularly hard time maintaining their cultural identity and often feel like outsiders in both the American Indian and white cultures. In response, hundreds of programs nationwide are fighting addiction by

Constraints

American Indians and Alcohol Use: Facts and Fictions

Alcohol consumption is a serious problem among many American Indians. The rate of alcohol-related deaths is six times higher among American Indians than among whites (Kington and Nickens, 2001).

American Indians under age 35 are about ten times more likely than other U.S. residents to die from alcohol-related problems such as liver disease. They are also about three times more likely to commit suicide because of alcohol use. In addition, more than half of violent crimes among American Indians involve drinking by both the victim and the offender (Greenfeld and Smith, 1999; Brenneman et al., 2000; Wissow, 2000).

Although alcohol abuse is a problem in any community, May (1999) notes that there are many stereotypes and myths about "the drunken Indian." In reality,

■ There is wide variation in the prevalence of drinking from one tribal group to another.

■ About 75 percent of alcohol-related deaths are due to sporadic binge drinking rather than chronic alcoholism.

■ Serious injuries (such as car accidents) due to alcohol often result in death because many Indians live in rural, remote environments where medical care is far away or unavailable.

According to many tribal leaders, several major beer companies have targeted American Indians with their marketing strategies. The poorest reservations often accept sponsorship from brewing companies for annual tribal fairs and rodeos.

Stop and Think . . .

• Should businesses that sell alcohol be banned in American Indian communities that don't want them? Or do such restrictions jeopardize "free enterprise"?

• Alcohol commercials dominate most television sports programs. Should they also be banned, especially in states with high American Indian populations?

reinforcing American Indian cultural practices and values (Sanchez-Way and Johnson, 2000; Sagiri, 2001).

One out of four American Indians lives below the poverty level. American Indians often have higher joblessness rates than do other racial-ethnic groups. On many reservations, unemployment rates run about 50 percent and sometimes up to 90 percent (Vanderpool, 2002).

Substandard housing is common, especially on reservations. Many homes are overcrowded and lack kitchen facilities (including stoves and refrigerators) and indoor plumbing (Bonnette, 1995a, 1995b).

Many people believed that the gambling casinos springing up on American Indian reservations would lift poor American Indians out of poverty. They were wrong. Only half of the 561 federally recognized tribes operate the nearly 300 casinos, which generate $23 billion a year in revenue. A few tribes with casinos located near big cities have hit the jackpot. Some members haul in as much $900,000 annually and still get up to $20,000 of federal aid per person. But 80 percent of American Indians haven't received a penny (Bartlett and Steele, 2002a, 2002b; National Indian Gaming Commission, 2006).

Why not? Some large tribes, such as the Navajo, oppose gambling for religious reasons. In other cases, in order to increase their own profits, the council of tribal leaders that controls official membership refuses to recognize certain individuals as members of the tribe. Non–American Indian investors have become billionaires by underwriting the initial costs of buying land and starting up the casinos, and are pocketing 40 percent of the profits (Barlett and Steele, 2002a, 2002b).

Despite the greed and corruption associated with them, casinos have created jobs, economic stability, and political power for some American Indians. Among other benefits, gambling profits have enabled tribes to fund health clinics, new schools, sanitation systems, services for the elderly and youth, and similar programs. In addition, some tribes have used gambling revenues to build or run enterprises such as malls, vacation resorts, community colleges, apparel companies, and power plants and to provide housing for low-income families (Gerdes et al., 1998; Fixico, 2001).

Strengths of the American Indian Family

Strengths of the American Indian family include "relational bonding," a core behavior that is built on widely shared values such as respect, generosity, and sharing across the tribe, band, clan, and kin group. Harmony and balance involve putting community and family needs above individual achievements. Another strength is a spirituality that sustains the family's identity and place in the world (Stauss, 1995; Cross, 1998).

In some cases, tribe members have worked patiently over several generations to develop self-sufficient industries. In the remote village of Mekoryuk, Alaska, for example, Inuit women collaborated with an anthropologist at the University of Alaska–Fairbanks to begin a knitting cooperative that transforms the downy wool of musk oxen into warm and lightweight clothes.

The knitters, ranging in age from 9 to 90, work in their homes in several villages and sell the products by mail order. The women don't get rich, but the knitting keeps them out of poverty. It also passes traditional skills on to younger generations, as the women incorporate ancient patterns from traditional Inuit culture into their knitting (Watkins, 2002).

Gaming profits from the Mystic Lake Casino, owned and operated by the Shakopee Mdewakanton Sioux Indians in Minnesota, have enabled the tribe to endow a program in Native American Studies at Augsburg College and to support Indian arts and the American Indian Dance Theatre. The casino also provides jobs for non-Indians, who make up more than half of its employees.

Making Connections

■ Many American Indian languages are becoming extinct. Is this a normal part of a group's acculturation into a host society that should be accepted? Or should the languages be preserved?

■ American Indians run tax-free gambling enterprises. Should African Americans have the same opportunities, especially because they lost their inheritances when they were brought to this country from Africa as salves?

Latino Families

Latino families are diverse. Some trace their roots to the Spanish and Mexican settlers who established homes and founded cities in the Southwest before the arrival of the Pilgrims. Others are immigrants or children of immigrants who arrived in large numbers around the turn of the twentieth century (see Chapter 3).

Spanish-speaking people from Mexico, Ecuador, the Dominican Republic, and Spain differ in their customs and in their experiences in U.S. society. We focus here primarily on characteristics that Latino families share, noting variations among different groups where possible.

Family Structure

About 65 percent of Latino children live in two-parent families, down from 78 percent in 1970 (see *Figure 4.3;* see, also, Lugaila, 1998). Shifting social norms, economic changes, and immigration patterns have altered the structure of many Latino families. Couples are more likely to divorce, and there are more out-of-wedlock births. In addition, some young Latino children may be more likely to live with relatives than parents because new immigrants depend on family sponsors until they can become self-sufficient (Garcia, 2002; see, also, Chapters 11 and 15).

Gender Roles and Parenting

Gender and parenting roles vary on factors such as how long a family has lived in the United States, whether the wife or mother works outside the home, and the extent of the family's acculturation into U.S. society. Many Latino families, especially new immigrants, must grapple with new gender and parenting roles that are very different from those in their homeland.

GENDER ROLES Latino men often suffer the stereotype of *machismo,* a concept of masculinity that emphasizes characteristics such as dominance, aggression, and womanizing (see Chapter 3). The mainstream press often ignores such positive elements of *machismo* as courage, honor, *respeto* (a respect for authority, tradition, and family), *dignidad* (avoiding loss of dignity in front of others), and close ties with the extended family.

since you asked

Are Latinas dominated by "macho" men?

The female counterpart of *machismo* is *marianismo. Marianismo,* associated with the Virgin Mary in Catholicism, expects women to remain virgins until marriage and to be self-sacrificing and unassuming (De La Cancela, 1994; Mayo, 1997; see, also, Chapters 5 and 7).

Some scholars contend that *machismo* is a ludicrous stereotype: Many Latino men participate in domestic work and child rearing instead of acting like macho tough guys who are domineering husbands and fathers. Among recent Dominican immigrants, for example, many husbands share some housework and consult their wives about expensive purchases (Pessar, 1995; González, 1996).

On the other hand, some researchers report that even wives who work outside the home are often subordinate to men and are expected to follow traditional family roles. In a study of Puerto Rican families, for example, Toro-Morn (1998) found that working mothers were primarily responsible for the care of the home and the children. And in a study of Central American workers, Repak (1995) found that men in working-class households balked at sharing household responsibilities and child care even when their wives worked full time outside the home.

PARENTING Most Latino parents, like other parents, are caring and affectionate and expect their children to be successful. They teach their children to be obedient, honest, and respectful, both at home and outside the home. There are socioeconomic differences, however. Like their white counterparts, middle-class Latinos who have acculturated to U.S. society tend to be more permissive in raising their children (Harwood et al., 2002).

Even when they're in the labor force, most Latinas devote much of their lives to bearing and rearing children. As one Latina said, "To be valued [in our community] we have to be wives and mothers first." Parenting and marital conflicts sometimes erupt, however, because mothers are often overloaded by the demands of caring for their families and working outside the home (Segura, 1994; DeBiaggi, 2002).

Fathers don't do nearly as much parenting as mothers. Nevertheless, they're warm and loving with their children. And compared with white fathers, Latino fathers are more likely to supervise and restrict their children's TV viewing, regulate the types of programs they watch, and require them to finish their homework before going outside to play (Toth and Xu, 2002; see, also, Chapter 12).

Familism and Extended Families

For many Latino households, familism and the strength of the extended family have traditionally provided emotional and economic support. In a national poll, for example, 82 percent of Latinos, compared with 67 percent of the general U.S. population, said that relatives are more important than friends ("The ties that bind," 2000).

FAMILISM *Familism*, you recall, refers to family relationships that take precedence over individual well-being (see Chapter 3). The family serves as an essential support system, providing emotional and economic help. Sharing and cooperation are key values. Familism is often a response to historical conditions of economic deprivation. Many Mexican American families, for example, survive only because they have the support of immigrants who arrived earlier (Baca Zinn and Wells, 2000).

Some researchers claim that social support increases with each generation living in the United States. Others have found that familism may be declining because of high separation and divorce rates, a decrease in married-couple families, and a lack of economic resources—all factors that erode support networks (Hurtado, 1995; Vega, 1995; Taylor, 2002).

EXTENDED FAMILIES Many Latino families include aunts and uncles, grandparents, cousins, in-laws, godparents, and even close friends. The extended family exchanges a wide range of goods and services, including child care, temporary housing, personal advice, nursing, and emotional support. Some Mexicans practice "chain migration," in which those already in the United States find employment and housing for other kin who are leaving Mexico (López, 1999; Sarmiento, 2002).

The importance of extended families varies by place of residence and social class. For example, a study of Mexican families in Texas concluded that "among economically advantaged Mexican Americans in urban centers, the extended family is not central to the routines of everyday life" (Williams, 1990: 137). In very poor communities where the family has been decimated by unemployment, drugs, or AIDS, social agencies and community-based organizations sometimes become the new extended family, taking the place of grandparents and other family members (Abalos, 1993).

Being Bilingual

Among many recent immigrant families, young children often have more responsibilities than U.S.-born children. Because children learn English faster than their parents, they often take on adult roles. According to one researcher,

> I see a lot of situations where [Salvadoran and Guatemalan] parents will take a young child to get their gas installed, to ask why their services were shut off, to pay the bill. . . . In that sense the children play a different role from other children because they are secretaries or assistants to their parents in order for the family to function (Dorrington, 1995: 121).

Generally, being bilingual in English and Spanish has a positive effect on educational attainment. According to a recent national study, for example, young Latinos who reported rarely speaking Spanish with their friends are more likely to attain a high school diploma or college degree than those who speak Spanish almost always with their friends. However, the greater use of Spanish with parents increases academic success, largely because such interactions encourage school performance (Blair and Cobas, 2006).

To strengthen their cultural ties and preserve their language, many Latino parents send their children "home" to spend summers with relatives. A teen from the Dominican Republic says that he looks forward to such trips. "Here in school, I speak mainly English. When I'm in my country, I'm speaking Spanish and I'm happy" (Blumberg, 2005: 13).

Economic Well-Being and Poverty

According to historian Kevin Starr, "The economy of the Sun Belt and California would collapse without Hispanics. They are doing the work of the entire culture," from harvesting the nation's food supply to providing much-needed workers at hotels, restaurants, and construction sites (cited in Chaddock, 2003: 1, 3).

ECONOMIC SUCCESS Like that of black families, the number of middle-class Latino families has increased.

Almost one in three earns $50,000 a year or more (see *Figure 4.6*), up considerably from 7 percent in 1972.

Keep in mind that there is a great deal of variation among Latino families. Almost 37 percent of Cuban families earn this much, compared with 31 percent of Mexican American and 32 percent of Puerto Rican families (U.S. Census Bureau, 2006).

Economic success depends on a number of inter-related factors, including U.S. immigration policies and political relations with the country of origin, the timing of migration, the skills that immigrants bring with them, and the deterioration of urban neighborhoods that are available for residential and business development.

In the case of Cuban immigrants, all these variables were just right in the late 1950s. The U.S. government, hoping to weaken Fidel Castro's power, extended Cuban exiles a "generous welcome." Unlike *any* other group of immigrants in history, Cuban refugees received government subsidies for housing, magnanimous refugee programs that provided job training and intensive English classes, college scholarships, and other resources (Suro, 1998).

Many of the Cubans came from a middle- or upper-middle-class background. They had *human capital* (such as high educational levels and entrepreneurial skills), worked hard to develop rundown and abandoned Miami neighborhoods, and became politically active (Pérez, 1992). In contrast, none of the other Latino immigrants have received such assistance, regardless of their human capital resources.

This doesn't mean that all Cuban Americans are wealthy and all other Latinos are poor. There is wide variation among Latino subgroups. About 20 percent of all Latino families live below the poverty line. Of these, 68 percent are Mexican, 17 percent are Central and South American, 12 percent are Puerto Rican, and only 3 percent are Cuban (U.S. Census Bureau, 2006).

POVERTY In many cases, according to one Latino researcher, "The family that is doing the right thing is still falling behind. We have people working, people married, and yet we see poverty increasing" (Fletcher, 1997).

Why do many Latino families have high poverty rates? Many recent immigrants who were professionals in their native land find only low-paying jobs (such as delivering food for restaurants, cleaning buildings, or working as cashiers in retail stores). They don't have enough time both to work and to learn the language that would help them gain the accreditation they need to practice as doctors, lawyers, and accountants ("Living humbled . . . ," 1996).

Other recent immigrants and U.S.-born Latinos have low educational levels. Almost one-third don't have a high school degree. Some drop out of high school because they're failing; some are forced to work to support their families. Others say they drop out because public schools marginalize them, disrespect their culture, and make them feel "like a dumb Mexican" (Headden, 1997; U.S. Census Bureau, 2006).

A number of Latinos have few skills and lack the kinds of work experience that employers want. Therefore, they are likely to earn entry-level salaries in lower-skilled jobs. During recessions, including that of the early 2000, even second-generation young Latinos suffered unemployment rates as high as 10 percent. Darker-skinned Latinos, especially, face discrimination in the labor market (Espino and Franz, 2002; Lowell, 2002). Day laborers are among the most abused workers in America (see the box "Mexican Day Laborers in America").

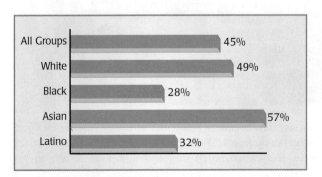

FIGURE 4.6 **Households with Annual Incomes of $50,000 or More, 2004**

SOURCE: Based on DeNavas-Walt et al., 2005, Table A-1.

Strengths of the Latino Family

Despite their economic vulnerability, many Latino families are resilient and adaptive. Family networks protect their members' health and emotional well-being. Many immigrants demonstrate incredible internal resources in coping with economic hardship, learning a new language, and shaping their own solutions in adjusting to a new environment (Alfaro et al., 2006; DeGarmo and Martinez, 2006).

The ability of Latino families to transmit traditional values about familism has often offset the negative impact of prejudice and discrimination, drug use, and other risky behavior among many adolescents. As in black families, parental socialization, which emphasizes

Changes

Mexican Day Laborers in America

Day laborers gather in a Home Depot parking lot in Freeport, N.Y., waiting for work. The construction business on Long Island, once dominated by local whites, now relies heavily on Latino immigrants.

Angelo earned $100 for 16 hours of work at a Los Angeles construction site. Antonio stacked boxes at a Chicago warehouse for 10 hours and wasn't paid at all. Both Angelo and Antonio are *los jornaleros,* Mexican slang for "day laborers."

Day laborers are people who are paid for work on a daily or short-term basis. They often congregate on street corners before dawn and wait for employers to drive by and offer them work. When an employer drives up, the men swarm around the SUV or pickup truck to be noticed and hired for the day.

Day laborers are a common sight in California and the Southwest. Increasingly, they are also working in Chicago and other cities and suburbs along the East Coast. Some researchers estimate that there are more than 100,000 of these workers across the United States, making up only a fraction of the 11 million undocumented immigrants in the country.

Day labor offers no health benefits, no job security, no overtime, and payment in cash. The employers get cheap labor, tax-free. And the workers get work.

Day laborers are overwhelmingly Mexican men who speak little English and have no more than a sixth-grade education. The 80 percent who are undocumented immigrants are especially vulnerable to unscrupulous employers, homeowners, and contractors. Most are underpaid, are paid less than they were promised, or don't get paid at all.

Day laborers can earn as much as $1,069 in a good month and as little as $341 in a typical bad month. Many send a large portion of their earnings home; others use the money to smuggle relatives across the U.S. border.

Day laborers handle toxic materials without proper safety equipment, perform dangerous work, and suffer injuries on the job. They possess the very traits that we celebrate—self-reliance, hard work, and raising income for their families—yet they are "widely used, abused, and despised" (Valenzuela, 2000; Rectanus and Gomez, 2002; Bazar and Armour, 2005; Garcia, 2006).

Stop and Think . . .

- Because they work hard at jobs that most Americans don't want, why do you think that day laborers are "widely used, abused, and despised"?

- Some activist groups are pressuring elected officials to punish the local employers who hire day laborers. Others argue that day laborers are exploited and should be protected because they provide much-needed cheap labor. How do you feel?

Groups of Latino men surround the car of a potential employer looking for possible work opportunities outside a 7-Eleven in Herndon, Virginia. Many construction businesses, once dominated by local whites, now rely heavily on Latino immigrants.

ethnic pride and identity, protects many Latino children from anger, depression, and, in some cases, violence (Strait, 1999; Quintana and Vera, 1999; Phinney et al., 2001).

Asian American Families

Asian Americans encompass a wide range of cultures and traditions. They come from at least 26 countries of East and Southeast Asia (including China, Taiwan, Korea, Japan, Vietnam, Laos, Cambodia, and the Philippines) and South Asia (including India, Pakistan, and Sri Lanka). They follow different religions, speak different languages, and use different alphabets. Asian Americans also include Native Hawaiians and other Pacific Islanders from Guam and Samoa.

Chinese are the largest Asian American group (2.3 million), followed by Filipinos (1.9 million) and Asian Indians (1.7 million). Combined, these three groups account for 58 percent of all Asian Americans (Barnes and Bennett, 2002).

Regardless of their country of origin, Asian American families feel pressure to adapt to U.S. culture. Some of the changes they experience are in family structure, gender roles, and parent–child relationships.

Family Structure

Asian American family structures vary widely depending on country of origin, time of arrival, past and current immigration policies, whether the families are immigrants or refugees, and the parents' original socioeconomic status. Almost 11 percent of Asian American and Pacific Islander families have six or more members, compared with 5 percent of families nationally. Average household size varies across groups: 5.1 for Cambodians, Hmong, and Laotians, for example, but only 2.5 for Japanese families (McLoyd et al., 2001).

Asian American families are likely to be extended rather than nuclear. They might include parents, children, unmarried siblings, and grandparents. Most children grow up in two-parent homes (see *Figure 4.3*). Female-headed homes, whether because of divorce or out-of-wedlock birth, are much less common among Asian Americans than in other groups.

Gender Roles

Gender-role socialization is very traditional in many Asian American families. In Chinese American families, for example, many parents rely more heavily on girls than on boys to perform domestic chores (Fuligni et al., 1999).

Some groups, especially Asian Indians, practice semi-arranged or arranged marriages. Others—especially if they've been in the United States for several generations—follow U.S. practices of open courtship (see Chapters 6 and 9).

Many Asian Americans follow Confucianism, which endorses a patriarchal social structure. This structure instructs women to obey their father, husband, and oldest son. The woman thus derives her status through her role as a wife, mother, or daughter-in-law. The man, in contrast, is head of household, principal provider, decision maker, and disciplinarian (Yu, 1995; Chan, 1997).

Women are more likely to be equal partners in some Asian American groups than in others. Filipino culture historically has had a less patriarchal gender role structure than other groups: Husbands and wives share financial and domestic decision making. Generally, Filipino husbands and wives tend to have egalitarian relationships (Espiritu, 1995).

In contrast, Korean, Asian Indian, Hmong, and Vietnamese families, among others, follow traditional gender roles, even if the wife is in the work force. Large numbers of Asian American mothers are employed because a double income is necessary for economic survival. In some cases, a woman may work outside the home to support the family while the man pursues an education or job training (Kibria, 2002; Min, 2002; Purkayastha, 2002).

In many cases, working outside the home has not decreased the wife's homemaker role. The wife is still expected to cook, clean the house, and take care of the children. She bears these double roles regardless of length of residence in the United States (Kim and Kim, 1998; Chen, 1999).

Tensions often arise as the husband's traditional role of breadwinner shifts. Especially in working-class families, two-paycheck couples may be working at more than one job or working irregular hours. They have little time for each other, their children, or household tasks, and stress builds (Fong, 2002).

Parents and Children

In many Asian American families, the strongest family ties are between parent and child rather than between spouses. Parents sacrifice their personal needs in the interests of their children. In return, they expect *filial piety*: respect and obedience toward one's parents (Chan, 1997).

FAMILY VALUES As with the Latino emphasis on *familism*, to Asian Americans the family is more important than the individual. Among Indian Asian families, traditional Hindu values regard kinship ties as more important than individual interests (Chekki, 1996).

In a similar vein, the Vietnamese saying *mot giot mau dao hon ao nuoc la* ("one drop of blood is much more precious than a pond full of water") reflects the belief that family solidarity is more important than relationships with people outside the family. Even when extended kin don't live together, they may cooperate in running a family business, pool their income, and share certain domestic functions, such as meal preparation (Glenn and Yap, 2002).

Filipino ideology teaches that revealing a family problem to an "outsider"—whether a friend, teacher, or counselor—creates gossip and brings shame (*hiya*) and embarrassment to the family. Such "confessions" imply that parents are doing a bad job of raising their children. On the other hand, bottling up problems may lead to loneliness, depression, and suicidal thoughts (Wolf, 1997).

DISCIPLINE Asian American parents exercise more control over their children's lives than non–Asian American parents. They use guilt and shame rather than physical punishment to keep their children in line and to reinforce the children's strong obligations to the family. In Chinese American families, for example, *guan* ("to govern") has a positive connotation. *Guan* also means "to care for" or "to love." Therefore, "parental care, concern, and in-

volvement are synonymous with a firm control and governance of the child" (Chao and Tseng, 2002: 75; Fong, 2002).

Vietnamese parents expect obedience from both sons and daughters. Parents enforce discipline more strongly among girls than among boys, however, even in the use of corporal punishment. The Vietnamese ideal of "the virtuous woman" expects girls to live up to higher behavioral standards than boys (Zhou and Bankston, 1998; Saito, 2002).

Many Asian American parents are indulgent, tolerant, and permissive with infants and toddlers. As the child approaches school age, however, the parents expect greater discipline and more responsibility in grooming, dressing, and completing chores (Chan, 1997).

Most parents don't tolerate aggressive behavior and expect older children to serve as role models for their younger siblings. Parents also teach their children to conform to societal expectations because they are concerned about what other people think, both within and outside the Asian American community.

Many parents not only pressure their children to excel in school but also may endure extreme hardships—even selling their house—to ensure the best college opportunities for their children (Fong, 2002). The box "How to Be a Perfect Taiwanese Kid" describes the emphasis on academic achievement.

The ability of Asian American families to succeed despite historical discrimination and exclusion has cre-

---

Multicultural Families

How to Be a Perfect Taiwanese Kid

Many immigrant parents—Latino, Middle Eastern, and African—emphasize education as the route to upward mobility and success. The value of education is embodied in the Chinese proverb, "If you are planning for a year, sow rice; if you are planning for a decade, plant trees; if you are planning for a lifetime, educate people." For many Asian American parents, securing a good education for their children is a top priority (Zhou and Bankston, 1998; Pollard and O'Hare, 1999).

By excelling in school, the child brings honor to the family. Educational and occupational successes further enhance the family's social status and ensure its economic well-being as well as that of the next generation (Chan, 1999). The following tongue-in-cheek observations about how to be the perfect Taiwanese kid (Ng, 1998: 42) from

the parents' perspective would apply to many other Asian American families as well:

1. Score 1600 on the SAT [Scholastic Aptitude Test].
2. Play the violin or piano at the level of a concert performer.
3. Apply to and be accepted by 27 colleges.
4. Have three hobbies: studying, studying, and studying.
5. Go to a prestigious Ivy League university and win a scholarship to pay for it.
6. Love classical music and detest talking on the phone.
7. Become a Westinghouse, Presidential, and eventually a Rhodes Scholar.
8. Aspire to be a brain surgeon.
9. Marry a Taiwanese American doctor and have perfect, successful children (grandkids for *ahma* and *ahba*).
10. Love to hear stories about your parents' childhood, especially the one about walking 7 miles to school without shoes.

Asian American youths, such as Wendy Guey of West Palm Beach, Florida, often win national spelling bees and science contests. Guey won the 69th annual competition by correctly spelling " vivisepulture." (I had to look it up, too.)

ated problems. Their reputation for being a "model minority," for example, has both helped and hindered their progress.

The Model Minority: Fictions and Facts

Recently, a *Washington Post* article heralded the opening of a Korean-owned Super H Mart, which was billed as "Northern Virginia's newest supermarket extraordinaire." Among other things, it would compete with the big chain grocers, expand Korean-owned stores outside mom-and-pop inner-city ethnic enclaves, and prove that hardworking immigrants can be successful in U.S. society (Cho, 2003). Do you think such stories encourage its readers to stereotype *all* Asian American families as the "model minority"?

since you asked

Are Asian American children really more self-disciplined and higher achieving than other American children?

FICTIONS ABOUT THE MODEL MINORITY Asian American families have the highest median income in the country (see *Figure 4.5*). Such figures are misleading, however. Many Asian American households are larger than average, as you saw earlier, and include more workers. In addition, lumping all Asian Americans together as a "model minority" ignores many subgroups that are not doing well because of low educational levels and language barriers.

The most successful Asian Americans are those who speak English relatively well *and* have high educational levels. As in the case of Latinos, many recent Asian American immigrants with top-notch credentials from their homeland experience underemployment in the United States. For example, some Korean doctors work as hospital orderlies and nurses' assistants because they can't support a family at the same time that they prepare for the English-language test and the medical exam in their field of specialization (Jo, 1999).

Even when Asian Americans are employed in professional jobs—as architects, engineers, computer systems analysts, teachers, and pharmacists—they are not in the upper management levels (Hope and Jacobson, 1995). The "Dangers of the Model Minority Myth" box describes some negative effects of the "model minority" image on Asian Americans and on American society in general.

FACTS ABOUT THE MODEL MINORITY Why have many Asian American families become successful? There are three major factors.

First, the U.S. Immigration and Naturalization Service screens immigrants, granting entry primarily to those who are the "cream of the crop." For example, nearly 66 percent of Filipino immigrants are professionals, usually nurses and other medical personnel, and nearly two-thirds of all Asian American Indian professionals in the United States have advanced degrees beyond college. Also, foreign-born professionals are usually willing to work the long hours demanded by public hospitals and to work for lower salaries (Adler, 2003).

Second, the mixture of Buddhist and Confucian values and traditions resembles the traditional middle-class prerequisites for success in America. All three ideologies emphasize hard work, education, achievement, self-reliance, sacrifice, steadfast purpose, and long-term goals.

Asian American and American traditions differ in at least one important way, however. Whereas American values stress individualism, competition, and independence, Buddhist and Confucian traditions emphasize interdependence, harmony, cooperation, and pooling of resources. For example, many Korean immigrants have been able to secure capital to start a small business through *kae* (or *kye*), a credit rotation system in which

Multicultural Families

Dangers of the Model Minority Myth

In recent years, many Asian American and other scholars have debunked the stereotypical notion of Asian Americans as a "model minority." Petersen (1966: 21) first used the phrase "model minority" when he described Japanese Americans as an unparalleled success story:

By any criterion that we choose, the Japanese Americans are better than any other group in our society, including U.S.-born whites. They have established this remarkable record, moreover, by their own almost totally unaided effort. Every attempt to hamper this progress resulted only in enhancing their determination to succeed.

There are six dangers in endorsing the model minority stereotype (Do, 1999: 118–22):

Danger 1: The model minority image distorts and ignores the differences within Asian American communities. Although Vietnamese Americans, for example, share many cultural characteristics and customs, they are a diverse group in terms of time of arrival, educational levels, English proficiency, and support received after landing on U.S. shores.

Danger 2: The model minority stereotype creates tension and antagonism within and across Asian American subgroups. If recently arrived immigrants aren't as successful as their predecessors, there must be some-

thing wrong with them. Other immigrants have done very well, after all.

Danger 3: Model minority images can lead to verbal and physical assaults. White supremacist groups, who resent many Asian Americans' educational and occupational accomplishments, often target Asian Americans with hate crimes, including murder.

Danger 4: The model minority myth camouflages ongoing racial discrimination in U.S. society by blaming the victim. If some groups—such as blacks, Latinos, and American Indians—don't succeed, it must be their own fault rather than the fault of U.S. policies or racism.

Danger 5: As with any stereotype, the model minority image denies its members' individuality. Although many Asian American students are interested in teaching, social work, dance, and theater, they are often pressured to pursue careers in law, medicine, engineering, dentistry, computer science, or the biological sciences.

Danger 6: The model minority myth deprives individuals of necessary social services and monetary support. Asian Americans typically are excluded from many civil rights policies, such as affirmative action programs, because they are labeled as "achievers" (Ancheta, 1998).

Stop and Think . . .

- Why do you think these myths about Asian Americans as a model minority are so widespread?

- How do such myths and stereotypes affect our relationships with Asian Americans in classes, at work, and in Asian American–owned businesses?

---

about a dozen families donate $1,000 or more to help a shopkeeper set up a new business (Yoon, 1997).

The rotating savings and credit organization is common to many ethnic groups: Ethiopians call it *ekub*, Bolivians call it *pasanaqu* (to "pass from hand to hand"), and Cambodians call it *tong-tine*. All operate on the same basic principles: Organize a group of close friends, agree on how much and how often to pay into the kitty, and determine how the money will be apportioned, whether by lottery or according to need. The winner can use the funds to start a business, pay for a wedding, put a down payment on a home, or pay for college tuition (Suro, 1998).

A third reason for many Asian American families' success is pretty straightforward: They usually work harder than their non–Asian counterparts. For example, many Asian American students are active in ex-

tracurricular activities—such as school clubs, athletics, and community service. Yet they typically spend twice as much time on homework as other American students, and less time watching television, socializing with friends, or working after school (Saito, 2002).

Strengths of the Asian American Family

As in the case of Latino families, researchers continuously emphasize that Asian American families vary significantly in their country of origin, time of immigration, ability to speak English, and other factors. Generally, however, the strengths of Asian American families include stable households in which parents encourage their children to remain in school and offer personal support that reduces the stress produced by discrimination and leads to better emotional health (Barringer et al., 1993; Leonard, 1997).

Traditional Asian American families are changing. Still, many young adults want to maintain the close-knit character of their family life, which emphasizes cooperation, caring, and self-sacrifice (Kibria, 1994; Zhou and Bankston, 1998).

Middle Eastern Families

What do the following well-known people have in common: consumer advocate Ralph Nader, singer and *American Idol* judge Paula Abdul, heart surgeon Michael De Bakey, Heisman Trophy winner Doug Flutie, Senators George Mitchell and John Sununu, and Tony Shalhoub of the popular *Monk* television program? All are Middle Eastern Americans of Arab descent.

The term *Middle East* refers to "one of the most diverse and complex combinations of geographic, historical, religious, linguistic, and even racial places on Earth" (Sharifzadeh, 1997: 442). The Middle East encompasses about 30 countries. They include Turkey, Israel, Iran, Afghanistan, Pakistan, and a number of Arab nations (such as Algeria, Egypt, Iraq, Jordan, Kuwait, Lebanon, Palestine, Saudi Arabia, Syria, and the United Arab Emirates).

Of the almost 19 million people in the United States who speak a language other than English or Spanish at home, almost 11 percent speak Middle Eastern languages such as Armenian, Arabic, Hebrew, Persian, or Urdu (U.S. Census Bureau, 2006). As in the case of Asian American families, Middle Eastern families make up a heterogeneous population that is a "multicultural, multiracial, and multiethnic mosaic" (Abudabbeh, 1996: 333).

Family Structure

As in other ethnic groups, Middle Eastern family structures vary. However, many share similar values and attitudes about family life.

FAMILY SIZE "Wealth and children are the ornaments of this life," says the Qur'an, the sacred book of Muslims. In traditional Middle Eastern societies, not having children is a reason for great unhappiness. A study of a working-class Arab American community in Dearborn, Michigan, found that 38 percent had five or more children (Aswad, 1994).

The number of children declines, however, among people who are U.S. born and members of higher so-

Tony Shalhoub plays the neurotic but brilliant crime investigator in the popular television series, Monk. *Shalhoub's father emigrated from Lebanon as an orphan and married a Lebanese-American woman. Shalhoub, who had nine brothers and sisters, was born in Green Bay, Wisconsin, in a Lebanese-American community. He has turned down numerous scripts that he felt had racist overtones.*

cioeconomic classes. U.S.-born Arab American women have low fertility rates: just under two children per lifetime (which is lower than the average among all U.S. women). Many women postpone childbearing and have fewer children because they pursue college and professional degrees and have high employment rates (Kulczycki and Lobo, 2001).

NUCLEAR AND EXTENDED FAMILIES Most Middle Eastern children (84 percent) live with both parents, compared with 71 percent of all American children. Middle Eastern families frown on divorce. Iranians, for example, view divorce as a calamity (*bala*) and equate it with an "unfortunate fate" that should be avoided at all costs.

Although divorce rates for U.S.-born Middle Eastern families are increasing, the percentages are much lower than the national average (almost half of all marriages). Unless a parent is a widow or a widower, single parenthood is seen as abnormal (Aswad, 1997; Hojat et al., 2000).

Nuclear families are the norm, but extended family ties are important. "The typical Lebanese," for example, "views family as an extension of him or herself" (Richardson-Bouie, 2003: 528). Households composed of parents and children maintain close contact with relatives. These relationships include financial, social, and emotional support.

Whenever possible, Middle Eastern families try to bring relatives from their homeland to stay with them over long periods to attend U.S. colleges and universities, to work, or just to visit. According to a young Algerian woman, her 26-year-old female cousin lived with their family for six years while attending school. Both women had strict curfews (Shakir, 1997).

One of my Turkish students told his classmates that his American-born parents "kicked me down to the basement" because a visiting uncle was to use his bedroom for the next year or so. The students were appalled. He simply shrugged: "Relatives are important in Turkish families."

Marriage and Gender Roles

Many Middle Eastern families value close and reciprocal ties between husbands and wives. Marriage is often a "family affair," and gender role expectations are usually clearly delineated.

since you asked

Has assimilation changed Middle Eastern families?

MARRIAGE Marriage is endogamous (see Chapter 1), favoring marriage between cousins in some groups and, in general, between people from the same national group. Marriage is a sacred ceremony and is regarded as central to the family unit.

Marriage is usually a contract between two families and is rarely based on the Western concept of romantic love. Marriages are often arranged or semi-arranged in the sense that children can turn down their parents' choices of a suitable mate.

Some of these practices are changing and they vary from one group to another. Among Iranians, Lebanese, and Palestinians, especially those from upper and middle-class families, young adults tend to choose their own marital partners but usually seek parental approval. Others visit their homelands to meet prospective partners that their kin (especially mothers and aunts) have singled out for marriage (Jalali, 1996).

GENDER ROLES Middle Eastern cultural attitudes mandate distinct gender role expectations. Men have been socialized to be the providers for the family and to protect their wives, children, and female kin. A "good" husband, then, supports his family and makes decisions that promote the family's well-being. In most cases, the husband is the highest authority in the family and has the final decision on any family issues (Aswad, 1999; Joseph, 1999).

Women anchor the family's identity. A "good" wife takes care of the home and children, obeys her husband, and gets along with her in-laws. She doesn't challenge her husband, especially in public, and doesn't work outside the home, especially when the children are young. Although men have many privileges, women have considerable influence and status in the domestic area (Simon, 1996).

A wife should always act honorably and do nothing that humiliates her husband and relatives. Premarital sex and extramarital affairs are out of the question because they bring shame to the family and kin. According to some young women, such gender role expectations are comforting rather than restrictive because they protect women from assaults and competition for dates (Shakir, 1997).

Gender roles are changing, however. Many Middle Eastern women must work out of economic necessity. The women who are most likely to be employed, however, at least among Arab Americans, are those without children at home. In effect, then, patriarchal systems dictate that Middle Eastern women in some groups can be in the labor force only when they don't have traditional responsibilities such as raising children (Read, 2004).

Divorce rates are low but increasing. And as families become more Americanized, there are more conflicts between parents and children.

Parents and Children

According to an Arabic saying, "To satisfy God is to satisfy parents." Satisfying parents means following the family's customs and traditions, respecting one's cultural identity, and living up to gender role expectations.

ETHNIC IDENTITY Parents and children usually have strong bonds. In a study of Arab Canadian teenagers, for example, nine out of ten respondents said that they talk to their parents, usually the mother, about their personal lives and problems (Abu-Laban and Abu-Laban, 1999).

This trust and confidence reflects the Middle Eastern value in which parents are a resource. Parents also teach their children to feel a lifelong responsibility to their siblings and parents and to respect their aunts, uncles, cousins, and grandparents (Ajrouch, 1999).

Parents reinforce ethnic identity by encouraging their children to associate with peers from their own culture. Armenian children, for example, attend language school on weekends. Here adolescents not only learn their language but also associate with Armenian peers who have similar cultural values (Phinney et al., 2001).

GENDER ROLE EXPECTATIONS Many Middle Eastern parents have a double standard in dating and curfews. Girls have many more restrictions in both areas. Girls are guarded because husbands want a virgin bride and not "damaged goods" (see Chapter 1). Brothers have every right to scold or threaten their sisters if they "misbehave" or act in any way that could tarnish the family name.

Although boys are expected to marry within their ethnic group, they have much more freedom to date, both inside and outside their group. According to a Lebanese mother, "We just feel the boy can take care of himself. If a boy goes out with a girl, nobody's going to point a finger at him." In contrast, a girl who dates or dresses "the wrong way" will ruin her reputation and dishonor the family's name (Simon, 1996; Ajrouch, 1999).

Girls are expected to perform traditional domestic chores and serve men. Some girls accept these roles, but others complain. According to a young Lebanese woman,

> So many times I would be asked to fix my brother's bed. I was told, "He is a boy." And I would say, "He has arms and legs." Or sometimes he would be sitting, and he would say, "Go get me a glass of water." I would say, "Never! Get your own." My family would say to me, "Your head is so strong, it cannot be broken with a hammer" (Shakir, 1997: 166).

The double standards create conflict between daughters and their parents. Middle Eastern teenage girls who spend much time with their American friends, especially, balk at the restrictions on dating. These and other disagreements can strain intergenerational relationships.

Prejudice and Discrimination

All ethnic families have experienced prejudice and discrimination (see Chapter 3). Middle Eastern families, however, have suffered a large share of verbal and physical assaults because of the U.S. government's combative relations with the Middle East, the September 11, 2001, terrorist attacks, and, most recently, the war in Iraq.

Despite increased diversity of the U.S. population, Middle Eastern children are often ridiculed because of their "funny names" and "strange behavior" (such as not attending proms because Islam discourages dances). In other cases, patients may distrust Middle Eastern physicians and other qualified practitioners, especially since 9/11, because the patients suspect that the health providers might be terrorists who would purposely endanger a patient's health (Marvasti and McKinney, 2004).

Most Middle Eastern families, including the Muslim women shown here, demonstrated solidarity with other Americans after the September 11, 2001, terrorist attacks on the United States.

The number of workplace discrimination complaints to the Equal Employment Opportunity Commission more than quadrupled three months after the September 11 terrorist attacks. The complainants, many of whom were Arab Americans, said that they had been fired without any notice or explanation (Conlin, 2001; Grimsley, 2001).

Still others experienced harassment, hate crimes, and even death:

■ An Arab American citizen, the father of eight children, was shot to death at a convenience store where he worked in Fresno, California. This was one of five murders that the Arab-American Anti-Discrimination Committee attributed to the September 11 attacks.

■ Muslim American and Arab American women—many recognizable by their distinctive head scarves, or *hijabs*—became targets of violence even though they were middle-class professionals. For example, a young cashier at a Staples store in Westbury, New York, threw a credit card back at an Arab American woman.

■ Some teachers implied that all Muslims are terrorists. Some classmates harassed U.S.-born Middle

Eastern children with comments such as "Go back where you belong." As a result, many children were afraid to reveal their Middle Eastern heritage (Benet, 2001; Breslau, 2001).

These and other instances of prejudice and discrimination have a negative impact on parents and their children. Nevertheless, Middle Eastern families—like African Americans, American Indians, Latinos, and Asian Americans—show enormous resilience in overcoming obstacles.

Strengths of the Middle Eastern Family

In many ways, Middle Eastern children have the best of two worlds. Because they're bicultural (and many are bilingual), they understand their own culture as well as American culture. When ethnic identity, strong family ties, and religion tie children to their communities, they can cope with prejudice and discrimination. Most important, perhaps, many Middle East families have extended kin networks and relatives whom they can count on during hard times (Hayani, 1999).

Making Connections

■ If you're a member of a racial-ethnic family, what do you see as its major strengths? What about its problems?

■ How do the media reinforce the image of the model minority? Also, how do children's and adult movies (like *Aladdin* and *The Mummy*) portray Middle Eastern people, especially Arabs?

Interracial and Interethnic Relationships and Marriages

In 1997, professional golfer Tiger Woods said he was "Cablinasian," a word he'd made up as a boy, because he was one-eighth Caucasian, one-fourth black, one-eighth American Indian, one-fourth Thai, and one-fourth Chinese. Many blacks were upset that Woods seemed to downplay his African American roots, but Woods maintained that he was embracing all parts of his multicultural heritage. Even former President Bill Clinton announced that he, too, was a multiracial American because some of his ancestors were American Indians.

Interracial and Interethnic Relationships

One of the big news stories from the 2000 Census was that California is now a "minority majority" state, meaning that whites make up less than half of the state's population (Kent et al., 2001). Not all people identify themselves with only one racial or ethnic group, however.

GROWING MULTIRACIAL DIVERSITY As you saw earlier in this chapter, the 2000 Census allowed people to mark more than one race and ethnicity for the first time. Those checking more than one "box" could choose any of 126 categories and combinations.

Almost 98 percent reported only one race. But one in 40 Americans calls herself or himself the product of two or more racial groups. About 4 percent of children under age 18 were identified as multiracial, compared with 2 percent of adults. Almost a third of those reporting two or more races were Latinos (Jones and Smith, 2001). The next highest percentages included combinations of whites and other racial-ethnic identities (see *Figure 4.7*).

According to an Italian and Irish man and his black wife who live in Hawaii and have a biracial daughter, "You ask a Hawaiian what race they are and you'd get 20 different races" (Fears, 2001: A8). That's an exaggeration, but Hawaii has the largest proportion of people—21 percent—who identify themselves as two or more races, followed by Alaska and California (5 per-

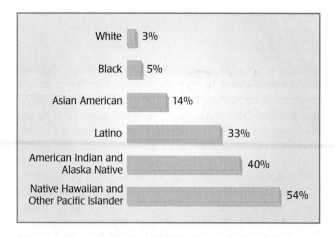

FIGURE 4.7 **Percentage of Americans Who Identify with More Than One Race**

Note: Of the 281.4 million population in 2000, 2.4 percent identified themselves with two or more races. Only 0.1 percent said they were three or more races.

SOURCES: Based on Jones and Smith, 2001, Tables 4 and 5.

cent each), Puerto Rico (4 percent), and Arizona and Washington (almost 4 percent each) (Jones and Smith, 2001).

REACTIONS TO INTERRACIAL RELATIONSHIPS Of all the people who reported being more than one race, 42 percent were children under age 18. These "mixies," as they sometimes call themselves, experience emotions ranging from self-confidence to self-hatred (Jones and Smith, 2001; see, also, Chapter 12).

Interracial dating is fairly common (see Chapter 8). Nonetheless, interracial couples encounter everything from discrimination to acceptance. In a recent survey, whites were more likely than other groups to feel that people should marry only within their own race. There were striking differences by age, however. Only 17 percent of people between ages 18 and 29, compared with 68 percent of those age 65 and over, felt that it's better to marry someone of your own race (*Race and Ethnicity . . .*, 2001).

These are attitudes. What about behavior? How do people react to dating or marrying across racial and ethnic lines?

When a national survey asked couples how often they encountered discriminatory behavior such as stares or pointing, 25 percent of black–white couples said "never," compared with 9 percent of Latino–white couples and 5 percent of Asian–white couples. Such behavior varies greatly by region, however. In the West, where percentages of multiracial couples are high, biracial couples are less likely to be "marked" than in regions, such as the South, where interracial relationships are more likely to be stigmatized (*Race and Ethnicity . . .*, 2001).

One of the world's top golfers, Tiger Woods, recently married a Swedish model. Do such marriages reduce the pool of eligible mates for well-educated, attractive, and successful African American women? Or do they encourage greater acceptance of interracial marriages?

Interracial and Interethnic Marriages

Laws against *miscegenation* (marriage or sexual relations between a man and a woman of different races) existed in America as early as 1661. It wasn't until 1967, in the U.S. Supreme Court's *Loving v. Virginia* decision, that antimiscegenation laws were overturned nationally. Interracial and interethnic marriages reflect *exogamy* (and *heterogamy*): marrying outside of one's particular group (see Chapters 1 and 8).

since you asked

Do most Americans marry outside of their ethnic-racial groups?

PREVALENCE OF RACIAL-ETHNIC INTERMARRIAGES Rates of racial-ethnic intermarriages have increased slowly, from 0.7 percent in 1970 to 5.4 percent of all married couples in 2000 (Fields and Casper, 2001).

Thus, about 95 percent of all marriages are between women and men of the same race or ethnicity.

When people think about racial intermarriage, they generally assume that it's between blacks and whites. This is a misconception. Of the 3 million racial-ethnic intermarriages, the outmarriage rates are lower for whites and blacks than for Latinos, Asian Americans, and American Indians (see *Table 4.1*). Whereas black men are more likely to marry white women than women in other racial-ethnic groups, white men are more likely to marry Latino, Asian American, and American Indian women (and in that order) than African American women (Fields and Casper, 2001).

Why have racial-ethnic intermarriages increased? And why do the rates vary across and within racial-ethnic boundaries? There are a number of reasons. Let's begin with proximity.

PROXIMITY We tend to date and marry people whom we see on a regular basis. Greater opportunity for interracial contact through housing, schools, work, and leisure activities may result in more racial-ethnic intermarriages (Kalmijn, 1998; see, also, Chapter 8).

TABLE 4.1

Racial-Ethnic Intermarriages by Sex

Racial/Ethnic Group	Men	Women
White		
Number	43.8 million	43.6 million
Percentage married out	3.4	2.9
Black		
Number	4.1 million	3.9 million
Percentage married out	8.4	3.3
Latino		
Number	5.2 million	5.3 million
Percentage married out	15.0	17.2
Asian American		
Number	1.9 million	2.2 million
Percentage married out	9.9	21.3
American Indian		
Number	351,000	371,000
Percentage married out	52.3	53.9
Total		
Number	55,352,000	55,352,000
Percentage married out	5.4	5.4

Note: These data tabulate the race of spouses for persons married and living with a spouse. For example, 43.8 million white men and 43.6 million white women were married and living with a spouse in 2000.

SOURCE: Adapted from Farley, 2002, Table 1.1.

The military, one of the most integrated of all U.S. institutions, seems to set the stage for dating and interracial marriage. White men who have served in the military are three times more likely to marry black women than are white men who have never served. White women who have served are seven times more likely to marry outside their racial group than are those who have never served ("Interracial marriages . . . ," 1997).

AVAILABILITY OF POTENTIAL SPOUSES We sometimes marry outside of our racial-ethnic group because of a shortage of eligible spouses. Because the population is so small, for example, an overwhelming 80 percent of U.S.-born Arabs have non-Arab spouses. In contrast, intermarriage rates among Latinos and Asian Americans have decreased since 1990—for both women and

men—because the influx of new immigrants has provided a larger pool of eligible mates (Farley, 2002; Kulczycki and Lobo, 2002).

Some demographers predict, however, that by 2100 more than half of all Asian Americans, Pacific Islanders, and Latinos will have intermarried (Edmonston et al., 2002). Because many children are multiracial, the racial divides that exist now will presumably be much less important in the future.

ACCULTURATION The racial-ethnic groups that are most acculturated to U.S. society are also most likely to intermarry. For example, the Asian Americans who are less likely to out-marry are those who live in ethnic enclaves, do not speak fluent English, and have lived in the United States a short time (Shinagawa and Pang, 1996).

Among Japanese Americans, in contrast, intermarriage rates are high because many families have been in the country for four or five generations, have acculturated, and are generally more accepting of intermarriage. In addition, the number of Japanese Americans is small compared with those of other Asian American groups. This decreases the opportunities for Japanese Americans to find a desirable mate within their own group (Hwang et al., 1994; Rosenfeld, 2002).

CHANGING ATTITUDES An increase in interracial marriages also reflects changing attitudes. American approval of interracial marriage rose from 4 percent in 1958 to a whopping 65 percent in 2002 (*Marriage between Blacks and Whites*, 2002).

Whites are less accepting of all racial-ethnic intermarriages than are members of other groups, however. According to a recent survey, 46 percent of white respondents said that people should "marry someone of their own race," compared with 21 percent of African Americans, 29 percent of Latinos, and 30 percent of Asian Americans (*Race and Ethnicity*, 2001).

An Ohio pastor refused to allow a wedding in his church when he learned that the white bride's groom was black. And, according to one white bride, her parents accepted her Puerto Rican husband because they thought he was Italian ("Interracial wedding . . . ," 2000; Fears and Deane, 2001).

Even though, as a group, African Americans are more accepting than whites of interracial marriages (including those between whites and blacks), many disapprove. With a significant shortage of marriageable African American men, many black women feel betrayed or deserted when a black man marries a white woman. Some black leaders also feel that mixed marriages weaken black solidarity (see Chapter 8).

Asian American parents also have mixed feelings about outmarriages. They often encourage their children to marry within their own group to preserve "lineage purity" and avoid the clash of values (about child rearing, hard work, and respect for elders, for example) that intermarriage with "mainstream America" often brings.

Asian American parents are often more accepting of marital partners *within* Asian American groups. According to a Chinese American writer and artist, for example, his mother's initial dismay that he was dating a non-Chinese woman evaporated when the mother learned that he was seeing a Korean American woman. The mother saw Koreans as physically similar to the Chinese and felt that many of the woman's values would be similar to her son's (Kibria, 1997).

Making Connections

- One of every five babies born in Sacramento, California, is multiracial. Could we conclude, then, that Sacramento is one of America's most integrated cities? Or not?

- Are racial-ethnic intermarriages desirable because they reflect an acceptance of "other" groups? Or do they dilute cultural heritages?

Conclusion

The racial and ethnic composition of American families is *changing*. There has been an influx of immigrants from many non-European countries. The increase in the numbers of African American, American Indian, Asian American, Latino, and Middle Eastern families is expected to continue in the future.

As you've seen in this chapter, there are many variations both between and within racial-ethnic groups in family structure, extended kinship networks, and parenting styles. This means that families have more *choices* outside the traditional, white, middle-class family model.

These choices often are steeped in *constraints*, however. Even middle-class racial-ethnic minorities confront stereotypes and discrimination on a daily basis. Because many children are multiracial, they must live in at least two cultural and social worlds. These worlds become even more complicated, as you'll see in the next chapter, because gender roles also play an important role in every family's daily life.

Summary

1. U.S. households are becoming more diverse in their racial and ethnic composition. Demographers project that if current immigration and birth rate trends continue, by 2050 only half of the U.S. population will be white.

2. Many Americans are ambivalent about the high rates of immigration to the United States. Some are grateful that immigrants provide important work at both the low-wage and professional levels. Others worry about national security and "diluting our national identity."

3. Latino, African American, Asian American, Middle Eastern, and American Indian families are considered minority groups. One of the most important characteristics of a minority group is its lack of economic and political power relative to the dominant group.

4. Black families are very heterogeneous. They vary in kinship structure, values, and social class. Despite

such variations, African American families are the subject of many myths.

5. American Indian families are complex and diverse. They speak many languages, practice different religions and customs, and maintain a variety of economic and political styles. Because of assimilation into mainstream U.S. society, a number of tribes are losing their language and customs.

6. Latino families vary in a number of ways, including when they settled in the United States, where they came from, and how they adapted to economic and political situations. In addition, family structure and dynamics vary greatly by social class and degree of assimilation.

7. Asian American families are even more diverse than American Indian and Latino families. Asian American family structures vary depending on the family's origin, when the immigrants arrived, whether their homeland was ravaged by war, and the socioeconomic status of the parents.

8. Middle Eastern families come from about 30 countries. Although they speak many languages and practice different religions, most place a high value on nuclear and extended families, teach traditional gender roles, and reinforce their children's ethnic identity.

9. The number of multiracial Americans is increasing. Much of this population consists of children under age 18.

10. Rates of interracial and interethnic marriage have been increasing slowly since 1967. Some of the reasons for the growing number of these marriages include proximity in school and workplaces, greater public acceptance of racial-ethnic intermarriage, acculturation, and a shrinking pool of eligible marriage partners in some groups.

Key Terms

assimilation 86
cultural pluralism 86
acculturation 86
minority group 89

racial group   90
ethnic group   90
racial-ethnic group   90
prejudice   91

discrimination   91
racism   94
racial socialization   94
infant mortality rate   95

Taking It Further

Race and Ethnicity Resources on the Internet

The first site, **American Studies Web,** is very comprehensive, containing national and international materials on groups such as African Americans, Asian Americans, American Indians, and Latinos. The other URLs provide links to specific racial-ethnic groups.

American Studies Web
http://lumen.georgetown.edu/projects/asw

WWW Virtual Library: American Indians
www.hanksville.org/NAresources

Asian American Studies WWW Virtual Library
coombs.anu.edu.au/WWWVL-Asian Americanstudies.html

African Studies Center
www.africa.upenn.edu/Home_Page/mcgee.html

Arab-American Affairs Homepage

www.arab-american-affairs.net

Hispanic Resources on the Web

http://homepages.ed.ac.uk/huwl/resources/resources.html

Interracial Voice

www.webcom.com/~intvoice

And more: www.prenhall.com/benokraitis provides sites containing information about teaching tolerance, international migration, minority health, civil rights legislation, hate sites, and numerous URLs of sites dealing ethnic minority groups in the United States.

Investigate With Research Navigator

Go to www.researchnavigator.com and enter your LOGIN NAME and PASSWORD. For instructions on registering for the first time, view the detailed instructions at the end of the Chapter 1. Search the Research Navigator™ site using the following key terms:

acculturation
prejudice
discrimination

Norman Rockwell, "The Shiner." Printed by permission of the Norman Rockwell Family Agency. Copyright © 1953 The Norman Rockwell Family Entities.

Outline

Socialization and Gender Roles

Data Digest

- Nearly a billion people in the world are illiterate; **two-thirds of them are women.**

- Of the world's 115 million children **who do not receive a primary education,** 78 percent are girls.

- In only 22 countries do women represent 25 percent or more of elected legislators, and this number has decreased since the early 1990s. **The figure for the United States (15 percent) is lower** than those for many other countries, including Sweden (45 percent), Cuba (28 percent), Vietnam (27 percent), and Mexico (16 percent). In two countries—Kuwait and the United Arab Emirates—there are no women in the legislature.

- White men comprise only **33 percent of the U.S. population.** Yet they account for 97 percent of school superintendents, 94 percent of the U.S. Congress, 92 percent of Fortune 500 chief executive officers, 90 percent of daily newspaper editors, 88 percent of college presidents, 86 percent of the Fortune 1000 board seats, 85 percent of partners in law firms, 85 percent of tenured professors, and 84 percent of state governors.

- Nationally, 26 percent of first-year undergraduate men and 16 percent of undergraduate women feel that "the activities of married women **are best confined to the home and family.**"

Sources: Schemo, 2002; Strupp, 2002; Center for American Women and Politics, 2005; Joyce, 2005; UNICEF, 2005; Zakaria, 2005; "Students," 2006.

Do you know what would have happened if there had been Three Wise Women instead of Three Wise Men? They would have asked for directions, arrived on time, helped deliver baby Jesus, cleaned the stable, made a casserole, brought practical gifts, and there would be peace on Earth. Does this anecdote stereotype women and men? Or do you think that it contains a kernel of truth?

In this chapter we examine gender roles: how we learn them and how they affect our marriage and family relations. Let's begin with a look at gender myths and some of the nature–nurture debates that often fuel such myths. First, however, take the quiz in the "Ask Yourself" box to see how much you already know about women and men.

Gender Myths and Biological Puzzles

Many Americans think that men and women are very different. Both sexes often describe men as aggressive, courageous, and ambitious. In contrast, they see women as emotional, talkative, patient, and affectionate (see Table 5.1).

TABLE 5.1

The Top Ten Personality Traits Ascribed to Men and Women

Trait	More True of Men	More True of Women
1. Aggressive	68%	20%
2. Courageous	50	27
3. Ambitious	44	33
4. Easygoing	55	48
5. Intelligent	21	36
6. Creative	15	65
7. Patient	19	72
8. Talkative	10	78
9. Affectionate	5	86
10. Emotional	3	90

SOURCE: Newport, 2001: 34.

Ask Yourself

A Gender Quiz: Are Women and Men Different?

True	False	
☐	☐	1. Women are the weaker sex.
☐	☐	2. Boys are more group-centered, active, and aggressive than girls.
☐	☐	3. Women are more emotional than men.
☐	☐	4. Women talk more than men.
☐	☐	5. Women suffer more from depression.
☐	☐	6. Women are more likely than men to divulge personal information.
☐	☐	7. Men smile more often than women.
☐	☐	8. Women and men don't care whether a baby is a boy or a girl ("Just as long as it's healthy").
☐	☐	9. Most women are confident about managing their financial affairs.
☐	☐	10. A heart attack is more likely to be fatal for a man than for a woman.

(The answers to this quiz are on p. 125.)

Do these traits characterize your family members and friends? Probably not. Your mom may be aggressive and ambitious and your dad emotional and talkative. Or both may be aggressive, emotional, or talkative, depending on the situation. And either or both parents may change over the years.

We tend to associate stereotypically female characteristics with weakness and stereotypically male characteristics with strength. We may criticize women for being "emotional," for example, but praise men for being "aggressive."

Consider, also, how often we describe the same behavior differently for women and men:

- He's firm, but she's stubborn.

- He's careful about details, but she's picky.

- He's honest, but she's opinionated.

- He's raising good points, but she's "bitching."

- He's a man of the world, but she's "been around."

Because we don't differentiate between sex and gender, we often ignore the importance of the social context that produces and maintains these stereotypes. It's therefore important to understand these two basic concepts.

The Difference between Sex and Gender

Although many people use *sex* and *gender* interchangeably, these terms have distinct meanings. Sex and gender are related, but sex is a biological designation whereas gender is a social creation that teaches us to be masculine or feminine as we perform various roles.

SEX Sex refers to the biological characteristics with which we are born: our chromosomal, anatomical, hormonal, and other physical and physiological attributes. Such biological characteristics determine whether you have male or female genitalia, whether you will menstruate, how much bodily hair you will have and where it will grow, whether you're able to bear children, and so on.

Although sex influences our behavior (such as shaving beards and buying bras), it does *not* determine how we think, feel, and act. We learn to be feminine or masculine through our gender, a much more complex concept than sex.

GENDER Gender consists of learned attitudes and behaviors that characterize people of one sex or the other. Gender is based on social and cultural expectations rather than on physical traits. Thus, whereas we are *born* either male or female, we *learn* to be either women or men because we associate conventional patterns of behavior with each sex.

If you've shopped for baby cards, you might have noticed that most of the cards for girls are pink while those for boys are blue. The cards usually portray the baby girls as playing with their toes, sitting in a bubble bath, or gazing at a mobile hanging above their crib. The cards for boys usually depict sports-related items such as baseballs, toys such as train sets, and even laptops.

You also might have noticed how many baby cards describe female infants as "dear," "sweet," "cute," or "cuddly;" male infants are described as "a special joy," "a pride," and "a precious gift." What's the message in these cards? It's that female infants are passive and ornamental whereas male infants are active and involved.

GENDER ROLES One of the functions of the family is to teach its members appropriate social roles (see Chapter 1). Among the most important of these are **gender roles:** the characteristics, attitudes, feelings, and behaviors that society expects of females and males.

We learn to become male or female through interactions with family members and the larger society. In most societies, for example, men are expected to provide shelter, food, and clothing for their families while women are expected to nurture their children and to tend to the family's everyday needs (see Chapters 12 and 13).

Social scientists often describe our roles as gendered. *Gendered* refers to the process of treating and evaluating males and females differently because of their sex:

> To the extent that women and men dress, talk, or act differently because of societal expectations, their behavior is gendered. To the extent that an organization assigns some jobs to women and others to men on the basis of their assumed abilities, that organization is gendered. And to the extent that professors treat a student differently because that student is a man or a woman, their interaction is gendered (Howard and Hollander, 1997: 11).

The fact that we learn gender roles doesn't mean that we can't change them. Many women now pursue college degrees and contribute to the family's finances; men participate more in raising children and doing housework than they did in the past.

GENDER IDENTITY Early in life, children develop a **gender identity,** a perception of themselves as either masculine or feminine. Most cultures teach gender identity early. Indian and Mexican baby girls have pierced ears, for example, and toddler hairstyles and clothing differ by sex. Gender identity, which typically corresponds to a person's biological sex, is learned in early childhood and usually remains fixed throughout life.

The Nature–Nurture Debate: Is Anatomy Destiny?

Most social scientists differentiate among sex, gender, and gender roles. If gender roles are learned, they argue, they can also be unlearned. However, other social scientists and biologists believe that differences in the behavior of women and men reflect innate biological characteristics, not social and cultural expectations. This difference of opinion is often called the *nature–nurture debate* (see *Table 5.2*).

since you asked

When people refer to "nature versus nurture," what are they talking about?

How Important Is Nature?

Those who argue that nature (biology) shapes behavior point to four kinds of evidence: developmental and health differences between men and women, research on the effects of sex hormones, sex differences in some parts of the human brain, and unsuccessful attempts at sex reassignment. Let's look at each of these briefly.

DEVELOPMENTAL AND HEALTH DIFFERENCES There are some documented biological differences between men and women. For example,

- Boys are more likely to suffer from genetic disorders, such as night blindness, myopia (nearsightedness), hemophilia, and glaucoma.

- The senses of smell and taste are more acute in women than in men, and hearing is better and lasts longer in women than in men.

- Although women are better than men at warding off viral and bacterial infections, they are much more susceptible to autoimmune diseases such as lupus.

- Women have a higher risk than men of developing diabetes (a major contributor to endometrial cancer, adult blindness, and cardiovascular disease).

- Some conditions, such as migraine headaches, are more common in women whereas others, including some kinds of skin cancer, are more common in men (McDonald, 1999; Sugg, 2000; Kreeger, 2002a, 2002b).

EFFECTS OF SEX HORMONES Scientists don't know why women and men differ, but they believe that hormones provide part of the explanation. All males and females share three sex **hormones:** chemical substances secreted into the bloodstream by glands of the endocrine system. These hormones are *estrogen* (dominant in females and produced by the ovaries), *progesterone* (present in high levels during pregnancy and also secreted by the ovaries), and *testosterone* (dominant in males and produced by the testes). All these hormones are produced in minute quantities in both sexes before puberty.

After puberty, varying levels of these hormones in males and females produce different physiological changes. For example, testosterone, the dominant male sex hormone, strengthens muscles but threatens the heart. It triggers the production of low-density lipoprotein, which clogs blood vessels. Therefore, men are at twice the risk of coronary heart disease as are (premenopausal) women. The dominant female sex hormones, especially estrogen, make blood vessels more elastic and strengthen the immune system, making females more resistant to infection (Wizemann and Pardue, 2001).

TABLE 5.2

The Nature–Nurture Debate

Nature	Nurture
Differences in male and female beliefs, attitudes, and behavior are	Differences in male and female beliefs, attitudes, and behavior are
Innate	Learned
Biological, physiological	Psychological, social, cultural
Due largely to heredity	Due largely to environment
Fairly fixed	Very changeable

SEX DIFFERENCES IN THE BRAIN In some cases, gender identity may be inconsistent with a person's biological sex. *Transgendered* is an umbrella term that describes people who adopt a gender identity that differs from their sex at birth. *Transvestites*, for example, are men and women who dress in clothing of the opposite sex.

Transgendered individuals also include *transsexuals*, people who feel that their gender identity is out of sync with their anatomical sex. They often describe themselves as feeling "trapped in the wrong body" (Devor, 1997).

About one person in 350,000 believes that she or he was born in a body of the wrong sex (Gorman, 1995). Some undergo surgery (which costs about $70,000), but others opt for only hormonal treatments. In one of the earliest and most publicized cases, in the 1970s, Richard Raskind, a married man with two children who was a highly ranked tennis player and a respected ophthalmologist, underwent surgery and became Renee Richards.

No one knows the reasons for transsexualism. Autopsies of six male-to-female transsexuals found that a tiny brain structure that controls sexual function was more like that of a woman than like that of a man. Most recently, a team of Swedish researchers found that the brains of transsexual men develop differently than those of heterosexual men during pregnancy because of a higher flow of some hormones, especially estrogen. Thus, some researchers suggest that structures in the brain—that is, nature—may account for transsexualism (Zhou et al., 1995; Henningsson et al., 2005).

Others argue that most transsexuals are gay men who are so feminine that they want to become women. According to this perspective, sex differences in the brain have nothing to do with transsexualism (Bailey, 2003).

UNSUCCESSFUL SEX REASSIGNMENT Some scientists point to unsuccessful attempts at sex reassignment as another example favoring the nature-over-nurture argument. Since the 1960s, John Money, a highly respected psychologist, has published numerous articles and books in which he maintained that gender identity is not firm at birth but is determined as much by culture and nurture as by hormones (see, for example, Money and Ehrhardt, 1972).

Several scientists have challenged such conclusions, however. As the box "The Case of John/Joan" shows, Money's most famous sex reassignment experiment does not support his contention that infants born as biological males can be successfully raised as females.

Dr. Ben Barres, a neurobiologist at Stanford University's Medical Center, underwent sex surgery. He says that, "By far, the main difference I have noticed is that people who don't know I am transgendered treat me with much more respect" than when he was a woman. "I can even complete a whole sentence without being interrupted by a man." (On the right is a photo of Dr. Barres as a bridesmaid in 1988.)

How Important Is Nurture?

Most social scientists maintain that culture, or nurture, shapes human behavior. They often point to four sources of data to support their argument: cross-cultural variations in gender roles, international differences in male violence rates, a rise in female violence, and successful sex assignment cases.

CROSS-CULTURAL VARIATIONS IN GENDER ROLES In a classic study, anthropologist Margaret Mead (1935) observed three tribes that lived within short distances of each other in New Guinea and found three different combinations of gender roles. Among the Arapesh, both men and women were nurturant with their children. The men were cooperative and sensitive and they rarely engaged in warfare.

Choices

The Case of John/Joan

In 1963, twin boys were being circumcised. The penis of one of the infants was accidentally burned off. Encouraged by John Money, a medical psychologist at Johns Hopkins Hospital, the parents agreed to reassign and raise "John" as "Joan." Joan's testicles were removed a year later to facilitate feminization, and when she was older, further surgery would be done to construct a full vagina.

Money reported that the twins were growing into happy, well-adjusted children of opposite sexes. The case set a precedent for sex reassignment as the standard treatment for 15,000 newborns with similarly injured genitals (Colapinto, 1997).

In the mid-1990s, however, Milton Diamond, a biologist at the University of Hawaii, and Keith Sigmundson, a psychiatrist with the Canadian Ministry of Health, conducted a follow-up of Joan's progress that showed that the sex reassignment had not been successful.

Almost from the beginning, Joan refused to be treated like a girl. When Joan's mother dressed her in frilly clothes as a toddler, Joan tried to rip them off. She preferred to play with boys and with stereotypical boys' toys such as machine guns. People in the community said that she "looks like a boy, talks like a boy" (Colapinto, 1997: 70).

Joan had no friends, and no one would play with her. "Every day I was picked on, every day I was teased, every day I was threatened," she said (Diamond and Sigmundson, 1997: 300).

When she was 14, Joan rebelled and stopped living as a girl: "She refused to wear dresses and now favored a tattered jean jacket, ragged cords and work boots. Her hair was unwashed, uncombed and matted" (Colapinto, 1997: 73). She urinated standing up, refused to undergo vaginal surgery, and decided that she would either commit suicide or live as a male.

When her father finally told her the true story of her birth and sex change, John recalls that "all of a sudden everything clicked. For the first time things made sense and I understood who and what I was" (Diamond and Sigmundson, 1997: 300).

Joan had a mastectomy at the age of 14 and underwent several operations to reconstruct a penis. Now called John, he was able to ejaculate but experienced little "erotic sensitivity." At age 25 he married a woman several years older than he was and adopted her three children. He committed suicide in 2004 at the age of 38.

Most recently, several Johns Hopkins scientists followed 14 boys who had been surgically altered as infants and raised as girls. The infants had a rare disorder, occurring once in every 400,000 births, in which the penis was small or nonexistent, despite the presence of testicles.

Five of the boys were happily living as girls. The others were living as males or had had "reassigned" themselves, taking on boys' names and dressing in masculine clothes (Reiner and Gearhart, 2004).

In contrast to Money's theories, then, some scientists maintain that John's case is evidence that gender identity and sexual orientation are largely innate. Nature, they argue, is stronger than nurture in shaping a person's sexual identity.

Stop and Think . . .

- What would you do if you had to make a decision about a child's sex reassignment?
- Because some boys who had been surgically altered are happily living as girls, can scientists conclude that gender identity and sexual orientation are largely innate?

Answers to "A Gender Quiz: Are Women and Men Different?"

1. **False.** Although infant mortality rates vary by race and ethnicity, the death rate for male infants is 22 percent higher than the rate for female infants. And, on average, women live about five years longer than men do.

2. **True.** Boys' play is typically hierarchical, group-centered, competitive, physical, and aggressive. Girls engage in more reciprocal, verbal, and cooperative kinds of play.

3. **False.** Both sexes are equally emotional, but men and women express their feelings differently. Men may "churn" more internally whereas women "externalize" (act out) their emotions through facial and verbal expressions.

4. **False.** In most situations, men tend to talk more and at greater length than women.

5. **True.** Women are two to three times more likely than men to suffer from depression. Women's societal roles affect their happiness, and unhappiness, in turn, can affect brain functions. In addition, women's brains produce less of the feel-good chemical serotonin.

6. **False.** Both sexes self-disclose by divulging personal information but are more comfortable doing so with women than with men.

7. **False.** Women smile significantly more than men. Women are expected to do "emotion work." Smiling is one way to restore harmony and reduce tension when people disagree.

8. **False.** In a recent Gallup poll, 55 percent of men but only 32 percent of women said that if they could have only one child, they would prefer a boy.

9. **False.** About 67 percent of American women say that they have little knowledge about financial affairs or how to manage and invest their money.

10. **False.** A heart attack is more likely to be fatal for a woman than for a man. Women with heart disease are less likely than men to be diagnosed correctly or treated promptly and are less likely to be sent for cardiac rehabilitation.

SOURCES: Sugg, 2000; Misra, 2001; Mathews et al., 2002; Vaccarino et al., 2002; Vakili et al., 2002; Wood, 2002; LaFrance et al., 2003; "Financial experience . . .," 2006.

The Mundugumors were just the opposite. Both men and women were competitive and aggressive. Neither parent showed much tenderness, and both often used physical punishment to discipline the children.

The Tchumbuli demonstrated the reverse of Western gender roles. The women were the economic providers. The men took care of children, sat around gossiping, and spent a lot of time decorating themselves for tribal festivities. Mead concluded that attributes long considered either masculine (such as aggression) or feminine (such as nurturance) were culturally—rather than biologically—determined.

Those of you who are familiar with Mead's publications may know that some anthropologists have challenged her findings regarding sexual behavior in Samoa (for example, see Freeman, 1983, and Shankman, 1996). The New Guinea study, however, hasn't elicited any similar controversies.

Contemporary cultures and subcultures also vary widely in how people perform gender roles. As you saw in Chapter 4, for example, black couples are more egalitarian than white couples or recent immigrants from Asia or the Middle East.

CROSS-CULTURAL VARIATIONS IN MALE VIOLENCE If men were biologically predisposed to be aggressive, rates of violent acts, such as homicide, by males would be similar in all societies. Instead, male homicide rates vary widely from one country to another (see *Figure 5.1*). In addition, rates of deadly assault can change over time because they reflect factors such as attitudes about crime, law enforcement policies, and the extent of poverty in the population (Krug et al., 2002).

Male violence and aggression are more likely to occur in patriarchal societies than in matriarchal ones. In a **patriarchy**, men hold the positions of power and authority—political, economic, legal, religious, educational, military, and domestic. In a **matriarchy**, in contrast, women control cultural, political, and economic resources and, consequently, have power over men.

Scholars doubt that truly matriarchal societies have ever existed. Some cultures, however, exercise much more control than others over women's behavior. In some Middle Eastern countries, for example, women (but not men) are killed if they dishonor the family by engaging in premarital or extramarital sex (see Chapter 7). As the box "The Worldwide War against Women"

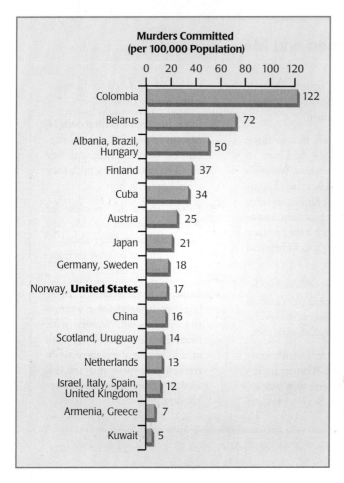

FIGURE 5.1 **Deadly Assaults by Males in Selected Countries**

SOURCE: Based on Krug et al., 2002, Table A-7.

shows, patriarchal societies practice discrimination and violence against women because cultural and religious values, customs, and laws relegate women to second-class citizenship. This does not mean, however, that *all* men are aggressive and *all* women are nonviolent.

A RISE IN FEMALE VIOLENCE Generally, male crime rates are much higher and more serious than women's. Of all individuals who are arrested, 77 percent are men. They make up 82 percent of those arrested for violent crimes and 69 percent of those arrested for property crimes. Between 1994 and 2003, however, 18 percent of those arrested for violent crimes—including murder, robbery, and other assaults—were women, up from 8 percent in 1994, while the percentage of arrestees who were men decreased (Federal Bureau of Investigation, 2004). Although the rates of violent acts committed by women are much lower than the rates of such acts com-

mitted by men, such data show that women are *not* innately nonviolent.

One in three juveniles arrested for violent crimes is female. Some scholars feel that the higher arrest rates reflect police officers' tougher stance toward girls: "If [girls] engage in even minor violence, they are perceived as being more vicious than their male counterparts" (Chesney-Lind and Pasko, 2004: 52).

Others argue that girls are actually becoming more violent. Researchers speculate that the change may reflect girls' increased likelihood of being exposed to violence on a daily basis and the fact that girls have learned to express their anger by striking out rather than being passive (Prothrow-Stith and Spivak, 2005).

SUCCESSFUL SEX ASSIGNMENT As you saw earlier, some scientists cite the John/Joan case as evidence of the imprint of biology on gender roles and identity. Others maintain that successful sex assignments of hermaphrodites demonstrate the powerful effects of culture.

Hermaphrodites—also known as *intersexuals*—are people born with both male and female sex organs (internal and/or external). (The term *hermaphrodite* comes from the names of the Greek gods Hermes, a male, and Aphrodite, a female.) The incidence of ambiguous genitalia—so that the sex of the newborn is not immediately apparent—is about 1 in every 8,000 to 10,000 births (O'Mara, 1997).

Typically, parents of such infants choose a sex for the child and pursue surgical and hormonal treatments to change the ambiguous genital organs. The parents raise the child in the selected gender role: The name is male or female, the clothes are masculine or feminine, and the child is taught to behave in gender-appropriate ways. Such sex assignments, most of which are successful, suggest that socialization may be more important than biology in shaping a child's gender identity.

What Can We Conclude about the Nature–Nurture Debate?

What does all this information tell us, ultimately, about the nature–nurture debate? Several things. First, women and men exhibit some sex-related genetic differences. Boys, for example, are more likely to suffer from genetic defects, physical disabilities, mental retardation, reading disabilities, and school and emotional problems. There is no evidence, however, that boys' (or girls') hormones *cause* physical or behavioral maladies.

Second, cross-cultural research shows much variation in the characteristics that are typically ascribed to

Cross-Cultural Families

The Worldwide War against Women

Women make up half the world's population, do two-thirds of the world's work, earn one-tenth of the world's income, and own one-hundredth of the world's property. And women are mistreated in many countries around the world. For example:

- *Afghanistan:* In the countryside, tribal leaders deploy religious police to enforce stringent controls on women's behavior. Many girls cannot attend school, and laws dictate that families murder their own women if they have been "dishonored" by rape during a war. One in seven mothers dies in childbirth.
- *China:* A culture that values boys more than girls, China has used advances in sonogram technology to help prospective parents identify—and abort—female fetuses. Despite official condemnation of this practice, the gap between the number of male and female births is widening (see Chapters 7 and 8).
- *Nigeria:* The penal code allows a man to "correct" his wife as long as the "correction" does not leave a scar or necessitate a hospital stay of 21 days or more.
- *India and Pakistan:* If a groom and his family decide that a bride's dowry is too small, she may be persecuted or burned to death. Abortion of female fetuses is still widespread in India.
- *Latin America:* A macho culture pervades most countries in Latin America, unofficially condoning wife abuse, rape, and other forms of violence against women.
- *Morocco:* If a woman commits adultery, the law permits her husband to maim or kill her as punishment. Adulterous husbands are not punished.
- *Norway:* Even though women dominate the political scene, they are still hired last, fired first, paid less than men, and held back from the top jobs.
- *Pakistan:* In some regions, tribal council elders order (and sometimes participate in) gang rapes of girls to avenge a brother's (real or imagined) crime. Domestic violence, acid throwing, burning, "honor" killings, and sex trafficking of young girls are common.
- *Russia:* Wife-beating is not against the law; approximately 15,000 wives are killed by their husbands each year.

- *Saudi Arabia:* A divorced woman may keep her children until they are 7 years old. After that, though she may visit them, they are raised by the father's relatives.
- *South Africa:* Every 83 seconds a woman is raped. Domestic work is the primary occupation for black women, and the average salary earned by women is about $80 a month.
- *Thailand:* Young rural women are kidnapped or bought from their parents for prostitution. An estimated 1 million women work in Thai brothels.
- *Turkey:* In some regions, young girls are killed by their fathers or brothers because they have shamed the family by going out with boys or marrying someone from a different sect.
- *Britain:* The police believe that 117 women from Middle Eastern and South Asian countries were murdered in 2004 because they "dishonored" their families by refusing arranged marriages or dating men before marriage.
- *United States:* On average, women earn 75 percent of what men earn in the same jobs, and a woman with several years of college earns less, on average, than a man who is a high school dropout.
- In war-torn countries around the world, hundreds of thousands of women and children have been victims of mass rape, torture, and genital mutilation (for example, in *Bangladesh, Burundi, Cambodia, Liberia, Peru, Rwanda, Somalia,* and *Uganda*).

Some women have been raped more than a hundred times. Reports of large-scale organized rape have come from the countries that made up the former *Yugoslavia,* where at least 20,000 women and girls were raped during the first few months of the war that followed the country's dissolution in 1992.

SOURCES: Neft and Levine, 1997; Goodsmith, 2000; Dauer, 2002; Itano, 2002b; "Pakistani girl describes . . .," 2002; *State of the World's Mothers,* 2003; Brandon, 2005; U.S. Census Bureau, 2006.

Stop and Think . . .

- Why do many countries, including the United States, tolerate violence against women?
- Do you think that women would experience greater equality if more legislators and heads of state were women?

men and to women (see *Table 5.1*). Gender roles may be the result of a cascade of biological, genetic, family, and peer influences that vary widely across cultures and subcultures within a society (Lippa, 2002).

Finally, nature and nurture clearly interact to explain our behavior. Parenting, for example, has a strong effect on children's behavior despite their genetic makeup. A child with a difficult temperament—irritability, hostility, or aggressiveness—can become more sociable and learn self-control if his or her parents are continuously patient and loving (see Chapter 12).

Many researchers contend that genes are turned on or off by socialization: "A particular gene can have a different effect, depending on the environment" (Sapolsky, 2000: 68). Although identical twins are the same genetically, for example, they may differ dramatically in personality, aggression, and mental disorders, depending on environmental factors such as parental behavior and peer influences (Sinha, 2004; Brendgen et al., 2005). In effect, then, nature and nurture are connected.

Living Gendered Lives

There are more similarities than differences between the sexes. Males and females have similar cognitive skills, memory abilities, and abstract problem-solving aptitudes. In addition, parents usually express love to their children in very similar ways (Day, 2002). Despite these similarities and regardless of our personal preferences or abilities, most of us accommodate our behavior to gender-role expectations, in a process that West and Zimmerman (1987) call "doing gender."

We "do gender," sometimes consciously and sometimes unconsciously, by adjusting our behavior and perceptions according to the gender and age of the person with whom we are interacting. By the time we reach adulthood, we experience society-wide inequalities such as unequal incomes, unequal responsibilities in child care, and significant differences in political and economic power. But if there are more similarities than differences between men and women, why is this the case? Gender socialization theories provide some of the answers.

How We Learn Gender Roles

A common misconception is that our gender roles are carved in stone by about age 4. In fact, gender roles change throughout the life course. Before we can understand how such change occurs, we need to examine, briefly, three of the major perspectives on gender-role learning: social learning theory, cognitive development theory, and feminist approaches.

Cooking with his dad teaches a young boy that domestic work is an acceptable activity for men. Such activities also increase interaction and closer relationships between fathers and their children.

Social Learning Theory

The central notion in **social learning theory** is that people learn attitudes, beliefs, and behaviors through social interaction. The learning occurs as a result of reinforcement, imitation, and modeling (Bandura and Walters, 1963; Lynn, 1969).

Reinforcement occurs when we receive direct or indirect rewards or punishments for particular gender role behaviors. For example, a little girl who puts on her mother's makeup may be told that she is cute, but her brother who does the same thing will be scolded ("boys don't wear makeup"). Children also learn gender roles through indirect reinforcement. For example, if a little boy's male friends are punished for crying, he will learn that "boys don't cry."

Children also learn to behave as boys or girls through *observation* and *imitation*. Although children may not be

since you asked

Are people automatically masculine or feminine as a result of being born male or female?

directly rewarded or punished for "behaving like boys" or "behaving like girls," they learn about gender by watching who does what in their families. A father who is rarely at home because he's always working sends the message that men are supposed to earn money. A mother who is always complaining about being fat sends the message that women are supposed to be thin.

Because parents are emotionally important to their children, they are typically a child's most powerful *role models*. Other role models include caregivers, teachers, friends, and celebrities. According to a multiethnic study of Los Angeles adolescents, teenagers who said that their role model was someone they knew (a parent, relative, friend, or doctor outside the family) had higher self-esteem, higher grades, and lower substance use than peers whose role models were sports figures, singers, or other media characters. The researchers concluded that role model selection can have a positive or negative outcome on a teenager's psychosocial development (Yancey et al., 2002).

Cognitive Development Theory

In contrast to social learning theories, **cognitive development theory** argues that children acquire female or male values on their own by thinking, reasoning, and interpreting information in their environment. According to this perspective, children pass through a series of developmental stages in learning gender-appropriate attitudes and behavior.

By the age of 3 or 4, a girl knows that she is a girl and prefers "girl things" to "boy things" simply because she likes what is familiar or similar to herself. By age 5, most children anticipate disapproval from their peers for playing with opposite-sex toys, and avoid those toys as a result. After acquiring masculine or feminine values, children tend to identify with people of the same sex as themselves (Kohlberg, 1969; Maccoby, 1990; Bussey and Bandura, 1992).

According to cognitive development theory, children use cues to evaluate the behavior of others as either gender appropriate ("good") or gender inappropriate ("bad"). Eventually, they become sex-typed because they accept cultural definitions of gender appropriateness and reject behavior that does not match their sex (Bem, 1993).

Sex typing may become more rigid during adolescence. At that time, young people often feel compelled to conform to their peers' **gender-role stereotypes**—the belief and expectation that both women and men will display definite traditional gender-role characteristics. Gender-role stereotypes may become more flexible during adulthood. Generally, however, people who have internalized sex-typed standards tend to expect stereotypical behavior from others (Hudak, 1993; Renn and Calvert, 1993).

Feminist Approaches

Feminist theories differ from other perspectives in several ways. First, many feminist scholars view gender as a social role: a role that is socially constructed because it is taught carefully and repeatedly. Consequently, one's *gender script*—how society says you're supposed to act based on your sex—becomes "so natural as to be seen as an integral part of oneself" (Fox and Murry, 2001: 382). For example, a study of preschoolers concluded that educational institutions channel children's behavior into "appropriate" gender scripts. Even though boys' play often was much noisier than girls', the teachers told girls to be quiet or use a "nicer" voice three times more often than they told boys to do so. In effect, girls and boys were learning gender scripts at an early age (Martin, 1998).

Second, feminists argue that gender scripts result, over time, in macro-level power differences and inequality in the home and elsewhere. Because many parents follow traditional gender scripts, they interact differently with their sons and daughters. For example, a study of middle-class parents and their sixth- and eighth-grade children found that the parents—especially fathers—used less scientific language with their daughters than with their sons. The girls and boys were equally interested in science, were confident about their abilities, and earned the same grades in scientific subjects. However, the parents assumed that the sons were more interested in science and provided them with more resources and support (Tenenbaum and Leaper, 2003).

Finally, feminists maintain that if people change women's and men's traditional roles, behavior will also change. If, for example, boys are taught to cook and clean, they are more likely to do so in adulthood. If girls are taught to be independent, they are more likely to fend for themselves instead of relying on a man for economic support.

Making Connections

- Drawing on your experiences and your knowledge of people of both sexes, do you think that women and men are similar? Or different?

- Think about how you were raised. Who played a major role in teaching you what it means to be "masculine" or "feminine"? What happened, if anything, when you broke "the rules"?

Who Teaches Gender Roles?

We learn gender roles from a variety of sources. The most important are parents (and other adult caregivers), peers, teachers, books, and popular culture.

Parents

Parents usually are a child's first and most influential socialization agents. Many parents treat male and female infants differently from birth. They hold girls more gently and cuddle them more. Fathers, especially, are more likely to jostle and play in a rough-and-tumble way with boys (Parke, 1996). Parents also shape their children's gender roles through differential treatment in several important ways, including talking, setting expectations, and providing opportunities for various activities.

since you asked

Why are parents critical in shaping our gender roles?

TALKING Parents often communicate differently with boys than with girls, starting at a very early age. Even when babies are as young as 6 to 14 months, mothers often speak differently to their children. They talk more to their daughters and sons and comfort and hug their daughters more often. This suggests that girls are "supposed" to interact with other people and to be more verbal. In contrast, mothers talk less often with boys, giving them more room to explore their environment on their own, teaching and reinforcing a sense of independence. Thus, even babies receive different gendered messages months before they start to speak (Clearfield and Nelson, 2006).

Fathers tend to use more directives ("Bring that over here") and more threatening language ("If you do that again, you'll be sorry") with their sons than with their daughters. Mothers tend to ask for compliance rather than demand it for both sons and daughters ("Could you bring that to me, please?"). These parental differences send the message that men are more authoritative than women.

By the time they start school, many boys use threatening, commanding, and dominating language ("If you do that one more time, I'll sock you"). In contrast, many girls seek agreement and cooperation ("Can I play, too?") (Shapiro, 1990).

SETTING EXPECTATIONS When parents *expect* their daughters to do better in English and their sons to excel in math and sports, they provide the support and advice that enable the children to do so. This sex-stereotypical

encouragement builds up the children's confidence in their abilities and helps them master the various skills (Eccles et al., 2000).

The ways that parents divide up household tasks also influence the gender typing of their children. Even when mothers work outside the home or parents try to be egalitarian, household chores are gendered—between parents themselves and between children. Parents typically assign child care and cleaning to daughters and maintenance work to sons. Girls are also given these duties much earlier in childhood and adolescence than boys (Leaper, 2002). These gender-stereotyped responsibilities lay the foundation for role differences in adulthood (as you'll see shortly).

Mothers start criticizing their children's—especially their daughters'—weight and physical appearance in elementary school. And throughout adolescence, fathers make more appearance-related comments to their daughters than to their sons (Schwartz et al., 1999; Smolak et al., 1999). Such gender-typed expectations may result in negative body images and eating disorders in girls (see Chapter 14).

PROVIDING OPPORTUNITIES Here's what one of my students said when we were discussing this chapter:

> *Some parents live their dreams through their sons by forcing them to be in sports. I disagree with this but want my [9-year-old] son to be "all boy." He's the worst player on the basketball team at school and wanted to take dance lessons, including ballet. I assured him that this was not going to happen. I'm going to enroll him in soccer and see if he does better (Author's files).*

Is this mother suppressing her son's natural talent in dancing? We'll never know because she, like many parents, expects her son to perform gender roles that meet with society's approval.

During childhood and adolescence, parents provide children with activities and opportunities that our culture defines as gender appropriate. Boys often get toys that demand more space (such as trains and car sets); girls usually receive dolls or dollhouses, which take up less space. Also, boys' toys (such as footballs and basketballs) encourage leaving the home; girls' toys (such as play vacuum cleaners and play ovens) are designed to be used in the home (Knapp and Hall, 1992).

Many parents systematically restrict opportunities for fun and learning when they pressure children to choose "girls' stuff" or "boys' stuff." Because, in general, "boys' stuff" is more interesting than "girls' stuff," parental pressure for girls to play with sex-stereotypical toys diminishes the daughters' cognitive skills and reduces their interest in "active" toys and activities.

Parents are important agents of socialization. This three-year-old may be inspired to follow in his father's occupational footsteps.

Fathers, especially, are still more likely to stress the importance of a career or occupational success for their sons than for their daughters. As a result, parents are more likely to provide opportunities for their sons than for their daughters to attend computer summer camps, more likely to explain science exhibits to their sons than to their daughters, and more likely to pressure boys to attend college (Crowley et al., 2001; Kladko, 2002).

Toys, Sports, and Peers

Toys, sports, and peer groups are also important sources of socialization. Few encourage gender-neutral attitudes and behavior.

TOYS From an early age, play with toys is generally sex-typed. Girls' sections of catalogs and toy stores are swamped with cosmetics, dolls and accessories, arts and crafts kits, and housekeeping and cooking wares. In contrast, boys' sections feature sports equipment, building sets, workbenches, construction equipment, and toy guns (see the box "Are Children's Toys Becoming More Sexist?").

Barbie was the top-selling toy in the twentieth century. According to many critics, the problem with Barbie dolls is that they idealize unrealistic body characteristics such as large breasts, a tiny waist, and small hips (see

Table 5.3). One of the results is that that many girls and women try to achieve these fictional expectations through diets (that include eating disorders) and cosmetic surgery (see Chapter 14).

Male action figures have grown increasingly muscular over the years. GI Joes, for example, have biceps that are twice as large as those of a typical man and larger than those of any known bodybuilder. These action figures (and comic strip heroes) put boys at risk of developing the "Barbie syndrome"—unrealistic expectations for their bodies. As a result, some researchers maintain, increasing numbers of men are becoming preoccupied with working out and taking dangerous drugs such as anabolic steroids (Pope et al., 1999; see, also, Chapter 14).

SPORTS Many parents encourage sports for both their daughters and their sons. Athletic activities are healthy, give children a chance to develop self-confidence and team skills, and may lead to college athletic scholarships.

The share of women among all intercollegiate athletes increased from 28 percent in 1982 to almost 42 percent in 2001 (Clayton, 2002). Despite considerable progress, female athletes still face numerous institutional barriers. They play in inferior facilities, stay in low-quality hotels on the road, eat in cheaper restaurants, get smaller promotional budgets, and have fewer

TABLE 5.3		
Real Women and Barbie		
	Average Woman	Barbie
Height	5' 4"	6'
Weight	145 lbs.	101 lbs.
Dress size	11–14	4
Bust	36–37"	39"
Waist	29–31"	19"
Hips	40–42"	33"

SOURCE: Data cited in *Anorexia Nervosa and Related Eating Disorders, Inc.,* 2006.

Changes

Are Children's Toys Becoming More Sexist?

Many of my students feel that most children's toys are considerably more "unisex" than they were during the 1980s and the 1990s. Are they right?

According to sociologists Caryl Rivers and Rosalind Barnett (2005), large toy stores have returned to "selling girls on primping and passivity" and portraying boys as active and creative. For example,

- Toys "Я" Us catalogs offer no pictures of girls on its sports page or of girls playing with cars and trucks. Boys, meanwhile, are seen playing basketball or with an electronic hockey game.
- Pages devoted to building sets feature boys playing with Legos, Tinker Toys, and Lincoln Logs. Girls are offered Cinderella Castle blocks and a cheap toddler block set. On a learn-and-create page, boys play with toy trains while girls "seem delighted with a glitter dream dollhouse."
- No boys are pictured on the dolls page, where you can find items such as a Cinderella carriage, a Barbie primp-and-polish styling head for hairdos, a Holly-wood party limo, and scores of Barbies.
- The aisles of most American toy stores or toy departments have the same gender-coded sections as in the

past. Hot items for girls are the big-eyed Bratz dolls (which are even more overtly sexual than Barbie) and sport navel-baring tops, hooker boots, and miniskirts.

- A growing trend is makeovers for girls 5 to 13 in local shopping malls, sponsored by a group known as Club Libby Lu. The club counselors create fancy hairstyles and apply sparkly makeup to the little girls, who wind up looking like beauty pageant contestants.
- After protests from some teenage girls, Abercrombie & Fitch removed a T-shirt with "Who needs brains when you have these?" emblazoned across the wearer's chest. But the company still sells girls' T-shirts with such logos as "Available for parties," "Do I make you look fat?" and "Blondes are adored, brunettes are ignored."

Stop and Think . . .

- Do you agree with the writers who contend that toys are becoming more sex-typed?
- Why do many parents endorse makeovers for little girls? What messages are they sending their daughters and sons?

---

assistant coaches. And when colleges and universities cut their athletic budgets, women's sports are usually the first to go (Bradley-Doppes, 2002; Flores, 2002).

The visibility of tennis superstars such as Serena and Venus Williams gives the false impression that minority girls and women have unprecedented opportunities in sports. In fact, most black women don't play sports at all and have access primarily to basketball and track because they don't grow up in suburban neighborhoods or attend schools that offer lacrosse, soccer, rowing, swimming, or a variety of other sports. Even then, less than 3 percent of minority female athletes receive scholarships to play sports in the top schools and divisions (Suggs, 2001).

Asian American, American Indian, and Latina athletes are even less likely to participate in college sports. Many Latinas grow up in communities where girls and women are expected to avoid "unfeminine" activities like competitive sports. Some exceptions—athletes such as softball players Kristy Aguirre, Felicia Delgado, and Laura Rodriguez—credit their athletic success to their

parents, especially their fathers, who enrolled them in church sports programs as preschoolers and encouraged their athletic development (Williams, 2002).

Only a handful of women and minority men own professional leagues or serve as athletic directors or coaches. A recent study gave colleges an "F" for not hiring female and minority athletic directors. Women now coach only 45 percent of women's teams, down from 99 percent in the 1970s. In the Division 1 colleges (those with the highest sports sponsorship, sports attendance records, and financial aid awards), only 5 percent of the athletic directors are members of minority groups, and only 7 percent are women (Lapchick, 2003). Thus, female and minority athletes have few role models.

PEERS By as early as age 2, most toddlers are learning to interact with peers. One of the most widely recognized social characteristics of childhood is young children's preference for same-sex play partners. The more time boys spend with other boys, the greater the likelihood that they

Katie Brownell, 11, a Little League pitcher who pitched a perfect game on May 14, 2005, holds up her jersey, which she is donating to the National Baseball Hall of Fame in Cooperstown, N.Y. She honed her skills playing with her two older brothers and has a .714 batting average. She persevered even though her male teammates told her to stick to softball "like the other girls."

will learn to be rough, aggressive, competitive, and active. The more time girls spend with other girls, the more likely they are to be cooperative rather than assertive, to play quiet games, and to be less physical in their play than boys. Thus, the more both girls and boys play with same-sex partners, the more likely they are to participate in gender-typed play (Martin and Fabes, 2001).

Especially when sex hormones kick in, adolescents develop a strong interest in members of the opposite sex. In our society, being "popular" is essential. Being disliked by one's peers may lead to feelings of isolation, loneliness, and alienation. But trying to be popular can also have negative effects. Boys and girls who hang out with peers who bully, for example, tend to do more bullying themselves. If girls want to join the "inner circle" of the "queen bees," they may bully even their closest friends by tormenting them with gossip and

sarcastic comments (Cassidy and Asher, 1992; Wiseman, 2002; Espelage et al., 2003).

Teachers and Schools

Teachers and schools send a number of gender-related messages to children. These messages follow boys and girls from preschool to college.

ELEMENTARY AND MIDDLE SCHOOLS In elementary and middle schools, boys usually get more time to talk in class, are called on more often, and receive more positive feedback than do girls. Teachers are more likely to give answers to girls or to do the problems for them but to expect boys to find the answers themselves. Expecting more from boys increases their problem-solving abilities, decision-making skills, and self-confidence in finding answers on their own (Sadker and Sadker, 1994).

Even when their behavior is disruptive, "problem girls" often receive less attention than do either boys or "problem boys." Teachers tend to emphasize "motherwork" skills for girls, such as nurturance and emotional support. Although both sexes are evaluated on academic criteria, such as work habits and knowledge, teachers are more likely to also evaluate girls on nonacademic criteria such as grooming, and personal qualities such as politeness and appearance (Martin, 1998).

since you asked

How do teachers affect our gender roles?

Despite our current era of "grrl power," girls still write stories about romance whereas boys write about action and adventure. For example, a study of eighth-grade students found that both sexes expected girls to write about "mushy stuff" and boys to write about sports and violence, even though the school encouraged teachers to promote egalitarian gender roles (Peterson, 2002).

HIGH SCHOOL In high school, guidance counselors, who play an important role in helping students make career choices, may be particularly guilty of sex stereotyping. Even well-intentioned counselors often steer girls into

vocational training, such as secretarial work or data processing, rather than college preparatory programs. And during summer vacations, teachers and counselors often help boys, but not girls, find jobs (Gerber, 2002).

In some college preparatory programs, counselors and teachers advise girls to take courses in the social sciences and humanities rather than mathematics or the physical sciences. For example, according to Dr. Suzanne Franks, founding director of the Women in Engineering and Science Program at Kansas State University, some middle and high schools dismiss nontraditional opportunities for girls as inappropriate:

> We contacted a school in Western Kansas to notify them of an opportunity to send some of their middle school girls on an industry tour we were sponsoring, where the girls could meet women engineers and scientists and see what they did for a living. We were flatly turned down, with the explanation being "I can assure you that none of our girls would be interested in such a thing" (Personal correspondence, October 9, 2002).

COLLEGE   Women earn almost 58 percent of all bachelor's degrees. Still, most women college students focus on traditional female-dominated disciplines such as home economics, social work, teaching, and nursing (U.S. Census Bureau, 2006).

Some people argue that women pursue these low-paying areas because they want to do so. Others maintain that women aren't exposed to science and math courses that might pique their interest in male-dominated fields like engineering and computer science (Margolis and Fisher, 2002).

Books and Textbooks

Historically, children's books have portrayed female characters as using household objects (cooking utensils, brooms, sewing needles) and male characters as mastering tools used outside the home (shovels, plows, construction equipment) (Crabb and Bielawski, 1994). Although many of these books were published in the period from the 1950s to the 1990s, they are still popular with young readers and reinforce sex-stereotypical images of women and men.

Nonstereotypical books are more readily available than ever before, especially for preschoolers. Very young children are generally open to stories that describe nontraditional male roles, such as boys playing with dolls (Etaugh and Liss, 1992). If parents or teachers tend to stereotype gender roles, however, children will not be exposed to these resources.

Early exposure to gender-neutral information is essential in removing gender blinders because many educational materials continue to depict men's and women's roles very narrowly. As the box "Do Books and Textbooks Stereotype Women and Men?" shows, high school and college textbooks are still gendered in their portrayal of the sexes.

Popular Culture and the Media

Media myths and unrealistic images assault our gender identity on a daily basis. A few examples from advertising, newspapers and magazines, television, and music

Much advertising in the United States and other Western countries uses sexy images of women to sell everything from cars to soap, in this case. Many people have praised Dove for featuring "normal-sized" women with "real curves." Others question whether the models are representative of the average American woman and what soaps and lotions have to do with women "cavorting" on giant billboards in their bra and panties.

Constraints

Do Books and Textbooks Stereotype Women and Men?

Many textbooks in colleges and professional schools ignore women or present them in stereotypical ways. Mendelsohn and her associates (1994) analyzed more than 4,000 illustrations in 12 anatomy and physical diagnosis textbooks used in medical schools. The anatomy textbooks used illustrations of male bodies more than twice as often as illustrations of female bodies. In the texts on physical diagnosis, the illustrations of women were largely confined to chapters on reproduction, falsely implying that female and male physiology differs only in reproductive organs.

The researchers concluded that "women are dramatically underrepresented in illustrations of normal, nonreproductive anatomy" and that "males continue to be depicted as the norm or the standard. As a result, students may develop an incomplete knowledge of normal female anatomy" (p. 1269).

Most recently, a team of researchers examined the number of women physicians who have published articles in the six most prominent medical journals since 1970. The researchers concluded that there is still a huge "gender gap" because fewer than 29 percent of the articles are authored by women. Also, the higher the medical journal's prestige, the less likely that women are the authors (Jagsi et al., 2006).

A self-proclaimed "teacher and therapist" maintains that nature intends girls primarily for having and nurturing children. He contends that by age 10 the development of a girl's brain causes her to be concerned about being pretty and popular, and she has a "natural" drive to "connect" with others (Gurian, 2002).

The author declares unequivocally that the structure of most girls' brains makes it difficult for them to grasp subjects such as calculus and physics and that women lack natural technical ability. He argues that if they put too much emphasis on achievement and careers, girls will suffer lifelong misery. Teachers "lined up" to buy his books (Rivers, 2002).

A study of the ten best-selling self-help books found that half the books promote stereotypical behavior. The books maintain that female independence and assertiveness could jeopardize their relationships with men. The books also describe men as being *inherently* success- or achievement-oriented and rarely advise men to improve their relationships with women (Zimmerman et al., 2001).

Stop and Think . . .

- Think about your high school and college history textbooks. How many discussed gender issues? How many described men's lives beyond wars, politics, and inventions?

- If teachers believe that girls' brains are hardwired for relationships and men's for success, how do such attitudes shape girls' and boys' behavior?

- Women physicians are less likely than men to publish articles in prominent medical journals. Do you think that the women's lower publication rates influence our information about women's health? Or do you feel that the author's sex is irrelevant in the medical data that we get?

---

videos illustrate how the media reinforce sex stereotyping from childhood to adulthood.

ADVERTISING Much of the advertising aimed at children creates and strengthens stereotypes. Minority children are often faces in a crowd, or they promote products as "cool" or trendy. Black children routinely appear in commercials that plug sports and music, reinforcing the stereotype that African Americans are "natural" in sports and music—and, by default, "not natural" in educational and other pursuits (Bang and Reece, 2003).

Many media critics maintain that magazine ads are more sexist than ever, especially during televised sporting events. In beer commercials, for example, half of the camera shots focus on women's breasts, buttocks, and crotches—instead of their entire bodies. In addition, advertisers can now change photographs with computers—for example, elongating bodies or putting one woman's head on another woman's body. Such alterations present unrealistic images of a "perfect" woman that—despite many men's fantasies—don't exist in reality, even among supermodels (Hall and Crum, 1994; Kilbourne, 1999).

Victoria's Secret—in catalogues, commercials, and ads—is not about lingerie but "the sheer sexual objectification of women." For example, an ad for the new perfume *Basic Instinct* portrays a woman with disheveled hair ("in a sexy way, of course") and a little black dress whose straps are falling off her shoulders. Her hands are tied behind her back and she has been thrown to the ground, implying rape. The perfume's name suggests that a woman's basic instinct is to play the part of a sexual victim. In other cases, images of "corporate" women flaunting their cleavage make it clear that femininity means sexiness, not intellectual or professional competence (Janson, 2005).

One result of such ads is that many women, especially white women, are unhappy with their bodies (Smith, 2004). In breast size, for example,

- Surgery for breast implants surged from 32,000 in 1992 to almost 253,000 in 2004.

- From 2002 to 2003, the number of girls 18 and younger who got breast implants nearly tripled, from about 4,000 to almost 12,000.

- Women are choosing ever-larger breast implants (Boodman, 2004; Kreimer, 2004; Roan, 2005).

Between 1985 and 2000, the Food and Drug Administration (FDA) received almost 130,000 reports of adverse effects of breast implants, some of which resulted in death due to blood loss and other surgery problems ("Breast implants," 2002; Kaufman, 2002). Nevertheless, and even though the surgery is expensive (about $7,000 on average), increasing numbers of women, including teenagers, are risking their health to have larger breasts.

Why? A major reason is that many American women want to appeal to men who think big breasts are sexy. However, about 75 percent of the women who get breast implants are already married; for them, large bosoms may be a symbol of femininity and enhance their self-esteem as "real women." In contrast, physicians aren't offering men penis implants to appear more masculine or to increase their self-confidence.

NEWSPAPERS AND MAGAZINES

Newspapers routinely ignore women. A survey of 104 national and local newspapers found that in 3,500 front-page stories, male sources outnumbered female sources almost three to one. Men were more likely to be quoted in stories about politics, business, parenting, religion, and science. Women were more likely to be cited in stories about health, home, food, fashion, travel, and ordinary people ("Newspaper content . . .," 2001). Thus, even though women have the greatest responsibility for child rearing, men are quoted as parenting "experts."

Magazines that emphasize women's appearance (such as *Cosmopolitan*, *Glamour*, and *Vogue*) hold the largest share of the magazine market. About 60 percent of women read such "women's magazines" during the year, compared with just 7 percent who read business or financial magazines. Although ad pages and dollars for all magazines have declined, they have increased for the top women's magazines (Wellner, 2002). In effect, then, women are exposed to more beauty ads and traditional images of femininity than ever before.

TELEVISION AND OTHER SCREEN MEDIA Children spend much more time in front of the television set and other screen media (video games, videotapes, DVDs, computers, and movies) than they do interacting with their parents, family members, teachers, or friends. According to two national studies, the typical American child spends almost seven hours *a day* watching television. Twenty-eight percent of preschool children aged 2 to 5 and 60 percent of adolescents have television sets in their bedrooms (Roberts et al., 1999; Woodard and Gridina, 2000).

What do children see about gender roles when they watch television or movies? About 73 percent of all

Charlie and the Chocolate Factory *was a popular film, but some people criticized the movie for its all-white cast of kids.*

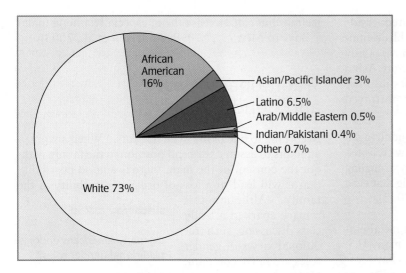

FIGURE 5.2 **Racial Diversity of Prime Time Characters on Television**

SOURCE: Glaubke and Heintz-Knowles, 2004, Figure 1.

or how family members perceive reality and react to it (see Chapter 2).

The National Organization for Women (NOW) sees few reasons to celebrate most of television's prime-time portrayals of women and minorities. After examining all the prime-time programs on ABC, CBS, FOX, NBC, UPN, and WB, the NOW study concluded, among other things, that

▨ **White men rule television** (see *Table 5.4*).

▨ **Studios follow the "Jennifer Aniston Rule."** At least 140 women on TV are white, young, model-thin, and conventionally beautiful, compared with just 31 women who appear to wear a size 10 or larger.

characters on prime-time television are white and nearly two-thirds of all characters are male (see *Figure 5.2*).

These proportions have remained the same since 1999. Thus, although 40 percent of American youth age 19 and under are minorities, "few of the faces they see on television represent their race or cultural heritage." Also, girls are much less likely than boys to see women in leading roles "that offer positive, strong, and competent role models" (Glaubke and Heintz-Knowles, 2004).

Are movies different? According to a recent study of the top-grossing G-rated animated and live actions films for children between 1990 and 2004, only 28 percent of the speaking characters were female. Most of the movies and cartoons were dominated by male characters and male stories. Minority males (whether boys or parents) were hard to find even though minority men make up at almost a third of the U.S. population.

In addition, almost twice as many minority males (62 percent) as white males (38 percent) were portrayed as physically aggressive, violent, and dangerous. The study concluded that such disproportionate numbers "offer young children a transparent message that being male and white is not just the norm, but preferable," and that white males are presented as more trustworthy than their minority counterparts (Kelly and Smith, 2006).

Although popular, how true to life are television "reality" shows in their portrayal of families? In both *Nanny 911* and *Supernanny,* outsiders tell parents what they are doing "wrong" in raising their kids. But socialization is never that simple. Symbolic interactionists would point out that strangers don't understand a family's complex history, its communication patterns,

TABLE 5.4

What Roles Do Women Play in Television?

According to the National Organization for Women (NOW), prime-time television typically casts men rather than women in leading roles across numerous institutional areas. Besides NOW's list, consider whether or not women have made any inroads that are not stereotypical in more recent shows such as *House, Boston Legal, Desperate Housewives,* and other programs that you usually watch.

Occupation	Programs in Which Men Dominate
Heads of government	24, Spin City, The West Wing
The military	JAG
Investigative agencies	The Agency, Alias, The X-Files
Police and crime labs	The District, Law & Order: Criminal Intent, Law & Order: Special Victims Unit, NYPD Blue, CSI
Hospitals	ER, Scrubs
Radio stations	Frasier, Once & Again
Schools	Boston Public, The Simpsons
Factories	George Lopez
Department stores	The Drew Carey Show
Space exploration	Star Trek: Enterprise

SOURCE: Based on Bennett, 2002.

■ **Blacks, whites, and others are segregated.** Aside from the handful of shows centered on black families, racial and ethnic diversity is minimal. Only *George Lopez* includes Latinos, and four Asian American actresses play supporting roles in other shows. There are no regular characters portrayed by American Indian actors.

■ **Women are very similar.** If you are a middle-aged woman, a lesbian, a Latina, a woman with a disability, overweight, or a low-income mom struggling to get by, "good luck finding programming that even pretends to reflect your life" (Bennett, 2002).

Although some directors cast a "mix" of racial-ethnic actors, this isn't always the case. Because many U.S. kids aren't white, for example, some observers have criticized movies like *Charlie and the Chocolate Factory* for casting only white actors in the main children's roles (Silver-Greenberg, 2005). Thus, even children's movies that are supposed to appeal to a wide audience still exclude racial-ethnic children from the main roles.

MUSIC VIDEOS Another dominant source of much sex-stereotypical programming is music videos. In the years since the advent of Music Television (MTV) in 1981, a number of researchers have found that music videos are rife with sex, sexism, drugs, and violence (Strasburger and Wilson, 2002).

A study of the 20 most popular music videos on MTV found that more than 25 percent of the videos emphasized female breasts, legs, or torsos. Almost two-thirds of the videos featured women as props—for example, as background dancers. Whereas half the female props were seminude or dressed in revealing clothes, 75 percent of the male props were fully dressed. Moreover, violent music lyrics don't cause aggressive thoughts and

✲ Making Connections

■ Some people feel that sitcoms (such as *Everybody Loves Raymond* and *The Bernie Mac Show*) degrade men by portraying them as lovable but insensitive doofuses. Others maintain that most viewers don't take such shows very seriously. What do you think?

■ Think about the MTV videos you've watched over the years. Did they influence your thoughts about women, men, sex, drugs, or violence?

■ To decrease advertisers' influence on children, many European countries have banned TV ads on children's television programs. Should the United States do the same?

feelings but can increase them, especially among males ("Boys to Men . . .," 1999; Anderson et al., 2003).

Traditional Views and Gender Roles

According to one of my male students, "When a woman attempts to assume the head position in the family without the consent of the man, there is a good possibility that it will lead to a loss of order and stability in the family." Although this remark sparked a lively class discussion, such traditional views of gender roles are fairly common. Here are a few more examples:

since you asked

Do many Americans endorse traditional gender roles?

■ The Southern Baptist Convention doctrine opposes female pastors and says wives should submit to their husbands. An official recently sent 25 missionaries a deadline to sign this document or face dismissal.

■ In a national study, 50 percent of recent Latino immigrants and 23 percent of "highly assimilated" immigrants felt that "the husband should have the final say in family matters."

■ Kansas state senator Kay O'Conner, an elected official, stirred up a controversy when she said that there was no reason to celebrate the passage of the Nineteenth Amendment, which allowed women to vote. She believes that mothers should stay home to rear their children and that "the man should be the head of the family."

■ Several best-selling pop psychologists maintain that women have a "primal need" to be mothers and to be supported by men and that wives should "surrender themselves" to their husbands because a man should be the boss of the family (Doyle, 2001; "Baptist missionaries . . .," 2003).

Instrumental and Expressive Roles

Do you ever read the "Blondie" comic strip? If not, you (and I) may be in the minority. Created in 1930, the strip appears in more than 2,300 newspapers in 55 countries and is translated into 35 languages. It is consistently among the five most popular newspaper comics nationally (Gardner, 2005).

Why is Blondie so popular after more than 75 years? Even though Blondie now runs a catering business and her husband, Dagwood, uses a computer at the office, their gender roles haven't changed very much. Blondie still does the housework while Dagwood eats and naps. But while some may complain about these stereotypical roles, Blondie and Dagwood offer stability "in an age of social upheaval, rocked by divorce and dysfunction. They're still together after all these years" (Gardner, 2005: 16).

Many critics view structural-functionalist descriptions of traditional gender roles as outmoded (see Chapter 2). Still, many people apparently identify or agree with Blondie and Dagwood's instrumental and expressive roles. Let's take a closer look at these two types of roles.

INSTRUMENTAL ROLES Traditionally, *instrumental role players* (husbands and fathers) must be "real men." A "real man" is a procreator, a protector, and a provider. He must produce children because this will prove his virility, and having boys is especially important because they will carry on his family name.

The procreator must also be a protector. He must be strong and powerful in ensuring his family's physical safety. The provider keeps working hard even if he is overwhelmed by multiple roles like "the responsible breadwinner," "the devoted husband," and "the dutiful son" (Gaylin, 1992; Betcher and Pollack, 1993).

If the traditional man is a "superman," the traditional woman is an only slightly more modern version of the "true woman" you met in Chapter 3. Many women have internalized gender expectations and try to live up to them. For example, a study of students in two middle schools found that intelligent female students—regardless of social class and across all racial groups—lived up to the traditional definition of girls: pretty and polite but not too aggressive, not too outspoken, and not too smart. Young women often "dumbed down" to be popular with male and female peers and with some teachers (Orenstein, 1994).

EXPRESSIVE ROLES Traditionally, *expressive role players* (wives and mothers) provide the emotional support and nurturing qualities that sustain the family unit and support the husband/father. They should be warm, sensitive, and sympathetic. For example, the expressive role player consoles a teenage daughter when she breaks up with her boyfriend, encourages her son to try out for Little League, and is always ready to comfort a husband who has had a bad day at work.

A good example of women's expressive roles is that of kinkeeper. This role is often passed down from mother to daughter. Kinkeepers are important communication links between family members. They spend a lot of time maintaining contact with family members, visiting friends and families, organizing family reunions, or holding gatherings during the holidays or for special events like birthdays and anniversaries. They also often act as the family helper, problem solver, or mediator (Rosenthal, 1985).

Benefits and Costs of Traditional Gender Roles

Traditional gender roles have both benefits and costs (see *Table 5.5*). These roles may be chosen consciously or they may be a product of habit, custom, or socialization. Remember, too, that traditional relationships vary. In some, the partners feel loving and committed; in others, they feel as though they are trapped or sleepwalking.

BENEFITS Traditional gender roles provide stability, continuity, and predictability. Because each person knows what is expected, rights and responsibilities are clear. Husbands and wives don't have to argue over who does what: If the house is clean, she is a "good wife;" if the bills are paid, he is a "good husband."

Using the exchange model (see Chapter 2), if the costs and benefits of the relationship are fairly balanced and each partner is relatively happy, traditional gender roles can work well. As long as both partners live up to their role expectations, they are safe in assuming that they will take care of each other financially, emotionally, and sexually.

Some women stay in traditional relationships because they don't have to make decisions or take responsibility when things go wrong. An accommodating wife can enjoy both power and prestige through her husband's accomplishments. A good mother not only controls and dominates her children but can also be proud of guiding and enriching their lives (Harris, 1994).

When a traditional husband complained about his traditional wife's spending too much money, the wife composed and gave her husband the following "help wanted" ad:

I need someone full time who is willing to be on call 24 hours a day, seven days a week. Sick leave only when hospitalization is required. Must be able to cook, clean house, do laundry, care for children, feed and clean up after dog, do yard work, mow lawn, shovel snow, do shopping, do menu planning, take out trash, pay bills, answer phone and run errands. Must be able to pinch pennies. Also must be a friend and companion. Must be patient and cannot complain. If you are interested, please leave a

TABLE 5.5

Some Benefits and Costs of Traditional Gender Roles

For Men. . .		For Women. . .	
Benefits	Costs	Benefits	Costs
• A positive self-image in being the provider	• Loss of identity in the case of unemployment	• Not having to juggle employment and domestic tasks	• Loss of financial security if there's a separation or divorce
• Little marital stress in climbing a career ladder because the wife takes care of the kids and the home	• Little time with wife or children	• Time to focus on the husband–wife relationship	• Often being alone because the husband is working long hours or makes numerous out-of-town trips
• Doesn't have to do much, if any, housework or child care	• Wife may feel unappreciated	• Lots of time with children	• Feeling useless when children leave home
• Has a sexual partner who isn't stressed out by having a job and caring for the family	• Wife may feel taken for granted because she should always be available for sexual intercourse	• Nurturing a husband and children and enjoying their accomplishments	• Feeling like a failure if the children aren't successful, or feeling isolated and helpless if the husband is abusive

message. I will contact you when I feel like talking. Speak only when you have something to say that might interest me. Otherwise, shut up and get to work.—C. L. in Utah ("Want ad proves . . . ," 1997).

This "ad" provides a good example of how men benefit from traditional marriages. That is, traditional wives don't nag their husbands about sharing domestic chores. In addition, the wives benefit because they don't have the tension of being pulled in many directions—such as juggling jobs and housework. Such clearly designated duties can decrease both partners' stress.

COSTS Traditional gender roles have their drawbacks. Although many traditional families try to scale down their standard of living, a sole breadwinner is under a lot of economic pressure: "When mothers quit work to care for babies, fathers must shoulder unbearable stress to provide for more dependents" (Alton, 2001: 20).

The dutiful worker, husband, and father may feel overwhelmed by his responsibilities and may be unhappy with his life. A traditional man may believe that he never quite lives up to the standard of manhood. Although he has not failed completely, he may feel that he has not succeeded, either (Gaylin, 1992).

Sometimes the seemingly distant man is quiet because he is continuously worried about the family's economic well-being. Because many men's definitions of themselves are based on the breadwinner role, losing a

job can send some men into severe depression, frustrated rages that end in violence, and even suicide (Kaufman, 1993; Liu, 2002).

In terms of costs, a traditional wife can expect little relief from never-ending tasks that may be exhausting, monotonous, and boring. Besides being taken for granted by their husband and children, women who play traditional gender roles may assume that being taken for granted is natural and normal.

And what are her options if she's miserable? Traditional values such as being nurturant, dependent, and submissive can discourage some women from leaving abusive relationships. If she's been out of the work force for a number of years, she might be worse off after a divorce. Or a woman who has left all the money matters to her husband may find after his death that he did little estate planning and that their finances are in disarray (see Chapters 14, 15, and 17).

Gender-role stereotypes reflect another cost of traditional roles. The box "Should *You* Enroll in These Classes?" offers a tongue-in-cheek look at such stereotypes.

WHY DO TRADITIONAL GENDER ROLES PERSIST?

Traditional gender roles persist for two main reasons. First, they are profitable for business. The unpaid work that women do at home (such as housework, child rearing, and emotional support) means that companies don't have to pay for child-care services or counseling

Applying What You've Learned

Should You Enroll in These Classes?

Humor fulfills a number of functions, including relieving tension and expressing an opinion on a controversial or sensitive topic. Consider this list of "college seminars for sexist men and women." Do the suggested courses contain a kernel of truth? Or are they stereotypes?

Seminars for Men
1. You, Too, Can Do Housework
2. Easy Laundry Techniques
3. Get a Life—Learn to Cook
4. Spelling—Even You Can Get It Right
5. How to Stay Awake after Sex
6. Garbage—Getting It to the Curb
7. How to Put the Toilet Seat Down
8. Combating Stupidity

Seminars for Women
1. You, Too, Can Change the Oil
2. Elementary Map Reading
3. Get a Life—Learn to Kill Spiders
4. Checkbook Balancing—Even You Can Get It Right
5. How to Stay Awake during Sex
6. Shopping in Less Than 16 Hours
7. How to Close the Garage Door
8. Combating the Impulse to Nag

for stressed-out male employees.

If there is only one breadwinner, many men may work extra hours without additional pay to keep their jobs. Thus, companies increase their profits. If women feel that their place is in the home, they will take part-time jobs that do not provide benefits, will work for less pay, and will not complain. This increases the corporate world's pool of exploitable and expendable low-paid workers.

Second, traditional roles maintain male privilege and power. If women are seen as not having leadership qualities (see *Table 5.1*), men can dominate political and legal institutions. They can shape laws and policies to maintain their vested interests without being challenged by women who are unhappy with the status quo.

Contemporary Gender Roles in Adulthood

In 1993, the Ms. Foundation for Women launched "Take Our Daughters to Work Day," a day when parents would take their daughters to work to encourage girls to expand their career aspirations. In 2003, the

foundation decided to include boys and the event was renamed "Take Our Daughters and Sons to Work Day."

Why the change? To urge parents of both sexes—as well as employers—to think about ways to balance

Army Pfc. Lori Piestewa was the first female American soldier killed in combat in Iraq and the first U.S. military mother to die in war. She is also believed to have been the first American Indian woman killed while fighting for the U.S. military. Here, Piestewa's older daughter, 4, attends a memorial service for her mom with her grandparents, who are raising the girls.

work and family life. According to the president of the Ms. Foundation, "Women are not going to get equality in public life until men can participate equally in private life" (Tergesen, 2003: 105).

Many women's private and public roles have changed dramatically in the last two decades. Today, nearly 68 percent of married mothers are in the labor force, compared with 50 percent in 1970 (U.S. Census Bureau, 2006). Has women's employment changed gender roles at home? Not much.

Gender Roles at Home: Who Does the Work?

Heloise Cruise (of "Hints from Heloise") once said, "I think housework is the reason most women go to the office." Employment, however, rarely lightens women's domestic workload because many men continue to dodge housework and child care responsibilities.

since you asked

If there's greater equality between men and women these days, why are women still doing more housework than men?

THE "SECOND SHIFT"

In many cases, one of the major sources of tension is that many fathers do not participate in the *second shift*—the household work and child care tasks that many mothers face after coming home from work. Increasingly, more couples say that they share these tasks, especially cooking and grocery shopping, about equally. In shopping for groceries and children's clothing, for example, men were the principal purchasers in 21 percent of all households in 2002, up from 13 percent in 1985 (Fetto, 2002).

In these and other areas, however, there's still quite a difference between women and men. According to the best and most recent estimates, women spend almost twice as much time performing tasks related to family care as men. The amount of time women spend doing housework declined from 27 hours per week in 1965 to less than 16 hours in 1995; the time spent by men increased from 5 to 10 hours per week. Wives still perform most traditionally feminine tasks whereas men do household labor on a more sporadic basis. For the most part, however, neither employed women nor full-time homemakers are doing as much housework as was typical in the past (Robinson and Godbey, 1999; Bianchi et al., 2000). Instead, most of us have adapted to messier and dustier homes.

It's surprising that men do any housework at all; women's magazines continue to treat domestic work as a gender-specific task. *Martha Stewart Living*—a magazine targeted at women—has published special editions devoted entirely to tips on laundering, ironing, and storing clothes properly. And the lead cover story of *Real Simple* magazine devoted space to instructing women (not men) on how to achieve a more sparkling sink (McGrath, 2003).

CHILD CARE AND DOMESTIC CHORES In child care, the amount of time women spend caring for children decreased from six to five hours a week between 1965 and 1995, mainly because employed mothers use child care services. The amount of time spent by men remains much the same—about two hours a week. As you'll see in Chapter 12, many men still believe that child care is "women's work."

There is also a discrepancy between women's and men's perceptions of their domestic contributions. Many men don't feel that women have as much responsibility for household tasks as women say they do (see *Figure 5.3*). Conflict over who does how much housework may lead to communication problems or, ultimately, to separation and divorce (see Chapters 10 and 15).

Even when men share some of the work, women feel more responsible for caring for the home and children:

Dr. Kalpana Chawla, 41, immigrated to the United States from India in the 1980s and became an astronaut in 1994. She was one of seven astronauts who died on the space shuttle Columbia *when it broke apart and burst into flames over Texas on February 1, 2003.* Columbia *was just 16 minutes away from a safe landing in Florida.*

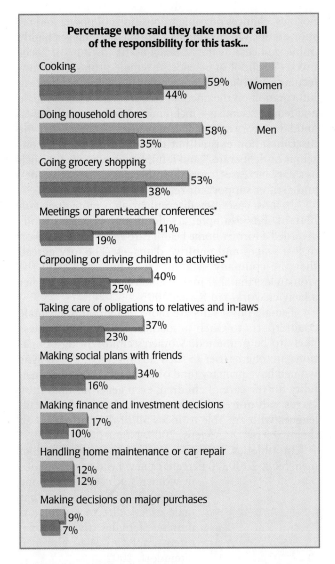

Percentage who said they take most or all of the responsibility for this task...

Cooking
59% Women
44%

Doing household chores
58% Men
35%

Going grocery shopping
53%
38%

Meetings or parent-teacher conferences*
41%
19%

Carpooling or driving children to activities*
40%
25%

Taking care of obligations to relatives and in-laws
37%
23%

Making social plans with friends
34%
16%

Making finance and investment decisions
17%
10%

Handling home maintenance or car repair
12%
12%

Making decisions on major purchases
9%
7%

FIGURE 5.3 She Says, He Says
Question: "Thinking of your relationship with your spouse or partner, I'd like to ask you about your roles with respect to a number of responsibilities in your relationship. For each item I read, please tell me whether you take all the responsibility for that item, you take most but not all the responsibility, or your spouse or partner takes all the responsibility . . ."

*Asked of respondents who are part of a couple in a household and have children.

Note: All questions were asked of respondents who are part of a couple in a household.
SOURCE: Survey by Peter D. Hart Research Associates for Shell Oil, January 7–13, 2000. Adapted from table in *Public Perspective,* July/August 2000, p. 27.

More women than men kept track of doctor's appointments and arranged for kids' playmates to come over. More mothers than fathers worried about a child's Halloween costume or a birthday present for a school friend. They were more likely to think about their children while at work and to check in by phone with the babysitter (Hochschild and Machung, 1989: 24).

In addition, women sometimes complain that men's participation is often peripheral:

I'm always amused when my husband says that he'll "help" me make our bed. I guess he "helps" because he feels making the bed is my responsibility, not his, even though we both sleep in it. When I mow the lawn, it's no big deal. But when he occasionally helps make the bed or does the dishes, he expects a litany of thank-you's and hugs (Author's files).

A heavier housework load combined with full employment means that women often experience greater stress than men. Because they have either more responsibility or a greater share of the domestic work, women often "multitask"—for example, write checks while returning phone calls or responding to e-mail. In addition, women do more of the tedious household chores, such as scrubbing the toilet, whereas men prefer to tend to their children and do "fun" things with them like going to the movies or playing video games.

FATHERS AND CHILDREN After her parents divorced, Ianna moved in with her father in San Diego, California. When she was five he gave her a rod and took her out on a fishing boat for the first time. By age 11, Ianna outfished most adult men, including landing a 35-pound yellowtail. She plays with and collects dolls but says that her numerous fishing awards are "cool" (Benning, 2005).

Ianna's fishing talents wouldn't have blossomed if her dad had ignored them. Indeed, many of today's fathers think they're doing a better parenting job than their fathers did. In a national poll, for example, 55 percent of fathers said that being a parent is more important to them than it was to their own fathers, 61 percent said they understand their children better than their own fathers did, and 70 percent said they spend more time with their children than their fathers spent with them (Adler, 1996).

Fathers may feel very close to their children and be affectionate with them, but they are still less involved in child care than mothers. Despite their positive self-evaluations, most fathers still spend little time with their children. When they do so, and as in previous years, most of their primary child-care activities are recreational (playing, reading) rather than the "custodial" time that mothers mainly put in (feeding, dressing) (Robinson and Godbey, 1999).

Gender Roles in the Workplace

Although there has been progress toward greater workplace equality, we still have a long way to go. In the United States, the average male employee still doesn't have options for flexible schedules, paternity leaves, or extended absences for "household matters." And women often feel that they have to postpone or forgo having children if they want to pursue a career.

We'll examine family and work roles at some length in Chapter 13. Here we'll briefly consider sex discrimination and sexual harassment—two work-related gender inequities that affect women, men, their partners, and their families.

SEX DISCRIMINATION When someone asked a top executive why there are so few high-ranking women in the advertising industry, he replied that it's because they aren't good enough. Women don't deserve to be promoted, he said, because their roles as caregivers and childbearers prevent them from working hard and succeeding in top positions (Bosman, 2005).

Such attitudes result in a *glass ceiling,* an unofficial and discriminatory barrier that limits women's and minorities' chances of rising to positions of power and responsibility. One example of the glass ceiling is a highly publicized case at the Massachusetts Institute of Technology's School of Science. A female professor of molecular biology spent several years collecting information on the unequal resources provided to male and female scientists—including salaries, research funds, and laboratory space. The university admitted that the discrimination existed but that it had not been "conscious or deliberate," and it implemented remedies such as salary increases, more desirable teaching assignments, and greater support for research (Wilson, 1999).

In most cases, sex discrimination is more open and blatant. For example, a federal jury in Minneapolis awarded a former home health care executive $1 million in lost wages and punitive damages. The jury agreed that the company, Mallinckrodt Inc., had paid the woman less than her male counterparts while giving her a heavier workload (Cruz, 2003).

Female physicians are more likely than their male counterparts to teach in medical schools but are less likely to be promoted. Women's child-rearing obligations are one barrier to their advancement. As long as women have primary (and often nearly total) responsibility for the care of children, even generous maternity leaves will not enable them to catch up to male colleagues who are able to focus all of their attention on their careers (De Angelis, 2000; Nonnemaker, 2000).

In athletics, women consistently fare worse than men. Since 2000, 90 percent of new head coaching jobs in women's athletics have gone to men. Why? Some say that male athletic directors, who outnumber females five to one, often simply prefer to hire men (Steindorf, 2002).

SEXUAL HARASSMENT Sexual harassment is any unwelcome sexual advance, request for sexual favors, or other conduct of a sexual nature that makes a person uncomfortable and interferes with her or his work. Harassment includes touching, staring at, or making jokes about a person's body, unreciprocated requests for sexual intercourse, rape, and any other form of unwanted sex.

A landmark Supreme Court decision in 1986, *Meritor Savings Bank v. Vinson,* ruled that sexual harassment violates

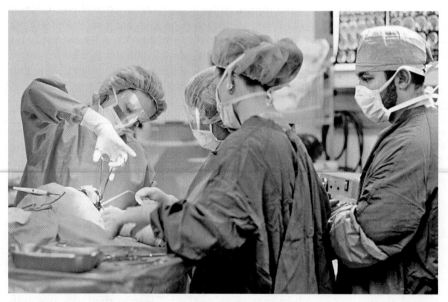

Increasing numbers of men are pursuing such traditionally-female occupations as nursing while more women are becoming physicians, including brain surgeons, a traditionally male-dominated occupation.

federal antidiscrimination laws. Sexual harassment in the workplace had a generally low profile, however, until the Senate confirmation hearings for Clarence Thomas, a candidate for the U.S. Supreme Court in October 1991. Sexual harassment suddenly received national media coverage when Anita Hill, a law professor at the University of Oklahoma, testified that in the early 1980s Thomas had sexually harassed her while he was her supervisor and the director of the Equal Employment Opportunity Commission (EEOC). Despite the allegations, Congress approved Thomas's appointment to the U.S. Supreme Court.

Very few women complain about or sue for sexual harassment. In most cases, especially in lower-level positions, they tolerate the abuse because they don't want to lose their jobs. In other cases, even when women have some financial resources, they know that a lawsuit will take seven to eight years to settle and might cost them at least $300,000. Therefore, few women have the money or energy to pursue sexual harassment lawsuits.

The cases in which women have sued illustrate the types of sexual harassment that they've encountered. For example,

- A California jury awarded six female employees $30 million because a manager at a Ralph's supermarket chain terrorized them for more than a year. The manager used foul language and racial slurs, threw telephones and 12-pack sodas at them, and touched them inappropriately.

- Lutheran Medical Center in Brooklyn, New York, agreed to pay more than $5.4 million to settle complaints by 51 current and past employees that a doctor sexually harassed them during pre-employment physical examinations. The suit accused the physician of touching the women's breasts and genitals needlessly and making lewd comments about their sexual and dating habits.

- The EEOC has had more complaints about the fast-food industry than any other sector. Among other incidents, a store manager raped a 14-year-old employee, some of the young women were repeatedly called "bitch," some have had their breasts fondled or their buttocks slapped, and others have encountered continuous obscene comments and gestures ("Harassment in the Supermarket," 2002; Retsinas, 2003; Sanchez, 2003).

Some men say that they are confused about what sexual harassment is. They claim that they don't see the difference between flirting or complimenting someone and behavior that is called sexual harassment. This is nonsense. If someone says "stop it" and you don't, it's sexual harassment. (We'll look at the prevalence, consequences, and legal ramifications of sexual harassment in more detail in Chapter 13).

Religion and Gender Roles

Religion influences gender roles and behavior, especially within the family. In the Middle East, for example, a popular version of Barbie is the Fulla doll. Fulla is dark-eyed and dark-haired, wears a black *abaya* (a robe that covers the body from head to toe) and matching head scarf, comes with a pink prayer mat, and will never have a boyfriend doll like Barbie's Ken. Fulla "flies off the shelves" because she reflects "Muslim values": She's honest, loving, and caring, and she respects her mother and father (Zoepf, 2005: A4). Most important, Fulla wears clothing that is deemed appropriate for women in many parts of the Middle East.

PARENTING U.S. dolls don't advocate particular religious values. However, religion shapes gender and family roles in many other ways. For example, the Ten Commandments teach children to honor their parents and married couples to be faithful to each other.

A study of Catholics, mainline Protestants (such as Episcopalians, Methodists, and Lutherans), and evangelical Protestants (such as Southern Baptists and Assemblies of God) found that in all these faiths, fathers were more likely than those with no religious affiliation to spend more time with their children. The former were more likely to interact with their children (including working on projects, talking, and helping with reading or homework), have family dinners, and participate in youth-related activities such as sports, school functions, and religious youth groups (Wilcox, 2002; Chatters and Taylor, 2005).

DOMESTIC ROLES Religion also shapes the division of labor in the home. In evangelical households, wives, including those who work outside the home, spend four to five more hours per week performing tasks that are traditionally defined as women's work (cooking, cleaning, and laundry). Even though some feminist evangelicals have challenged such gendered housework, many female evangelicals believe that it is divinely ordained that men provide for and protect the family and that women support men by taking on most of the household responsibilities (Bartkowski, 2001; Ellison and Bartkowski, 2002; Gallagher, 2003).

ROLE MODELS At religious colleges and universities, some female faculty members feel that their expected gender roles are constraining. Often there are few full-time faculty members at these institutions who are women. Those who are hired may feel alienated because many Christian colleges constantly remind female students that once they get married and have children, "God does not expect them to work outside the home" (Mock, 2005). In effect, then, some of these women faculty wonder if they're effective in providing their female students with role models to which they will aspire after college.

Gender and Communication

Sociolinguist Deborah Tannen (1990, 1994) proposes that women and men have distinctive communication styles that include different purposes, different rules, and different ways of interpreting communications. For example, Tannen says, women are more likely than men to use "rapport-talk," a way of establishing connections and negotiating relationships. They are most concerned with how people feel and with making people feel comfortable.

In contrast, men are more likely to use "report-talk," a way of showing knowledge and skill and holding center stage through storytelling, joking, or giving information. For example, if a man comes home and his wife asks, "How was your day?" she probably expects rapport-talk in response (such as office gossip). Often, however, she will get report-talk: "Fine. Had some problems but got 'em straightened out." Not hearing what she expects, the woman may be miffed, and her husband probably won't understand why she's upset. (We'll examine differences between women's and men's communication patterns in more detail in Chapter 10).

Making Connections

- Why do you think reality shows about families, such as *Nanny 911*, are so popular? Because parents get good advice that changes their behavior? Because we want quick fixes for complex socialization issues? Or other reasons?

- Some of my students maintain that instrumental and expressive roles no longer exist. Others argue that both roles are alive and well. Think about your parents, your spouse or partner, or your friends. Does their behavior reflect instrumental and expressive roles? What about you?

Current Gender Roles: Changes and Constraints

Most women and men, especially if they are employed, share the same concerns and want the same things in life. For example, both sexes worry about inadequate health care and retirement security, lack of fairness and respect in the workplace, and limited family medical leave and child care.

Despite these similarities, there are still a number of differences between men's and women's gender roles. Employed mothers, especially, consistently report more stress than men in their everyday lives. Some attribute such stress to role conflict. Others argue that our society—and feminism in particular—is creating strain by waging a "war" against boys and men.

since you asked

Is U.S. society waging a "war" against boys and men?

Role Conflict

As gender roles change, most of us are bound to encounter **role conflict**: the frustration and uncertainties that a person experiences when confronted with the requirements of two or more roles that are incompatible with each other. College students often experience role conflict because it is difficult to meet course requirements, especially if students register for a "full load" but also work 20 or more hours per week. The role conflict increases if the student also has young children or cares for an aging parent.

Faculty members also grapple with role conflict. Many have evening classes and feel guilty because they must hire baby sitters to care for their young children. Women faculty, especially, often feel emotionally drained because it's difficult to keep up both with parental and academic roles such as teaching, grading exams, meeting with students, presenting talks at professional conferences, and meeting research deadlines.

Mothers who work full time report being exhausted by juggling their job and family responsibilities. Some men complain, however, that their wives' house cleaning standards are too high, that they add unnecessary "finishing touches" (such as rewiping the kitchen table after the husband has cleaned it), or that the women grumble that the husband "dressed the kids funny" (Coltrane, 1996; "Motherhood today . . .," 1997).

As a result, men may feel unappreciated or inadequate and take on fewer housework and child-care responsibilities. Women, on the other hand, maintain that men should have higher standards and do domestic tasks "right." Such disagreements intensify some of the strain that characterizes changing gender roles.

Role conflict is grueling for both sexes. It can produce tension, hostility, aggression, and stress-related physical problems such as insomnia, headaches, ulcers, eating disorders, teeth grinding, anxiety attacks, chronic fatigue, nausea, weight loss or gain, and drug and alcohol abuse (Weber et al., 1997).

Are We Waging a War against Boys and Men?

A *Business Week* cover, "The New Gender Gap," shows a picture of a young girl, arms crossed, smiling smugly while a young boy looks sad and forlorn. The cover story then maintains that from kindergarten to graduate school, boys are now "the second sex"—far behind girls in education, less likely to participate in extracurricular activities, more likely to commit suicide, and so on. There have also been several well-publicized books claiming that girls (and women) are mean and vicious creatures (see Chesler, 2002; Simmons, 2002; Wiseman, 2002).

Is U.S. society neglecting boys? Or do these concerns signal a backlash against some of the gains that girls and women made in the 1980s and 1990s?

CONCERN ABOUT MEN'S AND BOYS' DEVELOPMENT
Since the mid-1990s, a small but vocal number of clinical psychologists, journalists, and other writers have argued that many boys are "in trouble." Among other things, boys make up 67 percent of the students in special education classes, are more likely than girls to suffer from attention deficit disorders, lag behind girls in reading scores, create more disciplinary problems in school, and are more likely than girls to be both perpetrators and victims of crime. In some cases, the authors blame feminists for encouraging girls to succeed while ignoring boys (Garbarino, 1999; Kindlon et al., 1999; Nikkah and Furman, 2000; Sommers, 2000).

A BACKLASH AGAINST GIRLS' AND WOMEN'S PROGRESS
Critics respond that accusations of biases against males are unwarranted and unsupported. It's true that the educational gender gap has widened. Nationally, a larger share of women than men now earns college degrees (see *Figure 5.4*). Also, the percentage of undergraduate men—in all racial-ethnic categories and across all income groups—has decreased since 1995 (King, 2003).

Do these numbers mean that male students are at a disadvantage? No. The traditional gender gap in the

Many people dismiss female athletes as "unfeminine," "butch," or "less powerful" than men. How accurate are such adjectives in describing most female athletes, like Serena Williams, pictured here?

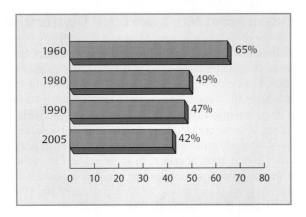

FIGURE 5.4 **Where are the College Men?**

Source: Based on U.S. Department of Education, 2005, Table 246.

national mathematics and science scores of 17-year-olds has narrowed, but males still outperform females. And if girls are enjoying more success, perhaps they've earned it: "While the girls are busy working on sweeping the honor roll at graduation, a boy is more likely to be bulking up in the weight room . . . playing *Grand Theft Auto: Vice City* on his PlayStation2, or downloading rapper 50 Cent on his iPod" (Conlin, 2003: 76).

A study of the long-term trends in education concluded that the "hysteria" about boys from so-called experts is little more than hype because girls are doing better rather than boys doing worse. Among other things, men are enrolling in higher education in greater numbers than ever before and earning degrees at historically higher rates (Mead, 2006).

In college, "Dean's lists are dominated by women while probation and dismissal lists are dominated by men" (Bolduc, 2005). Even though women generally have better academic records than men, many college administrators admit that they often give preference to men. Numerous colleges have offered men special privileges to entice them to their campuses. Some admissions offices are "more forgiving of the occasional B or even a C" in a male's high school transcript. Others have targeted special mailings to high school boys that include photos and descriptions of new science and math buildings, beefed-up athletic scholarships, sports programs, and superb athletic facilities. Some college presidents, especially at private colleges, have admitted enrolling men at higher rates than women even though women are usually stronger candidates (Clayton, 2001; Hong, 2004; Marklein, 2005).

Although many girls are succeeding in school, they are twice as likely as boys to suffer from depression, they make up 90 percent of the teens with eating disorders, and they have caught up with—and sometimes even surpassed—boys in smoking, taking drugs, and drinking alcohol (see Chapter 14).

For girls, pressure to have sex begins at age 12 and comes from both boys and girls. White and Asian American girls, especially, report increasing pressure to fit in, take drugs, drink, and be popular and cool. In addition, one-fourth to one-third of girls have been sexually victimized (ranging from sexual harassment to rape) by the time they finish high school (Haag, 1999; see, also, Chapter 7).

Instead of girl- and women-bashing, many researchers propose, we should look at the evidence, especially in adulthood. For example,

- Men dominate powerful positions in education, government, and the economy (see "Data Digest").

- Among full-time workers, women with college degrees earn about $38,500 per year compared with almost $33,300 for men with only a high school degree (U.S. Census Bureau, 2006).

- About 29 percent of women in the military say that they have experienced sexual assault by their peers or officers. The percentage is even higher in U.S. military academies (Tessier, 2003; *Report of the defense task force. . .*, 2005).

- Although women have been earning Ph.D.s for several decades, the percentage of female full professors in Western countries ranges from a low of 5 percent in Ireland to a high of only 23 percent in the United States (Bollag, 2002b; Curtis, 2005).

Another way to look at women's progress is to note the number of "firsts" you read or hear about when you pick up the newspaper or turn on the news. Recently, for example, Brown University hired its first woman (and African American) as president, House Democrats elected their first female minority leader, and Ford Motor Company named its first female executive vice president. In other countries, Germans elected their first female Chancellor and Jamaica elected its first female prime minister. When we no longer hear about such "firsts," we can be more confident that there is greater equality between men and women.

Is Androgyny the Answer?

Some social scientists feel that **androgyny** may be the solution to sexist gender roles. In androgyny, both masculine and feminine characteristics are blended in the same person.

According to Bem (1975), who did much of the pioneering work on androgyny, our complex society requires that people have both kinds of characteristics. Adults must be assertive, independent, and self-reliant, but they must also relate well to other people, be sensitive to their needs, and give them emotional support.

Androgyny allows people to play both instrumental and expressive roles. According to social psychologist Carol Tavris (2002: B8), both men and women demonstrate humanity's "graces and furies":

> Both are equally likely to be empathic, kind, altruistic, and friendly and to be mean, hostile, aggressive, petty, conformist, and prejudiced. Both sexes can be competitive or cooperative, selfish or nurturant, loving parents or indifferent ones—and reveal all of those qualities on different occasions.

Androgyny might be especially beneficial for men. Many men might stop being workaholics, relax on weekends, refrain from engaging in risky sexual behavior (to demonstrate their sexual prowess), live longer, and stop worrying about being "real men." If we felt more comfortable when children display nontraditional gender traits, assertive girls and nonaggres-

Women in Kenya, Africa, acquired a right to vote only in 1963 but now constitute 54 percent of the country's voting population. In both tribal villages and urban centers, women line up to vote for important issues such as the right to inherit money and property.

sive boys would be happier and emotionally healthier (Martin, 1990).

There is still greater disapproval of boys than of girls who reject traditional gender roles. Do you think that androgyny might take some of the pressure off men, giving them more freedom to be and do whatever they want? Or do you think that androgynous men would be dismissed as wimps and sissies?

A Global View: Variations in Gender Roles

Because each culture has its own norms and values, the degree of equality between men and women differs widely from one society to another. Such cross-cultural variations constitute some of the best evidence that gender roles are learned rather than innate.

There is no easy way to compare the status of women around the world. Still, the Gender Development Index (GDI) is a measure that sheds some light on women's status and quality of life. The GDI is based on key indicators including life expectancy, educational attainment, and income. It also measures "intentional commitment to equality principles and policies" (Seager, 2003: 12). As *Figure 5.5* shows, most of the world's women live in countries that rank from "medium" to the "bottom 10 countries" on the GDI. Let's begin with the "top 10 countries"—those that have the greatest equality between women and men.

since you asked

Are there countries where women are better off than in the United States?

Top Ten Countries

The United States, Canada, Australia, Japan, Iceland, the Scandinavian countries, the Netherlands, and Belgium rank highest on the GDI. Being in the top ten doesn't mean that women live in paradise, however. As you've seen throughout this chapter, there is great inequality between women and men in the United States and other industrialized countries in power, income, and privilege.

There's also wide variation among the top ten countries on several indicators. In the proportion of elected female government officials, for example, Sweden ranks at the top, with 55 percent women, compared with only 32 percent in the United States. Even then, Swedish women undergraduates report sexual harassment, and women faculty members—only 11 percent of whom are tenured—complain about widespread discrimination in awarding of postdoctoral fellowships, hiring practices,

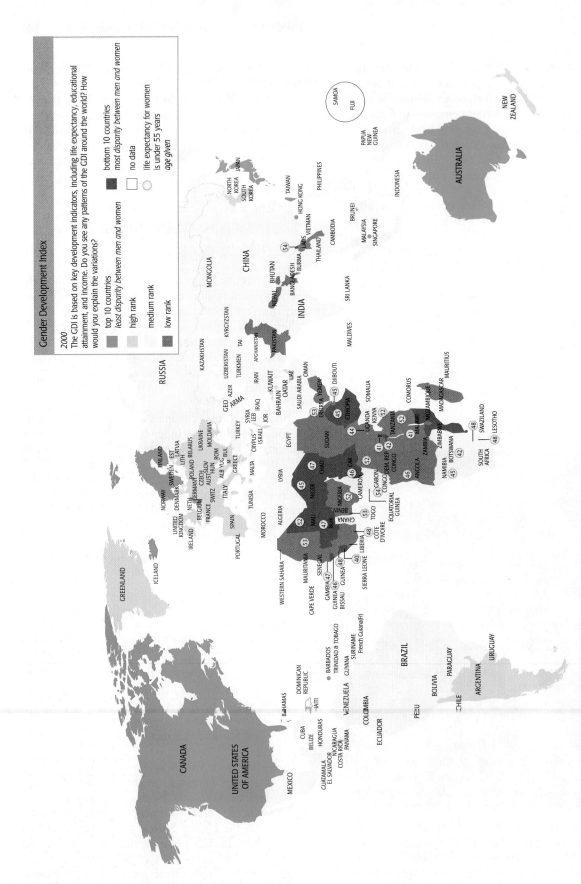

FIGURE 5.5 The State of Women around the World

SOURCE: Seager, 2003: 12–13.

The map legend reads:

Gender Development Index

2000
The GDI is based on key development indicators, including life expectancy, educational attainment, and income. Do you see any patterns of the GDI around the world? How would you explain the variations?

top 10 countries
least disparity between men and women

high rank

medium rank

low rank

bottom 10 countries
most disparity between men and women

no data

life expectancy for women
is under 55 years
age given

150

and promotion criteria (Bollag, 2002a, 2002b; Seager, 2003).

In Japan, women comprise more than half of the work force but hold only 9 percent of all managerial positions. Full-time working women earn only 65 percent of what men earn (Gender Equality Bureau, 2000).

High-Rank Countries

The countries that rank high in gender development include Greenland, most of the European countries, South Korea, Chile, Argentina, Uruguay, Greece, and several countries in the Middle East (Israel, Kuwait, and the United Arab Emirates).

Again, women and men are not fully equal in these societies. Some of the high-rank countries have positive characteristics such as high female literacy rates, low maternal mortality rates, and high percentages of female university students. Yet domestic violence is widespread: 68 percent of women in the United Kingdom and 53 percent of women in Portugal report having experienced physical abuse by a male partner, and in Israel wives are killed by their husbands at a rate of one every nine days (Seager, 2003).

Middle-Rank Countries

The middle-rank countries are primarily those in Central and South America, northern and southern Africa, Russia, and much of the Middle East. Especially in Islamic cultures, there is a great deal of variation in women's roles in the family, education, politics, and employment opportunities. Each country interprets women's rights under Islam somewhat differently, and within each country social class is a determining factor in women's privileges.

In the Arab world, the overall female literacy rate is more than 50 percent, but it ranges from a low of 30 percent in Iraq to a high of almost 100 percent in Jordan. In some countries (including Kuwait, Indonesia, China, Thailand, and Saudi Arabia), thriving sex industries are fed by a steady supply of young women— mostly from Bangladesh, India, the Philippines, Sri Lanka, and other poor countries where the women cannot find employment. The unsuspecting women are told that they are accepting overseas jobs as maids or domestic laborers. Instead, they are forced into prostitution (Farley, 2001; Elson and Keklik, 2002).

Women's well-being and rights are mixed in other middle-rank countries as well. In South Africa, 84 percent of women are literate but rapes of infants and very young children are widespread. According to one survey of rape victims, 38 percent of young girls said that

a schoolteacher or principal had raped them. Child labor, child prostitution, and child pornography are pervasive (Human Rights Watch, 2003; *State of the World's Mothers*, 2003).

Low-Rank Countries

The low-rank countries include Pakistan and several Middle Eastern countries as well as a number of African societies. In much of Africa, women's life expectancy is well under 55 years (see *Figure 5.5*). Early death results primarily from AIDS but also reflects high rates of death during childbirth because of poor nutrition, the scarcity of trained health personnel, and murder by husbands after marriage. In African countries, female literacy rates range from a low of 28 percent in Senegal to a high of 71 percent in Zambia. In Nigeria, women can be stoned to death for infidelity or, in the case of divorced women, having sexual relations without having remarried. In addition, an estimated 37 percent of girls aged 15 to 19 are forced to wed against their wishes (Rosen, 2003; *State of the World's Mothers*, 2003).

In Pakistan, only 28 percent of the women are literate. In some regions, tribal councils decree that a young woman can be raped in revenge for a crime committed by a brother or other male family member. When a girl turns 15 or 16, she usually weds in an arranged marriage and leaves school to start having babies. In some poor regions, it's common for fathers to marry off 18-year-old girls to 80-year-old men to settle a "blood debt"—making amends for having wronged someone (Sarwar, 2002).

Bottom Ten Countries

The lowest-ranked countries on the GDI are 11 countries in Africa, including Ethiopia, Niger, and Sierra Leone. Here, women have short life expectancies for the same reasons as women in the low-rank African societies.

In these countries, women's literacy rates range from a low of 8 percent in Niger to a high of only 47 percent in Malawi. Women's participation in government is negligible and as low as 1 percent in Niger. Rates of sex trafficking of women to other countries are especially high in Ethiopia, Niger, and Burkina Faso (*State of the World's Mothers*, 2003).

Some of these countries are struggling to improve women's status. In Mozambique, for example, 70 percent of the country's schools were destroyed during 16 years of civil war. Although 80 to 90 percent of the elementary-school-age children are now in school, in rural areas most girls drop out by age 12 to marry.

Some parents worry that if their daughters go to school, they might be lured into prostitution or be sexually abused by teachers. And in many regions there are not enough teachers or classrooms. Even when there are teachers, there aren't enough desks or books and there are no blackboards (Itano, 2002a).

Conclusion

The past 25 years have seen the beginning of dramatic *changes* in some aspects of gender roles. More people today say that they believe in gender equality and unprecedented numbers of women have entered colleges and the labor force.

But do most people really have more *choices*? Women have become increasingly resentful of the burden of both domestic and economic responsibilities, especially in a society that devalues them and their labor. Men, although often freed from the sole-breadwinner role, feel that their range of choices is narrowing as women compete with them at work.

Significant change in gender roles elicits *constraints* for both sexes at every level: personal, group, and institutional. Those who benefit the most from gender-role inequality resist giving up their privileges and economic resources. In the next chapter we examine how changes in gender roles affect love and intimate relationships.

Summary

1. *Sex* and *gender* are not interchangeable terms. Sex refers to the biological characteristics we are born with. Gender refers to the attitudes and behavior that society expects of men and women.

2. Scholars continue to debate how much of our behavior reflects nature (biology) or nurture (environment). Although biology is important, there is little evidence that women are naturally better parents, that men are naturally more aggressive, or that men and women are inherently different in other ways than anatomy.

3. Traditional gender roles are based on the beliefs that women should fulfill expressive functions and that men should play instrumental roles.

4. Traditional roles have both positive and negative consequences. On the positive side, men and women know what is expected of them. On the negative side, traditional roles often create stress and anxiety and seriously limit choices.

5. A number of theoretical perspectives try to explain how we learn gender roles. Social learning theory posits that we learn gender roles by reward and punishment,

imitation, and role modeling. Cognitive development theory maintains that children learn gender identity by interacting with and interpreting the behavior of others. Feminist approaches argue that we learn gender roles through gender scripts that parents, especially, endorse.

6. We learn gender role expectations from many sources—parents, peers, teachers, and the media. Many of these socializing influences continue to reinforce traditional male and female gender roles.

7. During much of our adult life, our activities are sex-segregated. Typically, men and women play different roles in the home and the workplace.

8. Men and women tend to communicate differently. These differences are often unintentional, but they may create misunderstandings.

9. Some writers contend that boys are ignored and devalued whereas girls are supported. Others argue that girls' and women's progress toward closing gender gaps has been exaggerated.

10. There is wide variation among cultures in gender roles. Many societies are male-dominated; others are much more progressive than the United States.

Key Terms

sex *121*
gender *121*
gender roles *121*
gender identity *121*
hormones *122*

transgendered *123*
transsexuals *123*
patriarchy *126*
matriarchy *126*
social learning theory *128*

cognitive development theory *129*
gender-role stereotypes *129*
sexual harassment *144*
role conflict *146*
androgyny *148*

Taking it Further

Socialization and Gender Roles Material Online

There are hundreds of gender-related Internet resources. Some of the most comprehensive and interesting Web sites include the following:

Women's Studies/Women's Issues Resource Sites offers hundreds of e-mail lists related to women, Websites around the world, and dozens of topical subsections on gender topics.
http://research.umbc.edu/~korenman/wmst/links.html

The Men's Bibliography provides almost 13,000 references to material about men, gender roles, masculinity, and sexuality.
http://mensbiblio.xyonline.net

Women of Color Web focuses on issues related to feminism, sexuality, and reproductive health and rights, as well as writing by and about women of color in the United States.
www.hsph.harvard.edu/grhf/WoC

International Gender Studies Resources offers general and specific bibliographies and filmographies on issues pertaining to women and gender in Africa, Asia, Latin America, and the Middle East and Arab countries and among minority cultures in North America and Europe.
http://globetrotter.berkeley.edu/GlobalGender

WWWomen: The Premier Search Directory for Women Online includes material on such topics as women in business, feminism, lesbians, publications, women's resources, science and technology, women's sports, and women throughout history.
www.wwwomen.com

Women's Resources on the NET includes dozens of links to sites dealing with women and politics, international women's agencies and global statistics, education resources for girls, and advocacy and academic organizations.
www.wic.org/misc/resource.htm

And more: www.prenhall.com/benokraitis offers resources on health and genetics, guidelines for nonsexist language, women's e-news sources, The Movie Mom's Guide to Family Movies, Girl Tech sites, men's centers, several international sites, information on dowry deaths, sexual harassment resources, and a gallery of the most negative ads about women; it also invites you to calculate how much unequal pay will cost you over your lifetime if you're a woman.

Investigate with Research Navigator

Go to www.researchnavigator.com and enter your LOGIN NAME and PASSWORD. For instructions on registering for the first time, view the detailed instructions at the end of the Chapter 1. Search the Research Navigator™ site using the following key terms:

gender roles
role conflict
sexual harassment

Outline

6

Love and Loving Relationships

Data Digest

- **Love is great for business.** On Valentine's Day, Americans spend more than $400 million on roses, purchase more than $600 million worth of candy, and send more than 1 billion cards (compared with 150 million on Mother's Day). In 2005, men spent an average of $218 on Valentine's Day gifts compared with $146 for women.

- More than half of all American adults (52 percent) believe in love at first sight and **almost 75 percent believe in "one true love."**

- **Men are more likely than women to initiate romantic e-mail.** Of the people who engage in online chats, 64 percent—most of them men—say they experience "online chemistry."

- **Does love make life "richer or fuller"?** "Yes" say 37 percent of people born between 1965 and 1980 compared with only 9 percent of those born before 1930.

- **Should women propose to men?** Yes, according to 77 percent of men but only 63 percent of women.

Sources: Carlson, 2001; Yin, 2002; Alvear, 2003; White, 2003; Armstrong, 2004; Soukup, 2005.

Many of the most popular movies have been about love: first love (*Titanic*), obsessive love (*Fatal Attraction*), self-sacrificing love (*The Bridges of Madison County*), love that survives obstacles (*My Big Fat Greek Wedding*), and falling in love with someone from "the wrong side of the tracks" (*Pretty Woman*). Love means different things to different people. As the box "On Love and Loving" shows, love has been a source of inspiration, wry witticisms, and even political action for many centuries.

In this chapter we explore the meaning of love, why we love each other, the positive and negative aspects of love, and how love changes over time. We also look at some cross-cultural variations in people's attitudes about love. Let's begin with friendship, the root of love.

Loving and Liking

Love—as both an emotion and a behavior—is essential for human survival. The family is usually our earliest and most important source of love and emotional support (see Chapter 1). It is in families that we learn to love ourselves and, consequently, to love others.

since you asked

Is it possible to love someone you don't like?

Self-Love

Actress Mae West once said, "I never loved another person the way I loved myself." Although such a statement may seem self-centered, it's actually quite insightful. Social philosopher Erich Fromm (1956) saw self-love, or love for oneself, as essential for our social and emotional development and as a prerequisite for loving others.

Social scientists describe self-love as an important basis for self-esteem. People who like themselves are more open to criticism and less demanding of others. Those who don't like themselves may not be able to reciprocate friendship. Instead, they constantly seek love relationships that will bolster their own poor self-image (Casler, 1974).

Changes

On Love and Loving

Throughout the centuries many writers have commented on the varieties, purposes, pleasures, and pain of love. Here are some examples:

- **Jesus (4 B.C.–A.D. 29):** "A new commandment I give unto you, that ye love one another."
- **I Corinthians 13:4–7:** "Love is patient and kind; love is not jealous or boastful; it is not arrogant or rude . . . Love bears all things, believes all things, hopes all things, endures all things."
- **William Shakespeare (1564–1616):** "To say the truth, reason and love keep little company together nowadays" (from *A Midsummer Night's Dream*).
- **Hindustani proverb:** "Life is no longer one's own when the heart is fixed on another."
- **Abraham Cowley (1618–1667):** "I love you, not only for what you are, but for what I am when I am with you."
- **Ninon de Lenclos (1620–1705):** "Much more genius is needed to make love than to command armies."
- **Irish saying:** "If you live in my heart, you live rent-free."
- **Elizabeth Barrett Browning (1806–1861):** "How do I love thee? Let me count the ways. I love thee to the depth and breadth and height my soul can reach."
- **Henry Wadsworth Longfellow (1807–1882):** "Love gives itself; it is not bought."

- **Japanese saying:** "Who travels for love finds a thousand miles only one mile."
- **William Thackeray (1811–1863):** "It is best to love wisely, no doubt; but to love foolishly is better than not to be able to love at all."
- **Robert Browning (1812–1889):** "Take away love and our earth is a tomb."
- **Benjamin Disraeli (1804–1881):** "The magic of first love is our ignorance that it can ever end."
- **Marlene Dietrich (1901–1992):** "Grumbling is the death of love."
- **Turkish proverb:** "When two hearts are one, even the king cannot separate them."
- **Anonymous:** "Nobody is perfect until you fall in love with them."
- **Che Guevara (1928–1967):** "The true revolutionary is guided by a great feeling of love."
- **John Lennon (1940–1980):** "All you need is love."
- **Katherine Hepburn (1907–2003):** "Sometimes I wonder if men and women really suit each other. Perhaps they should live next door and just visit now and then."
- **Cher (1946–):** "The trouble with some women is that they get all excited about nothing—and then marry him."
- **Jay Leno (1950–):** "Today is Valentine's Day—or, as men like to call it, Extortion Day!"

Love and Friendship

Do you like people whom you don't love? Sure. Do you love people whom you don't like? No—at least not in a healthy relationship. In his classic research on "the near and dear," Keith Davis (1985) identified eight important qualities of friendship:

■ **Enjoyment.** Friends enjoy being with each other most of time. They feel at ease with each other despite occasional disagreements.

■ **Acceptance.** Friends accept each other the way they are. They tolerate faults and shortcomings instead of trying to change each other.

■ **Trust.** Friends trust and look out for each other. They lean on each other during difficult times.

■ **Respect.** Friends respect each other's judgment. They may not agree with the choices the other person makes, but they honor his or her decisions.

■ **Mutual support.** Friends help and support each other. They do so without expecting something in return.

■ **Confiding.** Friends share experiences and feelings. They don't gossip about each other or backstab.

■ **Understanding.** Friends are sympathetic about each other's feelings and thoughts. They can often "read" each other without saying very much.

■ **Honesty.** Friends are open and honest. They feel free to be themselves and say what they think.

Love includes all these qualities and three more—sexual desire, priority over other relationships, and caring to the point of great self-sacrifice. A relationship can start off with friendship and develop into love. It's unlikely, however, that we can "really" love someone who isn't a friend. Love, like friendship, is a process that develops over time.

But just what is love? What attracts lovers to each other? And are lust and love similar?

What Is Love?

Love is an elusive concept. We have all experienced love and feel that we know what it is. When asked what love is, however, people give a variety of answers. According to a nine-year-old boy, for example, "Love is like an avalanche where you have to run for your life." And according to a six-year-old girl, "Love is when mommy

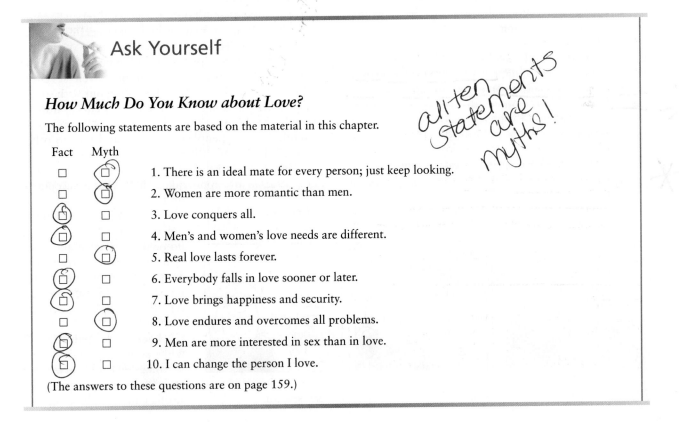

Ask Yourself

How Much Do You Know about Love?

The following statements are based on the material in this chapter.

all ten statements are myths!

Fact	Myth	
☐	☑	1. There is an ideal mate for every person; just keep looking.
☐	☑	2. Women are more romantic than men.
☑	☐	3. Love conquers all.
☑	☐	4. Men's and women's love needs are different.
☐	☑	5. Real love lasts forever.
☑	☐	6. Everybody falls in love sooner or later.
☑	☐	7. Love brings happiness and security.
☐	☑	8. Love endures and overcomes all problems.
☑	☐	9. Men are more interested in sex than in love.
☑	☐	10. I can change the person I love.

(The answers to these questions are on page 159.)

sees daddy on the toilet and she doesn't think it's gross." Before you read any further, test your general knowledge about love in the box "How Much Do You Know about Love?"

Some Characteristics of Love

During the war in Iraq, a U.S. soldier wrote his 15-month-old daughter a letter that said, in part, "You are the meaning of my life. You make my heart pound with joy and pride. No matter what happens to me or where we go, you will always know that I love you." The letter was found on the soldier's body when he died in the crash of a Black Hawk helicopter shot down by insurgents (Zoroya, 2005).

As the letter illustrates, parental love is strong and deep. Still, people often make a distinction between "loving someone" (family members, relatives, and friends) and "being in love" (a romantic relationship). Both types of love, nonetheless, are multifaceted, based on respect, and often demanding.

LOVE IS MULTIFACETED Love has many dimensions. It can be romantic, exciting, obsessive, and irrational. It can also be platonic, calming, altruistic, and sensible. Love defies a single definition because it varies in degree and intensity and in different social contexts. At the very least, and as you will see shortly, love includes caring, intimacy, and commitment.

LOVE IS BASED ON RESPECT Although love may involve passionate yearning, respect is a more important quality. If respect is missing, the relationship is not based on love. Instead, it is an unhealthy or possessive feeling or behavior that limits the lovers' social, emotional, and intellectual growth (Peele and Brodsky, 1976).

LOVE IS OFTEN DEMANDING Long-term love, especially, has nothing in common with the images of in-fatuation or frenzied sex that we get from movies, television, and romance novels. These misconceptions often lead to unrealistic expectations, stereotypes, and disillusionment.

In fact, real love is closer to what one author calls "stirring-the-oatmeal" love (Johnson, 1985). This type of love is neither exciting nor thrilling but is usually mundane and unromantic. It means paying bills, scrubbing toilet bowls, being up all night with a sick baby, and performing myriad other tasks that aren't very sexy.

Some partners take turns stirring the oatmeal. Others break up or get a divorce. Whether we decide to tie the knot or not, why are we attracted to some people and not others?

What Attracts People to Each Other?

Many people believe in "true love," that "there's one person out there that you're meant for," and that destiny will bring us together (see "Data Digest"). Such beliefs are romantic but unfounded. Cultural norms and values, not fate, bring people together. We will never meet millions of potential lovers because they are "filtered out" by formal or informal rules on partner eligibility due to factors such as age, race, social class, religion, sexual orientation, health, or physical appearance (see Chapter 8).

Beginning in childhood, parents indirectly encourage or limit future romances by living in certain neighborhoods and selecting certain schools. Even during the preteen years, group practices and expectations shape romantic experiences. For example, even seventh-graders have "rules," such as not going out with someone their friends don't like, or telling parents as little as possible for as long as possible because "Parents nose around, get into people's business, and talk to other parents" (Perlstein, 2005: 33).

Although romance may cross cultural or ethnic borders, criticism and approval teach us what is acceptable and with whom. All societies—including the United States—have "rules" about homogamy (dating and marrying within one's group) and exogamy (dating and marrying someone outside an "acceptable" group) (see Chapters 1 and 4).

Even if we "fall in lust" with someone, our sexual yearnings will not lead most of us to "fall in love" if there are strong cultural taboos against

it. These taboos explain, in part, why we don't always marry our sexual partners.

Do Lust and Love Differ?

Lust and love differ quite a bit. Regan and Berscheid (1999) differentiate between sexual arousal (or lust), sexual desire, and love—especially romantic love. They describe *sexual arousal* as a physiological rather than an emotional response, one that may occur either consciously or unconsciously (see Chapter 7). *Sexual desire*, in contrast, is a psychological state in which a person wants "to obtain a sexual object that one does not now have or to engage in a sexual activity in which one is not now engaging" (p. 17).

Sexual desire may or may not lead to *romantic love*. Once desire evaporates, disillusioned and disappointed lovers will wonder where the "spark" in their relationship has gone and may reminisce longingly about "the good old days."

This does not mean that sexual desire *always* culminates in sexual intercourse or that romantic love and love are synonymous. Married couples may love each other even though they rarely, or never, engage in sexual intercourse for health and other reasons. Regardless of the nature of love, healthy loving relationships reflect a balance of caring, intimacy, and commitment.

Caring, Intimacy, and Commitment

As you'll see later in this chapter, people fall in love for many reasons: Because they are physically attracted to each other, have shared interests, seek companionship, or simply want to have fun. In any type of love, however, caring about the other person is essential.

since you asked

Can there be intimacy without sex?

Caring

Love includes *caring*, or wanting to help the other person by providing aid and emotional support (Cutrona, 1996). Although we often use metaphors for love such as "I'm crazy about you" or "I can't live without you,"

Answers to "How Much Do You Know about Love?"

All ten statements are myths. Eight or more correct answers indicate that you know a myth when you hear one. Otherwise—watch out!

1. We can love many people, and we can love many times. This is why some people marry more than once.

2. Men fall in love more quickly, are more romantic, and suffer more intensely when their love is not returned.

3. Because almost one out of two marriages ends in divorce, love is not enough to overcome all problems and obstacles. Differences in race, ethnicity, religion, economic status, education, and age can often stifle romantic interest.

4. As in friendship, both men and women want trust, honesty, understanding, and respect from those they love.

5. Love can be genuine but not last forever. People today live much longer, the world is more complex, and even marital partners change as they mature and grow older.

6. Some people have deep-seated emotional scars that make them suspicious and unloving; others are too self-centered to give love.

7. Love guarantees neither happiness nor security. As you'll see shortly, love doesn't "fix" people who are generally insecure or anxious about themselves or their relationships.

8. People who love each other make sacrifices, but emotional or physical abuse should not be tolerated. Eventually, even "martyrs" become unhappy, angry, depressed, and resentful.

9. During the romantic stage, both women and men may be more interested in sex than in love. As love matures, both partners value such attributes as faithfulness, patience, and making the other person feel wanted.

10. You can only change yourself. Trying to change someone usually results in anger, resentment, frustration, and unhappiness.

these terms of endearment may not be translated into ongoing, everyday behavior such as valuing your partner's welfare as much as your own.

Caring means responding to the other person's needs. If a person sees no evidence of warmth or support over time, there will be serious doubts that a partner *really* loves her or him.

This doesn't mean that a partner should be submissive or docile. Instead, people who care about each other bolster each other's self-esteem and offer encouragement when there are problems. When a person is sensitive to a partner's needs, the relationship will become more intimate and will flourish.

Intimacy

Although definitions of intimacy vary, all of them emphasize feelings of closeness. In his analysis of couples, for example, P. M. Brown (1995: 3) found that people experience *intimacy* when they

- Share a mutual emotional interest in each other
- Have some sort of history together
- Have a distinct sense of identity as a couple
- Hold a reciprocal commitment to a continued relationship
- Share hopes and dreams for a common future

Still other writers distinguish among three kinds of intimacy—*physical* (sex, hugging, and touching), *affective* (feeling close), and *verbal* (self-disclosure). They also point out that physical intimacy is usually the least important of the three (Piorkowski, 1994).

Self-disclosure refers to communication in which one person reveals his or her honest thoughts and feelings to another person with the expectation that truly open communication will follow. In intimate relationships, people feel free to expose their weaknesses, idiosyncrasies, hopes, and insecurities without fear of ridicule or rejection (P. M. Brown, 1995).

Lovers will reveal their innermost thoughts, and marital partners feel comfortable in venting their frustrations because their spouses are considered trustworthy, respectful, and their best friends or confidantes. Self-disclosure does *not* include nagging, which decreases intimacy. If you pick at your partner, you're saying "I'm better than you. Shape up." Most people resent nagging because it implies superiority.

Intimacy includes more than the relationship between two adults. It is also a bond between children and parents, adult children and their parents, children and stepparents, children and grandparents, and so on. Even though much research has emphasized the role of the mother in intimate ties with children, a father's love is just as important. If a father is close to his children, he can play a crucial role in their development of self-esteem, their emotional stability, and their willingness to avoid drugs and other risky behavior (Rohner and Veneziano, 2001).

In adult love relationships, intimacy increases as people let down their defenses, learn to relax in each other's company, and find that they can expect reciprocal support during good and bad times (Josselson, 1992). Caring and intimacy, in turn, foster commitment.

Commitment

Many of my students, especially women, complain that their partners are afraid of "the big C"—commitment. The ultimate commitment is marriage, but as our high divorce rates show, marriage and commitment don't always go hand in hand (see Chapter 15).

Commitment is a person's intention to remain in a relationship "through thick and thin." Mutual commitment can arise out of (1) a sense of loyalty and fidelity to one's partner; (2) a religious, legal, or moral belief in the sanctity of marriage; (3) continued opti-

mism about future rewards—emotional, financial, sexual, or otherwise; and (4) strong emotional attachments, dependence, and love. Many people end their relationships, even if they still love each other, if they feel that mutual commitment is not increasing (P. M. Brown, 1995; Fehr, 1999; Sprecher, 1999).

In a healthy relationship, commitment has many positive aspects, such as affection, companionship, and trust. Each partner is available to the other not just during times of stress but day in and day out. Even when we're tempted to be unfaithful if our partners don't pay as much attention to us as we'd like or if we feel overwhelmed with daily responsibilities, committed partners will persevere during rough times.

Commitment in a secure relationship is not a matter of "hearts and flowers." Instead, it is behavior that demonstrates—repeatedly and in a variety of situations—that "I'm here, I will be here, I'm interested in what you do and what you think and feel, I will actively support your independent actions, I trust you, and you can trust me to be here if you need me" (Crowell and Waters, 1994: 32).

Making Connections

- How are your friendships similar to and different from your love relationships? If you can have many friends, can you also be in love with several people at the same time?

- How many times have you been in love? Were your feelings similar in all cases? Or did they change as you grew older?

Some Theories about Love and Loving

Why and how do we love? Biological explanations tend to focus on why we love. Psychological, sociological, and anthropological approaches try to explain how as well as why.

since you asked

Is love due to "raging hormones"?

The (Bio)Chemistry of Love

Biological perspectives maintain that love is grounded in evolution, biology, and chemistry. Biologists and some psychologists see romance as serving an evolutionary purpose: drawing men and women into long-

term partnerships that are essential to child rearing. On open and often dangerous grasslands, for example, one parent could care for offspring while the other foraged for food.

When lovers claim that they feel "high" and as if they are being swept away, it's probably because they are. A meeting of eyes, a touch of hands, or a whiff of scent sets off a flood of chemicals that starts in the brain and races along the nerves and through the bloodstream. The results are familiar: flushed skin, sweaty palms, and heavy breathing (Ackerman, 1994).

Natural amphetamines such as dopamine, norepinephrine, and phenylethylamine (PEA) are responsible for these symptoms. PEA is especially effective; it revs up the brain, causing feelings of elation, exhilaration, and euphoria:

> No wonder lovers can stay awake all night talking and caressing. No wonder they become so absent-minded, so giddy, so optimistic, so gregarious, so full of life. Naturally occurring amphetamines have pooled in the emotional centers of their brains; they are high on natural "speed" (Fisher, 1992: 53).

PEA highs don't last long, though, which may explain why passionate or romantic love is short-lived.

What about love that endures beyond the first few months? According to the biological perspective, as infatuation wanes and attachment grows, another group of chemicals, called *endorphins*, which are chemically similar to morphine and reside in the brain, takes over. Unlike PEA, endorphins calm the mind, eliminate pain, and reduce anxiety. This, biologists say, explains why people in long-lasting relationships report feeling comfortable and secure (Walsh, 1991; Fisher, 2004).

Medical researchers contend that the loss of a loved one ("a broken heart") may be linked to physical problems. According to brain images and blood tests, traumatic breakups can release stress hormones that travel to cells in one part of the brain. The resulting stress can bring on chest pain and even heart attacks (Najib et al., 2004; Wittstein, 2005).

There are two major problems with biological perspectives. First, they typically rely on tiny samples of volunteers (nine to 17 people, in some cases), and usually only women. Second, chemicals (like dopamine) that apparently trigger intense romantic love are also found in gamblers, cocaine users, and even people playing computer games. Thus, it's not clear how hormones "cause" love.

Sociological perspectives—and some psychological theories—claim that culture, not PEA, plays the role of Cupid. The social science theories that help us understand the components and processes of love include

In 2005, Japan's Princess Sayako, 36, gave up her royal status to marry a commoner— an urban planner who was her childhood friend. The Princess took driving lessons and practiced supermarket shopping in preparation for her new life.

attachment theory, Reiss's wheel theory of love, Sternberg's triangular theory of love, Lee's research on the styles of loving, and exchange theories.

Attachment Theory

Attachment theory proposes that our primary motivation in life is to be connected with other people because this is the only true security we will ever have. British psychiatrist John Bowlby (1969, 1984) asserted that attachment is an integral part of human behavior "from the cradle to the grave." Adults and children benefit by having someone look out for them—someone who cares about their welfare, provides for their basic emotional and physical needs, and is available when needed.

American psychologist Mary Ainsworth (Ainsworth et al., 1978), one of Bowlby's followers, assessed infant–mother attachment in her classic "strange situation" study. In both natural and laboratory settings, Ainsworth created mild stress for an infant by having the mother temporarily leave the baby with a friendly stranger in an unfamiliar room. When the mother returned, Ainsworth observed the infant's behavior toward the mother and the mother's reactions to that behavior.

Ainsworth identified three infant–mother attachment styles. She characterized about 60 percent of the infants as *secure* in their attachment, with sensitive and responsive mothers. The babies showed some distress when left with a stranger, but when the mother returned, they clung to her for just a short time and then went back to exploring and playing.

About 19 percent of the infants displayed *anxious/ambivalent* attachment styles when their mothers were inconsistent—sometimes affectionate, sometimes aloof. The infants showed distress at separation but rejected their mothers when they returned. The remaining 21 percent of the infants, most of whom had been reared by caregivers who ignored their physical and emotional needs, displayed *avoidant* behavior when their mothers returned after an absence.

Some of the infant attachment research has been criticized for relying almost exclusively on laboratory settings instead of natural ones and for not addressing cross-cultural differences in child-rearing practices (see Feeney and Noller, 1996). Despite such criticisms, some researchers propose that adult intimate relationships reflect these three attachment styles.

Using a "love quiz" based on Ainsworth's three attachment styles, Cindy Hazan and her associates interviewed 108 college students and 620 adults who said they were in love (Hazan and Shaver, 1987; Shaver et al., 1988). The respondents were asked to describe themselves in their "most important romance" using three measures:

- *Secure style:* I find it easy to get close to others and am comfortable depending on them and having them depend on me. I don't often worry about being abandoned or about someone getting too close to me.

- *Avoidant style:* I am somewhat uncomfortable being close to others; I find it difficult to trust them completely and to depend on them. I am nervous when anyone gets too close and when lovers want me to be more intimate than I feel comfortable being.

- *Anxious/ambivalent style:* Others are reluctant to get as close as I would like. I often worry that my partner doesn't really love me or won't want to stay with me. I want to merge completely with another person, and this desire sometimes scares people away.

The researchers also asked the respondents whether their childhood relationships with their parents had been warm or cold and rejecting. *Secure adults* (about 56 percent of the sample), who generally described their parents as having been warm and supportive, were more trusting of their romantic partners and more confident of a partner's love. They reported intimate, trusting, and happy relationships that lasted an average of 10 years.

Anxious/ambivalent adults (about 20 percent) tended to fall in love easily and wanted a commitment almost immediately. *Avoidant adults* (24 percent of the sample) had little trust for others, had the most cynical beliefs about love, and couldn't handle intimacy or commitment.

Several studies have tracked attachment styles from toddlerhood to adulthood and have found that attachment styles can change over the life course regardless of a person's early childhood experiences. If, for example, we experience disturbing events such as parental divorce, the breakup of a relationship, being dumped a few times in succession, or our own divorce, we may slip from a secure to an avoidant style. Alternatively, positive experiences can change a person from an avoidant to a secure attachment style (Kirkpatrick and Hazan, 1994; Lewis et al., 2000; Hollist and Miller, 2005).

Therefore, "the view that children's experiences set attachment styles in concrete is a myth" (Fletcher, 2002: 158). Instead, critics point out, events such as divorce, disease, and financial problems are far more important in shaping a child's well-being by age 18 than any early bonding with his or her mother (Lewis, 1997; Hays, 1998; Birns, 1999).

Reiss's Wheel Theory of Love

Sociologist Ira Reiss and his associates proposed a "wheel theory" of love (see *Figure 6.1*) that generated much research for several decades. Reiss describes four stages of love: rapport, self-revelation, mutual dependency, and personality need fulfillment (Reiss, 1960; Reiss and Lee, 1988).

In the first stage, partners establish rapport based on similar cultural backgrounds, such as upbringing, social class, religion, and education (see Chapter 1 on endogamy). Without this rapport, according to Reiss, would-be lovers would not have enough in common to establish an initial interest.

In the second stage, self-revelation brings the couple closer together. Because each person feels more at ease in the relationship, she or he is more likely to discuss hopes, desires, fears, and ambitions and to engage in sexual activities.

FIGURE 6.1 **The Wheel Theory of Love**
Reiss compared his four stages of love to the spokes of a wheel. As the text describes, a love relationship begins with the stage of rapport and, in a lasting relationship, continues to build as the wheel turns, deepening the partners' rapport, fulfillment, and mutual dependence and increasing the honesty of their self-revelation.

Source: Based on Reiss, 1960: 139–45.

In the third stage, as the couple becomes more intimate, the partners' *mutual dependency* increases: They exchange ideas, jokes, and sexual desires. In the fourth and final stage, the couple experiences *personality need fulfillment.* The partners confide in each other, make mutual decisions, support each other's ambitions, and bolster each other's self-confidence.

Like spokes on a wheel, these stages can turn many times—that is, they can be repeated. For example, partners build some rapport, then reveal bits of themselves, then build more rapport, then begin to exchange ideas, and so on.

The spokes may keep turning to produce a deep and lasting relationship. Or, during a fleeting romance, the wheel may stop after a few turns. The romantic wheel may "unwind"—even in a single evening—if the relationship droops because of arguments, lack of self-disclosure, or conflicting interests.

Sociologist Dolores Borland (1975) modified the wheel theory, proposing that love relationships can be viewed as "clocksprings" like those in a watch. Like clocksprings, relationships can wind up and unwind several times as love swells or ebbs. Tensions, caused by such events as pregnancy and the birth of a child, may wind the spring tightly. If the partners communicate and work toward a common goal, such tensions may solidify rather than sap the relationship. On the other hand, relationships can end abruptly if they are so tightly wound that the partners cannot grow or if one partner feels threatened by increasing or unwanted intimacy.

Others note that both the wheel theory and the clockspring theory ignore the variations in intensity between stages of a relationship. People may love each other, but the intensity of their feelings may be high on one dimension and low on another. For example, a couple may have rapport because of similar backgrounds but may experience little personality need fulfillment because one partner is unwilling to confide in the other (Albas and Albas, 1987; Warner, 2005).

Sternberg's Triangular Theory of Love

Instead of focusing on stages of love, psychologist Robert Sternberg and his associates (1986, 1988) have proposed that love has three important components: intimacy, passion, and decision/commitment:

- *Intimacy* encompasses feelings of closeness, connectedness, and bonding.

- *Passion* leads to romance, physical attraction, and sexual consummation.

- *Decision/commitment* has a short- and a long-term dimension. In the short term, partners make a decision to love each other; in the long term, they make a commitment to maintain that love over time.

According to Sternberg, the mix of intimacy, passion, and commitment can vary from one relationship to another. Relationships thus range from *nonlove,* in which all three components are absent, to *consummate love,* in which all the elements are present.

Even when all three components are present, they may vary in intensity and over time for each partner. Sternberg envisions these three components as forming a triangle (see *Figure 6.2*). In general, the greater the mismatching of dimensions, the greater the dissatisfaction in a relationship.

Let's use Jack and Jill to illustrate this model. If Jack and Jill are "perfectly matched" (*Figure 6.2A*), they will be equally passionate, intimate, and committed, and their love will be "perfect." Even if the degree to which each of them wants intimacy and commitment varies a little, they may still be "closely matched" (*Figure 6.2B*).

If both are about equally passionate, but Jack wants more intimacy than Jill does, and Jill is unwilling to

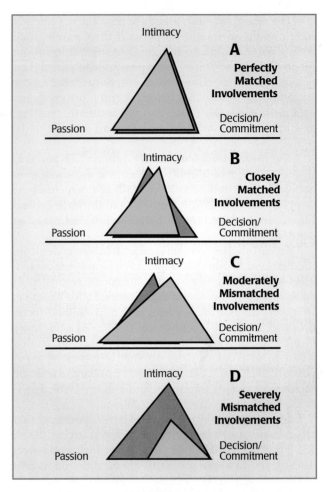

FIGURE 6.2 The Triangular Theory of Love
This theory of love suggests how people can be very close on some dimensions but very far apart on others.

SOURCE: Adapted from Sternberg, 1988.

make the long-term commitment that Jack wants, they will be "moderately mismatched" (*Figure 6.2C*). And if they want to marry each other (make a commitment), but Jill is neither as intimate nor as passionate as Jack, they will be "severely mismatched" (*Figure 6.2D*).

Some find this theory useful for counseling purposes. If, for instance, people recognized that love encompasses more than just passion—which is actually a fleeting component of love—there would be fewer unfulfilled expectations and less disappointment. A decline of passion is normal and inevitable if a relationship moves on to commitment, which creates a more stable union than just "being in love" (García, 1998).

Like the other perspectives we've discussed, the triangular theory of love has limitations. "Perfectly matched" exists only in Disney movies. Also, love varies depending on one's marital status. Intimacy and passion are much stronger in casual dating, for example, than in marriage. Commitment, on the other hand, is much higher among married couples than among dating or engaged couples (Lemieux and Hale, 2002).

Lee's Styles of Loving

Canadian sociologist John Lee (1973, 1974) developed one of the most widely cited and studied theories of love. According to Lee, there are six basic styles of loving: eros, mania, ludus, storge, agape, and pragma, all of which overlap and may vary in intensity (see *Table 6.1*).

EROS Eros (the root of the word *erotic*) is love of beauty. Because it is also characterized by powerful physical attraction, eros epitomizes "love at first sight." This is the kind of love, often described in romance novels, in which the lovers experience palpitations, lightheadedness, and intense emotional desire.

Erotic lovers want to know everything about each other—what she or he dreamed about last night and what happened on the way to work today. They often like to wear matching T-shirts and matching colors, to order the same foods when dining out, and to be identified with each other as totally as possible (Lasswell and Lasswell, 1976).

TABLE 6.1

Lee's Six Styles of Love

	Meaning	Major Characteristics
Eros	Love of beauty	Powerful physical attraction
Mania	Obsessive love	Jealousy, possessiveness, and intense dependency
Ludus	Playful love	Carefree quality, casualness; fun-and-games approach
Storge	Companionate love	Peaceful and affectionate love based on mutual trust and respect
Agape	Altruistic love	Self-sacrificing, kind, and patient love
Pragma	Practical love	Sensible, realistic

SOURCES: Adapted from Lee, 1973, 1974.

MANIA Characterized by obsessiveness, jealousy, possessiveness, and intense dependency, **mania** may be expressed as anxiety, sleeplessness, loss of appetite, headaches, and even suicide because of real or imagined rejection by the desired person. Manic lovers are consumed by thoughts of their beloved and have an insatiable need for attention and signs of affection.

Mania is often associated with low self-esteem and a poor self-concept. As a result, manic people typically are not attractive to individuals who have a strong self-concept and high self-esteem (Lasswell and Lasswell, 1976).

LUDUS Ludus is carefree and casual love that is considered "fun and games." Ludic lovers often have several partners at one time and are not possessive or jealous, primarily because they don't want their lovers to become dependent on them. Ludic lovers have sex for fun, not emotional rapport. In their sexual encounters, they are typically self-centered and may be exploitative because they do not want commitment, which they consider "scary."

STORGE Storge (pronounced "STOR-gay") is a slow-burning, peaceful, and affectionate love that "just comes naturally" with the passage of time and the enjoyment of shared activities. Storgic relationships lack the ecstatic highs and lows that characterize some other styles.

Sex occurs late in this type of relationship, and the goals are usually marriage, home, and children. Even if they break up, storgic lovers are likely to remain good friends. Because there is mutual trust between them, temporary separations are not a problem. In storgic love, affection develops over the years, as in many lasting marriages. Passion may be replaced by spirituality, respect, and contentment in each other's company (Murstein, 1974).

AGAPE The classical Christian type of love, **agape** (pronounced "AH-gah-pay"), is an altruistic, self-sacrificing love that is directed toward all humankind. Agape is always kind and patient and never jealous or demanding, and does not seek reciprocity. Lee points out, however, that he did not find an outright example of agape during his interviews.

Intense agape can border on masochism. For example, an agapic person might wait indefinitely for a lover to be released from prison, might tolerate an alcoholic or drug-addicted spouse, or might be willing to live with a partner who engages in illegal activities or infidelity (Lasswell and Lasswell, 1976).

PRAGMA Pragma is rational love based on practical considerations, such as compatibility. Indeed, it can be described as "love with a shopping list." A pragmatic person seeks compatibility on characteristics such as his or her background, education, religious views, occupational interests, and recreational pursuits. If one person does not work out, the pragmatic person moves on, quite rationally, to search for someone else.

Pragmatic lovers look out for their partners, encouraging them, for example, to ask for a promotion or finish college. They are also practical when it comes to divorce. For example, a couple might stay together until the youngest child finishes high school or until both partners find better jobs (Lasswell and Lasswell, 1976).

Researchers have developed dozens of scales to measure Lee's concepts of love (see Tzeng, 1993). Use the "What Do *You* Expect from Love?" box to reflect on some of your attitudes about love.

Exchange Theory

Social scientists often describe love as a *social exchange process* (see Chapter 2). Romantic and long-term love relationships involve social exchanges in the sense that they provide rewards and costs for each partner. If the initial interactions are reciprocal and mutually satisfying, a relationship will continue. If, however, our needs are mismatched (see *Figure 6.2*) or change drastically over time, our love interests may wane or shift between adolescence and later life.

LOVE DURING ADOLESCENCE Exchange theory is especially helpful in explaining why romantic love is short-lived among adolescents. Adolescent love is usually intense but also self-centered. Because adolescents are still "finding themselves," they often form relationships with peers who offer many benefits and few costs ("I can call him whenever I'm lonely" or "I'm hookin' up with a knockout cheerleader this weekend").

LOVE DURING ADULTHOOD As we mature, our perceptions of rewards and costs usually change. We might decide, for example, that nurturing a relationship with someone who's patient and confident outweighs the benefits of being with someone who's "a good catch" or "a knockout" but is controlling and self-centered.

 ## Applying What You've Learned

What Do You *Expect from Love?*

Use this scale to examine your own and your partner's feelings. If you've never been in love or don't have a partner now, answer in terms of what you think your responses might be in the future. There are no wrong answers to these statements; they're designed simply to increase your understanding of different types of love. For each item, mark **1** for "strongly agree," **2** for "moderately agree," **3** for "neutral," **4** for "moderately disagree," and **5** for "strongly disagree."

Eros

1. My partner and I were attracted to each other immediately after we first met.
2. Our lovemaking is very intense and satisfying.
3. My partner fits my standards of physical beauty and good looks.

Ludus

4. What my partner doesn't know about me won't hurt him/ her.
5. I sometimes have to keep my partner from finding out about other partners.
6. I could get over my partner pretty easily and quickly.

Pragma

7. In choosing my partner, I believed it was best to love someone with a similar background.
8. An important factor in choosing my partner was whether or not he/she would be a good parent.
9. One consideration in choosing my partner was how he/she would affect my career.

Agape

10. I would rather suffer myself than let my partner suffer.
11. My partner can use whatever I own as she/he chooses.
12. I would endure all things for the sake of my partner.

Storge

13. I expect to always be friends with the people I date.
14. The best kind of love grows out of a long friendship.
15. Love is a deep friendship, not a mysterious, passionate emotion.

SOURCES: Lasswell and Lasswell, 1976, pp. 211–24; Hendrick and Hendrick, 1992a, 1992b; Levesque, 1993, pp. 219–50.

LOVE DURING LATER LIFE We also weigh the costs and benefits of love later in life. In a national survey of people age 60 and over, 90 percent said that they wanted a romantic partner who had moral values, a pleasant personality, a good sense of humor, and intelligence ("Half of older Americans. . .," 1998).

The survey found several distinct differences between men and women, however. Most women were interested in financial security while most men wanted partners who were interested in sex. Men (67 percent) were more likely than women (48 percent) to want a partner with "a terrific body." Because older women are less likely than men to be affluent, the women may see the "benefits" of a love relationship differently than men (see Chapters 8 and 17).

Making Connections

- Return to *Figure 6.2* and think about your current love relationship. (If you are not currently involved with someone, reflect on a past relationship.) Are you and your partner "matched" in intimacy, passion, and commitment? Or is any one of these characteristics not important in your relationship?

- Think about Lee's styles of loving (*Table 6.1*). Do you and your partner have similar or different attitudes about love? If your styles of loving differ, does this create problems, or does it make the relationship more interesting? Did your past relationships break up because your partner's style of loving was different from yours?

Functions of Love and Loving

One historian argues that love is dysfunctional because it creates high divorce rates. That is, because many Americans are in love with love, their unrealistic expectations result in unhappiness and the dissolution of marriages (Coontz, 2005). In contrast, a number of researchers and family practitioners believe that love is at the core of healthy and well-functioning relationships and families. Love fulfills many purposes that range from ensuring human survival to providing opportunities for recreation.

since you asked

Why is love important?

Love Ensures Human Survival

In a tongue-in-cheek article, one writer suggested that romantic love is a "nuisance" and "a nasty trick played upon us by nature to keep our species going," especially during the childbearing years (Chance, 1988: 23). In fact, love *does* keep our species going. Because children can be conceived without love, there is no guarantee that people who engage in sex will feel an obligation to care for their offspring and make sure they survive. Unlike sex, love implies a commitment. By promoting an interest in caring for helpless infants, love ensures the survival of the human species.

Love Prolongs Life

Babies and children who are deprived of love may develop a wide variety of problems—depression, headaches, physiological impairments, and psychosomatic difficulties—that sometimes last a lifetime. In contrast, infants who are loved and cuddled typically gain more weight, cry less, and smile more. By age five, they have higher IQs and score higher on language tests (Hetherington et al., 2005).

Perhaps the most dramatic example of the effects of lack of love is suicide. People who commit suicide often feel socially isolated, rejected, unloved, or unworthy of love. Suicide is far more prevalent among divorced people than among married people. Divorced people also tend to suffer more serious illnesses and more chronic disabling conditions than do married people (see Chapters 10 and 14).

Love doesn't guarantee that we'll live to be 100, of course. Instead, researchers suggest, there is a link between loving relationships and living longer.

Love Enhances Our Physical Health

Numerous studies show a connection between our emotions and our physical well-being. About 25 percent of people who visit a doctor have physical symptoms that are probably due to their emotional state (Roan, 2003).

Chronic stress, whether due to a demanding job or to an unloving home life, elevates blood pressure. Arguing or just thinking about a fight also raises blood pressure. People in unhappy marriages may be less healthy because stress can change the levels of certain hormones in the blood and weaken the immune system. As a result, people who are stressed out face a higher risk of heart disease and other illnesses (Kiecolt-Glaser and Newton, 2001; Cacioppo et al., 2002; Glynn et al., 2002).

The family is usually our earliest and most important source of love and emotional support.

According to a highly-respected heart physician, love is good medicine:

Love and intimacy are at the root of what makes us sick and what makes us well. . .People who feel lonely are many times more likely to get cardiovascular disease than those who have a strong sense of connection and community. I'm not aware of any other factor in medicine—not diet, not smoking, not exercise, not genetics, not drugs, not surgery—that has a greater impact on our quality of life, incidence of illness, and premature death. In part, this is because people who are lonely are more likely to engage in self-destructive behavior (Ornish, 2005: 56).

In contrast, positive feelings can contribute to better health. Friends, family, and positive relationships over a lifetime can help counteract the normal wear and tear of life as we age. People in their 70s who have had a lot of supportive friends, good relationships with their parents and spouses, and little criticism from their spouses and children suffer from fewer risk factors for diseases and death, including high blood pressure, high cholesterol levels, and abnormal blood sugar metabolism (Seeman et al., 2002).

Love Improves the Quality of Our Lives

Love fosters self-esteem. From a solid basis of loving family relationships, children acquire the confidence to face the world outside the family (Bodman and Peter-

son, 1995). Terminally ill patients and paraplegics often report that they can accept death or cope with their disabilities when they are surrounded by supportive, caring, and loving family members and friends (see Chapter 17).

Not having a secure base of love, on the other hand, can lead to aggression, hostility, diminished self-confidence, and emotional problems. At least half of all teenage runaways are escaping a home where there is no love, as evidenced by violence, abuse, or incest. Battered wives become suspicious, fearful, and bitter (see Chapter 14).

Love Is Fun

Without love, life is "a burden and a bore" (Safilios-Rothschild, 1977: 9). Even though love can be painful, it is also enjoyable and can be exciting.

It is both comforting and fun to plan to see a loved one, to travel together, to write and receive e-mail messages and exchange presents, to share personal activities, to have someone care for you when you are sick or grumpy, and to know that you can always depend on someone for comfort, support, and advice.

Overall, love and intimacy are critical for our emotional and physical well-being. In contrast, isolation, loneliness, hostility, anger, depression, and similar feelings often contribute to suffering, disease, and premature death.

Experiencing Love

When we discuss this chapter, I ask my students a simple question: "Who do you think is in love with someone right now?" Most say that people who are in love are probably young women who are dating or living with a boyfriend. Wrong on all counts. According to a recent national poll, those who say that they are "in love" are most likely to be married men between the ages of 30 and 49 (see *Figure 6.3*).

Why do so many of us assume that only young unmarried adults, especially women, are the most likely to seek and experience love? Among other reasons, we're inundated with Hollywood images of love that have nothing to do with real life. Movies rarely portray love between married couples. Instead, most movies and television shows emphasize sex rather than love, especially among young adults of unhappily-married couples (see Chapter 5).

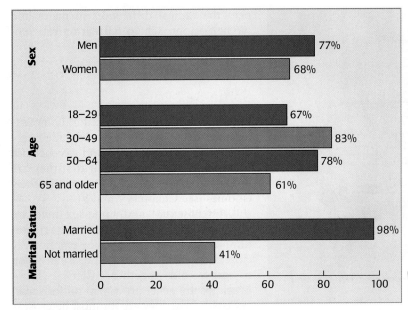

FIGURE 6.3 **Who's in Love?**
This Gallup poll asked people, "Would you say you are—or are not—in love with someone right now?" Here are the responses of the 72 percent who said "yes."

SOURCE: Based on Saad, 2004.

For most people, caring, trust, respect, and honesty are central to love. There are some differences, however, in the ways that men and women conceive of love and express it. And although heterosexuals and homosexuals share many of the same feelings and behaviors, there are also some differences in their experiences of love.

Are Women or Men More Romantic?

During a recent online discussion, Emily, one of my students, wrote:

> It's important to distinguish the truly romantic men from the "What-do-I-need-to-do-to-get-her-in-bed" romantic men. Truly romantic men do things for you that take a substantial amount of time and energy and involve some sacrifice on their part. For example, for Valentine's Day my boyfriend spent hours making me an absolutely beautiful Valentine's Day card. That meant more to me than dinner at a fancy restaurant (Author's files).

Many of the female students in class felt that Emily's boyfriend was an exception. Contrary to such popular opinion, however, many men seem to fall in love faster and are more likely than women to initiate romantic e-mail exchanges (see "Data Digest").

According to a national poll, 17 percent of men compared with 14 percent of women think about a past love every day. And almost one in four men (24 percent), compared with only one in 10 women (11 percent), say that they have been in love five or more times since they turned 18. Men are also just as likely as women to believe that "True love lasts forever" and that there is only one person "out there" who's meant for them (Covel, 2003; Popenoe and Whitehead, 2003).

Both women and men tend to link love and sex in their romantic relationships (Hendrick and Hendrick, 2002). Women are more likely to expect some of the trappings of romantic love, however. For example, whereas 62 percent of men say that "just spending time together" would be an ideal Valentine's Day celebration, 53 percent of women would probably break up with someone who didn't give them a gift (Yin, 2002; Christenson, 2003).

Do such data suggest that women are more materialistic than men in their love relationships? Or that women are more likely than men to see gifts as tangible proof of a partner's affection? For example, one of women's biggest complaints is that the men who profess to love them are reluctant to marry. Women sometimes belittle men for being "commitment dodgers," "commitment phobics," "paranoid about commitment," and "afraid of the M word" (Crittenden, 1999; Millner and Chiles, 1999). Romance and commitment are different, however. Men can be very romantic but not see love as necessarily leading to marriage (see Chapter 9).

Are Women or Men More Intimate?

Some years ago, advice columnist Ann Landers sparked a nationwide controversy when she reported that many women prefer being touched, hugged, cuddled, and kissed over having sexual intercourse. When women complain about a lack of intimacy, they usually mean that the man doesn't communicate his thoughts or feelings. Many men believe that such expectations are unfair; they feel that they show intimacy through sex. Whereas many women want to feel close emotionally before being sexual, many men assume that sex is the same as emotional closeness (Piorkowski, 1994).

since you asked

Are men more interested in sex than women?

Edward Leedskin, born in Latvia in 1887, was engaged to marry his one true love. His 16-year-old sweetheart cancelled the wedding just one day before the ceremony. Heartbroken, Leedskin immigrated to the United States. Filled with obsession and undying passion, he labored for over 28 years to build "Coral Castle," a monument dedicated to his lost love, in southern Florida. Leedskin was just 5 feet tall and weighed only 100 pounds but used blocks of coral rock, some weighing as much as 30 tons, without any human assistance or modern machinery.

Love relationships and intimacy are complex. For wives, intimacy may mean talking things over. For husbands, as the box "Do I Love You . . .?" shows, it may mean *doing* things (such as taking care of the family cars). According to one woman, Eddie, her husband, shows his love through "small, everyday courtesies":

> *Eddie cleans the bugs off my windshield so I don't have to. He removes all his favorite cassettes from the tape deck in the car and puts mine in before I go to work. . . . At home, he makes sure I have my favorite bottled water in the fridge . . . (Ann Landers, 2001:3D).*

Although men and women may show affection differently, there are more similarities than differences between them in their attitudes toward love. In a study based on Lee's typology (see *Table 6.1*), Montgomery and Sorell (1997) analyzed the attitudes of people aged 17 to 70. They found that *both* women and men valued passion (eros), friendship and companionship (storge), and self-sacrifice (agape). As a result, Montgomery and Sorell criticized the shallowness of popular books, such as Gray's *Men Are from Mars, Women Are from Venus,* that trum-

pet "the radical differences in men's and women's approach to partnering relationships" (p. 60).

Same-Sex Love

Homophobia, fear and hatred of homosexuals, has decreased in the last decade or so. One result is that lesbians and gay men are more likely to openly admit that they are lovers and to participate in commitment ceremonies (see Chapters 7 and 9).

Heterosexual and same-sex love are very similar. Regardless of sexual orientation, most partners want to be emotionally close, expect faithfulness, and usually plan to grow old together (Clark, 1999). Breakups are generally as painful for same-sex partners as they are for most heterosexual couples. A few years ago, for example, one of my best students was devastated when his partner left. The student's grades plummeted because he was unable to concentrate on his courses. He became depressed and wanted to drop out of college. Thanks to counseling and supportive friends, he finished his senior year and graduated with honors.

One of the biggest differences between heterosexual and same-sex love is that lesbians and gay men are usually criticized for showing their affection in public. Otherwise, there are more similarities between men and women than between heterosexuals and gays in how they express sexual love (see Chapter 7).

Barriers to Experiencing Love

A number of obstacles can block our search for love. Some are *macro-level*—for example, the impersonality of mass society, demographic variables, and our culture's emphasis on individualism. Others are *micro-level*—such as certain kinds of personality characteristics and family experiences.

Understanding some of these barriers can give us more choices and more control over our decisions and our lives. Recognizing some of the macro-level hurdles, especially, can help us accept some constraints that we can't change.

MASS SOCIETY AND DEMOGRAPHIC FACTORS Our society's booming technologies—such as answering ma-

If a partner gets fed up with their "me, me, me" self-focus, narcissists aren't bothered by breaking up. Because they have already been cheating, they can link up right way with another "trophy" romance waiting in the wings. In some cases, narcissists can be dangerous. If they feel rejected—even outside of dating relationships—they can become angry, aggressive, and even violent (Campbell et al., 2002; Twenge and Campbell, 2003).

Jealousy: Trying to Control Love

A few years ago, a 78-year-old great-grandmother killed her 85-year-old ex-boyfriend. She shot him in the head four times as he read a newspaper in a senior citizens' home. She was angry that their year-long romance was ending and that the man had found another companion. "I did it, and I'd do it again!" she shouted to the police (Bluestein, 2005).

since you asked

Is intense jealousy a proof of one's love?

Typically, and regardless of age, people experience *jealousy* when they believe that a rival is competing for a lover's affection. The jealous person feels threatened and is suspicious, obsessive, angry, and resentful. Some people are even jealous when their partner spends time with family members or relatives, or in pursuing hobbies (Brehm, 1992; Hanna, 2003).

WHY ARE LOVERS JEALOUS? It bears repeating that love flourishes when it is based on trust and respect. In contrast, jealousy is usually an unhealthy manifestation of insecurity, low self-confidence, and possessiveness (Douglas and Atwell, 1988; Farrell, 1997). All of us have some of these traits, so why are some of us more jealous than others?

Jealous people tend to depend heavily on their partners for their own self-esteem, consider themselves inadequate as mates, and feel that they are more deeply involved in their relationship than their partner is. For example, college students who grew up in homes characterized by continual parental conflict or rejecting, overprotective parents are more likely than others to report jealousy and fears of abandonment in their love relationships (Hayashi and Strickland, 1998).

In some cases, people who are jealous have been or are still unfaithful to their partners. They distrust a partner because of their own cheating. In other cases, jealousy is triggered by rivalry. A staple of sitcom romances is that a little bit of jealousy is good for a relationship: It reminds a partner not to take the loved one for granted. In reality, jealousy is hostile and destructive.

ARE WOMEN OR MEN MORE JEALOUS? There is ongoing debate about this question. According to evolutionary psychologists, jealousy evolved a million or so years ago. Men worried about sexual infidelity because if they were cuckolded, they might unknowingly end up raising someone else's child rather than passing on their own genes.

In contrast, women were more concerned about their partners' emotional than sexual entanglements. If a man became emotionally attached to other women, who would bring home the food and ensure their children's survival? Thus, according to evolutionary psychologists, twice as many men as women report being more upset by imagining their partners' "enjoying passionate sexual intercourse" with other people than by imagining their partners' "forming a deep emotional attachment" (Buss et al., 1996; Buss, 2000).

Some researchers have criticized evolutionary perspectives for forcing respondents into an "either/or" answer: "Do you feel more threatened with sexual *or* emotional infidelity?" In addition, some critics maintain, evolutionary approaches have relied on samples of college students, whose responses are not representative of the larger population (DeSteno et al., 2002).

Others contend that evolutionary studies are limited because they ask only hypothetical questions ("How would you feel *if* your partner were unfaithful?"). When Harris (2003) asked people (other than college students) about their *actual* experiences, she found that men and women—whether heterosexual or gay—were more jealous of emotional than of sexual infidelity.

Harris speculates that people are more jealous about a mate's emotional affairs for two reasons. First, they blame themselves ("Maybe I don't satisfy her or him sexually"). Second, they see an emotional affair as more threatening because it could develop into a long-term relationship that may produce offspring who compete for the father's affection and resources.

JEALOUSY AND STALKING Some jealous lovers become obsessed with the desired partner. They constantly daydream about him or her, make numerous phone calls, send flowers, cards, gifts, and love letters, or continuously check up on a partner's whereabouts.

Stalking—behaviors (such as telephone harassment and surveillance) that invade a person's privacy and cause fear—is a serious problem. California passed the first antistalking law in 1990. By the mid-1990s, all 50 states had adopted similar legislation. Unfortunately, these laws rarely discourage suitors (almost always men) from threatening, harassing, or even killing those who reject them.

We often hear about people who stalk celebrities—like the man who scaled the eight-foot wall around pop

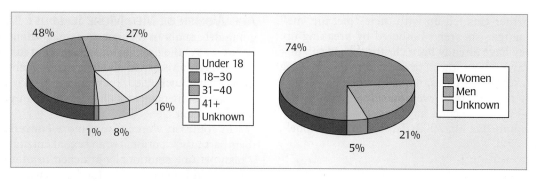

FIGURE 6.4 **Who are the Victims of Cyberstalking?**
SOURCE: Working to Halt Online Abuse, 2006.

star Madonna's property or the woman who broke into the home of talk show host David Letterman. However, most stalking involves average people: 8 percent of women and 2 percent of men have been stalked in their lifetime. About 87 percent of all stalkers are men who hound women ("Stalking," 2005).

Cyberstalking is threatening behavior or unwanted advances using e-mail, instant messaging, and other electronic communications devices. Many chat rooms may evolve into offline stalking, including abusive or harassing phone calls, vandalism, threatening or obscene mail, trespassing, and physical assault ("Working to Halt Online Abuse," 2006).

Cyberstalking has been increasing. And, as in offline stalking, the majority of cases involve former intimates, most of the victims are women (see *Figure 6.4*), and the stalkers are generally determined to control the woman. Cyberstalking is sometimes more dangerous than offline stalking because the perpetrators can be anywhere in the country, can post inflammatory messages on bulletin boards and in chat rooms, and electronic communications are difficult to trace (U.S. Department of Justice, 2001b).

IS JEALOUSY UNIVERSAL?
Although it is widespread, jealousy is *not* universal. Surveying two centuries of anthropological reports, Hupka (1991) found two types of cultures: In one type, jealousy was rare (for example, the Todas of southern India); in the other, jealousy was common (for example, the Apache Indians of North America).

Toda culture discouraged possessiveness of material objects or people. It placed few restrictions on sexual gratification, and it did not make marriage a condition for respecting women. In contrast, Apache society prized virginity, paternity, and fidelity. While a man was away from home, for example, he had a close relative keep secret watch over his wife and report on her behavior when he returned.

Based on the variations he found in different cultures, Hupka concluded that jealousy is neither universal nor innate. Instead, jealousy is more common in societies in which women are regarded as "property" and where expressing jealousy is culturally acceptable.

Filmed in 1987, Fatal Attraction *has become a "modern classic" in dramatizing some of the negative effects of stalking.*

Other Types of Controlling Behavior

Jealousy is not the only type of unhealthy, controlling behavior that may occur in love relationships. Threatening to withdraw love or creating guilt feelings can be deeply distressing. Inflicting severe emotional and physical abuse can also be devastating.

"IF YOU LOVED ME . . ." One of the most common ways of pressuring people to have sex (especially by men) is to accuse a partner of not loving them: "If you *really* loved me, you'd show it."

People threaten to withdraw love to manipulate other kinds of behavior as well. Faculty members hear many accounts of students who choose majors they hate because they don't want to disappoint parents who in-sist that they must become a doctor, a lawyer, an accountant, and so on. I've seen women drop out of college because their husbands or boyfriends blamed them of "always studying" instead of taking care of the house, preparing dinner on time, and being free on weekends.

Essentially, controlling people want power over others. They use "love" to manipulate and exploit those who care about them. With pressure and ultimatums, they force their partners or family members to sacrifice their own interests to please the controller and make him or her happy.

Controllers are not all alike: "A wealthy executive may use money and influence, while an attractive person may use physical allure and sex" to manipulate others (Jones and Schechter, 1992: 11). Moreover, as the box "If This Is Love, Why Do I Feel So Bad?" shows, controllers

Ask Yourself

If This Is Love, Why Do I Feel So Bad?

If you feel bad, what you're experiencing may be *control*, not love. Controllers use whatever tactics are necessary to maintain power over another person: nagging, cajoling, coaxing, flattery, charm, threats, self-pity, blame, insults, or humiliation.

In the worst cases, controllers may physically injure and even murder people who refuse to be controlled. As you read this list, check any items that seem familiar to you. Individually, the items may seem unimportant, but if you check off more than two or three, you may be dealing with a controller instead of forging your own choices in life.

- ☐ My partner calls me names: "dummy," "jackass," "whore," "creep," "bitch," "moron."
- ☐ My partner always criticizes me and makes even a compliment sound like a criticism: "This is the first good dinner you've cooked in months."
- ☐ Always right, my partner continually corrects things I say or do. If I'm five minutes late, I'm afraid my partner will be mad.
- ☐ My partner withdraws into silence, and I have to figure out what I've done wrong and apologize for it.
- ☐ My partner is jealous when I talk to new people.
- ☐ My partner often phones or unexpectedly comes by the place where I work to see if I'm "okay."
- ☐ My partner acts very cruelly and then says I'm too sensitive and can't take a joke.
- ☐ When I try to express my opinion about something, my partner either doesn't respond, walks away, or makes fun of me.
- ☐ I have to account for every dime I spend, but my partner keeps me in the dark about our bank accounts.
- ☐ My partner says that if I ever leave he or she will commit suicide and I'll be responsible.
- ☐ When my partner has a temper tantrum, he or she says it's my fault or the children's.
- ☐ My partner makes fun of my body.
- ☐ Whether my partner is with us or not, he or she is jealous of every minute I spend with my family or other relatives or friends.
- ☐ My partner grills me about what happened whenever I go out.
- ☐ My partner makes sexual jokes about me in front of the children or other people.
- ☐ My partner throws things at me or hits, shoves, or pushes me.

SOURCE: Based on Jones and Schechter, 1992: 16-22.

use a variety of strategies to dominate and control a relationship. They may also switch strategies from time to time to keep the controlled person off balance.

THE GUILT TRIP People often use guilt to justify actions that have nothing to do with love. Some parents, especially, rely on love and guilt to influence their children's behavior: "If you cared about me, you'd go to college. I've made a lot of sacrifices to save up for your education"; or "If you marry that Catholic [or Jew or Protestant], how can I face Father Mulcahey [or Rabbi Katz or Mr. Beirne] again!"

The guilt trip does not end when children become young adults. Older parents and relatives sometimes use guilt to manipulate middle-aged children. One of the most disabling guilt trips is the "affection myth," in which children are taught that love is synonymous with caregiving. Children and grandchildren may feel that, regardless of their own circumstances, they must care for needy elderly family members at home. As a result, younger family members sometimes endure enormous stress, even though their elderly relatives would get much better medical care at a good-quality nursing facility (see Chapter 17).

In other situations, married couples or couples who are living together try to control a person through a sense of obligation: "If you are the right kind of person, you will take care of me and never leave. Can't you see how much I care about you?" (Harvey and Weber, 2002: 90). Such comments reflect emotional blackmail, not love.

EMOTIONAL AND PHYSICAL ABUSE People sometimes use love to justify severe emotional or physical neglect and abuse. A partner who is sarcastic or controlling or a parent who severely spanks or verbally humiliates a child is not expressing love for the child's "own good," as they often insist. They are simply being angry and brutal. Violence is *never* a manifestation of love (see Chapter 14).

"The most insidious aspect of family violence" is that children grow up unable to distinguish between love and violence and believe "that it is acceptable to hit the people you love" (Gelles and Cornell, 1990: 20). The film *What's Love Got to Do with It?*, based on singer Tina Turner's biography, portrays Turner as enduring many years of violence because she believed that doing so proved her love and commitment to her husband, Ike.

OTHER "PERVERSE" REASONS FOR LOVE Some people are in love for "dubious and downright perverse reasons" (Solomon, 2002). In many cases, we profess love for someone even though we are really afraid of being alone or coping with changes (such as meeting new people after breaking up). Or we might stay in a bad relationship because we want to avoid a partner's hostility after breaking up.

In other cases, we don't want to hurt someone's feelings by telling them we don't love them. And if we promise to "love, honor, and obey" (although many couples have substituted "cherish" for "obey" in their marital vows), we feel an obligation to love our spouse even though our love has dwindled over the years (or we never really loved him or her to begin with). In addition, is it realistic to promise to love someone for the next 50 to 60 years—especially if their behavior becomes offensive or abusive?

Unrequited Love

In unrequited love, one does not reciprocate another's romantic feelings. Why not? First, a person may "fall upward" in love. That is, someone who's "average" in appearance may fall in love with someone who's gorgeous. People tend to choose partners who are similar to themselves in dating and marriage (see Chapter 8). Therefore, love for someone who is much better looking may go unrequited.

The rebuff is especially painful if the person senses that physical appearance is the major reason for being cast aside (Baumeister and Wotman, 1992). We often hear both women and men complain that the object of their affections "never took the time to get to know me." These accusations imply that other characteristics such as personality, intelligence, and common interests should be more important than looks.

Second, love may be unrequited when only one of the partners wants to progress from hooking up or casual dating to a serious romance. It can be very upsetting, even traumatic, to realize that the person one is dating, and perhaps having sexual relations with, is in the relationship "just for the fun of it" (as with ludic lovers, including narcissists) and does not want to become more serious or exclusive.

Some people wait, sometimes for years, for someone to return their love. They assume that the situation "is bound to get better" (Duck, 1998). Forget about it. It's emotionally and physically healthier to let go of an unrequited love and develop relationships with people who care about you.

Making Connections

- Are you a narcissist? If not, have you ever gone out with a narcissist? If so, how long did the relationship last? Did you enjoy the relationship in some ways?

- Have you ever dumped someone? If so, how did you cut the strings? Or, if you were the one who was dumped, how did you deal with the situation?

How Couples Change: Romantic and Long-Term Love

Romantic love can be both exhilarating and disappointing. In contrast, long-term love provides security and constancy. Let's begin with some of the characteristics of romantic love.

Some Characteristics of Romantic Love

Romantic love is usually a passionate and dizzying experience:

■ Lovers find it impossible to work, study, or do anything but think about the beloved.

■ Their moods fluctuate wildly; they are ecstatic when they hope they might be loved, despairing when they feel that they're not.

■ They find it impossible to believe that they could ever love again.

■ They fantasize about how their partner will declare his or her love.

■ They care so desperately about the other person that nothing else matters; they are willing to sacrifice anything for love.

■ Their love is "blind," and they idealize each other (Tennov, cited in Hatfield, 1983: 114).

Romantic love is intense, emotional, passionate, and sometimes melodramatic (see *Table 6.2*). Romantic love can also be self-absorbed and self-serving. As you saw earlier, for example, narcissists enhance their own self-esteem rather than express interest in their partner ("Tell me what else you like about *me*" versus "How are *you* doing?").

People from other cultures often see romantic love as bizarre and frivolous, but those in Western countries take it very seriously (see "Data Digest"). Romantic love is considered the most legitimate reason for dating, living together, getting married, or getting a divorce ("the spark is gone"). Romantic love thrives on two beliefs—love at first sight and fate.

since you asked

If you don't feel romantic about your partner, can you still be in love with him or her?

LOVE AT FIRST SIGHT Romantic love was less common in the United States in the 1800s than it is today for several reasons: Life expectancy was shorter, living in isolated towns and homes made it difficult to meet a variety of lovers, and most people did not live long enough to fall in love more than once. Today, with increased life spans, greater geographic mobility, and high divorce rates, we may fall in love with many people during our lifetime.

More than half of Americans believe in love at first sight but such beliefs decrease with age and experience.

TABLE 6.2

How Would You Describe Passionate Love?

Over the years, Professor Sharon L. Hanna (2003: 288-289) has asked her students at Southeast Community College in Lincoln, Nebraska, to describe passionate love as if they were writing "an all-consuming romantic novel." Here are some of the students' contributions. Does any of this sound familiar? What other descriptions would you add?

Survival

"I can't live without you."

"I'm nothing without you."

"If you ever leave me, I'll die."

Physical sensations

"Love feels zingy, and you get dingy."

"I just melt when you look at me."

Walking on air or clouds, weak knees, dizziness

Palpitating heart, shortness of breath; can't eat, sleep, or think

Perfection

"No one has ever loved like this before."

"It's perfect. You're perfect."

"Nothing will ever go wrong."

Exaggerated promises

"All I need is you."

"I'd do anything for you."

"I'll never look at another man (or woman)."

Exclusivity and possessiveness

"You're the only one for me."

"You belong to me and I belong to you."

"I'm jealous and you're jealous, and that means we're in love."

"Just the two of us. Nothing else matters."

By permission of Johnny Hart and Creators Syndicate, Inc.

People who are now in their 70s are less likely than those in their 20s to believe that love is as good as people expect (see "Data Digest"). People who are in a romantic relationship report being happier than those who aren't. Still, people who are older—and especially those who have been married a while—are more likely to view love as a commitment rather than as a series of "thrills" or "highs" (Dush and Amato, 2005; see, also, Chapter 10).

FATE Some people see fate as an important component of romantic love. Songs tell us that "you were meant for me" and "that old black magic has me in its spell." In reality, fate has little to do with romance. Romantic love is typically ignited not by fate but by such factors as similar socioeconomic background, physical attractiveness, and a need for intimacy (Shea and Adams, 1984; Benassi, 1985).

day after day, year after year. Thus, it's easier to fall in love than it is to stay in love.

Second, romantic love is self-centered, whereas long-term love is altruistic. Romantic lovers are often swept away by their own fantasies and obsessions, but lasting love often requires putting the partner before oneself and making him or her feel cherished.

Third, romance is typically short-lived because love changes over time. Flaws that seemed "cute" during a whirlwind courtship may become unbearable a year after the wedding. For example, his dumpy furniture may have seemed quaint until she realized that he refuses to spend any money on home furnishings. And values, especially religious values, become increasingly important after the birth of the first child (Trotter, 1986).

Fourth, long-term love grows and develops whereas romantic love is typically immature. Romantic lovers often feel insecure about themselves or the relationship. As a result, one of the partners may demand constant attention, a continuous display of affection, and daily "I love you" reassurances (Dilman, 1998). Most of us appreciate tokens of love, verbal or behavioral. However, never-ending and self-absorbed commands such as "prove to me that you love me" can become tedious and annoying.

Love in Long-Term Relationships

Where most people go astray is in equating romance with love, not realizing that it's only a steppingstone. Romance draws people together and "jumpstarts" love, but it often fizzles because it's narrow and needy (Brander, 2004).

Some characteristics of romantic and long-term love overlap. Both reflect such attributes as trust, understanding, and honesty (see *Figure 6.5*). There are also some striking differences.

First, romantic love is simple, whereas lasting love is more complicated. It takes much less effort to plan a romantic evening than to be patient with a partner

Unique to Romantic Love	Common to Both	Unique to Long-Term Love
• Romantic Walks • Obsession • Longing • Candlelit Trysts • Going Out For Dinner • Picnics and Sunsets • Playfulness • Fantasy • Physical Attraction • Loss of Sleep • Ecstasy	• Trust • Caring • Communication • Honesty • Friendship • Respect • Understanding • Having Fun Together • Passion (but More Intense in Romantic Love)	• Patience • Independence • Putting Other before Self • Possibility of Marriage • Making Other Feel Wanted

FIGURE 6.5 **Romantic Love and Long-Term Love: Similar but Different**
If you are currently in a relationship with someone, try to rate that relationship according to the characteristics shown here. Is your relationship one of romantic love? Or long-term love? What about other relationships between people you know?

SOURCE: Based on Fehr, 1993, pp. 87–120.

Fifth, companionate (storgic) love is most characteristic of long-term relationships compared with passion and game-playing in romantic love. Those who are the happiest describe their love as companionate (characterized by feelings of togetherness, of connectedness, sharing, and supporting each other) or committed. Committed partners, ruled by the head as much as the heart, are faithful to each other and plan their future together (Hecht et al., 1994).

Finally, demographic variables play a role in sustaining love. For example, an analysis of two national polls found an association between socioeconomic status and long-term relationships: "Having enough income to be out of poverty may alleviate financial problems enough to reduce stress and thereby facilitate feelings of love" (Smith, 1994: 34). So, although money may not buy love, its absence can cause couples to fall out of love.

What does long-term love look like? Here's one description:

Happy couples have similar values, attitudes, interests, and to some degree, personality traits. They also share a philosophy of life, religion, vision, or passion that keeps them marching together in spite of minor differences . . . They are autonomous, fairminded, emotionally responsive individuals who trust one another and love spending time together . . . Because they are separate selves, they also enjoy spending time apart to solidify their own individuality without feeling threatened by potential loss or abandonment (Piorkowski, 1994: 286).

For more ideas on how to achieve a satisfying, lasting relationship, see the box "Helping Love Flourish."

Choices

Helping Love Flourish

Several family practitioners (Hendrix, 1988; Osherson, 1992) have suggested some "rules" for creating a loving environment. Although these rules do not guarantee everlasting love, they are worth considering:

■ Relationships do not just happen; we create them. Good relationships are the result of conscious effort and work.

■ One partner should be pleased, rather than threatened, by the other partner's successes or triumphs.

■ A lover is not a solution to a problem. Love may be one of life's greatest experiences, but it is not life itself.

■ Love is about acceptance: Being sympathetic to another's flaws and cherishing the person's other characteristics that are special and lovable. People who feel loved, accepted, and valued are more likely to treat others in a similar manner.

■ Lovers are not mind readers. Open communication is critical.

■ It's not what you say but what you do that maintains love.

■ Stable relationships are always changing. We must learn to deal with both our own changes as individuals and the changes we see in our mates.

■ Love is poisoned by infidelity. If a loved one is deceived, it may be impossible to reestablish trust and respect.

■ Blame is irresponsible. It discourages communication, makes people feel angry, and damages self esteem.

■ Love does not punish but forgives. It may be difficult to forget occasional cruel words or acts, but forgiveness is essential in continuing a healthy relationship.

■ Even though partners are very close, they must respect the other person's independence and his or her right to develop personal interests and other friendships.

A Global View

Although people in all known societies have intimate and loving relationships, the meaning and expression of love varies from one culture to another. In Western societies that emphasize individualism and free choice, love may or may not result in marriage. In cultures that stress the group and the community, arrangements between families are more important than romantic love.

Romantic Love

In the United States, love hasn't always been the basis for getting married. The early colonists believed that marriage was far too important to be based on love; politics and economics, not romance, were the key factors in selecting an appropriate partner. It was only in the early twentieth century that people came to expect marriage to be based on love, sexual attraction, and personal fulfillment (Coontz, 2005; see, also, Chapter 3).

Because romantic love exists in at least 89 percent of societies, it constitutes "a universal, or at the least a near-universal" phenomenon. A number of studies in China, Hong Kong, Taiwan, and Hawaii have found that many people, especially the young, believe in passionate love (Jankowiak and Fischer 1992; Doherty et al., 1994; Cho and Cross, 1995; Goodwin and Findlay, 1997).

Romance is least important in societies where kin ties take precedence over individual relationships. In Burma, India, and Mexico, college students said that storgic, agapic, and pragmatic love are more desirable than manic, erotic, and ludic love styles. In much of China, similarly, love is tempered by recognition that a match would need parental approval. In Saudi Arabia and some other Middle Eastern countries, public embracing between men and women is taboo, and the sexes cannot mix in public (Leon et al., 1994; Moore, 1998).

Many Arab nations celebrate Valentine's Day "with much fanfare." In 2002, however, Saudi Arabia officially banned Valentine's Day and prohibited stores from selling red roses and displaying tokens of affection. A year later, Iranian police ordered shops in Tehran to remove heart-and-flower decorations, images of couples embracing, and other "corrupt" materials that symbolize "decadent" Western holidays ("Valentine's a 'Worthless' Day?," 2002; "Police in Iran . . .," 2003).

"Arranged Love"

In the United States and other Western countries, people become engaged and then inform family and friends of "the good news." Worldwide, a more typical pattern is **arranged marriage,** in which parents or relatives choose their children's partners. It is expected that the partners' love for each other will grow over time.

In many countries, arranged marriages are the norm because respect for parents' wishes, family traditions, and the kin group are more important than romantic love. Thus, the well-being of the community is valued more highly than the feelings of the individual. In fact, people in many societies find American beliefs about dating and romance at least as strange as some Americans find the concept of arranged marriages (see the box "Modern Arranged Marriages in India").

Arranged marriages vary quite a bit. In some African countries, fathers who are poor may force daughters as young as 10 years old into marriages with men in their 60s and 70s in exchange for cattle or to pay a loan (see Chapter 10). In other parts of Africa, too

Although many marriages in India are still arranged (see text), "Bollywood" films are very popular. These movies feature romantic love, passion, infatuation, and even obsession. Why do you think that the films are so popular?

Cross-Cultural Families

Modern Arranged Marriages in India

In India the majority of marriages are arranged by parents or elders: "There has never been any room for romantic marriage in Indian society on the line of Western societies" (Singh, 2005: 143). Loyalty of the individual to the family is a cherished ideal. To preserve this ideal, marriages have traditionally been carefully arranged so that young men and women will avoid selecting mates that the family deems unsuitable.

In some cities, however, traditional aspects of arranged marriages are combined with nontraditional methods for finding prospective spouses (Pasupathi, 2002). For example, every Sunday the newspapers are filled with classified ads inviting inquiries about "smart, well-educated, professional boys" and "really beautiful, homely, university graduate girls." ("Homely" in India does not mean that a woman is unattractive but that she would be a good homemaker.)

There are variations in different regions and social classes, however. Although educated, upper-middle-class women are allowed to marry whomever they want, many opt for arranged marriages. One young woman explained: "Love is important, but it's not sufficient." She asked her parents to research and solicit proposals from parents of men with a good education and earning potential who were refined, intellectual, and good human beings. She is reportedly happily married to a man whom she had met just three times before their engagement. In other cases, children have "veto power" over undesirable candidates.

A 1976 study of upper-middle-class women in northern India found that 39 percent said love was essential for marital happiness. Two decades later, that figure had fallen to 11 percent. Among urban professionals polled in another survey, 81 percent said their marriages had been arranged, and 94 percent rated their marriages as "very successful" (Lakshmanan, 1997).

Why are arranged marriages attractive in much of India? For one thing, shy people can end up with a good partner. Also, parents and relatives seem to do a good job in choosing mates.

Arranged marriages are popular because they offer stability. Unlike "love marriages," arranged marriages last longer because the couple's families stand behind them: "If the relationship between the couples is about to go haywire . . . parents of both spouses make concerted efforts to resolve the crisis" (Singh, 2005: 144).

Arranged marriages persist, also, because of family ties. Even financially independent couples usually live with the husband's parents. As a result, similar backgrounds and compatibility with in-laws are more important than in the West. The advantage is that there tends to be much family support if a marriage runs into trouble.

Stop and Think . . .

- Why are arranged marriages less fragile than marriages based on love?

- In arranged marriages, factors such as social class and religion are seen as more important than romantic love or physical attraction. If Americans endorsed "arranged love," do you think that our divorce rates would decrease?

much love between spouses is seen as disruptive because the couple may withdraw from their responsibilities to the community (Regis, 1995).

In arranged marriages in Sri Lanka, men and women who fall in love usually let their parents know their choices in advance. In Turkey, about 52 percent of women live in arranged marriages, but there is a trend toward "love marriages" among younger, better-educated, and urban women. In Canada, some second-generation Muslim Pakistani women are "rebelling" against arranged marriages. Others participate willingly because they can't find a suitable partner on their own or feel that their parents know best (de Munck, 1998; Zaidi and Shuraydi, 2002; Nauck and Klaus, 2005).

Love is important in all societies. It may manifest itself differently in various cultures and historical eras, but "overall, people are more similar than different" (Hendrick and Hendrick, 2003: 1065).

Making Connections

- Have you ever experienced love at first sight? If so, was the person similar to you in physical appearance or very different? How long did the love last? Why do you think that some people are more likely than others to fall in love at first sight?

- Some of my students—including those in their 30s and 40s—feel that long-term relationships are "pretty boring" because there's no romance in them. Do you agree?

Conclusion

When love is healthy, it *changes* how we feel about ourselves and others. Love can inspire us and motivate us to care for family members, friends, and lovers. Love also creates *choices* in the ways in which we may find happiness during dating, marriage, and old age. There are *constraints,* however, because we sometimes confuse love with jealousy or controlling behavior.

Love is essential to human growth and development, but it is often shrouded in myths and hampered by formidable barriers. For those who are willing to learn and to work at it, love is attainable and can be long-lasting. Do love and sex go together? Not always. We examine this and related issues in the next chapter.

Summary

1. Love is a complex phenomenon that varies in degree and intensity in different people and social contexts. Minimally necessary for a loving relationship are willingness to accommodate the other person, to accept his or her shortcomings, and to have as much concern about his or her well-being as about one's own.

2. Friendship is the root of love. Friendship and love share such characteristics as trust, respect, honesty, and mutual support.

3. Caring, intimacy (including self-disclosure), and commitment form the foundations of love. These characteristics strengthen relationships and help love flourish.

4. There are many approaches to understanding love and loving: Attachment theory proposes that warm, secure, loving relationships in infancy are essential to forming loving relationships in adulthood; Reiss described four stages of love; Sternberg focused on the relationships between passion, intimacy, and decision/commitment; Lee identified six styles of loving; and exchange theorists see love as a series of mutually beneficial transactions.

5. Love serves many functions, and people fall in love for a variety of reasons. Availability of partners is one factor. Others include the desire to have children, the drive for survival of the species, quality of life, inspiration, and just plain fun.

6. Despite popular beliefs, men are usually more romantic than women and suffer more when a relationship ends. Women are more likely to express their love verbally and to work at a relationship, but they are also more pragmatic about moving on when love goes awry. There are more similarities than differences, however, between women's and men's love relationships.

7. There are many obstacles to love. Macro-level barriers include the depersonalization of mass society, demographic factors, the double standard, our society's emphasis on individualism, a negative view of gay and lesbian love, and family pressures. Micro-level obstacles include personality characteristics and childhood experiences.

8. Several kinds of negative and controlling behavior can kill love. Narcissism and jealousy are usually destructive and sometimes even dangerous. Other harmful behaviors include threatening a partner with the withdrawal of love, making the partner feel guilty, and causing physical and emotional pain.

9. Although romantic love can be exhilarating, it is often short-lived and can be disappointing. In contrast to romantic love, long-term love is usually secure and constant and adapts over the life course.

10. There is a great deal of variation among cultures in how people express love. Some societies embrace love. Others view love as less important than marrying someone who meets with the approval of parents and kin.

Key Terms

self-disclosure *160*	ludus *165*	pragma *165*
eros *165*	storge *165*	homophobia *170*
mania *165*	agape *165*	arranged marriage *180*

Taking It Further

Love and Romance in Cyberspace

Want to find out how romantic you are? Whether you and your partner are compatible? Here are a few self-assessment sites and other links that you might enjoy:

Romance on the Air provides an *Interactive Romantic Survey* to help you see how romantic you really are. It also includes *Romantic Stories for Some Inspiration,* a humor section, and an advice column.

members.aol.com/wakkarotti/romance.htm

Words of Love has an engaging array of Shakespeare's sonnets, songs, and witticisms about love.

www.randomhouse.com/wordsoflove

Valentines on the Web is "Dedicated to the One I Love." Netters can send Valentine cards that include both Web-sites and personal messages.

home.aristotle.net/valentines

Love Test, constructed by Betty Harris and Jim Glover, will remind you of Sternberg's and Lee's measures of love. You can take the *Concept of Love* quiz or the *Experience of Love* questionnaire and receive an "analysis" of your (and your partner's) love styles after you submit the answers. It's fun!

dataguru.org/love/lovetest/findings

TheRomantic.com offers "1000s of Creative Ideas & Expert Advice on Love, Dating & Romance."

http://www.theromantic.com

And more: www.prenhall.com/benokraitis provides numerous other sites that deal with topics covered in this chapter. Some offer resources for victims of stalking. Others are great diversions when you need a break from studying or writing papers: love quizzes, a collection of loving and nasty valentines that Victorian Americans sent to their lovers and ex-lovers, and several anti–Valentine's Day URLs.

Investigate with Research Navigator

Go to www.researchnavigator.com and enter your LOGIN NAME and PASSWORD. For instructions on registering for the first time, view the detailed instructions at the end of Chapter 1. Search the Research Navigator™ site using the following key terms:

intimacy
attachment theory
love

Outline

Sexuality and Sexual Expression Throughout Life

Data Digest

- About 56 percent of adolescents ages 13 to 18 say that they want to **abstain from sex until they marry.**

- Among adolescents, 28 percent of girls and 32 percent of boys **have had sexual intercourse before age 15.**

- **Teenagers are delaying sex.** In 2002, 30 percent of females ages 15 to 17 had had sex (compared with 37 percent in 1988), and 31 percent of males had done so (compared with 50 percent in 1988).

- Among those ages 15 to 44, 6 percent of men and 11 percent of women **have had sexual contact with a same-sex partner** at least once.

- At age 70 and older, 87 percent of men and 63 percent of women **engage in sexual activities** (including kissing and self-stimulation) at least once a week.

- Worldwide, **42 million people are living with HIV.** In 2005, more than 3 million died of AIDS, including 570,000 children under 15. The largest number of deaths was in sub-Saharan Africa (2.4 million).

Sources: Abma et al., 2004; AARP, 2005; Mosher et al., 2005; UNAIDS/WHO, 2005.

In the movie *Annie Hall,* a therapist asks two lovers how often they have sex. The character played by Woody Allen answers, "Hardly ever, maybe three times a week." The character played by Diane Keaton replies, "Constantly, three times a week."

As this anecdote illustrates, sex is more important for some people than others. Besides physical contact, sex provides an opportunity to express loyalty, passion, and affection.

Culture shapes our sexual development, attitudes, and actions. As a result, there are significant differences from one society to another in defining what is "normal" or "abnormal." In addition, sexual behavior changes throughout life and varies over the years. Before

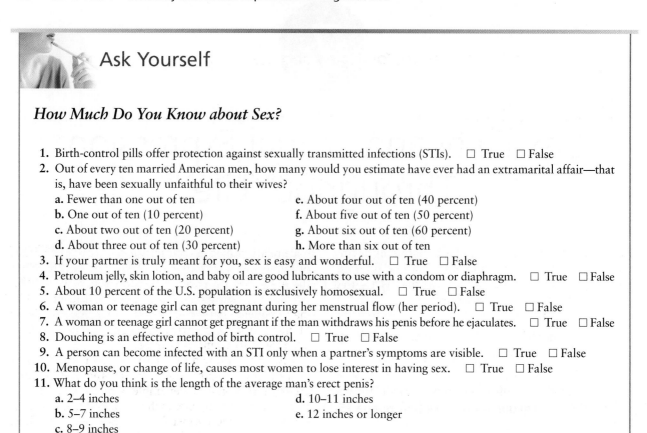

Ask Yourself

How Much Do You Know about Sex?

1. Birth-control pills offer protection against sexually transmitted infections (STIs).   ☐ True   ☐ False
2. Out of every ten married American men, how many would you estimate have ever had an extramarital affair—that is, have been sexually unfaithful to their wives?
   - **a.** Fewer than one out of ten
   - **b.** One out of ten (10 percent)
   - **c.** About two out of ten (20 percent)
   - **d.** About three out of ten (30 percent)
   - **e.** About four out of ten (40 percent)
   - **f.** About five out of ten (50 percent)
   - **g.** About six out of ten (60 percent)
   - **h.** More than six out of ten
3. If your partner is truly meant for you, sex is easy and wonderful.   ☐ True   ☐ False
4. Petroleum jelly, skin lotion, and baby oil are good lubricants to use with a condom or diaphragm.   ☐ True   ☐ False
5. About 10 percent of the U.S. population is exclusively homosexual.   ☐ True   ☐ False
6. A woman or teenage girl can get pregnant during her menstrual flow (her period).   ☐ True   ☐ False
7. A woman or teenage girl cannot get pregnant if the man withdraws his penis before he ejaculates.   ☐ True   ☐ False
8. Douching is an effective method of birth control.   ☐ True   ☐ False
9. A person can become infected with an STI only when a partner's symptoms are visible.   ☐ True   ☐ False
10. Menopause, or change of life, causes most women to lose interest in having sex.   ☐ True   ☐ False
11. What do you think is the length of the average man's erect penis?
    - **a.** 2–4 inches
    - **b.** 5–7 inches
    - **c.** 8–9 inches
    - **d.** 10–11 inches
    - **e.** 12 inches or longer
12. Which of the following STIs do experts call "the silent epidemic"?
    - **a.** scabies
    - **b.** genital herpes
    - **c.** syphilis
    - **d.** chlamydia

(Answers are on page 187.)

you read any further, take the "How Much Do You Know about Sex?" quiz.

Sexuality and Human Development

Sexuality is much more complex than just physical contact. Among other things, it is the product of our sexual identity, sexual orientation, and sexual scripts.

Sexual Identity

Our *sexual identity* consists of our awareness of ourselves as male or female and the ways in which we express our sexual values, attitudes, feelings, and beliefs. It is part of how we define who we are and what roles we play. Sexual identity involves placing oneself in a category created by society (such as female and heterosexual) and learning, both consciously and unconsciously, how to act as a person in that category.

Sexuality is a multidimensional concept that incorporates psychological, biological, and sociological components such as sexual desire, sexual response, and gender roles (Bernhard, 1995). *Sexual desire* is the sexual drive that makes us receptive to sexual activity. *Sexual response* encompasses the biological aspects of sexuality, which include experiencing pleasure or orgasm. *Gender roles* reflect the behavior that women and men enact according to culturally prescribed expectations (see Chapter 5).

In a typical situation, a man may be aroused by a woman's cleavage because our society considers breasts sexy (sexual desire), may experience an erection (sexual

Answers to "How Much Do You Know about Sex?"

Scoring the test:
Each question is worth 1 point. Score each item and add up your total number of points. A score of 11 or 12 is an "A," 9 or 10 a "B," 8 a "C," 7 a "D," and below 7 an "F."

Correct answers:
1. false, 2. c, 3. false, 4. false, 5. false, 6. true, 7. false, 8. false, 9. false, 10. false, 11. b, 12. d.

response), and may then take the initiative in having sexual intercourse with a woman whom he finds attractive (gender roles). But what if the man is aroused by other men rather than by women?

Sexual Orientation

Our sexual identity incorporates **sexual orientation**, a preference for sexual partners of the same sex, the opposite sex, or both sexes:

- **Homosexuals** (from the Greek root *homo,* meaning "same") are sexually attracted to people of the same sex. Male homosexuals prefer to be called *gay;* female homosexuals are called *lesbians. Coming out* is a person's public announcement of a gay or lesbian sexual orientation.

- **Heterosexuals,** often called *straight,* are attracted to partners of the opposite sex.

- **Bisexuals,** sometimes called *bis,* are attracted to members of both sexes.

Although most people are sexually attracted to others, **asexuals** lack any interest in or desire for sex.

Sexual orientation isn't as clear-cut as most people believe it to be. Asexuality may be a temporary condition because of the effects of medications. Bisexuals may be attracted to people of both sexes but engage in sexual behavior primarily with women or with men. Some people who identify themselves as heterosexual might fantasize about having a same-sex experience. And homosexuals who haven't come out may have sexual intercourse only with heterosexual partners because they fear the consequences of violating cultural norms (Kinsey et al., 1948).

In what one author has described as being "on the down low," black men who sometimes sleep with other men see themselves as "straight" and don't disclose their male relationships to their female sex partners, friends, or family members (King, 2004). But black men aren't the only ones who are on the down low. White men who are married and hold high-ranking leadership jobs may frequent chat rooms and use such code words as "bimm" (bisexual married male) and "m4m" (married male for married male) (Vargas, 2004).

Because of down low activities, some researchers now question whether men who say they are bisexual aren't, in fact, gay. For example, a recent study found that men (but not women) who identified themselves as bis were aroused by members of the same sex. Thus, men who claim to be bisexual are probably gay but may be ambivalent about their homosexuality or are simply staying in the closet to avoid being stigmatized by their partners, families, and friends (Rieger et al., 2005).

Although heterosexuality is the predominant sexual orientation worldwide, homosexuality exists in all societies (see the box "Homosexuality in Non-Western Cultures"). Many gays and lesbians deny or try to suppress their sexual orientation because our society is still characterized by heterosexism. **Heterosexism** is the belief that heterosexuality is superior to and more "natural" than homosexuality.

According to some estimates, about 2 percent of Americans are *transgendered* (Gorman, 1995). This term encompasses several groups:

- *Transsexuals:* people who are born with the biological characteristics of one sex but choose to live their life as a member of the opposite sex—either by consistently cross-dressing or by surgically altering their sex (see Chapter 5).

- *Intersexuals:* people whose medical diagnosis at birth is not clearly male or female.

- *Transvestites:* people who cross-dress at times but don't necessarily consider themselves to be a member of the opposite sex.

Cross-Cultural Families

Homosexuality in Non-Western Cultures

In their classic studies, Ford and Beach (1972) examined data on 190 societies in Oceania, Eurasia, Africa, North America, and South America. They drew three conclusions about homosexuality: (1) Social attitudes toward homosexuality are widely divergent; (2) homosexuality occurs in all societies, regardless of societal reactions; and (3) males seem more likely than females to engage in homosexual activity.

Despite many attempts to repress homosexuality, especially by Western missionaries, homosexuality is common today in many parts of Africa. For example, woman-to-woman marriage has been documented in more than 30 African populations, including at least nine groups in southern Africa (Carrier and Murray, 1998).

In China, both homosexuality and bisexuality date back to at least the Bronze Age. An estimated 100 million Chinese, or 7 percent of the country's population, are gay. Although Chinese officials disapprove of homosexuality, Chinese psychiatrists have recently stopped classifying homosexuality as a mental disorder. Some gays and lesbians have celebrated "weddings," although these marriages are not recognized legally (Hinsch, 1990; Chu, 2001; "*Reuters* highlights . . . ," 2002).

Homosexuality is tolerated more in some countries than in others. For example:

- In Egypt and many African countries, gays can be stoned, imprisoned, or killed (Wax, 2005).
- Nigeria's laws prescribe a 14-year imprisonment for homosexuals (Modo, 2005).
- In Afghanistan, homosexuality—including with young boys—has "long been a clandestine feature of life," even though it is not practiced openly (Smith, 2002: 4).
- Although gays aren't prosecuted, two-thirds of South Koreans believe that homosexuality is wrong and sinful. Because Confucian beliefs stress the continuity of families along bloodlines, homosexuality threatens a family's permanence (Prusher, 2001).
- There is considerable variation in Latin America. Gay relationships are fairly open in some cities. In other cases, government and university officials define homosexuality as an illness that can and should be "cured" (Parker and Cáceres, 1999; Chauvin, 2002).

Transgendered people include gays, heterosexuals, bisexuals, and men and women who don't identify with any specific gender category.

Transgendered people are becoming increasingly more visible and accepted. A few years ago, for example, San Francisco approved health insurance to cover sex change operations, hormonal treatments, and any related costs. And Australia has become the first country in the world to issue a passport that lists a person's sex as "indeterminate" (Butler, 2003).

WHAT DETERMINES SEXUAL ORIENTATION? No one knows why we are heterosexual, gay, or bisexual. *Biological theories* maintain that sexual orientation has a strong genetic basis. Some studies have found that if one member of a pair of twins is homosexual, the other twin is more likely to be homosexual if he or she is an identical twin than if he or she is a fraternal twin. Because identical twins have identical genes, these studies suggest that a particular region of the X chromosome may hold a "gay gene" (Bailey and Pillard, 1991; Bailey et al., 1993; Burr, 1996).

since you asked

Do we inherit our sexual orientation?

Like their heterosexual counterparts, most gay and lesbian parents are proud of their children and offer loving homes. In this Gay Pride Parade in New York City, fathers demonstrate their committed role as parents and affirm their identity as homosexuals.

Many cities, including Baltimore, Maryland (pictured here), have used billboards to discourage teen sex and, consequently, teen pregnancy.

"feature a mix of scantily clad starlets and bawdy humor but go to some lengths to avoid being labeled as pornography." According to some critics, magazines like *Men's Health* and *Men's Fitness* are more about sex than about physical health (Kuczynski, 2001; Carr and Hays, 2003).

Many women's magazines also sell sex. Nearly every article and ad in *Cosmopolitan* is about sex. *Redbook* and *Mademoiselle* also have a heavy dose of articles about sex (e.g., "35 sexy new ways to touch your man"). Even magazines that target young teenage and preteen girls, such as *YM*, often have sex-related articles ("Look summer sexy") (King, 2002; see, also, Chapter 5).

MOVIES Rating systems are not strictly enforced (few moviegoers are stopped from seeing R-rated films, for example), and videos are accessible to people in most age groups. Also, film ratings have become more lenient. Since 1992, many films that were rated PG-13 ("Parents strongly cautioned") are now rated PG ("Parental guidance suggested"). Because of this "ratings creep," it is commonplace for adolescents and even younger children to get much of their sex information from movies (Thompson and Yokota, 2004).

Much of the portrayal of sex in movies does not reflect real life. Because marital sex is rarely portrayed, movies give the impression that only sexual activities outside of marriage are common or enjoyable. Also, the emphasis on casual sex sends the message that there is no connection between sex and commitment (Brown et al., 2002).

TELEVISION Sex is a staple in most television shows, ranging from 28 percent of reality shows to 96 percent of soap operas (see *Figure 7.3*). *How* and *how much* sex is portrayed on television has changed. Today, 70 percent of all shows contain some sexual content, up from 56 percent in 1998. Shows that depict sexual intercourse have also increased—from 7 percent in 1998 to 11 percent in 2005 (Kunkel et al., 2005).

Does sex-saturated TV content affect behavior? A national study of 12- to 17-year-olds found that the 10 percent of adolescents who watched the most sexually related content were twice as likely to engage in sexual intercourse a year later as were those who saw the least amount of sexual content. It's not clear whether the adolescents who are most interested in becoming sexually active are also most likely to watch sexually explicit TV shows. Nevertheless, nearly three out of four teens ages 15 to 17 say that viewing sex on TV influences the sexual behavior of kids their age (Collins, 2005; Kunkel et al., 2005).

Many people criticize sex on television because the programs rarely portray the negative aspects of casual or unprotected sex, which can result in STIs or unwanted pregnancies. But television can also be a positive force in sexual socialization. For example, in one episode of *Friends*, a very popular sitcom, a female character told her former boyfriend that she was pregnant with his child. He exclaimed, "But we used a condom!" When researchers surveyed youth ages 12 to 17 who

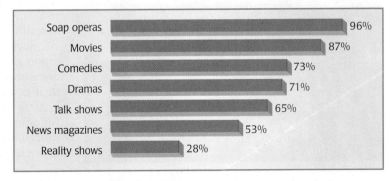

FIGURE 7.3 **Percentage of TV Shows with Sexual Content**

Note: *Sexual content* ranges from talk about sex to kissing to sexual intercourse.

SOURCE: Kunkel et al., 2003.

saw the episode, 65 percent of the viewers remembered the connection between pregnancy and condom failure. More important, one in 10 of the viewers said that they had talked with an adult about the effectiveness of condoms after seeing this episode (Collins, 2005).

THE INTERNET The Internet can be a source of unwanted information about sex. For example, when we access our e-mail we often find that much of it consists of spam (unsolicited commercial e-mail sent to a large number of addresses). Every day, it seems, spam messages urge us to enlarge our breasts or penis or to view pornography.

Another problem related to Internet use is filters that block access to legitimate sex-related information. As access to the Internet expands, more and more young people are turning to the Web as a source of health information. Among the most common topics searched are pregnancy, birth control, HIV/AIDS, and other STIs, but efforts to block pornographic sites often block access to nonpornographic sex-related sites as well. The Children's Internet Protection Act of 2000 requires that schools and libraries use Web-browsing filters to block pornographic content or risk losing federal funds.

Nationally, from 23 to 60 percent of the blocked sites include information about herpes, birth control, safer sex, and gay health. The barred sites also include information about women's health and STIs maintained by medical journals and government agencies (Richardson et al., 2002; Rideout et al., 2002). It's also not clear how many parents who use filtering products prevent their children from accessing accurate information from these sites.

From Sex Education

As you just saw, many parents do *not* teach their children about sex. And the media and popular culture often bombard people with unrealistic portrayals of sexuality. Consequently, many schools and community groups have assumed responsibility for teaching children and adolescents about sex.

since you asked

Why is sex education by schools controversial?

About 93 percent of U.S. adults approve of schools providing sex education, an increase from 65 percent in 1970. Even though only 15 percent of parents want an abstinence-only curriculum, this is what 35 percent of public school districts provide (Kelly, 2005).

A major reason for this situation is that in 2001 the Bush administration established a federal program to fund only abstinence curricula. Even when schools provide comprehensive sex education classes, they vary quite a bit—from a total of two hours in one school to a full semester in an adjacent school. And in some schools athletic coaches, rather than teachers, teach sex education classes (Walker, 2003; Kelly, 2005).

Some faith-based programs offer information on a variety of topics in addition to abstinence, including homosexuality, STIs, masturbation, and oral sex. A very vocal minority of parents, however, headed primarily by conservative religious groups, oppose sex education in schools. These groups, as well as organizations such as "Priests for Life," argue that sex education in schools will encourage young children to become interested in sex, increase promiscuity, and result in abortions (Clarkson, 2002).

Such fears are unfounded. Several national studies report that teenagers at high schools that provide condoms and instruction in condom use are less likely than their counterparts to engage in risky sex or to report lifetime or recent sexual intercourse (Blake et al., 2003; Johnson et al., 2003). It may be that teens who are informed about condoms (and the potential consequences of not using them) are less likely to have sex impulsively.

"Just say no" abstinence-only approaches rarely work. Many teens are already sexually active, and 88 percent of middle- and high school students who pledge to remain virgins until marriage end up having premarital sex anyway (Brückner and Bearman, 2005; Fortenberry, 2005).

At King Junior High School in Berkeley, California, the 9th grade "social living" class includes instruction in sexual anatomy. Do you think teachers should provide this information? Or should parents be responsible for educating their children about sexuality?

A national study of students in grades 7 through 12 found that almost half of those who had reported taken a virginity pledge denied having done so a year later. Some may have lied about taking the pledge in the first place, but most had become sexually active (Rosenbaum, 2006).

It's also not clear why many of the abstinence-only groups oppose giving teenagers information about condoms and birth control. If teens are *really* going to abstain from sex until marriage, why should sex education change their behavior?

Which sex education programs are most effective? Those that teach adolescents critical thinking skills by:

- Including activities that tell young people how to resist peer pressure to engage in sex

- Focusing on specific issues, such as delaying the initiation of intercourse or using protection

- Providing accurate information about the risks of unprotected intercourse

- Involving students in small-group discussions, role playing, and real-world exercises such as locating contraceptives in local drugstores and visiting family planning clinics

- Addressing the problem of social and media pressure to have sex (such as advertising that uses sex to sell products or the "lines" men typically use to persuade someone to have sex)

- Including open discussions about homosexuality to address students who are struggling with their sexual orientation (Kirby et al., 1994; "Issues and answers . . . ," 2001)

The most successful sex education programs train adolescents to serve as peer counselors. They also discuss sexual feelings and behavior as a normal part of human development rather than focusing only on danger and disease (Ehrhardt, 1996; Rust, 2000).

Making Connections

- How did you learn about sex? Were the "facts" you obtained accurate?

- What kind of sex education classes, if any, did you have in middle school and high school? Did the classes influence your sexual behavior?

Sexual Behaviors

Many of us have fairly conventional sex lives. For example, most U.S. adults have one or no sex partners during any given year (see *Figure 7.4*). Keep in mind that sex is not just sexual intercourse. Sexual expression encompasses many other behaviors, including autoeroticism and oral sex.

Autoeroticism

Autoeroticism refers to arousal of sexual feeling without an external stimulus. Two of the most common forms of autoeroticism are sexual fantasies and masturbation.

SEXUAL FANTASIES Most of us, regardless of our age or marital status, have sexual fantasies. Men are more likely than women to have sexual fantasies. Such fantasies often mirror differences in gender roles (see Chapter 5). Women's fantasies, for example, are typically romantic, passive, and submissive. Compared with women, men are more likely to fantasize about a large number of partners and encounters that won't lead to a relationship (Battan, 1992; Geer and Manguno-Mire, 1996).

Even when women fantasize about "unusual" sex practices, they are less likely to engage in them in real life. In one national survey, for example, twice as many men as women said that they had acted out such fantasies as incest, sex with defecation, sadomasochism, or sex with an animal (Patterson and Kim, 1991).

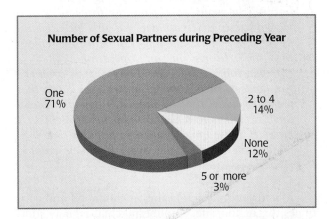

FIGURE 7.4 Sex Is Largely Monogamous
Although this nationwide U.S. survey of sexual behavior is now a decade old, the data are still considered the most authoritative available. These findings surprised many people. Why do you think this was the case?

SOURCE: Based on Laumann et al., 1994: 177–80; 369.

According to scientists, sexual fantasies are emotionally and psychologically healthy. They can provide a safety valve for pent-up feelings or a harmless escape from boring, everyday routines: "to be covered in whipped cream and wrestle my lover, then the loser has to lick it off" or "having sex on the 50-yard line at a sold-out football game" (Patterson and Kim, 1991: 79).

Fantasies can also boost our self-image because we don't have to worry about penis or breast size, height, or weight. Because we have total control in producing and directing the fantasy, we can change or stop it whenever we want (Masters et al., 1992).

MASTURBATION When asked about what sex would be like in the future, comedian Robin Williams said: "It's going to be you—and you." **Masturbation** is sexual self-pleasuring that involves some form of direct physical stimulation. It may or may not result in orgasm. Masturbation typically includes rubbing, stroking, fondling, squeezing, or otherwise stimulating the genitals. It can also involve self-stimulation of other body parts, such as the breasts, the inner thighs, or the anus.

since you asked

Is masturbation unhealthy?

Early in the twentieth century, masturbation was branded as a source of damage to the brain and nervous system. It was believed to cause a variety of problems, such as bad breath, blindness, deafness, acne, and heart murmurs. Some physicians treated masturbation with recommendations for prayer or exercise. Others went much further:

> *"Treatment" for boys included piercing the foreskin of the penis with wire, applying leeches to the base of the penis, or cutting the foreskin with a jagged scissors. "Treatment" for girls included applying a hot iron to the thighs or clitoris or removing the clitoris in an operation called a clitoridectomy. Adults could buy various commercial devices, such as metal mittens, an alarm that went off when the bed moved, rings with metal teeth or spikes to wear on the penis at night. . . . Some of these horrors were so popular that they were advertised in the Sears-Roebuck catalog (Wade and Cirese, 1991: 46).*

Masturbation often begins in childhood and continues throughout life. Prepubertal children may stimulate themselves without realizing that what they are doing is sexual. For example, one girl learned when she was 8 years old that she could produce an "absolutely terrific feeling" by squeezing her thighs together (Nass et al., 1981). Thus, many children discover masturbation accidentally.

More than three times as many men as women report masturbating at least once a week. Black men (60 percent) are twice as likely as whites, Latinos, and Asians to say that they have never masturbated (Laumann et al., 1994). It's not clear whether masturbation rates among African American men are lower than among other groups because black men have traditionally viewed masturbation as an admission of inability to seduce women or whether this activity reflects only men in lower socioeconomic groups (Belcastro, 1985; Timberlake and Carpenter, 1990).

Like fantasies, masturbation fulfills several needs: It can relieve sexual tension, provide a safe means of sexual experimentation (avoiding disease and unwanted pregnancy), and ultimately transfer valuable learning to two-person lovemaking. Masturbation can be as sexually satisfying as intercourse, and it does not hinder the development of social relationships during young adulthood or create problems in a marriage (Leitenberg et al., 1993; Kelly, 1994).

Oral Sex

In January 1998, President Clinton wagged his finger at the television audience and proclaimed that "I want to say one thing to the American people. I want you to lis-

"I'd like a page 15 followed by a page 28 please!"

© www.CartoonStock.com

ten to me. I'm going to say this again: I did not have sexual relations with that woman, Miss Lewinsky. . . . Never. These allegations are false." It turned out, however, that Monica Lewinsky (a White House intern) and former President Clinton routinely had oral sex.

Like many teenagers and college students, President Clinton apparently defined oral sex as not *really* sex. Some writers call this behavior "outercourse," a way of rationalizing sexual behavior because it's "almost sex" and an alternative to sexual intercourse (Harvey and Weber, 2002; Kamen, 2002).

Oral sex includes several types of stimulation. **Fellatio** (from the Latin word for "suck") is oral stimulation of a man's penis. **Cunnilingus** (from the Latin words for "vulva" and "tongue") is oral stimulation of a woman's genitals. Fellatio and cunnilingus can be performed singly or simultaneously. Simultaneous oral sex is sometimes called "69," indicating the physical positions of the partners.

Adolescents are more likely to have oral than vaginal sex. By age 17, for example, 13 percent of males and 11 percent of females have had oral sex but not vaginal intercourse (Mosher et al., 2005). In many other age groups, oral sex is almost as common as vaginal intercourse. By age 44, most people have had vaginal intercourse, but 90 percent of men and 88 percent of women have experienced oral sex (see *Figure 7.5*).

Some people find oral sex pleasurable or engage in it to please their partner. Others complain about the odors (although bathing solves the problem for both sexes), do not enjoy it, or find it revolting. According to a female college student, for example, oral sex is like "blowing your nose in my mouth" (Wade and Cirese, 1991: 334).

Oral sex, like many other sexual behaviors, depends on personal preference. Many people don't realize, however, that sexual diseases can be transmitted orally. Oral sex can result in syphilis, gonorrhea, and herpes, as well as papilloma virus, which can cause cervical cancer (Halpern et al., 2000; Schvaneveldt et al., 2001).

Sexual Intercourse

Most people assume that sexual intercourse refers to heterosexual, vaginal-penile penetration. In fact, the term applies to any sort of sexual coupling, including oral and anal. *Coitus* specifically means penile-vaginal intercourse. Unless noted otherwise, we will use *sexual intercourse* to refer to coitus.

VARIATIONS BY AGE AND MARITAL STATUS Some adolescents begin to be sexually active in their early teens (see "Data Digest"). On average, however, the first heterosexual intercourse takes place between the ages of 16 and 17 for both sexes.

Average frequency of sexual intercourse peaks between ages 25 and 34 and then declines over the years. Over time, as you'll see shortly, people develop other priorities in maintaining a family or a relationship.

Married couples and cohabitants have much higher rates of sexual intercourse than single people do. For example, about 25 percent of singles, compared with only 11 percent of married people have sexual intercourse only a few times a year (Laumann et al., 1994). Such figures challenge popular perceptions of "swinging singles." Having an easily accessible partner, such as in marriage or cohabitation, seems to have the largest impact on the frequency of sexual activity.

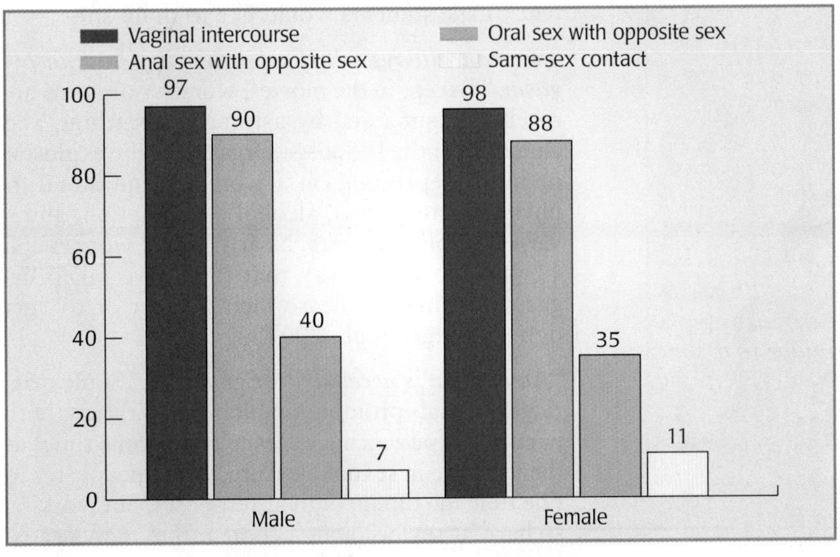

SEX AND THE GENDER GAP Overall, women report an average of six sex partners in their lifetimes, compared with 20 for men. A better measure is the median, the midpoint between the high and low scores, because a small number of individuals—especially men—report having had 99 or more sex partners (Langer et al., 2004). Whether we use averages or medians, men have almost

FIGURE 7.5   Types of Sexual Contact
Percentage of U.S. males and females 25–44 years of age who have had each type of sexual contact, 2002.

SOURCE: Adapted from Mosher et al., 2005, Figure 4.

three times as many sex partners as do women (see *Figure 7.6*).

Only 34 percent of women, compared with 70 percent of men, say that they think about sex every day. And although women express satisfaction with their sex lives, only 59 percent say that they enjoy sex "a great deal," compared with 83 percent of men (Langer et al., 2004).

These differences are probably due to gender roles. Women are more likely than men to be balancing jobs and domestic responsibilities and therefore have less time to think about and enjoy sex (see Chapter 5). Also, traditional male sexual scripts focus on sex as recreational, whereas traditional female sexual scripts focus on feelings, emotions, and commitment. Although our sexual scripts have become more egalitarian, many people still follow traditional scripts. As comedian Jay Leno quipped, "According to a new survey, 76 percent of men would rather watch a football game than have sex. My question is, why do we have to choose? Why do you think they invented halftime?"

SOME MYTHS ABOUT SEX AND SEXUAL RESPONSE

Fantasies, sounds, smells, touch, sexy pictures, dreams, hearing the person we love say "I love you," and a variety of other stimuli can arouse our sexual feelings. Our **sexual response** is our physiological reaction to sexual stimulation. Sexual response can vary greatly by age, gender, and health. Despite these variations, there are a number of myths about sex and sexual response that many people believe:

- *"Withdrawal is an effective birth control method."* In males, the first responses to sexual stimulation are swelling and erection of the penis. The penis may emit several drops of fluid that are not semen but may contain sperm cells. If this fluid is discharged while the penis is in the vagina, the woman can be impregnated. Thus, withdrawal before ejaculation may not prevent conception.

- *"Erections, ejaculations, and orgasms are connected."* Penile erections, ejaculations, and orgasms do not occur simultaneously because they are affected by different neurological and vascular systems. Thus, men who argue that a penile erection must be followed by ejaculation during sexual intercourse lest they suffer dire consequences ("blue balls") are, quite simply, wrong. There is no evidence that any man has ever died of a "terminal erection." Many partners are fully satisfied by tender sexual activities that do not necessarily include orgasm.

- *"The bigger the penis, the better the sex."* One of some men's biggest concerns is that their penis isn't big enough to stimulate women during intercourse (Reinisch and Beasley, 1990). There is no association between clitoris, breast, or penis size and orgasm. Similarly, there is no evidence for the belief that, compared with white men, African American men have larger penises, greater sexual capacity, or an insatiable sexual appetite (although some of my black male students would like to think so).

- *"We can always tell if a partner has had an orgasm."* Except in the movies, women's orgasms are rarely accompanied by asthmatic breathing and clutching of the bedposts. Orgasm can be explosive or mild, depending on a woman's emotional or physical state, stress, alcohol consumption, and a variety of other factors. Nearly half of women and 11 percent of men say that they have faked orgasms, mainly to please their partner or to "get done" (Langer et al., 2004).

- *"An orgasm is necessary for good sex."* Some marriage manuals promote simultaneous orgasm (both partners experiencing orgasm at the same time) as the ultimate in sexual pleasure. Many people try to fine tune the timing of their responses, but working so hard at sex becomes a chore rather than a satisfying experience. Although simultaneous orgasm can be exhilarating, so can independent orgasms. An estimated 5 to 10 percent of women never experience an orgasm yet enjoy sex throughout the life course (Lloyd, 2005).

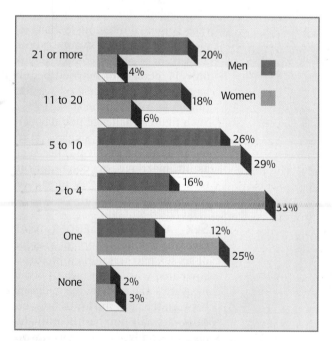

FIGURE 7.6 Over a Lifetime, Men Have More Sex Partners than Women.

SOURCE: Based on Langer et al., 2004, p. 4.

Sexuality Throughout Life

We may love dozens of people over our lifetime. We'll have sex with very few of them, however. We might also have sex with people whom we don't love. There can be many sexual relationships during the life course, and a diversity of sexual unions. There is also another option: abstinence.

Virginity and Abstinence

The terms *abstinence* and *virgin* have several meanings. One definition, which many religious groups endorse, refers to the absence of *all* types of sexual activity. For scientists, a virgin is someone who has never had vaginal-penile intercourse. And people are not abstainers if they engage in sexual activities such as petting (fondling various parts of the body, especially the breasts and genitals) and anal or oral sex.

Although sexual activity is widespread, virginity is not a cultural dinosaur. About 12 percent of all women age 18 and older had their first sexual intercourse after marrying (comparable numbers are not available for men) (Abma et al., 1997).

In 1990, 46 percent of teens in grades 9 to 12 said that they had not had sexual intercourse. By 2002, the number had increased to 54 percent (Abma et al., 2004).

There are numerous explanations for early sexual intercourse among adolescents (see *Table 7.1*). But why are some teens more likely to abstain than others? Also, why do many adults go without sex?

WHY TEENS ABSTAIN FROM SEXUAL INTERCOURSE

There are several possible explanations for the decline of teen sexual intercourse in recent years. The reasons range from abstinence movements to family dynamics, but only some of these reasons are supported by scientific data.

since you asked

Do abstinence pledges work?

First, some credit the abstinence movement, especially religious and medical groups that advocate chastity for either moral or health reasons. Since 1993, numerous church groups have encouraged kids to publicly sign chastity-until-marriage pledges. The media have publicized such pledges with headlines like "Abstinence Pledges Work."

Such headlines are wrong. Abstinence pledges postpone intercourse only for 14- and 15-year-olds, and only for about 18 months. And when the pledgers break their promise, they are less likely than nonpledgers to use contraceptives. Also, rates of sexually transmitted

---

TABLE 7.1

Factors Related to Early Sexual Intercourse among Adolescents

- Alcohol or other drug use
- Delinquent behavior
- Dating before age 16 or involvement in a committed relationship
- Having a low grade point average or dropping out of school
- Frequent moves that divert parental attention and decrease parental supervision; adolescents sometimes use sex to establish new friendships or combat loneliness
- Parental divorce during adolescence
- Poverty
- Physical or sexual abuse at home or by relatives
- Minimal parental monitoring of teens' activities and friends
- Permissive parental values toward sex, including a parent who cohabits or entertains overnight guests
- Lack of neighborhood monitoring of adolescents, especially teens

---

disease are similar for pledgers and nonpledgers ages 18 to 24 (Bearman and Brückner, 2001; Brückner and Bearman, 2005).

Second, some argue that sex education programs have decreased adolescents' tendency to engage in sexual intercourse. When comprehensive education includes both abstinence and contraceptives, adolescents are more informed about their options and act more responsibly.

The Bush administration, however, has pumped money into abstinence-only programs. One of the results is that teens and young adults in abstinence-only programs are more likely to become pregnant because they know little about contraception. For example, a study of college students found that the students who broke their pledge were less likely to use a condom during their first sexual experience than were students who did not promise to abstain from sex. According to the researcher, "If you're making a pledge to remain a virgin, it would be very inconsistent to carry a condom around with you. So when the desire to have intercourse comes up . . . people find themselves unprepared" (Angela Lipsitz, cited in Mundell, 2003; see, also, Risman and Schwartz, 2002).

Third, and as you've already seen, many teenagers now substitute "outercourse," including oral sex, for sexual intercourse. Oral sex may be one of the major reasons for the decline in sexual intercourse.

Why is oral sex so acceptable? Many adolescents feel that oral sex isn't "real sex," is less intimate and less dangerous than intercourse, and doesn't violate their morals or religious views about abstaining from sex until marriage (Halpern-Felsher et al., 2005). In effect, then, adolescents are sexual, but they have redefined their idea of sex.

Finally, family dynamics—such as child–parent "connectedness" and good communication—may delay sexual initiation. Religious affiliation may also have an effect on early sexual activity. For example, teens—particularly girls—who grow up in families with strong religious views are less likely to have sex than are less religious teens. Dating, however, increases the likelihood of sexual intercourse regardless of the girl's religious views (Rodgers, 1999; Kirby, 2001; Meier, 2003).

WHY ADULTS ABSTAIN FROM SEXUAL INTERCOURSE

Major reasons for adult abstinence include not having a partner, bad luck in the dating game, divorce, or widowhood. Situational factors can also encourage abstinence. Unlike food, sleep, and shelter, sex is not necessary for physical survival. Sexual relationships can certainly be satisfying and rewarding, but neither virginity nor abstinence is fatal.

Sex and Adolescents

The first sexual experience can be happy and satisfying. It can also be a source of worry, disappointment, or guilt:

> My first time was very unpleasant. The boy I was with rushed and fumbled around and then came so fast it was over before it started. I thought, "What's so great about this?" For weeks afterward, I was afraid I had V.D. and had bad dreams about it (Masters et al., 1992. 226).

The tasks adolescents face as they navigate through unknown sexual waters are formidable: They must forge an identity that includes culturally dictated gender-role expectations. They must learn about sexual and romantic relationships. They must also develop a set of sexual values.

Many adolescents have sexual intercourse before they have accomplished these tasks. At age 15, 25 percent of girls and 30 percent of boys have had sexual intercourse (Holt et al., 2003). By the twelfth grade, almost half of all high school students have done so.

The rates are higher for black and Latino adolescents than for their white counterparts. For example, about 14 percent of high school seniors have had four or more sex partners; the highest rates are among African American and Latino males (see *Figure 7.7*).

REASONS FOR ADOLESCENT SEX

"Raging hormones," the old explanation for adolescent sex, is more fiction than fact. Although adolescents who mature early are likely to become sexually active at a younger age than their later-maturing peers, young people's interest in sex is affected by a variety of factors.

For young girls, sex still occurs most often in the context of close, romantic relationships. For example, 75 percent of girls ages 15 to 19 had their first sex with someone with whom they were "going steady" (Abma et al., 2004). Although there are no comparable national data for men, some smaller studies suggest that young males are more casual about sex and may "go steady" to get sex (see Chapter 7).

One reason for early premarital sex, you recall, especially for boys, is *peer pressure*. One in three boys

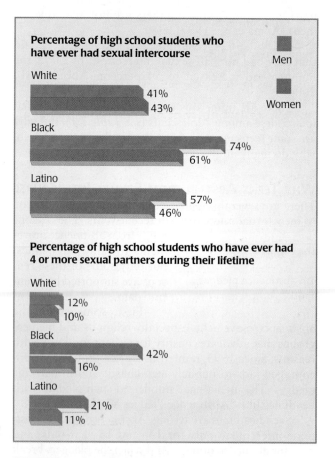

FIGURE 7.7 Sexually Experienced Teens, 2003

SOURCE: Based on Grunbaum et al., 2004, Table 42.

ages 15 to 17 say that they feel pressure to have sex, compared with 23 percent of girls (Holt et al., 2003).

Boys as young as 13 brag about their sexual prowess (although most are lying) and ridicule friends who have not "scored." Boys may even challenge a friend to "prove his manhood." Girls are likely to have fewer partners and to engage in sex to keep or to please their boyfriends (Sprecher and McKinney, 1993; Holt et al., 2003).

Parental factors also play an important role in whether a teen engages in early premarital sex. As you saw earlier, young teens (those between ages 14 and 16) are less likely to engage in sexual intercourse and have fewer partners if their mothers, in particular, monitor their activities, maintain good communication, and have strict attitudes about adolescent sex.

Parental monitoring doesn't guarantee abstinence, however. One-third of 12-year-olds, for example, report that they recently attended a party where no adults were in the house. By age 14, this percentage increased to 51 percent for boys and 42 percent for girls. In about half of the sexual encounters, an adult was "around" (Albert et al., 2003). Thus, teens are often having sex at home, just down the hall from a parent.

Environmental variables also influence how early sexual intercourse occurs. Teens who are more likely to engage in sexual activities are those who live in single-parent or remarried families, have more opportunities for sex (as in steady dating), associate with delinquent peers, use alcohol and other drugs, or have been sexually abused (Whitbeck et al., 1999; Lindberg et al., 2000).

Even seasons affect the age at which young people first have sex. The first sexual intercourse of teens in grades 7 through 12 is most likely to occur during two seasonal "peaks." One, in June (the "summer vacation effect"), occurs between people who are not in a romantic relationship but go to the prom, have a lot of free (and unsupervised) time at the end of the school year, and wear fewer and less restrictive clothes. The second peak, in December ("the holiday season effect"), occurs between adolescents in romantic relationships. The holidays seem to encourage lovemaking because they are bathed in romantic "trimmings" such as mistletoe and Christmas movies about people falling in love (Levin et al., 2002).

Cultural attitudes and expectations also influence teens' sexual experiences. Young Latino males, for instance, are much more likely than Latinas to report that they've had sexual intercourse and that they've had more partners (see *Figure 7.7*). The double standard that we discussed earlier in this chapter and in Chapters 5 and 6 probably explains some of the gender differences.

Two concepts that are common in Latin American cultures promote female premarital abstinence: *verguenza*

("shame"), which connotes embarrassment about body parts and the notion that "good" girls should not know about sexuality, and *marianismo* (from the name of the Virgin Mary), which reflects values related to chastity, purity, and virtue. If young Latinas endorse these cultural values, they are likely to delay sexual activity (Liebowitz et al., 1999). As immigrants become assimilated into U.S. culture, their children often internalize peer values and behaviors that encourage early sexual intercourse (see Chapter 4).

FORCED SEXUAL INTERCOURSE Nationwide, 13 percent of female and 6 percent of male high school students said that they have had sex against their will. Black and Latino students (10 percent and 9 percent, respectively) were more likely than white students (7 percent) to have been forced to have sexual intercourse. About 18 percent of those whose first sex occurred at age 14 or younger said that it was involuntary (Grunbaum et al., 2002; Abma et al., 2004).

For young girls, the most common factors associated with unwanted sex include the mother's having an abusive boyfriend, illicit drug use (by the parent, the victim, or the nonparental abuser), lack of parental monitoring in the home, a history of sexual abuse in the victim's family, and the victim's living apart from her parents before age 16. Adolescent boys report unwanted sexual touching (kissing, petting, fondling) and a romantic partner's threatening to withhold love (Small and Kerns, 1993; Christopher and Kisler, 2004).

Sex and Singles

Women and men are staying single longer for a variety of reasons—higher education, military service, and careers. Postponing marriage increases the likelihood of premarital sex. Divorced and widowed individuals may find a new sexual partner whom they may or may not marry (see Chapter 8).

Premarital sex isn't limited to Western nations. For example, 70 percent of Beijing residents say that they had sexual relations before marriage, compared with just 16 percent in 1989 (Beech, 2005).

WHO INITIATES SEXUAL CONTACT? Traditional sexual scripts dictate that the man should initiate sexual contact because "nice girls don't." But many young women have become more assertive than in the past. Instead of sitting around at home, they frequent singles bars and clubs, or call, e-mail, or text message men on cell phones. They also invite sexual contact in other ways, such as going to a man's apartment or dorm room. In steady dating relationships, women may touch or stroke a partner or make sensuous comments about his appearance to arouse him (O'Sullivan and Byers, 1993).

Many young women rationalize intercourse in the same way that earlier generations justified petting ("It's O.K. if I love him"). The growing number of women who have casual sex when "hookin' up," however, suggests that these traditional views are changing (see Chapter 8).

WILL YOU STILL LOVE ME TOMORROW? Maybe. Young people, especially women, view casual sex less favorably than they did a generation ago. In 1980, for example, 50 percent of first-year college students said that "if two people really like each other, it's all right for them to have sex even if they've known each other for a short time." In 2005, 45 percent of first-year college students (58 percent of the men and 34 percent of the women) agreed with this statement (*Chronicle of Higher Education*, 2006).

And will you respect me tomorrow? Not if we're having casual sex, according to some researchers. Many men still have a double standard. They often judge sexually permissive women as terrific for casual dates or as regular sexual partners but unacceptable for long-term commitments or as marriage partners (see Chapter 8).

Stereotypes and double standards are more common in some social contexts than in others. Many women consume alcohol both in private (parties, dates) and public (sporting events). In bars, many men perceive women drinkers as "loose" and "sexually easy," especially if they dress in a "provocative" manner. As one man said, appearance increases the risk of aggression: "Some girls whose boobs are hanging out, skirts up to here, no underwear on, you know something's going to happen" (Parks and Scheidt, 2000: 936). In contrast, men feel free to dress and act any way they want without being labeled as "loose."

ARE SINGLES HAPPY WITH THEIR SEX LIVES? Nationally, 53 percent of young singles (under age 30) report being "very satisfied" with their sex lives, compared with 77 percent of people who are married or in a committed relationship. Singles have less sex than people who are married or cohabiting. Sexually active young singles are also twice as likely as other adults to worry about contracting AIDS or some other sexually transmitted disease (Langer et al., 2004).

Sex in Marriage

Most married couples are happy with their sex lives. Increasingly, however, couples report that being tired and stressed out affects their sexual behavior.

FREQUENCY OF SEX "I got married," says one guy to another, "so that I could have sex three or four times a week." That's funny," says his buddy. "That's exactly why I got divorced." There are many similar jokes about married people not having enough sex. In fact, about 40 percent of married people have sex with their partner two or more times a week. This rate is twice as high as for singles (Laumann et al., 1994).

In terms of indirect measures of sexual frequency, such as condom sales, the highest rates are among married couples with children under age 12 and under age 6 (26 percent and 15 percent, respectively) (Fetto, 2003). This suggests that couples with young children are sexually active.

Among some couples, frequency of sexual intercourse may remain constant or even increase over the years. Among others, the nature of their sexual expression may change: Intercourse may become less frequent, but fondling and genital stimulation (with or without orgasm) may increase.

GEECH®   **by Jerry Bittle**

Overall, the frequency of marital sex typically decreases over time. As a marriage matures, concerns about earning a living, making a home, and raising a family become more pressing than the desire for lovemaking.

Consciously or not, some married women, especially mothers, avoid sex because they're angry:

Mad that he would never think to pick up diapers or milk on his way home . . . He doesn't help around the house enough or with the kids. He sees the groceries sitting on the counter. Why doesn't he take them out of the bag and put them away? (Deveny, 2003: 45, 46).

In most cases, marital sex decreases in frequency because couples are overworked, are anxious about the economy, and devote much of their time to raising kids. About 23 percent of adults say that simply being tired day after day has sapped their sex lives (National Sleep Foundation, 2005).

QUALITY OF SEX Although the frequency of sex decreases, the longer people are married the more likely they are to report that they are very satisfied with their sex life. Sex is especially satisfying if both spouses feel—in terms of exchange theory—that their rewards and costs are similar and that they have a mutually satisfying emotional relationship (Call et al., 1995; Lawrance and Byers, 1995; Waite and Joyner, 2001).

Married people are happier with their sex lives than either single people or cohabitants (Laumann et al., 1994). These findings support the notion, discussed in Chapter 6, that sexual intercourse is more than just the sexual act—it also involves intimacy, commitment, and love.

The false notion that most married couples have unhappy sex lives has become big business. We have become so obsessed with this subject that sex manuals are constantly on best-seller lists. Most recently, for example, one writer insists that having sex about once a month is synonymous with a "sexless" or "sex starved" marriage (Weiner-Davis, 2003).

Newsmagazines and pharmaceutical companies are fanning such opinions to increase sales. Less frequent marital sex is neither unusual nor abnormal. Even young married couples report that companionship is often more important than sexual passion. As one man stated,

On my list [sex] would come fourth. Marriage, as far as I'm concerned, is friendship and companionship; that ranks first. Then there's consideration for one another, and then trust, and then fourth I'd say your physical relationship. And those three that come before hopefully enhance what you experience in your physical relationship (Greenblatt, 1983: 298).

Sex During the Middle Years

As we mature, our sexual interests, abilities, and responses change. While a majority of adults age 45 and older agree that a satisfying sexual relationship is important, it's not their top priority. Good spirits, good health, close ties with friends and family, financial security, spiritual well-being, and a good relationship with a partner are all rated as more crucial than a fulfilling sexual connection (Jacoby, 2005). Our priorities shift, in part, because of the physiological changes that accompany aging.

MENOPAUSE Early in the twentieth century many women died, often in childbirth, long before they experienced **menopause,** the cessation of the menstrual cycle and the loss of reproductive capacity, or "the change of life," as it was once called. *Perimenopause,* also a normal phenomenon, usually precedes menopause. Whereas menopause typically begins in a woman's mid-40s to early 50s, perimenopause can begin in the early 40s and last four to five years.

The symptoms of both perimenopause and menopause include hormonally induced "hot flashes" (a sudden experience of overall bodily heat, sometimes accompanied by sweating), irregular menstrual cycles with uncharacteristically heavy or light bleeding, mood changes, fatigue, migraine headaches, backaches, insomnia, loss or increase of appetite, diarrhea or constipation, and urinary incontinence (Northrup, 2001). Because of these changes, one of my older students "defines" menopause as "Everyone around you suddenly has a bad attitude."

Some (lucky) women hardly notice that they are going through menopause. Hot flashes affect about 75 percent of all women, but they usually last only a few minutes. Even when the symptoms are severe, most women do not consider menopause a crisis but a liberating time of life: Many enjoy sex more because they are no longer bothered by menstruation, the need for contraception, or the fear of pregnancy (Fisher, 1999).

MALE CLIMACTERIC It is unclear whether there is a **male climacteric** or change of life analogous to female menopause. Testosterone production declines with age. But, unlike women, men do not lose their reproductive capacity. Some men in their late 70s have fathered children.

Only a small percentage of men experience nervousness, depression, decreased sexual performance (which often can be treated medically), inability to concentrate, irritability, and similar problems. It may be that the male "change of life" is a more general "midlife crisis" in which men look back over their lives and feel distress at not having achieved what they had planned (Gould et al., 2000).

Although some spouses in their middle years are dissatisfied with their sex life, they represent a minority of all marriages. Couples who have no children living at home and don't have to care for elderly parents are freed from time-consuming responsibilities. They have more time, energy, and privacy for talking, intimacy, and sex. Thus, "the empty nest may actually be a love nest" (Woodward and Springen, 1992: 71; Edwards and Booth, 1994).

The older women and men are, the more likely they are to say that qualities such as making them feel important or feeling loved go beyond sex. Nevertheless, there are several gender gaps in later life.

Sex and Later Life

An 80-year-old husband says, "Let's go upstairs and make love." His 75-year-old wife replies, "Pick one, dear. I can't do both." This is one of my elderly aunt's favorite jokes. Despite such jokes, many men and women remain sexually active into their 70s, 80s, and beyond.

SEXUAL ACTIVITY Sexual activity among older people declines but doesn't disappear, especially for those with a regular partner. For example,

- About half of 50- to 59-year-old men and 43 percent of women have sexual intercourse at least once a week.

- Among 60- to 69-year-olds, 36 percent of men and 24 percent of women have sexual intercourse at least once a week.

- At age 70 and older, 22 percent of men and 14 percent of women have sexual intercourse at least once a week.

- At age 70 and older, 54 percent of men and 27 percent of women engage in sexual touching or caressing; 8 percent of men and 2 percent of women have oral sex (AARP, 2005).

Lowered activity—or inactivity—isn't a problem if both partners have a loving and committed relationship (Marsiglio and Greer, 1994).

In a study of the sexual practices of 202 men and women ages 80 to 102 (that's right, 102!), 47 percent of the respondents were having sexual intercourse and 34 percent engaged in oral sex. Also, 88 percent of the men and 71 percent of the women still fantasized or daydreamed about the opposite sex (Bretschneider and McCoy, 1988; Jacoby, 1999).

HEALTH AND SEXUALITY It's not until about age 70 that frequency of sexual activity, in both men and women, begins to decline significantly. This generally results from poor health and habits. Smoking, alcoholism, heart disease, prostate problems, and vascular illnesses can decrease sexual desire and activity in both sexes.

For women, the drop in estrogen levels after menopause can decrease sexual desire and make sex painful because the walls of the vagina become thin and dry. In addition, especially for women, a mix of stress, anger, or a cooling relationship can dampen sexual desire. Some illnesses, such as diabetes and arteriosclerosis, as well as some medications for high blood pressure, can cause impotence in older men (Butler and Lewis, 1993; McKinlay and Feldman, 1994).

Despite these difficulties, older men and women engage in sex and enjoy it. A reporter asked a 90-year-old woman who married an 18-year-old man, "Aren't you afraid of what could happen on the honeymoon? Vigorous lovemaking might bring on injury or even a fatal heart attack!" She smiled and replied, "If he dies, he dies!"

MORE DOUBLE STANDARDS AND SEXUAL SCRIPTS Whereas gray-haired men in their 60s are considered "distinguished," their female counterparts are just "old." Men are not under the same pressure as women to remain young, trim, and attractive. When comparing her own public image with that of her actor husband, Paul Newman, actress Joanne Woodward remarked, "He gets prettier; I get older."

The aging process may enhance a man's desirability because he has more resources and power. In contrast, an older woman may be regarded as an asexual grandmother: "Because attractiveness is associated with feelings of well-being, a perceived decline in appearance can be particularly devastating for women" (Levy, 1994: 295–96).

As in earlier stages of life, older men's sexual scripts usually focus on intercourse and orgasm. Older women are more interested in relational and nongenital activities such as hugging and holding hands. Such differences may explain why 40 percent of older men but only 15 percent of older women without regular sex partners rate their sex life at the bottom of the satisfaction scale (B.K. Johnson, 1996; Jacoby, 2005).

As people age, the biggest impediment to sex, especially for widows or divorcees, is a "partner gap." Because our culture frowns on liaisons and marriages between older women and younger men but approves of matches between older men and younger women, single older women have a small pool of eligible sexual partners. In contrast, married women over age 70 report being both sexually active *and* sexually satisfied (Matthias et al., 1997; see, also, Chapters 6, 9, and 17).

Making Connections

- Have you ever been pressured to have sex? How did you react? What advice would you give younger people who would like to resist such pressure from their friends and girlfriends or boyfriends?

- What kind of sex do you enjoy most? Least? Why? If you haven't had sexual intercourse yet, do you fantasize about it?

- How would you feel if your widowed 80-year-old parent, grandparent, or great-grandparent had an unmarried sexual partner?

Sexual Infidelity

Someone once quipped, "When a woman steals your husband, there is no better revenge than to let her keep him." This may be good advice for both women and men, especially in the long run, but few people heed it. Among other things, people don't always define "stealing" a partner in the same way.

What Is Sexual Infidelity?

Some people use the terms *affair, infidelity, adultery, unfaithful,* and *extramarital sex* interchangeably. Others define infidelity more broadly as "a breach of trust, a betrayal of a relationship, a breaking of an agreement" in *any* committed relationship—married or not (Pittman, 1990: 20).

Extramarital sex is more damaging than other forms of infidelity because a partner breaks a civil contract that's legally binding. Many are also breaking a religious promise to be faithful.

EMOTIONAL INFIDELITY   Emotional and online infidelity can be devastating to both married and unmarried couples. Almost one out of four American women feels that a sexual act is not necessary for a person to be unfaithful; lust is enough to qualify (see *Table 7.2*).

Many therapists agree that affairs do not have to include sexual intercourse. According to Glass (2002), the "new infidelity" is any betrayal of the expectation of emotional or sexual exclusivity in a committed relationship. Thus, Glass maintains, emotional infidelity includes secrecy (meeting someone without telling your spouse or partner), emotional intimacy (confiding things you haven't told your spouse or partner), and even "sexual chemistry" (being mutually attracted to someone else).

ONLINE INFIDELITY   You might have noticed that only 42 percent of men but 64 percent of women consider a virtual tryst (cybersex) to be cheating (see *Table 7.2*). If most of these people will never meet each other, what harm is done?

Although the people involved may never meet, some cyber-affairs may eventually break up a marriage or a relationship. In almost 30 percent of cyber-affairs,

TABLE 7.2

Is This Infidelity?

Percentage of people who strongly agree that the following acts constitute infidelity in a committed relationship:

	Men	Women
Intercourse with another man or woman	88%	94%
Oral sex with another man or woman	85	93
Fondling another man or woman	78	88
Kissing another man or woman	51	69
Telephone sex	48	69
Cybersex	42	64
Holding hands with another man or woman	35	48
Lustfully thinking about another man or woman	17	23
Flirting with another man or woman	16	21
Looking at another man or woman	6	6

Do you see any differences between women's and men's responses? Do you agree that telephone sex and cybersex constitute infidelity?

SOURCE: Covel, 2003: 16.

Desperate Housewives, a television show that focuses largely on extramarital sex, has been a hit since it first aired in 2004. Why?

the relationship escalates from e-mail to telephone calls to personal contact (Greenfield, 1999).

Some practitioners believe that Internet romances are betrayals because they reflect emotional infidelity: People share personal information (including comments about marital dissatisfaction), become more secretive, and may spend more time with a cyberlover than with a spouse or partner (Young, 2001). Because online infidelity violates a trust, it can elicit hurt, anger, depression, and insecurity.

since you asked

Is online sex harmless?

How Common Is Sexual Infidelity?

A few years ago, a happily married mother of two designed a new line of greeting cards for people involved in affairs. Many people were appalled because they felt that such cards romanticize infidelity, encourage affairs, and celebrate a negative behavior that wreaks havoc in marriages and other committed relationships (Siegel, 2005).

The entrepreneur defended herself. She said that she "had done a lot of research" and found that half of all married people had had affairs (Kiehl, 2005). Her numbers were wrong. Maybe her "research" was based on watching *Desperate Housewives* or other television morning shows that interview clinicians who work with troubled couples and conclude that "at least" half of all married people have cheated.

A survey that included both married and unmarried couples found that 29 percent had been unfaithful to a partner at some time (Covel, 2003). Extramarital sex, however, is *not* a common occurrence. Although it makes great fodder for talk shows, national surveys show that most Americans are faithful. In one such study, when researchers asked people whether they had *ever* had extramarital sex, 16 percent said yes (21 percent of men and nearly 13 percent of women) (Morin, 1994).

A more recent national study confirms these figures. In all committed relationships, married and unmarried, 16 percent of the partners admit to having cheated, but the numbers are higher for men (21 percent) than for women (11 percent) (Langer et al., 2004).

These numbers may seem high, especially when 80 percent of Americans believe that marital infidelity is "always wrong," up from 70 percent in 1970 (Ali and Miller, 2004). But year after year, my students refuse to believe that most married people are faithful because of their personal experiences. For example,

"I work as a bartender part-time and hang out in bars on the weekends. I watch people leave my bar all the time and all I can think of is his poor wife waiting at home."

"I find it hard to believe that only 16 percent of married people have cheated. Most are lying."

"A lot of men, single or married, think with their penis. You'll never convince me that only about 20 percent of men have cheated on their wives" (Author's files)

Why Are Spouses and Partners Unfaithful?

Popular magazines routinely imply that it's the woman's fault if a man is unfaithful. The articles offer advice on how to please a husband or boyfriend, such as having cosmetic surgery, losing weight, buying sexy lingerie, preparing romantic dinners, and not nagging. Magazines very rarely advise a husband to please his wife so that *she* will not be tempted to have an affair.

The complex reasons for adultery include both macro- and micro-explanations. Although they overlap and are often cumulative, let's look at them separately for greater clarity.

MACRO-REASONS Among the many macro-explanations for extramarital sex, several are especially significant:

1. *Economic problems* place strains on families. Unemployment, underemployment (employment below

a person's level of training and education), and lay-offs can create pressures that may increase the incidence of sexual infidelity. Husbands and wives who must work different shifts or are separated because of military duty or frequent business trips may develop intimate relationships with others.

2. *The purpose of marriage* has changed for many people. Although procreation is still important, today many couples marry primarily for companionship and intimacy (see Chapter 1). When these needs are not met, outside relationships may develop.

3. *The anonymity of urban life* provides opportunities for and conceals adultery more easily than is the case in small towns, where people are more likely to know one another.

4. Because today people *live longer*, marriages can last as long as 60 years, increasing the chances for conflict, dissatisfaction, and infidelity.

5. Because there are more women in the workplace and they have more contact with men, there is *greater opportunity for sexual infidelity*. In one survey, for example, 22 percent of the unfaithful men said that they couldn't pass up "a perfect opportunity" to have sex with an available woman. About 37 percent of the women and men who cheated said that they did so with a co-worker (Covel, 2003; Langer et al., 2004).

6. New *technology* has increased opportunities for cyber-flirting. People can sneak down to their computers and engage in cyber-affairs while their spouse or other partner is sleeping (Gardner, 2004).

MICRO-REASONS There are also a number of micro-explanations for sexual infidelity:

1. *The need for emotional satisfaction* may propel people into extramarital sex. Women who are unfaithful often feel that their husbands do not communicate with them and have no time for them except in bed. According to one woman, "We shared nothing but sex. He never wanted to talk to me about his work, or about mine, or go anywhere, or do anything. It . . . was like going to bed with a stranger" (Wolfe, 1981).

2. Sometimes people have "flings" to decrease *loneliness*. In one survey, 22 percent of the women said that loneliness was their top reason for having an affair (Covel, 2003).

3. Sexual infidelity is an *ego-enhancer*. As people grow older, some may try to prove to themselves that they are still physically and socially desirable and at-tractive. As one unfaithful wife said, "He tells me my skin is soft. He makes me feel sexy again" (Ali and Miller, 2004: 49).

4. Sexual infidelity reflects a *social exchange*. Men who are involved in extramarital affairs are generally older and have much higher incomes than their female partners. Often they are the woman's boss or mentor. Aging but powerful men get sex in exchange for a younger woman's attraction to their status, power, prestige, or wealth.

5. People sometimes have extramarital sex as a form of *revenge or retaliation* against a spouse for involvement in a similar activity or "for some sort of nonsexual mistreatment, real or imagined, by the spouse" (Kinsey et al., 1953: 432).

6. An extramarital relationship may provide a *way out of marriage*. Some people might deliberately initiate an affair as an excuse to dissolve an unhappy marriage (Walsh, 1991).

Consequences of Sexual Infidelity

In 2001, Jesse Jackson, a highly respected civil-rights leader, admitted that his mistress was pregnant with his child. More recently, the wife of New Mexico state senator Carlos Cisneros hit him on the head with a hammer after she found him in bed with another woman. The Boeing Corporation forced its president and chief executive officer to resign after it became known that he had an extramarital affair with a company executive. Company leaders decided that the affair showed "poor judgment" in his personal life that might also affect his professional decisions. And, in a rare move, the Army relieved one of its 11 four-star generals of his command because he had committed adultery, a violation of the Uniform Code of Military Justice. The general wasn't the first offender, but the Army decided to send the message that it wouldn't tolerate extramarital affairs at any level (Clemetson and McRoberts, 2001; Torres, 2005; White, 2005).

Only about 10 percent of adulterous relationships end in marriage, and the average length of an affair is a year (Patterson and Kim, 1991). In other words, affairs most often end rather than endure.

What are the consequences of these short-lived affairs? One clinician describes the discovery of a spouse's affair as the "emotional equivalent of having a limb amputated without an anesthetic" (McGinnis, 1981: 154). The injured spouse typically feels deceived, betrayed, and depressed. The aggrieved person may also experience doubts about his or her own desirability, adequacy, or worth.

Because extramarital affairs rarely end in marriage, a man may not support his lover's child or children in case of a pregnancy. Moreover, both men and women may be justifiably concerned about contracting or infecting a partner with STIs, especially HIV/AIDS.

Marriage counselors point out that most extramarital affairs devastate the entire family. They can have an especially negative impact on children, who often feel insecure and confused, particularly if the marriage collapses because of the affair. Because very young children are self-centered, they may feel that they are somehow to blame for what has happened (see Chapter 15).

Extramarital sex also has broad structural implications for society as a whole. Group solidarity is necessary for a society's survival. Because family members depend on one another for emotional support, their unity and cohesiveness can be threatened by sexual "intruders."

Making Connections

■ Do you think that emotional infidelity, including cybersex, is a form of sexual infidelity? Or is it just a harmless romantic game (the ludic love discussed in Chapter 6)?

■ One of the most common questions for advice columns like *Dear Abby* is whether a co-worker, friend, relative, or family member should tell someone about a partner's or spouse's sexual infidelity. What would you advise people to do? Or, what have you done in such situations?

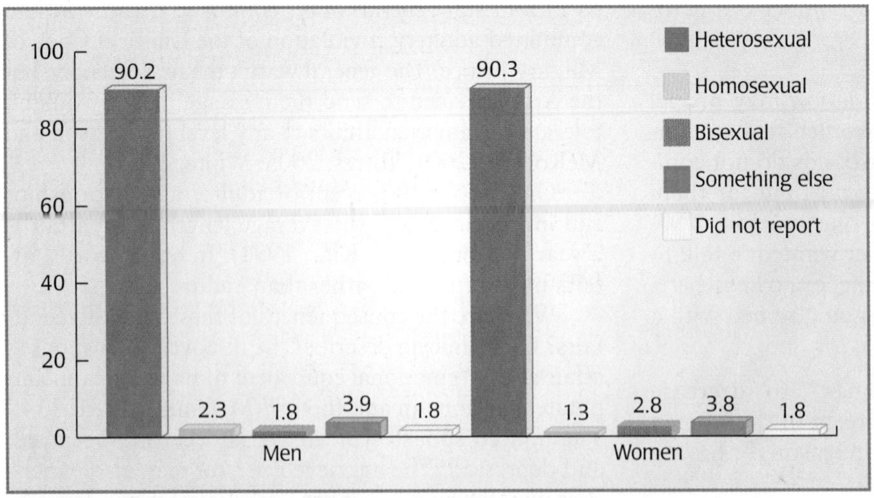

Gay, Lesbian, and Bisexual Sex

Although the percentage of gays and bisexuals in the U.S. population is small, their sexual activities have triggered a wide range of public reactions. Let's begin with a look at the extent of homosexuality in the United States.

The Extent of Homosexuality

How many gay men, lesbians, and bisexuals are there in the United States? No one knows for sure, largely because it's difficult to define and measure sexual orientation. Researchers generally measure the extent of homosexuality by simply asking people whether they identify themselves as heterosexual or gay, lesbian, or bisexual (GLB). About 8 percent of Americans identify themselves as homosexual or bisexual (see *Figure 7.8*). However, 18 percent have had same-sex sexual contact (Mosher et al., 2005).

Same-Sex Behavior

Except for penile-vaginal intercourse, gay couples do everything that heterosexuals do. Their sexual activities include kissing, caressing, hugging, nipple stimulation, oral and anal sex, and other nongenital touching or foreplay.

Lesbian sexual activities include cunnilingus, manual masturbation, body-to-body rubbing of breasts or clitorises, and slow, sensual body caressing. Although some lesbians report using dildos, the most popular activities include oral sex and nongenital acts such as kissing. Like heterosexuals, homosexuals use a variety of positions to achieve sexual satisfaction, and not all couples participate in or enjoy all sexual activities (King, 2002).

Societal Reactions to Homosexuality

Societies vary greatly in their responses to homosexuality. Some are punitive, many are tolerant, and some (such as New Guinea) have included homosexual relations in puberty ceremonies (Herdt, 1997). In

FIGURE 7.8 **Sexual Orientation**
Percent distribution of men and women 18–44 years of age: United States, 2002.

SOURCE: Mosher et al. 2005, Figure 8.

since you asked

Are Americans more accepting of homosexuality than in the past?

the United States, societal reactions range from homophobia to growing acceptance of gays and lesbians.

HOMOPHOBIA Fear and hatred of homosexuality, or **homophobia**, is less overt today than in the past but is still widespread. Some parents have blocked health curricula in public schools that discuss homosexuality. Others have demanded the right to pull their kindergarten children out of classes that use books containing pictures of same-sex parents (Simon, 2005).

Homophobia often takes the form of *gay bashing:* threats, assaults, or acts of violence directed at homosexuals. Of the more than 9,000 hate crimes reported to U.S. law enforcement agencies in 2005, nearly 16 percent of the victims were GLBs (Federal Bureau of Investigation, 2005).

Who is most likely to be homophobic? Men (56 percent), people age 65 and older (57 percent), those who have never known anyone who's gay (47 percent), and people with a high school education or less (57 percent) (*Inside*-OUT . . . , 2001).

Sheryl Swoopes of the Women's National Basketball Association (WNBA) was the first "superstar" to come out of the closet, in 2005, while still playing.

A college education does not guarantee acceptance of homosexuality, however. For example, Boston University's chancellor ordered a secondary school operated by the university to disband a support group for gay and lesbian students. And in a survey of 14 college campuses, 36 percent of the GLB undergraduates had experienced harassment. Of these, 20 percent said they feared for their safety—even at colleges with strong GLB support groups (Kiernan, 2002; Rankin, 2003).

Minority GLBs are most likely to encounter prejudice and discrimination. Asian American lesbians feel that they face additional obstacles. They rarely appear in the mainstream or GLB media because of the stereotype that there are no gay Asians. They cannot come out to their families because "women are not seen as sexual beings" in some Asian cultures. Coming out would bring shame on the parents because relatives, friends, and other members of Asian communities view GLBs as abnormal. These women also experience more verbal and physical assaults because they are "triple rejects"—women, Asian, and lesbian (Foo, 2002).

INCREASING ACCEPTANCE The percentage of Americans who believe that homosexuality is an acceptable way of life increased from 43 percent in 1977 to 57 percent in 2005 (Saad, 2005). Still, many people are divided on the issue. About 56 percent of Americans oppose legalizing homosexual unions, but large numbers feel that gay men and lesbians should have equal rights in job opportunities and protection against hate crimes (see *Figure 7.9*).

Numerous municipal jurisdictions, corporations, and smaller companies now extend health-care coverage and other benefits to the partners of their gay and lesbian employees. Many states allow gay partners to jointly adopt children on the same basis as unmarried couples. Large numbers of colleges and universities offer health and other benefits to gay and lesbian couples, offer courses or programs in gay and lesbian studies, and provide funding for gay student clubs. And there are at least 3,000 gay-straight alliances (GSAS)—clubs for gay and gay-friendly kids—on high school campuses, up from just 100 in 1997 (Cloud, 2005; see, also, Chapter 11).

In late 1999, the Vermont state supreme court ruled that same-sex partners should have the same rights as married couples. Some of these rights include joint ownership of homes and other property, a share of the partner's medical or life insurance, inheritance rights, and survivors' benefits if a partner dies. Since then, several other states have passed similar legislation. (We'll examine civil unions in Chapter 9.)

Commercial television has also come a long way in its portrayal of gays and lesbians. In an episode of the

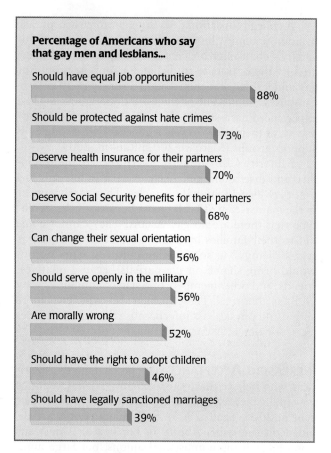

FIGURE 7.9 Attitudes about Gay and Lesbian Rights
SOURCES: Based on *Inside*-OUT . . . , 2001, and Saad, 2005.

hurdles in their families and communities because of cultural, religious, and generational differences (see Chapters 8 and 9).

Making Connections

■ How would you react if your best friend told you she or he was gay? What if one of your parents did so? Your brother or sister? Your adolescent daughter or son? Or, if you're gay and have come out, how did other people react?

■ How does gay bashing affect all of us and not just the victims?

Sexually Transmitted Infections, HIV, and AIDS

Sexual expression is not always smooth and carefree. *Appendix B* provides information about sexual problems, dysfunctions, and their treatment. Here we'll briefly examine STIs—diseases, infections, and illnesses that are conveyed almost solely through sexual intercourse.

STIs

Sexually transmitted infections (STIs) are diseases that are spread by contact, either sexual or nonsexual, with body parts or fluids that harbor specific microorganisms (generally bacterial or viral). (STI corresponds to but has recently replaced another frequently used term, **sexually transmitted disease,** or STD.) The term *sexually transmitted* indicates that sexual contact is the most common means of spreading infections.

PREVALENCE There are approximately 15 million new cases of STIs in the United States every year. STIs affect women and men of all backgrounds and economic levels. However, nearly half of all STIs occur in people under 25 years of age.

There are at least 50 types of STIs (see *Appendix E* for more information about some of these diseases, their symptoms, and their treatment). Today *syphilis* is the least common STI; the most common is *chlamydia*, a bacterial infection, followed by *gonorrhea* (see *Figure 7.10*).

EFFECTS OF STIs Most of the time, STIs cause no symptoms, particularly in women. Even when there are no symptoms, however, a person who is infected can pass the diseases on to a partner. STIs can cause cancer,

popular 1970s show *Marcus Welby, M.D.,* Dr. Welby advised a patient to suppress his homosexual tendencies in order to be a good husband and father. Since the mid-1990s, in contrast, a multitude of gay characters have appeared in major or secondary roles on prime-time TV in popular programs like *Friends, Mad about You, Spin City, Ellen, Will & Grace, Dawson's Creek, Chicago Hope, ER, The Simpsons,* and *Queer Eye for the Straight Guy,* among others. In 2005, *Brokeback Mountain*—a movie about gay cowboys—received the Golden Globes award for best motion picture of the year.

Does such programming reflect progress? Some think so, but others are offended. Ambivalence about homosexuality is especially evident in religious institutions. Some denominations have welcomed gays as members and ordained GLB ministers and even bishops ("A first . . . ," 2003). Others—Episcopal, Lutheran, Methodist, Presbyterian, and United Church of Christ—find themselves polarized and divided over homosexuality. Ethnic gay men and lesbians face additional

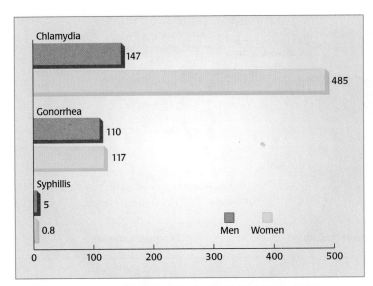

FIGURE 7.10 Cases of Selected STIs in the United States, 2004
These figures are conservative because many people don't realize that they're infected and don't seek medical care. The actual rates are about four to five times higher.

SOURCE: Based on Centers for Disease Control and Prevention, 2005b.

birth defects, miscarriages, and in some cases death. Untreated chlamydia can cause permanent damage to the reproductive organs, often resulting in infertility in women and sterility in men. Gonorrhea can result in infertility in men. A baby born to an infected mother may become blind.

since you asked

Can all STIs be "cured"?

Without early screening and treatment, 10 to 40 percent of women with gonorrhea develop pelvic inflammatory disease (PID). PID can result in infertility in women and life-threatening (ectopic) pregnancy when, for example, the fertilized egg implants itself in the fallopian tube rather than the uterus. The tube can rupture and, without surgical intervention, cause death.

Human papilloma virus (HPV) causes *genital warts,* which infect an estimated 1 million Americans each year. In addition to genital warts, certain types of HPV cause cervical cancer and other genital cancers. There is treatment but no cure for herpes or genital warts.

HIV and AIDS

One of the most serious (and still fatal, in many cases) STIs is the **human immunodeficiency virus (HIV),** the virus that causes AIDS. **Acquired immunodeficiency syn-** drome **(AIDS)** is a degenerative condition that attacks the body's immune system and makes it unable to fight a number of diseases, including some forms of pneumonia and cancer.

PREVALENCE First reported on June 5, 1981, AIDS had taken the lives of almost 525,000 Americans by the end of 2004. An estimated 1.2 million people are living with AIDS. Almost 43,000 new HIV infections are reported each year (Centers for Disease Control and Prevention, 2005a).

Although AIDS death rates have been decreasing, some populations have become more vulnerable to the virus. As *Figure 7.11* shows, the HIV epidemic is highest among men, African Americans, and men having sex with men (MSM).

HOW HIV SPREADS Although childbirth and breast milk can pass on HIV, the most common infections are through sexual contact and other behaviors that transmit blood and semen:

- **Anal sex.** A major reason why gay men have high rates of HIV/AIDS is that they engage in anal sex. This practice causes rectal bleeding, which permits the passage of HIV from one person to another.

- **Oral sex.** A partner who has bleeding gums, cuts, or sores in the mouth or throat can transmit HIV.

- **Sharing needles.** Drug users often share a needle to inject drugs. People who are infected with HIV can infect others by sharing needles.

- **Drug use.** Using any kind of drug, including alcohol and marijuana, can impair one's judgment. For example, alcohol consumption among teens lowers the likelihood that they'll use contraceptives during sex. The rate of methamphetamine (meth) use has tripled since 2001, especially among MSM. Because meth increases arousal and reduces inhibitions, often prompting users to seek sex with multiple partners, meth use heightens the risk of contracting HIV (Markowitz et al., 2005; Ornstein, 2005).

- **Multiple partners.** A sexual liaison exposes people to a "chain" of past partners. Anyone in the chain who is infected can transmit HIV to numerous later partners (Bearman et al., 2004).

Some myths about HIV transmission still linger. According to the best possible information, none of the following transmit HIV: insect bites, sweat, tears, sneezing,

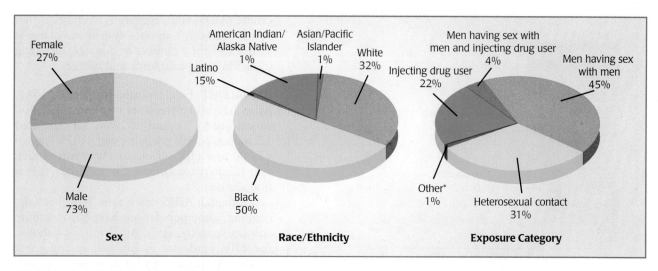

FIGURE 7.11   U.S. Adults Living with HIV/AIDS, 2004

*Includes hemophilia, blood transfusion, and risk not reported or not identified.

SOURCE: Based on Centers for Disease Control and Prevention, 2005a.

coughing, food preparation, toilet seats, blood donations, or a swimming pool that uses chlorine.

Why STIs Are Spreading

Why are STI rates rising? As in other situations, there are both macro-level constraints and micro-level choices. Let's look at a few examples.

In terms of macro reasons,

1. Some groups *aren't informed about infectious diseases.* For example, the number of HIV-positive people older than 50 has been "rising sharply." Many older people are sexually active, but older women, especially, are not concerned about becoming pregnant, don't think they're at risk, and don't insist that their partners wear condoms (Zwillich, 2005).

2. *Assimilation increases risky behavior.* Latino adolescents who have been in the United States for a generation are more than twice as likely as recent immigrants to be sexually active. As immigrants become more Americanized, they lose "the healthy immigrant effect," which includes avoiding drugs that increase the likelihood of risky sexual behavior and having unprotected MSM (Adam et al., 2005; Flores and Brotanek, 2005; Ramos, 2005).

3. *Poverty spreads infections.* African American women and men are six times more likely to be in-

fected with chlamydia than whites. Half of all HIV-infected people are African Americans.

Why are there such wide disparities among racial and ethnic groups? Minorities are less likely to get early screening. HIV-positive women tend to be unemployed, depend on public assistance, exchange sex for drugs, and have many sexual partners. Minority women in poor neighborhoods, where there is often a scarcity of eligible men, usually select sexual partners from the same high-risk neighborhood (Miller et al., 2004; Adimora and Schoenbach, 2005; Sternberg, 2005).

Individual characteristics and choices also spike infection rates. For example,

1. As you saw earlier, both adults and adolescents *know a lot less about sex than they think they do.* The lack of information and misinformation increases the chances of a sexual infection. The parents who are the most likely to have medically inaccurate information are politically conservative and hold very negative views about condoms and oral contraceptives. The more positive teens' attitudes about contraception are, the more likely they are to use it (Brückner et al., 2004; Eisenberg et al., 2004).

2. The less we know about sex, the more likely we are to believe that "*it won't happen to me.*" A national study of boys ages 15 to 17 found that 53 percent believed that a condom should fit tightly, leaving

no space at the tip (Rock et al., 2005). A tight fit increases the chance of breakage and semen escaping during intercourse.

3. *Attitudes and behavior don't always mesh.* About 84 percent of sexually active adults ages 18 to 35 said that they take the necessary precautions to protect themselves against sexually transmitted diseases. Their actions didn't reflect their beliefs: 82 percent said that they never use protection against STIs for oral sex, 64 percent never use protection for anal sex, and 47 percent never use protection for vaginal sex. Also, 93 percent said that their current partner did not have a STI, but about one-third had never discussed the issue with their partners (Lilleston, 2004).

4. *Some people simply lie.* A study conducted by the Centers for Disease Control and Prevention found that 43 percent of black men, 26 percent of Latino men, and 7 percent of white men reported being on the down low. Down low men are lying to women. Many MSM are also dishonest: Approximately 58 percent avoid testing because they are afraid of learning that they have HIV or worry that others will find out about the results (Sifakis et al., 2005; Wahlberg, 2005).

5. *Heterosexual women are especially vulnerable.* They are more than twice as likely as men to become infected with HIV, for several reasons. First, the genital surface exposed to the virus is much larger in women than in men. Second, vaginal secretions from an HIV-infected woman are believed to be less potent than an infected man's semen, which is capable of packing high concentrations of the virus. Third, a man's exposure to the virus is limited to the duration of sex, but semen remains in a woman's body after intercourse. Fourth, many women are not aware that their male partners are gay. Finally, many women—especially those at low income levels but 56 percent of college women as well—believe that they won't contract HIV or other STIs. As a result, they don't use condoms even when they have multiple sex partners (Nicolosi et al., 1994; Yarnall et al., 2003).

Some of the macro-level reasons for the spread of infectious diseases filter down to the micro level. For example, if teenagers don't get accurate information about sex, they are less likely to use condoms, to use them correctly, or not to use dental dams during oral sex. In other cases, people take more chances because of medical technology. Some older MSM have returned to risky sexual behavior because they feel "condom fatigue" and believe that AIDS treatment will keep them alive until they become "old and unattractive" (Halpern-Felsher et al., 2005; McClain, 2005).

Preventing STIs

Most Americans think that they'll never contract an STI. For example, a national survey of college students ages 18 to 22 (and living away from home) found that 73 percent of those who were sexually active had unprotected sex (Society for Adolescent Medicine, 2004). The rates for students on commuting campuses may be even higher because they're more autonomous and can do pretty much what they want, even if they live with their parents. This means that millions of college students may be increasing their risk of contracting sexually transmitted diseases if one partner is infected.

Many women are uninformed or silent about STIs and HIV/AIDS. In a recent survey of women ages 18 to 49, 60 percent said that they had never discussed STD or HIV testing with their current partner. One in six women had withheld sexual health information from a health-care provider because they were embarrassed. Most women didn't know that STDs don't have immediate symptoms or that they can lead to certain cancers, and most thought (mistakenly) that a Pap smear tests for STIs ("National sexual health survey . . . ," 2003).

Finally, as noted throughout this chapter, many adolescents have little information about STIs, including

Africa has the highest rates, worldwide, of adults and children who die of AIDS. To combat the spread of HIV infection, many government officials, public health experts, and community activists have worked together to inform communities about HIV/AIDS using brochures, billboards, and door-to-door visits. Here, an HIV/AIDS educator addresses youth in Uganda.

about how casual sex can lead to serious health consequences (Carter, 2003).

Conclusion

One of the biggest *changes* since the turn of the century is that we are better informed about our sexuality. Today we have more *choices* in our sexual expression, and most people recognize that sexuality involves more than just the sex act. Instead, sexuality has emotional, intellectual, spiritual, and cultural as well as biological components.

But there are also a number of *constraints*. We are often unwilling to give young people the information they need to make thoughtful decisions about sex. Gay men and lesbians still face discrimination and harassment because of their sexual practices. And our health and lives and the lives of our children are threatened by the rising incidence of STIs and HIV infection.

HIV/AIDS. Therefore, trusted adults—parents, teachers, and other community members—must become more informed themselves and then talk frankly with youth

These changes have significant effects on both women and men in their search for suitable marriage partners and other long-term relationships. We'll look at some of these issues in the next several chapters.

Summary

1. Our sexual lives affect our families and marriages from birth to death. Regardless of age or marital status, sexual expression plays an important role throughout life.

2. Human sexuality is complex and incorporates several components, including sexual identity, sexual orientation, and gender roles. Biological theories maintain that genes and sex hormones determine sexual preference, whereas cultural theories emphasize social and environmental factors.

3. Although we like to think that our sexual behavior is spontaneous, sexual scripts shape most of our sexual activities, attitudes, and relationships.

4. Most of us do not learn about sex in the home. Much of our information, and misinformation, comes from peers and the media. Although there are variations from one state to another, many sex education programs are being funded generously only if they emphasize abstinence-only approaches.

5. Sexual activity encompasses many behaviors other than sexual intercourse, such as fantasies, masturbation, petting, and oral sex.

6. Adolescent girls are more likely to romanticize sex, whereas adolescent boys typically see sex as an end in itself. The reasons for early premarital sex include early puberty, peer pressure, environmental factors, and cultural expectations.

7. Marital sex typically decreases over the course of a marriage, but married couples enjoy a variety of other sexual activities in addition to intercourse.

8. Despite many stereotypes about sexuality and aging, people age 70 and older continue to engage in sexual activities, including intercourse, masturbation, and sexual fantasy.

9. Gay and lesbian partners experience many of the same feelings as do heterosexuals, and face some of the

same problems in their relationships. Major factors that differentiate gay and lesbian couples from heterosexual couples are society's disapproval of homosexual practices and their consequent lack of legal rights in many areas.

10. Although today more people are informed about STIs, HIV, and AIDS, many still engage in high-risk be-haviors such as sharing drug needles, having sex with many partners, and not using condoms. The rates of new HIV infections are especially high among male–male couples, minorities, and heterosexual women.

Key Terms

sexual orientation   *187*
homosexual   *187*
heterosexual   *187*
bisexual   *187*
asexual   *187*
heterosexism   *187*
sexual script   *190*
autoeroticism   *201*
masturbation   *202*

fellatio   *203*
cunnilingus   *203*
sexual response   *204*
menopause   *209*
male climacteric   *209*
homophobia   *215*
sexually transmitted infections
   (STIs)   *216*

sexually transmitted diseases
   (STDs)   *216*
human immunodeficiency virus
   (HIV)   *217*
acquired immunodeficiency syndrome
   (AIDS)   *217*

Taking It Further

Everything You've Ever Wanted to Know about Sex

American Experience: The Pill explores some of the issues surrounding the creation of the Pill and the many ways in which it transformed the lives of women and American culture.
http://www.pbs.org/wgbh/amex/pill/index.html

National Abstinence Clearinghouse offers resources and material that encourage premarital abstinence.
www.abstinence.net

Centers for Disease Control and Prevention provides health information, publications, international data, and links to numerous health-related sites dealing with HIV, AIDS, and other STIs.
www.cdc.gov

SIECUS (Sexuality Information and Education Council of the United States) develops and disseminates information about sexuality education and responsible sexual behavior.
www.siecus.org

Kaiser Family Foundation is a wonderful source of information about sexuality, sex-related surveys, and sexual health. It also provides daily, weekly, or monthly e-mail alerts on a number of issues and recent news releases about sex and current research on sex.
www.kff.org

And more: www.prenhall.com/benokraitis includes numerous sites dealing with safer sex, world statistics and maps on HIV and AIDS, decreasing teen pregnancy, menstruation, female genital mutilation, men's and women's sex-related health issues, and tips on reviving your sex life.

Investigate with Research Navigator

Go to www.researchnavigator.com and enter your LOGIN NAME and PASSWORD. For instructions on registering for the first time, view the detailed instructions at the end of the Chapter 1. Search the Research Navigator™ site using the following key terms:

homosexuals
sexually transmitted diseases
double standard

Outline

Choosing Others: Dating and Mate Selection

Data Digest

■ Among twelfth-grade students, **those who said that they never date** increased from 14 percent in 1991 to 25 percent in 2003.

■ In 2004, 25 percent of all **never-married adults** were between the ages of 30 and 44.

■ Among all singles, **only 16 percent say that they are looking for a romantic partner.** Even among those who are seeking relationships, about half had been on no more than one date in the previous three months.

■ About 63 percent of Americans say "I love you" to their pet every day; **90 percent would not consider dating someone who didn't like their pet.**

■ In 2005, more than 22 million Americans—about 14 percent of all Internet users—**visited online dating sites,** 37 percent of singles have used dating Websites, and 17 percent say that they entered long-term relations or married someone they met online.

Sources: Fetto, 2002; "Dating," 2005; Juarez, 2006; Rainie and Madden, 2006; Sullivan, 2006; U.S. Census Bureau, 2006.

Someone once joked that dating is the process of spending a lot of time and money to meet people you probably won't like. Yet some of the most popular television programs are *Elimidate, Get the Hook Up, Blind Date, Dismissed,* and *Change of Heart.* Why are these shows so popular?

Singlehood has its advantages (see Chapter 9). Most of us, however, seek intimacy with a lifelong partner. Regardless of what words we use—"dating," "going out," "hookin' up," "having a thing," or "seeing someone"—mate selection is a process that, we hope, will result in finding an intimate partner or marriage mate.

As the box "Courting throughout U.S. History" shows, dating is a recent invention. It emerged in the United States in the twentieth century and became a well-established rite of passage in the 1950s. How we date has changed, but why and whom we date and why

Changes

Courting throughout U.S. History

Contrary to what we might think, young people in colonial America often experienced premarital sex. As a young woman wrote passionately to her lover,

O! I do really want to kiss you. How I should like to be in that old parlor with you. I hope there will be a carpet on the floor for it seems you intend to act worse than you ever did before by your letter. But I shall humbly submit to my fate and willingly, too, to speak candidly (Rothman, 1983: 401).

There were also practical considerations. In colonial New England, an engaged woman's parents conducted economic negotiations with the family of her fiancé, and most young men could not even think about courtship until they owned land. They were advised to "choose by ears, as well as eyes" and to select women who were industrious, hardworking, and sensible. Affection was expected to blossom into love after marriage.

Many women were very down-to-earth about courtship. A New York woman wrote,

I am sick of all this choosing. If a man is healthy and does not drink and has a good little handful of stock and a good temper and is a good Christian, what difference can it make to a woman which man she takes? (Ryan, 1983: 40–41).

Before the Industrial Revolution, most courtship took place within the hustle and bustle of community life. Young people could meet after church services, during picnics, or at gatherings such as barn raisings and dances. Buggy rides were especially popular: There was no room

in the buggy for a chaperone, and "the horse might run away or lose a shoe so that one could be stranded on a lonely country road" (McPharlin, 1946: 10).

At the turn of the twentieth century, especially among the middle classes, gentlemen "called" on women. A woman or her mother invited a suitor to visit at the woman's home, and other family members would be present. If the relationship proceeded toward engagement, the couple enjoyed some privacy in the parlor (Bailey, 1988).

With the advent of bicycles and telephones, parlor sofas and porch swings were quickly abandoned. People began to use the term *dating,* which referred to couples setting a specific date, time, and place to meet. When the automobile came into widespread use in the early 1920s, dating took a giant step forward. "The car provided more privacy and excitement than either the dance hall or the movie theater, and the result was the spread of petting" (Rothman, 1984: 295). Young people now had the mobility to meet more frequently, informally, and casually.

Until the early 1970s, dating reflected a strict and gendered code of etiquette. Men initiated dates and paid all the expenses. Women waited to be "asked out" and provided companionship (and sometimes sex) during a date.

Stop and Think . . .

- Did the colonists have the right idea in being "practical" about courtship? Or should courtship always involve searching for a "soul mate"?

- Talk to your parents, grandparents, or other relatives about dating in the 1950s and 1960s. What were some of the advantages of these dating rituals? What about the disadvantages?

---

we break up have been fairly constant over time. Let's begin with the question of how often people date.

How Often Do We Date?

Many traditional college students (those who are living on campus and under age 25) dismiss **dating**—the process of meeting people socially for possible mate se-

lection—as "old fashioned" because "there's no time, no money, and no need" (Wolcott, 2004: 11). Dating may be dead on many traditional college campuses, but this is not the case elsewhere.

A majority of Americans age 18 and older either are dating or would like to (see "Data Digest"). Dating has declined among people under age 18, but 27 percent of high school seniors say that they date frequently (see

since you asked

Is dating "dead"?

Figure 8.1). It's not clear, however, what teenagers mean by "dating." For many teenagers, and unlike their parents, a "formal date" may mean little more than meeting a girlfriend or boyfriend at a mall (Denizet-Lewis, 2004).

Dating, in the formal sense, has decreased even among people age 65 and older because many of them subscribe to online dating sites. At age 75, for example, a retired Sears Roebuck manager has dated 50 women whom he has met online since his wife died five years earlier. "There's a lot of choice and a lot of possibility," he says happily (Saillant, 2004: A1).

Why Do We Date?

The reasons for dating seem self-evident. Dating is more complex than just getting together, however. Sociologists describe the dating process as a **marriage market** in which prospective spouses compare the assets and liabilities of eligible partners and choose the best available mate.

Everyone has a "market value," and whom a person "trades" with depends on one's resources. Like most other choices we make, dating involves taking

risks with the resources we invest. The more valuable the "catch" we seek, the more likely we are to devote time and money to looking attractive, accommodating the partner's personality or interests, or getting along with her or his family and friends. In contrast, "one-night stands" entail few risks (assuming that the partners don't contract STDs and the woman doesn't become pregnant) and little investment of resources.

Also, people might use their resources differently depending on whether the relationship is new or "settling in." As one of my students observed, people may invest more time than money in a partner if they are no longer in the "trading" stage in the marriage marketplace:

> *It's very expensive to date. When two people are in a comfortable relationship, they tend not to go out as much. The quiet nights at home are considerably less expensive than extravagant nights on the town. The longer you date someone, the less need there is to impress that person with fancy dinners and costly dates (Author's files).*

Dating fulfills a number of specific functions that enhance people's emotional development and ultimately contribute to the needs of the larger society (see Chapter 1). These functions vary according to the person's age, social class, and gender. Dating functions can be either *manifest*—the purposes are visible, recognized, and intended—or *latent*—the purposes are unintended or not immediately recognized (see Chapter 2). Keep in mind that these functions often overlap.

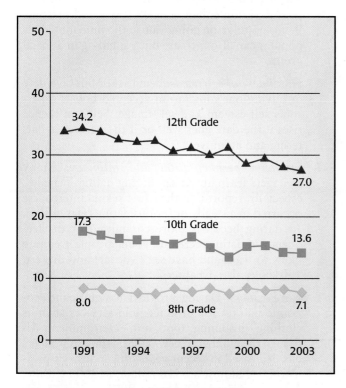

FIGURE 8.1 How Often Do Teenagers Date?

Source: ChildTrends Data Bank, 2005.

Manifest Functions of Dating

Dating fulfills several important manifest functions:

- *Maturation:* Whether young people are interested in the opposite sex or the same sex, dating sends the message that an adolescent is reaching puberty. She or he becomes capable of engaging in developmental tasks such as emotional intimacy outside the family and, quite possibly, sexual expression (see Chapter 7).

- *Fun and recreation:* Going out with people we like relieves boredom, stress, and loneliness. As more people postpone marriage (see Chapter 9), dating has become an important recreational activity.

- *Companionship:* Regardless of one's age, dating can be a valuable source of companionship. It can also

since you asked

Why are my parents so critical of many of the people I date?

ease the heartbreak of being widowed. One of my students described her 72-year-old mother as being very depressed after the death of her husband, to whom she had been married for 50 years, until she "met a wonderful man and they started socializing."

■ *Love and affection:* Dating provides a socially accepted way of enjoying intimacy. Among college students, for example, both women and men say that they initiated a first date because they were in love and wanted a caring and serious relationship (Clark et al., 1999). The relationship may fizzle, but dating is an avenue for getting closer to another person.

■ *Mate selection:* Whether people admit it or not, dating is usually a search for a marital partner. Adolescents often become angry if their parents criticize their dates with remarks like "We don't want you to marry this guy" or "She's not good enough for you."

The Wodabe, a nomadic West African tribe, value male beauty. The men perform a dance, showing off the whiteness of their teeth and eyes, to compete for honor and selection as the most beautiful man by women of the tribe at an annual festival.

The teenager's impatient rebuttal is usually "I'm not going to marry him (her). We're just going out!"

Parents are often judgmental because they know that dating *can* lead to marriage. Young people are "comparison shopping," acquiring knowledge about what kinds of people they are attracted to and may want to marry (Whyte, 1990). In contrast, as you'll see shortly, there is little need for dating in cultures in which parents influence their children's mate selection through such customs as arranged marriages (see, also, Chapters 5 to 7).

Latent Functions of Dating

Dating also fulfills several important latent functions:

■ *Socialization:* Through dating, people learn about expected gender roles, family structures that are different from their own, and different attitudes, beliefs, and values. This kind of learning may be especially valuable for adolescents, who can test and hone their self-confidence and their communication skills in one-on-one settings (Berk, 1993; see, also, Chapters 1, 5, and 7).

■ *Social status:* Going out with an attractive or successful person enhances one's status and prestige. Being popular or going out with someone who's popular can also increase one's standing in a social group.

■ *Fulfillment of ego needs:* Being asked out on a date or having one's invitation accepted boosts a person's self-esteem and self-image. Self-confidence rises if the date goes well or if the partner is flattering and attentive.

■ *Sexual experimentation and intimacy:* Many teenagers learn about sex during dating. Females, especially, report that their first sexual intercourse occurred in a steady or serious dating relationship. As dating becomes more committed or the frequency of dating increases, young people are more likely to want and have sex (Michael and Bickert, 2001; see, also, Chapter 7).

■ *Big business:* Dating provides a significant economic market for products and services such as clothing, grooming, food, and entertainment. Although the number of new online dating subscribers has decreased in recent years, this industry's profits totaled almost a $516 million in 2005 (Rouse, 2002; Musgrove and Ahrens, 2005).

Manifest and latent dating functions may change over time. As people mature, status may become less relevant and companionship more important, especially if the dating partners are planning to get married.

The Dating Spectrum

Unlike a few generations ago, dating today is distinct from courtship and may or may not end in marriage. Between adolescence and the altar, most people initially get an overview of the marriage market by getting together in groups of prospective partners, then pair off, and ultimately go with one person. Although traditional dating is still widespread, there are a number of newer forms of getting together, as well as some combinations of traditional and contemporary dating.

Traditional Dating

The *traditional date*, which predominated through the 1970s, is still a fairly formal way of meeting potential spouses. In traditional dating, males and females follow clear, culturally defined gender role scripts, at least among the middle classes. The girl waits to be asked out, the boy picks her up at her home, and she is almost always late, giving Mom and Dad a chance to chat with the boy. The boy has specific plans for the evening, pays for everything, and brings her home before curfew.

Some older television programs, such as *Happy Days* and *The Brady Bunch*, though idealized, portray this type of date. Men pay for the date, but what exactly are they buying? A good time, perhaps. Or female companionship. But there is always "an uncomfortable undercurrent of sexual favors lurking in the background" (Stone and McKee, 2002: 70). Although the expectation is unstated, members of both sexes often assume that the woman will show her gratitude in some way—usually through a goodnight kiss, petting, or intercourse.

CULTURAL VARIATIONS ON TRADITIONAL DATING

The popularity of traditional dating is particularly evident in formal events such as *coming-out parties* or debutante balls, where young women, usually of the upper classes, are "introduced to society" (Kendall, 2002). Other cultural rites of passage include the *bat mitzvah* for girls and the *bar mitzvah* for boys in Jewish communities. These rituals mark the end of childhood and readiness for adult responsibilities and rights, including dating.

In one ritual of the Latino quinceañera, the young woman's father slips on her first pair of high heels.

In many Latino communities, the *quinceañera* (pronounced kin-say-NYE-ra) is a coming-of-age rite that celebrates a girl's entrance into adulthood on her fifteenth birthday. *Quince* (pronounced KEEN-say) means fifteen in Spanish. The *quinceañera* is an elaborate and dignified religious and social affair given by the girl's parents. It begins with a Catholic Mass and is followed by a reception at which 14 couples (each couple representing one year in the girl's life before the *quince*) serve as her attendants.

The event includes a traditional waltz in which the young woman dances with her father, a champagne toast, and the tossing of a bouquet to the boys to determine who will win the first dance with the young woman. The girl may be allowed to date boys after her *quinceañera*. There is no comparable rite of passage for Latino boys.

The *quinceañera* "can be as elaborate as the finest wedding and as expensive and as time consuming to organize" (Garcia, 2002: 73). Because the celebration reflects pride in one's heritage, even working-class parents save money for years to host a typical party, which costs between $10,000 to $20,000 for gowns, photographers, the banquet hall, music (often a mariachi band), limos, food, and party favors. A new magazine, *Quince Girl*, provides fashion and other advice to the more than 400,000 Latinas in the United States who turn 15 every year.

To meet the need of preparing for the *quinceañera*, many large retail and bridal stores carry a large selection of gowns and accessories. Royal Caribbean offers seven-day *quinceañera* cruises out of Miami (at $850 to $1,200 per person) that are booked solid into the next year. And, perhaps as a sure sign that this event is an important ceremony, a *Quinceañera Barbie* is available in toy stores throughout the nation (Song, 2003; Miranda, 2004).

GOING STEADY Going steady and "getting pinned" were common in the 1930s and became especially popular after World War II. A couple was "pinned" when a young man gave his fraternity pin to his girlfriend as a symbol of his affection and commitment. *Going steady*, which often meant that the partners were seeing only each other, usually came after a couple had had a number of dates, and it sometimes preceded engagement (Tuttle, 1993).

Typically, however, going steady was short-lived. As one teenage girl explained, "Going steady doesn't have to mean you're madly in love. . . . It just means you like one boy better than the rest" (quoted in Breines, 1992: 116). Going steady reduced many of the anxieties associated with traditional dating: It allowed emotional and sexual intimacy without a long-term commitment and gave a "hands-off" message to possible competitors.

A modern version of going steady is "going with" or "going together." For many middle-school students, "goin' with" signals the transition from childhood to adolescence. Although the couples are not planning to get engaged, they are also not seeing others. "Goin' with" sometimes starts before puberty, even though the relationships of fourth-, fifth-, and sixth-graders usually break up after a few weeks (Merten, 1996; Albert et al., 2003). For older adolescents, such liaisons may last for months or even years.

The advantage of "goin' with" is having a stable relationship when many other things in life are changing and unpredictable (such as physiological changes, divorcing parents, and preparation for college or a job). The disadvantage is that such relationships discourage adolescents from meeting new people—especially when they are experiencing many developmental changes in a short period (see Chapter 2).

Contemporary Dating

Contemporary dating falls into two general categories: *casual dating*, which includes hanging out, getting together, "pack dating," and "hooking up"; and *serious dating*,

since you asked

Why is casual dating so popular?

which can lead to cohabitation, engagement, and marriage.

HANGING OUT Parents and adolescents in many American homes engage in a familiar dialogue:

Parent:	Where are you going?
Teenager:	Out.
Parent:	What will you do?
Teenager:	Just hang out.
Parent:	Who will be there?
Teenager:	I don't know yet.
Parent:	When will you be back?
Teenager:	I'm not sure.
Parent:	Leave your cell phone on, please.

Whether *hanging out* occurs on a neighborhood street corner, at a fast-food place, or in a mall, it is a time-honored adolescent pastime. A customary meeting place may be set, with people coming and going at different times. Or, once a group gets together, the members decide what they want to do and the information is quickly spread by e-mail, instant messaging (IM), or phone text messages. Hanging out is possible both because many parents respect their teenagers' privacy and independence and because most 16- and 17-year-olds have access to cars.

GETTING TOGETHER *Getting together* is more intimate and structured than hanging out. A group of friends meet at someone's house, a club, or a party. Either males or females can organize the initial effort, and the group often pools its resources, especially if alcohol or other drugs are part of the activities. Because participants are not dating, there is a lot of flexibility in meeting people.

Getting together typically involves "floating." The group may meet at someone's house for a few hours, decide to go to a party later, spend a few hours at a mall, and wind up at another party. Adolescents see getting together as normal and rational—"You get to meet a lot of people" or "We can go someplace else if the party is dead"—but it concerns many parents. Even if teenagers call home from the various locations, parents worry that the gatherings can become unpredictable or dangerous because of drug use.

Getting together is a popular form of dating for several reasons. Because the activities are spontaneous, there is little anxiety about preparing for a formal date or initiating or rejecting sexual advances. The experience is less threatening emotionally because the participants don't have to worry about finding a date or

MOTHER GOOSE & GRIMM   *BY MIKE PETERS*

getting "stuck" with someone (like a blind date) for the whole evening.

It also relieves females of sexual pressure because they may help organize the get-together, share in the expenses, and come alone or with friends (rather than as part of a couple). People may pair off, participate in the group as a couple, or gradually withdraw to spend more time together, but there is less pressure to have a date as a sign of popularity.

Finally, getting together decreases parental control over the choice of friends. Parents usually don't know many of the adolescents in the group and are less likely to disapprove of friendships or compare notes with other parents.

"PACK DATING" Whereas traditional dating and early marriages are common on some campuses, especially in the South and Midwest, many undergraduates socialize in unpartnered groups, or *pack dating* (also called "group dates" on many campuses):

> *They go out to dinner in groups, attend movies in groups and at parties dance in a circle of five or six. The packs give students a sense of self-assurance and identity, but keep them from deeper, more committed relationships (Gabriel, 1997: 22).*

Pack dating may be popular for several reasons. If college students don't expect to marry until their 30s, socializing in small groups provides recreation without the pressure of making a commitment or becoming romantically involved. Also, because increasing numbers of students hold down jobs while taking heavy course loads, many feel that they don't have the time and energy to find dates or to maintain one-on-one relationships.

"HOOKING UP" *Hooking up* (or "hookin' up") refers to physical encounters, no strings attached. "Hooking

up" is a vague term that can mean anything from kissing and genital fondling to oral sex and sexual intercourse. Several studies at colleges have found that between 60 and 84 percent of the students had hooked up at one time or another. At many high schools, hooking up is more common than dating. Hooking up commonly, but not always, takes place when both people are drinking. They might also hook up with casual friends or a former girlfriend or boyfriend (Denizet-Lewis, 2004; McGinn, 2004).

Hooking up has its advantages. It's cheaper than dating. Also, it's intentionally vague. Because no one knows for sure what, if anything, happened, women can avoid getting a bad reputation for being "loose" or "easy." Most important, it's assumed that hooking up requires no commitment of time or emotion: "A girl and a guy get together for a physical encounter and don't necessarily expect anything further" (Wolcott, 2004: 11).

Hooking up also has disadvantages. Because it's ambiguous, hooking up can create insecurity:

> *If you can "hook up" with someone occasionally at a party but not be "hanging out" with them; or be "seeing" someone, but not "dating"; or "talking to" someone, but not really "having a conversation," how does a girl know when she's headed toward something serious, already there or, for that matter, when a relationship has ended? (Stepp, 2003: F1).*

In addition, hookups aren't always as impersonal as people expect them to be. In a survey of college women, many said that hookups made them feel sexy and desirable. However, about 64 percent also said that they later felt awkward, exploited, or disappointed. Others felt confused because they didn't know what to expect next or whether a guy would call again (Glenn and Marquardt, 2001).

Traditional–Contemporary Combinations

Several dating patterns incorporate both traditional customs and contemporary trends. For example, 85 percent of adults feel that it's okay for women to ask men out on dates, and 40 percent of women have done so ("Come here often?," 2002). Even though it's now more acceptable for members of either sex to initiate a date or to invite someone to a prom or dinner, many gender scripts remain remarkably traditional (see Chapter 5).

PROMS AND HOMECOMING PARTIES *Proms* and *homecoming parties* are still among the most popular and traditional dating events (Best, 2000). As in the past, they are formal or semiformal. Women receive corsages, men are typically responsible for transportation and other expenses, and both men and women, but especially women, invest quite a bit of time and money in preparing for these events.

Contemporary changes in the characteristics of proms include "turnabout" invitations (those extended to men by women) and dining out beforehand with a large group of couples. Couples might prolong the event by holding a group sleepover (presumably chaperoned by parents), staying out all night and returning after breakfast, or continuing the festivities into the weekend at a nearby beach or other recreational area.

DINNER DATES One of the most traditional forms of dating, the *dinner date,* is still popular today, particularly among adults who are in their thirties or older. According to a national survey, 52 percent of women and 57 percent of men said that they preferred a "nice dinner" as a first date (*2006 Dating Trends Survey,* 2006).

Dinner dates, like first dates of any kind, are still highly scripted. The man typically initiates the date, drives the car, opens doors, and starts sexual interaction (such as kissing the woman goodnight or making out). The women spends a good deal of time on her appearance, depends on the man to make the plans, and often responds to a sexual overture rather than making the first move. Thus, making a "good impression" early in the dating relationship is still largely synonymous with playing traditional gender roles. As in the past, men are much more likely than women to initiate a first date, including a dinner date, because they are more interested in sexual intimacy than are women (Rose and Frieze, 1993; Regan, 2003).

The rise of the women's movement in the 1970s led to the custom of *going Dutch,* or splitting the costs of a date. Sharing dating expenses frees women to initiate dates and relieves them from feeling that they should "pay off" with sex.

When women ask men out, however, the rules about who picks up the check aren't clear. About half of Americans feel that the

person who initiated the date should pay for it, but more than one-third think that the man should *always* pay for the date. Thus, the "rules" are vague: "Some men tell tales of women who ask them out and then expect them to pick up the tab" (Campbell, 2002: 4).

Perhaps the least gender-typed dating, at least on first dates, is between same-sex partners. A study of lesbians and gay men found little gender typing compared with heterosexual dating: Both partners participated more equally in orchestrating the date, maintaining the conversation, and initiating physical contact. There was also less concern about appearance (Klinkenberg and Rose, 1994). Because there are no recent studies of same-sex dating, however, it's not clear whether these behaviors have changed.

Dating Later in Life

Dating after divorce or after being widowed can be both therapeutic and intimidating. It can enhance one's self-esteem, decrease loneliness, and involve reassessing one's strengths and weaknesses as one forges new relationships. Dating can also provide companionship while one is still grieving a spouse's death.

Dating can also be daunting. A recently divorced person may be bitter toward the opposite sex, or a parent may worry about a child's reactions to her or his dating. Widowed people may be nervous about reentering the marriage market, feel guilty about their ro-

Fatima Haque and her friends in Fremont, California, may have invented a new American ritual: the all-girl Muslim prom. It is a response to Muslim religious and cultural beliefs in which dating, dancing with or touching boys, or appearing without wearing a hijab is not permitted.

Monica Almeida/The New York Times

mantic yearnings, and experience anxiety about their physical appearance or sex appeal.

However, many divorced and widowed people establish new and satisfying relationships through dating (see Chapters 15 and 17). Some seek out their teen heartthrobs online, rekindle the old flame, and marry. Not all reunions have a happy ending, of course. People change over the years, and our memories of our "first love" are highly romanticized. For example, the class Don Juan is still attentive, but now he's also bald and fat, has bad breath, and cheats on his wife. In other cases, however, sparks fly again and both partners see the same person they had loved, just older (Russo, 2002).

Making Connections

■ What do *you* mean by "hookin' up"? If you or your friends' hookups included sex, what were the benefits and costs?

■ Many teenagers and young adults feel that hooking up decreases the artificiality and pressure of dating. Some maintain, however, that such recreational sex means less romance, less excitement, less passion, and less intimacy because many women are giving out "free samples" (Mansfield, 2004). What do *you* think?

Meeting Others

The quest for love involves a variety of creative strategies. On Friday evenings, for example, Wal-Mart runs a "Singles Shopping" campaign in all of its 91 stores in Germany. The singles get a big bright red bow to attach to their shopping cart or shopping basket to signal their availability. "Flirting points" around the stores are stacked with "romantic" merchandise such as chocolates, wine, and cheese. It's not clear how successful the matchmaking has been, but in some stores 300 to 400 people take part every week. Because of its popularity, Wal-Mart has implemented "Singles Shopping" at its stores in Puerto Rico, South Korea, and Britain (Bhatnagar, 2005).

At some American bars, singles can scope out other people using video monitors scattered around the room. Using a joystick, they can zoom in for a better look, send the "target" a message, and then meet at a private booth in the bar (Hamilton, 2002).

Many of us meet our dating partners through friends and family members. But there are many other avenues for finding a mate, including clubs, college classes, matchmaking by your sister-in-law, and recreational activities such as hiking, bicycling, and bowling. Other common ways of meeting a prospective spouse range from personal classified ads to online dating sites.

Personal Classified Advertisements

Personal classified advertisements used to be published in the back pages of "smutty" magazines. Now mainstream newspapers as well as suburban, religious, and local newspapers also carry personal ads.

Advertisers are usually very "selective" in their self-descriptions because both sexes "are quite conscious of the cultural scripts" that females and males expect. Because women know that men want attractive partners, they emphasize their appearance and femininity. Men, aware of women's expectations, describe their success, professional status, or "caring" and "sensitive" nature. Single women rarely mention having children because men might not be willing to support children from a previous marriage (Ahuvia and Adelman, 1992; Raybeck et al., 2000).

Such findings suggest that most women and men barter with the qualities that they see as most important in the marriage market. Because many men value youth and attractiveness, women often describe themselves as "sexy" or "curvaceous." Because women want a man with high status and earning potential, many men emphasize being "college-educated," a "homeowner," or a "professional" (Dunbar, 1995).

The advantages of classified ads include anonymity, low cost, time savings, and numerous applicants. A major disadvantage is that advertisers often exaggerate their attributes. As one of my male students said, "I called her because she said she was gorgeous and intelligent. She was neither."

Mail-Order Brides

Some American men seeking wives use mail-order services that publish photographs and descriptions of women, usually from economically disadvantaged regions such as Russia, Ukraine, and other Eastern European and South Asian countries.

Most of the men are white, college-educated, and anywhere from 20 to 50 years older than the young brides they seek. Complaining that American women are "too independent, too demanding, and too critical," the men typically want women with relatively little education and who are raised in cultures in which a married woman is expected to be a subservient homemaker. Many U.S. brokers adorn their sites with photos of bikini-clad women and market the women as quiet, submissive, and easily controlled (Scholes and Phataraloaha, 1999; Weir, 2002; Terzieff, 2006).

An estimated 4 percent of the 100,000 to 150,000 women seeking U.S. husbands find them. Because the mail-order bride business is unregulated, there's no way of knowing how many of these marriages are successful. Often, however, the American Prince Charming turns out to be an abusive "monster." Some have murdered their wives; some have beaten, choked, and raped their brides; and others control their spouses by denying them any contact with their families at home or with their American neighbors. In the first lawsuit of its kind nationwide, in 2004 a Maryland jury awarded a mail-order bride from Ukraine $430,000 in damages. Her husband had beaten her over a period of several years, even while she was breastfeeding their child, and told her that she would be deported if she left him (Hanes, 2004).

Beginning in 2006, the International Marriage Broker Regulation Act required U.S. men seeking a visa for a prospective bride to disclose any criminal convictions for domestic violence, sexual assault, or child abuse. Broker agencies are angry about the law, but its enforcement is weak. Most of the women stay in abusive relationships and don't report assaults because they speak broken English, have no money and no friends in the United States, don't know that they can leave abusive husbands without being deported, and fear that their families will blame them, and not their husbands, for a breakup (Milbourn, 2006; Terzieff, 2006).

Professional Matchmakers

In Shanghai, China, a 25-year-old lawyer has become wealthy by finding virgin brides for at least 50 men who are millionaires. Although hundreds of women sent in applications, complete with photos and personal information, others have denounced such matchmaking as crass and insulting. According to one woman, for example, "People's beauty derives from their inner qualities, not their virginity. Those girls have sold themselves like cheap merchandise" (French, 2006: A4).

In the United States, online dating is booming (see "Data Digest"). Despite its popularity, some find the process too time-consuming, are disappointed with the results, or want more privacy. As a result, professional matchmaking services and training programs are thriving. In New York City, for example, a husband-and-wife team moonlights as matchmakers for Muslim singles; they work directly with individuals rather than being hired by a woman's parents (Campbell, 2005).

These matchmakers charge only a small amount for their service—$50 per introduction, plus a $50 one-time registration fee—but typical matchmaking fees are considerably higher. For example, one New York enterprise, Serious Matchmaking Incorporated, charges fees beginning at $20,000 for an initiation fee, plus $1,000 for a one-year membership that includes 12 dates. The services consist of an "image consultant" who suggests wardrobe changes (for both women and men) and a trip to a bridal shop so that a woman can visualize herself getting married. In addition, members must be willing to date imperfect people who aren't "soul mates" and to be less "picky" in choosing a mate. Many of the consultants themselves are single and haven't yet found a marriage mate. After spending thousands of dollars with a consultant, one woman said that she eventually met "her man" through an online dating service at a cost of $160 (Marder, 2002; Thernstrom, 2005).

How successful are matchmakers in finding mates? They may be better at getting rich than they are at marrying people off. For example, Daniel Dolan, a Harvard-trained corporate lawyer, has become a multimillionaire after setting up and franchising his "It's Just Lunch" (IJL) matchmaking service. The purpose of IJL is to set up busy professionals with meetings over lunch. The brochures and online advertising claim that "dating experts" thoughtfully pair up people based on personality, appearance, and goals (Fass, 2004).

Many participants, however, have complained about numerous problems. Nationally, for example, both women and men said that they wasted $1,200 to $1,500 for a year's membership fees because they had only one or two dates (and both were "disastrous"); IJL never met their basic dating criteria (such as age, distance, weight, interests, health, not smoking, and not having children); members did not receive refunds when dates didn't show up; and IJL sales representatives didn't return calls involving complaints, or pressured people to accept dates that they didn't want because "your criteria are unrealistic" or "inflated" ("It's Just Lunch," 2006).

Speed Dating

Recently, one of my friends participated in an 8-Minute Dating encounter at a local restaurant. He and 13 other guys attended an event at which they met 14 women. The participants went from one table to another, spending 8 minutes chatting with each person. At the end of an hour or two, they "graded" one other. If two people chose each other and wanted to meet, the organizer of the event e-mailed contact information to both parties.

This is an example of the fast-growing *speed dating* industry that emerged in 1999. The purpose of speed dating is to allow people to meet each other face to face,

During this speed dating event in New York City, dozens of singles spend five to ten minutes with each "date." Event organizers send contact information by e-mail if the participants choose each other.

within a short period, to decide whether there is mutual interest in another date.

Since 1999, speed dating has spawned a number of companies that serve heterosexuals, gays, and a variety of ethnic and age groups. Because American Muslims are prohibited from dating at all before marriage, speed dating (known as *halal* dating) offers the opportunity for women and men to meet each other while being chaperoned. A young sheikh, or religious leader, usually leads a group discussion about the importance of marriage before the participants break up into speed dating groups (Al-Jadda, 2006).

Speed dating has several advantages. It is inexpensive (about $30 per function), takes little time, guards against stalking because the participants use only their first names, usually draws people from the same region, and avoids the awkwardness of blind dates. Some people initially feel embarrassed or uncomfortable about attending ("What if someone I know is there?"). According to the events' organizers, however, more than half of the participants meet someone with whom there is mutual interest in another date (Morris, 2003).

Speed dating also has several disadvantages. Because the participants engage in only a few minutes of conversation, they often rate potential partners on very superficial criteria such as appearance rather than more substantive traits such as values and lifestyle. Also, people who are shy may be crossed off someone's list even though they may be wonderful marriage mates over the long term (see Chapter 6).

Cyberdating

Millions of people are turning to the Internet to find romance and dates (see "Data Digest"). They can subscribe to discussion groups and chat rooms, "meet" thousands of potential partners, and discuss anything from radishes to romance. There are more than 800 online dating sites, and new ones keep popping up. Some of the largest—such as Match.com, Yahoo! Personals, and Matchmaker.com—have from 10 million to 50 million profiles in their databases (Williams, 2004).

since you asked

Is it a good idea to try to find a date online?

Numerous dating sites—and many are free—now exist for almost every imaginable group. A few examples include Jdate.com (for Jewish singles), Planet Out.com (for gays, lesbians, and bisexuals), TheSpark.com (for people with a weird sense of humor), OnlyFarmers.com, CatholicSingles.com, AsianFriendFinder.com, and BlackPlanetLove.com. Sites like MuslimMatch.com help hundreds of thousands of Muslims worldwide find partners with similar Islamic views and levels of religious commitment (Armario, 2005).

Online dating is novel, and even exciting, because it involves a "coexistence of opposing features that cannot be found in offline relationships." There is a "detached attachment" that "presents an entirely different ball game in the field of personal interactions." The physical distance coupled with emotional closeness triggers contradictions that make romantic relationships more intense but also less stable (see *Table 8.1*).

Online dating has both benefits and costs. A major advantage of online dating is its accessibility and low cost. A fee of $20 to $25 a month provides instant access to tens of thousands of eligible singles, and subscribers can sift candidates based on height, age, income, mutual interests, and dozens of other traits. Singles who felt isolated can have up to three dates a week while corresponding with several dozen people at the same time.

Another advantage of electronic liaisons is that subscribers can use code names and remain anonymous as long as they wish. Because physical appearance is in the background, verbal intimacy can lead to enduring relationships or even marriage. Match.com, for example claims credit for 1,300 marriages since it started in 1995 ("Romance on the Web," 2003).

People age 55 and older are the fastest-growing group of users of online dating services. One reason for this is that the youngest baby boomers turned 60 in 2006, have high divorce rates, and are now looking for new mates. The Internet can be especially helpful to older women: Many don't have the same dating opportunities as men or find that men their age are looking

TABLE 8.1

The Contradictory Nature of Online Dating

Online dating involves a new type of romantic relationship with a combination of close and remote characteristics. How do the opposing characteristics create both excitement and disappointment?

Distance	**Immediacy**
People may not know each other's geographic location or live thousands of miles apart.	There is emotional closeness and a feeling that the other person is in the same room.
Lean communication	**Rich communication**
Lack of nonverbal communication (such as body language) provides less information about feelings.	People may chat many times a day about a variety of issues.
Anonymity	**Self-disclosure**
It's easy to conceal information or to lie.	People often share intimate information and reveal very personal feelings.
Sincerity	**Deception**
The more time people spend chatting with each other, the more open they become about themselves and interested in the other person.	It's easy to lie and to misrepresent oneself.
Continuity	**Discontinuity**
People communicate regularly, day or night, without worrying about how they look, and may always be on each other's minds.	People can suddenly decide not to communicate or to terminate a relationship without any explanation.
Little physical investment	**Considerable emotional investment**
Online dating involves little money or time (compared with a dinner date, for instance), and no obligation to participate in various activities.	People usually devote a lot of mental energy to getting to know each other, keeping a relationship going, or suffering when there's no response.

SOURCE: Based on Ben-Ze'ev, 2004: 27–51.

for younger women. Among those age 55 and older, only 14 percent of women, compared with 22 percent of men, say that their most important reason for dating is to find a marriage mate, but members of both sexes are seeking companionship in their later years (Johnston, 2005; Wilkinson, 2005; Kantrowitz, 2006; see, also, Chapter 17).

Cyberdating also has its downside. Some complain that the dating sites have "a whole population of rebound people" who have not recovered from breakups. And some "hot" prospects simply disappear with no explanation after weeks of intensive e-mailing. In other cases, after rekindling romances with past sweethearts, some people have had extramarital affairs with them or have divorced their spouses (Mahoney, 2004; Dotinga, 2005).

Another disadvantage is that electronic romances can be deceptive and superficial. As with classified personal ads, people may be dishonest or have a very high opinion of themselves. Women tend to lie about their age and weight ("Her photo must've been taken 10 years and 40 pounds ago"). Men tend to lie about their weight, height, income, and occupation. Moreover, about 20 percent of online daters are married men (Brooks, 2003; Fernandez, 2005).

Rejected suitors may start stalking or harassing their love interests. In addition, people who use the Internet to find real-life sex partners are much more likely to have engaged in risky behavior. As a result, people who seek sex using the Internet are at greater risk of contracting STDs and HIV infection (McFarlane et al., 2000; Booth, 2005).

Many women who feel that they've encountered lying and cheating men online are fighting back. Websites like DontDateHimGirl.com, ManHaters.com, and TrueDater.com are dedicated to outing men who are married or on the down low (see Chapter 7) or who lie about their personal characteristics (such as age, educational attainment, and weight). Some men have been outraged by such public accusations, but few have contested the charges (Alvarez, 2006).

Making Connections

■ How do *you* meet other eligible singles? Or are you waiting for Cupid to come to you?

■ Millions of people have paid up to $350 for a two-day weekend workshop on how to snag a date (Stout, 2005). Is successful dating teachable? Or do most people land good dates through a trial-and-error process?

■ Have you or your friends ever tried online dating? If so, were you happy with the results? If you've never cyberdated, why not?

Choosing Whom We Date: Choices and Constraints

Many Americans believe that "I can date anyone I want." This is a myth. Most of us select dating partners and marry people who are similar to ourselves because filtering processes shape and limit our choices.

Homogamy and Filter Theory: Narrowing the Marriage Market

Theoretically, we have a vast pool of eligible dating partners. In reality, our field of potential partners is limited by our culture. According to **filter theory,** we sift eligible people according to specific criteria and thus narrow the pool of potential partners to a small number of candidates (Kerckhoff and Davis, 1962). *Figure 8.2* depicts the filter theory of mate selection.

The major filtering mechanism is homogamy. Often used interchangeably with the term *endogamy* (see Chapters 1 and 4), homogamy refers to dating or marrying someone with similar social characteristics, such as ethnicity and age. Some of the most important filtering variables are propinquity, physical appearance, and social characteristics such as race or ethnicity, religion, age, social class, and values.

PROPINQUITY Geographic closeness, or propinquity, is one of the first filters that shapes whom we meet, get to know, interact with frequently, and subsequently date

and marry. After all, we can't meet, date, and marry someone we have never met.

Despite the mushrooming business in personal ads, singles bars, and cyberdating, most people who are currently in serious long-term relationships or marriage met through family and friends or in a work or school setting (see *Table 8.2*). Although workplace dating can create problems, 33 percent of adults have dated a co-worker. And a growing number of cities have gay neighborhoods where men and women easily meet potential partners at the grocery store, the library, or church (Yin, 2002; Sullivan, 2006).

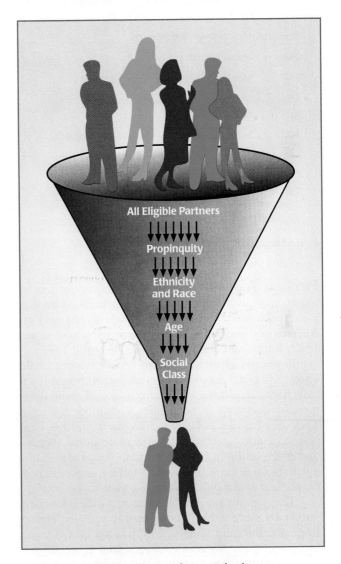

FIGURE 8.2 The Filter Theory of Mate Selection
According to filter theory, most of us narrow our pool of prospective partners by selecting people we see on a regular basis who are most similar to us in terms of such variables as age, race, values, social class, sexual orientation, and physical appearance.

TABLE 8.2

Most People Find Each Other Offline

In a national study of Internet users, the researchers found that most of the people in marriages and long-term relationships first met each other offline. So if your mom, classmate, best friend, or co-worker wants to fix you up with someone, go for it!

38%	Met at work or school
34%	Met through family or friends
13%	Met at a nightclub, bar, café, or other social gathering
3%	Met through the Internet
2%	Met at church
1%	Met by chance, such as on the street
1%	Met because they lived in the same neighborhood
1%	Met at a recreational facility like a gym
1%	Met on a blind date or through a dating service
6%	Met in a variety of other ways, such as growing up together

SOURCE: Madden and Lenhart, 2006: 6.

PHYSICAL APPEARANCE Once propinquity brings us together, looks matter. A number of studies show that men and women choose partners whose physical attractiveness is similar to their own (Berscheid et al., 1982; Kalick and Hamilton, 1986; Feingold, 1988).

Physically attractive people benefit from a "halo effect": They are *assumed* to possess other desirable social characteristics such as warmth, sexual responsiveness, kindness, poise, sociability, and good character. They are also seen as likely to have more prestige, happier marriages, greater social and professional success, and more fulfilling lives. In reality, life satisfaction is much the same for both attractive and less attractive people (Brehm et al., 2002; Olson and Marshuetz, 2005).

Throughout the world, men (regardless of their looks) are more likely than women to want an attractive mate (Buss and Schmitt, 1993). In the United States and many other Western countries, and especially for women, attractiveness is synonymous with slimness and youth.

The pressure to "look good" begins as early as middle school. Overweight girls ages 12 to 18 are less likely than their thinner counterparts to date. In adulthood, a woman's physical attractiveness is a key reason for being asked out on a first date. It's not surprising, then, that in 2005 almost 12 million teenage girls and women (up from 2 million in 1997) underwent cosmetic surgery to enlarge their breasts, reshaped their noses and ears, and endured liposuction (Cawley, 2001; American Society for Aesthetic Plastic Surgery, 2006).

Businesses are delighted by women's obsession with their looks. According to one marketing analyst, "Anything with the words 'age defying' sells." As a result, we can be seduced into believing that we've halted or slowed the aging process by using a variety of products, and most of those products target women. Among them are Rembrandt Age Defying toothpaste, Age Defiance hosiery, Clairol's Revitalizing Age-Defying Color System, Oil of Olay Age Defying Daily Renewal Cream, and Revlon's Age Defying eye color (Mayer, 1999).

Physical attractiveness may also have some costs. In a study of black women, for example, some of the respondents felt that a good-looking woman might make a man feel so insecure that he would not approach her because "people assume you already have enough candidates." Many of the women also felt that "the guys want to show you off because an attractive woman increases a man's status in his friends' eyes" (Sterk-Elifson, 1994: 108). If some men treat attractive women as trophies instead of serious choices for marriage, the women

Men assign more importance to physical attractiveness than women do, but members of both sexes tend to choose partners whose degree of attractiveness closely matches their own.

may have a large pool of dating partners but few serious suitors.

Culture matters, too, in perceptions of beauty. Several Nigerian communities prize hefty women and "hail a woman's rotundity" as a sign of good health, beauty, and a family's wealth. Teenage girls spend several months in a "fattening room" eating starchy food such as yams, rice, and beans. The fattening room is a centuries-old rite of passage from girlhood to womanhood. Some younger women are starting to abandon this ancient practice because of community campaigns to lose weight for health reasons. Still, many girls and women still follow the custom (Soares, 2006).

ETHNICITY AND RACE More than any other group, African American women face what one black journalist calls a "marriage crunch": "The better educated we are, the less likely we are to meet brothers who can match our credentials. The more successful we are, the less likely we are to meet brothers who can match our pocketbooks" (Chambers, 2003: 136).

About 12 percent of African American men in their 20s and early 30s are in prison or jail. Since 1976, nearly twice as many black women as black men have earned bachelor's, doctoral, and professional degrees (in such fields as medicine, law, and theology). Thus, many well-educated and successful black women find that they have "priced themselves out of the market" for finding a mate (Harrison and Karberg, 2003; U.S. Census Bureau, 2005).

since you asked

Why do some African Americans disapprove of interracial dating?

Unlike the situation portrayed in the film *How Stella Got Her Groove Back*, most successful black women are unlikely to find happiness with a man who is 20 years younger than they are or one who's not intimidated by their achievements (Cose, 2003). What choices do these women have? Some are staying single; others are interdating.

About 55 percent of Americans have *interdated*—gone out with a member of another racial or ethnic group (Wellner, 2005). Interdaters are more likely to be men than women and more likely to be Asian American or African American than Latino or white (see *Figure 8.3*).

The amount of interdating also depends on a person's social networks. Among college students, for example, those who are most likely to develop interethnic and interracial romantic relationships have close friends

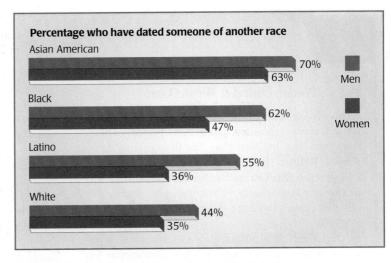

FIGURE 8.3   Dating People of Another Racial/Ethnic Group
Overall, about 4 in 10 Americans report having dated someone of another race or ethnicity. A companion survey found that more than two-thirds of these relationships were "serious romantic relationships."

SOURCE: *Washington Post*/Henry J. Kaiser Family Foundation/Harvard University survey, 2001; table presented in Fears and Deane, 2001, p. A4.

who are ethnically diverse and who support interdating across ethnic or racial boundaries. As an Asian American female stated, "Currently, I'm in a relationship with a Caucasian. Three of my close friends are also in interethnic relationships" (Clark-Ibáñez and Felmlee, 2004: 300).

Interdating has increased, but some groups don't embrace the change. As the box "Why I Never Dated a White Girl" shows, for example, a number of African Americans endorse homogamy and disapprove of interracial dating. (We'll examine interracial and interethnic dating more closely later in this chapter.)

RELIGION Religion can also play a major role in dating and mate selection. All three of the major religions practiced in the United States—Catholicism, Protestantism, and Judaism—have traditionally opposed interfaith marriages in the belief that they weaken individuals' commitment to the faith. Church leaders, for example, often advise Mormon adolescents to date only within their own religion. One reason for such a policy is that only Mormons are allowed to participate in the highly valued marriage ceremony in a Mormon temple (Markstrom-Adams, 1991).

The Roman Catholic Church encourages interfaith couples to ensure that their children will be raised as Catholics. And some Jews consider intermarriage a serious threat to Jewish identity and culture. As a result, many Jewish congregations do an "exemplary job of providing opportunities for unmarried people to get to

Multicultural Families

Why I Never Dated a White Girl

Although interdating is fairly common (see *Figure 8.3*), it is still controversial. For example, 41 percent of black teens who have interdated say that their parents disapproved (Wellner, 2005).

Lawrence Otis Graham (1996: 36–56) explains why he's never dated a white woman and, presumably, why other black men shouldn't either:

- **Objection 1:** When black leaders or advocates marrying outside the race, such decisions demonstrate less commitment to black people and our causes.
- **Objection 2:** We fear that intermarrying blacks are making a statement to black and white America that black spouses are less desirable partners and are therefore inferior.
- **Objection 3:** Interracial marriage undermines our ability to introduce our black children to black mentors and role models who accept their racial identity with confidence and pride.
- **Objection 4:** Because it diffuses our resources, interracial marriage makes it difficult to build a black America that has wealth, prestige, and power.

- **Objection 5:** We worry that confused biracial children will turn their backs on the black race once they discover that it's easier to live as a white person.
- **Objection 6:** Today's interracial relationships are a painful reminder of a 250-year period in black American history when white people exploited our sexuality.

Interracial and interethnic couples encounter negative reactions on a fairly regular basis. One of the most common reactions is being stared at, particularly in public places. In the service sector, waiters or waitresses, gas station attendants, convenience store clerks, sales staff in retail outlets, and even other customers are often rude or hostile (McNamara et al., 1999; see, also, Chapter 4).

Stop and Think . . .

- Do you agree with Graham's reasons for not dating and marrying outside the African American community?
- Graham states why he feels that interracial dating and marriage are dysfunctional. Think back to the discussion of manifest and latent functions of dating at the beginning of the chapter. Are there ways in which interdating is functional?

---

know one another" to promote religious and ethnic endogamy (Glenn, 2002: 55).

Many young people choose religious colleges that promote traditional values regarding dating, gender roles, and sexual abstinence. Some prohibit dating, "steady company keeping," and public displays of affection, including hugging and kissing. A vast majority become engaged by the spring of their senior year ("ring by spring") and marry shortly after graduation (Riley, 2005).

AGE In some African countries, girls under age 15 are often married off to men who may be 30 or 40 years older. Americans are age-endogamous because they tend to marry within the same age group. Typically the man is a few years older than the woman. Among people who are currently dating, a large majority (68 percent) say that they would not marry a man who is 10 or more years younger than they are; 65 percent of men say that they would not marry a woman who is 10 or more years older than they are (*2006 Dating Trends Survey,* 2006; see, also, Chapter 10).

Men often seek younger women because they want to have families. In some cases, however, a woman may find that a much older man may be unwilling to have children, especially if he has a family by a previous marriage or is expected to share in the child-rearing responsibilities. Large age differences may also lead to generation gaps in attitudes about lifestyle, such as music preferences, recreation, and family activities.

Some recent research in Europe and the United States suggests that successful women who have their own resources sometimes seek younger, attractive men with few assets but who can be "molded" (Moore et al., 2006). There's little evidence, however, that such unions are widespread, at least so far.

SOCIAL CLASS Most people date and marry within their social class because they and their partners share similar attitudes, values, and lifestyles. Even when people from different racial and ethnic groups intermarry, they usually belong to the same social class (Kalmijn, 1998).

Talk show host Larry King is almost the same age as the father of his seventh wife, Shawn. Why are most families and friends less likely to approve of age heterogamy in mate selection if the woman is 25 to 30 years older than the man?

workers rarely meet each other in the workplace because they occupy different physical spaces and have different schedules. At colleges and universities, for example, staff and maintenance workers are often housed in different buildings or floors and rarely interact. If we add religion, age, and physical appearance to the mix, homogamy reduces the number of eligible dating partners even further.

VALUES Mate selection methods may have changed, but has there been a corresponding change in the values that shape our choices? College students' responses in three widely spaced studies—1939, 1956, and 1967—didn't change much (Hudson and Henze, 1969). Students said that they wanted partners who were dependable, emotionally stable, intelligent, sociable, and good-looking. They sought partners with pleasing dispositions, good health, and a religious background and social status similar to their own.

The characteristics of the "ideal partner" had changed only somewhat by the late 1990s. As the box "What Are the Most Important Qualities in a Mate?" shows, both sexes are remarkably similar in valuing traits such as mutual attraction, good character, emotional maturity, and a pleasant disposition.

What has changed since 1939 is that chastity is now one of the least important characteristics for both sexes. And, in contrast to 1939, members of both sexes now rank "good financial prospect" higher. According to several recent surveys, both men and women say that having a steady job, a good credit history, and being financially responsible are even more important than sexual compatibility in sustaining a dating relationship (Kristof, 2006; *2006 Dating Trends Survey,* 2006).

Homogamy narrows our pool of eligible partners. Increasing numbers of people, however, are expanding their marriage markets through heterogamy.

Many of us face strong pressures to date people of similar (or preferably higher) social standing. Despite the popularity of films like *Pretty Woman,* in which a powerful business mogul marries a prostitute, very few of the rich and powerful marry outside their social group (Kendall, 2002).

The New York Times wedding page provides a good example of class consciousness. The *Times* emphasizes four things—college degrees, graduate degrees, career path, and parents' professions. Thus, couples from lower socioeconomic levels rarely see their engagement or wedding announcement in the *Times* or other national newspapers (Brooks, 2000).

Parents may not have to exert pressure on their children to marry someone of "their own kind" because communities are typically organized by social class. Schools, churches, and recreational facilities reflect the socioeconomic status of neighborhoods. It is highly unlikely that children living in upper-class neighborhoods will even meet children from middle-class, much less working-class, families.

One researcher has described colleges and universities as "matrimonial agencies" that are arranged hierarchically because students at Ivy League, private, state-supported, and community colleges have few chances to meet one another. Because they influence their children by encouraging them to attend college and helping them choose a school, many parents further narrow their dating choices in terms of social class (Eckland, 1968).

Finally, social class interacts with other variables to promote homogamy. Blue-collar and white-collar

Heterogamy: Expanding the Marriage Market

As U.S. society becomes more diverse and multicultural, many people are dating and marrying across traditionally acceptable boundaries. Whether we complain about

Applying What You've Learned

What Are the Most Important Qualities in a Mate?

What do you feel are the most important traits in a date or prospective mate? Are there any qualities that you would add to this list? Any that you would omit?

Order of Priority	Men Want	Women Want
1	Mutual attraction and love	Mutual attraction and love
2	Dependable character	Dependable character
3	Emotional stability, maturity	Emotional stability, maturity
4	Pleasant disposition	Pleasant disposition
5	Education, intelligence	Education, intelligence
6	Good health	Desire for children, home
7	Sociability	Ambition, industriousness
8	Good looks	Sociability
9	Desire for home, children	Good health
10	Ambition, industriousness	Similar educational background
11	Refinement, neatness	Good financial prospects
12	Similar religious background	Refinement, neatness

SOURCE: Based on Buss et al., 2001.

the changes or like them, mate selection processes *are* changing because of heterogamy.

HETEROGAMY Often used interchangeably with the term *exogamy* (see Chapter 1), heterogamy refers to dating or marrying someone from a social, racial, ethnic, religious, or age group that is different from one's own. Most societies, for example, prohibit dating or marriage between siblings and between children and their parents, aunts and uncles, or other relatives. In some countries, such as India, rules of exogamy forbid marriage between individuals of similarly named clans, even though the families live several hundred miles apart and have never met (Gupta, 1979).

Although mate selection options are still limited by homogamy, for many people they are increasing throughout the life cycle rather than just during early adulthood. These options are especially evident in same-sex, social class, interfaith, and interracial relationships.

SAME-SEX RELATIONSHIPS Most societies still define a marriage as valid only if it is between a man and a woman. Nevertheless, several countries now allow same-sex partners to marry while others recognize same-sex civil unions as legitimate in the sense that the partners can enjoy the same legal benefits as heterosexual couples.

In the United States, Vermont permits civil unions in which gay partners have many of the same rights as heterosexuals. In 2003, a Massachusetts court ruled that gays can marry. The following year, however, the state's legislature began a process of enacting an amendment to the state constitution that would ban marriage between gay and lesbian partners. Because constitutional amendments must be approved by voters, the issue won't be decided before this textbook is published. We'll examine same-sex marriages and civil unions in Chapter 9. For now, suffice it to say that recognizing gay relationships increases heterogamy by not limiting dating to opposite-sex partners.

SOCIAL CLASS RELATIONSHIPS As you saw earlier, most of us marry within our social class. In open class societies like the United States, however, our dating and mate selection can move us up or down the social ladder. **Hypergamy** involves "marrying up" to improve one's overall social standing. Because the United States is still a race-conscious society, minority women, especially, can improve their social status by marrying a white man, even though the man has a lower educational level than the woman (Fu, 2001; Tsai et al., 2002).

Hypogamy, in contrast, involves "marrying down" in social class. As women postpone marriage to pursue educational and career goals, they often find that "Mr.

TABLE 8.3

But Is He Smart?

Percentage of single Americans who say that the following characteristics are "extremely important" or "very important" to them when looking for a mate.

	High School or Less	Some College	College Graduate
Intelligent	66%	86%	90%
Funny	65	73	75
Attractive	32	36	37
Athletic	10	12	16
Wealthy	8	4	5

SOURCE: Adapted from Gardyn, 2002: 37.

Right"—a man with credentials similar to theirs—just isn't available when they're ready to settle down (Whitehead, 2002). As a result, some women "marry down."

Although hypergamy used to describe most women in the past, this is no longer the case. Increasing numbers of educated women make more money than their dating partners and do not have to rely on marriage for financial security or upward mobility. Because gender role scripts still dictate that women and not men be hypergamous, many men feel intimidated by "high-powered" women and don't date or marry them (Dowd, 2002).

About 90 percent of the most highly educated singles say that finding a partner who is intelligent is extremely or very important, compared with only 66 percent of those with a high school degree (see *Table 8.3*). Intelligence and being a college graduate aren't synonymous, of course. Many singles, however, use formal education as a proxy for intelligence. Note also that wealth is much less important than intelligence.

INTERFAITH RELATIONSHIPS Historically, religion has been an important factor in dating and mate selection in the United States and many other countries. Now, however, interfaith marriages—and especially interfaith dating—are common in the United States. About 47 percent of Jewish-born U.S. adults, for example, had intermarried by 2001 (Shapiro, 2004).

Religion is less influential than race and ethnicity in determining whom we date and marry. For example, only 56 percent of long-term part-

nerships and 72 percent of marriages are between people with the same religious affiliation (Laumann et al., 1994). Race and ethnicity, in contrast, play a major role in whom we date and marry.

INTERRACIAL AND INTERETHNIC RELATIONSHIPS Although more than half of Americans have interdated, racial intermarriage is much less common. The rate of interracial marriage has increased slowly, from less than 1 percent in 1970 to 5.4 percent in 2000 (see *Figure 8.4*). The highest percentage of those who marry outside of their racial and ethnic groups are American Indians, Latino males, and Asian American women (see Chapter 4).

The percentage of black–white marriages is low—only 20 percent of all interracial marriages. These low rates suggest that social norms against white–black marriages are still much stronger than norms against marriages among other racial and ethnic groups (Lee and Edmonston, 2005; U.S. Census Bureau, 2006).

However, black men are three times more likely than black women to marry a member of another racial or ethnic group. Why? Interracial dating still reflects a double standard. For example, black journalists such as Ellis Cose (1995) have criticized black women but not black men for dating interracially.

Outside of the double standard, why are African American women less likely than African American men to marry outside their group? Generally, intermarriage rates tend to increase with education (Lee and Edmonston, 2005). Black women, as a group, are more likely

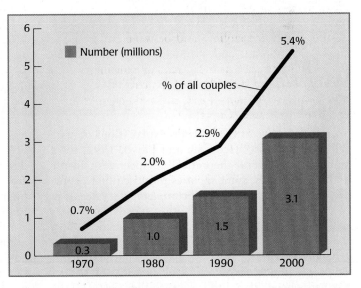

FIGURE 8.4 Interracial Marriages Have Increased in the United States
SOURCE: Lee and Edmonston, 2005 (Figure 1).

than their male counterparts to obtain college and graduate degrees. Thus, it's not clear why many African American women are less likely than their African American men to intermarry.

Some scholars suggest that there may be a continuum of explanations for higher interracial marriages among black men than black women. These explanations include structural factors like the decline in segregationist policies that has increased interracial contact, psychological factors that involve black men's associating attractiveness with whiteness, and exchange theories which posit that African American men experience "a boost in self-esteem" because they believe that their white partners have a higher social status (Craig-Henderson, 2006).

Although a continuum helps explain why interdating has increased overall, it still doesn't answer why the rates differ for African American men and women. Mate selection theories provide further insights.

Making Connections

■ Think about the people that you've dated or someone you've married. Do you agree that the filter theory influenced your behavior? If so, which variables were most important?

■ Some people maintain that interracial dating and marriage is healthy because such practices will break down some of the racial-ethnic barriers in our society. Others argue that interracial relationships will dilute our cultural heritage. How do *you* feel?

Why We Choose Each Other: Theories of Mate Selection

Sociologists have offered various explanations of mate selection processes (see Cate and Lloyd, 1992, for a summary of several theoretical perspectives). In the 1950s and 1960s, some theories proposed that people are drawn to each because of *complementary needs;* in other words, opposites attract (Winch, 1958). This and similar perspectives have fallen out of scientific favor because they are not supported by empirical data (Regan, 2003).

since you asked

If "opposites attract," why do people tend to marry partners who are similar to themselves?

As you saw earlier, filter theory proposes that social structure limits our opportunities to meet people who are very different from us. In this sense, the sifting process that narrows the pool of eligible candidates is largely unconscious and often beyond our control. What influences our decision to stay in a relationship or to move on? Exchange theory and equity theory suggest that satisfaction is a key factor in weighing our mate selection investments and liabilities.

Dating as Give and Take: Social Exchange Theory

According to social exchange theory, people are attracted to prospective partners who they believe will provide them with the best possible "deal" in a relationship (see Chapters 2 and 6). This may not sound very romantic, but social exchange theorists propose that costs and rewards form the basis of most relationships.

Social exchange theory posits that people will begin (and remain in) a relationship if the rewards are higher than the costs. *Rewards* may be intrinsic characteristics (intelligence, a sense of humor), directly rewarding behavior (sex, companionship), or access to desired resources (money, power). *Costs,* the "price" paid, may be unpleasant or destructive behavior (insults, violence) or literal losses (money, time). The box "Am I Seeing the Wrong Person?" offers advice from practitioners for filtering out undesirable candidates as you look for a long-term relationship.

Historically, because women were expected to bear children and be homemakers, physical attractiveness was one of the few assets they could offer in the marriage market. Men, on the other hand, had a variety of resources—including money, education, and power—and therefore had more dating options. Today, as more women earn college degrees and establish careers, they are increasing their assets and can be more selective in dating relationships. As a result, however, both sexes have a smaller pool of eligible partners.

As they compete for jobs, women's values about desirable traits in men are changing. Although they are interested in men who are competent workers and high earners, women today are also concerned about finding a partner who will share housework and child-rearing responsibilities (see Chapters 5 and 10). Economic security is as important as companionship and communication. Men who dismiss such characteristics as unimportant are less desirable partners; many women view such men as wanting one-sided relationships in which they get all the rewards and have few or no costs.

Ask Yourself

Am I Seeing the Wrong Person?

Because often "love is blind," many people overlook serious flaws and marry Mr. or Ms. Wrong. Here are some red flags that should alert you to possible problems.

- **Don Juans and other sexual predators.** Men admit using a variety of "lines" to persuade women to have sex. These Don Juans will *declare their love for you* ("I don't want to have sex with you—I want to make love to you"), *flatter you* ("You're one of the most beautiful women I've ever seen," "I've never met anyone like you before"), *make meaningless promises* ("Our relationship will grow stronger," "I swear I'll get a divorce"), *threaten you with rejection* ("Our relationship really needs to move on," "If you loved me, you would"), *put you down* if you refuse ("You're really old-fashioned"), or *challenge you* to prove that you're "normal" ("Are you frigid?" "Are you gay?").

- **Incompatibility of basic values.** Initially, it may be exciting to be with someone who's very different. In the long run, however, serious differences in values may jeopardize a relationship. If your partner likes to curl up with a mystery novel but you want to go out with friends every weekend, you may be in for trouble.

- **Rigid sex roles.** If your partner wants you to be a full-time homemaker and parent but you want a career, there may be strain.

- **Emotional baggage.** If your partner often talks about an ex-partner—comparing you with her "saintly" dead husband or his past lovers—she or he is living in the past instead of getting to know you.

- **Extreme jealousy and violent tendencies.** Stay away from someone who is possessive, jealous, or violent. Such characteristics as a bad temper, frequent angry outbursts, constant criticism, and sudden mood swings will not decrease in the future.

- **Substance abuse.** Someone who is addicted to alcohol or other drugs is the wrong choice for a mate. Watch for such things as slowed responses, slurred speech, glassy eyes, extreme mood swings, or failure to keep dates.

- **Excessive time spent with others.** Does your partner spend several nights a week with others while you spend time alone? If your partner is always on the phone, or if family "emergencies" often come before your needs, there will probably be similar conflicts in the future.

- **Mr. Flirt and Ms. Tease.** If your partner is flirtatious or a sexual tease, watch out. Flirting may be entertaining at first, but not over the long run.

- **Lack of communication.** Good communication is essential for a good relationship. Feelings of boredom, evidence of your partner's disinterest, or finding that you have little to talk about may signal serious communication problems that will decrease intimacy.

- **Control freaks.** Does your partner always try to change or control you or the relationship? Do you constantly feel criticized, judged, scrutinized, and corrected, especially in public? If so, stay away.

- **Blaming others for problems.** It's always someone else's fault if something goes wrong ("My boss didn't appreciate me" instead of "I was fired because I always came in late").

SOURCES: Powell, 1991; Collison, 1993; Kenrick et al., 1993.

Dating as a Search for Egalitarian Relationships: Equity Theory

According to equity theory, an extension of social exchange theory, an intimate relationship is satisfying and stable if both partners see it as equitable and mutually beneficial (Walster et al., 1973). Equity theory advances several basic propositions:

- The greater the perceived equity, the happier the relationship.

- When people find themselves in an inequitable relationship, they become distressed. The greater the inequity, the greater the distress.

- People in an inequitable relationship will attempt to eliminate their distress by restoring equity.

Equity theory reflects the American sense of "fair play," the notion that one has a right to expect a reasonable balance between costs and benefits in life. If we give more than we receive, we usually become angry. If we receive more than our "fair share" of benefits, we may feel guilty. In each case, we experience dissatisfaction with the relationship. We try to decrease the distress and restore equity by changing our contributions, by persuading a partner to change his or her contributions, or by convincing ourselves that the inequity doesn't exist (Miell and Croghan, 1996).

Consider Mike and Michelle, who were initially happy with their dating relationship. Among other exchanges, she helped him with his calculus and he helped her write a paper for a sociology class. Mike and Michelle spent as much time as possible together and shared similar extracurricular interests. By the end of the semester, however, Michelle was still helping Mike with his calculus assignments but Mike was no longer available to help Michelle with her sociology papers because he had joined the swim team. According to equity theory, Mike might feel guilty and increase his help, or Mike and Michelle will have to "renegotiate" their contributions. If the distress is too great, one or both will break up the relationship.

Judgments about equity can vary, depending on the stage of the relationship. As two people get acquainted, severe inequity usually ends further involvement. Once a relationship enters a stage of long-term commitment, people tolerate inequality—especially if they plan to marry—because they are optimistic about the future. Later in most long-term relationships, however, and especially as people face transitions (such as parenthood), perceived inequities can increase stress and dissatisfaction (Sprecher, 2001).

A Global View: Mate Selection Across Cultures

Mate selection is an important process, but societies around the world vary considerably in how they negotiate the marriage market. A few of these variations involve differences between modern and traditional approaches, exogamy and endogamy, and free choice versus arranged marriages.

Modern and Traditional Societies

Most countries do not have the "open" courtship systems that are common in Western nations. Many factors—such as wealth, age, and values—promote traditional mate selection arrangements.

WEALTH Money can play an important role in mate selection. In some Mediterranean, Middle Eastern, and Asian societies, the **dowry**—the money, goods, or property that a woman brings to a marriage—is still an important basis for mate selection. Women with large dowries have a competitive edge in attracting the "best" suitors. If the bride's family fails to meet dowry expectations, their newlywed daughter may face onerous responsibilities in her new household, as well as violence and even death.

Despite modernization, use of the dowry in many parts of India is becoming more widespread, and the amount is increasing. Even though the Indian government has legally outlawed the dowry system, the practice still flourishes. Many women who disapprove of dowries in principle regard them as necessary for attracting the most desirable men and as a way for young couples to obtain consumer goods (Srinivasan and Lee, 2004).

Whereas a dowry is a payment by the family of the bride, a *bride price* is the required payment by the family of the groom. The payment varies from a few cattle to a thousand dollars or more. Some have criticized the bride price for treating women as property and for discouraging marriage among unemployed men. However, many defend the custom. For example, Africans argue that paying for a bride bonds families and decreases the likelihood of wife abuse. In Afghanistan, a bride price

Every Sunday, parents gather in a park in Nanjing in east China's Jiangsu province to find girlfriends and boyfriends for their unmarried children. Parental matchmaking has become more aggressive because many urban Chinese youths, often in their mid- to late-twenties, are busy with careers and are geting married at older ages than the previous generations.

ensures a man's getting a virgin (sometimes as young as 11 years old) who will till fields, tend livestock, and bear children. In return, the bride's family delivers the girl from hunger and pays off some debts (Bearak, 2006; Calvert, 2006).

AGE The minimum age at which people may marry varies widely from one country to another. In industrialized societies, the minimum age at marriage may be 16 or 18. In traditional societies in Africa, parents can betroth a baby girl to a friend's 4-year-old son or before the girl is 10 years old, or to a man who may be 20 or 30 years older than the girl (Wilson et al., 2003; Modo, 2005).

The minimum age at marriage is also low in many Middle Eastern countries. Only recently, for example, Iran passed a bill that permits girls to be married at age 13 (instead of 9) and boys at the age of 15 (instead of 14) without court permission. Female lawmakers saw the change as a major advance in protecting very young girls from early marriage ("Iranian arbitrating body . . . ," 2002).

VALUES Many modern societies, including the United States, accept love as the basis of mate selection. Thus, Americans and people in many other industrialized countries, including Scandinavia and the Netherlands, consider intimate relationships (such as living together) that don't result in marriage as acceptable and "normal" (van Dulmen, 2003; Trost and Levin, 2005).

In traditional societies, customs are more important than love in mate selection. As you've just seen, wealth and age may be important factors in deciding who marries whom. Gender roles are also important in finding a mate. In some parts of India, for example, even some college-educated women take courses that encourage them to be submissive. The courses instruct women to think of prospective husbands as "gods" because men "are the cornerstone of society," and to always obey future in-laws because "the mother-in-law and father-in-law are never wrong" (Lancaster, 2004).

Exogamy and Endogamy

Mate selection also varies according to exogamy and endogamy norms. Exogamy, as you recall, involves marrying outside one's family or kin group, while endogamy refers to marrying someone within one's social group, such as a person of the same race, religion, or social class (see Chapter 1).

EXOGAMY In industrialized societies, both laws and custom prohibit people from marrying someone within her or his family. In the United States, many states don't allow marriages between first cousins (see Chapter 1). Especially if people don't have prospective marriage

mates within their own social group, they marry "outsiders." In Argentina, for example, people married outside of their ethnic boundaries when immigration rates decreased and there were fewer prospective mates of the same nationality (Jelin, 2005).

ENDOGAMY In many societies, mate selection is endogamous. In Afghanistan, for example, there is an old saying that "a marriage between cousins is the most righteous because the engagement was made in heaven." And across the Arab world, an average of 45 percent of married partners are related to each other (Kershaw, 2003; Aizenman, 2005).

Endogamy has its advantages. In India, for example, endogamous mate selection ensures that people marry within their social class and can pass down their wealth to a kin group. In Turkey, endogamy ensures strong and continuing family ties (Nauck and Klaus, 2005; Singh, 2005).

Endogamy also has costs. In Cuba—and despite the government's formal policy of racial heterogeneity—racist beliefs about black inferiority and racial purity discourage people from seeking partners with lighter or darker skin colors. In Sri Lanka, classified ads for marriage partners

In a number of developing societies, marriage is often a transaction among families. The younger the bride, the higher the price she fetches. A father uses the bride price to ward off poverty, buy farm animals, and pay off debts. In most cases, the young girl is younger than the man's children and may be subservient to his other wives. Pictured here, in Afghanistan, Ghulam Haider, 11, is to be married to Faiz Mohammed, 40. She had hoped to be a teacher but was forced to quit her classes when she became engaged.

ask respondents to indicate their caste because educated people don't want to mate with people from lower socioeconomic groups (Roschelle et al., 2005; Magnier, 2006).

Endogamy can also increase the chances of passing down diseases. In some parts of Saudi Arabia, for example, where blood relatives range from 55 to 70 percent of married couples, inbreeding produces several genetic disorders, including thalassemia (a potentially fatal blood disease), sickle cell anemia, spinal muscular atrophy, diabetes, deafness, and muteness. Educated Saudis have begun to pull away from the practice, but the tradition of marrying first cousins "is still deeply embedded in Saudi culture." And in Afghanistan, where first-cousin marriages are common because women are prohibited from mingling with unrelated men, doctors are finding that children have a higher chance of being born with birth defects and diseases, such as brain disorders and mental retardation, that might be inherited (Kershaw, 2003; Aizenman, 2005).

Free Choice and Arranged Marriages

Mate selection processes also differ in terms of free choice versus arranged marriages. As you saw earlier, filter theory argues that people in industrialized societies, including the United States, are limited in their selection of dating and marriage mates. Still, open dating offers people more choices than do arranged marriages.

In arranged marriages, the family or community is more important than the individual. Although arranged marriages are disappearing in many traditional societies, they still play an important role in numerous cultures. In Islamic societies, especially, arranged marriages increase solidarity between families. If, for example, a newly-wed couple experiences problems, family members might intervene to resolve some of the conflicts.

since you asked

Do arranged marriages work better than dating in finding a mate?

Small groups of Saudi and other Middle Eastern women are challenging some strict restrictions on dating (see Chapter 5). However, many young Asian Muslims who live in the United States believe in arranged marriages. Among other things, they feel that dating undermines girls' self-respect. As one Muslim teenager commented about her best friend, who is not Islamic, "She is always tortured about whether her boyfriend likes her or not, if she is fat, attractive, how many silly Valentine's cards she gets. I couldn't go through all of that. It's crazy" (Alibhai-Brown, 1993: 29).

Arranged marriages aren't paradise, however. In poor nations like Afghanistan, parents arrange marriages between daughters and older men who are able to afford the $500 to $1,500 dowry. Thus, a 14-year-old girl may be given in marriage to a 60-year-old married man with grown children. To escape such arranged or unhappy marriages, girls and young women sometimes douse themselves with fuel and set themselves on fire. One regional hospital in Afghanistan has at least 100 such cases every year, and the numbers have been rising (Reitman, 2002).

Arranged marriages often involve marrying a first cousin as the "top choice." In 2002 alone, 250 Pakistani girls born in Great Britain were lured home to visit but were then coerced into marrying first cousins or other men. If a father or uncle takes away the girl's passport and isolates her, she has little legal recourse or chance of escaping. Islam does *not* allow forced arranged marriages. Instead, these are social and cultural practices in societies where men dominate and can force girls and women to marry against their will "to preserve culture and lineage" (Tohid, 2003: 7).

In some traditional societies, men sometimes abduct women and force them into marriage (see the box "If She Says "No" . . ."). Although such practices are rare, they show that many women still have few choices regarding whom they can marry.

Some societies are trying to maintain their traditional mate selection processes; others are changing. In some cases, these changes are the result of a shortage of women. In others, a rising number of women who pursue higher education and careers are postponing marriage.

How Mate Selection Methods Are Changing

Some countries in Asia and the Middle East are experiencing changes in the ways that people meet and select mates. In Pakistan, for example, many young adults use the Internet to find prospective mates. Others participate in television shows that try to connect "soul mates" rather than relying on arranged marriages (Riccardi, 2004).

India and China are experiencing a glut of single men and a scarcity of single women. In both countries, the preference for boys has led to the killing of millions of female infants and the deaths of many others as a result of neglect—poor nutrition, inadequate medical care, or desertion. Unmarried women have become scarce. Men in some poor rural regions of China often rely on a booming trade of kidnapped women from Vietnam and North Korea as a source of wives (Hudson and den Boer, 2004; see, also, Chapter 5).

China has responded to the preponderance of males by implementing some Western-style mate selection methods, including newspaper and magazine ads and Internet "singles" services. In Beijing, on any

Cross Cultural Families

If She Says "No," Just Kidnap Her

In some parts of Turkey, males abduct women for a number of reasons: to get a bride even though her family disapproves, to avoid dowries that the bride's family can't afford, or when both sides of the family have other mates in mind.

In some other societies, men simply kidnap women who refuse to marry them. One example is Kyrgyzstan, a country to the west of China that broke away from the Soviet Union in 1991. Even though the practice has been illegal for many years, more than half of Kyrgyzstan's married women were snatched from the street by their husbands. This custom, *ala kachun*, translates roughly into "grab and run."

Some women don't mind *ala kachun* because it's a form of elopement, but many see it as a violent act because they are taken against their will. Once a kidnapped girl or woman has been kept in the abductor's home overnight, her virginity is suspect, her reputation is disgraced, and she will find it difficult to attract a husband of her choice.

Many men in Kyrgyzstan rationalize the kidnappings. For example, snatching a woman is easier and cheaper than paying the standard "bride price," which can be as much as $800, and "Men steal women to show that they are real men." And according to an old Kyrgyz saying, "Every good marriage begins in tears." That is, women are expected to adjust to the marriage.

The threat of abduction begins to haunt women in their teenage years. Some rarely leave their homes. Some women attending universities wear wedding bands or head scarves to fool men into thinking that they are already married.

Sources: Smith, 2005; Nauck and Klaus, 2005.

Stop and Think . . .

- Some women adapt to *ala kachun*. In effect, then, is this mate selection practice fairly harmless?
- Although kidnapping women is illegal in Kyrgyzstan, the law is not enforced. What does this tell us about patriarchal societies?

of four days each week hundreds of parents go to one of the city's three parks to play matchmaker, whether the children like it or not. Anxious that in their mid-20s their children are still unmarried because they are in fast-track jobs and don't have time to date, the parents are determined to find mates for them. They come prepared with photos and computer printouts describing the adult child and his or her desired mate. For example, "Male, 28 years old, 1.72 meters tall [about 5′ 6″], a junior college graduate from an upper-middle class family, seeking a shorter woman between 16 and 23 years of age, with a high school degree, a stable income, and a Beijing residence permit" (Epstein, 2005: 1A).

Alarmed by the low rates of mating and procreation among its college-educated singles, Singapore may be the only city in the world that has a government-run dating service. The matchmaking includes subsidized mixers, trips, "marriage awareness" seminars, and speed dating (Murphy, 2002).

In Japan and Korea the mating game has also changed, in part because more women are acquiring a college education, finding jobs, postponing marriage, or preferring to remain single. Japan has one of the highest average ages of marriage in the world: 29 years for men and 26 years for women. To retain the loyalty of unmarried employees in the under-40 age bracket, several companies have engaged matrimony brokerage

firms to act as matchmakers for those seeking a spouse. Matchmaking companies are thriving, generally, because many men are eager to learn how to date, court, and select a wife (Thornton, 1994).

But a growing number of college-educated Japanese women are looking for husbands abroad. Thousands have signed up with matchmaking agencies that screen American and European men. According to a 35-year-old women who works at a top trading firm,

They treat you like equals, and they don't hesitate to express mutual feelings of respect. I think Western men are more adept [at such things] than Japanese men. I think they see women as individuals (Richardson, 2004: 1).

In 2005, one in five marriages in Taiwan were to a foreigner. Most were to women from China, Vietnam, and other Southeast counties who met their husbands through marriage brokers. Men in rural towns, especially, have difficulty finding a wife locally who "will keep house and bear children without complaint" and who will care for her in-laws when they get old. Because of language barriers, abuse, and cultural differences, 40 percent of the marriages break down within five years. Other wives develop friendships with brides from their own countries and adjust (Montlake, 2006).

In some parts of Spain, the Dominican Republic, Ecuador, and Colombia, women are scarce because they've left home to work in cities. To help men find mates, some enterprising farmers have organized "Cupid crusades." Women who are disenchanted with city life board a bus and spend a day with a group of bachelors: "Lonely hearts mingle over roasted lamb and a halting *pasodoble,* or two-step." An event usually lasts eight hours; the women pay $10 apiece and the men $30. Some of these encounters result in marriage (Fuchs, 2003).

Harmful Dating Relationships: Power, Control, and Sexual Aggression

A few years ago, one of my best students, Jennifer, dropped by my office to apologize for missing an exam and a week of classes. I listened quietly as she fumbled with excuses: "I was sick. . . . Well, actually, my mom was sick. . . . I've been having car problems, too." She then burst into tears and showed me a bruise around her neck. Her boyfriend had been abusing her for some time but now had tried to strangle her.

So far we've focused on the positive side of dating: how people meet each other and what qualities they look for in marital partners. Dating also has a dark side. As in Jennifer's case, going together can be disappointing and even dangerous. Some major problems in dating, such as control and manipulation, may lead to violence. We can recognize risk factors for sexual aggression and date rape, however, and seek solutions.

Power and Control in Dating Relationships

Why do so many women still sit around waiting for their "boyfriends" to call even when they are in steady relationships? Sociologist Willard Waller's (1937) *principle of least interest* is useful in explaining power in many dating relationships.

PRINCIPLE OF LEAST INTEREST According to Waller, males have more power than females because they are usually the partner with the least interest. The person with more power is less dependent on others, is less interested in maintaining the relationship, and as a result, has more control. Conversely, the person with less power—usually the female—is more likely to be dependent, to try to maintain the relationship, and, often, to be exploited as a result (Lloyd, 1991; Sarch, 1993).

GENDER DIFFERENCES Men often maintain power and control during a dating relationship through direct strategies such as assertion, aggression, and discussion; women more often choose indirect strategies such as hinting, withdrawing, or attempting to manipulate a partner's emotions. According to a national study of single, never-married people between ages 18 and 30, women were more likely than men to keep tabs on their partners, make the men do what they want, and generally set the rules for the relationship. And, increasingly, girls are becoming more physically aggressive and violent both within and outside of dating (Christopher and Kisler, 2004; Garbarino, 2006).

Women's manipulation and control of men is the topic of a popular self-help book, *The Rules* (Fein and Schneider, 1996), that's still cited by many journalists and counselors. The authors encourage women to scheme and maneuver men to obtain marriage proposals. Some of "the rules" include not calling the man, rarely returning his calls, and always ending phone calls first to maintain control of the relationship.

Because *The Rules* was a best-seller, one might conclude that women are desperate to get married even if dating involves conniving and manipulating men. Tricks and dishonesty are *not* a sound basis for marriage or a long-term relationship for either men or women, however (see Chapter 6). The box "How Abusers Control Dating Relationships" examines some coercive tactics in more detail.

Aggression and Violence in Dating Relationships

Control often increases as a relationship progresses from casual to more serious dating. Men are much more likely than women to use physical force and sexual aggression to get their own way or to intimidate a partner. Women can also be physically and emotionally abusive, however (Christopher and Kisler, 2004; Prothrow-Stith and Spivak, 2005).

since you asked

Are men or women more guilty of dating violence?

DATING VIOLENCE Dating violence is widespread. Consider the following statistics:

■ About 42 percent of adolescents in the sixth through twelfth grades have experienced dating violence. Of these, 65 percent reported that the violence was mutual, 20 percent said that they were

Constraints

How Abusers Control Dating Relationships

Both men and women try to control relationships. Although the following categories describe the experiences of women who have been victims, men are also subject to abusive dating relationships.

- **Jealousy and blaming:** Blaming is often based on jealousy; almost anything the partner does is considered provocative. For example, a man may criticize his partner for not being home when he calls or for talking to another man. He may say he loves her so much that he can't stand for her to be with others, including male friends.

- **Coercion, intimidation, and threats:** Abusers may coerce compliance by threatening their partners. An abuser says things like "I'll break your neck" or "I'll kill you," and then dismisses them with "Everybody talks like that." Abusers also threaten to commit suicide or to attack a partner's family.

- **Isolation:** Typically, abusers spend a lot of time and energy watching their victims. They accuse family and friends of "causing trouble." Abusers may deprive victims of a phone or car or even try to prevent them from holding a job. If these isolating techniques work, they break the partner's ties with other friends and increase dependence on the abuser.

- **Physical abuse:** Violent acts range from slaps and shoves to beatings, rape, and attacks with weapons.

Many abusers manage to convince a partner, on each violent occasion, that "I really love you" and "This will never happen again," but it does. And in some cases the last time the abuser strikes, he or she kills.

- **Emotional and verbal abuse:** Emotional abuse is very powerful. Insults, which attack a person's feelings of independence and self-worth, are generally intended to get the partner to succumb to the abuser's demands ("Don't wear your skirt so short—it makes you look like a hooker"). The abuser often says or implies that she had better do what the partner wants or be left without anyone.

- **Sexual abuse:** Conflicts about sex can lead to violence. Often a male abuser decides whether to have sex, which sex acts are acceptable, and whether or not the couple will use condoms or other contraceptive devices.

SOURCES: Gamache, 1990: Rosen and Stith, 1993; Shackelford et al., 2005.

Stop and Think . . .

- Have you, your friends, or relatives experienced any of these forms of abuse? How did you react?
- Do you think that we can really love someone we're afraid of?

perpetrators, and 15 percent said that they were victims (Gray and Foshee, 1997).

- Nationwide, 9 percent of high school students had been hit, slapped, or physically hurt on purpose by their boyfriend or girlfriend in the 12 months preceding the survey (Eaton et al., 2006).

- One in five young women experiences rape (either completed or attempted) during college. In 80 to 90 percent of the cases, the victims and assailants know each other (Karjane et al., 2005).

- Among adults, women are six times more likely than men to experience dating violence ("Dating violence," 2000).

- Among all adults age 18 and older, almost 22 percent of women and 3 percent of men have been raped by a current or former date, boyfriend, or girlfriend. Almost 82 percent of the male victims had been raped by another male (Tjaden and Thoennes, 2006).

- A study of more than 13,000 university students in 32 nations found that almost a third of the female as well as male students physically assaulted a dating partner in the 12 months preceding the survey (Straus, 2006).

Dating violence is rarely a one-time event. Apparently, many women interpret the violence as evidence of love. According to a domestic violence counselor, "With so little real-life experience, girls tend to take jealousy and possessiveness to mean 'he loves me'." In some cases, couples who stay in abusive relationships seem to have accepted violence as a legitimate means of resolving conflict. It is almost as if they are testing the strength of their relationship: "If we can survive this, we can survive anything" (Lloyd, 1991; L. Harris, 1996).

Although rates of violence among gay and lesbian couples are similar to those among heterosexuals, they're highly underreported. In some cases, gays don't report dating or other violence for fear of increasing homophobia. In other cases, and until recently, 13 states had sodomy laws. Therefore, gays could be prosecuted for having same-sex intercourse rather than being protected from an abusive partner (Hoffman, 2003; see, also, Chapter 9).

ACQUAINTANCE AND DATE RAPE Women are especially vulnerable to acquaintance and date rape. **Acquaintance rape** is rape of a person who knows or is familiar with the rapist. Acquaintance rapists may include neighbors, friends of the family, co-workers, or someone whom the victim meets at a party or get-together.

One female in seven attending the nation's military academies has been sexually assaulted since becoming a cadet or midshipman, and more than half have experienced some form of sexual harassment on campus. These women reported few of the incidents of sexual harassment and only a third of the assaults. Most of the women don't report the attacks because they're afraid of being seen as weak or that their military careers would be ended (U.S. Department of Defense, 2005).

Date rape is unwanted, forced sexual intercourse in the context of a dating situation; the victim and the perpetrator may be on a first date or in a steady dating relationship. Nationally, women are more likely to be raped by a date or an acquaintance than by a spouse or ex-spouse, a stranger, or a live-in partner (see *Figure 8.5*). One of the reasons date rape is so common, and one of the reasons it comes as a great shock to the victim, is that typically the rapist seems to be "a nice guy"—polite, clean-cut, and even a leader in the community or on campus.

Factors Contributing to Date Violence and Date Rape

There are many reasons for dating violence and date rape. Some of the most important explanations include family violence, gender-role expectations, peer pressure, secrecy, and use of alcohol and other drugs.

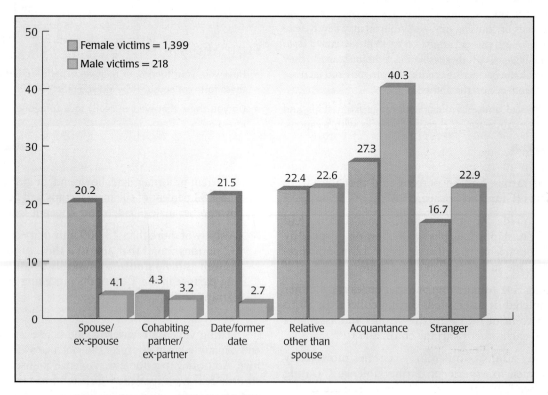

FIGURE 8.5   Rape Victims and Victim-Offender Relationships

Note: Percentages by sex exceed 100 because same victims were raped by more than one person.
SOURCE: Tjaden and Thoennes, 2006, Exhibit 13.

FAMILY VIOLENCE AND GENDER-ROLE EXPECTATIONS

A number of researchers have found an association between family violence and dating violence. Dating violence is more common among partners who had punched, shoved, or otherwise abused a sibling than among those who had not. Such violence is compounded by growing up in a family in which children see parent-to-parent violence or experience parent-to-child violence. Seeing that aggression produces compliance increases the likelihood of being both an assailant and a victim during courtship (Foshee et al., 1999; Noland et al., 2004).

Some attribute violence to *misogyny*, or hatred of women. Dating violence and date rape are ways of striking out against women (especially independent and self-confident women) who challenge men's "right" to control them.

Remember our discussion of narcissists—people who love themselves more than anyone else—in Chapter 6? Narcissistic men are especially likely to use sexual coercion during dating. They can become aggressive and even commit rape because they feel entitled to sexual gratification that they want and expect (Bushman et al., 2003).

Generally speaking, men who commit date rape hold traditional views of gender roles, seeing themselves as in charge and women as submissive. They initiate the date and pay the expenses, and often claim that women lead them on by dressing suggestively. Traditional men, especially, can be sexually aggressive and not feel guilty about it because "She deserved it" or "Women enjoy rough sex." Some college men who commit date rape also have stereotypical views of women's sexual behavior. For example, they are socialized to believe that women initially resist sexual advances to preserve their reputation and, because of this, prefer to be overcome sexually. In addition, some men believe that if a woman is "a tease" or "loose," she is asking for sex (Christopher, 2001; Sampson, 2002).

Women are more likely than men to blame themselves for dating violence because females are socialized to accept more responsibility for relationship conflict than males. In one study, both male and female college students saw the woman as encouraging or being responsible for acquaintance rape because women should "know better" than to visit men in their apartments or "lead men on" through heavy petting (Szymanski et al., 1993; Lloyd and Emery, 2000).

PEER PRESSURE AND SECRECY Peer pressure is one of the major reasons why some people are violent and why many partners stay in abusive dating relationships. "The pressure to date is fierce,"

and having any boyfriend is considered better than having none. Teens who date are seen as more popular than those who don't (L. Harris, 1996).

Peer pressure may be even more greater in college. In some cases, fraternity members and male athletes cover up incidents of sexual abuse—especially when it occurs during and after a party—instead of reporting the violence. Women can also be sexually coercive. In a study of 165 men and 131 women—all of them new members of fraternities or sororities—34 men and 36 women said that they had experienced unwanted sexual contact. Most of the male victims reported giving in to sexual arousal or verbal pressure by women. The women were more likely to have been subjected to physical force or plied with alcohol or drugs (Larimer et al., 1999; Sampson, 2002).

Secrecy protects abusers. Most teenagers remain silent about abusive relationships because they don't want their friends to put pressure on them to break up. They rarely tell their parents about the abuse because they are afraid of losing their freedom, don't want their parents to think they have poor judgment, or are trying to figure out what to do on their own (M. Harris, 1996).

Women who are members of minority racial or ethnic groups may endure dating violence for several interrelated reasons. Young Asian/Pacific women, for instance, may be torn between duty to their values of virginity and family honor and accommodating the men they are dating. When violence occurs in a secret dating relationship, there is additional pressure to prevent parents from learning about both the violence and the relationship itself. The secrecy intensifies the woman's

Parties provide a good avenue for meeting other singles. Drinking too much, however, may pave the way for trouble later in the evening, especially for women (see text).

feeling of responsibility for the violence (Yoshihama et al., 1991; Foo, 2002).

USE OF ALCOHOL AND OTHER DRUGS Although they are not the cause, alcohol and drugs play a large role in sexual assaults. In more than 75 percent of college rapes, the offender, the victim, or both had been drinking. Many college students deny any relationship between alcohol consumption and sexual aggression. Men say that they can control themselves, and women feel that they can resist unwanted sex. However, alcohol lowers inhibitions against violence and reduces a woman's ability to resist a sexual assault. In some cases, men admit that their strategies include getting women drunk to get them into bed (Nurius et al., 1996; Sampson, 2002).

Since the mid-1990s, a growing number of college women have reported being raped after their drink was spiked with Rohypnol (also known as "roofies," "rope," and a variety of other street terms). When it is slipped into any beverage, Rohypnol's sedating effects begin within 20 minutes of ingestion and usually last more than 12 hours. Rohypnol has been called the "date-rape drug" and the "forget me pill" because women who have been knocked out with roofies have blacked out, been raped, and had no memory of what happened. When mixed with alcohol or narcotics, Rohypnol can be fatal ("Rohypnol," 2003).

A more recent "rape drug" is GHB, or gamma hydroxybutyrate, a liquid or powder made of lye or drain-cleaner that's mixed with GBL, gamma butyrolactone, an industrial solvent often used to strip floors. GHB is an odorless, colorless drug that knocks the victim out within 30 minutes. The coma-like effects of GHB last from three to six hours. As recently as 1994—when the drug was still new—there were only 56 GHB-related emergency room cases nationwide. By 2001, the number had jumped to 3,340 (Lloyd, 2002a).

Consequences of Dating Violence and Date Rape

Most dating violence and date rape occurs in situations that seem safe and familiar. This is why these behaviors often come as a great shock to the victim, who cannot believe what is happening.

Violence and rape violate both body and spirit; they can affect every aspect of the victim's life. *Even though they are not responsible for the attack,* women often feel ashamed and blame themselves for the rape. Fear of men, of going out alone, and of being alone becomes part of their lives, as do anger, depression, and sometimes inability to relate to a caring sexual partner. *Table 8.4* lists other consequences of courtship violence and date rape.

TABLE 8.4

Emotional and Behavioral Difficulties Experienced by Victims of Courtship Violence or Date Rape

- General depression: Symptoms include changes in eating and sleeping patterns and unexplained aches and pains. Depressive symptoms may prevent women from attending classes, completing courses, or functioning effectively on the job.

- Feelings of powerlessness, helplessness, vulnerability, shame, and sadness.

- Loss of self-confidence and self-esteem, which may increase the likelihood of future sexual assaults.

- Changes in the victim's behavior in an intimate relationship and attitudes toward sexual relationships in general.

- Irritability toward family, friends, or co-workers.

- Generalized anger, fear, anxiety, or suicidal thoughts.

- Inability to concentrate, even on routine tasks.

- Development of dependence on alcohol or drugs.

- Unwanted pregnancy.

SOURCES: Benokraitis and Feagin, 1995; Larimer et al., 1999; Silverman et al., 2001.

Some Solutions

Because violent behavior and rape are learned behaviors, they can be unlearned. Solutions are needed on three levels: individual, organizational, and societal.

On the *individual level*, less than 5 percent of college students report completed and attempted rapes to campus authorities and/or the police. On the *organizational level*, several federal laws require colleges to report rape and other sexual assaults. Only 37 percent of colleges comply fully with these laws. Even when assaults are reported, the perpetrators are rarely suspended or dismissed. If colleges and law enforcement agencies prosecuted sexual violence, it would decrease (Karjane et al., 2005).

To make a serious dent in the incidence of dating violence and date rape, however, we must also change *societal attitudes and beliefs* about violence and about male and female dating roles. The traditional notion that it is the woman's job to maintain the tone of a relationship often leads women to blame themselves when things go wrong and to overlook, forgive, or excuse men's sexual aggression.

Breaking Up

Social scientists use numerous terms for breaking up, including "uncoupling," "disengagement," and "relationship dissolution." In plain English, we dump someone or vice versa. According to one poll, nearly half of American adults have gotten the romantic heave-ho at least twice during their lifetime, and 22 percent say that they have been dumped by significant others six to ten times (Mundell, 2002).

since you asked

If "breaking up is hard to do," why do so many couples break up?

A classic song tells us that "breaking up is hard to do." It is, sometimes. According to college students in both the United States and Korea, for example, "relatedness" (feeling close to other people) is more important than money, pleasure, and self-esteem (Sheldon et al., 2001). Why, then, do so many couples break up?

Why We Break Up

There are numerous reasons for breaking up dating and other intimate relationships that include both micro-level and macro-level factors:

- *Individual (micro) reasons* include communication problems, different interests, emotional and physical abuse, obsessive "love" and controlling behavior, mismatched love and sexual needs, self-disclosure that reveals repulsive attitudes, disillusionment, lowered affectionate behavior, infidelity, and "freeloading" rather than making a commitment (Forward, 2002; Harley, 2002; Regan, 2003).

- *Structural (macro) reasons* include moving away, economic recessions that trigger unemployment and arguments about finances, and societal reactions that disapprove of relationships between young partners, young men and older women, couples from different racial or ethnic and religious backgrounds, and same-sex partners (Martin, 1993; Regan, 2003).

How We React

Breakups are usually very painful, but people respond in different ways. Women, for example, are usually more devastated by cheating than men—who feel that betraying a friend is a greater offense than sexual infidelity. And, as you might expect, people who have fewer "chips" on the marriage market are more upset by dating breakups than those who have many options because they're sexy, successful, or attractive (Feldman et al., 2000; Schmitt and Buss, 2001).

Getting upset is one of the most common reactions to breakups because we may not know why we were rejected. Explaining the reasons for a breakup provides a sense of closure—"a cathartic purging of feeling guilt, anger, depression, loneliness, insecurity, and confusion" (Regan, 2003: 174).

Men seem to get over breakups more quickly than women do. Shortly after a breakup, for example, 42 percent of men and 31 percent of women start dating someone else (Fetto, 2003).

Is Breaking Up Healthy?

Absolutely. Disagreements and conflict are part and parcel of any close relationship, especially before marriage. Breaking up a dating or cohabiting relationship is much less complicated than breaking up a marriage (see Chapter 15).

Recall that one of the important functions of dating and courtship is to filter out unsuitable prospective mates. Thus, breaking up is a normal process. It can also be a great relief to end a bad relationship (see Chapter 6).

If anything, breaking up should probably occur more often than it does because most people don't "circulate" enough before getting married (Glenn, 2002). Ending a dating relationship provides opportunities to find a mate who may be more suitable for marriage. In addition, breaking up opens up a larger pool of eligible and interesting partners as we mature and become more self-confident before deciding to marry.

Making Connections

- Some women stay in violent dating relationships because they have a "caretaker identity": They feel responsible for the man's behavior or want to "rescue" him from his problems (Few and Rosen, 2005). Have you known women who fit this description? Why do you think men are less likely to take on such caretaking roles?

- Some people feel that breaking up on e-mail or text messages is tacky. Others argue that these are quick and painless ways to end a relationship (Noguchi, 2005). What do *you* think?

Conclusion

We have more *choices* in mate selection today than ever before. A broad dating spectrum includes both traditional and contemporary ways to meet other people.

These choices emerge within culturally defined boundaries, or *constraints,* however. Factors that determine who selects whom for a partner come into play long before a couple marries and despite the romantic notion that "I can date anyone I want." Most people feel pressure to date and mate people who are similar to themselves. Some partners must also deal with aggression and violence.

One response to our array of choices and constraints in mate selection is to postpone marriage. In fact, a significant *change* today is the decision of many people to stay single longer, the subject of the next chapter.

Summary

1. Sociologists describe the dating process as a marriage market in which prospective spouses compare the assets and liabilities of eligible partners and choose the best available mate. In this sense, we "trade" with others, depending on what resources we have.

2. Dating fulfills both manifest and latent functions. Manifest functions of dating include recreation, companionship, fun, and mate selection. Latent functions include socialization, social status, sexual experimentation, and meeting intimacy and ego needs.

3. Forms of dating have changed over the years. Many adolescents and young adults, especially, have forsaken traditional dating for more informal methods such as "getting together," "pack dating," and "hookin' up."

4. Adults use a variety of mate selection methods to meet a potential spouse, including personal classified ads, marriage bureaus, computerized services, and the Internet.

5. Much of our dating and mate selection behavior is shaped by homogamy—rules that define appropriate mates in terms of race, ethnicity, religion, age, social class, values, and other characteristics.

6. Our pool of eligible partners expands when we seek mates from outside our own religious, racial, or ethnic group.

7. Social exchange theory and equity theory suggest that dating partners seek a balance of costs and benefits in a relationship. The relationship is most satisfying when it is seen as egalitarian.

8. Unlike the United States and some other Western nations, most countries around the world do not have "open" courtship systems. Rather, marriages are often arranged by families and restricted to members of the same culture, religion, or race. The selection methods are changing in many traditional societies, however.

9. Although dating is typically fun, there are also many risks and problems. Women, especially, are often victims of sexual pressure and aggression, violence, and date rape. The reasons for such victimization include power differences between men and women, peer pressure and secrecy, and the use of alcohol and other drugs.

10. Ending a relationship may be painful, but it also provides opportunities for finding a better mate.

Key Terms

dating 224
marriage market 225
filter theory 234
homogamy 235

propinquity 235
heterogamy 240
hypergamy 240
hypogamy 240

equity theory 242
dowry 244
acquaintance rape 250
date rape 250

Taking It Further

Meeting People Online and Avoiding Date Violence on Campus

Here are a few sites that are free, offer a free trial membership, or include interesting links to a variety of national, international, religious, and travel sites for "single and romance-minded individuals":

Meet Me Online

www.meetmeonline.com

SingleSites.com

www.singlesites.com

Yahoo! Personals

personals.yahoo.com

The following sites provide valuable information about campus crime statistics and prevention of campus violence, contain links to sites dealing with acquaintance and date rape, and offer a variety of resources to assist victims of violence:

The Sexual Assault Resource Agency

http://www.sexualassaultresources.org

Dating Violence Resource Center

http://www.ncvc.org/ncvc/main.aspx?dbID=DB_DatingViolenceResourceCenter101

National Teen Dating Violence Prevention Initiative (American Bar Association)

http://www.abanet.org/unmet/missionstatement.html

Security on Campus, Inc.

http://www.securityoncampus.org

And more: www.prenhall.com/benokraitis contains sites dealing with interracial and intercultural relationships, the *quinceañera,* how to avoid marrying a jerk, speed dating, interfaith family resources, and several URLs on breaking up—politely or more bluntly—if she or he "just doesn't get it."

Investigate with Research Navigator

Go to www.researchnavigator.com and enter your LOGIN NAME and PASSWORD. For instructions on registering for the first time, view the detailed instructions at the end of the Chapter 1. Search the Research Navigator™ site using the following key terms:

date rape
dowry
homogamy

Outline

Singlehood, Cohabitation, Civil Unions, and Other Options

Data Digest

- The number of **single people** (never married, divorced, and widowed) increased from 37.5 million in 1970 to 100 million in 2005.

- The **never married** make up the largest and fastest-growing segment of the single population. The proportion of adults who have never been married rose from 15 percent in 1972 to 24 percent in 2003.

- The proportion of households consisting of **one person living alone** increased from 17 percent in 1970 to 26 percent in 2005.

- The number of **unmarried-couple households** has grown—from only 1.1 percent of couples in 1960 to 9 percent in 2004.

- Over 60 percent of unmarried-couple households include **one or more children under age 18.**

- An estimated 702,000 households are made up of **same-sex partners.**

Sources: Smith and Gates, 2001; Fields, 2004; Hobbs, 2005; U.S. Census Bureau, 2006; U.S. Census Bureau News, 2006.

A couple who had been dating for several years went out to a Chinese restaurant for dinner. After studying the menu, the man turned to the woman and asked, "How would you like your rice: fried or boiled?" She looked him straight in the eye and replied, "Thrown." Sound corny? Maybe not.

Most people eventually make that "love connection" and marry. Until then—or if the relationship fizzles—today there is more freedom than ever before to pursue other alternatives. This chapter examines four nontraditional living arrangements: singlehood, cohabitation, gay households, and communal residences. We'll look at other nonmarital households, such as single parents and widowed people, in later chapters.

Before reading further, take "A Quiz about Singles." It asks how much you know about unmarried people and provides a preview of the chapter.

Ask Yourself

A Quiz about Singles

True	False	
☑	☐	**1.** Men are more likely to live alone than women.
☑	☐	**2.** The age group with the largest number of people who live alone is between ages 25 and 34.
☒	☐	**3.** Living together is a good way to find out whether partners will get along in marriage.
☐	☒	**4.** Women and men who live together typically share housework and other domestic tasks.
☐	☐	**5.** The percentage of never-married people is higher for whites than for Latinos.
☐	☐	**6.** Most singles are happier than most married people.
☐	☐	**7.** About the same percentage of people live in unmarried-couple households as in married-couple households.
☐	☐	**8.** Utah has the lowest percentage of same-sex households.
☐	☐	**9.** Rates of domestic violence are lower among gay couples than among straight couples.
☐	☐	**10.** Most elderly people have numerous options in deciding where to live.

Answer: All the answers to the "Quiz about Singles" are false.

The Single Option

You'll recall that many people are anxious about the state of the family today (see Chapter 1). They fear that marriage is disappearing, especially because of the increase in single people (see "Data Digest"). Are such concerns warranted?

Are Americans Opting Out of Marriage?

Today more people than in the past are choosing not to marry, are living together, or are raising children alone. As a result, according to some social scientists, there is "a marriage problem" in the United States (Wilson, 2002).

After reading this chapter, you can decide for yourself whether we have a marriage problem or not. It's certainly true, however, that more people than ever feel that being single is an attractive option (see "Data Digest"). This doesn't mean that singles will never marry. Instead, many young adults are simply marrying at later ages.

Many Singles Are Postponing Marriage

Many people are pursuing a college education, preparing for a job or career, and spending more time in recreational or other activities before settling down. As a result, many of us are marrying later than our parents or grandparents did.

In 1970, the median age at first marriage was 21 for women and 23 for men. By 2005, it had risen to 26 for women and over 27 for men, the oldest ages at first marriage ever recorded by the U.S. Census Bureau (see *Figure 9.1*). (Remember that the *median* represents the midpoint of cases. Thus, half of all men were 27 or older and half of all women were 26 or older when they first got married.)

From a historical perspective, the present tendency to delay marriage is the norm, especially for men. Men's median age at first marriage was only slightly lower in 1890 than it was in 2000 (26 and 27, respectively). The median for women has increased more noticeably, how-

since you asked

Why are my parents constantly asking me when I'm going to get married?

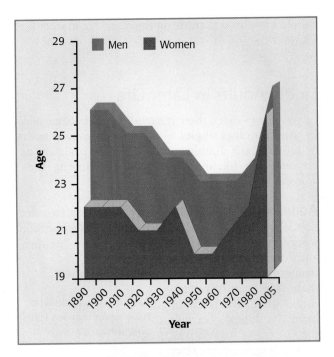

FIGURE 9.1 At What Age Do Men and Women First Marry? As the text points out, the median age of first marriage for men was almost the same in 2000 as in 1890, but the median for women has dramatically risen since 1960.

SOURCE: Based on data from Saluter, 1994, Table B; Saluter, 1996, Table A-33; and U.S. Census Bureau News, 2006.

ever, especially since 1960 (20 in 1960 and 26 in 2005) (see *Figure 9.1*).

For people of both sexes, the younger age at first marriage in the 1950s and 1960s was a historical exception rather than the rule. As you saw in Chapter 3, World War II delayed many marriages. When the soldiers came back, there was a surge of weddings. Throughout the 1950s, the United States tried to regain "normalcy" by encouraging both women and men in their late teens or early twenties to marry and have babies. Young couples themselves wanted to marry and form families after men returned from the war.

In the late 1960s, feminists, especially, began to question women's traditional roles both within and outside the family. Over the last few generations, both women and men have thought more consciously and deliberately about when and whom to marry (see Chapters 2, 5, and 6).

Although being single has become more acceptable, many people still feel pressure to marry. Some of my students complain that "if you're not married by the time you're 30, people think there's something wrong with you. My family and friends are constantly telling me to get married." Unmarried women, especially, often dread family get-togethers because they are asked over and over again whether they are dating "someone special." Parents drop not-so-subtle hints about having grandkids. Invitations to friends' weddings pile up. And "bridesmaid dresses stare back at single women when they open their closet doors" (Hartill, 2001: 15).

The older singles are, the more often friends and relatives badger them about their marriage plans. Others complain of feeling invisible and not being invited to social or family activities with married couples unless it's to be "fixed up" with one of the couple's single friends (Campbell, 2001). Despite such pressure, more people are single than ever before.

The never-married constitute only one cluster of a very diverse group of singles. In fact, many unmarried Americans don't identify with the word "single" because they are parents, have partners, or are widowed.

The Diversity of Singles

There are several kinds of singles: those who are postponing marriage, the small percentage who will never marry, the currently unmarried who are divorced or widowed but may be looking for new partners, and lesbians and gay men, who are still legally barred from marrying. In addition, people's living arrangements may vary greatly, from living alone during part of one's adult life to singlehood in later life.

Single Adults in General

Singlehood reflects more dimensions than simply not being married. Singlehood can be either freely chosen or unintentional as well as either enduring or temporary:

- *Voluntary temporary singles* are open to marriage but place a lower priority on searching for mates than on other activities, such as education, career, politics, and self-development. This group includes men and women who cohabit.

- *Voluntary stable singles* include people who have never married and are satisfied with that choice, those who have been married but do not want to remarry, those who are living together but do not intend to marry, and those whose lifestyles preclude the possibility of marriage, such as priests and nuns. Also included are single parents—both never married and formerly married—who are not seeking mates and are raising their children alone or with the help of relatives or friends.

Some people delay marriage longer than others. Hugh O'Brian, TV's Wyatt Earp star during the 1950s, married for the first time at age 81. He married his girlfriend of 18 years, age 54.

- *Involuntary temporary singles* are those who would like to be married and are actively seeking a mate. This group includes people who are widowed or divorced and single parents who would like to get married.

- *Involuntary stable singles* are primarily older divorced, widowed, and never-married people who wanted to marry or remarry but did not find a mate and now accept their single status as permanent. This group also includes singles who suffer from some physical or psychological impairment that limits their success in the marriage market (Stein, 1981).

A person's position in these categories can change over time. For example, voluntary temporary singles may marry, divorce, and then become involuntary stable singles because they are unable to find another suitable mate. In this sense, the boundaries between being single and being married are fairly fluid for most people. For a much smaller number, singlehood is constant either because it's a choice or because some people have little to trade on the marriage market (see Chapter 8).

Single Adults in Later Life

As one grows older, there is a tendency to become pickier. And for older singles who date and want to marry or remarry, the double standard still favors men, decreasing the likelihood of marriage among older women.

AGING AND THE DOUBLE STANDARD In mate selection, aging women are typically seen as "over the hill," whereas aging men are often described as "mature" and "distinguished." Older women are also more likely than older men to remain single after divorcing or being widowed because they are caring for relatives, primarily aging parents (see Chapter 17).

since you asked

Are elderly people who have never married lonely and unhappy?

There is little research on older people who have never married, probably because only 3 percent of men and women age 65 and over fall into this category (U.S. Census Bureau, 2006). Some are isolated and others have many friends, some wish they were married, and others are glad they're single.

SOME ADVANTAGES AND DISADVANTAGES OF BEING SINGLE IN LATER LIFE Some see the never-married elderly as lonely and unhappy. Marriage may be satisfying, but it also means limiting one's freedom:

> When I was a little girl and, later on, an adolescent, it never occurred to me that I would not meet the man of my dreams, get married, and live happily ever after. Now, at fifty-four, it seems unlikely, though not impossible, that this will happen. Not only do I live alone but I actually like it. I value my space, my solitude, and my independence enormously and cannot [imagine] the circumstances that would lead me to want to change it (Cassidy, 1993: 35).

On the positive side, never-marrieds don't have to deal with the trauma of widowhood or divorce. Many develop extensive networks of friends and relatives. They work, date, and engage in a variety of hobbies, volunteer work, and church activities and often have lasting relationships with friends and siblings.

Some singles live with others, some alone. Let's look briefly at who lives alone and why.

Home Alone

Because more than 90 percent of all Americans marry at least once, marriage is still the norm. Household size has been shrinking, however. In 1900, nearly half of the U.S. population lived in households of six or more people (Hobbs and Stoops, 2002). A century later, more than one in four Americans is living alone (see *Figure 9.2*). Who are these people living alone? And what explains the rise in solitary living?

Who Is Living Alone?

Singlehood is widespread, and singles are a diverse population. Nevertheless, we can identify some patterns in terms of sex, age, and race and ethnicity.

SEX AND AGE More women (15 percent) than men (11 percent) live alone. Of all age groups, older Americans are the most likely to live alone: about 31 percent in 2003. In their later years, women are more likely than men to live alone (see *Figure 9.3*). On average, women live about five years longer than men. If they enjoy good health and have enough income, they can care for themselves into their eighties and even their nineties (Fields, 2004; see, also, Chapter 17).

RACE AND ETHNICITY Of all people who are living alone, more than 80 percent are white. Members of racial-ethnic groups are more likely to live in extended-family households because of values that emphasize caring for family members and pooling financial resources (U.S. Census Bureau, 2005a; see, also, Chapter 4).

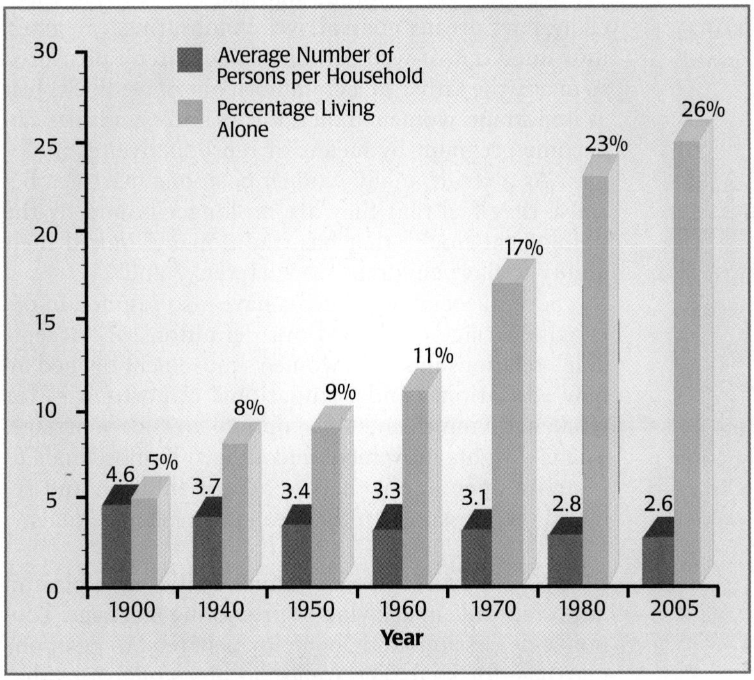

Why Do People Live Alone?

Rachel, one of my graduate students, recently bought a townhouse in a nice neighborhood. Rachel is 32, has a good job as a bank manager, has no children, and hopes to marry. But, she says, "I'm not going to put off making this investment until Mr. Right comes along."

Rachel's reasons for living alone echo those of many other singles her age. Many Americans choose to live alone because *they can afford it*. In fact, single women are second only to married couples in the number of homes they buy, and 30 percent of them are under age 35 (Paul, 2002).

since you asked

Why do many people prefer to live alone?

A second and related reason is that *our values emphasize individualism*. Most unmarried Americans of all ages are highly involved in their families but prefer to live alone if they can afford to. Living alone offers more privacy and freedom than living with parents or others (see Chapters 1, 3, 4, and 8).

Third, living alone varies at *different stages of life*. People who are living alone include young adults, like Rachel, who have decent-paying jobs and can afford an apartment or house. Separated, divorced, and widowed people also often live alone (Hobbs, 2005).

A fourth reason for living alone is that Americans are *living longer and healthier lives,* making it possible for them to live independently after retirement. Even before retirement, being healthy means that people can live by themselves instead of moving in with others.

Finally, and perhaps most important, many people are living alone because they are postponing marriage or deciding not to marry. That is, they have *more options, including singlehood*. As Rachel said, she doesn't want to put her life on hold "until Mr. Right comes along."

FIGURE 9.2 The Shrinking Household
Both the decline in the average number of people per household and the rapidly rising numbers of people living alone have contributed to a smaller contemporary household.

SOURCE: Hobbs and Stoops, 2002; U.S. Census Bureau News, 2006.

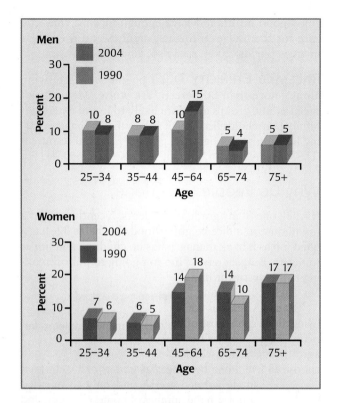

FIGURE 9.3 Living Alone: 1990 and 2004
As these data show, older women are much more likely than older men to be living alone in their middle and later years, especially after age 74. How would you explain these differences?

SOURCE: Based on U.S. Census Bureau, 2006, Table 67.

Making Connections

- There are several kinds of singles. Are *you* single? Why? Are you single voluntarily or involuntarily?

- Do you or your friends live alone? Why? What are some of the positive and negative aspects of not living with other people?

Why More People are Single

Many Americans will tell you that they are single because they are not in love and are still waiting for "the right person." Despite what people say, being single—especially for those who are postponing marriage—reflects an interplay of macro-level factors that affect demographic variables, which, in turn, influence individual (micro-level) decisions (see *Figure 9.4*). Let's begin with some of the macro-level factors that delay the decision to marry.

Macro-Level Factors

A number of macro-level variables—over which we have little or no control—affect our decisions about matrimony. A few examples include war, technology, social movements, the economy, and gender roles.

WAR, TECHNOLOGY, AND SOCIAL MOVEMENTS

Marriage rates tend to drop during war. In Afghanistan, for example, decades of war killed, handicapped, or psychologically traumatized many men, leading to a shortage of potential husbands. After the U.S. invasion of Iraq in 2003, many couples—especially in Baghdad, the capital—postponed weddings because "mornings are flavored with explosive powders, where people are meeting death every day." In the quieter areas in the north and south, in contrast, nuptial ceremonies blossomed because they signaled "a belief in future" (Roug, 2005).

Technological advances in contraceptive techniques, especially the Pill, have decreased rates of unplanned pregnancies and "shotgun marriages." Women, especially, have greater control over childbearing, can avoid unwanted out-of-wedlock births, and aren't pressured to marry the father of a child born out of wedlock. Just as important, women in their forties and even fifties can become pregnant by means of reproductive technologies. As a result, many women postpone marriage because they feel that they are no longer bound by the "biological clock" that has traditionally limited their ability to have children (see Chapters 7 and 11).

Several social movements have also resulted in delayed marriage or shaped our definitions of "acceptable" relationships. The women's movement opened up new educational and occupational opportunities for women, giving them career options outside marriage. The gay rights movement encouraged homosexuals to be more open about their sexual orientation and relieved the pressures on them to marry heterosexuals.

ECONOMIC FACTORS

Economic realities also play an important role in delaying or promoting marriage. Economic depressions and unemployment tend to postpone marriage for men. The well-paid blue-collar jobs that once enabled high school graduates to support families are mostly gone. The job prospects for some college-educated men are also worsening rather than improving. In contrast, economic opportunities, as well as the belief that a person has access to those opportunities, encourage men to marry (Landale and Tolnay, 1991; see, also, Chapter 13).

The effects of employment on women's tendency to marry are somewhat contradictory. Being employed increases a woman's chances of meeting eligible men and may enhance her attractiveness as a potential contributor to a household's finances. On the other hand, women with high salaries may be unwilling to settle down with men who earn less than they do (Hacker, 2003; see, also, Chapter 8).

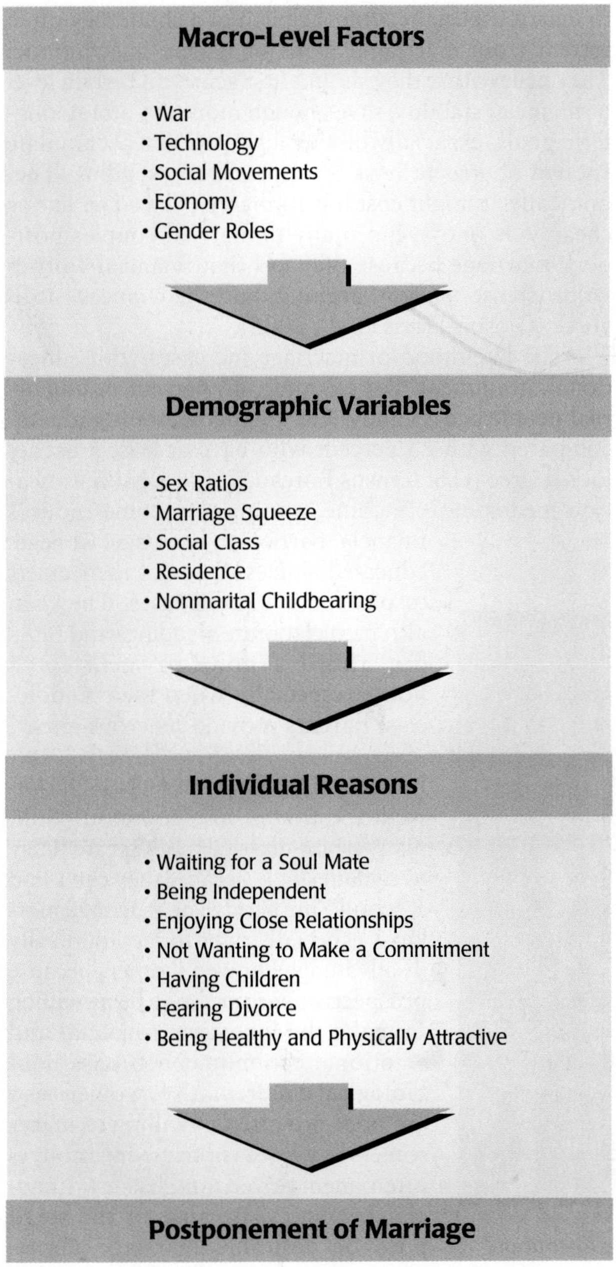

Macro-Level Factors

- War
- Technology
- Social Movements
- Economy
- Gender Roles

Demographic Variables

- Sex Ratios
- Marriage Squeeze
- Social Class
- Residence
- Nonmarital Childbearing

Individual Reasons

- Waiting for a Soul Mate
- Being Independent
- Enjoying Close Relationships
- Not Wanting to Make a Commitment
- Having Children
- Fearing Divorce
- Being Healthy and Physically Attractive

Postponement of Marriage

FIGURE 9.4   Some Reasons for Postponing Marriage

GENDER ROLES Technological and economic transitions affect gender roles. As gender roles change, so do attitudes toward marriage and self-sufficiency. With the advent of washing machines, cleaning services, frozen foods, wrinkle-resistant fabrics, and 24-hour one-stop shopping, for example, men are no longer dependent on women's housekeeping (Coontz, 2005).

Women aren't rushing into marriage, either. Because the stigma once attached to "living in sin" has largely vanished, many women choose to cohabit and have babies outside marriage. In other cases, because it's difficult to juggle a career and a family, many women have chosen to advance their professional lives before marrying and starting a family.

Demographic Influences

Macro-level factors delay marriage. Demographic shifts (such as changes in the sex ratio and the marriage squeeze), social class, and nonmarital childbearing also help explain the large proportion of singles.

THE SEX RATIO The sex ratio, expressed as a whole number, is the proportion of men to women in a country or group. A ratio of 100 means that there are equal numbers of men and women; a ratio of 110 means that there are 110 men for every 100 women.

The biological norm is for about 95 girls to be born for every 100 boys. Male infants, however, have a naturally higher mortality rate (see Chapter 5). As a result, by early childhood the numbers of boys and girls are roughly equal. In the United States, the sex ratio is around 100 until later in life. In the 75- to 84-year-old age group, for example, the ratio is 92 because women tend to live longer than men (see Chapters 17 and 18).

In some countries, the sex ratio is skewed from birth. For example, the sex ratio is 118 in China, 113 in the Caribbean and South Korea, 108 in India (126 in the Punjab region), and 105 in Latin America. The sex ratios of other countries are disproportionately female rather than male: 92 in sub-Saharan Africa, 94 in North Africa, and 96 in Central America (Sharma, 2001; Seager, 2003; Eberstadt, 2004).

These uneven sex ratios result from a variety of factors. In countries like China and India, there is a preference for boys, who will carry on the family name, care for elderly parents, inherit property, and play a central role in family rituals. As a result, hundreds of thousands of female infants die yearly because of neglect, abandonment, infanticide, and starvation. Others are aborted after ultrasound scanners reveal the sex of the child (Eberstadt, 2004; Dogra, 2006).

According to some estimates, as many as 10 million female fetuses might have been aborted in India in the last 20 years. An Indian law passed in 1994 forbids doctors from revealing the sex of a fetus to its parents because of the common practice of "sex-determined abortions." However, only a few districts in some of the wealthy districts where the ratios of girls to boys are at their lowest have begun to enforce the law (Baldauf, 2006; Gentleman, 2006).

In Africa, there are more women than men because of civil wars and AIDS deaths. In Central America, there are more men than women because women often migrate to other countries—such as the United States—for jobs (see Chapters 4 and 7).

THE MARRIAGE SQUEEZE

A **marriage squeeze** is a sex imbalance in the ratio of available unmarried women and men. Because of this imbalance, members of one sex can be "squeezed" out of the marriage market. The squeeze may result from wealth, power, status, education, age, or other factors that diminish the pool of eligible partners.

Is there a marriage squeeze in the United States? Yes. There are large numbers of never-married people, especially men, in almost all age categories and most racial-ethnic groups (see *Figure 9.5*). If we add to the pool the 156 million people who were unmarried because of divorce, separation, or being widowed during 2000, the marriage market appears to be very large. However, homogamy narrows the pool of eligible mates. In addition, many women in their middle years experience a marriage squeeze because men their age are looking for much younger women (see Chapter 8).

Many countries are experiencing a much more severe marriage squeeze. Men in China, India, Korea, Taiwan, the Middle East, and other regions face a scarcity of young, single women because of skewed sex ratios. There are dozens of "bachelor villages" in China's poorer regions where men can't find wives. As a result, there is a booming trade in kidnapped women who are brought to China as wives (Pomfret, 2001; see, also, Chapter 8).

SOCIAL CLASS

Although low-income couples expect to marry, especially after the birth of a child, they often retreat from marriage. A major reason is economic: They believe that they should first achieve a certain level of financial stability, save enough money to attain long-term goals (especially buying a house), and accumulate enough savings to host a "respectable" wedding. Theoretically, it might cost less to marry ("Two can live as cheaply as one"), but many unmarried couples postpone marriage because they feel that financial worries will increase tension, arguing, and the chances of divorce (Gibson-Davis et al., 2005).

The likelihood of marriage increases with educational attainment. For example, 82 percent of unmarried people age 25 and older are high school graduates compared with 23 percent who have at least a bachelor's degree (U.S. Census Bureau, 2005a). More education means more income, and more income reduces financial barriers to marriage. College-educated singles can pool their assets to pay for living expenses. They can also plan elaborate weddings and often can afford a down-payment for a house, especially when their middle-class parents provide generous gifts.

NONMARITAL CHILDBEARING

Out-of-wedlock births are common. Still, many never-married mothers are likely to remain single because they can't find a "good" husband. The marriage market is especially tight for economically disadvantaged unwed mothers because prospective partners may be unwilling to make the long-term financial and emotional commitment to raise non-biological children. Also, women who are poor are often unwilling to marry someone who has little education, is often unemployed, and has few financial resources. Because of the small pool of desirable marriage mates, many of these women cohabit rather than marry (Qian et al., 2005).

India has one of the lowest sex ratios in the world because of female infanticide. This photo shows mothers with newborn sons in the Dhanduha village of the Punjab region. Only one girl was born here in the last six months.

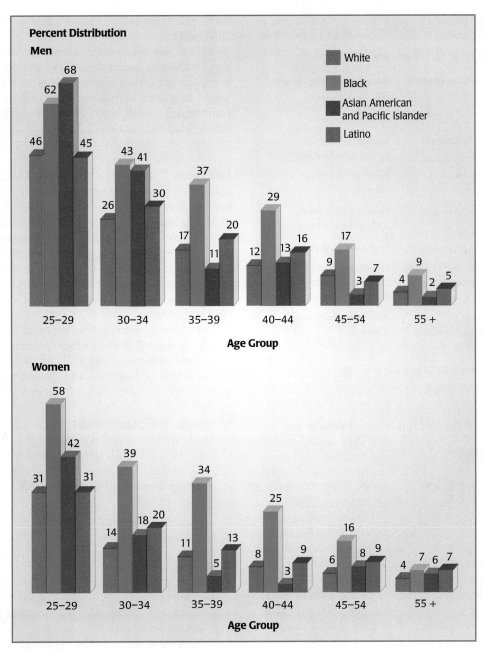

FIGURE 9.5   Who Has Never Married?

SOURCE: Kreider and Fields, 2002: 8.

Individual Reasons

Although marriage offers many benefits, there are also incentives for being single (see *Table 9.1*). Both choices and constraints shape our attitudes and behavior about getting married or staying single. Let's begin with waiting to find an ideal partner, a "soul mate."

WAITING FOR A SOUL MATE Many singles delay marriage because they are waiting to meet their "ideal mate" or "true love." In a study of never-married young singles ages 20 to 29, an overwhelming 94 percent agreed with the statement that "when you marry you want your spouse to be your soul mate, first and fore-

TABLE 9.1

Benefits of Marriage and Singlehood

Benefits of Getting Married	Benefits of Being Single
Companionship	Privacy, few constraints, independence
Faithful sexual partner	Varied sexual experiences; cohabitation
Dependability, love	Exciting, changing lifestyle
Sharing mutual interests	Meeting new friends with different interests
Pooling economic resources	Economic autonomy
Social approval for "settling down" and producing children	Freedom from responsibility to care for spouse or children
Becoming a part of something larger than self	A need for independence

SOURCES: Based on Stein, 1981; Carter and Sokol, 1993.

most." Another national survey of never-married single adults ages 18 to 49 found that 79 percent believed that they would eventually find and marry their "perfect mate" (Edwards, 2000; Whitehead and Popenoe, 2001).

since you asked

Am I going to find my soul mate?

Some people feel that waiting for a "super relationship" is unrealistic because a marriage involves more than emotional intimacy. If a person decides that a partner is no longer a soul mate, for example, she or he will become disillusioned and bail out. Also, the longer one waits to marry, the smaller the pool of eligible partners, especially among the never-married (Peterson, 2003; see, also, Chapter 8).

Others contend that waiting for a soul mate isn't necessarily starry-eyed: "Perhaps more than ever before, young people have an opportunity to choose a partner on the basis of personal qualities and shared dreams, not economics or 'gender straitjackets'" (Rivers, 2001).

BEING INDEPENDENT One of the biggest advantages of being single is independence and autonomy. Members of both sexes can do pretty much what they please. According to a 32-year-old male newscaster, "You don't have to worry about commitments to your career [affecting] your commitment to a family. I'm not

ruling out marriage. . . . There's just no rush" (Wilson, 2001: D1).

When a 43-year-old freelance writer and yoga instructor decides to travel, she does so freely: "She packs her bags, gets on a plane, and goes hiking through Spain, mountain biking in Death Valley or touring the Caribbean" (Fallik, 2001). As one of my 29-year-old female students once said, "I don't plan to marry until my feet have touched six of the seven continents."

ENJOYING CLOSE RELATIONSHIPS A common reason for getting married is companionship (see *Table 9.1*). Singles who are delaying marriage rely on peers rather than a spouse for support and companionship. Especially in large cities, singles have close friends (sometimes called "urban tribes") with whom they socialize. They may meet weekly for dinner at a neighborhood restaurant, sometimes travel together, move one another's furniture, and paint one another's apartments (Watters, 2003).

In addition, many singles are quite involved in family life. Some still live with their parents. Others spend much time with nieces and nephews. Women, especially, devote much of their time and resources to supporting other family members (see Chapters 5 and 12).

MAKING A COMMITMENT There are more never-married men than women in most age groups (see *Figure 9.5*). Why, then, do so many women complain that "there's nothing out there"? One reason is that many men simply don't want to get married:

> *Ed . . . is a charming, handsome, 48-year-old Washington, DC, lobbyist who plans evenings that most women just fantasize about. His dates may involve box seats at a performance of Tosca, champagne served during the intermission, dinner at the best Italian restaurant. . . . What Ed is not planning is a long-term relationship: "I have had four very important relationships," he says. "Each one lasted about three years, but at a certain point the woman wanted marriage and I didn't" (Szegedy-Maszak, 1993: 88).*

There's an old joke about single guys: "My girlfriend told me I should be more affectionate. So I got two girlfriends!" Some family practitioners feel that men are the foot-draggers—especially when there's an abundance of girlfriends—because there's little incentive for men to marry (Pittman, 1999).

Because of the greater tolerance for premarital sex, most men can have sex and intimate relationships without getting married. Many men also put off marriage because of stagnant wages and job losses. They view marriage as a major economic responsibility that they don't want to undertake (Ooms, 2002; see, also, Chapter 7).

HAVING CHILDREN Couples often marry because they plan to raise a family. Nearly 70 percent of Americans, however, disagree with the statement that "the main purpose of marriage is having children" (Popenoe and Whitehead, 2003). Also, just 37 percent of Americans say it is "very important" that an unwed couple marry when the couple has a child together (Saad, 2006). Because cohabitation and out-of-wedlock parenting are widely accepted, singles of all ages feel less pressure to get married.

Though still small in number, women age 35 and older are the fastest-growing group of unwed mothers. Some people call middle-class, professional, unmarried women who intentionally bear children "single mothers of choice" (Mattes, 1994; see, also, Chapter 11).

Most of these women's *first* choice is to marry and *then* have children, however. As one 35-year-old mother said, "You can wait to have a partner and hope you can still have a baby. Or you can choose to let that go and have a baby on your own" (Orenstein, 2000: 149). Even

QUALITY TIME   Gail Machlis

The *Quality Time* cartoon by Gail Machlis is reprinted by permission of Chronicle Features, San Francisco, California.

if a woman finds a soul mate, he may not want to participate in child care and other domestic activities that many women now expect men to share (see Chapter 5).

FEARING DIVORCE Divorce or prolonged years of conflict between parents can have a negative effect on young adults' perceptions of marriage. Many stay single as long as possible because they worry about divorce. If children have grown up in homes where parents divorced one or more times, they are wary of repeating the same mistake. As one 21-year-old woman stated, "My father left my mother when I was 6. I don't believe in divorce" (Herrmann, 2003). A 32-year-old man who works for a publishing company is in no rush to marry for similar reasons: "I would say you can never be too choosy. . . Most of my friends' parents are not together anymore or on their second marriages (Hartill, 2001: 17).

Others feel that marriage doesn't necessarily improve people's lives or relationships. According to one of my thirty-something male students (with whom many of his classmates agreed),

> *If you have issues before marriage, you're going to have those same issues after marriage. If you marry someone else with issues, instead of one person being miserable, you have two. Many of my friends who are married aren't happy. Some are considering divorce. I feel no need to jump into a marriage (Author's files).*

Many singles are postponing marriage because they see it as a sacred institution that should last forever rather than "just a piece of paper." According to a 24-year-old short-order cook who lives with his girlfriend, "Marriage is a big step. . . I don't want to be one of those couples that gets married and three years later gets a divorce" (Gibson-Davis et al., 2005: 1309). Thus, many singles are hesitant about matrimony not because they don't believe in marriage but because they fear divorce (see, also, Chapter 15).

BEING HEALTHY AND PHYSICALLY ATTRACTIVE Emotional and physical health and physical appeal also affect singlehood. In the marriage market, most men are initially drawn only to attractive women. On a scale of 10, men who are a 2 or a 3 go after attractive women who have better options. In these mismatches, "men pursue prizes beyond their grasp, when they could be perfectly content with someone who isn't viewed as a great catch. So these men lose, not only by failing to get what they covet but also in a chance for a happy ending" (Hacker, 2003: 191). People with physical or emotional problems are also more likely to remain single longer or not marry at all (Wilson, 2002; see, also, Chapters 7 and 8).

Singles in large cities go to many nightclubs to meet people. Despite the racial and ethnic diversity, many still can't find a mate.

Racial and Ethnic Singles

Among some racial and ethnic groups, the unmarried population has increased significantly during the last few generations. Why? Although there are many reasons, structural factors as well as attitudes and values explain some of the changes. Let's look at some of these singles more closely, beginning with African Americans.

since you asked

Why are so many African Americans single?

African Americans

Compared with other groups, blacks are most likely to be single (see *Figure 9.6*). Many African Americans are postponing marriage, but an even higher proportion may never marry (see *Figure 9.5* on the percent of black men and women age 55 and over who have never married).

STRUCTURAL FACTORS A major reason for the high percentage of never-married black women is the shortage of marriageable African American men. This shortage reflects many structural factors. Deteriorating employment conditions, especially in urban areas, often discourage young African American men from getting married. Occupational hazards in dangerous jobs have claimed many black men's lives. Mortality rates for heart disease are almost three times higher for blue-collar workers—many of whom are black—than for managerial and professional groups, at least in part because of a lack of preventive medical care. In addition, a disproportionately large number of urban black men in their twenties and early thirties are in prison or jail (Ooms, 2002; Hill, 2005; see, also, Chapters 4 and 8).

As a group, black men earn more than black women in every occupation. There are more college-educated black women than college-educated black men, however (see Chapters 8 and 13). Many middle-class men are already married, and women are reluctant to "marry down." In a memorable scene in the movie *Waiting to Exhale*, the black women lament the marriage squeeze (though not in those words) and consider the merits and problems of marrying hardworking black men in lower socioeconomic levels.

VALUES AND ATTITUDES Homogamy generally limits the pool of eligible mates across social classes and regardless of race (see Chapter 8). Some of my black, "thirty-something" female students have stated emphatically, "I'm making a lot of sacrifices to be in college while working full time. I don't think a man will appreciate what I've accomplished unless he's gone through the same [expletive deleted]!"

Because of their relative scarcity, many lower-class African-American men don't see marital commitment as necessary. Some middle-class black men may simply screen out assertive, independent, or physically unappealing women because they benefit from a large pool of eligible romantic partners. And like many whites, blacks whose parents have divorced tend to shun marriage (Bulcroft and Bulcroft, 1993; Davis et al., 2000).

Attitudes about social mobility also affect singlehood. Many middle-class black parents emphasize educational attainment over early marriage. As a result, black women who pursue higher education may place a higher priority on academic achievement than on developing personal relationships. Others have tight social schedules because they devote most of their time to successful businesses and to community activities (Jones, 1994; Perry et al., 2003).

Latinos

Latinas are generally less likely than black women to experience a shortage of marriageable partners. Nevertheless, singlehood is also increasing among Latinos (see *Figure 9.6*). Although there are variations among sub-

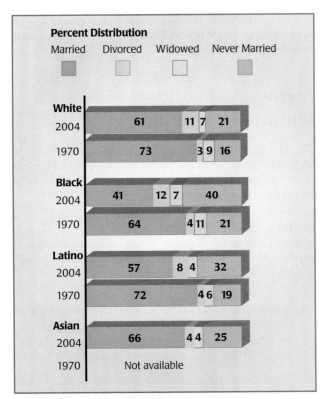

Percent Distribution

FIGURE 9.6 Changes in Marital Status, by Race and Ethnicity, 1970 and 2004.
The percentage of people who are married has decreased while the percentage of divorced and never-married people has increased, especially among blacks.

SOURCE: Based on Saluter, 1994: vi, and U.S. Census Bureau, 2006, Table 50.

groups, structural factors and attitudes explain some of the overall increases in the numbers of Latino singles.

STRUCTURAL FACTORS On average, the Latino population is much younger than the non-Latino population. As a result, a higher percentage of Latinos have not yet reached marriageable age. Large numbers of Mexicans who are migrating to the United States for economic reasons are postponing marriage until they can support a family. If people are undocumented (illegal) or are migrant workers, it's difficult for them to marry. In addition, low-paying jobs and high unemployment rates can delay marriage or increase the number of single people through high divorce rates (Baca Zinn and Pok, 2002).

Although their marriage rates are high, many Cuban American women remain single after divorce because the remarriage market is more favorable for men than for women. Men have more education, higher incomes, and other resources that attract prospective mates (Pérez, 2002).

VALUES AND ATTITUDES Familism, as you saw in previous chapters, encourages marriage and having children. In the Cuban community, for example, because of the emphasis on the importance of marriage and children, marriage rates are high and divorce rates are low. The latter have been increasing, however, as second and third generations have assimilated American values and behaviors (Pérez, 2002).

Many Puerto Rican women and men have moved away from familistic values because the relationships between families in Puerto Rico and the United States have weakened. Even though some familistic values have changed, many Puerto Rican women still have extensive kinship networks both in the United States and in Puerto Rico. As a result, Puerto Rican women may remain single because family members are helping them to raise and financially support out-of-wedlock children (Toro-Morn, 1998; Carrasquillo, 2002).

Whether people marry also depends on family reactions. For example, familial support (encouragement and approval) increases marriage among white women but not Latinas. It may be that Latino family members are more likely than their Anglo counterparts to dampen a daughter's romance by getting too involved (butting in) (Umaña-Taylor and Fine; 2003).

Asian Americans

Asian Americans and Pacific Islanders have some of the lowest singlehood rates. At ages 35–39, for example, only 11 percent of the men have never married, compared with 17 percent of white men, 20 percent of Latino men, and 37 percent of black men (see *Figure 9.5*).

As noted in previous chapters, it's important not to lump all Asian Americans into one group because doing so obscures important differences between subgroups. Although there is very little information about these singles, the available research suggests that Asian Americans share some values—such as a strong belief in the importance of marriage and family—that explain the low number of singles in these groups.

STRUCTURAL FACTORS Intermarriage decreases singlehood rates, especially among Asian American women (see Chapter 4). Marrying outside of one's own group reflects several structural factors, such as group size, sex ratios, and acculturation. For example, because Japanese Americans have been in the United States for many generations and the pool of eligible partners is small, their intermarriage rates are high (Takagi, 2002). These high rates suggest that Japanese Americans are less likely to be single because they decrease their marriage squeeze by choosing partners from a large pool.

Acculturation can also increase the number of singles. Despite the emphasis on family and marriage, many Asian Americans are experiencing higher divorce rates. Korean Americans born in the United States, for example, have a higher divorce rate than their immigrant counterparts. American-born Korean women, in particular, are more ready to accept divorce as an alternative to an unhappy marriage (Min, 2002). One of the results of acculturation, then, is a larger number of women and men who are single.

VALUES AND ATTITUDES Interracial marriages reflect a variety of individual factors. For example, college-educated Asian American women can maximize their social status by marrying the most advantaged men, regardless of race or ethnicity. Also, those who seek men with the most egalitarian attitudes toward women may marry outside of their particular group (Tsai et al., 2002; Ishii-Kuntz, 2004; see, also, Chapter 8 on mail-order brides).

Cultural values can also decrease the number of singles. You may recall that many Asian American households see the family as the core of society. Among Chinese Americans, for example, divorce rates are much lower than in the general population. Divorced women find it difficult to survive economically and are not readily accepted in the community (Glenn and Yap, 2002). As a result, many women avoid divorcing and becoming single again at almost all costs.

Other Racial/Ethnic Groups

American Indian women are more likely than men to be single because they are separated, widowed, or divorced. In addition, widowhood is more common among American Indian women than among black and white women because American Indian men are likely to die earlier than black or white men because of poor health and alcohol-related deaths, such as fatal car accidents and homicides (Yellowbird and Snipp, 2002; see, also, Chapter 4).

Some of the available data suggest that there are more singles among Indian Asian Americans and Middle Eastern Americans because of rising divorce rates. Outside of acculturation, however, it's not clear why this is the case. We need much more re-

search on both of these groups to understand how many singles there are and why some marry whereas others postpone marriage.

Myths and Realities about Being Single

The late comedian Rodney Dangerfield once quipped "My wife and I were happy for twenty years. Then we met!" Being married has many advantages, but some of its benefits have been exaggerated or romanticized, as the joke implies. Here are some of the most popular myths about singlehood (Cargan and Melko, 1982):

since you asked

Are most single people selfish and self-centered?

1. *Singles are tied to their mother's apron strings.* In reality, there are few differences between singles and marrieds in their perceptions of and relationships with parents and other relatives.

2. *Singles are selfish and self-centered.* In reality, singles often make more time for friends than married people do, and they tend to be more active in community service.

3. *Singles are well-off financially.* A number of single professionals and young college graduates in high-tech jobs are affluent, but more singles than mar-

Single women and men often work long hours at their jobs, sometimes because they want to advance their careers but sometimes because they're perceived as being less burdened with home and family responsibilities.

rieds live at or below the poverty level. In general, married couples are better off financially because both partners work.

4. *Singles are happier.* Although singles spend more time in leisure activities such as attending movies, eating in restaurants, and going to clubs, they are also more likely to be lonely, to be depressed when they are alone, and to feel anxious and stressed.

5. *There's something wrong with people who don't marry.* There's nothing wrong with being or staying single. Many singles simply feel that the disadvantages of marriage outweigh the benefits.

In terms of personal well-being, single men have the most problems, married men the fewest. Compared with married men, single men have higher mortality rates and a higher incidence of alcoholism, suicide, and mental health problems. This may be due to married men's family responsibilities, which leave them less time and money to engage in high-risk behaviors such as using alcohol or other drugs. Wives often urge their husbands to have annual physical checkups, may prepare nutritious meals, and are generally concerned about preventing illness among family members (Rowe and Kahn, 1997; see, also, Chapter 10).

On a day-to-day basis, however, single women encounter more problems than do single men. Single women, who often live alone, are more likely than their married counterparts to be mugged, burglarized, or raped. Professional women who travel must often take extra safety precautions because they are more vulnerable than single men.

Unmarried people of both sexes face a number of prejudices. They are often accused of being "immature" or "flighty" ("When are you going to put down roots?" "Are you *ever* going to settle down?"). In addition, they may be given more responsibilities at work because they are viewed as having more free time. For example, some single professional women complain that they are often expected to do "little extras" at work: "to serve on more committees, to volunteer for more overtime, or to give up more holidays and weekends—because they are perceived as having nothing better to do" (Cejka, 1993: 10).

✦ Making Connections

- ■ Why are you, your classmates, and friends single rather than married? Or married rather than single? Are there any racial/ethnic variations?

- ■ What would you add to the discussion of the advantages and disadvantages of being single?

Cohabitation

When they moved in together, Susannah, 24, and James, 29, had been dating for more than a year. Then their daughter, Elizabeth, was born. But the Albuquerque, New Mexico, couple was not ready to take the big step into matrimony. "We want to make sure we're doing the right thing," says Susannah, who also has a 4-year-old daughter from a previous marriage (Kantrowitz and Wingert, 2001: 46).

Susannah and James are an example of **cohabitation,** a living arrangement in which two unrelated people are not married but live together and usually have a sexual relationship. The U.S. Census Bureau sometimes calls cohabitants **POSSLQs** (pronounced "possel-kews"), "persons of the opposite sex sharing living quarters" ("shacking up," in plain English). Unmarried couples also include same-sex relationships, a topic we'll cover shortly.

Cohabitation Trends and Characteristics

To the delight of some people and the dismay of others, cohabitation isn't a passing fad. Some sociologists describe cohabitation as "reshaping American families" because it questions conventional ideas about what constitutes a family. Since it is based on emotional rather than legal ties, "Cohabitation is a distinct family form, neither singlehood nor marriage. We can no longer understand American families if we ignore it" (Brown, 2005: 33).

THE GROWTH IN COHABITATION The number of heterosexual unmarried couples in the United States has increased tenfold—from about 0.4 million in 1960 to more than five million in 2005 (see *Figure 9.7*). This number increases by at least another 594,000 if we include same-sex partners. Of all unmarried couples, about 1 in 9 (11 percent of all unmarried-partner households) are gay men or lesbians (Simmons and O'Connell, 2003).

These data probably undercount the number of cohabiting couples for several reasons. The Census Bureau doesn't tabulate all unmarried couples in a household but only the "householder" who rents or owns the residence and her or his unmarried partner. Thus, there may be numerous cohabiting couples that aren't counted. Also, unmarried couples—both gay and straight—may be reluctant to disclose that they are living together. Instead, they may describe themselves as roommates, friends, or girlfriends and boyfriends. Others, who feel that they're in a common-law marriage, often don't describe themselves as "unmarried partners" (Gates and Ost, 2004; Manning and Smock, 2005).

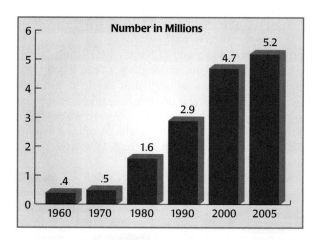

FIGURE 9.7 **Cohabiting Couples in the United States, 1960–2005**

Note: These figures represent two adults of the opposite sex.
SOURCE: Based on U.S. Census Bureau, Current Population Survey, March and Annual Social and Economic Supplements, 2005 and earlier, Table UC-1, 2006, www.census.gov/population/socdemo/hh-fam/uc1.pdf (accessed September 17, 2006).

Keep in mind, also, that only 9 percent of the population is cohabiting at any time. In contrast, married couples maintain 52 percent of all households (Fields, 2004).

DURATION Most cohabiting relationships are short-lived: About one-half end within one year, and over 90 percent end by the fifth year. When these relationships end, 44 percent result in marriage (Lichter et al., 2006).

Whether a cohabiting relationship ends in marriage or a breakup depends, among other things, on *why* people are living together. Those with the lowest levels of commitment are the most likely to split up (see *Table 9.2*).

Types of Cohabitation

Cohabitation serves many purposes and varies at different stages of the life course. The most common types are dating cohabitation, premarital cohabitation, and cohabitation that is a trial marriage or a substitute for a legal marriage.

DATING COHABITATION Some people drift gradually into **dating cohabitation**, which occurs when a couple that spends a great deal of time together eventually decides to move in together instead of living apart while dating. Thus, dating cohabitation is essentially an alternative to singlehood. The decision may be based on a combination of reasons, such as convenience, finances, companionship, and sexual accessibility. Such couples are unsure about the quality of their relationship, and there is no long-term commitment (Manning and Smock, 2005).

Especially among young adults, there is more **serial cohabitation**, living with one partner for a time and then with another. Because dating cohabitation is similar to being single, partners might terminate one cohabiting relationship and then move in with someone else. Even if there's an unplanned pregnancy, the man, especially, may decide to "move on" to another cohabiting arrangement (Wartik, 2005).

PREMARITAL COHABITATION For many people, premarital cohabitation is a step between dating and marriage. In **premarital cohabitation**, the couple is testing the relationship before making a final commitment. They may or may not be engaged, but they have definite plans to marry. Just 19 percent of Americans in 1988 said that they had lived with their spouse before marriage, compared with 37 percent in 2002 (Jones, 2002b). Thus, increasing numbers of Americans are cohabiting before marriage.

TABLE 9.2

Does Cohabitation Lead to Marriage?

Type of Cohabitation	Percentage of Couples	After 5 to 7 Years		
		Split Up	Cohabiting	Married
Dating cohabitation	29%	46%	21%	33%
Premarital cohabitation	46	31	17	52
Trial marriage	15	51	21	28
Substitute marriage	10	35	40	25

SOURCE: Adapted from Bianchi and Casper, 2000.

TRIAL MARRIAGE In a **trial marriage,** the partners want to see what marriage might be like—whether marriage to each other or to someone else. This type of living together is similar to premarital cohabitation, but the partners are less certain about their relationship. Such "almost married" cohabitation may be especially attractive to partners who doubt that they can deal successfully with problems that arise from differences in personalities, interests, finances, ethnicity, religion, or other issues.

SUBSTITUTE MARRIAGE A **substitute marriage** is a long-term commitment between two people without a legal marriage. Motives for substitute marriages vary widely. For example, one or both partners may be separated but still legally married to someone else, or may be divorced and reluctant to remarry. In some cases, one partner may be highly dependent or insecure and therefore prefer any kind of relationship to being alone. In other cases, the partners may feel that a legal ceremony is irrelevant to their commitment to each other (see Chapter 1).

Cohabitation is more complex than these four classifications suggest. Especially where children are involved, cohabitation can include two biological parents, one biological parent, or an adoptive parent. In addition, one or both partners may be never married, divorced, or remarried. These variations can create very different relationship dynamics, a topic that researchers are just beginning to explore.

Who Cohabits?

Cohabitants are a diverse group. Even though many characteristics of cohabitants overlap, there are some general patterns in terms of age, gender, race and ethnicity, social class, and other traits.

AGE Many people think that college-age students are the largest group of cohabitants. In fact, only 20 percent of all cohabitors are 24 years of age or younger. A majority, 56 percent, is between 25 and 44 (Fields, 2004).

Among cohabitants who are in their mid-30s to mid-40s, one or more partners may be divorced and involved romantically but not interested in remarrying. Compared with their younger counterparts, older cohabitants (those age 50 or older) report significantly higher relationship quality and stability but view their relationship as an alternative to marriage or remarriage rather than as a prelude to them. Older people are typically not having or raising children, an important reason for marriage among younger couples (King and Scott, 2005).

The cohabitation rate for people age 65 and older has increased significantly—from less than one percent in 1960 to three percent in 2003 (Fields, 2004). Many

Many cohabiting couples like this one are raising children from previous relationships as well as having their own cildren.

demographers expect these numbers to climb as baby boomers age and Americans in general stay healthy and live longer.

In many cases, seniors cohabit because remarriage may mean giving up a former spouse's pension, Social Security, and medical insurance. A 72-year-old woman who lives with her 78-year-old partner, for example, has no intention of getting married because she'd lose her late husband's pension: "My income would be cut by $500 a month if I got married, and we can't afford that" (Silverman, 2003: D1). In other cases, older couples avoid remarriage because of unpleasant divorces in the past or because their grown children fear that they will be displaced in their parent's affection—and especially their will (Greider, 2004).

GENDER By age 30, half of all U.S. women have cohabited. When it comes to living with a man, daughters often follow their mother's lead: Young adult women whose mothers cohabited are 57 percent more likely than other women to cohabit. Also, women whose mothers have a college degree or more are significantly less likely to cohabit than are women whose mothers have less than a high school education. In this sense, attitudes about cohabitation—especially among women—may be transmitted from one generation to another (Mellott et al., 2005).

As a result of the shortage of marriageable men, many low-income black women don't want to marry because they feel that their live-in partners will be unemployed, unfaithful, or not responsible in caring for children. Low-income white and Puerto Rican single mothers don't marry their partner, similarly, if they see the man as a poor provider or immature even though "he is the love of my life" (Jayakody and Cabrera, 2002; Edin and Kefalas, 2005).

RACE AND ETHNICITY The highest rates of cohabitation occur among American Indians/Native Alaskans and African Americans (about 17 percent for each group), and the lowest rates among Asian Americans (almost 5 percent) (see *Figure 9.8*).

Although Latinos have relatively low cohabitation rates, some scholars expect these numbers to rise. As the children of immigrants become more Americanized, especially those who are economically disadvantaged may "retreat from marriage" and enter cohabiting relationships. Even now, Latinos and blacks are more likely than whites to approve of cohabitation. In addition, many Latinos come from countries in Latin America and Central America that have extremely high cohabitation rates compared with the United States (Oropesa and Landale, 2004).

SOCIAL CLASS Race, ethnicity, and gender intersect with social class in explaining cohabitation. However, cohabitation is more common among people at lower educational and income levels. For example, 60 percent of women with no high school diploma or general equivalency diploma (GED) cohabit, compared with 38 percent of women with a bachelor's degree or higher. Men—especially African American men—are more likely to cohabit than to marry if their earnings and educational levels are low. Men who are employed full time, especially those in professional and semiprofessional occupations, are more likely to marry their live-in partners than are unemployed men (Bumpass and Lu, 2000; Gorman, 2000; Wu and Pollard, 2000; Schoen and Cheng, 2006).

A number of studies show that economic circumstances reduce the odds of getting married. Although cohabitors see the quality of a relationship as critical for marriage, so are finances (Lichter et al., 2003; Xie et al., 2003; Carlson et al., 2004).

Many low-income men may want to marry but don't do so because they feel that they can't support a family. Many black women, as you saw earlier, are unwilling to marry men with erratic employment records and low earnings. Women in low-income groups yearn for "respectability and upward mobility" (including home ownership and financial stability). They don't marry their current boyfriend, however, if they feel that the man won't achieve economic stability (Ooms, 2002).

Across all ethnic groups, three out of four cohabitants say that "Everything's there except money." Money problems delay marriage for several reasons: One does not marry if the couple is struggling financially or in debt, the male partner cannot provide for the family, or lack of money creates stress and conflict. In addition, even a modest wedding may pose a serious obstacle to marriage for working-

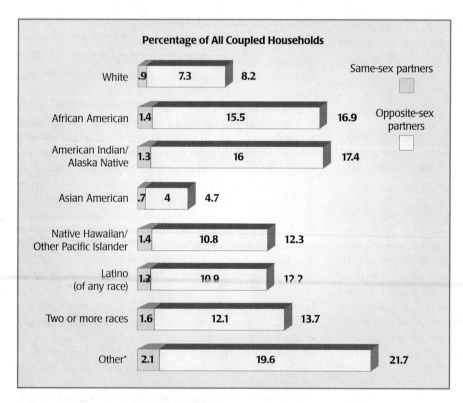

FIGURE 9.8 Who Is Living Together?
*"Other" includes "some other race alone" and Latino/white combinations of ethnicity but not race.

SOURCE: Simmons and O'Connell, 2003, Figure 3.

and middle-class young adults: "Ben, a 30-year-old railroad conductor, said he did not know how he would come up with $5,000 for a wedding, exclaiming, 'Weddings are expensive!'" (Smock et al., 2005: 688).

RELIGION Religious values also affect cohabitation rates. In the United States, the most religious Americans—those who attend church weekly—are less than half as likely to cohabit as those who seldom or never attend church because they believe that premarital cohabitation increases the odds of divorce. Teenage girls who attend religious schools and religious services at least once a week are less likely to cohabit than those without such experiences (Houseknecht and Lewis, 2005).

A large percentage of American teenagers—nearly 7 in 10—support the idea of couples living together before marriage. And about half of religious teenagers (those who have attended church or synagogue in the last seven days) approve of cohabitation. Such widespread acceptance, especially among adolescents, suggests that because so many teens have grown up with a cohabiting parent or have experienced the divorce of their parents, "wedding vows may no longer mean as much" (Lyons, 2004; Cunningham and Thornton, 2005).

The Benefits and Costs of Cohabitation

Even though rates of cohabitation and acceptance of the practice are growing, this topic is usually one of the most controversial in my classes. Some of my students feel that living together is immoral while others argue that it's financially practical. As in any other relationship (including dating and marriage), cohabitation has both advantages and disadvantages.

BENEFITS OF COHABITATION The benefits of cohabitation include the following:

- Couples have the emotional security of an intimate relationship but can also maintain their independence by having their own friends and visiting family members alone (McRae, 1999).

- Couples can dissolve the relationship without legal problems, or they can leave an abusive relationship more freely (DeMaris, 2001).

- Couples who postpone marriage have a lower likelihood of divorce because being older is one of the best predictors of a stable marriage (see Chapter 15).

- Cohabitation can help people find out how much they really care about each other when they have to cope with unpleasant realities such as a partner who doesn't pay bills or has different standards of hygiene from theirs.

- Among unmarried people age 65 and over, cohabitation may increase the chances of receiving care that is usually provided by spouses (Chevan, 1996).

- Cohabitants don't have to deal with in-laws (Silverman, 2003).

- Even at lower socioeconomic levels, children can reap some economic advantages by living with two adult earners instead of a single mother. A single mother of two children who earns $15,000 a year gets an earned income tax credit of $41,000. If she marries a man making $10,000 year, the benefit drops to $2,100 (Kalil, 2002).

COSTS OF COHABITATION Cohabitation also has disadvantages. The costs of cohabitation include the following:

- Unlike married couples, cohabitants have few legal rights. There's no automatic inheritance if a partners dies without having made a will, for example.

- Some partners experience a loss of identity or a feeling of being trapped. For example, they may feel restricted from participating in activities with friends.

- Women in cohabiting relationships do more of the cooking and other household tasks than many married women do, especially when the cohabiting man is not committed to the relationship (Coley, 2002; Ciabattari, 2004).

- Compared with married couples, cohabitants have a weaker commitment to their relationship, have lower levels of happiness and satisfaction, report more alcohol problems, and are more likely to be unfaithful (Treas and Giesen, 2000; Waite, 2000).

- Spouses who cohabit before marriage demonstrate more negative behaviors (such as trying to control the partner's thoughts or feelings, verbal aggression, and anger) than spouses who don't cohabit (Cohan and Kleinbaum, 2002).

- Cohabitation dilutes intergenerational ties. Compared to their married peers, the longer people live together, the less likely they are to give or receive help from their parents, turn to their parents in an emergency, and be involved in extended family activities. Parents might sometimes avoid contact because they are unsure of their roles when their children cohabit (Eggebeen, 2005).

■ U.S. laws don't specify a cohabitant's responsibilities and rights. For example, it's usually more difficult to collect child custody payments from a cohabiting father than from a married father (or mother) (see Chapter 11).

Often, after reading this section, students raise an important question: Should my girlfriend or boyfriend and I live together? Speaking sociologically, there's no simple answer to this question. Some of the research, however, suggests issues that you should think about before or during cohabitation (see the box "Should We Live Together?").

Even though cohabitation has benefits and costs, many cohabitants are convinced that it leads to better marriages. Is this true? Or is it wishful thinking?

Does Cohabitation Lead to Better Marriages?

No, it doesn't. Generally, couples who live together before marriage have higher divorce rates than those who do not live together before marriage (Bramlett and Mosher, 2002).

Although divorce rates are higher for those who cohabit than for people who don't live together before marriage, there are variations across racial and ethnic groups. Divorce is more likely for white women than for black and Mexican American women who have cohabited before marriage, for example (Phillips and Sweeney, 2005).

Except for short-term premarital cohabitation, why is living together generally associated with a higher risk of divorce, especially for white women? So far there's no single answer, but many sociologists feel that there may be a *selection effect* or a *cohabitation experience effect*. Most recently, some believe that an *inertia effect* also helps explain why living together has negative marital outcomes.

THE SELECTION EFFECT   The selection effect refers to the fact that people who cohabit before marriage have different characteristics than people who do not. Some cohabitants are poor marriage partners because of drug problems, inability to handle money, trouble with the law, unemployment, sexual infidelity, or mental health problems. In addition, cohabitants are less likely than noncohabitants to put effort into the relationship, less likely to compromise, tend to have poorer communication skills, and have doubts about their partner or about marriage as a sacred bond. It may be these characteris-

tics that later lead to divorce (McRae, 1999; Cohan and Kleinbaum, 2002; Dush et al., 2003).

THE COHABITATION EXPERIENCE EFFECT   The experience of cohabitation itself may lead to marital instability. Through cohabitation, people may come to accept the temporary nature of relationships and to view cohabitation as an alternative to marriage. Cohabitants who are independent and used to having their own way, for example, may be quick to leave a marriage (DeMaris and MacDonald, 1993).

Serial cohabitation may be especially harmful to marital stability. People who leave cohabiting relationships may be more willing to dissolve other relationships, including marriage: "People's tolerance for unhappiness is diminished, and they will scrap a marriage that might otherwise be salvaged" (Popenoe and Whitehead, 2002: 5).

THE INERTIA EFFECT   Some cohabitants drift into marriage. After moving in together, a couple often makes numerous decisions that make it more difficult to break up—splitting the finances, buying furniture, spending less time with friends, and even having a child. Once a couple has lived together and shared possessions, pets, or children, and has invested time in the relationship, they may be more open to the possibility of marriage. Instead of making a conscious decision and commitment, however, the couple may slide into marriage because of inertia ("We might as well get married because there's no reason not to") (Stanley and Smalley, 2005).

Troubled marriages that begin with cohabitation often reflect selection, experience, and inertia effects. In terms of *selection*, people might choose "risky" partners (those who use drugs or are hard to live with, for example) because they think a cohabitation relationship will be easy to break up. In terms of *experience*, the couple may also have poor communication and problem-solving skills that carry over into marriage. Despite these and other difficulties, marriage that "just sort of happens" may be short-lived because of *inertia* effects.

Some research suggests that women who limit their cohabitation to a future husband do not experience a higher risk of divorce. For the most part, however, there is little evidence that those who cohabit before marriage have stronger marriages than those who do not (Teachman, 2003; Popenoe and Whitehead, 2006).

How Does Cohabitation Affect Children?

Since 1960, there has been an increase of over 900 percent in the number of cohabiting couples who live with children. In fact, nearly half of all children today will

Applying What You've Learned

Should We Live Together?

Most people live together because they're unwilling to make a long-term commitment or are uncertain about whether they want to marry. Such doubts are normal and should probably arise more often than they do (see Chapter 8, especially, on breaking up).

A few social scientists are adamantly opposed to the practice of living together. According to Popenoe and Whitehead (2002), for example,

■ *You should not live together at all before marriage* because there is no evidence that cohabitation leads to better or stronger marriages. People should not live together unless they've already set a wedding date.

■ *Don't make a habit of cohabiting* because multiple experiences of living together decrease the chances of marrying and establishing a lifelong partnership.

■ *Limit cohabitation to the shortest possible period of time.* The longer you live together with a partner, the more likely it is that you, your partner, or both will break up and never marry.

■ *Don't consider cohabitation if children are involved.* Children need parents over the long term. In addition, children are more likely to be abused by cohabitants than by biological parents.

On the other hand, people who live together give rational reasons for doing so:

■ *Economic advantages:* "We can save money by sharing living expenses."

■ *Companionship:* "We are able to spend more time together."

■ *Increased intimacy:* "We can share sexual and emotional intimacy without getting married."

■ *Easy breakups:* "If the relationship doesn't work out, there's no messy divorce."

■ *Compatibility:* "Living together is a good way to find out about each other's habits and character."

■ *Trial marriage:* "We're living together because we'll be getting married soon" (Olson and Olson-Sigg, 2002; Solot and Miller, 2002; Sassler, 2004).

So where does this leave you? You might use exchange theory (see Chapters 2 and 6) in making a decision. List the costs and benefits and then decide what you want to do.

Stop and Think . . .

• If you live with someone (or have done so in the past), why? What would you advise other people to do?

• Look at *Appendix F* ("Premarital and Nonmarital Agreements"). Have you discussed any of these topics with someone you've lived with in the past or now?

---

spend some time in a cohabiting family before age 16 (Bumpass and Lu, 2000).

Cohabitation isn't an ideal arrangement for most children. As with marriage, cohabitation has a negative effect on children if the parents are poor, psychologically distressed, or unhappy. Children living with two biological cohabiting parents fare somewhat better than those with "social fathers" (mothers' boyfriends). Social fathers are less involved in the children's emotional and physical well-being than are married fathers (Kalil, 2002; Manning, 2002).

since you asked

Are children of married parents better off than those of cohabiting couples?

For the most part, however, children who grow up with cohabiting couples—even when both are biological parents—tend to have worse life outcomes than those who grow up with married couples. For example, children living in cohabiting households

■ Experience more domestic violence because of the cohabiting men's lower investment in the relationship and because many women tolerate the assaults (Cunningham and Antill, 1995).

■ Are more likely to be poor: When unmarried couples break up, men's household income drops by 10 percent while women lose 33 percent; the percentage of women living in poverty increases from 20 percent to 30 percent while men's poverty level remains relatively unchanged at about 20 percent (Avellar and Smock, 2005).

■ Live in households in which the partners spend more on adult goods such as alcohol and tobacco and less on child-related goods such as health and education than do married parents (DeLeire and Kalil, 2005).

■ Have more academic, emotional, and behavioral problems because of poverty or because one or both adults experience more parenting problems than do married couples (Manning and Lamb, 2003; Brown, 2004; Seltzer, 2004a).

Besides these difficulties, children often suffer the consequences of serial cohabitation or a parent's breakup with a partner. About 75 percent of children born to cohabiting parents see their parents split up before they reach age 16, compared with 33 percent of children born to married parents. The breakups increase already existing problems such as poverty for women and their children. Because cohabiting relationships are so unstable, they often aggravate personal and social difficulties for children, including behavior problems and poor academic performance (Popenoe and Whitehead, 2002; Raley and Wildsmith, 2004).

Although couples say that they've found their "true love," most cohabitation is short lived. Thus, many family practitioners and attorneys advise people who live together to draw up premarital and nonmarital agreements that will safeguard each person's assets.

Cohabitation and the Law

A few years ago, a sheriff in North Carolina fired a dispatcher because she would not marry her live-in boyfriend. North Carolina is one of seven states that have laws prohibiting cohabitation (the others are Virginia, West Virginia, Florida, Michigan, Mississippi, and North Dakota). Most of the laws are at least 200 years old and rarely enforced. In this case, however, the sheriff felt that the dispatcher's live-in arrangement was immoral and decided to enforce the law. More recently, legislators in North Dakota voted to uphold a law that can be used to prosecute unmarried couples who cohabit (Hartsoe, 2005).

Even when states don't prosecute cohabitants, unmarried couples and their children have very little legal protection. A full 70 percent of children living with a cohabiting couple are the offspring of one of the partners, yet they have few of the automatic rights and privileges enjoyed by children of married parents (Scommegna, 2002; see, also, Chapter 16).

According to many legal experts, cohabitants' best protection in financial matters is to maintain separate ownership of possessions. Cohabiting partners should not have joint bank accounts or credit cards. Shared leases should also be negotiated before the partners move in together. If partners buy real estate together, they should spell out carefully, in writing, each person's share of any profit. Cars should not be registered in a woman's name just to escape the high insurance premiums commonly charged men under 25. If there is an accident, the woman will be liable even if the man was driving.

Health insurance plans that cover a spouse rarely extend to an unmarried partner. And if a partner dies and leaves no will, relatives—no matter how distant—can claim all of his or her possessions. Cohabiting couples' best course is to put everything possible in writing. If a couple has children, both partners must acknowledge biological parenthood in writing to protect the children's future claims to financial support and inheritance (Mahoney, 2002).

Discussing legal matters may not seem very romantic when people love each other. But when a cohabiting relationship ends, the legal problems can be overwhelming. Many attorneys recommend that cohabitants draw up a contract similar to a premarital document. *Appendix F* describes some of the complex issues that cohabitants are likely to encounter.

Do such "rules" apply to all cohabiting couples? No. According to some financial experts, middle-aged and older couples should probably live together rather than marry or remarry (see the box "Does Living Together Make More Sense Than Marriage?").

Cohabitation: A Global View

Cohabitation has been around for a long time, but its prevalence and the government benefits available to co-habitants vary widely from one country to another.

PREVALENCE Cohabitation is common in Latin America and the Caribbean—especially in Cuba, the Dominican Republic, Ecuador, Panama, and Venezuela—and less common in Africa and Asia. In China, an estimated one-third of all couples cohabit. About two-thirds of these unions occur in the countryside and constitute "early marriages" between adolescents who are below the legal minimum age for marriage—20 for women, 22 for men (Neft and Levine, 1997).

Although living together is still frowned upon in some southern European countries, such as Greece and Portugal, it has lost its social stigma elsewhere. In Britain, for example, over 75 percent of first partnerships are cohabiting. Of all out-of-wedlock births, one-third are in cohabiting households. In Australia, 71 percent of couples live together before marriage (Qu and Weston, 2001; Seltzer, 2004b).

Cohabitation rates have risen dramatically in the last decade and are highest in industrialized countries. There is a great deal of variation among nations, however. Cohabitation is most common in the Nordic countries of Denmark, Sweden, and Finland, where up to one-third of the population has cohabited. Sweden is the only country where there are more first births within cohabiting unions than within marriages. The lowest cohabitation rates are in Italy (14 percent), Ireland (12 percent), Portugal (9 percent), Greece (8 percent), and Japan (3 percent) (Kiernan, 2002, 2004).

The reasons for cohabitation also vary from one country to another. For example, more than 75 percent of cohabitations end in marriage in Belgium, Switzerland, Finland, and Slovenia, compared with only 36 percent in Canada. Thus, cohabitation is primarily a prelude to marriage in some countries but an alternative to marriage in others (Heuveline and Timberlake, 2004).

GOVERNMENT BENEFITS As more and more couples live together before or instead of marrying, some countries have extended cohabitants many of the same rights as those enjoyed by married couples. Argentina, for example, grants pension rights to spouses in common-law marriages. Canada provides the same rights and benefits (such as child support) to children whether they are born to married or unmarried couples. Other countries, including Australia, require equal sharing of property when cohabiting relationships break up (Neft and Levine, 1997; Le Bourdais and LaPierre-Adamcyk, 2004).

Many nations offer single women economic security regardless of marital status. In Sweden, for example,

Constraints

Does Living Together Make More Sense Than Marriage?

Many people, especially young adults, say that they cohabit to save money—for example, by pooling the costs of housing, electric bills, and cable. People who are older and have accumulated possessions might be better off cohabiting rather than marrying for several reasons:

- *Liability:* If you get married, you've also married your partner's debts. In contrast, unmarried people can keep their finances separate, can maintain their individual credit ratings, and don't risk losing everything if a cohabiting partner is sued.

- *Inheritance:* Unlike a married couple, unmarried partners aren't automatically entitled to receive an inheritance from their partner. This is important if a cohabiting partner wants to preserve the inheritance of children from a previous marriage.

- *Social Security:* Widows and widowers are eligible for Social Security and pension survivor benefits from a deceased spouse.
- *Financial aid:* A single parent may find it easier than a married couple to get financial aid for a child's education because the income of one parent, rather than two, will affect the child's eligibility to receive financial support (Reeves, 2005).

Stop and Think...

- Do you agree that cohabiting—rather than marrying—makes a lot of sense, especially for people who are no longer raising young children?
- Do you think it's "fair" or not that financial aid favors children of cohabiting rather than married couples?

all parents, married or unmarried, receive a children's allowance from the state, and divorced and single mothers are entitled to cash advances on child-support payments if a child's father fails to pay. Norway's policies are similar.

Many European countries give children born within and outside marriage the same inheritance and other rights. There is more ambivalence about the rights and responsibilities of cohabiting adults. After biological relationships have been established, Sweden, France, Norway, and Great Britain grant cohabiting parents the same obligations and rights as married couples. In Germany and Italy, in contrast, the father can gain some rights to guardianship but not necessarily to custody (Kiernan, 2002, 2004).

Making Connections

■ Look back at *Table 9.2* on page 273. Are there other types of cohabiting couples that you can think of? For example, what about being indifferent to marriage?

■ A few years ago, the prestigious American Law Institute (2002) created a stir when it proposed that cohabitation be legalized. Unmarried couples would have the same rights and responsibilities as married couples regarding inheritance, child custody, debts, alimony, and health insurance, for example. Do you agree with this proposal?

Gay and Lesbian Couples

Regardless of our sexual orientation, most of us seek an intimate relationship with one special person. Because legal marriage is still rare for them, most homosexuals must turn to cohabitation.

Gay and Lesbian Relationships

Gay and lesbian couples come in "different sizes, shapes, ethnicities, races, religions, resources, creeds, and quirks, and even engage in diverse sexual practices." An estimated 29 percent of gay men and 44 percent of lesbians currently have steady romantic partners. In addition, many households are headed by same-sex partners (Black et al., 2000; Stacey, 2003: 145; see, also, "Data Digest").

Like heterosexuals, homosexual cohabitants must work out issues of communication, power, and household responsibilities. If there are children from previous marriages, gay and lesbian partners, like

heterosexual parents, must deal with custody and child-rearing issues (see Chapter 12).

LOVE AND COMMITMENT Most lesbians and gay men want an enduring love relationship. Gender, however, seems to shape a couple's values and practices more powerfully than does sexual orientation. Lesbian and heterosexual women, for example, are less competitive and more relationship-oriented than gay or heterosexual men. In addition, both lesbian and straight women are more likely than either gay or straight men to value their relationships more than their jobs (Huston and Schwartz, 1995; Stacey, 2003).

In 2003, *The New York Times* announced that it would begin running same-sex commitment notices, joining 70 other U.S. newspapers that had already adopted the policy. Having an engagement or wedding notice in a newspaper is a simple rite of passage that most heterosexuals don't think about twice. For lesbian and gay couples, it's a significant step in proclaiming their love and commitment publicly (Venema, 2003).

POWER AND DIVISION OF LABOR A majority of gay and lesbian couples report having equal power in their relationship. When power is unequal, however, and as social exchange theory predicts, the older, wealthier, and better-educated partner usually has more power. The "principle of least interest" is also pertinent. As in heterosexual couples, the person in the gay couple who is less involved in the relationship and is less dependent has more power (Patterson, 2001; see, also, Chapter 8).

Gay life is not divided into "butch" and "femme" roles. One partner may usually perform most of the "feminine" activities, such as cooking, whereas the other performs most of the "masculine" tasks, such as car repair. The specialization typically is based on individual characteristics, such as skills or interests, rather than on traditional husband–wife or masculine–feminine gender roles (Peplau et al., 1996; Kurdek, 2004).

PROBLEMS AND CONFLICT Like heterosexual cohabitants, gay and lesbian couples experience conflicts in four areas. In terms of *power*, all couples are equally likely to argue about finances, inequality in the relationship, and possessiveness. They are also equally likely to complain about such *personal flaws* as smoking or drinking, driving style, and grooming. Couples are similar in being unhappy with some aspects of *intimacy*, especially sex and demonstrating affection. Both groups are also equally likely to criticize partners who are *physically absent*, usually because of job or education commitments. Suspicion may be more common among gay and lesbian cohabitants, however, because their previous lovers are likely to remain in their social support networks, increasing the possibility of jealousy and resentment (Kurdek, 1994, 1998).

Violence is more prevalent among gay male couples than among either lesbian or heterosexual cohabitants. Compared with 8 percent of heterosexual couples, for example, 15 percent of gay cohabiting men reported being raped or physically assaulted by a male partner, and 11 percent reported being the victim of such violence by a lesbian partner (Tjaden and Thoennes, 2000).

It's not clear why the violence rates among gay male cohabitants are so high. One explanation may be that gay men have internalized the cultural belief that aggression is an acceptable "male" way of solving conflict, even in intimate relationships. Another reason may be that gay men are more likely than lesbians to be rejected by their family and friends and to strike out against intimate partners when there are problems.

RACIAL-ETHNIC VARIATIONS Gay and lesbian couples often get less social support from family members than do heterosexual couples. The greatest rejection may come from racial-ethnic families, whose traditional values about marriage and the family are often reinforced

Davic Dietz, left, kisses his husband Karl Paulnack, while displaying their Massachusetts Certificate of Marriage moments after the two were wed on May 20, 2004. They've had a committed relationship for 12 years.

by religious beliefs. In some faiths, homosexual behavior is considered aberrant or a sin (Hill, 2005).

In African American, Asian American, Latino, and Middle Eastern communities, family members are expected to marry and to maintain the traditional family structure (see Chapter 4). Many racial-ethnic groups also have strong extended-family systems. A gay family member may be seen as jeopardizing not only intrafamily relationships but also the extended family's continued strong association with the ethnic community (Morales, 1996; Liu and Chan, 1996; Mays et al., 1998).

Lesbian and gay couples might encounter additional problems because the partner comes from the "wrong" religion, racial-ethnic group, or social class. Even if both partners are "out" to their family and relatives, the family might exclude a partner in subtle ways, such as inviting the heterosexual son-in-law of two years, but not the lesbian partner of 15 years, to be in a family picture (Clunis and Green, 2000).

The War over Same-Sex Marriage

The institution of marriage has changed legally over several centuries. It was only after the Civil War that African Americans were allowed to marry. It was only in 1967 that a U.S. Supreme Court decision allowed interracial marriage (see Chapter 1). And until recently, same-sex couples were prohibited everywhere in the world. (Other terms for same-sex marriage include "gay marriage," "homosexual marriage," and "same-gender marriage.")

THE DEFENSE OF MARRIAGE ACT In 1996, President Bill Clinton signed the Defense of Marriage Act, which bans federal benefits for spouses (such as Medicare) unless the couple is in "a legal union between one man and one woman as husband and wife." The act also states that no U.S. state or territory has any legal duty to respect a marriage between homosexuals, even if such a marriage is valid in another state.

The Defense of Marriage Act was a significant piece of legislation because 1,049 federal laws base rights and privileges on marital status. Under these laws, only married heterosexual couples enjoy a variety of benefits, including a spouse's Social Security payments, housing and food stamps, veterans' and other military services, employment benefits, naturalization, and even privacy protection (General Accounting Office, 1997).

Since 1996, 37 states have passed similar Defense of Marriage Acts that ban same-sex marriages. This means that gays, unlike heterosexuals, don't have such rights as inheritance, child custody and visitation, adoption, and even the right to make funeral arrangements for a partner who has died.

CIVIL UNIONS Same-sex couples who are not recognized by law as married can enter into civil unions (sometimes also called "domestic partnerships" and "registered partnerships"). Civil unions entitle the couple to some of the same legal benefits as married couples, such as health benefits and adoption rights.

In about 25 countries, same-sex marriages are registered partnerships rather than official marriages. They were first legalized in Denmark in 1989 and most recently in the Czech Republic and Slovenia (2006) and Switzerland (2007). Although the partners can't marry in church, they have most of the same legal rights as married and unmarried heterosexual couples.

In the United States, Vermont was the first state to recognize civil unions between same-sex couples. According to Vermont's 1999 legislation, gay and lesbian couples could take advantage of more than 300 benefits that previously were available only to married couples, such as the ability to make medical decisions for their partners. Since then, Connecticut, Hawaii, Washington, DC, Maine, New Jersey, and many local jurisdictions in California and other states have implemented similar laws.

Although the overall percentage is still small, about 31 percent of employers—especially at large companies—now offer domestic-partner benefits, including health packages, bereavement leave, relocation and adoption assistance, life insurance, and employee discounts. In addition, 74 percent of the 50 most prestigious four-year colleges offer domestic-partner health benefits (Herrschaft, 2005).

Many same-sex couples argue, however, that civil union legislation isn't enough. Besides causing them to be denied federal benefits, they maintain, their inability to marry results in their being treated as second-class citizens.

SAME-SEX MARRIAGE In 2004, Massachusetts became the first state to legalize same-sex marriage. Finally, according to a Boston physician who had lived with her partner for nine years, "we're fully equal, fully recognized by the state" (Gardner, 2004: 12). As this book goes to press, however, Massachusetts voters could still overturn the law by voting against the state constitutional amendment that allows same-sex marriage.

Worldwide, the number of countries that has legalized same-sex marriages has grown slowly and now includes the Netherlands, Belgium, Canada, Spain, and South Africa. Twelve countries (Australia, China, Ireland, Portugal, and the United Kingdom, among others) are debating the issue.

Unlike people in other countries that have legalized same-sex marriages, Americans are ambivalent about this issue. About 88 percent say that homosexuals should have the same rights as heterosexuals in the workplace, up from 56 percent in 1977. However, only 39 percent feel that same-sex marriages should be legalized. Almost 6 out of 10 teens who are opposed to same-sex marriages say that homosexuality is due to upbringing and could be changed (Newport, 2006; Saad, 2006).

SOME CONTROVERSIES ABOUT SAME-SEX MARRIAGE

Many people, including gay men and lesbians, have mixed feelings about same-sex marriage. On the "against" side—and even though ministers, rabbis, and even priests have performed marriage ceremonies—many religious groups and individuals feel that same-sex marriage would legitimize "sinful" relationships that reflect a decline in family values. Also, same-sex marriages can provoke family tensions and divisiveness when family members feel that such unions are "just wrong" (Calvert, 2003; Armstrong, 2004).

since you asked

Why is same-sex marriage so controversial?

For the most part, however, gay activists support campaigns to legalize same-sex marriage. If gay marriages were legal, for example, family members and relatives could not contest inheritance by a gay partner. Gay couples would be entitled to the same hospitalization or bereavement leaves as married couples. Being able to marry would allow same-sex couples the same federal benefits and protections, such as Medicare, immigration laws, and joint filing of tax returns. Also, same-sex marriages would stabilize homosexual relationships, especially among gay men, and decrease the number of sexually transmitted infections that result from casual sex (King and Bartlett, 2006; see, also, Chapter 7).

Many businesses also endorse same-sex marriage. After Massachusetts legalized such marriages in that state, for example, some entrepreneurs said that they could bring in an additional $300 million just for the weddings. The profits from out-of-state guests, honeymoons, and tourism would be much higher (Symonds and Hempel, 2004).

Making Connections

- Should your state (unless it's done so already) pass legislation to legalize same-sex marriage?

- What do you think are some of the advantages and disadvantages of same-sex marriage? Are the costs and benefits different for gays and straights?

Communal Living Arrangements

Communes are collective households in which children and adults from different families live together. The adults may be married or unmarried. Some communes permit individual ownership of private property; others do not. There is a great deal of historical variation in the economic, sexual, and decision-making rights in communes.

Communes in the Past

Communes are not a modern invention. They have existed since 100 B.C.E. The popularity of communal living has fluctuated in the United States, but the number of people living in communes has never exceeded more than a tenth of 1 percent of the entire population (Kantor, 1970).

Both nineteenth-century and contemporary communes have varied greatly in structure, values, and ideology. In the nineteenth century, communes wrestled with the issue of monogamy and resolved the issue in very different ways. One group, the Icarians, made marriage mandatory for all adult members. Others, such as the Shakers and Rappites, required everyone, including married couples, to live celibate lives. Still others practiced free love, permitting sexual intercourse with all members, married or not (Muncy, 1988).

Most communes have been short-lived. Often the members were unwilling to give up their autonomy or private property. There was also conflict and jealousy regarding sexual relationships. Other groups dwindled because of a lack of new members. For example, most of the buildings of the Shakers in Maine and other states have been turned into tourist attractions and museums

---

Choices

Growing Old, but Not at Home

Almost 95 percent of Americans age 75 and older want to remain in their home as long as possible (Lichtenstein et al., 2006). When doing so isn't possible, older people have more housing options today than in the past. Here are some of the most common alternatives for older people who can't or don't want to "age in place":

■ *Retirement communities* offer apartments for residents who are mobile and can take care of themselves. These communities offer a variety of social and recreational activities, meals in a central dining room, and housekeeping services. There may be entrance fees (up to $40,000), and rents can vary widely (up to $4000 a month).

■ *Homesharing* involves two or more people sharing a home or apartment. Each person has a private bedroom but shares a kitchen and other living spaces. Some homeowners seek this arrangement to avoid living alone or to supplement their income by taking in a boarder.

■ *Elderly cottage housing opportunities (ECHOs)* are small, portable "cottages" that can be placed in the back or side yard of a single-family home, usually the home of an adult child. These units typically cost $35,000 or more.

■ *Continuing care retirement communities (CCRCs)* offer several housing options and services, depending

on a resident's needs. Typically, people begin by living independently in their own apartment. Later they may move to an assisted-living facility or nursing home on the same grounds. CCRCs are usually out of the financial reach of many older people because they have large entrance fees and expensive monthly charges. The fees and rents can be as high as $500,000 a year.

■ *Assisted-living facilities* provide housing, group meals, personal care, recreation, social activities, and limited nursing care (such as administering medications) in a residential setting. Residents often pay about $4000 a month.

■ *Board and care homes* are smaller in scale than assisted-living facilities. They provide a room, meals, and help with daily activities. These homes often are unlicensed, cost $400–$3000 a month, and might be supported by Supplemental Security Income (SSI), which helps people with low incomes.

Stop and Think . . .

• Where do your elderly parents, grandparents, or other relatives live? What kinds of choices and constraints have they experienced in their living arrangements?

• When you look at some of these housing options, what do they tell you about social class and "aging comfortably"?

or the land has been given to preservation groups (W. L. Smith, 1999; Llana, 2005).

Contemporary Communal Living

Communal living is common on college campuses. For example, fraternities, sororities, and houses that are rented and shared by five or six students fulfill many of the social and economic functions that characterize all communes.

A new program, Co-Abode, matches low-income single mothers in subsidized housing. The mothers live together and split household bills, divvy up chores, care for each other's children when they want to shop, and chat daily. Children often share a room. The housing is usually in safe neighborhoods with good school districts, and an outreach program provides the mothers with referrals "for everything from dentists to lawyers and credit counselors" (Wolcott, 2003: 14).

At the other end of the age continuum, a growing proportion of older people are experimenting with communal living as an alternative to moving in with children or living in a nursing home. When older people can't live alone because of physi-

since you asked

When I'm elderly and can't live alone anymore, what choices will be open to me?

cal problems or dementia (see Chapter 17), they have increasing housing options. As the box "Growing Old, but Not at Home" illustrates, many elderly people live in "communities" that provide medical, emotional, and physical care, functions traditionally performed by the family. The elderly thus have more options than before, but *only* if they have high incomes.

Conclusion

There have been a number of *changes* in relationships outside, before, and after marriage. Some of our *choices* include staying single longer, cohabiting, forming same-sex households, participating in communal living arrangements, or not marrying at all. Thus, larger numbers of people are single for a greater portion of their lives.

Our choices are not without *constraints,* however. For example, many U.S. laws do not encourage or protect most of these relationships. Despite the growing numbers of unmarried people, marriage is not going out of style; it is merely occupying less of the average adult's lifetime.

Although there is less pressure to marry, most of us will do so at least once in our lives. In the next chapter we examine the institution of marriage.

Summary

1. Diverse lifestyles have always existed, but in the past 20 years the number of alternative family forms has increased, including singlehood, cohabitation, gay households, and communal living arrangements.

2. Average household size has been shrinking since the 1940s. A major reason for the decrease is the growing number of people who are postponing marriage and living alone.

3. More people are postponing marriage because there is greater acceptance of cohabitation and out-of-wedlock children.

4. Singles constitute an extremely diverse group. Some have been widowed, divorced, or separated; others have never been married. Some singles choose their status, whereas others are single involuntarily.

5. There are many reasons why the numbers of singles have increased since the 1970s. Some of the reasons are macro, some are demographic, and some reflect personal choices.

6. Cohabitation has boomed since the 1960s. Although most cohabitation is short-lived, in some cases it is a substitute for legal marriage. Like other living arrangements, cohabitation has both advantages and disadvantages.

7. There is no evidence that cohabitation leads to more stable or happier marriages. Cohabitants have higher divorce rates than noncohabitants, and men typically benefit more from cohabitation than women do.

8. For the most part, cohabitation is disadvantageous for children. Some of the negative effects include do-

mestic violence, poverty, and behavioral and academic problems.

9. Legal factors often dictate living arrangements. Same-sex marriage is prohibited in all states except Massachusetts (as this book goes to press). Still, gay and lesbian partners have fewer options than do heterosexuals.

10. Communal living arrangements have changed since the turn of the twentieth century and even since the 1970s. They are less numerous and less popular today, but they still fulfill the economic and social needs of many people, especially elderly adults.

Key Terms

sex ratio 264
marriage squeeze 264
cohabitation 271

POSSLQ 272
dating cohabitation 272
serial cohabitation 272

premarital cohabitation 273
trial marriage 273
substitute marriage 273

Taking It Further

Learn More about Nonmarried Living Arrangements

There are a number of informative Internet sites on heterosexual cohabitation, same-sex households, and communal living arrangements. Here are a few:

The Alternatives to Marriage Project has a wide variety of information, statistics, and legal guides about and for unmarried people.
www.unmarried.org

Cohabitation: Living Together provides numerous sites that offer financial advice, results of national polls, and the pros and cons of living together before or instead of marriage.
http://dating.about.com/people/dating/msubcohab.htm

Queer Resources Directory contains almost 26,000 files, including links to "Queers and Their Families."
www.qrd.org

The Cohousing Network provides information about "collaborative housing that attempts to overcome the alienation of modern subdivisions."
www.cohousing.org

Law.com is a valuable resource on cohabitation rights, prenuptial agreements, and many other issues relevant to nonmarital living arrangements.
www.law.com/index.html

And more: www.prenhall.com/benokraitis includes links to sites of national organizations that lobby for singles' rights, information about the status of same-sex marriage legislation, collaborative housing options, and lists of government agencies, higher education institutions, and private-sector employers that offer domestic partnership benefits.

Investigate with Research Navigator

Go to www.researchnavigator.com and enter your LOGIN NAME and PASSWORD. For instructions on registering for the first time, view the detailed instructions at the end of the Chapter 1. Search the Research Navigator™ site using the following key search terms:

cohabitation
same-sex marriage
counseling

Outline

10

Marriage and Communication in Committed Relationships

Data Digest

- Among high school seniors, 82 percent of girls and 70 percent of boys say that **having a good marriage and family life is "extremely important"** to them.

- About 77 percent of men, compared with 63 percent of women, think **it's acceptable for women to propose to men.**

- In 1980, **a typical American wedding** cost $4,000. Today, it costs about $23,000. Some 27 percent of couples pay for the wedding themselves.

- About 61 percent of couples **omit the word "obey" from their vows,** but 83 percent of brides take their husband's name.

- Nearly 2.3 million marriages are performed annually (more than 6,000 a day). By age 30, **three-quarters of U.S. adults have been married.**

- More than 88 percent of Americans say that **they are "completely satisfied" or "very satisfied" with their marriage.**

Sources: Armstrong, 2004; Glenn, 2005; Kiefer, 2005; "For Richer or Poorer," 2005; Martin, 2006; Popenoe and Whitehead, 2006; U.S. Census Bureau, 2006.

On April 12, 1919, a young couple drove off (in a Model T Ford) to Jeffersonville, Indiana, because the bride-to-be, 14, was under the legal age to get married in Kentucky, their home state. In 2002, the same couple—William, 104, and Claudia Lillian Ritchie, 98—celebrated their 83rd wedding anniversary. When reporters asked them the secret to their long marriage, Mr. Ritchie said that they loved each other, there was a lot of give and take, and "We didn't have very many arguments" (Davis, 2002).

Most people agree that marriage isn't what it used to be, but how much do you really know about marriage? Find out by taking "A Marriage Quiz."

In this chapter we discuss marital expectations and rituals, consider various types of marriages and how they change over the years, and examine communication

Ask Yourself

A Marriage Quiz

True	False		
☑	☐	**1.**	The vast majority of today's mothers want a full-time career.
☐	☐	**2.**	Men and women are equally likely to say that they are happily married.
☐	☐	**3.**	The best single predictor of overall marital satisfaction is the quality of the couple's sex life.
☐	☐	**4.**	Overall, married women are physically healthier than married men.
☐	☐	**5.**	The keys to long-term marital success are good luck and romantic love.
☐	☐	**6.**	Marriages are much more likely to end in divorce today than 20 years ago.
☐	☐	**7.**	A husband is usually happier if his wife is a full-time homemaker than if she is employed outside the home.
☐	☐	**8.**	Having children typically brings a couple closer together and increases marital happiness.
☐	☐	**9.**	"No matter how I behave, my partner should love me because he/she is my spouse."
☐	☐	**10.**	If the wife is employed full time, the husband usually shares equally in housekeeping tasks.
☐	☐	**11.**	Husbands usually make more lifestyle adjustments in marriage than wives do.
☐	☐	**12.**	"If my spouse loves me, he/she should know what I want and need to make me happy."

Scoring the Marriage Quiz

All the items are false. The more "true" responses you gave, the more you believe in myths about marriage. The quiz is based on research presented in this chapter, Popenoe, 2002, and Coontz, 2006.

---

processes that can strengthen or undermine intimate relationships within and outside of marriage. Let's begin by looking at why people tie the knot.

Why Do People Marry?

When someone announces, "I'm getting married!" we respond with "Congratulations!" rather than "How come?" In Western societies, we assume that people marry because they love each other. We marry for a variety of reasons, however. Some are more conscious than others, and some are positive while others can be negative.

since you asked

Because it's easier to live with someone, why do people marry?

Positive Reasons for Getting Married

Positive motives encourage marital stability. Although these reasons don't *guarantee* that a marriage will last, they increase the odds of staying together, especially during rough times.

LOVE AND COMPANIONSHIP The single greatest attraction of marriage is continuous, intimate companionship with a loved one. Even though a couple may experience conflict, the partners have similar interests and enjoy each other's company (Bradbury et al., 2001).

CHILDREN A traditional reason for getting married is to have children. Because marriage is a social institution (unlike singlehood and cohabitation), most societies have laws and customs that protect children within marriage but not outside of it (see Chapter 9).

Many of India's high-income families have expensive weddings that invite up to 1,000 guests and last about a week. Most weddings are less lavish, but many families follow century-long nuptial traditions. In this photo, for example, Muslims in the Kashmir region of India surround a groom as he goes to his in-laws' house to fetch his bride.

ADULT IDENTITY Developmental theory, you recall, asserts that family members progress through various stages during the life course (see Chapter 2). Finding a job and being self-sufficient marks adulthood. So does marriage. Getting married says "I am an adult" to the community. A man who married at age 28 recalls,

> *You've made it to the next level, you've finally grown up. . . . Once I was married, it really suited me. I've found this with a lot of my married friends—you just feel more solid. You have a definite position in the world (Paul, 2002: 80).*

COMMITMENT AND PERSONAL FULFILLMENT An overwhelming number of Americans believe that marriage should be a lifelong commitment (see *Figure 10.1*). Commitment includes sexual fidelity.

Marriage connects people. The happiest couples report that they help each other, spend time together, and feel emotionally close. Moreover, those who believe that the quality of a marriage depends on determination and hard work are more likely to report having good marriages than couples who believe that relationships depend on fate, luck, or chance (Myers and Booth, 1999; Olson and Olson, 2000).

CONTINUITY AND PERMANENCE Whereas much of life is unpredictable, marriage promises stability. We ex-

pect a spouse to be a constant source of support and understanding in a shifting and changeable world.

Marriage also offers a sense of permanence and continuity by establishing one's own family. According to one of my students, "Whenever we look at our kids, my husband and I think about the wonderful things they might achieve someday. And I'm really looking forward to being a grandma."

However unintentionally, we may also marry for one or more "wrong" reasons.

Negative Reasons for Getting Married

Negative motives usually derail a marriage. They may be very functional in the sense that they fulfill a purpose (see Chapter 1). Often, however, negative reasons for matrimony lead to misery or divorce.

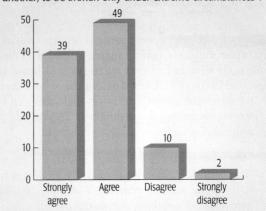

In a recent survey here's how Americans responded to the item "Couples who marry should make a lifelong commitment to one another, to be broken only under extreme circumstances":

Strongly agree	Agree	Disagree	Strongly disagree
39	49	10	2

In the same survey, almost 22 percent of Americans said that it's unrealistic to expect a couple to remain married to each other for life. How might you explain such inconsistent attitudes—that marriage is a lifelong commitment but that it's unrealistic to expect people to be married to each other for life?

Note: Respondents who refused to answer or said "don't know" were excluded from the base of percentages.

FIGURE 10.1   Should Marriage Be a Lifelong Commitment?

SOURCE: Based on Glenn, 2005, p. 29.

In recent years, it's become more common for couples to break from tradition when planning their weddings. Here, this bubbling bride and groom have an underwater marriage at their favorite scuba diving spot.

SOCIAL LEGITIMACY Getting married to "legitimate" an out-of-wedlock baby is one of the worst reasons for marrying (even though many religious groups would probably disagree). Often, the partners are young, one or both may not want to marry, and the couple may have only sex in common.

SOCIAL PRESSURE Sometimes parents are embarrassed that their children haven't married, and well-meaning (married) friends feel that marriage will bring happiness (see Chapter 8). Even if parents have been divorced, they project their own desires on their children by encouraging marriage. According to a 26-year-old media consultant, for example,

> *My mother was in her sixties and single. Even after her own two divorces, she was by no means turned off by the idea of marriage; in fact, she wanted more than anything to marry again . . . . Even though she didn't say it outright, she worried that I would become one of "those" women—thirty-five, lonely, careerist, with a cat and a studio apartment . . . (Paul, 2002: 58).*

ECONOMIC SECURITY When we were in graduate school, one of my friends, Beth, married a successful businessman because he was wealthy. Within a few months, Beth was staying at the library longer and longer because she dreaded going home to be with her husband. Their marriage lasted two years.

Marrying someone just for her or his money won't sustain a marriage. Among other things, a partner may be stingy and watch every penny after the wedding. One or both partners may be laid off and use up their savings very quickly. Or, even if you marry someone who's rich and then get a divorce, in most states you'll have a difficult time getting any of the money if you've been married less than 10 years (see Chapter 15).

REBELLION OR REVENGE Young people sometimes marry to get away from their parents. They flee their families for a variety of reasons: Physical, verbal, or sexual abuse; conflict between the parents or with a stepparent; or a yearning for independence. Even when the reasons for getting away from one's family are valid, rebellion is a weak foundation for marriage.

In other situations, people marry on the rebound: "I'll show Jeff that other guys love me even if he dumped me." Such marriages are bound to fail because revenge doesn't solve any problems. Since the ex-partner doesn't care, an "I'll show him (or her)" attitude is meaningless.

PRACTICAL SOLUTIONS TO PROBLEMS We sometimes marry for other "wrong" reasons because we're seeking practical solutions to a dilemma. Dating can be a disappointing series of experiences (see Chapter 8), and some people hope that marriage will give them an "escape hatch" from their problems. It won't, of course, because marriage is more complicated and more demanding than singlehood.

Most of us have heard stories about people who marry because they want a "helpmate"—someone to put them through medical or law school, share expenses in a new business, care for kids after divorce or widowhood, and so on. Such marriages typically are short-lived because they create more problems than they solve.

Regardless of our reasons for tying the knot, what do most of us expect from marriage?

What Do We Expect From Marriage?

Marriages are very personal, but they don't occur or exist in a vacuum. Many wedding rituals and practices reinforce the idea that marriage is a fusion of lovers

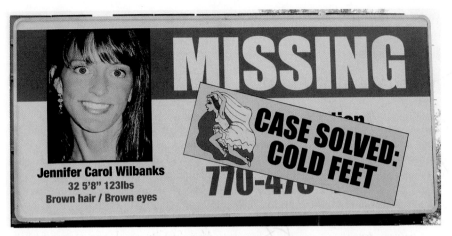

In 2005, Jennifer Wilbanks faked her abduction four days before the wedding and triggered a massive search (including billboards in this photo) and intensive media coverage. The wedding, which would have involved 14 groomsmen, 14 bridesmaids, and 600 guests was apparently too much for her to handle. This "runaway bride" later admitted that she took a cross-country bus trip to Albuquerque, New Mexico. She's signed contracts with publishers and movie producers. She's also suing her former fiancé for a half million dollars for selling the story to the media without her permission.

who make a lifelong commitment to each other. Some people are more guarded, however, and prepare prenuptial agreements. Let's begin with a look at the marriage rituals that presumably cement a marriage.

Marriage Rituals

Marriage is a critical rite of passage in almost every culture. In the United States, the major events that mark the beginning of a marriage are engagement, showers and bachelor or bachelorette parties, and the wedding itself.

since you asked

Why are wedding ceremonies important?

ENGAGEMENT Traditionally, an **engagement** formalizes a couple's decision to marry. According to the *Guinness Book of Records,* the longest engagement was between Octavio Guillen and Adriana Martinez of Mexico, who took 67 years to make sure they were right for each other. Most engagements are at least 65 years shorter.

Whether or not a couple follows traditional customs, an engagement serves several functions:

- It sends a "hands-off" message to others.

- It gives both partners a chance to become better acquainted with their future in-laws and to strengthen their identity as a couple.

- It provides each partner with information about a prospective spouse's potential or current medical problems (through blood tests, for example).

- It legitimates secular or religious premarital counseling, especially if the partners are of different religions or racial and ethnic backgrounds.

- It signals the intent to make the union legal if the couple has been living together or has had a child out of wedlock.

At a *bridal shower,* female friends and relatives "shower" a bride with both personal and household gifts and commemorate the beginning of a new partnership. At a *bachelor party,* the groom's friends typically lament their friend's imminent loss of freedom and celebrate one "last fling." Some women also have *bachelorette parties* that include anything from dinner with female friends to a male stripper show.

Many men now participate in the preparations for their wedding. About 80 percent attend bridal shows, give their opinions about flowers, produce original wedding invitations on their computers, and make menu choices. According to one wedding planner, "I've had grooms call me five or six times a day about small details months before their weddings" (Caplan, 2005: 67).

THE WEDDING In 2001, in an annual ceremony in Seoul's Olympic Stadium, the Reverend Sun Myung Moon, founder of the Unification Church, married 30,000 couples from more than 100 countries, including the United States. Reverend Moon matched the couples—all of whom were strangers—by age and education. Although there are no accurate statistics, some estimate that the divorce rate for these couples is about 75 percent (Baker, 2000; Lampman, 2001).

Most weddings are more traditional. The wedding ceremony typically reinforces the idea that the marriage commitment is a sacred, permanent bond. The presence of family, friends, and witnesses affirms the acceptance and legitimacy of the union. Even when the partners are very young, a wedding marks the end of childhood and the acceptance of adult responsibilities. The box on "Some Cherished Wedding Rituals" illustrates the historical origins of some of our current marriage conventions.

Changes

Some Cherished Wedding Rituals

Most of our time-honored customs associated with engagement and marriage, such as rings and the honeymoon, originally symbolized love and romance. Many were designed to ensure the fertility of the couple and the prosperity of their household.

Some, however, also reflected the subordinate position of the woman in the union. For example, the Anglo-Saxon word *wedd,* from which "wedding" is derived, was the payment for the bride made by the groom to her father. Thus, a wedding was literally the purchase of a woman. Here are some others:

- Before the twelfth century, the *best man* was a warrior friend who helped a man capture and kidnap a woman he desired (usually from another tribe).
- *Carrying the bride over the threshold* isn't simply a romantic gesture. Originally, it symbolized the abduction of a daughter who would not willingly leave her father's house.
- After a man captured (or bought) a bride, he disappeared with her for a while in a *honeymoon* so that her family couldn't rescue her. By the time they found the couple, the bride would already be pregnant. In America, around 1850, the honeymoon was usually a wedding trip to visit relatives. The safety and comfort of the railroad popularized more distant honeymoons.
- The *engagement ring* symbolized eternity. The medieval Italians favored a diamond ring because they believed that diamonds were created from the flames of love.
- Soldiers of ancient Sparta first staged *stag parties:* The groom feasted with his male friends on the night before the wedding. The function of this rite of passage was to say goodbye to the frivolities of bachelorhood while swearing continued allegiance to one's comrades despite being married.
- In the 1890s, the friend of a newly engaged woman held a party at which a Japanese parasol, filled with little gifts, was turned upside down over the bride-to-be's head, producing a shower of presents. Readers of fashion pages, learning of this event, wanted *bridal showers* of their own.
- In medieval times the wedding party's *flower girl* carried wheat to symbolize fertility. Perhaps for symmetry, the male *ring bearer* also appeared during the Middle Ages.
- In biblical times, the color blue symbolized purity. In 1499, however, Anne of Brittany set the pattern for generations to come by wearing a white wedding gown for her marriage to Louis XII of France. The *white bridal gown* came to symbolize virginity and is still worn by most first-time brides even though they aren't virgins.
- The first *wedding ring* was made of iron so that it wouldn't break. The Romans believed that a small artery or "vein of love" ran from the third finger to the heart and that wearing a ring on that finger joined the couple's hearts and destiny.
- The ancient Romans baked a special wheat or barley cake that they broke over the bride's head as a symbol of her hoped-for fertility. The English piled up small cakes as high as they could, and the bride and groom tried to kiss over the cakes without knocking the tower over; success meant a lifetime of prosperity. The cakes evolved into a *wedding cake* during the reign of England's King Charles II, whose French chefs decided to turn the cakes into an edible "palace" iced with white sugar.
- *Tying shoes to the car bumper* probably came from ancient cultures. For example, the Egyptians exchanged sandals at a wedding ceremony to symbolize a transfer of property or authority. A father gave the groom his daughter's sandal to show that she was now in his care. In an Anglo-Saxon wedding, the groom tapped the bride lightly on the head with the shoe to show his authority. Later, people began throwing shoes at the couple, and somehow this evolved into the current practice.

SOURCES: Based on Kern, 1992; Ackerman, 1994; Bulcroft et al., 1999.

In 2001, in a ceremony in Seoul's Olympic Stadium, the Reverend Sun Myung Moon, founder of the Unification Church, married 30,000 couples. Brides and grooms who could not be present were represented by photographs held by their future spouses. Reverend Moon conducts such mass marriages every year.

Does a marriage last longer if the wedding ceremony is traditional rather than nontraditional (such as performing the marriage in an exotic location or in a simple civil ceremony)? There are no national data, but family practitioners emphasize that the ceremony is far less important than the marriage. If couples and their parents go into debt to pay for an elaborate wedding, both groups may experience strained relationships. Also, ignoring future in-laws before and after a marriage can alienate prospective family members who might be very supportive—emotionally and financially—when the couple runs into problems (Kiefer, 2005; Silverman, 2006).

Many brides are swept off their feet by merchandising and spend at least a year planning a "perfect," often extravagant wedding ceremony (see "Data Digest"). Increasingly, however, attorneys are advising both women and men to invest some of their time in creating prenuptial agreements just in case the marriage fizzles after a few years.

Love and Prenuptial Agreements

Prenuptial agreements are common among the very wealthy. Although most people don't create "prenups" because doing so seems unromantic and little property is involved at the start of most marriages, 20 percent of couples do so ("For Richer or Poorer," 2005).

As *Appendix F* shows, prenuptial agreements cover numerous topics—from how many times partners expect to have sexual intercourse to trusts and wills. These contracts also include agreements about disposing of premarital and marital property, whether the couple will have children (and how many), the children's religious upbringing, who buys and wraps presents for relatives, and whether there will be combined or "his" and "her" savings and checking accounts.

Some of the arguments about prenuptial agreements are similar to those about cohabitation contracts. If there are children from a first marriage, or if one partner has considerable assets, the contract makes ending a bad marriage less complicated. Because women usually are the ones who suffer financially after a divorce, a contract gives them some legal protection (see Chapters 9 and 15).

Those who oppose prenuptial agreements feel that such documents set a pessimistic tone for the marriage. Also, if the contract is executed in a state other than the one where it was drawn up, the couple will experience legal problems. Moreover, because people change over time, the contract may not reflect their future viewpoints.

Regardless of how people feel about prenuptial agreements, both scholars and family practitioners maintain that most of us don't know very much about the people we marry (see Chapter 8). The box "Before You Say 'I Do'" suggests some questions that couples should discuss before tying the knot, including whether or not to draw up a legal premarital contract.

✸ Making Connections

◾ If you're single, do you want to get married? If so, why? If you're married, did you marry for the "right" reasons, the "wrong" reasons, or a combination of reasons?

◾ Do you think that prenuptial agreements are a good idea or not? Read *Appendix F* before deciding.

Types of Marriages

When someone asked a happily married couple to what they owed their successful marriage of 40 years, the husband replied, "We dine out twice a week—candlelight, violins, champagne, the works! Her night is Tuesday; mine is Friday."

As this anecdote suggests, happily married couples aren't joined at the hip. Instead, marriage reflects considerable diversity in relationships both in the United States and in other countries.

Types of Marriage in the United States

On the basis of a study of 400 "normal," upper-middle-class marriages (the partners ranged in age from 35 to 55), Cuber and Haroff (1965) identified five types of

Applying What You've Learned

Before You Say "I Do"

Some scholars contend that the best way to decrease divorce rates is to be more selective in choosing our marital partners (Glenn, 2002). In doing so, we should spend more time planning a marriage than planning a wedding. Here are some questions that committed partners who are planning to marry might discuss:

- What do you hope to contribute to our marriage?
- How often do you like to have time to yourself?
- Will you want to change your name after marrying?
- Which holidays will we spend with which family?
- Do you or your family have a history of any diseases or medical problems?
- What goals do you have in your career?
- Do you get along with co-workers?
- How much free time spent away from one another is acceptable?

- What makes you angry?
- What do you consider cheating or infidelity?
- Is religion important to you?
- Are you in debt?
- What would you do with an extra $10,000?
- Do you have to make any child support or alimony payments?
- How often do you plan to cook and clean?

SOURCE: Based on Outcalt, 1998: 14–138.

Stop and Think . . .

- What would you add to this list of questions?
- Instead of using such self-help lists, should couples seek premarital counseling? Or are the self-help lists sufficient?

---

marriage. Some were happy and some were not, but all endured.

- In a **conflict-habituated marriage**, the partners fight, both verbally and physically, but do not believe that fighting is a good reason for divorce. They feel that feuding is an acceptable way to try to solve problems, and they thrive on their incompatibility. Usually the reason for the conflict is minor and the partners seldom resolve their disputes.

since you asked

If a couple is fighting all the time, should they get a divorce?

- In a **devitalized marriage,** the partners were deeply in love when they married. As the years go by, they spend time together—raising the children, entertaining, and meeting community responsibilities—but begin to do so out of obligation rather than love. They get along and, as a result, do not consider a divorce. Although one or both partners may be unhappy, they are both resigned to staying married.

- In a **passive-congenial marriage,** the partners have a low emotional investment in the marriage and few expectations of each other. Fairly independent, they achieve satisfaction from other relationships, such as those with their children, friends, and co-workers. They often maintain separate activities

and interests. Passive-congenial couples emphasize the practicality of the marriage over emotional intensity.

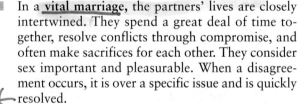

- In a **vital marriage,** the partners' lives are closely intertwined. They spend a great deal of time together, resolve conflicts through compromise, and often make sacrifices for each other. They consider sex important and pleasurable. When a disagreement occurs, it is over a specific issue and is quickly resolved.

- In a **total marriage,** which is similar to a vital marriage, the partners participate in each other's lives at all levels and have few areas of tension or unresolved hostility. Spouses share many facets of their lives; they may work together or have the same friends and outside interests. This type of marriage is more encompassing than a vital marriage.

Finding that approximately 80 percent of the marriages they studied fell into the first three categories, Cuber and Haroff characterized these as *utilitarian marriages* because they appeared to be based on convenience. The researchers called the last two types *intrinsic marriages* because the relationships seemed to be inherently rewarding. In their study, vital marriages accounted for 15 percent of the population and total marriages for only 5 percent.

Benjamin Franklin and his wife, Deborah, presumably had a close marriage. During 18 of their 44 years of marriage, however, they lived apart because Franklin represented the United States at the royal court of French King Louis XVI. According to some historians, Franklin enjoyed his LAT marriage (see text) because he was a "babe magnet" who was surrounded by adoring women. His wife, loyal to the end, tolerated Franklin's sexual "dalliances."

The Cuber–Haroff typology and others are useful in showing that there are many types of marriages and marital relationships (see, for example, Olson and Olson, 2000). Often, however, the research is based on middle-class and upper-middle-class couples that are probably not representative of most U.S. marriages.

Some Cross-Cultural Variations in Marriage Types

Marriage forms vary across cultures. Some couples live in LAT (living apart together) relationships because of economic or personal reasons. In China, for instance, growing numbers of rural husbands are going to urban areas to look for jobs. The men work temporarily in nearby cities to bring cash back home while their wives stay on the land. In these LAT marriages, "the husband works in town and the wife plows the field" (Sheng, 2005: 108).

In some Scandinavian countries, similarly, some LAT couples are married but have moved apart to save the relationship. They live in separate homes because "too many quarrels and too much irritation would have made the relationship deteriorate." Some maintain such arrangements indefinitely. For others, the LAT separation "might turn out to be the first step toward a calm divorce" (Trost and Levin, 2005: 358). In other marital forms, custom and tradition take precedence over personal options and even laws (see the box "Forced to Marry before Puberty").

Marital Success and Happiness

When a journalist interviewed couples celebrating their fiftieth or later wedding anniversaries, she found some common characteristics: mutual respect, common goals, supportive spouses, and a focus on communication and problem solving rather than on winning battles. Disagreements did occur, but they were toned down. As a 77-year-old woman said about her husband,

> *In all our 55 years, he has rarely gotten angry. If I get angry about something, we have a little argument, and he'll say something funny to me. I'll have to laugh and there goes the argument. Laughter has always been a big part of our life (Licht, 1995: 19).*

Researchers usually measure marital success according to "marital stability" and "marital satisfaction." *Marital stability* refers to whether a marriage is intact and whether the spouses have ever suggested divorce to each other (Noller and Fitzpatrick, 1993; Holman et al., 1994). *Marital satisfaction* refers to whether a husband or wife sees their marriage as good. In assessing the quality of relationships, researchers have used such concepts as adjustment, lack of distress, contentment, happiness, and success (Fincham and Bradbury, 1987; Glenn, 1991).

Are Married Couples Happy?

Since 1973, the University of Chicago's National Opinion Research Center has asked nationally representative samples of Americans to rate their marital happiness. The percentage saying that they're "very happy" has decreased somewhat since the 1970s but remains above 60 percent (see *Figure 10.2*). In a more recent national study, 69 percent of the respondents said that their marriages were "very happy" (Glenn, 2005).

Because happiness is a self-reported and highly subjective measure, it's impossible to know how respondents define happiness. Do they mean a "passive-congenial" marriage? Acceptance of the status quo because "things could be worse"? Better than being alone? Or something else?

Although the measures are subjective, many of the findings have been fairly consistent. For example, both marital stability and marital satisfaction tend to be higher for whites than for African Americans, for those with a college education or higher, for those who say that they are religious, and for those who married after age 20 instead of during their teens.

At least some of these variables reflect economic stress. Marital happiness decreases when couples experience poverty, job loss, and financial problems. All

Cross-Cultural Families

Forced to Marry before Puberty

When she was 11, Mwaka's father married her to a man in his forties to repay a $16 debt. The father had borrowed the money from his neighbor to feed his wife and five children. In another case, a father gave his daughter Rachel, 12, to a 50-year-old acquaintance in exchange for a bull.

In some rural pockets throughout sub-Saharan countries—from Ghana to Kenya to Zambia—such forced marriages are fairly common. Because custom decrees that children in patriarchal tribes belong to the father, girls as young as 10 years old can be traded as marriage partners—sometimes to men in their sixties—to finance a brother's wedding, to educate sons, to buy food or cattle, or to settle debts:

The consequences of these forced marriages are staggering: adolescence and schooling cut short; early pregnancies and hazardous births; adulthood often condemned to subservience. The list has grown to include exposure to HIV at an age when girls do not grasp the risks of AIDS (LaFraniere, 2005: A1).

For the most part, government officials have been unsuccessful in protecting the girls because many marriages are governed not by civil law but by traditional customs in which "the control is with the man." In some African countries, such as Malawi, forced marriages are becoming more common in communities that have been hard hit by famine. According to a director of social welfare services, "Households that can no longer fend for themselves opt to sell off their children to wealthier households" (LaFraniere, 2005: 1A).

Stop and Think. . .

- How does forced marriage, especially for young girls, reflect and reinforce men's superior status in patriarchal societies? Who gains from such practices?
- Is forced marriage—regardless of a girl's age—inhumane, as some women's rights advocates claim? Or does every society have the right to establish its own rules about marriage?

these events are more likely for couples at lower socioeconomic levels, of whom a disproportionate number are African American (Bradbury and Karney, 2004; Lewin, 2004; Smock, 2004; Glenn, 2005).

Higher socioeconomic status contributes to marital well-being, but it doesn't guarantee either stability or satisfaction. Individual factors are also important in shaping the quality of a marriage.

What's Important in a Successful Marriage?

Is there a recipe for an enduring and happy marriage? Researchers have been searching for an answer to this question for decades. Despite what advice manuals say, there are no 10, 12, or 20 steps for living happily ever after. Social scientists have uncovered some aspects of marital relations that describe satisfying and stable marriages, however.

since you asked

Is there a formula for a happy marriage?

COMPATIBILITY Initially, people are attracted to each other because of similar attitudes, values, and beliefs. Similar social backgrounds (such as ethnicity, religion, and education) decrease major interpersonal differences that can lead to conflict and disagreements (see Chapter 8).

After marriage, personality becomes increasingly important in maintaining a relationship. Couples are happier when they have similar personalities and emotional "wavelengths." Unlike dating, marriage requires regular interaction and extensive coordination in dealing

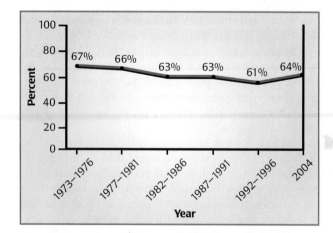

FIGURE 10.2 Percentage of Married People Age 18 and Older Who Said That Their Marriages Are "Very Happy"

SOURCES: Based on Smith, 1999, Table 9, and General Social Survey, 2004.

with the tasks, issues, and problems of daily living (Whyte, 1990; Luo and Klohnen, 2005).

Despite popular opinion, couples who play together don't necessarily stay together. Couples who participate together in leisure activities (such as watching television or going for a walk) that only one spouse likes become dissatisfied over time. Women, especially, are likely to engage in recreational activities that only their husbands enjoy. The more time women spend in those activities, the more likely they are to end up being unhappy with their marriage (Crawford et al., 2002; Gager and Sanchez, 2003).

FLEXIBILITY Our relationships are never 100 percent compatible. One spouse may be better organized or more outgoing than the other, for example. Happily

married couples, however, are more likely than their unhappy counterparts to discuss how to handle and adjust to such differences (Olson and Olson, 2000).

At the beginning of this chapter, the husband of the longest-married couple in the world said that their marriage had lasted so long because "It's a lot of give and take." Happily married people are flexible and compromise rather than trying to control their spouses or insisting on doing everything their own way. Flexible partners often accommodate the other person's needs and enjoy doing so (Schwartz, 2006).

POSITIVE ATTITUDES Spouses who like each other "as a person" and a good friend have happier marriages. Couples whose marriages begin in romantic bliss are especially prone to divorce because it's difficult to maintain

Ask Yourself

How Close Is Our Relationship?

All marriages and other long-term relationships go through difficult times. When we feel valued by our partner, however, positive feelings overcome hurtful moments. This short quiz will give you an idea of whether you and your partner appreciate each other.

True	False	
☐	☐	1. I look forward to spending much of my free time with my partner.
☐	☐	2. At the end of the day, my partner is glad to see me.
☐	☐	3. My partner is usually interested in hearing my views.
☐	☐	4. We enjoy talking to each other.
☐	☐	5. We have fun together.
☐	☐	6. We are spiritually compatible.
☐	☐	7. We share the same basic values.
☐	☐	8. We have many of the same dreams and goals.
☐	☐	9. Even though our activities are different, I enjoy my partner's interests.
☐	☐	10. Despite busy schedules, we make time for each other.
☐	☐	11. My partner tells me when he or she has had a bad day.
☐	☐	12. We make decisions together, including how to spend our money.

SOURCES: Based on Gottman and Silver, 1999, and Schwartz, 2006.

Scoring

Give yourself one point for each true answer. If you score 10 or above, your marriage (or relationship) is strong. If you score below 10, your marriage (or relationship) could use some improvement.

such intensity. Couples who marry after a whirlwind courtship are quickly disillusioned because they're saddled with fantasies and unrealistic expectations about married life (Pittman, 1999; Ted Huston, cited in Patz, 2000). The "How Close Is Our Relationship?" quiz may help you determine whether you and your spouse (or other partner) have positive attitudes about each other.

COMMUNICATION AND CONFLICT RESOLUTION

Compared with unhappy couples, happy couples recognize and work at resolving problems and disagreements. Sometimes conflict resolution means backing off because one or both partners are hurt or angry. For example, a salesperson who has been married 36 years advises,

> *Discuss your problems in a normal voice. If a voice is raised, stop. Return after a short period of time. Start again. After a period of time both parties will be able to deal with their problems and not say things that they will be sorry about later (Lauer and Lauer, 1985: 23).*

Couples that have been happily married 50 years or longer say that resolving conflict is a key ingredient for marital success. For example, "When differences arise, resolve them through discussion"; "Talk out problems, work out mutual solutions, and compromise"; "You must never go to sleep bad friends"; and "You must never be afraid to say 'sorry'" (Kurland, 2004; "Secret to Wedded Bliss," 2005).

EMOTIONAL SUPPORT

According to happily married couples, emotional support is much more important than romantic love. Some of their comments about trust, cooperation, and respect are instructive:

> *He makes me feel smart, pretty, capable, and cherished (Married 21 years).*

> *I asked my husband why he thought our marriage was a success. He said it was because we don't "compete with each other" and because we "respect each other's independence." I agree (Married 33 years).*

> *Whatever we had was ours, not yours or mine. We rarely borrowed money and paid all bills on time (Married 60 years) (Mathias, 1992: B5; Kurland, 2004: 65).*

In contrast, partners in unhappy marriages keep trying to change each other to fulfill their own needs. They often become frustrated and angry when their efforts fail. Instead of cooling off and thinking a problem through, as the salesperson quoted earlier advises, the partners react when they're upset. For example, a 103-year-old man who recently celebrated his eightieth wedding anniversary advised, "When a woman is upset, keep quiet."

Such advice is equally useful for a wife whose husband is angry. Even if hostile and sarcastic comments don't lead to verbal or physical abuse, they are unhealthy in a marriage.

How Does Marriage Affect Health?

Actress Zsa Zsa Gabor once said, "Husbands are like fires: They go out when unattended." Most American husbands must be forest fires because, according to much research, they are usually very well attended.

The Health Benefits of Marriage

Some writers describe marriage as having "medical power" (Waite and Gallagher, 2000). Overall, married people are generally healthier and happier than people

Reprinted with special permission of King Features Syndicate.

since you asked

Are married people healthier than those who are single?

who are single, divorced, or widowed. Married people have lower rates of heart disease, cancer, stroke, pneumonia, tuberculosis, cirrhosis of the liver, and syphilis. They attempt suicide less frequently and have fewer automobile accidents than do singles. They are less likely to suffer from depression, anxiety, and other forms of psychological distress. Married people are also less likely to say that they are sick, to be disabled, to visit a doctor, or to be hospitalized than are unmarried people (Horwitz et al., 1996; Wickrama et al., 1997; Schoenborn, 2004. We'll examine the economic benefits of marriage in Chapter 13).

Why is there a general positive association between marriage and physical and psychological well-being? The two major sociological explanations have to do with selection and protection.

THE "SELECTION EFFECT" Some researchers claim that married people are healthier than their unmarried counterparts because of a "selection effect." Healthy people are attracted to other healthy people and are more desirable marriage partners than people who are less healthy. In contrast, sick people tend to marry other sick people. This may be because they share similar emotional stresses and lifestyles, including poor diets and alcohol usage (Booth and Johnson, 1994; Wilson, 2002).

THE "PROTECTION EFFECT" Other researchers maintain that it's not mate selection, but marriage itself, that makes people healthier. Receiving emotional, social, and physical support from a spouse improves one's general health and life span by reducing anxiety and preventing or lessening depression. Marriage may also decrease risky activities and encourage healthy behaviors. For example, married people (especially men) are more likely to quit smoking and less likely to drink heavily, to get into fights, or to drive too fast—risks that increase the likelihood of accidents and injuries (Murray, 2000; Kiecolt-Glaser and Newton, 2001).

And when one partner becomes ill, the physical and emotional support that a spouse provides during recuperation after surgery or other medical treatment can help speed recovery. Such support, however, typically comes from wives rather than from husbands and results in gender differences in health.

Gender and Health

A number of studies show that married women are less healthy than married men. On average, women live longer than men. Still, unlike husbands, many wives experience depression and other health problems.

WHY HUSBANDS ARE HEALTHY Many married men enjoy "emotional capital" because wives provide nurturing and companionship. Men routinely report that their greatest (and sometimes only) confidantes are their wives, whereas married women often talk to close friends and relatives. Thus, husbands can depend on their wives for caring and emotional support, but wives often look outside the marriage for close personal relationships (Steil, 1997; Maushart, 2002).

Wives tend to encourage behaviors that prolong life, such as regular medical checkups. Marriage also often introduces lifestyle changes that reduce some of men's bad habits:

> *Being married involves new sets of responsibilities, mutual caring, intimacy, and increased adult contacts, as well as less time spent in bars and at parties frequented by singles—the "singles scene," where a lot of smoking, drinking, and illicit drug use tend to take place (Bachman et al., 1997: 172).*

If husbands work long hours, there's no effect on their wives' health. If wives work more than 40 hours a week, however, their husbands are significantly less healthy than other married men because they depend on their wives (even those who work long hours) to take care of their well-being, both physically and emotionally (Stolzenberg, 2001).

A review of almost 35 years of research found that a stable marriage is only one of seven factors that affect men's longevity. The other factors included alcohol use, drug abuse, smoking, exercise, coping mechanisms for stress, and depression (Cole and Dendukuri, 2003). Thus, marriage alone does not work miracles in extending married men's lives.

The one recent negative health indicator for married men is weight. Compared with both married women and other males, married men are more likely to be overweight or obese (see *Figure 10.3*). The weight problems may be due to a number of variables, such as having a sedentary job, not exercising, eating high-fat meals (especially at work), or consuming alcohol (which is high in calories). Regardless of the reasons, being overweight or obese increases married men's chances of dying early due to heart disease, diabetes, or other medical problems.

WHY WIVES ARE LESS HEALTHY Women typically are more attuned than men to the emotional quality of marriages. They work harder if the marriage is distressed, have many domestic responsibilities even if they work outside the home, have little time to "unwind," and neglect their own health while caring for family members, including their husbands (Kiecolt-Glaser and Newton, 2001).

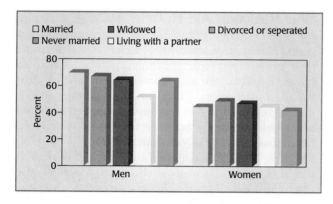

FIGURE 10.3 **Married Men are Most Likely to be Overweight or Obese**

Note: *Overweight* or *obese* is defined as a body mass index (BMI) greater than or equal to 25. BMI is based on one's height and weight.

Source: Schoenborn, 2004, Figure 5.

Employed wives—especially those with children—are at especially high risk for depression. They often feel overwhelmed by the chronic strain of meeting the needs of their husband and children while also working full time (Nolen-Hoeksema et al., 1999).

According to a recent national survey, African American men benefit more from marriage than do African American women. Married black women report poorer physical health than unmarried black women, married or unmarried black men, and white married couples (Blackman et al., 2005).

Why does the health of African American women suffer once they marry? So far, there's no single explanation. Black wives who are employed may experience more stress at work because of discrimination. Besides their work roles, many African American women often care for elderly relatives or the children of kin who are incarcerated, have more household responsibilities than their husbands, and may have to cope with an unfaithful husband. Because of all these stresses, African American women often don't make the time to visit doctors and, generally, don't take care of themselves because they are too busy meeting the needs of their children, husband, and in-laws (Shatzkin, 2005).

Marital Quality and Health

Marriage itself isn't a magic potion that makes us healthier and happier. The *quality* of our marriages is much more important for our health than simply getting or being married.

MARRIAGE AND LIFE SATISFACTION Many of us feel that marriage will make us happier than we are. That's not the case. Married people are happier than unmarried people because marriage *improves* an already happy life. People who are very satisfied with life and have a rich social network of family members, friends, and co-workers have little to gain from marriage. On the other hand, people who are lonely and dissatisfied with life can get companionship by marrying (Lucas et al., 2003).

TROUBLED MARRIAGES The quality of the marriage is critical for our emotional and physical well-being. Among other things, a spouse may increase stress levels. Over the years, stress can contribute to higher blood pressure, which, in turn, leads to heart disease. Emotional stress can also create psychological and physical problems that affect the spouses' work roles. A wife might "medicate" herself with pills and a husband might turn to alcohol to decrease the stress (Barnett et al., 2005; "Medical Memo. . . ," 2005).

People who are unhappy in their marriages don't always end up in divorce court. Instead, they may experience marital burnout.

Marital Burnout

Marital burnout is the gradual deterioration of love and ultimate loss of an emotional attachment between partners. The process can go on for many years. In marital burnout, even if the spouses share housework and child care, one spouse may not give the other emotional support. One spouse may complain that the other isn't confiding his or her innermost thoughts and feelings or doesn't want to discuss problems (R. J. Erickson, 1993; Kayser, 1993).

Marital burnout can develop so slowly and quietly that the couple is not aware of it. Sometimes one partner hides dissatisfaction for many years. At other times both partners may ignore the warning signs (see the box "Am I Heading toward Marital Burnout?"). Social exchange theory (see Chapter 2) suggests that when the costs in the relationship become much greater than the benefits, the couple will probably seek a divorce.

Marital Roles

When people marry, they have certain expectations about their marital roles. **Marital roles** are the specific ways in which married couples define their behavior and structure their time. Even if the partners have lived together before marriage, they experience changes when they marry. Who will do what housework? Who's responsible for paying the bills? Who's in charge of which child care tasks?

Constraints

Am I Heading toward Marital Burnout?

All marriages have ups and downs. Checking off even as many as seven of the following items doesn't necessarily mean that your marriage is in trouble. However, the more items you check, the wiser you may be to look further into these symptoms of marital burnout. The earlier you recognize some of these symptoms, according to some health practitioners, the better your chances of improving your marriage.

■ You've lost interest in each other.

■ You feel bored with each other.

■ There's a lack of communication; neither of you listens to the other.

■ You seem to have little in common.

■ Deep down, you want a divorce.

■ There's a lack of flexibility: You can no longer compromise with each other.

■ Minor irritations become major issues.

■ You no longer try to deal honestly with important issues.

■ You find yourself making family decisions alone.

■ You have no desire for physical touching of any kind.

■ Your relationships with other people are more intimate than your relationship with your spouse.

■ The children have begun to act up; they have frequent problems at school, get into fights with friends, or withdraw.

■ One of you controls the other through tantrums, violence, or threats of suicide or violence.

■ You are both putting your own individual interests before the good of the marriage.

■ You can't talk about money, politics, religion, sex, or other touchy subjects.

■ You avoid each other.

■ One or both of you subjects the other to public humiliation.

■ You have increasing health problems, such as headaches, back pain, sleeplessness, high blood pressure, recurring colds, or emotional ups and downs.

■ One or both of you is abusing alcohol or other drugs.

■ Shared activities and attendance at family functions decrease.

■ One or both of you is irritable and sarcastic.

■ You are staying in the relationship because it is easier than being on your own.

SOURCES: Based on Stinnett and DeFrain, 1985; Kayser, 1993.

Stop and Think . . .

• Have you experienced marital burnout? If so, what, if anything, did you do about it?

• Why do you think that many married couples—especially those who have been married at least 50 years—never experience marital burnout?

"His and Her Marriage"

More than 30 years ago, sociologist Jessie Bernard (1973) coined the phrase "his and her marriage." She argued that most men and women experience marriage differently. Because men make fewer adjustments to marriage than women, Bernard wrote, "his marriage is better than hers."

NEW ROLES Whether his marriage is better than hers is debatable. However, much research supports Bernard's observation that there are many gender differences in married life (Nock, 1998). Consider the process of identity bargaining, in which newly married partners adjust their idealized expectations to the realities of living together. In **identity bargaining,** partners

negotiate adjustments to their new roles as husband and wife.

In these negotiations, gender—rather than age, personality, intelligence, or employment, for example—is generally the best predictor of marital roles. According to sociologist Susan Maushart (2002), wives contribute 100 percent of the husband care—the myriad tasks of physical and emotional nurture that she calls "wifework." Wifework includes

since you asked

Why do newlyweds seem to have so many problems?

■ Performing up to three-quarters of the unpaid household labor.

- Assuming total responsibility for the husband's emotional caretaking (from organizing his underwear drawer to arranging his social life).

- Taking full responsibility for child care drudgework (laundry, meals, shopping) so that he can enjoy leisure time (games, sports, watching television with the kids).

- Monitoring his physical well-being (providing a healthful diet, making medical appointments).

- Preparing meals tailored to his taste, appetite, and schedule.

- Maintaining his extended family relationships (buying presents, sending thank-you notes, staging and catering family gatherings).

Maushart contends that there is no reciprocal "husbandwork" in many marriages in which husbands maintain their wives' well-being.

MORE ROLES Marriage also increases the number of roles that each partner performs, thereby raising the potential for role conflict (see Chapter 5). If both partners are employed, for example, they may feel strain in living up to extended family members' expectations to visit or spend time together. Or, in the case of one of our friends, the wife's father assumed that his new son-in-law would be "glad" to spend Saturdays on the father-in-law's home improvement tasks. The son-in-law resented the intrusion on his weekend activities but felt that he couldn't refuse.

Couples also add more roles if they associate with one (or both) of the partner's friends, attend her or his religious services, or join new community organizations. Some women must take on the most demanding role of all—that of mother—very quickly because as many as 13 percent of women are pregnant when they marry (Abma et al., 1997). A man must also cope with the multiple roles of husband and father.

Variations in Domestic Roles

Domestic work includes two major activities: housekeeping (cooking, cleaning, laundering, outdoor work, repairs) and child rearing. Domestic work varies according to such factors as age, stage of life, employment (see Chapter 13), gender, the presence of children, race and ethnicity, and social class. Let's look at a few of these variables.

GENDER Although men's domestic work has increased since the 1970s, married women still do at least twice as much housework as men do. This means that wives

TABLE 10.1

How Much Time Do Wives and Husbands Spend on Housework Each Week?

Wives Report	Husbands Report
26 hours for self	18 hours for self
13 hours for husband	25 hours for wife

SOURCE: Based on Lee and Waite, 2005, Table 2.

spend the equivalent of almost two full days more on housework than their husbands each week (Lee and Waite, 2005).

Husbands, however, overestimate the amount of housework they do (see *Table 10.1*). It's not clear whether this is because men are comparing themselves to their fathers (who did very little) or whether they include occasional domestic tasks as "housework" (such as driving the kids to athletic practices or paying bills) (Coltrane, 2000).

EMPLOYMENT Husbands whose wives work outside the home perform more household tasks, largely because their wives are not home to do "their share." However, men are less likely to increase the time they spend doing housework if the wife earns more than the husband. A couple in which the wife earns more than her husband is still considered "deviant." As a result, women may do more housework to maintain the traditional gender role expectation that women *should* do more housework than men. Otherwise, the husband is seen as economically dependent on his wife and "not really a man" (Evertsson and Nermo, 2004; Davis and Greenstein, 2004; see, also, Chapter 13).

In two-earner working-class families in which both partners grew up in traditional homes where household tasks were sex-segregated, marital quality may be higher when the household labor is *not* collaborative. The woman may not want to give up control of traditionally female tasks, including housework. Men may sometimes resent being asked to do traditionally female household tasks, feeling that their time and energy should be focused on breadwinning (Helms-Erikson, 2001).

THE PRESENCE OF CHILDREN Although child rearing is highly rewarding, it's also a 24-hour, 7-day job that's physically exhausting and emotionally draining. When couples have children, mothers increase their household work by almost 23 tasks per day compared with six tasks per day for fathers. Even when wives work full time, they are three times more likely than husbands to perform "dirty tasks" such as changing the baby's diaper and doing the laundry. And as the number of children increases, so does women's share of child rearing and housework (Coltrane, 2000; Huston and Holmes, 2004; Perry-Jenkins et al., 2004).

Are the differences in such child-rearing tasks "unfair"? And are mothers more likely than fathers to feel that men aren't doing enough? It depends on the fathers' participation. If, for example, fathers of infants perform some of the unpleasant tasks (such as changing diapers and not just giving baths) or take on more household chores, spouses tend to see such divisions of labor as fair and experience few conflicts about domestic tasks (Feeney and Noller, 2002).

RACE AND ETHNICITY Men's housework roles often vary by race and ethnicity. For example, employed Latino and African American men spend more time doing household tasks than employed white men do, including such typically female tasks as meal preparation, dishwashing, and house cleaning (see Chapter 4).

Even so, men and women do not share household work equally. Although Latinas, Asian, and African American women have a long history of full-time work outside the home, they still bear a disproportionate share of housework and child care. In two-earner families, for example, black men do only one-third as much household work as women do (Kamo and Cohen, 1998; Kim, 1999).

Although their wives do the major share of child care tasks, some Latino husbands report being much more involved in child rearing than their own fathers were. While there is little sharing of family work in many Latino families, most men and women don't see the wife's much higher contributions as unfair because of cultural values about traditional gender roles (López, 1999; DeBiaggi, 2002; see, also, Chapter 4).

SOCIAL CLASS The division of household labor also varies by social class. The higher a wife's socioeconomic status, the more likely it is that her husband will help with family tasks. Wives with high incomes get more help from their husbands than do wives who are employed at the lower end of the occupational scale (Perry-Jenkins and Folk, 1994; Davis and Greenstein, 2004).

One or more factors may be at work here: Educated, professional women may have more authority in the home, women with high-powered jobs may be required to spend longer hours at work, and successful self-employed women may feel more comfortable asking their spouses for help. In addition, college-educated women tend to be married to college-educated men, who are more likely to endorse gender equity and who tend to do more of the domestic work than men with less education (Coltrane, 2000).

Domestic Roles and Marital Quality

Men are usually happy in their marriage when there's greater equality in decision making but not in housework. Women are happier when there's greater equality in decision making *and* when both spouses share more equally in housework responsibilities (Amato et al., 2003).

Mothers, especially, are least satisfied with their marriages when they have a disproportionate share of domestic and child care responsibilities, have little decision-making power, and do most of the "emotional work" to develop or maintain intimacy. The sense of carrying an unfair burden (rather than the actual amount of work) creates anxiety, erodes the women's emotional and psychological well-being, and increases the risk of depression (Erickson, 2005; Wilcox and Nock, 2006).

Doing an unfair share of housework is also costly to men:

> *If men want the pleasure of living with women and children they are going to have to shape up. All work and no play may have made Jill too dull to understand a football game but all play and no work will make Jack that most vulnerable of creatures, a redundant male (Greer, 1999:136).*

Although such words seem harsh, many women end marriages that they feel they can't mend. Especially in the case of employed women, there's little motivation to stay in marriages in which the costs are significantly and continuously greater than the rewards (see Chapter 5).

What happens when there's a gender gap in domestic roles? In time, women feel worn out and may become dissatisfied with the marriage (Piña and Bengston, 1993). In one case, the gender gap resulted in an essay that has become a classic (see the box "Why I Want a Wife)."

Making Connections

- One writer, you recall, contends that "wifework" characterizes most marriages. Do you agree that there are no comparable "husbandwork" roles?

- Unequal housework increases men's marital satisfaction but decreases women's. How can married couples resolve this dilemma? What's worked for you, for example?

Changes
Why I Want a Wife

The essay excerpted here has been reprinted more than 200 times in at least 10 different countries (Brady, 1990). Written by Judy Brady [then Judy Seiters] in 1972, the article satirizes the traditional view of woman as wife and mother:

I am a wife. . . . Why do I want a wife? . . . I want a wife who will work and send me to school . . . and take care of my children. I want a wife to keep track of the children's doctor and dentist appointments [and] . . . mine, too. I want a wife to make sure my children eat properly and are kept clean. . . . I want a wife who takes care of the children when they are sick, a wife who arranges to be around when the children need special care because . . . I cannot miss classes at school. . . .

I want a wife who will take care of my physical needs. I want a wife who will keep my house clean . . . pick up after me . . . keep my clothes clean, ironed, mended, replaced when need be, and who will see to it that my personal things are kept in their proper place so that I can find what I need the minute I need it. I want a wife who cooks the meals, a wife who is a good cook. I want a wife who will plan the menus, do the necessary grocery shop-

ping, prepare the meals, serve them pleasantly, and then do the cleaning up while I do my studying. I want a wife who will care for me when I am sick and sympathize with my pain. . . .

I want a wife who . . . makes love passionately and eagerly when I feel like it, a wife who makes sure that I am satisfied. And, of course, I want a wife who will not demand sexual attention when I am not in the mood. . . . I want a wife who assumes the complete responsibility for birth control, because I do not want more children. . . .

When I am through with school and have a job, I want my wife to quit working and remain at home so that my wife can more fully and completely take care of a wife's duties.

My God, who wouldn't want a wife?

Stop and Think . . .

- Do you think that this excerpt is outdated, or does it still describe many married women's roles today?
- Write a paragraph or two that would parallel this essay on "Why I Want a Husband."

How Marriages Change Throughout the Life Course

When I read the literature on marriage and think about my own marriage, the key word is probably "adjustment." From a developmental perspective, people perform different roles and learn new tasks as a marriage develops its own structure and identity. Throughout the life course, we must adjust, adjust, adjust—to agreeing on specific goals, to marital changes, and to disagreements and conflict. The adjustments begin with the first year of marriage and continue until we die.

The Early Years of Marriage

The bridal media bombard women with merchandise. Many people spend more on a wedding than the cost of a four-year degree at an average-priced state college (see "Data Digest"). Because most couples don't attend pre-

marital classes, what happens after the romantic wedding ceremonies are over?

AFTER THE VOWS The first year of marriage involves basic adjustments. After the wedding, the groom takes on the new and unfamiliar role of husband. Brides, especially, often experience "marriage shock." Unlike their husbands, many women must take on such "wifely" roles as pleasing the husband's family and friends and being the "emotional guardian" of the marriage (Heyn, 1997). Many experience a "wedding postpartum":

When . . . you find that your new husband blows his nose in the shower, few brides escape feeling some degree of disillusionment. You know then you're not at the champagne fountain anymore. Even though you weren't expecting perpetual bubbly from your marriage, the reality can be startling (Stark, 1998: 88).

It takes some women up to a year to feel comfortable with their new married name and the new identity of "wife" that it brings (Nissinen, 2000).

A second adjustment involves putting a mutual relationship before ties with others. Couples must strike a balance between their relationships with their in-laws and their own marital bond. Parents (especially mothers) who fear losing contact with their married children sometimes create conflict by calling and visiting frequently and "meddling" in the couple's life (Greider, 2000; Viorst, 2003).

SETTLING IN If both partners grew up in families in which the parents were responsive to each other's emotional needs, they have good role models. They are more successful at weathering the effects of marital stress over time (Sabatelli and Bartle-Haring, 2003; Umberson et al., 2005).

Two-paycheck newlyweds—especially those who marry after a long period of independence—must make the transition from "my" money to "our" money. Adjusting to a joint bank account isn't always easy because most people aren't used to pooling their money. In addition, the couple will have to reach a consensus about paying off college loans, credit card debt, mortgage payments (if she just bought a house and he hasn't, for example), and saving for the future. And what if she's a spender and he's a saver?

Marriage and Children

One of the most important functions of the family is to socialize children to become responsible and contributing members of society (see Chapters 1, 4, and 5). In some countries, teens marry at an early age and are considered adults. In Western societies, including the United States, adolescents are dependent on their parents until their late teens and even into their mid- or late twenties. This means that couples spend much of their married life raising their offspring (see Chapter 11).

YOUNG CHILDREN Socializing children takes enormous time and patience. Families with young children spend much of their time teaching them rules, showing them how to live up to cultural expectations, and inculcating such values as doing well at school, following the rules, being kind, controlling one's temper, doing what one is asked, being responsible, and getting along with others (Acock and Demo, 1994).

In general, and as you'll see shortly, marital satisfaction tends to decrease after a couple has children. Most parents experience more frequent conflicts and disagreements after having children than do childless spouses. On the other hand, many couples who marry before their out-of-wedlock child is born enjoy being married. Compared with their unmarried counterparts, after the first year of marriage they report greater financial security, a stable home life, and optimism about both spouses being good parents (Crohan, 1996; Timmer and Orbuch, 2001).

ADOLESCENTS Raising adolescents is difficult. Besides all the usual developmental tasks associated with the physical changes of puberty and emotional maturation, contemporary adolescents face more complicated lives than ever before. Both parents and children may have to cope with divorce, parental unemployment, and such dangers as violence and drugs in their schools and neighborhoods (Cotten, 1999). We'll return to the adolescent years in Chapter 12.

The potential for family stress often increases as adolescents begin to press for autonomy and independence. Conflict sometimes occurs not necessarily because of the children but as a result of a dip in the parents' happiness due to marital burnout or communication problems. Sometimes changes occur suddenly because of geographic moves. Depending on the breadwinner's

In 2005, the British monarchy granted Prince Charles permission to marry Camilla Parker Bowles, his long-time mistress. Prince Charles became the first heir to the throne to marry a divorced woman. Prince Charles was married to Princess Diana in 1981 but they divorced in 1996. The couple had two sons and a stable but unhappy marriage with little communication.

(usually the father's) occupation and career stage, family members may have to adjust to a new community and form new friendships (see Chapter 13).

Marriage at Midlife

Like their younger counterparts, couples in their midlife years (between ages 45 and 65) must continually adapt to new conditions. The most common adjustments involve intergenerational ties, relationships with in-laws, the empty nest syndrome, and the boomerang generation.

INTERGENERATIONAL TIES Our family of origin, you recall, plays a significant role in shaping our values and behavior over the life course (see Chapter 1). Couples may be ambivalent about their intergenerational relationships, however. When families meet for holidays and celebrations, grandparents and other relatives may criticize the parents about how they discipline their children, especially teenagers. Married couples may be torn between pleasing their parents or their spouses. Spouses may also experience strain about accepting help, especially financial assistance, from their parents because such assistance may obligate them in the future (Beaton et al., 2003).

RELATIONSHIPS WITH IN-LAWS There are numerous jokes about mothers-in-law ("Hey guys, looking for a great gift for your mother-in-law on Mother's Day? Why not send her back her daughter!"). In contrast, we rarely, if ever, hear father-in-law jokes. Why?

First, women—not men—typically arrange family gatherings for both their own and their husband's family (Lee et al., 2003). If in-laws are unhappy with the get-togethers, they usually blame the wife and not the husband.

Second, most husbands are mute when their wives encounter in-law problems. This "silent male syndrome" often reflects two male versions of staying out of in-law (especially mother-in-law) conflicts. In one response, the husband tries to avoid the problem by maintaining that "We're all reasonable people." If the wife has problems, she must be the one who's being "unreasonable." The second response by many husbands is that their wives are "making a mountain out of a mole hill." Thus, instead of supporting their wives, many husbands shrug off in-law problems as "hers" and not "mine" (Ehrlich, 2000).

Negative relations with in-laws can decrease marital satisfaction. Even after 20 years of marriage, in-laws can intrude on a couple's marriage and create problems by treating a daughter-in-law or son-in-law with disrespect, openly criticizing how the couple raises their children, and making demands on the married couple, such as spending all holidays together (Bryant et al., 2001; Doherty, 2001).

THE "EMPTY NEST SYNDROME" Social scientists used to characterize middle-aged parents as experiencing the *empty-nest syndrome*—depression and a lessened sense of well-being, especially among women—when children leave home. Some parents, especially mothers who have devoted their lives to bringing up children, feel "empty" and "useless" when their kids fly from the nest.

In fact, the children's departure gives many married couples a chance to relax and to enjoy each other's company:

> *Now that our . . . son is away [at college] we can talk about subjects that interest only us without having to consider whether he feels left out. We can talk about people he doesn't know without explaining who they are. . . . [Or we can] simply eat in companionable silence without the pressure to use mealtime for interacting with our kids (Rosenberg, 1993: 306–07).*

In many cases, then, both parents experience a sense of freedom and easing of responsibility (Antonucci et al., 2001).

Children who leave the nest sometimes return, however. In fact, many middle-aged parents have to live with a "boomerang generation" that keeps flying back to the nest.

THE BOOMERANG GENERATION A recent phenomenon is the **boomerang generation,** young adults who move back into their parents' home after living independently for a while. In the case of a weak economy, low income, divorce, or the high cost of housing, many young adults move back into their parents' home or never leave it in the first place. Parents try to launch their children into the adult world, but, like boomerangs, some keep coming back.

since you asked

Am I a member of the "boomerang generation"?

Boomerang kids can have either a positive or a negative impact on their parents' marital life. Co-residence, for example, has a more negative influence on remarried parents than on parents in their first marriage because of unresolved tensions in the home. As one mother stated,

> *I did like it [living together with my daughter] when she was in a good mood and she was playful. This was far and few between, though. The stress caused by her relationship with her stepfather was especially disruptive to the family (Mitchell and Gee, 1996: 446).*

Marital satisfaction also diminishes when a child returns home several times. The multiple returns prevent some parents from enjoying the greater intimacy, privacy, and freedom to pursue new interests that they expected when their children left home. Marital satisfaction increases, however, if the children have a good relationship with their parents during co-residence. The children can provide assistance, emotional support, advice, and companionship. Thus, they can improve the overall quality of family relationships (Willis and Reid, 1999).

Marriage in Later Life

Many older couples describe their marriage as the best years of their lives. They have developed trust and intimacy over the years, enjoy each other's company, and are happier than their younger counterparts. Couples continue to make adjustments in later life, however, as is evidenced by the "U-shaped curve," retirement, and health issues.

THE U-SHAPED CURVE A number of studies have found a U-shaped curve in marital satisfaction over the life cycle. Initially, romantic love produces a high degree of excitement and attraction in marriage. Marital satisfaction decreases because of the strain caused by family life-cycle events, especially having and raising children. When the children grow up and leave home, marital satisfaction usually increases (Glenn, 1991).

The U-shaped curve varies by ethnicity, gender, and age, however. In a longitudinal study of three generations of Mexican Americans, for example, Markides and his colleagues (1999) found that midlife marital satisfaction declined for women but remained about the same for men. After their children leave home, the researchers suggest, Mexican American women may feel that something is missing from their motherhood role and their marriage. In addition, older Mexican American women often bear the burden of caring for extended family members. Thus, caretaking responsibilities may continue well past midlife and into old age, reducing marital satisfaction.

RETIREMENT Many older couples report an upturn in marital happiness. They have few unresolved issues, settle conflicts more effectively than their younger and middle-aged counterparts, and savor the rewards of a long-term friendship.

Retirement typically brings more time to enjoy each other's company. Gender roles usually don't change very much. Husbands continue to do most of the "male" chores but may take on large-scale projects such as remodeling. Although men might do more shopping, women still invest much of their time in "female" chores such as food preparation, laundry, and cleaning the house (Charles and Carstensen, 2002). The biggest change in later life for both sexes is physical decline.

HEALTH AND WELL-BEING The marital quality of older couples, whether one or both are retired, depends quite a bit on the partners' health. Sexual expression remains an important element in long-term marital relationships, though more so for men than for women. Older spouses who feel valued are happier and live longer than unhappy older couples (Vinick, 2000; Tower et al., 2002; see, also, Chapter 7).

A decline in health often impairs marital quality. Depression, for example, is the most common illness in aging populations. The depressed spouse may have problems communicating and making decisions and may get angry quickly. The nondepressed spouse may feel confused, frustrated, and helpless (Sandberg et al., 2002). If a spouse needs long-term care, whether at home or in a nursing facility, the caregiver undergoes tremendous stress. And if a spouse is widowed, she or he may have to forge new relationships (see Chapter 17).

Power and communication issues affect marital quality throughout the life course. Most of these issues are similar whether people are married or single.

Communication: A Key to Successful Relationships

People who have been married a long time usually give very similar reasons for the success of their long-term relationship: "We never yelled at each other," "We joked around a lot," "We treated each other with respect," "We tried to be patient," and "We accepted what we couldn't change about each other." Effective verbal and nonverbal communication is essential to any committed relationship, not just marriage.

What Is Good Communication?

Our most intimate relationships are within the family. Being able to express thoughts and feelings and to listen are critical components of all close relationships. Let's begin by looking at some of the major goals of effective communication in intimate relationships.

COMMUNICATION GOALS A major goal of effective communication is developing ways of interacting that are clear, nonjudgmental, and nonpunitive. A second important goal is resolving conflicts through problem solving rather than coercion or manipulation. Very little can be gained "if someone tells us how we are *supposed* to feel, how we are *supposed* to behave, or what we are *supposed* to do with our lives" (Aronson, 1995: 404).

Good communication conveys *what* we and others feel. It incorporates different approaches that are equally valid (as when people agree to disagree). Effective communication also establishes an atmosphere of trust and honesty in resolving—or at least decreasing—conflict. An important first step in successful communication is self-disclosure.

SELF-DISCLOSURE Self-disclosure is telling another person about oneself and one's thoughts and feelings with the expectation that truly open communication will follow (see, also, Chapter 6). *Reciprocity* is important if self-disclosure is to be an effective aspect of communication and conflict resolution. In terms of exchange theory, reciprocal self-disclosure increases partners' liking and trusting each other, eliminates a lot of guesswork in the relationship, and helps balance costs and benefits.

Women tend to disclose more than men do but to hold back when they anticipate an uncaring, unemotional, or otherwise negative response. Men tend to disclose more to women than to men. They often don't disclose, however, when they feel that they will get an emotional (rather than an objective and dispassionate) response (Arliss, 1991).

Disclosure can be either beneficial or harmful, depending on whether the reaction is supportive or worsens already negative feelings. Disclosure is beneficial under four conditions (Derlega et al., 1993):

- *Esteem support* can reduce a person's anxiety about troubling events. If the listener is attentive, sympathetic, and uncritical, disclosure can motivate people to change significant aspects of their lives.

- A listener may be able to offer *information support* through advice and guidance. For example, people who are under stress may benefit by knowing that their problems are not due to personal deficiencies.

- Disclosure can provide *instrumental support* if the listener offers concrete help, such as shopping for food or caring for the children when the partner is sick.

- Even if a problem is not easily solved, listeners can provide *motivational support*. For example, if a husband is distressed about losing his job, his wife can encourage him to keep "pounding the pavement" and assure him that "we can get through this."

When is self-disclosure detrimental? If feedback is negative, disclosure may intensify a person's already low self-esteem. (Disclosure: "I'm so mad at myself for not sticking to my diet." Response: "Yeah; if you had, you'd have something to wear to the party tonight.")

Where self-esteem is strong, even negative feedback will not be devastating. One of my students, in her mid-fifties, said that she was anxious about attending an honors banquet for students with outstanding GPAs because "I'll look like everyone's grandmother." Expecting support, she asked her husband to attend the ceremony with her because she felt "out of place." He replied, "Well, just don't go. Everyone will wonder what an old lady is doing there and no one will hire you, anyway." (She attended alone, had a wonderful time, and accepted a job offer by the end of the summer. She also divorced her husband a year later.)

Self-disclosure is risky. People gain "information power" through self-revelation that they can then use against a partner ("Well, you had an affair, so you have no right to complain about anything"). If the self-disclosure is one-sided, it sends the message that "I don't trust you enough to tell you about my flaws" (Galvin

DILBERT reprinted by permission of United Feature Syndicate, Inc.

and Brommel, 2000). If a trust is violated, partners are unlikely to reveal intimate information about themselves in the future.

Do men and women differ in self-disclosure and other communication patterns? And if they differ, is the interaction innate or learned?

Sex Differences in Communication

In recent years, "communication" has become a buzzword to summarize problems in male–female relationships. We'll first consider some of the studies that suggest that men and women speak differently. Then we'll examine some of the research which shows that communication variations aren't biologically based but reflect differences in gender roles and power.

since you asked

Do women and men communicate differently?

WOMEN'S SPEECH Because women tend to use communication to develop and maintain relationships, *talk is often an end in itself*. It is a way to foster closeness and understanding. A second important characteristic of women's speech is the *effort to establish equality*. Thus, women often encourage a speaker to continue by showing interest or concern ("Oh, really?" or "I feel the same way sometimes"). Or they may use affirmation, showing support for others ("You must have felt terrible" or "I think you're right").

Women often ask questions that *probe for greater understanding* of feelings and perceptions ("Do you think it was deliberate?" or "Were you glad it happened?"). Women also do *conversational "maintenance work."* They may ask a number of questions that encourage conversation ("Tell me what happened at the meeting").

Another quality of women's speech is a *personal, concrete style*: Women often use details, personal disclosures, and anecdotes. By using concrete rather than vague language, women's talk clarifies issues and feelings so that people are able to understand and identify with each other. *References to emotions* ("Wasn't it depressing when . . .?") personalize the communication and makes it more intimate.

A final feature of women's speech is tentativeness. This may be expressed in a number of ways. *Verbal hedges* ("I kind of feel you may be wrong") and qualifiers ("I may not be right, but . . .") modify, soften, or weaken other words or phrases. Men often give direct commands ("Let's go"), whereas women appear to show uncertainty by hedging ("I guess it's time to go").

Women also use more *verbal fillers*—words or phrases such as "okay," "well," "you know," and "like"—to fill silences. *Verbal fluencies*—sounds such as "mmh," "ahh," and "unhuh"—serve the same purpose. Women use fillers and fluencies much more frequently when talking to men than when talking to other women (Pearson, 1985; Lakoff, 1990; Fitzpatrick and Mulac, 1995).

MEN'S SPEECH A prominent feature of men's speech is *instrumentality*; men tend to use speech to accomplish specific purposes ("Give me three reasons why I should . . ."). They often focus on problem solving: getting information, discovering facts, and suggesting courses of action or solutions. Thus, for men, speech is more often the *means to an end* rather than the end itself.

Masculine speech is also characterized by *exerting control* to establish, enhance, or defend personal status and ideas by asserting oneself and, often, challenging others ("I'll need more information to make a decision").

Men are much less likely than women to offer empathic remarks ("That must have been very difficult for you"). Men are also less likely to express sympathy or to divulge personal information about themselves.

Another feature of men's communication is *conversational dominance*. In most contexts, men tend to dominate the conversation, speaking more frequently and for longer periods. They also show dominance by interrupting others, reinterpreting the speaker's meaning, or rerouting the conversation. Men tend to express themselves in assertive, often absolutist, ways ("That approach won't work").

Compared with women's talk, men's language is typically more forceful, direct, and authoritative; tentativeness is rare. Finally, men are more apt to *communicate in abstract terms* ("What about using another paradigm?"), a reflection of their more impersonal, public style (Tannen, 1990, 1994; Roberts, 2000).

GENDER ROLES, COMMUNICATION, AND SOCIAL CONTEXT Some researchers consider the "female speech" and "male speech" dichotomy to be stereotypical. The notion that women and men come from "two cultures" (or, worse yet, from two planets) ignores the importance of gender roles and social context.

Gender roles shape communication. Many men don't communicate in intimate relationships because they are accustomed to being "stress absorbers" and stoics. Although the noncommunicative male is missing an opportunity for intimacy, he is protecting his loved ones from "the disappointment, frustrations, and fears that are part and parcel of his daily work life" (Nowinski, 1993: 122). Instead of focusing on disturbing feelings, many men may turn to alcohol or drugs.

Social context is also important in understanding gender communication styles. Men are more likely to use "men's speech" when interacting with women in general than with their wives. Husbands decrease the interaction distance between themselves and their wives by adopting a more "feminine" style in conversations. Women, in contrast, tend to maintain the same "women's speech" both with their husbands and with men in general (Fitzpatrick and Mulac, 1995).

Communication Problems

Despite our best intentions, many of us don't communicate effectively. Because communication involves *both* partners, we can't control or change our partner's interaction, but we can recognize and do something about our own communication style. Common communication problems include a variety of issues, ranging from not listening to using the "silent treatment."

NOT LISTENING Both partners may be so intent on making their point that they are simply waiting for their turn to speak rather than listening to the other person. Consider a nondiscussion with my husband that occurred while I was revising this textbook several years ago:

> Me: "I haven't had time to do any Christmas shopping yet."
>
> My husband: "I think you should get a new computer. What about a Mac this time?"
>
> Me: "And I'll probably be writing Christmas cards in February."
>
> My husband: "You'd probably be better off with a laptop than a desktop."
>
> Me: "I'll never finish these revisions on time. What I need is a clone."
>
> My husband: "Will the kids be home for dinner tonight?"

Body language conveys powerful messages about listening and interacting. How is this guy ignoring his partner's body language?

This everyday exchange illustrates the common pattern of partners talking but not communicating. One of the most important components of communication is *really* listening to the other person instead of rehearsing what we plan to say when he or she pauses for a breath. Listening and responding are especially critical when partners discuss relationship problems.

NOT RESPONDING TO THE ISSUE AT HAND If partners are not listening to each other, they will not be able to address a problem. There are three common miscommunication patterns. In *cross-complaining,* partners present their own complaints without addressing the other person's point:

> Wife: "I'm tired of spending all my time on the housework. You're not doing your share."
>
> Husband: "If you used your time efficiently, you wouldn't be tired" (Gottman, 1982:111).

In *counterproposals,* a spouse ignores a partner's suggestions and presents his or her own ideas. In *stonewalling,* which is much more common among men than among women, one of the partners may "Hmmmm" or "Uh-huh," but he or she really neither hears nor responds; it's as though the partner has turned into a stone wall (Krokoff, 1987; Gottman, 1994). If a partner is addicted to alcohol or drugs, for example, she or he might refuse to talk about the problem:

> *Whenever someone brings up the [alcohol] issue, he proclaims that they are making a big deal about nothing, are out to get him, or are just plain wrong. No matter how obvious it is to an outsider that the addict's life may be falling apart, he stubbornly refuses to discuss it. If that does not work, he may just get up and walk out (Nowinski, 1993: 137).*

BLAMING, CRITICIZING, AND NAGGING Instead of being listened to and understood, partners may feel neglected or unappreciated. They feel that their spouse or partner magnifies their faults, belittles them, accuses them unjustly, and makes them feel worthless and stupid. The criticism may escalate from specific complaints ("The bank called today and I was embarrassed that your check bounced") to more global and judgmental derision ("Don't you know anything about managing money?!").

The blamer is a faultfinder who criticizes relentlessly and generalizes: "You never do anything right," "You're just like your mother/father." In blaming and criticizing, a partner uses sophisticated communication skills to manipulate a more vulnerable partner

(Gordon, 1993; Burleson and Denton, 1997). If I'm an effective blamer, for example, I can probably convince you that our budget problems are due to *your* over-spending rather than to *my* low salary.

SCAPEGOATING Scapegoating is another way of avoiding honest communication about a problem. By blaming others, we imply that our partners, not we, should change. We may be uncomfortable about being expressive because we grew up in cool and aloof families. Or we might be suspicious about trusting people because a good friend took advantage of us. Regardless of the reasons, blaming parents, teachers, relatives, siblings, or friends for our problems is debilitating and counterproductive (Noller, 1984).

COERCION OR CONTEMPT Partners may be punitive and force their point of view on others. If this works, coercive behavior, which is related to scapegoating, can continue. Contempt can also be devastating. The most visible signs of contempt are insults and name-calling, sarcasm, hostile humor, mockery, and body language such as rolling your eyes, sneering, and curling your upper lip (Gottman, 1994).

As you saw in the "Am I Heading toward Marital Burnout?" box, some of the red flags include efforts to control a partner through tantrums, violence, or threats of suicide or violence. In addition, one partner may subject the other to public humiliation.

THE SILENT TREATMENT People communicate even when they are silent. Silence in various contexts, and at particular points in a conversation, means different things to different people. Sometimes silence saves us from "foot-in-mouth" problems. Not talking to your spouse or partner, however, builds up feelings of anger and hostility. Initially, the "offender" may work very hard to make the silent partner feel loved and to talk about a problem. Eventually, however, the partner who is getting the silent treatment may get fed up, give up, or look for someone else (Rosenberg, 1993).

Power and Conflict in Relationships

Power and conflict are normal and inevitable in close relationships. Both shape communication patterns and decision making. The person who has the power to make decisions often influences many of the dynamics in marriage and in nonmarital relationships.

Sociologists define **power** as the ability to impose one's will on others. Whether we're talking about a dating relationship, a family, or a nation, some individuals and groups have more power than others.

THEORIES OF POWER Some scholars use *resource theories* to explain marital power. Typically, the spouse with more resources has more power in decision making. Thus, a husband who earns more money than his wife or has more control over household finances has more power (Vogler and Pahl, 1994).

Resources are often interrelated. For example, people with high incomes often also have more education or higher occupational status. As women increase their resources through paid work, they become less dependent on their husbands or cohabiting partners and more powerful in demanding that household chores and child care be shared.

SOURCES OF POWER Power is not limited to tangible things such as money. Love, for example, is an important source of power. As you saw in Chapter 8, the *principle of least interest* explains why, in a dating relationship, the person who is less interested is more powerful than the committed partner. In marriage, similarly, if you are more committed to your marriage than your spouse is, you have less power. As a result, you may defer to your partner's wishes, do things you don't want to do, or avoid expressing negative feelings.

Other nonmaterial sources of power include access to information or particular abilities or talents. For example, husbands often have more decision-making power about how to spend money on expensive things, such as houses or cars, because they are typically more knowledgeable about financial matters, investments, and negotiating contracts. In traditional households, the wife may have more power than the husband in furnishing a home or raising children. The wife usually devotes more time to reading informational material, shopping, or becoming familiar with neighborhood professionals, such as pediatricians and dentists, who provide important services.

CONFLICT AND COMMUNICATION *Conflict* refers to discrete, isolated disagreements as well as chronic relationship problems. All partners and families, no matter how supportive and caring they are, experience conflict. A study of married couples found that the majority of participants reported an average of one or two "unpleasant disagreements" per month (McGonagle et al., 1993; Canary et al., 1995).

Comedian Phyllis Diller's quip, "Don't go to bed mad. Stay up and fight!" is actually insightful. Conflict is not in itself a bad thing. If partners recognize it and actively attempt to resolve it, conflict can serve as a catalyst to strengthen relationships. Before considering coping techniques, let's look at some common reasons that couples fight.

Are all celebrity marriages doomed to fail? No. Some, like actress Renee Zellweger (left), married country star singer Kenny Chesney after a whirlwind romance and split up four months later. Others, like Jon Bon Jovi (right) who formed a rock-and-roll band in the 1980s, is still married to his high school sweetheart. They've been married since 1989 because, Bon Jovi jokes, "My wife tells me that if I ever decide to leave, she is coming with me."

What Do Couples Fight About?

Money is at the top of the list of the things couples fight about. Other common areas of disagreement are housework, fidelity, children, and privacy (see, also, Chapter 15 on divorce).

Money

In a national survey, 84 percent of couples said that money creates tension in their marriage and 15 percent said that they fight about money several times a month or more (Regnier and Gengler, 2006).

One reason married couples argue about money is that they don't know or even agree on how much they have. Disagreements arise because wives overstate debt and husbands overstate income. These dissimilar views of the family's finances increase conflict (Zagorsky, 2003).

Although arguments typically erupt over specific expenditures, they are often really based on different values. Because of different financial priorities, both married and unmarried couples lie about their spending habits (see *Figure 10.4*).

Housework

As you saw earlier, women and men often have different attitudes about household work. If they cannot compromise, especially when both partners are employed, tension may rise and quarrels become more frequent.

Fidelity

Fidelity is another common source of friction. For unmarried couples, the most common violations include having sexual intercourse outside the relationship, wanting to date others, and deceiving the partner. As you saw in Chapter 7, extramarital affairs and cybersex are the most serious types of betrayal. Married and unmarried couples also argue about other violations of trust and commitment, such as lying, betraying confidences, and gossiping (Jones and Burdette, 1994; Metts, 1994).

Children

Children are wonderful and sometimes strengthen a marriage (see Chapter 12). They also create stress, tension, and conflict. In addition to feeling stress because of the demands children make on them, partners may have different philosophies about such issues as discipline,

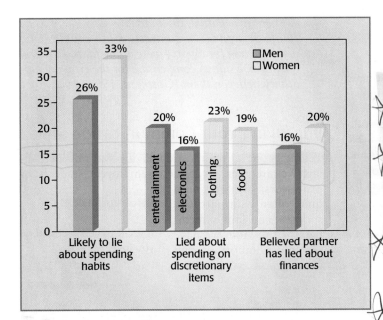

FIGURE 10.4 Love, Lies, and Money

Sources: Based on Singletary, 2005; "Stats & Facts . . ." 2005.

the importance of teaching young children self-control, and the kinds of responsibilities a child should have.

As more spouses (and some partners) collaborate in child rearing, there are more opportunities for clashes between different approaches to child-rearing. For example, although a wife may expect her husband to take on more child care tasks, she may also resent his insistence on making decisions about the child's playmates, bedtimes, or curfews. Children are especially likely to be a source of conflict in remarriages (see Chapter 16).

Privacy

Most of us need and value privacy. No matter how close a couple is, the partners can run into problems if they don't respect each other's privacy, including having the physical space and time to be alone. For example, many men have workshops not because they produce great furniture but because it gives them a place to be alone.

Many couples fight about privacy because they equate it with secrecy, but privacy and secrecy are not synonymous. For example, some couples never open each other's mail or e-mail not because they are afraid a partner may get a letter or message from a lover but because they respect each other's privacy.

How Do Couples Deal with Conflict?

It bears repeating that conflict is a normal part of life. What may *not* be normal or healthy is the way a family handles conflict.

COMMON WAYS OF COPING WITH CONFLICT

Families typically use four techniques to end—though not necessarily resolve—conflict: submission, compromise, standoff, and withdrawal.

Submission. One person submits to another; the conflict ends when one person agrees with or goes along with the other.

Compromise. Partners find a middle ground between their opposing positions; each must give in a little to accept a compromise. The compromise can be suggested either by a partner or by a third party.

Standoff. The disputants drop the argument without resolving it; they agree to disagree and move on to other activities. No one wins or loses, and the conflict ends in a draw.

Withdrawal. When a disputant withdraws, he or she refuses to continue the argument, either by "clamming up" or by leaving the room. Among the four techniques, withdrawal is the most disruptive of family interaction because there is no resolution of the conflict (Vuchinich, 1987).

since you asked

When someone argues with me, should I withdraw?

Except for compromise, these aren't the best ways to resolve conflict.

EFFECTIVE WAYS OF HANDLING CONFLICT

One of the biggest myths about interpersonal relationships is that it's okay to "say what's on your mind" and "let it all hang out." Some partners unleash "emotional napalm" to "blow off some steam" (Noller and Fitzpatrick, 1993: 178).

Displaced rage, unbridled attacks, and physical aggression aren't normal ways of handling conflict. On the other hand, denying the existence of conflict can destroy a relationship. Couples who confront their problems may be unhappy in the short term but will have a better relationship in the long run. Otherwise, the anger and bitterness will fester.

Both researchers and family practitioners have suggested effective ways of dealing with anger and strife, including guidelines for "fighting effectively" (see the box "Ground Rules for Fair Fighting"). Such rules don't ensure a resolution. Because they are based on negotiation and compromise, however, they offer partners a better chance of developing more constructive ways of dealing with conflict.

Productive Communication Patterns

Over time, communication problems can erode intimate relationships. It takes time to forge good communication networks.

Psychologist John Gottman interviewed and studied more than 200 couples over a 20-year period. He found that the difference between lasting marriages and those that split up was a "magic ratio" of five to one—that is, five positive interactions between partners for every negative one:

As long as there was five times as much positive feeling and interaction between husband and wife

as there is negative, the marriage was likely to be stable over time. In contrast, those couples who were heading for divorce were doing far too little on the positive side to compensate for the growing negativity between them (Gottman, 1994: 41).

Improving Your Communication Style

Yelling is one of the most damaging ways of interacting. We rarely scream at guests, employers, students, or professors. Yet we do so quite often with partners, spouses, and family members, with whom we have our most important and

since you asked

Is it OK to yell at someone you love?

Choices

Ground Rules for Fair Fighting

Therapists, counselors, and researchers maintain that arguing the issues is healthier than suffering in silence. Clinicians who work with unhappy couples offer the following advice for changing some of our most destructive interaction patterns:

1. Don't attack your partner. He or she will only become defensive and will be too busy preparing a good rebuttal to hear what you have to say.

2. Avoid ultimatums; no one likes to be backed into a corner.

3. Say what you really mean and don't apologize for it. Lies are harmful, and apologetic people are rarely taken seriously.

4. Avoid accusations and attacks; do not belittle or threaten.

5. Start with your own feelings. "I feel" is better than "You said." Focus on the problem, not on the other person.

6. State your wishes and requests clearly and directly; don't be manipulative, defensive, or sexually seductive.

7. Limit what you say to the present. Avoid long lists of complaints from the past.

8. Refuse to fight dirty:

   ■ No *gunnysacking*, or keeping one's complaints secret and tossing them into an imaginary gunnysack that gets heavier and heavier over time.

   ■ No *passive-aggressive behavior*, or expressing anger indirectly in the form of criticism, sarcasm, nagging, or nitpicking.

   ■ No *silent treatment*; keep the lines of communication open.

   ■ No *name-calling*.

9. Use humor and comic relief. Laugh at yourself and the situation but not at your partner. Learning to take ourselves less seriously and to recognize our flaws without becoming so self-critical that we wallow in shame or self-pity can shorten fights.

10. Strive for closure as soon as possible after a misunderstanding or disagreement by resolving the issue. This prevents dirty fighting and, more important, it holds the partners to their commitment to negotiate until the issue has been resolved or defused (Crosby, 1991a; Rosenzweig, 1992).

Stop and Think . . .

- According to Hendrickson (1994), "a good fight is an essential ingredient" in building a good marriage. Do you agree? Or does keeping silent and sidestepping conflict increase affection and respect?

- Have you ever used similar "rules for fair fighting" in your own relationships? If so, what were the results?

longest-lasting relationships. "Hollering is just part of my personality" is no excuse for obnoxious behavior that injures other people.

According to researchers and practitioners, couples can increase positive communication and decrease negative interaction patterns in the following ways:

Ask for information. If your partner has a complaint ("I never get a chance to talk to you because you're always busy"), address the issue. Don't be defensive ("Well, if you were around more often, we could talk"); find out why your partner is upset.

Don't generalize. Accusations like "You always do X" increase anger and tension.

Stay focused on the issue. Don't bring up past events and old grudges. If you're discussing spending habits, focus on the items that were purchased recently.

Be specific. A specific complaint is easier to deal with than a general criticism. "You never talk to me" is less effective than "I wish we could have 30 minutes each evening without television or the kids."

Keep it honest. Honesty not only means not lying, it means not manipulating others. Do not resort to bullying, outwitting, blaming, dominating, or controlling. Do not become a long-suffering martyr. Truthfulness and sincerity reinforce mutual trust and respect.

Make it kind. Some people use "brutal honesty" as an excuse for cruelty. Temper honesty with positive statements about your partner.

Express appreciation. Thanking your partner for something he or she has done will enhance both the discussion and the relationship.

Use nonverbal communication. Nonverbal acts, such as hugging your partner, smiling, and holding his or her hand, can sometimes be more supportive than anything you might say.

Above all, just listen. Sharpen your emotional communication skills by being really interested in what your partner is saying rather than always focusing on yourself (Knapp and Hall, 1992; Gottman and DeClaire, 2001).

Making Connections

- Think about the conflicts you've experienced with a partner or spouse during the last year or so. What were most of the disagreements about?

- When you and your partner argue, how do you react? How does your partner respond? Do you resolve the conflict? Or does it smolder until the next eruption?

Family Therapy and Marriage and Relationship Programs

Because conflict is inevitable, family therapy and counseling have become a booming industry. Indeed, the number of couples who take premarital tests (which cost up to $500) to determine whether they should marry increased steeply—from 100,000 couples in 1993 to 800,000 in 2004 (Barry, 2005).

Since 2001, the Bush administration has spent $300 million a year on "marriage strengthening" efforts, especially for low-income couples. In 2006, Congress approved $100 million a year for five years for marriage and relationship education (MRE) for high school classes, marriage skills training programs, and a variety of divorce reduction programs. Do therapy and MRE work? The data are mixed.

MARRIAGE EDUCATION PROGRAMS ARE EFFECTIVE

Some studies show that professional and experienced counselors can help couples identify their strengths and weaknesses and improve their relationship. For example, a review of 23 studies of programs for engaged couples concluded that the programs were generally effective. They produced immediate gains in communication processes, conflict management skills, and overall relationship quality that lasted from six months to three years (Carroll and Doherty, 2003).

To determine the effectiveness of MRE programs, a team of scholars examined 13,000 research articles on marriage education, counseling, and therapy programs. Of the 39 studies that were "of the highest quality" scientifically, MRE programs had only a "moderate" effect on improving relationships and a "small" effect on improving communication (Reardon-Anderson et al., 2005).

Despite such modest effects, some scholars point out that MRE programs may provide benefits that studies haven't measured. Some of these benefits might include working on a relationship, deciding not to marry (thus preventing a divorce), and seeking help for an unhealthy and abusive relationship (Ooms, 2005).

MARRIAGE EDUCATION PROGRAMS DON'T WORK

In one survey, people ranked marriage counseling at the bottom of the list of programs designed to improve relationships. Part of the problem is that "almost anyone can hang out a shingle as a marriage counselor" (Kantrowitz and Wingert, 1999). And, as you saw in Chapter 2, the authors of some of the best-selling self-help books include "therapists" who have been divorced at least twice, are estranged from their children, and know less about communication than you or I do.

Many counselors have internalized cultural stereotypes about how women and men should behave based on traditional gender roles (Wright and Fish, 1997). For example, one of my students who sought premarital counseling concluded that it was "a lot of bull":

An older woman in my church told me, in so many words, to put up with whatever my fiancé would throw my way. She said that men run wild but eventually get tired or old and will settle down. She told me that good Christian women stay with their husbands even though they're miserable (Author's files).

Summary

1. Marriage, an important rite of passage into adulthood, is associated with many traditions, rituals, and rules. Many of the rituals reflect historical customs.

2. There are several types of marriage. Most endure despite conflict over such issues as parenting, communication, finances, sex, and religious attitudes.

3. What people consider to be "very important" in marriage hasn't changed much over the years. Both men and women consider love, sexual fidelity, and the ability to discuss feelings to be the most important elements of a good marriage.

4. Marriage generally increases a person's physical and mental health. Married women, however, are less likely to enjoy good health than are married men.

According to one highly regarded family therapist, marital therapists do more harm than good. Many are incompetent. Others remain neutral instead of dealing with a couple's problems, or else they undermine the union ("If you're not happy, why do you stay in the marriage?") (Doherty, 2002).

Researchers also criticize MRE programs because they are expensive and there's little evidence that there are any long-term positive effects. Most important, the programs ignore broad social forces—such as unemployment and poverty—that undermine relationships and marriages by creating financial problems (Halford et al., 2002; Ooms, 2005).

Conclusion

Someone once said that marriages are made in heaven, but the details have to be worked out here on earth. Working out those details is an ongoing process throughout a marriage or other committed relationship. The biggest sources of conflict and *change* are disagreements over money, household work, and communication problems.

Different *choices* can have different consequences. Deciding to have a more egalitarian division of domestic work and child-rearing responsibilities, for example, can diminish some of the *constraints* that many women (and some men) encounter as they juggle multiple roles. Also, deciding to interact more honestly can result in more effective communication and greater interpersonal satisfaction.

Despite the constraints, marriage is one of the most important rites of passage for almost all of us. Another is parenthood, our focus in the next two chapters.

5. Men and women often experience marriage differently. Some of these differences reflect differences in the status of men and women in society and the organization of household and child care tasks.

6. Marriage changes throughout the life course. In general, having children decreases marital satisfaction, but satisfaction increases again when grown children leave the home. Over the years, families adjust to raising young children, communicating with adolescents, and enjoying the empty-nest and retirement stages.

7. Communication is a key to successful intimate relationships. Self-disclosure is an important element of effective communication, but couples should recognize that disclosing all of their innermost thoughts might be detrimental rather than helpful.

8. Most marriages that break down do so not because of conflict but because couples fail to cope adequately with disagreements. Such negative coping strategies as complaining, criticizing, being defensive, and stonewalling may lead to a partner's isolation or withdrawal.

9. Conflict is unavoidable and normal. It is unrealistic to expect communication to cure all marital problems.

Nevertheless, effective communication can decrease the power struggles and hostility that can lead to breakups in marriages and other committed relationships.

10. Marriage and relationship education is booming. Some maintain that such programs are effective; others argue that the costs outweigh the benefits.

Key Terms

engagement *291*
conflict-habituated marriage *294*
devitalized marriage *294*
passive-congenial marriage *294*

vital marriage *294*
total marriage *294*
marital burnout *300*
marital roles *300*

identity bargaining *301*
boomerang generation *306*
self-disclosure *308*
power *311*

Taking It Further

Wedding Bells and Marriage Bytes

If you are planning to marry (or remarry) or just want to improve communication with your partner, here are some informative sites.

Town and Country Wedding Registry has fashions, planning advice, and a free service that helps couples set up Web pages announcing their weddings and wedding registries.

tncweddings.com

Gay Wedding Planners offers same-sex couples around the country complete wedding packages for a civil union ceremony or "a grand wedding event."

www.gayweddingplanners.com

Indiebride, a site for the "independent-minded bride," explores "the highs, the lows, and the complexities" of weddings and marriage.

indiebride.com

Iowa State University Extension offers guidelines for communication about finances, worksheets, and other resources.

extension.iastate.edu/financial/management.html

Marriage Support provides information and encouragement to married and unmarried people who want to improve their relationship skills. The site includes bulletin boards, a relationship satisfaction quiz, and other resources.

www.couples-place.com

The **National Healthy Marriage Resource Center** is an information clearinghouse. Its goals is to help couples gain the knowledge and skills to build and sustain a healthy marriage.

www.healthymarriageinfor.org

As Long as We Both Shall Live presents a photographic essay of couples that have been married 40 years or longer.

www.longmarriedcouples.com

And more: www.prenhall.com/benokraitis offers numerous links to engagement and wedding sites (including those for same-sex marriages), honeymoon ideas, several sites that scramble family names and provide a list of suggestions for those who want a "new" surname after marriage that reflects both sides of the family, and the National Marriage Project at Rutgers University.

Investigate with Research Navigator

Go to www.researchnavigator.com and enter your LOGIN NAME and PASSWORD. For instructions on registering for the first time, view the detailed instructions at the end of Chapter 1. Search the Research Navigator™ site using the following key terms:

marriage
communication
counseling

Outline

To Be Or Not To Be A Parent: More Choices, More Constraints

Data Digest

- In a national study of first-year college students, 76 percent said that **having children is an "essential" or "very important" objective** in their lives.

- The **number of births** in the United States decreased from 4.2 million in 1990 to 4.1 million in 2004.

- In 2004, **88 percent of births to teenage women were out of wedlock,** compared with 52 percent of births to women in their early twenties.

- The number of **adoptions of foreign-born children** increased from 7,093 in 1990 to nearly 28,000 in 2005.

- About 14 percent of **women have babies they don't want,** up from 9 percent in 1995.

- The **number of childless women** ages 40 to 44 has almost doubled—from 10 percent in 1976 to 19 percent in 2004.

Sources: Chandra et al., 2005; Dye, 2005; Hamilton et al., 2005; "Students," 2006; U.S. Department of State, 2005.

A successful physician in his fifties took his 80-year-old mother to a performance at the Metropolitan Opera in New York City. They were making their way out the lobby doors to the physician's Mercedes when his mother turned to him and asked: "Do you have to go to the bathroom, dear?"

As this anecdote suggests, parenthood lasts forever. We may change colleges, buy and sell houses and cars, switch careers, and marry more than once, but becoming a parent creates a lifelong commitment to our children. According to one author, "The way I bring up my children affects my grandchildren, too" (Ostrowiak, 2001:18). That is, having a child also shapes future generations and relationships.

Although today we are freer to decide whether to have children, our choices are more complicated than in the past. Most people can decide when to have children and how many. Women can postpone parenthood longer than ever before, sometimes even after menopause. We can become parents despite problems that prevent normal conception or birth. And we can decide to remain child free altogether. We cover all these possibilities in this chapter.

Parenthood is a process. *Having* children—through childbirth or adoption—is not the same as *raising* children. This chapter focuses primarily on the biological, economic, and social aspects of *becoming* a parent (or not). The next chapter examines the child-rearing roles, activities, and responsibilities of being a parent. Let's begin by looking at the choices that couples have.

Becoming a Parent

We sometimes hear about mothers, usually unmarried teenagers, who abandon their newborn infants. Overwhelmingly, however, most people have children because they really want them. A couple may discuss family size before getting married, set up a savings account for their children's college education, enroll in a health insurance plan that will cover pregnancy costs, and even buy a house to accommodate the family they plan.

Almost half of all pregnancies in the United States are unintended (Chandra et al., 2005). Whether planned or not, a couple's first pregnancy is an important milestone. Pregnancies are "family affairs": Both parents typically worry about the developing baby and look forward to its birth with great anticipation. The reactions of both partners to pregnancy can vary, however:

■ *Planners* actively discuss the issue, having jointly decided to conceive a child. They are typically jubilant about becoming pregnant. As one wife said, "When the doctor called with the news that I was pregnant, I was so excited I wanted to run out in the street and tell everybody I met."

■ *Acceptance-of-fate* couples are pleasantly surprised and quietly welcoming of a child, even though they have not planned the pregnancy. Often, such couples have unconsciously or intentionally made an unspoken agreement to become pregnant by using contraceptive methods only sporadically or not at all.

■ *Ambivalent couples* have mixed feelings before and after conception and even well into the pregnancy. As one wife noted, "I felt confused, a mixture of up and down, stunned, in a daze." Ambivalent couples decide to have the baby because one partner feels strongly about having a child and the other complies. Or the pregnancy might be unintended, but one or both partners don't believe in abortion.

■ In *yes–no couples* one partner may not want children, even late in the pregnancy. Typically, the wife decides to go ahead with the pregnancy regardless of what her husband thinks, and the pregnancy sometimes causes a separation or divorce. Or, in the case of unmarried teenage couples, the father may simply stop seeing the woman after she becomes pregnant (Cowan and Cowan, 2000: 33–45).

It's not surprising that many couples are ambivalent about parenthood. After all, parenthood involves costs as well as benefits.

The Benefits and Costs of Having Children

Some people weigh the pros and cons of having a baby. Many don't. Emotions, after all, play a role in deciding to have a baby. Speaking both emotionally and practically, what are some of the benefits and costs of becoming a parent?

BENEFITS One of our thirty-something neighbors recently had their first baby. When I asked Matt how they were doing, he exclaimed, "There's nothing like it! She's the most gorgeous baby in the world!" Matt's reaction is fairly typical. For example, 96 percent of first-time parents in a national survey said that they were "in love" with their baby, and 91 percent reported being "happier than ever before" ("Bringing up baby," 1999).

Couples often feel that their lives would be incomplete without children. According to many parents, children bring love and affection; it's a pleasure to watch them grow; they bring joy, happiness, and fun; they create a sense of family; and they bring fulfillment and a sense of satisfaction (Gallup and Newport, 1990).

Unlike those in many other countries, most parents in the United States don't expect their children to care for them in their old age (see Chapters 17 and 18). Instead, many say that having children brings a new dimension to their life that is more fulfilling than their job, their relationships with friends, or their leisure activities. Most couples place a high priority on raising happy, healthy children. Even new parents who are struggling with a colicky infant (whose abdominal distress causes frequent crying) delight in the baby's social and physical growth.

COSTS Parenthood isn't paradise. To begin with, having and raising children is expensive. *Figure 11.1* shows a typical year's expenses for a child 1 or 2 years old in husband–wife middle-income families. Middle-income families (those earning an average of $57,400 a year)

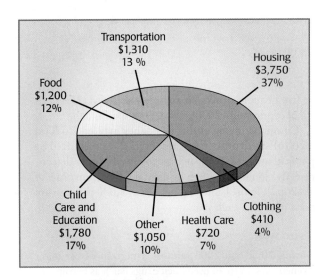

FIGURE 11.1   What a Middle-Income Family Spends during the First Two Years of a Child's Life
In 2005, families earning $43,200 to $72,600 spent, on average, $10,220 per year on each child under 2. This amount does not include the costs of prenatal care or delivery.

*Includes personal-care items, entertainment, and reading materials.

SOURCE: Based on Lino, 2006, Table ES1.

spend about 20 percent of their earnings on a child every year from the child's birth to age 17 (Lino, 2006).

Child-rearing costs are much higher, especially in low-income families, if a child is disabled or chronically ill or needs specialized care that welfare benefits don't cover. And if one or both parents are laid off, they usually lose any medical benefits for themselves or their children (Lukemeyer et al., 2000; see, also, Chapter 13).

Becoming a parent has other economic and social costs. Many women pay a "mommy tax": Their unpaid work at home doesn't count toward Social Security pensions, they often forgo educational opportunities, and they are more likely than men or childless women to live in poverty in old age or after a divorce (Crittenden, 2001).

Contrary to what many people think, it is *not* selfish to consider economic costs before having a child. In fact, it is selfish *not* to do so because a child raised in a poverty-stricken home may suffer lifelong disadvantages. One problem may be finding suitable housing. Large houses are expensive, low-income families often have fewer housing options, and some rental units exclude children or limit their number. Indeed, some towns have gone to court to limit new housing construction to two-bedroom homes. Presumably, such restrictions will keep out large families and the residents can avoid paying higher taxes to build and maintain schools (Folbre, 1994; Mansnerus, 2003).

Children also have emotional costs. While most parents report being "in love" with their baby, first-time parents, especially, experience anxiety or fatigue: 56 percent say that they are stressed and worn out; 52 percent are afraid of doing something wrong; and 44 percent are unsure about what to do "a lot of the time" ("Bringing up baby," 1999).

As parents become more focused on the child, interpersonal relationships may deteriorate. Many mothers report feeling strain when attempting to balance their job and household responsibilities. Others feel that their husbands become more distant emotionally—even though they're devoted fathers—because the wife spends most of her time caring for the infant (see Chapter 10).

Men also experience conflict after the birth of the first child. Although many would like to be involved fathers, they are still expected to be full-time breadwinners. As a result, they may work long hours, rarely see the baby, and feel that they're missing out on the parenting experience. New parents may take out their frustrations on each other: "For couples who thought that having a baby was going to bring them closer together, this is especially confusing and disappointing" (Lupton and Barclay, 1997; Cowan and Cowan, 2000: 18).

The Joys and Tribulations of Pregnancy

Pregnancy can be exciting and joyful, particularly when it is planned and welcomed. For both prospective parents, it can deepen feelings of love and intimacy, and it can draw them closer as they plan for the family's future. At the same time, pregnancy—especially the first pregnancy—can arouse anxiety about caring for the baby properly and providing for the growing child economically.

The expectant mother usually experiences numerous discomforts. In the first trimester (three-month period), she may have frequent nausea, heartburn, insomnia, shortness of breath, painful swelling of the breasts, and fatigue. She may also be constantly concerned about the health of her *fetus* (the term for the unborn child from eight weeks until birth), especially if she or the baby's father has engaged in any high-risk behaviors (see the box "Having Healthier Babies").

The second trimester can be thrilling because the mother begins to feel movements, or *quickenings*, as the fetus becomes more active. *Sonograms* (diagnostic imaging produced by high-frequency sound waves) can reveal an image of the baby and its sex.

On the downside, backaches may become a problem, and fatigue sets in more quickly. In her third trimester, a woman may start losing interest in sex,

Applying What You've Learned

Having Healthier Babies

Will your current lifestyle affect your baby's health in the future?

Most babies are born healthy. If people engage in high-risk behaviors, however, their baby can be born with a variety of problems. Many are due to the parents' lifestyle rather than to genetic diseases or other disorders.

Smoking

Smoking cuts off the supply of oxygen to the baby's brain, impairs the baby's growth, and is linked to spontaneous abortion, premature birth, low birth weight, and childhood illness. Low birth rate is conventionally defined as less than 2500 grams, or 5 pounds, 8 ounces.

Low birth rate (which affects 7 percent of all newborns) increases the infant's chances of sickness, retarded growth, respiratory problems, infections, low intelligence, learning problems, poor hearing and vision, and even death (Cornelius and Day, 2000).

Fetuses of women who smoke 10 or more cigarettes per day are three times more likely to have genetic abnormalities than are fetuses of nonsmokers. By age 2, these children are more likely than those of nonsmoking mothers to show problem behavior such as defiance, aggression, and poorer social skills. In addition, children of women whose mothers and maternal grandmothers smoked during pregnancy are almost three times more likely to develop asthma by age five (de la Chica, 2005; Li et al., 2005; Wakschlag et al., 2006).

Alcohol

Human infants experience a "brain growth spurt" that starts in the sixth month of the pregnancy and continues for two years after birth. During this period, a single drinking binge—lasting four hours or more—can permanently damage the brain of the unborn child (Ikonomidou et al., 2000).

Birth defects associated with prenatal alcohol exposure can occur in the first three to eight weeks of pregnancy, before a woman even knows that she's pregnant. One out of every 29 women who know they're pregnant reports "risk drinking" (seven or more drinks per week,

or five or more drinks on any one occasion) ("Fetal alcohol syndrome," 2000).

Chronic drinking during pregnancy may lead to **fetal alcohol syndrome (FAS)**, a condition characterized by physical abnormalities such as congenital heart defects, defective joints, and often by mental retardation (Baer et al., 2003). In the United States, about 8,000 children are born with FAS each year.

Drugs

During 2002 and 2003, almost 5 percent of pregnant women ages 15 to 44 used illicit drugs (such as heroin, cocaine, morphine, and opium). Mothers who use illicit drugs are likely to have infants who are addicted. The baby may experience problems such as prenatal strokes, lasting brain damage, seizures, premature birth, retarded fetal growth, and malformations ("Substance Use . . . ," 2005).

Obesity and Eating Disorders

Women who are obese or overweight before becoming pregnant are at a much higher risk than normal-weight women of having infants with birth defects such as spina bifida, heart abnormalities, and other problems. Researchers suspect that obese women suffer from nutritional deficits—due to poor eating habits—that result in diabetes and health-related problems for infants. Pregnant teenagers with poor diets can hurt their baby's bone growth because the fetus is not getting enough calcium (Chang et al., 2003; Watkins et al., 2003).

Infectious Diseases

Infectious diseases can cause numerous problems. A woman who contracts German measles during the first three months of pregnancy may give birth to a deformed or retarded child.

Sexually transmitted infections (STIs) can also be dangerous or fatal to an unborn child. A woman with gonorrhea may give birth to a baby who becomes blind after passing through the infected birth canal. Herpes or syphilis can result in a spontaneous abortion, a stillborn birth, or a baby who is brain-damaged, deformed, blind, or deaf. Finally, and perhaps most serious of all, a parent with HIV can pass the deadly disease on to a fetus (see Chapter 7).

which becomes awkward and difficult because of her ever-larger abdomen. She begins to retain water and may feel physically unattractive and clumsy. Once-simple, automatic tasks, like tying shoelaces or retrieving something that has fallen on the floor, may require assistance.

Vaginal births may be quick, or they may be long and exhausting. Sometimes they're not possible and a woman has a *cesarean section* (surgical removal of the baby from the womb through the abdominal wall), which afterwards is more painful for the mother and entails a longer period of recovery. Both vaginal births and cesarean sections often involve bloody discharge for several weeks. Infections and fevers are also common.

Effects of Parenthood on Both Mother and Father

Parenthood is steeped in romantic misconceptions. And often we expect too much of mothers and ignore fathers. An infant will respond to *any* person, mother or father, who is a consistent source of stimulation, love, attention, and comfort:

> The father is usually larger than the mother, his voice is deeper, his clothes are not the same and he moves and reacts differently. Furthermore, parents differ in odor and skin texture. The father and mother offer the child two different kinds of persons to learn about as well as providing separate but special sources of love and support . . . For example, the infant may prefer the mother when hungry or tired and the father when seeking stimulation or more active play (Biller, 1993: 12).

MOTHERS AND THEIR NEWBORNS There is a widespread myth that an instant "bonding" occurs between a mother and her newborn baby (see Chapter 6). In reality, it is not only mothers but also fathers, siblings, grandparents, and friends who have an effect on children.

since you asked

Is there an immediate bonding between a mother and her newborn?

Historically and in most cultures, many adults, not just mothers, have nurtured children. Because responsibility for the baby's care tends to fall heavily on new mothers, however, they often feel frustrated or stressed out and experience a decline in marital satisfaction (Twenge et al., 2003).

Many women experience **postpartum depression**—"the blues" that appear after the birth of a baby. Some of this depression may be caused by chemical imbalances. The sudden drop in estrogen and progesterone levels as the concentrations of these hormones in the placenta are expelled with other afterbirth tissue may have a depressive effect.

The high levels of the body's natural painkillers, called *beta-endorphins,* produced by the mother during labor also drop after birth. As a result, the mother may experience postpartum depression. Newborn infants need frequent feeding and almost constant care, which may also contribute to fatigue and depression. In addition, using alcohol or tobacco increases the likelihood of depression both during and after pregnancy (Marcus et al., 2003).

Despite physical pain, postpartum depression, and wondering whether they'll ever get two hours of uninterrupted sleep again, most mothers are elated with their infants. Many new mothers (and sometimes fathers) can spend hours describing the baby's eating schedule, every yawn and facial expression, and even the bowel movements of the "cutest and most intelligent baby you've ever seen."

FATHERS AND THEIR NEWBORNS Our society tends to stress the importance of mothers over that of fathers, especially in caring for infants. But fathers as well as mothers are important for infants' emotional development. Fathers are just as effective at soothing crying babies, for example, and playing with them (Diener et al., 2002).

Like mothers, many fathers worry about being good parents. Even when they feel anxious, many men think that their task is to be calm, strong, and reassuring—a gender stereotype. Their tendency to keep their worries to themselves may increase the tension and distance between the partners. The couples who fare best are those who can listen sympathetically to each other without expecting immediate solutions (Cowan and Cowan, 2000).

Fatherhood often enhances maturity: "Being a father can change the ways that men think about themselves. Fathering often helps men to clarify their values and to set priorities" (Parke, 1996: 15).

New fathers express loving and affectionate emotions that are good for them and for babies. Many fathers also forge stronger links with their own parents, who may be supportive grandparents (Johnson and Huston, 1998). From a developmental perspective, fatherhood is an important transition in a man's life course (see Chapter 2).

Some men's transition to fatherhood is problematic. They may become abusive because of increased financial responsibilities, the emotional demands of new familial roles, and the restrictions that parenthood brings (Schecter and Ganely, 1995; see, also, Chapter 14).

Becoming a parent seems to be an individual decision, but that's not entirely the case. Although most people have a choice about conception, childbearing also reflects what's going on in society and how it changes over time. Consider childbearing patterns in the last century.

How Many Children Do You Want?

The United States, though well behind China and India, is the world's third largest country. Our population is growing faster than that of any other developed country because of high immigration rates (see Chapter 4). **Fertility**, the number of live births in a population, is another important driving force in U.S. population growth.

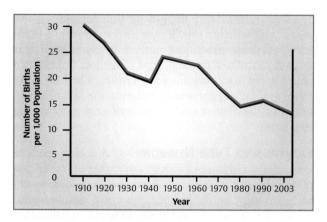

FIGURE 11.2 **Births in the United States, 1910-2003**

SOURCE: Martin et al., 2005.

How U.S. Fertility Patterns Have Changed

Except for the baby boom "blip" of the 1950s, the U.S. birth rate (the number of live births annually per 1,000 population) has been declining steadily since the turn of the twentieth century—from 30.1 in 1910 to 14.1 in 2003 (see *Figure 11.2*). Demographers often use the **total fertility rate (TFR)** to measure the average number of births to women in a population. In the early 1900s,

U.S.-born white women had an average TFR of 3.5 children, compared with 2.0 children in 2003 (Kent and Mather, 2002; Martin et al., 2005).

Why Fertility Patterns Have Changed

Much of the decrease in birth rates is due to a combination of macro-level societal factors and micro-level individual practices (see *Figure 11.3*). People have more choices on the individual level if a society provides incentives for reducing fertility rates.

MACRO-LEVEL FACTORS Although there are many reasons for lower birth rates, especially in industrialized countries, two related factors are improvements in contraceptive methods and more opportunities in higher education. Since the early 1960s, oral contraceptives have allowed women to space their pregnancies and delay motherhood. Because women have also had greater access to higher education, they have been able to choose other roles besides the traditional ones of wife and mother (Kent and Mather, 2002).

Second, advances in medicine and hygiene have lowered infant mortality rates. Families no longer have to have six children because three or four will die before their first birthday. As a result, family size has decreased. In 1900, for example, 45 percent of all households were

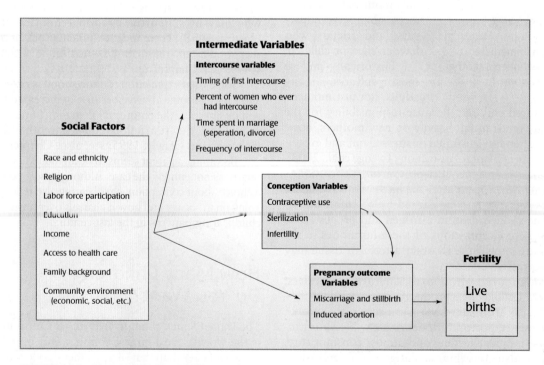

FIGURE 11.3 **Factors Affecting Fertility**

SOURCE: Chandra et al., 2005, Figure 1.

President Vladimir Putin, upset that the population in Russia is declining, has doubled monthly child support payments (about $55) and is paying women who have a second child $9,200 (the average monthly incomes are about $330). So far, the new incentives don't seem to be working. Why do you think this is the case?

made up of five or more people, compared with only 11 percent of households in 2000 (Hobbs and Stoops, 2002).

A third reason for lower birth rates reflects economic changes. As the incomes of many men under age 30 fell dramatically in the 1970s and 1980s, many wives sought employment to be able to afford the lifestyle to which they were accustomed. As women joined the work force, many postponed having children. Postponing parenthood also means that women have fewer years in which to become pregnant (Macunovich, 2002).

MICRO-LEVEL FACTORS Social factors alone don't explain fertility. We also make choices, such as how often we have sexual intercourse, whether or not we use effective contraception, or whether we decide to end a pregnancy through abortion (see *Figure 11.3*). And, as you saw earlier, our lifestyles can have negative outcomes such as miscarriages or stillbirths.

Macro- and micro-level factors are often interrelated in explaining birth rates. For example, one reason for our falling fertility rates reflects a combination of attitudes and economic factors such as relative income. **Relative income** is a person's earning potential compared with his or her desired standard of living. Couples need a higher income if they want to own a new BMW rather than an old Ford, for instance.

Variations by Race and Ethnicity

Birth rates are higher for Latinas than for other women in almost all age groups (see *Figure 11.4*). Within this population, however, fertility rates range from a high of 106 for Mexican American women to a low of 57 for Cuban American women. Most Mexicans who have recently emigrated from rural areas value large families. Children perform important economic functions, including contributing to the family's income, sometimes as migrant workers. In contrast, Cuban Americans are predominantly middle class, have low unemployment rates and more education, and do not depend on children to augment family income (Hamilton et al., 2003; see, also, Chapter 5).

Why are fertility rates higher for some racial and ethnic groups and subgroups than for others? Two important factors are education and sexual practices.

EDUCATION A woman's schooling has a profound effect on the number of children she has. Those with more education are more likely to desire and give birth to fewer children, to use contraceptives more effectively, to marry later, and to postpone childbearing. Over a lifetime, for

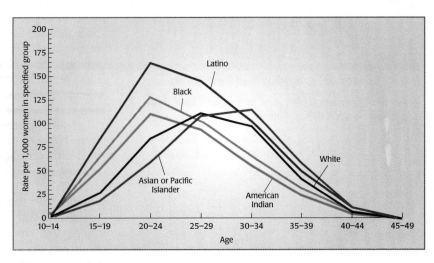

FIGURE 11.4   U.S. Birth Rates, by Race, Ethnicity, and Age, 2003

SOURCE: Martin et al., 2005, Figure 4.

example, women who have at least a bachelor's degree are much less likely than those with no high school diploma to bear three or more children (see *Table 11.1*).

The highest birth rates among Asian American and Pacific Islander women are for those ages 30 to 39 (see *Figure 11.4*). This may be because Asian American women—especially Japanese women and Filipinas—tend to postpone childbearing until they've completed college and have attained professional degrees (see Chapter 5).

SEXUAL PRACTICES Young Latinos and African Americans typically begin sexual activities earlier than their white and Asian American counterparts. They also tend to have more partners and to not use contraception (see Chapter 7). All these behaviors increase the number of births during the teenage years and over a lifetime.

As you will see later in this chapter, some African American youth have babies on purpose to fill an emotional void in their lives. Compared with white communities, black communities also tend to be more accepting of out-of-wedlock births and more likely to oppose abortion.

Spacing Pregnancies

How often women have babies also affects birth rates. According to a recent analysis of more than 11 million pregnancies in the United States, Europe, and developing nations, better family planning could prevent thousands of infant deaths each year. Getting pregnant less than 18 months after giving birth and spacing children more than five years apart sometimes raises the risk of complications such as premature births and low birthweight. In the case of close spacing, pregnancy and nursing use up nutrients in a woman's body. If she becomes

pregnant before those nutrients are replaced, the next infant may suffer. It's not clear why, on average, intervals longer than five years may cause problems. The researchers speculated that time could diminish a woman's reproductive capacity and lead to less viable fetuses (Conde-Agudelo et al., 2006).

About 21 percent of U.S. women give birth a second time within 24 months of the first birth. Closer spacing of children is more common among women with lower levels of education and income, especially those living below the poverty level (Chandra et al., 2005). Thus, once again, social class affects a woman's chances of having healthy babies.

Comparisons with Other Countries

Family size varies significantly around the world. Although there are many reasons for these variations, let's consider two issues: birth rates and infant mortality.

BIRTH RATES In Milan, Italy, a 32-year-old woman who is part of a two-career married couple has a 3-year-old son and doesn't plan to have more children. She enjoys spending time with her son, adding, "It doesn't make sense to have three children just to tuck them in at night" (Bruni, 2002).

This woman is similar to many others around the world who are planning to have few, if any, children. A country needs a 2.1 TFR to replace those who die. Many countries' TFRs are well below this level, including Ukraine, Russia, Poland, China, and Thailand. In contrast, some countries have high TFRs, especially in many of the developing African nations and Afghanistan (see *Table 11.2*).

U.S. birth rates are high compared with those for other industrialized countries. Unlike other western nations, the United States has high immigration rates, and many of the immigrants—especially Mexicans—are young, in their child-bearing years, and value large families. Yet the United States has implemented few family-friendly policies that ease the burden of combining work and child-rearing responsibilities (see Chapter 12).

As birth rates fall, some governments become concerned about future labor pools. Japan has funded public fertility treatments and matchmaker services to increase the birth rate. Spain has decreased the cost of utility bills for large families, has policies to help young couples buy homes, and is creating thousands of preschools and nursery schools to accommodate working parents. And, most recently, France has doubled the tax credit for in-home child care and offered discounts on transportation and retail products for families with more than two children (Bruni, 2002; Kakuchi, 2004; Kent and Haub, 2005).

TABLE 11.1

Education, Ethnicity, and Birth Rates

Percent of women, 22–44 years of age, who have three or more children over a lifetime

	No High School or GED*	Bachelor's Degree or Higher
African American	64%	12%
Latinas	48%	12%
White	39%	13%

*General Educational Development high school equivalence diploma.

Source: Based on Chandra et al., 2005, Table 3.

TABLE 11.2

Family Size Varies Around the World

	Children Born per Woman*
Some Countries with the Highest Birth Rates	
Niger (West Africa)	8.0
Guinea-Bissau and Mali (West Africa)	7.1
Somalia and Uganda (East Africa)	6.9-7.0
Afghanistan and four countries in Africa	6.8
Some Countries with the Lowest Birth Rates	
Belarus, Czech Republic, Poland, Ukraine (Eastern Europe)	1.2
Bosnia-Herzegovina, Slovenia (Southern Europe)	1.2
Taiwan, Republic of China (East Asia)	1.2
Latvia, Lithuania, Hungary (Eastern Europe), and Russia	1.3
Birth Rates of Some Industrialized Countries	
South Korea (East Asia)	1.2
Japan and Greece, Italy, and Spain (Southern Europe)	1.3
Austria, Switzerland (Western Europe)	1.4
Canada	1.5
Norway, Denmark, and Sweden (Northern Europe)	1.8
France (Western Europe)	1.9
United States	**2.0**

*This is the total fertility rate (TFR), or the average total number of children born per woman during her lifetime.

SOURCE: Based on Haub, 2005.

The reasons for the plunging birth rates in many countries are similar to those in the United States: More women are studying longer, working, and then marrying later, which doesn't necessarily include having a baby. Men are equally likely to postpone marriage and children because success at finding and keeping a job is unpredictable.

INFANT MORTALITY Even though the United States is the richest country in the world, it has a high **infant mortality rate,** the number of babies under one year of age who die per 1,000 live births in a given year. While the health of infants in many countries is improving, U.S. babies now face an increased risk of dying before reaching their first birthday. In 2004, for example, the United States, with an infant mortality rate of 7.0, ranked 28th among industrialized countries such as Singapore (2.5) and Japan (3.2.), and well above developing countries such as the Czech Republic (4.1) (U.S. Department of Health and Human Services, 2004; Haub, 2005).

The leading causes of infant mortality are physical birth defects (due to genetic disorders, a toxic intrauterine environment, and unknown factors) and very low birth weight. Newborns that weigh less than 3 pounds 4 ounces are about 100 times more likely to die by age one than are infants of normal birth weight. Since 1999, there has been an increase in infants born weighing less than 1 pound 11 ounces for women ages 20 to 24 and for white, black, and Latina mothers (MacDorman et al., 2005).

Overall, the infant mortality rate for African Americans is double that for the general population (14.3) and is higher than that of any other ethnic group. These high rates probably reflect lack of prenatal care, which can result in pregnancy complications; lifestyle choices such as smoking and using drugs; and specific medical problems such as diabetes and hypertension (MacDorman et al., 2005; Bogart, 2006; Hoyert et al., 2006).

since you asked

Why does the United States have a higher infant mortality rate than other developed nations?

Making Connections

- If you don't have children, do you plan to have them in the future? If no, why not? If yes, at what age? And how many?

- If you're a parent, what have been the major benefits and costs of having children?

- Look back at *Figure 11.4.* How would you explain the high fertility rates of Latinas ages 20 to 24? Why do you think that the fertility rates of black women ages 30 and over are generally lower than those of women in most other groups? How might you explain the much higher fertility rates of Asian and Pacific Islander women after age 29?

Postponing Parenthood

"Babies vs. Career!" exclaimed a recent *Time* magazine cover. The cover story expressed alarm that so many women have put careers before having babies. Most of the articles discussed fertility problems and implied that childless women (not men) are selfish and too career-oriented (see Gibbs, 2002).

The numbers of first-time older mothers are rising. In the early 1970s, only 4 percent of American women having their first babies were age 30 or older. Since then, the numbers of women who had their first baby in their thirties and forties has increased substantially: 25 percent for women ages 30 to 34, 36 percent for women ages 35 to 39, and 70 percent for women ages 40 to 44 (Ventura, Martin, et al., 2000; Hamilton et al., 2003). Thus, despite *Time*'s sensational coverage, most women are postponing parenthood rather than avoiding it.

Many men, similarly, are having children later in life. The majority of children continue to be born to men ages 20 to 34. Between 1980 and 2003, however, the rate of births among men ages 40 to 44 went up 32 percent, and the rate for those ages 45 to 49 rose 21 percent. For men ages 50 to 54, the rate of increase was 9 percent (Martin et al., 2005).

Why Are Many People Postponing Parenthood?

Both micro- and macro-level factors affect decisions to postpone parenthood. You'll notice as you read this section that women are usually much more likely than men to feel constrained in deciding whether and when to have children.

MICRO-LEVEL FACTORS Being single, you recall, has many attractions, including independence, the opportunity to develop a career, and more time for fun (see Chapter 9). There are similar micro-level reasons for postponing parenthood:

■ Daunting jobs and careers make it more difficult to meet prospective mates (see Chapter 8).

■ Many single women don't want to conceive or adopt a child on their own. According to a 43-year-old woman whose mother raised her and her siblings, "The hardest thing you can be is a single, working mom" (Peterson, 2002: 2D).

■ Many couples don't want nannies or child care centers to raise their children. They delay having children until they feel that one of them (usually the wife) can be a stay-at-home parent.

■ Both women and men want to build equity in homes, put some money aside, and save for retirement before having children (Poniewozik, 2002).

■ Women who enjoy their jobs and need the money to boost their family's income are often reluctant to struggle with balancing child rearing and paid work (see Chapter 13).

MACRO-LEVEL FACTORS On the macro level, economic and reproductive factors seem to play the biggest role in postponing parenthood:

■ In periods of economic recession and high unemployment rates, many young men don't have the resources to start a family.

■ Young married couples living with their parents may postpone childbearing because they don't want to make already crowded living conditions even worse.

■ Disturbed by the current high divorce rate, some young couples delay parenthood until they feel confident that the marriage will work.

■ Advances in reproductive technology, as you'll see shortly, have reduced many women's concerns about their "biological clock" and finding a mate.

■ Women and men are delaying childbearing because the United States—especially compared with many European countries—has abysmal family leave policies, no national child care programs, and rigid work schedules.

One of the major reasons for many women's delaying having children is that the best years for childbearing (when women are young) coincide with the best years for establishing a career. A woman who starts having babies at age 25, for example, will have a difficult time competing in the labor market with younger men and with women 10 or 20 years later. According to a fashion designer, 33, who dropped her X-Girl clothing line after having a baby when she was 26, "How can you come back at 36 or 37 and say, 'I'm here, guys—snap, snap, let me start another line of hip-hop clothing'?" (Poniewozik, 2002: 58).

Some Characteristics of Older Parents

"My parents had me in their mid-forties. They were always too tired to attend many of the school functions or to take me to baseball games."

"My mother had me when she was 45 and that was in 1973. I'm living proof that older moms are good parents."

As these comments by some of my students show, many of us have strong opinions about the age at which people should have kids.

since you asked

Are there any advantages to having children after age 40?

Like most other options in life, being an older parent has both advantages and disadvantages.

ADVANTAGES Women who give birth for the first time between ages 22 and 34 have healthier babies than those who have babies during their teenage years or after age 40. The latter may experience more problems in conceiving a child. However, mothers in their teens are more likely than their older counterpart to have babies with birth defects and to experience infant deaths: They often have poor nutrition, don't obtain adequate prenatal care, or engage in unhealthy lifestyles that include smoking and using alcohol and other drugs (Mirowsky, 2005).

Compared with younger mothers, older mothers are more likely to be married and highly educated. They also tend to work in professional occupations and to have high family incomes (Bachu, 1993). Higher incomes decrease stress because the family has more resources in raising a child.

Older mothers tend to feel more self-assured, more ready for responsibility, and better prepared for parenthood than do younger women. Younger mothers sometimes feel trapped by having a baby because they still want to party, go out with friends, and have a good time (Maynard, 1997).

Men who postpone parenthood usually enjoy more advantages and have fewer constraints than women do. Most men do not face sex discrimination in the workplace, they earn higher salaries, and they have better health benefits. Thus, they are less likely to worry about not having the resources to raise children later in life. According to one of my students, for example, having an older dad "made life wonderful for me:"

> *I am the youngest of four. I was only 7 years old when my dad retired. He spent a lot of time with me. He invested well and made financial decisions that were beneficial for the entire family. I think his age played a big part in having the means to make his family comfortable and raising his children without any financial burdens (Author's files).*

With fewer economic concerns, men remarry more often and sometimes, after a divorce, support children from two families (see Chapter 16). Also, because their careers are better established, older fathers may have more flexibility to spend their nonwork hours and weekends with their families. Older fathers can spend more time with their children and form strong emotional bonds with them because they are often more relaxed—especially if they are financially secure and don't have to work as aggressively at a career (Carnoy and Carnoy, 1997).

DISADVANTAGES Although older parents may be more patient, mature, and financially secure, there are some drawbacks to delaying parenthood. Pregnant women in their forties are at greater risk of having a baby with Down syndrome than are women in their thirties. Even beyond health risks, there are some practical liabilities in becoming a parent at age 49:

> *At 52, you'd be coming out of the "terrible twos" and hosting play groups for toddlers. As you turned 55, your child would start kindergarten and you'd qualify for dual memberships in the PTA and the American Association of Retired Persons (AARP). At 60, you and your spouse would be coaching soccer. . . . By the time you hit 70, you'd be buried under college tuition bills. And if your child delayed marriage and family like you did, you might be paying for a wedding when you were 80 and babysitting for your grandchildren at 90 (Wright, 1997: E5).*

A 16-year-old daughter of an almost-60-year-old mother feels that the "huge generation gap" has led to greater conflict because of their different attitudes and values ("How late is too late?" 2001). Moreover, some women who have waited to have children find that it is too late to have as many as they wanted.

Older mothers, especially those who have risen to powerful but demanding executive positions, may feel

Chris Britt/Copley News Service © 1997.

especially guilty about splitting their time between their family and their employer and thus "cheating" both (see Chapter 13). At one point or another, many midlife parents are mistaken for Grandma or Grandpa. Some laugh it off, but others bristle at such errors (Crandell, 2005). Finally, postponing parenthood may mean that parents will never get to see their grandchildren.

You see, then, that there are many reasons for postponing childbearing—especially for women who seek more options in education and jobs. However, millions of Americans have fewer choices because they are infertile.

Infertility

Infertility is generally defined as inability to conceive a baby after 12 months of unprotected sex. Infertility affects about 15 percent of all couples of reproductive age. Although infertility rates have been fairly stable since the mid-1960s, the likelihood of infertility increases as people delay childbearing. For example, the rate of infertility for couples between ages 30 and 34 is more than 50 percent greater than for those between ages 25 and 29 (Mosher and Pratt, 1991; Chandra et al., 2005).

since you asked

What causes infertility?

There are many reasons for infertility, and the reactions are typically quite distressing. First, let's look at some of the reasons for infertility.

Reasons for Infertility

Infertility is due about equally to problems in males and females; each sex independently accounts for about 40 percent of cases. Approximately 20 percent of infertile couples are diagnosed as having *idiopathic infertility*. In plain language, doctors simply don't know what's wrong.

Until recently, most infertility research focused almost exclusively on women. For years people believed that the major reason for female infertility was aging. Although it is true that our reproductive organs age faster than other parts of our body, people of either sex can be infertile.

FEMALE INFERTILITY The two major causes of female infertility are failure to ovulate and blockage of the fallopian tubes. A woman's failure to *ovulate*, or to produce a viable egg each month, may have a number of causes, among them poor nutrition, chronic illness, and drug abuse. Very occasionally, lack of ovulation may be attributed to psychological stress (Masters et al., 1992).

The *fallopian tubes* carry the egg—whether or not it has been fertilized—from the ovaries to the uterus. The fallopian tubes can be blocked by scarring caused by **pelvic inflammatory disease (PID)**, an infection of the uterus that spreads to the tubes, the ovaries, and surrounding tissues. PID, in turn, is often caused by sexually transmitted diseases like chlamydia.

Chlamydia, a bacterial infection that is often called "the silent epidemic" because it exhibits no symptoms in 75 percent of women and 33 percent of men, is a rapidly rising cause of PID. Once diagnosed, this infection is easily cured with antibiotics (see Chapter 7 and *Appendix E* for more information about sexually transmitted diseases).

Another major reason for women's infertility is **endometriosis**, a condition in which the tissue that forms in the endometrium (the lining of the uterus) spreads outside the womb and attaches itself to other pelvic organs, such as the ovaries or the fallopian tubes. Although the cause of endometriosis is not known, some researchers believe that women with endometriosis have certain malfunctioning genes that prevent an embryo from attaching to the uterine wall (Kao et al., 2003). Endometriosis can lead to PID, uterine tumors, and blockage of the opening to the uterus.

Excessive exercise or rapid weight loss can also decrease the production of reproductive hormones. Regular use of vaginal douches and deodorants that contain certain chemicals may kill sperm or inhibit their ability to fertilize an egg (Fogel and Woods, 1995; DeLisle, 1997).

MALE INFERTILITY Male infertility often results from "sluggish" sperm or a low sperm count. Since 1938 the sperm counts of men in the United States and 20 other countries have plunged by an average of 50 percent (Swan et al., 1997).

Chemical pollutants might play a major role in male infertility. For years men have been more likely than women to work in environments in which they come into contact with toxic chemicals or are exposed to other hazardous conditions (Kenen, 1993).

Other possible causes of low sperm counts include injury to the testicles or scrotum, infections such as mumps in adulthood, testicular varicose veins that impede sperm development, undescended testes (the testes normally descend from the abdominal cavity into the scrotum in about the eighth month of prenatal development), endocrine disorders, and excessive consumption of alcohol, marijuana, narcotic drugs, or even some prescription medications. The sperm of chronic smokers (men who have smoked four or more cigarettes a day for at least two years) are on average 75 percent less fertile than those of nonsmokers (Nagourney, 2005).

Numerous studies report that long-distance bicycle riding or tight-fitting underwear can lower sperm counts. Spending many hours each week on a bike saddle with a high "nose" can create enough pressure on the perineum (the area between the anus and the pubic bone) to damage the artery—sometimes permanently—that supplies blood to the penis (Schrader, 2005).

Prolonged and frequent use of saunas, hot tubs, and steam baths may also have a negative effect because sperm production is sensitive to temperature. In the case of obese men, excess fat in the genital area could raise the temperature of the testicles, reducing the quality and quantity of sperm (Bhattacharya, 2003).

Sperm quality and the speed at which sperm travel toward an egg also decline in men over 50 (Marcus, 2003). In this sense, men may also have a "biological clock" that decreases their fertility as they age.

Reactions to Infertility

Although people respond to infertility differently, many couples are devastated. In most societies, including the United States, two cultural norms about procreation dominate. One is that all married couples *should* reproduce; the other is that all married couples *should want to* reproduce (Veevers, 1980).

For many women, then, infertility becomes "an acute and unanticipated life crisis" that involves stigma, psychological distress, grief, guilt, and a sense of violation. As one woman said, "It's a slap in the face. I feel like I'm isolated in a prison . . . no one understands how horrible this is" (Whiteford and Gonzalez, 1995: 29; McQuillan et al., 2003).

Though well intentioned, potential grandparents' expectations exert pressure to carry on the family line ("Do you think that I will have a grandchild before I die?"). The fact that generational continuity will come to an end may reinforce a woman's feelings of being a "failure" when she doesn't conceive:

> My husband is Italian and for the 10 years that we've been married, I have known that his having a son has been important to him, and my not being able to deliver has been a real difficult thing for me to deal with. . . . My mother-in-law has been pushing for a grandchild since the day we got married (Whiteford and Gonzalez, 1995: 34).

Many women, concerned that people will see them in a new and damaging light, engage in "information management" (Goffman, 1963). They may avoid the topic whenever possible, or they may attribute the problem to a disease such as diabetes or kidney trouble, taking the focus off specific reproductive disorders.

Because male infertility may be considered a defect in masculinity, women often accept responsibility for infertility themselves:

> When I tell them we can't have children, I generally try to leave the impression that it's me. I may mutter "tubes you know" or "faulty plumbing" (Miall, 1986: 36).

Marital satisfaction can decrease if women blame themselves or bury their feelings instead of seeking their partner's emotional support. Coping with infertility is especially difficult if men distance themselves by making light of the situation or acting as if nothing is wrong (Peterson et al., 2006).

For many couples, infertility is socially isolating: "It often becomes difficult to socialize with family and friends whose conversation gravitates to the joys (or miseries) of parenthood." They may also avoid events ranging from family holidays that include infants and children to baby showers for pregnant co-workers (Shapiro, 2005: F15-F16).

Some infertile couples, however, enjoy vicarious parenthood through contact with children of relatives and friends. Others become increasingly involved in work-related activities and even begin to regard their childlessness as an advantage.

Some couples accept infertility as a fact of life and remain childless. A much larger group tries to adopt.

Making Connections

- What are some of the advantages and disadvantages of having children during one's twenties rather than during one's forties?

- Are people's reasons—especially women's—for postponing having children valid? Or are they being selfish and self-centered in delaying childbearing?

- As *Table 11.2* shows, the United States has the highest fertility rate among developed countries. Why, then, do people often criticize married couples who don't have children?

Adoption: The Traditional Solution to Infertility

At one time, 80 percent of U.S. babies born out of wedlock were given up for adoption. This rate has dropped to about 2 or 3 percent because today most unwed mothers keep their babies.

How Many Children Do Americans Adopt?

An estimated 2.1 million children, or about 8 percent of all children in the United States, live with adoptive parents. Of these, nearly 18,000 are foreign-born. However, adoption touches many other lives. A recent survey estimates that 65 percent of Americans have experience with adoption through their family or friends. Moreover, four in 10 Americans say that they have considered adopting a child (*National Adoption Attitudes Survey*, 2002; Kreider, 2003).

Of the 560,000 foster children nationwide, at least 122,000 are eligible for adoption because their biological parents are dead or missing, have been found unfit, or have legally surrendered their rights to their children. Many of these children are hard to place, however, because they are sick, physically handicapped, biracial, nonwhite, emotionally disturbed, HIV-positive, or "too old" ("*Child welfare outcomes . . .*," 2000; Adams, 2005).

Whether we arrive by birth or adoption, none of us chooses our family. Adoptive families, however, often experience "intrusions" that biological parents don't (Melosh, 2002). Some of the most controversial issues include transracial and open adoptions. There are also misgivings about adoptions by same-sex partners and international adoptions.

Transracial Adoption

Transracial adoptions are controversial. Advocates, including some social workers, maintain that many African American or biracial children, especially those with emotional or physical handicaps, would remain in foster homes until age 18 if white parents did not adopt them (Altstein, 2006). Others disagree.

since you asked

Are transracial adoptions a good idea?

WHY PEOPLE SUPPORT TRANSRACIAL ADOPTIONS

Proponents of transracial adoption argue that insistence on same-race adoption has decreased adoptions of black children by about 90 percent (Furgatch, 1995). In addition, some critics contend that promoting foster care instead of transracial adoptions is self-serving because it protects social service jobs: "The more kids in foster care, the more money states get from the federal government for their overall programs, since 50 percent of foster care funds go to administrative costs, including social worker salaries" (Spake, 1998: 31).

When white adoptive families encourage them to participate in multicultural and multiracial activities, children in transracial adoptions do well. If anything, some black adoptees complain, their white parents tried too hard to educate them about their heritage, turning dinner-table conversations into lectures on African American history (Simon, 1993; Simon and Alstein, 2000).

Although children adopted across cultures can benefit from learning about their birth culture, doing so is not a prerequisite for healthy psychological development. For example, strong family ties and good peer relationships are more important to the children's well-being than identifying with one's birth culture (Baden, 2001).

WHY PEOPLE OPPOSE TRANSRACIAL ADOPTIONS

The National Association of Black Social Workers, among others, has strongly opposed transracial adoptions because the children "are alienated from their culture of origin" and "dislodged from the ethnic community" (Kissman and Allen, 1993: 93).

The Multiethnic Placement Act of 1994 makes it illegal to deny transracial adoption. Many African American (and some white) social workers find ways to get around the law, however. They believe that every child has the right to a permanent home with a family of the same race and that a white parent, "no matter how skilled or loving, could do irreparable harm to the self-esteem of a black child" (Furgatch, 1995: 19). Some black social workers also question the wisdom of placing African American children with white parents who may not provide the children with the strategies they need to deal with everyday episodes of racism, prejudice, and discrimination.

Open and Closed Adoption

Another controversial issue is open adoption. **Open adoption** is the practice of sharing information and maintaining contact between biological and adoptive parents throughout the child's life. In a **closed adoption**, all information is confidential and the birth parents, adoptive parents, and children have no contact and do not exchange identifying information.

In a third option, **semi-open adoption**, sometimes called *mediated adoption*, there is communication between the adoptee and the adoptive and biological parents, but it takes place through a third party (such as a caseworker or attorney) rather than directly. *Table 11.3* provides some of the pros and cons of each of these adoption methods.

By late 2006, 23 states provided open access to adoption records. Some birth mothers feel that such laws

TABLE 11.3

The Pros and Cons of Adoption Types

	Closed Adoptions	**Semi-Open Adoptions**	**Open Adoptions**
Pros	• *Birth parents* have a sense of closure and can move on with their life. • *Adoptive parents* are safe from the interference or co-parenting by birth parents. • *Adopted children* are safe from unstable or emotionally disturbed birth parents.	• *Birth parents* can maintain privacy while providing some information. • *Adoptive parents* have a greater sense of control than is usual in closed or open adoptions. • *Adopted children* don't fantasize about birth parents.	• *Birth parents* can develop a relationship with the child as she or he grows. • *Adoptive parents* have a better understanding of the child's history. • *Adopted children* are less likely to feel abandoned ("Why did you place me for adoption?") and can increase their circle of supportive adults.
Cons	• *Birth parents* may experience more distress because they lack information about the child's well-being. • *Adoptive parents* don't have access to much medical information about the birth family. • *Adopted children* may experience identity confusion because their physical traits differ from those of their adoptive parents.	• *Birth parents* may experience more distress about the decision because they are in contact with the adoptive family. • *Adoptive parents* may have to deal with troubling communications (letters, e-mail) between birth parents and an adopted child. • *Adopted children* may want more information than third parties are willing to divulge.	• *Birth parents* may be disappointed if the adoptive family fails to meet all their expectations. • *Adoptive parents* may have difficulties dealing with emotionally disturbed birth parents. • *Adopted children* may feel rejected if contact with birth parents ceases, or they may play their birth and adoptive families against each other.

SOURCES: Based on Grotevant, 2001; National Adoption Information Clearinghouse, 2002.

violate their right to privacy, especially when the birth resulted from a rape or violent relationship. A birth mother who is now in her late fifties said that the adoption "was the most searingly painful time of my life." Being contacted by the biological child would renew past traumas that she has struggled to forget. Adopted children argue, however, that they have a right to information about their biological parents, even if a biological parent doesn't want to be contacted. Some adult adoptees contend, for example, that they want to find out about health problems that have shown up in their own children and that may reflect genetic factors (Collins, 2005; National Adoption Information Clearinghouse, 2006).

Adoption by Same-Sex Partners

As this book goes to press, Florida, Mississippi, and Utah ban adoptions by lesbians and gay men. Other states—including Nebraska, Arkansas, Missouri, and

New Hampshire—prevent gays from adoption or becoming foster parents, even though there are no laws to prohibit such adoptions. Also, seven southern states have introduced bills to bar gay men and lesbians from adopting children (Paulson, 2006).

Although same-sex partners don't have adoption rights in many states, some professional groups have endorsed such policies. A few years ago, for example, the American Academy of Pediatrics announced its support for lesbians and gay men adopting children as well as their partners' children. According to the Academy, "A growing body of scientific literature demonstrates that children who grow up with 1 or 2 gay and/or lesbian parents fare as well in emotional, cognitive, social, and sexual functioning as do children whose parents are heterosexual" (Perrin, 2002: 341).

In 2005, President Bush opposed gay adoption because "the ideal is where a child is raised in a married family with a man and a woman." Nevertheless, about 40 percent of adoption agencies have placed children with gay or lesbian parents. These agencies feel that placing children in loving and responsible families is more important than whether the parents are heterosexual or homosexual (Carey, 2005; "Expanding Resources for Children . . . ," 2006).

International Adoption

Because the waiting period for adopting a child from overseas is only one or two years, compared with seven to 10 years for adopting a child in the United States, Americans have increasingly turned to international adoptions. In the past decade, about 170,000 U.S. families have adopted children from China, Eastern Europe, Central America, and India (Tyre, 2005).

A large number of intercountry adoptions are successful because the adoptees are infants (as in China) or come from well-managed foster-care systems (as in South Korea). Many infants from other countries, however, have a variety of diseases and problems, such as parasites, malnutrition, tuberculosis, asthma, and neurological damage. Especially in Russia, many infants suffer from developmental lags because of prenatal exposure to alcohol (McGuiness and Pallansch, 2000; Oleck, 2000).

Because there are no international adoption standards or accreditation criteria, prospective parents may face unexpected obstacles in the adoption process (see the box on "The Politics of International Adoption").

Babies and children are orphaned in many countries. About 300,000 of these orphans are in Romania. Because there are few facilities, a number of children may have to share a crib, such as those pictured here. Even teenagers may be crowded into cribs because there are no available beds.

Some Rewards and Costs of Adoption

People who are thinking about adoption should do much more research than rely on a few pages of a textbook. As in the case of having a biological child, as you saw earlier, there are rewards and costs in adopting a child.

SOME REWARDS OF ADOPTION The most obvious benefit is that adoptive parents and abandoned children find people to love. Most single parents are women, who tend to adopt girls or older, nonwhite, or mentally handicapped. Without adoption, many of these children would grow up in foster homes rather than in a stable environment.

Compared with children raised in foster homes or by never-married mothers, adopted children are economically advantaged, more likely to complete high school and hold a skilled job, and less likely to use drugs, commit crimes, or be homeless as adults (Bachrach et al., 1990; Spake, 1998). In fact, some of the most notable people in the United States and elsewhere have been adopted. They include

- Playwrights and authors (James Michener, Edgar Allen Poe, and Leo Tolstoy)

- Actors (Shari Belafonte-Harper, Ted Danson, Melissa Gilbert, and Ginger Rogers)

- Past U.S. presidents and first ladies (Gerald Ford, Herbert Hoover, and Nancy Reagan)

- Civil rights leaders and politicians (Jesse Jackson and Newt Gingrich)

- Entrepreneurs (Steve Jobs, co-founder of Apple Computer; Tom Monaghan, founder of Domino's Pizza; and Dave Thomas, founder of Wendy's)

Biological and adoptive parents are very similar. Both groups use positive rather than negative discipline (such as praising rather than spanking), emphasize desirable behavior in their children (such as doing well in school), and expect their children to complete college. Thus, adoptive parents function quite well and "at least as well as their biological counterparts" (Borders et al., 1998).

SOME COSTS OF ADOPTIONS Adoption also has disadvantages. Adoptive parents sometimes worry that a teenage girl who has not had prenatal care or used drugs could deliver a baby who may later have health problems. Adoptive parents must also have to sort out their feelings about having their own child versus adopting someone else's. And, about 3 to 8 percent of adoptions are dissolved because the adoptive parents can't cope

Cross-Cultural Families

The Politics of International Adoption

Most international adoptions are successful. However, enthusiastic parents often are uninformed and unprepared for some of the risks.

In some countries, such as Russia, agencies say that a child is in good health, but after adoption the parents find that the child has one of a wide range of illnesses. These include hepatitis B, tuberculosis, intestinal parasites, congenital heart defects, brain damage, and other maladies that U.S. physicians find difficult to treat. On the other hand, since 1991 the Russian government has restricted U.S. adoptions of Russian children because about a dozen of those children have died at the hands of abusive American parents. Thus, although Russians don't adopt the 700,000 orphans in their country, they are also unwilling to have them adopted by foreign parents (Brink, 1994; Finn, 2005; Pertman, 2005).

Even though there are thousands of orphans in Eastern Europe, it is not easy to adopt them. Some couples describe "endless" bureaucratic obstacles and legal systems that are hostile to intercountry adoptions. Agencies may "forget" about a promised adoption because of a last-minute higher offer from a flourishing black market in illicit adoptions. In some cases, prospective parents have arrived in Eastern European countries only to find that adoption and immigration policies have been changed while they were en route.

Prospective parents may have to pay bribes, called "contributions," to private agencies, religious groups, and government offices, both in the United States and abroad, that profit from adoptions. Attorneys or adoption agencies in the United States have sometimes collected up to $20,000 from parents, promising them, for example, a healthy baby from Eastern Europe, but never delivered (Weir, 2000; Ambrose and Coburn, 2001).

In India, American and European families adopt about 800 babies a year, compared with 1,200 in-country adoptions. Some Indian organizers have recently blocked international adoptions. They argue that poor families often raise their sons (because of the cultural value placed on boys) but sell their infant daughters to orphanages for as little as $20. The orphanages, in turn, make the babies available to foreign applicants who pay more for a child than do Indians seeking to adopt (Bonner, 2003).

Since 1991, American families have adopted more than 55,000 Chinese children, almost all girls. With U.S. couples eager to adopt, child-trafficking rings have emerged in China. They abduct female infants, including those wanted by their families, and sell them to orphanages for about $450. The orphanages then place the children for adoption, many going to U.S. families, in exchange for "mandatory contributions" of $3,000 per baby, a sum nearly twice the average per capita income in China (Clemetson, 2006; Goodman, 2006).

Stop and Think . . .

- However unintentionally, are Americans who turn to international adoptions encouraging child trafficking in some countries?
- There are thousands of U.S.-born children languishing in foster homes. Should our government forbid international adoptions until most of these children have been adopted?

with the child's severe behavior problems (Daly, 1999; Festinger, 2002).

Should adoptive parents be allowed to change their minds after the adoption has been finalized? In a recent survey, 23 percent of Americans said "yes," 59 percent said "no," and 19 percent weren't sure (Hollingsworth, 2003). Some argue that adoptive parents make a commitment and should deal with the problems instead of returning a child. Others contend that keeping a child whom parents don't love might create even more problems for both the parents and the child.

While some people adopt children, others turn to reproductive technologies. In fact, the number of infants born each year in the United States through artificial reproductive technology is higher than that of U.S.-born infants who are adopted.

Medical and High-Tech Solutions to Infertility

With advances in genetic research, our ability to alter the course of nature has expanded greatly. New genetic technologies have generated some difficult medical, legal, and ethical questions. Before considering these issues, let's look at the most common medical and high-tech treatments for infertility.

Medical Treatments for Infertility

Medical treatments include *artificial insemination* and *fertility drugs*. Artificial insemination is the most common treatment for men with low sperm counts. Fertility drugs improve the chance of conception in infertile women.

ARTIFICIAL INSEMINATION Artificial insemination, sometimes called *donor insemination (DI)*, is a medical procedure in which semen is introduced artificially into the vagina or uterus at about the time of ovulation. The semen, taken from the woman's husband or from a donor, may be fresh or it may have been frozen. Artificial insemination was first performed successfully in the 1970s and was followed by a normal pregnancy and birth. The current success rate is close to 20 percent (King, 2002).

For single women, artificial insemination offers a means of having children without waiting for Mr. Right to come along. Moreover, some couples prefer artificial insemination to adoption because the woman wants to experience a pregnancy and birth, or one or both parents want to contribute to the child's genetic makeup.

The use of fertility drugs—especially popular among white, educated, middle-class women—has resulted in multiple births, including quintuplets.

Prospective parents can browse a catalogue and choose a sperm donor by eye and hair color, nationality, blood type, height, and profession. (There is an extra charge for the sperm of Ph.D.s, doctors, and attorneys.) According to one man in Southern California who donated sperm to help cover living expenses while in medical school, "I could fill a banquet hall with 'my' children." Because donors are typically anonymous, half-siblings might meet and mate, not knowing that they have the same biological father and may share the same health problems (Romano, 2006; Streisand, 2006).

FERTILITY DRUGS If a woman is having difficulty becoming pregnant, her physician will try **fertility drugs,** medications that stimulate the ovaries to produce eggs. In 1997, a couple from Carlisle, Iowa, became the parents of the first septuplets ever born alive. The mother had been taking a fertility drug. For religious reasons, the couple refused to undergo a process known as *selective reduction:* aborting some of the fetuses to give the others a better chance to develop fully. An estimated two-thirds of triplets, quadruplets, and quintuplets are the result of increased use of fertility-enhancing drugs or a combination of drugs and other reproductive technologies (Ventura, Martin, et al., 2000).

Fertility drugs have a high success rate: 50 to 70 percent. A major concern, however, is that multiple births increase the chances of babies being born prematurely and having a low birth weight. As a result, the babies may end up with major health problems and lifelong learning disabilities (Elster et al., 2000).

High-Tech Treatments for Infertility

Infertile couples have more options than ever before through **assisted reproductive technology (ART),** a general term that includes all treatments or procedures that involve the handling of human eggs and sperm to establish a pregnancy. The Centers for Disease Control and Prevention (CDC) estimates that ART accounts for more than 1 percent of all U.S. births (*2003 Assisted reproductive technology . . . ,* 2005).

About 15 percent of U.S. women have received some type of infertility treatment since the introduction of ART in 1981. Success rates vary, declining significantly after age 40. Still, the number of infants born using ART has increased steadily from about 60,000 in 1996 to 120,000 in 2003 (*2003 Assisted reproductive technology . . . ,* 2005).

Many ART techniques are risky, and success rates are modest—about 30 percent. The most common of these techniques is in vitro fertilization.

IN VITRO FERTILIZATION In vitro fertilization (IVF) involves surgically removing eggs from a woman's ovaries, fertilizing them in a petri dish (a specially shaped glass container) with sperm from her husband or another donor, and then transferring the resulting embryos into the woman's uterus. (An *embryo* is the developing organism up to the eighth week of pregnancy.)

Louise Brown, the first in vitro baby (*in vitro* is Latin for "in glass") was born in England in 1978 and celebrated her 25th birthday in 2003. IVF is an outpatient procedure conducted at nearly 400 clinics in the United States alone. More than 1 million children worldwide owe their birth to this procedure (Mestel, 2003).

Although IVF is a miracle for many couples, it has drawbacks. Because more than one egg is usually implanted to increase the chances of success, nearly half of all women using in vitro procedures have multiple births. Multiple-birth babies are ten times more likely than single babies to be born prematurely, with a low birth weight, and/or with poorly developed organs. As with fertility drugs, a low birth weight subjects infants to medical risks ranging from lung disease and brain damage to infant death (Mitchell, 2002; Wood et al., 2003).

IVF is expensive, time-consuming, painful, and can be emotionally exhausting. Despite the difficulties and expense, egg donation is a growing enterprise at

Choices

Motherhood after Menopause

The National Center for Health Statistics defines the childbearing years as between ages 15 and 44. During the last decade or so, however, a number of women have had children after menopause:

- In 1994, a 59-year-old British woman who was artificially impregnated at a clinic in Italy gave birth to twins.

- In 1994, a 62-year-old Italian woman gave birth to a healthy boy after being implanted with a donated egg fertilized with her husband's sperm.

In 2004, Aleta St. James gave birth to her twins just three days before her 57th birthday. She is believed to be the oldest woman in America to give birth to twins.

- In 1996, a 63-year-old woman became the world's oldest known mother after an anonymous donor's egg was fertilized with sperm from her husband and implanted in her uterus. The woman was 69 in 2002 and received child care help for her five-year-old daughter from her 90-year-old mother.

- In 2002, a woman had twin boys at age 55, using eggs from a woman in her 20s.

- In 2006, a 57-year-old woman in New York City who conceived through IVF gave birth to twins.

A study of 77 postmenopausal women (ages 50 to 63) who had borne children through IVF found that they were doing well (Paulson et al., 2002). Several countries, however, including France and Italy, have passed laws barring postmenopausal women from artificial impregnation. The countries view such practices as immoral and dangerous to women's health.

Stop and Think . . .

- Some people feel that it's irresponsible for a menopausal woman to have children because she might not live to see the children grow up. Do you agree?

- If we bar women in their fifties from getting pregnant, should we also require vasectomies of men who father children in their fifties, sixties, and later?

hundreds of clinics nationwide. Increasingly, even women who have gone through menopause have become pregnant using a younger woman's donated eggs that are fertilized with sperm from the older woman's husband or from another donor. Although a woman's ovaries cease egg production after menopause, her other reproductive organs remain viable (see the box "Motherhood after Menopause").

SURROGACY In **surrogacy**, a woman who is capable of carrying a pregnancy to term serves as a substitute for a woman who cannot bear children. Usually, the surrogate is artificially inseminated with the sperm of the infertile woman's husband, and if she conceives, she carries the child to term. In some cases, the infertile couple's egg and sperm are brought together in vitro and the resulting embryo is implanted in a surrogate, who carries the child for them.

Some people believe that a major risk associated with surrogacy is that the surrogate mother might decide to keep the baby. Such battles are rare. Nevertheless, surrogacy raises complicated questions about kinship. Is a grandmother who gives birth to her grandson the boy's grandmother or his mother, for example?

Surrogacy is illegal in some countries, such as Austria, Germany, Spain, Sweden, and Norway. Other countries—France, Denmark, and the Netherlands—prohibit payments to surrogate mothers. U.S. laws vary from one state to another. Arizona, New Jersey, and Michigan ban surrogacy completely, whereas others allow it under certain conditions.

A growing number of childless people, including Americans, have made India a top destination for surrogacy. In the United States, surrogate mothers are typically paid $15,000, and agencies claim another $30,000. In India, the costs range from $2,500 to $6,500. Because surrogacy isn't widely accepted in India, the women and their families live in neighboring villages to keep the pregnancy a secret (Chopra, 2006).

Why do the women do it? A major reason is money. For example, Mehli, 32 and a mother of three children, will deliver a healthy baby and hand the newborn over to an American couple:

> She'll be paid about $5,000, a bonanza that would take her more than six years to earn on her salary as a schoolteacher. "I might renovate or add to the house, or spend it on my kids' education or my daughter's wedding," Mehli said (Chu, 2006: A1).

Some criticize such practices as "reproductive tourism" that exploits poor women by "renting their wombs, cheap," and risks their lives because of the possible complications of pregnancy and childbirth. Others argue that the service improves the family's standard of living (where the average income is about $500 a year) and that the doctors provide high-quality care. There are also cultural reasons for being a surrogate: Indian society views producing offspring as an almost sacred obligation, Hindu teachings promise rewards in the next life for good deeds performed on earth, and the mothers empathize with childless parents. For example, according to a surrogate mother who has two children and will give birth to another for an Indian couple, "I'll be happy because they'll be blessed with a child" (Chu, 2006: A1).

PRENATAL TESTING Preimplantation genetic diagnosis (PGD) is a recent ART procedure that enables physicians to identify genetic diseases in the embryo, such as cystic fibrosis or Down syndrome, before implantation. PGD allows a couple to choose only healthy embryos for transfer into a woman's uterus.

Some critics fear that PGD will increase abortion rates because of "imperfect" embryos and open the door to a "new eugenics" as parents customize their babies for anything "from tissue type to eye color, broad shoulders, to extreme intelligence." On the other hand, many researchers feel that PGD will eventually produce embryos that are free of fatal diseases and that this new technology is fertility's "new frontier" (Healy, 2003; Jones, 2003).

Genetic Engineering: Its Benefits and Costs

Genetic research and biotechnology have been a blessing for many couples, but some people wonder whether scientists are going too far (see the box "So What's Next? Pregnant Men?"). Some worry that genetic manipulation, because it "meddles" with nature, is unethical and detrimental to society. Others feel that the benefits outweigh the costs.

since you asked

Does genetic engineering benefit primarily the wealthy?

THE BENEFITS OF GENETIC ENGINEERING Genetic engineering has been valuable in detecting prenatal genetic disorders and abnormalities. Two diagnostic procedures that have become fairly common are amniocentesis and chorionic villus sampling. In **amniocentesis**, which is performed in the twentieth week of pregnancy, a needle is inserted through the abdomen into the amniotic sac, and the fluid is analyzed for such abnormalities as Down syndrome and spina bifida (an abnormal opening along the spine).

Changes
So What's Next? Pregnant Men?

In the movie *Junior,* a scientist loses funding for his research and implants a fertilized egg in his own body to test a wonder drug that ensures healthy pregnancies.

In real life, there are some problems. Men don't produce the appropriate hormones. Men don't have ovaries and therefore don't produce eggs. And they don't have wombs.

However, hormones can be injected. And perhaps wombs may not be necessary. Abdominal pregnancies—those occurring outside the womb—are rare, but they do happen about once in every 10,000 pregnancies.

An abdominal pregnancy may occur when the placenta, which is produced partly by the fetus, attaches to something other than the womb. In August 1979, for example, George Poretta attempted to perform an appendectomy on a Michigan woman who was suffering from stomach cramps. "I opened her up expecting to find an appendix," Poretta said, "and there was this tiny foot." The baby, a boy, weighed 3 pounds 5 ounces (Teresi, 1994: 55).

Both male and female abdomens offer a similar environment for impregnation, including a membrane, called the *omentum,* that encloses abdominal organs in which, theoretically, a fertilized egg could become implanted. Thus, fertilizing an egg in vitro and inserting the developing embryo through a small incision in the abdominal cavity could produce a male pregnancy (Peritz, 2003).

Scientists have recently turned stem cells from both female and male mice into eggs (Hübner et al., 2003). This research suggests that even men might have the biological capacity to produce eggs.

Stop and Think . . .

- Should we continue to develop technology that will allow men to become pregnant and deliver babies? Or is such research a sci-fi nightmare?

- One of the advantages of creating human eggs, and using the same process that researchers use to create mouse eggs, is that there would be no need for donors. What are some possible disadvantages?

The same information can be produced at ten weeks by **chorionic villus sampling (CVS).** A catheter inserted through the vagina removes some of the *villi* (fingerlike protrusions) from the *chorion* (the outer membrane that surrounds the amniotic sac). The chief advantage of detecting abnormalities early is that parents can decide on an abortion early in the pregnancy. Both these tests have risks, though low (about 1 to 2 percent of all cases), of spontaneous abortions and possible deformities (Boodman, 1992).

Besides detecting prenatal abnormalities, genetic engineering produces children who are usually as healthy as children born naturally. In addition, because some women experience infertility due to cancer treatments, they can freeze their eggs before chemotherapy and doctors can later reimplant those eggs to produce healthy babies (Hobson, 2004; Shevell et al., 2005).

THE COSTS OF GENETIC ENGINEERING Medical treatments for infertility are limited to affluent couples because the procedures are expensive and rarely covered by insurance programs. For example, repeated IVF attempts can easily cost up to $100,000 (Weil, 2006). Because only the rich can afford genetic engineering, the technology doesn't benefit all social classes.

There is also concern about such issues as parents' and scientists' right to "manufacture" babies, creating "designer babies" by choosing genes for a child's hair color and height; parents' right to reject imperfect fetuses; and the rights of both parents and embryos. Suppose that both parents of a fertilized egg that has been frozen die. Who's responsible for the frozen embryo? Should it be destroyed because the parents are dead? Should it be given to relatives? Put up for adoption? Turned over to doctors for medical research?

Since the birth of the Iowa septuplets in 1997, many fertility experts have criticized physicians for not limiting the number of embryos implanted during IVF to two or three because "the human uterus is not meant to carry litters" (Cowley and Springen, 1997: 66). Triplets, quadruplets, and quintuplets are 12 times more likely than other babies to die within a year. Many suffer from respiratory and digestive problems. They're also prone to a range of neurological disorders, including blindness, cerebral palsy, and mental retardation.

In 1999, in the first known birth of its kind in the United States, a California woman had a baby using sperm that had been retrieved from her husband 30 hours after he died unexpectedly of an allergic reaction. The physician who extracted the sperm cells did so to allay the family's stress and grief. Medical ethicists wondered, however, whether it's appropriate to give birth to a child whose father is dead ("Woman gives birth . . . ," 1999).

Some parents conceive children to use the tissue from the umbilical cord to provide life-saving cells for a sick sibling. They might certainly love the new baby as much as the other children. The question is whether it's ethical to bear babies primarily so that their tissue can be used to help other children in the family.

Finally, how many parents can a baby have? If lesbian moms split up, for example, who has parenthood rights: the sperm donor, the egg donor, the mother who bears the child, or all three? And who are the parents of a child who has a sperm donor, an egg donor, a surrogate mother, and a stepparent who adopts the child?

Making Connections

- In several European countries—including Britain, Sweden, Norway, and the Netherlands—it's illegal to sell anonymous donor sperm. Should the United States pass similar laws, even if the number of donors decreases?

- PGD allows people to select the sex of their offspring. Should prospective parents have such choices? Or should they be grateful that they have a healthy baby, regardless of the infant's sex?

- A team of researchers in Japan has created "virgin" births in mice using two eggs and no sperm (Kono et al., 2004). Do you think that such research will create more options in the future? Or that we shouldn't blur the biological lines between female and male reproduction?

Having Children Outside Marriage

In 2001, a Wisconsin Supreme Court judge "banned" a father of nine who owes child support from having more children unless he could prove that he would support all his offspring. The man has four sons and five daughters, ages three to 16, born to four different mothers. Since then, a national study has found that the states with the strictest child support enforcement laws have decreased their rates of out-of-wedlock births by as much as 20 percent (Price, 2001; Plotnick et al., 2004).

It's not clear whether tougher child support laws prevent pregnancies or encourage marriage. However, we typically associate having children outside marriage with women, not men. As a result, almost all the research focuses on out-of-wedlock births to females rather than males. We begin with a general description of nonmarital childbearing and then consider some differences between older single mothers and teens.

Some Characteristics of Nonmarital Childbearing

In 1950, only 3 percent of all births were to unmarried women. By 2004, there were 1.5 million births to unmarried women, accounting for almost 36 percent of all births in the United States (Hamilton et al., 2005).

Why has the rate of out-of-wedlock births increased? The reasons encompass a multitude of decisions and complex processes that stretch across a person's lifetime. At all ages, for example, women are more likely to have out-of-wedlock births if they don't see marriage as a prerequisite for parenthood and if they feel that family members will provide support, including child care (Schoen and Tufis, 2003). The mother's race and ethnicity, educational level, and age also affect nonmarital birth rates.

WHAT IS THE PURPOSE OF HAVING CHILDREN?

©2006 CREATORS SYNDICATE, INC. www.creators.com

IT'S THE ONLY WAY TO LEARN HOW TO USE THIS iPod.

By permission of John L. Hart FLP and Creators Syndicate, Inc.

VARIATIONS BY RACE AND ETHNICITY Nonmarital birth rates vary widely among different racial and ethnic groups (see *Figure 11.5*). And since 1990, nonmarital birth rates have increased for white women (from 24 to 29 per 1000 unmarried women ages 15 to 44) and Latinas (from 90 to 92), and decreased for black women (from 91 to 66) (Martin et al., 2005).

There is also much variation *within* groups. Among Asians and Pacific Islanders, for example, 6 percent of births are to unmarried Chinese women compared with almost 20 percent for Filipinas and 51 percent for Hawaiian women. Among Latinas, births to unmarried women range from 25 percent for Cuban women to 60 percent for Puerto Rican women (Ventura, Martin, et al., 2000).

VARIATIONS BY EDUCATIONAL ATTAINMENT Education is also related to out-of-wedlock births. Less than 5 percent of all nonmarital births are to college-educated women. Unmarried women with less than a high school diploma are at least three times more likely to have a baby than unmarried women with some college (Ventura et al., 1995; Musick, 2002).

Educated women usually have more job opportunities, greater awareness of family planning, and more decision-making power in their relationships. They are also more likely to marry late, to postpone their first pregnancy, to allow more time between births, and to have fewer children. And if college-educated women have out-of-wedlock births, they have more financial resources to raise their children.

VARIATIONS BY AGE Contrary to popular belief, teenagers have lower out-of-wedlock birth rates than older women. While teenage nonmarital birth rates started to decline in 1994, those for women ages 20 to 39 continued to increase (see *Figure 11.6*). Still, almost 83 percent of births to teenagers are out of wedlock (Hamilton et al., 2005). Let's look at unmarried older mothers before turning to teen moms.

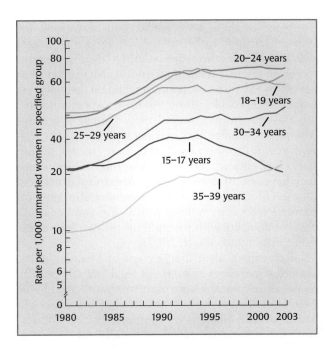

FIGURE 11.6   Birth Rates for Unmarried Women, by Age of Mother, 1980–2003

Note: Rates are live births per 1,000 unmarried women ages 15–44.
SOURCE: Based on Martin et al., 2005.

SOURCE: Martin et al., 2005, Figure 5.

Unmarried Older Mothers

We usually hear more about unmarried teenage mothers than about older unmarried mothers. Between 1980 and 2003, however, the proportion of births to unmarried women ages 20 to 29 increased and was higher than the proportion for unmarried teens (see *Figure 11.6*).

WHY THE RATES HAVE INCREASED A major reason for the increase in births to unmarried women is the rise in cohabitation. People often assume that out-of-wedlock births create mother-only families. In fact, fully 40 percent of such births now occur in cohabiting families. In addition, half of all nonmarital births are second or later births, and 25 percent are third or later births, primarily to women who are not teenagers (Wu et al., 2001).

Because many cohabiting couples see themselves as a family and there's little stigma attached to out-of-wedlock births, there's little incentive to "legitimate" children by getting married. Whether they are cohabiting or not, among unmarried women ages 22 and older, 35 percent of those with no high school diploma and 25 percent of those with a high school diploma report using no contraceptives, compared with 8 percent of those with a college degree or higher (Chandra et al., 2005).

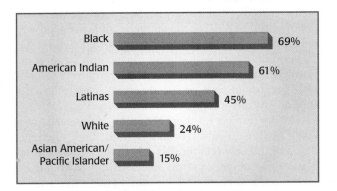

FIGURE 11.5   Percent of Births to Unmarried Women, by Race and Ethnicity, 2003

Some of these women may still be waiting for Prince Charming rather than "settling" for a partner who doesn't meet their expectations. Others don't want to marry because their boyfriend or live-in partner is unemployed or won't support the children. Even if these women—especially those in lower socioeconomic groups—want to wed, their chances of doing so are low. Among other things, they may not want to sacrifice welfare income (however modest) to marry men with similarly low educational or occupational achievement, they have less time to meet a prospective partner, and they usually are not attractive to economically better-off partners who don't want to provide for another man's child or compete with the child for the mother's attention (Lichter and Graefe, 2001).

Remember, also, that, except in Massachusetts, same-sex marriages still are not legal (see Chapter 9). Same-sex relationships are more acceptable than in the past, but lesbians who have children have no choice but to be counted among the "unmarried older women" statistics that include out-of-wedlock births.

CONSEQUENCES FOR CHILDREN AND ADULTS The poverty rate among never-married mothers is twice that of divorced mothers and 12 times higher than that of married-couple families. Child support enforcement has increased during the past decade. Nevertheless, the rate of support is never higher than 27 percent for never-married mothers in all age groups (Bartfeld and Meyer, 2001; see, also, Chapters 13 and 15). This means that many never-married mothers and their children live in poverty or near poverty.

Nonmarital childbearing decreases the likelihood of getting married. At age 14, for example, girls who have given birth out of wedlock are 58 percent more likely to have never married by age 35 than girls who have not born a child out of wedlock. And with each additional such child, the likelihood of marrying declines (Lichter and Graefe, 2001; Upchurch et al., 2001).

Unmarried Teenage Mothers

Many teenagers now frequently refer to out-of-wedlock parents as "baby mamas" and "baby daddies" instead of "parents." Such language suggests that births to unmarried adolescents are acceptable, at least among many teens (Kane, 2006).

Although teenage out-of-wedlock birth rates are very high, they've been declining (see "Data Digest" and *Figure 11.6*). How can we explain both trends? And how do nonmarital births to adolescents affect the children?

since you asked

Why are teenager out-of-wedlock birth rates so high?

WHY THE RATES HAVE DECREASED There are a number of reasons for the decrease in nonmarital teen birth rates. Many teenagers are less sexually active than in the past, especially those ages 15 to 17 (Abma et at., 2004).

Some community leaders feel that pro-abstinence movements explain much of the decline in teenage births. Others maintain that candid school sex education programs account for the drop in both teenage sex and teen births because teens are more likely to use contraceptives (Davis-Packard, 2000; Kirby, 2002).

Contraception is the prevention of pregnancy by behavioral, mechanical, or chemical methods. Between 1995 and 2002, the percentage of never-married females ages 15 to 19 who never used contraceptives decreased from almost 30 percent to 17 percent. However, about one-third of both female and male teens report not receiving any instruction about contraceptive methods before age 18 (Abma et al., 2004). (*Appendix D* describes the most common contraceptives, including their usage, effectiveness, and possible problems.)

Another factor may be the long period of economic expansion during the 1990s. As more jobs with good pay became available, some teens postponed pregnancy and parenthood (Ventura, Curtin, et al., 2000). According to a sex education researcher who directs a teen pregnancy prevention program in New York City, the best contraceptive is providing teens with a climate in which "they grow to believe that they are capable of success" and will have opportunities in the future (Marks, 2002: 3).

Although nonmarital teen birth rates have declined, they are higher in the United States than in any other industrialized nation. And regardless of how well-intentioned they are, most unwed teens simply don't have the resources and maturity to raise happy, healthy children.

ADOLESCENTS AND PARENTHOOD A surprisingly low number of teens say that they would be "very upset" if they experienced a pregnancy (see *Figure 11.7*). Some teenagers intentionally have a baby to satisfy emotional or status needs. "Babies may become a sought-after symbol of status, of passage to adulthood, of being a 'grown' woman" (Anderson, 1990: 127; see, also, Davies et al., 2004). This pseudo-adulthood offers adolescents some status without requiring them to be completely responsible because parents or social service agencies usually support the teen mothers and their offspring.

Many teenage mothers are emotionally needy as a result of abuse, neglect, or molestation. They often feel that a brand new relationship—with the baby—will replace or reshape existing relationships with kin, a boyfriend, and peers. In addition, if young teens fail in school, they often feel that they can succeed at motherhood (Mauldon, 2003; see, also, Chapter 14).

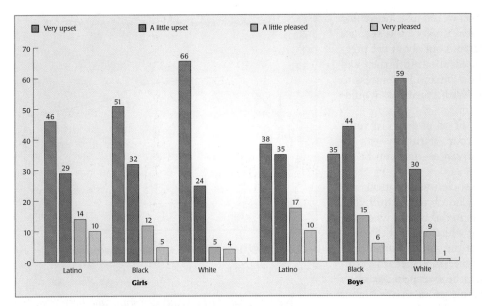

FIGURE 11.7   How Teenagers Feel About Getting Pregnant
A national survey asked almost 20 million never-married teens, 15 to 19 years old, how they would feel "If you got pregnant now/got a girl pregnant now." How might you explain the variations by sex and race-ethnicity?

SOURCE: Based on Abma et al., 2004, Table 32 Supplement.

led to many problems in my life. I personally believed that somehow I was dealt a hand less than others and so I perceived that other people were entitled to more. I can see the difference in the attitude and confidence of my daughter, who is being raised with both of her [married] parents (Author's files).

Although rates of out-of-wedlock birth in the United States are high, they'd be much higher if teens and older women didn't have access to abortion. Some people see abortion as sinful; others feel that it's a responsible way to avoid parenthood, both inside and outside marriage.

Such expectations are rarely fulfilled. Most teens from lower socioeconomic backgrounds live in dangerous neighborhoods or with violent partners and therefore must constantly worry about themselves and their children. Adolescent mothers, whether married or not, experience more pregnancy and delivery problems, have less healthy babies than adult mothers, and about 80 percent live in poverty. They are also more likely than their nonparenting counterparts to use tobacco, alcohol, and other drugs and to suffer from stress and depression (Hellerstedt, 2002; Miller, 2002).

On a more personal level, here are some comments from a few of my students, both white and African American:

I had my first son out of wedlock when I was 17. I had many struggles—finances, housing, jobs, and education. I did not plan to have him but he was conceived and I decided to have him. I was often angry with myself and his father. I had my second son after getting married. That's why I'm in school right now—to make life better for my sons. I have learned that being married can give you and your children some stability.

I was born out of wedlock when my mom was 18 and always had a yearning for my parents to be together. I didn't feel secure because money was always a problem. Understanding my worth was critical and

Abortion

A few years ago, a 15-year-old girl in Texas tried to abort her twins by hitting herself. When that didn't work, she asked her boyfriend, 17, to repeatedly step on her abdomen until she miscarried. She escaped punishment because, under Texas and federal laws, a woman cannot be charged for causing the death of her own fetus. Her boyfriend, however, was convicted of two counts of murder and sentenced to life in prison (Cook, 2005).

In 2003, President George W. Bush signed the Partial Birth Abortion Bill. Where are the women making decisions about their bodies and reproductive rights?

Proper usage of contraception would have prevented this tragedy. The couple didn't seek an abortion because they didn't want their parents to find out about the pregnancy and didn't know what to do about it. If they had been better informed about abortion and had access to family planning services, the boyfriend probably wouldn't be in prison.

Abortion is the expulsion of an embryo or fetus from the uterus. It can occur naturally—as in *spontaneous abortion,* or *miscarriage*—or it can be induced medically.

Practiced by people in all societies, abortion was not forbidden by the Catholic Church until 1869. The United States outlawed abortion in the 1800s, when the practice was widespread among white, married, Protestant, American-born women in the middle and upper classes. Upper-middle-class white men became concerned that the country would be overpopulated by members of "inferior" new ethnic groups with higher birth rates (Mohr, 1981; see, also, Chapter 3).

Incidence of Abortion

Half of all pregnancies in America are unintended: Some are unwanted at the time of conception or at any time in the future, while others are "mistimed" because they occur sooner than the woman wanted. About half of the unintended pregnancies end in abortion. Ultimately, more than one-third (35 percent) of American women will have had an abortion by the time they reach age 45 (Boonstra et al., 2006).

In 2002, 1.3 million U.S. women (2 percent of all women) terminated pregnancies by abortion. The *abortion rate,* or the number of abortions per 1000 women ages 15 to 44, increased during the 1970s but has steadily decreased since 1980 (see *Figure 11.8*).

Who Has Abortions?

Abortion is most common among women who are young (in their twenties), white, and never married (see *Figure 11.9*). Proportionately, however, African American women are more than three times as likely as white women to have an abortion, and Latinas are 2.5 times as likely (Guttmacher Institute, 2005a).

These variations reflect social class rather than racial-ethnic differences. Since 1987, the major reason for abortion (74 percent of all cases) has been a financial inability to support the baby. About 57 percent of women who have abortions live well below the poverty level (Guttmacher Institute, 2005b; Boonstra et al., 2006). They feel that having an unwanted baby would plunge them deeper into poverty and create even more parenting problems. For example, here's how a 25-year-old mother of two children, separated from her husband, explained her decision for an abortion:

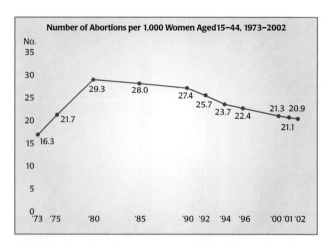

FIGURE 11.8 **U.S. Abortion Rates Have Decreased**
SOURCE: Guttmacher Institute, 2005a.

Neither one of us is really economically prepared. For myself, I've been out of work for almost two years now. I just started, you know, receiving benefits from DSS [Department of Social Services] and stuff. And with my youngest child being three years old, and me . . . constantly applying for jobs for a while now . . . And with the father . . . let's just say I don't think he needs another one (Finer et al., 2005: 114).

In effect, then, many women seek an abortion not because they're selfish or because it's "convenient," but because they feel a responsibility to maintain economic stability and to care for the children they already have or might have.

About 70 percent of the women who have abortions are Catholics and Protestants, and about 8 percent belong to "other" religious groups, especially "born-again Christians." Only 22 percent of women who have had abortions identify themselves as having no religious affiliation. This number may be low, however, because many women who have abortions are reluctant to claim a religious affiliation out of guilt (Guttmacher Institute, 2005b).

Is Abortion Safe?

Anti-abortion groups maintain that abortion endangers a woman's physical and emotional health. Safety can be measured on two levels: physical and emotional.

PHYSICAL HEALTH On the physical level, a legal abortion in the first trimester (up to 12 weeks) is safer than driving a car, using oral contraceptives, undergoing sterilization, or continuing a pregnancy (see *Table 11.4*). Abortions performed in the first trimester pose virtually no long-term risk of problems such as infertility, miscarriage, birth defects, or preterm or low-birth-weight delivery (Boonstra et al., 2006).

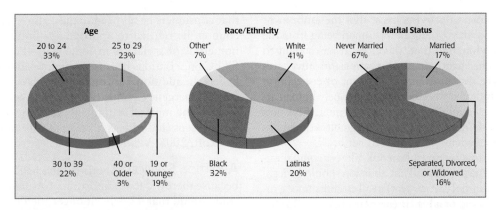

FIGURE 11.9   Who Has Abortions?

*Other includes Asian/Pacific Islanders, American Indians and Alaska Natives.

Source: Based on Guttmacher Institute, 2005b.

EMOTIONAL HEALTH In terms of emotional health, the data are mixed. Several studies have found no evidence that abortion has long-term negative psychological consequences. In fact, women who abort an unwanted pregnancy report less depression than those who give birth to an unwanted or unplanned baby. Without abortion, many young single mothers would have closely spaced children, which would increase the economic stress they experience and place their children at greater risk for abuse and neglect (Westhoff et al., 2003; Schmiege and Russo, 2005).

since you asked

Is abortion dangerous?

Several other studies show that abortion temporarily decreases some women's psychological health. Low-income women who have an abortion, for example, are more depressed than low-income women who deliver a baby, although the depression may also reflect poverty. It's also not clear whether the depression is due to the most recent abortion or to having had multiple abortions over time (Reardon et al., 2003; Boonstra et al., 2006).

All the studies are limited because about half of all women conceal their abortion histories from interviewers and medical practitioners (Koop, 1989). We know less about how women react to abortions in the short and long term than we do about why abortion rates have decreased.

Why Have Abortion Rates Decreased?

More women are having unwanted babies (see "Data Digest"). Why, then, have abortion rates decreased? There are several reasons, ranging from personal attitudes to structural factors such as politics and laws.

ATTITUDES ABOUT ABORTION Although abortion has been legal since the U.S. Supreme Court's *Roe* v. *Wade* ruling in 1973, it is a fiercely controversial issue in the United

TABLE 11.4

Abortion Risks in Perspective

Activity	Chance of Dying
Motorcycling	1 in 1,000
Illegal abortion	1 in 3,000
Driving a car	1 in 6,000
Power boating	1 in 6,000
Legal abortion after 20 weeks	1 in 11,000
Continuing a pregnancy	1 in 14,300
Oral contraceptive use (smoker)	1 in 16,000
Playing football	1 in 25,000
Sexual intercourse (risk of pelvic infection)	1 in 50,000
Legal abortion (13 to 15 weeks)	1 in 60,000
Oral contraceptive use (nonsmoker)	1 in 63,000
Tubal ligation	1 in 67,000
Using an intrauterine device	1 in 100,000
Vasectomy	1 in 300,000
Tampons (risk of toxic shock syndrome)	1 in 350,000
Legal abortion (9 to 10 weeks)	1 in 500,000
Legal abortion before 9 weeks	**1 in 1 million**

Sources: Finer and Henshaw, 2003; Guttmacher Institute, 2005b.

States. Anti-abortion activists insist that the embryo or fetus is not just a mass of cells but a human being from the time of conception, and that, therefore, it has a right to live. On the other hand, many abortion rights advocates believe that the organism at the moment of conception lacks a brain and other specifically and uniquely human attributes, such as consciousness and reasoning. Abortion rights proponents also believe that a pregnant woman has a right to decide what will happen to her body.

According to a recent Gallup poll, almost equal numbers hold extreme positions: That abortion should be legal (24 percent) or illegal (20 percent) in all circumstances, including rape, incest, or a life-threatening condition for the mother. A larger number (55 percent), however, support abortion, but with some limits. These divergent opinions have been fairly consistent since 1975 (Saad, 2003).

CONTRACEPTIVES As much as 43 percent of the decline in abortions since 1994 can be attributed to the use of "emergency contraction" (EC) (Guttmacher Institute, 2005a). Sometimes called "morning-after" birth control, oral contraceptive pills taken within 72 hours after sexual intercourse prevent implantation of the fertilized ovum in the uterine wall. About half of the 3 million unintended pregnancies in the United States each year could be prevented with morning-after pills (Stenson, 2002; Boonstra et al., 2006).

Morning-after pills are controversial, however. Opponents claim that they are *abortifacients*, substances that cause termination of pregnancy. Proponents maintain that they are contraceptives because they prevent pregnancy and abortion.

Despite the controversy, the Bush administration has allowed Medicare to cover prescriptions for sexual enhancement drugs such as Viagra for men but has blocked women's access to emergency contraceptives. And, even though President Bush's scientific advisors recommended

The Chinese government has successfully reduced its population growth by promoting its one-child policy, as seen in this billboard on an apartment building.

that consumers be allowed to purchase EC pills over the counter, he refused to approve this policy. As a result, numerous pharmacists in some states have declined to fill EC prescriptions because of their religious or personal beliefs. In addition, just one in three hospitals routinely offers emergency contraception to sexually assaulted women and medical staff members at one in 10 hospitals never discuss EC with assaulted patients (Sonfield, 2004; Rockoff, 2005; Van Riper and Hellerstedt, 2005).

ABORTION SERVICES Abortion rates have also decreased because there are fewer abortion providers. A California study found that 42 percent of certified nurse-midwives and 24 percent of physician assistants want training in abortion. Because of domestic terrorism by anti-abortion activists, however, few doctors perform abortions. For example, the number of abortion providers has declined by 11 percent since 1996; 87 percent of U.S. counties and 31 percent of metropolitan areas have no abortion facilities. If a woman doesn't have the resources to travel to another state, she has little choice except to bear an unwanted or unplanned baby (Finer and Henshaw, 2003; Hwang et al., 2005; Boonstra et al., 2006).

LAWS AND POLICIES South Dakota hasn't had any doctors that provide abortion since 1997. In 2006, this state's legislature passed a law—designed to overturn *Roe v. Wade*—that makes it a felony for any doctor to perform any abortion, even in cases of rape and incest—except to save the life of a pregnant woman. Even though the law violates *Roe v. Wade*, pro-abortion groups have not challenged it so far (Nieves, 2006).

South Dakota isn't the only state that has set limits on abortion. In 2005, other states passed a total of 52 new laws that restrict abortion. For example,

- 46 states allow doctors to refuse to provide an abortion (regardless of the reason).

- 34 states require some type of parental involvement in a minor's decision to have an abortion.

- 33 states have made it more difficult or more expensive for poor women and teenagers to obtain contraceptives and related family planning services.

- 32 states require women to receive preabortion counseling (which may include viewing gory films about aborted fetuses).

- 13 states allow the sale of "Choose Life" license plates; most of the proceeds go to anti-abortion groups and are used to pay for advertisements opposing abortion (Guttmacher Institute, 2005b; "'Choose life' license plates," 2006; Tumulty, 2006).

The Bush administration has also funded at least 4000 crisis pregnancy centers (CPCs). CPC staff—usually volunteers with no professional training—try to discourage girls and women from having abortions by "playing gruesome videos depicting bloody fetuses, withholding pregnancy-test results, and even pressuring her to sign adoption papers" (Kashef, 2003: 18).

According to several recent studies, most of CPCs advertise themselves as "women's centers" and "clinics." When women arrive expecting a full range of services, the "staff" tell the women that having an abortion increases the risk of breast cancer, causes sterility, and leads to suicide and "post-abortion stress disorders." Such false and misleading information represents "inappropriate public health practices" (National Abortion Federation, 2006; United States House of Representatives, 2006).

Abortion in Other Countries

Although the United States is the third largest country in the world, it accounts for only 3 percent of all abortions worldwide. Whether the procedure is legal or not, women throughout the world have abortions. Some countries, such as El Salvador, Chile, and Colombia, ban abortion regardless of the circumstances. As a result, many women use abortion-inducing methods that can be fatal, such as clothes hangers, ingesting fertilizers and caustic car battery acids, or having abortions performed in unsanitary conditions and by unskilled providers (Guttmacher Institute, 2005b; Yin, 2005; Hitt, 2006).

Making abortion illegal and prosecuting women doesn't lower abortions rates. Instead, many women who have unsafe abortions die as a result. The Bush administration has funded U.S. anti-abortion groups to advocate their work overseas. Some critics wonder whether such funding is responsible, however, because the groups promote having children rather than endorsing family-planning programs, sex education, and

⚙ Making Connections

■ Are you for or against abortion? What are the reasons for your position?

■ Many Americans (like you, perhaps) assume that *Roe v. Wade* will continue to provide women with choices about abortion. How would you feel if the U.S. Supreme Court overturned this law?

■ Do children have a right *not* to be born if the parents know that the child will be severely disabled? Are parents irresponsible if they don't abort a child who will always depend on others for care or may die at an early age?

access to birth control—especially for families that can't support their children (Human Rights Watch, 2005).

In 1979 China, confronted with overwhelming population growth, instituted a policy that permits every family to have only one child. The means used to enforce the one-child policy include forcing women to get abortions and undergo sterilization. The policy has reduced China's rapid population growth, but some families have gotten around the policies in various ways. For example, because there are no penalties for multiple births, some women have taken fertility drugs to have more babies in a single birth. China has banned using fertility drugs but enforcement is virtually nonexistent (Beech, 2005; "China: Drug bid. . . . ," 2006).

Child Free by Choice

American author Edgar Watson Howe once said that families with babies and families without babies feel sorry for each other. Just as some couples make a conscious decision to have a child, others decide not to have children. The desire to have children is not universal. According to one nationwide survey, 4 percent of respondents said that they did not have children, did not want them, or were glad they had none (Gallup and Newport, 1990). The percentage of women still childless at ages 40 to 44 (most of whom subsequently remain childless) has increased in recent years (see "Data Digest").

since you asked

Are childless couples self-centered?

Many couples without children prefer to call themselves "child free" because "childless" implies a lack or a loss. "Child free," in contrast, connotes freedom from the time, money, energy, and responsibility that parenting requires (Paul, 2001).

A few years ago, economist Sylvia Ann Hewlett (2002) created a stir when she contended that many professional women pay a huge price by pursuing a career: They end up childless. According to a recent survey, however, 72 percent of the women disagreed that being a mother is the key to a full life (Center for the Advancement of Women, 2003).

People have many reasons for being child free. Often, educated and successful men and women simply don't want kids:

Non-parents never have to budget for diapers or college educations. They can make decisions about where to live without worrying about the quality of local schools or which pediatricians offer weekend hours. They can even experience parenthood vicariously through nieces, nephews, and friends' children—but only if they choose to (Crispell, 1993: 23–24).

This freedom may well be one of the reasons that childless couples say they're very happy. Women report enjoying stimulating discussions with their husbands, shared projects and outside interests, a more egalitarian division of household labor, more time and energy for work and volunteering, and freedom from the troubling child–parent relationships that they themselves encountered (Somers, 1993; Safer, 1996; Casey, 1998).

Some couples remain child free because of inertia or indecision. When couples disagree about having a child, for instance, the partner who wants a child postpones further discussion, sometimes indefinitely (Thomson, 1997).

Others marry later in life and decide not to have children. As one husband said, "I didn't want to be 65 with a teenager in the house" (Fost, 1996: 16). Some are teachers or other professionals who work with children but like to "come home to peace and quiet and a relaxing night with my husband" (May, 1995: 205). For others, marriage is a precondition for parenthood:

A thirty-five-year-old divorced Black attorney who had grown up in a "secure two-parent family" wanted to have children as a part of a committed relationship with "two on-site, full-time loving parents." She had two abortions because the men involved "weren't ready for the responsibility of fatherhood," and she did not want to be a single mother (May, 1995: 193).

Some feel that it's irresponsible to bring more children into an already-crowded world. Some don't think they're suited for parenthood because they feel that they'd be impatient with offspring. Others simply don't want to structure their lives around children's activities and school vacations and to worry about how a child will turn out (see Bulcroft and Teachman, 2004, for a discussion of theories of childlessness).

Although today the general public is much more accepting of child free couples than in the past, some people are still suspicious of couples without children: "Through-out the culture, motherhood is celebrated while childlessness is promoted as a sorry state" (Morell, 1994: 1).

Child free couples are often seen as self-indulgent, selfish, self-absorbed, workaholics, less well-adjusted emotionally, and less sensitive and loving than couples with children. They have even been stereotyped as "weirdos," "child haters," or "barren, career-crazed boomers" (Arenofsky, 1993). In fact, people who don't marry are lonelier later in life than those who don't have children (Zhang and Hayward, 2001).

Why do these stereotypes about child free couples exist? Perhaps couples with children resent childless couples because the latter have (or seem to have) more freedom, time, money, and fun. As you will see in the next chapter, raising children is not an easy task, and parents often feel unappreciated. Thus, a child free life can sometimes be very attractive.

Conclusion

Attitudes about becoming a parent have *changed* greatly, even during the last generation. There are more *choices* today than in the past, including postponing parenthood, becoming pregnant despite infertility, and having children outside of marriage.

These choices are bounded by *constraints*, however, and many expectations about parenthood are contradictory. We encourage young adults to postpone parenthood, yet are still somewhat suspicious of people who decide to remain child free. We are developing reproductive technologies that help infertile couples become pregnant yet do little to eliminate hazardous work environments that increase people's chances of becoming infertile and of giving birth to infants with lifelong physical and mental disabilities.

In addition, the high costs of reproductive technologies limit their availability to couples at the lower end of the socioeconomic scale. Despite such contradictions, however, most people look forward to raising children, our focus in the next chapter.

Summary

1. Parenthood is an important rite of passage. Unlike other major turning points in our lives, becoming a parent is permanent.

2. There are both benefits and costs in having children. The benefits include emotional fulfillment and personal satisfaction. The costs include a decline in marital satisfaction, problems in finding adequate housing, and generally high expenses.

3. Fertility rates in the United States have fluctuated in the past 70 years but are still relatively low. Birth rates are higher for Latinas than for other women, but there are intragroup variations.

4. Postponing parenthood is a common phenomenon. Remaining childless as long as possible has many attractive features, including independence and building a career. There are also costs, such as finding it difficult or impossible to have biological children later in life.

5. Approximately 15 percent of all couples are involuntarily childless. The reasons for infertility include

physical and physiological difficulties, environmental hazards, and unhealthy lifestyles.

6.   Couples have a variety of options if they are infertile, including adoption, artificial insemination, and a number of high-tech procedures, such as in vitro fertilization and surrogacy.

7.   Some ongoing issues in the area of adoption include the rights of the biological father, transracial adoption, and open adoption.

8.   Contrary to popular belief, women in their 20s have higher rates of nonmarital childbearing than do teenagers. The percentages of teenagers who are un-

married mothers have been decreasing but vary by race and ethnicity. There are both micro- and macro-level reasons for the surge in out-of-wedlock births among older women.

9.   Improved contraceptive techniques and the availability of abortion have resulted in fewer unwanted births. The incidence of abortion has declined since 1990, but abortion continues to be a hotly debated issue in the United States.

10.   Couples who decide not to have children are still a minority, but remaining child free is becoming more acceptable.

Key Terms

fetal alcohol syndrome (FAS)   *322*
postpartum depression   *323*
fertility   *324*
total fertility rate (TFR)   *324*
relative income   *325*
infant mortality rate   *327*
infertility   *330*
pelvic inflammatory disease (PID)   *330*
chlamydia   *330*

endometriosis   *331*
open adoption   *333*
closed adoption   *333*
semi-open adoption   *333*
artificial insemination   *336*
fertility drugs   *336*
assisted reproductive technology
   (ART)   *336*
in vitro fertilization (IVF)   *337*

surrogacy   *338*
preimplantation genetic diagnosis
   (PGD)   *338*
amniocentesis   *339*
chorionic villus sampling (CVS)   *339*
contraception   *342*
abortion   *344*

Taking it Further

Planning and Creating Families

There is a wealth of information about family planning on the Internet. Some of these sites include the following:

Child Trends, Inc. is a research organization that provides information about a variety of family-related issues, including nonmarital birth.

www.childtrends.org

RESOLVE National Home Page provides information and support on infertility.

www.resolve.org

National Adoption Information Clearinghouse is a comprehensive resource for adoption statistics, a literature

database, agency and support group lists, and dozens of links to specific areas of adoption, such as open adoption, transracial adoption, and the costs of adopting.

www.calib.com/naic

Nature magazine offers online articles about the legal and ethical issues surrounding reproductive technology, among other topics.

www.nature.com

And more: www.prenhall.com/benokraitis provides sites dealing with adoption, sperm banks, planned parenthood, voluntary childlessness, information about "morning-after" contraception, and a guide to understanding depression during and after pregnancy.

Investigate with Research Navigator

Go to www.researchnavigator.com and enter your LOGIN NAME and PASSWORD. For instructions on registering for the first time, view the detailed instructions at the end of Chapter 1. Search the Research Navigator™ site using the following key terms:

fertility patterns
infertility
parental rights

Outline

Raising Children: Promises and Pitfalls

Data Digest

■ Congress recognized Mother's Day as a **national holiday** in 1914. Father's Day became an official holiday in 1972.

■ A **full-time stay-at-home mother would earn about $135,000 a year** if paid for all her work.

■ 76 percent of U.S. adults **approve of spanking** to discipline a child. This percentage has been fairly consistent since 1946, when 72 percent approved.

■ **60 percent of women return to work within six months of giving birth,** and 46 percent return to work within three months.

■ The **most stressed people in America** are working mothers: 65 percent say that they have little time to relax, compared with 55 percent of working dads and 27 percent of two-income couples with no children.

■ **The number of parents who report never talking with their child about drugs doubled** from 6 percent in 1998 to 12 percent in 2004.

■ 73 percent of parents say that **today's kids are too focused on buying things.**

Sources: Fields et al., 2001; Jones, 2002a; Lyons, 2004; Partnership for a Drug-Free America, 2004; Tyre et al., 2004; Carroll, 2006; Wulfhorst, 2006.

Want to practice some parenting skills? For the "mess exercise," smear peanut butter on the sofa and curtains, or place a fish stick behind the couch and leave it there all summer. For the "grocery store exercise," borrow one or two small animals (goats are best) and take them with you as you shop. Always keep them in sight, and pay for anything they eat or damage.

A Swahili proverb says that a child is both a precious stone and a heavy burden. Child rearing is both exhilarating and exhausting, a task that takes patience, sacrifice, and continuous adjustment. There are many rewards, but no guarantees.

In this chapter we examine some of the central issues of child rearing, such as parenting styles in a variety of families and social classes, parents' impact on their children's development, and child care. Let's begin by looking at contemporary parenting roles.

Contemporary Parenting Roles

Becoming a parent is a major life change. Even before they are born, children affect their parents. Most prospective parents are emotionally and financially invested in planning for their child's arrival. Months before the baby is born, they begin to alter their lifestyles. Many shop for baby clothes and nursery furniture, and child-rearing manuals pile up on their nightstands.

The mother may forgo Big Macs and increase her intake of calcium-rich dairy or soy products and fresh vegetables. "Parenthood effects" may also include eliminating cigarettes, alcohol, and other drugs by pregnant women (and often by their partners) that may continue after childbirth (Bachman et al., 1997).

A Parent Is Born

Infants waste no time in teaching adults to meet their needs. Babies are not merely passive recipients of care; they are active participants in their own development:

This 4-year-old girl seems as engrossed in filling her dump truck as she might be in dressing a doll. If parents and other caretakers don't steer children toward sex-stereotypical activities, both girls and boys enjoy a variety of games and toys.

The infant modulates, regulates, and refines the caretaker's activities. . . . By fretting, sounds of impatience or satisfaction, by facial expressions of pleasure, contentment, or alertness he . . . "tells" the parents when he wants to eat, when he will sleep, when he wants to be played with, picked up, or have his position changed. . . . The caretakers, then, adapt to him . . . (Rheingold, 1969: 785–86).

Rather than simply performing parental roles, people *internalize* them: "We absorb the roles we play to such a degree that our sense of who we are (our identities) and our sense of right and wrong (our consciences) are very much a product of our role-playing activities" (LaRossa, 1986: 14).

Internalizing the parental role changes both partners. As people make the transition to parenthood, they help each other learn the role of parent, deal with the ambiguity of what constitutes a "good" parent, and share in the care of their child.

Parenting does *not* come naturally. It is neither instinctive nor innate. Especially with the first child, most of us muddle through by trial and error. Many people are so anxious about being perfect parents that they often turn to "experts" for advice. Some of the advice can be valuable, especially on topics such as physical care of the baby. Unfortunately, as you'll see later in this chapter, even some "experts" promote myths that have become widely accepted.

Rewards and Difficulties of Parenting

Just as there are benefits and costs of having children, there are also benefits and costs of raising them: "Parenting varies, being enormously satisfying and seemingly easy at times as well as confounding, difficult, and burdensome at other times" (Arendell, 1997: 22). Employed mothers and fathers, especially, are experiencing a "time crunch" because their parenting roles have expanded (Schor, 2002).

Sociologists often use *role theory* to explain the interactions among family members. A *role,* you recall, is a set of expected behavior patterns, obligations, and privileges (see Chapter 1). Theoretically, every role has culturally defined rights and responsibilities. In practice, however, role strain may occur as norms or role expectations change.

ROLE STRAIN Role strain involves conflicts that someone feels *within* a role. The role of student often reflects role strain. For example, professors encourage students to think creatively and critically. On the other hand, they also tell students to "concentrate on the study questions I gave you" or "give me the facts, not your opinions."

Almost all people experience role strain because many inconsistencies are built into our roles. Four factors contribute to parents' role strain: unrealistic role expectations, decreased authority, increased responsibility, and high parenting standards.

UNREALISTIC ROLE EXPECTATIONS Many mothers and fathers experience problems because of unrealistic and one-sided expectations of parenting roles. Just as students accept the fact that some professors are better than others, most of us accept occasional mistakes from lawyers, social workers, and other professionals. Parents, however, expect and are expected to succeed with every child, and may feel guilty if they "fail."

DECREASED AUTHORITY Many parents experience role strain because they feel that they have less authority in raising kids than was generally true in the past. For example, parents have fought state laws to educate their children at home or to take terminally ill children off life-support systems when there is no possibility of recovery. Parents must also compete with television and other media in teaching their children values, a topic we'll address later (Elkind, 2002; see, also, Chapter 5).

INCREASED RESPONSIBILITY Parental authority has decreased, but responsibility has increased. If parents raised several children and one ran away from home, relatives and friends would feel that these "good" parents had had one "bad apple." In contrast, many professionals (such as psychiatrists and social workers) often automatically assume that children do not run away from good homes. Therefore, they maintain, there must be something wrong with the parents. Such judgments increase parents' feelings of anxiety and role strain.

Some counties have passed "parental responsibility" laws that make parents liable for damage caused by their child, whether it's a minor offense such as graffiti or a serious offense such as homicide (Schrof, 1999). Thus, parents—rather than such influences as peers or the media—are held accountable for a child's misbehavior.

HIGH PARENTING STANDARDS Parents have no preparation for their difficult role, yet they must live up to high standards. We receive more training to get a driver's license than we do to become parents. In contrast to previous generations, parents are now expected to be informed about medical technologies, to watch their children closely for early signs of physical or mental abnormalities, and to consult with specialists immediately if they detect learning problems.

There's also a feeling that the division of labor in families should be equal. This is rarely the case, however. Instead, many mothers and fathers experience contradictions in their child-rearing responsibilities.

Motherhood: Ideal versus Realistic Roles

New mothers often face enormous pressures and role strain. The myth that mothering "comes naturally" creates three problems. First, it assumes that a good mother will be perfect if she simply follows her instincts. Second, it implies that there's something wrong with a mother who doesn't devote 100 percent of her time to child rearing. Third, it discourages the involvement of other adults, especially fathers.

since you asked

Does being a good mother come naturally?

Almost 61 percent of children under age 18 live with two employed parents. Nevertheless, mothers continue to do most of the child rearing and housework. Both employed and stay-at-home mothers spend more time caring for their children than their own mothers did (Fields, 2004; Bianchi et al., 2006; see, also, Chapters 5, 10, and 13).

Even though many mothers are working harder than ever before at raising kids, they feel considerably more anxious about not living up to an idealized vision of "perfect motherhood." Some conservative social scientists have blamed employed mothers for everything from misbehavior by preschoolers to problems of adolescents (see Wilson, 2002).

Others contend that the media, especially, have generated a "new momism": a highly romanticized, yet demanding, view of motherhood in which standards for success are impossible to meet. For example, many newspaper articles insist "that women are the best caretakers of children, and that to be a remotely decent mother, a woman has to devote her entire physical, psychological, emotional, and intellectual being, 24/7, to her children" (Douglas and Michaels, 2004: 4).

In recent years, magazine covers have featured celebrity moms (such as Julia Roberts, Brooke Shields, and Britney Spears) who have chic maternity clothes, perfect hairdos and makeup, expensive baby products, and of course, nannies: "When the beautiful people embrace parenting, it becomes sexy." Despite this "gloss" on motherhood, the situation is very different for the typical mother: "Real mothers are still worn out by broken sleep, worries about how to split their time between paying work and child-rearing, and what to do about child care" (Fisher, 2005). The problem is that many "real" mothers compare themselves to celebrity moms and feel inadequate and unattractive as a result.

Mommy myths and traditional gender roles can be harmful. Even when women don't compare themselves to celebrities, traditional gender roles idealize the mother role and expect fathers to step aside in child

"Mommy's not complaining, honey. Don't call your lawyer!"

per a squiggly baby on a changing table. . . . But first-time fathers who work outside of the home . . . [are expected] to know how to be dads instantaneously, and this unrealistic expectation causes problems (Marzollo, 1993: 10).

Gerson (1997) suggests that there are three types of fathers:

- *Breadwinner fathers* see themselves as primary earners, even if their wives work outside the home. They view fatherhood mainly in economic terms and prefer a wife who takes responsibility for domestic tasks and child care.

- *Autonomous fathers* seek freedom from family commitments and distance themselves—usually after a marital breakup—from both their former spouse and their children. (Examples include "deadbeat dads," who don't provide economic or emotional support after a marital breakup.)

- *Involved fathers* feel that "good fathering" includes extensive participation in the daily tasks of child rearing and nurturing. Although these fathers don't necessarily share equally in their children's care, they forge satisfying relationships with their wives and children.

When mothers are employed, fathers are an important source of care for young children (see *Figure 12.1*). They are more likely to provide care if they work evening and weekend shifts or if they are unemployed. Fathers in low-income families are also more likely to take care of their children than are fathers in middle-class families because child care costs constitute a large proportion of a poor family's budget: 35 percent, compared with 6 percent for middle-class families (Smith, 2000).

Many fathers want to be close to their children, but with long commutes and demanding employers, they may have little time to do so. What happens when fathers encounter such contradictions? They usually place a lower priority on parenting. More than 90 percent of mothers and fathers say that both parents should be equally involved in most child-rearing tasks. In reality, only 17 percent of fathers discipline their children, 14 percent play with them, 24 percent give them emotional support, 27 percent monitor their play or friends, and 58 percent provide basic care that may include everything from changing diapers to preparing the children's meals (Bianchi, 2001).

Why are parenting roles so lopsided? Even when people have "modern" views about gender roles, stereotypical attitudes linger. In a national survey, for exam-

rearing. Such "maternal gatekeeping" decreases a father's involvement in his children's lives. If, for example, mothers believe that men aren't capable parents, they may limit the father's accessibility to children such as not encouraging him to interact with the children or to respond to phone calls from the child's teacher or doctor (McBride et al., 2005).

Generally, the greater the father's participation in raising children, the greater the mother's satisfaction with her own parenting and the marriage (Johnson and Huston, 1998; see, also, Chapters 5 and 10). But how much do fathers contribute to child rearing?

Fatherhood: Ideal versus Realistic Roles

Fathers, like mothers, experience role strain. They may have very little opportunity to learn parenting skills, especially during the first year of a baby's life:

An old joke for musicians goes like this: A young man asks an older musician, "How do I get to Carnegie Hall?" The older man answers, "Practice, my son, practice." You can say the same for fatherhood. It takes practice to know how to handle a crying baby in the middle of the night and to dia-

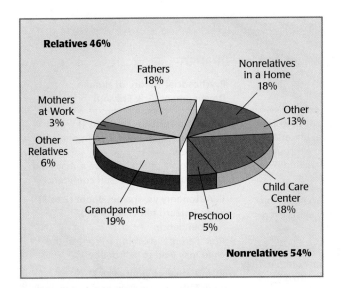

FIGURE 12.1 **Who's Minding the Kids?**

SOURCE: Based on Overturf Johnson, 2005, Table 3.

ple, 27 percent of men and 20 percent of women said that they don't believe men are as competent parents as women (Fetto, 2006).

If both partners believe that the mother is innately more nurturing, the father may back off while the mother deepens her emotional connection with the children. As fathers step back, the idea that mothers have a natural connection is perpetuated, mothers take on more child-related tasks, and fathers are often left out. In contrast, fathers who nurture their children have more egalitarian views of gender roles: They value women's

Making Connections

- Who did most of the child-rearing when you were growing up? Was your mom or your dad more influential during your childhood? If you have children now, who does most of the parenting?

- A mother in London, England, wrote an essay for the *Daily Mail* newspaper entitled "Sorry, But My Children Bore Me to Death!" She said, among other things, that motherhood is tedious because she "hates" changing diapers, reading bedtime stories, and driving her children to numerous activities every day. She received a lot of "hate mail," but a number of mothers agreed with her (Soriano, 2006). Should this mom never have had children? Or should parents, especially mothers, be more open about some of the negative aspects of having and raising children?

economic contributions and are more attuned to what their wives and children need (Cowdery and Knudson-Martin, 2005; Matta and Knudson-Martin, 2006).

Parents are the primary socialization agents (see Chapters 1 and 5). How do they influence their children's development over time? Theorists have offered various answers to this question.

Some Theories of Child Development

Social scientists have proposed a number of theories to explain child development. Three perspectives have been especially influential. George Herbert Mead (1934, 1938, 1964) focused on social interaction as the core of the developing human being. Jean Piaget (1932, 1954, 1960) was interested in the child's cognitive development: the ability to think, reason, analyze, and apply information (see Chapter 5). Erik Erikson (1963) combined elements of psychological and sociological perspectives to create a theory that encompasses adulthood as well as childhood. Refer to *Table 12.1* as we look briefly at these major theories.

since you asked

What helps a child develop into a mature, productive adult?

Mead's Theory of the Social Self

George Herbert Mead (1863–1931) saw the *self* as the basis of humanity that develops not out of biological urges but as a result of social interaction. For Mead, the newborn infant is a *tabula rasa* (the Latin phrase for a blank slate), with no inborn predisposition to behave in any particular way. It is only as the infant interacts with other people, Mead said, that she or he begins to develop the necessary attitudes, beliefs, and behaviors to fit into society.

The child learns first by imitating the behavior of specific people, such as parents, sisters, and brothers. As the child matures, he or she learns to identify with the *generalized other*—roles that many people fulfill (e.g., "Doctors help sick people"). When the child has learned the significance of roles, according to Mead, she or he has learned to respond to the expectations of society (see Chapter 5).

Piaget's Cognitive Development Theory

Jean Piaget (1896–1980) was interested in the growing child's efforts to understand his or her world, to learn how to adapt to that world, and to develop an independent

TABLE 12.1

Some Theories of Development and Socialization

Theory of the Social Self (George Herbert Mead)	Cognitive Development Theory (Jean Piaget)	Psychosocial Theory of Human Development (Erik Erikson)
Stage 1: Imitation (roughly birth to 2) The infant does not distinguish between self and others. She or he learns behavior by mimicking significant others (primarily parents, but also siblings, teachers, and peers). **Stage 2: Play (roughly 2 to 6)** As children begin to use language and continue to interact with significant others, they distinguish between "self" and "other." The child learns social norms, especially that she or he is expected to behave in certain ways. The child also begins to understand other roles in "let's pretend" and other kinds of play. **Stage 3: Games (roughly 6 and older)** As children grow older and interact with a wider range of people, they learn to respond to and fulfill social roles. They learn to play multiple roles and to participate in organized activities (the "generalized other").	**Sensorimotor stage (birth to 2)** The child develops a physical understanding of her or his environment through touching, seeing, hearing, and moving around. The child learns the concept of object permanence (e.g., a toy exists even when it is out of sight). **Preoperational stage (2 to 7)** Children learn to use symbols. For example, they learn to represent a car with a block, moving the block around. They learn to use language to express increasingly complex ideas. However, they still have difficulty seeing things from another person's viewpoint. **Concrete operational stage (8 to 12)** Children learn to discern cause and effect: They can anticipate possible consequences of an action without having to try it out. They begin to understand the views of others. They also understand that quantities remain the same even when their shape or form changes (e.g., a fixed amount of liquid poured into a tall, thin glass and into a short, wide one is the same, even though it looks different in differently shaped containers). **Formal operational stage (13 and older)** Children can reason using abstract concepts. They can understand future consequences and evaluate the probable outcomes of several alternatives. They can evaluate their own thoughts and consider major philosophical issues, such as why pain and suffering exist.	**I. Trust vs. mistrust (birth to 1)** *Task:* To develop basic trust in oneself and others. *Risk:* A sense of abandonment may lead to mistrust and lack of self confidence. **II. Autonomy vs. shame, doubt (2 to 3)** *Task:* To learn self-control and independence. *Risk:* Parental shaming to control the child may lead to self-doubt. **III. Initiative vs. guilt (4 to 5)** *Task:* To learn new tasks and pursue goals aggressively. *Risk:* Feeling guilty for having attempted forbidden activities or been too aggressive. **IV. Industry vs. inferiority (6 to 12)** *Task:* To develop an interest in productive work rather than just play. *Risk:* Failure or fear of failure may result in feelings of inferiority. **V. Identity vs. identity confusion (13 to 19)** *Task:* To achieve a sense of individuality and of having a place in society. *Risk:* Making important decisions may lead to confusion over who and what one wants to become. **VI. Intimacy vs. isolation (20 to 30)** *Task:* To achieve close ties with others and fulfill commitments. *Risk:* Inability to take chances by sharing intimacy may result in avoiding others or in isolation. **VII. Generativity vs. self-absorption (31 to 64)** *Task:* To establish and guide the next generation—especially one's children—to create ideas and products. *Risk:* Inability to bear children or create ideas or products may lead to stagnation. **VIII. Integrity vs. despair (65 and older)** *Task:* To feel a sense of satisfaction and dignity in what one has achieved. *Risk:* Disappointments and unrealized goals may lead to feelings of alienation or despair.

identity. In his four major developmental stages, Piaget traced the acquisition of such abilities as differentiating oneself from the external world, learning to use language and symbols, understanding the perspective of another person, and learning to think and reason in abstract terms about the past, the present, and the future.

Piaget believed that children play an active role in learning, processing information, and seeking knowledge. He emphasized that although some children learn faster than others, they must pass through the same four stages, at similar ages, and in the same order. Once children have mastered the tasks of one stage, they move on to the next, which is more difficult.

Erikson's Psychosocial Theory of Development

Erik Erikson (1902–1994) is one of the few theorists whose explanation of human development encompassed the entire lifespan rather than just childhood and adolescence. In each of Erikson's eight stages, the developing person faces a specific challenge, or "crisis," that presents both tasks and risks.

The outcome of each "crisis" determines whether the individual will move on successfully to the next stage. For example, a person may leave the first stage having learned to trust other people, such as parents or caregivers, or else unable to count on anyone. For Erikson, resolving each of these "crises" is the responsibility of the individual, but successful development also reflects the person's social relationships with family members, peers, and others.

The important point in all three of these theories is that children grow and mature by learning to deal with new expectations and changes. A child who feels loved and secure has a good chance of developing into a reasonably happy and productive member of society, one of the family's major socialization functions (see Chapter 1).

These and other theories give us some insight into children's development but say nothing about different parenting approaches. How do mothers and fathers perform parenting tasks? And what are the most effective parenting styles and forms of discipline?

Parenting Styles and Discipline

Parents differ greatly in their child-rearing approaches. Let's look at some general parenting styles and then more specific beliefs about discipline.

Parenting Styles

Although adolescents might think that their parents have little or no effect on them, parenting styles make a big difference in how a child turns out. A **parenting style** is a general approach to interacting with and disciplining children. Psychologist Diana Baumrind (1968, 1989, 1991) has identified four parenting styles: authoritarian, permissive, authoritative, and uninvolved.

since you asked

Is spanking effective in disciplining children?

These four styles vary on two dimensions: support and control (*see Figure 12.2*). *Support,* sometimes called responsiveness, refers to the amount of affection, acceptance, warmth, and caring that a parent provides to a child. *Control,* sometimes called demandingness, is the degree of flexibility a parent shows in guiding a child's behavior. Control ran range from offering suggestions to physical abuse.

AUTHORITARIAN PARENTING Parents who use an **authoritarian style** are often very demanding, rigid, and punitive. They expect absolute obedience from their children and often use forceful measures to control their behavior. Verbal give-and-take is rare because the child is expected to accept parental authority without question ("You'll do it because I said so").

Authoritarian parents typically show their children little warmth and support. The parents may be experiencing stress due to low income and other factors, such as racial discrimination. In addition, psychological factors like depression increase the likelihood of punitive parenting styles. Children from these homes are often irritable,

Many parents spend hundreds of dollars on educational toys, as for this 11-month-old child, to increase their intelligence. Do these toys work? Or are parents wasting their money?

Bill Wingell/The New York Times.

	Parental support is...	Parental control is...	Example
Authoritarian	Low	High	"You can't have the car on Saturday because I said so."
Permissive	High	Low	"Sure; you can borrow the car whenever you like."
Authoritative	High	High	"You can borrow the car after you've picked up your sister from soccer practice."
Uninvolved	Low	Low	"I don't care what you do; don't bother me."

FIGURE 12.2   Four Common Parenting Styles

moody, and unfriendly (Giles-Sims et al., 1995; Jackson et al., 1998; Bluestone and Tamis-LeMonda, 1999).

A recent study also suggests that authoritarian parenting styles can lead to overweight children. For example, strict mothers who commanded their children to "Clean your plate or else!" were five times more likely than more flexible and permissive parents to have children who were overweight by the time the children entered the first grade (Rhee et al., 2006).

PERMISSIVE PARENTING In the **permissive style**, parents are warm, responsive, and undemanding. They place few requirements on their children for orderly behavior or household tasks. According to one observer, permissive kids (and their parents) are "downright annoying": "I never expected prissy public behavior at a clothing store for toddlers, but an astounding number of preschool-age children were pulling clothes off hangers and onto the floor while their mothers smiled absently at them" (Klein, 2006). Other examples of permissive parenting are evident in television shows such as *Nanny 911* or *Supernanny:* four-year-olds who are still using baby bottles or diapers, school-age children who hit their parents, and siblings who are constantly kicking or hitting each other.

Instead of setting boundaries, permissive parents are indulgent. They don't bully or tyrannize their children, but adolescents raised in indulgent households are often less mature, more irresponsible, and less able to assume leadership positions. They are also more likely to be rebellious and impulsive, and to have behavior problems such as fighting and losing their temper (Wolfradt et al., 2003; Aunola and Nurmi, 2005).

AUTHORITATIVE PARENTING Parents who use the **authoritative style** are demanding. They impose rules and standards of behavior, but they are also responsive and supportive. These parents encourage autonomy and self-reliance, and tend to use positive reinforcement rather than harsh punishment.

Unlike authoritarian parents, authoritative parents encourage verbal give-and-take and believe that the child has rights. Although they expect disciplined conformity, they typically don't hem the child in with heavy-handed restrictions. Instead, they are open to discussing and changing rules in particular situations when the need arises.

One of the most consistent research findings is that authoritative parenting styles produce children who are self-reliant, achievement-oriented, and more successful in school. Authoritative fathers, especially, help adolescents resist peer pressure to use drugs (Dorius et al., 2004; Eisenberg et al., 2005).

UNINVOLVED PARENTING In the **uninvolved style**, parents are neither supportive nor demanding because they're indifferent. They spend little time interacting with their children and know little about their whereabouts or interests.

Uninvolved parents can also be rejecting: They typically ignore a child as long as she or he doesn't interfere with the parents' activities. The most extreme examples include neglectful parents who lock their children in their bedrooms or strap them down for hours while visiting friends or going to nightclubs (Meyer and Oberman, 2001).

Children from these homes are often immature, withdrawn, or underachieving. They often show signs of a variety of psychological and behavioral problems, such as drug use and bullying. Because these children are used to doing what they want, they may become rebellious when confronted with demanding teachers or other authority figures (Pellerin, 2005).

WHICH PARENTING APPROACH IS MOST EFFECTIVE?
Although there are some exceptions, a number of studies show that healthy child development is most likely in authoritative families, in which the parents are consistent in combining warmth, monitoring, and discipline. Compared with adolescents whose parents are permissive or authoritarian, children from authoritative households have better psychosocial development, higher school grades, greater self-reliance, lower levels of delinquent behavior, and are less likely to be swayed by harmful peer pressure (to use drugs and alcohol, for example) (Gray and Steinberg, 1999; Barnes et al., 2000; National Center on Addiction and Substance Abuse, 2003).

Authoritarian, permissive, and authoritative parenting styles often overlap. Immigrant Chinese mothers, for example, use a combination of parenting roles. They might

Cross-Cultural Families

Parenting in Japan

Japanese parents' approach to parenting is considerably different from that of U.S. parents. Most Americans value individualism, independence, and initiative, and raise their children to be self-reliant. The Japanese value loyalty to family and community over personal success. Respect for authority and obedience are taught in the home and reinforced in school (Fukuzawa and LeTendre, 2001).

Japanese child rearing is based on the concept of *amae* (pronounced ah-mah-eh), a sense of complete dependence based on the desire for love and caring. Many mothers spend every waking hour with their infants, often sleep with their babies, pick them up whenever they cry, and cater to their every whim.

Most American parents think this kind of behavior will spoil a child and discourage independence and self-reliance. In contrast, the Japanese feel that keeping children happy will motivate them to be cooperative later in life. *Amae*-based care and guidance are continued in the schools, where children are rewarded for cooperative behavior and teamwork.

Although Japanese fathers are often absent from home, the father's authority is reinforced in daily mother–child interactions:

"Since my husband is gone most of the time, my son really needs a role model to be a strong and responsible man. That's why I remind him constantly of what a diligent, dedicated, responsible, and great father he has.

I also tell my daughter that it is important for her to find a hard-working man like her father who earns a comfortable living for the family." This is from a homemaker–mother whose 9-year-old daughter and 6-year-old son see their father on the average of 4 minutes a day (Ishii-Kuntz, 1993: 59).

Because provider and father roles are synonymous, co-workers or family members may criticize Japanese men who reduce their work hours to be at home with their children. Because many fathers devote themselves to their jobs, mothers have complete authority in the home: "It's motherhood, not wifehood, that gives a woman a sense of accomplishment and it's the children around which the family revolves" (Diggs, 1998: 49).

Stop and Think . . .

- Rates of violence, such as homicide, are much higher in the United States than in Japan (see Chapters 1 and 5). Do you think that *amae* can explain these differences?
- What advantages and disadvantages do you see in American versus Japanese parenting approaches?

seem authoritarian because they have high expectations about academic success, but they are also warm, nurturing, and supportive (Gorman, 1998; see, also, Chapter 4).

Parenting styles also reflect cultural values. For many recent Latino and Asian immigrants, for example, authoritarian parenting produces positive outcomes, such as better grades. This parenting style is also more effective in safeguarding children who are growing up in communities with high levels of crime and drug peddling (Brody et al., 2002; Pong et al., 2005).

Some people believe that parenting is difficult in the United States because our cultural values (such as competition, independence, and success) encourage individuality rather than conformity. In other cultures, parental values emphasize cooperation rather than independence (see the box "Parenting in Japan").

Discipline

In 1994, a woman was shopping in a grocery store in Woodstock, Georgia, when her 9-year-old son, who reportedly was picking on his sister, talked back to his mother. The mother slapped him. Fifteen minutes later, in the parking lot, a police officer summoned by a store employee arrested the mother and charged her with cruelty to children, a felony that carries a jail sentence of 1 to 20 years.

Many parents were outraged. Why should the police intrude in a private family matter? And what's wrong with slapping or spanking kids? The incident fueled a national debate over how Americans should discipline their children.

Children must learn discipline because self-control is *not* innate. Many parents feel that both verbal and corporal punishment are legitimate forms of discipline.

VERBAL PUNISHMENT A national study found that almost all parents, in all socioeconomic groups, used verbal and psychological aggression to control or change their children's behavior (Straus and Field, 2003):

- 50 percent yelled, screamed, and shouted at their infants and 1-year-old children, and 90 percent did the same with children ages 4 to 17.

- 33 percent swore at their children, and 17 percent admitted calling them names (such as "dumb" or "lazy").

- 20 percent threatened, at least once, to kick the child out of the house.

These percentages are probably low because many parents don't want to admit that they attack their children verbally. Also, because the incidents are so common and "normal," parents don't remember all of them.

CORPORAL PUNISHMENT About 94 percent of American parents have spanked their children by the time they are 3 or 4 years old. About 35 percent discipline their infants by slapping a hand or leg; pinching; shaking; hitting the buttocks with a hand, belt, or paddle; or slapping the infant's face. Hitting the child with a belt or paddle is most common for children ages 5 to 12 (28 percent). More than half of parents have hit their children at age 12, a third at age 14, and 13 percent at age 17. Parents who hit teenagers do so an average of about six times a year (Straus and Stewart, 1999).

Corporal punishment is more prevalent among low-income parents, in the South, for boys, and by mothers, especially younger white mothers (those under age 33). Overall, older parents are less likely to use physical punishment than are younger parents. It could be that older parents face less stress at work because their jobs or careers are better established, they feel more self-assured, they are more ready to take on parenting responsibilities, and they have more resources—such as time and money—with which to engage their children in activities that relieve boredom (Day et al., 1998; Walsh, 2002; see, also, Chapter 11).

DOES CORPORAL PUNISHMENT WORK? Spanking vents a parent's anger and frustration, but does physical punishment change a child's behavior? Several studies of 2- and 3-year-olds found that parents who use reasoning and back it up with physical and nonphysical punishment have well-behaved children (Larzelere et al., 1998; Holden et al., 1999).

However, most research shows that corporal punishment increases the child's aggression and misbehavior. In a study of preschool-age children, for example, children whose mothers threatened, insulted, spanked, or yelled at them were more likely to be disobedient and disruptive when they entered school. An analysis of 88 studies conducted over 62 years concluded that spanking children can make them temporarily more compliant but increases the risk that they will become aggressive, antisocial, and chronically defiant (Spieker et al., 1999; Gershoff, 2002a).

A team of researchers who surveyed mothers in China, India, Italy, Kenya, the Philippines, and Thailand found that the greater use of physical discipline was associated with more child aggression. Even when cultural norms approved of spanking, the children who were punished physically were more likely to get into fights, to bully other children, and to be generally more anxious and fearful than children who were not punished physically (Lansford et al., 2005).

Many researchers and pediatricians maintain that physical punishment is a futile disciplinary method (see the box "Is Spanking Effective or Harmful?"). Increasingly, childrearing experts recommend nonphysical forms of punishment, such as removing temptations to misbehave, making rules simple, being consistent, setting a good example, praising good behavior, and disciplining with love and patience instead of anger. These anti-spanking proponents maintain that nonphysical discipline has better long-term effects than physical punishment (Gibson, 1991; Simons et al., 1994).

WHAT'S A PARENT TO DO? According to many family counselors, it's important not to discipline too early. Children under 6 years old are curious and eager to learn (see *Table 12.1*). Parents can often avoid problems by guiding their children's exploration and interest in new activities instead of yelling "Stop that!" or "I told you not to touch that!"

Effective discipline involves more than rewards and punishments. Children need three types of inner resources if they are to become responsible adults: positive feelings about themselves and others, an understanding of right and wrong, and alternatives for solving problems. The "Applying what you've Learned" box lists 10 building blocks that parents can use to establish these inner resources in their children.

We've touched on some variations in parents' disciplinary methods. How do race, ethnicity, and social class affect these and other parenting aspects?

Making Connections

- According to one of my students, "Spank while they're little so the law doesn't later." Do you agree or disagree with this general philosophy?

- Recently, parents in Houston, Texas, kept warning their three young sons to behave. When the parents became fed up with the boys' constant fighting, cussing, and obscene gestures, they sold all their Christmas toys on eBay and took down the Christmas tree. Are such disciplinary measures more effective than spanking? Or are they emotionally harsher than physical punishment?

Choices

Is Spanking Effective or Harmful?

Fifteen nations—including Austria, Croatia, Cyprus, Denmark, Germany, Hungary, Israel, Italy, Latvia, and the Scandinavian countries—have made it illegal for parents to spank their children. In contrast, many adults in the United States support spanking (see "Data Digest").

Advocates feel that spanking is effective, prepares children for life's hardships, and prevents misbehavior. They feel that spanking is acceptable if it is age-appropriate, used selectively, and to teach and correct rather than as an expression of rage (Trumbull and Ravenel, 1999; Larzelere, 2000; Baumrind et al., 2002).

Some pediatricians feel that a "mild" spanking (one or two spanks on the buttocks) is acceptable when all other discipline fails, but that slapping a child's face is abusive. Others argue that spanking and all other types of physical punishment are unacceptable. They maintain that children who are spanked regularly, from as early as 1 year old, face a higher risk of developing low self-esteem, depression, alcoholism, and aggressive and violent behavior, and later, physically abusing their own spouse and children (Straus and Yodanis, 1996; Whipple and Richey, 1997; Swinford et al., 2000).

Some researchers have offered a variety of reasons for not spanking or hitting children:

■ *Physical punishment sends the message that it's okay to hurt someone you love or someone who is smaller and less powerful.* A parent who spanks often says, "I'm doing this because I love you." Thus, children learn that violence and love can go hand in hand and that hitting is an appropriate way to express one's feelings.

■ *No human being feels loving toward someone who hits her or him.* A strong relationship is based on kindness. Hitting produces only temporary and superficially "good" behavior based on fear.

■ *Unexpressed anger is stored inside and may explode later.* Anger that has accumulated over many years may erupt during adolescence and adulthood, when the person feels physically strong enough to express it.

■ *Spanking can be physically damaging.* It can injure the spinal column and nerves and even cause paralysis. Some children have died after mild paddlings because of undiagnosed medical problems.

■ *Physical punishment deprives the child of opportunities to learn effective problem solving.* Physical punishment teaches a child nothing about how to handle conflict or disagreements (Hunt, 1991; Straus, 2001; Marshall, 2002).

Stop and Think . . .

- When you were a child, did your parents spank you? If so, how did you feel?
- Some people feel that spanking is synonymous with hitting. Do you agree?
- Should the United States ban spanking? Or would such laws interfere with parenting decisions?

Variations by Ethnicity and Social Class

As you've seen in previous chapters, ethnicity and social class intersect and shape our family life. Although both variables overlap, how does parenting vary in racial-ethnic families?

Parenting across Racial-Ethnic Families

We looked at socialization practices across a number of racial-ethnic families in Chapter 4. Some specific child-rearing tasks include spending time with children and monitoring their activities.

SPENDING TIME WITH CHILDREN One important characteristic of a child's well-being is the type and amount of interaction that occurs between the child and his or her parents. Interaction includes reading to children and taking them on outings.

Reading is an important activity, not only because it stimulates a child's cognitive and intellectual abilities but also because it's a way for parents to spend time with their youngsters. Latino parents are less likely to read to their young children than are African American, Asian American, and white parents (see *Table 12.2*).

Another way to spend time with children is to take them on outings to a park, playground, zoo, or to visit friends or relatives. Such trips provide opportunities for parents to talk to their children and get to know them.

Applying what you've Learned

Some Building Blocks of Effective Discipline

As you read these guidelines, think about what worked for you when you were growing up. If you're a parent, which of these "rules" do you think are most effective? And what would you add to this list?

- *Show your love.* You can express your love not only through a warm facial expression, a kind tone, and a hug but also by doing things with your children, such as working on a project together, letting them help with grocery shopping, and reading their favorite books. When children feel loved, they want to please their parents and are less likely to engage in undesirable behaviors.
- *Be consistent.* Predictable parents are just as important as routines and schedules. A child who is allowed to do something one day and not the next can become confused and start testing the rules.
- *Communicate clearly.* Ask children about their interests and feelings. Whenever possible, encourage them. Constant nagging, reminding, criticizing, threatening, lecturing, questioning, and demanding make a child feel dumb or bad.
- *Understand problem behavior.* Observe a problem behavior and look for a pattern that may explain why; for example, a child becomes unusually cranky when tired or hungry. Children may also have behavioral

problems because their parents are experiencing a stressful event, such as divorce.
- *Be positive and patient.* Sometimes children act up because they want attention. Patience and approval of good conduct encourage children to repeat the positive behavior.
- *Set up a safe environment.* Children are doers and explorers. Removing hazards shortens the list of "no's," and changing play locations relieves boredom and prevents destructive behavior.
- *Make realistic rules.* Set few rules, state them simply, and supervise closely. Don't expect more than your child can handle; for instance, don't expect a toddler to sit quietly during long religious services.
- *Defuse explosions.* Try to avert temper tantrums and highly charged confrontations (for example, distract feuding preschoolers by involving them in other activities).
- *Teach good problem-solving skills.* Children under 4 years of age need very specific guidance in solving a problem and positive reinforcement for following suggestions.
- *Give children reasonable choices.* Don't force them to do things that even you wouldn't want to do (such as eating a vegetable they hate). Removing children from the play area when they misbehave, and giving them a choice of other activities, is often more effective than scolding or punishing (Goddard, 1994; Rosemond, 2000).

White children under 12 years old have more outings than either black or Latino children, regardless of social class. For example, even in high-income families, white children have an average of 14 outings with a parent during a month, compared with 12 for black children and 10 for Latino children (Lugaila, 2003).

There may be several explanations for these racial and ethnic variations in parental reading and outings. One is marital status. Many single parents who work have less time and energy to interact with their children. In multigenerational homes, mothers may be caring for older family members and also depend on their children, sometimes as young as 8 years old, for caregiving (see Chapter 17). As a result, these parents may be less aware of their children's needs and devote less time to activities such as reading and outings (Jambunathan et al., 2000). Moreover, recent immigrants who don't speak English well may be uncomfortable with or unaware of recreational opportunities outside the home.

TABLE 12.2

How Often Do Parents Read to Their Kids?

Percentage of Children Never Read to Last Week

Race or Ethnicity of Child	Children 1 or 2 Years Old	Children 3 to 5 Years Old
White	5	4
Black	11	13
Asian and Pacific Islander	19	11
Latino	24	17

SOURCE: Based on Lugaila, 2003, Table 3.

MONITORING CHILDREN'S ACTIVITIES African American and Latino fathers typically supervise their children's activities more closely than do white fathers. Recent Asian immigrants are also more likely to monitor their children than are U.S.-born parents. As children acculturate, parental supervision and control decrease because many adolescents conform to the values of their peer group rather than those of their family (Willie and Reddick, 2003; Coltrane et al., 2004; see, also, Chapter 4).

In monitoring television viewing, a major source of recreation for children, parents often impose three rules: the types of programs, times of day, and number of hours the child may watch. About 70 percent of white, black, Asian American, and Latino parents report setting such rules for children ages 6 to 11. These rules vary by social class, however. As a parent's educational level increases, so do restrictions on television viewing. For example, 67 percent of parents with a high school degree or less, compared with 78 percent of parents with a college degree, restrict television watching for children ages 6 to 11 (Fields et al., 2001; Lugaila, 2003).

Parenting and Social Class

Many racial and ethnic parenting approaches reflect social class variations. That is, middle-class parents, regardless of race and ethnicity, are more similar to each other than to low-income and high-income parents in their child-rearing practices.

Many schools, as at the Amistad Academy in Connecticut, are encouraging minority dads, grandfathers, and uncles to visit schools and become more involved in their children's education.

Social scientists typically measure social class using **socioeconomic status (SES)**, an overall rank of an individual's position in society based on income, education, and occupation. Sociologists have delineated as many as nine social classes in America (see Warner and Lunt, 1941). For our purposes, low-SES families are those living just above or below the poverty level, middle-SES families are those in blue-collar and white-collar occupations, and high-SES families are professionals and higher.

since you asked

How does social class affect parenting?

LOW-SES FAMILIES Most low-SES parents, especially recent immigrants, must grapple with numerous obstacles. Macro-level stressors such as poverty, unemployment, and racism often create interpersonal conflict (Galvin and Brommel, 2000; Fuligni and Yoshikawa, 2003). Besides living in violent neighborhoods, children in such families have little physical space at home and usually attend schools that are overcrowded and underfunded.

Compared with middle-SES parents, low-SES parents typically give their infants fewer opportunities for daily stimulation and appropriate play materials (Bornstein, 2002). Although many school-related activities are free, parents may lack the time, energy, health, and economic resources to encourage children to participate in extracurricular activities.

Children are especially vulnerable in low-income families in which the parents also have mental health problems, are unemployed, or experience psychological distress. These children are less likely to be successful in school (in basic language, math, and reading skills) by age 7 and 8, and more likely to experience cognitive problems (Votruba-Drzal, 2003).

Depression is higher among economically disadvantaged mothers than higher income mothers because of poverty and unhappy relationships. Because depressed mothers are more likely to use harsh discipline strategies or none, the children are more likely to act out and get into trouble at school and in the community as early as the third grade (Moore et al., 2006).

Despite meager resources, many low-SES parents raise happy and healthy kids. In family activities, for example, almost 25 percent of parents living at or below the poverty level read to their children at least once a week. And despite their economic insecurity, more than 73 percent of low-income parents say that the family works together when problems arise (Lugaila, 2003; Orthner et al., 2004).

The same proportion of parents (59 percent) in low- and high-SES families would like their children to get a college education and believe they will do so (Lugaila, 2003). Despite poverty, then, many low-income parents have the same values and aspirations for their children as higher-income parents.

MIDDLE-SES FAMILIES Middle-SES parents have more resources (money, time, education) to enhance their children's emotional, social, and cognitive development. Many working- and middle-class men feel that they show their commitment to parenthood by staying in their jobs—even jobs they hate—to provide for their families. Such fathers furnish the resources for children to pursue educational or cultural opportunities at summer camps or through music lessons and sports. Such activities often avoid the possible harmful influences of "bad friends." Economically disadvantaged parents aren't able to provide such advantages (Ambert, 1997).

Middle-SES mothers talk to their infants more, and in more sophisticated ways, than do low-SES mothers. Such conversing facilitates children's self-expression. Middle-SES parents are also more likely than lower-SES parents to seek professional advice about child development (Bornstein, 2002).

HIGH-SES FAMILIES The more money parents have, the more they can spend on education, health care, reading materials, and other expenses that enhance their children's life chances. From birth to age 17, a high-income family ($109,000 income a year) spends $280,000 on a child, compared with $190,000 for a middle-income family ($58,000 income a year) and $139,000 for a low-income family ($27,000) a year (Lino, 2006). Thus, a child from a high-income family enjoys considerably more material resources from birth until late adolescence than does a child in a middle- or low-income family.

Parents in high-SES families read to their children more often and provide more outings. Their children are involved in more extracurricular activities that broaden their self-confidence, knowledge base, and physical and intellectual abilities. For example, 20 percent of children ages 6 to 17 in low-SES homes participate in sports, compared with 41 percent of children in high-SES households (Lugaila, 2003).

Children's activities are expensive. Many require special clothing and equipment, hotel and restaurant bills during tournaments outside local areas, assorted costs such as car maintenance and gas, and flexibility in work schedules so children can be transported to events. Such expenses are "negligible" for high-income families, affordable for many middle-class parents, but daunting for low-income families (Lareau, 2003).

Most of us associate child rearing with childhood and adolescence. In fact, however, parenting continues until both parents die. Because people live much longer than in the past, thereby creating multigenerational families, parenting often spans the entire life course.

Changes Over the Life Course

Raising children from infancy to adulthood requires a variety of adjustments over time. Because constructive or hurtful parenting behavior is often passed down to the next generation, understanding the changes that take place over the life course can improve family relationships (Chen and Kaplan, 2001).

Parenting Infants and Babies

Expecting a baby is very different from *having* a baby. The first year of a child's life can be very demanding. Infants need what LaRossa (1986: 88) calls "continuous coverage": "They need to be talked to, listened to, cuddled, fed, cleaned, carried, rocked, burped, soothed, put to sleep, taken to the doctor, and so on."

Infancy, the period of life between birth and about 18 months, encompasses only a small fraction of the average person's lifespan but is a period of both extreme helplessness and enormous physical and cognitive growth. Parents spend twice as much time with infants as they do with children in elementary school (Bornstein, 2002).

Because parents are on call 24 hours a day, they typically have little time to relax. Instead, stress and fatigue set in.

OK, SO MAYBE WE'VE ALL OVERSCHEDULED OUR KIDS A LITTLE...

6-22
©2006 CONEQU
SPEEDBUMP.COM
DIST. BY CREATORS SYND. INC.

THE DEMANDS OF INFANTS Infants communicate hunger or discomfort by crying and "fussing." Both parents experience frustration when they can't soothe a crying infant. Mothers, especially, may feel inadequate and experience strain and a decline in marital satisfaction (Crnic and Low, 2002).

Parents should recognize that crying is the most powerful way for a baby to get attention. Babies cry during the first few months for a variety of reasons. They may be unable to digest cow's milk if they are bottle-fed; if they are breast-fed, they may want to suckle even if they are not hungry; they may be in pain due to ear or urinary tract infections; they may be uncomfortable because of an allergy or other condition; they may be wet or soiled; or they may simply want some company (Kitzinger, 1989).

Sometimes parents bring colicky babies to bed with them because "bed sharing" quiets the infant and promotes family companionship. Breast-feeding mothers find bed sharing more convenient. Although bed sharing is common throughout much of the world, it's a new trend in the United States. The percentage of babies sleeping with a parent or another caregiver at least part of the night rose from 6 percent in 1993 to 13 percent in 2000. Bed sharing is more common among Asian Americans (32 percent) and African Americans (31 percent) than among Latinos (13 percent) and whites (10 percent) (Willinger et al., 2003).

Should parents sleep with their infants and babies? Although most pediatricians are neutral on this question, others feel that bed sharing can increase the risk of the infant's falling out of bed, suffocating, or being injured or killed by a parent (especially one who's been drinking) who rolls over onto the baby (Stein, 2003).

FATIGUE AND STRESS Babies are demanding. As a father of a newborn commented, "Going out for a quick beer, staying late at work, being spontaneous—all that stuff is history" (Blanchard, 1999–2000: 20). As the workload increases, parents have less time for each other.

Mothers, in particular, are often exhausted by child care. Those who are employed outside the home are tired and may temporarily lose interest in sex. Even though many wives accommodate their husbands' sexual overtures, they experience a loss of desire. Part of the disinterest may be due to fatigue or to hearing the baby crying in the next room (Walzer, 1998).

Parental characteristics often affect stress levels. Mothers who are more withdrawn, anxious, or depressed generally experience greater stress during their children's infancy. Mothers are often insecure about their parenting skills and need support from their partner, such as positive statements and discussions about the difficulties of parenting (Mulsow et al., 2002).

Some of the insecurity associated with parenting comes from "experts" who give contradictory advice or reinforce misconceptions. Parents can protect themselves by recognizing some common myths about babies.

MYTHS ABOUT BABIES Some of the ideas parents have about child development, especially from self-help books and talk shows, reflect common misperceptions about the baby's early years (Segal, 1989). Here are some of the most widespread myths about babies:

1. *Myth 1: You can tell in infancy how bright a child is likely to be later on.* A baby's early achievements—such as reaching, sitting, crawling, or talking—are rarely good indicators of intelligence. For example, early agility in building with blocks or imitating words has almost no relationship to later performance in school.

2. *Myth 2: The more stimulation a baby gets, the better.* Babies can be overstimulated, agitated, or even frightened into withdrawal by constant assaults on their senses by an intrusive rattle, toy, or talking face. Millions of parents buy "enrichment" products such as flash cards and educational software for children as young as 6 months ("Your baby will learn the numbers 1–20!" according to some ads). Others play classical music all day or play cassette tapes in the baby's crib that are supposed to teach the baby French or German (MacDonald, 2003).

   Classical music and language tapes are a waste of money because there's no evidence that they increase a baby's intelligence. Although positive stimuli are better than none, parents can have a very beneficial effect by just talking to their infants (Garrison and Christakis, 2005).

3. *Myth 3: Parents who pick up crying babies will spoil them.* It's impossible to spoil a child who is under 1 year old. Crying is the only way a baby can tell parents that he or she is hungry, uncomfortable, or sick. Parents should pick up their baby as much as they want and not worry about discipline at such a young age (Bornstein, 2002).

4. *Myth 4: Special talents surface early or not at all.* Many gifted children do not recognize or develop their skills until adolescence or even later. For example, jazz musician Louis Armstrong was a neglected and abandoned child. It was only years later, when he was living in the New Orleans Colored Waifs Home for Boys, that he was taught to play an instrument, and his talent was ignited.

5. *Myth 5: Parental conflicts don't affect babies.* Babies as young as 1 year old understand the facial

These kindergartners seem very attentive to their teacher's instructions on how to use a computer. If they're loved and supported by their parents and families, children are more likely to meet this and other challenges successfully.

expressions and voice tones of people around them and react accordingly. Thus, parental yelling or arguing affects a baby (Mumme and Fernald, 2003).

These and other myths create unnecessary anxiety and guilt for many parents because they set up false expectations or unrealistic goals.

Although many parents experience strain, relationships can also become richer after a child is born. As the baby starts sleeping through the night and the parents develop a schedule, life (including sex) usually returns to normal. It just takes time.

Parenting Children

The quality of relationships with adults and other caregivers has a profound impact on a child's development. Most parents realize this and spend a lot of physical and emotional energy, as well as financial resources, to ensure their children's well-being.

DAILY INTERACTION The majority of children under 6 years old interact with their parents quite a bit. About 75 percent have dinner with one or both parents every day, and 70 percent receive parental praise three or more times a day ("Good for you" or "Way to go"). In 2001, children ages 3 to 12 spent an average of 31 hours per week with their mothers and 23 hours with their fathers compared with 25 and 19 hours, respectively, in 1981 (Sandberg and Hofferth, 2001; Lugaila, 2003).

Although many parents still view child rearing as primarily the mother's responsibility, fathers in intact families spend 67 percent as much time with children as mothers on weekdays and 87 percent as much on weekends. Fathers' child-rearing involvement increases for school-age children, especially in sports, outdoor activities, hobbies, and television or video viewing (Yeung et al., 2001).

PARENTS' AND CHILDREN'S INPUTS Child rearing reflects both parental inputs and children's temperaments. Children as young as 3 or 4 years old who are routinely exposed to "complex language" (rather than baby talk) are more likely to develop important language skills. Parents who encourage their 3-year-old children's curiosity (such as exploring their environment) and speaking improve the children's cognitive abilities. And children age 13 and younger who spend time in family activities and have regular bedtime schedules have fewer behavior problems than other children (Huttenlocher et al., 2002; Raine et al., 2002).

Although parents shape a child's environment, each baby arrives in the world with its own genes, physical appearance, temperament, and personality. Even children in the same family can differ greatly. Some children are easier to satisfy and soothe and have a happy demeanor. Others are more cautious and shy. Still others are difficult to please and seem constantly unsatisfied (Ambert, 2001).

There can be considerable differences even between identical twins in personality and behavior. One of my colleagues tells the story of his twin girls, who received exactly the same dolls when they were 3 years old. When the parents asked the girls what they would name the dolls, one twin chattered that the doll's name was Lori, that she loved Lori, and she would take good care of her. The second twin muttered, "Her name is Stupid," and flung the doll into a corner. By adolescence, identical twins can be very different emotionally even though they are the same age, gender, ethnicity, and social class; live in the same community; attend the same school; and share the same genetically-based traits (Crosnoe and Elder, 2002; Lytton and Gallagher, 2002).

Despite children's different temperaments, parents have similarly high expectations of them. Some, however, overmedicalize and overprogram their offspring.

THE MEDICALIZATION OF CHILDHOOD Many researchers are concerned that, increasingly, physicians and parents are overmedicating their children. A study of 200,000 children ages 2 to 4 found that almost 2 percent were receiving stimulants (such as Ritalin), antidepressants (such as Prozac), or tranquilizers. About 4 percent of children ages 5 to 14 took Ritalin. By age 20, children might be taking a range of potent drugs that have been tested only on adults (Zito et al., 2000; Zito et al., 2003).

Antipsychotic drugs like Zyprexa and Risperdal are given as "quick fixes" to kids who "act out." Clonidine, a blood pressure medication, is now being given to children with attention deficit hyperactivity disorder (ADHD) and even to "sleep resistant" babies. Since 1997, prescription spending for children has risen faster than spending for any other group, including seniors. Many of the drugs have had adverse side effects, including an increase in suicidal thoughts, reduced bowel control, heart problems, and even death. Some researchers feel that the medications are unnecessary because many "unruly" preschoolers may be misbehaving due to stressors such as divorce, neglect, or harsh parenting styles rather than ADHD (Diller, 1998; Cordes, 2003).

In 2002, psychiatrists prescribed antipsychotic drugs to children and adolescents at five times the rate they did in 1993. A third of the children—primarily white boys—were diagnosed as having "behavior disorders" and received new drugs that were usually given only to adults. Because the drugs are largely untested, no one knows how the drugs will affect children in the long run (Olfson et al., 2006).

THE OVERPROGRAMMING OF CHILDHOOD Many children age 12 and under lead very structured lives. Children today have 6 hours a week of free play time, compared with almost 10 hours in 1981 (Karasik, 2000). As a result, many children have much more hectic schedules than in the past.

China has been successful in reducing its population growth by enforcing a one-child-per-family policy. However, some "onlies" fare better than others depending on the parents' social class. For example, at the Beijing Intelligence and Capability Kindergarten, violin is optional but golf is mandatory. Tuition and fees run about $6,000 a year, double the income of the average Beijing household.

Structured activities increase children's self-confidence and provide valuable interpersonal interactions. On the other hand, they can also interfere with play time and sleep. Many parents have no idea that their children are overbooked: Kids are three times more likely to feel time-deprived as their parents believe they are. Some children don't mind. Others complain that their days are filled with "a mad scramble of sports, music lessons, prep courses, and then hours of homework" (Weiss, 2001).

Only Children, Birth Order, and Siblings

Although parents often insist that they treat all their children alike, this isn't true, nor should it be, because the requirements of parenting differ for only children and for children who are born first, second, or later. For children, birth order brings different advantages and disadvantages. Siblings also affect children's development.

ONLY CHILDREN Being an only child is not unusual; today 20 percent of children are "onlies." Over the years, attitudes toward only children haven't changed much. Many people believe that only children are spoiled, selfish, and self-centered (Boodman, 1995).

Only children sometimes wish they had had siblings. One grandmother remembers,

> Even though I loved being an only child, there was always this moment of loneliness when I walked home from school with my best friend and her sister. At the last corner they walked down one street to their house, and I had to walk down the other alone. I always wished I had a sibling to walk the rest of the way (McCoy, 1986: 119).

For the most part, "onlies" aren't very different from children who grow up with siblings. They are no more selfish or maladjusted and are as likely to be successful in college and careers, have happy marriages, and be good parents. They do well in school, have higher IQs than children with siblings, and tend to be more self-confident and popular among their peers. They are also more likely to have better verbal skills and to finish high school and go to college (Polit and Falbo, 1987; Blake, 1989).

Famous onlies who have excelled in various fields include Hans Christian Andersen (writer), Leonardo da Vinci (artist and scientist), Albert Einstein (scientist), Clark Gable (actor), Elvis Presley (singer), and Jean-Paul Sartre (philosopher and writer). One of the reasons that only children may be more successful than children with siblings is financial assets. In larger families, parental resources must be divided among a larger number of siblings. As a result, the children often have lower levels of educational attainment and achievement (Travis and Kohli, 1995; Baydar et al., 1997).

BIRTH ORDER Children are onlies until another baby is born. How does the arrival of a sibling affect parenting? Generally, parents experience less difficulty with the second-born than with the firstborn, mainly because they are more experienced, know more about the second-born's everyday activities, and are still focusing on the first child's transition to adolescence. Later-born children probably get away with more because they receive less parental attention than the firstborn (Whiteman et al., 2003).

In many families, firstborns seem more driven, ambitious, and successful. Parents tend to encourage firstborn children to pursue interests that could lead to a prestigious career such as becoming a doctor. Parents are usually more relaxed and open with younger children and allow them to develop interests that are artistic or oriented to the outdoors (Leong et al., 2001).

Even when children's intelligence and the parental attention they receive are similar, why do some get ahead as adults while others struggle to survive financially? Except for affluent families, larger families have fewer resources for the second, third, and later children. There is also is a "pecking order" among siblings, due more to larger social forces than to individual personalities. For example, a firstborn may be less successful if a parent dies or deserts the family, if remarriage improves the later-born children's financial situation, if parents are more supportive of boys' education than of girls', or if later-born children are born during better economic times (Conley, 2004; Wichman et al., 2006).

SIBLINGS Regardless of a family's socioeconomic status, children seem to benefit from growing up with one or more siblings. Although they may fight, brothers and sisters develop social skills for resolving conflict that are useful outside the home. Unlike onlies and step-siblings, full siblings are better able to form and maintain friendships, to get along with people who are different, to express feelings in a positive way, and to show greater sensitivity to other people's feelings (Downey and Condron, 2004).

Parenting Teenagers

Adolescence is a time of tremendous change. Teenagers are establishing their own identity and testing their autonomy as they mature and break away from parental supervision, a healthy process in human development (see Erikson's stages in *Table 12.1*).

CHANGES IN PARENT–CHILD RELATIONSHIPS A good parent–child relationship may shift suddenly during adolescence. As children enter the seventh and eighth grades, there may be conflict over such issues as relationships, money, and spending time with friends.

since you asked

Why is parenting teenagers sometimes so difficult?

As teenagers become more independent, increasingly interested in peers, and more likely to confide in friends, parents may feel rejected and suspicious. The most difficult part of parenting adolescents, according to some mothers, is dealing with their changing moods and behavior: "She used to chatter incessantly on car rides; now . . . "What's new in school today?" you ask. "Nothing," she answers" (Patner, 1990: C5). One mother dragged her 13-year-old son to a local hospital for a battery of tests: She was convinced that he had a hearing problem because he never seemed to respond to what she was saying (Shatzkin, 2004).

For many years, people attributed such dramatic changes to "raging sex hormones." Some scientists now think that there may be a link between a teen's baffling behavior and a surge of hormones in the brain. As the teenage brain develops, it's flooded with chemicals,

Some teenagers are happy that "car chips" help parents locate them in an emergency. Others complain that such technology gives parents too much control. So, what should parents do?

including hormones, that "influence everything from emotion and cognition to driving too fast down dark roads." What's going on? Among other chemical changes, teenagers start to secrete melatonin—one of the brain's sleep chemicals—up to two hours later than they did when they were younger. One of the results is that teens stay up later, have a harder time "getting up at dawn to get to high schools that begin ridiculously early," and are cranky because they're sleep deprived (Strauch, 2003: 141, 209).

Regardless of the sources of change, normal adolescent development can strain a marriage. In most cases, the husband and wife are experiencing stresses in their relationship, at work, and with extended family members. Parenting teenagers adds to marital role strain but doesn't necessarily cause it. Instead, "the seeds of parents' individual and marital problems are sown long before their first baby arrives" and continue through the child's adolescence (Cowan and Cowan, 2000: ix; see, also, Grych, 2002; Schoppe-Sullivan et al., 2004).

Because of the seemingly overnight changes in many adolescents' behavior, language, clothes, and music, parents sometimes view their children as "aliens from another planet" (Danesi, 2003). Teenagers often do things that are silly or dangerous, but are parents too anxious about raising adolescents?

ARE TEENAGERS GETTING A RAW DEAL?
Yes and no. One of the reasons parents worry about their teenagers or see them as moody, rebellious, and difficult is that such stereotypes pervade popular culture and self-help books. For example, when was the last time you watched the news and saw a positive story about a teenager?

A study of 59 self-help books for parents of adolescents found that 20 percent characterized adolescence as a period of "storm and stress or turmoil," and 42 percent projected negative stereotypes about adolescence as "turbulent," "a struggle," and a period of "conflict" that parents need to "survive." Even worse, some of the books, written by parents with no profes-

TABLE 12.3

Teens at High Risk for Substance Abuse

According to the National Center on Addiction and Substance Abuse (2003), almost one in four U.S. teens is at "high risk" for substance abuse:

- 25 percent smoke.
- 94 percent have tried alcohol, and 43 percent drink alcohol in a typical week.
- 42 percent get drunk at least once a month.
- 79 percent have friends who use marijuana.
- 69 percent know a friend or classmate who uses acid, cocaine, or heroin.
- 71 percent have tried marijuana.
- 57 percent could buy marijuana in one hour or less.

sional training, consist of anecdotes about parent–adolescent conflicts that are "little better than good fiction about family life" (Smith et al., 2003: 178).

Some parental nervousness about teenagers is warranted, however. Many teens have high rates of sexually transmitted infections, have many partners, and don't use condoms (see Chapter 7). And according to a recent national survey, 21 percent of teens ages 12 to 17 are at "high risk" and another 34 percent are at "moderate risk" for substance abuse (see *Table 12.3*).

Teenagers' substance abuse is influenced by many factors, including peers who smoke or drink as well as parents who smoke or abuse drugs, are unmarried, and engage in ongoing conflict (Gritz et al., 2003; National Center on Addiction and Substance Abuse, 2003).

Simply telling teens "to do" or "not to do" something is much less effective than being a good role model. And instead of giving teens undeserved praise,

parents can boost their psychological and emotional well-being by teaching them good social skills: positive behaviors (such as being considerate to others), self-control, taking the initiative in developing social relationships, and using constructive strategies (such as discussion) to resolve conflict (Zaff et al., 2002).

GENDER DIFFERENCES IN PARENTING TEENAGERS

Parents differ in their relationships with their children. Some children get along better with their mother, some with their father, and others report no difference.

Although many studies find that adolescents generally feel closeness (warmth, acceptance, and affection) with both parents, many feel closer to their mothers than to their fathers. According to a recent survey, when asked which parent deserves the most thanks for all that they do, 44 percent of teens said "Mom," 50 percent said "both parents are equally deserving," and only 4 percent said "Dad" (Fetto, 2006). Mothers probably get higher ratings because they are more likely than fathers to express love through compliments, praise, and support (Hosley and Montemayor, 1997).

Employed parents often experience **role overload,** a feeling of being overwhelmed by multiple commitments. Nearly half of American parents feel that they don't spend enough time with their children, although only 5 percent of teens feel this way. Fathers of adolescents, especially, worry that the amount of time they spend at work is robbing them of the last opportunity to get to know their children before the youngsters go off to college or jobs (Crouter et al., 2001; Mazzuca, 2004; Milkie et al., 2004).

Most adolescents manage to reach adulthood without major problems. In fact, between ages 18 and 25, the average young adult (especially women) shows significantly lower levels of depressive symptoms, higher levels of self-esteem, and a greater sense of psychological well-being. These improvements are highest among families with well-educated parents and among young adults who suffer only short periods of unemployment. Over time, however, people in their mid-20s are happier than they were at age 18 because they have married or formed new friendships (Galambos et al., 2006).

Teenagers who fare best have interrelated traits that some psychologists have labeled "the 5 Cs:" competence, confidence, connection, character, and caring (Steinberg and Lerner, 2004). As teens withdraw from the family, their parents try to keep in touch with them. Others take more drastic measures (see the box "Should Parents Track Their Teens?").

Constraints

Should Parents Track Their Teens?

In a recent national survey of teens ages 13 to 17, 44 percent said that they plan to raise their own children pretty much as their parents did. Of the 55 percent who said that they would do things differently, the largest number (18 percent) felt that their parents were too strict and controlling (Mazzuca, 2004).

Increasingly, parents are using high-tech methods to track everything from where their children are driving to what they buy and whether they show up for classes. One gadget is a cell phone that transmits location data. Another device is a debit-like card used at school lunch counters. The car chip and the Global Positioning System (GPS), installed in a vehicle, monitor speed, distance, and driving habits.

Parents contend that such high-tech devices increase their teens' safety, especially because kids will act more responsibly if they know they're being watched. Some teenagers don't mind the monitoring because it cuts down on the need to constantly "check in." According to one 17-year-old, for example, his mom simply presses a "locate" button on a cell phone to see where he is (Harmon, 2003).

Many teens, however, complain that they feel like prisoners. "It's annoying," grumbles a 15-year-old who has been caught in a few places where he wasn't supposed to be. "It gives parents too much control." Some college students have simply left their GPS-enabled cell phones under their dorm room beds when they went off with friends ("High-tech gadgets...," 2005).

Stop and Think...

- Do tracking devices keep teens safer? Or do they intrude on adolescents' privacy?

- Parents are accountable, even legally, for their teens' behavior. So should parents keep tabs on their children? Or should teens be allowed to learn from their mistakes, as their parents did?

Even though many parents enjoy their teenagers, they look forward to the end of child rearing. Often, however, children bounce back to the parental nest in young adulthood and later. According to one joke, "I childproofed my house, but they still get in."

Parenting in the Crowded "Empty Nest"

Robert Frost wrote: "Home is the place where, when you have to go there, they have to take you in." Almost 18 million young adults ages 18 to 34 who live with their parents apparently agree.

In the 1960s and 1970s, sociologists almost always included the "empty-nest" stage in describing the family life cycle (see Chapter 2). This is the stage in which parents, typically in their 50s, find they are alone at home after their children have married, gone to college, or found jobs and moved out.

The pendulum has swung back, however, especially for white middle-class families. Today young adults are living at home longer than was generally true in the past.

since you asked

What do people mean when they talk about the "boomerang generation"?

And there is a new group of young adults, the *boomerang generation,* who move back into their parents' home after having lived independently (see Chapter 10). Some journalists have called this group "adultolescents" because they're still "mooching off their parents" instead of living on their own. This stage of life isn't solely an American phenomenon. The English call such young adults "kippers" ("kids in parents' pockets eroding retirement savings"). In Germany, they are "nesthockers" (literally translated as "nest squatters"), in Italy "mammone" (young men and women who won't give up Mamma's cooking), and in Japan "freeter" (young adults who job hop and live at home) (van Dyk, 2005).

BACK TO THE NEST Although most young adults leave the parental nest by age 23, the proportion of adults ages 25 to 34 who are living with parents increased from 9 percent in 1960 to nearly 17 percent in 2000 (Fields and Casper, 2001). Twice as many men as women in this age group are living with their parents (see *Figure 12.3*).

Who are the boomerangers? Among the middle classes, men, especially, are not moving out or are returning home because they are delaying marriage and don't feel a need to establish their own homes. Others enjoy the comforts of the parental nest: "Some parents find they have an adult on their hands who still wants Mom to cook his meals and do his laundry . . ." (Large, 2002: 4N).

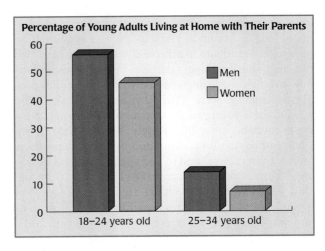

Percentage of Young Adults Living at Home with Their Parents

FIGURE 12.3 **Who Lives at Home?**

Note: The total number is 13.8 million for ages 18–24 and almost 4.1 million for ages 25–34.

SOURCE: Based on Fields, 2004, Table 7.

One of my male students, in his late 20s, may be representative of other men his age who enjoy living at home: "My mom loves my living with her. She enjoys cooking, cleaning my room, and just having me around. I don't pitch in for any of the expenses, but we get along great because she doesn't hassle me about my comings and goings. I have lots of freedom without worrying about bills."

Women also move back with doting parents who support them financially. A 29-year-old elementary-school teacher moved into her parents' home in a retirement community in Cape Cod, Massachusetts, because her $1,400-a-month apartment in Boston didn't have air-conditioning, a dishwasher, or a washing machine. She now enjoys golf and tennis privileges, yoga classes, a fancy clubhouse, and her parents' Jacuzzi bathtub—all at the parents' expense. A 32-year-old woman moved home with her parents because, among other things, her dad fills her gas tank and maintains her car and her mom packs home-cooked lunches for her to take to work. Both parents pay many of her credit-card expenses. And because the daughter has complained about being disturbed while she sleeps, dad grinds his coffee beans at night instead of at 5 A.M. and mom has stopped doing laundry, including the daughter's, early in the morning or late at night (Rich, 2005; White, 2005).

Macro-level factors also encourage a larger number of young adults to stay home or move back. Student loans, low wages, soaring house prices, divorce, credit card debt, and jumping from job to job until they find "meaningful" work have made it harder for young middle-class adults to maintain the lifestyles that their parents created. And the transition to adulthood gets tougher the lower you go on the economic and educational ladder. About 20 years ago, it was possible for a high school graduate to achieve a middle-class standard of living. That's no longer the case. Instead, young adults now need a college degree to be where blue-collar people the same age were 20 or 30 years ago (Côté, 2000).

Do these young adults save up the money while living at home to move out? Rarely. Without the responsibility of paying bills, many boomerangers have more money than they're used to and spend it instead of saving: "Most of their needs are taken care of by Mom and Dad. Many twenty-somethings are living at home, but if you look, you'll see flat-screen TVs in their bedrooms and brand-new cars in the driveway" (Grossman, 2005: 51–52).

RELATIONSHIPS BETWEEN PARENTS AND BOOM-ERANGERS How do adult children and parents get along, especially when they're living under the same roof? Some parents report that they are tolerant of but unhappy with the return of their children. There is often conflict about clothes, helping out, use of the family car, and the adult child's lifestyle. The average parent spends at least $12,200 a year to support a young adult. This may not sound like much, but it may be about 20 percent of a parent's retirement income. Parents whose adult children suffer from mental, physical, or stress-related problems or are unemployed or unwilling to help with household expenses experience greater stress than do parents whose children don't have these difficulties (Paul, 2003; Ramachandran, 2005).

The biggest problems arise if the adult children are unemployed or if grandchildren live in the home. College-educated fathers, especially, are angry about children who move back home instead of living on their own. This may result in part from the fathers' higher expectations for their children's success. Single mothers who move back into their parents' homes are often unhappy because the parents are likely to interfere with the mother's child-rearing practices (Aquilino, 1997).

Other research shows that co-residence brings mutual assistance. For example, adult children and their older parents often benefit by sharing some household expenses and child care, especially if they respect each side's privacy (Estess, 1994).

On an anecdotal level, some of my students feel that there are many mutual payoffs to living at home. For example, "After my dad died, my mom wanted me to live at home because she was always a stay-at-home mom and was very lonely"; "My dad still treats me like a ten-year-old, but I take care of him and he helps me pay my tuition and looks after my kids when I'm in class or at work"; and "I'm not happy about my parents' telling me that they disapprove of some of my friends, but they also cheer me up when I feel down."

Parenting in Later Life

The majority of parents (62 percent) provide some form of help to at least one of their adult children. Parents are most likely to give advice (46 percent), and about one-third assist with child care and household tasks. Although monetary help is less common, such assistance varies. For example, low-income adult children are significantly more likely to receive financial help from a parent than their better-off siblings. Also, parents are more likely to help children who live close to them and those with whom they have a good relationship (Zarit and Eggebeen, 2002).

Although they don't expect to do so, a number of grandparents find themselves raising grandchildren in their later years, especially if the parents are on drugs, in prison, or have mental health problems. Grandparents often pitch in, but they're not always happy to do so. Most would prefer to spend their time in recreational activities or visiting friends rather than raising grandchildren or great-grandchildren (see Chapter 17).

You see, then, that whether people are married, unmarried, or single, they parent their children throughout the life course. What about same-sex parents? Are their child-rearing practices similar to or different from those of heterosexual parents?

Making Connections

- Think about how your parents or guardians raised you. Did the parenting differ in terms of your parents' gender or your siblings' birth order? If you're an only child, are you glad or not that you had no brothers or sisters?

- Is it "fair" or not for adults to move back home (or never move out) when their parents have looked forward to an "empty nest"?

Parenting in Lesbian and Gay Families

Nationally, 33 percent of female same-sex couples and 22 percent of male same-sex couples live with children under 18 years old. The actual figures are probably much higher because census data don't count single gay men and lesbians who are raising children (Simmons and O'Connell, 2003; Gates and Ost, 2004).

since you asked

How do gay and lesbian families differ from heterosexual families?

Lesbian mothers who work outside the home often have to struggle, just as heterosexual parents do, to be able to spend quality time with their children.

In most respects, lesbian and gay families are like heterosexual families: The parents must make a living, family members may disagree about the use of space or money, and they must all develop problem-solving skills. Gay and lesbian parents face the added burden of raising children who will often experience discrimination because of their parents' sexual orientation (Goldberg and Sayer, 2006; see, also, Chapters 6, 7, and 8).

Children with Lesbian and Gay Parents

In many cases, children feel that having same-sex parents is "no big deal." According to one 8-year-old, for example, "I just say I have two moms—'Mom' and 'Mamma Sheri.' They're no different from other parents except that they're two girls" (Gilgoff, 2004: 42).

In other cases, especially during adolescence, children may try to hide the information from their friends:

> *High school was the hardest. My brother and I would never allow Mom and Barb to walk together or sit next to each other in a restaurant. We wouldn't have people spend the night; if we did have friends over, we would hide the gay literature and family pictures (McGuire, 1996: 53).*

Despite the particular difficulties that children in gay families face, their peer and other social relationships are similar to those of children raised in heterosexual families. A number of studies of adolescents growing up with same-sex parents have concluded that what matters is not the gender of parents but the quality of their relationships with their children. Adolescents whose parents have close and satisfying relationships are likely to do better in school and have

few behavioral problems (Stacey and Biblarz, 2001; Wainright et al., 2004).

Lesbian and gay parents often do a better job of managing their anger than heterosexual couples do. They are more likely to use discussion instead of physical punishment to discipline their children. Only 15 percent of gay and lesbian parents use corporal punishment, compared with 60 percent of heterosexual parents. One of the reasons may be that lesbian and gay parents tend to be highly educated: Almost half have graduate degrees (Nanette Silverman, cited in Schorr, 2001). As you saw earlier, high-SES parents are less likely than low-SES parents to hit or spank their children.

Parents with Gay and Lesbian Children

About one-third of youth ages 15 to 19 do not tell their parents that they are lesbian, gay, or bisexual (D'Augelli et al., 2005). When children do come out, many heterosexual parents are initially negative because they think that their children could be heterosexual if they wanted to be. Most Asian parents, for example, view homosexuality as a chosen lifestyle, "an undesirable indulgence of individual freedom in the United States" (Leonard, 1997: 148). A child who once was familiar now appears to be a stranger. Parents may also be concerned about being stigmatized themselves.

Negative feelings are frequently followed by strong feelings of guilt and failure in their parenting roles. A common question is "Where did we fail?" Some parents may break off contact with their children, try to convince them to change their sexual preference, or ignore the issue. Over time, others accept the child's homosexuality (Barret and Robinson, 1990; Savin-Williams and Dubé, 1998).

Regardless of their sexual orientation, mothers and fathers who are consistently and positively involved in their children's lives help them grow up with a strong sense of self, a feeling of security, and a host of other positive characteristics. Parents can also stunt their children's development.

Parents' Impact on Child Development

Recently, a school superintendent in Lebanon, Pennsylvania, proposed that teachers grade parents on how involved they are in their children's education. Some parents were furious because they felt that being judged by their children's teachers would be demeaning. Others thought it was a good idea because many parents aren't on top of their children's academic progress ("Report cards for parents . . . ," 2003). Whether it's education or other areas, parents can have both positive and negative effects on their children.

Parents' Positive Impact

Parents play many roles: social initiators, mediators, advisors, and managers, to name a few. "Good" parents provide guidance and economic support and develop a healthy emotional relationship with their children that includes love, caring, listening, and respect (Waller, 2002; Parke et al., 2003).

An important adult responsibility is to set guidelines or rules that teach children the difference between right and wrong and what kinds of behaviors are acceptable. Much research supports the idea that setting clear limits is a critical element in shaping children's judgment and developing a conscience (Brown et al., 2001).

Setting guidelines includes establishing routines and rituals. Especially during times of stress and transition, routines and rituals improve family relationships and well-being. Routines get things done and promote a sense of order and reciprocal expectations. Rituals, such as dinnertimes and birthday celebrations, enhance family members' sense of stability and belonging to the group (Fiese et al., 2002).

As you saw earlier, parents who spend time with their children experience greater warmth and closeness. They are more likely to report that their teenagers have fewer mental health problems, greater academic motivation, and fewer emotional difficulties. In addition, many parents who participate in religious activities with their children have more cohesive family relationships, lower levels of conflict, and children with fewer behavioral problems (Flouri and Buchanan, 2003).

Most parents are responsible and have a beneficial effect on their children. In other cases, parenting styles or lack of parenting jeopardize children's well-being.

Parents' Negative Impact

Parents' negative impacts on their children can be grouped into two broad categories. *Acts of commission* are cases in which irresponsible behaviors result in poor outcomes. *Acts of omission* are behaviors whose absence can be detrimental to development.

Recently, a 54-year-old middle-class father was arrested for soliciting a prostitute for his teenage son because he had caught the boy looking at pornographic Web sites and adult magazines. The father said that he wanted to provide a remedy for the son's "sexual frustration." Most acts of commission don't end in an arrest, but they can still have negative effects. For example,

■ Children whose parents smoke are twice as likely to begin smoking between the ages of 13 and 21. Second-hand smoke is also detrimental to children's health (Hill et al., 2005; Pyle et al., 2005).

■ Children of alcohol-abusing fathers have more symptoms of anxiety, depression, and temper tantrums than their counterparts. By age 5, they are also more likely to have behavioral problems such as cheating, swearing, and physically attacking other children (Jaffee et al., 2003).

■ Children who grow up in households in which parents constantly argue and fight have sleep problems, are emotionally insecure, and as teenagers and adults are more likely to engage in drug and alcohol abuse, smoking, risky sexual behavior, and antisocial behavior (Cummings et al., 2006; Davies et al., 2006; El-Sheikh et al., 2006).

■ One out of four U.S. parents allow their teens to drink at home with their parents present. About 32 percent of teens say that their parents provide the alcohol (American Medical Association, 2005).

■ American teens are the fattest in the industrialized world. The rate of overweight adolescents has risen sharply since 1976 (see *Figure 12.4*), and increases the chances of diabetes, stroke, heart disease, arthritis, and some cancers in adulthood. Most of the increase is due to parents' allowing children to eat fast food, snacks, and sugary sodas as well as permitting sedentary lifestyles (Lissau et al., 2004; Johnston et al., 2006).

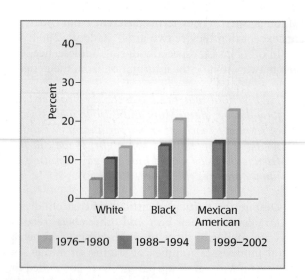

FIGURE 12.4 Percentage of Overweight Children, by Ethnicity, 1976–2002

Note: The data are for children ages 6–18.
SOURCE: Based on Johnston et al., 2006, p. 30.

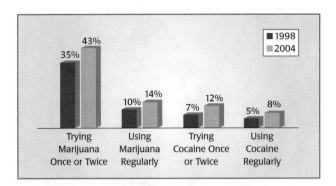

FIGURE 12.5 Fewer Parents See Drug Use as Risky
Compared with 1998, today's parents are more likely to see "slight" or "no risk" in health if teenagers try or use marijuana or cocaine. Why do you think that parents' attitudes have changed?

SOURCE: Partnership for a Drug-Free America, 2004, p. 5.

Parents can also be guilty of acts of omission when they don't live up to their responsibility of raising happy, healthy children. Whether these behaviors are intentional or not, they can have dire long-term consequences. For example,

- Poor nutrition in the first few years of life lead to lower IQ levels, which, in turn, lead to antisocial and aggressive behavior through age 17 (Liu et al., 2004).

- Many parents lament that their kids are self-centered, self-absorbed, and out of control. However, 30 percent buy their children top-of-the-line brands (even when they can't afford the clothes and products) and 75 percent say that they rarely ask their children to do household chores (Tyre et al., 2004).

- About one in five teenagers have tried painkillers such as Vicodin or OxyContin to get high. Kids who learn about the risks of drugs at home are up to 50 percent less likely to use drugs, but only 31 percent of teens say that their parents have ever talked to them about the risks of taking drugs, including nonprescription cold or cough medicine (Partnership for a Drug-Free America, 2006).

- Many parents have lax attitudes about drugs. Since 1998, for example, there has been a significant increase in the number of parents who see little or no risk in their children's using marijuana or cocaine (see *Figure 12.5*). Such perceptions may be due to the parents' coming of age when drug use was at its peak: "Many of them got high, some regularly, and they're doing just fine. They assume their children will follow the same path" (Marks, 2005: 4).

- Even though parental conversations with college-bound students about not drinking are effective in reducing alcohol consumption, many parents don't have such discussions (Turrisi et al., 2001).

Parenting, then, can be harmful to many children's health. Is nonparental child care a better alternative for these and other families?

Making Connections

- Much research shows that sexual orientation has little effect on children's well-being. Why, then, are many people opposed to gay and lesbian parenting?

- Think about your own parents. What positive impacts did they have on you? What about negative influences?

Child Care Arrangements

The Reverend Jesse Jackson reportedly said, "Your children need your presence more than your presents." Many parents, especially absentee fathers, spend little time with their children. Some latchkey kids must fend for themselves after school until a parent comes home from work. In many other cases, employed parents must rely on child care outside the family.

Absentee Fathers

Some people believe that one of the most serious problems facing contemporary families is that the United States is becoming an increasingly fatherless society:

> *Tonight, about 40 percent of American children will go to sleep in homes in which their fathers do not live. Before they reach the age of eighteen, more than half of our nation's children are likely to spend at least a significant portion of their childhoods living apart from their fathers. . . . Never before have so many children grown up without knowing what it means to have a father (Blankenhorn, 1995: 1).*

Absentee fathers can have a negative impact on their children from birth to young adulthood. Two disadvantages of a father's absence are economic deprivation and little, if any, social support.

ECONOMIC DEPRIVATION Half of families headed by single mothers live below the poverty line, compared with 10 percent of two-parent families (see Chapter 13). Although many single-mother families were poor even before the father left, his departure reduces a child's economic resources even further. Economic problems, in turn, affect the quality of a neighborhood and its schools, the mother's ability to pay for child care, and the child's access to enriching after-school and summer programs.

LACK OF SOCIAL SUPPORT Compared with children raised in single-mother households, those raised in single-father homes are less well behaved at school, are less successful at getting along with others, and put forth less effort in class (Downey et al., 1998; Carlson, 2006).

Single mothers sometimes get financial and other support from "social fathers," male relatives and mothers' boyfriends who are like fathers to the children. Male relatives, especially, can enhance children's cognitive abilities by giving them books, reading to them, and spending time with them (Jayakody and Kalil, 2002). If social fathers leave or move away, however, the children lose access to such resources.

Latchkey Kids

Demographers sometimes refer to families in which both parents are employed full time as **DEWKS,** or dual-employed with kids. As the proportion of DEWK families has increased, so has the number of latchkey children.

There's nothing new about children being on their own at home. The phrase *latchkey children* originated in the early 1800s, when youngsters who were responsible for their own care wore the key to their home tied to a string around their neck. Today **latchkey kids** are children who return home after school and let themselves in to an empty house or apartment, where they are alone and unsupervised until their parents or another adult comes home.

The number of latchkey kids has almost doubled since the 1970s. Almost 6 million children 5 to 14 years old (15 percent of children in this age group) care for themselves on a regular basis before or after school. On average, children spend six hours per week in self-care, typically until a parent returns from work (Overturf Johnson, 2005).

Who are the children who are home alone? The older children are, the more likely they are to be latchkey kids. For example, 1 percent of children in self-care are 5 or 6 years old, compared with 39 percent of 14-year-olds. Employment rather than family structure influences self-care. That is, in both married-couple and single-mother homes, about 20 percent of elementary-school children spend some time in self-care if the parents are employed. White 5- to 14-year-olds are nearly twice as likely as their African American and Latino peers to spend time in self-care (Overturf Johnson, 2005).

Millions of "latchkey kids" return from school to an empty house, where they must wait two to four hours until an adult or other caretaker arrives. Most schools don't provide after-school care. In other cases, parents—especially single mothers—can't afford expensive after-school programs.

Most children enjoy being home alone, savoring the independence. They watch television, play, read, and do homework and some chores. Others are nervous about being by themselves, don't structure their time, don't do their homework, or invite friends over, against house rules. Some researchers believe that most 6- to 9-year-olds are not ready to care for themselves regularly, and certainly less able than older children to deal with household emergencies (Belle, 1999; Vandivere et al., 2003).

Child Care

Few issues make working parents as anxious as choosing child care. Parents experience stress because they worry about their children's safety and the possibility of their engaging in risky behavior when unsupervised (Barnett and Gareis,

since you asked

Are child care centers harmful to young children?

2006). The greatest concern is for preschoolers because they are least able to fend for themselves.

CHILD CARE PATTERNS AND CHARACTERISTICS You'll recall that the majority of children under age 5 with employed parents receive care from nonrelatives, especially at child care centers and in providers' home (see *Figure 12.6*). The arrangements vary, however, depending on such factors as the availability of care, its costs, the hours of child care programs, and race and ethnicity (Capizzano and Adams, 2000b).

Nationally, black parents are more likely than white and Latino parents to use child care centers, while Latino parents are more likely to depend on relatives (see *Figure 12.6*). Latino parents are probably less likely to use child care centers because many are recent immigrants who do not speak English and aren't aware of child care facilities, because little care is available nearby, because they cannot afford the costs, or, in the case of undocumented immigrants, because they aren't eligible for state programs that subsidize child care (Capps et al., 2005).

Higher-income families are more likely to use child care arrangements, including child care centers, than are lower-income families. Nationally, the average cost of a child care center for children under age 5 is about $6,000 a year (Overturf Johnson, 2005). The costs are higher for infants and for young children living in metropolitan areas. According to one of my students, for example, "I pay almost $8,000 a year for my 10-month-old son, and it isn't easy to also pay for my tuition and books." It's sometimes more expensive to send a toddler to a "mediocre" child care center than to pay the tuition at a community college or a four-year public college or university.

Some companies, such as Stride-Rite (a shoe manufacturer) in Cambridge, Massachusetts, have implemented programs that combine elder care and child care.

EFFECTS OF CHILD CARE ON CHILDREN AND PARENTS Daycare is a controversial issue. Those with conservative perspectives, especially, are critical of employed mothers who place their children in child care. They maintain that working mothers are responsible for juvenile delinquency, children's poor performance in school, childhood obesity, and a host of other maladies, including playground accidents (Eberstadt, 2004).

Such accusations increase mothers' feelings of guilt, but are they valid? No. For example, children are considerably more likely to be abused by relatives than by daycare workers, preschool children are almost twice as likely to be injured on playground equipment at home as in other locations (including child care centers), and the death rate among children receiving care in private homes is 16 times greater than the rate for children in child care centers (U.S. Consumer Product Safety Commission, 2001; Wrigley and Dreby, 2005).

A number of studies report that a well-run child care center has positive effects on children's social and cognitive development. In high-quality daycare, even children from low-income families outscore more advantaged children on IQ tests by the time they enter kindergarten. The higher the quality of child care in the first three years of life—among children from both poor and

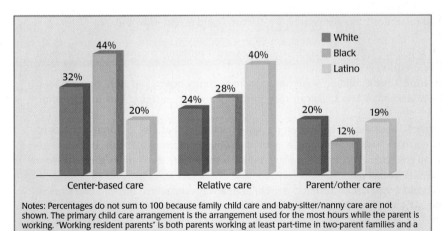

Notes: Percentages do not sum to 100 because family child care and baby-sitter/nanny care are not shown. The primary child care arrangement is the arrangement used for the most hours while the parent is working. "Working resident parents" is both parents working at least part-time in two-parent families and a single parent working at least part-time in single-parent families.

FIGURE 12.6 Child Care Arrangements for Children Under 5, by Ethnicity

SOURCE: Adapted from Capizzano et al., 2006, Figure 2.

middle-income families—the greater the child's language abilities and school readiness skills such as counting and knowing the alphabet (NICHD . . . , 2003; Loeb et al., 2005).

The benefits of high-quality child care may continue into adulthood. Throughout their school years, children from low-income families who are in high-quality daycare are less likely to get into trouble or to drop out of school. They have better language and mathematical skills and higher academic achievement than their counterparts in a provider's home, and are also more likely to attend college (Campbell and Ramey, 1999; Reynolds et al., 2001).

Good child care centers also help employed parents. Low-income mothers, especially, benefit from state subsidies for child care services. The mothers can not only get off welfare but can also comply with employers' requests for overtime and work schedules that might include night shifts or working on weekends. In the long term, these mothers may be promoted to better-paying positions that improve their and their children's lives (Press et al., 2006; see, also, Chaudry, 2004).

The daycare centers with the best results are small and have high staff-to-child ratios (see the box "How Can I Find a Good Child Care Program?"). Good child care providers often quit, however, because they earn among the lowest wages: about $17,000 a year, less than pet groomers. Few receive health insurance or retirement benefits. Consequently, 30 percent of day-care workers leave their jobs within a year (Zuckerman, 2000).

Good child care isn't a question of money but of priorities. It would take about $30 billion a year to cover the costs of high-quality child care for all U.S. families. This sum is nothing compared with the tax cuts and Social Security benefits that total almost $230 billion annually—mainly benefiting the affluent—that the Bush administration has provided in recent years. In addition, the war in Iraq will cost at least $1 trillion before it ends (Warner, 2005; Zuckerman, 2006).

Because of state budget cuts, many low-income families aren't eligible for child care programs, must endure long waiting lists, and are subject to high co-payments that they can't afford. Even though it's the richest

Ask Yourself

How Can I Find a Good Child Care Program?

Following are some questions that will help you evaluate the day-care programs you visit. Some are questions to ask of the administrators, teachers, and staff, as well as other parents. Others are questions to ask yourself as you mull over the information you've gathered.

1. *What is the staff–to-child ratio?* The best programs have enough staff members on hand so that children get plenty of attention. Suggested staff–to-child ratios are 1 to 3 for infants, 1 to 10 for 5- and 6-year-olds, and 1 to 12 for children over 6.
2. *What is the staff turnover rate?* If half the staff members leaves every year, it probably means that they are paid extremely low wages or feel that the program is not run well.
3. *How do the staff and children look?* If the children seem unhappy, have runny noses, and seem passive, look elsewhere. If the staff members seem distant or lackadaisical, they probably are not engaging kids in interesting projects.
4. *How well equipped is the facility?* There should be interesting indoor activities that give children a choice of projects, as well as ample playground space with swings, jungle gyms, and other exercise equipment. If there is no adjacent outdoor area, do the children go regularly to a park or playground? Is the facility clean and organized? Does it have a range of toys, books, materials, and activities?
5. *What are the safety regulations and hygienic practices?* Are children always accounted for when they arrive and leave? Are staff trained in first aid? What are the policies about children who take medications (for allergies, for example)?
6. *Is the director of the center willing to have you talk to other parents who use the center?* Better yet, does the center have video cameras so you can log on from work or home? The "Taking It Further" section at the end of this chapter provides Internet sites for accessing a wealth of information about child care facilities.

country in the world, the United States lags far behind other industrialized countries—such as Japan, France, Germany, and Sweden—where the government runs preschool and child care centers or pays up to 90 percent of child care costs (Forry and Walker, 2006; see, also, Chapter 13).

Current Social Issues and Children's Well-Being

Government officials often proclaim that children are our most precious resources, tomorrow's leaders, and so on. Do public policies and parenting behavior contradict such noble sentiments? Let's look at the effects of electronic media on children, some of the risks that children face, and foster care.

since you asked

Are U.S. children better off today than in the past?

The Impact of Electronic Media

The typical American child is saturated with electronic media (see Chapters 5 and 7). The American Academy of Pediatrics and many child development experts recommend that children under age 2 be kept away from all screen media to encourage creative play and interaction with parents. Still, 68 percent of children under 2 view two to three hours of television daily—years before they even ask for TV. Some experts have criticized even the highly respected *Sesame Street* as "downright irresponsible" for recently producing a new DVD series targeted at children ages 6 months to 2 years. Electronic media can be educational, but parents often use them as nannies: "My two-year-old daughter will play a game for an hour or more at a time. I'm sure she's learning something" (Garrison and Christakis, 2005; Oldenburg, 2006).

Because few television programs have educational content, some scholars feel that parents have an overly positive view of the impact of television on young children. Especially in homes where the television is always on, and even if no one is watching, parents of children under age 6 spend less time reading to children and these children have lower reading skills than those who have limited access to television, DVDs, videos, and other electronic media (Vandewater et al., 2005; Rideout and Hamel, 2006).

On average, seventh- to twelfth-graders spend almost seven hours a day with media compared with about two hours each with parents and friends, and less than one hour per day doing homework (see *Figure 12.7*). Because of multiple activities (such as hanging out with parents and watching TV at the same time), children are actually exposed to about 8.5 hours of media content a day, more than the equivalent of a full-time job (Rideout et al., 2005).

How healthy is the ever-expanding presence of electronic media in children's everyday environment? Much depends on factors such as age, content, parental monitoring, and the frequency of an activity (see Bremer, 2005, for a review of some of this literature).

Generally, children and adolescents who watch a lot of television (more than two hours daily) do poorly in school because TV viewing displaces reading and homework. Having a bedroom television set, especially, increases viewing, which, in turn, decreases academic success. As early as the third grade, children with their own TV sets score lower in math and reading than those without their own sets. Computer access, especially when children use the Internet for homework, improves both reading and math scores (Borzekowski and Robinson, 2005; Hancox et al., 2005; Zimmerman and Christakis, 2005).

Adolescents who are heavy television viewers start drinking alcohol at an earlier age, largely because commercials link alcohol to normal, everyday life. In addition, a major concern is that electronic media (especially TV, cartoons, music, and music videos) desensitize

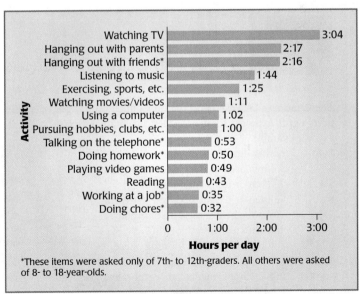

FIGURE 12.7 Media Time and Other Activities in a Child's Typical Day

Source: Rideout et al., 2005: 38.

children to violence and increase the likelihood that adolescents will become sexually active. Advisory labels on CDs have little effect because a vast majority of teens, 74 percent, say that they ignore the labels in their purchase decisions (Collins et al., 2005; Ellickson et al., 2005; Kirsh, 2005; Mika, 2005; Ward and Friedman, 2006; see, also, Chapters 5 and 7).

Electronic media can also provide many benefits. About 87 percent of U.S. youth ages 12 to 17 use the Internet, up from 73 percent in 2000. As teenagers grow older, they tend to be less interested in diversions like online games and more likely to use the Web for homework, health and religious material, and information about colleges or jobs (Lenhart et al., 2005).

Children at Risk

Life is improving for many American children. They are smoking less, graduating from high school in larger numbers, and are less likely to die of firearm injuries or to have an out-of-wedlock baby (Federal Interagency Forum . . . , 2005).

There's also some bad news. As you saw earlier and in Chapter 11, U.S. childhood obesity rates have exploded since 1980, the infant mortality rate is twice as high among blacks as among whites, and the number of low-birthweight babies has risen. About 89 percent of children have health insurance coverage at some point during the year, but this means that 11 percent—almost 9 million kids—don't. About 22 percent of children of

low-income immigrants have no health coverage at all. In addition, housing for more than one in three U.S. households with kids is physically inadequate, crowded, or costs more than 20 percent of the household's income (Capps et al., 2005; Federal Interagency Forum . . . , 2003; 2005; see, also, Chapter 13).

If children are our most precious resource, we are squandering our assets (see the box "One Day in the Life of America's Children"). Compared with other industrialized countries, the United States is least effective in protecting its children against gun violence and has the highest child poverty rates. It is also the *only* industrialized nation in the world that does not provide guaranteed prenatal care for every pregnant woman (Children's Defense Fund Action Council, 2005).

Foster Care

The growth of poverty, child abuse, and parental neglect has increased children's out-of-home placements, including care by relatives, residential treatment facilities, group homes (which house a number of children), and shelters for runaways. The most common out-of-home placement is the **foster home,** in which parents raise children who are not their own.

PREVALENCE OF FOSTER HOMES An estimated 800,000 children are in foster care at some point during the year, almost three times as many as in 1987. In contrast, there are only 144,000 available foster homes. About 119,000

Choices

A Day in the Life of America's Children

The Children's Defense Fund Action Council (2005) reports a grim existence for many American children. Every day, for example,

1	mother dies in childbirth.
4	children are killed by abuse or neglect.
5	children or teens commit suicide.
8	children or teens are killed by firearms.
77	babies die before their first birthday.
177	children are arrested for violent crimes.
375	children are arrested for drug abuse.
1,186	babies are born to unmarried teen mothers.
1,900	public school students are corporally punished.
2,341	babies are born to mothers who are not high school graduates.
2,385	babies are born into poverty.
16,964	public school students are suspended.

Stop and Think. . .

- The United States ranks first in the world in defense expenditures, gross national product, health technology, and numbers of millionaires and billionaires. Why, then, are we first among 16 industrialized nations in the proportion of children living in poverty?

- Consider how many politicians discuss child-related issues, such as spending less than 1 percent of the nation's budget for children's needs (Children's Defense Fund, 2002). Does their ignoring such topics affect your vote?

children in foster care are waiting to be adopted. This means that hundreds of thousands of children end up in group homes, temporary detention, and psychiatric wards awaiting placement, a wait that can last months or even years (Children's Defense Fund, 2005).

Recent years have seen a dramatic growth in kinship care, sometimes called *relative foster care*. In 2005, 23 percent of children in foster care lived with relatives, up from 18 percent in 1986 (Barbell and Freundlich, 2001; Children's Defense Fund, 2005). Some children in foster homes do well. Most, however, experience problems.

PROBLEMS OF FOSTER HOMES In theory, foster homes are supposed to provide short-term care until children can be adopted or returned to their biological parents. In reality, many children go through multiple placements and remain in foster care until late adolescence.

Approximately 25 to 30 percent of the children who are returned to their biological parents are soon back in foster care. Children who are older or have behavioral or emotional problems are most likely to bounce from home to home. In this sense, the foster care system may sometimes worsen children's already significant physical and mental health problems. Also, many experience fear, anger, and a sense of loss: They don't know what will happen in the future and miss seeing their family and relatives (Whiting and Lee, 2003).

Foster children are especially disadvantaged in attaining a higher education. About 150,000 are qualified, but only 30,000 attend college. Of those in college, only 5 percent finish. The high dropout rate is due to a number of interrelated factors. For example, the youth don't have adults, especially parents or foster parents, who encourage them to succeed; they often lack the skills they need to function on their own (such as living independently) because they have sometimes lived in as may as 10 foster homes and have attended as many schools; and may suffer from depression or anxiety because of the traumatic feelings of abandonment and living apart from their families (Wolanin, 2005).

BENEFITS OF FOSTER HOMES The obvious benefit of foster homes is that many children experience physical

and emotional safety: "We had some parents that we could trust [and] . . . they care about me" or "You don't get beat, they teach you the right way to do stuff, they teach you not to lie, stuff like that" (Whiting and Lee, 2003: 292).

Foster parents often make sure that the kids in their care get the medical and mental health services they need. Instead of being in a group home, where many kids have severe behavioral problems, a child in a foster home usually lives with "healthy" adults (Wiltenburg, 2002).

The typical foster parent, usually a woman, is paid little (about $400 a month for a child age 2). Although this might sound like a hefty amount to some people, foster parents typically use their own income to pay for many expenses. For many, being a foster parent is a labor of love. For example, according to a Latina who lives in a modest home in a working-class neighborhood in Arizona, "For children who have nothing, at least I've been able to give them a home and security for a while" (Vanderpool, 2004: 3).

Conclusion

As this chapter shows, there have been numerous *changes* in raising children in the last decade or so. Many fathers are more interested in helping to raise their children. On the other hand, there are more at-risk children and a widespread need for high-quality day care.

Parents face many micro- and macro-level *constraints*. The most severe problems are generated by political and economic conditions. Even though the United States is one of the wealthiest countries in the world, the number of American children who live in poverty and who are deprived of basic health care and other services has increased since 1980.

Socioeconomic status, race, ethnicity, and other factors shape parental *choices*. Gay and lesbian, minority, and working-class parents, for example, have to struggle to raise happy, healthy children. In the next chapter we address the economic constraints and choices that many families confront.

Summary

1. Infants play an active role in their own development and socialization. Parenting is not a "natural" process but a long-term, time-consuming task that must be learned through trial and error rather than formal training.

2. Among the major theories of child development and socialization are Mead's theory of the social self, Piaget's theory of cognitive development, and Erikson's psychosocial theory of development over the life cycle.

3. Many parents experience problems in raising children because they have unrealistic expectations and believe many common myths about child rearing.

4. Social scientists have identified four broad parenting styles: authoritarian, permissive, authoritative, and uninvolved. These styles often vary in different racial and ethnic groups and social classes.

5. Corporal punishment is a controversial issue. Although many parents maintain that physical punishment is necessary, most educators argue that there are more effective disciplinary methods than spanking, slapping, or verbal putdowns.

6. Parenting stretches across the life course. Largely for economic reasons, adult children are staying in their parents' home longer and often returning after living independently, sometimes with their own children.

7. In general, gay and lesbian parenting is similar to heterosexual parenting. For example, all parents must make a living and develop effective problem-solving strategies.

8. Parents are usually the most important people in their children's lives. Parenting can be stressful, however, if the father is not involved in a constructive way, if very young children are latchkey kids, and if child care is expensive, low quality, or otherwise inaccessible.

9. Most parents are responsible and have a beneficial effect on their children. Poor parenting styles or lack of parenting can also jeopardize children's well-being.

10. One response to at-risk families is to place children in out-of-home care, especially foster homes. Although many foster homes are beneficial, some create more problems than they solve.

Key Terms

Taking It Further

Parenting Resources

There are many great parenting sites. Here are a few examples.

Preparing for Parenthood offers both humorous and serious information on anticipating and coping with parenthood.
www.sowashco.k12.mn.us/lake/PK/html/PFP.HTML

Zero to Three offers excellent material on promoting young children's social, emotional, and intellectual development.
www.zerotothree.org

Family.Com provides a unique directory of regional activities for kids and families.
www.family.go.com

CYFERNet provides practical, research-based information on children, youth, and families from the Cooperative Extension Services of universities in all 50 states.
www.cyfernet.org

The Children's Bureau promotes "the safety, permanency, and well-being of children." Some of the resources include national clearinghouses and up-to-date information on adoption and foster care.

www.acf.hhs.gov/programs/cb

The National Child Care Information Center offers a wealth of information, including a link to Child Care Resources on the Internet, which provides links to at least 100 sites dealing with child care issues.

www.nccic.org

And more:

www.prenhall.com/benokraitis provides numerous links to parenting newsletters from professional and government organizations, sites dealing with single parenting, online journals, discussion groups about pregnancy and expectant parents, national parent information centers, sites targeted at fathers and children with disabilities, and resources for families of various racial and ethnic groups with young children.

Investigate With Research Navigator

Go to www.researchnavigator.com and enter your LOGIN NAME and PASSWORD. For instructions on registering for the first time, view the detailed instructions at the end of Chapter 1. Search the Research Navigator™ site using the following key terms:

child care
parenting
Erik Erikson

Outline

Balancing Work and Family Life

Data Digest

■ In 2005, **the median income for all U.S. households** was $46,326: $61,094 for Asian Americans, $50,784 for whites, $35,967 for Latinos, and $30,858 for African Americans.

■ **If the $5.15 hourly minimum wage had risen at the same rate as CEO compensation** since 1990, it would be $23.03.

■ In 2004, 55 percent of **mothers of children 1 year of age or younger were employed,** down from 59 percent in 1998 but up from 31 percent in 1976.

■ **Only 34 percent of American adults say that today's children will be better off financially** than their parents, down from 55 percent in 1999.

■ The percentage of Americans **who worry about not having enough money to pay normal monthly bills** (such as healthcare and energy costs) increased from 44 percent in 2001 to 52 percent in 2006.

■ The **average number of vacation days** after being on the job for one year varies widely, from 30 to 31 days in Denmark and Finland to 6 in Mexico. The average number of vacation days for employees in Canada, Japan, and the United States is 10 days.

Sources: "Who gets the most time off," 2000; Dye, 2005; DeNavas-Walt et al., 2006; Jeffery, 2006; Jones, 2006a; Taylor et al., 2006b.

Pamela Gallina, 45, recently got a job because "We're so much worse off today than we were five years ago:"

> While she hasn't racked up debt, Gallina also hasn't been able to save. . .Though her house has appreciated nicely, her expenses have soared and her husband's raises haven't kept pace. She shells out $171 a month for electricity and $2.79 a gallon for home heating oil, about double what she paid a few years ago ("Median income. . . ," 2006: 3E).

Economic issues are critical to a family's well-being. You'll see in this chapter that many mothers experience wage inequality, family roles have changed as parents juggle employment and domestic responsibilities, and work policies often hurt rather than help families. Let's begin with a brief look at some macro-level factors that affect family life.

The Big Picture: Work and Family in Society

Many people, like the Gallinas, feel that they have to run as fast as they can to maintain a modest standard of living. Because of an increase in income inequality, poverty, and homelessness in the past 20 years, some families fell out of the race no matter how fast they ran. A growing number of families has watched the race from their penthouses.

Social Class and Income

A *social class,* you'll recall, is a category of people who have a similar standing or rank based on wealth, education, power, prestige, and other valued resources (see Chapter 1). **Wealth** is the money and economic assets that a person or family owns. It includes property (such as real estate, stocks and bonds, retirement and savings accounts, and personal possessions such as cars and jewelry) and income. **Income** is the amount of money a person receives, usually through wages or salaries, but it can also include rents, interest on savings accounts, dividends on stocks, or the proceeds from a business.

Although there is no across-the-board definition of social class, the U.S. Census Bureau currently differentiates among upper-, middle-, and lower-income families (see *Figure 13.1*). You'll notice that middle-income families cover quite a large range, from only $15,000 a year to almost $75,000 a year. Someone who earns $35,000 a year is usually very different from someone who earns $70,000 a year in occupation, education, prestige, access to better housing, retirement benefits,

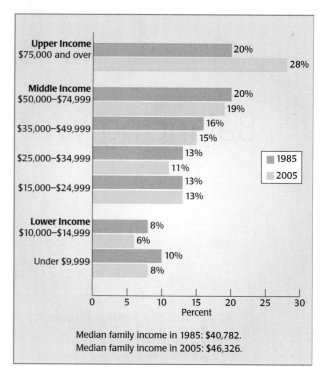

FIGURE 13.1   Is the Number of Middle Class Families Shrinking?

SOURCE: Based on DeNavas-Walt et al., 2005, Table A-1.

and being able to buy goods and services (such as a home computer, an iPod, and high-quality medical care).

The methods used to measure social class vary (see Chapter 12), but most researchers agree on two points. One is that income inequality is greater in the United States than in any other Western industrialized nation. The other is that the rich are getting richer, the middle classes are struggling, and the poor have gotten poorer.

THE RICH ARE GETTING RICHER The degree of wealth inequality in the United States is staggering. The top 1 percent of households have nearly a third of the entire nation's wealth. The lowest 50 percent of families hold only 3 percent of all wealth. The richest 20 percent of American households have more than half of the nation's total family income, up from 44 percent in 1967 (Kennickell, 2003; Mishel et al., 2006).

When the stock market declines, as it did during 2000 and 2001, wealthy families don't notice much of a difference. In 2002, for example, the average chief executive officer's salary alone (excluding stock, bonuses, and so on) was almost $7 million a year—282 times the average worker's pay of $26,267. A typical American today produces about 80 percent more, per hour of work, than did his or her counterpart 30 years ago. Still, corporate earnings rise at a double-digit pace while the wages and

David Sadat of New York works full time at the Broadway 99 Cent Store in Harlem. After paying rent, he has little left to live on. The number of full-time workers who live in poverty has climbed in the past 20 years.

salaries of employees increase by a paltry 2 percent a year (Francis, 2003b; Petruno, 2005; Trumbull, 2005).

THE MIDDLE CLASS IS STRUGGLING

Some middle-class households have enjoyed higher incomes and have moved into higher income brackets. For the most part, however, this hasn't been the case. Between 2001 and 2004, for example, middle-class families with incomes of less than $34,000 a year, accounting for 40 percent of such families, saw their "net worth" decrease by 13 percent. The number of jobs has increased since 2001, but most are in the low-paying service sector, such as retailing (Wal-Mart clerks) and health (nursing home aides). Even at successful companies with good reputations, such as the United Parcel Service (UPS), most of the record profits have gone to executive salaries rather than employee wages (Bernasek, 2004; Bucks et al., 2006).

Most Americans spend more time on the job than workers almost anywhere else in the industrialized world (see *Figure 13.2*). Americans now spend the equivalent of two more 40-hour weeks a year than the Japanese, who have long been viewed as a nation of "workaholics." U.S. workers also have fewer vacation days

than do workers in most other countries (see "Data Digest").

Most Europeans get four to five weeks of paid vacation a year. About 25 percent of U.S. workers in the private sector do not get any paid vacation time; another 33 percent take only a seven-day vacation, including a weekend. Some company leaders maintain that Americans should take more time off, but many workers feel they can't afford to do so: Some worry about catching up on projects while others fear that taking longer vacations might jeopardize their jobs (Egan, 2006).

American workers, especially those in the middle class and below, are justified in being concerned about meeting their basic financial needs. The share of American workers with company pension plans slipped from almost 40 percent in 1980 to 20 percent in 2003 (Revell, 2003). Many people who had retired are going back to work:

> *When he retired 20 years ago to south Florida, Jack Baum expected to enjoy the relaxing coastal life with his wife. Now in his 80s, he claims to be the oldest employee at the Hallandale Beach Wal-Mart. "We've had to scrimp and save and work, work, work," he says while stocking needles and threads in the sewing aisle (Scherer, 2003: 1).*

THE WORKING CLASS IS BARELY SURVIVING

Whereas many middle-class households are managing to stay afloat, numerous working-class families are clinging to

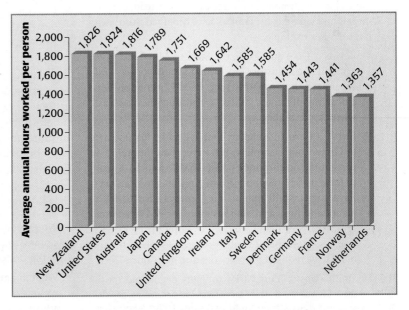

FIGURE 13.2 **Working Hours in Industrialized Countries, 2004**

SOURCE: Based on Organization for Economic Co-operation and Development, *OECD Employment Outlook,* 2005: Statistical Annex, Table F, www.oecd.org (accessed September 16, 2006).

a sinking ship. Overall, 38 percent of Americans say that their biggest financial problem is meeting basic survival needs such as housing, transportation, utilities, and healthcare. Lower-income groups that earn less than $30,000 a year are especially concerned about meeting these costs (Newport and Carroll, 2006).

Most of the reasons for the dire financial predicament of working-class families—who range from skilled blue-collar workers (such as auto mechanics) to minimum wage workers—are macro level. First, the number of so-called smokestack industries and assembly lines that used to employ many production workers has declined, or companies have upgraded their production methods so that they use robots or computerization instead of human labor. Hourly manufacturing pay is still high ($31 an hour in the automotive industry), but such jobs are scarce (Trumbull, 2005).

Second, a number of U.S. manufacturers have relocated to developing countries because of their low labor costs. Manufacturing workers in China earn an average of only $1,182 per year. In Nicaragua, English-speaking employees who call Americans to collect debts for hospitals and credit-card companies earn about $400 a month, triple their minimum wage. Such *offshoring* (usually called *outsourcing*) keeps prices down at home but also reduces the number of jobs. About 700,000 U.S. jobs have been outsourced to India alone during the last few years (Fleeson, 2003; Harman, 2005).

Third, the entire structure of the economy has changed. Many high-paying, goods-producing indus-

Constraints

Does Corporate Welfare Help Working-Class Families?

In 1996, the Clinton administration ended welfare for most poor people, but not for corporations. Corporate welfare takes many forms: tax discounts, cash grants, training funds, low-cost loans and leases, free buildings, and free land. A number of states, counties, and cities offer generous business incentives with the understanding that the companies that move there will create new jobs, especially among low-wage earners. Instead, corporations and high-income families have benefited from such largesse. For example,

■ Between 1994 and 1996, the State of Maryland gave London Fog Industries Inc. funds to train workers and subsidized their monthly rent. In 1997, London Fog closed the plant and moved its production overseas, where labor is cheaper.

■ BMW, a German company that assembles luxury cars in Greer, South Carolina, has never paid the state's 5 percent tax on corporate profits. BMW pays $1 a year to lease its $36 million piece of land. In addition, taxpayers spent $40 million on a runway for BMW's planes and furnished millions more for BMW worker "training," including whitewater rafting trips for executives. More than 200 other companies in South Carolina have received property tax discounts since 1997.

■ Sunlite Casual Furniture Company negotiated more than $8 million in state incentives for promising to create 900 jobs in Paragould, Arkansas. The jobs never materialized.

■ Fruit of the Loom, a clothing manufacturer, obtained more than $10 million in tax breaks from the State of Louisiana before it closed several plants there and laid off more than 4,000 employees over a three-year period.

■ Rite Aid Corporation laid off 600 employees and closed a West Virginia distribution center that had received more than $2 million in low-cost loans.

■ Fulcrum Direct, owner of a children's playclothes industry, shut down in New Mexico and laid off 700 workers after costing the state $1 million in training funds.

Who profits from the corporate welfare packages that many states offer? Three groups: companies that can increase their profits, well-paid consultants who represent businesses in negotiations, and politicians who are elected for promising to bring jobs into poor and working-class neighborhoods (Hetrick, 1994; Henry, 1999; Hancock, 1999a, 1999b).

Stop and Think . . .

• Would you be willing to pay about twice as much for clothes, food, and other products if they were produced in the United States?

• What, if anything, should be done to reduce corporate welfare?

tries have been replaced by service industries that pay only the minimum wage ($5.15 an hour). Currently, 5 percent of Americans age 25 and over earn the minimum wage or less. Yet the hourly wage necessary to support a family of four is close to $18 in areas where housing costs are high (Economic Policy Institute, 2003; U.S. Department of Labor, 2005).

Finally, a number of states support **corporate welfare,** an array of direct subsidies, tax breaks, and indirect assistance that the government has created for the special benefit of some businesses, especially corporations. The box "Does Corporate Welfare Help Working-Class Families?" examines this issue more closely.

Many working-class families are a paycheck away from poverty. Millions of other families move in and out of poverty or are chronically poor, even if they are employed (see, for example, Kennedy, 2005).

Poverty

In 2002, Linda Lay, the wife of the late former Enron CEO Ken Lay, appeared on NBC's *Today* show and wailed, tearfully, that her family was in financial ruin: "There's nothing left," she lamented, "other than the home we live in" (Eisenberg, 2002: 38). At the time,

their five-bedroom high-rise condo in Houston was worth at least $8 million.

In one national survey, 21 percent of respondents with annual household incomes of less than $20,000 described themselves as "haves," whereas 6 percent of those making more than $75,000 a year saw themselves as "have-nots" (Parmelee, 2002). How is it that someone with an $8 million condo sees herself as poor while people with an income of less than $20,000 a year view themselves as "haves"? (Before reading any further, take the quiz "How Much Do You Know about Poverty?")

WHAT IS POVERTY? There are two ways to define poverty: absolute ("What I need") and relative ("What I want"). **Absolute poverty** is not having enough money to afford the most basic necessities of life, such as food, clothing, and shelter. A person or family that can't get enough to eat, lives in inadequate housing, or suffers poor health faces a life-threatening existence. For example, the $17,530 earned by the average Wal-Mart employee in 2005 was $1,820 below the poverty line for a family of four (Jeffery, 2006).

Relative poverty is an inability to maintain an average standard of living. People who experience relative poverty may feel poor compared with a majority of others in society, but they have the basic necessities to survive.

Ask Yourself

How Much Do You Know about Poverty?

True	False	
☐	☐	1. The number of Americans living in poverty has decreased since 2000.
☐	☐	2. Most Americans could get out of poverty if they had a job.
☐	☐	3. Most poor people in the United States are white.
☐	☐	4. According to the federal government, a family of four is poor if it earns less than $25,000 a year.
☐	☐	5. The majority of poor children in the United States are African American.
☐	☐	6. The U.S. child poverty rate is higher than in most of the world's industrialized countries.
☐	☐	7. Single fathers are as likely to be poor as single mothers.
☐	☐	8. The poverty rate of the elderly is lower than that of any other age group.
☐	☐	9. Since 2000, working families make up a rising share of all poor families.
☐	☐	10. Single men and veterans have been the fastest-growing groups of homeless people.

The answers to this quiz are on the next page.

Answers to the quiz "How Much Do You Know about Poverty?"

1. *False.* The number of Americans living in poverty has increased since 2000 (see, especially, *Figure 13.3* and the related discussion).

2. *False.* Most Americans living in poverty are too young, too old, or incapable of working due to physical or mental illness or disability. Nearly two-thirds have to depend on someone else in the household to make a living. More than half of unemployed husbands in poor married-couple families are ill or disabled; the remainder are unable to find work, are going to school, or are retired (Lamison-White, 1997).

3. *True.* Most poor people are white, but most white people aren't poor (see text).

4. *False.* The federal government's poverty threshold is much lower (see text).

5. *False.* White children comprise the largest group of children living in poverty, even though black and Latino children are disproportionately likely to be poor (see text).

6. *True.* The U.S. child poverty rate is about 20 percent. This rate is much higher than that of many other countries: under 3 percent in Denmark and Finland; under 8 percent in France, Sweden, Belgium, and France; and less than 11 percent in the Netherlands, Germany, and Austria. Even some developing countries have much lower child poverty rates than we do (7 percent in the Czech Republic, 9 percent in Hungary, and 13 percent in Poland) (UNICEF, 2005).

7. *False.* Female-headed households are twice as likely to be poor as male-headed households (see text).

8. *True.* The poverty rate for Americans age 65 and older has been among the lowest nationally because of government programs such as Medicare and Medicaid (see text and Chapters 17 and 18).

9. *True.* The number of poor families that include at least one worker has risen from 54 percent in 1989 to 65 percent (McNichol and Springer, 2004).

10. *False.* The fastest-growing group of homeless people is families with children (see text).

THE POVERTY LINE In 1965, the U.S. government adopted an official poverty line to designate people living in absolute poverty. The **poverty line** is the minimum level of income that the government considers necessary for individuals' and families' basic subsistence.

since you asked

What's a "poverty line?"

To determine the poverty line, the Department of Agriculture (DOA) estimates the annual cost of food that contains the minimum nutrients required for survival. The federal government then multiplies this figure by three to cover the minimum cost of clothing, housing, and other necessities. Below this line, one is considered officially poor and is eligible for government assistance (such as food stamps and health care). The poverty line also measures the extent of poverty in the United States: almost 13 percent of the population, or nearly 37 million people, in 2005 (see *Figure 13.3*).

The poverty level doesn't include the value of non-cash benefits such as food stamps, medical services (Medicare and Medicaid, for example), and public housing subsidies. The poverty line, which was $19,806 in 2005 for a family of four (two adults and two children), changes every year to reflect changes in the cost of basic goods and services.

Some policy analysts feel that official poverty rates are inflated because the amount of money needed for subsistence varies drastically from one region of the country to another. They also argue that too many families rely on government programs instead of working harder.

Others claim that the poverty level is unrealistically low. For example, a single parent with two children is defined as poor if she or he earned $15,735 in 2005. To afford basics (food, clothing, shelter, and utilities), however, such families need between $20,000 and $40,000, depending on the region where they live (Bernstein et. al., 2000). There's quite a gap, then, between the official poverty line and what a family requires for basic necessities.

Poverty isn't random. Instead, children, the elderly, women, and racial-ethnic minorities are disproportionately poor.

CHILDREN AND THE ELDERLY Children make up only 26 percent of the U.S. population but 35 percent of the poor. Nearly one out of every five children under age 18 lives in poverty. In contrast, people 65 and over account

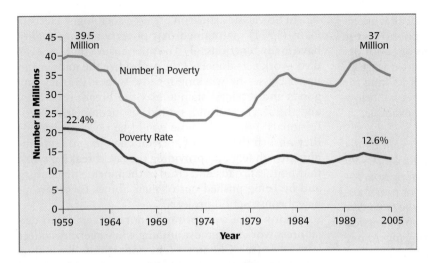

FIGURE 13.3 **Poverty in the United States, 1959–2005**

SOURCE: DeNavas-Walt et al., 2006, Figure 4.

for 12 percent of the total population and 10 percent of the poor (DeNavas-Walt et al., 2006).

The poverty rate of older Americans has never been lower, but that of children has risen. Although government programs for the elderly have kept up with the rate of inflation, since 1980 many welfare programs for children have been reduced or eliminated. About 40 percent of *all* children will experience poverty at some point in their lives because their families move in and out of poverty over time (Kacapyr, 1998).

Most children living in poverty—4.2 million—are white. However, in proportion, 9 percent of white children are poor, compared with 31 percent of black children, 28 percent of Latino children, and 11 percent of Asian and Pacific Islander children (Proctor and Dalaker, 2003).

WOMEN Single mothers and their children make up a large segment of the poor. Poverty rates are higher for single-female households (29 percent) than for single-male households (13 percent) or married-couple families (6 percent). Even with one or more workers, female-headed households are twice as likely to be poor as male-headed households (Proctor and Dalaker, 2003).

Researcher Diana Pearce (1978) coined the term **feminization of poverty** to describe the growing number of women and their children who are poor. There are several reasons for the feminization of poverty. Unmarried teen mothers have little *human capital,* or work-related assets such as education, job training, experience, and specialized skills. Others, as you'll see shortly, work in low-paying jobs, have been laid off, and experience job and wage discrimination.

Some men desert their biological children, wives, and girlfriends. Divorce also pushes many mothers into poverty. Ex-husbands and absent fathers typically offer very little support to women and children, especially if the father is poor or unemployed (see Chapters 9, 12, and 15).

RACIAL-ETHNIC MINORITIES Less than half the poor people in the United States are white (44 percent). Most white people are not poor, however. As *Figure 13.4* shows, proportionately more racial-ethnic minorities are poor, given their numbers in the general population (see Chapter 1).

During economic recessions, African Americans and Latinos are particularly vulnerable to layoffs because they often fall victim to "last hired, first fired" policies. (See Chapter 4 for a discussion of poverty in Latino subgroups.) Because many racial-ethnic minorities have a smaller cushion of wealth, on average, than whites do, extended unemployment takes a bigger toll. In some cases, accepting a job for only half of the previous salary can depress many families' incomes to just above the poverty level (Cauthen and Lu, 2003).

Many families are poor even when both parents work full time, year-round. Parental employment may reduce poverty but not eliminate it.

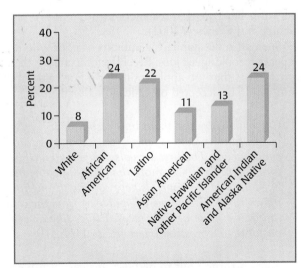

FIGURE 13.4 **Percentage of Families Living in Poverty by Race and Ethnicity, 2004**

SOURCE: Based on DeNavas-Walt et al., 2005, Table 4.

THE WORKING POOR Almost 40 percent of all workers now fall into the category of the working poor (Proctor and Dalaker, 2003). The U.S. Department of Labor defines the **working poor** as people who spend at least 27 weeks a year in the labor force (working or looking for work) but whose family or personal incomes fall below the official poverty level (Beers, 2000). For example,

> *Donna Chambers works at a job that sounds decent enough: assistant manager at the Broadway 99 Cent store in Harlem, N.Y. She puts in long hours—often six days a week. Yet the mother of two doesn't earn enough to always put food on the table: She frequently gets free groceries from food pantries. She has no health insurance. She's struggling to pay an outstanding medical bill . . . Housing alone consumes most of Chambers's income, which averages $1,000 a month (Francis, 2000: 1, 9).*

Although many people think that the working poor are simply looking for government handouts, this is not the case. In fact,

- 12 percent are full-time, year-round workers.

- 12 percent are single mothers who work full-time, year-round.

- 27 percent are employed during part of the year (Beers, 2000; Proctor and Dalaker, 2002).

WHY ARE PEOPLE POOR? Why does the United States, one of the wealthiest countries in the world, have such high poverty rates? According to several polls, more than half of all Americans feel that the poor don't believe in hard work, lack motivation, and are lazy (Lichter and Crowley, 2002).

Such attitudes ignore the millions of poor who are desperately looking for jobs. Recently, for example, there were rumors that job applications for a Ford assembly plant would be accepted on Chicago's North Side:

> *Chicagoans by the thousands responded, turning out in bitterly cold weather for a shot at gainful employment. The first arrivals showed up well before dawn. By 7 A.M. more than 2,000 people had lined up, and the hopefuls kept coming throughout the morning. They shivered, and tears from the cold ran down some of their faces. It was like a scene out of the Depression (Herbert, 2003: A23).*

The rumors turned out to be false. Instead of job applications, there was an "orientation session" to identify candidates who might be qualified for low-paying jobs that might materialize in the distant future.

In his classic article on poverty, sociologist Herbert Gans (1971) maintained that poverty and inequality have many functions: (1) The poor ensure that society's dirty work gets done; (2) they subsidize the middle and upper classes by working for low wages; (3) they buy goods and services (such as day-old bread, used cars, and the services of old, retired, or incompetent "professionals") that otherwise would be rejected; and (4) they absorb the costs of societal change and community growth (e.g., by providing the backbreaking work that built railroads and cities in the nineteenth century and by being pushed out of their homes by urban renewal construction projects).

Many employers profit from poverty. Latino day laborers work for almost nothing while agencies collect hefty fees (see Chapter 4). Corporations like Labor Ready, the nation's top employer of temporary manual labor, makes $1 billion in annual revenues by recruiting homeless workers and then paying them below-minimum wages and illegally charging them for safety gear (such as gloves and goggles) and a 5 percent fee for payments in cash (Cook, 2002).

Convenience stores in many poor neighborhoods routinely advance cash to their customers at interest rates of about 20 percent for a two-week loan. If the debt can't be repaid, it's rolled over—for another 20 percent. Thus, within a few months, the borrower owes three times more money than the amount borrowed and lives "dangerously close to the edge of destitution" (Shipler, 2004; see, also, Acs and Nichols, 2005).

One of the most devastating consequences of poverty is homelessness. Even when people work, they can find themselves at risk of losing their homes.

Many African-Americans feel that they're losing their construction jobs to the influx of undocumented Mexican immigrants who are willing to work for much lower wages.

Most of the people who lost their homes after Hurricane Katrina in 2005 were low-income African Americans, especially single women with children. Government officials spent $177 million a day on the war in Iraq but didn't provide the funding to help the poorest families in New Orleans, Louisiana.

Homeless Families

While Michelle Kennedy was living in her car with her three children in Belfast, Maine, she parked someplace different each night so no one would notice them. She instructed the children to tell anyone who asked that they were "staying with friends" ("Striving to keep. . . ," 2006: 11A).

Kennedy and her children are among the many "hidden" homeless who are not counted by researchers. The uncounted include people who live in automobiles, have makeshift housing (such as boxes and boxcars), or stay with relatives for short periods. According to the best estimates, about 3.5 million people, a third of whom are children, are likely to experience homelessness in a given year. This translates to approximately 1 percent of the U.S. population (National Coalition for the Homeless, 2005a).

CHARACTERISTICS OF THE HOMELESS Families are the fastest-growing group of homeless people. Families with children account for 40 percent of the homeless population, up from 34 percent in the late 1990s. Forty-two percent of the children in these families are under the age of five, and 84 percent live in single-mother families (Burt et al., 1999; National Coalition for the Homeless, 2005a).

Homelessness is not confined to cities. In parts of rural Illinois, for example, women with children and men with families make up more than half of the 180,000 homeless people in the state (Gardner, 2003).

WHY FAMILIES ARE HOMELESS Homelessness results from a combination of factors, some of which are beyond people's control, such as mental illness or physical disability, eroding job opportunities, and a decline in wages and public assistance. Other factors include poverty, lack of education, lack of marketable skills, unemployment, domestic violence, substance abuse, and the inability of relatives and friends to provide social and economic support during crises (National Coalition for the Homeless, 2005b).

One of the biggest reasons for homelessness is the lack of affordable housing. Because rents are high and housing assistance is in short supply, the most vulnerable renters are the working poor. The average American must earn $16.00 an hour—about three times the minimum wage—to afford a modest apartment (see *Table 13.1*).

We've examined some macroeconomic changes that affect American families. How do families cope with these changes on a daily basis?

Making Connections

- What role do personal decisions play in financial problems? For example, should schools teach such topics as budgeting, credit card debt, and saving money?

- What do you think can be done to reduce the numbers of homeless children? Or is it impossible to do anything at all?

Adapting to Economic Changes

Across the country, many families are struggling to survive. They have adopted a variety of techniques, including taking low-paying jobs, working shifts, doing part-time work, and working overtime. If these tactics fail, they find themselves among the unemployed.

Low-Wage Jobs and Shift Work

One writer described the United States as "a nation of hamburger flippers" because of the explosion of low-wage jobs in recent decades (Levine, 1994). While the minimum wage hasn't budged since 1996, Congress voted itself eight pay raises (totaling almost $32,000 per member) between 1997 and 2005 ("What's at stake?. . . , 2006). In contrast, about 25 percent of families with children work regularly but can't make ends meet.

LOW-WAGE JOBS Who are the low-income working families? About 60 percent have at least one full-time,

---

TABLE 13.1

Where Can Low-Income Families Afford Decent Housing?

Below are the hourly wages (the "housing wage") that a person working full time must earn to rent a modest but "decent" two-bedroom unit at the area's fair market rent (FMR) and using no more than 30 percent of his or her gross income. If you live in Massachusetts, for example, you must earn $21.88/hour to rent a livable two-bedroom apartment—excluding utility costs. You can explore the FMR values in your state by clicking on www.nlihc.org/oor2005 and then searching by county, metropolitan area, or rural area.

Least Affordable	Housing Wage for Two-Bedroom FMR
District of Columbia, Hawaii, Massachusetts, California, and New Jersey	More than $20.00
New York, Maryland, Connecticut, Rhode Island, and New Hampshire	Between $18.00 and $19.99
Most Affordable	
North Dakota, South Dakota, Wyoming, Montana, Oklahoma, Kentucky, Alabama, and Mississippi	Between $10.00 and $11.00
Arkansas, West Virginia, and Puerto Rico	Between $7.00 and $9.99

SOURCE: Based on National Low Income Housing Coalition, 2005.

---

year-round worker; the average wage is about $9.00 an hour; 72 percent have at least a high school education; 70 percent are native born; and 80 percent are in either married-couple or multiple-adult families (Acs and Loprest, 2005).

Almost half of full-time workers have no health insurance. Some receive no health benefits because small-business owners can't afford both wages and health benefits. When employers decrease health coverage to maintain high profit margins, many workers simply can't afford the cost of insurance offered by employers or private companies (Golden et al., 2006; "Employee compensation," 2006).

Low-wage work is also getting harder. For example, housekeepers (who earn less than $18,000 a year on average) at many of the nation's fanciest hotels are experiencing more arm, shoulder, and lower-back injuries. They now typically lift king-size mattresses (which weigh 115 pounds) up to 200 times a day, must bend to scrub dozens of large tubs and Jacuzzis every day, and have greater workloads because each room requires more tasks, such as changing more pillowcases, cleaning hair dryers, and washing coffeepots (Greenhouse, 2006).

SHIFT WORK In many countries, workers are needed almost around the clock because business is being conducted somewhere almost every hour of the day, including weekends. In the United States, two in five people work weekends, evenings, or nights. Almost 15 percent of full-time wage and salary employees work such nonstandard hours. This shift work is more common among men than among women, African Americans, and people in service occupations (see *Figure 13.5*).

Most reasons for shift work reflect the nature of the job. For example, police, firefighters, nurses, truck drivers, and hotel workers are needed around the clock. Others work night or evening shifts due to personal preference (12 percent); because child care by a spouse, partner, or relative is available during those hours (16 percent); because the worker couldn't get a better job (8 percent); or because the job offered better pay (7 percent) (U.S. Bureau of Labor Statistics, 2005c).

Shift work is higher among families with preschool-age children than among other types of families. Single mothers with only a high school diploma are especially likely to be locked into evening and night-shift jobs because they work as cashiers, nursing home aides, waitresses, and janitors—positions that are most likely to require nonstandard work hours (Presser and Cox, 1997).

How does shift work affect families? When both parents work shifts, husbands and wives may rarely see each other or their children:

My husband works a 9-to-5 shift, and I work from 6 P.M. until 2:30 A.M. We have done this for 12 years because with three kids, it helps save the cost of child care. I average four hours of sleep a night. My husband comes home after an eight-hour day of work, has dinner with the kids, helps with their homework, takes care of baths and reads them stories at bedtime. I wake up, get the kids off to school, clean the house, do the laundry, start dinner and prepare for another night of work. I barely see

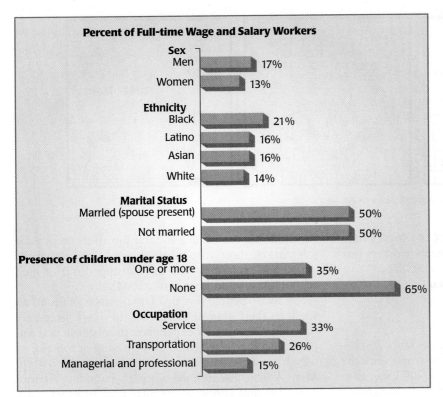

Percent of Full-time Wage and Salary Workers

Sex	
Men	17%
Women	13%
Ethnicity	
Black	21%
Latino	16%
Asian	16%
White	14%
Marital Status	
Married (spouse present)	50%
Not married	50%
Presence of children under age 18	
One or more	35%
None	65%
Occupation	
Service	33%
Transportation	26%
Managerial and professional	15%

FIGURE 13.5 Who Works Shifts?

Source: Based on U.S. Bureau of Labor Statistics, 2005c, Tables 4 and 5, and the author's calculations.

my older kids, and my husband and I have no so-cial life. . . . As soon as he walks in the door from work, I walk out ("Night shift . . . ," 1996: 3D).

Both parents and children usually suffer even if only one parent has shift work. For example, the children tend to do less well in school because a parent is not available to supervise homework; preschool children, especially, experience more emotional and behavioral problems because they receive less parenting; and the parents report more depressive symptoms, such as feeling angry and sometimes withdrawing from family life. These and other strains, especially among low-wage workers, increase the likelihood of parental conflict and divorce (La Valle et al., 2002; Swanberg, 2005; Strazdins et al., 2006).

Too Little Work or Too Much

Many families face an economic dilemma: An increasing number of jobs are only part time. On the other hand, some employees are required to work unwanted overtime hours.

PART-TIME JOBS About 17 percent of all employed people work part time (defined as working less than 35 hours a week). Of these part-timers, 61 percent are women. Although 75 percent of part-timers are "voluntary" because they don't want to work more hours, 25 percent are involuntary because they can't find suitable full-time employment (U.S. Department of Labor, 2005).

The percentage of part-time employees, voluntary or not, is likely to increase because employers can save money by not providing health care or other benefits to part-timers. According to an internal memo sent to Wal-Mart's board of directors, for example, the vice president for health benefits recommended reining in costs by hiring more part-time workers and not hiring unhealthy people (Greenhouse and Barbaro, 2005).

OVERTIME DEMANDS At the other extreme is the demand by some employers that experienced workers, especially those in production jobs, work more overtime hours. For employers, paying for overtime is less expensive than hiring and training new people. The most common violation is failing to pay hourly wage earners time-and-a-half when they work more than 40 hours a week—or failing to pay them anything at all for the extra hours worked (Shatzkin, 2000).

Skilled and highly educated salaried employees are especially likely to work long hours. Among those in professional, technical, or managerial jobs, more than 33 percent of men and 17 percent of women now put in 50-hour-plus weeks, compared with 20 percent of men and 7 percent of women in other occupations. College graduates are four times more likely to work long hours than those with a high school degree or less. Some are compensated for their overtime but most are not (Jacobs and Gerson, 1998).

During weak economic times, many employers wring more work out of their full-time workers instead of hiring additional employees. Because many people are afraid of losing their jobs, they don't protest. Many workers are silent, even when they make only $40,000 a year after being laid off from a $130,000-a-year job.

DILBERT reprinted by permission of United Feature Syndicate, Inc.

Companies can squeeze more out of employees than ever before because they know that many workers fear being laid off (Conlin, 2002; Kadlec, 2003).

Unemployment

According to some economists, job losses since 2001—especially in the private sector—are the worst since the Great Depression (Bernstein and Mishel, 2003; see, also, Chapter 3). The unemployed include such diverse groups as people who have been laid off or fired, who have quit their job, or who are about to begin a new job. Overall, more than half the unemployed have been laid off.

Unemployment hits some people and sectors harder than others. Historically, unemployment rates have been about twice as high among African Americans as among whites. One of the reasons, as you saw earlier, is that black youth are less likely than other groups to have the human capital that would enable them to compete successfully for jobs. In addition, nearly 90 percent of those who lost jobs were in manufacturing. Because African Americans have been employed in manufacturing more than in other sectors, unemployment hits blacks harder than whites (Gottschalck, 2006).

Unemployment figures (about 5 percent in 2006) are artificially low because they don't count discouraged and underemployed workers. Families in all racial-ethnic groups include both types of workers.

since you asked

Are official unemployment numbers accurate?

DISCOURAGED WORKERS Unemployment figures are misleading because they ignore **discouraged workers,** or what some call the "hidden unemployed." The discouraged worker wants a job and has looked for work in the preceding year, but has not searched recently because she or he believes that job-hunting efforts are futile.

There are millions of discouraged workers. Among them are retirees, mothers who have been taking care of their kids but can't find a suitable job after entering the job market, those who refuse to work for a minimum wage, and teenagers who have dropped out of high school (Davey and Leonhardt, 2003).

Why do people give up? Usually they've found no work in their area of expertise; they lack necessary schooling, training, or experience; they believe that employers have rejected them as too young or too old; or they have experienced other types of discrimination. Many young discouraged workers, including African American and Latino males, may turn to illegal ways of making a living because they lack the skills and education that many employers seek (Soltero, 1996).

UNDEREMPLOYED WORKERS Unemployment rates are also misleading because they ignore **underemployed workers.** The underemployed include people who have part-time jobs but would rather be working full time, as well as those who accept jobs below their level of job experience and education credentials. Women, particularly those with children, are more likely than men to suffer from underemployment because of problems in finding and affording good child care services.

Another large group of underemployed workers are professionals (engineers, physicists, and chemists)—especially men in their fifties—who are laid off when corporations want to increase their profits. Companies can hire two young college graduates for the price of one senior-level employee, and they often do so.

EFFECTS OF UNEMPLOYMENT Regardless of social class, unemployment is typically overwhelming. It can trigger a vicious "chain of adversity" that includes financial strain, depression, loss of personal control, decreased emotional functioning, and poorer physical health. Even two years after finding a new job, people still report negative effects such as insecurity and lowered self-esteem. Those who are less educated experience greater financial hardship, a loss of control, and lower self-confidence than their counterparts with higher educational levels (Broman et al., 2001; Price et al., 2002).

Millions of men, like this steelworker who was laid off in 2001, are turning down low-wage jobs. Instead, this couple is scraping by on her salary, taking out a second mortgage, and depleting the family's savings.

have very high-paying jobs and expect equally high job security in the future, it's not clear how one-earner families can expect to be well off financially.

Juggling Family and Work Roles

The high proportions of high school and college women who say that they expect to marry, have children, and work are right on target, because many will have to work to support themselves and their families. In fact, the widespread employment of mothers is often cited as one of the most dramatic changes in family roles that occurred during the twentieth century. Except for a brief period after the end of World War II, the numbers of working women have been increasing steadily since the turn of the twentieth century (see *Table 13.2*).

An even more dramatic change has been the increase in the numbers of employed mothers with infants (see "Data Digest"). Historically, African American mothers were more likely than any other group to be employed, but the gap between black and white women has closed (see *Figure 13.6*).

People who lose their jobs also lose health coverage. In many cases, banks repossess houses because the couple or individual can no longer afford the monthly mortgage payments. About 56 percent of families cut back on spending for food, 33 percent cut off or delay their education, and 26 percent move in with relatives or friends (National Employment Law Project, 2003).

Sometimes, unemployment is so stressful that couples divorce. In other cases, they hold on, hoping for better times. The situation would be much worse for many families if women weren't employed.

Women's Participation in the Labor Force

Many young adults expect to work and raise children simultaneously. In a nationwide survey of colleges, for example, 75 percent of first-year students said that being very well off financially was "very important" or "essential"; 76 percent felt the same way about raising a family. However, 26 percent of the men and 16 percent of the women said that "the activities of married women are best confined to the home and family" ("Attitudes and characteristics . . . ," 2006). Unless they

since you asked

Why do so many mothers of young children work outside the home?

TABLE 13.2			
Women and Men in the Labor Force, 1890–2005			
	Percentage of All Men and Women in the Labor Force		*Women as a Percentage of All Workers*
Year	Men	Women	
1890	84	18	17
1900	86	20	18
1920	85	23	20
1930	82	24	22
1940	83	28	25
1945	88	36	29
1947	87	32	27
1950	87	34	29
1960	84	38	33
1970	80	43	37
1980	78	52	42
1990	76	58	45
2005	74	60	44

SOURCE: U.S. Department of Labor, 2005.

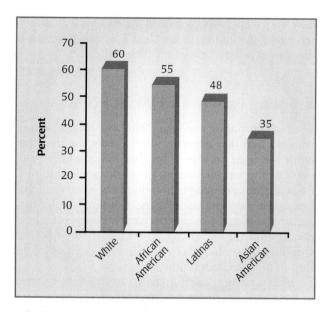

FIGURE 13.6 **Percentage of Employed Mothers with Infants**

SOURCE: Based on Dye, 2005, Table 4.

Why Do Women Work?

The two principal reasons that women work outside the home are the same as men's reasons—personal satisfaction and to support themselves and their dependents. Work usually adds meaning to life. The opportunity to succeed at tasks and to be rewarded for competence enhances self-esteem, which, in turn, increases overall well-being. This is especially true for people who enjoy their work or are employed in stimulating, rewarding jobs.

The purchasing power of families has declined considerably. After adjusting for inflation, for example, the median income for men under age 44 is significantly lower than it was in 1970 (Bucks et al., 2006). It's not surprising, then, that seven out of 10 mothers with young children are in the labor force. Although the need for a creative outlet motivates some women to work, in most cases women are employed because of economic necessity. The box "Variations in the Working Mother Role" examines motherhood and employment more closely.

Most working mothers can't afford to stay home. They are single parents, can't take unpaid maternity leaves for financial reasons, or are married to men with

Changes

Variations in the Working Mother Role

Employed mothers reflect a variety of motivations. Here are four general categories (Moen, 1992: 42–44):

■ *Captives* would prefer to be full-time homemakers. These mothers may be single parents who are sole breadwinners, wives of blue-collar workers whose incomes are insufficient to support the family, or middle-class wives who find two salaries necessary to maintain a desired standard of living. Captives find their multiple responsibilities overwhelming and remain in the labor force reluctantly.

■ *Conflicted* mothers feel that their employment is harmful to their children. They are likely to leave the work force while their children are young, and many quit their jobs when they can afford to do so. Conflicted mothers include many Latinas whose husbands support their wife's employment as long as she fulfills all housework and child care duties despite her outside job. Many of these women quit their jobs as soon as the husband secures better-paying work (Segura, 1994).

■ *Copers* are women with young children who choose jobs with enough flexibility to accommodate family needs. As a result, they often settle for minimally demanding jobs that offer lower wages and fewer benefits, and in the long run they forgo promotions, seniority advantages, and pay increases.

■ *Committed* mothers have both high occupational aspirations and a strong commitment to marriage and family life. As the section on dual-earner families shows, however, mothers who can afford good child care and are free to pursue careers are still a minority.

Stop and Think . . .

• Which group of mothers, if any, has freely chosen to work outside the home?

• Do these categories also describe employed fathers?

There are many husband-wife businesses in which both partners, like these owners of a photo store, work together to support themselves and their families.

low-paying jobs. Today, only 27 percent of women quit their job around the time of the birth of their first child, compared with 63 percent between 1961 and 1965 (Smith et al., 2001).

The biggest recent increases in stay-at-home moms have occurred among women whose families earn at least $50,000 a year and college-educated women who are confident about reentering the workforce. Even when there are infants at home, employment rates are appreciably higher for women with graduate or professional degrees (70 percent) and college degrees (60 percent) than for women or who are high school graduates (52 percent) or are not high school graduates (36 percent) (Conlin et al., 2002; Dye, 2005).

Women who have invested more time in their education return to work more rapidly because they have a greater commitment to their careers, can command higher salaries, and have more work experience than do women with fewer years of schooling. In addition, they have the resources to purchase child care services, especially if their husbands are also employed.

Does It Pay for Women to Work Outside the Home?

The answer depends on a number of factors, especially the woman's marital status, ethnicity, and educational level, and whether she has young children. In a two-income family—especially if the woman's wages are much lower than her husband's—taxes, child care costs, clothing, and car maintenance costs can gobble up much of the family income.

Especially since 2005, transportation costs are higher than ever. For example, Ana Lopez, 48—a housekeeping manager at a hotel in Miami Beach—her hus-

band, and their young son moved out of the metropolitan area to be able to afford a decent house. It used to cost her about $30 a week to fill up her "aging Toyota 4Runner." Since gas prices have surged, she pays $80 a week. This means that nearly 13 percent of her $32,000 annual income goes for gas, up from 5 percent a few years ago. Because her family needs her income, Ana continues working outside the home, but the family has made numerous sacrifices. They no longer go to the movies, she has given up manicures and trips to the beauty salon, she buys tilapia for $2.99 a pound instead of her favorite fish, salmon, for $7 a pound, and she spends more time visiting friends who live within walking distance (Pogrebin, 2006).

Unlike middle-class mothers (whether married or single), those from lower socioeconomic groups have to work to support their children. And when women hit "glass ceilings" by not being promoted or are laid off, increasing numbers start their own businesses. Between 1997 and 2002, for example, the number of women-owned businesses, many of them one-person enterprises (most in health care and retail trade), grew by 20 percent, twice the national average for all businesses. Minority women own about a quarter of these firms. African American women are more likely than any other group of women to encounter obstacles such as obtaining financing to start a business. Nevertheless, about 68 percent of these enterprises have survived the ups and downs of business cycles (Nance-Nash, 2005; U.S. Census Bureau, 2006).

Employed mothers and stay-at-home moms aren't the only options. There are several other possibilities that reflect a couple's economic resources and personal choices.

Making Connections

- In a recent national survey, 48 percent of Americans said that mothers with preschoolers shouldn't work outside the home (Gerson, 2003). Do you agree?

- Is a woman with a college degree "wasting" her education by being a homemaker? Or not?

New Economic Roles Within Marriage

In Chapter 5 we examined the traditional male breadwinner–female homemaker roles. There are currently two variations on the traditional division of labor within marriage: the two-person single career and the stay-at-home dad.

The Two-Person Single Career

In the **two-person single career**, one spouse, typically the wife, participates in the partner's career behind the scenes, without pay or direct recognition. The wives of many college professors, for example, support their husband's career by entertaining faculty and students, doing library research, helping to write and edit journal articles or books, and grading exams.

The best public example of the two-person single career is that of the First Lady, who often enjoys considerable power and influence behind the scenes. Most recently, Nancy Reagan influenced her husband's staffing decisions, Barbara Bush criticized her husband's opponents, Hillary Rodham Clinton promoted her husband's domestic policies and defended him during his sexual scandals, and Laura Bush endorsed improvements in teaching (Allgor, 2002).

The military is an especially "greedy institution" that imposes numerous demands on family life. Whether they live on military installations or at home, the wives of soldiers on active duty must often sacrifice their own interests to support their husband's role. Families stationed overseas must cope with missing their friends, being separated from extended family, and being marginalized by peers after returning to the United States (Smith, 1991; Segal and Harris, 1993; McFadyen et al., 2005).

Many middle-class homemakers are proud of their husbands' accomplishments and gain a sense of fulfillment from helping them. Some wives, however, complain that a two-person career is very stressful and that they undergo burnout as commonly as their high-powered husbands do. For example, they are constantly involved in activities such as entertaining and organizing fund-raising events, besides running a household and raising their children.

Stay-at-Home Dads

In the movie *Daddy Day Care*, Eddie Murphy is an unemployed father who starts a "guy-run" day-care center with a buddy. Stay-at-home dads (or *househusbands*, as they were called in the 1990s) are the rare men who stay home to care for the family and do the housework while their wives are the wage earners.

PREVALENCE An estimated 143,000 stay-at-home dads care for their children while their wives work outside the home. Among all married two-parent families, less than 1 percent of the fathers are stay-at-home dads during a given year (U.S. Census Bureau, 2006).

since you asked

Are stay-at-home dads common?

REASONS Being a stay-at-home dad is usually a temporary role. Some men take on the role by default; they are unemployed or are not working because of poor health or disability. Others are retired, have remarried much younger women who are employed, or want a "second chance" to watch a child grow up in a second (or even third) marriage (Gutner, 2001).

Sometimes graduate students who are supported by their wives take on a modified housekeeping role, doing household chores between classes and studying at the library. And, especially at well-financed private colleges and universities, some male faculty take advantage of generous one-year family leaves to care for their children while the mother works (Latessa, 2005).

Many of these middle-class men have wives who earn more than they do and have greater job security, better health care benefits, and in some cases, high-powered jobs. Of the 187 participants at *Fortune* magazine's Most Powerful Women in Business Summit, for example, a third had househusbands. A number of the stay-at-home dads took early retirement from high-level executive positions, were wealthy, and often hired a nanny to assist with child care (Morris, 2002).

Staying home with the kids is harder for men who don't feel that they have a choice. After being laid off, for instance, a systems engineer, 43, cared for his 3-year-old son. However, being a stay-at-home dad, even for a short time, was a jolt to his ego because "I've been programmed all my life to be a provider" (Morris, 2002: 94).

BENEFITS AND COSTS Being a full-time dad is a mixed blessing. Some fathers find childrearing a joy because they are more intimately involved with their kids: "I know my son's and daughter's friends. I know everything they like and dislike. I have the chance to be there to answer questions" (Barovick, 2002: B10). Parents also don't have to worry about the quality of day-care or after-school programs.

On the other hand, some stay-at-home-dads are concerned about losing their business skills and their "professional place in line." Some feel unappreciated by their working wives, who may complain that the house is a mess or that people view them as "nonachievers" professionally (Baldauf, 2000).

In most families, parents don't have the choice of staying home with their children. Instead, both partners work either part time or full time, and sometimes both.

Two-Income Families

After 61 years as a traditional housewife and mother, in the late 1990s the comic-strip character Blondie opened a catering business. Blondie and Dagwood's shift to a two-income marriage reflects what has been happening

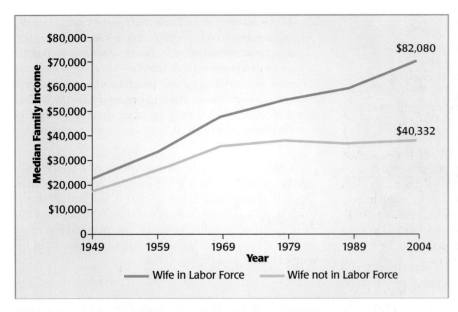

FIGURE 13.7 **Median Family Income When Women Work, 1949–2004**

Source: U.S. Census Bureau, 2002 and 2005. "Historical Income Tables—Families," Tables F-13 and F-14, www.census.gov (accessed September 11, 2003, and May 13, 2006.)

sist of middle-aged people who are paying for their children's college education, saving for their own retirement, and sometimes helping low-income aging parents (Warren and Tyagi, 2003; see, also, Chapter 17).

Having two wage earners raises the family's standard of living, however. And if a husband's income is low or he is laid off, his wife's financial support relieves some of the pressure on him to be a provider. In many ethnic groups that rely on unpaid family members' participation to create and run a small business, much of the discretionary income may be invested in the entrepreneurship rather than increasing a family's standard of living in the short term (Wong, 1998; see, also, Chapter 4).

in many U.S. families. There are several types of two-income families: dual-earner and dual-career couples, trailing spouses, commuter marriages, and marriages in which wives earn more than their husbands.

Dual-Earner versus Dual-Career Families

In the past 50 years, the proportion of married women in the labor force has almost tripled. When wives work full time, the median family income can be twice as high as when they stay home (see *Figure 13.7*). The higher income characterizes both dual-earner and dual-career families.

DUAL-EARNER COUPLES In dual-earner couples, both partners work outside the home. They are also called *dual-income, two-income, two-earner,* or *dual-worker* couples. These couples make up 62 percent of all married couples (U.S. Census Bureau, 2005).

Despite their two incomes, dual-earner families are seldom affluent. Only a small fraction has much **discretionary income,** money remaining for other purposes after the costs of basic necessities like food, rent, utilities, and transportation have been paid.

Even though the dual-earner family brings in 75 percent more (inflation-adjusted) income than the one-earner family of a generation ago, it still has less discretionary income. Many dual-earner families con-

DUAL-CAREER COUPLES In dual-career couples, both partners work in professional or managerial positions that require extensive training, a long-term commitment, and ongoing professional growth. The better educated the couple, the more hours they work.

Only about 5 percent of two-income families are dual-career couples. Usually, but not always, their incomes are well above average. Married women in such professions as law, medicine, high-level management, or college teaching remain a small group among dual-earner couples as a whole. Because such women are less likely to have children, dual-career families with children make up a tiny percentage of all two-income families. Although no national data are available, perhaps only 1 to 2 percent of dual-career couples have children.

The most common source of stress for dual-career couples is role overload, especially when their children are young. To achieve their career goals, both partners often feel driven to work very hard for long hours. Having a strong professional identity along with a commitment to family life requires ongoing coping and effective conflict resolution skills (Bird and Schnurman-Crook, 2005).

Role overload—for all two-income couples who juggle work and family responsibilities—can lead to increased health risks; decreased productivity; increased tardiness, absenteeism, and turnover; and low morale at work (see Chapter 12). On the positive side, two-income parents feel that they provide responsible adult role models for their children and that their children

are more independent and less "needy" than they would be if only one parent worked (Barnett and Rivers, 1996).

Many couples, especially those in middle or higher classes, opt for a one-earner family. Some, as you saw earlier, include a stay-at-home mom who leaves the labor force to raise the children. Others include trailing spouses who hope to find work after moving to a new city or state.

Trailing Spouses

Some companies provide employment assistance for the **trailing spouse,** the partner who gives up his or her work and searches for another position in the location where the spouse has taken a job. Most don't, however.

WHO'S THE TRAILING SPOUSE? Male trailing spouses—only 10 to 15 percent of all trailing spouses—fall into five categories: (1) men who can't find suitable employment in their present location; (2) men with "portable" professions, such as photographers, computer programmers, and engineers; (3) men who take pride in and accommodate their wives' relocation because of job offers; (4) men with blue-collar skills, such as construction workers, who are used to changing jobs; and (5) laid-off managers and executives whose wives are climbing the corporate ladder (Cohen, 1994; "The big picture," 2000).

In most cases, the wife is the trailing spouse because of traditional gender roles in which wives are expected to accommodate husbands' work roles (see Chapter 5). According to a faculty member, for example, about 90 percent of her male Ph.D. students apply for almost every job that "remotely matches their qualifications," even if it would require moving to a different location, compared with only 50 percent of their female counterparts:

Many intelligent and talented women substantially reduce their chances for career success, prestige, and financial security by being unwilling to participate in a national job search—usually because the men in their lives don't want to move. We rarely see male graduate students severely limiting their job searches because of their partners' desires (Williams, 2001: B20).

Often, income is the best predictor of who the trailing spouse will be. As a wife's income increases, both in absolute terms and relative to that of her husband, she tends to play a greater role in deciding whether the family will move. Typically, however, the husband has more influence because his income is usually higher than his wife's (Bielby and Bielby, 1992).

WHAT ARE THE BENEFITS AND COSTS FOR TRAILING SPOUSES? The most obvious benefit of being a trailing spouse is that the main provider can increase his or her income and job opportunities. Especially when women hit glass ceilings, their only option for a better job may require relocation.

There are also many drawbacks to being a trailing spouse. Moving is usually much harder on wives than on husbands. Most husbands continue to perform similar tasks in new locations and maintain contact with colleagues through meetings and conferences. Wives often lose contact with friends, are concerned about the children's adjustment to a new environment, and feel lonely and isolated. In addition, a majority of wives who had been employed feel anxiety about the loss of their jobs (Frame and Shehan, 1994).

Many female instructors who are adjunct faculty members are trailing spouses. They often move with their spouses, hoping to find a full-time teaching position at the new location. Instead, often they must piece together a string of part-time teaching jobs. Says one: "After nearly two years of driving 65 miles each way to teach for less than $10,000 a semester, the truth was apparent: My car was going the distance, but my career and my spirits were in neutral" (Carroll, 2003: C4).

Another part-time instructor describes being a trailing spouse as an "esteem-crushing nightmare." The pay is low, health insurance is nonexistent, there is zero opportunity for advancement, and the wife becomes the full-time partner's caretaker, handling everything from grocery shopping to home repairs (Taz, 2005).

Because of such difficulties, many couples don't or won't relocate. Instead, they try to pursue their independent careers in commuter marriages.

Commuter Marriages

In a **commuter marriage,** married partners live and work in different geographic areas and get together intermittently, such as over weekends. Demographers report that there are over a million commuter marriages in the United States, an estimate that doesn't include unmarried people in long-term relationships (Large, 2006).

WHY DO THEY DO IT?   There are several reasons for commuter marriages. First, if one partner (usually the wife) sees that relocation will have negative effects on her employment prospects, she may decide not to move. Second, if both partners have well-established careers in different cities, neither may be willing to make major job sacrifices after marriage. Third, a commuter marriage may create less stress on the family because it avoids uprooting teenage children or elderly parents. Fourth, when jobs become scarce, financial security is an important factor in launching a commuter marriage. As you saw earlier, many professional and high-skilled workers are working multiple jobs to save for the future. Some of these jobs may involve living apart during part of the week or on weekends.

Finally, racial-ethnic couples may feel that commuter marriages are the only possible route to occupational success. Black dual-career commuter marriages have risen in response to exclusionary employment practices. Although they increase career options and social mobility, black commuter marriages also take a toll. Like their white counterparts, many black couples experience strain in their interpersonal relationships, child–parent interactions, community life, and friendship networks (Jackson et al., 2000).

BENEFITS   What are the advantages of commuter marriages? Long-distance couples feel that they can devote more attention to their work during the week and that they learn to appreciate and make the most of the time they have together. Each person is more independent and can take advantage of time alone to pursue hobbies or recreational interests that the other partner might not enjoy. As one writer noted, "She can watch all the foreign movies she wants and eat sushi for lunch and dinner" (Justice, 1999: 12).

COSTS   Commuter marriages also have disadvantages, one of which is financial. The costs of frequent airplane flights and maintaining two residences can be very high. The commuting partner may feel isolated from community and social relationships, a situation that can lead to extramarital relationships on the part of either partner. Moreover, the stay-at-home parent may resent the weekend parent, who is shouldering little of the parenting responsibility (Belkin, 1985; Justice, 1999).

Many commuting partners work 14- to 18-hour days during the week, live in hotel rooms or small apartments, and subsist on TV dinners or deli sandwiches. (During two periods when my husband and I had a commuter marriage, for example, his typical dinner for several years was a salad, a can of tuna, and a bagel because the expenses for maintaining our two homes were high.) Besides feeling lonely, parents also report feeling helpless if something goes wrong at home. For example, a father said that one of the worst moments of his life was when he was paged—800 miles from home—with the message that his 6-year-old daughter had had to have stitches in her forehead after an accident at school (Stiehm, 1997).

Whether a two-income marriage involves long-distance commuting or not, women continue to earn less than men. There are also an increasing number of families in which the wife earns more than her husband.

When Wives Earn More

Almost a third of women earn more than their husbands, up from 24 percent in 1987 (U.S. Department of Labor, 2005). They typically work full time year-round as professionals or managers. The majority has no children at home, and most have at least a college degree. In other cases, as profits in farming and ranching communities have decreased, wives who work as county treasurers, as tax assessors, or in other public offices also earn more than their husbands (Belsie, 2003).

since you asked

Are husbands happy if their wives earn more than they do?

In some cases, women's higher incomes may be short term. For example, a wife's income may be higher only for a year or so because her husband has been laid off, on a short-term disability leave, or pursuing a college or graduate degree.

EFFECT ON MARITAL HAPPINESS   According to one national poll, 41 percent of Americans agreed that "it is much better for everyone involved if the man is the achiever outside the home and the woman takes care of the home and family." One in four said that it is "generally not acceptable" for a woman to be the major wage earner in a marriage (Tyre and McGinn, 2003: 49).

Are husbands happy when their wives make greater contributions to the family income? Not always. If a husband holds traditional views about being the primary provider, an increasing salary gap tends to decrease the husband's marital satisfaction. He may feel overshadowed and resent lighthearted comments by friends and co-workers like "Boy, you've got it made!"

In contrast, increases in a woman's income generally enhance her feelings of marital happiness and psychological well-being (Brennan et al., 2001; Jervey, 2005).

Men are usually pleased when their wife's income increases—up to a point. Even husbands with fairly egalitarian attitudes tend to become gloomier, suffer more headaches, and generally feel more pressured and stressed if their wife's income increases by a larger percentage. For example, men don't feel glum if their wife gets a 10 percent raise as long as they also get a raise of 10 percent or more (Rogers and DeBoer, 2001).

EFFECT ON MARITAL ROLES Despite exchange and resource theories (see Chapters 2 and 10), there is usually little impact on marital power when wives earn more than their husbands do. Couples typically ignore the income differences or minimize them by having joint bank accounts and contributing equally to household expenses. They often stick to traditional roles in public, however: The husband picks up the tab at restaurants and pays for the groceries, for example.

To compensate for not meeting the cultural expectation of being the primary breadwinner, the husband may avoid "feminine" activities or not do them well. If the wife is sympathetic and doesn't want to threaten his masculinity further, she may do more of the housework to support his self-esteem (see Chapter 10).

One sociologist describes such situations as "deviance neutralization." That is, couples violate traditional gender-role expectations if the wife's earnings are higher and the husband is economically more dependent on his wife. To neutralize such deviant identities, husbands may do less housework and wives may do more than their share (Greenstein, 2000).

High-earning wives typically enjoy a more equitable division of labor in the home than their lower-income counterparts do, but they often still bear the larger burden of housework and child care (the "second shift" discussed in Chapters 5 and 10). They may see this as fair because they tend to judge their success as wives and mothers by how much they do around the house rather than by how much they earn. Others are afraid

---

Making Connections

- If you, your friends, or your parents are two-income couples, do you and they experience more benefits or more stresses?

- If women earn more than their husbands, should husbands do more of the housework and child care than their wives? What about cohabiting couples?

---

of exercising their decision-making power because doing so might threaten their husbands' masculinity and, consequently, the relationship. Thus, gender, rather than the woman's income, often reinforces the husband's marital power (Tichenor, 2005).

Work and Family Dynamics

Employment affects the family in many ways. Most important, of course, work keeps many families out of poverty. Work roles also have an impact on the quality of a marriage, the division of household labor, and how a couple handles stress.

Marital Quality and Family Life

Work and family have both positive and negative "spillover effects" in the sense that one affects the other. Marital quality, however, is more influential than work. If people are happily married, their job satisfaction increases, and strong marital ties can "buffer" job stress. If there is marital discord, job satisfaction generally decreases for both women and men (Grzywacz et al., 2002; Rogers and May, 2003).

since you asked

Does work have a different effect on women's and men's family life?

Leisure time has increased for some Americans, but not for employed parents. Even then, relaxation is gendered. Men who spend more time at work have less free time but don't feel as rushed as women do. Mothers, especially, feel that their free time is too deeply entangled with caregiving to be "the pause that refreshes." Unlike most men, women feel more rushed because they compress housework into fewer hours and replace their free time with child-centered leisure activities (Mattingly and Sayer, 2006).

Especially when they are employed, wives of men who are away for most of the week because of work-related travel sacrifice their leisure time for the husband's emotional health. For example, a study of trucking and fishing families found that the mothers undertook all the household tasks (including household repairs and paying bills) and worked extra hard during the week so that their husbands could relax when they came home. Ensuring that men enjoyed their leisure time at home significantly reduced the women's free time throughout the week (Zvonkovic et el., 2005).

Despite the views of many conservative writers, women's employment does *not* undermine marriage. Instead, marital conflict significantly increases the likelihood that wives will enter the labor force, work more hours per week, or seek more training for a promotion. If the discord continues or gets worse, employed women have more resources to survive economically after divorce (Rogers, 1999; see, also, Chapter 15).

Division of Household Labor

Although men's participation in family work has increased, women continue to perform the lion's share (see Chapters 5 and 10). What are some of the variations by social class and ethnicity?

SOCIAL CLASS VARIATIONS A longitudinal study in Great Britain, Germany, and the United States concluded that dual-earner couples adapt their division of household labor when women enter the labor force. When wives get a full-time job, husbands increase their domestic work by around 2 hours per week and wives reduce theirs by about 4 to 8 hours a week. Thus, although the division of domestic work is far from equal, husbands do slightly more and wives do a lot less (Gershuny et al., 2005).

Some middle-class employed mothers report feeling closer to their children and being "good" mothers when they do more of the daily child care chores than fathers do (for example, taking children to the park and day-care). In most cases, however, women, but not men, are less satisfied with their marriages if they are unhappy about their husband's small contribution to housework and child care (Ehrenberg et al., 2001; Stevens et al., 2001).

Working-class families, especially when the spouses are over age 40, experience greater conflict over family work than do middle-class families. Worn out from completing one shift at work and a second shift at home, wives may feel entitled to their husbands' full participation in domestic labor:

"Sure, he helps me out. . . . He'll give the kids a bath or help with the dishes. But when I ask him. He doesn't have to ask me to go to work every day, does he? Why should I have to ask him?" (Rubin, 1994: 87).

Some men, on the other hand, feel that their wives' complaints are unreasonable and unfair:

The men . . . feel embattled and victimized on two fronts—one outside the home, the other inside. When their wives fail to appreciate them, the men feel violated and betrayed. "You come home and you want to be appreciated a little. But it doesn't work that way, leastwise not anymore," complains a twenty-nine-year-old drill press operator (Rubin, 1994: 87–88).

If men have jobs that are tedious or unrewarding, being expected to do housework may create marital conflict. Because married men tend to work longer hours than their full-time employed wives, wives' demands that they do more household work may seem especially oppressive (Perry-Jenkins and Folk, 1994).

RACIAL-ETHNIC VARIATIONS The division of household labor varies not only by social class but also by race and ethnicity. As you saw in Chapter 4, African American men are more likely than men of other racial-ethnic groups to cook, clean, and care for children. The greater participation in family work might reflect the historical exclusion of black men from many jobs:

"My mother worked six days a week cleaning other people's houses, and my father was an ordinary laborer, when he could find work, which wasn't very often," explains a thirty-two-year-old father of two children. "So he was home a lot more than she was, and he'd do what he had to do around the house. The kids all had to do their share, too" (Rubin, 1994: 92).

Black men's greater involvement in housework might also reflect a "socialization for competence." Many African American parents, especially employed mothers, expect all children to participate in household chores at a young age, including laundry, cooking, and cleaning, and to take turns doing so. In adulthood, men expect their offspring to do the same (Penha-Lopes, 2006).

The more resources a woman has, the more likely it is that family work will be divided more equitably. For example, a study of Latino families found that wives who earned less money, worked fewer hours, held less prestigious jobs, had less education, or were much younger than their husbands were most likely to feel responsible for all the housework and child care (Valdez and Coltrane, 1993). Also, Asian and Latino men who are least likely to share in family work are those who live in ethnic neighborhoods where there is strong support for traditional gender roles, even when the wife works outside the home (see Chapters 4 and 12).

Stress

All of us experience stress for a variety of reasons, but the most common sources of stress are money, work, and family-related issues (see *Figure 13.8*). More women (51 percent) than men (43 percent) say that they are stressed out because they worry about finances, the family's health, and the children's well-being ("Americans engage . . . ," 2006).

Stress affects both our physical and mental health. A majority of American adults who experience stress

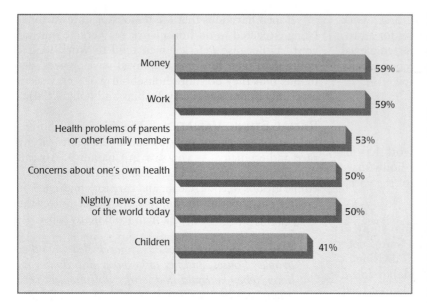

FIGURE 13.8 Leading Sources of Stress for Americans

SOURCE: Based on "Americans engage. . . ," 2006.

report such symptoms as anxiety, depression, fatigue, irritability, anger, sleep problems, obesity, and lack of motivation or energy. Many families cope with life's stresses by attending religious services, trying to find solutions, and talking to family members and friends. Others, however, use alcohol and other drugs, smoke, or overeat ("Americans engage . . . ," 2006).

Although parents may feel stressed, most children see their parents as loving and responsive. In a national study of third- through twelfth-graders, for example, Galinsky (1999) asked the children to "grade" both their mothers and their fathers on "making me feel important and loved." Most of the children (72 percent) gave their mothers an A and 67 percent gave their fathers an A. There was no difference in the grades the children gave to employed mothers and to those who stayed home or the grades they gave to mothers who worked part-time or full-time.

The greatest stressors for the dual-earner family stem from work-related tensions. For example, when parents experience job stress and role overload, they are more demanding, withdrawn, and negative when interacting with their children. Parental job stress may also be associated with a child's poor academic achievement or behavioral problems in school. It can also lead to child abuse (Piokowski and Hughes, 1993; Parcel and Menaghan, 1994). The box "Juggling Competing Demands in Dual-Earner Families" offers some suggestions for dealing with some of the problems that families encounter.

Conventional wisdom says that money can't buy happiness. Maybe not, but people with higher incomes are

happier (see *Figure 13.9*). As the late American entertainer Sophie Tucker once observed, "I've been rich and I've been poor—and believe me, rich is better."

Inequality in the Workplace

The media often romanticize employed women: They present images of perfectly groomed women, briefcases in hand, chairing important meetings or flying across the country, cell phones and laptops in action. In reality, the majority of working women have much less exciting jobs. They are also much more likely than men to encounter income discrimination, limited opportunities for advancement, and sexual harassment. All these difficulties affect the family's interpersonal and economic well-being.

The Mommy Track and the Daddy Penalty

In a work that has become a classic, Felice Schwartz (1989) divided women managers into two groups: those on the career-primary track and those on the career-and-family track. The *career-primary women,* who sacrifice

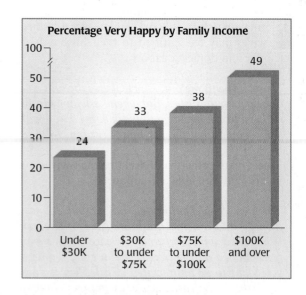

FIGURE 13.9 Does Money Buy Happiness?

SOURCE: Taylor et al., 2006a, p. 3.

Applying What You've Learned

Juggling Competing Demands in Dual-Earner Families

As you read these suggestions for balancing work and family life, think about other strategies that have worked for you, your parents, or your friends.

- *Emphasize the positive.* Concentrate on the benefits you get from having a job: personal fulfillment, a higher standard of living, and providing more cultural and educational opportunities for your children.
- *Set priorities.* Because conflicts between the demands of family and job are inevitable, establish principles for resolving clashes. For example, parents might take turns staying home with sick children.
- *Be ready to compromise.* Striving for perfection in family and job responsibilities is unrealistic. Instead, aim for the best possible balance among your various activities, making compromises when necessary. For example, homes don't have to be immaculate.
- *Separate family and work roles.* Many mothers, especially, feel guilty while at work because they are not

with their children. And when they are at home, they feel guilty about not working on office assignments. If you must work at home, set time limits for the work and enjoy the rest of the time with your family.
- *Organize domestic duties.* Resolve domestic overload by dividing family work more equitably between adults and children. Many families find it useful to prepare a weekly or monthly job chart in which everyone's assignments are clearly written down. It's also useful to rotate assignments so that everyone gets to do both the "better" and the "worse" jobs.
- *Cultivate a sharing attitude.* Sit down with your partner periodically and discuss what you can do to help each other in your roles at home and at work. Most of us are happier when our spouses and partners provide a sounding board or offer encouragement.
- *Maintain a balance between responsibilities and recreation.* If you are both working to improve your standard of living, use some of your extra income to enjoy life. Otherwise, you'll have little energy left for activities that will make life more enjoyable (Beck, 1988; Crosby, 1991b).

family and children for upward mobility, are identified early and groomed for top-level positions alongside ambitious men. In contrast, *career-and-family women,* who are viewed as wanting to spend more time at home, are recruited for part-time work. The latter arrangement, quickly dubbed the **mommy track** by the media, is a slower track or even a sidetrack for women who want to combine a career with child rearing.

Many feminists contend that the mommy track is still flourishing. For example, women make up 46 percent of the work force (see *Table 13.2*), but men still hold more than 95 percent of the top management jobs in America's largest corporations (see Chapter 5). Although there are some very successful women in business (such as Meg Whitman, who built eBay into a multimillion-dollar online flea market), women receive only 4 percent of the estimated $20 billion that venture capitalists invest in funding start-up companies (McDonald, 2000).

According to economist Heather Boushey, many women also experience a "mommy wage gap." For the first child a woman has, her wages are 2 percent to 10

percent lower than those of nonmothers. For the second child, they are 4 percent to 16 percent lower than those of women with no children (cited in Kleiman, 2005). The reasons for the mommy wage gap are unclear, but they may reflect employers' beliefs that mothers are more likely than nonmothers to leave their jobs to care for children or to be distracted by family problems.

Some researchers also argue that corporations are penalizing the husbands of women who work outside the home, a phenomenon that the media call the **daddy penalty.** For example, married men whose wives aren't employed earn about 31 percent more per hour than never-married men, but men married to women with a full-time job earn only 3 percent more. Thus, having a wife who devotes most of her time to raising the kids and other housework frees men up to work longer and harder. In effect, corporate prejudice in favor of traditional families produces a "double whammy": "The dual-career wife earns less than she would if she were her husband, and her husband earns less than he would if she were not working" (Harris, 1995: 27; Chun and Lee, 2001).

The Wage Gap

In 2005, women who worked full time year-round had a median income of $32,168, compared with $41,965 for men. This means that women earn 77 cents for every dollar men earn. For many ethnic minorities, the situation is even worse. Although Asian American and Pacific Island women earn 80 cents for every dollar men earn, African American women earn only 69 cents and Latinas earn only 57 cents for every dollar men earn.

since you asked

Why do women earn less than men, even when their jobs are almost identical?

On average, a woman with a college degree earns only slightly more per week than a man with an associate degree ($792 and $788, respectively). Stated differently, *the average woman must work almost four extra months every year to make the same wages as a man* (U.S. Bureau of Labor Statistics, 2005a; Joyce, 2006; Webster and Bishaw, 2006).

WHAT IS THE WAGE GAP? This income difference is the **wage gap** (sometimes called the *gender wage gap*). Although the wage gap can be partially explained by differences in education, experience, and time in the workforce, a significant portion is the result of sex discrimination in hiring, promotion and pay, bias against mothers, and occupational segregation. For example, two-thirds of all American women are still crowded into 21 of the 500 occupational categories (WAGE, 2006).

Over a lifetime, the average woman who works full time and year round for 47 years loses a significant amount of money because of the wage gap: $700,000 for high school graduates; $1.2 million for college graduates; and over $2 million for women with a professional degree in business, medicine, or law (Murphy and Graff, 2005).

The wage gap is even more costly than these figures suggest. Because raises are typically based on a percentage of one's annual income, the lower the wages, the lower the raises and possible savings. Lower wages and salaries also reduce women's purchasing power and quality of living. Imagine, for example, what you could do with an extra $6,000 a year if you're a female college graduate! In addition, lower wages result in lower monthly Social Security payments after retirement (Horn, 2006; see, also, Chapters 17 and 18).

Sometimes a woman's income is lower than a man's, *even when the man doesn't work*, because many unemployed men still have income from unemployment, disability, pensions, and investments (Krafft, 1994). This means that a single mother in a low-paying job may live just above the poverty level while a man enjoys a much higher standard of living without working at all.

Men earn more than women in almost every occupational category. (The only exception is black women, who make up 3 percent of all black workers in construction and earn slightly more than black men in construction jobs but it's not clear why.) Also, the wage gap tends to increase at the higher-paying managerial and professional levels. If we think about earnings as a ladder, white and Asian men are on top, then black men, followed by Latinos. At the bottom of the ladder are women, with Latinas faring worse than any of the other groups (see *Figure 13.10*). We see, then, that sex *and* race or ethnicity intersect in the workplace.

Many conservatives, both women and men, blame women for the wage gap:

> *Women have made enormous workplace gains, but they earn less because of their own choices, not because of discrimination. They choose to be teachers, or child care providers, or mothers, even though they earn less. Then they compound the pay-gap by opting out of the labor force at times or by scaling back their career ambitions—and sometimes work schedules—for personal reasons (Grimsley, 2000: E3).*

According to numerous studies, however, gender, not "choices," explains much of the earnings difference between women and men. That is, a wage gap remains even when women work full-time over a lifetime and when women and men have the same education, number of years in a job, seniority, marital status, number of children, and are similar on numerous other factors (Goyette and Xie, 1999; "Summary of recent studies . . .," 2000; Holden, 2001; Fogg, 2003).

As you can see in *Figure 13.11* on page 411, for example, male nurses, who make up only 8 percent of the profession, earn more than female nurses, who far outnumber them. The same is true in other traditionally female jobs, such as social work and elementary-school teaching. Because all these occupations have been traditionally "female" for decades, it can't be argued that men earn more because of seniority, higher educational levels, or more work experience. And, as one of my students commented, "I didn't choose to be a mother. Because men can't have babies, why should working women be penalized?"

COMPARABLE WORTH: A SOLUTION FOR THE WAGE GAP Some women have tried to remedy the wage gap by filing individual or *class action suits*, legal proceedings that are brought by one or more people but represent the interests of a larger group. According to some estimates, corporations alone paid more than $1.2 *billion* between 2000 and 2004 to settle wage discrimination claims. In 2004, for example, Boeing (a manufacturer of commercial planes and military aircraft)

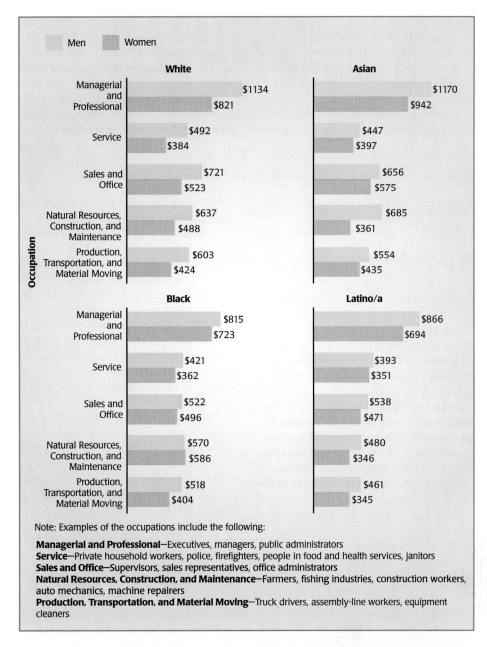

FIGURE 13.10   Median Weekly Earnings of Full-Time Workers, by Sex and Ethnicity, 2005

SOURCE: Based on unpublished data, personal correspondence, U.S. Bureau of Labor Statistics, Division of Labor Force Studies, 2006.

agreed to pay between $40 and $72 million; Morgan Stanley (a financial services company) agreed to pay $54 million; and Abercrombie & Fitch (a clothing company) agreed to pay $50 million to settle gender and racial discrimination lawsuits (Murphy and Graff, 2005; Horn, 2006).

Such lawsuits are costly and unnecessary. According to the concept of **comparable worth,** men and

women should receive equal pay for doing work that involves similar skills, effort, responsibility, and work conditions. If employers instituted comparable worth policies, the benefits would far outweigh the costs. In 1982, for example, the State of Minnesota implemented comparable worth for its public-sector employees, phasing in the program over a number of years. By 2002, women who worked for the state earned about 97 cents for every dollar men made, and overall personnel costs were less than 3 percent of the total state budget. Comparable worth not only cuts women's poverty rate in half but also gives women more purchasing power, which strengthens the economy (Murphy and Graff, 2005; Horn, 2006; see, also, Chapter 18).

There is no country in the world where women's average earnings equal those of men. However, the size of the wage gap varies enormously from one country to another. As the box "Women are Cheap Labor around the World" shows, the United States is not the only nation that exploits women in the workplace.

Employment inequality hurts all families. Many women and some men must also endure work-related abuses such as sexual harassment.

Cross-Cultural Families

Women Are Cheap Labor around the World

Occupational sex segregation and wage disparities between men and women are the norm in most countries. The United States ranks 46th out of 58 countries in women's economic opportunities (such as equality in private-sector employment) and well below a number of developing countries such as Costa Rica, China, and Poland (Lopez-Claros and Zahidi, 2005).

U.S. corporations with plants in developing countries where labor is cheap are among the worst offenders, but many other governments also practice sex discrimination. Countries with the biggest wage gaps in manufacturing, where many women work, include Bangladesh (where women earn 50 percent of what men earn), Brazil

This girl, age 12, living in Nepal in southern Asia, had been working as an indentured servant (for about $50 a year) to pay her family's debts. She was allowed to stay home after the family had a pig to raise and sell.

(54 percent), Japan (56 percent), Malaysia (58 percent), and Jordan (62 percent) (Seager, 2003).

In Kuwait, one of the wealthiest countries in the Middle East, Filipino maids normally put in exhausting 14-hour days as domestic servants and earn about $150 a month. Hundreds of thousands of poor women are sent to work as domestic servants in middle- and upper-class homes in Europe, Japan, the Middle East, the United Kingdom, and the United States. Both the Philippine government and recruiting agencies reap tremendous profits by providing employers in these "host" countries with extremely cheap service workers, who are often mistreated and required to work in appalling conditions (Chang, 2000; Prusher, 2000).

Even countries that promote women's rights in many areas still lag in the workplace. In Norway, for example, women who are full-time workers earn 71 percent of what men earn. The pay gap is also wide in several other counties, including Ireland (65 percent), Russia (70 percent), Canada (73 percent), and Germany (76 percent) (Seager, 2003).

Multinational corporations that move their production to countries with abundant and cheap labor reap huge profits. In China, for example, 3 million young women work for wages as low as 12 cents an hour to make sporting goods and toys to be sold in the United States and Canada. Nike's $5 billion empire has been built by exploiting labor in poor countries like China, Indonesia, and Vietnam. Workers receive less than three dollars a day, child labor is common, people aren't paid for working overtime, and many women suffer sexual and verbal abuse (Dixon, 1996; MacAdam, 2003).

Stop and Think . . .

- How does the wage gap affect all families, and not just women?
- Why is achieving gender equality in work such a grindingly slow process, especially in such "progressive" countries as the United States?

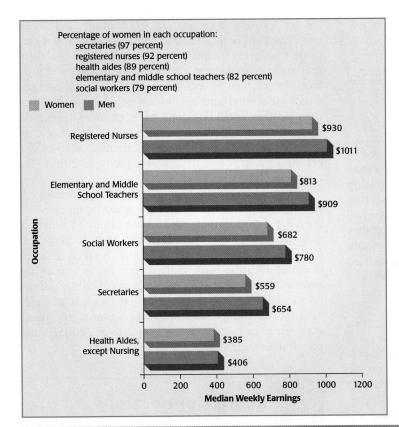

Percentage of women in each occupation:
   secretaries (97 percent)
   registered nurses (92 percent)
   health aides (89 percent)
   elementary and middle school teachers (82 percent)
   social workers (79 percent)

Women   Men

Registered Nurses — $930 / $1011

Elementary and Middle School Teachers — $813 / $909

Social Workers — $682 / $780

Secretaries — $559 / $654

Health Aides, except Nursing — $385 / $406

(x-axis: Median Weekly Earnings, 0 to 1200; y-axis: Occupation)

Sexual Harassment

Before reading any further, take the "Do You Recognize Sexual Harassment?" quiz to see how attuned you are to this issue.

Sexual harassment became illegal and a form of sex discrimination in 1964 (Title VII of the Civil Rights Act of 1964) and again in the 1980 Equal Employment Opportunity Commission (EEOC) guidelines. According to the EEOC, the fastest-growing area of employment discrimination complaints is sexual harassment, with almost 200,000 complaints filed with the EEOC between 1992 and 2005.

As you saw in Chapter 5, sexual harassment includes the following:

■ *Verbal behavior* (such as pressures for dates or demands for sexual favors in return for hiring, promotion, or tenure, as well as the threat of rape)

FIGURE 13.11 **Median Weekly Earnings in Traditionally Female Occupations, by Sex, 2005**

SOURCE: Based on U.S. Department of Labor, 2005, Table 39.

Ask Yourself

Do You Recognize Sexual Harassment?

Is it sexual harassment if:

Yes No

☐ ☐   **1.** An employee uses e-mail to send sexual jokes to co-workers.

☐ ☐   **2.** An employee continues to ask a co-worker to go out on dates despite repeated refusals.

☐ ☐   **3.** Employees tell bawdy jokes to co-workers who enjoy them in nonworkplace settings.

☐ ☐   **4.** A male employee frequently brushes up against female employees "accidentally."

☐ ☐   **5.** Male and female co-workers repeatedly talk about their sexual affairs and relationships at the office.

☐ ☐   **6.** A cashier in a restaurant greets each customer by calling him or her "Honey" or "Dearie."

☐ ☐   **7.** A male supervisor tells a female employee "You look very nice today."

☐ ☐   **8.** Employees put up pornographic material on company bulletin boards or in lockers.

☐ ☐   **9.** Employees or supervisors make frequent comments to co-workers about sexually explicit material in the media (films, television, magazines).

☐ ☐   **10.** At the end of a staff meeting, a male manager says to two female secretaries, "Why don't you girls clean up this room?"

(The answers to these questions are on page 413.)

■ *Nonverbal behavior* (such as indecent gestures and displaying posters, photos, or drawings of a sexual nature)

■ *Physical contact* (such as pinching, touching, and rape)

Sexual harassment in the workplace is a display of power that is usually perpetrated by a boss and directed at a subordinate. Because men dominate positions of power, it is far more likely that a harasser will be a man than a woman. The superior–subordinate relationship of perpetrator and victim also accounts for the fact that women often fail to report incidents of harassment. The women feel that nothing will be done and that they risk losing their jobs if they complain. Teenage girls are especially vulnerable. They often tolerate unwanted comments and touching by coworkers and supervisors because they view them as romantic overtures rather than as sexual harassment (Joyce, 2004).

Some people claim that there is a fine line between sexual harassment and flirting or simply giving a compliment. Wrong. If someone says "stop it" and the perpetrator doesn't stop, it's sexual harassment. Most people know—both instinctively and because of the other person's reaction—when sexual attentions are unwelcome.

Sexual harassment can be very costly, both emotionally and financially, to its victims. What many people don't realize is that sexual harassment constitutes wage discrimination because repeated harassment can cause employees (usually women) to leave or lose their jobs and, consequently, forfeit potential raises and promotions. Victims of sexual harassment may also experience emotional and behavioral problems that affect their families, including depression; changes in attitude toward sexual relationships or in sexual behaviors; irritability toward family members, friends, or co-workers; and alcohol and drug abuse (WAGE, 2006; see, also, Chapter 5).

Sexual harassment is also expensive for employers and companies. In 2004 alone, for example, some of the biggest corporations paid women almost $3 million to settle sexual harassment lawsuits. Most recently, the California Supreme Court ruled that even consensual sleeping with the boss, male or female, is sexual harassment because it may result in favoritism (such as promotions and pay increases) that treats women as "sexual playthings" and penalizes women (and men) who refuse to sleep with the boss (Dolan, 2005; Murphy and Graff, 2005).

Making Connections

■ Are women and men too accepting of gender wage gaps? If you're a male, how would you feel if your mother, daughter, wife, or partner was earning only 77 percent or less than a man in a comparable position?

■ Have you, your friends, or members of your family ever observed or experienced sexual harassment? If so, what did you or they do about it?

Families and Work Policies

How family-friendly are workplace policies? Pregnancy discrimination laws are supposed to protect workers and their jobs, and family leave policies have made it easier to care for newborns and sick family members. On the other hand, child and elder care provisions and welfare reform leave much to be desired (see Chapters 17 and 18).

The Pregnancy Penalty

Pregnancy discrimination cuts across all occupations. For example,

■ A driver for a valet service in Mesa, Arizona, was fired because "pregnant women are susceptible to

In 2004, a Burger King in St. Louis settled a sexual harassment lawsuit for $400,000. The money was paid to seven high school female employees whose boss had subjected them to groping, vulgar sexual comments, and demands for sex.

Answers to "Do You Recognize Sexual Harassment?"

1. Repeated instances could meet the legal definition of sexual harassment if they create an offensive and hostile work environment.

2. Yes.

3. No.

4. Yes.

5. No, if no one else is around and the talk is consensual. It could be if a passerby finds such talk offensive.

6. No, if the comments are directed at both sexes and aren't intentionally derogatory or degrading.

7. No.

8. Yes; this creates a hostile work environment.

9. Yes.

10. No, but it's a sexist comment.

SOURCES: Based on Langelan, 1993; Coolidge, 1998.

cramps and nausea while driving customers around, which might result in accidents and lawsuits."

- A supervisor at a restaurant chain in New York was fired after becoming pregnant because, according to her (male) manager, "it was going to be a challenge to be a single parent and to continue the job."

- An executive vice president of marketing and communication at a national corporation in Wisconsin was fired three days after informing the CEO that she was pregnant. She brought suit and eventually settled for $450,000 in lost wages (Donnelly, 2003; Woznicki, 2005).

The federal Pregnancy Discrimination Act of 1978 forbids employers with more than 15 workers to fire, demote, or penalize a pregnant employee. Some state laws extend this protection to companies with as few as four employees. Despite such protections, the EEOC reports that charges of pregnancy discrimination are increasing. Claims have risen 33 percent in recent years. In 2005, nearly 4500 women filed complaints that they had been fired, demoted, or had some of their responsibilities taken away from them when their employers learned that they were pregnant ("Pregnancy discrimination charges," 2006).

This is just the tip of the iceberg. Between 1996 and 2000, for example, almost 5 percent of women (about 288,000 employees) reported being laid off while pregnant or within 12 weeks after giving birth (Overturf Johnson and Downs, 2005). Thus, only a fraction of the women who are victimized by pregnancy-related job discrimination ever take action. Many aren't aware of their rights; others don't have the resources to pursue lengthy lawsuits.

Family and Medical Leave Policies

One of the most important pieces of U.S. legislation having to do with families is the 1993 Family and Medical Leave Act (FMLA). This law allows eligible employees to take up to 12 weeks of unpaid annual leave, with continuation of health benefits, after the birth or adoption of a child, to care for a seriously sick family member, or to recover from their own illnesses. The box "A Tour of the Family and Medical Leave Act" provides a closer look at these rights.

BENEFITS OF THE FMLA The most obvious benefit of family leave policies is that many employees should no longer lose their jobs because of sickness, childbirth, or parental leave. Also, most employees, except for the top 10 percent, are guaranteed the same job or an equivalent job when they return. The FMLA defines an "equivalent" position as one with the same pay, benefits, and working conditions and "substantially similar" duties and responsibilities. Most important, because the FMLA is law, employees don't have to depend on the supervisor's good will for leave.

Many parents, especially mothers, stitch together paid leave (such as sick days and vacations) to cover childbirth and caring for an infant for a few weeks or longer. The percentage of women who had some paid leave increased from 37 percent in 1981 to 42 percent in 2000. Most companies, especially those with 1,000 or more employees, fund this pay through a general temporary disability insurance (TDI) plan that provides partial wage replacement for maternity-related leaves, but only for mothers (Bond et al., 2005; Overturf Johnson and Downs, 2005).

Choices

A Tour of the Family and Medical Leave Act

Workers who know their rights under the Family and Medical Leave Act (FMLA) are more likely to take advantage of its benefits.

Who is covered? Any employee is eligible for 12 weeks of leave if she or he has worked at least 1,250 hours during a 12-month period—roughly the equivalent of 25 hours a week—at a company or work site that employs at least 50 people.

The highest-paid 10 percent of employees must be granted a leave like all other employees. However, members of this group are not guaranteed a job on return if their absence causes "substantial and grievous economic injury" to their employer.

What are the purposes of leave? An employee may take family or medical leave for the birth or adoption of a child and to care for a newborn; to care for a spouse, child, or parent with a serious illness; or to recuperate from a serious illness that prevents the employee from working.

Who pays for the leave? The employee pays for the leave. A company may require or allow employees to apply paid vacation and sick leave to the 12 weeks of family leave, but it does not have to pay workers who take leave.

When should the employer be notified? In foreseeable cases, such as a birth, adoption, or planned medical treatment, 30 days' verbal or written notice is required. When that's impossible (for example, if a baby is born earlier than expected), the employer must be notified as soon as possible, generally within one or two business days. Employers may ask for medical proof that a leave is needed.

Must the leave be taken all at once? No. For example, the leave can be used to shorten the workweek when an employee wants to cut back after the birth of a child. Medical leave can also be taken piecemeal (to accommodate weekly appointments for chemotherapy treatments, for instance).

What if you feel that your rights have been violated? Any local or regional office of the U.S. Department of Labor's Wage and Hour Division, Employment Standards Administration, will accept complaints, which must be filed within two years of the alleged violation. Private lawsuits must also be filed within two years of the violation.

According to a recent Supreme Court ruling (*Nevada Department of Human Resources v. Hibbs*), state employees can now sue agencies that violate the FMLA.

Stop and Think . . .

- In contrast to the United States, 17 other industrialized countries—and even some developing countries, such as Senegal—have provided 12 to 72 weeks of paid parental leave since 1989 (Ruhm and Teague, 1997; Heymann, 2002). Why don't we do the same?

- Many U.S. employers now cover some paid maternity (but not paternity) leave under disability insurance. Why is pregnancy a "disability"? And why are men excluded from such "disability insurance"?

LIMITATIONS OF THE FMLA The biggest problem is that the 60 percent of U.S. employees who work in companies with fewer than 50 employees are not covered by the FMLA. Small companies are much less likely than larger ones to provide employee benefits such as health insurance, paid sick leave, and disability insurance. Thus, the FMLA ignores millions of employees who already have limited benefits. In addition, the many workers in part-time, temporary positions (most of whom are women) are excluded from family leave policies.

A second problem is that 30 percent of employers with 50 or more employers offer fewer than 12 weeks of unpaid family leave, a violation of the FMLA. It's not clear whether the employers are simply unaware of the law or violate it deliberately. In fact, 90 percent of businesses report that they incur no additional costs by providing unpaid leave or actually increase their profits through higher employee morale and productivity (Smith et al., 2001; Bond et al., 2005).

A third problem is that the FMLA is of little help to many parents because it involves unpaid time off and covers only major illnesses, which typically necessitate a hospital stay. In most cases, children don't need hospitalization but instead have frequent routine illnesses. As the number of higher-paid jobs decreases, many working parents can't afford to take any unpaid leave (Phillips, 2004).

Finally, employees and employers may disagree about what constitutes "equivalent" jobs or "substantially similar" responsibilities. For example, does a person have an "equivalent" job if it involves driving an extra 30 minutes to work to an unfamiliar office at a less desirable location?

IS THE FMLA GENDERED? About 46 percent of employers say that they offer women at least some replacement pay for maternity leave but only 13 percent provide similar benefits for paternity leave. Also, 9 percent of companies say that any employee, male or female, can use *flextime* (allowing workers to change their daily arrival and departure times) to accommodate parenting responsibilities (Bond et al., 2005).

As you saw earlier, about 5 percent of women report having been laid off during or after a pregnancy. In private companies with 50 or more employees, 39 percent of the workers feel that using flextime and family leave policies jeopardizes their prospects for advancement. And in a survey of Fortune 500 senior executives, 44 percent said that employee requests for leave time, especially by men, would have a negative impact on their chances of promotion (Bond et al., 2005; Miller and Miller, 2005).

Employers may label men who use flextime or paternity leave as not fully dedicated to their job or career. And with downsizing always threatening to reduce the number of available jobs, "few male employees want to send a signal that they are less than 100 percent devoted to their jobs" (Saltzman, 1993: 66). In response, many men avoid paternity leave and instead use vacation and sick days to spend time with their wives and newborns.

Sweden offers some of the most generous parental leaves in the world—15 months of paid leave. On average, however, fathers use only 1 to 2 months, especially if they work in male-dominated occupations, for small companies, and in jobs where other fathers haven't used much paternity leave. Similarly, "Women at male-dominated workplaces may be called into question if they take a long parental leave, and they may thus have difficulties sustaining their work position"

(Bygren and Duvander, 2006: 370). Thus, even in the most "progressive" countries, family leave is gendered.

Care for Dependents

One of the most serious problems facing families today is inadequate day care for young children. And increasingly families are confronting the need to provide services for elderly parents. What, if anything, are businesses and government doing to help families care for their dependents?

CHILD CARE As you saw in Chapter 12, high costs, poor quality, and long waiting lists are just some of the obstacles that confront working parents who seek safe and reliable care for their children. "The search for quality nonparental care for young children is daunting at best and can reach crisis proportions at worst, because our nation currently lacks a policy that ensures reliable, affordable, appropriate care for all children who need it" (Piokowski and Hughes, 1993: 193).

Unlike almost all other industrialized countries, we have no national child care program. Some companies that tout child care assistance actually do little more than provide a list of child care providers in the area. Only 7 percent of employers with 50 or more workers provide child care at or near the workplace (Bond et

Sales representatives, like this mother, can often work from home, which enables them to interact with their children more frequently.

Changes

Working at Home: Still Not a Paradise

The average American spends more than 100 hours each year traveling to and from work ("Americans spend...," 2005). This means that if we work for 35 years, we'll spend about 5 percent of our life simply commuting to work. To decrease both travel time and conflicts between work and family roles, people can *telecommute*, or work from home through computer hookups to an office.

In 2006, 32 percent of U.S. employees worked from home at least two days a week, up from 9 percent in 1995. Most were in managerial, professional, and sales jobs; about equal percentages were women and men; and the higher the educational level, the greater the likelihood of telecommuting ("Work at home in 2004," 2005; Jones, 2006b).

On the *positive side,* many telecommuters spend less money on clothes, have a more flexible work schedule, and have reduced the cost of child care. Some report that working at home brings the family closer together. A parent is available when a child returns after school, and family members sometimes get involved in business tasks. Often, companies permit telecommuting to retain talented employees who prefer to work from home.

On the *negative side,* some telecommuters miss their co-workers and feel that nothing can replace face-to-face communication. Others worry that telecommuting might make them less visible to managers who award promotions and raises (Heubeck, 2005).

Telecommuting can also decrease the quality of family time. Some parents resent interruptions or distractions while they're working, worry that they can't leave job stress at the office, or find that it's hard to separate their family and business lives.

Noise from children, pets, and appliances may also decrease productivity and create tension at home. Some people are also concerned that the costs of telecommuting may be screened more carefully by the Internal Revenue Service and increase the risk of audits (Learner, 2002).

Stop and Think . . .

- During 2005 and 2006, gasoline prices soared. Do you think that such costs affect employees' decisions to work for a company that allows telecommuting? Or not?

- Have you or your friends ever telecommuted or done paid work at home? If so, what were the advantages and disadvantages?

al., 2005). Because most companies charge their employees for day-care services, many low-wage workers are unable to pay even the reduced costs that companies offer. (Chapter 18 describes innovative child care facilities that some companies have implemented.)

Working at home, or *telecommuting,* is one of the newest flexible work styles that allow parents to combine both work and child-rearing. As the box "Working at Home: Still Not a Paradise" shows, however, telecommuting has both benefits and costs.

ELDER CARE The FMLA does not include elder care. Most businesses rarely provide or subsidize elder-care leave, but about 79 percent of all companies say that they offer employees time off to care for elderly parents without jeopardizing their jobs (Bond et al., 2005). It's not clear, however, how much of that "time off" includes paid leave. Probably very little, because family members—especially women—provide most elder care and often have to quit their jobs to do so (see Chapter 17).

Programs for Poor Families

The United States is the only one among 19 wealthy nations with a double-digit poverty rate (Smeeding et al., 2000). Unlike the United States, countries such as Germany, Italy, and the Netherlands have less poverty because they have higher minimum wages, guaranteeing that full-time workers' children will not be poor. What help is available for the poor? Not much. In 1996, Congress passed the Personal Responsibility and Work Opportunity Reconciliation Act (PRWORA) that changed the welfare system. PRWORA was targeted almost entirely at poor, mother-only families.

since you asked

How has welfare reform affected families?

The central feature of PRWORA was the replacement of Aid to Families with Dependent Children (AFDC) with block grants. The states set their own eligibility criteria and benefit levels. Three other important changes included the following: (1) Federal money cannot be used to provide cash assistance to unmarried women under age 18 or children born to mothers who are already receiving assistance; (2) adults are expected to work after receiving welfare for two years; and (3) a family cannot receive cash assistance for more than a total of five years.

PRWORA advocates are delighted that some families have left the welfare rolls. Critics argue, however, that PRWORA scapegoats poor, unmarried (and especially black) mothers and their children instead of focusing on macro-level problems such as widespread economic inequality, jobs that don't provide decent wages and benefits, and a growing poverty rate among young two-parent families. Especially because minimum wages can't sustain families, many parents who are no longer on welfare are still living barely above the poverty level (Sidel, 1998; McKernan and Radcliffe, 2006).

Most developed countries have greatly reduced child poverty because of priorities and values rather than affordability. In much of Europe, for example, "the well-being of the child and the mother is usually the foremost value, and the absent father's willingness and ability to pay are of secondary concern" (Rainwater and Smeeding, 2003: 137). In contrast, some scholars contend, the goal of PRWORA was not to reduce poverty or suffering but the governments' responsibility for improving the well-being of all U.S. citizens (Miles and Fowler, 2006; Segal, 2006).

Conclusion

Because many families lack sufficient economic resources, they have very few *choices* in the workplace. Macro-level economic *changes* have created numerous *constraints* that often present dilemmas for families. Incomes have not kept up with inflation, so more household members have to work. This cuts into family time and creates stress, which can contribute to illness, absenteeism, and layoffs. The more successful employed women and men are, the more difficult it is for them to find time for family activities.

Many parents, especially single mothers, can't afford child care because it is too expensive. But without child care, they can't get the training for jobs that will pull them out of poverty. Many of the same economic forces also have an impact on family violence, a topic we examine in the next chapter.

Summary

1. Social class and economic resources play a major role in what happens to families. Affluent families are getting richer, an increasing number of middle-class families are experiencing lower income, and the number of poor families is growing.

2. Some political analysts feel that poverty rates are exaggerated because they ignore noncash benefits from the government, such as housing subsidies and medical services. Most researchers, however, maintain that the proportion of people living in poverty is underestimated because the amount of money needed for subsistence varies drastically by region and because the U.S. Census Bureau undercounts the poor.

3. Although there are no exact figures, about 3.5 million people are homeless in a given year. About a third of the homeless are children.

4. Economic recessions and stagnant incomes have resulted in more dual-earner families. There is a great deal of variation in these families, however, in terms of social class and willingness to relocate or to have a commuter marriage.

5. The widespread employment of mothers was one of the most dramatic changes in family roles in the twentieth century.

6. Employment affects the family in many ways. Regardless of whether the results are positive or negative, work roles influence the duration and quality of a marriage and the division of household labor.

7. Because of economic changes and the increasing number of employed mothers with young children, many families encounter serious child care problems.

8. One of the biggest problems employed women face is the gender gap in wages and salaries. Pregnancy discrimination and sexual harassment make the situation even worse.

9.   Although the Family and Medical Leave Act is supposed to protect an employee's job during illness and maternity and paternity leave, many employers still provide only limited coverage.

10.   Welfare reforms have done little to lift most families out of poverty. In fact, many families are worse off than ever before.

Key Terms

wealth *386*	working poor *392*	trailing spouse *402*
income *386*	discouraged worker *396*	commuter marriage *403*
corporate welfare *389*	underemployed worker *396*	mommy track *407*
absolute poverty *389*	two-person single career *399*	daddy penalty *408*
relative poverty *389*	dual-earner couple *401*	wage gap *408*
poverty line *390*	discretionary income *401*	comparable worth *409*
feminization of poverty *391*	dual-career couple *401*	

Taking it Further

Combining Family and Work More Effectively

The Internet offers much information on how to improve working conditions and family life. Some of these sites include the following:

U.S. Department of Labor home page provides a cornucopia of data and practical information about employment, workplace illnesses, and employee benefits. www.bls.gov

U.S. Department of Labor Women's Bureau home page offers statistics, advice on hiring someone to work in your home, and much data on women in the workplace. www.dol.gov/dol/wb

The Families and Work Institute conducts research on the changing work force and examines family policies. www.familiesandwork.org

The **Pew Research Center** features numerous (and very readable) research reports and analyses on families and work.

http://pewresearch.org

The **Urban Institute** analyzes policies and evaluates programs that affect working families and poverty.

http://www.urban.org

The **National Coalition for the Homeless** is dedicated to preventing and ending homelessness. This site offers a wealth of resources, including suggestions about getting involved at the local, state, or national level.

www.nationalhomeless.org

And more: www.prenhall.com/benokraitis includes sites dealing with the economic situation worldwide, reports on U.S. workers, advice about family finances, information about how to calculate your personal gender wage gap online, FMLA research, resources for at-home-dads and stay-at-home moms, and more.

Investigate with Research Navigator

Go to www.researchnavigator.com and enter your LOGIN NAME and PASSWORD. For instructions on registering for the first time, view the detailed instructions at the end of Chapter 1. Search the Research Navigator™ site using the following key terms:

underemployment
family leave
household labor

Outline

Family Violence and Other Health Issues

Data Digest

■ Between 1994 and 2004 the rate of **reported child abuse or neglect decreased** from 15.2 to 11.9 per 1,000 children.

■ Of all **intimate partner homicides,** 76 percent of the victims are women.

■ Nearly **43 percent of women who are physically assaulted by an intimate partner are injured,** compared with 20 percent of men.

■ Almost **30 percent of U.S. children live in partner-violent families.**

■ The **cost of child maltreatment** is almost $95 billion a year. The costs are both direct (such as hospitalization and law enforcement) and indirect (such as juvenile delinquency and adult criminality).

■ Each year, spouses, adult children, or close acquaintances **injure about 36,000 people age 65 or older and kill about 500.**

Sources: Klaus, 2000; Fromm, 2001; Rennison, 2003; Fox and Zawitz, 2003; McDonald et al., 2006; U.S. Department of Health and Human Services, 2006.

Recently the Newark, New Jersey, police, alerted by suspicious neighbors, were horrified by what they found. Two little boys, ages 4 and 7, were locked in the basement of their home:

The children were starving and filthy, their bodies covered with excrement and burn marks. A day after finding the boys in the basement, police discovered the body of a third child, stuffed inside a plastic container. . . . The 7-year-old boy, a twin, *had been dead for more than a month. Investigators described the body as so withered and stiff it was "mummified" (Smalley and Braiker, 2003: 32).*

According to the police, the boys had also been sexually assaulted over a number of years by relatives and their mother's boyfriends.

Families can be warm, loving, and nurturing, but they can also be cruel and abusive. Over a lifetime, we are more likely to be assaulted or killed by a family member than by a stranger: "That violence and love can coexist in a household is perhaps the most insidious aspect of family violence, because we grow up learning that it is acceptable to hit the people we love" (Gelles, 1997: 12).

This chapter examines the different forms of domestic violence, describes its prevalence, and discusses why people who say that they love each other are so abusive. We then turn to other family health issues, such as drug abuse, depression, suicide, and eating disorders. We'll end the chapter with a look at some successful prevention and intervention strategies.

Marital and Intimate Partner Violence

Marital and intimate partner violence is pervasive in U.S. society. In a recent national survey, 20 percent of women and 3 percent of men said that they had been physically assaulted by a current or former spouse, cohabiting partner, or date at least once in their lifetime (Rennison, 2003). These numbers are probably conservative because many people are too ashamed or afraid to report the victimization.

Types of Domestic Violence

Intimate partner violence may be physical, sexual, or emotional. *Physical violence* includes such behaviors as throwing objects, pushing, grabbing, shoving, slapping, kicking, biting, hitting, beating, choking, threatening with a knife or gun, or using a knife or gun. In *sexual abuse,* a person is forced to have sexual intercourse or take part in unwanted sexual activity (such as anal or oral sex).

Emotional abuse (both psychological and verbal), is equally harmful. Scorn, criticism, ridicule, or neglect by loved ones can be emotionally crippling. Listen to a 33-year-old mother of two children: "He rarely says a kind word to me. The food is too cold or . . . too hot. The kids are too noisy. . . . I am too fat or too skinny. No matter what I do, he says it isn't any good. He tells me I am lucky he married me 'cause no one else would have me" (Gelles and Straus, 1988: 68).

The Prevalence and Severity of Domestic Violence

Women's victimization by intimate partners decreased slightly between 1993 and 2001, but the numbers are still high and are considerably higher than those for men (see *Figure 14.1*). During this period, women were five times more likely than men to experience violence by an intimate partner. In fact, almost 85 percent of all

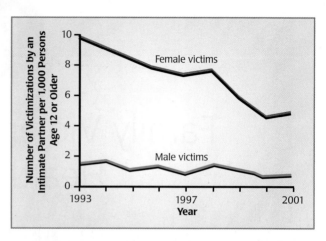

FIGURE 14.1   **Violence Rates by an Intimate Partner, by Sex, 1993–2001**

SOURCE: Rennison, 2003.

attacks by intimate partners are against women (Rennison, 2001).

Men are more likely than women to engage in repeated violence against their partners. Women are also more likely to experience serious physical injuries because they are usually smaller than their partners and more likely to use their fists rather than weapons. Pregnant women are especially vulnerable. Homicide ranks second, after auto accidents, as a leading cause of death for women during pregnancy or within one year after giving birth. Sexual and physical violence usually go hand in hand during pregnancy. Injury and death rates are especially high for unmarried women under age 20 who are black, poor, and have received no prenatal care (Chang et al., 2005; Koenig et al., 2006).

Most victims of intimate homicide are killed by their spouses (see *Figure 14.2*). Although homicide rates for husbands who were victims decreased by 75 percent, those for wives almost tripled between 1976 and 1995 (Puzone, 2000).

We'll examine why women's victimization rates are much higher than men's shortly. First, however, let's look at some of the characteristics of domestic violence.

Characteristics of Violent Households

Who batters? There is no "typical" batterer, but some characteristics are common to abusers (see *Table 14.1*). Some reflect macro-level influences, such as unemployment and poverty. Others are due to micro-level factors such as drug abuse. The more risk factors, the more likely the violent behavior.

In general, both male and female abusers tend to be young, poor, unemployed, divorced or separated, often

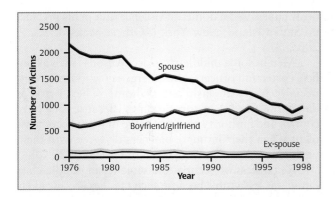

FIGURE 14.2 **Homicides of Intimates, by Relationship of Victim to Offender**

SOURCE: Rennison and Welchans, 2000: Figure 2.

use alcohol and other drugs, and may have observed a father or other male using violence to resolve conflicts. Typically, however, abusive relationships reflect a combination of these and other factors. They also vary across groups in terms of gender, age, marital status, race and ethnicity, social class, and status incompatibility.

since you asked

Is there *one* major reason for domestic violence?

GENDER Women are much more likely than men to experience domestic violence (see *Figure 14.1*). In violent crimes such as sexual assaults and assaults with a weapon, only 3 percent of those experienced by men, compared with 19 percent of those experienced by women, involve an intimate partner. In homicides, and across all racial-ethnic groups, women are almost twice as likely as men to be murdered by an intimate partner (Paulozzi et al., 2001; Catalano, 2004).

AGE In general, younger rather than older people are more likely to be the victims and perpetrators of domestic violence. Younger women generally experience higher rates of intimate partner violence than older women. For example, women ages 16 to 24 are the most likely to be abused by their intimate partners. In every age category, however, women are more likely than men to be murdered by an intimate partner. Among people ages 35 to 49, for instance, 38 percent of homicide victims are women compared with 6 percent of men (Rennison, 2001).

Teen mothers are especially likely to experience domestic violence for several years after a child's birth. Much of the violence probably results from financial responsibilities that the couple can't manage. As a result, there may be stress, conflict, and violence (Harrykissoon et al., 2002).

MARITAL STATUS Women who are separated from their husbands—especially women ages 20 to 34—experience higher violence rates than do married, divorced, widowed, or never-married women. The next-highest rate is for divorced women (Rennison, 2001).

Many separated and divorced women experience high rates of partner abuse because their husband or ex-husband is determined to control his partner, past or present. Men are also considerably more likely than women to commit "familicide." That is, they murder their wife and children before committing suicide. Although women kill their children, they rarely commit familicide (Websdale, 1999).

RACE AND ETHNICITY Across all racial-ethnic groups, domestic violence is directed more against women than men. Among females, American Indian women report

TABLE 14.1

Risk Factors Associated with Domestic Violence

- There are social-class differences, especially if the woman's education or income level is higher than the man's.
- The couple is cohabiting rather than married.
- The male partner is more likely to be the victim if his race or ethnicity differs from the woman's.
- The man is sadistic, aggressive, or obsessively jealous.
- The man has threatened, injured, or killed a family pet.
- One or both partners grew up seeing one parent hit the other.
- One or both partners is divorced and remarried or the current union is a common-law marriage.
- The man is unemployed and the woman is employed.
- The man is a high school dropout.
- The family's income is below the poverty line.
- The man is under age 30.
- Either or both partners abuse alcohol and other drugs.
- The man has assaulted someone outside the family or committed some other violent crime.
- The family is socially isolated from neighbors, relatives, and the community.

SOURCES: Bachman, 1994; Gelles, 1995; Hutchison, 1999; MacMillan and Gartner, 1999; Tjaden and Thoennes, 2000; Thompson et al., 2006.

the highest abuse rates (38 percent), and Asian American women report the lowest (15 percent) (see *Figure 14.3*).

Although national data are useful, they should be interpreted cautiously, for several reasons. First, there are still no data on domestic violence *within* ethnic-racial groups, such as possible variations within Latino and Asian American subgroups and American Indian tribes. Another problem is that the police are more likely to report domestic violence among blacks than similar violence among other groups. Third, and as you'll see shortly, recent immigrants are reluctant to report domestic violence. Finally, it's difficult to untangle the effects of race, ethnicity, and social class.

SOCIAL CLASS Although domestic violence cuts across all social classes, it is most common in low-income families. Women living in households with annual incomes less than $7,500 a year are nearly seven times more likely to be victimized by an intimate partner than women living in households with an annual income of at least $75,000 (Macomber, 2006).

The most likely abusers and victims are those who marry at a young age or who cohabit. Violence escalates if one or both partners abuse drugs, are unemployed, live in poverty, and have more children than they can afford to raise (DeMaris et al., 2003; Frias and Angel, 2005; Hill, 2005).

Violence does not occur only in low-income families, of course. A few years ago, for example, the authorities arrested a police lieutenant who had pressed his service revolver to the back of his wife's head, threatening to kill her. He was upset because his wife had come home with a regular cake instead of an ice cream cake for his 47th birthday. The lieutenant had previ-

ously supervised a domestic violence unit in his precinct on Staten Island, New York ("Officer accused. . . . ," 2005).

Men in some middle-class occupations (such as police, correction officers, and emergency workers) are especially likely to lash out at home. They work in dangerous or violent surroundings. Because they have control and authority at work, some of them become violent when their intimate partners disagree with them or don't meet their expectations (Melzer, 2002).

Regardless of occupation, violence in middle-class families is less visible because such families are less likely to live in crowded housing where neighbors call the police during fights. Moreover, their physicians are often reluctant to report domestic violence injuries to the police or social service agencies.

Husbands in higher socioeconomic families also abuse their wives. The attorney-husband of a 50-year-old Colorado woman appeared to be a pillar of the community. According to his wife of 28 years, however, he hit her, threw her down the stairs, and tried to run over her. "One night in Vail," she said, "when he had one of his insane fits, the police came and put him in handcuffs. . . . My arms were still red from where he'd trapped them in the car window, but somehow, he talked his way out of it" (Ingrassia and Beck, 1994: 29).

STATUS INCOMPATIBILITY According to resource theory, women with more assets (such as education) are more likely to have egalitarian relationships with their partners in decision making and to command more respect (see Chapters 10, 12, and 13). However, a growing number of studies report that status compatibility may be a more important factor in explaining partner violence.

When couples have *status compatibility*, they are fairly similar on variables such as education, income, and economic contributions to the household. In *status reversal*, women are higher than men on one or more such measures.

Status reversal often increases the likelihood that a woman will experience partner violence. When men have fewer economic resources than their wives, they may engage not in physical abuse but in emotional abuse (such as put-downs, threats of physical violence, and limiting the woman's movements). Especially when men have traditional views about gender roles and equate masculinity with being the primary breadwinner, they are more likely to use physical violence to compensate for their lack of income. In both types of situations, the men try to restore their control and dominance over their partner through emotional or physical abuse (Kaukinen, 2004; Atkinson et al., 2005).

There is some evidence, however, that the relationship between status incompatibility and domestic vio-

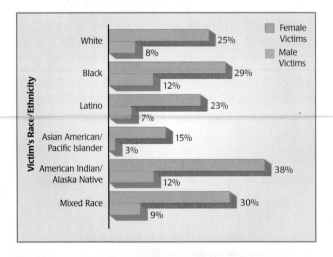

FIGURE 14.3 Percentage of People Victimized by an Intimate Partner in Lifetime, by Sex and Race/Ethnicity

SOURCE: Based on data in Tjaden and Thoennes, 2000: Exhibits 6 and 7.

lence varies by social class. For example, low-income, single, unmarried women who found jobs and left welfare reported less domestic abuse. The reasons may include having more bargaining power, less household stress and conflict over finances, less time spent with the abuser, and support from caseworkers who intervene in domestic violence (Gibson-Davis et al., 2005).

Marital Rape

Marital rape (sometimes also called *spousal rape* or *wife rape*) is an abusive act in which a man forces his wife to have unwanted sexual intercourse. Marital rape has been a crime in all states since 1993. However, 30 states grant a *marital rape exemption*. That is, they do not prosecute a rape case if the man is actually living with the woman (married or not) or if the wife is mentally or physically impaired, unconscious, or asleep during the act (Bergen, 2006).

Even in states that don't grant such exemptions, offenders are rarely prosecuted. A wife may have difficulty proving that a rape occurred if she shows no visible signs of having been forced, such as bruises or broken bones. Some husbands use physical force, but many rely on other forms of coercion such as threatening to leave or to cheat on a wife (Hines and Malley-Morrison, 2005).

Although an estimated 20 percent of women nationwide have been raped by their spouses or ex-spouses, very few report these crimes. A traditional wife, believing that she has no choice but to perform her "wifely duty," may accept the situation as normal, especially if her husband does not use a weapon or threaten her with physical harm (Michael et al., 1994; Tjaden and Thoennes, 2006).

The Cycle of Domestic Violence

Since 1978, state governors have granted clemency to more than 125 women who were convicted of killing their abusers. The women were pardoned based on the defense of **battered-woman syndrome,** a condition that describes a woman who has experienced many years of physical abuse and feels incapable of leaving her partner. In a desperate effort to defend themselves, such women sometimes kill the abuser.

The battered-woman syndrome is controversial because, some argue, abused women have the option of leaving the abusers instead of killing them. Others maintain that a "cycle theory of battering incidents" supports the battered-woman syndrome defense. According to this theory, a tension-building phase leads to an acute battering incident. This is followed by a period of calm until the cycle starts again (Walker, 1978, 2000).

PHASE ONE: THE TENSION-BUILDING PHASE In the first phase of the cycle, when "minor" battering incidents occur, the woman tries to reduce her partner's anger by catering to him or staying out of his way. At the same time, the battered woman often feels that her partner's abuse is justified: "When he throws the dinner she prepared for him across the kitchen floor, she reasons that maybe she did overcook it, accidentally. As she cleans up his mess, she may think that he was a bit extreme in his reaction, but she is usually so grateful that it was a relatively minor incident that she resolves not to be angry with him" (Walker, 1978: 147). Although the victim hopes that the situation will change, the tension typically escalates, the man becomes more brutal, and the woman is less able to defend herself.

PHASE TWO: THE ACUTE BATTERING INCIDENT Abusers often have a Dr. Jekyll and Mr. Hyde personality in which the rational and gentle Dr. Jekyll changes, unpredictably, into an unreasonable and brutal Mr. Hyde. In the second phase, Mr. Hyde emerges, exploding in rage and beating or otherwise abusing his partner. Thus, the woman's feelings fluctuate:

> . . . I have two responses to Stu because I am responding to two different people, or two different parts of one person. There's the Stu who is very thoughtful and gentle and kind, and then there's the brutal and hostile Stu (Strasser, 2004: 210).

Some women who have lived with abuse for a long time actually anticipate this phase and trigger the violent incident to get it over with. They often deny the severity of their injuries and refuse to seek medical treatment. One woman who wanted to go to a family party with her husband and sensed that an acute battering incident was about to occur deliberately provoked it during the week so that by the weekend her husband would be pleasant for the party (Walker, 1978).

PHASE THREE: CALM (THE "HONEYMOON PHASE") Mr. Hyde becomes the kindly Dr. Jekyll in the third phase, begging the woman's forgiveness and promising that he will never beat her again: "He manages to convince all concerned that this time he means it; he will give up drinking, seeing other women, visiting his mother, or whatever else affects his internal anxiety state. His sincerity is believable" (Walker, 1978: 152).

If the victim has been hospitalized because of her physical injuries, the man often deluges her with flowers, candy, cards, and gifts. He may also get his mother, father, sisters, brothers, and other relatives to plead his case to her. They build up her guilt by telling her that he would be devastated if she left him and that a father should not be separated from his children. Because most

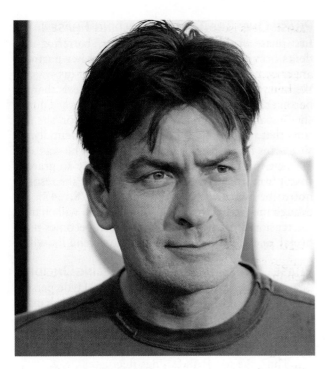

Actor Charlie Sheen pleaded "no contest" to physically abusing his former girlfriend. He received two years probation, must pay $2,800 in fines and restitution, attend counseling sessions, and perform 300 hours of community service.

battered women hold traditional values about love and marriage, the wife convinces herself that *this* time he'll *really* change.

Because he is now loving and kind, the battered woman believes that "the good man," the one she loves, will honor his tearful promises to change. After a while, the calm and loving behavior gives way to battering incidents, and the cycle starts all over again, often including marital rape.

Why Do Women Stay?

Walker theorized that the cycle of violence results in *learned helplessness:* The woman becomes depressed, loses her self-esteem, and feels incapable of seeking help or escaping the abusive rela-

since you asked

Why do many battered women stay with their partners?

tionship. It's not clear whether these characteristics reflect personality traits that battered women possessed before they met the abusers, whether they are the result of the abuse, or whether they are a combination of both (Rathus and O'Leary, 1997).

Still, the obvious question is "Why do these women stay?" Despite the common tendency to think of abused

women as passive punching bags, 87 percent of abused wives and female partners seek help at medical facilities, including hospital emergency rooms. Many rely on family, friends, and shelters to leave the batterers safely and permanently (Goetting, 1999; Tjaden and Thoennes, 2000).

Some women, like one of my students, find the courage to leave only when they suddenly realize that the abusive relationship is harming their children:

> *John never laid a finger on our daughter but struck me in front of her. . . . I cringe to remember but at the time I chose to believe that what Sheri saw wasn't affecting her. One afternoon when I heard Sheri banging and yelling, I rushed to her room. . . . Sheri was hitting her doll and screaming four-letter words she often heard her father yell at me. She was just starting to talk, and that was what she was learning. That moment changed our lives forever. . . . I left John that night and never went back (Author's files).*

There is no single reason why some women don't leave violent relationships. Instead, there are multiple and overlapping explanations.

NEGATIVE SELF-CONCEPT AND LOW SELF-ESTEEM

Most batterers convince their partners that they are worthless, stupid, and disgusting: "Behind a closed door, a man calls a woman a 'slut' and a 'whore.' He tells her that she is too fat, too sexy or too frumpy, that she is 'a poor excuse for a mother,' a worthless piece of dirt" (Goode et al., 1994: 24).

Such tyranny is effective because in many cultures a woman's self-worth still hinges on having a man. Sometimes women are willing to pay any price to hold on to the relationship because they believe that no one else could love them.

BELIEF THAT THE ABUSER WILL CHANGE One

woman, her cheek still raw from her husband's beating, said, "I'm still in love with him, and I know he's going to change as soon as he gets past these things that are troubling him."

Our society has long nurtured the myth that women are responsible for changing men into kind and loving beings. Consider the message in the popular Walt Disney film *Beauty and the Beast.* The woman is taken captive and isolated from her friends and family. The Beast turns into a prince only after Beauty stays with him and says that she loves him despite his cruelty, threats, breaking furniture, and acting like a beast.

Many women stay in violent relationships because they are seduced by the Cinderella fantasy. The woman believes that, sooner or later, the abuser will change and she and Prince Charming will "live happily ever after." As a result, millions of women stay in an abusive relationship because they hope to "rehabilitate" the man rather than break up the family (Sontag, 2002).

A college professor remained married to a batterer for 12 years because she believed that her husband would eventually change back to being "a good man": "Before we married, my husband seemed to be the perfect man—kind, gentle, romantic, admiring of me and my academic successes." She clung to this illusion for over a decade even though the battering began three weeks after they married, when she learned that she was pregnant (Bates, 2005: C1).

ECONOMIC HARDSHIP AND HOMELESSNESS Because many abused women do not work outside the home or have few marketable skills, they see no way to survive economically if they leave the abuser. For example, an award-winning high school coach in Baltimore stabbed his wife 10 times with a screwdriver, leaving her partially paralyzed. The wife pleaded with the judge *not* to send the husband to jail. Ironically, she wanted him to keep working so his health insurance could pay for treating her injuries; she had worked part time and had no medical benefits (Shatzkin, 1996).

Many batterers keep their wives in economic chains. Nothing is in the woman's name—not checking or savings accounts, automobiles, or homes. Because most abusers isolate their victims from friends and relatives, the women have no one to turn to. Moreover, those who might give battered women a place to stay are afraid that they might endanger their own family. Without resources, some abused women who do leave become homeless (Browne, 1993; Choice and Lamke, 1997).

Women often have nowhere to go. Hundreds are turned away from shelters for battered women every day because of overcrowding and underfunding. In Missouri, for example, almost 4,300 women were turned away from shelters in 2004 alone because there was not enough space (Gonnerman, 2005).

NEED FOR CHILD SUPPORT Leaving a man or filing charges against him may push a woman and her children into poverty. Many women believe that even an abusive husband (and father) is better than none. As one of my students, a former abused wife who eventually left her husband, once said in class, "This man brings in most of the family's income. Without him, you can't pay the rent, buy the groceries, or pay the electric bills. If he goes to jail, he'll probably lose his job. And then what will you and the kids do?"

SENSE OF SHAME OR GUILT Strong cultural factors may also keep a woman from leaving an abuser. In some Asian American communities, especially, there is strong pressure not to bring shame or disgrace on the family by exposing problems such as domestic violence. Women in rural areas are especially isolated: There are no shelters, their wages range from $5.15 to $6.95 an hour, and the women are afraid that disclosing abuse to co-workers or supervisors will bring gossip and shame on the family (Swanberg and Logan, 2003).

BLAMING THEMSELVES Battered women often feel that somehow they have brought the violence on themselves. Men who batter may be well-respected professional athletes, community leaders, or attorneys. The women start thinking that because the men have a "good" reputation, it must be their fault when the men are abusive at home (Parameswaran, 2003).

This is particularly likely if women have seen their mothers

The Clothespin Project, a program started in Cape Cod, Massachusetts, in 1990, is a way for women affected by violence to express their emotions and remember those who have been murdered. The concept is simple: "Let each woman tell her own story and hang it out for all to see. It's a way of airing society's dirty laundry."

or grandmothers suffer similar treatment: "One woman whose bruises from her husband's beatings were clearly visible was told by her grandmother, 'You have to stop provoking him. You have two children, and the bottom line is you have nowhere to go. If he tells you to shut up, shut up!'" (Goode et al., 1994: 27).

Thus, a tradition is passed on. Women feel they are responsible for preventing male violence, and if they don't succeed, they believe that they must accept the consequences. Moreover, because some priests, ministers, and rabbis remind a woman that she is married "for better or for worse," religious women may feel guilty and sinful for wanting to leave (Jones, 1993; Hines and Malley-Morrison, 2005).

FEAR Fear is a *major* reason for staying in an abusive relationship. Some men threaten to kill the woman, her relatives, and even the children if the woman tries to escape. Several directors of battered women's shelters have told me that it is not unusual for husbands to track down their families from as far away as 1,000 miles and threaten violence to get them to return.

Even when women go to court to protect themselves, they may find that the judge does not take domestic violence seriously. Consider this courtroom experience:

> [The judge] took a few minutes to decide on the matter. . . . He said, "I don't believe anything that you're saying . . . because I don't believe that anything like this could happen to me. If I was you and someone had threatened me with a gun, there is no way that I would continue to stay with them. . . . Therefore, since I would not let that happen to me, I can't believe that it happened to you." When I left the courtroom that day, I felt very defeated, very defenseless, very powerless, and very hopeless (Maryland Special Joint Committee, 1989: 3).

Such reactions are not as dated as you might think. Some judges take domestic violence seriously, but others still view it as little more than "marital spats" (Ptacek, 1999).

THE HOME BECOMES A PRISON Both emotional and physical abuse trap the battered woman in her home.

Applying What You've Learned

Some Warning Signs of Domestic Violence

There are numerous clues to the potential for violence before it actually occurs. How many of these "red flags" do you recognize in your or your friends' relationships?

■ *Verbal abuse:* Constant criticism, ignoring what you are saying, mocking, name-calling, yelling, and swearing.

■ *Sexual abuse:* Forcing or demanding sexual acts that you don't want to perform.

■ *Disrespect:* Interrupting, telling you what you should think and how you should feel, putting you down in front of other people, saying ugly things about your friends and family.

■ *Isolation:* Trying to cut you off from family and friends, monitoring your phone calls, reading your mail or e-mail, controlling where you go, taking your car keys and cell phone.

■ *Emotional withholding or neglect:* Not expressing feelings, not giving compliments, not respecting your feelings and opinions.

■ *Jealousy:* Very possessive, calling constantly or visiting unexpectedly, checking the mileage on your car, doesn't want you to work because "you might meet someone."

■ *Unrealistic expectations:* Expecting you to be the perfect mate and meet his or her every need.

■ *Blaming others for problems:* It's *always* someone else's fault if something goes wrong.

■ *Rigid sex roles:* Expecting you to serve, obey, and always stay home.

■ *Extreme mood swings:* Switching from sweet to violent in minutes or being very kind one day and very vicious the next.

■ *Cruelty to animals and children:* Killing or punishing pets brutally. May expect children to do things that are far beyond their ability or tease them until they cry.

■ *Threats of violence:* Saying things like "I'll break your neck" and then dismissing them with "I didn't really mean it" or "Everybody talks like that."

■ *Destruction of property:* Destroying furniture, punching walls or doors, throwing things, breaking dishes or other household articles.

■ *Self-destructive behavior:* Abusing drugs or alcohol, threatening self-harm or suicide, getting into fights with people, causing problems at work (such as telling off the boss).

With little chance of escaping, the victim becomes a prisoner. The man is the ultimate authority, and she is punished if she disagrees with him. She must follow his "house rules" about not leaving the house or even making phone calls without his permission. In some cases, he takes the phone with him when he leaves for work. She has no control over her body, is isolated from her friends and relatives, and is watched constantly (Avni, 1991; Gonnerman, 2005).

All these factors help explain why many women stay in abusive relationships: "Staying may mean abuse and violence, but leaving may mean death. A bureaucracy may promise safety, but cannot ensure it. For many battered women, this is a risk they cannot take" (Englander, 1997: 149–50).

Domestic violence takes different forms, but the goal is always the same: control of the partner through fear and intimidation. The box "Some Warning Signs of Domestic Violence" provides clues to potential problems.

Women Who Abuse Men

In 2003, a highly publicized case drew attention to violence by women against men. A jury in Houston, Texas, sentenced a 45-year-old dentist to 20 years in prison for killing her husband, an orthodontist. The wife ran over her husband several times with her Mercedes-Benz after finding him with his mistress, a former receptionist. The case received prominent national attention because the incident involved an upper-middle-class couple.

Some researchers and journalists have argued that women hit men as often as men hit women and that husband abuse is the most underreported form of marital violence. Even unmarried male victims, these writers contend, are reluctant to report assaults by their intimate partners (Steinmetz, 1978; Pearson, 1997; Felson and Paré, 2005).

Why are men less likely than women to report domestic violence? Many men, like women, think that assaults by an intimate partner are not a crime compared with assaults by strangers. Men may also be embarrassed about reporting domestic violence. According to some male victims, "society simply doesn't take the issue seriously . . . and men who claim such abuse are deemed wimps and laughed at" (Hastings, 1994: 1D; Felson and Paré, 2005).

Others maintain that focusing on male victims diminishes women's abuse. For example, women are 10 times more likely than men to be injured in domestic violence cases. Especially among married couples, assaults by husbands on wives are more frequent than assaults by wives on husbands (Gelles, 1997; Felson and Cares, 2005). In addition, battered men are less likely to be trapped in a relationship than are battered women because they have more economic resources. It's also easier for men to walk out of an abusive situation because, typically, women feel responsible for the children.

Even when the abuse is mutual, the outcomes are different. Although intimate partner violence has negative health consequences for women and men, women are much more likely than men to experience depression and substance abuse (Anderson, 2002). Moreover, partner violence often spills over into violence against children.

Making Connections

- Are learned helplessness and the battered-woman syndrome contradictory? That is, if a woman feels too beaten down to leave an abusive situation, why does she kill the batterer or hire someone else to do so?

- Look, again, at the "Applying What You've Learned" box on p. 428. Do any of these characteristics reflect your current relationship with an intimate partner? If so, what are you going to do about it?

Child Maltreatment

A few years ago, Andrea Yates, a suburban homemaker in Houston, Texas, filled the bathtub and drowned each of her five children, who ranged in age from 6 months

In 2001, Andrea Yates, a former high school valedictorian, nurse, and then full-time homemaker admitted drowning her five children in a bathtub. In her retrial in 2006, pictured here, the jury found her guilty by reason of insanity which means that she won't be executed under Texas law.

to 7 years: "It took a bit of work for her to chase down the last of the children; toward the end, she had a scuffle in the family room, sliding round on wet tile" (Roche, 2002: 44).

Abuse and killing of children is not a recent phenomenon. Among the Puritans, women were instructed to protect children "if a man is dangerously cruel with his children in that he would harm either body or spirit" (Andelin, 1974: 52). And men were not the only offenders: In 1638, Dorothy Talbie "was hanged at Boston for murdering her own daughter, a child of 3 years old" (Demos, 1986: 79).

In 1946, after observing unexplained fractures in children he had seen over the years, pediatric radiologist John Caffey suggested that the children had been abused. And in what may have been the first formal paper on the subject, in 1962 physician C. Henry Kempe and his colleagues published an article on the battered-child syndrome in the *Journal of the American Medical Association*. Nevertheless, only in recent years has child abuse become a major public issue.

What Is Child Maltreatment?

Child maltreatment includes a broad range of behaviors that place a child at serious risk or result in serious harm, including physical abuse, sexual abuse, neglect, and emotional abuse. This term involves either acts or failure to act responsibly by a biological parent, stepparent, foster parent, adoptive parent, caregiver, or other person who is supposed to care for a child. (I sometimes use the older term, **child abuse**, interchangeably with *child maltreatment*.)

since you asked

Is physical abuse more harmful than emotional abuse?

PHYSICAL ABUSE *Physical abuse,* one type of maltreatment that causes bodily injury to a child, includes beating with the hands or an object, scalding, and severe physical punishments. In a rare form of physical abuse called *Munchausen syndrome by proxy,* an adult (usually a white, middle-class mother who is knowledgeable about medicine or nursing) feigns or induces illness in a child to attract medical attention and support for herself and her child. Her motives include wanting to be the center of attention, trying to obtain tangible rewards such as money or charitable donations, and hoping to get her husband's attention. The mother may be needy and lonely or may have a mental problem (Rosenberg, 1997; Parnell and Day, 1998).

SEXUAL ABUSE *Sexual abuse* is a type of maltreatment that involves the child in sexual activity to provide sexual gratification or financial benefit to the perpetrator. Sexual abuse includes making a child watch sexual acts, fondling a child's genitals, prostitution, statutory rape (having sexual intercourse with a minor), forcing a child to engage in sexual acts for photographic or filmed pornography, and incest. This category also includes sexual assault on a child by a relative or stranger.

NEGLECT *Neglect* is failure by a parent or other caregiver to provide a child with life's basic necessities. In *medical neglect,* the caregiver doesn't provide the appropriate health care that will ensure the child's healthy development.

Most recently, some clinicians have included stimulation neglect and language neglect under the umbrella of child neglect. In *stimulation neglect,* parents don't cuddle and talk to their babies, don't take their children to the park (or other recreational spots), and don't play with or engage in activities that nourish the child's cognitive development (Cantwell, 1997).

Language neglect discourages the development of the child's communication skills, such as ignoring an infant's babbling, not reading to a child, and commanding young children ("Put this here" or "Don't do that") instead of conversing with the child and eliciting a response ("Where do you think we should hang this picture?") (Oates and Kempe, 1997). Neglectful caretakers are usually the child's parents but may also include people in residential centers for children or foster-care homes.

EMOTIONAL ABUSE *Emotional abuse,* sometimes referred to as *psychological maltreatment,* conveys to children that they are inferior, worthless, unloved, or unwanted. Verbal abusers devalue and reject their children with constant criticism, put-downs, and sarcasm (Briere, 1992; Brassard and Hardy, 1997).

More specifically, emotional maltreatment includes *spurning* (rejecting the child verbally and nonverbally), *terrorizing* (threatening to hurt, kill, or abandon the child), *isolating* (denying the child opportunities to interact with peers or adults inside or outside the home), and *exploiting* or *corrupting* (being a poor role model and permitting or encouraging a child's antisocial behavior) (Hart et al., 2003).

There are other forms of emotional abuse: parents who focus on their own problems and ignore those of their children, who use guilt and other manipulations to control children's lives, who subject children to unpredictable mood swings due to alcoholism and other drug abuse, and who frequently demand that children assume adult caretaking responsibilities (Forward, 1990; see, also, Chapter 17).

Here, Oprah Winfrey, one of the world's richest and most influential women, launches O: The Oprah Magazine, *one of her many successful enterprises. When she was nine years old, Winfrey's 19-year-old cousin started to molest her sexually. At age 14, she gave birth to a premature baby who died shortly after birth. Winfrey says that she was too confused and afraid to report the sexual abuse.*

Prevalence and Characteristics of Child Maltreatment

A few years ago, the Tampa, Florida, police arrested a mother and her boyfriend for locking up the woman's 7-year-old daughter in a room. They gave the girl so little food that she looked like a "walking skeleton." She weighed just 25 pounds, less than half the normal weight for a child her age ("Florida couple . . . ," 2002).

Rates of child maltreatment have decreased (see "Data Digest"), but there were about 872,000 confirmed cases in 2004. Because only a fraction of the total number of child victimizations is reported, it can be assumed that millions of American children experience abuse and neglect on a daily basis (U.S. Department of Health and Human Services, 2006).

What are some of the characteristics of the victims and offenders? And how many child maltreatment cases are fatal? Let's begin with the victims.

VICTIMS Although a child is often a victim of more than one type of maltreatment, the most common form of abuse is neglect (see *Figure 14.4*). From birth to age 18, girls (52 percent) are slightly more likely than boys (48 percent) to be neglected. Although children less than 1 year old account for 10 percent of all victims, victimization rates decrease as a child grows older (U.S. Department of Health and Human Services, 2006).

The rates decline not necessarily because maltreatment decreases, but for a variety of other reasons. For example, older children suffer injuries that medical personnel may not catch, neighbors and teachers are less likely to be attuned to and to report neglect, and caretakers may threaten children to be silent about abuse and neglect because "it's nobody else's business."

Victimization rates by race and ethnicity range from 2.9 per 1,000 children for Asian Americans to 19.9 per 1,000 for African Americans (see *Figure 14.5*). Overall, however, almost 54 percent of all victims are white, 25 are percent black, 17 percent are Latino, and 4 percent are Asian Americans, Pacific Islanders, or American Indians or Alaska Natives (U.S. Department of Health and Human Services, 2006). That is, child maltreatment percentages are highest among whites, but a disproportionate share of reported cases involves minority groups.

Although these differences among various groups are large, there is some evidence that reporting of child

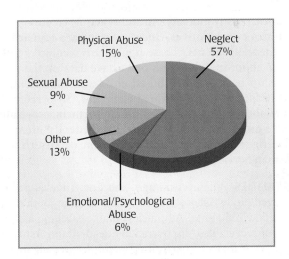

FIGURE 14.4 Types of Child Maltreatment: 2004
"Neglect" includes medical neglect (about 2 percent of these cases). "Other" includes abandonment, threats of harm to the child, and babies who are born drug-addicted.

SOURCE: Based on U.S. Department of Health and Human Services, 2006, Table 3-6.

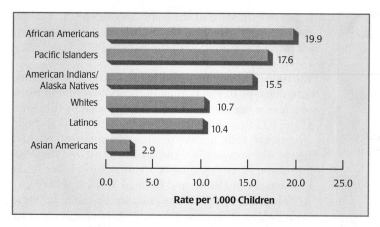

FIGURE 14.5 Child Victimization Rates, by Race/Ethnicity

SOURCE: U.S. Department of Health and Human Services, 2006, Figure 3-5.

abuse may be more common in poor and black families. In contrast, abuse in white, middle-class families is often underreported. According to a study of children under age 3, for example, doctors were twice as likely to miss evidence of abuse in children from white, two-parent families as in children from minority, single-parent families. The researchers attributed the misdiagnoses to physicians' lack of training (such as recognizing head traumas) and especially to discomfort about casting suspicion on parents who seem to be "solid citizens" (Ards et al., 1998; Jenny et al., 1999).

PERPETRATORS About 79 percent of people who abuse children are parents. A majority (58 percent) are women, mostly mothers. An additional 7 percent of perpetrators are relatives, and 4 percent are unmarried partners of parents. These figures are incomplete because about half the states don't have data on the relationship between the abused child and the offender. According to other national estimates, 38 percent of child abusers are women's intimate partners, especially white men in their mid- to late 20s (Federal Bureau of Investigation, 2004; U.S. Department of Health and Human Services, 2006).

FATALITIES A few years ago, the Los Angeles police charged Holly Ashcroft, 21, a college student, with murder and child abuse. A homeless man, searching a trash bin for recyclables, discovered her dead infant. Ashcroft had given birth to her full-term son by herself in her off-campus apartment. She then put him in a cardboard box and left him to die (Trounson and Wride, 2005).

Homicide is the leading cause of death among infants and the rates have almost doubled since 1970. Of the 993 children who died of abuse in 2004, 45 percent were under age one. Each day about four children die

because of maltreatment (Peddle et al., 2002; U.S. Department of Health and Human Services, 2006).

The Ashcroft case attracted national attention, probably because the offender was white and middle class, had delivered the baby by herself, and none of her college friends or family knew that she was pregnant. In contrast, most mothers who kill their infants are unmarried teenagers, Latinas or black women, have dropped out of high school, already have one or more children, and have a history of mental illness ("Infant homicide," 2003).

About 79 percent of child deaths are caused by one or both of the child's parents. Almost one-third of the offenders are mothers acting alone (see *Figure 14.6*). The first two months of an infant's life are usually the most deadly. A young mother may know little about parenting and be unable to cope with the constant crying of a normal infant. As one of my students said, "My daughter had colic and she cried all night long for three months. I thought I'd go crazy." Mothers often kill their children during infancy, whereas fathers are more likely to murder children age 8 and older (Greenfeld and Snell, 1999; Paulozzi and Sells, 2002).

It's not clear why fathers are more likely than mothers to kill older children. Although there are no national data, the higher rates of these murders may result from men's greater likelihood, as discussed earlier, of killing the entire family—including a wife, ex-wife, or girlfriend—before committing suicide or fleeing prosecution.

Many researchers maintain that "official" child victimization rates are far too low. For example, a study of homicide records for children age 10 and younger in North Carolina found that the number of children who died at the hands of parents or other caregivers was un-

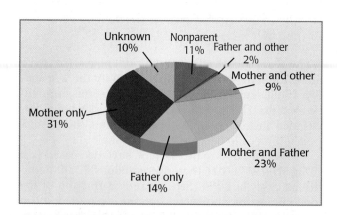

FIGURE 14.6 Who Kills Children?

SOURCE: U.S. Department of Health and Human Services, 2006: Figure 4-2.

derreported by nearly 60 percent. The numbers of child deaths from maltreatment may be four times higher than those reported every year (Herman-Giddens et al., 1999; "Child fatalities fact sheet," 2000).

Sexual Abuse and Incest

Sexual abuse makes up 9 percent of child maltreatment cases. Nearly three-quarters of the abusers are family members, friends, or neighbors (U.S. Department of Health and Human Services, 2006).

Like those for other child maltreatment, sexual abuse rates are much higher than those reported to law enforcement agencies and child protective services. Nationally, 8 percent of all adults say that they were sexually abused as children. A study of southwestern American Indians found that 49 percent of females and 14 percent of males had experienced childhood sexual abuse, mostly by family members and relatives. A study of Latinas in Los Angeles County found that 33 percent of respondents had experienced sexual abuse before age 18. Of the alleged perpetrators, 96 percent were male, and more than 50 percent were family members (Robin et al., 1997; Romero and Wyatt, 1999; Zielinski, 2005).

Sodomy, sexual assaults with objects, forcible fondling, and incest affect up to 8 percent of children age 12 and younger. Most of these crimes are committed by parents or adult family members. Nationally, an estimated 21 percent of adolescents who run away from home do so to escape sexual abuse (Finkelhor and Ormrod, 2000; Hammer et al., 2002).

Most cases of reported incest are between fathers and daughters or stepfathers and stepdaughters. The rarest forms of sexual abuse, estimated to account for 1 percent of all cases, are between sons and fathers and sons and mothers (Masters et al., 1992).

The incest taboo, which forbids sexual intercourse between close blood relatives, is a cultural norm in almost all known societies (see Chapter 1). In the United States, *incest* is defined by law as sexual intercourse or marriage between nuclear family members, as well as between uncles and nieces, aunts and nephews, grandparents and grandchildren, and often, first cousins and half-siblings. Some of my former students, who are now social workers in isolated rural areas, say that incest is "much more common than people think." The abuse is difficult to prove, however, because the children are afraid to talk to anyone about the experience. One of the results of underreporting is that many people refuse to believe that incest is a serious problem (see the box "Myths and Facts about Incest").

Although the personality traits of people who commit incest vary greatly, offenders share some common characteristics. Sexual offenders often have low self-esteem and lack self-control. Incest offenders are usually "narcissistic, uninhibited men who believe that their own sexual impulses must be fulfilled" (Hanson et al., 1994: 197).

Typically, a man who abuses his child or children starts doing so when the child is between 8 and 12 years old, although in some cases the child is still in diapers. The father may select only one child (usually the oldest daughter) as his victim, but it is common for several daughters to be victimized, either sequentially or simultaneously over the years.

Many incestuous men convince their daughters that the attacks are really expressions of affection ("This is how daddies show their love"). Others intimidate their victims with promises of physical retaliation against the victim and other family members. They threaten that they will be arrested or the family will break up if the incest is reported. Children remain silent out of fear and guilt because they feel that they are somehow responsible for the abuse. According to some researchers, as long as children are nurtured almost exclusively by women, men are likely to view their children—especially daughters—as sexual objects rather than as their flesh and blood to be cared for and protected (M. T. Erickson, 1993).

Because most women trust their partners, a mother may blame incest on the onset of adolescence or a response to other difficulties, such as school problems or peer interactions. One mother, for example, interpreted her 4-year-old daughter's resistance to the mother's going to work as resentment rather than as fear of being left alone with her sexually abusive father. Other mothers may suspect incest but not intervene because they themselves are battered, have extremely low self-esteem, or suffer from mental illness (Jacobs, 1990; Elbow and Mayfield, 1991).

Why Do Adults Abuse Children?

There are many reasons for child maltreatment. Some of the most important are substance abuse, family size, poverty, partner abuse, and divorce.

SUBSTANCE ABUSE A number of studies have linked child abuse with the parents' substance abuse. Children whose parents abuse alcohol and other drugs are three times more likely to be abused and almost five times more likely to be neglected ("Child welfare and chemical dependency . . . ," 2001).

Alcohol-abusing parents usually have poor ing skills: They typically don't give their childr tional support or monitor them. As a result, th haven't learned social control, lack social

Constraints

Myths and Facts about Incest

Forcing, coercing, or cajoling a child into an incestuous relationship is one of the most devastating things an adult can do to a child. Even when family members are aware of incestuous behavior in the family, most neither report it nor try to stop it. Why? Because they believe in myths like the following:

■ *Myth:* Children lie about incest.

■ *Fact:* Children rarely lie about incest. Most are too young to know the significance of the sexually exploitative acts they describe.

■ *Myth:* Children fantasize about incest. Every daughter fantasizes a romantic relationship with her father; every son imagines a romantic relationship with his mother.

■ *Fact:* A child wants and needs love and caring from a parent, not sexual intimacy.

■ *Myth:* If a child is not coerced, it is not incest.

■ *Fact:* Regardless of whether a child has been verbally seduced or violently raped, incest is a crime.

■ *Myth:* If a child experiences pleasurable feelings during the encounter, the incest isn't harmful.

■ *Fact:* A child's physiological excitement as an automatic response to sexual manipulation is one of the most damaging effects of incest. It can cause confusion and feelings of guilt or complicity.

■ *Myth:* The younger the victim, the less traumatic the incest.

■ *Fact:* Incest is traumatic at *any* age. People who recall incestuous experiences vividly describe feelings of pain and humiliation.

■ *Myth:* Incest happens only in poor, disorganized, or unstable families.

■ *Fact:* Incest is more likely to be discovered in poor, disorganized, or unstable families because these families often come to the attention of social service agencies. Incest also occurs in many seemingly "normal" middle-class families.

■ *Myth:* Fathers turn to their daughters for warmth and nurturance that have been denied them by their wives.

■ *Fact:* The majority of men who are guilty of incest have received plenty of nurturance from their mothers, wives, and other women.

■ *Myth:* Incest is usually punished by incarceration.

■ *Fact:* Perpetrators are rarely charged or imprisoned, largely because a child's testimony is seldom accepted as evidence of incest. In addition, solid physical evidence is rarely available because the event is not reported and investigated quickly enough.

■ *Myth:* A child can be seductive and thus is often responsible for the adult's sexual arousal.

■ *Fact:* Children are *never* responsible for adults' sexual arousal or physical assaults.

SOURCES: Tamarack, 1986; Faller, 1990; Adams et al., 1994; Wilson, 2006.

---

often begin using alcohol themselves at an early age ("Alcohol and health," 2000).

FAMILY SIZE Children from larger families (with four or more children) often experience more abuse and neglect than do children from smaller families. Additional children, especially closely spaced children in large families, result in additional tasks and responsibilities and more worry about finances (Belsky, 1993).

POVERTY Most abusive homes are experiencing economic stress and poverty. Children from families with annual incomes under $15,000 are 26 times more likely than children from families with annual incomes above $30,000 to be abused or neglected. Low-income teen

mothers may be more abusive than older mothers because of a variety of factors such as substance abuse, inadequate information about a child's developmental needs, and poor parenting skills (Gaudin et al., 1996; U.S. Department of Health and Human Services, 1996).

PARTNER ABUSE Child maltreatment is also more common in homes in which the woman is abused. The greater the amount of violence toward a partner, the greater the probability of child abuse, especially by the male. Noting that 70 percent of wife beaters also physically abuse their children, Kurz (1993) posits that family violence, including child maltreatment, is a direct outcome of men's attempts to maintain control over the powerless members of the family—women and children.

DIVORCE The period just after divorce may make child maltreatment more likely because parental conflict and family tension are high. For example, the custodial parent may be changing residences, working longer hours, and experiencing more turmoil. Parents who are already stressed may react abusively to infants who, also affected by the parents' emotional state, become more irritable and harder to soothe (see Chapters 12 and 15).

A COMBINATION OF FACTORS Generally, child maltreatment reflects a combination of variables. For example, infant maltreatment rates are seven times higher than the average for the general population when families have a number of risk factors, including poverty, the infant's low birth weight (which requires more caretaking), more than two siblings, and an unmarried mother (Wu et al., 2004).

Thus, even if parents insist that they love their children, love isn't enough. Whether the reasons are micro, macro, or a combination, child abuse has a very negative impact on children's lives.

How Abuse Affects Children

Some children manage to survive and do well despite growing up in abusive homes. Most, however, suffer the costs of domestic violence over the course of a lifetime.

Children who survive severe violence are often left with brain injuries. Infants who are shaken violently may suffer intracranial (within the brain) bleeding.

Abused infants may have feeding and sleeping disorders, fail to thrive, or exhibit persistent lethargy, hyperactivity, or irritability. And children who are neglected may experience poor physical growth, including underdevelopment of the brain and problems in intellectual and speech development (Anda et al., 2001; Kernic et al., 2002).

Whether abuse is physical, emotional, or sexual, children often suffer from a variety of physiological, social, and emotional problems, including headaches, bedwetting, chronic constipation, difficulty communicating, learning disabilities, poor performance in school, and a variety of mental disorders. Children from violent families are often more aggressive than children from nonviolent families. Maltreatment doubles the probability of engaging in many types of crimes. Being abused or neglected as a child increases the likelihood of arrest as a juvenile by 59 percent, as an adult by 28 percent, and for a violent crime by 30 percent (Widom and Maxfield, 2001; Currie and Tekin, 2006).

Adolescents who experience maltreatment are more likely than their nonabused counterparts to engage in early sexual activity, have unintended pregnancies, suffer emotional and eating disorders, abuse alcohol and other drugs, and engage in delinquent behavior. In adulthood, abused children are twice as likely to be unemployed and in welfare programs. They are also more likely to be violent with their intimate partners (Ehrensaft et al., 2003; Zielinski, 2005).

Childhood experiences of abuse and neglect are linked with serious life-long problems. For example, the victims are at least five times more likely to experience

Hedda Nussbaum was the live-in lover of criminal attorney Joel Steinberg when he "adopted" infant Lisa (left). Six years later, battered beyond recognition by her "lover" (center), Hedda witnessed his arraignment for the murder of Lisa, whom he had begun to abuse as well. Doctors, teachers, and neighbors had noticed Lisa's bruises but did nothing. Late in 1987, Steinberg hit Lisa and left her lying on the floor, comatose. Lisa died three days later. Steinberg was convicted and jailed. Nussbaum, judged incapable of either harming or helping Lisa, began slowly to rebuild her life. She now spends much of her time giving lectures about the need to help battered women (right).

TABLE 14.2

Signs of Child Abuse

	Physical Signs	Behavioral Signs
Physical Abuse	• Unexplained bruises (in various stages of healing), welts, human bite marks, bald spots • Unexplained burns, especially cigarette burns or immersion burns • Unexplained fractures, lacerations, or abrasions	• Acts self-destructively • Withdrawn and aggressive, displays behavioral extremes • Arrives at school early or stays late, as if afraid to be at home • Is uncomfortable with physical contact • Displays chronic runaway behavior (adolescents) • Complains of soreness or moves uncomfortably • Wears inappropriate clothing to cover bruises
Physical Neglect	• Abandonment • Unattended medical needs • Lack of parental supervision • Consistent hunger, inappropriate dress, poor hygiene • Lice, distended stomach, emaciation	• Fatigue, listlessness, falling asleep • Steals food, begs from classmates • Reports that no caretaker is at home • Frequently absent or tardy • School dropout (adolescents)
Sexual Abuse	• Torn, stained, or bloody underclothing • Pain or itching in genital area • Difficulty walking or sitting • Bruises or bleeding from external genitalia • Sexually transmitted disease • Frequent urinary or yeast infections	• Withdraws or is chronically depressed • Is excessively seductive • Role reversal; overly concerned about siblings • Displays lack of self-esteem • Experiences drastic weight gain or loss • Displays hysteria or lack of emotional control • Has sudden school difficulties • Exhibits sex play or premature understanding of sex • Threatened by closeness, problems with peers • Is promiscuous • Attempts suicide (especially adolescents)
Emotional Maltreatment	• Speech disorders • Delayed physical development • Substance abuse • Ulcers, asthma, severe allergies	• Exhibits habit disorders (sucking, rocking) • Antisocial; is responsible for destructive acts • Displays neurotic traits (sleep disorders, inhibition of play) • Swings between passive and aggressive behaviors • Exhibits delinquent behavior (especially adolescents) • Exhibits developmental delay

SOURCE: Based on American Humane Association, 2001.

depression and 12 times more likely to attempt suicide. Physically abused adolescents are 12 times more likely to have alcohol and drug problems, and sexually abused adolescents are 21 times more likely to become substance abusers. As many as two-thirds of people in drug treatment programs report that they were abused as children (Putnam, 2006).

Incestuous relationships in childhood often lead to mistrust, fear of intimacy, and sexual dysfunctions in adulthood. *Table 14.2* summarizes some of the physical and behavioral signs that a child is being abused and needs protection.

Making Connections

■ Some people feel that emotional maltreatment—for both children and adults—is less harmful than physical abuse. Do you agree?

■ When child neglect occurs in lower socioeconomic families, are we, in effect, "blaming the victim"? For example, would neglect rates decrease if poor parents had decent-paying jobs? Or not?

Hidden Victims: Siblings and Adolescents

Violence between siblings and abuse of adolescents are less visible, primarily because the authorities are rarely notified. Such abuse, however, can be just as devastating as the other forms of domestic abuse we've examined.

Sibling Abuse

Sibling conflict is so common that many parents dismiss it as normal. But physical, emotional, and sexual abuse among siblings can leave lasting emotional scars.

PHYSICAL AND EMOTIONAL ABUSE Almost all young children hit a sibling occasionally. In one survey, over 80 percent of parents said that their children had engaged in at least one incident of sibling violence (such as kicking or punching) (Gelles and Straus, 1988). More recently, a national study found that almost 30 percent of children ages 2 to 17 had been physically assaulted by a sister or brother at least once (Finkelhor et al., 2005).

since you asked

Is hitting and teasing brothers and sisters a normal part of growing up?

Although most sibling conflict does not involve weapons, it can be very traumatic. Wiehe and Herring (1991) describe some common forms of sibling abuse:

- *Name-calling and ridicule:* Name-calling and ridicule are the most common forms of emotional abuse among siblings. Victims remember being belittled about things like their height, weight, looks, intelligence, or athletic ability. One woman is still bitter because her brothers called her "fatso" and "roly-poly" during most of her childhood. Another woman said, "My sister would get her friends to sing songs about how ugly I was" (p. 29).

- *Degradation:* Degrading people, or depriving them of a sense of dignity and value, can take many forms: "The worst kind of emotional abuse I experienced was if I walked into a room, my brother would pretend he was throwing up at the sight of me. As I got older, he most often would pretend I wasn't there and would speak as if I didn't exist, even in front of my father and my mother" (p. 35).

- *Promoting fear:* Siblings often use fear to control or terrorize their brothers or sisters. A woman in her 40s said that her siblings would take her sister and her into the field to pick berries. "When we would hear dogs barking, they would tell us they were wild dogs, and then they'd run away and make us find our own way home. We were only five or six, and we didn't know our way home" (p. 37).

- *Torturing or killing a pet:* The emotional impact on a child who loves an animal that a sibling tortures or kills can last for many years: "My second-oldest brother shot my little dog that I loved dearly. It loved me—only me. I cried by its grave for several days. Twenty years passed before I could care for another dog" (p. 39).

- *Destroying personal possessions:* Childhood treasures, such as favorite toys, can become instruments of emotional abuse: "My brother would cut out the eyes, ears, mouth, and fingers of my dolls and hand them to me" (p. 38).

Many children report that their parents rarely take physical or emotional abuse by siblings seriously: "'You must have done something to deserve it,' parents might say. My parents seemed to think it was cute when my brother ridiculed me. Everything was always a joke to them. They laughed at me. Usually their reply was for me to quit complaining—'You'll get over it'" (Wiehe and Herring, 1991: 22, 73).

However unintentionally, parents often promote sibling violence by yelling at their kids instead of teaching them how to resolve disagreements. Parents might also escalate the violence by treating children differently or having favorites. They may describe one child as "the smart one" or "the lazy one." Such labeling discourages siblings' respect for each other and creates resentment. The preferred child may target a "less preferred" sibling for maltreatment, especially when the parents aren't present (Updegraff et al., 2005).

A favored child may become abusive toward siblings because of his or her power and status in the family. A child's perception that she or he is less loved damages not only sibling relationships but also the child's self-image (Caffaro and Conn-Caffaro, 1998).

Sibling aggression is more dangerous than many parents think. About 10 percent of all murders in families are *siblicides*, killing of a sibling, and they account for almost 2 percent of all murders nationwide. The mean age of siblicide victims is 33 years, and the murder occurs during early and middle adulthood rather than during adolescence, as one might expect. Men are much more likely than women to be either offenders (88 percent) or victims (84 percent). The most common reason for siblicide is an argument between the perpetrator and the victim (Dawson and Langan, 1994; Underwood and Patch, 1999).

By not discouraging sibling violence, parents send the message that it's okay to resolve conflict through fighting. Children raised in such violent environments learn that aggression is acceptable not only between brothers and sisters but also with their own spouses and children (Gelles, 1997).

Sisters and brothers, like parents, play central roles in children's lives and in shaping family dynamics. When siblings are violent, the child learns that violence is a normal or acceptable way of dealing with others. Such perceptions increase the likelihood of bullying at school and aggression with friends and in dating relationships (Simonelli et al., 2002).

SEXUAL ABUSE Sexual abuse by a sibling is rarely an isolated incident. In most instances the episodes continue over time. They are often accompanied by physical and emotional abuse and may escalate. According to one woman,

> I can't remember exactly how the sexual abuse started but when I was smaller there was a lot of experimenting. My brother would do things to me like put his finger in my vagina. Then, as I got older, he would perform oral sex on me (Wiehe, 1997: 72).

Many respondents said that they had been sexually abused by brothers who were baby-sitting. Some used trickery: "At about age ten my brother approached me to engage in 'research' with him. He told me he was studying breast-feeding in school and needed to see mine. He proceeded to undress me and fondle my breasts" (Wiehe and Herring, 1991: 52).

Others threaten violence: "I was about twelve years old. My brother told me if I didn't take my clothes off, he would take his baseball bat and hit me in the head and I would die. I knew he would do it because he had already put me in the hospital. Then he raped me" (Wiehe and Herring, 1991: 55). Most children say nothing to their parents about sexual abuse, either because they are afraid of reprisal or because they think their parents won't believe them.

In most cases of sibling incest, older brothers molest younger sisters. Male and female roles in families in which sibling incest occurs are often shaped by rigid gender stereotypes. Girls generally perceive themselves as less powerful than their brothers. As a result of such gender-based power differences, an older brother and a younger sister are most at risk for sibling incest. As one woman explained,

> My brother was the hero of the family. He was the firstborn, and there was a great deal of importance placed on his being a male. My father tended to talk to him about the family business and ignore us girls. My mother would hang on every word my brother said. . . . If he ever messed up or did something wrong, my parents would soon forgive and

> forget. When I finally confronted them as a teenager about Shawn molesting me, at first they didn't believe me. Later, they suggested that I just get over it (Caffaro and Conn-Caffaro, 1998: 53).

Adolescent Abuse

Although the risks of family violence and child homicide decrease as children grow older, a staggering number of parents (or stepparents) abuse teenagers. As with abuse in early childhood, victimization during adolescence is the root of many problems later in life.

PREVALENCE OF ADOLESCENT ABUSE Many parents are physically and verbally abusive toward their children throughout the teen years. When adolescents fail to live up to their parents' expectations, the parents sometimes use physical force to assert control (see Chapter 12).

Of all child victims, an astounding 26 percent are ages 12 to 17. Within this age group, almost 22 percent have been sexually assaulted by a family member, including adult relatives (Kilpatrick et al., 2003; U.S. Department of Health and Human Services, 2006).

CONSEQUENCES OF ADOLESCENT ABUSE Some teenagers strike back physically and verbally. Others rebel, run away from home, withdraw, use alcohol and other drugs, become involved in juvenile prostitution and pornography, or even commit suicide (Estes and Weiner, 2002).

Compared with nonvictims, abused adolescents are twice as likely to be victims of other violent crimes, perpetrators of domestic violence, and substance abusers as adults. They are also almost three times more likely to commit serious property and violent crimes. Compared with 17 percent of nonvictim boys, 48 percent of boys who have been sexually assaulted engage in delinquent acts. About 20 percent of sexually assaulted girls engage in delinquency, compared with 5 percent of their nonvictim counterparts (Menard, 2002; Kilpatrick et al., 2003; Wasserman, 2003).

Another aspect of family violence that receives little attention is mistreatment of the elderly. Although elder abuse is less common than other forms of domestic violence, it is a serious problem.

Elder Abuse and Neglect

Baby boomers, now in their early 40s to late 50s, are often referred to as the **sandwich generation** because they must care not only for their own children but also for their aging parents (see Chapter 1). Most people in

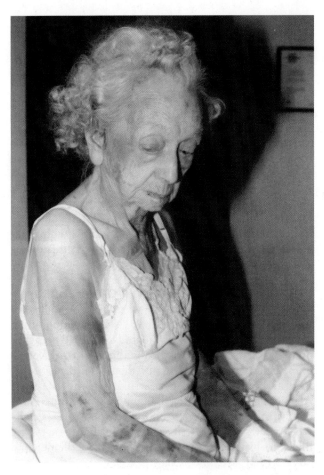

This 84-year-old woman suffered continuous physical abuse by a caregiver in the older woman's home. When arrested, the caregiver claimed that the woman had fallen out of bed.

the sandwich generation are remarkably adept at meeting the needs of both the young and the old. Others may abuse their children, their elderly parents and relatives, or both.

What Is Elder Abuse?

Elder abuse, sometimes also called *elder mistreatment,* includes the following:

- Physical abuse (such as hitting or slapping)

- Negligence (such as inadequate care)

- Financial exploitation (such as borrowing money and not repaying it)

- Psychological abuse (such as swearing at or blaming the elderly for one's own problems)

- Deprivation of basic necessities such as food and heat

- Isolation from friends and family, and

- Not administering needed medications (Decalmer and Glendenning, 1993; Carp, 2000).

Police officers who are guest lecturers in my classes describe some horrific cases of elder abuse or neglect. Some elderly people die of starvation, and their bodies aren't discovered for a year or more. A 71-year-old woman was left in bed for so long that her bedsores became infested with maggots.

Family members and acquaintances mistreat an estimated 5 percent of the elderly every year (see "Data Digest"). Some researchers call elder abuse "the hidden iceberg" because about 93 percent of cases are not reported to police or other protective agencies (National Center on Elder Abuse, 2005).

Cultural variations often shape family members' definitions of elder abuse. Some aging Asian Americans may see their sons' behavior as neglectful if they don't meet their filial obligation to provide for their parents' medical, transportation, financial, or emotional needs. Similarly, if daughters-in-law don't live up to cultural expectations to perform services for parents-in-law, they may be seen as emotionally or psychologically abusive (Chang and Moon, 1997).

Who Are the Victims?

Although most elder abuse is hidden, researchers estimate that 1 to 2 million Americans age 65 or older have been injured, exploited, or otherwise mistreated by a family member or caretaker. The rates for different types of maltreatment include physical abuse, 62 percent; abandonment, 56 percent; emotional or psychological abuse, 54 percent; financial abuse, 45 percent; and neglect, 41 percent (Tatara, 1998; National Center on Elder Abuse, 2005).

About 77 percent of elder abuse victims are white. Despite the revered role of grandparents among most minorities, elder maltreatment rates are also high among African Americans, Latinos, American Indians, and Asian Americans. A major difference is that whites are more likely to engage in physical abuse. Minority family members are more likely to be guilty of neglect, emotional abuse, and financial exploitation (like keeping much of the income from the elderly person's Social Security checks) (Malley-Morrison and Hines; 2004; Teaster et al., 2006).

About 66 percent of elder abuse victims are women and 43 percent are 80 or older. Elderly women are probably more likely than elderly men to be abused because they tend to live longer than men. Thus, women are more dependent on caretakers because they have few economic resources, experience poor health, and may command less authority and power with family members (Teaster et al., 2006; see, also, Chapters 5 and 17).

Who Are the Abusers?

Rosa is a 79-year-old widow who lives with Michael, her 52-year-old son. Michael moved in with his mother after a divorce in which he lost custody of his two children and ownership of his home. Within a few months of Michael's move, he assumed responsibility for Rosa's Social Security checks and meager pension. He did not allow her to see visitors and locked her in her room when he left the house. Neighbors who never saw Rosa became suspicious and called the police (Teaster et al., 2006).

since you asked

Is elder abuse more common in nursing homes than elsewhere?

Adult children like Michael are the largest group of abusers (53 percent), followed by the victim's spouse (19 percent). In fact, 90 percent of the abusers are family members (see *Figure 14.7*).

Why Do They Do It?

Why do family members mistreat the elderly? A number of risk factors, both micro and macro, increase the likelihood of elder abuse and neglect.

LIVING ARRANGEMENTS A shared living situation is a major risk factor for elder mistreatment. Sharing a res-idence increases opportunities for contact, tensions that can't be decreased simply by leaving, and conflicts that arise in everyday situations (Bonnie and Wallace, 2003).

SOCIAL ISOLATION Elder abuse is more likely in living arrangements where the family members don't have a strong social network of kin, friends, and neighbors. Care providers who don't have supportive networks to provide occasional relief from their caretaking activities experience strain and may become violent toward their elderly parents or relatives (Kilburn, 1996).

ALCOHOL ABUSE Alcohol use and abuse are common among abusers of the elderly. Daily alcohol consumption is more than twice as likely among those who abuse elders as among those who do not (Reay and Browne, 2001; Bonnie and Wallace, 2003).

IMPAIRMENT OF THE CAREGIVER OR THE CARE RECIPIENT A 70-year-old "child" who cares for a 90-year-old parent—a situation that is not uncommon today—may be frail, ill, or mentally disabled and thus unaware that he or she is being abusive or neglectful. Some elderly people suffer from dementia (deteriorated mental condition) after a stroke or the onset of Alzheimer's disease. They may pinch, shove, bite, kick, or strike their caregivers. Children or spouses, especially when they know little about debilitating diseases, are likely to hit back during such assaults (Pillemer and Suitor, 1991; see, also, Chapter 17).

DEPENDENCY OF THE OLDER PERSON ON CAREGIVER Elderly people who live with their children because they are too poor to live on their own may also suffer from incontinence, serious illness, or mental disabilities. They become physically as well as economically dependent on their caretakers. If the elderly are demanding, the caregivers may feel angry or resentful.

The dependency between the abuser and the victim is often mutual. Spouses, for example, may depend on each other for companionship. In the case of children and parents, although the abuser may need the older person for money or housing, the older parent needs the abuser for help with chores or to alleviate loneliness. If the adult child is still dependent on an elderly parent for housing or finances, she or he may mistreat the parent to compensate for the lack or loss of power (Payne, 2000).

MEDICAL COSTS AND STRESS Having to pay medical costs for an elderly relative may trigger abuse. Unlike low-income people, middle-class families are not eligible for admission to public institutions, yet few can afford the in-home nursing care and service that upper-class families can afford. As a result, cramped quarters and high expenses increase the caretakers' stress.

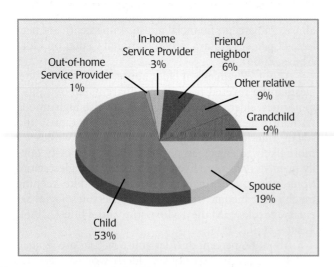

FIGURE 14.7 Relationship of Perpetrators and Victims of Elder Abuse

SOURCE: Based on Tatara, 1998: Figure 4-9.

PERSONALITY Sometimes personality characteristics of elderly people increase their risk of abuse. Chronic verbal aggression and hostility can spark physical and verbal maltreatment by a caretaker (Comijs et al., 1998).

In many cases, however, the violence begins early in a marriage and continues for decades. Some practitioners refer to this phenomenon as "domestic violence grown old." For example, women who grew up during the 1920s and 1930s were taught that "you married for life and you stuck things out," regardless of the husband's personality or behavior (France, 2006: 82).

INTERGENERATIONAL TRANSMISSION OF VIOLENCE

According to social learning theory (see Chapters 2 and 5), some victims of child abuse may grow up to be abusers, a pattern that is often described as *the cycle of violence.* Children who have learned to deal with conflict through abuse may do so themselves with their elderly parents or relatives (Bonnie and Wallace, 2003).

Making Connections

- Think about your or your friends' relationships with their brothers and sisters. Are the relationships abusive? Do the parents take sibling mistreatment seriously?

- There's an old saying: "Be nice to your children because they may be taking care of you some day." Does this saying illustrate the cycle of violence?

Violence Among Same-Sex Couples and Racial-Ethnic Immigrants

Compared with other families, there has been considerably less research on domestic violence in same-sex and immigrant households. Still, neither sexual orientation nor national origin deters abuse and neglect.

Same-Sex Couples

The prevalence of battering in lesbian and gay couples is about the same as it is for heterosexual couples, occurring in approximately 25 to 33 percent of all couples.

since you asked

Is abuse less common among same-sex and immigrant couples?

About 10 percent of men and 2 percent of women are violent with their same-sex partners (Rennison, 2001).

Much of the abuse tends to recur. For example, one researcher found that 54 of the 100 women in her study of lesbian couples said that they had experienced more than 10 abusive incidents during the course of the relationship. In almost 35 percent of cases, the birth mother's partner abused the children (Renzetti, 1992).

A study of 288 gay and lesbian batterers reported that all the men and women had been psychologically abused as children. About 93 percent of the men and 88 percent of the women said that they had experienced physical abuse during childhood (Farley, 1996).

Same-sex couples are often reluctant to report domestic violence. Many feel that the police don't take the abuse seriously. Others believe that such reports will increase the general public's negative views of homosexuality. Because treatment and support services for violent gay and lesbian households are minimal, children living in these families may be at especially high risk for future violence (Leventhal and Lundy, 1999).

Racial-Ethnic Immigrants

Although child maltreatment rates for Asian and Pacific Islander families are lower than those in the general population, the rates vary widely within subgroups. For example, a study in Washington state found that reported cases of child abuse ranged from about 15 percent for Cambodians, Filipinos, and Vietnamese to 3 percent or less for Japanese, Thai, and Guamanians.

These variations reflect a combination of factors. Relatively recent immigrants (like Cambodians) have more children, endure more economic stress because they lack marketable skills in an industrialized society, and use physical punishment to discipline children. In contrast, groups that have been in the United States for at least four generations (like the Chinese and Japanese) have acculturated: They are more likely to tolerate teenage girls' independence that violates traditional gender roles, are less likely to use physical punishment (which can result in abuse and be reported to protective agencies), and experience less economic stress because of higher educational levels and upward occupational mobility (Pelczarski and Kemp, 2006).

Immigrant women generally experience more domestic violence than their American-born counterparts do. For example, a recent study in New York City found that among victims of intimate partner homicides, 51 percent were foreign-born whereas 45 percent were born in the United States. In another study, 48 percent of Latinas reported that their partner's violence increased after they immigrated to the United States (cited in Family Violence Prevention Fund, 2006).

Recent immigrants rarely report domestic abuse. Women, especially those who don't speak English well, may not report marital violence because they fear being deported or ostracized by their community. Many tolerate violence because they don't know about or trust social service organizations that could provide help (Foo, 2002; Raj and Silverman, 2002).

South Asian immigrant women rarely report marital rape. Consenting to marriage generally means that the woman will be available for sexual intercourse, even when it's unwanted, because the man controls the marriage. Latinas may also be silent about marital rape because of cultural values that require them to remain loyal and to protect the man's honor and reputation, especially as a sign of the wife's "warmth and goodness" (Abraham, 2000; Vandello and Cohen, 2003).

Explaining Domestic Violence

Why are families violent? There are dozens of competing explanations based on medical, political, psychological, and criminological perspectives. Let's examine,

since you asked

Is there one explanation regarding why family members abuse each other?

briefly, five influential perspectives—patriarchy or male dominance theory, social learning theory, resource theory, exchange theory, and ecological systems theory. (You might want to refer to *Figure 2.1* on page 35 to refresh your memory of some of these perspectives.)

Patriarchy or Male Dominance Theory

Patriarchy or male dominance theory maintains that men's authority creates and condones domestic violence. Aggression against women and children, particularly female children, is common in societies where men have power, status, and privilege. In such "intimate terrorism," men control a partner or child (Johnson, 2005).

This perspective maintains that as long as cultural values encourage men to be controlling, dominant, competitive, and aggressive rather than nurturing, caring, and concerned for the welfare of others, men will continue to express their anger and frustration through violent and abusive behavior (see, for example, Birns et al., 1994). The box "Worldwide Male Violence against Women and Girls" illustrates some of the results of patriarchy.

Social Learning Theory

According to social learning theory, we learn by observing the behavior of others. For most people, the family is the first "school" of behavior, so to speak. Some people try to avoid the kind of violence that

they've experienced in the past. However, continuous exposure to abuse and violence during childhood increases the likelihood that a person will be violent as an adult (McKay, 1994).

Moreover, people learn and internalize social and moral justifications for abusive behavior. A child may grow up believing that the explanation "it's for your own good" is a legitimate reason for abusive behavior (Gelles and Cornell, 1990; see, also, Chapter 12).

So far, no one really knows whether or how much family violence is transmitted intergenerationally through modeling or imitation (see National Research Council, 1998, for a review of some of this literature). Modeling probably plays an important role in learning abusive behavior, but many children who grow up in violent households don't themselves become abusive.

Resource Theory

According to resource theory, men usually command greater financial, educational, and social resources than women do, so they have more power. Men with the fewest resources are the most likely to resort to abuse. For example, a man who has little education, holds a job low in prestige and income, and has poor communication skills may use violence to maintain his dominant position in a relationship or the family. Many women cannot assert themselves simply because they have even fewer resources than their partners (Babcock et al., 1993; Atkinson et al., 2005).

A decline of resources and the resulting stress can also provoke violence. If a man's contribution to earnings decreases relative to the wife's or the man experiences spells of unemployment, the woman is more likely to experience abuse. The situation can be aggravated by living in a disadvantaged neighborhood, having a large number of children, and refusal by the wife to work more hours outside the home (Fox et al., 2002).

Resource theory also helps explain nonmarital violence. If a woman feels that she has few resources to offer, she may be willing to date an abusive man just to have *someone*. Or, as you saw earlier, she may convince herself that she can reform the batterer. On the other hand, a woman who has more resources (such as money, a good job, or a college education) is often less willing to put up with abuse (see Chapters 8 and 13).

Exchange Theory

According to exchange theory, both victimizers and victims tolerate or engage in violent behavior because they believe that the benefits outweigh the costs. You'll recall that many battered women stay in an abusive relation-

Cross-Cultural Families

Worldwide Male Violence against Women and Girls

You've seen throughout this chapter that domestic violence is a serious problem in the United States. This is true elsewhere as well. Worldwide, at least one of every three women has been beaten, coerced into sex, or otherwise abused at some time in her life. The proportion of women who have suffered domestic violence at the hands of a male partner ranges from 15 percent in Japan to 71 percent in Ethiopia. As many as 33 percent of girls globally are forced into their first sexual experience.

In many parts of the world, both laws and customs permit male assaults against women. For example,

■ In Vietnam, 80 percent of women have experienced some form of violence. Men blame alcohol or temper for their violence, and the women, in the tradition of stoic Vietnamese womanhood, accept it as normal.

■ In the Islamabad region of Pakistan, in the last eight years more than 4,000 women have been doused with kerosene and burned by family members, predominantly in-laws or spouses. These "stove deaths" occur because the woman failed to give birth to a son, the husband wants to marry a second wife and can no longer support the first wife, there is long-running hostility with mothers-in-law, or almost any other disagreement between spouses and their relatives. Police usually call such attacks "suicides."

■ In Bolivia and Puerto Rico, 59 percent of battered women have been sexually assaulted by their partners; in Colombia, the figure is 46 percent.

■ In Australia, Aboriginal women and children are 45 times more likely to be victims of domestic violence than are non-Aboriginal women, and eight times more likely to be murdered. Some judges view such murders and rapes as "traditional culture that whites do well to ignore."

■ In Zambia, Africa, sexual attacks on girls, some as young as 8 years old, are common. As a result, HIV is spreading quickly among Zambian girls. Police and authorities rarely enforce laws forbidding sexual abuse.

■ A recent survey in Syria found that nearly one married woman in four has been beaten by her husband.

■ In Tanzania, Africa, about 500 elderly women who are accused of being witches are killed each year.

■ In Egypt, 96 percent of women in low-income neighborhoods have been beaten at least once by their husbands. A husband has the right to beat his wife if she talks to him disrespectfully, speaks to another man, spends too much money, or refuses to have sex with her husband.

■ In Britain, almost half of all women have been hit by a male partner, sexually attacked, or stalked.

■ In Japan, 10 percent of reported serious crimes are rapes. Japanese laws are usually lenient on rapists and batterers because such assaults are seen as domestic matters.

■ Studies from Australia, Canada, Israel, and the United States show that 40 to 70 percent of female murder victims are killed by their husbands or boyfriends; in contrast, about 5 percent of men are killed by their current or former female partners.

Even though India has legally abolished the institution of dowry, dowry-related violence is on the rise. More than 5,000 women are killed every year by their husbands and in-laws, who burn them in "accidental" kitchen fires if their ongoing demands for dowry before and after marriage are not met.

Sulfuric acid is a cheap and easily accessible weapon that can be used to disfigure and sometimes kill women and girls for reasons as varied as family feuds, inability to meet dowry demands, and rejection of marriage proposals. In Bangladesh, there are more than 200 acid attacks each year.

In several countries—including Bangladesh, Egypt, Iraq, Jordan, Lebanon, Pakistan, and Turkey—women are killed to uphold the "honor" of the family. Any reason—alleged adultery, premarital relationships (with or without sexual relations), rape, or falling in love with a person the family disapproves of—is enough justification for a male family member or relative to kill a woman.

Sources: "Domestic violence . . . ," 2000; Arthurs, 2002; Chelala, 2002; Krug et al., 2002; Terzieff, 2002; Lite, 2002; "Abuse spreads HIV . . . ," 2003; Kakuchi, 2003; Sandler, 2003; Morris, 2005; World Health Organization, 2005; "Egypt: Abused women . . . ," 2006; Zoepf, 2006.

ship for financial reasons. The rewards for perpetrators include release of anger and frustration and accumulation of power and control. They often spend little time in jail, and the women they abuse often take them back (Sherman, 1992).

Violence also has costs. First, it's possible that the victim will hit back. Second, a violent assault could lead to arrest or imprisonment and a loss of status among family and friends. Finally, the abuser may break up the family (Gelles and Cornell, 1990). However, if a patriarchal society condones male control of women and children, the costs will be minimal.

Ecological Systems Theory

Ecological system theory explains domestic violence by analyzing the relationships between individuals and larger systems like the economy, education, state agencies, and the community. For example, elder abuse is highest when there is a combination of micro and macro variables: Caretakers abuse drugs or have limited resources and experience stress, older people develop physical or mental disabilities, caregivers and the elderly are physically and socially isolated from a larger community, and there are few social service agencies that provide high-quality care.

Moreover, cultural values—including television programs and movies—that demean, debase, and devalue women and children promote and reinforce abusive behavior. For example, even if hip-hop music, especially "gangsta rap," doesn't actually cause physical abuse against women, the lyrics are "often chillingly supportive of rape and violence" (Hill, 2005: 185; see, also, Chapter 5).

Using Several Theories

Researchers rarely rely on only one theory of domestic violence because the reasons for human behavior, including violence, are complex. For example, resource theory suggests that men who have few assets in fulfilling a provider role are more likely to be violent toward their wives than are men with high incomes. However, men who have average incomes but lower educational and income levels than their employed wives may also resort to violence. Patriarchy or male dominance theory suggests that these men have less egalitarian views about decision making or that they "explode" when the wives pressure them to share more of the housework (Anderson, 1997). If we also consider personality variables and exchange factors, explaining family violence becomes even more complex.

Other Family Health Issues

Although abuse and violence can destroy a family, other health-related problems can also become crises. For example, many families must cope with long-term problems such as inappropriate use of steroids or other drugs, abuse, depression and suicide, and eating disorders such as anorexia and bulimia.

Drug Abuse

Recently, Eddie, a 22-year-old father of two young children, was rushed to the hospital. He died 10 days later, the result of having overdosed on a mix of pharmaceutical pills. Although his parents were shocked, his mother later said that "Eddie was not the first kid to die in this neighborhood from prescription drugs" (Leinwand, 2006). A number of drugs—whether legal or illegal—can create problems during both adolescence and adulthood.

ILLEGAL DRUGS An estimated 8 percent of Americans (over 19 million people) age 12 and older use illegal drugs. Those with the lowest usage rates are college graduates, employed adults, people living in rural areas, and women. Among racial-ethnic groups, American Indian youth have the highest usage rates and Asian Americans the lowest (see *Figure 14.8*).

Among youth between the ages of 12 and 17, girls have caught up with boys in illicit drug and alcohol use and have actually surpassed boys in cigarette smoking and prescription drug use. About 19 percent of American teenagers (almost 5 million) have taken prescription painkillers such as Vicodin or OxyContin or stimulants such as Ritalin or Adderall to get high. Some teens organize "pharm parties" ("pharm" being short for pharmaceuticals) where they down fistfuls of prescription drugs that they can easily get from their parents' medi-

since you asked

What's a "pharm party"?

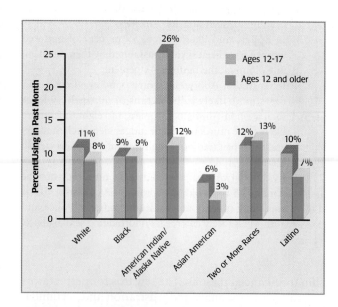

FIGURE 14.8 Illicit Drug Use, by Race/Ethnicity and Age, 2004

Source: Based on Substance Abuse and Mental Health Services Administration data, 2005.

cine cabinets (Partnership for a Drug-Free America, 2005; Office of National Drug Control Policy, 2006).

Researchers are especially concerned about the growing popularity of prescription-type drugs. The drugs were unknown to teenagers just a few years ago. In 2005, however, almost 24 percent of American high-school seniors said that they had used prescription drugs such as tranquilizers and sedatives. Like other illicit drugs, prescription-type drugs often "filter down" to middle-school students. The problem isn't just that children can easily become addicted to prescription drugs. These medicines can also send kids to the emergency room: They can lead to difficulty in breathing, a drop or rapid increase in heart rate, or impaired responses when driving (Banta, 2005; Johnston et al., 2006).

Marijuana is the most popular illegal drug (used by 6 percent of the U.S. population, about 15 million people). Short-term effects of marijuana use include problems with memory and learning, distorted perception, difficulty in thinking and problem solving, loss of coordination, increased heart rate, and anxiety (Substance Abuse and Mental Health Services Administration, 2005).

Although many users maintain that marijuana is less harmful than tobacco or alcohol, some researchers describe it as a "gateway" drug that leads to use of "harder" drugs. According to a study of fraternal and identical twins, for example, the twin who used marijuana before age 17 was five times more likely to later use cocaine, heroin, hallucinogens, sedatives, or alcohol (Lynskey et al., 2003).

About 1 percent of Americans (2 million people) use cocaine; of them, 567,000 use crack. An estimated 5 percent of women use illicit drugs, including cocaine, while pregnant. Exposure to cocaine has harmful effects on a child's cognitive development. At 2 years old, cocaine-exposed babies have lower memory scores, less language and problem-solving ability, and less motor control and coordination than other children their age (Singer et al., 2002; Substance Abuse and Mental Health Services Administration, 2005).

ALCOHOL Alcohol use increases with age: 2 percent at age 12, 20 percent at age 15, 36 percent at age 17, and 71 percent for people 21 years old. Among young adults ages 18 to 25, 21 percent admitted having driven under the influence of alcohol at least once during the year (Substance Abuse and Mental Health Services Administration, 2005).

Alcohol can cause greater damage to the brain development of people under 25 than to any other age group. The prefrontal region of the brain plays an important role in forming the adult personality and in controlling, planning, and monitoring behaviors. Because this part of the brain develops from childhood until early adulthood, adolescents need to drink only half as much as adults to suffer the same negative effects, such as learning and memory impairments ("Underage drinkers . . . ," 2002).

Adolescent drug use also leads to health problems in adulthood. Twenty years later, for example, people who had used drugs as teens report more health problems, including a higher incidence of respiratory problems such as colds and sinus infections; cognitive problems such as difficulty in concentrating, remembering, and learning; and headaches, dizziness, and vision problems. Besides other problems, alcoholics are five to ten times more likely than the general population to experience depression and to commit suicide (Brook et al., 2002; Preuss et al., 2003).

STEROIDS During the last few years, the media have focused on professional athletes, such as Barry Bonds, a superstar baseball player, who has been suspected of using steroids. Even before the Bonds controversy, several American Olympic athletes were banned from competition after testing positive for steroid use.

Steroids are synthetic hormones, most often testosterone, that improve physical appearance, muscle mass,

There have been suspicions that Barry Bonds, an outstanding batter, used performance-enhancing drugs. Some American athletes have been banned from the Olympics for using steroids.

and strength. When taken orally or injected, they increase the size and strength of muscles in just a few months. Among high school students, 3 percent of girls and 5 percent of boys have admitted using steroids (Eaton et al., 2006).

Athletes take steroids to improve their performance in sports, but the appeal of these substances is broader. Girls take steroids to lose weight, trying to emulate the body images they see in the media. Boys as young as 10, as well as high school students who do not play sports, are "bulking up simply because they want to look good" (Egan, 2002: A1).

Steroids can be dangerous. For men, side effects can include a decrease in testosterone production, a possibly irreversible shrinkage of the testicles, disinterest in sex, outbreaks of acne, increased facial and body hair, early balding, strokes and heart attacks, reduced sperm counts, liver disorders, kidney disease, a sharp increase in aggression, and, with heavy usage, the possible development of psychosis. For women, side effects include increased facial and body hair, a deepened voice, reduced breast size, and menstrual irregularities. Teenagers run the particular risk of permanent damage to their reproductive and skeletal systems. For example, one 13-year-old who had taken steroids for two years stopped growing at five feet (Fulz, 1991; Field et al., 2005).

As many Americans become fatter, they often turn to steroids and dietary supplements to achieve what is often unachievable. They don't realize, for example, that the images of male models in advertisements are often shaded to make their muscles look more defined. Similarly, the photos of female models can be brushed to make them appear slimmer and younger than they really are.

WHY ARE DRUG USE RATES SO HIGH? Although there are many reasons, such as poverty and peer pressure, parents play an important role in their children's drug use. Many middle-class parents, especially, rely on Ritalin and other drugs to control young children's behavior (see Chapter 12). And, as you saw earlier in this chapter, children who experience domestic violence—including physical and sexual abuse—are more likely to use drugs and alcohol in adolescence and adulthood than their nonabused counterparts.

Although even the most responsible parents can't prevent their children from trying drugs, many parents don't discuss drug use with their children or do so only superficially. According to one national survey, for example, 35 percent of parents, but only 14 percent of teenagers ages 14 to 17, said that the parents talked to their teenagers about drugs "a lot" (Schultz, 2000).

In a study of drug addicts in drug treatment centers in four states, 20 percent of the respondents said that their parents had introduced them to drugs. The parent–teen drug sharing cut across all racial lines and

was almost as pervasive in suburbs (17 percent) as in inner-city neighborhoods (22 percent) (Baldauf, 2000).

Other reasons for drug use include their easy availability, especially on the Internet, and a belief that some drugs (such as marijuana and prescription medicine) are safer than "street drugs" (such as heroin). Even when adolescents know that drug abuse is risky, they feel that they themselves won't experience any negative effects, including death because only "druggies" die (Partnership for a Drug-Free America, 2006; Valadez-Meltzer et al., 2005).

Depression and Suicide

Two major problems for families are depression and suicide. Both have negative impacts that affect kin and friends throughout the life course.

DEPRESSION Depression is a mental disorder characterized by pervasive sadness and other negative emotions that interfere with the ability to work, study, sleep, eat, and enjoy experiences that were formerly pleasurable (see *Table 14.3*).

Over a lifetime, 14 percent of adolescents and 15 percent of adults (ages 18 and older) have experienced at least one major depressive episode (one that lasts at least two weeks), but fewer than half ever seek treatment. In all age groups, twice as many women as men

TABLE 14.3

Symptoms of Depression

1. Persistent sadness, anxiety, or an "empty" feeling

2. Feelings of worthlessness, guilt, helplessness, hopelessness

3. Loss of interest or pleasure in usual hobbies and activities, including sex

4. Difficulty concentrating, remembering, making decisions

5. Fatigue and loss of energy

6. Restlessness, irritability

7. Changes in appetite and weight (weight loss or overeating)

8. Disturbed sleep (such as insomnia or sleeping much of the time)

9. Suicidal thoughts or attempts

10. Persistent physical problems such as headaches, pain, and digestive disorders that don't respond to treatment

suffer a major depressive episode every year. Although substance abuse doesn't "cause" depression, those who abuse alcohol and use illicit drugs are twice as likely to experience a major depressive episode as are nonusers (Bostic and Miller, 2005; Substance Abuse and Mental Health Services Administration, 2005).

SUICIDE Depression may lead to suicide. Among adults, suicide is the eleventh leading cause of death. It is the eighth leading cause of death for men even though women attempt suicide about three times more often than men do. Suicide rates are highest among white males, followed by American Indian men (Substance Abuse and Mental Health Services Administration, 2005; "Suicide: Fact sheet," 2006).

Suicide is the third leading cause of death among young people ages 15 to 24; 86 percent are men. Many men, especially adolescents, seem to have a harder time accepting breakups with their girlfriends. As a result, they may react violently against the woman or commit suicide in a final desperate act ("Suicide: Fact sheet," 2006; see, also, Chapter 8).

Young men ages 15 to 24 account for 64 percent of all suicides among American Indians. Some attribute such self-destructive behavior to acculturation. Instead of being anchored in native values that emphasize health and well-being, acculturation often leads to feelings of marginalization, loss of self-respect, and alienation from both Anglo and American Indian cultures. Other researchers suggest that the usage of alcohol and marijuana—rather than acculturation—increases the likelihood that American Indian adolescents will commit suicide and engage in other self-destructive behaviors such as interpersonal violence (Potthoff et al., 1998; "Suicide and suicidal behavior," 2000; "Suicide: Fact sheet," 2006).

Suicide attempts and completions are also rising for young Latinas. As they become more Americanized, Latinas (much more than teenage Latinos) develop a host of insecurities about appearance, academic success, peer popularity, family expectations, and sex. Especially in low-income families in which the parents don't speak English, teenage girls (more often than boys) may have the added burden of serving as translators on a daily basis. The teens also worry about the health of parents who may be struggling to make ends meet, and often find themselves in a push-and-pull match between meeting their parents' traditional expectations and fitting in with their U.S.-born friends (Flores et al., 2002; Eaton et al., 2006; see, also, Chapter 5).

Most recently, several studies have found an association between negative body image, depression, and suicide. Suicidal thoughts and attempts are much more common among teenagers who think they're too fat or too thin, regardless of how much they weigh. Teens who see themselves as either very fat or very skinny are twice

TABLE 14.4

Some Common Warning Signs of Suicide

- Withdrawal from family or friends
- Verbal expression of suicidal thoughts or threats, even as a joke
- Major personality changes
- Changes in sleeping or eating habits
- Drug or alcohol abuse
- Difficulty concentrating
- Violent or rebellious outbursts
- Running away
- Recent suicide of a relative or friend
- Rejection by a boyfriend or girlfriend
- Unexplained, sudden drop in quality of schoolwork or athletic interests
- Giving or throwing away prized possessions
- Sudden lack of interest in one's friends or usual activities
- Extreme and sudden neglect of appearance
- Eating disorders (very thin or overweight)

as likely to think about or attempt suicide as their normal-weight counterparts (Eaton et al., 2005; Dyl et al., 2006).

Most teenagers experience ups and downs as they mature. When, however, the downs become frequent, parents, friends, teachers, and relatives should seriously consider the possibility that the adolescent is planning suicide and should intervene when they show symptoms of suicidal behavior (see *Table 14.4*).

Eating Disorders: Anorexia and Bulimia

In 1994, former gymnast Christy Henrich died of multiple-organ system failure resulting from a history of anorexia nervosa and bulimia. She was 22 and weighed 60 pounds. Henrich, who missed making the 1988 U.S. Olympic team by 0.118 points, became concerned about her weight during a gymnastics meet where she overheard a judge say that she was too fat. At that time, she was 4 feet 11 and weighed 93 pounds (Lonkhuyzen, 1994).

since you asked

Why are so many adolescent girls practically starving themselves to death?

Anorexia nervosa, a dangerous eating disorder, is characterized by fear of obesity, the conviction that one is "fat," significant weight loss, and refusal to maintain one's weight within the normal limits for one's age and height. **Bulimia,** another eating disorder, is a cyclical pattern of eating binges followed by self-induced vomiting, fasting, excessive exercise, or use of diuretics or laxatives.

Although the numbers vary, at some point in their lives an estimated 4 percent of American women suffer from anorexia and another 7 percent from bulimia. Of all people affected by these disorders, 10 percent are male. Eating disorders can affect people of all ages, but 86 percent report onset of anorexia or bulimia before age 20 (Berkman et al., 2006; National Mental Health Association, 2006).

Anorexia may cause slowing of the heartbeat, loss of normal blood pressure, cardiac arrest, dehydration, skin abnormalities, hypothermia, lethargy, potassium

Is this model too thin? A prestigious fashion show in Madrid, Spain, created an uproar when it banned "overly thin models." Organizers said that models had to be within a healthy weight range (e.g., a 5' 9" woman would need to weigh at least 125 pounds.). According to the National Eating Disorders Association, in 1965 models weighed an average of 8 percent less than the typical U.S. woman; the average model now weighs 23 percent less than the average woman.

deficiency, and kidney malfunction. With treatment, about half of anorexics get better, about 40 percent remain chronically ill, and 10 percent die of causes related to the disease (Fichter et al., 2006).

Bulimia's binge-purge cycle can cause fatigue, seizures, muscle cramps, an irregular heartbeat, and decreased bone density, which can lead to osteoporosis. Repeated vomiting can damage the esophagus and stomach, cause the salivary glands to swell, make the gums recede, and erode tooth enamel.

Although most anorexics and bulimics are young middle-class white women, some researchers are finding that the number of Latinas and African American women with eating disorders is increasing, especially for binge eating. For example, a study of college students found that 5 percent of the Asian American women were bulimic. The numbers may be increasing because more minority women are seeking treatment instead of being secretive about their condition (Tsai and Gray, 2000; Striegel-Moore et al., 2003; Brodey, 2005).

As with most mental illnesses, eating disorders are due to a combination of cultural, psychological, and biological factors. Some parents of 3-year-olds say that their daughters eat enough (even when the girls are thin) but they encourage their sons to eat more to become big and strong even though 18 percent of the boys are overweight (Holm-Denoma et al., 2005).

Other cultural and psychological factors include a history of sexual abuse, low self-esteem, and cultural norms of attractiveness. For example, a study of girls ages 5 to 8 found that those who play with Barbie dolls rather than Emme, a doll with a more proportional body shape, had lower body esteem and a greater desire for a thinner body, laying the foundation for the development of eating disorders (Dittmar et al., 2006).

Girls who participate in competitive sports in which body shape and size are a factor (for example, ice skating, gymnastics, crew, and dance) are at three times greater risk for eating disorders than their peers. Anorexic men include models, actors, gymnasts, and jockeys, as well as young men in nonprofessional sports training who are trying to keep their weight down during competitions ("Facts about eating disorders," 2000; Morgan, 2002a).

Educator Jean Kilbourne, who has done pioneering work on the negative effects of advertising on women's body image, notes that women are conditioned to be terrified of fat: "Prejudice against fat people, especially against fat women, is one of the few remaining prejudices that are socially acceptable" (Kilbourne, 1994: 402). Consequently, the most common explanation of anorexia and bulimia is that women are trying to live up to a cultural ideal that equates thinness with beauty and success:

If I'm thin, I'll be popular. If I'm thin, I'll turn people on. If I'm thin, I'll have great sex. If I'm thin,

I'll be rich. If I'm thin, I'll be admired. If I'm thin, I'll be sexually free. If I'm thin, I'll be tall. If I'm thin, I'll have power. If I'm thin, I'll be loved. If I'm thin, I'll be envied (Munter, 1984: 230).

Body image obsession often leads to self-loathing, social isolation, and depression. The most serious outcome is suicide. People who have a distorted body image and think obsessively about their appearance are 45 times more likely to commit suicide than people in the general population (Phillips and Menard, 2006).

Researchers are now finding that about half of the risk for developing anorexia could be attributed to an individual's combination of genes and brain chemistry. If there is a genetic predisposition for anorexia, for example, the brain can reduce or overproduce chemicals, especially serotonin. Some scientists theorize that by eating less, anorexics reduce the serotonin activity in their brains, creating a sense of calm, even as they are about to die of malnutrition (Frank et al., 2005; Bulik et al., 2006). However, because eating disorders typically co-occur with other problems such as depression and sexual abuse, the relationship between genes and eating disorders is still tentative.

Most of my students feel pretty depressed after reading this chapter. It's also depressing, as an author, to read the research and summarize the results. However, many groups (and individuals) have been successful in implementing a variety of programs to decrease family violence and other crises.

Making Connections

- Should a parent who suspects his or her child of substance abuse use a home drug kit? Or would this create rebellion and more problems in the parent–child relationship?

- The number of men with eating disorders is increasing. Is this because men are becoming more concerned about their appearance? Because they are now more likely to seek help? Or other reasons?

Combating Domestic Violence and Other Family Crises

Few people know that in 2005 the U.S. Supreme Court watered down restraining orders against abusers. The Court ruled that it's "unrealistic" to expect police departments to enforce every restraining order. Thus, the courts are diluting some existing laws that have protected abuse victims.

Another major reason for the high family violence rates is that many people don't realize the extent of domestic violence. Once people are better informed, prevention and intervention strategies can reduce the maltreatment and other family crises.

since you asked

Is it possible to reduce partner and child abuse?

Raising Awareness about Domestic Violence

A recent study of partner violence concluded that "Domestic violence thrives on a social climate of secrecy, tolerance, and passivity." A greater public sense of responsibility and accountability and involvement in helping victims would increase the exposure and social control of partner violence against women (Gracia and Herrero, 2006: 767).

Public education efforts to raise awareness about domestic violence have typically been aimed at women. If such efforts leave men—especially young men—out of the conversation, there'll be little change. How do you stop a 30-year-old man from beating his wife? "Talk to him when he's 12," writes a journalism professor, and as often as possible, about not abusing girls (Voss, 2003).

On campuses, women should encourage their boyfriends and male friends to attend antiviolence meetings and lectures to raise men's awareness of the problem. Women can also encourage their fathers, brothers, and boyfriends to make an annual donation, however modest, to a local shelter for abused women and children.

Preventing Domestic Violence and Other Crises

Numerous organizations offer programs to prevent domestic violence and other family crises. For example, many schools and communities have implemented "keeping kids clean" programs that teach youth how to avoid risky behaviors and instruct parents in how to talk to their children more effectively about the dangers of drugs (Atkin, 2002).

Most children imitate their parents (see Chapter 5). If parents abuse drugs or are violent, children get the message that both behaviors are okay. As much of this chapter has shown, what's wrong with kids is usually not kids but their parents, caregivers, and other adults (see, also, Chapter 12).

Preschool programs can reduce the likelihood of child abuse. For example, for children of low-income parents who are involved in their children's preschool programs, the rate of maltreatment is 52 percent lower than the rate for children whose parents don't participate in such programs (Reynolds and Robertson, 2003).

The Watchful Shepherd (www.watchful.org), a non-profit organization founded in Pennsylvania, protects at-risk children with electronic devices that children can use to contact hospital emergency personnel when they feel threatened or fear abuse. An unexpected outcome is use of the device by parents who fear that they are losing control and might hurt their child unless someone intervenes.

Caseworkers usually have the right to obtain warrants to search the homes of suspected child abusers. Many don't do so, however, because of high caseloads and our cultural norms about not "intruding" on parents.

Intervening in Domestic Violence and Other Crises

Thousands of programs and laws are designed to intervene in family crises. Some are ineffective because the staff is overworked, the agency is underfunded, or the police and judges don't enforce laws against domestic violence. These programs and interventions have had some successes, however. For example,

- Abused women who obtain permanent (rather than temporary) court orders of protection are 80 percent less likely to be assaulted again.

- Counseling generally has little effect on a batterer's attitudes or behavior. Arrests, restraining orders, and intensive monitoring by police are far more effective.

- Kaiser Permanente, a national health maintenance organization, has launched a successful program that screens and treats domestic violence victims in emergency rooms and reports the abuse to police.

- Teen substance abuse programs that involve the entire family have a higher success rate than those that only treat the adolescent.

- Women who are treated for substance abuse during pregnancy are much more likely to have healthy babies than those who don't have prenatal care.

- Nurses and trained volunteers who visit low-income adolescent mothers and reinforce their parenting skills reduce the mothers' isolation and decrease child abuse by as much as 40 percent (Centers for Disease Control and Prevention, 2003; Jackson, 2003; Jackson et al., 2003; Vesely, 2005; Middlemiss and McGuigan, 2005; Paris and Dubus, 2005).

Although many programs have decreased rates of violence and other family crises, there are still numerous gaps. Recently, for example, a Maryland man who killed his poodle was sentenced to 15 days in jail. In contrast, a Vermont judge handed out only a 60-day jail sentence to a man who had repeatedly raped a 7-year-old girl until she was 10. A father who served four years in prison for raping his 5-year-old daughter still has visitation rights. And 70 percent of men who have battered their wives have convinced judges that the mother shouldn't have sole custody of their child (Waller, 2001; "Man who raped. . . ," 2002; Joyce, 2005). Because many judges are elected, you can vote them out of office.

Conclusion

Millions of U.S. families are experiencing negative *changes,* such as domestic violence, elder abuse and neglect, and high drug use among middle-school children and teenagers. This does not mean that the situation is hopeless, however. As people become more informed about these and other problems, they have more *choices* in accessing supportive community resources and legal intervention agencies.

These choices are sometimes eclipsed by a number of *constraints.* Laws are not always enforced, our society still tolerates much male violence, and social service agencies are too understaffed and underfunded to deal with many health-related problems. Besides violence and health issues, many families must also deal with separation and divorce, the topic of the next chapter.

Summary

1. People are more likely to be killed or assaulted by family members than by outsiders.

2. Although both men and women can be violent, abuse of women in intimate relationships results in much more serious physical and emotional damage than does abuse of men.

3. Women and children who are battered often suffer from low self-esteem and learned helplessness.

4. Women often don't leave abusive relationships for a number of reasons: poor self-concept, a belief that the man they love will reform, economic hardship, the need for child support, doubt that they can get along alone, fear, shame and guilt, and being imprisoned in their homes.

5. There are four major categories of child maltreatment: physical abuse, sexual abuse, neglect, and emotional maltreatment.

6. Child maltreatment results in a variety of physiological, social, and emotional problems. Many of these problems are long term and continue into adulthood.

7. The incidence of physical and sexual abuse among siblings and elderly abuse is greatly underreported.

8. The most influential theories of domestic violence and female victimization include patriarchy or male dominance theory, social learning theory, resource theory, exchange theory, and ecological systems theory.

9. Besides violence, families must grapple with other health-related issues such as substance abuse. Parental drug use, inappropriate use of steroids, depression, suicide, and eating disorders also affect many families.

10. To decrease domestic violence and other family crises, we must do a better job of informing people about the problems, provide successful prevention programs, and implement better intervention strategies.

Key Terms

marital rape *425*
battered-woman syndrome *425*
child maltreatment *430*
child abuse *430*

sandwich generation *438*
elder abuse *439*
steroids *445*
depression *446*

anorexia nervosa *448*
bulimia *448*

Taking it Further

Family Violence: Resources and Remedies

The National Coalition against Domestic Violence provides dozens of sites with information about women's shelters, counseling, legal aid, and other resources for dealing with domestic violence.
www.ncadv.org

The National Clearinghouse on Child Abuse and Neglect Information focuses on the prevention, identification, and treatment of child abuse and neglect.
www.calib.com/nccanch

The National Center on Elder Abuse describes and illustrates the various types of elder abuse and neglect. The site also suggests agencies and lists hotline phone numbers established by federal, state, and local governments.
www.elderabusecenter.org

The Bureau of Justice Statistics provides data and many reports on domestic violence, child abuse, and runaways.
www.ojp.usdoj.gov

The National Mental Health Association offers numerous fact sheets, research resources, and prevention programs dealing with a large number of mental health disorders, including anorexia and bulimia.
www.nmha.org

And more: www.prenhall.com/benokraitis provides links to abuse prevention centers, men's domestic violence home pages, state domestic violence laws, a "Wheel Gallery" of abuse, a test to evaluate whether you or someone you know has an eating disorder, and much more.

Investigate with Research Navigator

Go to www.researchnavigator.com and enter your LOGIN NAME and PASSWORD. For instructions on registering for the first time, view the detailed instructions at the end of Chapter 1. Search the Research Navigator™ site using the following key terms:

child maltreatment
elder abuse
eating disorders

Outline

15

Separation and Divorce

Data Digest

- Among Americans ages 18 and older, almost **94 percent believe that divorce is a serious problem in the United States.**

- About **1 in 5 American adults has divorced at least once.**

- On average, **first marriages that end in divorce last about 8 years.**

- **Among men who have ever been divorced,** 22 percent are white, 19 percent are African Americans, 13 percent are Latinos, and 9 percent are Asian Americans. The respective rates for women are 23 percent, 21 percent, 17 percent, and 11 percent.

- After a divorce, **85 percent of mothers have custody of their children.** This proportion has been constant since 1994.

- Of the **13.4 million custodial parents in 2002,** 7.9 million (59 percent) had some type of child support agreement.

Sources: Kreider and Fields, 2002; Grall, 2003; Glenn, 2005; Kreider, 2005.

When I was in college during the mid-1960s, divorce was rare. In hushed tones, adults described the few children whose parents were divorced as "poor dears" and their parents as "disgraceful." Today, most people view divorce as a normal event that may occur in a person's lifetime. Statistically, nearly two out of every five students reading this chapter probably come from divorced homes. Thus, both divorce rates and our reactions have changed dramatically within just one generation.

As you'll see in this chapter, divorce has both costs and benefits for adults and children. Let's begin by looking at separation, which usually precedes divorce.

Separation: Process and Outcome

Separation can mean several things. It may be a temporary time-out from a highly stressful marriage during which the partners decide whether to continue the marriage. One person may move out of the home in a trial separation, allowing the partners to see what living apart feels like.

Separation can also be a permanent arrangement because some religious beliefs don't allow divorce. Or a couple may seek a legal separation—that is, a temporary period of living apart, which is required by most states before the couple can be granted a divorce.

The Phases of Separation

Separation is usually a long and painful process that encompasses four phases: preseparation, early separation, midseparation, and late separation (Ahrons and Rodgers, 1987). Regardless of the duration of a particular phase and whether or not the partners go through all four stages, the process rarely occurs quickly. Typically, partners agonize for months or even years before making a final break.

PRESEPARATION During the *preseparation* phase, the partners may fantasize about what it would be like to live alone, escape from family responsibilities, or form new sexual liaisons. Although the fantasies rarely become reality, they can make separation or divorce seem appealing.

In the later stages of the preseparation phase, the couple splits up after a period of gradual emotional alienation. The partner who feels that a separation can end the unhappiness of one or both partners usually initiates the separation.

Even when people are considering separation (or have already made the decision), they often maintain a public pretense that nothing is wrong. The couple may attend family and social functions together, continuing rituals like holding hands right up until the actual separation.

Despite such outward appearances of tranquility, separation usually is traumatic, especially for the person who is left. He or she may feel guilty for causing the separation and may also experience anxiety, fear of being alone, and panic about the future.

EARLY SEPARATION The *early separation* phase is problematic because our society doesn't have clear-cut rules for this process. Many questions, both serious and trivial, plague the newly separated couple: Who should move out? What should the partners tell their family and friends? Should the child's teacher be notified? Who gets the new plasma TV?

In addition, the partners may be very ambivalent about leaving a marriage. They are confused and upset when their feelings fluctuate—as they usually do—between love and hate, anger and sadness, euphoria and depression, or relief and guilt.

Couples also must confront economic issues such as paying bills, buying the children's clothing, and splitting old and new expenses. The woman's economic survival may be a particularly difficult question. Even when she is employed outside the home, a wife typically earns much less than her husband (see Chapter 13). As a result, she faces a lower standard of living, especially if the children live with her. Some people get support from family and friends, but most must cope on their own.

MIDSEPARATION In the *midseparation* phase, the harsh realities of everyday living set in. The pressures of maintaining two households and meeting the children's emotional and physical needs mount, and stress intensifies. If family or friends don't help or if their help diminishes, the partners may feel overwhelmed, especially if there are additional stressors such as illness, unexpected expenses, a dependent elderly parent, or difficulties at work or while seeking a college or graduate degree.

Because of these problems, and especially when couples have been married at least 10 years, people may experience "pseudo-reconciliation." That is, the earlier preseparation expectations or fantasies may be followed by a sense of loss when partners don't see their children, by guilt over abandoning the family, and by disapproval from parents, relatives, or friends. As a result, partners may move back in together.

This second reunion rarely lasts. Soon the underlying problems that led to the separation in the first place

"It's National We're History Month."

surface again, conflicts reemerge, and the couple may separate again (Everett and Everett, 1994).

LATE SEPARATION In the *late separation* phase, the partners must learn how to survive as singles again. This stage may be especially stressful for men who have been raised with traditional gender role expectations. For example, men may become frustrated or angry when they can't or don't want to perform routine tasks like preparing a favorite dish or doing their own laundry.

Both partners often must deal with mutual friends who have a hard time accepting the separation. Some friends may avoid both partners because it threatens their perceptions of their own marriages. Others may take sides, which forces a separating couple to develop new friendships.

Finally, and perhaps most important, partners must help their children deal with anxiety, anger, confusion, and sadness. We'll return to this topic later in the chapter.

On the positive side, separating couples may experience "growth-oriented coping" (Nelson, 1994). For example, they may further their education, form new friendships, and enjoy a greater sense of independence and self-control.

Some Outcomes of Marital Separation

Not all separations end in divorce. Sometimes people reconcile and try to give their marriage a second chance:

> After 25 years of marriage, my dad just moved out one day and lived in another state for almost three years. Then one day they reconciled and that was that. They never talk about it but my mom once commented that having dad around was better than being alone, the utilitarian marriage we discussed in class a couple of weeks ago. I'm assuming they'll stay together because my parents recently celebrated their 31st wedding anniversary (Author's files).

SEPARATION AND RECONCILIATION Data on reconciliation are practically nonexistent. According to the most recent study, however, approximately 10 percent of all married U.S. couples (9 percent of white women and 14 percent of black women) who have separated have gotten back together (Wineberg and McCarthy, 1993).

since you asked

After a separation, does reconciliation work?

A national study of black women who had a successful reconciliation in their first marriage found that the decision varied by age. Women separating after age 23 were substantially more likely to reconcile than were younger women. The researcher attributed this difference to three reasons: Older women are more mature and more willing to make sacrifices in reuniting; they've invested more in the marriage than younger women have, especially if there are children; and they may feel that marriage should be a lifelong commitment (Wineberg, 1996). Although some couples reconcile, many separate but don't get a divorce.

SEPARATION WITHOUT DIVORCE Many people separate and even do the necessary paperwork, but about 6 percent never make the divorce official. Within five years, 97 percent of white women have moved from a separation to a divorce, compared with 77 percent of Latinas and only 67 percent of African American women (Bumpass et al., 1990; Bramlett and Mosher, 2002).

Why the variation among racial-ethnic groups? There's an old saying that people marry for love and divorce for money. If people, especially wives, don't have the money to get a divorce, the separation might last many years. Long-term separations are most likely among women who don't have a high school degree, have a low income, are not employed, and/or have one or more out-of-wedlock children (Bramlett and Mosher, 2002).

Although there are no national data, it's possible that low-income women with low educational levels have no incentive to pay the costs of a divorce because their husbands may be unemployed and unable to pay for child support. In most cases, however, separations end in divorce.

SEPARATION AND DIVORCE Divorce, the legal and formal dissolution of a marriage, is not a new phenomenon. The Code of Hammurabi, written almost 4,000 years ago in ancient Mesopotamia, permitted termination of a marriage. (What was once Mesopotamia is currently composed of Iraq and parts of Syria and Turkey.) Among the nobility, especially, divorce was apparently as easy for women as for men:

> If she was careful and was not at fault, even though her husband has been going out and disparaging her greatly, that woman, without incurring any blame at all, may take her dowry and go off to her father's house (J. Monk, cited in Esler, 1994).

Many centuries later, in 1830, some researchers were alarmed that divorce rates had been increasing and that marriage was no longer "a permanent and lifelong state" (Thwing and Thing, cited in Reiss, 1971: 317). By the early twentieth century, a number of men ended their marriage by deserting rather than seeking a legal divorce.

Trends in Divorce

CNN talk show host Larry King has been to the altar six times. Actor and singer Billy Bob Thornton has had five marriages. As this book goes to press, model Christie Brinkley, 52, has separated from her fourth husband, and actor Tom Cruise, 44, is planning to wed a third wife. As some older students might recall, actress Elizabeth Taylor divorced seven men between 1962 and 1996. Are such celebrities typical of the average American? Not at all.

Are Current U.S. Divorce Rates Alarming?

Talk show hosts and many journalists often report that one in two U.S. marriages end in divorce. This rate is highly misleading because it is based on the number of people who divorce in a given year. In fact, roughly one in five Americans age 15 and over has ever been divorced (see "Data Digest"). Historically, the divorce rate has never exceeded about 41 percent in a given year (Kreider, 2005).

Whether current divorce rates are alarming or not depends on one's perspective. In an ideal world, couples would have a happy marriage until one of the spouses died. On the other hand, divorce rates are considerably lower than those proclaimed, incorrectly, by the mass media and many marriage proponents (see Chapters 1 and 2). In fact, U.S. divorce rates have decreased.

Divorce Rates Have Decreased

The U.S. divorce rate rose steadily throughout the twentieth century (see *Figure 15.1*). The small peak in the early 1950s, after the end of World War II, has been attributed to divorces among people who had married impulsively before the soldiers left for war. When the men returned, the couples found that they had nothing in common. War-related family stress also increased divorce rates (see Chapter 3).

since you asked

Are U.S. divorce rates the highest in the world?

In the mid-1960s, divorce rates began to climb. They reached a plateau and remained there for a while, but started dropping in 1995. In effect, divorce rates are *lower* today than they were between 1975 and 1990 (Schoen and Canudas-Romo, 2006).

It's not clear why this is the case. Perhaps more people are seeking premarital counseling and working harder to save their marriages. On the other hand, the recent lower divorce rates may reflect the growing number of

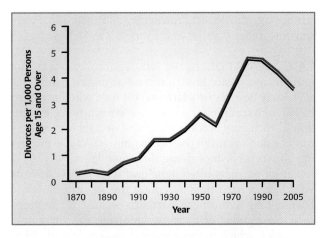

FIGURE 15.1 **Divorce in the United States, 1870–2005**

SOURCES: Plateris, 1973; U.S. Census Bureau, 2002; Munson and Sutton, 2006.

couples who cohabit and postpone marriage. That is, many cohabiting couples in "trial marriages" break up instead of getting married and then divorcing. In a sense, then, remaining single has the effect of decreasing divorce rates (see Chapter 9). However, while U.S. divorce rates have decreased, those in many other countries have increased (see the box "Divorce around the World").

Most people want to marry and to stay married. In a recent nationwide survey, for example, 79 percent of the adult respondents said that one of life's major goals was "having one marriage partner for life" (Rapaport, 2000). Despite such goals, divorce occurs and is a painful milestone in many people's lives.

The Process of Divorce

Like separations, few divorces are spontaneous, spur-of-the-moment acts. Instead, the divorce process is usually spread over a long period during which the couple gradually redefines their relationship and their expectations of each other. In navigating this transition, many people go through a number of stages. One widely cited process is Bohannon's (1971) six "stations" of divorce: emotional, legal, economic, coparental, community, and psychic.

since you asked

Can a divorced couple remain friends?

Emotional Divorce

The *emotional divorce* begins before any legal steps are taken. One or both partners may feel disillusioned, unhappy, or rejected. The person who eventually initi-

Cross-Cultural Families

Divorce around the World

One of the most consistent global changes has been a rise in divorce rates during the last 30 years or so. Russia has the highest divorce rate in the world—more than one out of two marriages ends in divorce. U.S. divorce rates are slightly lower than Russia's but two to three times higher than those for some other industrialized countries, such as Switzerland, Canada, France, Israel, Germany, Japan, and the Scandinavian countries.

Some of the lowest divorce rates (from less than 1 percent to 15 percent of all marriages) are in Albania, Italy, Portugal, Spain, Turkey, and some countries in Eastern Europe and many in Africa. Religious and traditional values may account in part for these low rates.

The Philippines, a predominantly Roman Catholic country, is one of the few nations that prohibits divorce, even though a marriage can be easily annulled on psychological grounds. The Mediterranean island state of Malta is the only other nation in the world that forbids divorce.

One of the reasons divorce rates are rising around the world is that since the 1970s many countries—both industrialized and developing—have liberalized their divorce laws. Getting a divorce in Cuba is as easy as a trip to the notary public: Couples pay $4 and are divorced within 20 minutes. Some believe that such liberal divorce laws fuel one of the world's highest divorce rates—there are almost 70 divorces for every 100 marriages in Cuba, particularly among young couples. Divorce is a quick and simple process because people have few possessions and there isn't much property to divide.

Divorce laws have also changed in much of the Islamic world. For example, once a rare phenomenon, divorce now occurs in one-third of all marriages in Kuwait and is common in many Nigerian cities. Among Muslims, the husband may obtain a divorce by merely repeating the phrase "I divorce thee" to his wife three times in front of witnesses. The couple can reconcile within three months, but if they do not, the marriage ends.

In some countries, such as Jordan and Egypt, women who divorce must forfeit any right to financial compensation, including alimony and the dowry their husband received at the time of the marriage. Turkey, in contrast,

entitles women to an equal share of joint assets in the event of a divorce.

Regardless of the country, women usually take the initiative in seeking a divorce, and they do so for remarkably similar reasons. In South Korea, for example, almost half of all marriages end in divorce within the first three years of marriage. The most common reasons for divorce, in order of priority, are adultery by the husband, domestic violence, failure to provide adequate financial support, and disappearance of the husband for more than three years.

Sources: Al Naser, 2005; Amaro, 2005; Katz and Lavee, 2005; Mburugu and Adams, 2005; Modo, 2005; Nauck and Klaus, 2005; Sheng, 2005; Singh, 2005; Trost and Levin, 2005; United Nations Economic Commission for Europe, 2005; Wiseman and Nishiwaki, 2005.

Stop and Think . . .

- Are divorce rates everywhere too high? What are the advantages and disadvantages, especially for women and children, in having greater access to divorce?

- In the past, Chinese couples vowed to remain married to each other "even if the seas run dry and the rocks crumble." Divorce rates in China have jumped because more people, especially young women, have jobs and refuse to tolerate infidelity. Do you think that more liberal divorce laws, in China and elsewhere, will encourage husbands to be more loving, faithful, and attentive?

ates the divorce may feel that the marriage was never "right" to begin with, that the partners were mismatched, or that they were living a lie:

> I came to realize that there had been a very long time when we really had no life together. We just sort of shared a house, and sort of took care of the kids together. But mostly I did that with the kids and he went and did his thing, and we were sort of this phony family for friends and neighbors and the relatives (Hopper, 2001: 436).

Spouses may be aloof or polite, despite their anger, or they may become overtly hostile, making sarcastic remarks or hurling accusations at each other.

The emotional divorce often progresses through stages, from a beginning phase to an end phase (Kersten, 1990). In the *beginning phase,* spouses feel disappointment in each other but hope that the marriage will improve.

During the *middle phase,* their feelings of hurt and anger increase as efforts to correct the situation seem unsuccessful. The partner who is less happy begins evaluating the rewards and costs of leaving the marriage.

In the *end phase,* one of the partners stops caring and detaches emotionally from the other. Apathy and indifference replace loving, intimate feelings. Even when people don't hate each other, it may be too late to rekindle the marriage:

> I knew I was going to die if I didn't get out of this marriage. We couldn't talk. We buried our feelings until there was nothing between us except the shell of a life. I was depressed for a long time before I got the courage to leave. I think I must have been grieving for years. It was so sad. He is not a bad person (Gold, 1992: 45).

Many couples delay the divorce as long as possible. For example, a national study of people age 40 and older found that 17 percent had postponed getting a divorce for at least five years, primarily "because of the children" (Montenegro, 2004).

In the short term, according to many lawyers, there's a lull in divorce initiations from Thanksgiving until the New Year because many couples put on a happy face and celebrate the holidays for the sake of their family. After New Year's, the attorney's phone "rings off the hook" as one of spouses resolves to end a troubled marriage (Heslam, 2006). Even though some couples turn to counseling and marital therapy, as you'll see later in this chapter, most seek legal advice to end the marriage.

Legal Divorce

The *legal divorce* is the formal dissolution of a marriage. During this stage, couples reach agreements on such issues as child custody and the division of property and other economic assets.

In part because divorce is an adversarial procedure during which each partner's attorney tries to maintain the upper hand, the process is rarely trouble free. For example, the partner who does not want the divorce may try to forestall the inevitable end of the marriage or get revenge by making demands that the other spouse will find hard to accept, such as getting custody of the family dog.

Some issues may include **alimony** (sometimes called *spousal maintenance*). Other conflicts involve **child support**—monetary payments by the noncustodial parent to the custodial parent to help pay for child-rearing expenses. Because spouses often disagree on what is fair and equitable, they may use money to manipulate each other into making more concessions ("I'm willing to pay child support if you agree to sell the house and split the proceeds").

Even after a divorce is legal, couples may experience ambivalence: "Did I really do the right thing?" or "Should I have been satisfied with what I had?" Such doubts are normal, but some family clinicians caution divorcing parents not to reveal their ambivalence to their children, who may become confused or anxious, or deny the reality of divorce and fantasize about reconciliation (Everett and Everett, 1994).

Sometimes people have divorce parties, like this one, to celebrate the end of an unhappy marriage. Do you think that such ceremonies help people get closure on a divorce?

Economic Divorce

During the *economic divorce,* the couple may argue about who should pay past debts, property taxes, and expenses for the children, such as braces. Thus, conflict over financial issues may continue long after the legal questions have been settled. In addition, the partners may try to change the child-support agreement or not make the required payments.

Most financial planners now advise couples who are contemplating divorce to think about their retirement funds because they are often among the largest assets to be divided. They also urge prospective divorcees to go to court and renegotiate payments, especially for child support, when there are downturns in the economy. In doing so, couples may be involved in an economic divorce for several decades if their children are very young at the time of the divorce.

Coparental Divorce

The *coparental divorce* involves agreements about legal responsibility for financial support of the children, their day-to-day care, and the rights of the custodial and non-custodial parents in spending time with them. As you'll see shortly, conflict during this period may be short lived or long term, depending on how well the parents get along.

Community Divorce

Partners also go through a *community divorce,* during which they inform friends, family, teachers, and others that they are no longer married. Relationships between grandparents and grandchildren often continue, but in-laws may sever ties. The partners may also replace old friendships with new ones, and they typically start dating again (see Chapter 16).

Psychic Divorce

In this final stage, the couple goes through a *psychic divorce* in which the partners separate from each other emotionally and establish separate lives. One or both spouses may undergo a process of mourning. Some people never complete this stage because they can't let go of their pain, anger, and resentment, even after they remarry. Recently, some couples have held "divorce ceremonies" to help them finalize the divorce symbolically and publicly. Although still rare, such ceremonies "ask the partners to offer apologies to each other and seek forgiveness for the hurt they have inflicted" (Tesoriero, 2002: F11).

Not all couples go through all six of Bohannon's stations. Also, some couples may experience some stages, such as emotional and economic divorce, simultaneously. The important point is that divorce is a *process* that involves many people, not just the divorcing couple, and may take time to complete. Moreover, because people differ, divorcing couples may respond to each other in varying ways, as the box "How Divorced Parents Relate Can Make All the Difference" illustrates.

Making Connections

- Based on your own experiences, how well do Bohannon's six stations describe divorce? Would you add other stages, for example? Or feel that some are considerably more important than others?

- According to one divorce attorney, even happily married couples should prepare for a divorce, especially financially. One example includes making regular deposits into a private account that a spouse won't notice (Fogle, 2006). Is such advice offensive? Or is it practical and realistic—"just in case"—especially for women?

Why Do People Divorce?

Social scientists explain divorce rates on three levels: macro or societal; demographic; and micro or interpersonal. As you read this section, keep in mind that these various factors often overlap. As *Figure 15.2* shows, macro variables influence demographic variables, which, in turn, may lead to specific problems that end a marriage.

Macro-Level Reasons for Divorce

There are many macro-level reasons for divorce. Five important reasons involve social institutions, social integration, gender roles, cultural values, and technology.

SOCIAL INSTITUTIONS Changes in legal, religious, and family institutions have affected divorce rates. The economy also plays an important role.

All states have **no-fault divorce** laws so that neither partner need establish guilt or wrongdoing on the part of the other. Before no-fault divorce laws, the partner who initiated the divorce had to prove that the other was to blame for the collapse of the marriage because of adultery, desertion, or physical and mental cruelty, for example.

Choices

How Divorced Parents Relate Can Make All the Difference

Because divorcing spouses are often angry, hurt, or bitter, many divorces are hostile and painful. As the following five styles of relating to each other suggest, the more civility partners can maintain in their postdivorce relationship, the more productive their relationships will be, both with each other and with their children (Ahrons and Rodgers, 1987; Gold, 1992).

Perfect Pals A very small group of divorced spouses share decision making and child rearing much as they did in marriage, and many feel that they are better parents after the divorce. These former spouses may even spend holidays together and maintain relationships with each other's extended families.

Cooperative Colleagues Although most divorced spouses do not consider themselves good friends, some are able to cooperate. Working together often takes effort, but they accept their roles as parents and believe that it is their duty to make mutually responsible decisions about their children.

Cooperative parents want to minimize the trauma of divorce for their children and try to protect them from conflict. Such parents are willing to negotiate and compromise on some of their differences. They may also consult counselors and mediators to resolve impasses before going to court.

Angry Associates These divorced couples harbor bitter resentments about events in their past marriage as well as the divorce process. Some have long and heated battles over custody, visitation rights, and financial matters, for example. These battles may continue for many years after the divorce.

Fiery Foes Some divorced spouses are completely unable to coparent. Such partners are incapable of remembering any good times in the marriage, and each emphasizes the wrongs done by the other. Children are caught in the middle of the bitter conflict and are expected to side with one parent and regard the other as the enemy.

One parent, usually the father, sees the children less and less often over the years, and both parents blame each other for this declining contact. As in the case of "angry associates," legal battles sometimes continue for years after the divorce.

Dissolved Duos Unlike the battling "fiery foes," the partners break with each other entirely. Noncustodial parents may "kidnap" the children, or a partner may leave the area where the family has been living.

In some cases, one partner, usually the man, actually disappears, leaving the other partner with the entire burden of caring for the family. The children have only memories and fantasies of the vanished parent.

Stop and Think . . .

- Think about yourself, your parents, or your friends. Do any of these five styles characterize your or their divorces?
- Why, in most cases, are few parents "perfect pals" and "cooperative colleagues"? If parents say that they really care about children, why do so many use them as pawns in divorce struggles?

Couples can now simply give "irreconcilable differences" or "incompatibility" as a valid reason for divorce.

The increasing number of people entering the legal profession and the growth of free legal clinics has also made divorce more accessible and inexpensive. Because divorce cases account for one-third of all civil lawsuits, they provide millions of jobs for lawyers, judges, and other employees of the legal system. If a divorcing couple has had a long-term marriage, accountants may spend several years (and charge up to $50,000) disentangling property rights and accumulated marital property.

In child-custody disputes, attorneys may hire marriage counselors, psychologists, education specialists, medical personnel, clergy, social workers, and media-tors. Although not everyone who wants a divorce can afford all these services, their very availability sends the message that divorce is acceptable and that many professionals are eager to "help."

Changes in the institution of the family and in the economy have also affected divorce rates. As the United States shifted from a preindustrial to an industrial society, family members became less dependent on one another financially and for recreation. And as more people moonlight or work evening and weekend shifts, many couples experience more stress and spend less time together (see Chapters 1 and 13).

Nonstandard work schedules and long hours at work can increase tension. Fatigue, demanding child-rearing responsibilities, and job instability (such as mov-

Macro-Level Reasons

- Changing Social Institutions
- Low Social Integration
- Changing Gender Roles
- Cultural Values
- Technology

Demographic Variables

- Parental Divorce
- Age at Marriage
- Premarital Childbearing
- Race and Ethnicity
- Religion
- Education
- Income
- Prior Cohabitation
- Marital Duration

Interpersonal Problems

- Extramarital Affairs
- Violence
- Substance Abuse
- Conflict over Money
- Disagreements about Raising Children
- Lack of Communication
- Irritating Personality Characteristics
  (Critical, Nagging, Moody)
- Annoying Habits
  (Smoking, Belching, etc.)
- Not Being at Home Enough
- Growing Apart

DIVORCE

FIGURE 15.2   Some Causes of Divorce

To combat the high divorce rates among active-duty soldiers and officers, the military offers numerous weekend retreats and marriage education classes. Here, a group of Marine wives in Camp Pendleton, California, discuss the difficulties of daily life while their husbands are in the Middle East. Such support groups help spouses deal with stress, loneliness, anxiety, and other issues such as maintaining an effective family plan and how to adjust a budget and save money.

ing from job to job) can increase the likelihood of divorce (Presser, 2000; Ahituv and Lerman, 2004).

SOCIAL INTEGRATION At the turn of the twentieth century, French sociologist Émile Durkheim maintained that people who are integrated into a community are less likely to divorce, commit suicide, or engage in other self-destructive behaviors. A number of contemporary social scientists agree that **social integration**—the social bonds that people have with others and with the community at large—discourages divorce.

The great diversity of subcultures, languages, and religious practices in the United States has decreased social integration. We now also have looser bonds to the community that help explain the high divorce rates. For example, divorces of first marriages are more likely in communities with high unemployment, low median family income, and high poverty levels. Stress often leads to conflict, disagreements, and splitting up. In contrast, more affluent neighborhoods can strengthen shaky marital bonds by providing a variety of services for adults and children that connect people to one another and to the community during stressful periods (Bramlett and Mosher, 2002).

Whether married couples are happy or not isn't the issue. Instead, according to many contemporary social scientists, people who live in communities and societies that are more socially integrated are more likely to stay married.

GENDER ROLES American women are twice as likely as men to initiate a divorce. Some are escaping abusive marriages. For others, getting a divorce can increase the likelihood that a father who has abandoned his family can be tracked down for child-support payments. Women are also more likely to initiate a divorce in states where they feel that they have a good chance of getting sole custody of the children (Brinig and Allen, 2000).

Changing gender roles, especially employed women's growing economic independence, have mixed effects on divorce rates. Women with more resources—those with college degrees or good jobs, for example—are filing for divorce instead of living with a husband who is emotionally distant, adulterous, a substance abuser, or who refuses to share domestic tasks. If women are economically self-sufficient, they don't have to tolerate such behavior (Hacker, 2003; see, also, Chapters 5, 7, and 14).

A wife's employment can also have a stabilizing effect on a marriage. Especially in a marriage in which both spouses are satisfied with the division of domestic tasks, her income increases the family's financial security and raises its standard of living (Schoen et al., 2002; Rogers, 2004).

CULTURAL VALUES American attitudes and beliefs about divorce have been changing. Some observers feel that Americans are increasingly emphasizing individual happiness rather than family commitments. As people pursue self-fulfillment, some argue, they betray the spouses who love them because of a "narcissistic greed for personal happiness" that leads them to seek a divorce (Pittman, 1999).

The women's movement of the late 1960s challenged the traditional belief that women should stay in unhappy or abusive marriages. Throughout the 1970s and 1980s, many therapists and attorneys not only sent the message that "divorce is okay" but flooded the market with self-help books on how to get a divorce, how to cope with loneliness and guilt after a divorce, how to deal with child-custody disputes, and other legal issues. And television programs like *Divorce Court* show viewers that divorce is an everyday occurrence.

But some attitudes toward divorce are shifting. Compared with the 1970s, for example, women with at least a college degree now have considerably more "restrictive" attitudes, feeling that divorces should be harder to get. This change may be due to many women's greater ability to choose partners with stable jobs, as well as their greater commitment to marriage because marriage works better for the "haves" than for the "have-nots" (Martin and Parashar, 2006).

TECHNOLOGY Technological advances like the Internet have made divorce more accessible. Many people now go online to save money and time and avoid the emotional clashes that can play out in lawyers' offices. Some online do-it-yourself divorces cost as little as $50 for all the necessary court forms and documents.

Some critics contend that the online services invite impulsiveness. People who have used the services, however, say that the decision to seek a divorce is always agonizing but the online accessibility saves money on legal fees. According to one proponent of online services, "You're not going to get divorced because it's on special offer" (O'Donnell et al., 1999: 8).

Although there are no national data, some researchers suspect that online dating that results in marriage may be especially likely to end in divorce. Many online daters are likely to "jump the gun" because they want to marry. They often don't know each other well, rush into marriage, and then discover that they have little in common or that one of the partners lied about his or her background (Gamerman, 2006; see, also, Chapter 8).

Demographic Variables and Divorce

Many demographic variables also help explain why certain couples are prone to divorce. Some of the most important factors are having divorced parents, age at marriage, premarital childbearing, the presence of children, race and ethnicity, social class, and religion.

PARENTAL DIVORCE If the parents of one or both partners in a marriage were divorced during childhood, the partners themselves are more likely to divorce. Because children of divorced parents are less able to afford college (which tends to delay marriage), they are more likely to marry early. And the younger partners are when they marry, the more likely they are to divorce (Wolfinger, 1999, 2000; Glenn, 2005).

Some researchers have proposed that children of divorced parents have high divorce rates because they are less willing than others to tolerate unhappy marriages. Other researchers have argued, instead, that many children of divorced parents have trouble making the kind of commitment that is necessary for marital success (Glenn, 2005). It's not clear, however, whether the lack of commitment is due to parental role models, a general suspicion that happy marriages are impossible, a higher likelihood of cohabiting (which increases divorce rates), or social class (see Chapter 9).

AGE AT MARRIAGE A number of studies have found that early age at marriage—especially under age 18—increases the chances of divorce. In fact, early marriage may be one of the strongest predictors of divorce. After 10 years of marriage, for example, 48 percent of first marriages of women under age 18 have dissolved, compared with 24 percent of first marriages of women who were at least age 25 at the time of the marriage (Kurdek, 1993; Bramlett and Mosher, 2002).

Why do young spouses have high divorce rates? Sometimes, if young couples are experiencing problems, parents and relatives who disapproved of the marriage may encourage divorce. In most cases, however, young couples are not prepared to handle marital responsibilities. Among other things, they complain that their spouses become angry easily, are jealous or moody, spend money foolishly, drink or use drugs, or get into trouble with the law (Booth and Edwards, 1985).

PREMARITAL PREGNANCY AND CHILDBEARING Women who conceive or give birth to a child *before* marriage have higher divorce rates than women who conceive or have a child *after* marriage. Divorce is especially likely among adolescent parents, who generally lack the education or income to maintain a stable family life (Garfinkel et al., 1994; Teachman, 2002).

PRESENCE OF CHILDREN The presence of preschool children, especially firstborn children, seems to increase marital stability. This may reflect the fact that some couples stay together for the sake of the children. In addition, the presence of young children may make the divorce process more costly, both emotionally and financially (Previti and Amato, 2003).

The risk of divorce is low when the youngest child is under 3; it reaches a plateau as the youngest child passes through ages 7 to 12, peaks when the children are in their teens, and drops sharply after the last child reaches age 17. When children are older, especially during the teen years, couples may have fewer incentives to stay together. In some cases, problems with adolescent children worsen already strained marital relationships, and the marriage may fall apart (Heaton, 1990; Waite and Lillard, 1991; see, also, Chapters 12 and 16).

RACE AND ETHNICITY Divorce rates vary by race and ethnicity. After 10 years of marriage, for example, 20 percent of Asian American women's first marriages have dissolved, compared with 32 percent for white women, 34 percent for Latinas, and 47 percent for black women (see *Figure 15.3*).

One of the most consistent research findings is that blacks are more likely than people in any other racial-ethnic group to divorce. Since 1960, divorce rates among African Americans have been almost 76 percent higher than those among whites and Latinos, and nearly twice as high since 1980. These differences persist at all income, age, educational, and occupational levels (Rank, 1987; White, 1991; Saluter, 1994). The box "Why Are African American Divorce Rates High?" examines some of the reasons for these findings.

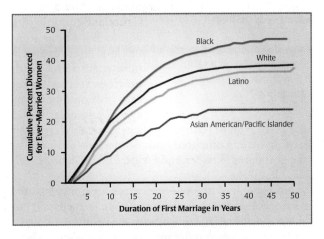

FIGURE 15.3 **Divorce among Racial-Ethnic Groups**
SOURCE: Kreider and Fields, 2002: Figure 5.

Multicultural Families

Why Are African American Divorce Rates High?

Race and ethnicity don't "cause" divorce. Other macro, demographic, and interpersonal factors are at work. One of the reasons for higher marital dissolution rates among blacks is their higher rates of teenage and premarital pregnancies. As you saw earlier, a woman who bears her first child out of wedlock or within seven months of marriage has a higher risk of separation or divorce.

Another reason for the high divorce rate among blacks is poverty. Because African Americans are disproportionately poor, they are more likely to experience financial strain and male unemployment, problems that often lead to divorce in all kinds of families.

African American men, especially those age 40 and older, are more likely than whites and Latinos to experience a major illness. If the man has lost his job or the family doesn't have health insurance, an illness can aggravate marital problems.

Some researchers also suggest that divorce may be more acceptable among African Americans. Divorce may be less stressful because the community offers divorcing partners social support. During painful life events like divorce, African American families and churches provide love, services, money, and other resources.

Low Asian American divorce rates, on the other hand, reflect a combination of variables. Recent immigrants, for example, are likely to endorse traditional values that encourage staying married, even if there is domestic violence. Moreover, birth rates for unmarried Asian American women are low, another factor that decreases the risk of divorce.

SOURCES: Hill, 2003; Willie and Reddick, 2003; Costigan et al., 2004; Montenegro, 2004; see, also, Chapters 4, 13, and 14.

Stop and Think. . .

- Some of my African American students contend that discussions of high black divorce rates are racist ("You white folks are always emphasizing the negative"). Do you agree? And do such comments indicate that most Americans, including blacks, still see divorce as deviant rather than as normal?

- One recent national study concluded that risk factors such as age at marriage, education, premarital childrearing, and region of residence explain little of the overall difference between white and black divorce rates because there are many unknown variables (Sweeney and Phillips, 2004). What might be some of the unknown variables that researchers haven't taken into account?

SOCIAL CLASS Low educational attainment, high unemployment rates, and poverty increase separation and divorce rates. A number of social scientists have commented on a "divorce divide" between people with a bachelor's degree or higher and those with a high school education or less. For example (and consistent with previous studies), a recent poll of Americans age 18 and older found that 24 percent of four-year college graduates have ever been divorced compared with 36 percent of non–college graduates (Kreider and Fields, 2002; Glenn, 2005; Carroll, 2006).

since you asked

Why do college graduates have lower divorce rates than those with less education?

Do people with college degrees have more stable marriages because they're smarter? No. Rather, going to college postpones marriage, with the result that college graduates are often more mature, experienced, and capable of dealing with personal crises when they marry. They have higher incomes and better health care, which reduce stress due to financial problems. Also, some of the characteristics required for completing college (such as persistence, dependability, and responsibility) also increase the likelihood of having a stable marriage (Kreider and Fields, 2002; Glenn, 2005).

RELIGION People who say that religion is important to them experience lower separation and divorce rates than do less religious individuals. Spouses who follow the same religion or convert to the other spouse's religion at marriage are more likely to reconcile after a separation. Religious similarity may be important to marital stability because it reflects the compatibility of the partners' traditions, values, and feelings of community (Wineberg, 1994; Bramlett and Mosher, 2002).

Being religious doesn't guarantee marital stability, of course. All of us know ardently religious couples who have divorced while couples who are not religious have celebrated their fiftieth wedding anniversary. Generally, however, people who are religious are more likely to persevere in a marriage, even if it's unhappy.

Interpersonal Reasons for Divorce

Macro and demographic variables affect interpersonal reasons for divorce. Because we live longer than people did in the past, a married couple may spend a significantly longer period of time together. Thus, there is a greater chance that, over the years, the partners may grate on each other's nerves. Or macro-level factors such as unemployment can create strain and aggravate existing annoyances.

Still, there are many individual reasons for divorce. Most overlap, as when a lack of commitment leads to infidelity, verbal or physical abuse, or poor communication. Although financial difficulties create conflict for both spouses, women give more reasons for their divorces than men do (see *Figure 15.4*). These differences explain why women are more likely than men to initiate a divorce.

People grow apart for many reasons, but some problems are especially likely to break up a marriage. Four common stressors are unrealistic expectations, conflict and abuse, infidelity, and communication problems.

UNREALISTIC EXPECTATIONS People now have fewer children and more time to focus on their relationship as a couple, both while the children are living at home and after they move out. One of the results is a greater chance that one of the spouses will become disillu-

sioned. Wives, especially, may expect to be continuously told that they are loved or appreciated. Or couples may compare themselves with unrealistic images in films and on television and conclude that their marriage isn't as idyllic as it should be (see Chapters 1, 5, and 10).

CONFLICT AND ABUSE Nationally, arguments and conflict are major reasons for divorce for both sexes (see *Figure 15.4*). The seeds of dissatisfaction are often sown years before a marriage. A strong predictor of divorce is negative interaction before marriage. Unless people change their interaction patterns (and they usually don't), marital distress grows, increasing the likelihood of divorce (Clements et al., 2004).

Sometimes the conflict escalates into abuse, especially for wives. For example, 42 percent of women but only 9 percent of men said that domestic violence was a major reason for divorce. Among those age 40 and older, 23 percent of women, compared with only 8 percent of men, said that verbal, physical, or emotional abuse was "the most significant reason for the divorce" (Montenegro, 2004; Glenn, 2005).

INFIDELITY Cheating is another major reason for divorce, especially for women (see *Figure 15.4*). Many men claim that they're unfaithful because they're unhappy with their sex life, but there's little evidence to support such complaints. Nationally, for example, only 2 percent of men and women say that sexual incompatibility or poor sexual performance was the most important reason for a divorce (Montenegro, 2004; see, also, Chapter 7).

COMMUNICATION Communication problems derail many marriages (see Chapters 5 and 10). Some researchers can predict whether a newlywed couple will still be married four to six years later by observing not *what* they say but *how* they say it. Couples that stay together listen to each other respectfully even when they disagree, don't start discussions with accusatory statements ("You're lazy and never do anything around the house"), and have more positive interactions than negative ones. Lasting relationships may not be blissful, but the communication isn't venomous (Gottman, 1994).

There are other reasons for divorce, but they're not at the top of the list. Although many couples stay in a marriage for the sake of the children, disagreements about how to raise and discipline children can trigger a divorce. Money is another source of conflict in marital breakups. Wives grow disillusioned if their husband can't find or hold a job. Unemployed or low-paid men, who already feel inadequate, complain that their wives' nagging

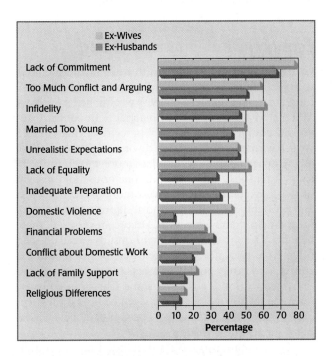

FIGURE 15.4 Why People Get a Divorce, by Sex

Source: Glenn, 2005: Figure 19.

about bills makes them feel even worse (Hetherington and Kelly, 2002; Stanley et al., 2002; Montenegro, 2004).

It bears repeating that interpersonal difficulties often reflect demographic or macro-level factors. For example, many black divorced men report that financial strain created or aggravated existing communication problems. As one divorced father said, "I worked too much and spent little time at home. . . . It is ironic that my efforts to provide for my family made me vulnerable to charges of being distant and uncaring" (Lawson and Thompson, 1999: 65).

Making Connections

■ Some people send humorous greeting cards to announce their divorce. A smaller number hold "divorce ceremonies" to celebrate their marital breakup. Are these methods tasteless or effective ways of getting some closure on divorce?

■ Think about the people you know who have experienced a divorce. Were the reasons macro, demographic, interpersonal, or a combination?

How Divorce Affects Adults

In the film *The First Wives Club*, three middle-aged women get revenge on their ex-husbands for dumping them for younger girlfriends. Among other stereotypes, the husbands are portrayed as cads, the wives are presented as innocent victims, and getting even is fun.

In real life, divorce is usually an agonizing process for both sexes, at all socioeconomic levels, and regardless of race or ethnicity. Divorce has significant effects in at least three areas of a couple's or family's life: physical, emotional, and psychological well-being; economic and financial changes; and child-custody and child-support arrangements.

Physical, Emotional, and Psychological Effects

Divorced people are worse off than married people in many ways. They report greater social isolation, economic hardship, and stress. They also have less social support and less satisfying sex lives (Mastekaasa, 1997; Waite et al., 2002; see, also, Chapter 7).

The psychic divorce described earlier may continue for many years. Even when both partners know that their marriage cannot be salvaged, they are often ambivalent. They may fluctuate between a sense of loss and a feeling of freedom; they may have periods of depression punctuated with spurts of happiness. The box "Do You Know Someone with Divorce Hangover?" examines some of the adjustments that newly divorced people face.

Initially, divorced people of both sexes experience emotional problems, but they tend to react differently: Women report more depression while men report more alcohol abuse and smoking. Such reactions reflect cultural norms about gender roles. That is, in our society women typically express stress by turning inward, while men are more likely to engage in high-risk behaviors. An individual's emotional health usually improves when he or she forms a new relationship, especially by cohabiting or remarrying (Johnson and Wu, 2002; Simon, 2002; Martin et al., 2005).

It's not clear, however, whether divorce lowers people's well-being, whether preexisting problems (such as depression and alcohol abuse) lead to divorce, or whether there's a combination of factors. Some people are prone to psychological or interpersonal problems before divorce but exhibit additional problems afterward. For example, an aggressive husband may become physically abusive with new partners after a divorce. In other cases, long-standing problems such as infidelity and substance abuse play a major role in dissolving a marriage (Amato, 2002; Lucas, 2005).

Economic and Financial Changes

Generally, marriage builds wealth while divorce depletes it. For example, a national study of people ages 41 to 49 found that, on average, a couple's wealth increases about 16 percent for each year of marriage. In contrast, divorced couples lose about 77 percent of their shared wealth within five years of the divorce (Zagorsky, 2005).

Married couples accumulate more wealth for a variety of reasons: They maintain one household instead of two, save more money, invest more of their income, and probably work harder and seek promotions to pay for their children's education. Divorce reverses all these benefits. Despite their best intentions, divorced couples often have two mortgages, two sets of household expenses, and rarely pool their assets to pay for their children's educational costs. At some Christian colleges, staff and faculty members may even be fired if they separate or divorce, increasing a person's financial instability (Simpson, 2006).

Gender can also have a dramatic impact on a divorced person's economic status. As one accountant noted, "The man usually walks out with the most valu-

Applying What You've Learned

Do You Know Someone with Divorce Hangover?

In a "healthy" divorce, the ex-spouses must accomplish three tasks: letting go, developing new social ties, and, when children are involved, redefining parental roles. Often, however, divorced partners suffer from "divorce hangover" (Walther, 1991; Everett and Everett, 1994).

In each of the following statements, fill in the blanks with the name of someone you know who has just gone through a divorce. If you agree that many of these statements describe a friend or acquaintance, you know someone with divorce hangover.

Sarcasm When someone mentions the ex-spouse, _____ is sarcastic or takes potshots at the former partner. The sarcasm may be focused on the marriage in particular or unsupported generalizations: "All men leave the minute their wives turn 40" or "All women are just after their husband's money."

Using the children _____ tries to convince the children that the divorce was entirely the other person's fault and may grill the children for information about the other parent.

Lashing out _____ may try to assert control in such ways as making unreasonable demands (for example, refusing joint custody) or blowing up at a friend because the ex-spouse was invited to a party.

Paralysis _____ can't seem to get back on track like going back to school, getting a new job, becoming involved in new relationships, or finding new friends.

Sometimes it's even hard for _____ to get up in the morning and go to work, clean the house, or return phone calls.

Holding on The ex-spouse's photograph still sits on _____'s piano, and his/her clothing or other former possessions remain in view, keeping the ex-spouse's presence alive in _____'s daily life.

Throwing out everything _____ may throw away things of value—even jewelry, art, or priceless collections—that are reminders of the ex-spouse.

Blaming and finding fault Everything that went wrong in the marriage or the divorce was someone else's fault, _____ maintains: the ex-spouse, family, friends, kids, boss, and so on.

Excessive guilt _____ feels guilty about the divorce, regardless of which partner left the other. _____ buys the children whatever they want and gives in to the children's or ex-spouse's demands, however unreasonable they may be.

Dependency To fill the void left by the ex-spouse, _____ leans heavily on other people, particularly new romantic involvements.

Divorce can be devastating when it results in a loss of emotional and sexual intimacy, identity as part of a couple, financial security, self-esteem, friends, possessions, predictability, and even a home. Confronting these symptoms of divorce hangover can help a divorced person recognize and begin to overcome such losses.

---

able asset, earning ability, while the woman walks out with the biggest cash drain, the kids and house" (Gutner, 2000).

ALIMONY Alimony is less common than in the past, but it still exists. In some states, even if the wife is employed and the couple is childless, the higher earner, who is usually the man, may pay up to a third of his salary to his ex-wife for several years if they've been married longer than 10 years or if she is deemed physically or emotionally unhealthy.

GENDER According to some observers, no-fault divorce has done more harm than good to many women. Because

both partners are treated as equals, each, theoretically at least, receives half of the family assets, and the ex-wife is expected to support herself regardless of whether she has any job experience or work-related skills. Even though the couple's combined wealth decreases, the economic well-being of mothers declines by 36 percent and the financial status of fathers improves by 28 percent after a divorce. Whether a couple has children or not, the woman must often fight for a portion of her ex-husband's retirement income, which he earned during the marriage (Bianchi et al., 1999; Tergesen, 2001).

AGE A woman's age can also affect her income after a divorce. In 1979, homemaker Terry Hekker published

In 1997, Lorna Wendt, the wife of a wealthy General Electric corporate executive, rejected a $10 million settlement after her husband of 32 years sought a divorce. Ms. Wendt went to court, arguing that she was worth more as a full-time homemaker because she had raised their children single-handedly, entertained her husband's business associates, and made numerous business-related trips to 40 countries in support of her husband's career. The judge awarded her half the marital estate—worth about $100 million. In 1998, Wendt founded the Institute for Equality in Marriage (www.equalityinmarriage.org) to help women in similar circumstances.

a best-selling book that attacked career women and encouraged women to devote their lives to being full-time wives and mothers. Twenty years later, her husband presented her with divorce papers on their fortieth anniversary and left her for a younger woman. Hekker, who had raised five children, was devastated. Although she had no income and no marketable skills, the judge in her divorce case suggested that—at age 67—she go for job training. Hekker ended up selling her engagement ring to pay for roof repairs, got a job at a salary of $8,000 a year, and started living on food stamps. Her ex-husband, meanwhile, was vacationing in Mexico with his new lover. Hekker's current project is writing a book that warns young women to learn how to support themselves instead of being full-time homemakers (Harris, 2006).

Hekker is fairly representative of many divorced women. The proportion of women ages 55 to 60 who divorced jumped from less than 5 percent in 1970 to almost 19 percent in 2002. In addition, 22 percent of divorced women over 65 live in poverty. And because older women are less likely to remarry than are older men, their poverty rates are expected to increase. Remember, also, that millions of "career women" are now turning to full-time homemaking. If there is a divorce 20 or 30 years later, it is debatable whether they can reenter the job market as easily as they think, especially because new technologies demand up-to-date and high-level skills in most occupations (Haider et al., 2003; see, also, Chapter 12).

Many younger women's incomes plunge because in 85 percent of all divorce cases the children live with the mother (Grall, 2003). Even if both parents have child custody rights, child support payments rarely meet the mother's and children's living expenses. Let's look at child custody first and then examine child support issues.

Custody Issues

Children often are caught in the middle of custody battles:

> **Mark, age eight:** "I don't think either one of them should get me. All they ever do is fight and yell at each other. I'd rather live with my grandma."

> **Mary, age ten:** "I hate going to my dad's because every time I come back I get the third degree from Mom about what we did and who was there and whether Dad did anything wrong or anything that made us mad. I feel like a snitch."

> **Robin, age seven:** "Mom wants me to live with her and Dad wants me to live with him. But I want to live with both of them. Why do I have to choose? I just want us to be happy again."
> (Everett and Everett, 1994: 84–85).

Custody is a court-mandated ruling as to which parent will have the primary responsibility for the welfare and upbringing of a couple's children. Children live with a custodial parent, whereas they see the noncustodial parent according to specific visitation schedules worked out in the custody agreement. Because approximately 90 percent of all divorces are not contested, most child custody cases are settled out of court (Clarke, 1995).

In some cases, fathers get child custody by default: The biological mother doesn't want to raise the children, child protective agencies seek the father's involvement, or a child wants to live with the father. Even when they don't expect or want custody, some fathers, including those living in impoverished communities, often enjoy raising their children: "It's the best part of who I am," according to one father. However, they must often rely on kin for childrearing support because of inflexible work schedules and low wages (Hamer and Marchioro, 2002: 126).

TYPES OF CUSTODY There are three types of custody: sole, split, and joint. In **sole custody** (about 81 percent of cases), one parent has sole responsibility for raising the child; the other parent has specified visitation rights. Parents may negotiate informally over such things as schedules or holidays, but if they disagree, the legal custodian has the right to make the final decisions.

In **split custody** (about 2 percent of cases), the children are divided between the parents either by sex (the mother gets the daughters and the father gets the sons) or by choice (the children are allowed to choose the parent with whom they want to live).

In **joint custody**, sometimes called *dual residence* (about 16 percent of cases), the children divide their time between their parents, who share in decisions about their upbringing. In another 1 percent of cases, custody is awarded to someone other than the husband or wife, such as a relative (Clarke, 1995).

There are two types of joint custody. In *joint legal custody*, both parents share decision making on such issues as the child's education, health care, and religious training. In *joint physical custody*, the court specifies how much time children will spend in each parent's home.

Most recently, researchers have been using the term **co-custody** when parents share physical and legal custody of their children equally. This newer term is especially appropriate because many fathers, especially, are pushing for equal physical and legal custody.

PROS AND CONS OF CO-CUSTODY Co-custody is a heated issue because fathers' rights groups and many women are on opposite sides of the battlefield. The issue is especially complex because studies show that co-custody has mixed outcomes for both adults and children.

since you asked

Should divorced parents share custody of the children?

Proponents of co-custody advance several arguments:

- Many men say that they want to care for their children. Men have formed organizations such as Fathers United for Equal Justice to lobby for co-custody laws in almost every state.

- Much research indicates that the father's involvement–whether married, unmarried, or divorced—is essential to children's development.

- Co-custody eases the economic burdens of parenting, particularly for mothers.

- Because, on average, divorced fathers have higher incomes than divorced mothers, they can provide more resources for their children.

- Fathers are more likely to honor court-mandated child support and alimony payments if they have equal child-rearing rights (Hetherington and Stanley-Hagan, 1997; Sayer, 2006).

Opponents contend that co-custody does more harm than good:

- Constantly shuttling children between two homes can create instability and confusion as well as disrupt school attendance and academic performance.

- Children may have to deal with more parental conflict because parents who argued frequently during marriage continue to do so after a divorce (about child-rearing practices, discipline, or religious upbringing, for example).

- Co-custody usually decreases child support payments to mothers, who earn less than fathers do.

- Co-custody gives men more rights than responsibilities: They have more legal control and decision-making power, while mothers provide most of the children's emotional and routine physical care.

- Co-custody makes it possible for men who abused their wives or children before the divorce to continue doing so (Wolchick et al., 1996; Comerford, 2005; Kernic et al., 2005).

Finally, some observers feel that there is a gender bias in the court system. When custody is contested, for example, courts sometimes apply a double standard: "Often, men are judged by the availability of other child care, from a second wife to a girlfriend, while women are evaluated based on their own, personal ability to be with a child, ignoring the presence of a grandmother or a babysitter" (Feldmann and Goodale, 1995: 18).

WHAT SHOULD COURTS DO? So far, Iowa and Maine have passed legislation that gives parents co-custody if a parent requests it. Judges who deny such requests must explain their reasons.

Men's rights groups have been pushing for similar laws in other states because, they contend, a child should have two "real parents" instead of "one parent and one visitor." Women who resist such legislation argue that noncustodial fathers show little evidence of taking their parenting roles seriously. Many are "Disneyland dads" who are more likely to engage in leisure activities with their children (picnics, movies, sports) than to participate in school events or to supervise homework (Stewart, 2003).

Many family court judges also dislike co-custody. Some want more flexibility in deciding each case according to what they think is best for children. Others feel that co-custody arrangements are often temporary and may wind up in court again. For example, an ex-spouse who remarries may spend more time with a new partner or stepchildren than with the children from his previous marriage. Or a divorced parent may get a new job in another state or one with different work hours that requires extensive babysitting services. Co-custody is also unlikely to succeed if neither parent has a full-time job or both have unstable work histories (Gardner, 2004; Juby et al., 2005).

Some research shows that co-custody works well if both parents act like adults, cooperating with each other and encouraging the children to respect both parents. If there is little conflict between the parents and both parents manage the separate households, set rules, and supervise their offspring, most children adjust to joint custody with few problems (Bauserman, 2002; Lee, 2002).

CUSTODY AMONG GAY PARENTS Resolving child custody disputes among same-sex couples can be difficult because laws vary from one state to another. In Vermont, for example, which recognizes civil unions, both partners have child custody rights. If a partner moves to a state that doesn't recognize civil unions, however, the court might rule against both joint custody and visitation for one of the partners, even when both have drawn up detailed legal contracts.

What constitutes a parent among homosexual couples—biology, legal agreements, a relationship, or whether a person acts like a parent? In two recent cases in which lesbian couples split up, the California Supreme Court ruled that same-sex partners are entitled to co-custody despite the absence of legal adoption or a biological connection (such as not bearing the child after artificial insemination). In a third case, the Court required an employed partner to pay child support to the mother, who was a full-time homemaker, even though the partner had argued that "I'm not the children's father" (Paulson and Wood, 2005; Willing, 2005).

Some people maintain that if marriages among same-sex couples were legal, couples that split up could have a "clean divorce." Until then, most gay parents must face ongoing problems and court battles involving custody rights and responsibilities.

CHILD ABDUCTION Some parents who don't get custody abduct their children. **Child abduction** is the taking or keeping of a child by a family member in violation of a custody order, a decree, or other legitimate custodial right. The estimated 203,900 children who were victims of a family abduction in 1999 (the most recent year for these statistics) "represent a large group of children caught up in divisive and potentially disturbing family dynamics" (Hammer et al., 2002: 9).

Of all "missing" children, 1.3 million (9 percent) were abducted by a parent. In family abduction cases, 44 percent of the children are younger than age 6 and 53 percent are snatched by their biological father. In most cases, the custodial parent knows the ex-spouse's and children's whereabouts. In 6 percent of cases, however, the parent who abducts the child or children "disappears" (Hammer et al., 2002; Sedlak et al., 2002, 2005).

Child custody is a prickly issue. Child support is even more volatile and can have negative outcomes over the life course.

Child Support

When couples separate or divorce, child support can be a critical issue. Let's begin by looking at who pays and who gets child support.

WHO PAYS CHILD SUPPORT? Nearly half of all men neither see nor support their children after a divorce. In fact, two-thirds of noncustodial fathers spend more on car payments than they do for child support. Others ignore their children entirely, including not sending them birthday presents (Garfinkel et al., 1994; Sorensen and Zibman, 2000).

Of the almost 13 million non-custodial parents, 59 percent are supposed to pay child support. There is a variety of reasons for not seeking court-ordered child support, such as informal agreements, the other parent's inability to pay, not wanting contact with the other parent, or problems establishing a father's paternity or whereabouts. A parent may also avoid seeking child support because the child stays with the other parent part of the time or because the "legal hassles" seem overwhelming, especially for mothers with low educational levels (Grall, 2003; Huang and Pouncy, 2005).

When parents provide financial support, the large majority are white, male, those with a legal child support agreement, at least high school graduates, live above the poverty level, and make payments for only one child (see *Figure 15.5*). The two most common methods of child support are through wage withholding (34 percent) and direct payment to the other parent (32 percent) (Grall, 2005).

WHO GETS CHILD SUPPORT? In 2004, the child support program served almost 16 million children. Women

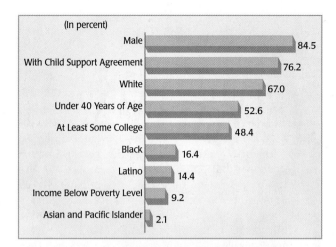

FIGURE 15.5 **Who Provides Financial Child Support, by Selected Characteristics**

Source: Adapted from Grall, 2005: Figure 2.

made up 85 percent of all custodial parents. Among custodial mothers, 56 percent were white, 27 percent black, and 15 percent Latinas (Grall, 2003; Turetsky, 2005).

The average annual amount of child support is minimal: $3,192 to custodial mothers and $2,881 to custodial fathers. One reason the sums are so low is that many fathers do not pay the full amount of financial support. In 2002, for example, only 45 percent of mothers received the full amount, 30 percent received partial payments, and 25 percent received nothing. On aver-

age, a father had not paid almost $5,200 of the child support due (Grall, 2003).

Nationally, child support payments provide only 15 percent of a family's total income. If a mother is poor, however, an average payment of $3,000 a year accounts for 40 percent of the family's total income. Thus, the poorer a mother is, the more she depends on child support. The proportion of custodial parents and their children living below the poverty level decreased from 33 percent in 1993 to 23 percent in 2001. Still, custodial mothers are twice as likely as custodial fathers to be poor (Grall, 2003; Center for Law and Social Policy, 2004).

Custodial mothers receive about 63 percent of the child-support payments that are due them. Even then, the amounts vary. For example, custodial mothers with the lowest payments are African American, have never been married, and are high school dropouts (see *Figure 15.6*). These data suggest that women with greater resources, such as a college degree, are able to collect more financial support, may have ex-husbands who can provide more support, or are more aggressive about getting court-ordered awards.

Some noncustodial parents also provide noncash support. More than half of all custodial parents, typically mothers, receive birthday, holiday, or other gifts (58 percent), clothes for the children (39 percent), food and groceries (29 percent), medical assistance other than health insurance (19 percent), or partial or full payments for child care or summer camp (10 percent) (Grall, 2003).

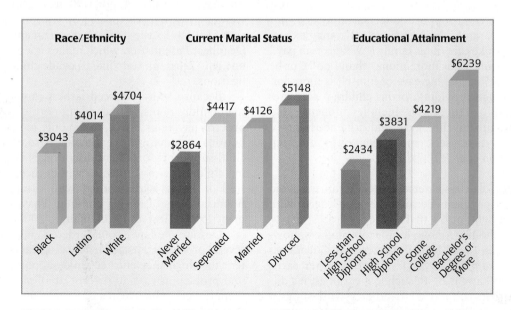

FIGURE 15.6 **Average Yearly Child-Support Payments Received by Custodial Mothers: 2001**

Source: Based on Grall, 2003: Table 5.

CHILD SUPPORT AND VISITATION Child support increases when there's parental involvement, especially joint custody and visitation rights. About 77 percent of custodial parents, most of whom are mothers, receive full or partial support payments, compared with 56 percent of those without shared custody or visitation rights (Grall, 2003).

Both interpersonal and other micro variables help explain why noncustodial parents, especially the majority of fathers, don't comply with child-support orders. According to Nuta (1986), for example, nonpaying fathers fall into four major categories:

- The *parent in pain* may feel shut out of the family and distance himself physically or emotionally from his children. He may even rationalize his distancing ("She turned them against me"). Other fathers are angry if they feel that their visitation rights are unfair.

- The *overextended parent* is overburdened with financial obligations. Anxious to get out of a marriage as soon as possible, he may agree to pay more support than he can afford. He may remarry and, unable to support two families, fail to provide for the children of his first marriage (Manning et al., 2003). Or he may become ill and unemployed and thus unable to make the child-support payments.

- The *vengeful parent* uses child support as a form of control. He may use nonpayment to change a visitation agreement or to punish his wife for initiating the divorce.

- The *irresponsible parent,* representing the greatest number of child-support dodgers, simply does not take his parental duties seriously. He may expect others to take care of his family ("Welfare will pay" or "Her family has more money than I do"), or he may think that taking care of himself is more important than providing for his children. The irresponsible parent often includes noncustodial parents with psychological and drug abuse problems who do not seek employment or cannot keep a job (Dion et al., 1997).

Many middle-class parents, especially fathers, avoid child-support payments because they don't agree with the visitation rights or feel that their ex-spouse is squeezing them for money. Among low-income fathers, however, many are "dead broke" rather than "deadbeat dads." For example, a typical divorced father earns about $17,000 a year. With such low earnings, it's difficult for fathers to meet court-ordered child-support payments that might consume 65 percent of their wages (Talvi, 2002).

Fathers4Justice, a social movement that began in Great Britain, has become popular in the United States. The fathers, both unmarried and divorced, demand better access to their children.

ENFORCEMENT OF CHILD SUPPORT Since the 1980s, federal legislation has established a number of laws to enforce court-ordered child-support awards. In 1984, Congress passed the Child Support Enforcement Amendments, which require states to deduct payments from delinquent parents' paychecks and tax returns. The Family Support Act of 1988 mandates periodic reviews of award levels to keep up with the rate of inflation. In 1998, the federal government passed the Deadbeat Parents Act, which makes it a felony for anyone who crosses a state line to evade child-support obligations.

Because many divorced fathers rarely provide for their children outside of child support, enforced court-ordered payments often are the only monetary contributions that many fathers make. Also, strengthening child-support enforcement discourages men from having children with women to whom they are not married or living with women who cannot share the financial costs of raising children (Paasch and Teachman, 1991; Aizer and McLanahan, 2005).

Despite the laws, court-ordered child support has several problems. First, states vary a great deal in the extent to which they enforce child-support laws. A second problem is that 30 percent of all parents, most of them fathers, who live in a different state than their ex-spouse can evade legal action because of local policies. According to a journalism professor in North Carolina, for example, it's been very difficult to collect any child support from her husband despite the Deadbeat Parents Act:

> *The county I filed with notifies nonpaying parents of legal action against them by putting a letter clearly marked from the child-support enforcement office into the U.S. Postal Service. The nonpayer can stall proceedings by simply not signing the letter's return-receipt card (Elmore, 2005).*

A third problem with child-support enforcement is that federal and state budgets change with the political administration in power. In 2006, for example, a Congress that was dominated by conservatives cut federal funding for child-support enforcement by at least $5 billion over the next 10 years, a 20 percent reduction. Unless the states make up these funds, and it's unlikely that they will do so, uncollected child-support payments will total $17 billion by 2016 (Turetsky, 2006).

DOES CHILD SUPPORT IMPROVE CHILDREN'S LIVES?

Of course, you might be thinking. The answer isn't this clear cut, however, because it depends on a number of variables, such as how much a parent pays and the family's social class.

Researchers who argue that child-support enforcement is "an investment that works" point to numerous advantages. For example, especially for poor mothers who are employed, child support is the second largest source of income for their families. In low-income families, getting child support may mean staying out of poverty. Fathers in low-income families are also more motivated to find a job and to stay employed longer. Among all families, fathers who make regular child-support payments are more involved with their children and the payments may reduce further conflict between the parents (Turetsky, 2006).

Other researchers are more skeptical. They note, for example, that most low-income, never-married fathers—especially those who have been in prison or have few marketable skills—can't support themselves, much less their children. As a result, they may avoid their children altogether. Some fathers, regardless of social class, just don't want to be involved with their children, even when they make some of the court-ordered child-support payments. Also, many fathers assume, often correctly, that a chunk of their child support pays for the administrative costs of the child-support bureaucracy rather than going to their children (Malm and Geen, 2006; Sayer, 2006).

Some scholars also feel that enforcing child-support payment laws will alleviate but not end poverty in sin-

gle-mother homes. For example, poverty among divorced mothers and never-married mothers will diminish only when women's earnings are comparable to those of men (Amott, 1993; see, also, Chapters 5 and 13).

Making Connections

▨ Judges have vast discretion in divorce proceedings, which vary from state to state and from case to case. The American Law Institute has proposed, instead, that a court should grant child custody to parents in proportion to the amount of time they spent caring for a child before divorce. Do you agree with this proposal?

▨ Some of my students argue that Nuta's description of nonpaying fathers (p. 472) should include custodial mothers, especially those who are vengeful. Others claim that fathers are the greatest offenders. What do you think?

▨ Some states have passed laws that include college expenses in setting child-support payments (Morgan, 2002b). Do such laws give an unfair advantage to children from divorced families compared with those from intact families?

How Divorce Affects Children

One of the most controversial issues is whether divorce is beneficial or harmful for children. An important "protective" factor is how the parents interact and handle the divorce (see the box "Children of Divorce"). The more civilized and mature the divorce, the easier it is on children.

Absent Fathers

About 15 percent of fathers get custody of their children. In the remaining cases, the mothers have custody and the fathers have visitation rights. In the years following a divorce, 31 percent of noncustodial fathers have no contact with their children and only a third see their children at least once a week. Nonresident mothers are more likely than nonresident fathers to maintain contact with their children through letters, telephone calls, and extended visits. Only 18 percent of biological fathers who don't reside with their adolescents are involved in the children's lives, such as

Constraints

Children of Divorce

How couples deal with divorce can have long-term effects on their children. After interviewing adult children of divorce about their memories of their parents' divorce and their current behaviors and lifestyles, Fassel (1991) found five types of divorce and their effects on children:

The Disappearing Parent Suddenly one parent leaves the home, and the children receive little explanation beyond "Your mother and I were divorced today." Adult children who recalled this situation had often grown up suspicious of people, fearing that their partners, too, would leave them.

The Surprise Divorce In this situation, parents often seemed close and open with each other, but without any warning, one filed for divorce. Adult children recalled feeling shock, bewilderment, and anger that the parent who left disrupted what they had thought was a happy family. As they grow up, such children may avoid intimate relationships because they expect a partner, like the parent who left, to be unpredictable or undependable.

The Violent Divorce Spouse abuse and, sometimes, child abuse cause many divorces. Children in such a setting don't learn how to manage anger because their role models could not handle it. The children often repress conflict for fear of violence, or they grow up believing that fighting is a way to test intimacy and to get their partner's attention.

The Late Divorce When parents stay together "for the children's sake," they often create an environment of veiled criticism and threats, unspoken anger, and even hatred. Many children in such homes learn to suppress their feelings to survive. Some equate love with suffering in silence; others may become cynical about the possibility of having a good relationship with anyone.

Protect-the-Kids Divorce Some well-intentioned parents may decide to protect their children by withholding information about the real reasons for their divorce. They don't accuse each other, they communicate, and each listens respectfully as the other talks to the children about the divorce. Dishonesty can be harmful. In one case, for example, a couple told their children that their father felt the need to explore, to be free, and to see the world. When, many years later, the children learned that their father was gay, they felt betrayed and angry.

Stop and Think. . .

- How can divorcing couples avoid these negative outcomes for their children?

- Based on your or your friends' and classmates' experiences, what are the top three ways that parents can minimize the negative effects of divorce on children?

discussing important decisions, attending their activities, and knowing their friends (Stewart, 1999; Hetherington and Kelly, 2002; Grall, 2003).

How important is a noncustodial father's involvement to his children's well-being? The findings are mixed. There is much evidence that a father's child support benefits the children's educational achievement. These children are more likely to focus on academic pursuits, to finish high school, and to enter college. Regular payments may also increase children's academic well-being because mothers, feeling more financially secure, are better able to deal with school-related problems (Baydar and Brooks-Gunn, 1994; Amato and Gilbreth, 1999).

There is less evidence that visits from a noncustodial father have beneficial effects on the child's emotional and behavioral well-being. Within a few years, children adapt to their father's absence, and some behavioral problems, especially among boys, decrease (Mott et al., 1997).

Children (and mothers) are better off having minimal contact with nonresident fathers if the father is abusive, fights with his ex-wife, or has other problems. Some fathers abuse alcohol, some may be too depressed after a divorce to maintain meaningful ties with their children, and some may have developed closer relationships with new partners and the partner's children (Aseltine and Kessler, 1993; King, 1994).

Divorced fathers can also enhance their children's development. For example, fathers who maintain close ties with their offspring can reestablish the children's trust in the fathers and other adults. Maintaining ties with one's children takes time and effort, however. Family practitioners suggest that fathers take specific steps to ensure the continuity of their relationship with their children:

■ A father should be guided by his child's developmental needs. For example, because toddlers' sense of time is different from that of adults and their memories are shorter, it's better for a father to make frequent brief visits than to make longer but less frequent visits. On the other hand, older children who are settled comfortably in social and school activities need more flexible visitation schedules.

■ If possible, a father should live close to his children, especially when they are young. And regardless of whether he and his former wife are friendly, he should not stop seeing his children. He should be with his children whenever he can, whether he's changing their diapers or helping them with their homework.

■ A father should pay child support regularly. Skipping payments not only deprives the child of resources but also lowers the father's self-respect. At the same time, a father should not overindulge his children; children of *all* ages expect a parent to establish limits for them (Pruett, 1987).

Although divorce is often difficult for all concerned, the rewards are immeasurable when a father perseveres in maintaining close ties with his children.

Parents as Peers

A 23-year-old daughter once complained to "Dear Ann," the advice columnist, that her divorced mother had started to treat her less like a daughter and more like a girlfriend: "She has told me some hair-raising stories about her sexual escapades, and now she keeps pressing me for details about my sex life. . . . I don't want to hear all the personal stuff she tells me" (Dear Ann, 2001: C7).

As this example illustrates, divorced parents sometimes make the mistake of treating their children like peers. Particularly if the children are bright and verbal, a parent may see them as being more mature than they really are. Mothers often share their feelings about a wide range of personal issues. They may express bitterness toward their ex-husband, anger at men in general, or frustration over financial concerns or social isolation.

In response, the child may console the parent and appear concerned and caring, but may also feel anger, resentment, sadness, or guilt. According to one 15-year-old girl, for example,

> Don't look to kids for emotional support. I was going through so much of my own emotional hell that my mom leaning on me was the last thing that I wanted, and it made me very, very resentful of her. My mom tried to use me as her confidant for all the bad stuff my dad did to her, but she refused to see that he was still my dad, and I still loved him (S. Evans, 2000: C4).

Many adults say that as children they often felt the need to protect their divorcing parents emotionally, especially their mother. Instead of talking to their parents, who were preoccupied with nursing their own wounds, the children often turned to siblings or friends or tried to deal with their problems alone (Marquardt, 2005).

Still, some researchers maintain that the mother–child "lean on me" relationship sometimes works well. For example, a study of some first-year college students concluded that mothers' depending on their children for emotional support during and after a divorce contributed to a sense of closeness. Another

Divorced fathers can maintain close relationships with their children by seeing them as often as possible, setting rules, discussing problems, and providing guidance.

study found that divorced parents' confiding in their adolescents had no negative effects unless the parent showed weakness, vulnerability, and a need for the adolescent to be strong—to be the parent's caretaker (Buchanan et al., 1996; Arditti, 1999).

Regardless of the message parents think they're conveying to their children, an especially sensitive or responsible child (often a girl) who is "parentified" during a divorce may find it difficult to focus on her (or his) own individual growth:

> Often the only time Mom talked to Dad, and vice-versa, was through messages sent through me. Even my brother and sister used me as a courier in getting the things they wanted. . . . I would feel an overwhelming sense of loneliness and desperation in my struggles to keep the peace and save the family. . . . I believe I went far away to college unconsciously, but once I was here, I suffered from guilt in abandoning my family duties. . . . Now after three years I still feel anger and sadness and loneliness when I see that it is once again my duty to restore the harmony in the family (Brown and Amatea, 2000: 180).

What Hurts Children During and After Divorce?

A large number of studies have shown that, compared with their counterparts in married families, children from divorced families experience a variety of difficulties, including lower academic achievement, behavioral problems, a lower self-concept, and some long-term

The Squid and the Whale *is one of the few films that examine the difficulties that divorce creates for both children and their parents.*

health problems (Thornberry et al., 1999; Furstenberg and Kiernan, 2001; see also, Amato, 2002, for a summary of some of this research).

since you asked

Can children benefit from their parents' divorce?

Most negative effects of divorce are short term, but others last longer. Why do some children adjust to their parents' divorce better than others? Let's begin by looking at predivorce difficulties.

PARENTAL PROBLEMS BEFORE A DIVORCE Typically, divorce crystallizes rather than creates long-standing family problems. That is, partners who divorce are more likely to have poor parenting skills and high levels of marital conflict or to suffer from persistent economic stress well before a separation or divorce occurs (Furstenberg and Teitler, 1994).

Parents in these predivorce families are less involved in their children's education, have lower expectations of their children, little discussion of school-related issues, and low attendance at school events. Besides poor academic progress, the children exhibit behavior problems and low self-concept at least three years before the divorce (Sun, 2001).

PARENTAL CONFLICT AND HOSTILITY Often it is not the divorce itself but parental attitudes during and after the divorce that affect children's behavior and perceptions about family life. The end of a highly conflicted marriage typically improves children's well-being. Freed from anxiety, stress, and depression, their mental health improves and their antisocial behavior decreases. In fact, children with parents in high-conflict marriages fare worse as adults than those from families in which high conflict has ended in divorce. The latter are less likely to feel caught in the middle when their parents argue, don't feel as much pressure to take sides, and experience less stress when feuding parents finally break up (Amato and Afifi, 2006).

On the other hand, divorces that dissolve low-conflict marriages may have negative effects on children. The children see the divorce as unexpected, unwelcome, and a source of turmoil and instability in their lives. Because nearly two-thirds of divorces end low-conflict marriages, some scholars question whether these marriages should be dissolved (Amato, 2003; Strohschein, 2005; Glenn and Sylvester, 2006).

Overall, within two to three years of a divorce, most adults and children adapt to their new lives reasonably well *if* they are not confronted with continued or new stresses. Still, the "echoes of divorce" can linger for many years. For example, youths from divorced families are more likely than their counterparts to select

According to many studies (see text), it is not the divorce itself but parental conflict during and after a divorce that is most damaging to children.

partners—often also from divorced families—who are impulsive, socially irresponsible, and who have a history of antisocial behaviors such as alcohol and drug abuse, trouble with the law, problems in school and work, and an unstable job history (Hetherington, 2003).

QUALITY OF PARENTING Children do not develop difficulties simply because their parents get a divorce. As one of my students remarked in class, "It wasn't my parents' divorce that left the most painful scars. It was their inability to be effective parents afterward."

Children's adjustment to divorce depends, to a great extent, on the quality of parenting they experience after the marriage ends. Because, as you saw earlier, many children lose touch with their fathers, a sense of loss can continue into adulthood.

If noncustodial fathers don't take their parenting role seriously, mere contact or even sharing good times together may not contribute to children's development. However, if these fathers play an authoritative role (such as listening to their children's problems, giving advice, and working together on projects), fathers and children report a close relationship (Amato and Gilbreth, 1999).

Twenty years after their parents' divorce, 62 percent of children say that their relationship with their father had improved or remained stable over time. It's not

custody that affects the quality of the relationship but a combination of pre- and postdivorce factors, especially continued conflict between the parents, a father's low involvement with his children in the early years of a divorce, and a father's quick remarriage (Kelly and Emery, 2003; Ahrons, 2004).

ECONOMIC HARDSHIP Although a divorce may reduce domestic conflict, the financial problems usually increase, especially for women. As you saw earlier, the mother's income usually drops by about a third after the divorce. Men's income typically increases, with estimates ranging from 8 percent to 41 percent. Men's income increases for a number of reasons: not having physical custody of the children, not complying with child support orders, having higher-paying jobs than their ex-wives do, and often taking some of the family's wealth—such as stocks and bonds—with them after the divorce (Sun and Li, 2002; Barber and Demo, 2006; Sayer, 2006).

In the first two years following divorce, family income falls 30 percent for children of white mothers and 53 percent for children of African American mothers. A major reason for this difference is that white mothers receive 10 times as much child support as black women do. The long-term economic costs of divorce are especially pronounced for black women because they are less likely to remarry and more likely to divorce after a remarriage (Page and Stevens, 2005; see, also, Chapter 16).

These income differences have a clearly negative impact on children's well-being. The financial drop may create more stress at home, decrease the children's access to enriching summer programs and camps, and make it more difficult to afford college tuition. The children may have to move (often to a poorer and more dangerous neighborhood), change schools, and get used to a new community (South et al., 1998).

CUMULATIVE EFFECTS OF DIVORCE Divorce is disruptive when it increases the chances of negative outcomes for parents and children over the life course. If divorce interferes with continued schooling, for example, this disadvantage cumulates through life, affecting occupational status, income, and economic well-being. People with low levels of educational attainment and high levels of economic hardship are at higher risk for depression in adulthood and more likely to experience unhappy or unstable interpersonal relationships (Chase-Lansdale et al., 1995; Ross and Mirowsky, 1999).

Divorce increases the probability that a woman will experience economic pressures and psychological depression. This strain and emotional distress tend to reduce the quality of her parenting. Reductions in the quality of parenting, in turn, increase a child's risk of emotional and behavioral problems and poor developmental outcomes. In addition, children may have to live with a parent whom they don't get along with and lose access to a parent with whom they've had a good relationship (South et al., 1998; Videon, 2002).

A divorce can also have negative consequences for subsequent generations through a process that some scholars call the **intergenerational transmission of divorce.** When grandparents divorce, for example, the second generation experiences lower educational attainment and problematic relationships: "These outcomes in turn become the causes of similar problems in the third generation" (Amato and Cheadle, 2005: 204).

Despite all these stressors, 80 percent of children from divorced homes navigate through troubled waters and "eventually are able to adapt to their new life and become reasonably well adjusted" (Hetherington and Kelly, 2002: 228). Among other things, children fare well if protective factors are at work during and after the divorce.

What Helps Children During and After Divorce?

The biggest advantage of divorce, as you saw earlier, is that it decreases the amount of stress that children undergo in a high-conflict, quarrelsome home. The children who experience the least negative effects are those who receive support from friends, neighbors, and schools, especially when their parents are self-absorbed or depressed. Even if a nonresident parent isn't around, the most effective custodial parents provide many protective factors, such as warmth, responsiveness, monitoring, involvement in the children's activities, and keep the children out of parental battlegrounds (Rodgers and Rose, 2002; Leon, 2003).

According to researchers and family clinicians, parents can lessen some of a divorce's negative effects in many ways:

- They can reassure the children that both parents will continue to love and care for them, emphasizing that they will remain actively involved with them and that the children will always be free to love both parents.

- They should not be afraid to talk about their feelings. Talking sets the stage for open communication between parents and their children. Parents can discuss their unhappiness and even their anger, but they should not blame the other parent because this will force the children to take sides.

- They should emphasize that the children are not responsible for problems between their parents,

pointing out that each adult is divorcing the other partner but not the children.

- They should reassure the children that they will continue to see their grandparents on both sides of the family.

- The noncustodial parent, usually the father, must maintain an ongoing relationship with the children. When noncustodial fathers maintain stable and frequent visitation, they give more advice to their children, and their adolescents are more satisfied and less likely to experience depression.

- More than anything else, teenagers and young adults say that they want to talk about their feelings and experiences freely and openly with significant people in their lives such as parents, teachers, coaches, and clergy (Barber, 1994; Harvey and Fine, 2004).

Making Connections

- What long-term effects of divorce, if any, have you experienced in your own life or observed in someone close to you?

- Should divorced parents treat their children as peers or as children?

- Do you think it's possible for parents to break the intergenerational transmission of divorce cycle?

Some Positive Outcomes of Separation and Divorce

Much of this chapter has looked at the harmful effects of divorce on adults and children. In response to such negative outcomes, some groups are proposing that no-fault divorce be eliminated and that divorce laws be made tougher (see the box "Should It Be Harder to Get a Divorce?"). Does divorce have any positive effects?

In a highly publicized book, *The Unexpected Legacy of Divorce,* Wallerstein and her colleagues (2000) advised parents to stay in unhappy marriages to avoid hurting their children. However, that well-intentioned advice was based on a clinical study of a small group of highly dysfunctional divorced families. In contrast, most divorced couples and their children adjust and function well over time.

since you asked

Should parents stay in an unhappy marriage for the sake of the children?

Should It Be Harder to Get a Divorce?

According to a recent national study, almost 59 percent of Americans feel that "Society would be better off if divorces were harder to get." On the other hand, in a national study of people age 40 and older, 64 percent of men and 76 percent of women said that they had made "absolutely the right decision" to divorce (Montenegro, 2004; Glenn, 2005).

Some people claim that the switch to no-fault divorce has led to an increase in the divorce rate in the United States and other countries. Others point out that divorce rates started increasing years before no-fault legislation was passed in the 1970s. In effect, no-fault laws simply ratified, symbolically, changes in societal values about marriage and divorce that had already occurred (Nakonezny et al., 1995; Rodgers et al., 1997; Glenn, 1997).

In the late 1990s, the Covenant Marriage Movement tried to make divorce more difficult. Those who signed the covenant gave up the right to no-fault divorce. A couple promised to live together "forever," and divorce was allowed only for a limited number of reasons (including adultery, a felony conviction, abuse, and abandonment) or after a two-year separation. Irreconcilable differences were not grounds for divorce.

Only Arkansas, Arizona, and Louisiana passed covenant marriage bills. In at least 21 other states, such bills were introduced but did not pass.

Here are a few arguments on each side of this issue:

Make Getting a Divorce More Difficult

- Simply discussing the covenant marriage option would encourage couples to take their vows more seriously and to seek counseling.

- It's too easy to get a divorce.
- Couples break up over little things because divorce is "no big deal."
- No-fault divorces disregard the interests of children.
- Ending no-fault divorce would give more rights to the partner who doesn't want a divorce.

Leave Current Divorce Laws Alone

- Covenant marriages could trap people whose spouses suffer from alcoholism or hurt low-income families who can't afford counseling.
- Getting a divorce is already difficult, complicated, expensive, and stressful.
- Many couples seek therapy to keep the marriage together and stay in destructive relationships for many years.
- Children fare worse in high-conflict two-parent families than in loving single-parent families.
- Ending no-fault divorce could keep children in high-conflict homes longer and make divorce even more adversarial.

Stop and Think . . .

- Would you enter a covenant marriage if it were available in your state?

- Should we make it harder to get a divorce? Harder to get married? Both? Or should we leave things the way they are?

The major positive outcome of divorce is that it provides options for people in miserable marriages. If a divorce eliminates an unhappy, frustrating, and stressful situation, it may improve the mental and emotional health of both ex-spouses and their children. Divorced parents who take joint-custody arrangements seriously, maintain good communication with their children and each other, and receive support from family, friends, and the community report being physically and mentally healthier than other divorced parents (Golby and Bretherton, 1998).

In addition, and as you saw earlier, parental separation is better for children, at least in the long run, than remaining in an intact family where there is continuous conflict. Divorce can also offer parents and children opportunities for personal growth, more gratifying relationships, and a more harmonious family life (Hetherington and Kelly, 2002).

How do divorced people fare, emotionally and socially, after a divorce? During the first year, about 70 percent express doubts or ambivalence about the breakup and continue to be angry. By two years after the divorce, the problems diminish. After 10 years, most divorced people have built a satisfying new life. Many women, especially, report being more competent, better adjusted, and more fulfilled. Those who return to school or work often meet and marry men from higher socioeconomic backgrounds and say that their later marriages are more successful than their first ones (Hetherington, 2003).

Both sexes cite gains after a divorce, but women are more likely to do so than men. Women are especially likely to say that they enjoy their new-found freedom, developing their own self-identity, and not having to answer to a domineering husband (Montenegro, 2004). According to one woman, "Divorce is a happy word: I've found things that I truly love to do instead of doing things that my husband or my family thought I should do. I have hobbies and interests; I have great joy in the ways I spend my time" (Orenstein, 2000: 233).

Divorced men also report benefits such as spending more money on themselves or their hobbies, being better off financially (because they rarely support their ex-spouses or children), having more leisure time, and dating numerous partners (Montenegro, 2004). As one African American author advises black men, "While the break-up may mean broken dreams, it doesn't have to mean broken homes. It may present fresh opportunities for men to reassess their lives and learn from their mistakes. And, perhaps, they won't stumble over the same rocks" (Hutchinson, 1994: 113).

Children and young adults experience positive outcomes after their parents' divorce, but only under certain conditions: if the parents have joint custody, if the parents are civil, if the children are comfortable staying in both parents' homes and can spend a lot of time with their dad, if a parent's relocation doesn't disrupt the children's everyday life, and if the parents (especially fathers, who usually have more income than mothers) support their children financially while they are in college (Fabricius, 2003; Warshak, 2003).

These empirical studies echo many of the experiences of my students. For example,

Sometimes a marriage just doesn't work out. I know because I stayed in an unhappy marriage for eleven years for the children's sake, hoping that things would work out. I gave 150 percent, but still nothing changed. To this day, nothing has changed between my ex-husband and me but he sees the kids every day and all of us are happier and healthier individuals (Author's files).

Counseling, Marital Therapy, and Divorce Mediation

Counseling, marital therapy, and mediation can help some families get through divorce or even avoid it. These and other strategies and interventions aren't always beneficial, however.

Counseling and Marital Therapy

According to some estimates, every year over 3 percent of the nation's 57.3 million married couples see a marriage or family therapist or a mental health professional for marital problems. The average cost is about $80 for a one-hour session (Jayson, 2005).

How effective are counseling and marital therapy? It's difficult to answer this question because there have been no scientific national studies that have measured the results. Some argue that counseling and marital therapy are better than nothing, especially if couples seek help within a few years of experiencing problems. Others contend that much counseling and therapy can do more harm than good (Doherty, 1999; Shadish and Baldwin, 2005).

since you asked

Does counseling and marital therapy work?

ADVANTAGES Counseling can be useful, especially if therapists serve as impartial observers rather than favoring one side or the other (as attorneys do). Counselors can help couples and families decrease some difficulties such as constant conflict and parenting problems. Thus, therapists can help married and divorcing parents build stronger relationships with each other and with their children.

Family practitioners assist divorcing couples and families in a number of ways: They individualize treatment programs, help parents learn to coparent as effectively as possible, help children cope with fears such as losing the nonresidential parent permanently, provide information on remarriage and its potential impact on the children and ex-spouse, and organize a variety of support networks (Leite and McKenry, 1996).

DISADVANTAGES Two years after ending counseling, 25 percent of couples are worse off than they were when they started. After four years of counseling or therapy, up to 38 percent are divorced (Gilbert, 2005).

Why does much counseling and therapy fail? Many therapists are untrained and inexperienced, and may feel overwhelmed by a couple's or family's problems. And, despite similar training, in every occupation some

Many divorced parents, especially fathers, stay in touch with their children using webcam.

people are more skilled than others at what they do (Doherty, 2002).

Some critics contend that many professional marriage counselors and therapists, instead of being neutral, promote marriage as a superior family form (compared with cohabitation or single-parent households, for example). Thus, they foster a life-long commitment to marriage and do everything they can to discourage divorce. Such "faith-based values" may be beneficial for some traditional couples, but not for those where one of the major sources of conflict may be domination of the wife by a controlling husband who expects her to sacrifice her needs to satisfy his or the children's (Leslie and Morton, 2004).

Also, not all marriages are salvageable. As you saw in Chapters 8 and 10, some of us choose the wrong partner and for the wrong reasons. In such cases, a separation or divorce may be a more effective strategy for resolving conflict than counseling and therapy.

Increasingly, many jurisdictions are ordering divorcing parents to attend educational seminars with professional counselors before going to court. The purpose of the sessions is not to convince parents to stay together but to teach them about their children's emotional and developmental needs during the divorce. In other cases, counseling is a preliminary step before meeting with a mediator.

Divorce Mediation

In **divorce mediation,** a trained arbitrator helps the couple come to an agreement. Issues that may be resolved in this way include custody arrangements, child support and future college expenses, and the division of marital property (such as a house, furniture, stocks, savings and retirement accounts, pension plans, cars, debts, and medical expenses). Although most mediators are attorneys or mental health professionals, accountants and others may also be trained as mediators.

ADVANTAGES Mediation will not eliminate the hurt caused by separation and divorce, but it has several advantages (see Hahn and Kleist, 2000, for a review of the conditions under which mediation is the most effective). First, mediation increases communication between spouses and decreases angry confrontations that don't resolve anything.

Second, mediation generally reduces the time needed to negotiate a divorce settlement. A mediation settlement typically takes a few months; a divorce obtained through a court proceeding may take two to three years.

Third, mediated agreements generally make it easier to accommodate changes as the children grow older. For example, as a child's activities and schedule change from, say, a Saturday morning ballet lesson at age 8 to Wednesday night driving lessons at age 15, the parents can negotiate schedule changes without resorting to costly and time-consuming requests for changes in court-ordered arrangements.

Finally, mediation prevents children from being pawns or trophies in a divorce contest. The mediator's approach is "What arrangements are best for you, your spouse, and your children?" There is no room for the adversarial stance, "Which of you will win the children?"

DISADVANTAGES Mediation doesn't work for everyone. If one partner is savvier about finances than the other, for example, the less informed spouse may be at a disadvantage. In addition, an aggressive or more powerful spouse (who is usually the husband) can be intimidating.

Another problem is that mediators may be unschooled in issues pertaining to children. Because the parent, not the child, is the client, mediation may not always be in the child's best interests (Wallerstein, 2003).

Conclusion

Greater acceptance of divorce in the late twentieth and early twenty-first centuries has created *change* in family structures. Indeed, separation and divorce seem to have become "an intrinsic feature of modern family life rather than a temporary aberration" (Martin and Bumpass, 1989: 49). As this chapter shows, a large segment of the adult population flows in and out of marriage during the life course.

This means that people have more *choices* in leaving an unhappy marriage. Often, however, parents don't realize that what are choices for them may be *constraints* for their children, who often feel at fault, guilty, and torn between warring parents.

If parents handled divorces in more rational and civilized ways, many children would be spared the emotional pain and economic deprivation that they now suffer. Some of the pain that both parents and children experience may become even greater after parents remarry, the topic of the next chapter.

Summary

1.   A separation is a temporary or permanent arrangement that precedes a divorce. In most cases, separation is a lengthy process involving four phases: preseparation, early separation, midseparation, and late separation.

2.   Marital separation leads to one of three outcomes: divorce, long-term separation, or reconciliation. The outcomes of marital separation often vary by race, ethnicity, and social class.

3.   Divorce rates increased rapidly in the 1970s, reached a plateau in the 1980s, and have decreased since the mid-1990s. Whereas in the past many marriages ended because of death or desertion, during the twentieth century divorce became the most common reason for marital dissolution.

4.   Nearly twice as many women as men file for divorce. Some women want to legalize a husband's emotional or physical absence. Others are more independent economically and thus less inclined to tolerate their husbands' extramarital affairs or other unacceptable behaviors.

5.   Divorce is often a long and drawn-out process. In most divorces, people go through one or more of six stages: the emotional divorce, the legal divorce, the eco-nomic divorce, the coparental divorce, the community divorce, and the psychic divorce.

6.   The many reasons for divorce include macro-level factors such as changing gender roles, demographic variables such as marriage at a young age, and interpersonal factors such as unrealistic expectations and infidelity.

7.   Divorce has psychological, economic, and legal consequences. Because child-support awards typically are very low, many women and children plunge into poverty after a divorce.

8.   There are three types of child custody: sole, split, and joint. Although most mothers receive sole custody, joint custody is becoming more common.

9.   Divorce is harmful to most children. Many of the problems that lead to marital disruption begin many years before the legal breakup.

10.   Counseling and divorce mediation are alternatives to the traditional adversarial approach that is typical of legal processes. Mediated divorces tend to be less bitter and less expensive and offer each partner more input in child-custody decisions.

Key Terms

separation   *454*
divorce   *455*
alimony   *458*
child support   *458*
no-fault divorce   *459*

social integration   *461*
custody   *468*
sole custody   *469*
split custody   *469*
joint custody   *469*

co-custody   *469*
child abduction   *470*
intergenerational transmission of
    divorce   *478*
divorce mediation   *481*

Taking It Further

Help and Information about Divorce on the Internet

The Divorce Support Page contains links to many sites on divorce, custody, and mediation, as well as information about divorce laws and professionals in each state.
www.divorcesupport.com

The **Association for Conflict Resolution** can refer you to a divorce mediator in your area.
www.acrnet.org

The **Human Development and Family Life Education Resource Center** of Ohio State University provides online bulletins on topics such as divorce and noncustodial fathers, guides for parents helping children with divorce, and a Website for adolescents whose parents are divorcing.
www.hec.ohio-state.edu/famlife/index.htm

Dads at a Distance suggests ideas and activities for strengthening long-distance relationships with children.
www.daads.com

Divorce Helpline is aimed at helping couples reduce conflict and stay out of court, and includes materials that can minimize the need for a lawyer.
www.divorcehelp.com

And more: www.prenhall.com/benokraitis provides links to bulletin boards where people can post divorce-related questions, lobby groups whose goal is to reform divorce laws, state-by-state information about divorce, chat rooms, academic resources, and online do-it-yourself divorce sites.

Investigate With Research Navigator

Go to www.researchnavigator.com and enter your LOGIN NAME and PASSWORD. For instructions on registering for the first time, view the detailed instructions at the end of the Chapter 1. Search the Research Navigator™ site using the following key search terms:

child custody
divorce
separation

Outline

16

Remarriages and Stepfamilies

Data Digest

- The U.S. Census Bureau estimates that **stepfamilies will outnumber traditional nuclear families** by the year 2007.

- **One out of three Americans** is now a stepparent, a stepchild, a stepsibling, or some other member of a stepfamily.

- Within three years of divorce, **50 percent of people remarry.** Remarriage rates are highest among white women and lowest among black women.

- About 3 percent of Americans have been **married three or more times.**

- Fewer than 5 percent of all **remarried couples have three sets of children:** yours, mine, and ours.

Sources: Bramlett and Mosher, 2002; Kreider and Fields, 2002; Kreider, 2005.

Even with high divorce rates, most people aren't disillusioned about marriage. Indeed, many remarry, some more than once. When this happens, the resulting family relationships can be intricate. Listen to a woman who married a widower describe her multifaceted family relationships shortly before the marriage of her stepdaughter. Both had children from previous marriages:

Ed will be my stepson-in-law, but there's no simple way to state the relationships between his daughter, Amy, and me. . . . Amy becomes my husband's stepgranddaughter, his daughter's stepdaughter, his granddaughters' stepsister or his son-in-law's daughter. But to me, the linguistic link is truly un-

wieldy: my husband's stepgranddaughter, my stepdaughter's stepdaughter, my stepgrandchildren's stepsister! (Borst, 1996, p. 16).

Because not all remarried couples have children from previous marriages, we'll sometimes examine remarriage and stepfamilies separately. Quite clearly, though, the two family forms overlap.

This chapter examines the prevalence and characteristics of remarriages and stepfamilies, their varied structures, how stepfamilies develop, key relationships in stepfamilies, and some characteristics of happy stepfamilies. Let's begin with dating and cohabitation, two activities that often lead to remarriage or forming a stepfamily.

Being Single Again: Dating and Cohabitation

After a divorce, singles soon become involved in *courtship*, the ways in which people seek and select a mate (see Chapter 8). Like those who seek to marry for the first time, divorced singles rely on two courtship avenues—dating and cohabitation—to meet and choose another mate. Unlike their earlier experiences, however, both of these courtship processes are now more complicated.

Dating after Divorce

Often people start dating again even before a divorce is legally final. To insulate themselves from the pain of divorce, many people rush into another relationship: "It's not unusual to see women and men frantically dating in the first year after their separation, trying to fill the void with an intense new love or even with just another warm body" (Ahrons, 1994: 65).

Dating after a divorce, including among older people, provides couples with companionship.

If the partners are young and have not been married very long, reentering the "dating scene" is fairly easy. Dating may be more awkward for those who have been married a long time because they don't know what to expect. For example, one of my friends, a woman who divorced after 12 years of marriage, wanted to pursue new relationships but was very anxious about dating: "Am I supposed to pay for myself when we go to dinner? Should I just meet him at the restaurant, or do men still pick women up? What if he wants to jump into bed after the first date?"

As people age, they may become more concerned about their physical appearance. Feeling nervous about intimacy is a big reason for staying on the dating sidelines. According to a 53-year-old recently divorced man, for example, "Even I don't like looking at me naked anymore" (Mahoney, 2003).

Although all dating couples—whether or not they have been married previously—often express similar concerns, people who have not dated for many years are often more apprehensive. They tend to feel that their dating skills are "rusty." They are often less self-confident in approaching new relationships because they believe they "failed" in their marriages. Some may avoid dating altogether, while parents who date frequently may feel guilty about being less available to their children.

Cohabitation: An Alternative to Dating after a Divorce

Some divorced people prepare for marriage by living together. More cautious about entering a new marriage, they consider cohabitation a way of testing a relationship, especially if children are present. Breaking up may increase the children's stress, but the couple avoids another unsuccessful marriage.

Half of all remarriages begin with cohabitation. In fact, living together is more common after a divorce than before a first marriage (Xu et al., 2006).

Cohabitation, rather than dating, is especially appealing to older adults:

> *Their social scripts for dating may be outdated, and they may feel foolish, nervous, or uncertain about what to do. . .Especially those who had been married for many years may be more comfortable setting up housekeeping with a partner than dating (Ganong and Coleman, 2004: 72).*

Especially if there are children, combining two households may be more familiar and simpler than contending with the ups and downs of dating.

Cohabitation can hasten matrimony because most adults court for only brief periods before plunging into

In many cultures, remarriages are based on practical considerations rather than love. For example, after the deadly 2004 tsunami in Indonesia, young women came from their home villages to marry thousands of hard-working fishermen whose wives and children had perished.

a remarriage. Some people may rush through the courtship process because they feel that they are running out of time or are desperate for financial or child-rearing help. Others may feel that they don't need as much time to get to know each other because they have learned from past mistakes. As you'll see later in this chapter, high redivorce rates show that such assumptions are often wrong.

Living together can also delay remarriage. If cohabitors move from one relationship to another over a number of years, it will take a long time to select a marriage partner. Or if one or both people are reluctant to marry, cohabitation may lead to a long-term relationship. Such *de facto* stepfamilies are on the rise in the United States and Europe. They include children from a past marriage and those born to the cohabiting couple (Ganong et al., 2006; Xu et al., 2006).

Not all courtship ends in a remarriage. Some stepfamilies are formed through remarriage, but others are cohabiting stepfamily households, some lasting longer than others.

Forming a Stepfamily

There isn't a single pathway in forming a stepfamily. Sometimes couples cohabit over decades. And because same-sex marriage is still illegal in the United States, lesbians and gay men may form stepfamilies through long-term committed relationships in which one or both partners raise children from previous unions.

Most couples, however, form stepfamilies through remarriage—usually after a divorce but sometimes after widowhood. Before we look at remarriage, what, exactly, is a stepfamily?

What Is a Stepfamily?

In the past, sociologists defined a *stepfamily* as a household in which at least one of the *spouses* had a biological child from a previous marriage. Currently, sociologists are defining the term more broadly to include a greater diversity of families (Ganong and Coleman, 2004; Pasley and Moorefield, 2004).

since you asked

Do stepfamilies include unmarried partners?

A **stepfamily** is a household in which two adults are biological or adoptive parents (heterosexual, gay, or lesbian), with a child from a previous relationship, who elect to marry or to cohabit. As in the case of defining *family* (see Chapter 1), not everyone would agree with this definition because it includes cohabitors. Nevertheless, this definition is more inclusive because it encompasses nontraditional stepfamilies. One large group consists of low-income households in which one or both adults have never been married but the family functions very much like a "traditional" stepfamily (Bumpass et al., 1995).

Sometimes journalists and social scientists use terms such as *reconstituted family* and *binuclear family* interchangeably with *stepfamily*. However, *reconstituted* and *binuclear* are awkward and confusing, and family sociologists rarely use these terms (Kelley, 1996; Ganong and Coleman, 2004).

Some researchers use *blended family*, but the leaders of some stepfamily organizations disagree. For example, according to Margorie Engel (2000), a past president of the Stepfamily Association of America, stepfamilies don't "blend." Instead, there are more parents, children have divided loyalties, and stepfamilies must develop new and unfamiliar roles for all their members, both adults and children.

How Common Is Remarriage?

Remarriage has spawned a huge industry of services, magazines, and books. *Bride Again* magazine, for example, aimed at "encore brides" who marry again and again, is booming.

The U.S. remarriage rate is the highest in the world. Nearly 85 percent of Americans who divorce remarry, half of them within three years. About 13 percent of women and men have been married twice, and 3 percent have married three or more times (Kreider and Fields, 2002; Kreider, 2005).

The high divorce and remarriage rates have important implications for family structure and family roles in the future. For example, whereas 70- to 85-year-olds today have 2.4 biological children on average, by 2030 that group will average only 1.6 biological children but will have twice as many stepchildren as they do now (Wachter, 1997).

This means that the baby boom generation will have to rely more on stepchildren and stepgrandchildren rather than biological children and biological grandchildren for caregiving when they reach age 75 or older. If adult children perceive current and former stepparents to be family, it is more likely that they will provide them with help and financial support in later life (Schmeeckle et al., 2006). So, be nice to your stepchildren. (We'll examine aging and caregiving in Chapter 17.)

Cohabitation, divorce, remarriage, and stepfamilies have created a variety of family structures. Despite the variations, researchers have uncovered some common characteristics of remarried couples and stepfamilies. We'll look at remarriages first and then examine stepfamilies.

Characteristics of Remarried Couples

Many factors affect people's decision to remarry. Among the most common are age, gender, race and ethnicity, social class, and the presence of children. These variables usually interact to explain remarriage rates.

Age and Sex

For both sexes, divorce usually doesn't last long. The average age of a first remarriage is 33 for women and 35 for men. Of those who have ever been married, 46 percent of women and 37 percent of men ages 30 to 49 have remarried; of those 50 and older, 15 percent of women and 20 percent of men have been married three or more times (see *Figure 16.1*).

Historically, men remarried sooner, more of them remarried, and they were more likely to remarry more than once than women did. Some of these patterns may be changing, however. The percent of people who have remarried is very similar for both sexes—17 percent for women and 16 percent for men (Kreider, 2005). The major difference is that by age 50, men are more likely than women to have been married at least twice.

The women who are most likely to remarry are those who married at a young age the first time, have few marketable skills, and want children (Wu, 1994).

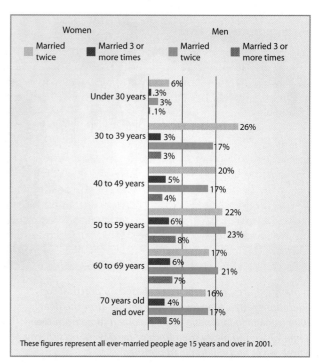

FIGURE 16.1 Percent of Americans Who Have Remarried, by Age and Sex
Source: Based on Kreider, 2005: Table 3.

These women are especially attractive to older divorced or widowed men who want a traditional wife to "spark" their lives. For example, Antonio, a 40-year-old divorced man who married Marisa, 22, says that he loves his new life despite the family complexity and having a child that remarriage has created:

> "She was like a Barbie to me," recalls Antonio, a department manager at a Target store. . . . Marisa's attentions made him "feel young again," he said. . . . One of his daughters from his first marriage is two years younger than his second wife. Another daughter has married his wife's brother—making her both his daughter and sister-in-law. "We're all one happy family," he says, bouncing his toddler son on his lap (Herrmann, 2003: 6).

Remarriage rates are high for both sexes age 50 and over, especially men (see *Figure 16.1*). Older women, especially those who seek to remarry, may be attractive to older men because neither partner has children in the home that may create conflict. Also, the woman may be willing to devote her time to taking care of her husband instead of pursuing a job or higher education. If older women have few economic resources, and as the pool of eligible mates grows smaller, they might make hasty choices because they don't want to be alone in their aging years (see Chapter 17).

The older a woman is, the harder it is for her to attract a man for marriage and remarriage. In each age group, because men tend to choose women who are younger and women tend to choose men who are older, the pool of eligible (and acceptable) marriage partners expands for men but shrinks for women (see Chapters 7 and 8).

Overall, U.S. remarriage rates have decreased since the early 1970s (Norton and Miller, 1992). A major reason for the decline may be the increase in cohabitation. According to a recent national study of Canadians (who are similar to Americans in many ways), after a divorce, the most prevalent choice for a second union is cohabitation rather than remarriage. For example, among people whose marriage was not preceded by cohabitation, 10 years after a separation or divorce, 60 percent had formed other relationships, with 41 percent choosing cohabitation and only 19 percent choosing remarriage. If people had lived together before a previous marriage, they were even more likely to cohabit rather than remarry, especially men (Wu and Schimmele, 2005).

Race and Ethnicity

Overall, African Americans are slightly more likely than whites to remarry, and Asian Americans are most likely to marry only once (see *Figure 16.2*). African Americans are also more likely than members of other groups to separate without divorcing and tend to remain single longer after a divorce (see Chapter 15).

since you asked

Why do African American women have lower remarriage rates than women in other racial-ethnic groups?

African American women, however, are less likely to remarry after a divorce than are black men or women in other racial-ethnic groups. Five years after divorce, for example, the probability of remarriage is 58 percent for white women, 44 percent for Latinas, and only 32 percent for black women (Bramlett and Mosher, 2002).

Why do African American women have lower remarriage rates? The reasons are similar to those that explain low first marriage rates. That is, college-educated black women have a small pool of eligible partners because many college-educated black men are marrying women with lower educational levels and some are marrying and remarrying across racial-ethnic boundaries (see Chapters 8 and 10).

Because of the large pool of eligible partners, many black men marry younger and less educated women, who exchange their youth and attractiveness for an older man's economic security. In addition, black

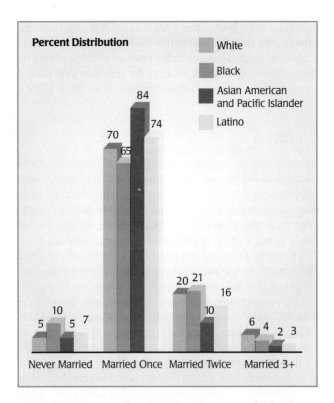

FIGURE 16.2   How Often We Marry, by Race and Ethnicity
Note: These figures show the number of times people age 45 and over have married.

Source: Kreider and Fields, 2002: Figure 3.

women with low socioeconomic status have little to gain if they marry men who are unemployed or who have few economic prospects for the future (see Chapters 9 and 10).

Social Class

In general, the more wealth a divorced man has, the more likely he is to remarry. In the marriage market, men tend to be "worth more" than women of the same age because they are usually financially better off. Divorced women, on the other hand, often have severe financial problems. For many women, then, the surest way to escape poverty is to remarry. Not surprisingly, less-educated, low-income divorcees are more likely to remarry than are divorced women who are older, highly educated, and financially independent (Folk et al., 1992; Ganong and Coleman, 1994; see, also, Chapter 15).

Men with high educational attainment are more likely to remarry than are women with a similar education. Although women with higher socioeconomic standing are more eligible remarriage candidates and are likely to attract more desirable marriage partners, they have less to gain from remarriage because they are often economically independent. Moreover, highly educated women have a smaller pool of eligible mates to choose from because they may be unwilling to marry someone from a lower socioeconomic level (Wu, 1994).

Children

Because of high divorce rates and the increase in out-of-wedlock childbearing, many adults contemplating a new relationship are already parents. The presence of children from previous relationships affects parents' decision to remarry or not. Some child free people find a ready-made family appealing, but others don't.

Because divorced men rarely have custody of their children, they are usually freer to socialize and to date. Divorced mothers, in contrast, may be busy earning a living or seeking only someone who can help provide financial stability and economic advantages for their children. Children may also decrease parents' interest in finding a new partner: They want to keep their single mothers to themselves or dislike their parents' dating partners (Schmiege et al., 2001; Ganong and Coleman, 2004).

Custodial mothers sometimes rush into a new marriage because they want their children to have a father figure and a male role model. Men, on the other hand, may see mothers as less attractive dating partners because they don't want to take on parental responsibilities.

Although the presence of children generally lowers the likelihood of remarriage, this isn't always the case. Young children might encourage dating and remarriage to replace an absent parent, especially a divorced father who never sees them. Older children who are living on their own may want a divorced or widowed parent to find a new companion, especially if remarriage won't decrease their inheritance. In addition, custodial fathers are likely to remarry, to marry custodial mothers, and to maintain a traditional family structure (Goldscheider and Sassler, 2006).

Like divorce, remarriage is a process rather than a one-time act. And, like divorce, remarriage involves a series of stages.

Making Connections

- Do you agree that the definition of stepfamilies should include cohabitors and people who have never married?

- Besides variables such as age and social class, what else affects remarriage rates? Think about religion, physical attractiveness, and the influence of family and friends, for example.

Remarriage as a Process

Remarriage is generally much more complicated than a first marriage or a divorce. The remarriage process may involve a series of steps similar to Bohannon's six stations of divorce (Goetting, 1982; see, also, Chapter 15). As with divorce, the stages of remarriage aren't necessarily sequential, and not every couple goes through all of them or with the same intensity. If partners can deal successfully with each stage, however, they are more likely to emerge with a new identity as a couple.

since you asked

How do first marriages and remarriages differ?

Emotional Remarriage

The emotional remarriage stage is often a slow process. Besides physical attraction, a divorced person establishes a commitment to and trust in a new partner. Because many people feel inadequate after a divorce, this stage often involves concern that the remarriage might fail.

In addition, remarriages are emotionally intricate because roles aren't clear. What are a spouse's responsibilities to new relatives? If the husband's ailing mother wants to move in with her son, for example, should the second wife be willing to care for her?

Psychic Remarriage

People's identity changes from that of a single individual to that of part of a couple after they remarry. Because social status and personal identity are independent of marital status for many men, a shift in marital status does not require an extreme change in personal identity.

The identify shift may be more difficult for women. For a traditional woman, the psychic remarriage represents recovery of a valued identity as a wife. A nontraditional woman, on the other hand, may worry about the loss of her highly valued independence.

Community Remarriage

People often change their community of friends when they remarry. During this stage of remarriage, they may sever close personal ties that they established after a divorce and lose valuable friendships.

In addition, people may move to another community after a remarriage. Such moves may entail meeting new neighbors, going to a different church, and sometimes changing the children's schools. These transitions often loosen ties with previous friends and social networks.

Filling the role of the stepparent may be easier when stepchildren are grown than when they are very young.

Parental Remarriage

The parental remarriage involves developing relationships between a partner and the children of the new spouse. If the children's other biological parent still plays an active role in their lives, the stepparent may have to overcome many hurdles. He or she cannot assume the role of father or mother but must behave as a nonparent, deferring to the biological parent's rights.

In some families, the biological nonresidential father may step aside as the stepfather moves in. If divorced fathers live close to their biological children, however, they maintain ties through telephone calls or visits. Because there are no guidelines for this cooperation, the parental remarriage stage can lead to confusion and frustration for biological parents, stepparents, and children.

Especially when one or both partners have children from previous marriages, there may be little time to develop workable and comfortable marital relationships and to cement a husband–wife bond. Instead, both marital and parental roles must be assumed simultaneously, and this may lead to conflict between the partners and between one or both partners and the children.

Economic Remarriage

Remarriage reestablishes a marital household as an economic unit. The main problems during this stage may stem from the presence of children from a former marriage. For example, a biological father's child-support payments may become unpredictable after a custodial mother remarries. The biological parent, usually a father, often feels less financial responsibility for the children regardless of the stepfather's income level.

Another source of economic instability is the unpredictable nature of the needs of the husband's children, who typically live with their biological mother. The possibility of unexpected expenses, such as dentists' and doctors' fees, can cast a financial shadow over the biological father's remarriage.

There may also be disagreements about the distribution of resources: If his daughter is taking ballet lessons, should the stepfather also pay for his stepson's tennis lessons? If the noncustodial parent is not honoring child-support payments, should the stepparent provide the money for recreational, educational, and social expenses for the children?

Legal Remarriage

Because the legal system does not delineate remarriage responsibilities, people are left to struggle with many problems on their own (Skinner and Kohler, 2002; Hans, 2002). For example, the remarriage raises questions such as which wife deserves a man's life and accident insurance, medical coverage, retirement benefits, pension rights, and property: the former wife, who played a major role in building up the estate, or the current wife? Which children should a remarried father or mother support, especially when it comes to high costs such as those of a college education—his, hers, or theirs?

Most schools and other public institutions typically don't recognize a stepparent as a legal parent. Usually, school registration forms, field trip permission slips, and health emergency information are requested of biological parents, not stepparents. The message, whether intended or not, is that only biological parents count.

Even when there is a will, many state inheritance laws do not include stepchildren. In most states, stepchildren may have to go to court and battle biological children even when a stepparent has left the estate or other assets to a stepchild.

Some couples cope with the remarriage stages and move on. Others don't. Whether remarried couples succeed or fail, they must deal with new issues that people in first marriages don't have to confront.

Making Connections

■ If you, your parents, or friends have remarried, which of the remarriage stages were the most problematic? Why?

■ How are the remarriage stages even more complicated if one or both partners is still adjusting to a divorce?

How First Marriages and Remarriages Differ

First marriages and remarriages differ in several important ways. Family composition tends to vary more in remarriages, role expectations are less defined, family members in remarriages may be at different points in their life cycles, and stress factors pile up as the stepfamily tries to readjust to its additional family relationships. People who remarry may also look for spouses who offer more than their first partners did in terms of communication, income, or companionship.

since you asked

Why are remarriages often more complicated than first marriages?

Family Composition

Remarriages often result in myriad new relationships and a dramatic change in family composition. Children may suddenly find themselves with **half-siblings**—brothers or sisters who share only one biological parent—as well as stepsiblings, stepgrandparents, and a host of other relatives. As a result, the children's experiences may change radically. For example, they may have to share their biological parent's time, as well as their physical space, with stepsiblings. Listen to one 8-year-old:

> We feel like guests in Jim's house. We are careful of what we do. It is like we are the intruders. And I feel very bad that we took Tommy's room. They fixed up a room for him in the basement, with posters and all, but he's still mad at us for taking his room (Fishman and Hamel, 1981: 185).

Remarriage creates a unique set of issues because it combines people from at least two families. Imagine the transition involved when a custodial mother marries a custodial father and the couple then decides to have their own children. Each partner's children from the former marriage may fear that new children will be loved more or receive more attention because they belong to both parents rather than to just one or the other.

A child who travels between two homes may feel left out of some everyday activities and treats. According to one 12-year-old, for example, "I get jealous when I come back to my mom's and see candy wrappers laying around and I didn't get any" (Hamilton, 2002: J2).

For their part, the parents may worry about dividing their attention between three sets of children so that none of them feels left out. To complicate matters further, ex-spouses and ex-grandparents may want to have input into the new family, input that may not be welcomed by the remarried spouses.

Role Expectations

The absence of role expectations for stepfamilies creates perplexing questions. For example, should stepparents have as much authority over children as the children's biological parents do? Should a noncustodial parent who has visitation rights have the same decision-making authority regarding his or her children that a custodial parent does? And should a child born to a remarriage have more legal rights than the stepchildren?

Role expectations are especially fuzzy when it comes to the extended family. Past and current in-laws and grandparents may be unsure how to treat their "instant" new family members. For example, step-grandparents may feel awkward around their new grandchildren and avoid them or overindulge them to show that they're not playing favorites (LeBey, 2004).

Stages of the Life Course

People who remarry sometimes find that they and their children are at different stages of the family life course. As a result, their goals may conflict. For example, a man with young adult children from his first marriage who is planning for his retirement may marry a younger woman who is looking forward to starting a family. Or his new wife may be an older woman who has already raised her family and now looks forward to a career:

> Claire and Sydney had been married for 4 years. Sydney had two adult children, ages 25 and 27, who had never lived with the couple, and Claire had a daughter who was 18 and in college. Sydney was a computer expert who had risen from working in the field as a technician to heading the marketing department for a large and successful electronics firm. He now had a month's vacation each year and looked forward to retirement in 10 years. Sydney wished to purchase a vacation home on a lake, as he had spent a number of years "dreaming about retiring there and fishing to his heart's content."
>
> Claire, on the other hand, had gone to work at the telephone company to support herself and her daughter after her divorce. Now that she and Sydney were married, she had been able to return to school and study to be a nurse. She was employed at a local hospital, loved her work, and hoped to become a supervisor before long. She worked var-

ious shifts and had little time off. Claire's favorite way to relax was to read or knit. . . . [but she also] liked to go dancing or to the movies in the evenings. Claire and Sydney worked out many of the stresses of their relationship arising from the joining of their two family groups, but they began to argue over weekend plans and future arrangements (Visher and Visher, 1988: 161–62).

On the other hand, an older man may look forward to remarriage and a new set of biological children. If he's at the top of his career ladder and economically secure, for example, he has time to enjoy watching his "new" children grow up and to participate in their upbringing. Also, his much younger second (or third) wife might encourage him to pursue recreational activities (such as skiing or socializing with friends) that he missed during his first marriage because of the struggle to pay bills and raise children.

People who remarry sometimes seek someone who is more successful, more supportive, or more attractive than the ex-spouse. The most appealing mates are often

Changes

Trophy Wives and Trophy Husbands in Remarriages

In the late 1980s, *Fortune* magazine ran a cover story on the "trophy wives" for whom, the story said, chief executive officers (CEOs) were trading their loyal, self-sacrificing, matronly, child-rearing wives. The thinner, younger, and flashier trophy wives were sexier and more socially skilled. They pampered their husbands and never criticized them, spent money on them rather than hoarding it for the children's education, and generally made the CEO feel like the king of the castle (Connelly, 1989).

Because many of these women were successful in their own right (many were well educated and had thriving small businesses of their own), they enhanced the man's status without overshadowing his success. The trophy wives also spent a lot of time on their appearance. Nancy Brinker, 42, the third wife of Norman Brinker, 58, who founded the Steak and Ale and Bennigan's restaurant chains and was the CEO of Chili's restaurant chain, said, "I work out one hour a day at aerobics, I diet rigorously, and I play polo with my husband. . . . Norman likes me to look good" (Connelly, 1989: 54).

Unlike the first wife, who is busy caring for the children, the trophy wife has the time and connections to improve her husband's reputation: "She totes him to small dinner parties, opera galas, museum benefits, and auctions for worthy causes, getting her husband to cough up something suitable in the way of a donation" (Connelly, 1989: 54).

Older men who are narcissistic are especially drawn to young and successful women. If these men feel that they married well below their social status the first time, they enjoy watching "the guys who are eating their hearts out" when the husbands show off their new "powerhouse brides" (Siegel, 2004).

Most important, the trophy wife has the advantage of being glamorous, independent, and available because she is not saddled with the husband's children: "The CEO now wants a playmate, someone who is free to travel with him and have fun" (Connelly, 1989: 61).

The husband can play father when he wants to rather than when he must. His children need not interfere in his or his trophy wife's economic or romantic life: "Having pots of money may ease the burden of not being there because the CEO can afford to fly the kids out to see him and go on exciting vacations with them" (Connelly, 1989: 61).

Some successful women are now seeking trophy husbands in their second or third marriage: "The basic criterion is this: No matter how successful a woman is in her profession, he is at least her equal, and maybe her better. He has three or more of the five attributes that tend to accompany achievement: fame, prestige, power, brains, and money" (Finke, 1994: 37, 39).

When television's Diane Sawyer married Academy Award–winning director Mike Nichols, the media claimed that "they hadn't so much wed as 'acquired' each other." Moreover, "Kennedy cousin Maria Shriver brought home perhaps the only thing she could find bigger than her famous family—Arnold Schwarzenegger" (Finke, 1994: 40).

Stop and Think . . .

- Do only wealthy people and celebrities have trophy wives and trophy husbands? Or have such remarriages occurred among people you know?

- If a partner has children, what are the advantages of marrying a trophy husband or wife? What are the disadvantages?

older men who don't have custody of their children. The box "Trophy Wives and Trophy Husbands in Remarriages" examines this phenomenon at the higher socioeconomic levels of American society.

Stress and Resources

Remarriage creates stresses that traditional first marriages rarely face. Among other things, as you'll see shortly, remarriage involves trying to combine several families, jealousy when biological parents or stepparents seem to favor some children over others, children having to move and leave their friends when a parent remarries, and half-siblings who don't get along.

Remarriage also provides resources. Children have more adults who care about them, may experience less conflict between biological parents who were always fighting, and step-grandparents who may be delighted to add more grandkids to the fold. According to one adolescent, for example, the bright side of stepfamilies is having two Christmases, two vacations, and two birthday celebrations every year (Crosbie-Burnett and McClintic, 2000; Hamilton, 2002).

Couple Dynamics in Stepfamilies

A well-known song tells us that "love is better the second time around." Often, however, people have fantasies about the second marriage that have nothing to do with reality.

since you asked

Why do many remarried couples divorce?

Myths about Remarriage

Some couples are more realistic than others in how they think about a remarriage. Here are the most common myths that "can promote dangerous stepfamily expectations" (Hetherington and Kelly, 2002: 174):

- *The Nuclear Family Myth:* Believers of this fantasy expect family members to love and feel close to one another, children to show deference to parents, and "discomforting appendages" (such as a nonresidential parent) to disappear. Even in long-lasting stepfamilies, tight-knit relationships are not the norm.

- *The Compensation Myth:* The new mate is expected to be everything the problematic old mate wasn't—kind, sensitive, responsible, and true. But people prefer to be who they are; when pushed to be someone else, they often become angry and resistant.

- *The Instant Love Myth:* Believing marriage to be a form of parental entitlement, new stepparents presume an intimacy and authority that they have yet to earn. The instant love myth often produces disillusionment even faster than the nuclear family myth.

- *The Rescue Fantasy:* Stepparents think that they will "shape those kids up" and rescue them from a negative or lenient custodial parent. Custodial fathers expect the stepmother to take over responsibility for the care and nurturing of a stepchild, something a stepmother may be unable or unwilling to do because of employment, personality, or other factors.

Some couples continue to nurture these myths and fantasies, and eventually break up. Others become more down-to-earth and work on building satisfying relationships between themselves and the stepchildren.

Marital Roles and Power

Remarried couples report sharing decision-making more equally than they did during their first marriage. The partners have a more egalitarian relationship because they believe that unequal power was a major problem in their first marriage and don't want to repeat the mistake (Ganong et al., 2006).

Another reason for more equitable power in remarriages may be that women feel obligated to earn income to help support their children from a previous relationship. Mothers are especially likely to work outside the home when they recognize that men may be reluctant to bear the full financial responsibility for the stepchildren. Because such women provide more economic resources, they are likely to have greater decision-making authority in the remarriage (Ganong and Coleman, 2004).

Shared power doesn't always mean that partners share household tasks equally. Although remarried husbands do more housework than do husbands in first marriages, domestic work is based on traditional gender roles, and remarried women do most of the domestic labor and child-rearing (Deal et al., 1992; Pyke and Coltrane, 1996).

After a divorce, women who were employed in low-skilled jobs may seek partners who appreciate stay-at-home wives and have the money to support such choices. In other cases, women enjoy their child care and domestic responsibilities, consider themselves to be good mothers, and neither need nor want parenting help from their partners. In such situations, the partners follow traditional gender roles: She does the housework and child care while he makes the major financial decisions (Pyke, 1994; Bray and Kelly, 1998).

"Sometimes I wonder if it would've been better having one big marriage instead of a lot of little ones."

Remarriage Quality

The data on marital satisfaction are mixed. Although people in first marriages report greater satisfaction than do remarried spouses, the differences are small. Especially if the remarried parents have a stable relationship and the mother feels that the children's life is going well, remarried mothers benefit psychologically from remarriage and are happier than divorced mothers (Vemer et al., 1989; Demo and Acock, 1996).

Other researchers report that remarried spouses are more likely to express criticism, anger, and irritation. The disagreements generally center on issues related to stepchildren, such as discipline, rules, and the distribution of resources (Coleman et al., 2002).

Negative interactions between remarried partners probably result from the strain and change associated with the new marriage and stepfamily formation. In the first few years of marriage, stress could reflect the same poor communication and problem-solving skills that led to a previous divorce. Remarriages may also suffer from increased stress caused by the behavior problems of young adolescent children (Bray, 1999).

Remarriage Stability

About 60 percent of remarriages end in divorce. The average duration of first marriages is approximately 8 years. The average duration of second marriages that end in divorce is about the same—8 years for women but slightly higher for men, 9 years. Third marriages that end in divorce typically last about 5 years (Clarke, 1995; Kreider, 2005).

When age is factored in, however, second marriages may be more stable than first ones. For example, the most lasting remarriages are between people age 45 or older in which both partners have been married previously. Older people may choose their second mate more carefully, may have more resources to make the marriage work, or may be reluctant to divorce again (Clarke and Wilson, 1994).

Why do remarried people divorce? First, those who marry as teenagers and remarry at a young age are more likely to divorce after a second marriage (Wilson and Clarke, 1992). This may reflect a lack of problem-solving skills or immaturity in dealing with marital conflict.

Second, people most likely to redivorce see divorce as a "quick" solution for marital dissatisfaction. Remarriages are more fragile because people don't have clear rules, they have dissimilar values and interests, and there may be greater conflict in remarriages. Disagreements over stepchildren also increase redivorce rates (Booth and Edwards, 1992; Pyke, 1994).

Third, women who have a child between marriages are more likely to divorce. *Intermarital birth* (giving birth between marriages) may force a newly married couple to cope with an infant rather than devote time to their relationship (Wineberg, 1991).

Finally, remarriage instability may reflect a lack of commitment and a failure to maintain family boundaries. Having survived one divorce, people may feel that another divorce is a ready remedy for an unhappy marriage. Thus, they may exert less effort to make the remarriage work or they may be unwilling to invest the time and energy to try to resolve problems (Ihinger-Tallman and Pasley, 1987).

Remarried couples must also deal with more boundary maintenance issues than people in first marriages. For example, people in remarriages often have to insulate themselves against interference from ex-spouses and ex-in-laws. Remarried couples must also devote more effort to establishing boundaries with new family members and new relatives, especially if one of the partners is a custodial parent (Browning, 1994).

The Diversity and Complexity of Stepfamilies

Stepfamilies come in many shapes and sizes. We'll look at various types of stepfamilies first, consider the unique challenges of gay and lesbian families, and then examine some of ways in which stepfamilies differ from nuclear families.

since you asked

What are the biggest problems that arise in stepfamilies?

Types of Stepfamilies

When a couple forms a stepfamily, new family networks emerge. These new networks are often traced through a **genogram,** a diagram showing the biological relationships among family members. The genogram in *Figure 16.3* shows the possible family systems that are created when two previously married parents marry each other.

Although they vary in parent–child relationships, there are three basic types of stepfamilies:

- In the **mother–stepfather family,** all the children are biological children of the mother and stepchildren of the father.

- In the **father–stepmother family,** all the children are biological children of the father and stepchildren of the mother.

- In the **joint stepfamily,** at least one child is the biological child of both parents, at least one child is the biological child of only one parent and the stepchild of the other parent, and no other type of child is present.

Stepfamilies can be even more complicated. In a *complex stepfamily,* both adults have children from previous marriages. And in *joint step–adoptive families* and *joint biological–step–adoptive families,* at least one child is a biological child of one parent and a stepchild of the other parent, and one or both parents have adopted at least one child. Nor does the term *complex stepfamily* take account of the relationships between cohabitors, one or both of whom may have been married and have children from previous unions.

The concept of stepfamily could also be expanded to include the increasingly common situation in which an unmarried mother and her child move in with a man who is not the child's biological father. Thus, families can be fairly simple, composed of only a biological parent and his or her children and a stepparent. They can also be complex and include stepparents, stepsiblings, half-siblings, and a combination of stepparents, stepsiblings, and half-siblings. The latter combination accounts for over 2 percent of all stepfamilies (Fields, 2001).

Gay and Lesbian Stepfamilies

Gay and lesbian stepfamilies share the problems of all other stepfamilies, but the difficulties often are aggravated by the parent's and stepparent's sexual orientation. Berger (1998) suggests that lesbian and gay stepfamilies encounter triple stigmatization. First, they are stigmatized for their homosexuality, which many

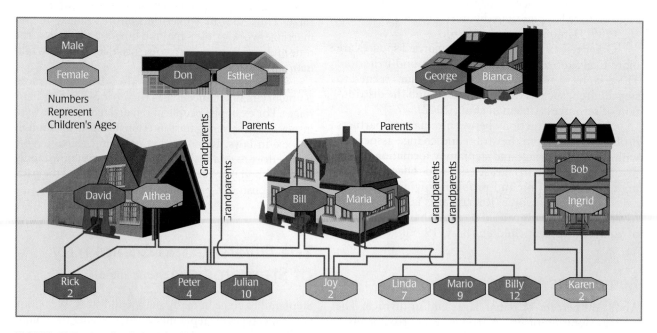

FIGURE 16.3 Stepfamily Networks
Each set of parents of our target couple, Bill and Maria, are grandparents to at least two sets of children. For example, Maria's parents are the grandparents of her children with her former husband, Bob (Billy, Mario, and Linda) and of her child with Bill (Joy). Depending on the closeness of the relationship Bill maintains with his former wife, Althea, however, Maria's parents might play a grandparental role to Peter and Julian, Bill and Althea's boys, as well.

SOURCE: Based on Everett and Everett, 1994: p. 132.

people view as immoral. Second, gay and lesbian step-families are still seen as deficient compared with nuclear families because they don't have adult role models of both sexes. Last, gay men, especially, criticize parenthood in the homosexual community because "the gay culture should emphasize the primacy of the couple relationship" rather than parenting.

Despite such obstacles, there is evidence that lesbian stepfamilies are resilient and as diverse as heterosexual stepfamilies. According to Wright (1998), for example, lesbian stepfamilies reflect three distinct stepparent roles:

▪ In the *co-parent family*, the nonbiological mother is a supporter of and helper and consultant to the biological mother, an active parent of the children, and a dedicated and committed family member.

▪ The *stepmother family* parallels heterosexual stepmother families. That is, the lesbian stepmother performs most of the traditional mothering tasks, but the biological mother (like the biological father in heterosexual families) retains most of the decision-making power.

▪ In the *co-mother family*, both mothers have equal rights and responsibilities in everyday decisions and child-rearing tasks.

Characteristics of Stepfamilies

Most children under age 18 live with their biological parents (see *Table 16.1*). Among stepfamilies, the most common form is mother–stepfather. Across racial-eth-nic groups, African American children and American Indian children are most likely to live in a mother–step-father family.

Stepfamilies may look like intact nuclear families because they are composed of married adults and children living in the same household. However, they differ from nuclear families in many ways that make step-parenting more difficult.

1. *The structure of stepfamilies is complex.* It bears repeating that stepfamilies create new roles: step-parents, stepsiblings, half-siblings, and stepgrand-parents. Note that this structure does not make stepfamilies better or worse than nuclear families; they are simply different.

   Stepfamilies offer the possibility for many different kinds of family ties, including relationships with uncles, aunts, and cousins. Ties between step-grandparents and their stepgrandchildren range from no contact to close relationships, depending largely on the investment the stepgrandparents make in those relationships (Cherlin and Furstenberg, 1994).

2. *A stepfamily must cope with unique tasks.* The stepparent may struggle to overcome rejection because the children may still be grieving over the breakup of the biological family, or the stepparent may disagree with the biological parent about discipline and rules (Hetherington and Kelly, 2002).

   One of the most common tasks is redefining and renegotiating family boundaries. This may in-

TABLE 16.1

Children Living with Two Parents in Biological, Step, and Adoptive Families, by Race/Ethnicity

	White	African American	Latino	American Indian and Alaska Native	Asian American and Pacific Islander
Children living with two parents[1]	36.8 million	4.4 million	7.1 million	667,000	2.2 million
Percentage living with					
Biological mother and father	88	83	91	81	92
Biological mother and stepfather	7	12	6	9	3
Biological father and stepmother	2	2	2	4	1
Adoptive mother and father	1	1	—[2]	5	4
Other combinations[3]	1	1	1	1	—

[1]Includes unmarried mothers and fathers.

[2]A dash represents less than 1 percent.

[3]These combinations include adoptive parents, biological parents, and stepparents.

SOURCE: Based on Fields, 2001: Table 2.

It is important in stepfamilies to make sure that all the children receive love and attention. If signs of jealousy appear, both parents should listen to the children's concerns and try to understand them.

clude making "visiting" children feel welcome and working out "turf" problems:

Consider the stepfamily in which the husband's three children rejoined the household every 3–4 days for a few days' time. The house was small, and the mother's three children who lived in the household had to shift where they slept, where they put their clothes, and where they could go to relax or to be alone to accommodate the extra family members. Bedrooms became dormitories, and the continual chaos created tension and instability for everyone (Visher and Visher, 1993: 241).

In such situations, it is difficult to develop clear and consistent rules about property rights and private spaces for each family member.

3. *Stepfamilies often experience more stress and conflict than nuclear families.* As the previous example illustrates, much of the stress in stepfamilies is due to the vagueness and the "lack of fit" with cultural norms that, however unrealistic, define the "ideal" family. Ambiguity may decrease as family members adjust to new roles and lifestyles. The sense that the family doesn't fit the ideal model may decrease as family functioning improves.

A major source of tension is the fact that family members must adjust to each other all at once rather than gradually, as in a nuclear family. Stress may come from several sources. More people make more demands, parents may differ on how to discipline children, one partner may feel excluded from the relationship between her or his spouse and the spouse's biological children, or there may not be enough resources to meet the larger family's needs (Whitsett and Land, 1992).

4. *Stepfamily integration typically takes years rather than months.* The age and sex of the children and the type of stepfamily (whether there is a stepmother or stepfather and whether there are children from one or both previous marriages) can affect adjustment. As "The Stepfamily Cycle" box shows, it may take as long as eight years for a couple to consolidate their family and to work as a team. And if they have a new baby or there are unexpected problems such as unemployment or a death in the family, the process may take even longer.

5. *Important relationships may be cut off or end abruptly, and others spring up overnight.* As you saw in Chapter 15, many fathers have no contact with their children after a divorce. Moreover, siblings sometimes are split between parents and may rarely see one another. Children are especially distressed if a parent's wedding announcement comes as a surprise:

One divorced father awakened his children one morning, asked them to get dressed, and drove them to the courthouse where he married a woman they had only recently met. The children were shocked and felt betrayed that they were not allowed to know that their father was serious about this woman and wanted to marry her. The woman also had a child, so that by 10 P.M. these children went to bed in a house that now included a new stepmother and a new stepsister. The children were not happy about it (Knox and Leggett, 1998: 184).

According to both researchers and clinicians, children should be given plenty of notice about an impending remarriage. The new partner and the children should get to know each other over the course of a year or two, go on vacations and have meals together, and just "hang around the house," getting to know one another (Bray and Kelly, 1998; Knox and Leggett, 1998).

6. *There are continuous transitions and adjustments rather than stability.* In a stepfamily, the people living in a household can change continuously. The boundaries between who is a member of a stepfamily and who is not are sometimes blurry. For example, is the new spouse of a child's noncustodial parent part of the child's family? And who decides the answer to this question?

Many families agree to have flexible boundaries so that at any age, including during adulthood,

Changes

The Stepfamily Cycle

Clinician Patricia Papernow (1993: 70–231) divides the process of becoming a stepfamily into three major stages. The early stage is characterized by fantasies, confusion, and slowly getting to know the other family members; in the middle stage, the family begins to restructure; and in the late stage the family achieves its own identity.

The Early Stages: Getting Started without Getting Stuck

Stage 1: Fantasy. Most remarrying couples start out with the fantasy that they will love the children of the person they love and be loved by them, and that they will be welcomed into a ready-made family. They see themselves as filling voids for the children, their spouses, and themselves.

Children in new stepfamilies also have fantasies that may encompass a mixture of hope and fear. Some children still hope that their biological parents will be reunited. Or they may fear losing or hurting one of their own parents if they come to love a stepparent.

Stage 2: Immersion. Chaos and confusion often characterize this stage. Biological parents, children, and stepparents may see problems differently. Stepparents may feel left out of the biological parent–child unit and may experience jealousy and resentment.

Biological parents are often caught in the middle. Some exhaust themselves trying to meet everyone's needs and make the stepfamily work; others ignore the difficulties. Particularly in the latter case, the children may feel lost or rejected. Some respond with angry outbursts; others withdraw.

Stage 3: Awareness. Members of the stepfamily get to know each other. Stepparents can learn about the children's likes and dislikes, their friends, and their memories without trying to influence the children.

Biological parents can try to find the right balance between overprotecting children and asking too much of them. Children should be encouraged to look at the positive aspects of the stepfamily, such as the parents' love.

The Middle Stages: Restructuring the Family

Stage 4: Mobilization. Many stepfamilies fall apart at this critical stage. The stepparent's task is to identify a few essential strategies for change (such as holding family meetings to deal with difficult issues) and make a sustained effort to communicate them to other family members while respecting the biological unit.

The biological parent's task is to voice the needs of her or his children and ex-spouse while supporting and addressing the stepparent's concerns. Children should voice their own needs to ease the pressures created by their conflicting loyalties.

Stage 5: Action. In this stage, the stepfamily can begin to make some joint decisions about how the family will operate. The stepparent begins to play a more active role in the family, and the biological parent doesn't feel the need to be all things to all people.

The Later Stages: Solidifying the Stepfamily

Stage 6: Contact. In this stage, family members begin to interact more easily. There is less withdrawal and more recognition of each other's efforts. The stepparent has a firm relationship with the spouse and has begun to forge a more intimate, authentic relationship with at least some of the stepchildren.

Stage 7: Resolution. Relationships begin to feel comfortable. The stepparent role is well defined and solid. Stepparents become mentors to some of their stepchildren. Other stepparent–stepchild relationships have achieved a mutually suitable distance.

In this stage, the adult stepcouple has become a sanctuary, a place to turn for empathy, support, and cooperative problem solving. The stepfamily finally has a sense of character and its own identity.

children have access to both of their biological parents and can move easily between households. If each child has parents who are divorced or remarried, there may be some difficulty in juggling individual needs, family traditions, and emotional ties between as many as four families.

7. *Stepfamilies are less cohesive than nuclear or single-parent households.* Stepchildren often feel closer to biological parents than to stepparents. As children grow up, they may also feel alienated because of differential economic support, as when only certain children in a stepfamily are supported during college. Or they may resent unequal favors and inheritance inequities bestowed by grandparents.

8. *Stepfamilies need great flexibility in their everyday behavior.* Varying custody and residential arrangements necessitate different daily or weekly routines. Moreover, within the household, the "expected" ways in which a family operates may not apply. For example, is the clarinet at Mom's house or Dad's? It's Amy's day to live at Mom's house, but over at Dad's they're going to play miniature golf.

The need for creativity and flexibility may decrease over time, but situations often arise (such as weddings, births, deaths, and holidays) that may require unusual solutions and arrangements. Should a noncustodial father who rarely visits his children pay for his daughter's wedding, or should her stepfather pay for it? If both the biological father and the stepfather are important in a young woman's life, who should walk down the aisle at her wedding? Both of them?

9. *Stepfamily members often have unrealistic expectations.* In one study of stepfamilies, 41 percent of partners said that they had remarried expecting that their stepfamily would become as close as a nuclear family. Many of the couples reported disappointment and astonishment when the everyday realities of stepfamily life were fraught with problems (Pill, 1990).

Stepfamilies often compare themselves with biological families and have idealized or naive expectations. There is no reason why members of the stepfamily—aside from the newly married adults—should automatically feel any sort of familial relationship or affection. It is physically and emotionally impossible for a stepfamily to mirror a biological family; there are simply too many players and too many new relationships. As you saw in the box on "The Stepfamily Cycle," stepfamilies must forge their own rules and identities.

10. *There is no shared family history.* The new stepfamily is a group of individuals who must develop meaningful, shared experiences. To do this, they must learn one another's patterns of communication (both verbal and nonverbal) and interaction. New stepfamily members often speak of culture shock: When their own behavioral patterns and those of other members of the household are different, they sometimes feel as if they are in an alien environment. For example, mealtimes and the meals themselves may be different from those they were used to in the past.

One way to ease some of the strangeness is to mesh rituals. In one remarried family, when a major holiday was approaching, family members were asked to suggest favorite foods. By preparing and serving these dishes, the new family honors some of the traditions of the previous families (Imber-Black and Roberts, 1993).

11. *There may be many loyalty conflicts.* Although questions of loyalty arise in all families, loyalty conflicts are intensified in stepfamilies. For example, suppose that a child in the stepfamily feels closer

Children in stepfamilies may often feel divided loyalties between their biological father, with whom they spend time periodically, their mother, and their stepfather.

to the noncustodial parent or to that parent's new spouse than to the biological and custodial parent or that parent's new spouse. Should these relationships be nurtured despite the resentment of the custodial parent or stepparent?

Moreover, a newly remarried adult must make a sustained effort to maintain loyalty to a new spouse despite loyalty to biological children. For example, when Gwen, who had lived with her mother and stepfather for nine years and then lived on her own while attending college, came back home for a time, her mother felt conflicted:

> Hugh [Gwen's stepfather] wants her to pay rent. I don't want her to. I feel that at this point in her life I would be a little more lenient than Hugh is. A lot of the difficulty is that she's been away for five years and now she's back in the fold. Hugh's a very rigid person—everything is preplanned and set up that way and that's the way you do it. I'm a little more loose (Beer, 1992: 133).

Gwen's mother's task was to find ways to help her daughter that did not diminish her loyalty to her husband. Had her husband been as "loose" as she was, adjustment might have been easier for this stepfamily.

12. *Roles of stepfamily members are often ambiguous.* A positive aspect of role ambiguity is that it provides freedom of choice: One may be able to play a variety of roles with different children and adults. For example, a stepparent who is willing to be a friend to the children, rather than a parent, can serve as a mediator when there is conflict between the children and the biological, custodial parent.

However, ambiguity creates problems because people don't always know what's expected of them or what to expect from others. A partner may want a spouse who offers support, not mediation, when he or she disagrees with the children.

When adults have problems, so do children. If adults are resilient and adjust, so do children. What, more specifically, are the everyday processes of living in stepfamilies?

Making Connections

- Did you grow up in a stepfamily? Looking at the list of 12 characteristics, which ones were most difficult for you or someone you know?

- What are some advantages of growing up in a stepfamily compared with a nuclear family?

Living in a Stepfamily

Stepparents don't have complete control over the relationships that develop in their new family. Often they must often overcome stereotypes and work very hard to merge members of several households into one.

Stereotypes about Stepfamilies

The *myth of the evil stepmother*, perpetuated in Western culture by classic tales such as "Cinderella," "Snow White," and "Hansel and Gretel," still exists. This myth, which depicts stepmothers as cruel, unloving, and abusive, has had a ripple effect over time. The harmful image persists even though many stepmothers neither wish nor expect to replace the stepchild's mother (Ganong and Coleman, 1997; Kheshgi-Genovese and Genovese, 1997; Orchard and Solberg, 1999).

Ex-wives who are still angry about a divorce sometimes refer to the stepmother as a witch in front of their children, deepening the rift between the stepmother and the stepchildren. Here's how one new stepmother, Melinda, describes her experiences when picking up her husband's sons at the custodial mother's house for weekend visits:

> When I first started picking up the boys, I could sense how much his ex-wife resented me as the "other woman" who broke up her marriage, even though they had started divorce proceedings before I met Clark. I would often see her peeking out of an upstairs window, looking at me with pure venom . . . As I sat there, I could hear the screaming accusations that his ex-wife was hurling at me in front of the boys (LeBey, 2004: 94–95).

Melinda and her husband, Clark, were raising her young daughter and their biological child and were experiencing financial difficulties. The boys from his previous marriage "ran wild" during weekends because Clark didn't impose any rules on their behavior. When the boys visited, Melinda, exhausted, was often "shrill, short-tempered, and angry. I was living up to the myth of the wicked stepmother." To make matters worse, Clark's parents often complained that their son had made an awful mistake by marrying "that woman," an intruder and home wrecker (LeBey, 2004).

To meet their husband's expectations, stepmothers often try to impose some kind of order on the household.

Many stepchildren become angry, resenting and resisting the rules:

> *In our most contentious stepfamilies, a real demonizing of the stepmother often occurred. We heard stepmothers described by some stepchildren as "evil," "malevolent," "wicked," or as "monsters," and nicknamed "Dog Face" or "The Dragon." Stepfathers rarely encountered this level of vitriol. Many well-intentioned but angry, discouraged, and defeated stepmothers gradually gave up and pulled out of the marriage (Hetherington and Kelly, 2002: 193).*

In contrast, the more recent *myth of instant love*, as you saw earlier, maintains not only that remarriage creates an instant family but that stepmothers will automatically love their stepchildren. In *The Sound of Music*, for example, Julie Andrews wins the affections of the seven von Trapp children within a few months. Remarried parents, especially women, expect such instant love because, according to the *myth of motherhood*, mothering comes easily and naturally to all women (Braverman, 1989; Quick et al., 1994; see, also, Chapters 5 and 12).

Members of a newly constituted family who believe all these myths may experience a high degree of stress as they try to adapt to new personalities, lifestyles, schedules, and routines. And considering the unrealistic views that people hold of the nuclear family, it's not surprising that the stepfamily suffers by comparison (Gamache, 1997; see, also, Chapter 1).

A woman who grew up believing that stepmothers are bad may try to become a "super stepmom." She may be especially frustrated if her stepchildren rebel despite all her sincere and self-sacrificing efforts. By the same token, a child who grew up with the same ideas about stepmothers may have negative expectations and may resist her attempts to develop a positive relationship. Thus, a self-perpetuating cycle is set in motion. The children expect the stepmother to be nasty, and as a result they will be aloof. Their unpleasant behavior may cause the stepmother to become more demanding and critical (Berger, 1998).

Parenting in Stepfamilies

About 7 percent of U.S. children live in stepfamilies. African American and American Indian children are most likely to live in stepfamilies and Asian American children least likely (see *Figure 16.4*).

Most stepfamilies face a number of issues when they attempt to merge two households after a remarriage. These include naming, sexual boundaries, legal

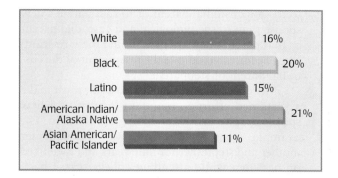

FIGURE 16.4 **Percentage of Children Living in Stepfamilies**
Sources: Based on Fields, 2001: Table 4.

issues, integrating the children into the family, establishing discipline and authority, helping children adjust to the new family form, and developing intergenerational relationships.

NAMING The English language has fairly clear terms for relationships in intact families, such as "father," "mother," "brother," and "daughter." Suppose, however, that the children want to call their stepfather "Dad." The biological children may feel threatened and annoyed by this if they don't accept their stepsiblings as "really" family. One of my friends admits that she feels pangs of anger and envy when her son calls his stepmother "Mom." Thus, bad feelings may result all around.

One stepmother was uncomfortable with her three young stepchildren's calling her by her first name (as her husband does) because it seemed impersonal and disrespectful. Here's her solution:

> *I did not want to confuse the children by asking them to call me "Mom," since they already have a mother. So, I came up with a name that worked— "Smom." It's now a year later, and the kids are completely comfortable calling me Smom. Even my husband's ex-wife calls me that. Sometimes, the kids have variations, like "Smommy" or "Smama." I'm happy, they're happy (Ann Landers, 2000: C11).*

The name children call a stepfather—whether he is married to or cohabiting with their mother—has special meaning for men. Actually hearing oneself called "Dad," as opposed to one's first name or "stepdad," is a sign of acceptance and belonging. Many men still remember first hearing "Daddy" or "Dad" as a thrilling and momentous occasion because the use of kinship terms goes hand in hand with a feeling of genuine fatherhood (Marsiglio and Hinojosa, 2006).

SEXUAL BOUNDARIES Our laws forbid sexual relations between siblings and between parents and children in biological families. However, there are rarely any legal restrictions on sexual relations between stepfamily members, either between stepchildren or between a stepparent and a stepchild.

Estimates of the extent of child abuse in stepfamilies vary, but researchers agree that children are at greater risk for both physical and sexual abuse if they live in a household with an adult who is not their genetic parent than if they live with both biological parents. When sexual abuse occurs, the perpetrator is typically a male, most likely a stepfather (Ganong and Coleman, 2004; Reading, 2006; see, also, Chapter 14).

Stepsiblings may also drift into romantic relationships that can damage family relationships. As the "Dealing with Sexual Boundaries in the Stepfamily"

box shows, one way to deal with such sexual problems is to prevent them in the first place.

LEGAL ISSUES Financial matters are more complicated in stepfamilies than in first marriages. Financial planners and marriage educators are nearly unanimous in urging people who are planning a second marriage to spell out their financial obligations to each other in a legally binding prenuptial agreement. The issues include whether to share financial responsibility for children from previous marriages, how to divide estates, whether to merge assets and liabilities, and how to divide property acquired before and after the marriage in case of divorce (Rowland, 1994; see, also, *Appendix F*).

Unless there is a prenuptial agreement that allows a "new" spouse to waive his or her rights to a share of an estate, children from a previous marriage may be

---

Applying What You've Learned

Dealing with Sexual Boundaries in the Stepfamily

Only some states forbid romantic relationships between nonbiological members of a stepfamily. The weakened incest taboo in the stepfamily makes rules less clear, and sexual liaisons can create confusion, anger, and a sense of betrayal.

The advice in this box is aimed at reducing the likelihood of a sexual relationship developing in a stepfamily. As you read this material, think about how you would explain why sexual attraction is much more common in stepfamilies than in biological families.

Practitioners Emily and John Visher (1982: 162–66) offer remarried partners these guidelines for dealing with sexuality in the stepfamily:

- Be affectionate and tender, but not passionate, with each other when the children are with you. Teenagers are particularly sensitive to open displays of affection because of their own emerging sexuality. Be aware of this sensitivity and forgo the kisses and embraces in the kitchen.
- Don't be sexually provocative. Walking around in a bra and underpants will counteract efforts to keep sexuality under control in your household, even when only younger children are around. Set a limit on teenagers' sexual behavior. The first time a teenager parades around the house scantily clad, for example,

he or she should be told to go back to his or her room and to dress properly. Be firm in setting limits for appropriate dress and behavior.
- Avoid roughhousing with children after they are 10 or 11 years old. This kind of behavior may become a physical turn-on between stepsiblings or between children and stepparents.
- Stop some forms of intimate behavior with children after they turn 10 or 11. For example, sitting on a stepfather's lap and showering him with kisses is inappropriate behavior for a teenage stepdaughter.
- If a teenager develops a crush on a stepparent, talk to him or her openly. Point out that the teen's affections are misplaced. Also, make it clear that there is a big difference between feelings and behavior. Just because people are attracted to others does not mean that they should act on their impulses.
- Rearrange the living space to cool off a sexual situation between stepsiblings. For example, avoid adjoining bedrooms and rearrange the bathroom sharing arrangements so that older children have more privacy and less temptation.
- Do not tolerate sexual involvement in your home. In one family, the adults asked the college-aged son to move out of the house because they were unwilling to accept his sexual relationship with his stepsister. Although stepparents can't control sexual attraction between stepsiblings, they can control what happens in their home.

practically disinherited even though this was not the parent's intention. Some biological children may resent their inheritance being divided with stepsiblings. In other cases, adult children feel devastated when an aging dad has a new wife and changes his will, leaving most of the deceased mother's jewelry and other personal belongings to his stepchildren (Cohn, 2005).

Legal experts advise setting up a trust fund to safeguard the biological children's or grandchildren's inheritance. Trusts allow parents to transmit gifts and inheritances to whomever they choose while they are alive or after their death. In addition, to minimize family friction, attorneys advise people to discuss their estate plans with those who will be affected by them (Spears, 1994).

DISTRIBUTING ECONOMIC RESOURCES The children of remarried fathers typically are at a financial disadvantage if they live with their biological mother. The stepchildren living with their remarried father may receive more support, such as loans, gifts, and health coverage. Loss of economic support can impoverish biological children and create hostility.

The partners must decide whether to pool their resources and how to do so. They may experience stress and resentment if there are financial obligations to a former family (such as custody awards, mortgage payments, or outstanding debts).

There may also be conflict about whose children should be supported at college or how wills should be written (e.g., whether the common property should be divided equally between the two families or among the children). Disagreements may range from seemingly petty issues, such as how much should be spent on birthday presents for relatives, to drastically different attitudes about whether money should be saved or spent.

Because men typically have more economic resources than women do, stepfathers may have more decision-making power in the new family. Sometimes men use money to control their wives' and children's behavior ("If you don't shape up, you can pay for your own car insurance next time"). This kind of manipulation creates hostility.

DISTRIBUTING EMOTIONAL RESOURCES Resources such as time, space, and affection must also be distributed equitably so that all the family's members feel content with the new living arrangements. Mothers sometimes are angry about spending much of their time and energy on live-in stepchildren but receiving few rewards:

My husband's kids don't see me as their mother. They shouldn't because I'm not. But I've gone out of my way to hold my tongue and do special things for them. It's as if whatever I do can be sloughed off, because I really don't count. I can do things for the kids and my husband gets the credit, not me. I resent them at those moments, and I resent him. It's really hard (Vissing, 2002: 193–194).

Although such difficulties are common, stepmothers are often "carpenters for damaged relationships" (Vinick, 1997). They may reestablish estranged ties between their husbands and his biological children by urging their husbands to make phone calls or by calling themselves, sending invitations for visits and family get-togethers, and buying children's birthday presents. Biological mothers can strengthen ties between their children and stepfathers by encouraging them to spend time together. As one mother said, "I'd send them off to the movies or to a park. They had to form a relationship without me intervening" (Wolcott, 2000: 16).

DEVELOPING PARENT–CHILD RELATIONSHIPS Children from stepfamilies usually show less emotional, social, and familial adjustment than do children from nuclear families. As a result, children in single-mother and remarried households are more likely than children in nuclear families to have emotional and behavioral problems, a topic that we'll examine shortly (see Hetherington and Stanley-Hagan, 2002, for a summary and review of some of this research).

Relationships with stepchildren are often more difficult for stepmothers than for stepfathers. Although stepfathers who don't monitor their stepchildren may have a long-term negative effect on the children's behavior, stepmothers may be less likely to have good relationships with their stepchildren because the

"You're right, I should spend more time with the kids. Which ones are ours?"

Medical Economics, January 25, 1993.

stepmother is more often the disciplinarian (Kurdek and Fine, 1993; MacDonald and DeMaris, 1996).

If the stepmother is at home more than her husband, she may be expected to be more actively involved in domestic duties, including raising the stepchildren. Regardless of the parent's gender, relations between children and parents in both intact and remarried homes are more positive when the parents include the children in decision making and are supportive rather than critical (Barber and Lyons, 1994; Crosbie-Burnett and Giles-Sims, 1994).

ESTABLISHING DISCIPLINE AND CLOSENESS Two of the biggest problems in stepfamilies are discipline and authority, especially in relationships between a stepfather and adolescent stepchildren. Teenagers complain, "He's not my father, and I don't have to listen to him." Stepfathers resent not being obeyed, both because they consider themselves authority figures and because they may be working hard to support the family.

Mothers often feel caught in the middle. Although they love their husbands, they may feel guilty for having married someone the children don't like, or they may disagree with the stepfather's disciplinary measures (Hetherington and Stanley-Hagan, 2002).

Whether they intend it or not, when parents find themselves forming strong relationships with the children of a new partner, they may feel that they are betraying their biological children. Similarly, children may feel guilty if they find themselves liking a stepparent better than a biological parent because the stepparent is more fun, more understanding, or easier to get along with (Papernow, 1993).

Regardless of age, visiting (nonresidential) children may feel awkward and uncomfortable. If the visits are intermittent, they may not develop a sense of belonging or fitting in. As you saw earlier, however, ensuring that each family member has a private physical space can lessen the alienation of visiting children.

Friendship is probably the best way to enhance step-relationships. If stepparents go slowly in approaching stepchildren, especially adolescents, they have a better chance of establishing discipline or setting rules. Some stepparents act as *quasikin*, a role midway between that of parent and friend. That is, they assume some of the functions of parents but let the biological parents make final decisions about their children. Maintaining a quasikin relationship can be tricky, however:

> *Stepparents must balance daily parenting activities such as getting children ready for school, giving allowances, and supervising household chores while taking a more distant stance when the stepchildren's parents are making major decisions about the children (Coleman et al., 2001: 263).*

Taking a quasikin role is easier with nonresidential (visiting) children than with custodial children and with older children than with younger children. This role is also more common among stepfathers than among stepmothers, who are often responsible for everyday monitoring and discipline.

Remarried partners sometimes have a child, hoping that the new addition will "cement" stepfamily bonds. A half-sibling rarely affects adolescents, however. As in other types of families, teens become more involved with friends and school activities than with siblings. If, however, stepparents shift all of their attention to the baby, they may become less involved with preadolescent children who need their attention (Stewart, 2005).

GENDER DIFFERENCES IN CHILDREN'S ADJUSTMENT Stepdaughter–stepfather relationships are usually more negative than those between stepsons and stepparents of either sex. Even when stepfathers make friendly overtures, stepdaughters may withdraw (Vuchinich et al., 1991).

One explanation for this distancing behavior is that daughters, who once had a privileged status in the family because they shared much of the authority in helping to raise younger children, may resent being replaced by someone with more power in the family. The stepdaughter–stepfather relationship may also be more distant because the stepfather has made sexual overtures or behaved in other inappropriate ways toward the stepdaughter (see Chapters 14 and 15).

Whatever the reasons for the problems girls experience in remarried families, the friction is often serious enough to cause adolescent girls to leave stepfamily households at an earlier age than do girls in either single-parent or intact homes. Stepdaughters also leave earlier to establish independent or cohabiting households (Kiernan, 1992; Goldscheider and Goldscheider, 1993).

Stepfathers, especially, need to be patient in establishing new relationships. In describing the gradual process of developing a relationship with the stepchild, one stepfather commented, "Brian is different now. At first he was reclusive and jealous and he saw me as infringing. It was a slow progression" (Santrock et al., 1988: 159). The box on "The 10 Commandments of Stepparenting" offers some guidelines for stepparents.

INTERGENERATIONAL RELATIONSHIPS Ties across generations, especially with grandparents and stepgrandparents, can be close and loving or disruptive and intrusive. After a divorce or during a remarriage, grandparents can provide an important sense of continuity for children at a time when many other things are changing. Although many children typically do not become as attached to their new stepgrandparents as they

Choices

The 10 Commandments of Stepparenting

All families, including stepfamilies, have to work hard to achieve a peaceful coexistence. Family practitioners (Turnbull and Turnbull, 1983; Visher and Visher, 1996) offer the following advice to stepparents who want to maintain harmony within the family:

1. **Provide neutral territory.** Most people have a strong sense of territoriality. Stepchildren may have an especially strong sense of ownership because some of their privacy has been invaded. If it is impossible to move to a new house where each child has a bedroom, provide a special place that belongs to each child.

2. **Do not try to fit into a preconceived role.** Be honest right from the start. Each parent has faults and peculiarities and the children will have to get used to these weaknesses. Children detect phoniness and will lose respect for any adult who is insincere or too willing to please.

3. **Set limits and enforce them.** One of the most difficult issues in stepfamilies is discipline. Parents should work out the rules in advance and support each other in enforcing them. Rules can change as the children grow older, but there should be agreement from the beginning on such issues as mealtimes, bedtimes, resolving disagreements, and household responsibilities.

4. **Allow an outlet for the children's feelings for the biological parent.** The stepparent should not feel rejected if a child wants to maintain a relationship with a noncustodial biological parent. Children's affection for their biological parents should be supported so that the children do not feel disloyal.

5. **Expect ambivalence.** Children's feelings can fluctuate between love and hate, sometimes within a few hours. Ambivalence is normal in human relationships.

6. **Avoid mealtime misery.** Many families still idealize the dinner hour as a time when family members have intelligent discussions and resolve problems. Although both parents should reinforce table manners, an unpleasant family mealtime should be ignored or avoided. Some suggested strategies include letting the children prepare their own meals and letting the father do some of the cooking.

7. **Do not expect instant love.** It takes time to forge emotional bonds; sometimes this never occurs. Most children under 3 adapt easily. Children over age 5 may have more difficulty. Some children are initially excited at having a new mother or father but later find that the words "I hate you" are potent weapons. A thick skin helps during this potentially hurtful time.

8. **Do not accept all the responsibility; the child has some, too.** Children, like adults, come in all types. Some are simply more lovable than others. Like it or not, the stepparent has to take what he or she gets. This does not mean assuming all the guilt for a troubled relationship, however.

9. **Be patient.** Good relationships take time. The first few months, and even six to seven years, are difficult. The support and encouragement of other parents who have had similar experiences can be invaluable.

10. **Maintain the primacy of the marital relationship.** The couple must remember that the marital relationship is primary in the family. The children need to see that the parents get along together, can settle disputes and, most of all, will not be divided by the children.

Stop and Think . . .

- Some of my students, especially those who are stepparents, feel that there should be a parallel list of "10 commandments" for stepchildren. Do you agree? Or do you think that peaceful coexistence is the adults' responsibility?

- If you were seeking a partner, would you use this list to screen a potential stepparent?

are to their biological grandparents, they can resent new grandparents who seem to neglect or reject them:

One twelve-year-old girl in our practice became angry and aggressive toward her two new and younger stepsiblings following their first Christmas holiday together, even though she had been very loving with them before that. Several weeks later she revealed to her father that she was hurt and disappointed because the stepsiblings received twice as many gifts from their grandparents as she did in total from everyone in the family (Everett and Everett, 1994: 140).

Children may feel anger and hostility when a parent or stepparent must go to court over such things as support payments owed by a child's biological father.

Reprinted with permission of the Daily Breeze © 2002.

Relations with paternal grandparents tend to decrease when a child lives with his or her mother after divorce and remarriage. When parents remarry, they tend to live farther away, have fewer visits with grandparents, and make fewer telephone calls (Lawton et al., 1994).

Such distanced behavior can decrease contact and closeness between grandparents and grandchildren. Even maternal grandparents may visit less often, call less often, and offer less baby-sitting time to remarried daughters than to married or divorced daughters. Intergenerational relationships, then, depend on how much effort the remarried partners and steprelatives put into maintaining or forging close family ties (Spitze et al., 1994; see, also, Chapter 17).

Some Effects of Stepfamilies on Children

Researchers have spent considerable time examining whether stepfamilies are beneficial or harmful to children. Among other variables, the results vary according to the family's socioeconomic status and degree of parental conflict.

HOW CHILDREN FARE The negative reactions of children (especially young children) are fairly short lived. Stepmothers and stepchildren usually establish good relationships within a few years (Hetherington and Clingempeel, 1992).

Some studies report that there are no emotional or behavioral differences between stepchildren and other children. Other studies show that about 20 percent of stepchildren are at risk for negative outcomes—a somewhat higher percentage than that of children living with both biological parents (Pasley and Moorefield, 2004).

Although the results are mixed, many studies show that children in stepfamilies don't fare as well as children in nuclear families. They tend to have more problems academically in grades, scores on achievement tests, school attendance, and high school graduation rates. Even though the family's economic resources increase after a remarriage, alternating residences during the school year raises a child's risk of dropping out of school or having problems with school authorities (Mekos et al., 1996; Teachman et al., 1996; Bogenscheider, 1997; Pong, 1997).

Compared with children in first-marriage families, stepchildren also exhibit more internalizing behavior problems, such as depression, and are at higher risk for emotional problems. Adolescent stepchildren also generally display more externalizing (acting out) behavioral problems, such as using drugs and alcohol, engaging in sexual intercourse, and having children out of wedlock (see Coleman et al., 2002, for a summary of some of this literature).

The most consistent findings on stepparent–stepchild relationships show that conflict between the biological parents create problems that often result in emotional and behavioral difficulties for the children (Ganong et al., 2006). Thus, as in biological and divorced families, children often suffer because adults can't seem to get along (see, also, Chapters 12 and 15).

Negative effects vary by ethnic group, however. For example, black teenage boys who live with stepfathers are significantly less likely to drop out of school, and black teenage girls with stepfathers are significantly less likely to become unmarried mothers than those in single-parent households. The income and role models that African American stepfathers provide may be critical in communities with few resources or minimal adolescent supervision (McLanahan and Sandefur, 1994).

Married stepfamilies, but not cohabiting ones, living in high-poverty neighborhoods often protect adolescent daughters. According to Moore and Chase-Lansdale (2001), daughters in stepfamilies are 92 percent less likely to have had sexual intercourse than daughters of single mothers. They are also less likely to have out-of-wedlock births. The researchers suggest that a mother's marriage increases the family's economic and social stability, support, and household maintenance and decreases many teenagers' risky sexual behavior.

THEORETICAL EXPLANATIONS FOR THE EFFECTS ON CHILDREN Studies that find variations in the effects of stepparenting on children propose several explanations for those differences. Although there are about a dozen theoretical perspectives, three of the most common are the cumulative effects hypothesis, risk and resilience theories, and social capital models.

In the *cumulative effects hypothesis,* children whose parents have had several partners over time had more internalizing and externalizing problems than children who lived with a parent who had remarried only once (Kurdek and Fine, 1993). That is, children who undergo multiple transitions experience more emotional and behavioral difficulties because the problems snowball.

Risk and resilience theories suggest that the effects of remarriage on children reflect both costs (risks) and benefits (resources that increase resilience). Remarriage can help single mothers escape from poverty. If children have a good relationship with a stepfather and a noncustodial father, they experience about the same number of problems as children from nuclear families. In addition, supportive schools and peers decrease the likelihood of adjustment problems. Children are less resilient, however, if the ex-spouses' "anger and acrimony undermine the happiness, health, and adjustment of family members" (Hetherington and Stanley-Hagan, 2000: 177; White and Gilbreth, 2001; Rodgers and Rose, 2002).

Social capital models maintain that children in stepfamily households have more problems than children in nuclear families if the parenting is inadequate. Children thrive when their "social capital" includes parents who are involved in school activities and homework, value learning, and there is minimal tension between the adults (Pong, 1997; Kim et al., 1999).

Making Connections

- Should stepparents be parents, friends, quasikin, or some combination of these roles?

- What kinds of traditions, rituals, and celebrations might stepfamilies implement to build a new identity for both stepchildren and stepparents?

Successful Remarriages and Stepfamilies

Many stepfamilies, as you've seen, encounter difficulties such as boundaries, cohesiveness, and conflicting loyalties that biological families rarely face. Yet we rarely hear about well-adjusted and happy stepfamilies. Although forging a civil relationship with an ex-spouse or new spouse and raising stepchildren is a daunting task, it can be done.

since you asked

What can stepparents do to make their new families more successful?

Some Characteristics of Successful Stepfamilies

In a review of the literature, Visher and Visher (1993) suggest that seven characteristics are common to remarried families in which children and adults experience warm interpersonal relations and satisfaction with their lives. Some of these characteristics, as you might expect, are the opposite of the problems we examined earlier.

First, successful stepfamilies *develop realistic expectations.* They have rejected the myth of instant love because they realize that trying to force friendship or love simply doesn't work. In addition, they don't try to replicate the biological family because they accept the fact that the stepfamily is "under construction." Teenagers who are beginning to rebel against authority are particularly sensitive to adult supervision. As one teenager in a stepfamily put it, "Two parents are more than enough. I don't need another one telling me what to do" (Visher and Visher, 1993: 245).

Second, adults in successful stepfamilies *let children mourn their losses.* These parents are sensitive to children's feelings of sadness and depression after their parents divorce. The stepparents also accept the children's expressions of fear, confusion, and anger, neither punishing them nor interpreting their reactions as rejection.

Third, the adults in well-functioning stepfamilies *forge a strong couple relationship.* This provides an atmosphere of stability because it reduces the children's anxiety about another parental breakup. It also gives children a model of a couple who can work together effectively as a team and solve problems rationally (Kheshgi-Genovese and Genovese, 1997).

Fourth, the *stepparenting role proceeds slowly.* A stepparent is catapulted into a parenting role, whereas a biological parent's relationship with a child develops over many years. One of the biggest mistakes that stepfathers make, usually with their wife's encouragement, is assuming an active parenting role too early in the marriage and presuming an intimacy and authority that they have not yet earned. Children might still be feeling the effects of "emotional divorce" even if their biological parents have recovered (see Chapter 15).

Fifth, except when young children are present, the *stepparent should take on a disciplinary role gradually.* As one of my students stated, "My stepfather wasn't ever in my face, which was good, because I would have been mad if he had tried to discipline me."

With teenagers, the biological parent should be the disciplinarian while the stepparent supports his or her rules ("What did your mom say about going to the

Which image of stepfamilies is probably more realistic—the one of the popular The Brady Bunch *television series, 1969–1974 (left), or the photo on the right?*

movies tonight?"). In successful stepfamilies, adults realize that relations between a stepparent and stepchildren can be quite varied: The stepparent may be a parent to some of the children, a companion to others, or just a good friend to all. And even if there are no warm interpersonal ties, it is enough that family members are tolerant and respectful of one another.

Sixth, successful *stepfamilies develop their own rituals.* They recognize that there is more than one way to do the laundry, cook a turkey, or celebrate a birthday. It is not a matter of a right or a wrong way. Instead, successful stepfamilies may combine previous ways of sharing household tasks or develop new schedules for the things they do together on the weekends. The most important criteria are flexibility and cooperation.

Finally, well-functioning stepfamilies *work out satisfactory arrangements between the children's households.* Adults don't have to like each other to be able to get along. In fact, it is useful for many adults to have a "business relationship" during such family events as holidays, graduations, and weddings. Many black families have flexible familial boundaries so that children feel welcome in several households regardless of biological "ownership." In addition, many African American families, including fictive kin, share material and emotional resources in raising children (Crosbie-Burnett and Lewis, 1993; see, also, Chapter 2).

The most successful stepfamilies have two sets of parents but one set of rules. They collaborate at school functions, parent–teacher meetings, and after-school activities. For example, if each child has a list in his or her backpack, both sets of parents can check off items (such as homework, musical instruments, and gym shorts) when the children move back and forth from house to house.

Communication is critical in successful stepfamilies. If adult relationships are strained, relying on e-mail, especially, can "take the 'feelings' out of communication. You can simply put the facts down, and you don't have to talk to the person" (Cohn, 2003: 13; Braithwaithe et al., 2006). In contrast, face-to-face interaction is more effective in stepchild–stepparent communication. Most important, adults should never criticize the children's biological parents or stepparents.

The Rewards of Remarriage and Stepparenting

Couples often say that their stepfamilies offer more benefits than their first marriage. Many feel they learned valuable lessons in their first marriage and that they have matured as a result of the experience. They feel that they know each other better than they knew their former spouse, talk more openly and more freely about issues that concern them, and are less likely to suppress their feelings.

Successful remarried couples say that they try harder, are more tolerant of minor irritations, and tend to be more considerate of each other's feelings than they were in their first marriages. They also report enjoying the new interests and new friends that a remarriage brings (Westoff, 1977).

Despite the ups and downs, a stepfamily gives its members opportunities that may be missing in an unhappy intact family. Because children see loving adults, they have a positive model of marriage (Rutter, 1994).

When remarried partners are happy, the children benefit from living in a satisfying household. A well-functioning stepfamily increases the self-esteem and well-being of divorced parents, and provides children who have minimal contact with noncustodial parents with a caring and supportive adult. In addition, the children's economic situation often improves after a parent, especially a mother, remarries (Pill, 1990; see, also, Chapter 15).

One of the greatest benefits of remarriage and stepparenting is that family members learn flexibility and more open attitudes about family issues and boundaries. Gender roles, for example, are less likely to be stereotypical because in well-functioning stepfamilies both parents typically earn money, write checks, do housework, and take care of the children (Kelley, 1992).

In many stepfamilies, the children benefit by having a more objective adult with whom to discuss problems, and they may be introduced to new ideas, different perspectives, and a new appreciation for art, music, literature, sports, or other leisure activities. Finally, if stepsiblings live together, they gain more experience in interacting, cooperating, and learning to negotiate with peers.

In some cases, children don't recognize the contributions of stepparents until they themselves are adults. One of my students, who admitted to being very rebellious and "a real pain" after her mother remarried, is now grateful that her stepfather didn't give up:

The best solution to mine and my stepfather's problems was age. As I am getting older and supporting myself more and more, I realize just how much my stepfather has done for me. Even though he is not my "real" dad, he is the only father I have known. He has provided me with food, clothes, an education, and a home. Growing up, I thought I had it so rough. I now realize that he's my friend. It's funny, but now I actually enjoy watching TV or a movie with my stepfather (Author's files).

Conclusion

As this chapter shows, there is life after separation or divorce. Of all the different marriage and family forms discussed in this textbook, stepfamilies are the most varied and complex. Thus, both children and adults must make many *changes* as family members adapt and work together.

Despite high redivorce rates, remarriage and stepparenting give people more *choices* in establishing a well-functioning and satisfying family life. Although stepfamilies must deal with many *constraints* after a remarriage, there are also numerous rewards in establishing a new household. The new households can be especially beneficial to families as parents and siblings become elderly, the topic of the next chapter.

Summary

1. After a divorce, dating and courtship patterns vary by age and gender. Most divorced people marry within four years after a divorce.

2. The most dramatic changes in family structure and composition result from remarriage and the formation of stepfamilies. More than 40 percent of marriages are remarriages for one or both partners.

3. Remarriage rates vary by sex, race and ethnicity, age, social class, and marital status. Men remarry more quickly than women do, remarriage rates are much higher for white women than for black women and Latinas, and women with low incomes and lower educational levels are the most likely to remarry.

4. Remarriage is a process with emotional, economic, psychic, community, parental, and legal aspects. Some of these stages involve children, whereas others don't.

5. There are several important differences between first marriages and remarriages. Among these differences are the composition of the family, the children's experiences, the roles of stepfamily members, family goals and objectives, and family structure.

6. Stepfamilies are very diverse in parent–child relationships and their ties to biological families. Stepfamilies can have three "sets" of children under the same roof, which may result in strained living arrangements.

7.   Stepfamilies still suffer from negative perceptions and stereotypes, even though much research shows that stepfamilies are similar to nuclear families in fulfilling basic family functions.

8.   Although stepfamilies perform many of the same functions as nuclear families, there is a number of unique tasks involved in merging two households after a remarriage. The most common include legal issues, integration of children into the family, and intergenerational relationships.

9.   Two major tasks for stepfamilies are establishing discipline and developing closeness. Although the data are mixed, stepfather–stepdaughter relations are more strained than those between stepsons and stepparents.

10.   Many couples who have remarried say that they know each other better, communicate more openly, and are more considerate of each other's feelings than they were in their first marriages. Thus, although there are problems in remarriages, there are also many rewards.

Key Terms

stepfamily   *487*
half-sibling   *492*

genogram   *496*
mother–stepfather family   *496*

father–stepmother family   *496*
joint stepfamily   *496*

Taking It Further

Getting Information and Support on the Internet

The **Stepfamily Association of America** provides information, support, and numerous articles about stepparenting.
www.stepfamilies.info

The **Children of Separation and Divorce Center, Inc.** describes itself as "an advocate and liaison for families in transition" and offers publications, parent seminars, newsletters, and suggestions for dealing with changes in family relationships.
www.divorceabc.com

The **Second Wives Club** serves stepmoms and second wives and offers resources that include articles, legal and practical advice, and information on finalizing custody arrangements.
www.secondwivesclub.com

CoMamas Association hopes to teach stepwives and their families how to develop cooperative and respectful relationships so that they can end their conflict and get along for the sake of the children.
www.comamas.com

The **Stepfamily Foundation** offers information on stepfamily research, counseling, and other resources.
www.stepfamily.org

The **American College of Trust and Estate Counsel** provides referrals to lawyers who draw up prenuptial agreements, trusts, and wills.
www.actec.org

And more:
www.prenhall.com/benokraitis offers resource directories, sites for legal referrals, online information about stepparent adoptions, Websites that provide support and solutions for stepfamilies, and a map of states where gay and lesbian stepfamilies are legally recognized.

Investigate with Research Navigator

Go to www.researchnavigator.com and enter your LOGIN NAME and PASSWORD. For instructions on registering for the first time, view the detailed instructions at the end of the Chapter 1. Search the Research Navigator™ site using the following key search terms:

stepfamilies
remarriage

Outline

17

Families in Later Life

Data Digest

- The **percentage of the U.S. population over age 65 has been increasing steadily:** 4 percent in 1900, 5 percent in 1920, 7 percent in 1940, 9 percent in 1960, and 13 percent in 2000. It is expected to grow to 20 percent by 2030.

- The **oldest old** (people age 85 and over) are a small but growing group. In 2000, this group made up 1.6 percent of the U.S. population, compared with 0.6 percent in 1900.

- The **average U.S. life expectancy** was 47 in 1900, 68 in 1950, and 78 in 2005 (80.7 years for women and 74.9 years for men).

- The **percentage of racial and ethnic minorities age 65 and older** in the U.S. population will increase from 16 percent in 2000 to 25 percent in 2030 and to 32 percent by 2050.

- More than **10 percent of American same-sex couples** consist of one partner age 65 or older.

- American **grandparents are raising or helping raise more than 6 million children,** a 30 percent increase in the last 15 years.

Sources: Smith, 2003; Fields, 2004; He et al., 2005; International Longevity Center, 2006; U.S. Census Bureau, 2006.

Although we age at different rates, today most Americans have longer and healthier lives than ever before. Many are mentally and physically active well into their 80s and beyond. For example,

- Emma Shulman, 92, recruits patients for Alzheimer's treatment at the New York University Medical Cen-

ter. Her boss says that it will take two or three people to replace her if she decides to retire.

- At 97, Martin Miller of Indiana works full time as a lobbyist on issues that concern older people.

- At 91, Hulda Crooks climbed Mount Whitney, the highest mountain in the continental United States.

513

■ Renowned chef Julia Child was in her fifties when she became famous for her televised expertise in French cuisine. In her eighties, she embarked on a new show featuring world-renowned chefs.

■ George Dawson, the grandson of slaves, learned to read at age 99 and co-authored a book at age 102 (see Dawson and Glaubman, 2000).

Are these people unusual? Probably. But as we continue into the twenty-first century, more older people are vigorous and productive. Before you read any further, take the quiz in the "Ask Yourself" box to see how much you already know about our aging population.

As this chapter shows, aging forges changes for older people, their families, and friends. Let's begin with a brief look at some demographic characteristics of our aging society.

Our Aging Society

In 1800, your chance of living to 100 was roughly 1 in 20 million; today it's 1 in 50 (Jeune and Vaupel, 1995). Despite the high incidence of illnesses like cancer and heart disease, more people are reaching age 65 than ever

before; American children born in 1990 have a **life expectancy** (the average length of time people of the same age will live) of 78 years. As a result, the number of *elderly* people age 65 and older is booming. (Many researchers use the terms *elderly, aged,* and *older people* interchangeably.)

since you asked

Why is the number of later-life families growing?

The Growth of the Older Population

The older population has been increasing steadily since 1900 (see "Data Digest"). While the number of older Americans has increased, the proportion of young people has decreased. By 2030 there will be more elderly people than young people in the United States (see *Figure 17.1*). As a result, the years of parent–child relationships will be prolonged. Many adult children will care for frail and elderly parents, and many young children will have not only great-grandparents but also great-great-grandparents.

Gerontologists—scientists who study the biological, psychological, and social aspects of aging—emphasize that the aging population should not be lumped

---

Ask Yourself

How Much Do You Know about Aging?

The items in this quiz refer to people age 65 and older.

True	False	
☐	☐	**1.** Older adults are generally more depressed than younger people.
☐	☐	**2.** Social contacts increase as people get older.
☐	☐	**3.** Most older people become preoccupied with memories of their youth and childhood.
☐	☐	**4.** The five senses (sight, hearing, taste, touch, smell) all tend to weaken in old age.
☐	☐	**5.** A majority of older people have no interest in, nor capacity for, sexual relations.
☐	☐	**6.** Retirement is usually more difficult for women than for men.
☐	☐	**7.** The older I get, the sicker I'll get.
☐	☐	**8.** Older people are usually more patient than younger people.
☐	☐	**9.** People age 85 and older are more likely to die of Alzheimer's than of any other disease.
☐	☐	**10.** Older people are more likely to commit suicide than teenagers or young adults.

The answers to this quiz are on page 516.

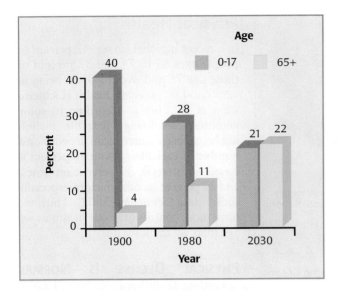

FIGURE 17.1 **The Young and the Old, 1900 to 2030**

SOURCE: U.S. Senate Special Committee on Aging et al., 1991: 9.

into one group. Instead, there are significant differences between the *young-old* (ages 65 to 74), the *old-old* (ages 75 to 84), and the *oldest-old* (age 85 and older) in living independently, working, and health care needs.

One of the fastest-growing groups is the oldest old, a population that increased from 100,000 in 1900 to 4.7 million in 2003. By 2030, this group will constitute almost 3 percent of the country's population. By 2010, about 129,000 people will be *centenarians,* or people who are 100 years old or older ("Older Americans 2000 . . . ," 2000; "Projections of the resident population . . . ," 2000; He et al., 2005).

The Gender Gap

As in most countries around the world, women live longer than men in the United States, and the proportion of women in the older population increases with age. Although women begin to outnumber men at about age 35, this gender gap widens at age 70 and older (see *Figure 17.2*).

Women tend to live longer than men for a variety of reasons, especially gender roles and lifestyles. Compared with men, women are more likely to seek medical attention, especially during their childbearing years, and to work in less dangerous jobs. Although

men have historically had higher mortality rates, the gap has narrowed during the last few decades. This change reflects women's increased smoking, use of alcohol and other drugs, and stresses related to multiple roles such as the "second shift" and caring for children and elderly family members (see Chapters 5, 10, 12, and 13).

Growing Racial and Ethnic Diversity

The older population is become more racially and ethnically diverse, reflecting changes in U.S. society over the last several decades. Our immigration rates are the highest in the world. Also, because many racial and ethnic groups have higher birth rates than whites do, the ethnic population age 65 and over is expected to grow from 16 percent in 2000 to 36 percent in 2050 (see *Figure 17.3*).

Life expectancy has increased for all groups over the years, but racial-ethnic differences remain. For example, older white Americans, especially women, have higher life expectancies than other groups. American Indians and Alaska Natives, especially men, have the lowest life expectancies (He et al., 2005).

Living longer and healthier lives has created millions of **later-life families,** families that are beyond the child-rearing years who have launched their children, or childless families who are beginning to plan for re-

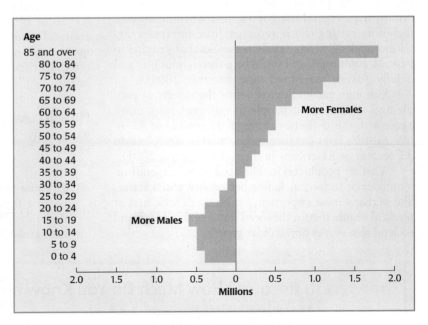

FIGURE 17.2 **Sex Ratio of Women and Men, by Age**

Note: The sex ratio is the number of men per 100 women (see Chapter 9).
SOURCE: He et al., 2005, Figure 2-20.

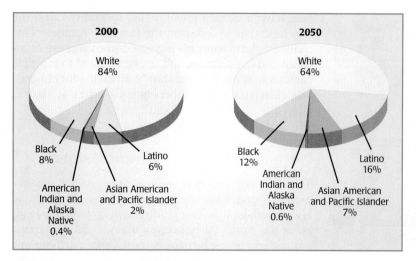

FIGURE 17.3 Population Age 65 and Older, by Race and Ethnicity, 2000 and 2050

SOURCE: "Older Americans 2000 . . . ," 2000: 4.

tirement. As later-life families age, they experience a variety of physical and social changes.

Health, Social Status, and Ageism

Orroli, a small town on the Italian island of Sardinia, has the world's highest percentage of centenarians. The inhabitants credit their long life to a number of reasons: unpolluted air; pure groundwater; a lean diet, especially homegrown vegetables; good genes; working all day, including raising sheep and pigs; little intermarrying with outsiders; strong family networks that provide financial, emotional, and social help throughout life; and a daily glass or two of red wine (Buettner, 2005).

Although gerontologists define the elderly as people age 65 and older, people in this age group don't agree with this definition. Instead, 45 percent of 65- to 69-year-olds consider themselves "middle-aged," as do 33 percent of Americans in their 70s (Gardyn, 2001).

Whether people feel middle-aged or old depends on a number of factors, including personality, social status, and perhaps most important, health. Let's look first at physical health, then at the social status of the elderly and societal stereotypes about older people.

Physical Health

In a recent national survey, 42 percent of people ages 65 to 74 and 32 percent of those age 75 and over reported being in very good or excellent health (Lichteinstein et al., 2006). According to some gerontologists, living a long life (including becoming a centenarian) depends on a number of variables: About 50 percent is based on lifestyle, 30 percent on genes, and 20 percent on other factors, especially social class (Schneider, 2002). Thus, we have more control over our health as we age than we think we do.

PHYSICAL DECLINE IS NORMAL
According to a 90-year-old retired diplomatic correspondent, a long life comes down to "keeping your heart pumping, your noodle active, and your mood cheery" (Roberts, 2001: 16). Researchers agree, but physical decline is normal and inevitable among people in all age groups.

A gradual process of physical deterioration begins early in life, affecting all the body's systems: Reflexes slow, hearing and eyesight dim, and stamina decreases. No matter how well tuned we keep our bodies, the parts eventually wear down. By age 85, for example, most people typically experience a considerable loss of lung capacity and muscle strength (see *Table 17.1*).

Some older people are healthier than others, of course. During and after his flight in space in 2000, for instance, 77-year-old John Glenn's heart rate was better than those of astronauts half his age ("Glenn's health . . . ," 2000).

HOW TO LIVE LONGER
We can't change our genes, but we can live longer by changing our lifestyles. For example,

- *Exercise physically.* Exercise increases blood and oxygen flow to the brain which, in turn, cleanses the body of impurities and decreases the risk of disease and death.

Answers to the quiz "How Much Do You Know about Aging?"

Odd-numbered statements are **false;** even-numbered statements are **true.**

The answers (discussed throughout this chapter) describe the aging population as a whole (even though there are exceptions).

The people of Sardinia, Italy, and Okinawa, Japan, have the largest percentage of centenarians in the world. The centenarians credit their long life to a lean diet and staying active, such as the elderly Okinawan women practicing their local dance pictured here.

- *Exercise mentally.* The brain is like a muscle that grows stronger with use. You can keep your brain fit by engaging in behaviors that increase thinking, such as playing board games, playing musical instruments, doing crossword puzzles, and reading.

- *Lose weight and don't smoke.* Among other diseases, smoking and obesity are linked to diabetes, heart disease, some cancers, and arthritis.

- *Watch what you eat.* Eating a diet that includes fruits, vegetables, whole grains, and nuts while avoiding food that contains saturated fats is healthy at any age. Well before we reach 65, fat concentrates around vital organs and increases the risk of disease.

- *Establish strong social networks.* Social relationships lower blood pressure (which decreases the risk of stroke) and reduces stress, anxiety, and depression (Redfearn, 2005; Tucker et al., 2005; Cohen, 2006; Manini et al., 2006).

Mental Health

In some illnesses, physical changes can lead to emotional and behavioral changes. Two of the most common mental health problems among older people are depression and dementia.

DEPRESSION Depression is a mental disorder characterized by pervasive sadness and other negative emotions that interfere with the ability to work, study, sleep, eat, and enjoy formerly pleasurable activities. Depression affects 15 percent of Americans age 65 and older compared with 18 percent of adolescents (Saluja et al., 2004; Federal Interagency Forum on Aging-Related Statistics, 2006).

Scientists believe that depression is due to a combination of genetic, personal history, and environmental factors. Older people who weather multiple stressful life experiences or crises (such as divorce, losing a job, or financial problems) are more likely to develop depression because the protein in their genes does not protect them from multiple emotionally difficult incidents. Medical illnesses such as a stroke, a heart attack, cancer, Parkinson's disease, and hormonal disorders can lead to depression. Depression can also be a side effect of some medications (Strock, 2002; Caspi et al., 2003).

Depression is one of the most common reasons for suicide among older people. Although suicide by younger people attracts more media attention and is the eleventh leading cause of death in the United States, elderly people are at a higher risk for suicide than any other age group. This is especially true for white males age 65 and older, who commit suicide at almost triple the national rate. Men in this age group are also eight times more likely to kill themselves than are women of the same age group, and have almost twice the suicide rate of men in all other age groups (see *Figure 17.4*). The suicide rates for the oldest-old white men, 51 deaths per 100,000 people, are almost five times the national rate of 11 per 100,000 Americans (National Center for Health Statistics, 2005).

It's not clear why depression and suicide rates for older white men are so high and increase steadily after age 65. There are probably multiple reasons, including social isolation and loneliness, a feeling of uselessness, financial hardship, multiple losses of loved ones, or chronic illness and pain. White men, especially those from higher socioeconomic levels, may fear becoming a

TABLE 17.1

Aging and Health

	Age			
	25	45	65	85
Maximum heart rate	100%	94%	87%	81%
Lung capacity	100%	82%	62%	50%
Muscle strength	100%	90%	75%	55%
Kidney function	100%	88%	78%	69%
Cholesterol level	198	221	224	206

SOURCE: Based on Begley et al., 1990: 44–48.

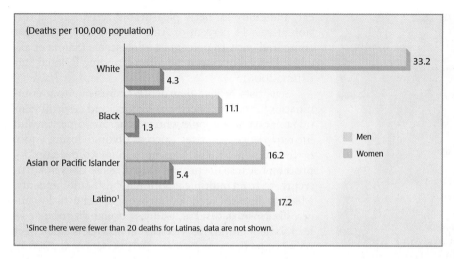

FIGURE 17.4   Suicide Rates Among People Age 65 and Over, by Race and Sex

Source: He et al., 2005, Figure 3-11.

burden to others and losing their control and dignity as their mental and physical capabilities diminish (De-Spelder and Strickland, 2005).

DEMENTIA **Dementia** is the loss of mental abilities that most commonly occurs late in life. Dementia increases with age, from about 8 percent of all people over age 65 to as many as 50 percent over age 85 (Brynes, 2001).

The most common form of dementia is **Alzheimer's disease,** a progressive, degenerative disorder that attacks the brain and impairs memory, thinking, and behavior. People age 65 and older are nine times more likely to die of heart disease than of Alzheimer's. Nevertheless, because Alzheimer's patients live an average of 10 years after the illness is diagnosed, the emotional and financial costs for family members can be devastating (American Health Assistance Foundation, 2006; Federal Interagency Forum on Aging-Related Statistics, 2006).

Medical researchers have linked Alzheimer's to genes that cause a dense deposit of protein and debris called "plaque," along with twisted protein "tangles" that kill nerve cells in the brain. According to neuroscientists, Alzheimer's spreads "like wildfire," destroying more and more brain cells as it progresses. After two years, the disease engulfs almost the entire brain in some patients (Reilly, 2000; Thompson et al., 2003).

The disease afflicts about 4.5 million elderly Americans—about 10 percent of those age 65 and older and 40 percent of those over 85. Some estimate that the number of patients with Alzheimer's will increase by 27 percent by 2020 and 300 percent by 2050, affecting about 14 million people (Hebert et al., 2003).

Unless a cure is found, medical researchers predict a future epidemic. According to the president of the Alzheimer's

Association, for example, "If left unchecked, it is no exaggeration to say that Alzheimer's disease will destroy the health care system and bankrupt Medicare and Medicaid" ("New Alzheimer's projections . . . ," 2003).

MEMORY LAPSE OR ALZHEIMER'S? During a recent interview, director Spike Lee commented that he must be getting old. When he watched one of his most recent movies, Lee said, "There was stuff I forgot we shot." When a reporter suggested that this might be a symptom of the early onset of Alzheimer's, Lee replied, "I've got Sometimers. Sometimes I remember and sometimes I forget" (Gostin, 2006: 70).

Like Lee, all of us experience memory slips such as misplacing car keys or cell phones, forgetting someone's name, or being unable to recall the name of a movie we saw a few weeks ago. The symptoms of Alzheimer's are much more severe (see the box "Ten Warning Signs of Alzheimer's Disease").

Until there are research breakthroughs, researchers suggest that the best way to prevent dementia is to exercise both the body and the mind. In a well-known study of elderly Catholic nuns, epidemiologist David Snowdon (2001) attributed their longevity and avoidance of Alzheimer's to "lives well lived" that were filled with mental and social activities, healthful eating, exercise, a positive outlook on life, and a variety of interests that included reading, knitting, and playing cards.

Some scientists are finding that depression and dementia (including Alzheimer's), which usually go hand in hand, may be due to the shrinkage of a certain area of the brain in old age. However, a number of studies report that regular exercise throughout life and avoiding obesity, especially during middle age, may prevent or at least delay the onset of dementia and even the forgetfulness often associated with normal aging (Whitmer et al., 2005; Simon et al., 2006; Wang et al., 2006). It appears, then, that our behavior can have a significant impact on how we age.

Social Status

We often hear that elderly people no longer have the respect they enjoyed in "the good old days." Historians point out, however, that the elderly did not necessarily enjoy respect and deferential treatment in the past.

Applying What You've Learned

Ten Warning Signs of Alzheimer's Disease

The Alzheimer's Association (www.alz.org) provides a list of symptoms that warrant medical evaluation. Have you seen any of these symptoms in family members or friends?

1. **Memory loss:** Although it's normal to forget names or telephone numbers, people with dementia forget such things more often and do not remember them later (for example, "I never made that doctor's appointment").
2. **Difficulty performing familiar tasks:** Not knowing the steps involved in preparing a meal, using a household appliance, or participating in a lifelong hobby.
3. **Problems with language:** Forgetting simple words. If someone with Alzheimer's can't find his or her toothbrush, for example, the person may ask for "that thing for my mouth."
4. **Disorientation to time and place:** Becoming lost on your own street, forgetting where you are and how you got there, and not knowing how to get back home.
5. **Poor or decreased judgment:** Dressing regardless of the weather, such as wearing several sweaters on a hot

day or very little clothing in cold weather. Showing poor judgment about money, such as giving away large amounts of money to telemarketers or paying for home repairs or products one doesn't need.
6. **Problems with abstract thinking:** In balancing a checkbook, for example, someone with Alzheimer's could forget completely what the numbers are and what should be done with them.
7. **Misplacing things:** Putting things in unusual places, such as an iron in the freezer or a wristwatch in the sugar bowl.
8. **Changes in mood or behavior:** Showing rapid mood swings—from calm to tears or anger—for no apparent reason.
9. **Changes in personality:** Becoming extremely confused, suspicious, fearful, or suddenly very dependent on a family member.
10. **Loss of initiative:** Becoming very passive, such as sitting in front of the television for hours, sleeping much of the time, or not wanting to engage in usual activities.

In colonial America, for example, treatment of the elderly depended very much on the person's wealth and social class. Church fathers gave wealthy and successful men in their thirties seats in the front row, but poor men in their seventies occupied seats near the back. Elderly women were rarely treated with respect, primarily because many were poor and powerless (Demos, 1986).

Still, the status of the elderly has generally declined since the turn of the twentieth century. Grandparents' influence on their children and grandchildren has diminished because families often live far apart. And because divorce and remarriage rates are high, in many cases familial ties have loosened. At family gatherings, for example, biological grandparents may have to compete with stepgrandparents (see Chapters 15 and 16).

Perhaps most important, whereas in many societies the elderly were once the source of all wisdom, contemporary advances in science, technology, and other areas have made some of the ideas of the elderly seem old-fashioned and outdated. According to some of my students, for example, grandparents are often appalled when their grandchildren highlight passages (often in a variety of colors) in textbooks because "I never did that when I was in school!"

In some cultures the elderly still maintain an influential position. For example, people in societies that endorse *familism* and filial piety, characterized by absolute obedience to the elderly and a sacred duty to support one's parents in their old age, are more likely to honor and respect the elderly. In many developing countries, older women enjoy more leisure because they delegate much of the domestic work to daughters or daughters-in-law, who defer to their knowledge and experience (Brown, 1992).

Ageism and Stereotypes

In 2001, 70-year-old Viktor Korchnoi won the elite Biel International Chess Festival in Switzerland, defeating another Russian champion, Peter Svidler, age 25. Korchnoi's victory surprised many chess fans because they assumed that younger contenders are smarter (Restak, 2002). Obviously, they were wrong.

FEAR OF AGING In our youth-oriented society, many people dread growing old. The late writer and feminist Betty Friedan, who died at the age of 85, admitted that her reaction to turning 60 was anything but jubilant:

> *"When my friends threw a surprise [birthday] party . . . I could have killed them all. Their toasts seemed*

[to be] . . . pushing me out of life . . . out of the race. Professionally, politically, personally, sexually . . . I was depressed for weeks" (Friedan, 1993: 13).

One of the best examples of negative attitudes about growing old is the deluge of anti-aging beauty products and services that flood stores and Internet sites. According to one physician, cosmetic surgery is a multi-million-dollar industry because many people don't want to look older than they are. In reality, cosmetic surgery doesn't restore your looks but is "repair work" for those who appear old prematurely because of lifestyle decisions such as sunbathing, smoking, alcohol and drug abuse, or lack of exercise (McDaniel, 2006).

Almost 3 million Americans got Botox injections in 2004—a 25 percent increase from 2003—to temporarily remove wrinkles from their skin. In the same year, Americans spent more than $20 billion on various anti-aging products (Zimbalist, 2005).

Do anti-aging products work? No. In one five-month period, for example, 40,000 people sent complaints to the Federal Trade Commission (FTC) after one e-mailing solicitor promised that his "human growth hormone" pills—at $80 a month—would regrow hair, remove wrinkles, increase muscle mass, reduce weight, and otherwise stop or reverse the aging process. An FTC attorney who settled some of the lawsuits remarked that "People would have gotten more growth hormone eating a steak" (Kirchheimer, 2005: 36).

According to scientists, there is no known way to stop, slow, or reverse human aging. Why, then, are anti-aging products and services so popular? One reason is that the U.S. Food and Drug Administration (FDA) doesn't regulate over-the-counter creams, lotions, herbal remedies, vitamins, and similar products. A major reason, however, is that many Americans fear aging in a society that celebrates youth. As a result, we spend billions of dollars every year on "anti-aging quackery, hucksterism, and snake oil" that promises a fountain of youth (Perls, 2004; Olshansky et al., 2004a, 2004b).

AGEISM In his classic book *Why survive? Being old in America,* physician Robert Butler (1975) coined the term **ageism** to refer to discrimination against people on the basis of age, particularly against the elderly. Among other things, Butler pointed out the persistence of the "myth of senility," the notion that if old people show forgetfulness, confusion, and inattention, they are senile.

If a 16-year-old boy can't remember why he went to the refrigerator, we say he's "off in the clouds" or in love; if his 79-year-old grandfather forgets why he went to the refrigerator, we're likely to call him senile. Our language is full of ageist words and phrases that stereotype and generally disparage elderly people: "biddy," "old bat," "old bag," "old fart," "old fogey," "fossil," "old goat," "old hag," "little old lady," "old maid," "dirty old man," "crotchety," "geezer," and "over the hill" (see Palmore, 1999, for examples of historical and current ageist terms and humor).

Although data show otherwise, many people continue to believe that older Americans are less intelligent, less competent, and less active than younger people. This view of the elderly is well illustrated by an experiment conducted by Patricia Moore, who wanted to know what it's like to be an older person in our society. As you can see from the box "Being Old in America," Moore found strong and pervasive negative attitudes and behaviors toward the elderly.

STEREOTYPES When you turn on the TV, what kinds of images of older people do you see? Most likely, those complaining about their health such as bladder problems, dentures, diabetes, and other diseases.

Children as young as 5 years old have negative stereotypes of older people and see them as incompetent. Young adults also have many stereotypes about getting old. For example, a recent national survey found that 66 percent of those ages 18 to 34 thought that most older people don't have enough money to live on. In fact, only 10 percent live below the poverty line and more than 25 percent are in high income brackets. Also, 61 percent of the respondents said that loneliness is a serious problem for older people, but only 33 percent of people age 65 and older feel this way (Kwong See and Rasmussen, 2003; Abramson and Silverstein, 2006).

The media also create and perpetuate negative images of aging. For example, less than 2 percent of prime-time television characters are age 65 or older, even though this group accounts for almost 13 percent of the population. Even then, only one-third of the older characters are women (International Longevity Center, 2006; see, also, Cruiksbank, 2003).

AGING AND PERSONALITY One of the most common stereotypes is that people become nasty as they age. In reality, most people's personalities are fairly stable throughout their lives (Belsky, 1988). If you're grumpy or unpleasant at 75, you were probably grumpy and unpleasant at 15, 35, and 55. Although work, marriage, and other life experiences do affect people, in general those who are hostile, anxious, or self-centered in their twenties are likely to be hostile, anxious, or self-centered in old age.

since you asked

Do most people tend to become nastier as they age?

Our personalities aren't set in cement, however. As people mature, they become more conscientious (organized and disciplined), more agreeable (warm and helpful), and less neurotic (prone to constant worry and emotional instability). As people become more aware

Constraints

Being Old in America

With the help of a professional makeup artist, Patricia Moore put on latex wrinkles and a gray wig, wore splints under her clothes to stiffen her joints, and put plugs in her ears to dull her hearing. Putting baby oil in her eyes irritated them and blurred her vision. "The look was that of eyes with cataracts, as the baby oil would float on the surface of the eyeball" (Moore and Conn, 1985: 56).

She used a special type of crayon, mixed with oil paint, to stain and discolor her teeth, and she gargled with salt to make her voice raspy. Then she "shuffled out" into the world to find out what it's really like to be old in America.

Over a three-year period, Moore found dramatic differences between the way people reacted to "Young" and "Old" Pat Moore. For example, as Old Pat, she went into a store to buy a typewriter ribbon. Ignoring her at first, the salesman finally approached her and was irritated when she was not sure what kind of ribbon she wanted, and impatient when she fumbled with the clasp on her handbag. Wordlessly, he gave her the change and dropped the package on the counter instead of handing it to her.

The next day, Young Pat, "sandy-blonde hair curled and falling on my shoulders, sunglasses and sandals," but wearing the same dress she had worn the day before, went to the same store to buy a typewriter ribbon. This time the salesman smiled and immediately offered her his assistance. When Pat pretended not to know what kind of ribbon she wanted, he was solicitous ("As long as you know it when you see it, you're all right").

When she fumbled with the clasp of the purse, saying, "Darn thing always gives me trouble," the salesman was amiable ("Well, better for it . . . to take a little longer to open than to make it easy for the muggers and the pickpockets"). He chatted as he counted out her change and opened the door because "it sticks sometimes."

What impressed Pat Moore was the way she accepted and internalized the negative responses. When she appeared to be 85 and people were more likely to push ahead of her in line, she didn't protest this behavior: "It seemed somehow . . . that it was okay for them to do this since they were undoubtedly busier than I was anyway. . . . After all, little old ladies have plenty of time, don't they?"

"Old Pat Moore."

Patricia Moore as herself.

Moore found that clerks assumed that she was hard of hearing, that she would be slow in paying for purchases, or that she would "somehow become confused about the transaction":

What it all added up to was that people feared I would be trouble, so they tried to have as little to do with me as possible. And the amazing thing is that . . . I absorbed some of their negative judgment about people my age. It was as if, unconsciously, I was saying . . . 'You're right. I'm just a lot of trouble. I'm really not as valuable as all these other people, so I'll just get out of your way as soon as possible so you won't be angry with me.' . . . I think perhaps the worst thing about aging may be the overwhelming sense that everything around you is letting you know that you are not terribly important any more" (Moore and Conn, 1985: 75–76).

Stop and Think . . .

- If you're an older student, do you identify with Moore's experiences? If you're a younger student, have you sometimes felt impatient with elderly people who fumble in checkout lanes or drive more slowly than you do?

- Talk to your parents, grandparents, or great-grandparents about whether they believe that, when one is aging, "everything around you is letting you know that you're not terribly important any more."

of the limited time they have left to live, they tend to focus more on positive thoughts, activities, and memories than do people ages 18 to 53 (Charles et al., 2003; Srivastava et al., 2003).

Contrary to the popular notion that people become more stubborn as they age, older people are usually more flexible than younger people. Older people are more likely to avoid confrontation and to be patient and less critical when there are interpersonal problems. In many stressful situations, older adults are more likely than young and midlife adults to do nothing rather than to argue or yell (Birditt and Fingerman, 2005; Birditt et al., 2005).

If some people seem harder to deal with as they age, it's often because they become less docile and submissive. When older people "suddenly" seem stubborn and defiant, they may simply be shedding some long-term inhibitions:

> *One of the greatest thrills of being a woman of 70 is having the luxury to be open about what I really think. When I was younger, I was so afraid of hurting people or worried about what they would think of me that I . . . kept my mouth shut. Now when I don't like something, I speak up . . . Age has made me more truthful. And that's one of the reasons that I feel better about myself now than I have at any other time in life (Belsky, 1988: 65–66).*

As people age, their family roles change. Retirement is a major transition for most adults. In U.S. society, it usually marks the end of the midlife years and entry into old age. Whether or not older people reenter the labor force (out of either choice or necessity) depends largely on many factors, such as economic factors, social class, and health.

Making Connections

- Over the past few decades, women have made great strides in education and the workplace (see Chapters 5 and 13). Why, then, do so many still spend millions of dollars every year for anti-aging products and services? And why are older men less likely to do so?

- Although dementia, including Alzheimer's disease, is incurable, many researchers are developing drugs to slow down the progression of the disease. Should we delay death by using drugs, even though doing so decreases the quality of life? Or should we let nature take its course?

Work, Retirement, and Family Life

Retirement, the exit from the paid labor force, is a recent phenomenon. Historians point out that in colonial America many people worked well past the age of 65. Men in their seventies hauled grain, transported rugs, and tanned leather. One man still worked in the coal mines at age 102. Those over age 65 who were in government positions (such as governors and their assistants) or were ministers who typically retained their offices until death, and some women worked as midwives well into their seventies (Demos, 1986).

since you asked

Why don't many people retire at age 65?

Older People Are Working Longer

Anthropologist Margaret Mead once said, "Sooner or later I'm going to die, but I'm not going to retire." True to her word, Mead authored and co-authored several books before she died at age 77. Like Mead, many people work until they die.

In 2004, 19 percent of men and 11 percent of women age 65 and over were in the labor force (Toossi, 2005). What many people don't realize is that many of these elderly employees are working full time. Moreover, the percentage of workers over 65 has increased considerably since 1995, especially for women (see *Table 17.2*).

The poverty rate for Americans age 65 and older dropped from 35 percent in 1959 to under 10 percent in 2004. This proportion is now lower than that for any other age group, including children (Federal Interagency Forum on Aging-Related Statistics, 2006; see, also, Chapter 13).

Why, then, are so many older Americans working well past age 65, either full time or part time? Some of the reasons include the following:

- **Social Security,** a public retirement pension system administered by the federal government, provides income to more than 90 percent of the elderly, but the benefits depend on how long people have been in the labor force and how much they have earned. Because Social Security replaces only 39 percent of the average older person's pre-retirement income, many must continue to work.

TABLE 17.2

Percentage of Older Americans Working Full Time, by Sex and Age: 1995 and 2005

	Men			Women		
Age	1995	2005	% Change	1995	2005	% Change
55–61	92	92	0	75	79	6
62–64	78	81	4	59	66	12
65	65	74	13	46	57	24
66–69	52	66	26	35	50	42
70+	44	52	17	30	39	32

Source: Gendell, 2006, Table 1.

- In 2000, the Social Security Administration eliminated penalties for working after age 65. Because people who reached their designated retirement age could receive full Social Security payments whether they were employed or not, many worked to supplement their income.

- The rapid growth of health care costs since the late 1990s led to reductions in employers' coverage of retirees, providing an incentive for older employees to work as long as possible.

- Since the early 1990s, many companies (especially in the steel, airline, and auto industries) have reduced or eliminated their employee pension plans. As a result, many older people, including baby boomers, plan to continue working indefinitely.

- Only 27 percent of workers age 40 and older and 50 percent age 65 feel confident that they will have enough money to live comfortably after they retire. And in all age groups—from age 18 to age 65 and older—about 48 percent worry that they won't be able to pay for medical costs after retirement. Such concerns are incentives for working as long as possible (Newport and Carroll, 2004; Gendell, 2006; Holley, 2006).

Some Americans continue to work into their seventies and even eighties. However, about half of adults ages 60 to 64 retire. This number increases to two-thirds for those ages 65 to 69. Only 1 in 10 adults works past age 69 (Butrica et al., 2006). Why do some retire while others keep on working?

Who Retires and Why?

The reasons for retirement vary. People who continue to work past age 65 are more likely to be self-employed. Because they don't have pension benefits and Social Security payments are usually low, they work out of economic necessity (Himes, 2001).

Four out of 10 retired workers leave their jobs sooner than they had planned: 47 percent cite health reasons, 44 percent point to job joss, and 9 percent care for an ailing family member. For example, an employee at IBM was laid off at age 60 and lost half of his expected pension. As a result, he reentered the work force, at less than half of his previous salary, to afford a "comfortable retirement." Because many large corporations, like IBM, have simply cut their promised pension plans, many employees must work after they expected to retire (Wild, 2005; Peterson, 2006).

Husbands and wives often coordinate their retirement plans and withdraw from the labor force at about the same time. They are less likely to retire before age 65, however, if one of the spouses has a health problem, and especially if the spouses aren't yet eligible for Social Security benefits. About 75 percent of adults ages 51 to 61 retire early because of health problems. In other cases, people continue to work if they have family responsibilities that include financially supporting adult children or frail parents. Women are especially likely to take an early retirement to care for elderly parents and in-laws (Johnson and Favreault, 2001; Johnson et al., 2006).

Variations in Retirement Income

The aged are an economically diverse group. The annual median income for people age 65 and over is almost $25,000, but there are wide differences: 30 percent have an annual income under $15,000 but 21 percent have an income of $50,000 or more (U.S. Census Bureau, 2006). There are also large variations by age, sex, marital status, and race and ethnicity.

AGE Median income decreases as people age (see *Figure 17.5*). The longer people live, the more likely they are to be poor. For example, 9 percent of people ages 65 to 74 live below the poverty line, compared with 12 percent of those age 75 and older. Some economists expect that poverty rates will increase among some groups, including high school dropouts, African Americans and Latinos, never-married women and men, divorced women, and the oldest old (He et al., 2005; Toder, 2005).

SEX In every age group, older women have a lower median income than men. For women age 65 and over, the

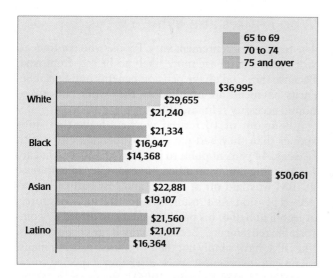

FIGURE 17.5 **Median Income of Older Households by Age and Race/Ethnicity, 2005**

Source: Based on U.S. Census Bureau, Current Population Survey, Annual Social and Economic Supplement, detailed tables, 2005, Table HINC-02.

median income is about $12,000 a year, compared with $21,100 for men in the same age group. Although women make up 57 percent of the population 65 and older, they account for 70 percent of the older people living in poverty. Many women live in poverty for more than half of their old-age years (He et al., 2005; "Older women workers. . . ," 2006).

More women (25 million) than men (19 million) receive Social Security benefits, largely because women live longer than men. Spousal benefits generally favor nonworking women. For example, a nonworking wife of a high-wage earner receives larger Social Security benefits than a woman who has been employed in middle-wage jobs most of her life (Favreault, 2005).

Women who have worked full time often were confined to low-paying jobs. As a result, their earnings were lower than those of men, even in comparable jobs. Besides lower earnings, women often have uneven employment histories: Many left their jobs periodically to raise children or to care for sick or elderly family members. Such interruptions and relatively lower earnings result in lower monthly benefits. In 2004, for example, the average Social Security benefit was $826 per month for retired women workers, compared with $1,077 for their male counterparts (Social Security Administration, 2006).

MARITAL STATUS Married couples have twice the median income of single men and more than twice that of single women. This difference characterizes every age group. Even at age 80 and older, when many people have depleted most of their savings, married couples

have an annual income of almost $28,000, compared with about $16,000 for single men and $12,000 for single women (Koenig and Mulpuru, 2003).

Widows age 65 and older are slightly less likely to be poor (16 percent) than are divorced (22 percent) or never-married women (21 percent). A major reason for this difference is that widows usually receive spousal and survivor benefits (Favreault, 2005).

RACE AND ETHNICITY Elderly whites and Asian Americans have much higher median incomes than do African Americans and Latinos (see *Figure 17.5*). About 8 percent of elderly whites live in poverty, compared with 20 percent of Latinos and 24 percent of African Americans (He et al., 2005).

Older women are poorer than their male counterparts in every racial group. The most vulnerable group is women age 65 and older who live alone: Almost 17 percent of white women and 41 percent of both African American women and Latinas live in poverty (He et al., 2005).

Retirement has an especially devastating impact on black women. Many have worked in low-paying clerical or service positions that provide minimal, if any, pensions. If their husbands had low-paying jobs or a sporadic employment history because of recessions and discrimination, the husbands' benefits may also be inadequate.

Retirement is an important role transition. Well before retirement, however, many adults take on another important role—that of a grandparent.

Making Connections

▪ Many women drop out of the labor force to raise children or to care for ill or aging relatives. In doing so, they forgo Social Security benefits later in life. Should the government compensate these women when they reach age 65?

▪ Almost four in 10 Americans plans to retire at age 59 or earlier, but less than half have calculated how much they need to save for a comfortable retirement (Barr, 2006). When do *you* plan to retire? How much retirement planning have you done? If you're already retired, is your income adequate?

Grandparenting

Grandparents are the glue that keeps a family close. They typically represent stability in family relationships and a continuity of family rituals and values. Grandparents often help their adult children with parenting (such as baby-sitting) and provide support during emergencies or crises, including illness and divorce (see Szinovacz, 1998, and Smith and Drew, 2002, for good summaries of grandparenting across racial-ethnic groups).

No matter how strict they were with their own children, many grandparents often serve as family mediators, advocates for their grandchildren's point of view, and shoulders to cry on. Because today's grandparents are generally healthier and wealthier than those of previous generations, they engage in a wide range of activities and spend a fair amount of money on their grandchildren.

African Americans and Latinos tend to become grandparents earlier than members of other groups. By age 65, however, 84 percent of all men and 80 percent of all women are grandparents (Himes, 2001). As with aging, grandparenting styles are diverse.

Grandparenting Styles

Grandparents usually take great pleasure in their grandchildren. The new role of grandparent gives their lives a sense of purpose and provides them with new experiences. There are a number of different grandparenting styles, however. Some of the most common are remote or detached, companionate and supportive, involved and influential, advisory and authoritative, and cultural transmitter.

since you asked

How do grandparenting roles differ?

REMOTE OR DETACHED In the *remote or detached* relationship, the grandparents and grandchildren live far apart and see each other infrequently, maintaining a largely ritualistic, symbolic relationship. For example, grandparents who are "distant figures" may see their grandchildren only on holidays or special occasions. Such relationships may be cordial but are also uninvolved and fleeting (Thompson and Walker, 1991).

Only about 3 percent of grandparents never see their grandchildren and never write to them. The biggest barrier to face-to-face contacts is living too far away. In other cases, grandparents are remote or detached because they're experiencing health problems or their grandchildren's busy schedule makes it difficult to get together (Davies and Williams, 2002).

Grandparents may be close to one grandchild but detached from others. Sometimes grandparents see a particular grandchild as "special" because of the child's personality, accomplishments, or respect for his or her grandparents. Not surprisingly, then, grandparents sometimes spend more time with some grandchildren than with others (Smith and Drew, 2002; Mueller and Elder, 2003).

This 5-year-old and her grandmother are attending the 1998 groundbreaking ceremonies for the Grandfamilies House in Dorchester, Massachusetts. This was the nation's first housing center designed for grandparents raising their grandchildren. For example, there are grab-bars in the bathrooms, safety covers on the electrical outlets, and a playground in the rear within easy view of caregivers. A live-in manager is available for emergencies and other needs. A coordinator organizes meetings, transportation, and services ranging from preschool and after-school child care to exercise and parenting classes for the grandparents.

Although they report feeling close to their great-grandchildren, great-grandparents often have remote relationships with them because they are in frail health, live far away, or feel that grandparents should play a more authoritative role. Great-grandparents may also have difficulty adapting to new situations such as divorce and remarriage, and often feel embarrassed, uncomfortable, or confused about great-grandchildren born in cohabiting relationships. As one great-grandparent said, "I guess I have two or three great-grandchildren, depending on how you look at it. My grandson is living with someone and they have a child" (Doka and Mertz, 1988: 196).

COMPANIONATE AND SUPPORTIVE The *companionate and supportive* style of grandparenting is the most common pattern. According to a national survey, most grandparents (68 percent) see a grandchild every one or two weeks. Eight in ten grandparents contact a grandchild by telephone at least once every couple of weeks, and 19 percent chat with a grandchild by e-mail every few weeks (Davies and Williams, 2002).

Supportive grandparents see their grandchildren often, frequently do things with them, and offer them emotional and instrumental support (such as providing money), but they don't seek authority in the grandchild's life. These grandparents are typically on the maternal side of the family, are younger, and have more income than other grandparents—characteristics that might encourage meddling—but they avoid getting involved in parental child-rearing decisions (Mueller and Elder, 2003).

Companionate grandparents generally don't want to share parenting and tend to emphasize loving, playing, and having fun. When visiting, grandparents and grandchildren usually spend their time eating together, watching TV shows, shopping for clothes or toys, playing sports, or attending church (Davies and Williams, 2002).

INVOLVED AND INFLUENTIAL In the *involved and influential* grandparenting style, grandparents play an active role in their grandchildren's lives. They may be spontaneous and playful, but they also exert substantial authority over their grandchildren, imposing definite—and sometimes tough—rules. Black grandmothers, especially, say that they are concerned with teaching their grandchildren the value of education, providing emotional support, and involving them in the extended family and community activities (Gibson, 2005).

In a recent national survey, 42 percent of the respondents who plan to move after retirement will do so to be closer to their families, especially grandchildren (Pulte Homes, 2005). Because many retirees may have another 20 healthy years ahead of them, the advantages of seeing their grandchildren grow up outweigh the disadvantages of moving to a new location.

Compared with past generations, many of today's grandfathers are more involved in their grandchildren's daily activities. According to a director of a child care center, for example, "We used to see grandfathers only at special events or in emergencies. Now, every day, grandfathers drive carpool, carry backpacks, and chat with teachers." Grandfathers are particularly influential in single-mother households. When grandfathers are involved, children (especially boys) have fewer social problems, are more self-confident, and do better academically (Zaslow, 2006).

In general, grandparents are more likely to be involved if their grandchildren are struggling in school. They are also twice as likely to be influential in their grandchildren's lives if they had close relationships with their own grandparents (Mueller and Elder, 2003).

ADVISORY AND AUTHORITATIVE In the fourth type of grandparenting, *advisory and authoritative,* the grandparent serves as an advisor, or what Neugarten and Weinstein (1964) call a "reservoir of family wisdom." The grandfather, who may be the family patriarch, may also act as a financial provider, and the grandmother often plays a crucial advisory role in the grandchildren's lives.

Especially when the mother is very young, the maternal grandmother may help the "apprentice mother" make the transition to parenthood by supporting and mentoring—but not replacing—her in the parenting role. The grandmother provides emotional, financial, and child care support until the "apprentice" shows that she is responsive to and responsible for the baby (Apfel and Seitz, 1991).

Many teenagers begin to break away from their families, including their grandparents, during high school. Still, many adolescents turn to their grandparents for advice or understanding. According to a 17-year-old boy, for example, "With my grandpa we discuss usually technical problems. But sometimes some other problems, too. He told me how to refuse to drink alcohol with other boys." A 16-year-old girl said that she and her grandmother go for walks and added, "I can tell her about everything" (Tyszkowa, 1993: 136). Sometimes the roles reverse, with teenage grandchildren helping their grandparents with errands or chores.

CULTURAL TRANSMITTERS Advisory grandparenting often overlaps with a fifth role, in which grandparents are *cultural transmitters* of values and norms. In American Indian families, for example, grandmothers often teach their grandchildren domestic chores, responsibility, and discipline that reflect tribal tradition. Grandfathers may transmit knowledge of tribal history and cultural practices through storytelling (Woods, 1996; see, also, Chapter 4).

Many recently arrived Asian immigrants live in extended families and are more likely to do so than any other group, including Latinos. Between 20 percent (Chinese) and 39 percent (Asian Indians) of Asian Americans age 55 years and older live with their grandchildren (Kamo, 1998).

In such co-residence, grandparents are often "historians" who transmit values and cultural traditions to their grandchildren even if there are language barriers. Chinese American grandparents, for example, help develop their grandchildren's ethnic identity by teaching them Chinese, passing on traditional practices and customs during holidays, and reinforcing cultural values such as respecting parents and other adults (Tam and Detzner, 1998; Tan, 2004).

Grandparents as Surrogate Parents

An emerging grandparenting role is that of *surrogate,* in which a grandparent provides regular care or replaces the parents in raising the grandchildren. About 5.6 million children live in a household run by a grandparent. Of the 1.4 million children being raised entirely by grandparents, many are white (see *Figure 17.6*). Contrary to the stereotype of the inner-city welfare mother who is raising her teenage daughter's baby, the majority of grandparent caregivers are white, own their own homes, and live in the suburbs (Fields, 2003, 2004).

The increase in grandchildren living with grandparents in these "skipped generation" homes results from many factors: higher drug abuse by parents, teen pregnancy, divorce, unemployment, a parent's mental illness, child maltreatment or abandonment, and the death or incarceration of parents. Three of the most common groups of surrogate grandparents are custodial, living-with, and day-care grandparents (Jendrek, 1994).

CUSTODIAL GRANDPARENTS *Custodial* grandparents have a legal relationship with their grandchildren through adoption, guardianship, or custody. Most take custody of a grandchild only when a situation becomes intolerable. For example, at age 75, actor George Kennedy and his wife, 68, adopted their 5-year-old granddaughter because the little girl's mother could not kick her drug habit. In other cases, grandparents adopt a grandchild after the death of one or both parents.

Many grandparents aren't eager to accept responsibility for their grandchildren. They do so, however, as a result of pressure from other family members or out of a sense of loyalty and duty. For many grandparents, the new responsibility may mean that they must give up work to provide care, whereas others find they have little or no time for their usual activities or friends (Cox, 2000).

Although custodial grandparents love their grandchildren, they often report a sense of powerlessness in not having a choice in the decision to become a parent at such a late stage in life. Those in low incomes, especially, experience financial hardship and psychological distress and may have physical health problems (Bachman and Chase-Landale, 2005).

Older custodial grandparents also worry about the long-term care of a child. According to an African American grandfather, "I won't live long enough to see her grow up because she [the grandchild] is still a baby. My wife might be around, but I probably won't be living to help her out. It worries me" (Bullock, 2005: 50).

LIVING-WITH GRANDPARENTS *Living-with* grandparents typically have the grandchild in their own home or, less commonly, live in the home of a grandchild's parents. Living-with grandparents take on child rearing responsibilities either because their children have not yet moved out of the house or because teenage or adult parents can't afford to live on their own with their young children.

In 2005, 8 percent of all American children lived with a grandparent. Of these 6.1 million children, 4.1 million lived in a grandparent's home and 1.9 million in a parent's home. In 75 percent of families with grandparents and grandchildren living together, a grandparent runs the household. About half of the grandparent-run families have both grandparents living with the grandchildren. A grandmother alone maintains most of the others (43 percent), while a grandfather alone maintains 7 percent of the families (Fields, 2003; "Grandparent's Day," 2006).

Grandparent-run households are more common among African Americans than among other groups. In these families, teenage children of single mothers have better outcomes than those who live in single-parent homes. Grandparents help young teen mothers, especially, by providing economic and emotional support in school, child care, and work, all of which are beneficial to their daughters and grandchildren's well-being (DeLeire and Kalil, 2002).

With the deployment of thousands of young parents to the war in Iraq, grandparents took on the care of grandchildren full or part time. The grandparents experienced a "double whammy"—looking after their grandchildren and worrying about their children's safety in Iraq or Afghanistan (Greider, 2003).

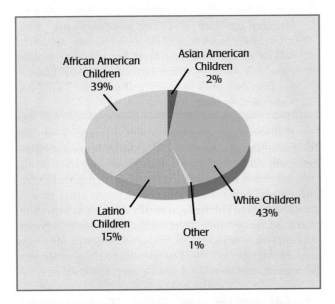

FIGURE 17.6 Grandparents Raising Grandchildren, 2002

SOURCE: Based on Fields, 2003: Table 3.

DAY-CARE GRANDPARENTS Because of the high cost of day care, in some families *day-care grandparents* assume responsibility for the physical care of their grandchildren, usually a daughter's, until the parents came home from work. These grandparents aren't casual baby-sitters, however. Some of the grandmothers quit their jobs to care for their grandchildren (Jendrek, 1994).

African American grandmothers are more likely than their Latina and white counterparts to provide full-time care from the child's birth to age 3. In all ethnic groups, grandparents are most likely to care for these young grandchildren if the mothers are 28 years old and younger, have full-time jobs, and work nonstandard hours such as evenings and weekends (Vandell et al., 2003).

Many grandmothers enjoy caring for grandchildren. However, they also experience stress and isolation, financial difficulties, and multiple roles that they hadn't expected to deal with in their later years (Rodgers and Jones, 1999).

These "nanny-grannies" often combine caregiving with careers and express emotions ranging from joy and satisfaction to fatigue and resentment. As one grandmother said, "It's very sad that after a lifetime of working full time, grandparents should have a second full-time job of caring for their grandchildren unpaid. . . . Something's wrong here" (Gardner, 2002: 16).

Some grandmothers are especially resentful because they are part of a sandwich generation that takes care of young grandchildren and elderly parents. Providing care is especially stressful if the grandchildren have emotional or behavioral problems and if the grandparent, usually a grandmother, is in poor health or has few financial resources to meet the grandchild's needs (Gattai and Musatti, 1999; Ingersoll-Dayton et al., 2001).

Grandparents and Divorce

Traditionally, divorce meant that a grandparent would have to establish new relationships with the ex-spouse or stepparent. More recently, family ties have shifted because grandparents themselves are getting a divorce.

GRANDPARENTS AND THEIR CHILDREN'S DIVORCE Divorce creates both opportunities and dilemmas for grandparents. Grandparents on the custodial side often deepen their relationships with children and grandchildren, especially when they provide financial assistance, a place to live, and help in child rearing. In contrast, grandparents on the noncustodial side typically have less access to their grandchildren.

Many custodial parents move after the breakup, increasing the visiting distance. Troubled postdivorce relationships often result in a loss of contact between grandchildren and some of their grandparents because the mother feels a closer relationship to her biological kin than to her in-laws (Ganong and Coleman, 1999).

In other cases, because of estrangement or a poor relationship with their child's ex-spouse, grandparents aren't allowed to see their grandchildren. Grandchildren sometimes become pawns, used to punish grandparents for real or imagined misunderstandings and slights.

If a custodial parent remarries, the noncustodial parent may drop out of the children's lives, making it awkward for the noncustodial grandparents to arrange visits with the grandchildren. However, if the custodial parent tries to maintain a relationship with the noncustodial grandparents and the ex-spouses don't "bad-mouth" each other, children can have strong relationships with noncustodial grandparents (Bray and Berger, 1990).

Sometimes grandparent–grandchild relationships become closer after the parents divorce or remarry. For example, if the mother gains custody of the children but receives little or no child support, she may move in with her parents. Baby-sitting while the mother works and being geographically close to the grandchildren can foster a close emotional relationship between grandparent and grandchild.

Often, grandparents can provide a safe haven for grandchildren whose divorcing parents are so emotionally distraught that they don't recognize their children's fears and worries:

> *Last night I was reading and Penny came out of the bedroom and she was crying a bit and I said "come sit on gramma's lap" and we cuddled. She was upset because she had wet her bed, so I changed her. Her father had gone away and she is afraid her mother will be going away, too. So I talked to her and reassured her that her mother wouldn't go away. Then I asked her if she'd like to get into bed with gramma and she said "yes" and then went to sleep (Gladstone, 1989: 71).*

A divorce can create unexpected financial burdens for grandparents, however. If grandparents anticipate being cut off from their grandchildren after the divorce, they may have to petition for visitation rights, thereby incurring legal expenses. In other cases, parents may provide financial help to children, especially daughters, to get a divorce. Such assistance often depletes the parents' savings. As one father noted, "I'm at the age where a lot of my friends are retiring, and I'm spending all my retirement savings on attorneys" (Chion-Kenney, 1991: B5).

GRANDCHILDREN AND THEIR GRANDPARENTS' DIVORCE About 33 percent of married people who were born between 1935 and 1944 have divorced by age 50. In 1960, under 2 percent of older men and women were divorced. In 2003, in contrast, 12 percent of men and 16 percent of women in their sixties were divorced. Because divorce rates among older people are increasing, many grandchildren will experience their grandparents' breakup (Kreider and Fields, 2002; He et al., 2005).

When grandparents split up, both they and their grandchildren may suffer. Grandparents who divorce don't have as much contact with their grandkids, feel less close to them, and consider the role of grandparent less important in their lives. Grandfathers, especially, have less contact, fewer shared activities, and higher levels of conflict with their grandchildren than do grandmothers who have divorced. However, grandparents who can maintain a good relationship with adult children despite a divorce will be able to establish strong ties to their grandchildren (King, 2003).

Grandparents' Visitation Rights

Whether an adult child is divorced or not, do grandparents have the right to visit a grandchild when the child's parents object? As rates of divorce, out-of-wedlock births, and drug use increased, states began passing laws bolstering the rights of grandparents when parents died, divorced, separated, or were jobless or disabled.

Now the pendulum is swinging back. Because of a perception that parents' rights have eroded, more than a third of the states have narrowed their visitation laws. In some states, for example, grandparents must prove that their visits are beneficial to the emotional, mental, or physical health of a grandchild.

Many parents welcome the changes because they have more control over grandparents' visitation and feel that they can decide what's best for their children. However, many groups argue that grandparents are part of an extended family and should have a right to visitation despite parents' objections, especially when high divorce rates fragment a family (Gearon, 2003).

✳ Making Connections

- What are the grandparenting styles in your family? Do they differ depending on the grandparent's age and gender, for example?

- Should grandparents sue for visitation rights with their grandchildren? Or respect a parent's decision even if they disagree?

Aging Parents and Adult Children

Most of us are living longer, but are our families happier? Let's examine this question in three areas—marital satisfaction, aging parents and adult child relationships, and sibling relationships in later life.

Marital Satisfaction

Marital relationships change as couples age. You'll recall that many family scholars have found a U-shaped pattern in marital satisfaction over the life course. That is, marital happiness is high in the early years, drops during the childrearing years, and then begins to rise after the children leave home (see Chapter 10).

Some researchers disagree. For example, a national study that documented marital happiness over nearly two decades found that marital satisfaction generally continued to decline after the empty nest period, even among couples that had been married for 30 to 50 years (VanLaningham et al., 2001).

Not all older couples experience a slump in marital satisfaction, of course. When a spouse has serious mental or physical health problems, the quality of the relationship becomes strained because of fatigue and stress, but this isn't true of healthy couples. Sexual

Love, intimacy, and companionship are just as important to older couples as they are to younger people.

intercourse typically declines over the years, but marital satisfaction remains high if couples are sexually intimate in other ways, such as touching, caressing, and showing affection (see Chapter 7).

Retirement can also affect marital happiness. As you saw earlier, health and financial security are the major factors in retirees' satisfaction with life. Among married couples, spouses are happier when they make joint decisions about the timing of retirement. For example, wives report less marital satisfaction if their already-retired husbands "push" them into retirement or are always underfoot (Szinovacz and Davey, 2005). "The Retired Husband Syndrome in Japan" box examines a particularly unhappy outcome of husbands' retirement.

Relationships Between Parents and Adult Children

Parenting becomes less important in most people's daily lives as couples age. Although parent–child relationships typically last a lifetime, they vary depending on a number of factors, such as geographic distance, amount of contact, emotional closeness, similar attitudes, and mutual assistance. For example, adult children who live nearby tend to have closer relationships with their aging parents than do those who live many miles away. These adult children often receive financial help and baby-sitting from their parents and reciprocate by providing assistance in household chores, especially yard work and home maintenance (Lin and Rogerson, 1995; Silverstein and Bengston, 2001).

Geographic closeness isn't the most critical factor that shapes intergenerational relationships, however. Parents tend to help children whom they see to be in need, especially those who are single, divorced, or widowed at a young age and if grandchildren are involved. For example, divorced daughters with child custody have more contact with their aging parents than married daughters do, and they often receive more help from their parents. Sons, on the other hand, receive more baby-sitting help from their parents when they are married than in other situations because the grandparents are involved with their grandchildren. If sons are divorced or cohabiting,

 ## Cross-Cultural Families

The Retired Husband Syndrome in Japan

In Tokyo, Sakura Terakawa, 63, describes her four decades of married life as a gradual transition from wife to mother to servant. Like most men of his generation, Terakawa's husband demanded strict obedience even though he spent his life almost entirely apart from her and their three children. He left home for the office just after dawn and stayed out late socializing after work. He even took most of his vacations with colleagues and clients.

Over the years, Terakawa developed her own life and her own way of doing things. She had many friends and enjoyed her life with her children.

Retirement cut the husband off from his long-time office social network, leaving him practically friendless. Within a few weeks of retirement, he forbade his wife to go out with her friends and criticized her meals and housework. She said she couldn't stand to look at her husband across the table and sat at an angle so she could stare out a window instead.

Within a few months, Terakawa developed stomach ulcers and polyps in her throat, her speech began to slur, and rashes broke out around her eyes. When doctors couldn't find a medical reason for the symptoms, they referred her to a well-known Japanese psychiatrist, who diagnosed the problems as stress-related "retired husband syndrome" (RHS).

The psychiatrist estimates that as many as 60 percent of the wives of retired men in Japan suffer from some degree of RHS. While 85 percent of soon-to-retire husbands are delighted by the idea of retirement, 40 percent of their wives describe themselves as depressed by the prospect. RHS may be one of the reasons that divorce rates among elderly Japanese couples have doubled since 1985.

Older wives are especially likely to experience RHS because the nature of Japanese family life has changed significantly over the past two decades. Members of younger generations are remaining single well into their forties, and newly-married couples, at least in urban areas, refuse to live with retired parents because they want more privacy. As a result, many older wives must deal with the "curse" of their husband's retirement alone (Faiola, 2005).

Stop and Think . . .

- Do you think that RHS is unique to Japan, or might it also be common in the United States?

- Japan has the fastest-growing aged population in the world (see Chapter 18). Is it possible, then, that RHS problems are exaggerated in Japan because of mass retirements? Or can we expect similar results in the United States as millions of baby boomers retire?

grandparents may see their grandchildren less often because the mother gets custody of the children or because the father remarries and starts a new family. In the latter case, the grandparents often split their time between their son's "old" and "new" families (Spitze et al., 1994; see, also, Chapters 15 and 16).

Parent–child relations are usually complex rather than positive, negative, or something in between. They often involve **intergenerational ambivalence**, contradictions that arise both from structured kinship roles and from personal emotions. For example, our society's gendered division of domestic work obligates women to care for aging parents and in-laws, as you'll see shortly. In such caregiving situations, a daughter or daughter-in-law may feel close to her aging parents or in-laws but may also resent their critical or demanding attitudes (Willson et al., 2003; see, also, Chapter 5).

Sibling Relationships in Later Life

About 80 percent of older people have siblings. Because brother–sister relationships usually last longer than any other family ties, they can be important sources of companionship and emotional support.

since you asked

Do siblings become closer as they age?

According to medical sociologist Deborah Gold (1989, 1990), sibling relationships in later life generally fall into five groups, the last two of which are negative:

- *Intimate siblings* are very close and consider each other to be best friends and close confidants. They help each other no matter what, and are in frequent contact.

- *Congenial siblings* feel close and see each other as good friends, but feel closer to a spouse or an adult child. They contact each other weekly or monthly but give help only when it doesn't conflict with their obligations to their spouse or children.

- *Loyal siblings* are available because of family bonds rather than affection or closeness. Disagreements don't erode the siblings' ties because they believe that family ties are important whether family members like each other or not.

- *Apathetic siblings* are indifferent, rarely think about each other, and have little contact with each other.

- *Hostile siblings* are angry and resentful, and have had negative ties for a long time. They spend considerable time demeaning each other and arguing about the past, inheritances, and so on.

Adult sibling relationships vary by race, sex, and other factors. For example, black siblings tend to have more positive relationships than white siblings, sisters tend to be closer than brothers, and married siblings have more in common than those who are divorced or child free (Quadagno, 2002; Atchley and Barusch, 2004).

Sibling relationships can change over time, especially during family crises. Over the years, for instance, a number of my students in their forties and fifties have said that their sibling relationships changed from apathetic to intimate when a parent, grandparent, or great-grandparent became ill and needed ongoing care. In other cases, divorce and widowhood often bring indifferent siblings closer together.

Whether they have children and grandchildren or not, aging couples can enjoy many years together because of our greater life expectancy. Sooner or later, however, family members must cope with another important life course event: the death of a loved one.

Sociologist Debra Umberson (2003:6–7) describes the death of a parent as "a turning point in the emotional, personal, and social lives of most adults—an event that initiates a period of substantial change and redirection in the way we see ourselves, our relationships to others, and our place in the world." She also notes that the death of a parent is a common cause of bereavement for adults in Western societies because by age 62, 75 percent of adults have lost both their parents.

Experiencing an aging parent's death can be life changing. The death of a spouse or a grandparent can also be devastating.

Dying, Death, and Bereavement

Woody Allen once said, "It's not that I'm afraid to die. I just don't want to be there when it happens." Although people who are very old and in poor health sometimes welcome death, most of us have difficulty facing death, regardless of our age and health.

Dealing with Death and Dying

How we deal with death depends on whether we are medical personnel treating the ill patient, relatives or friends of the patient, or the patient himself or herself. Each may have a different perspective on death and dying.

HEALTH-CARE PROFESSIONALS Physicians and other health-care professionals often use the term *dying trajectory* to describe how a very ill person is expected to die. In a *lingering trajectory*—for example, death from a terminal illness such as cancer—medical personnel do everything possible to treat the patient, but ultimately custodial care predominates. In contrast, the *quick trajectory* is an acute crisis caused by cardiac arrest or a serious accident. Staff typically work feverishly to preserve the patient's life and well-being, sometimes successfully.

When an elderly person suffers from a terminal illness such as advanced cancer, health-care professionals expect the patient to have a lingering death. Overworked hospital staff, especially, may respond to the patient's requests more slowly, place the patient in more remote wards, or even bathe and feed him or her less frequently. Family members, in contrast, typically expect their elderly relatives to be treated as painstakingly as any other patient.

A patient's perceived social worth can also influence the care that he or she receives. For example, elderly patients in private hospitals or those with high socioeconomic status often receive better care than do poor elderly patients or those in public hospitals (Hooyman and Kiyak, 2002).

PATIENTS, FAMILIES, FRIENDS Among the several perspectives on the dying process, probably the best known is that of Elisabeth Kübler-Ross (1969). Based on work with 200 primarily middle-aged cancer patients, Kübler-Ross proposed that there are five stages of dying:

- *Denial.* People may simply refuse to believe that they or a loved one are dying. For example, they may insist on having more tests or may change physicians.

- *Anger.* When denial is no longer possible, people may become angry and sometimes project their anger onto medical staff or others.

- *Bargaining.* The dying person sometimes tries to forestall death by making a deal with God: "If I can just live until my daughter's graduation, I'll make a large contribution to my church."

- *Depression.* When dying people recognize that death is imminent, depression may set in. They experience sadness, for instance, when they lose hair during radiation therapy or can no longer walk unaided. They may give away prized belongings or spend extra time with family members.

- *Acceptance.* When patients finally accept their approaching death, they may reflect on their lives and anticipate dying with quiet resignation.

Many have criticized this stage-based theory. Some claim that the stages are not experienced by everyone or in the same order. Others point out that the stages do not apply to the elderly. Because they are more accustomed to the sick role, many elderly people have had to confront the possibility of death for many years. For example, even before the onset of illness, elderly people may have had to give up activities such as driving, gardening, or climbing stairs.

Rather than deny death, some elderly may welcome it. Many have seen their spouses and friends die over the years, and they often view death as a natural part of life. They may even await death as an end to pain, sorrow, social isolation, dependency, and loneliness. In sum, the elderly may not experience Kübler-Ross's stages because they have been experiencing a "social death" over the course of many years (Retsinas, 1988).

Many people are personalizing their funerals. Here, mourners are treated to ice cream at the graveside of a man who had driven an ice cream truck for many years.

Multicultural Families

Death and Funeral Traditions among Racial-Ethnic Families

Despite acculturation, there are cultural, religious, and ethnic differences in how families cope with death. The variations include rituals, a display of emotion, the appropriate length of mourning, celebrating anniversary events, and beliefs about the afterlife. For example, many African American families give the deceased a "good sendoff" that includes buying the best casket the family can afford and a funeral in the home church with stirring songs and eulogies. In New Orleans, Louisiana, many African Americans have "jazz funerals" in which a procession of family and friends celebrate the life of the deceased on the way to the cemetery plot.

In many Middle Eastern families, traditional Muslim women display extreme emotions—crying, screaming, and pulling their hair—to express grief. Wearing black, Muslims usually mourn the death of a loved one for at least one year. They organize big gatherings of relatives and friends on the third day, the fortieth day, and one year after the death of a loved one.

Among many Mexican Americans, death brings family members and friends together even across geographic or psychological distances. Despite their heterogeneity, for Mexican American and other Latino families funeral rites often strengthen family values and ties in several ways:

- There is a common belief that it is more important to attend a funeral than to attend any other family event. The family and the community often attend the funeral and offer emotional support.
- The funeral reflects traditional family values of respect for elders, tradition, and the importance of the family.

Even if family members are not religious, they attend religious funerals.
- Socialization to death begins at a young age. Children attend wakes and funerals regularly and participate in memorial masses and family gatherings after the funeral.
- Many Mexican Americans cope with death through ritualistic acts such as a rosary, a mass, a graveside service, and the annual observance of All Souls' Day on November 2, which is more commonly known as the Day of the Dead (Día de los Difunios).

Recently, many cemeteries and mortuaries—whose directors are usually white—have adapted services to immigrant customs. For example, some funeral homes have removable pews so that Hindu and Buddhist mourners can sit on the floor. Funeral homes may also provide incense sticks and have common rooms where mourners can gather to snack and chat when funerals span several days.

Deceased Muslims are often propped on one shoulder inside their coffins so they face Mecca. Some funeral homes supply white shrouds, Egyptian spray perfume, and a particular soap that Muslims use to wash and dress the dead. Managers of funeral homes also make sure that women employees are working on days when female Muslims are washed in case an employee has to enter the preparation room.

Sources: Willis, 1997; Sharifzadeh, 1997; Murray, 2000; Martinez, 2001; Brulliard, 2006.

Stop and Think . . .

- How do some of these rituals differ from your family's? How are they similar?
- Talk to some of the international students on your campus or in class. How do their families cope with death? What kinds of rituals do the students practice?

Hospice Care for the Dying

Derived from the medieval term for a place of shelter and rest for weary or sick travelers, a **hospice** is a place for the care of dying patients. Because death seems imminent, a hospice provides pain control, gives patients a sense of security and companionship, and tries to make them as comfortable as possible. Hospice care is available in a variety of settings: patients' homes, hospitals, nursing homes, or other inpatient facilities.

In the hospice approach, physicians, nurses, social workers, and clergy work as a team to meet the physical, psychosocial, and spiritual needs of the patient and

his or her family and to give dying people full and accurate information about their condition. Hospice staff members work with family members and friends to help them deal with their feelings and sorrow.

Coping with Death

Bereavement is the process of recovery after the death of someone to whom we feel close. People who were close to the dead person are known as the *bereaved*. Grief and mourning are two common emotional reactions during bereavement.

GRIEF AND MOURNING Grief is the emotional response to loss. It usually involves a variety and combination of feelings such as sadness, longing, bewilderment, anguish, self-pity, anger, guilt, and loneliness, as well as relief.

The grieving process may last a few months or continue throughout one's lifetime. However long it lasts, grieving usually encompasses physical, behavioral, and emotional responses. In terms of behavior, for example, bereaved people may talk incessantly about the deceased and the circumstances of the death. Others may talk about everything but their loss because it's too painful to do so (DeSpelder and Strickland, 2005).

Mourning is the customary outward expression of grief. Mourning ranges from normal grief to pathological melancholy that may lead to physical or mental illness. Whether it's the death of a child, a parent, or a grandparent, most people don't "recover" and end mourning. Instead, they adapt and change (Silverman, 2000).

Coping with death varies in different social and cultural groups. Although many U.S. ethnic groups are acculturating to the values of mainstream society, traditional ceremonies reinforce family ties and religious practices (see the box "Death and Funeral Traditions among Racial-Ethnic Families").

PHASES OF GRIEF There are clusters or phases of grief (Hooyman and Kiyak, 2002). People generally respond *initially* with shock, numbness, and disbelief. After one of my elderly uncles died, for example, my aunt refused to get rid of any of his clothes because "he might need them when he comes back." The grieving person may be unable to sleep, lose interest in food, and not answer phone calls or even read sympathy cards because of an all-encompassing feeling of sorrow.

since you asked

How does grieving differ among people?

In the *intermediate stage* of grief, people often idealize loved ones who have died and may even actively search for them. For example, a widow may see her husband's face in a crowd. Recent widows or widowers may also feel guilty, regretting every lapse: "Why wasn't I more understanding?" "Why did we argue that morning?" Survivors may also become angry, blowing up at children and friends in a seemingly irrational way.

When the grieving person finally accepts the loss, disorientation, anguish, and despair may follow. The survivor may feel aimless—without interest, purpose, or motivation; unable to make decisions; and lacking in self-confidence.

The *final stage* of grief, recovery and reorganization, may not occur for several years, although many people begin to adjust after about six months. For the elderly, grieving is often more complex than it is for younger people because over a brief period an elderly person may experience the deaths of many people who were important to him or her.

DURATION AND INTENSITY OF GRIEF Death affects older people differently than it does younger people. A national study of couples age 65 and older found that up to 22 percent of spouses died within a year of being widowed. These "widower effects" (when a spouse dies shortly after being widowed) may reflect changes in the survivor's behavior, such as sleeping less, using sleep medications more often, consuming more alcohol, and losing weight. Even daily routines such as getting around, meal preparation, and household repairs may become more difficult both physically and emotionally (Christakis and Allison, 2006; Pienta and Franks, 2006; Utz, 2006).

For the most part, however, elderly bereaved individuals are very resilient. For example, almost half of those who have had satisfying marriages cope with the loss of their spouse with minimal grief: They accept the

THE WIZARD OF ID   **Brant parker and Johnny hart**

By permission of Johnny Hart and Creators Syndicate, Inc.

Choices

Helping Children Grieve

Because families are becoming increasingly complex and multigenerational, many children will experience the deaths not only of grandparents but also of great-grandparents, stepgrandparents, and other relatives. Here are some family practitioners' suggestions for helping children grieve:

■ **Encourage questions.** When someone dies, children usually want to know what has happened. Be honest and explain what the word "dead" means. Don't be afraid to say "I don't know" when you can't answer a question.

■ **Encourage the expression of feelings.** Encourage children to show their emotions. Talk about other people's feelings as well. For example, if Grandma seems to be angry, explain that it is not because the children did anything wrong but because Grandma is upset that the doctors couldn't save Grandpa's life (Nolen-Hoeksema and Larson, 1999).

Because children, like adults, vary in the degree to which they are comfortable in expressing feelings, some may prefer to write down their thoughts, make an album of photos of the loved one, or draw or paint pictures.

■ **Encourage participation in events after the death.** Tell the children about the events that will be taking place (wake, memorial service or funeral, and burial). Explain that these rituals are a way to say goodbye to the deceased but don't force children to participate in any activities if they are uncomfortable or are frightened to do so.

Instead, a child may prefer to commemorate the life of the deceased in his or her own way. For ex-

ample, "If . . . Erin and her grandmother used to play under a particular tree at Grandma's house, then maybe Erin would like to plant a similar tree at home in her own backyard" (Huntley, 1991: 41).

■ **Try to maintain a sense of normality.** To restore some semblance of security, try to follow the children's normal routine as closely as possible. During the first few months after the death, avoid making any drastic change, such as moving, unless it is absolutely necessary.

■ **Take advantage of available resources.** Schools, churches, and hospitals often offer children's support groups. When bereaved children get together, they become aware that they are not alone in their grief. Books written for children can be helpful, whether they are read by an adult to children or by the children themselves. When necessary, counselors who specialize in grief and bereavement can help both you and your child. Increasingly, the Internet is providing a way for people to seek solace after the death of a loved one (see "Taking It Further" at the end of the chapter).

Stop and Think . . .

• Most of my students, regardless of age, use euphemisms (such as "pass" and "pass on") instead of "died." Why? Do such euphemisms help us cope with death? Or do they imply that death isn't a normal part of life?

• What strategies have worked in your family in helping children grieve? Were any of them harmful to children?

death as part of life and take great comfort in their memories. About 10 percent are relieved at the death of a partner because they had been trapped in a bad marriage or had provided stressful caregiving for a number of years. About 16 percent experience chronic grief lasting more than 18 months, while 24 percent show an improvement in psychological well-being within a year or so after their partner's death (Mancini et al., 2006).

The duration and intensity of a person's grief depends on a number of factors, including the quality of the lost relationship, the age of the deceased person, whether the death was sudden or anticipated, and the quality of care the dying person received at the end

of his or her life (Carr et al., 2006). Three years after the death of her 89-year-old husband, for example, one of our family's friends is still experiencing enormous grief because she blames herself for not talking to his doctor more often during his routine physical examinations.

For many grieving people, holidays are especially difficult because they are so connected to family customs and rituals. The bereaved person may dread the normal festivities because everything—from cards and decorations to special meals and traditional music—may remind him or her of the loved one who has died. Counselors and therapists suggest that the bereaved not force themselves to participate in special family traditions if doing so is too painful (Thomas-Lester, 1994).

Adults sometimes don't realize that young children, especially, may be confused or experience grief over a death. Parents may be so involved in their own loss that they overlook a child's attachment to the person who has died. Some *thanatologists*—social scientists who study death and grief—encourage parents to talk about death with children openly and honestly (see the box "Helping Children Grieve").

Being Widowed and Single in Later Life

The death of a spouse often means not just the loss of a life companion but the end of a whole way of life. Friendships may change or even end because many close relationships during marriage were based on being a couple. Some ties, such as relationships with in-laws, may weaken or erode. In other cases, widowed individuals forge new relationships through dating and remarriage.

A small proportion (about 4 percent) of older people never marry. Another 7 percent of older men and 9 percent of older women remain single after a first or second divorce. As age increase, so does the proportion of the population who are widowed.

since you asked

Should widowed people begin dating soon after a spouse's death?

Who Are the Widowed?

There are more widows than widowers in all categories age 65 and over (see *Figure 17.7*). At age 75 and over, over 57 percent of men are married compared with only 21 percent of women. Among all racial-ethnic groups, African American widows age 85 and older comprise the largest proportion—87 percent compared with under 78 percent for Latinas, white and Asian American women (He et al., 2005).

There are three major reasons for the sex differences in widowhood. First, women tend to live longer than men (see "Data Digest"). Second, a wife typically is three or four years younger than her husband, which increases the likelihood that she will survive him. Third,

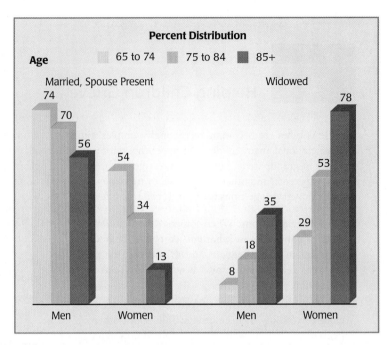

FIGURE 17.7   Widowhood Is More Common for Older Women Than for Older Men, 2003

SOURCE: Adapted from He et al., 2005, Table 6-2.

widowers age 65 and older are eight times more likely than women to remarry.

Facing Widowhood

A number of recently widowed older people exhibit depressive symptoms such as sadness, insomnia, loss of appetite, and dissatisfaction with themselves. As you just saw, however, many usually recover within a year or so, especially if they no longer experience the stress of caring for an ill spouse.

Insurance benefits, when they exist, tend to be exhausted within a few years after the husband's death. Financial hardships may be especially great for a woman who cared for her spouse during a long illness or depleted their resources during the spouse's institutionalization. Moreover, many older widows have few opportunities to increase their income substantially through paid employment because they were full-time homemakers and lack marketable skills.

Almost 11 million people age 65 and older who live alone are widowed; 75 percent are women (He et al., 2005). If they are healthy and financially self-sufficient, most older Americans, including the widowed, value their independence and prefer to live alone rather than moving in with their children. Others may feel isolated, especially when children or relatives live at a distance or rarely visit.

Forging New Relationships

Some widows and many widowers begin to date again within a few years of losing a mate. As a "Dear Ann Landers" letter shows, however, family members may disapprove:

> My brother died a year ago. He left behind his wife of 30 years and two grown children. Two months after his death, my sister-in-law removed all his clothes from the closet, as well as the wall photos of him and the trophies he had won. Eight months later, she began to date. This has been quite painful for the rest of his family. We don't understand why she is dating so soon ("Ann Landers," 2001: 3E).

Ann Landers told the writer to stop being "petty and mean-spirited" because the sister-in-law had grieved for nearly a year (and this was enough) and should be allowed to enjoy male companionship and to go on with her life.

Companionship is the most important reason for dating. Like younger people, older people enjoy having friends to share interests and whom they can call on in emergencies. After being widowed, older people who receive much emotional support from family and friends are less likely to want to date or to remarry than are those who are more isolated (Carr, 2004).

By age 85, only 34 percent of men are widowed, compared with 78 percent of women (see *Figure 17.7*). This is primarily because many older men have remarried. Especially if they have the resources to attract a new mate, and given the large pool of eligible women (those who are younger, widowed, divorced, or never married) and the shortage of men, it is easier for older men than for older women to remarry (see Chapters 8 to 10). In some cases, older people meet, date, and marry while living in retirement communities.

New partners can be important because love, intimacy, and sexual activity continue to be an important part of many older people's lives. Caregivers are even more vital in providing emotional and physical help as we age.

Family Caregiving in Later Life

One of my colleagues, Kathy, is a good example of the *sandwich generation* that's composed of midlife men and women who feel caught between meeting respon-

sibilities to their children and to their aging parents (see Chapters 1 and 13). Kathy and her husband are raising two children, ages 9 and 11, and have recently moved Kathy's mother, 76, into their home after she fell on the driveway and broke her hip.

Increasingly, the sandwich generation is morphing into a "club sandwich family" with four generations: children, parents, grandparents, and great-grandparents (Trafford, 2005). In this hierarchy, the parents are raising their children and may also be providing assistance to both grandparents and great-grandparents. Grandparents may be helping out their adult children, as you saw earlier, but also caring for great-grandparents or other frail, older relatives. Although some multigenerational ties create conflict, many of these families provide affection, help, and emotional as well as financial support.

Most of us don't realize that many family caregivers are children. A **caregiver** is a person, paid or unpaid, who attends to the needs of someone who is old, sick, or disabled. Nationally, about 1.4 million children between the ages of 8 and 18 (representing over 3 percent of all households) are caregivers for a parent, grandparent, or sibling. About 20 percent of these caregivers, most of whom are girls, say that their responsibilities have made them miss school and after-school activities and have kept them from doing their homework (Hunt et al., 2005).

Overall, however, most caregivers in later life are adults, like Kathy and her husband. In fact, today adult children provide more (and more difficult) care to more parents over much longer periods than their parents did in the so-called good old days.

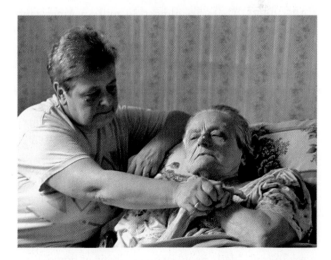

As life expectancy increases, many middle-aged adults find themselves caring for their aging parents. Most of the elder care is provided in the children's or the older person's home rather than in institutions such as nursing homes.

Who Are the Caregivers and Recipients?

As you might expect, the older we get, the more likely we are to need help. Most people who care for the elderly are women, however.

RECIPIENTS Among all people age 65 and older, about 21 percent (almost 9 million people) are considered frail because they have one or more physical, mental, emotional, or memory problems that interfere with activities of daily living (ADLs) or with instrumental activities of daily living (IADLs). ADLs include dressing, walking across a room, bathing or showering, eating (such as cutting up food), getting in or out of bed, and using the toilet (including getting up or down). IADLs include preparing hot meals, shopping for groceries, making phone calls, taking medications, and managing money (such as paying bills and keeping track of expenses) (Johnson and Wiener, 2006).

since you asked

Why are women usually the caregivers for elderly family members?

Many older people need occasional help with transportation, house maintenance, and other tasks. The frail elderly are the nation's most vulnerable population because the larger the number of ADL and IADL disabilities, the greater their reliance on caregivers for survival. The frail older population not in nursing homes or other institutions is disproportionately female (64 percent), age 80 or older (53 percent), white (83 percent), widowed (44 percent), and living alone (35 percent) (Johnson and Wiener, 2006).

CAREGIVERS There are almost 34 million Americans (16 percent of the adult population) who provide unpaid care to someone age 50 or older. A typical caregiver is female (61 percent), is approximately 46 years old, has at least some college education (66 percent), and spends an average of 20 hours or more per week providing care (79 percent). A majority of caregivers are married, and most have had to juggle work with caregiving responsibilities (National Alliance for Caregiving and AARP, 2004).

As in the case of providers for people age 50 and older, daughters and daughters-in-law are usually the caregivers of the frail elderly (see *Figure 17.8*). Even among the frail elderly themselves, most of the caregivers are wives because they live longer than men. On average, a caregiver provides about 25 hours of assistance per week to frail elderly people who are living at home. If an older person suffers from three or more ADL limitations, spouses typically provide 56 hours of care per week, and daughters and daughter-in-laws provide 33 hours per

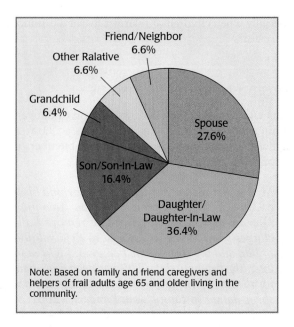

FIGURE 17.8 **Who Provides Care for the Frail Elderly?**

SOURCE: Johnson and Wiener, 2006, Figure 5.1.

week, even though at least half of the latter are employed full time (Johnson and Wiener, 2006).

Regardless of the older person's physical and emotional health, most frequently the caregiver is the female adult child who lives closest to the recipient of care or has the fewest career or family responsibilities. Even when they are employed full time, however, women are more likely than men to provide care, especially to parents and parents-in-law. Some scholars propose that these gender differences reflect broader cultural norms that assign caretaking tasks to women who are believed to be "naturally" more nurturing than men and who are expected to be "dutiful" (see Chapter 5).

Others maintain that the gender gap reflects structural factors such as employment. That is, women provide more caregiving to older adults because they are less likely than men to have lucrative, time-consuming, or satisfying jobs that they are unwilling to jeopardize. As a result, men in well-paying jobs are more likely to purchase help rather than take advantage of the Family and Medical Leave Act, which doesn't provide paid leave (Sarkisian and Gerstel, 2004; see, also, Chapter 13).

Across all racial and ethnic groups, caregivers are more likely to be women, people who are married or cohabiting rather than single or divorced, and those who are working rather than not employed. Overall, however, caregivers provide similar types of care and experience similar stresses regardless of their ethnic background, marital status, or other factors (National Alliance for Caregiving and AARP, 2004; Johnson and Wiener, 2006).

Midlife adults are not the only caregivers. For example, 19 percent of adult child caregivers are 60 or older and 24 percent of spouses who provide care are 80 or older. Spouses, especially, are struggling with their own health problems, with more than one in five experiencing at least several ADL and IADL disabilities (Johnson and Wiener, 2006).

Caregiving Styles of Adult Children

Families help their elderly members in different ways—financially, physically, and emotionally—but adult children still provide most of the assistance (see *Figure 17.8*). Because most of us grow up with brothers and sisters, how do siblings share the care? In one study, Matthews and Rosner (1988) found five primary types of caregiving for aging parents, some more cooperative than others.

ROUTINE HELP *Routine help* is the backbone of caring for older parents. The adult child incorporates assistance to the elderly parent into his or her ongoing activities and is regularly available to do whatever needs to be done. Routine involvement may include a wide range of activities: household chores, checking to see whether the person is all right, providing outings, running errands, managing finances, and visiting.

BACKUPS In a second style, siblings serve as *backups*. Although one person may give routine care to an aging parent, a brother or sister may step in when needed. For example, one sister explained, "I do what my sisters instruct me to do." She responded to her sisters' requests but did not initiate involvement. In other cases, a sibling may contact a "favorite child" when a parent refuses to do something that the routine caregiver thinks is necessary (such as taking medicine every day, regardless of its cost).

CIRCUMSCRIBED The *circumscribed* style of participation is limited but predictable and agreed upon. For example, one respondent said of her brother, "He gives a routine, once-a-week call." This call was important to the parent. The brother was not expected to increase his participation in the care of his parent, however.

Siblings who adopt this style can be counted on to help but make clear the limits on their availability. For example, in one family, a son who was a physician gave medical advice but was not expected to assume any other responsibility.

SPORADIC In contrast to the first three types of caregiving, the *sporadic* style describes adult children who provide services to parents at their own convenience. As one daughter said, "My brother comes when he feels like it to take Mother out on Sunday, but it's not a scheduled thing."

Some siblings don't mind this behavior, but others resent brothers and sisters who avoid the most demanding tasks:

> [My sister and I] were always very close, and we're not now. I don't think she comes down often enough. . . . She calls, big deal: that's very different from spending three to four hours a day. . . . She does not wheel my mother to the doctor, she does not carry her to the car, she does not oversee the help (Abel, 1991: 154).

DISASSOCIATION The last style is *disassociation* from responsibility altogether; this occurs when sisters and brothers know that they can't count on a sibling at all. In one family of three daughters, for example, the two younger sisters were routinely involved in helping their mother, whereas their older sister "was not included in our discussions or dealing with mother. . . . She doesn't do anything" (Matthews and Rosner, 1988: 188).

Siblings use personality, geographic proximity, employment, and other family responsibilities as excuses for not assuming caregiving responsibilities. Such justifications, however, may increase resentment among those who provide care (Ingersoll-Dayton et al., 2003).

Unequal caregiving burdens can create distance between siblings ("He never helps," or "I want to help but she rejects all my offers"). On the other hand, sisters and brothers sometimes overcome ancient grudges as they band together for their parents' sake. For example, they might make mutual decisions about an aging parent's living in a retirement community, share information about a parent's health, and work out visiting schedules for siblings who are geographically scattered (Russo, 2005).

The Satisfactions and Strains of Caregiving

Exchange theory suggests that caregivers experience both costs and benefits. Even though the costs of caring for older family members sometimes outweigh the benefits, especially for women in a sandwich generation with full-time jobs, caregiving can also be satisfying (Raschick and Ingersoll-Dayton, 2004).

CAREGIVING SATISFACTION Some people enjoy caregiving, believing that family relationships can be renewed or strengthened by helping elderly members. They see caregiving as a "labor of love" because of strong affection that has always existed in the family. For others, caregiving provides a feeling of being useful and needed. As one daughter said, "For me, that's what life's all about!" (Guberman et al., 1992: 611; Saldana and Dassori, 1999).

Caring for parents may be especially gratifying when it does not conflict with employment and the caregiver is not caring for other family members or relatives. Even when they have responsibilities to their own family, women often report that caregiving enhances their sense of self-worth and well-being, especially when family members help out (Martire et al., 1997).

CAREGIVING STRAINS Caretaking also creates stress and strain. Older people often need support at a time when their children's lives are complicated and demanding. Families are often unprepared for the problems involved in caring for an elderly person. In general, daily routines are disrupted, caregivers are confined to the home, and parent–child conflict may increase. Parents who are mentally impaired, can't perform basic daily self-care tasks, or engage in disruptive behavior are the ones who are most difficult to care for (Aranda and Knight, 1997; Dilworth-Anderson et al., 1999).

Financial burdens include not only the direct costs of medical care but also indirect costs such as lost income or missed promotions. Funds for services to reduce the strain on caregivers are limited. Women are more likely than men to quit their jobs or to decrease their work hours to provide care. Those who interrupt their employment to serve as parental caregivers generally receive fewer retirement benefits than other workers (National Alliance for Caregiving and AARP, 2004; Johnson and Wiener, 2006).

A troubled marital relationship may become more problematic with the added stress of assisting an aging parent. For many women, caring for many elderly relatives is not a single episode but continues throughout life. It may be necessary to care for elderly relatives, and the caregiving may be multilayered as an aging spouse, parents, in-laws, grandparents, and other elderly relatives need help sequentially or simultaneously.

Women, more often than men, feel especially worn out if their divorced parents live miles apart but count on their daughters for help as they age. And if their parents have remarried, adult children may feel torn. For example, should they help their mother take care of their stepfather, or should they help their stepmother care for their father?

A number of gay/lesbian relationships last well into retirement. This couple, ages 79 and 83, hold their marriage certificate issued in San Francisco, California, in 2004. They had been together for 51 years.

Other Support Systems

The family is an important caregiver for frail elderly people. The fact that only 5 percent are institutionalized—typically in nursing homes—shows that families are the primary source of assistance.

Many employers complain that the costs of elderly caregiving are expensive. In 2004, for example, the costs businesses bore because adult caregivers were absent, late, quit, or took unpaid leave totaled almost $34 billion (MetLife Mature Market Institute, 2006).

Although many employers gripe about the costs of caregiving, fewer than one in four U.S. businesses offer employees eldercare support services and benefits, such as flexible hours and telecommuting. Most employees don't even take unpaid leave because they believe that the workplace stigmatizes eldercare: "People are afraid that when their companies are downsizing, they'll be remembered for taking time off to care for their mothers" (Fleck, 2006: 19).

What are the options for most workers? Most formal support systems are expensive or limited to people who can walk, can take care of their physical needs, or don't suffer from dementia. For example, day care centers for the aged can cost over $1,000 a month, more than an average Social Security check pays. In 2004, the average monthly social security income for women was $784 and $1031 for men. Also, most older people don't have long-term care insurance that might pay for higher-quality nursing care.

Retirement communities are attractive options because they include health care, housekeeping, meals, and many other services. But how many older people can afford to pay at least $300,000 for a house or apartment and another $4,000 or so per month for annual maintenance and other fees? Similarly, assisted-living centers meet their residents' needs, but how many families can afford about $3,000 a month?

Unless an older person is financially destitute and qualifies for Medicaid (a federal government program for the poor), nursing homes are expensive. The average cost can be more than $5,000 a month, depending on the level of care. Moreover, high-quality nursing homes don't accept Medicaid recipients because government programs don't cover the costs (Kalb and Juarez, 2005).

From 1975 to 2004, Medicaid spent about $600 billion on long-term care of the elderly, with nearly 90 percent going to institutions. According to some analysts, Medicaid can save an average of $15,000 a year for each person who receives care at home instead of in a nursing home. Thus, there is increased pressure for families to provide more care for the elderly. About a dozen states, for example, have implemented programs that provide caregivers with respite care or allow families to purchase more of the goods and services they need for eldercare, including hospital-type beds and transportation costs (Feinberg et al., 2006; Lagnado, 2006).

So far, such options are largely limited to poor families and are not available to low-income and middle-class families. Some scholars also caution that expanding family-based assistance will increase the workloads of employed women, who are far more likely than employed men to care for the elderly (Sarkisian and Gerstel, 2004).

Conclusion

As this chapter shows, because of increased life expectancy many of us will have more *choices* in later life on how we will spend our "golden years." On the other hand, we will also face *constraints,* the most serious of which is how we will care for aging family members as longevity increases and health-related costs rise.

Another critical issue is how we will respond to the *changes* brought about by an aging population that has diverse social, health, and financial needs. Meeting family needs in the future is the focus of Chapter 18.

Summary

1. Our society is aging at an exceedingly rapid pace for several reasons, especially an increase in life expectancy.

2. Although there is great diversity in the aged population, people age 65 and over must confront similar issues, such as accepting changes in health, dealing with stereotypes, and adjusting to retirement.

3. One of the biggest changes in the last two or three decades has been the rapid growth of the multigenerational family. Because families now often span three or four generations, the importance of the grandparent role has increased.

4. There are five common grandparenting styles: remote, companionate, involved, advisory, and cultural transmitter. These styles often reflect factors such as the grandparents' age, physical proximity, and relationships with their adult children. In some cases, grandparents act as surrogate parents.

5. Divorce by their adult children creates both opportunities and dilemmas for grandparents. In some cases, relationships with grandchildren grow stronger; in others, especially for in-laws, ties become weaker.

6. All families must deal with the death of elderly parents. Physicians and other health-care professionals and families often view death differently.

7. Many families turn to hospice care, which makes the dying person more comfortable and provides companionship and pain control.

8. On average, women live about five years longer than men. Although most women outlive their husbands, both widows' and widowers' coping strategies typically involve adapting to a change in income and dealing with loneliness and the emotional pain of losing a spouse.

9. Today adult children provide more care (and more difficult types of care) to elderly parents over much longer periods than ever before. As our population ages, more disabled and frail Americans will need long-term care.

10. Some policy makers and health care organizations are pushing for more family care rather than institutionalization. Others caution that such changes will increase stress and domestic responsibilities, especially for employed women.

Key Terms

life expectancy *514*
gerontologist *514*
later-life family *515*
depression *517*
dementia *518*

Alzheimer's disease *518*
ageism *520*
Social Security *522*
intergenerational ambivalence *531*
hospice *533*

bereavement *533*
grief *534*
mourning *534*
caregiver *537*

Taking It Further

Aging on the Internet

There are an overwhelming number of aging-related resources on the Net. Here are a few URLs to whet your appetite:

Administration on Aging provides information about older people and services for the elderly, numerous links, fact sheets, and other resources.

www.aoa.gov

AARP's Internet Resources on Aging offers more than 900 links to a variety of topics, including employment, health, housing, Social Security, legal issues, and state and local sites.

http://www.aarp.org/internetresources

National Institute on Aging offers publications on topics related to health and aging and many links to caregiving sites.

www.nia.nih.gov

Senior Law Home Page includes materials on elder law, Medicare, Medicaid, estate planning, trusts, and the rights of the elderly and disabled.

www.seniorlaw.com

Senior Women Web offers many useful resources on grandparenting, politics, and health.

www.seniorwomen.com

Elder Wisdom Circle describes itself as "grandparents to the cyber-world." About 300 men and women, ages 60 to 97, answer questions and offer advice on a wide range of topics—relationships, parents, careers, depression, unrequited love, and so on.
www.elderwisdomcircle.org

And more: www.prenhall.com/benokraitis lists dozens of URLs for national organizations for seniors, grandparents' organizations, caregiver associations, home-care directories, health-related topics (such as Alzheimer's and vision loss), grief resources, health-care financing, locating reputable funeral organizations, e-mailing letters to loved ones after death, and much more.

Investigate with Research Navigator

Go to www.researchnavigator.com and enter your LOGIN NAME and PASSWORD. For instructions on registering for the first time, view the detailed instructions at the end of the Chapter 1. Search the Research Navigator™ site using the following key search terms:

caregiving
Alzheimer's disease
ageism

Outline

18

The Family in the Twenty-First Century

Data Digest

- By 2010, **couples with children under age 18** will make up 38 percent of all married-couple households, down from 47 percent in 1990.

- The **number of households headed by single mothers under age 25** is expected to increase by 44 percent, from 831,000 in 1995 to 1.2 million in 2010.

- The **number of single fathers** will grow an estimated 44 percent between 1990 and 2010 (to 1.7 million) but it will remain less than 2 percent of all households.

- **One-person households** are expected to rise from the current 24 percent to 27 percent in 2010.

- Between 2000 and 2004, **child poverty rates increased by 12 percent,** even though one or both parents were employed full time. These rates are expected to rise in the future because of the increase in the numbers of low-paid jobs.

- The **number of Americans age 65 and older increased** from 8 percent in 1950 to 12 percent in 2000. This group will account for 18 percent of the population by 2025 and 21 percent by 2050.

Sources: Miller, 1995; U.S. Census Bureau, 2002; Douglas-Hall and Koball, 2006; Shrestha, 2006.

Many scholars assume that the dynamic processes that have shaped the family in the past two decades will continue in the future. The family's importance has been a major theme throughout this book. In this chapter, we briefly consider the future of this institution, discussing its outlook in 6 areas: family structure, racial-ethnic diversity, children's well-being, health, economic concerns, and global aging.

Family Structure

It's likely that the current variations in family structures will increase in number and form in the future. We will probably see more households that are multigenerational and composed of unrelated adults, and more stepfamilies with his, her, and their children. The high number of divorces and remarriages may mean that senior citizens will depend as much (or more) on "stepkin" as on biological relatives to provide care (see Chapters 16 and 17).

since you asked

Will family structures change even more in the future?

In 2030, the oldest baby boomers will be in their eighties. Whether or not stepkin will support their elderly relatives will depend on geographic location and the degree to which parents and stepparents have close relationships with their children and stepchildren. If society's attitude toward homosexuals becomes more positive and domestic partners acquire more rights, especially the legalization of same-sex marriage, we may also see more families headed by lesbian and gay parents.

Despite these changes, there is no evidence that the institution of marriage will become extinct. As you saw in earlier chapters, although many people are cohabiting and many others are remaining single longer, about 93 percent of Americans marry at least once in their lifetime.

Although many of the family's functions have changed since the turn of the twentieth century (see Chapter 1), the family is still the primary group that provides the nurturance, love, and emotional sustenance that people need to be happy, healthy, and productive. Despite commuter marriages, increased work responsibilities, divorce, and other stressors, many Americans report that their family is one of the most important aspects of their lives (see Chapters 10 and 11).

Racial-Ethnic Diversity

One of the most striking changes in American society, the increase in racially and ethnically diverse families, is expected to continue in the future. Immigration and higher fertility rates among African Americans and some Asian American and Latino groups contribute to this change. These factors have also led to higher racial-ethnic intermarriage rates. Minorities account for 24 percent of the U.S. population, with an increase to 30 percent expected by 2020 (Population Reference Bureau, 1990; see, also, Chapter 4).

since you asked

How will immigration affect American families?

As minorities make up a larger share of the population and the labor force, they will have a greater impact on political, educational, and economic institutions. By 2025, for example, Latinos are expected to make up 48 percent of the population in New Mexico, 43 percent in California, 38 percent in Texas, and about 25 percent in Nevada and Florida.

Some predict that as the Latino population increases, its political power will grow. By 2030, we may find that minority youth are working to support a largely older, white population. If older white men continue to control the government and economy, such dominance, especially if discrimination persists, may increase racial-ethnic tension across generational lines (Morgenthau, 1997; see, also, Chapter 4).

Racial-ethnic communities will continue to grow and change during the twenty-first century. For example, whereas the most recent Asian Indian, Cambodian, and South American immigrants often live and work in interethnic areas of many large cities, Filipino and Korean American families have been moving to the suburbs and establishing communities where they have their own houses of worship and programs to teach their children their family's native language.

Children's Well-Being

A national study of U.S. families concluded that the United States, the most prosperous nation on earth, is failing many of its children:

Unfortunately, Andrew, you would still have to write thank-you notes even if Gramma and Grampa did have a modem.

The Quality Time Cartoon by Gail Machus is reprinted by permission of Chronicle Features, San Francisco, California.

Although many children grow up healthy and happy in strong, stable families, far too many do not. They are children whose parents are too stressed and busy to provide caring attention and guidance. They are children who grow up without the material support and personal involvement of their mothers and fathers. They are children who are poor, whose families cannot adequately feed and clothe them and provide safe, secure homes. They are children who are victims of abuse and neglect at the hands of adults they love and trust, as well as those they do not even know. They are children who are born too early and too small, who face a lifetime of chronic illness and disability. They are children who enter school ill prepared for the rigors of learning, who fail to develop the skills and attitudes needed to get good jobs and become responsible members of adult society. They are children who lack hope for what their lives can become, who believe they have little to lose by dropping out of school, having a baby as an unmarried teenager, committing violent crimes, or taking their own lives (National Commission on Children, 1991: vii–viii).

Such conclusions are well founded. Much of the research shows not only that the United States has abandoned many of its children but that the situation has been deteriorating since 1980. Moreover, some scholars argue, many adults are investing more in themselves and their personal pursuits than in raising their children (see Chapters 1, 12, and 13).

Some researchers describe American children as "the new poor" because poverty rates among children have increased (see "Data Digest"). Since 2000, children living in the Midwest have experienced the biggest increases in poverty largely because relatively well-paid manufacturing jobs (such as those in the auto industry) have been replaced with low-paying jobs in service industries that pay only a minimum wage (such as retail and restaurants). Children of immigrant parents in other regions are at especially high risk of living in poverty because many states do not offer programs such as food stamps and Medicaid (Douglas-Hall and Koball, 2006).

since you asked

Is children's well-being likely to increase or decrease in coming decades?

Many families have difficulty meeting basic survival needs, including housing, health care, and food. Almost 12 percent of children living below the poverty level experience "moderate" or "severe" hunger on a daily basis ("America's children . . . ," 2000).

Hunger and malnutrition rob children of their potential. Biologists and neurologists have found that physical nourishment determines the number of brain cells that children develop. In addition, stress activates hormones that can impair learning and memory and lead to problems in cognitive and behavioral development (see Chapter 12).

Family Policy

About 17 million children in the United States have absent fathers; each year 1 million children are born to unwed parents and another million are newly affected by divorce (see Chapters 11, 12, and 13). **Family policy**—the measures taken by governments to achieve specific objectives relating to the well-being of families—has improved many of these children's lives.

since you asked

Are U.S. government policies family-friendly?

One bright spot is child support policy. The first federal legislation to enforce child-support payment requirements was enacted in 1950, and additional bills were passed in 1965 and 1967, but the 1975 Office of Child Support Enforcement law was the first really significant piece of legislation in this area.

A new law, enacted in 1984, not only requires all states to establish offices of child-support enforcement but also provides federal reimbursement for nearly 75 percent of each state's enforcement costs. Whereas the 1975 act created the bureaucracy to enforce private child-support obligations, the 1984 Child Support Enforcement Amendments require states to adopt formulas and guidelines that the courts can use to determine such obligations. These amendments also require states to withhold pay from the wages and other income of noncustodial parents who are delinquent in their child support payments (Garfinkel et al., 1994).

In 1988, the Family Support Act strengthened the 1984 guidelines, requiring judges to provide a written justification if they violate state guidelines in any way. The act also instructs states to review and update child-support awards at least every three years. In addition, the legislation mandates that states withhold funds for child-support payment in all cases, not just those that are delinquent. States have varied quite a bit in enforcing the latter requirement, however (see Chapter 15).

Courts are also becoming more likely to recognize children's rights. In 35 states, for example, statutes specifically mandate that trial judges consider the presence or absence of domestic violence in child-custody disputes. Many divorcing women are afraid to testify against a batterer because they fear retaliation. However, trial judges who take domestic violence seriously are more likely to protect children from emotional and physical harm by not requiring joint physical and legal custody and not awarding visitation rights to the violent parent (Lehrman, 1996; see, also, Chapters 14 and 15).

Despite some progress, much U.S. family policy is less progressive than that of other major Western countries. Two of the largest gaps are in the areas of child care and parental leave.

Child Care

Few U.S. families can afford high-quality child care services (see Chapter 13). Compared with those of other industrialized countries, the United States' record in this area has been abysmal. Congresswoman Pat Schroeder of Colorado once remarked, "Under our tax laws, a businesswoman can deduct a new Persian rug for her office but can't deduct most of her costs for child care. The deduction for a thoroughbred horse is greater than that for children" (Gibbs et al., 1990: 42).

In contrast to the United States, 60 percent of child care in Japan is provided by the government, and both the government and most companies offer monthly subsidies to parents. One of the most successful programs is in France, where parents can enroll their children in a variety of child care centers, preschools, and special day-care homes run by the government. Tuition is free or minimal, adjusted according to the family income. Similar systems have been established in Denmark, Sweden, and other European countries (Shimomura, 1990; Clawson and Gerstel, 2002).

In Belgium, Italy, and Denmark, at least 75 percent of children ages 3 to 5 are in some form of state-funded preschool program, and in Germany, parents may deduct the cost of child care from their taxes. In Sweden, parents receive a subsidy for each child, and local communities organize and maintain high-quality child

A child care center in Denmark, where more than three quarters of children between ages 3 and 5 are in state-funded programs.

care centers, for which parents pay about 10 percent of the actual cost (Herrstrom, 1990).

Very few American companies provide any kind of child care assistance. Of employers with 50 or more workers, for example, only 3 percent offer parents any help with child care for school-age children on vacation, only 4 percent reimburse child care costs when employees must work late, and only 6 percent reimburse employees for some child care costs when they must travel overnight on business trips (Bond et al., 2005).

Parental Leave

Many countries have developed policies to help employed parents balance work and family responsibilities. In more than 30 developing countries, such as Angola and Ghana, parents can take paid infant-care leave. In the United States, the Family and Medical Leave Act, passed in 1993, provides only unpaid leave and only to some employees (Frank and Zigler, 1996; see, also, Chapter 13).

Unlike the United States, a number of industrialized nations provide generous parental leave benefits. In Sweden, each parent is entitled to 18 months' leave, paid for by the government. In Norway, mothers are entitled to 12 months off work with 80 percent pay or 10 months with full pay. The father can take almost all of the leave if the couple so chooses. In fact, fathers must take at least four weeks' leave or else those weeks will be lost for both parents. The leave is financed through taxes rather than paid for by employers ("Parenthood policies . . . ," 2006).

New mothers in the United Kingdom get six months' paid leave and the option of six months' further unpaid leave. The first six weeks are at 90 percent of pay and the next 20 at about $195 a week. New fathers are allowed two weeks' paid leave at a maximum of about $195 a week ("Parenthood policies . . . ," 2006).

In Austria, Canada, Denmark, Germany, and Hungary, fathers can share in some portion of parental leave. In most of these countries, extended parental leave carries with it the right to a wage-related benefit or a benefit is provided at a flat rate. In Finland, parents have a year of fully paid leave. They can choose among a guaranteed, heavily subsidized place in a child care center, a subsidy to help pay for in-home child care, or a cash benefit to provide support for an extended two-year parental leave at home to care for a child until her or his third birthday (Kamerman, 1996).

Because of the archaic parental leave policies in the United States, the lack of good child care facilities, and the increased numbers of women entering the labor force or higher education, battles over who should care for children will probably escalate. According to some researchers, such conflicts will decrease only when family policies take children and working parents seriously (Leach, 1994).

Health Issues

In many ways, Americans are healthier now than in the past. Resources for medical research, health care, and health education have improved the quality and quantity of health in the United States. Throughout the second half of the twentieth century, mortality rates decreased for leading causes, such as heart disease, stroke, and unintentional injuries (especially auto accidents). The death rates have remained about the same for cancer but have increased for chronic lower respiratory diseases (CLRD) (National Center for Health Statistics, 2005).

Rates of cigarette smoking dropped rapidly in the two decades following the first Surgeon General's report in 1964, but the rate of decrease has slowed in recent years. About 24 percent of men and 19 percent of women were smokers in 2003. Lung cancer, heart disease, and CLRD are all strongly associated with smoking.

Death rates due to heart disease and stroke declined, in part because of better control of risk factors (such as high blood pressure), improved access to early detection, and better treatment and care, including new drugs and greater usage of existing drugs. On the negative side, the rise in overweight and obesity has increased the risk of chronic diseases and disabilities, including heart disease, hypertension, diabetes, and back pain (National Center for Health Statistics, 2005).

A number of Americans are adopting healthier lifestyles. However, two health-related issues will probably continue to have a significant impact on families in coming years: unequal health care and a growing concern over the lack of a national health-care system.

Unequal Health Care

Health and health care vary by race-ethnicity, social class, geographic location, and other factors. In terms of race and ethnicity, for example,

- Minorities are less likely than whites to receive appropriate heart medicine or undergo bypass surgery, kidney dialysis or transplants, cancer treatment, or the newest treatments for HIV/AIDS.

- Minorities, even those with private health insurance, receive lower-quality care than do whites. This inferior treatment contributes to higher death rates and shorter lifespans.

- Black children under age 18 suffer more disabilities—such as asthma, diabetes, mental retardation, and learning difficulties—than their white counterparts because black children are more likely to grow up in poverty (Swift, 2002; Newacheck et al., 2003).

Some scholars are also finding health disparities between native-born African Americans and black immigrants from Africa, the Caribbean, and some nations in Central and Latin America. Upon arrival, African immigrants have lower rates of heart disease, cancer, hypertension, obesity, and overall chronic medical conditions than U.S.-born blacks. This health advantage drops with years of residence in the United States. The reasons for the decline are not entirely clear, but it may be due to a number of overlapping factors: assimilation and associated stresses, language barriers in accessing early screening and health care, and lack of social networks that can help immigrants navigate the health care system (Arthur, 2006; Ghassemi, 2006).

Generally, the higher one's socioeconomic status, the better one's health and health care. Recently, however, even some educated middle-class families with health insurance can't pay for health care costs. As many as 400,000 of these families file for bankruptcy each year because of medical expenses. Insurance companies are now shifting more costs to consumers in the form of limited coverage and much higher deductibles, co-payments, or premiums.

If there is a serious illness that requires expensive treatment or extended hospitalization, a family with health insurance might still pay as much as $40,000 a year in out-of-pocket expenses. If people become too sick to work, they often lose their jobs and health coverage. Few middle-class families can afford a $1,000 monthly premium for private health insurance, especially if the major provider loses her or his job (Himmelstein et al., 2005; Warren, 2005).

National Health Care

The United States is one of the few industrialized countries that has neither national health insurance nor a system that makes health care a right of all citizens. In 2004, 16 percent of Americans had no private or employer-sponsored health insurance. Despite the existence of government programs such as Medicaid and Medicare, almost 24 percent of the poor have no health insurance of any kind (see *Figure 18.1*).

Our chances of not having health insurance or inadequate coverage depend on our sex, age, and employment status. Women are slightly more likely than men to have health insurance because more of them live in families below the poverty line and thus qualify for Medicaid. Young adults ages 18 to 24 are more likely than people in any other age group to have no health insurance because they have part-time or low-paying jobs that offer

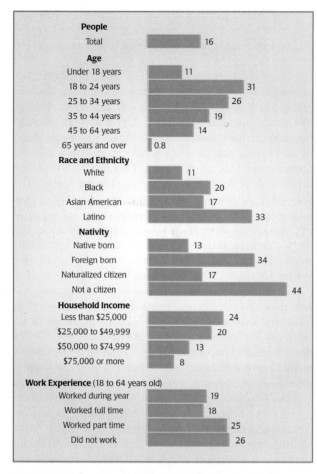

People	
Total	16
Age	
Under 18 years	11
18 to 24 years	31
25 to 34 years	26
35 to 44 years	19
45 to 64 years	14
65 years and over	0.8
Race and Ethnicity	
White	11
Black	20
Asian American	17
Latino	33
Nativity	
Native born	13
Foreign born	34
Naturalized citizen	17
Not a citizen	44
Household Income	
Less than $25,000	24
$25,000 to $49,999	20
$50,000 to $74,999	13
$75,000 or more	8
Work Experience (18 to 64 years old)	
Worked during year	19
Worked full time	18
Worked part time	25
Did not work	26

FIGURE 18.1   Percentage of Americans without Health Insurance, by Selected Characteristics, 2004

Source: Based on DeNavas-Walt et al., 2005, Table 7.

able healthcare. In the United States, the only country of the three that does not have a publicly funded healthcare system, Americans also rated the quality of healthcare in their country lower (48 percent) than did Britons (55 percent) or Canadians (58 percent) (McMurray, 2004).

since you asked

Why are drug prices lower in Canada than in the United States?

The Canadian health-care system has received much attention from the U.S. news media. Among other appealing characteristics, it requires little paperwork when a patient consults a doctor:

> *Several years ago I moved from the United States to Canada, and a few months later I had my first experience with a nationalized health-care system. After making my appointment with a physician who had been recommended to me by friends, I waited only a brief time to see the doctor and when we were finished I asked the receptionist whether there was anything I needed to do—I expected to pay a bill or fill out some forms or sign something. The receptionist seemed puzzled by my question and when I explained she said that there was nothing for me to do and that I could leave (Klein, 1993).*

Although often applauded as a model that the United States should adopt, the Canadian health-care system is not without problems. Some observers point out that government-run medicine, as practiced in Canada and England, is most effective when people's health problems are minor and they are able to wait for services. Also, high-tech resources such as sophisticated medical equip-

no health benefits. Stable, full-time employment improves a worker's chances of having continuous coverage.

Nationally, uninsured adults are nearly four times less likely to see a doctor when they need one than are people who have health coverage. About 12 percent of parents of uninsured children restrict their children's play because of fear of injuries (Lief, 1997; Robert Wood Johnson Foundation, 2006). Such restrictions clearly reduce a family's quality of life. Also, not seeing a doctor when necessary may lead to illnesses and diseases that cost taxpayers much more in the long run than would providing national health care for all families.

Canada: A Model Health Care System?

In a recent national survey, 61 percent of Canadians, 48 percent of Britons, but only 27 percent of Americans said that they were satisfied with the availability of afford-

Many older Americans travel to Mexico or Canada to buy less expensive prescription medicine. Why are the costs of drugs so high in the United States?

ment are often scarce in these countries. Hundreds of physicians have reportedly left Canada, most for the United States, because increased government interventions reduced their incomes and placed restrictions on where and how they could practice (Krauss, 2003).

Canadians often complain that they have difficulty getting an appointment for routine and ongoing medical care and experience long wait times for specialists. The government has placed a high priority on four areas: cancer therapy, cardiac surgery, knee and hip replacement, and cataract surgery. Nevertheless, patients who require these procedures may have to wait up to seven months because many provinces are experiencing shortages of doctors and other health-care professionals, high-tech equipment, facilities, and money (Canadian Institute for Health Information, 2006).

You have probably seen print or broadcast media coverage of older Americans traveling to Canada (or placing Internet orders with Canadian firms) to buy less expensive prescription drugs. Despite the Bush administration's promise to reduce the cost of prescriptions, drug prices—especially of brand-name drugs—have risen over 6 percent since 2004 and at five times the general inflation rate (Binder et al., 2006).

If Canadians can buy necessary drugs at reasonable prices, why can't Americans? According to Jane Bryant Quinn (2004: 31), a nationally known financial columnist, "The sainted American drug industry, together with the Bush administration, doesn't want you to have them":

The drug companies, defending their profits, employ "godfather" muscle. They've warned Canadian wholesalers and pharmacies not to sell to

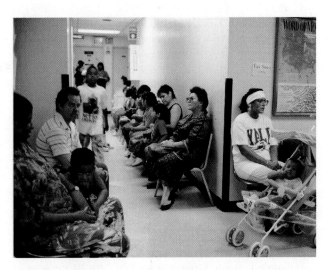

Many families that don't have health care coverage must spend long hours in the crowded waiting rooms of public clinics to receive medical treatment.

Americans by mail, and are cutting back supplies to those who dare.

Meanwhile, the administration is playing the fear card. Officials from the Food and Drug Administration will argue, at the drop of a hat, that Canadian drugs might be counterfeit, adulterated, mishandled, even a potential tool of international terrorism. Anthrax in a Paxil bottle. Funny, I recently spent a weekend in Canada and their pharmacies didn't look like Al Qaeda's caves to me.

Quinn's point is that Americans pay higher drug prices than Canadians do because our legislators support companies' greed for profits. Pharmaceutical manufacturers return the favor by making generous political campaign contributions.

Economic Concerns

Most Americans' income comes from employment (rather than investments or inherited wealth, for example). However, the traditional assumption that holding a job will keep a person out of poverty or off welfare rolls is becoming increasingly shaky.

Poverty

Much research shows that poverty, especially child poverty, is a serious problem in the United States. The United States also has higher child poverty rates than most other industrialized countries: 1 out of 5 U.S. children lives in poverty, compared with 1 out of 10 in Canada and Australia, 1 out of 25 in France, 1 out of 50 in Germany, and 1 out of 100 in Sweden (Danziger and Danziger, 1993).

In 2004, black and Latino children were more likely to be poor (33 and 29 percent, respectively) than white children (10 percent). Parents' work is the single most important factor in preventing child poverty. Work, in turn, is affected by economic conditions, especially a changing job market that doesn't need less-educated workers (Nichols, 2006).

According to some researchers, one of the reasons that U.S. poverty rates are high is that, except during the mid-1960s, the government has not developed a comprehensive antipoverty agenda. Danziger and Danziger (1993), for example, suggest that an integrated set of policies would include many components: improved education and training, subsidies to working-poor families, greater access to health care and child care, expanded support services for children and their parents (such as youth development programs and decent housing), elimination of labor-market practices that discriminate against minorities and women, and provision of employment opportunities for those who are unable to find jobs (see Chapters 4 and 13).

Most important, child and family poverty could be alleviated if parents had jobs that paid a living wage. For example, a head of household would have to earn $10.00 per hour (well above the $5.15 per hour minimum wage) and work full time, 52 weeks a year, to have an annual gross salary (before taxes) of $20,800, barely above the $20,474 income level defined by the federal government as the poverty level for a family of four (in 2005). How many full-time jobs pay $10.00 an hour to people with a high school education or less? Very few.

Welfare

Many Americans are direct or indirect recipients of some form of **welfare,** government aid to people who can't support themselves, generally because they are poor or unemployed. There are also many programs that benefit the middle class, the upper class, and corporations. For example, the middle class can take advantage of student loans, expensive farm subsidies that pay farmers not to raise certain crops, and loans to veterans (see Chapter 13).

THE WELFARE REFORM ACT In 1996, former President Clinton signed the Personal Responsibility and Work Opportunity Reconciliation Act (PRWORA, also called the "Welfare Reform Act"), which transferred control of federally financed welfare programs to the states. The law converts AFDC (Aid to Families with Dependent Children) to a block grant—a set amount of dollars—called Temporary Assistance to Needy Families (TANF), with a five-year lifetime limit on benefits for welfare recipients.

Under the law, cash assistance cannot exceed a period of five years, regardless of whether the family moves to another state or goes off welfare and returns later. In addition, after receiving two years of benefits, welfare recipients are required to work, enroll in on-the-job or vocational training, or do community service. Unmarried mothers under age 18 must live with an adult and attend school to receive welfare benefits.

Proponents of this law have argued that the best way to get people off welfare is to require them to work. Even if they can only find low-paying jobs, proponents maintain, welfare recipients will gain work experience and a job history, and will contribute to their own support (Mead, 1996).

Beyond some general guidelines, PRWORA gave states autonomy to set eligibility rules and determine how

Since the passage of the "Welfare Reform Act" in 1996 (see text), eligibility for food stamps has become stricter for some recipients, including able-bodied applicants, who are expected to work.

participants could meet work requirements. In addition, each state can use its funds for certain recipients who would not be covered by federal funds, furthering local options. As a result, states vary considerably in their welfare policies. In Alabama, for example, TANF applicants are required to register with the local employment office and apply for job openings in the region. Nevada, on the other hand, requires applicants to apply for a minimum of ten jobs a week. While thirteen states have a maximum TANF benefit of under $300 a month, six states allow $600 and above (Rowe and Giannarelli, 2006).

HAS WELFARE REFORM WORKED? Since 1996, the number of welfare recipients has plunged more than 60 percent, from 12.2 million to 4.4 million people. Does this mean that PRWORA has worked? The results are mixed.

Initially, welfare caseloads dropped by almost half because about 35 percent of families were deemed ineligible for assistance. In general, however, employment levels have increased. In 2004, for example, about 32 percent of adults on welfare were working. About 20 percent of welfare recipients have two or more characteristics that act as barriers to work, including limited education, little or no work experience, severe mental and physical disabilities, caring for young children, and language difficulties. Even so, the share of welfare recipients who worked despite two or more such barriers quadrupled, from 5 percent in 1997 to 20 percent in 1999. In 2002, in a weaker economy, the number dropped to 14 percent (Golden, 2005; Pear, 2006).

The welfare numbers have also decreased because many people don't apply for assistance. Millions of families don't take advantage of state support systems that provide working families with health insurance, food stamps, housing assistance, child care subsidies, or the Earned Income Tax Credit (EITC), which reduces or eliminates taxes for low-income workers. A number of eligible workers don't apply for such benefits for a variety of reasons: lack of knowledge, fear of deportation, complicated application processes, limited funding for child care subsidies, and the stigma of being on welfare (The Urban Institute, 2006).

A quarter of the recipients who left welfare by 2000 were back on the rolls in 2002. Compared with those who keep their jobs, people who return to welfare are much more likely to be in poor health, have low education levels, have young children, or fail to live up to job requirements such as showing up every day and being on time (Golden, 2005).

Many former welfare recipients work at low-wage jobs that average about $8.00 an hour. About 32 percent of low-income families cut or skip meals for financial reasons or worry about not being able to afford their next meal. About 31 percent of these families can't pay their rent, mortgage, or utility bills; 10 percent put off needed health care because they can't afford it (Golden, 2005).

There's some evidence that welfare reform has changed family structure, especially among lower-income and less-educated parents. For example, the share of children living in single-mother families decreased (from almost 22 percent of all children in 1997 to 19 percent in 2002), and the share living in cohabiting families rose from 5 percent to 6 percent. In addition, for mothers who had recently given birth, participation in six public assistance programs (such as TANF and food stamps) fell from 42 percent in 1996 to 29 percent in 2001. The decline may be due in part to an increase in the numbers of low-income women who are marrying or living with someone who has a job (Golden, 2005; Lugaila, 2005).

In mid-2006, the Bush administration issued sweeping new rules that require states to move much larger numbers of poor people from welfare to work. Under the new rules, for example, states must verify the numbers of hours that were actually worked. Also, 50 percent of adult welfare recipients in a state must be engaged in work or training by mid-2007 or face financial penalties that reduce the state's federal welfare grant. While the Welfare Reform Act gave states a large amount of discretion, the new rules limit states' flexibility. For example, the new rules define 12 acceptable types of work activity, such as vocational education training (up to 12 months in a lifetime), but not substance abuse treatment, caring for a disabled family member, or getting a GED—activities that in the past most states approved as legitimate preparation for work (U.S. Department of Health and Human Services, 2006). It's not clear how many states will be able to comply with the new rules.

CORPORATE WELFARE The cost of corporate welfare is much greater than that of assistance to poor families. The federal government has directly subsidized the shipping, railroad, and airline industries, along with exporters of iron, steel, textiles, paper, and other products. Since the late 1970s, the government has bailed out companies such as Chrysler Corporation, Penn Central, Lockheed, a number of petroleum companies, and hundreds of savings and loan banks that declared bankruptcy because of fraud, bad investments, or widespread embezzlement.

Corporate welfare programs cost taxpayers about $150 billion in 2002. Among the most egregious examples of corporate welfare is the Market Access Program. This program gives companies like Campbell Soup, Ralston Purina, and Gallo Winery millions of dollars every year to promote their goods overseas instead of borrowing from banks for investments abroad (Corporate Welfare Information Center, 2002).

Critics of such "corporate welfare queens" note that corporate welfare programs are supported both by U.S. presidents and Congress because the companies make large campaign contributions to both Democrats and Republicans. Recently, for example, Congress awarded $500,000 to improve a ballpark in a legislator's district in Virginia; $50 million for a five-acre indoor rainforest in Iowa; $2.2 million to improve the recreational facilities for a population of 1,570 people in North Pole, Alaska; and $500,000 to improve the sidewalks, lighting, and landscaping between two streets in Montezuma, Georgia. In return, the companies that were awarded the contracts for these projects made hefty contributions to members of Congress who were running for reelection (Williams and Middleton, 2004).

Because taxpayer dollars fund corporate welfare, there's less money available for financial assistance to poor, low-income, and middle-class families. Even a fraction of corporate welfare funds would go far to reduce poverty and eliminate the wage gap between women and men.

Comparable Worth

A chronic problem that contributes to women and children's economic vulnerability is the wage gap between women and men (see Chapter 13). The sex gap in pay stems from many factors, one of which is employment discrimination. Whatever their source, pay inequities have a negative impact on the family.

According to the concept of **comparable worth,** men and women should receive equal pay for doing work that involves comparable skills, effort, and responsibility and is performed under similar working conditions. Proponents of comparable worth argue that jobs can be measured in terms of such variables as required education, skills, experience, mental demands, and working conditions. Comparable worth policies also maintain that the inherent worth of a job—for example, its importance to society—can be quantified and measured.

since you asked

Will wage gaps between women and men persist in the future?

Assigning point values in these and other categories, investigators have demonstrated that, in several states, women were receiving much lower salaries than men even though their jobs scored comparable points. For example, a legal secretary was paid $375 a month less than a carpenter, but both received the same number of job evaluation points (U.S. Commission on Civil Rights, 1984).

Since 1984, a few states (such as Minnesota, South Dakota, New Mexico, and Iowa) have raised women's wages after conducting comparable worth studies. Although opponents argue that these kinds of adjustments are too costly, proponents point out that the cost of implementing pay equity in Minnesota came to less than 4 percent of the state's payroll budget but improved women's wages by more than 10 percent. As a result, about half a dozen states now have similar pay equity laws (Kleiman, 1993).

Such pay adjustments have affected only public-sector workers, however, because no U.S. law requires comparable worth in private business and industry. In contrast, comparable worth legislation has been enacted in half of the jurisdictions in Canada, a majority of which require that employers in both the public and private sectors set pay levels in accordance with comparable worth standards (Aman and England, 1997).

We've looked at how family structures, racial-ethnic diversity, family policy, and health and economic issues have changed since 2000. Another important topic is how an aging population—both in the United States and around the world—affects our choices and constraints now and will do so in the future.

Global Aging

The world's population is aging at an unprecedented rate. In 2000, almost 7 percent was 65 years old or older. By 2015, in some countries—such as Greece, Italy, Japan, and Sweden—over 21 percent of the population will be age 65 and older (see *Figure 18.2*).

The percentage of older people is important to any society because older people, especially the oldest old, depend on family, the government, or both for financial, physical, and emotional support (see Chapter 17). *Support ratios,* also called *dependency ratios,* present a broad view of the relative size of working- and dependent-age groups.

The **older support ratio** is the number of people age 65 and over per 100 people ages 20 to 64. In 2000, the

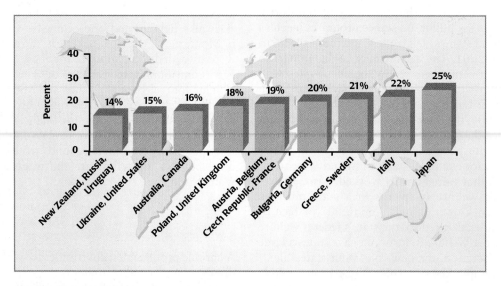

FIGURE 18.2 Global Aging, 2015

SOURCE: Based on Kinsella and Velkoff, 2001, Table 1.

older support ratio was 21, which indicates about one older person for every five working-age people. By 2030, this ratio is expected to be 36, which means that, unless older people go on working, fewer than three working-age people will be supporting each older person (see *Table 18.1*).

Our "graying world" is likely to affect both the young and the old in other ways as well. In the United States, for example, two emerging issues are the right to die and the competition for scarce resources.

The Right to Die

In Portland, Oregon, 65-year-old Steve Mason is ready for death. He suffers from terminal lung cancer that is spreading to his liver and brain. He has four small bottles of a lethal dose of barbiturates and plans to ingest the liquid when his breath is short and he feels too sick to eat or sleep. This isn't suicide, Mason says:

> *Suicide means a needless taking of life. When five doctors tell you nothing can be done, you are merely insuring that your life ends at the proper time. I don't want my daughters to see me wither away to 80 lbs. and have some night nurse shave my beard to get some tubing into my mouth (Roosevelt, 2005: 32).*

PHYSICIAN-ASSISTED SUICIDE Mason isn't alone in his plans to die on his own terms. Many elderly people commit suicide because they don't want to waste away in a hospital (see Chapter 17). Others have turned to physician-assisted suicide (PAS) for multiple reasons: Pain medications don't help, they have watched loved ones

since you asked

Do terminally ill people have a right to "die with dignity"?

TABLE 18.1

Older Support Ratios: 1980 to 2030

Year	Older Support Ratio
1980	19.9
1990	21.4
2000	21.1
2010	21.7
2020	28.4
2030	36.2

SOURCE: Based on He et al., 2005, Table 2-4.

become increasingly helpless over time, or they want control over their death. In other cases, people want to hasten their own death because of a severe loss of bodily functions. According to a daughter, for example, her elderly mother sought PAS because she was totally bedridden: "[Mother] was messing her sheets and stuff like this. She thought the quality of her life was appalling. She couldn't do anything. All she could do was lie in bed" (Pearlman et al., 2005).

In 1994, Oregon voters approved a referendum to legalize assisted suicide. The provisions of the Oregon proposal were fairly severe:

- Right to die decisions were limited to competent adults who were terminally ill; children were not eligible.

- The patient was required to make at least three requests to the physician—two verbally and one in writing—over the course of at least 15 days.

- A second physician had to make an independent diagnosis of both terminal illness and mental competence.

- If either physician felt that the patient was not emotionally stable, the process was to be stopped and the patient was to be referred to a psychiatrist or a clinical psychologist.

- If the two physicians agreed that the patient was both terminally ill and mentally stable, the patient was to have the prescription filled and to self-administer the drug. Patients who were not physically able to do this were not eligible for the "physician-aid-in-dying" process (Pridonoff, 1994).

The referendum passed, but the state appealed it. In 1997, the Supreme Court left it up to the states to decide the legality of doctor-aided suicide. Later that year, 60 percent of Oregon voters decided, a second time, to retain their Death with Dignity law. In 2005, the then-Attorney General John Ashcroft warned that Oregon doctors who persisted in PAS would lose their licenses. In 2006, however, the U.S. Supreme Court, ruling that Ashcroft had overstepped his authority, upheld Oregon's right to die law (Savage, 2006).

Despite the fears of its opponents, there is no evidence that legalization of Oregon's Death with Dignity Act has triggered widespread PAS. Between 1997 and 2005, for example, only 208 Oregonians took legal, lethal overdose prescriptions—out of almost 65,000 others who died of the same diseases (Roosevelt, 2005).

The debate over the right to die was triggered in 1990, when Dr. Jack Kevorkian built a "suicide machine" to help people suffering from chronic pain or terminal illnesses kill themselves. He had been acquitted of second-degree murder several times because he had only provided lethal drugs to patients rather than administering them.

In 1999, however, a Michigan judge sentenced Kevorkian to 10 to 25 years in prison because he had actually injected the drugs into the arm of a 52-year-old man suffering from amyotrophic lateral sclerosis (Lou Gehrig's disease). Kevorkian will be eligible for parole in 2007.

PUBLIC REACTIONS TO PHYSICIAN-ASSISTED SUICIDE

How do Americans feel about PAS? According to a recent Gallup poll, 69 percent said that they supported PAS if the patient and family requested it, up from 54 percent in 1947. Those most likely to support PAS were men, Catholics (rather than Protestants), liberals (rather than conservatives), whites, and people with college degrees or higher (Carroll, 2006).

In California, where opponents defeated assisted-suicide legislation in 1999, a national poll conducted in 2005 found that 70 percent of Californians agreed that "incurably ill patients have the right to ask for and get life-ending medication." More than two-thirds said that they would want their doctor to help them die if they were expected to live less than six months (Roosevelt, 2005). Because fewer than one in two registered voters actually vote—even in national elections—a minority of voters determine whether PAS and other legislation is passed even though a large majority of Americans support right to die laws.

Those opposed to the right to die movement are very persistent. They argue, among other things, that caregivers may pressure elderly people to end their lives, that older people's decisions may result from feelings of guilt about being a burden, that those considering PAS should be persuaded that much of their pain is treatable, and that physicians are responsible for extending rather than ending life (Veatch, 1995).

Despite such opposition, many elderly people and their families are becoming more vocal about a person's right to die with dignity, at home, and on his or her own terms. Organizations like Choice in Dying and Death with Dignity have reported widespread requests for information about living wills. A **living will** is a legal document in which a person can specify which, if any, life-support measures he or she wants in the event of serious illness and whether and when such measures should be discontinued.

Preparing such a document does not guarantee compliance, however. Physicians or hospitals may refuse to honor living wills if their policies support prolonging life at any cost, if family members contest the living will, or if there is any question about the patient's mental competence when the will was drawn up (Veatch, 1995). For these reasons and because state laws and policies vary widely, people who want living wills to be enforced should consult an attorney to minimize legal problems and to make sure that their wishes will be carried out.

Such demands for individual rights are bound to increase in the future. Because of their large numbers, baby boomers will probably be successful in challenging or encouraging the passage of right to die laws.

Competition for Scarce Resources

When the Social Security Act was passed in 1935, life expectancy in the United States was just below 62 years, compared with about 78 today (see Chapter 17). In the years ahead, the increasing numbers of older Americans will put a significant strain on the nation's health-care services and retirement income programs.

Older people "are one of the largest and politically best organized groups in the nation" (Crenshaw, 1992: 4). They vote in large numbers, follow issues carefully, and usually come to congressional hearings well prepared to defend their positions. As a result, the older population has considerable political clout.

AARP is one of the most powerful advocates for the elderly. It has over 35 million members, almost $340 million in assets, and more than 400,000 volunteers. Many other groups also lobby for older people, including the American Association of Homes for the Aging, the Gray Panthers, the National Association of

"I had another bad dream about Social Security."

Retired Federal Employees, the National Council of Senior Citizens, the National Council on the Aging, the Older Women's League, and the National Committee to Preserve Social Security and Medicare. It is not surprising, then, that the elderly have been successful in safeguarding and even increasing many of their benefits.

Although the elderly once had the highest poverty rates in the United States, they now have the lowest. In part because of the growth of Social Security and Medicare (which claim about one-third of the federal budget), in 2004 about 11 percent of the elderly had incomes below the poverty line compared with more than a third in 1959 (see Chapter 17).

Some observers have charged that older people have benefited at the expense of others, primarily children, because AFDC support has been cut while funding of programs for the elderly has increased. Remember, however, that although today's elderly, as a group, are better off financially than previous generations, there are specific pockets of poverty. For example, the poverty rate for elderly minorities is two to three times higher than for elderly whites. Poverty rates in the older population also increase dramatically with age: The older we get, the more likely we are to be poor (see Chapter 17).

The number of Americans who will be age 85 or older is expected to triple by 2030, and much of this population will have chronic health conditions that will increase their need for long-term care (Light, 1988). What will we do when our oldest old can't take care of themselves?

Some Possible Solutions

According to some researchers, we waste precious resources by providing care for dying elderly people to prolong their lives by a few months or years. This is especially true because many of these patients spend most of their time in intensive-care units, connected to feeding tubes and oxygen tanks. For example, Medicare spent almost $59,000 for each chronically ill patient in Los Angeles County in the last two years of his or her life, even though such "aggressive care" was an ordeal both for the patients and for their families (Wennberg et al., 2005).

One of the implications of such studies is that we're wasting money on hopeless end-of-life treatment instead of funneling it into other areas such as education, especially in low-income neighborhoods. As you saw earlier, as the older support ratio increases, we need well-educated people who can pay the expenses of our graying society.

Others feel that the competition for scarce resources between the young and the old can be lessened. For ex-

This 70-year-old stonemason is laying the foundation for a fountain in a public park.

ample, increasing the age at which one becomes eligible for old-age benefits from 65 to 70 would reduce the size of the elderly dependent population. Because people who will reach age 65 in coming years generally will be better educated and have more work-related skills than earlier generations, they are more likely to be productive employees well into their seventies. They may also offer an employer more skills than younger people, whose academic performance, as measured on standardized exams, appears to have diminished over the last few decades.

Because the rates of crime, substance abuse, out-of-wedlock births, and children living in poverty have increased, by 2010 large numbers of retirees will be depending on a small group of people in the labor force to support their Social Security and health-care benefits. Thus, some observers suggest that redefining "old age" would be beneficial to both the young and the old. If the definition of old age and the time of mandatory retirement were pushed up to age 70 or later, many productive older Americans could continue to work and contribute to Social Security. As a result, the burden of supporting an aging population would not fall wholly on younger workers.

Conclusion

Families in the twenty-first century are much more diverse in their racial and ethnic characteristics than those of earlier eras. It's difficult to predict whether this *change* will lead to greater cooperation or to further conflict. Because the United States is the only country in the world with such a heterogeneous mix of cultural groups, optimists argue that this diversity is healthy and will strengthen American communities.

The family in the twenty-first century will probably incorporate a wide variety of work and family roles. Because women's participation in the labor force is expected to increase, work and family functions will continue to overlap. The *constraints* of balancing domestic and work responsibilities are not expected to diminish, however. Consequently, women (and some men) may become more insistent in demanding family policies that put a higher priority on children, parenting, and the family.

Families in the twenty-first century will continue to have more *choices* than they did in the past. Divorce and remarriage are now common, and these options will probably continue in the future. In addition, as technological advances improve eyeglasses, hearing aids, wheelchairs, and other biomedical devices, many older Americans will be able to live independently instead of depending on care from others.

Summary

1. In the twenty-first century, some of the greatest changes in U.S. society will probably occur in 6 areas: family structure, racial and ethnic diversity, children's well being, health-related issues, economics, and meeting the needs of an aging population.

2. Family structures will continue to be diverse. Demographers predict that racial-ethnic diversity will increase because of increased immigration and higher fertility rates among African Americans and some Asian American and Latino families.

3. There is little evidence that the economic and emotional well-being of most U.S. children will improve very much in the future. The United States' child care and parental leave policies, for example, are backward compared with those of other industrialized nations. They are paltry even compared with those of some developing countries.

4. Health-care issues will probably be a major constraint on family life during this century. Two dominant issues will be unequal health care and the lack of a national health care program for all families.

5. There is little evidence that the economic problems of many families will decrease in the future. The United States has generous corporate welfare policies whereas programs for the poor typically provide access to low-paying jobs that don't include health benefits and that offer few opportunities for better wages.

6. As the world's population ages, right to die issues are becoming more prominent. In the United States, living wills are becoming more common, and some states are considering legalizing physician-assisted suicide.

7. In the future, there will probably be greater competition for resources between the young and the old. Because the elderly population is growing, is well organized, and has political power, issues that concern the elderly may be given higher priority than children's well-being.

8. Overall, in this century families will continue to have more choices than they did in the past, but there will also be many constraints.

Key Terms

family policy   *547*
welfare   *552*

comparable worth   *554*
older support ratio   *554*

living will   *556*

Taking It Further

Families and the Future

IDB Population Pyramids, provided by the U.S. Census Bureau, offers access to actual and projected population pyramids by age and sex for a variety of countries for 1997, 2025, and 2050.

www.census.gov/ipc/www/idbpyr.html

The **National Committee on Pay Equity** has information on gender wage gaps throughout the United States and the world.

www.pay-equity.org

The **U.S. Department of Health and Human Services** is an excellent source of information about children and families, aging, and federal rules governing welfare.

www.hhs.gov

The **Death with Dignity National Center** provides information for dying individuals to enable them to control their own end-of-life care.

www.deathwithdignity.org

Several sites explain the **Personal Responsibility and Work Opportunity Reconciliation Act of 1996;** they include the following:

www.urban.org

www.acf.dhhs.gov/programs/ofa/prwora96.htm

And more: www.prenhall.com/benokraitis provides sites dealing with the future of children's health, analyses of welfare reform, aging around the world, and prospective changes in retirement.

Investigate with Research Navigator

Go to www.researchnavigator.com and enter your LOGIN NAME and PASSWORD. For instructions on registering for the first time, view the detailed instructions at the end of the Chapter 1. Search the Research Navigator™ site using the following key search terms:

poverty
children's rights
family structure

Appendix A

Sexual Anatomy

The better you understand your own body, the more comfortable you may become with your sexuality. Also, remember that the word *intercourse* means "communication"; sexual intercourse is an activity in which two people communicate with each other through mutual bodily stimulation.

Female Anatomy

Collectively known as the **vulva** (Latin for "covering"), the external female genitalia consist of the mons veneris, labia majora, labia minora, clitoris, and vaginal and urethral openings. *Figure A.1* shows these structures and the internal female reproductive organs.

The **mons veneris** (Latin for "mount of Venus," referring to the Roman goddess of love) is the soft layer of fatty tissue overlaying the area where the pubic bones come together. Because of the many nerve endings in the mons area, most women find gentle stimulation of the mons pleasurable. Below the mons are the **labia majora** (major, or larger, lips) and **labia minora** (minor, or smaller, lips), outer and inner elongated folds of skin that, in the sexually unstimulated state, cover and protect the *vaginal* and *urethral* openings. The labia majora extend from the mons to the hairless bit of skin between the vaginal opening and anus, called the **perineum.** Located at the base of the labia minora are **Bartholin's glands,** which, during prolonged stimulation, secrete a few drops of an alkaline fluid that help neutralize the normal acidity of the outer vagina (sperm cannot survive in an acidic environment).

The **clitoris** (Greek for "hill" or "slope") develops from the same embryonic tissue as the penis and is extremely sensitive to touch. In fact, it is the only structure in either females or males whose only known function is to focus sexual sensations. Also highly sensitive are the labia minora, which meet at their upper end to form the **clitoral hood,** analogous to the male

foreskin (or *prepuce*), hiding all but the tip, or **glans,** of the clitoris.

The area between the two labia minora is sometimes called the **vestibular area** (Latin for "entrance hall") because it contains the entrance to the vagina. In sexually inexperienced females, or "virgins," a thin membrane called the **hymen** may partially cover the opening to the vagina. The urethral opening, also located in this area between the clitoris and the vaginal opening, is the outlet of the **urethra,** which carries urine from the bladder out of the body.

The internal female reproductive system consists of the vagina, uterus, fallopian tubes, and ovaries. The **vagina** (Latin for "sheath") is an internal structure located behind the bladder and in front of the rectum. It serves not only to receive sperm during sexual intercourse but as the passageway for a fully developed fetus at the time of birth.

The **uterus,** or womb, which holds and protects a developing fetus (see *Appendix C*), is connected to the vagina through its narrow end, called the **cervix.** The

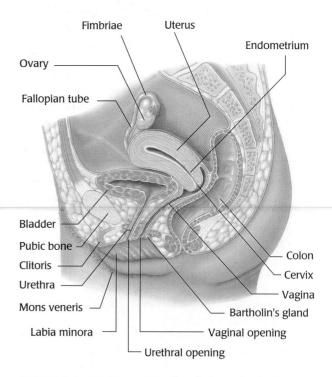

Fimbriae — Uterus

Endometrium

Ovary

Fallopian tube

Bladder

Pubic bone

Clitoris

Urethra

Mons veneris

Labia minora

Colon

Cervix

Vagina

Bartholin's gland

Vaginal opening

Urethral opening

FIGURE A.1 Side View of the Female Reproductive System

Appendix A is adapted from Bruce M. King, *Human Sexuality Today,* 4th ed. (Upper Saddle River, NJ: Prentice Hall, 2002), pp. 31–52. Adapted by permission of Prentice Hall, Upper Saddle River, New Jersey.

uterus has three layers: the innermost **endometrium,** in which a fertilized egg implants; a middle layer of muscles called the **myometrium,** which contract during labor; and an external cover called the **perimetrium.** Each month, after ovulation (see next paragraph), the endometrium thickens and becomes rich in blood vessels in preparation for the implantation of a fertilized egg. If fertilization does not occur, this tissue is sloughed off and discharged from the body as the menstrual flow.

Extending from each side of the uterus are the two fallopian tubes. The *fimbriae,* fingerlike structures at the end of each tube, brush against the **ovary,** which is the female sex gland. The ovaries, or gonads, are supported by ligaments on each side of the uterus and have two functions: to produce eggs (*ova*) and female hormones (*estrogen* and *progesterone*). Each month, in the process called *ovulation,* an egg is expelled from an ovary and picked up by the fimbriae, pulling it into one of the fallopian tubes. Fertilization, if it occurs, usually happens in the tube.

Male Anatomy

The external male genitalia are the penis and the scrotum. (The external and internal male reproductive organs are spongelike shown in *Figure A.2.*) The **penis,** which has both reproductive and excretory functions, consists of three parts: the body or shaft, the glans, and the root. Only the first two parts are visible. The *shaft* contains three parallel cylinders of spongelike tissue: two *corpora cavernosa,* or cavernous bodies, on top; and a *corpus spongiosum,* or "spongy body," on the bottom. The **glans** is the smooth, rounded end of the penis. The raised rim between the shaft and glans is the **corona,** the most sensitive to touch of any part of the penis. The **urethra,** which serves as a passageway for both urine and sperm, runs through the corpus spongiosum, and the urethral opening (*meatus*) is located at the tip of the glans.

The root of the penis is surrounded by two muscles (*bulbocavernous* and *ischiocavernosus*) that aid in both urination and ejaculation. (*Sphincter* muscles, which surround the urethra as it emerges from the bladder, contract during erection to prevent urine from mixing with semen.) The skin of the penis is very loose, to allow expansion during erection; unstimulated, the penis is about 3.75 inches long and 1.2 inches in diameter, but when erect it is about 6 inches long and 1.5 inches in diameter.

The sac located beneath the penis is called the **scrotum.** It holds the testicles outside the body cavity to protect the sperm, which can be produced only at a temperature about 5° F lower than normal body tem-perature. For this reason the skin of the scrotum has many sweat glands that aid in temperature regulation.

The male internal reproductive system consists of the testicles, a duct system that transports sperm out of the body, the prostate gland, the seminal vesicles that produce the fluid in which the sperm are mixed, and Cowper's glands.

The **testes,** or testicles (the male gonads), have two functions: The testes produce sperm (*spermatozoa*) and male hormones (*testosterone* and other *androgens*). Millions of new sperm are produced each day in several hundred *seminiferous tubules.*

Once produced, sperm pass through a four-part duct system (*epididymus, vas deferens, ejaculatory duct,* and *urethra*) before being expelled from the penis during ejaculation. Although an average ejaculation of semen contains about 300 million sperm, most of the volume of the ejaculate is fluid from the prostate gland and seminal vesicles. Among other substances, the **seminal vesicles** secrete fructose, prostaglandins, and substances. The **prostate gland** also secretes these substances, as well as a substance (fibrinogenase) that causes semen to coagulate temporarily after ejaculation, thus helping to keep it in the vagina. **Cowper's glands** are two pea-sized structures located beneath the prostate. They secrete a few drops of alkaline fluid that may appear at the tip of the penis before orgasm. Cowper's secretion neutralizes the normal acidity of the urethra, protecting sperm as they pass through the penis during ejaculation. Because Cowper's secretion often contains sperm, withdrawal of the penis just before ejaculation is a very unreliable method of birth control.

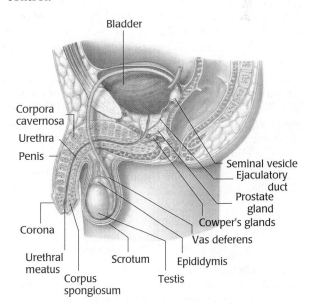

FIGURE A.2   Side View of the Male Reproductive System

Appendix B

Sexual Problems, Dysfunctions, and Treatment

There are many reasons for dissatisfaction with sex: poor general health, unhappiness with available sex partners, and not feeling loved by a partner. Most couples, at some time or other, may experience **sexual dysfunctions,** or conditions in which the ordinary physical responses of sexual function are impaired. Sometimes these problems are physiological, sometimes they are interpersonal, and sometimes they reflect a combination of both physiological and interpersonal factors. In general, serious sexual dysfunctions affect small numbers of people.

Male Sexual Dysfunctions

Erectile dysfunction, or **impotence,** is the inability to attain or maintain an erection. It is a rare man who does not experience this problem at least once in his lifetime. Impotence can occur at any age and can assume many different forms. Typically, the male with erectile dysfunction has partial erections that are too weak to permit insertion in the vagina. Sometimes firm erections quickly disappear when intercourse is attempted.

Impotence can have a negative effect on the female partner's self-esteem if she feels that she is not sexually desirable or is doing something wrong. Most continuing erectile dysfunctions have an organic basis, such as circulatory problems, neurological disorders (due to multiple sclerosis or spinal cord injury, for example), hormone imbalances, and infections or injuries of the penis, testes, urethra, or prostate gland. Diabetes, alcoholism, prescription medications (such as drugs for high blood pressure), and amphetamines, barbiturates, and narcotics can also cause erectile dysfunction.

Several other male dysfunctions are related to ejaculation. The most common of these dysfunctions is **premature ejaculation:** unintentional ejaculation before or while the male tries to enter his partner or soon after intercourse begins. An estimated 15 to 30 percent of all American men ejaculate prematurely on a regular basis. Whereas many female partners are understanding and accepting of the problem, others may feel angry, avoid sex, or seek another lover. Some men are not bothered, but others may question their masculinity. Some may experience heightened anxiety about performance, which in turn exacerbates the condition (Hock, 2007).

Many therapists believe that premature ejaculation is due to psychological factors. Others suggest that men who view women as sex objects are more likely to ejaculate prematurely, regardless of the woman's readiness. Other ejaculatory problems, such as the backward spurting of the semen into the bladder during orgasm, known as *retrograde ejaculation,* and ejaculation in the vagina only after a lengthy period and strenuous efforts (*retarded ejaculation*), or failure to ejaculate or achieve orgasm at all, may be caused by drug use, alcoholism, neurological disorders, or prescription medicines.

Female Sexual Dysfunctions

An estimated 1 to 30 percent of adult women are affected by **vaginismus,** or pain during penetration because of involuntary spasms of the muscles surrounding the outer third of the vagina (Hock, 2007). Vaginismus can be so severe that it prevents not only intercourse but even insertion of a finger or tampon. A woman's partner may deliberately avoid intercourse because vaginismus can be painful. Some men may become passive about sex, whereas others become impatient or openly hostile and may seek other sexual partners.

Vaginismus may have organic causes, such as poor vaginal lubrication, drugs that have a drying effect on the vagina (such as antihistamines, tranquilizers, or marijuana), diabetes, vaginal infections, or pelvic disorders. It can also reflect psychological difficulties, such as anxieties about intercourse, a fear of injury or harm to the internal organs, trauma (due to rape or abortion, for example), a strict religious upbringing in which sex was equated with sin, or fear of or hostility toward men. Such psychological problems are often treated by relaxation exercises followed by a gradual dilation of the vagina.

Another female sexual dysfunction is **anorgasmia:** the inability to reach orgasm. Anorgasmia, which used to be called frigidity, has several variations. In *primary anorgasmia,* a woman has never had an orgasm. In *secondary anorgasmia,* a woman who was regularly orgasmic at one time is no longer. And in *situational anorgasmia,* a woman is able to achieve orgasm only under certain circumstances, such as through masturbation.

Some anorgasmic women find that sex is satisfying and stimulating even though they have never experienced an orgasm. For others, the condition can lead to lowered self-esteem, a sense of futility, and depression. About 5 percent of cases of anorgasmia are attributed to organic causes. Orgasm can be blocked by severe chronic illness, diabetes, alcoholism, neurological problems, hormone deficiencies, pelvic disorders (due to infections, trauma, or scarring from surgery), or drugs (including narcotics, tranquilizers, and blood pressure medications). Other reasons for anorgasmia have an interpersonal basis. For example, women's most common sexual complaints include not getting enough sex because the partner gets tired too fast, intercourse does not last long enough, the partner is unskilled, the woman cannot readily lubricate because there is not enough foreplay, sex is boring ("same place, same time, same channel," according to one woman), or the timing is bad.

Finally, approximately 15 percent of adult women experience **dyspareunia,** or painful intercourse, several times a year. Another 1 to 2 percent are believed to have painful intercourse on a regular basis. Men, too, can experience dyspareunia (it is sometimes associated with problems of the prostate gland), but this disorder is believed to be much more common in women than in men. Like anorgasmia, female dyspareunia may be caused by any of a number of physical conditions, including poor vaginal lubrication, drugs, infections, diseases, and pelvic disorders.

Inhibited Sexual Desire

Both men and women can experience another common sexual problem, **inhibited sexual desire (ISD),** or a low interest in sex. Although the exact incidence of ISD is unknown, approximately 33 percent of the people who consult sex therapists do so because of ISD problems. It is important to remember that a low level of interest in sex is not uncommon. It creates a problem only when it becomes a source of personal distress. An extreme example of ISD is **sexual aversion,** in which people experience persistent or intense feelings of anxiety or panic in sexual situations and avoid sexual contact altogether. The causes of ISD are both organic and nonorganic. Organic factors include hormone deficiencies, alcoholism, kidney failure, drug abuse, and severe chronic illness. Nonorganic factors include fatigue, overwork, depression, and poor lovemaking skills.

Relationship Factors and Sexual Dysfunction

Personal and cultural factors play an important role in sexual expression. Many people do not realize that sex is not just a physiological response. Good or bad sex reflects the quality of our interpersonal relationships, especially in long-term situations. According to Wade and Cirese (1991), therapists typically encounter four interpersonal problems that are destructive to sexual relationships. The first is *anger and hostility.* Dissension and conflict are inevitable in any close relationship, but long-term resentments can sour erotic feelings and behavior.

A second destructive problem in interpersonal relationships is *boredom.* Boredom may be related specifically to sexual activity—it always takes place at the same time and in the same way—or it may reflect a general disinterest in the partner. Some people like sexual relations that are predictable; others become bored with predictability.

Third, *conflicting sexual expectations* can also be harmful to the relationship. One partner may demand oral sex, for example, but the other may find this activity repulsive.

Finally, *poor communication* is a constant problem in interpersonal relationships. Instead of saying what they want in sex, most people are reluctant to say anything, fearing to seem critical of the partner or to demand something they think the partner may not want to give. Suppressing their own needs may lead them to become angry and to strike out verbally at the partner ("You don't love me anymore"). Because many people find communicating about sex so difficult, they often deny the problem and allow it to fester.

Treating Sexual Problems

Because many sexual dysfunctions are caused by *organic* (physical or physiological) problems, a person experiencing such a dysfunction should first see a physician. If a thorough examination reveals no organic abnormalities, the physician may recommend that the person consult a psychiatrist or a psychotherapist. Be careful, however. Because sex therapy is largely an unregulated profession, people can offer their services with little more preparation than having attended a few workshops or reading a book. People seeking help should contact sex therapy centers that are affiliated with universities, medical schools, or hospitals. They can also seek advice about qualified therapists from local medical societies, psychological associations, or family physicians. Even when a clinician is trained and competent, people should feel free to change to a therapist who may be better suited to their temperament and personality.

Appendix C

Conception, Pregnancy, and Childbirth

About midway through a woman's menstrual cycle, an *ovum*, or egg, is released into the abdominal cavity, where it is picked up by the *fimbriae* at the end of one of the fallopian tubes. The ovum takes three to seven days to move through the fallopian tube to the uterus, and it is only during the first 24 hours after the egg leaves an ovary that it can be fertilized.

Conception

At orgasm during sexual intercourse, a man ejaculates into a woman's vagina 200 million to 400 million sperm, all of which attempt to pass through the cervix and uterus into the fallopian tubes. However, only a few thousand live long enough to complete the journey, and only about 100 to 1,000 reach the egg itself during its own journey through the tube (Hock, 2007). Because sperm can live for only 72 hours inside a woman's reproductive tract, the period during which conception can normally occur is extremely limited.

Appendix C is adapted from Bruce M. King, Human Sexuality Today, 4th edition (Upper Saddle River, NJ: Prentice Hall, 2002), Chapter 7. Adapted by permission of Prentice Hall, Upper Saddle River, New Jersey.

Conception takes place when one of the sperm penetrates the egg's surface. Within hours, spermatozoon (a single sperm cell) and ovum fuse to form a one-celled organism called a **zygote,** which contains the complete genetic code, or blueprint, for the new human life that has just begun. Shortly afterward, the zygote splits into two separate cells, then four, then eight, and so on. While this cell division continues, the organism journeys through the tube toward the uterus, a trip that transforms it into a hollow ball of cells called a **blastocyst.** At about 11 to 12 days after conception, the blastocyst, whose inner cell mass will become an embryo and whose outer layers will form structures to nourish and protect the growing fetus, burrows into the wall of the uterus in a process called **implantation.**

By about 14 days after conception, implantation is usually complete (see *Figure C.1*), and a series of connections between the mother and the **embryo**—the term for the developing organism after implantation—begins to form. The outer layers of the blastocyst begin to form the **placenta,** the organ that serves as a connection, or interface, between the infant's various systems and the mother's. One layer forms the **umbilical cord,** which connects the developing baby with the placenta. The **amnion,** a thick-skinned sac filled with fluid that surrounds and protects the baby from sudden movements and changes in temperature, and the **chorion,** which develops into the lining of the placenta, begin to form.

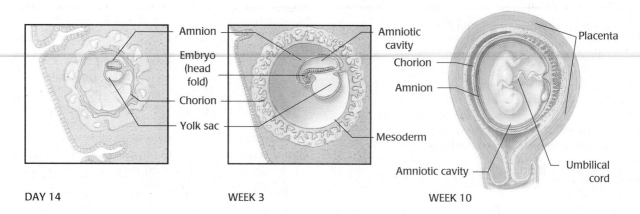

DAY 14   WEEK 3   WEEK 10

FIGURE C.1 Prenatal Development

Pregnancy

Pregnancy lasts an average of 260 to 270 days, or nine months. This time is divided into three-month periods called *trimesters.*

THE FIRST TRIMESTER Women exhibit a varying number of symptoms during the first three months of pregnancy. Breasts may begin to enlarge and become tender. Veins may begin to show on the breasts, and the *areolas* (the darker rings surrounding the nipples) may turn dark. Nipples may also become larger. Urination may increase in frequency, and bowel movements may no longer be regular. Many women feel tired and rundown. One of the more common symptoms of pregnancy is nausea. Although it is called "morning sickness," it can occur at any time of the day.

In the first trimester, the developing baby undergoes a great deal of change (see *Figure C.1*). After implantation, cell division continues, and portions of the organism begin to differentiate in an orderly fashion. Growth in the unborn child occurs from the head downward and from the center outward. In the embryo, three inner cell layers form specific parts of the body. The **ectoderm** forms the nervous system, skin, and teeth. The **mesoderm** forms the muscles, skeleton, and blood vessels. The **endoderm** forms the internal organs (such as lungs, liver, and digestive system).

In the third week of pregnancy, a central structure—the *neural tube*—becomes a dominant feature. This will become the central nervous system. By the end of the fourth week, the umbilical cord, heart, and digestive system begin to form. By eight weeks, all organs have begun to develop. The heart is pumping, and the stomach has begun to produce some digestive juices. From eight weeks until birth, the developing organism is called a **fetus**.

THE SECOND TRIMESTER In the fourth or fifth month of pregnancy, the movements of the fetus can be felt by its mother. The first experience of movement is called **quickening**. As her abdomen expands, red lines, or "stretch marks," may develop on the mother-to-be. The breasts begin to swell and may start to leak *colostrum,* a thick, sticky liquid that is produced before milk starts to flow. Water retention may cause swelling in the ankles, feet, and hands. Women may develop varicose veins or hemorrhoids. Morning sickness begins to diminish, which often brings an increase in appetite, and some women may experience heightened sexuality.

At this time, the fetus begins to make sucking motions with its mouth. In the fifth month, the fetus has a detectable heartbeat and will respond to sound. It also begins to show definite periods of sleep and wakefulness. In the sixth month, the fetus can open its eyes and will suck its thumb and respond to light. At the end of the second trimester, the fetus is almost a foot long and weighs well over a pound and a half.

THE THIRD TRIMESTER In the third trimester, walking, sitting, and rising become more difficult for the expectant mother, who may experience back pain as a result of the increasing burden she carries in her abdomen. The rapidly growing fetus puts pressure on the mother's bladder and stomach, often making urination more frequent. Indigestion, heartburn, gas, and constipation are also common complaints, and the active movements of the fetus may prevent restful sleep.

In the eighth month, the fetus's weight begins to increase dramatically. At the end of the eighth month, the fetus will weigh 4 to 6 pounds and will be 16 to 18 inches long. From this point on, the fetus will gain about 0.5 pounds per week. In the ninth month, the fetus will grow to about 20 inches in length and weigh 7 to 7.5 pounds, but these measurements vary widely. Shortly before birth (weeks or even hours before birth), the fetus will rotate its position so that its head is downward. This is called **lightening** because once the fetus's head has lowered in the uterus, pressure on the mother's abdomen and diaphragm is greatly reduced.

Complications of Pregnancy

Teratogens are agents that can cross the placental barrier and harm a fetus, such as diseases, drugs, or environmental pollutants. Until recently the placenta was thought to be a perfect filter that kept out all harmful substances, but now we know that hundreds of teratogens can invade the fetus's small world. Three things determine the harm that can be caused by teratogens: the amount of the agent, the duration of time of exposure of the fetus, and the fetus's age. Each part of the fetus's body has a time, or *critical period,* when it is most susceptible to damage. Although teratogens should be avoided at all times, most body parts are maximally susceptible to damage during the first eight weeks of development.

DISEASES Even the "weakened" disease organisms of certain vaccines can be harmful to a fetus if taken by the mother just before or during early pregnancy. Some strains of the flu, mumps, chicken pox, and other common diseases can also harm the fetus. One of the first teratogens to be discovered was the *rubella virus*, or German measles. A fetus exposed to rubella may be born blind, deaf, or intellectually impaired. A woman can be safely inoculated against rubella any time up to three months before becoming pregnant. Most types of *sexually transmitted diseases* can also affect a fetus or newborn baby.

PREECLAMPSIA A pregnant woman can also have a disease called **preeclampsia** (formerly called *toxemia*), whose symptoms include high blood pressure, excessive water retention, and protein in the urine. In about 5 percent of cases, the disease advances to *eclampsia*, which is characterized by convulsions and coma. Preeclampsia and eclampsia are among the leading causes of maternal and fetal death. The cause of preeclampsia is unknown. A low-salt diet, bed rest, and blood pressure medications are the usual treatments, but delivering the baby is the only cure.

RH FACTOR Most people's blood contains a protein called the **Rh factor.** If they do, they are "Rh positive"; if they don't, they are "Rh negative." The presence or absence of the Rh factor is determined genetically. In about 8 percent of pregnancies in the United States, the mother is negative and her baby is positive. Although this is not usually a dangerous situation in a first birth, antibodies may build up in the mother's blood and attack a second fetus who is also Rh positive. To prevent this, an injection should be given an Rh negative mother immediately after her first delivery to prevent the buildup of antibodies.

SMOKING Cigarette smoking is associated with an increased risk of miscarriage, complications of pregnancy and labor, preterm birth, lower birth weight, and higher rates of infant mortality. It has also been associated with an increased risk that the placenta will separate from the uterus too soon and with malformation of fetal organs such as the heart.

ALCOHOL The mother's use of alcohol during pregnancy can lead to physical deformities or mental retardation in the infant, a condition known as **fetal alcohol syndrome,** or **FAS** (see, also, Chapter 11). Alcohol can also cause the umbilical cord to collapse temporarily, cutting off oxygen to the fetus and causing a condition known as **minimal brain damage,** which has been associated with hyperactivity and learning disabilities. Even if a woman consumes only moderate amounts of alcohol, her baby still may develop health or emotional problems.

OTHER DRUGS Many drugs—whether illegal, prescription, or over-the-counter—can cross the placental barrier. Women who are addicted to heroin (or methadone) while pregnant will give birth to infants who are addicted as well. These infants must go through withdrawal and typically show such symptoms as fevers, tremors, convulsions, and difficulty in breathing. Even moderate cocaine use by a mother can result in her baby exhibiting low birth weight. "Crack babies" have a variety of sensorimotor and behavioral deficits, including irritability and disorientation. In addition, commonly used drugs such as antihistamines and megadoses of certain vitamins have proven to have harmful effects; for example, over-the-counter aspirin products taken in the last trimester can affect fetal circulation and cause complications during delivery.

ENVIRONMENTAL POLLUTANTS Substances such as heavy metals (lead and cadmium, for example) in drinking water can cause damage to the fetus. Physical deformities and mental retardation have been found in children whose mothers ate mercury-contaminated fish. Radiation and x-rays are also powerful teratogens, especially in the first trimester. Exposure to x-rays has been linked to increased risk of leukemia.

DETECTING PROBLEMS IN PREGNANCY The safest technique of examining the fetus in the womb for possible abnormalities is *ultrasound,* a "noninvasive" method in which sound waves are bounced off the fetus and the uterus. This technique is useful primarily in detecting structural problems. Other "invasive" techniques, those in which instruments are inserted into the womb or even the amniotic sac that holds the fetus, include *amniocentesis* and *chorionic villus sampling* (see Chapter 11), *celocentesis,* and *fetoscopy.* These methods can detect chromosomal problems, such as Down's syndrome, and certain diseases.

Childbirth

Labor is divided into three stages (see *Figure C.2*). In the initial, start-up stage, the woman's body prepares to expel the fetus from the uterus and into the outside world. This stage usually lasts from 6 to 13 hours. At this time, uterine contractions begin to push the baby downward toward the cervix, which undergoes **dilation**—widening—and **effacement**—thinning out. At first, contractions are far apart (one every 10 to 20 minutes) and last no more than 15 to 20 seconds, but eventually they begin to come closer together (1 to 2 minutes) and last longer (45 to 60 seconds or longer).

During labor, the thick layer of mucus that has plugged the cervix during pregnancy (to protect the developing baby from infection) is discharged, either

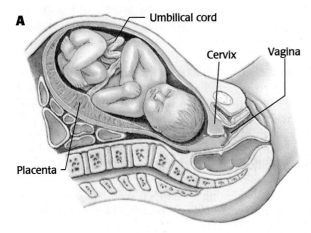

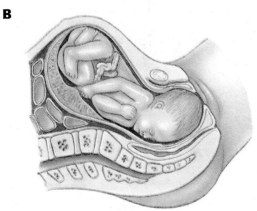

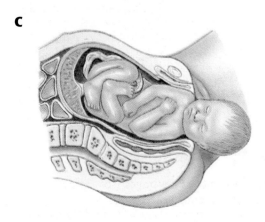

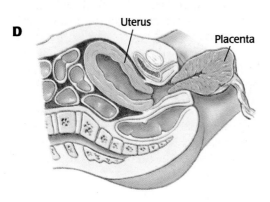

FIGURE C.2   The Stages of Labor
(A) The fetus is fully developed. (B) The first stage, dilation and effacement. (C) The second stage, expulsion. (D) The last stage, placenta detachment.

as a bloody plug that pops out like a cork or a little at a time. In 10 percent of cases, the amniotic sac will also break before labor begins, and the fluid gushes out (the "water breaks"). Labor usually begins within a day after this happens. If not, most physicians will induce labor with drugs in order to prevent contact with the outside world from causing infection in the fetus. Physicians sometimes break the amniotic sac on purpose to speed up labor.

The last part of the first stage of labor is called the *transition phase*. It takes place when the cervix is almost fully dilated (8 to 10 centimeters). Contractions are severe, and the woman may feel nauseous, chilled, and very uncomfortable. The transition phase usually lasts 40 minutes or less, and it marks the end of the initial stage of labor and the beginning of the next.

The second stage of labor, which concludes with the actual birth, begins when the cervix is fully dilated and the fetus begins moving through the birth canal. Contractions during this stage of labor are accompanied by an intense desire to push or "bear down," and they cause the opening of the vagina to expand. This stage lasts from 30 to 80 minutes, on average. Just before delivery, physicians often use a surgical procedure called an **episiotomy**, in which they make an incision from the lower portion of the vagina through the perineum to avoid tearing.

Crowning usually gives the first sight of the fetus. In most cases, the crown of its head appears at the opening of the vagina. In 2 to 4 percent of cases, a fetus will try to come through the birth canal feet or buttocks first, called a *breech birth*. Sometimes it is possible to turn the fetus, but often this situation necessitates a cesarean section (see next section). As the head is delivered, it is crucial to make sure the umbilical cord is not wrapped around the baby's neck. Suction is immediately applied to the baby's mouth and nose with a small rubber bulb to remove mucus so that the baby can breathe more easily. The head then turns, and the shoulders and the rest of the body come out rather quickly. A newborn will usually cry at birth. If not, the baby's back will be rubbed to start the baby breathing. The umbilical cord is clamped and cut about 1.5 inches from the baby's body; this stub will fall off in a few days, leaving what we call a *navel*.

In the third stage of labor the placenta detaches from the uterus and leaves the mother's body (along with other matter). Called the **afterbirth,** this stage usually lasts only 10 to 12 minutes. If even small pieces of the placenta stay in the uterus, infection and bleeding can occur. In this case, physicians use a procedure called *dilation* and *curettage,* or *D and C,* in which the cervix is dilated to allow access to the uterus, which is scraped clean. After the third stage of labor, the uterus normally contracts, returning eventually to its usual size.

CESAREAN SECTION A **cesarean section,** or *C-section,* involves the surgical delivery of a baby. In the past cesarean sections involved making a long vertical cut high on the abdomen through which the baby was delivered. Abdominal muscles run horizontally, however, so after these muscles have been cut, they are too weak to withstand the stress of labor in future pregnancies. Now physicians typically use a new type of incision that is horizontal and low on the abdomen (the "bikini cut"), which makes it possible to have normal (vaginal) deliveries in later pregnancies.

PREPARED CHILDBIRTH **Prepared childbirth** is the modern term for what was long called "natural childbirth": techniques first used in the 1930s by a British physician, Grantly Dick-Read, and later expanded by the French physician Fernand Lamaze. On the theory that much of the pain and fear experienced by women during childbirth was the result of being in a strange environment, surrounded by strangers, and not knowing what was going to happen next, these and other medical professionals began to teach expectant mothers—and ultimately their partners as well—about pregnancy, labor, and birth. In addition, such physical methods as relaxation training and breathing techniques can help make labor easier.

Appendix D

Birth Control and Disease Prevention Techniques

There are three primary questions to ask yourself when you choose a contraceptive, or birth control, technique. First, do you wish to prevent both pregnancy and the transmission of AIDS and other sexually transmitted diseases? The methods that are most effective in preventing pregnancy are not always those that are most effective in protecting against disease. If you are single and dating different people, your need to protect yourself against disease is very great. If you are married and certain of your and your spouse's faithfulness, your concern about pregnancy may take priority. Second, if you wish to prevent pregnancy, do you want only to postpone it or to rule it out permanently? The most effective method of contraception—other than abstinence—is sterilization by surgical means, and in most cases this is irreversible. Therefore, it is suitable only for those who are quite certain that they do not want (more) children. Third, do you need to consider such factors as religious restrictions? For example, the Catholic Church forbids artificial means of contraception. Your answers to these questions will help you sort through the various alternatives we discuss.

Appendix D is adapted from King (2002), Chapter 6, and Hock (2007), Table 5.1 Adapted by permission of Prentice Hall, Upper Saddle River, New Jersey.

Preventing Disease

Although spermicides that contain nonoxynol-9 not only kill sperm but have been shown to be effective against the bacteria and viruses that cause some STDs, spermicides reduce the risk of disease by only about 50 percent. The safest method of protection against disease is the latex rubber male condom used with a nonoxynol-9 spermicide.

Preventing Pregnancy

The chart that follows provides information on the most common contraceptive methods, giving a general description and data on the effectiveness of each method, its particular advantages, and its possible side effects. Note that two figures are given for effectiveness. The first, labeled "With Perfect Use," is the rate at which pregnancy will occur if the method is used precisely as prescribed. The second, labeled "With Typical Use," allows for the fact that people often do *not* use these products as they are instructed to do; a woman may forget to take a pill, or a man may wait too long to put on a condom. In general, the chart moves from the most effective to the least effective methods; slight discrepancies in the progression of effectiveness rates reflect the desire to keep male and female methods (for example, male and female condoms) or related methods (the three different "fertility awareness" methods) together.

Pregnancies Per 100 Women in First Year of Continuous Use				
Method	**With Perfect Use**	**With Typical Use**	**Advantages**	**Problems**
Voluntary Sterilization: A **vasectomy** is a male sterilization technique in which the vas deferens is tied off and cut, preventing passage of sperm through the male's reproductive tract. A **tubal ligation** is the procedure by which a woman's fallopian tubes are tied off or, more often, cut and tied. The procedure prevents passage of the egg, which simply disintegrates and is discharged during menstruation. The procedure is performed by **laparoscopy,** in which a long, tube-like instrument that transmits video pictures is inserted through a small incision; once the tubes are located, they are cauterized. Some doctors approach the fallopian tubes through the vagina (called a *culpotomy*).	0.1 for vasectomy; 0.2 for tubal ligation	0.2 for vasectomy; 0.4 for tubal ligation	Once done, many people report an increase in sexual desire because they no longer have to worry about pregnancy or contraceptive side effects; sexual relations can be completely spontaneous.	Surgical procedures always involve some risk, in part from the use of general anesthesia. Although it is sometimes possible to reverse vasectomy and, less often, a tubal ligation, sterilization should be considered permanent. Therefore, it should be used only by those who are quite sure they do not want any (or more) children.
Norplant: Norplant is a hormonal implant that offers contraceptive protection for up to 5 years. Six flexible silicone rubber tubes (or two rods), each about the size of a match, are inserted under the skin of the inside of a woman's arm, in a fanlike pattern. The tubes or rods contain levonorgestrel, a synthetic form of progesterone, that is slowly released over time and prevents pregnancy by inhibiting ovulation and thickening cervical mucus.	0.2	0.2	Believed by World Health Organization to be safer than the Pill because it contains no estrogen. Tubes can be removed at any time if a woman wants to conceive.	Spotting or irregular bleeding, weight gain, and headaches; less often, nervousness, dizziness, nausea, breast tenderness, and acne. However, more than 2/3 of users are very satisfied with this method.
Depo-Provera: Known as "the Shot," this injectable drug contains progestin. **Depo-Provera** works by preventing ovulation and lasts for 3 months. After discontinuation of the injections, it may take a woman from several months to a year to regain her fertility.	0.3	0.3	Avoids problem of pregnancy resulting from missing a daily dose, as with the Pill.	Initially thought to increase risk of several cancers, the drug is now approved by the World Health Organization. Some side effects are menstrual irregularities, fatigue and weakness, dizziness, and headaches.
The Pill: The most popular **Pill** combines synthetic estrogen and progesterone (progestins). It works by preventing ovulation, by inhibiting the buildup of the uterine lining necessary for implantation, and by keeping the cervical mucus thick and thus impeding the passage of sperm. A *minipill,* containing only progestin, has only the second and third of these actions and is for women who are breast-feeding or who cannot tolerate the side effects of the Pill's estrogen.	0.1 (Pill); 0.5 (minipill)	0.3	May reduce risk of cancer of endometrium, benign breast tumors, ovarian cysts, rheumatoid arthritis, and pelvic inflammatory disease. Alleviates premenstrual syndrome and menstrual pain and reduces menstrual bleeding.	Cardiovascular problems, particularly in women who smoke, are over 35, or have diseases such as diabetes or hypertension. May be less effective if antibiotics, analgesics, or tranquilizers are used at the same time. Backup methods must be used during the first month and whenever a woman forgets to take a pill.

Pregnancies Per 100 Women in First Year of Continuous Use (cont.)

Method	With Perfect Use	With Typical Use	Advantages	Problems
Some combination pills try to adjust the levels of progestins to mimic "natural" hormonal phases of the menstrual cycle, but manufacturers don't agree on what is "natural." The Pill is taken for 21 days and then discontinued for 7 to permit menstrual bleeding.				
Intrauterine Device (IUD): The **intrauterine device, or IUD,** is a small, plastic or metal device (of various shapes and sizes) that is placed in the uterus by a doctor. IUDs work primarily by impeding the transit of sperm, and a copper or progesterone coating further impairs this passage. The copper-coated IUD is effective for up to 10 years. Insertion of an IUD requires dilation of the cervical opening, which may be uncomfortable or painful. Doctors must be certain that a woman is not pregnant and does not have a sexually transmitted disease at the time of insertion, and they must use proper sterilization procedures to avoid infection.	0.6 (copper); 1.5 (progesterone)	0.8 (copper); 2.0 (progesterone)	97% of women who use the IUD have a favorable opinion of it. Progesterone coating decreases menstrual blood loss and pain. The IUD permits spontaneity in sexual relations.	Today's IUDS are generally regarded as safe, although they may cause spotting, bleeding, and infection and are sometimes expelled. Some earlier IUDs—the Dalkon Shield in particular—were associated with serious cases of pelvic inflammatory disease.
Condom: The best **condom** is a thin sheath made of latex rubber or polyurethane[a] that fits over the penis and thus traps sperm. It also prevents contact between the man's and woman's skin and membranes, thus preventing the spread of sexually transmitted diseases. The condom should be put on *as soon as the penis is erect.* If the condom does not have a nipple tip, the man should leave a little extra space at the tip of the penis to catch the ejaculate. He should also hold the base of the condom as he withdraws after intercourse. Condoms can be used only once and should not be stored for long periods of time in a warm place (such as a wallet) or where they are exposed to light. For greatest effectiveness, condoms should be used with a spermicide.	Less than 1.0 with spermicide; 3.0 without spermicide	12.0	Highly effective in reducing the spread of sexually transmitted diseases, including AIDS. Putting on a condom takes less time than inserting any female device, and spermicide application is less messy.	Some men will not use condoms because they say they are allergic to rubber or that condoms reduce their sensitivity. Others complain about lack of spontaneity. These disadvantages are far outweighed by the high rate of effectiveness of this method in preventing both conception and disease.
Diaphragm: A **diaphragm** is a shallow rubber cup with a flexible rim that fits snugly between the pubic bone and the back of the cervix, sealing the entrance to the uterus and preventing the passage of sperm. The diaphragm must be fitted by a doctor or health-care worker, and refitting may be needed after pregnancy or	6.0	20.0	Offers some protection against gonorrhea and chlamydia. Is inexpensive, lasting for several years (but should be checked regularly for defects). Is associated with very few serious risks to fertility or general health.	Possible infection if left in for a prolonged period of time. Some couples feel that insertion (if not done until sex play has begun) takes away from the spontaneity of sexual activity.

	Pregnancies Per 100 Women in First Year of Continuous Use (cont.)			
Method	**With Perfect Use**	**With Typical Use**	**Advantages**	**Problems**
weight changes of 10 pounds or more. For maximum effectiveness, it must be used with a spermicide and inserted no more than 2 hours before intercourse (lest the spermicide dissipate). More spermicide should be added (with an applicator) if intercourse is repeated. A diaphragm should be left in for 6 to 8 hours after intercourse to make sure no live sperm remain.				
Female Condom: The **female condom** is a 7-inch-long polyurethane pouch that is closed at one end, which is surrounded by a flexible metal rim, and open at the other, which is surrounded by a similar ring. The inner ring fits over the cervix, like a diaphragm, thus closing the entrance to the uterus; the outer ring covers part of the vulva. At present, the Reality Female condom is the only one on the U.S. market.	5.0–6.0	21.0	Thinner than male condoms, feels softer than rubber, and transfers heat. Some feel that it simulates bare-skin intercourse.	Much more expensive than male condom and, like it, can be used only once.
Cervical Cap: The **cervical cap** is another barrier device designed to prevent passage of sperm from the vagina into the uterus. Made of latex rubber, it is smaller and more compact than a diaphragm and resembles a large rubber thimble. It should be used with spermicide, and it fits over the cervix by suction. It is especially useful for women whose vaginal muscles have been relaxed by childbearing. Insertion and removal of the cap are more difficult than for the diaphragm, but it is more comfortable and can be left in for 48 hours. Women should make sure after intercourse that the cap has not dislodged.	8.0–10.0[b]	18.0	May offer some protection against gonorrhea and chlamydia.	Possible infection with prolonged use due to long exposure to secretions trapped by the cap. Currently recommended only for women who have normal Pap smears lest it adversely affect cervical tissues.
Spermicides: Spermicides are chemicals that kill sperm (nonoxynol-9 or octoxinol-9). Used alone, spermicidal foams and suppositories are more effective than jellies and creams, but for maximum effectiveness any of these should be used with a physical barrier method (e.g., condom, diaphragm). Spermicides must be placed in the vagina shortly before intercourse begins. They lose their effectiveness over time, so new spermicide must be inserted before each time a woman has intercourse.	6.0	21.0	Spermicides reduce the risk of some STDs, including AIDS, by killing bacteria and viruses. They may also reduce the risk of cervical cancer.	Several studies have found that nonoxynol-9–containing spermicides increase the risk of urinary tract infection. Some complain that they irritate the vagina or penis, detract from oral-genital sex, and interfere with spontaneity.

Pregnancies Per 100 Women in First Year of Continuous Use (cont.)

Method	With Perfect Use	With Typical Use	Advantages	Problems
Withdrawal: In **withdrawal,** or *coitus interruptus*, the male withdraws his penis just before reaching orgasm and ejaculates outside his partner's vagina. However, because sperm are found in the fluid secreted by the Cowper's glands just before a man ejaculates, this method is highly unreliable.	4.0	18.0	The withdrawal method is better than no method at all.	Highly ineffective compared with other methods. Also, withdrawal may not be very physically or emotionally satisfying for either partner.
Fertility Awareness: Fertility awareness (*natural planning* or *rhythm*) is based on predicting ovulation and identifying "safe days" in a woman's menstrual cycle. A woman can become pregnant only in the first 24 hours or so after ovulation; after that, the egg is overly ripe, and a sperm can't fertilize it. There are three variations of this method. The **calendar method** uses a formula to calculate the unsafe period based on the length of a woman's menstrual cycles. According to the **basal body temperature method,** or **BBT,** a couple should abstain from having sexual intercourse from the end of menstruation until 2 to 4 days after a temperature rise is noted (a woman's basal body temperature rises 24 to 72 hours after ovulation by a few tenths of a degree Fahrenheit). The **Billings method** attempts to pinpoint the time of ovulation by noting changes in the consistency of a woman's cervical mucus, which changes from white (or cloudy) and sticky to clear and slippery (like that of an egg white) 1 or 2 days before ovulation. The *symptothermal* method combines the BBT and Billings methods.	9.0 for calendar method; 9.0 for BBT; 3.2 for Billings	20.0+ for calendar method; 20.0+ for BBT; 20.0+ for Billings	Rhythm methods are usually considered to be safer than other contraception techniques and are acceptable to most religious groups.	All rhythm methods may be frustrating because they involve fairly long periods of abstinence from sex. However, chemical testing kits that will pinpoint the time of ovulation accurately enough to serve as contraceptives may soon be available for home use. To be effective, a method will have to predict ovulation at least 4 days in advance. Current products available, which predict 12 to 36 hours in advance, are useful only for couples who *want* to conceive.

[a]Do *not* buy condoms made of lamb intestine. These "skins" are porous, and HIV and other viruses and bacteria may easily penetrate through the tiny holes.

[b]In those who have not yet given birth.

Appendix E

HIV, AIDS, and Other Sexually Transmitted Infections

Sexually transmitted infections (once called *venereal diseases,* after the Roman goddess of love, Venus) are diseases that are spread either exclusively through sexual contact, such as chlamydia, gonorrhea, herpes, and human papillomavirus infection (genital warts), or primarily through sexual activity but by other means as well, such as HIV, hepatitis B, syphilis, and trichomoniasis. The chart on the following pages provides information on the symptoms, causes, and means of transmission of these diseases and their current forms of treatment and progress if left untreated. (STDs, with an emphasis on HIV and AIDS, are also discussed in Chapter 7.) Although there are probably more than 20 known STDs, these eight have the highest incidence and the most serious effects.

In the United States, there have been major outbreaks of STDs from time to time. The present epidemic situation can probably be attributed to several factors. First, the discovery of penicillin and other antibiotics about the time of World War II may have given some people a false sense of confidence, leading them to engage in sexual intercourse when previously they might have feared to do so. Second, the new feeling of sexual freedom given people by the arrival of the Pill and other reliable means of birth control may have lessened their attention to disease prevention. And third, because recent drug treatments have slowed the progression of HIV and AIDS, many people have become lax about using condoms (see Chapter 7).

Appendix E is adapted from King (2002), Chapter 5, and Hock (2007), Chapter 8. Adapted by permission of Prentice Hall, Upper Saddle River, New Jersey.

Disease and Symptoms	Incidence[a]	Cause	How Transmitted	Disease if Untreated	Current Treatments
Acquired Immunodeficiency Syndrome (AIDS): HIV may remain dormant for a time and then cause such flulike symptoms as diarrhea, fever, and other infections that linger on. In full-blown AIDS, diseases such as lymphoma, Kaposi's sarcoma, and pneumocystis carinii pneumonia appear.	40,000+	*Human immunodeficiency virus,* resident in semen, vaginal fluids, and blood.	Intimate sexual contact (anal or vaginal intercourse, occasionally oral sex), exposure to infected blood (sharing of needles among HIV drug users), mother-to-fetus transmission through blood.	AIDS is terminal, but death can be postponed and the quality of life improved with treatment.	Four *antiretroviral drugs* slow progression of HIV infection: zidovudine (AZT), didanosine (DDI), zalcitabine (DDC), and stavudine (D4T). Since 1996, new drugs known as protease inhibitors, used in combination with AZT and DDI, have been found to slow or reduce HIV in the bloodstream.
Chlamydia: In both men and women, irritation and burning of the urethra and a thin, clear discharge. However, many people have no symptoms in the initial stage.	3 million	*Chlamydia trachomatis* bacterium.	Sexual activity, contact between mucous membranes of infected person and those of another person.	In men, infection of prostate and epididymis and possible sterility. In women, *pelvic inflammatory disease,* leading to increased risk of tubal pregnancy and sterility. Babies born to infected women may have eye, nose, or throat infections.	Tetracycline, doxycycline, or an erythromycin. Some doctors are using newer drugs such as azithromycin.
Gonorrhea: Inflammation of urethra or vulva; discharge from penis or vagina; irritation during urination. Some men and many women show no initial symptoms.	650,000	*Neisseria gonorrhoeae* bacterium (often called *gonococcus*).	Almost exclusively through intimate sexual contact.	In men, inflammation of prostate, seminal vesicles, bladder, and epididymis; severe pain and fever; possible sterility. In women, pelvic inflammatory disease with severe abdominal pain and fever; possible sterility. Baby born to infected mother may become blind.	Ceftriaxone followed by tetracycline or an erythromycin. The bacterium is becoming resistant to many drugs.
Hepatitis B: Poor appetite, diarrhea, fever, vomiting, pain, fatigue, jaundiced or yellow tinge of skin and eyes, dark urine.	45,000+	HBC virus.	By infected blood or body fluids such as saliva, semen, and vaginal secretions. About half of U.S. cases are contracted sexually (commonest through anal sex); also by sharing drug-use needles, by	Serious, sometimes fatal liver disease.	No cure. Interferon is effective in about a third of patients; 90% of patients recover, but up to 10% remain infected and become carriers, infecting others.

Disease and Symptoms	Incidence[a]	Cause	How Transmitted	Disease if Untreated	Current Treatments
			blood transfusions, and by blood exchange between mother and fetus.		
Herpes: *Prodrome stage*—tingling, burning, itching of skin that contacted virus; *vesicle stage*—fluid-filled blisters, flulike symptoms, painful urination; *crusting-over stage*—sores develop scales and form scabs.	45 million	Herpes simplex virus types I and II. It is thought to cause oral herpes, II to cause genital herpes, but the symptoms and outcome of both types are the same.	Direct contact between infected site on one person and skin of another. One can get genital herpes from contact with a blister on a partner's lip or oral herpes from a genital sore. People can spread their own herpes from one site to another (such as the eyes) by touch.	Herpes is a leading cause of infectious blindness today. *Herpes encephalitis* is a rare disease of the brain that is often fatal. *Herpes meningitis* (inflammation of membranes covering brain and spinal cord) is also possible. In women, risks cancer of cervix. A baby may be infected during childbirth, suffering neurological, eye, skin, and internal organ damage.	No cure. Once you have herpes, the potential for another attack is always there. Acyclovir relieves symptoms and speeds healing during primary attack. Researchers are working on a herpes vaccine.
Human Papilloma Virus Infection: (Also *genital warts*). Some people have symptoms that only a doctor can detect; others develop cauliflower-like warts that cause itching, irritation, or bleeding. In males, warts usually appear on penis, scrotum, or anus and sometimes in the urethra; in females, on the cervix and vaginal wall, vulva, and anus.	5 million	Human papilloma virus (HPV) causes nongenital warts and other skin conditions; two types of HPV cause genital warts.	By sexual intercourse or sometimes oral–genital sex; highly contagious, and most common STD caused by viruses in the United States.	In women, HPV infection increases risk of cervical cancer. Cancer of the penis occurs, but is rare. Recurrence of symptoms of HPV infection is common.	No cure. External treatment with podophyllin; large warts may be removed surgically, internal ones by laser surgery. Cervical HPV infection is treated with cryotherapy (freezing). Vaccine to prevent HPV infection may be developed in the near future.
Syphilis: *Primary stage* begins with ulcerlike sore called *chancre*, usually on penis, cervix, lips, tongue, or anus, that is highly infectious but usually painless. Sore may disappear, but spirochete enters bloodstream and infection spreads throughout the body. In *secondary stage*,	7,000	*Treponema pallidum* bacterium (called the *spirochete*).	Majority of cases are transmitted by sexual contact. Spirochete can also pass directly into the bloodstream through a cut or scrape; thus one can get syphilis by merely touching the sores of an infected person.	If initial chancre is ignored it will disappear, but the person remains infected. In the third, *latent stage*, there are usually no symptoms although in about a third of victims large ulcers develop on skin and bones. In all cases bacteria continue their attack on the body's internal organs,	Spirochetes are easily eradicated with antibiotics; penicillin is still the most effective, although there are some indications that the bacterium may be becoming resistant to this agent.

Disease and Symptoms	Incidence[a]	Cause	How Transmitted	Disease if Untreated	Current Treatments
an itchless, painless rash spreads over the body; sores appear in moist areas around the genitals; other flu- and cold-like symptoms.				particularly the heart, blood vessels, and brain and spinal cord. Deafness, paralysis, insanity, and death often result.	
Trichomoniasis: In women a heavy vaginal discharge with a foul odor accompanied by severe vaginal itching.	5 million	One-celled protozoan, *Trichomonas vaginalis.*	Majority of cases are transmitted by sexual intercourse, but disease can be contracted from a wet toilet seat or by sharing towels (protozoan survives in urine and tap water for hours to days).	Can lead to adhesions in the fallopian tubes and sterility.	Metronidazole is the treatment of choice. However, this drug is under study as a possible carcinogen.

[a]Estimated new cases per year in the United States; based on 2004 data.

Appendix F

Premarital and Nonmarital Agreements

A premarital (also called a prenuptial or antenuptial) agreement is a contract between potential spouses that spells out the rights and expectations of the partners and determines how their property will be divided if they divorce. It specifies what is "yours, mine, and ours."

Most lawyers agree that never-before-married young people with few assets don't need a premarital agreement, but such contracts are recommended for couples marrying for the first time later in life, especially if they have pursued careers and have accumulated assets or remarry. Although some lawyers think that preparing a premarital agreement creates distrust and may damage the marriage, many others believe such pacts help ensure a successful marriage because both partners (and their children, if any) know what to expect in case there is a divorce or death.

I begin with some of the standard issues, especially property rights, covered by legal contracts and lawyers (see, for example, Winer and Becker, 1993; Dorf et al., 1996). I also include some items that would not be legally enforceable but that might be useful for couples who are planning to marry, as well as those living together, that "how-to" books written by lawyers often omit.

Premarital Property

- Do the partners plan to keep or dispose of premarital property (such as houses and land)?

- If the premarital property is kept or sold, how will the real estate profits be divided between the partners?

- If the premarital property increases in value over time, will both partners share the income that is generated when the property is sold?

Assets, Liabilities, and Income

- What is the income of both partners? What about savings, stocks, and other assets?

- Have both partners seen each other's tax returns?

- Who will be responsible for filing tax returns? Who will pay the taxes? How will refunds be distributed?

- Who is responsible for paying a partner's debts (such as college loans, credit card balances, and bank loans)?

- Should both partners hold all property jointly? Or should income, rents, profits, interest, dividends, stock splits, bank accounts, and other assets also be held separately by each partner?

Business or Investment Partnerships

- Should a spouse be a business partner, especially in a family-owned business?

- In a privately held corporation, should a spouse inherit stock or receive stock as part of a divorce settlement?

Disposition of Marital Property

- In case of death or divorce, will marital property go to the partner or the deceased partner's children?

- Will the property be sold? If so, how will the partners share the profits?

- What happens to such personal property as clothing, jewelry, collections (art, coins, stamps), recreation or sports equipment, expensive tools, or home maintenance equipment (such as lawn tractors)?

Life Insurance

- Do both partners have life insurance?

- What is the life insurance coverage? How much does each partner pay?

- Who is the beneficiary of the life insurance?

- Do both partners have documentation from the insurance company about the beneficiary?

Spousal Maintenance (Alimony)

- Will either partner receive alimony in case of divorce? If so, how much?

- Will alimony be paid in cash or through the disposition of property?

- Will alimony payments increase to keep up with inflation?

- How much should a spouse (typically a wife) be compensated if she has sacrificed her own career to support her husband's career or business?

Child Custody and Support

- If there is a divorce, who will have custody of the children?

- Will the custody be joint, split, or sole (see Chapter 15)?

- Who will be responsible for child support?

- What percentage of one's earnings is "reasonable" or "fair" for child support?

- Would both partners have the right to move to another state or country?

- Is either partner responsible for supporting children who attend college or trade schools after age 18?

Trusts and Wills

- If there are trust funds (such as leaving money or property to biological children), are these funds consistent with the terms of the will?

- Have all assets been listed in the will?

- Does the will list the beneficiaries of stock, bonds, and other income?

- Does the surviving partner have a right to live in the home even though she or he doesn't inherit the property?

- Does the surviving spouse have a right to choose a cemetery and burial decisions for the deceased partner?

- If the surviving spouse doesn't inherit the property, is there a monthly or annual allowance from the estate?

Although "lifestyle clauses" are not legally enforceable, they give partners a tool to disclose, examine, and specify expectations about their own and their partner's behavior. If people realize they cannot resolve major disagreements, they are preventing a future divorce by not getting married. Here are some topics that might be included in an informal nonmarital or premarital agreement:

Sex and Contraception

- What birth control methods will be used? Are both partners willing to abort an unwanted fetus?

- How does each partner define "sex" (sexual intercourse, cuddling, fondling)?

- How often do partners expect to have sexual intercourse?

- Are there any sexual acts that one partner considers demeaning or offensive?

- What happens if a partner loses interest in sexual intercourse?

- How serious is infidelity? How does each partner define "infidelity"?

Having and Raising Children

- Do both partners want children? If so, how many and at what intervals?

- Is attending religious services important? If so, how often? Should current or future children have a religious upbringing?

- If the woman keeps her surname, will the children have the father's or the mother's surname?

- Who is responsible for disciplining children? Does discipline include spanking, slapping, or hitting?

- Who will do the housework? What chores will each person perform?

Relatives and Friends

- How important is it to maintain contact with one's parents, siblings, or other relatives? If they live far away, is there a limit on long-distance phone calls?

- Which partner's parents should the couple visit, especially during the holidays?

- Is it important to celebrate relatives' birthdays, anniversaries, and other occasions? If so, who buys the cards and presents? Should there be a limit on gift-giving for births, birthdays, graduations, weddings, and other milestones?

- Can parents or other relatives live in the couple's home? Under what conditions and for how long?

- Who is responsible for caretaking an elderly or disabled parent or other relative?

- How important is socializing with friends? Is it acceptable for each partner to socialize with friends on her or his own? Can partners discuss their personal problems with friends or family members?

Financial Issues

- Should there be joint or separate savings and checking accounts? A combination?

- Can a partner do anything she or he wants with "his" or "her" separate checking or savings account?

- Who is responsible for paying the monthly bills?

- Who is responsible for preparing state and federal taxes?

- Do both partners agree that credit card debts are acceptable? If so, is there a limit on the amount of debt?

- Who decides whether and how much life insurance to buy? Who will be the beneficiaries?

- Who decides whether and when to invest in the stock market?

- If partners disagree about financial issues, how will the conflict be resolved?

Glossary

abortion The artificially induced or natural expulsion of an embryo or fetus from the uterus.

absolute poverty Not having enough money to afford the most basic necessities of life such as food, clothing, or shelter.

acculturation The process of adapting to the language, values, beliefs, roles, and other characteristics of the host culture.

acquaintance rape Unwanted, forced sexual intercourse, often in a social context such as a party; the rapist may be a neighbor, friend of the family, co-worker, or a person the victim has just met.

acquired immunodeficiency syndrome (AIDS) A degenerative disease caused by a virus that attacks the body's immune system and makes it susceptible to a number of diseases such as pneumonia and cancer.

agape Love that is altruistic, self-sacrificing, and directed toward all humankind.

ageism Discrimination against people on the basis of age, particularly against those who are old.

alimony Monetary payments made by one ex-spouse to the other after a divorce to support the latter's basic needs for survival.

Alzheimer's disease A progressive, degenerative disorder that attacks the brain and impairs memory, thinking, and behavior.

amniocentesis A procedure performed in the twentieth week of pregnancy, in which a sample of the amniotic fluid is withdrawn by a needle inserted into the abdomen; the fluid is analyzed for possible genetic disorders and biochemical abnormalities in the fetus.

androgyny A blend of culturally defined male and female characteristics.

anorexia nervosa A dangerous eating disorder characterized by fear of obesity, together with a distorted body image and the conviction that one is "fat," significant weight loss, and an absolute refusal to maintain weight within the normal limits for one's age and height.

artificial insemination An assisted reproductive technique in which male semen is introduced artificially into the vagina or uterus about the time of ovulation.

asexual Lacking any interest or desire for sex.

assimilation The conformity of ethnic group members to the culture of the dominant group, including intermarriage.

assisted reproductive technology (ART) A general term that includes all treatments and procedures that involve the handling of human eggs and sperm to produce a pregnancy.

attachment theory The notion that a warm, secure, and loving relationship is essential to human emotional growth and development.

authoritarian style An approach to parenting that is demanding, controlling, and punitive; emphasizes respect for authority, work, order, and traditional family structure; often uses punitive, forceful measures to control behavior.

authoritative style An approach to parenting that is demanding and controlling but supportive and responsive; encourages autonomy and self-reliance; generally uses positive rein-

forcement instead of punitive, repressive discipline.

autoeroticism Refers to arousal of sexual feeling without an external stimulus.

baby boomer A person born in the post–World War II generation between 1946 and 1964.

battered woman syndrome A condition in which women who have experienced many years of physical abuse come to feel incapable of making any satisfactory change in their way of life; recently used as a defense in cases in which such women have murdered their abusive husbands.

bereavement The period of recovery after the death of someone to whom we feel close.

bigamy The act of marrying one person while still legally married to another.

birth rate The number of live births per 1,000 population.

bisexual A person who is sexually attracted to members of both sexes.

boomerang generation Young adults who move back into their parents' homes after living independently for a while.

bulimia An eating disorder characterized by a cyclical pattern of eating binges followed by self-induced vomiting, fasting, excessive exercise, or the use of diuretics or laxatives.

bundling A courting custom in American colonial times in which a young man and woman, both fully dressed, spent the night in bed together, separated by a wooden board.

caregiver A person, paid or unpaid, who attends to the needs of someone who is sick or disabled.

child abduction Taking or keeping of a child by a family member in violation of a custody order, a decree, or other legitimate custodial right.

child abuse According to Public Law 93-237, the physical or mental injury, sexual abuse, negligent treatment, or maltreatment of a child under the age of 18 by a person responsible for the child's welfare.

child maltreatment A wide range of behaviors that place the child at serious risk, including physical abuse, sexual abuse, neglect, and emotional mistreatment.

child support Monetary payments by the non-custodial parent to the parent who has custody of children to help pay the expenses of raising the children.

chlamydia A sexually transmitted bacterial infection that can contribute to infertility by triggering pelvic inflammatory disease. The symptoms of chlamydia often go unnoticed.

chorionic villi sampling A procedure in which some of the villi, or protrusions, of the membrane that surrounds the embryo are removed by a catheter through the vagina and analyzed for abnormalities in the fetus.

clinical research The study of individuals or small groups of people who seek help for physical and/or social problems from mental health professionals.

closed adoption All the information is confidential and the triad of birth parents, adoptive parents, and children has no contact nor exchange any identifying information.

co-custody Parents share physical and legal custody of their children equally.

cognitive development theory A theory positing that children learn by interacting with their environment and, using the processes of thinking, understanding, and reasoning, by interpreting and applying the information they gather.

cohabitation A living arrangement in which two people who are not related and not married share living quarters and usually have a sexual relationship.

common-law marriage A nonceremonial form of marriage, established by cohabitation and/or evidence of consummation (sexual intercourse).

commuter marriage A marriage in which partners live and work in separate geographic areas and get together intermittently.

compadrazgo A Mexican American family system in which close family friends are formally designated as godparents of a newborn, participate in the child's important rites of passage, and maintain continuing strong ties with their godchild.

comparable worth A concept that calls for equal pay for men and women who are doing work that involves comparable skill, effort, responsibility, and work conditions.

conflict-habituated marriage A marriage in which the partners fight both verbally and physically but do not believe that fighting is a reason for divorce.

conflict theory A macro-level sociological theory that examines the ways in which groups disagree and struggle over power and compete for scarce resources and that views conflict and its consequences as natural, inevitable, and often desirable.

contraception The prevention of pregnancy by behavioral, mechanical, or chemical means.

corporate welfare An array of direct subsidies, tax breaks, and indirect assistance that the government has created for the special benefit of businesses.

cultural pluralism Maintaining aspects of immigrants' original cultures while living peacefully with the host culture.

cunnilingus Oral stimulation of a woman's genitals.

custody A court-mandated ruling as to which parent will have the primary responsibility for the welfare and upbringing of a child; the custodial parent cares for the child in her or his home, whereas the non-custodial parent may have specified visitation rights. *See also* joint custody.

daddy penalty A phenomenon in which men whose wives are employed outside the home are paid lower salaries than their counterparts whose wives are full-time homemakers.

date rape Unwanted, forced sexual intercourse in the context of a dating situation; victim and perpetrator may be on a first date or in a long-term dating relationship.

dating The process of meeting people socially for possible mate selection.

dating cohabitation A living arrangement into which people "drift" gradually.

dementia The loss of mental abilities that most commonly occurs late in life.

depression A mental disorder characterized by pervasive sadness and other negative emotions that interfere with the ability to work, study, sleep, eat, and enjoy once pleasurable activities.

developmental tasks Specific role expectations and responsibilities that must be fulfilled as people move through the family life cycle.

devitalized marriage A marriage in which the partners are initially in love, spend time together, and have a satisfying sex life but in time find they are staying together out of duty; because they see no alternatives, they do not consider divorce.

DEWKS (dual-employed with kids) A family in which both parents are employed full time outside the home.

discouraged worker An unemployed person who wants to work but who has recently given up the search for a position because of the belief that the job hunt is futile.

discretionary income Money remaining after essentials, such as rent or mortgage, food, utilities, and transportation costs, have been paid and that people can then spend as they please.

discrimination An *act* that treats people unequally or unfairly.

divorce The legal and formal dissolution of a marriage.

divorce mediation The technique and practice in which a trained arbitrator helps a divorcing couple come to an agreement and resolve such issues as support, child custody, and the division of property.

dowry The money, goods, or property a woman in traditional societies brings to a marriage.

dual-career couple Both partners work in professional or managerial positions.

dual-earner couple Both partners work outside the home.

ecological theory A theoretical perspective that examines the interrelationship between individuals' and family roles and environmental settings.

elder abuse Physical abuse, negligence, financial exploitation, psychological abuse, deprivation of necessities like food and heat, isolation from friends and relatives, and failure to administer needed medications to people age 65 or older.

endogamy A cultural rule requiring that people marry and/or have sexual relations only within their own particular group.

endometriosis A condition in which tissue spreads outside the womb and attaches itself to other pelvic organs, such as the ovaries or the fallopian tubes.

engagement The formalization of a couple's decision to marry and the last step in the courtship process.

equity theory A theoretical perspective which proposes that an intimate relationship is satisfying and stable if both people see it as equitable and mutually beneficial.

eros Love based on beauty and physical attractiveness.

ethnic group A set of people who identify with a common national origin or cultural heritage.

evaluation research Research that assesses the effectiveness of social programs in both the public and private sectors.

exogamy A cultural rule requiring that people marry outside of their particular group.

experiment A data collection method where the researcher investigates cause-and-effect relationships under strictly controlled conditions.

expressive role In structural-functional theory, the supportive and nurturing role of the wife or mother who must sustain and support the husband/father.

extended family A family in which two or more generations live together or in close proximity.

familism The notion that, within a given family, family relationships take precedence over the concerns of individual family members.

family Traditionally defined as a unit made up of two or more people who are related by blood, marriage, or adoption and who live together and form an economic unit. Defined in this book as an intimate environment in which (1) two or more people live together in a committed relationship; (2) the members see their identity as importantly attached to the group; and (3) the group shares close emotional ties and functions.

family life course development theory A micro-level theory that examines the changes that families experience over the lifespan.

family life cycle A series of stages, each focusing on a different set of events, that the family goes through from the early days of a marriage to the death of one or both partners.

family of orientation The family into which a person is born.

family of procreation The family a person forms by marrying and having or adopting children.

family policy The measures taken by governmental bodies to achieve specific objectives relating to the family's well-being.

family systems theory A theoretical perspective that examines the daily functioning and interactions of family members with each other and the larger society.

father–stepmother family A family in which all the children are biological children of the father and stepchildren of the mother.

fellatio Oral stimulation of a man's penis.

feminist theories Theoretical perspectives that analyze socially constructed expectations based on variables such as gender roles, social class, race, ethnicity, and sexual orientation.

feminization of poverty The growing proportion of women and their children who are poor.

fertility The number of live births in a population.

fertility drugs Drugs that stimulate ovaries to produce eggs.

fertility rate The number of births per year per 1,000 women of childbearing age (15 to 44).

fetal alcohol syndrome (FAS) Physical deformities and/or mental retardation in an infant caused by the mother's excessive use of alcohol during pregnancy.

fictive kin Nonrelatives who are accepted as part of a family.

field research A data collection method where researchers collect information by systematically observing people in their natural surroundings.

filter theory The theory that people in search of potential mates go through a process whereby they filter out eligible partners according to certain criteria and thus reduce the pool of eligibles to a relatively small number of candidates.

foster home A home in which a family raises a child or children who are not their own for a

period of time but does not formally adopt them.

gamete intrafallopian transfer (GIFT) A variation of in vitro fertilization in which eggs and sperm are artificially inserted into a woman's fallopian tube.

gender The socially learned attitudes and behaviors that characterize a person of one sex or the other; based on differing social and cultural expectations of the sexes.

gender identity An individual's emotional and intellectual awareness of being either male or female.

gender roles Distinctive patterns of attitudes, behaviors, and activities that society prescribes for females and males.

gender-role stereotype The belief and expectation that women and men each display rigid, traditional gender-role characteristics.

gender schema theory The theory that children develop information-processing categories that organize and guide their perceptions of cultural stimuli to develop a gender identity.

genogram A diagram of the biological relationships among family members.

gerontologist A scientist who studies the biological, psychological, and social aspects of aging.

grief The emotional response to loss.

half-sibling A brother or sister with whom one shares only one biological parent.

heterogamy Dating or marrying someone from a social, racial, ethnic, religious, or age group different from one's own.

heterosexism The belief that heterosexuality is superior to and more "natural" than homosexuality.

heterosexual A person who is sexually attracted to members of the opposite sex.

homogamy Dating or marrying someone who possesses similar social characteristics such as ethnicity, race, religion, age, and social class.

homophobia Fear and hatred of homosexuality.

homosexual A person who is sexually attracted to persons of the same sex.

hormones Chemical substances secreted into the bloodstream by glands of the endocrine system.

hospice A place for the care of the dying that stresses the relief of pain, companionship to dying patients, and making such patients comfortable.

human immunodeficiency virus (HIV) The virus that causes AIDS.

hypergamy Dating or marrying someone who is in a higher socioeconomic group than one's own.

hypogamy Dating or marrying someone who is in a lower socioeconomic group than one's own.

identity bargaining A stage in the evolution of a marriage in which partners readjust their idealized expectations to the realities of their life together.

incest Sexual intercourse between family members who are closely related. *See also* incest taboo.

incest taboo Cultural norms and laws that forbid sexual intercourse between close blood relatives, such as brother and sister, father and daughter, or mother and son.

income The amount of money a person receives, usually through wages or salaries, but can also include rents, interest on savings accounts, dividends on stock, or the proceeds from a business.

infant mortality rate The number of babies under one year of age who die per 1,000 live births in a given year.

infertility The inability to conceive a baby after 12 months of unprotected sex.

instrumental role In structural-functional theory, the "breadwinner" role of the husband or father, who must be hardworking, tough, and competitive.

intergenerational ambivalence Contradictions in relationships between parents and adult offspring that arise both from structured kinship roles and personal emotions.

intergenerational transmission of divorce The likelihood of divorce in later generations because an earlier generation passed down many of its problems.

intracytoplasmic sperm injection (ICSD) A procedure that involves injecting sperm directly into an egg in a laboratory dish to produce a pregnancy.

intrinsic marriage A marriage that is inherently rewarding.

in vitro fertilization (IVF) An assisted reproduction technique in which eggs are surgically removed from a woman's ovaries, fertilized with sperm from the woman's husband or a donor, and then the resulting embryos are transferred into the woman's uterus.

joint stepfamily A family in which at least one child is a biological child of both parents, at least one child is the biological child of one parent and the stepchild of the other parent, and no other "type" of child is present.

joint custody A custody arrangement in which the children divide their time between both parents; in *joint legal custody*, parents share decision making about the children's upbringing; in *joint physical custody*, the children live alternately and for specified periods in each parent's home.

kinship system A network of people who are related by marriage, blood, or adoption.

latchkey kids Children who return after school to an empty home and are alone and unsupervised until their parents or another adult arrives.

latent functions Functions that are not recognized or intended; present but not immediately visible.

later-life family A family that is beyond the years of child rearing and has launched the children or a childless family beginning to plan for retirement.

living will A legal document in which a person specifies what, if any, life-support measures she or he wishes to be provided with in the case of serious illness and if or when such measures should be discontinued.

ludus Love that is carefree and casual, "fun and games."

machismo A concept of masculinity that stresses such attributes as dominance, assertiveness, pride, and sexual prowess.

macro-level perspective A sociological perspective that focuses on large-scale patterns that characterize society as a whole.

male climacteric A "change of life" in men proposed by some as analogous to female menopause. More psychological than physiological, such a change affects only a small percentage of men and is not characterized by the cessation of reproductive capacity.

mania Love that is obsessive, jealous, and possessive.

manifest functions Functions that are recognized or intended and present in a clearly evident way.

marital burnout The gradual deterioration of love and, ultimately, the loss of an emotional attachment between marital partners.

marital rape An abusive act in which a husband forces his wife to engage in unwanted sexual intercourse.

marital roles The specific ways that people define their behavior and structure their time within the context of marriage.

marriage A socially approved mating relationship.

marriage market A courtship process in which prospective spouses compare the assets and liabilities of eligible partners and choose the best available mate.

marriage squeeze The oversupply of female baby boomers, born between 1945 and 1964, in relation to eligible males.

married singles Married partners who continue to live together, may be good friends, and may be sexually intimate but who, in many ways, have drifted apart.

masturbation Sexual self-pleasuring that involves some form of direct physical stimulation.

matriarchy A familial relationship in which the authority is held by the oldest female, usually the mother. Women control cultural, political, and economic resources and, consequently, have power over men.

matrilineal A kinship system in which children trace their family descent through their mother's line and property is passed on to female heirs.

menopause The cessation of the menstrual cycle.

micro-level perspective A sociological perspective that focuses on small-scale patterns of social interaction in specific settings.

minority group A group of people who may be treated differently or unequally because of their physical or cultural characteristics, such as gender, sexual orientation, religion, or skin color.

mommy track A slower or even a side track in business along which women managers who wish to combine both career and child rearing are expected to move.

monogamy The practice of having only one husband or wife.

mother–stepfather family A family in which all the children are biological children of the mother and stepchildren of the father.

mourning The customary outward expression of grief over the loss of a loved one.

no-fault divorce A divorce process in which neither partner need establish the guilt or wrongdoing of the other.

norm A culturally defined rule for behavior.

nuclear family A family made up of a wife, a husband, and their biological or adopted children.

older support ratio The number of people aged 65 and over per 100 people aged 20 to 64.

open adoption An adoption process that encourages the sharing of information and contact between biological and adoptive parents during the adoption process and throughout the adopted child's life.

parenting style A general approach to interacting with and disciplining children.

passive-congenial marriage A marriage in which partners with minimal emotional investment and expectations maintain independent spheres of interests and activities and derive satisfaction from relationships with others rather than from each other.

patriarchy A society or familial relationship in which the positions of power and authority—political, economic, legal, religious, educational, military, and domestic—are generally held by men.

patrilineal A kinship system in which children trace their family descent through their father's line and property is passed on to male heirs.

pelvic inflammatory disease (PID) An infection of the uterus that spreads to the fallopian tubes, ovaries, and surrounding tissues and produces scarring that blocks the fallopian tubes.

permissive style An approach to parenting that is highly responsive and warm, not demanding but sometimes manipulative; this approach encourages freedom of expression, autonomy, and internal control.

polygamy A form of marriage in which one woman or one man may have several spouses.

POSSLQs "Persons of the opposite sex sharing living quarters"; a U.S. Census Bureau household category.

postpartum depression Depression experienced by some women soon after childbirth; thought to be at least partially caused by chemical imbalances.

poverty line The minimum income level determined by the federal government to be necessary for individuals' and families' basic subsistence.

power The ability to impose one's will on others.

pragma Love that is rational and based on practical considerations, such as compatibility and perceived benefits.

prejudice An *attitude* that prejudges people, usually in a negative way.

preimplantation genetic diagnosis (PGD) A recent assisted reproductive technology that enables physicians to identify genetic diseases in the embryo, prior to implantation, before the pregnancy is established.

premarital cohabitation A living arrangement in which a couple tests its relationship before making a final commitment to get married.

primary group Important people, such as family members and close friends, characterized by close, long-lasting, intimate, and face-to-face interaction.

propinquity Geographic closeness.

qualitative research A data-collection process where researchers rely on observation and interviews and report their findings from the respondent's point of view.

quantitative research A data-collection process where researchers assign numbers to qualitative (nonnumeric) observations by counting and measuring attitudes or behavior.

racial group A category of people who share physical characteristics, such as skin color, that members of a society consider socially important.

racial-ethnic group A group of people with distinctive racial and cultural characteristics.

racial socialization A process where parents teach their children to negotiate race-related barriers and experiences in a racially stratified society and to take pride in their ancestry.

racism A belief that people of one race are superior or inferior to others.

relative income A person's earning potential compared to his or her desired standard of living.

relative poverty Not having enough money to maintain an average standard of living.

role Pattern of behavior attached to a particular status or position in society.

role conflict Frustration and uncertainty experienced by a person who is confronted with incompatible role requirements or expectations.

role overload A feeling of being overwhelmed by multiple commitments and not having enough time for oneself.

role strain Conflicts that someone feels *within* a role.

sandwich generation Midlife men and women who feel caught between the need to care for both their own children and their aging parents.

secondary analysis Analysis of data that have been collected by other researchers.

secondary group Groups characterized by relatively impersonal and short-term relationships and where people work together on common tasks or activities.

self-disclosure Open communication in which one person offers his or her honest thoughts and feelings to another person in the hope that truly open communication will follow.

semi-open adoption Sometimes refereed to as a *mediated adoption*, there is communication between the adoptive parents, birth parents, and adopted children, but through a third party (e.g., an agency caseworker or attorney) rather than directly.

separation A temporary period of living apart required by most states before a divorce is granted.

serial cohabitation Living with different sexual partners over time.

serial monogamy Marrying several people, one at a time; that is, marrying, divorcing, remarrying, divorcing again, and so on.

sex The biological—chromosomal, anatomical, hormonal, and other physical and physiological—characteristics with which we are born and that determine whether we are male or female.

sex ratio The proportion of men to women in a country or group.

sexual harassment Any unwelcome sexual advance, request for sexual favors, or other conduct of a sexual nature that makes a person uncomfortable and interferes with her or his work.

sexual orientation A preference for sexual partners of the same sex (homosexual), of the opposite sex (heterosexual), or of either sex (bisexual).

sexual response A person's physiological reaction to sexual stimulation.

sexually transmitted diseases (STDs) Diseases that are spread by contact with body parts or fluids that harbor what are usually bacterial or viral microorganisms.

sexually transmitted infections (STIs) Diseases that are spread by contact, either sexual or nonsexual, with body parts or fluids that harbor specific microorganisms (generally bacterial or viral). (Corresponds to but has recently replaced another frequently used term, **sexually transmitted diseases**, or STDs.)

sexual script Norms that specify what is acceptable and what is unacceptable sexual activity, identify eligible sexual partners, and define the boundaries of sexual behavior in time and place.

significant others People who play an important emotional role in a person's socialization.

social exchange theory A micro-level theory that proposes that the interaction between two or more people is based on the efforts of each to maximize rewards and minimize costs.

social integration The social bonds that people have with others and the community at large.

socialization The process of acquiring the language, accumulated knowledge, attitudes, beliefs, and values of one's society and culture and learning the social and interpersonal skills needed to function effectively in society.

social class A category of people who have a similar standing or rank based on wealth, education, power, prestige, and other valued resources.

social learning theory The notion that people learn attitudes and behaviors through interaction with the environment; learning may occur through reward and punishment or through imitation or role modeling.

Social Security A public retirement pension system administered by the federal government.

socioeconomic status (SES) An overall rank of people's positions based on income, education, and occupation.

sole custody A type of custody in which one parent has exclusive responsibility for raising a child and the other parent has specified visitation rights.

split custody A custody arrangement in which children are divided between the parents, usually female children going to the mother, males to the father.

stepfamily A household in which two adults are biological or adaptive parents (heterosexual, gay, or lesbian), with a child from a prior relationship, who elect to marry or to cohabit.

steroid A synthetic hormone, most often testosterone, that is taken to increase one's appearance, muscle mass, and strength.

storge Love that is slow-burning, peaceful, and affectionate.

structural-functional theory A macro-level theoretical perspective that examines the relationship between the family and the larger society as well as the internal relationships among family members.

substitute marriage A long-term commitment between two people without a legal marriage.

surrogacy An assisted reproduction technique in which a woman carries a pregnancy to term and serves as a substitute for a woman who cannot bear children. The substitute is either artificially inseminated by the husband of an infertile woman or is implanted with the woman's egg after it has been fertilized by the husband's sperm in vitro.

surveys Data-collection methods that systematically collect information from respondents either by a mailed or self-administered questionnaire or by a face-to-face or telephone interview.

symbolic interaction theory A micro-level theory that views everyday human interaction as governed by the symbolic communication of knowledge, ideas, beliefs, and attitudes.

theory A set of logically related statements that explain why a phenomenon occurs.

total fertility rate (TFR) The average number of children per woman in her lifetime.

total marriage A marriage in which the partners participate in each other's lives at all levels and have few areas of tension or unresolved hostility.

trailing spouse A spouse who resigns from a position to search for another job in the location where her or his spouse has accepted a job.

trial marriage People live together to find out what marriage might be like, with each other or someone else.

two-person single career An arrangement in which one spouse participates in the other's career behind the scenes without pay or direct recognition.

underemployed worker A person who holds part-time jobs but would rather work full time or who accepts jobs below his or her level of expertise.

uninvolved style A parenting approach in which parents are neither supportive nor demanding because they are indifferent.

utilitarian marriage A marriage based on convenience.

vital marriage A marriage in which spouses maintain a close relationship, resolve conflicts quickly through compromise, and often make sacrifices for each other.

wage gap The income difference between women and men (sometimes called the *gender wage gap*).

wealth The money and economic assets that a person or family owns, including property and income.

welfare Government aid to those who can't support themselves, generally because they are poor or unemployed.

working poor People who spend at least 27 weeks in the labor force (working or looking for work) but whose family or personal income falls below the official poverty level.

zygote intrafallopian transfer (ZIFT) A variation of in vitro fertilization in which a woman's eggs are fertilized by her husband's or a donor's sperm in vitro and are then transferred to the fallopian tube.

References

AARP. 2005. *Sexuality at midlife and beyond: 2004 update of attitudes and behaviors.* http://assets.aarp.org/rgcenter/general/2004_sexuality.pdf (accessed September 10, 2006).

A first, N.H. Episcopalians elect openly gay bishop as new leader 2003. *Baltimore Sun,* June 8, 10A.

ABALOS, D. T. 1993. *The Latino family and the politics of transformation.* Westport, CT: Praeger.

ABEL, E. R. 1991. *Who cares for the elderly? Public policy and the experiences of adult daughters.* Philadelphia: Temple University Press.

ABMA, J. C., G. M. MARTINEZ, W. D. MOSHER, AND B. S. DAWSON. 2004. Teenagers in the United States: Sexual activity, contraceptive use, and childbearing, 2002. *Vital and Health Statistics* (Series 23, No. 24). Hyattsville, MD: National Center for Health Statistics.

ABMA, J. C., G. M. MARTINEZ, W. D. MOSHER, AND B. S. DAWSON. 2004. Teenagers in the United States: Sexual activity, contraceptive use, and childbearing, 2002. National Center for Health Statistics, *Vital Health Statistics* 23 (24). www.cdc.gov/nchs/data/series/sr_23/sr23_024.pdf (accessed January 15, 2006).

ABMA, J., A. CHANDRA, W. MOSHER, L. PETERSON, AND L. PICCINO. 1997. *Fertility, family planning, and women's health: New data from the 1995 National Survey of Family Growth.* Washington, DC: National Center for Health Statistics. *Vital Health Statistics* 23 (19).

ABRAHAM, M. 2000. *Speaking the unspeakable: Marital violence among South Asian immigrants in the United States.* New Brunswick, NJ: Rutgers University Press.

ABRAHAMS, G., AND S. AHLBRAND. 2002. *Boy v. girl? How gender shapes who we are, what we want, and how we get along.* Minneapolis: Free Spirit.

ABRAMSON, A., AND M. SILVERSTEIN. 2006. *Images of aging in America 2004.* Washington, DC: AARP and the University of Southern California.

ABU-LABAN, S. M., AND B. ABU-LABAN. 1999. Teens between: The public and private spheres of Arab-Canadian adolescents. In *Arabs in America: Building a new future,* eds. M. W. Suleiman, 113–28. Philadelphia: Temple University Press.

ABUDABBEH, N. 1996. Arab families. In *Ethnicity and family therapy,* 2nd ed., ed. M. McGoldrick, J Giordano, and J. K. Pearce, 333–46. New York: Guilford.

Abuse spreads HIV among Zambian girls. 2003. BBC, Jan. 28. http://news.bbc.co.uk (accessed Feb. 4, 2003).

ACKERMAN, D. 1994. *A natural history of love.* New York: Random House.

ACOCK, A. C., AND D. H. DEMO. 1994. *Family diversity and well-being.* Thousand Oaks, CA: Sage.

ACS, G., AND A. NICHOLS. 2005. Working to make ends meet: Understanding the income and expenses of America's low-income families. The Urban Institute, September 20, www.urban.org (accessed May 10, 2006).

ACS, G., AND P. LOPREST. 2005. Who are low-income working families? The Urban Institute, September 20, www.urban.org (accessed October 25, 2006).

ACUNA, R. 1988. *Occupied America: A history of Chicanos,* 3rd ed. New York: Harper & Row.

ADAM, M. B., J. K. MCGUIRE, M. WALSH, J. BASTA, AND C. LECROY. 2005. Acculturation as a predictor of the onset of sexual intercourse among Hispanic and white teens. *Archives of Pediatrics & Adolescent Medicine* 159 (March): 261–65.

ADAMS, B. 1980. *The family.* Chicago: Rand McNally.

ADAMS, B. N. 2004. Families and family study in international perspective. *Journal of Marriage and Family* 66 (December): 1076–88.

ADAMS, B. N., AND R. A. SYDIE. 2002. *Contemporary sociological theory.* Thousand Oaks, CA: Pine Forge.

ADAMS, J. A., K. HARPER, S. KNUDSON, AND J. REVILLA. 1994. Examination findings in legally confirmed child sexual abuse: It's normal to be normal. *Pediatrics* 94 (Sep.): 310–17.

ADAMS, W. L. 2005. More than adoption. *Newsweek,* June 20, 54.

ADIMORA, A., AND V. SCHOENBACH. 2005. Social context, sexual networks, and racial disparities in rates of sexually transmitted infections. *Journal of Infectious Diseases* 191, S115–S122.

ADLER, J. 1996. Building a better dad. *Newsweek,* June 17, 58–64.

ADLER, S. M. 2003. Asian-American families. In *International encyclopedia of marriage and family,* 2nd ed., Vol. 2, ed. J. J. Ponzetti, Jr., 82–91. New York: Macmillan.

AHITUV, A., AND R. LERMAN. 2004. Job turnover, wage rates, and marital stability: How are they related? The Urban Institute, November www.urban.org (accessed July 5, 2006).

AHRONS, C. 1994. *The good divorce: Keeping your family together when your marriage comes apart.* New York: HarperCollins.

AHRONS, C. 2004. *We're still family.* New York: HarperCollins.

AHRONS, C. R., AND R. H. RODGERS. 1987. *Divorced families: A multidisciplinary developmental view.* New York: Norton.

AHUVIA, A. C., AND M. B. ADELMAN. 1992. Formal intermediaries in the marriage market: A typology and review. *Journal of Marriage and the Family* 54 (May): 452–63.

AINSWORTH, M., ET AL. 1978. *Patterns of attachment: A psychological study of the strange situation.* Hillsdale, NJ: Erlbaum.

AIZENMAN, N. C. 2005. In Afghanistan, new misgivings about an old but risky practice. *Washington Post,* April 17, A16.

AIZER, A., AND S. MCLANAHAN. 2005. The impact of child support enforcement on fertility, parental investment and child well-being. National Bureau of Economic Research, www.nber.org (accessed July 10, 2006).

AJROUCH, K. 1999. Family and ethnic identity in an Arab-American community. In *Arabs in America: Building a new future,* ed. M. W. Suleiman, 129–39. Philadelphia: Temple University Press.

AL NASER, F. 2005. Kuwait's families. In *Handbook of world families,* eds. Bert N. Adams and Jan Trost, 507–535. Thousand Oaks, CA: Sage.

AL-JADDA, S. 2006. Seeking love, American Muslim style. *Christian Science Monitor,* February 14, 9.

ALBAS, D., AND C. ALBAS. 1987. The pulley alternative for the wheel theory of the development of love. *International Journal of Comparative Sociology* 28 (3–4): 223–27.

ALBERT, B., S. BROWN, AND C. M. FLANNIGAN, EDS. 2003. 14 and younger: The sexual behavior of young adolescents. The National Campaign to Prevent Teen Pregnancy. www.teenpregnancy.org (accessed June 10, 2003).

Alcohol and health. 2000. U.S. Department of Health and Human Services. www.niaaa.nih.gov (accessed Sep. 19, 2003).

ALDOUS, J. 1996. *Family careers: Rethinking the developmental perspective.* Thousand Oaks, CA: Sage.

ALFARO, E. C., A. J. UMAÑA, and M. Y. BÁMACA. 2006. The influence of academic support on Latino adolescents' academic motivation. *Family Relations* 55 (July): 279–91.

ALI, L., AND L. MILLER. 2004. The secret lies of wives. *Newsweek,* July 12, 47–54.

ALIBHAI-BROWN, Y. 1993. Marriage of minds not hearts. *New Statesman & Society,* Feb. 12, 28–29.

ALLEN, W. R., AND A. D. JAMES. 1998. Comparative perspectives on black family life: Uncommon explorations of a common subject. *Journal of Comparative Family Studies* 29 (Spring): 1–10.

ALLGOR, C. 2002. *Parlor politics: In which the ladies of Washington help build a city and a government.* Charlottesville: University of Virginia Press.

ALMEIDA, R. V., ED. 1994. *Expansions of feminist family theory through diversity.* New York: Haworth.

ALTON, B. G. 2001. You think being a dad is a good deal? *Business Week,* Apr. 2, 20.

ALTORKI, S. 1988. At home in the field. In *Arab women in the field: Studying your own society,* eds. S. Altorki and C. E. El-Solh, 51–59. New York: Syracuse University Press.

ALTSTEIN, H. 2006. For adoption, leave race out of the discussion. *Baltimore Sun,* Jan. 25, 15A.

ALVAREZ, L. 2006. (Name her) is a liar and a cheat. *New York Times* (February 16): E1–E2.

ALVEAR, M. 2003. The annual rite: Dumbing down love. *Christian Science Monitor,* Feb. 14, 11.

AMAN, C. J., AND P. ENGLAND. 1997. Comparable worth: When do two jobs deserve the same pay? In *Subtle sexism: Current practices and prospects for change,* ed. N. V. Benokraitis, 297–314. Thousand Oaks, CA: Sage.

AMARO, F. 2005. The family in Portugal: Past and present. In *Handbook of world families,* eds. Bert N. Adams and Jan Trost, 330–346. Thousand Oaks, CA: Sage.

AMATO, P. 2004. The future of marriage. In *Vision 2004: What is the future of marriage?* eds., Paul Amato and N. Gonzalez, 99–101. Minneapolis, MN: National Council on Family Relations.

AMATO, P. R. 2002. The consequences of divorce for adults and children. In *Understanding families into the new millennium: A decade in review,* ed. R. M. Milardo, 488–506. Minneapolis: National Council on Family Relations.

AMATO, P. R. 2003. Reconciling divergent perspectives: Judith Wallerstein, quantitative family research, and children of divorce. *Family Relations* 52 (October): 332–339.

AMATO, P. R., AND J. CHEADLE. 2005. The long reach of divorce: Divorce and child well-being across three generations. *Journal of Marriage and Family* 67 (February): 191–206.

AMATO, P. R., AND J. G. GILBRETH. 1999. Nonresident fathers and children's well-being: A meta-analysis. *Journal of Marriage and the Family* 61 (Aug.): 557–73.

AMATO, P. R., AND T. D. AFIFI. 2006. Feeling caught between parents: Adult children's relations with parents and subjective well-being. *Journal of Marriage and Family* 68 (February): 222–235.

AMATO, P. R., D. R. JOHNSON, A. BOOTH, AND S. J. ROGERS. 2003. Continuity and change in marital quality between 1980 and 2000. *Journal of Marriage and Family* 65 (Feb.): 1–22.

AMBERT, A.-M. 1997. *Parents, children, and adolescents: Interactive relationships and development in context.* New York: Haworth.

AMBERT, A.-M. 2001. *The effect of children on parents,* 2nd ed. New York: Haworth.

AMBROSE, M. W., AND A. M. COBURN. 2001. Report on intercountry adoption in Romania. http://cb1.acf.dhhs.gov (accessed Aug. 8, 2003).

America's children: Key national indicators of well-being 2000. 2000. Washington, DC: Federal Interagency Forum on Child and Family Statistics.

American Community Survey. 2004. Data profile highlights. U.S. Census Bureau, American Fact Finder, www.census.gov (accessed Oct. 28, 2005).

AMERICAN HEALTH ASSISTANCE FOUNDATION. 2006. Alzheimer's disease research. www.ahaf.org (accessed August 13, 2006).

AMERICAN HUMANE ASSOCIATION. 2001. Answers to common questions about child abuse and neglect. www.americanhumane.org (accessed Oct. 3, 2003).

AMERICAN LAW INSTITUTE. 2002. *Principles of the law of family dissolution: Analysis and recommendations.* New York: Matthew Bender & Company.

AMERICAN MEDICAL ASSOCIATION. 2005. Adults most common source of alcohol for teens, according to poll of teens 13–18. August 8, www.ama-assn.org/ (accessed May 18, 2006).

AMERICAN SOCIETY FOR AESTHETIC PLASTIC SURGERY. 2006. Cosmetic surgery national data bank: Statistics. www.surgery.org (accessed March 11, 2006).

Americans engage in unhealthy behaviors to manage stress. 2006. APA Online, February 23, www.apa.org/ (accessed June 8, 2006).

Americans spend more than 100 hours commuting to work each year, Census Bureau reports. 2005. U.S. Census Bureau News, March 20, www.census.gov (accessed May 12, 2006).

AMOTT, T. 1993. *Caught in the crisis: Women and the U.S. economy today.* New York: Monthly Review Press.

An overview of abortion laws. 2006. State policies in brief, The Alan Guttmacher Institute, www.guttmacher.org (accessed May 3, 2006).

ANCHETA, A. N. 1998. *Race, rights, and the Asian American experience.* New Brunswick, NJ: Rutgers University Press.

ANDA, R. F., ET AL. 2001. Abused boys, battered mothers, and male involvement in teen pregnancy. *Pediatrics* 107 (Feb.): E19.

ANDELIN, H. 1974. *Fascinating womanhood: A guide to a happy marriage.* Santa Barbara, CA: Pacific.

ANDERSON, C., D. KELTNER, AND O. P. JOHN. 2003. Emotional convergence between people over time. *Journal of Personality and Social Psychology* 84 (May): 1054–68.

ANDERSON, E. 1999. *Code of the street: Decency, violence, and the moral life of the inner city.* New York: Norton.

ANDERSON, J. 1990. *The single mother's book: A practical guide to managing your children, career, home, finances, and everything else.* Atlanta: Peachtree.

ANDERSON, K. L. 1997. Gender, status, and domestic violence: An integration of feminist and family violence approaches. *Journal of Marriage and the Family* 59 (Aug.): 655–69.

ANDERSON, K. L. 2002. Perpetrator or victim? Relationships between intimate partner violence and well-being. *Journal of Marriage and Family* 64 (Nov.): 851–63.

ANGELL, M., R. D. UTIGER, AND A. J. J. WOOD. 2000. Disclosure of authors' conflicts of interest: A follow-up. *New England Journal of Medicine* 342 (Feb. 24): 586–87.

ANN LANDERS. 2000. *Washington Post*, May 9, C11.

ANN LANDERS. 2001. *Baltimore Sun*, Aug. 10, 3E.

Anorexia nervosa and related eating disorders, Inc. 2006. Statistics: How many people have eating disorders? January 16, www.anred.com (accessed August 7, 2006).

ANTONUCCI, T. C., H. AKIYAMA, AND A. MERLINE. 2001. Dynamics of social relationships in midlife. In *Handbook of midlife development*, ed. M. E. Lachman, 571–98. New York: Wiley.

APPEL, N. H., AND V. SEITZ. 1991. Four models of adolescent mother-grandmother relationships in black inner-city families. *Family Relations* 40 (Oct.): 421–29.

AQUILINO, W. S. 1997. From adolescent to young adult: A prospective study of parent-child relations during the transition to adulthood. *Journal of Marriage and the Family* 59 (Aug.): 670–86.

ARANDA, M. P., AND B. G. KNIGHT. 1997. The influence of ethnicity and culture on the caregiver stress and coping process: A sociocultural review and analysis. *The Gerontologist* 37 (3): 342–54.

ARDITTI, J. A. 1999. Rethinking relationships between divorced mothers and their children: Capitalizing on family strengths. *Family Relations* 48 (Apr.): 109–19.

ARDS, S., C. CHUNG, AND S. L. MYERS, JR. 1998. The effects of sample selection bias on racial differences in child abuse reporting. *Child Abuse & Neglect* 22 (Feb.): 103–16.

ARENDELL, T. 1997. A social constructionist approach to parenting. In *Contemporary parenting: Challenges and issues*, ed. T. Arendell, 1–44. Thousand Oaks, CA: Sage.

ARENOFSKY, J. 1993. Childless and proud of it. *Newsweek*, Feb. 8, 12.

ARIÈS, P. 1962. *Centuries of childhood.* New York: Vintage.

ARLISS, L. P. 1991. *Gender communication.* Upper Saddle River, NJ: Prentice Hall.

ARMARIO, C. 2005. More Muslims find online dating a good match. *Christian Science Monitor* January 19, 16.

ARMSTRONG, E. 2004. Gay marriages unite, and divide, families. *Christian Science Monitor*, May 20, 4–5.

ARMSTRONG, E. 2004. Should *she* pop the question? *Christian Science Monitor* (February 13): 1, 11.

ARONSON, E. 1995. *The social animal*, 7th ed. New York: W. H. Freeman.

ARTHURS, C. 2002. Most Vietnamese women abused. BBC, Oct. 22. http://news.bbc.co.uk (accessed Oct. 8, 2002).

ASELTINE, R. H., JR., AND R. C. KESSLER. 1993. Marital disruption and depression in a community sample. *Journal of Health and Social Behavior* 34 (Sep.): 237–51.

2003 Assisted reproductive technology success rates. 2005. U.S. Department of Health and Human Services, December, www.cdc.gov/ (accessed April 25, 2006).

ASWAD, B. C. 1994. Attitudes of immigrant women and men in the Dearborn area toward women's employment and welfare. In *Muslim communities in North America*, eds. Y. Haddad and J. Smith, 501–20. Albany: State University of New York Press.

ASWAD, B. C. 1997. Arab American families. In *Families in cultural context: Strengths and challenges in diversity*, ed. M. K. DeGenova, 213–47. Mountain View, CA: Mayfield.

ASWAD, B. C. 1999. Attitudes of Arab immigrants toward welfare. In *Arabs in America: Building a new future*, ed. M. W. Suleiman, 177–91. Philadelphia: Temple University Press.

ATCHLEY, R. C., AND A. S. BARUSCH. 2004. *Social forces and aging: An introduction to social gerontology*, 10th ed. Belmont, CA: Wadsworth.

ATKIN, R. 2002. Keeping kids "clean." *Christian Science Monitor*, Dec. 4, 11–13.

ATKINSON, M. P., T. N. GREENSTEIN, AND M. M. LANG. 2005. For women, breadwinning can be dangerous: Gendered resource theory and wife abuse. *Journal of Marriage and Family* 67 (December): 1137–48.

Attitudes and characteristics of freshmen at 4-year colleges, Fall 2005. *Chronicle of Higher Education*, Almanac Issue 2006–7, 53 (August 25): 18.

AUNOLA, K., AND J.-E. NURMI. 2005. The role of parenting styles in children's problem behavior. *Child Development* 76 (November/December): 1144–59.

AVELLAR, S., AND P. SMOCK. 2005. The economic consequences of the dissolution of cohabiting unions. *Journal of Marriage and Family* 67 (May): 315–27.

AVNI, N. 1991. Battered wives: The home as a total institution. *Violence and Victims* 6 (2): 137–49.

BABCOCK, J. C., J. WALTZ, N. S. JACOBSON, AND J. M. GOTTMAN. 1993. Power and violence: The relation between communication patterns, power discrepancies, and domestic violence. *Journal of Consulting and Clinical Psychology* 61 (1): 40–50.

BACA ZINN, M., AND A. Y. H. POK. 2002. Tradition and transition in Mexican-origin families. In *Minority families in the United States: A multicultural perspective*, 3rd ed., ed. R. L. Taylor, 79–100. Upper Saddle River, NJ: Prentice Hall.

BACA ZINN, M., AND B. WELLS. 2000. Diversity within Latino families: New lessons for family social science. In *Handbook of family diversity*, eds. D. H. Demo, K. R. Allen, and M. A. Fine, 252–73. New York: Oxford University Press.

BACHMAN, H. J., AND P. L. CHASE-LANSDALE. 2005. Custodial grandmothers' physical, mental, and economic well-being: Comparisons of primary caregivers from low-income neighborhoods. *Family Relations* 54 (October): 475–487.

BACHMAN, J. G., K. N. WADSWORTH, P. M. O'MALLEY, L. D. JOHNSTON, AND J. E. SCHULENBERG. 1997. *Smoking, drinking, and drug use in young adulthood: The impacts of new freedoms and new responsibilities.* Hillsdale, NJ: Erlbaum.

BACHMAN, R. 1994. *Violence against women: A national crime victimization survey report.* U.S. Department of Justice, Office of Justice Programs, Bureau of Justice Statistics. Fall.

BACHRACH, C. A., P. F. ADAMS, S. SAMBRANO, AND K. A. LONDON. 1990. Adoption in the 1980s. *Vital Health Statistics*, no. 181, Jan. 5, advance data. Hyattsville, MD: National Center for Health Statistics.

BACHU, A. 1993. Fertility of American women: June 1992. U.S. Census Bureau, Current Population Reports P20–470. Washington, DC: U.S. Government Printing Office.

BADEN, A. 2001. *Psychological adjustment of transracial adoptees: Applying the cultural–racial identity model.* Paper presented at the American Psychological Association, San Francisco, Aug. 2001.

BAER, J. S., P. D. SAMPSON, H. M. BARR, P. D. CONNOR, AND A. P. STREISSGUTH. 2003. A 21-year longitudinal analysis of the effects of prenatal alcohol exposure on young adult drinking. *Archives of General Psychiatry* 60 (Apr.): 377–86.

BAHR, K. S., AND H. M. BAHR. 1995. Autonomy, community, and the mediation of value: Comments on Apachean grandmothering, cultural change, and the media. In *American families: Issues in race and ethnicity*, ed. C. K. Jacobson, 229–60. New York: Garland.

BAILEY, B. 1988. *From front porch to back seat: Courtship in twentieth-century America.* Baltimore: Johns Hopkins University Press.

BAILEY, J. M., AND R. C. PILLARD. 1991. A genetic study of male sexual orientation. *Archives of General Psychiatry* 48 (Dec.): 1089–96.

BAILEY, J. M., R. C. PILLARD, M. C. NEALE, AND Y. AGYEI. 1993. Heritable factors influence sexual orientation in women. *Archives of General Psychiatry* 50 (Mar.): 217–23.

BAILEY, M. 2003. *The man who would be queen: The science of gender-bending and transsexualism.* Washington, DC: Joseph Henry.

BAILEY, W., M. YOUNG, C. KNICKERBOCKER, AND T. DOAN. 2002. A cautionary tale about conducting research on abstinence education: How do state abstinence coordinators define "sexual activity"? *American Journal of Health Education* 33 (Sep./Oct.): 290–96.

BAKER, L., T. H. WAGNER, S. SINGER, AND M. K. BUNDORF. 2003. Use of the Internet and e-mail for health care information. *Journal of the American Medical Association* 289 (May 14): 2400–2406.

BAKER, M. 2000. Adolphus gets married; soon he'll meet his wife. *Christian Science Monitor*, Feb. 15, 7.

BAKER, S. 2002. The coming battle for immigrants. *Business Week*, Aug. 26, 138, 140.

BALDAUF, S. 2000. More men forsake jobs to be full-time fathers. *Christian Science Monitor*, May 10, 1, 5.

BALDAUF, S. 2006. Indians crack down on gender abortions. *Christian Science Monitor*. March 31, 7.

BANDURA, A., AND R. H. WALTERS. 1963. *Social learning and personality development.* New York: Holt, Rinehart & Winston.

BANG, H.-K., AND B. B. REECE. 2003. Minorities in children's television commercials: New, improved, and stereotyped. *Journal of Consumer Affairs* 37 (Summer): 42–67.

BANNER, L. W. 1984. *Women in modern America: A brief history*, 2nd ed. New York: Harcourt Brace Jovanovich.

BANTA, C. 2005. Trading for a high. *Time*, August 1, 35.

Baptist missionaries must affirm doctrine. 2003. *The Guardian*, Apr. 16. www.guardian.co.uk (accessed Apr. 17, 2003).

BARBELL, K., AND M. FREUNDLICH. 2001. *Foster care today.* Washington, DC: Casey Family Programs.

BARBER, B. K. 1994. Cultural, family, and personal contexts of parent-adolescent conflict. *Journal of Marriage and the Family* 56 (May): 375–86.

BARBER, B. L., AND D. H. DEMO. 2006. The kids are alright (at least, most of them): Links between divorce and dissolution and child well-being. In *Handbook of divorce and relationship dissolution*, eds. M. A. Fine and J. H. Harvey, 289–311. Mahwah, NJ: Lawrence Erlbaum.

BARBER, B. L., AND J. M. LYONS. 1994. Family processes and adolescent adjustment in intact and remarried families. *Journal of Youth and Adolescence* 23 (Aug.): 421–36.

BARLETT, D. L., AND J. B. STEELE. 2002a. Playing the political slots. *Time*, Dec. 23, 52–63.

BARLETT, D. L., AND J. B. STEELE. 2002b. Wheel of misfortune. *Time*, Dec. 16, 42–58.

BARNES, A. S. 2000. *Everyday racism: A book for all Americans*. Naperville, IL: Sourcebooks.

BARNES, G. M., A. S. REIFMAN, M. P. FARRELL, AND B. A. DINTCHEFF. 2000. The effects of parenting on the development of adolescent alcohol misuse: A six-wave latent growth model. *Journal of Marriage and the Family* 62 (Feb.): 175–86.

BARNES, J. S., AND C. E. BENNETT. 2002. The Asian population: 2000. U.S. Census Bureau. www.census.gov (accessed Apr. 18, 2003).

BARNETT, R. C., AND C. RIVERS. 1996. *She works, he works: How two-income families are happy, healthy, and thriving*. Cambridge, MA: Harvard University Press.

BARNETT, R. C., and K. C. GAREIS. 2006. Parental after-school stress and psychological well-being. *Journal of Marriage and Family* 68 (February): 101–8.

BARNETT, R. C., A. STEPTOE, AND K. C. GAREIS. 2005. Marital-role quality and stress-related psychobiological indicators. *Annals of Behavioral Medicine* 30: 1 (36–43).

BAROVICK, H. 2002. Domestic dads. *Time*, Aug. 15, B4-B10.

BARR, S. 2006. Workers plan to retire, without a retirement plan. *Washington Post*, June 29, D4.

BARRES, B. A. 2006. Does gender matter? *Nature* 442 (July 13): 133–36.

BARRET, R. L., AND B. E. ROBINSON. 1990. *Gay fathers*. Lexington, MA: Lexington Books.

BARRET-DUCROCQ, F. 1991. *Love in the time of Victoria: Sexuality, class and gender in nineteenth-century London*. New York: Verso.

BARRINGER, H. R., R. W. GARDNER, AND M. J. LEVIN. 1993. *Asians and Pacific Islanders in the United States*. New York: Russell Sage Foundation.

BARRY, E. 2005. It must be love, but let's be sure. *Los Angeles Times*, May 21, A1.

BARTFELD, J., AND D. R. MEYER. 2001. The changing role of child support among never-married mothers. In *Out of wedlock: Causes and consequences of nonmarital fertility*, eds. L. L. Wu and B. Wolfe, 229–55. New York: Russell Sage Foundation.

BARTKOWSKI, J. P. 2001. *Remaking the godly marriage: Gender negotiation in Evangelical families*. New Brunswick, NJ: Rutgers University Press.

BATES, M. 2005. Tenured and battered. *Chronicle of Higher Education*, September 9, C1–C4.

BATTAN, M. 1992. *Sexual strategies*. New York: Putnam.

BAUMEISTER, R. F., AND S. R. WOTMAN. 1992. *Breaking hearts: The two sides of unrequited love*. New York: Guilford.

BAUMRIND, D. 1968. Authoritarian versus authoritative parental control. *Adolescence* 3, 255–72.

BAUMRIND, D. 1989. Rearing competent children. In *Child development today and tomorrow*, ed. W. Damon, 349–78. San Francisco: Jossey-Bass.

BAUMRIND, D. 1991. The influence of parenting styles on adolescent competence and substance use. *Journal of Early Adolescence* 11 (February): 56–95.

BAUMRIND, D., R. E. LARZELERE, AND P. A. COWAN. 2002. Ordinary physical punishment: Is it harmful? Comment on Gershoff (2002). *Psychological Bulletin* 128 (July): 580–89.

BAUSERMAN, R. 2002. Child adjustment in joint-custody versus sole-custody arrangements: A meta-analytic review. *Journal of Family Psychology* 16 (Mar.): 91–102.

BAYDAR, N., AND J. BROOKS-GUNN. 1994. The dynamics of child support and its consequences for children. In *Child support and child well-being*, eds. 1. Garfinkel, S. S. McLanahan, and P. K. Robins, 257–84. Washington, DC: Urban Institute.

BAYDAR, N., A. GREEK, AND J. BROOKS-GUNN. 1997. A longitudinal study of the effects of the birth of a sibling during the first 6 years of life. *Journal of Marriage and the Family* 59 (Nov.): 939–56.

BAZAR, E., and S. ARMOUR. 2005. Cities tackle day labor dilemma. *USA Today*, Oct 23, A3.

BEARAK, B. 2006. The bride price. *New York Times Magazine*, July 9, 45–49.

BEARMAN, P. S., AND H. BRUCKNER. 2001. Promising the future: Virginity pledges and first intercourse. *American Journal of Sociology* 106 (Jan.): 859–912.

BEARMAN, P. S., J. MOODY, AND K. STOVEL. 2004. Chains of affection: The structure of adolescent romantic and sexual networks. *American Journal of Sociology* 10 (July): 44–91.

BEATON, J. M., J. E. NORRIS, AND M. W. PRATT. 2003. Unresolved issues in adult children's marital relationships involving intergenerational problems. *Family Relations* 52 (Apr.): 143–53.

BECK, A. T. 1988. *Love is never enough: How couples can overcome misunderstandings, resolve conflicts, and solve relationship problems through cognitive therapy*. New York: Harper & Row.

BEECH, H. 2005. Enemies of the state? *Time*, Sept. 19, 56, 61.

BEECH, H. 2005. Sex, please—we're young and Chinese. *Time*, December 12, 61.

BEER, W. R. 1992. *American stepfamilies*. New Brunswick, NJ: Transaction.

BEERS, T. M. 2000. *A profile of the working poor, 1998*. U.S. Department of Labor, Bureau of Labor Statistics, stats.bls.gov (accessed Oct. 12, 2000).

BEGLEY, S., WITH M. HAGER AND A. MUIR. 1990. The search for the fountain of youth. *Newsweek*, Mar. 5, 44–48.

BELCASTRO, P. A. 1985. Sexual behavior differences between black and white students. *Journal of Sex Research* 21, 56–57.

BELKIN, L. 1985. Affording a child: Parents worry as costs keep rising. *New York Times*, May 23, C1, C6.

BELLAH, R. N., R. MADSEN, W. M. SULLIVAN, A. SWIDLER, AND S. M. TIPTON. 1985. *Habits of the heart: Individualism and commitment in American life*. Berkeley: University of California Press.

BELLE, D. 1999. *The after-school lives of children: Alone and with others while parents work*. Mahwah, NJ: Erlbaum.

BELSIE, L. 2001. An Iowa debate over newcomers. *Christian Science Monitor*, July 27, 1, 4.

BELSIE, L. 2003. More couples live together, roiling debate on family. *Christian Science Monitor*, Mar. 13, 1, 4.

BELSIE, L. 2003. Where do women out-earn men? Hint: not a city. *Christian Science Monitor*, Aug. 1, 12.

BELSKY, J. 1993. Etiology of child maltreatment: A developmental-ecological analysis. *Psychological Bulletin* 114 (Nov.): 413–34.

BELSKY, J. K. 1988. *Here tomorrow: Making the most of life after fifty*. Baltimore: Johns Hopkins University Press.

BEM, S. L. 1975. Androgyny vs. the tight little lives of fluffy women and chesty men. *Psychology Today*, Sep., 58–62.

BEM, S. L. 1993. *The tenses on gender: Transforming the debate on sexual inequality*. New Haven, CT: Yale University Press.

BEN-ZE'EV, A. 2004. *Love online: Emotions on the Internet*. New York: Cambridge University Press.

BENASSI, M. A. 1985. Effects of romantic love on perception of strangers' physical attractiveness. *Psychological Reports* 56 (Apr.): 355–58.

BENET, S. 2001. Muslim, Asian women target of insults, harassment. *Women's E-News*, Sep. 21. www.womensenews.org (accessed Sep. 21, 2001).

BENNETT, L. 2002. Watch out, listen up! 2002 feminist primetime report. National Organization for Women Foundation. www.nowfoundation.org (accessed May 23, 2003).

BENNETT, L., JR. 1989. The 10 biggest myths about the black family. *Ebony* (Nov.): 114–16.

BENNETT, R. L., ET AL. 2002. Genetic counseling and screening of consanguineous couples and their offspring: Recommendations of the National Society of Genetic Counselors. *Journal of Genetic Counseling* 11 (Apr.): 97–119.

BENNING, J. 2005. The girl's got guts. *Los Angeles Times*, Aug. 30, F6.

BENOKRAITIS, N. V., AND J. R. FEAGIN. 1995. *Modern sexism: Blatant, subtle, and covert discrimination*, 2nd ed. Upper Saddle River, NJ: Prentice Hall.

BENOKRAITIS, N. V., ED. 2000. *Feuds about families: Conservative, centrist, liberal, and feminist perspectives*. Upper Saddle River, NJ: Prentice Hall.

BERGEN, R. K. 2006. Marital rape: New research and directions. National Resource Center on Domestic Violence, February, pp. 1–13, www.vawnet.org (accessed June 4, 2006).

BERGER, R. 1998. *Stepfamilies: A multi-dimensional perspective*. New York: Haworth.

BERGLUND, H., P. LINDSTRÖM, AND I. SAVIC. 2006. Brain response to putative pheromones in lesbian women. *Proceedings of the National Academy of Societies* 103 (May 23): 8269–74.

BERGMAN, P. M. 1969. *The chronological history of the Negro in America*. New York: Harper & Row.

BERK, B. R. 1993. The dating game. *Good Housekeeping* (September.): 192, 220–21.

BERKMAN, N.D., ET AL. 2006. *Management of eating disorders*. Evidence Report/Technology Assessment No. 135. Rockville, MD: Agency for Healthcare Research and Quality.

BERLAND, G. K., ET AL., 2001a. Health information on the Internet: Accessibility, quality, and readability in English and Spanish. *Journal of the American Medical Association* 285 (May 23/30): 2612–21.

BERLAND, G. K., ET AL., 2001b. Evaluation of English and Spanish health information on the Internet. www.rand.org (accessed Aug. 8, 2001).

BERLIN, I. 1998. *Many thousands gone: The first two centuries of slavery in North America*. Cambridge, MA: Belknap Press of Harvard University.

BERNARD, J. 1973. *The future of marriage*. New York: Bantam.

BERNASEK, A. 2004. Jobs are back; too bad wages aren't. *Fortune*, May 3, 40, 42.

BERNHARD, L. A. 1995. Sexuality in women's lives. In *Women's health care: A comprehensive handbook*, eds. C. I. Fogel and N. F. Woods, 475–95. Thousand Oaks, CA: Sage.

BERNIER, J. C., AND D. H. SIEGEL. 1994. Attention-deficit hyperactivity disorder: A family and ecological systems perspective. *Families in Society: The Journal of Contemporary Human Services* (Mar.): 142–50.

BERNSTEIN, J., AND L. MISHEL. 2003. Labor market left behind. Economic Policy Institute, Washington, DC. www.epinet.org (accessed Sep. 13, 2003).

BERNSTEIN, J., C. BROCHT, AND M. SPADE-AGUILAR. 2000. *How much is enough? Basic budgets for working families*. Washington, DC: Economic Policy Institute.

BERNSTEIN, R. 2005. Foreign-born population tops 34 million, Census Bureau estimates. *U.S. Census Bureau News*, www.census.gov (accessed Nov. 1, 2005).

BERSCHEID, E., AND H. T. REIS. 1998. Attraction and close relationships. In *The handbook of social psychology*, 4th ed., eds. D. T. Gilbert, S. T. Fiske, and G. Lindzey, 193–81. New York: McGraw-Hill.

BERSCHEID, E., K. DION, E. WALSTER, AND G. W. WALSTER. 1982. Physical attractiveness and dating choice: A test of the matching hypothesis. *Journal of Experimental Social Psychology* 1, 173–89.

BEST, A. L. 2000. *Prom night: Youth, schools, and popular culture*. New York: Routledge.

BETCHER, W., AND W. POLLACK. 1993. *In a time of fallen heroes: The re-creation of masculinity*. New York: Atheneum.

BHATNAGAR, P. 2005. Lookin' for a cheap date? Try Wal-Mart. CNN/Money, April 8, http://money.cnn.com/2005/04/07/news/fortune500/walmart_dating (accessed April 12, 2005).

BHATTACHARYA, S. 2003. Obesity breaks up sperm DNA. www.newscientist.com, October 17 (accessed April 27, 2006).

BIANCHI, S. M. 2000. Maternal employment and time with children: Dramatic change or surprising continuity? Presidential address to the Population Association of America, Los Angeles, Mar. 24.

BIANCHI, S. M. 2001. *American families resilient after 50 years of change*. Washington, DC: Population Reference Bureau.

BIANCHI, S. M., AND L. M. CASPER. 2000. *American families. Population Bulletin* 55 (Dec.). Washington, DC: Population Reference Bureau.

BIANCHI, S. M., L. SUBAIYA, AND J. R. KAHN. 1999. The gender gap in the economic well-being of nonresident fathers and custodial mothers. *Demography* 36 (May): 195–203.

BIANCHI, S. M., M. A. MILKIE, L. C. SAYER, AND J. P. ROBINSON. 2000. Is anyone doing the housework? Trends in the gender division of household labor. *Social Forces* 79 (Sep.): 191–227.

BIANCHI, S. M., J. P. ROBINSON, and M. A. MILKIE. 2006. *Changing rhythms of American family life.* New York: Russell Sage Foundation.

BIELBY, W. T., AND D. D. BIELBY. 1992. I will follow him: Family ties, gender-role beliefs, and reluctance to relocate for a better job. *American Journal of Sociology* 97 (Mar.): 1241–67.

BILLER, H. B. 1993. *Fathers and families: Paternal factors in child development.* Westport, CT: Auburn House.

BILLINGSLEY, A. 1992. *Climbing Jacob's ladder: The enduring legacy of African-American families.* New York: Simon & Schuster.

BIRD, G. W., AND A. SCHNURMAN-CROOK. 2005. Professional identity and coping behaviors in dual-career couples. *Family Relations* 54 (January): 145–60.

BIRDITT, K. S., AND K. L. FINGERMAN. 2005. Do we get better at picking our battles? Age group differences in descriptions of behavioral reactions to interpersonal tensions. *Journals of Gerontology: Psychological Sciences and Social Sciences* 60 (May): P121–P128.

BIRDITT, K. S., K. L. Fingerman, AND D. M. ALMEIDA. 2005. Age differences in exposure and reactions to interpersonal tensions: A daily diary study. *Psychology and Aging* 20 (June): 330–340.

BIRNS, B. 1999. Attachment theory revisited: Challenging conceptual and methodological sacred cows. *Feminism & Psychology* 9 (Feb.): 10–21.

BIRNS, B., M. CASCARDI, AND S.-L. MEYER. 1994. Sex-role socialization: Developmental influences on wife abuse. *American Journal of Orthopsychiatry* 64 (Jan.): 50–59.

BISHOP, G. F., R. W. OLDENDICK, A. J. TUCHFARBER, AND S. E. BENNETT. 1980. Pseudo-opinions on public affairs. *Public Opinion Quarterly* 44 (Summer): 198–209.

BLACK, D., G. GATES, S. SANDERS, AND L. TAYLOR. 2000. Demographics of the gay and lesbian population in the United States: Evidence from available systematic data sources. *Demography* 37 (May): 139–54.

Black volunteers for AIDS studies may be hard to find. 2003. *Baltimore Sun,* Feb. 26, 5A.

BLACKMAN, L., O. CLAYTON, N. GLENN, L. MALONE-COLON, AND A. ROBERTS. 2005. The consequences of marriage for African Americans: A comprehensive literature review. Institute for American Values, www.americanvalues.org (accessed April 12, 2006).

BLAIR, S. L., and J. A. COBAS. 2006. Gender differences in young Latino adults' status attainment: Understanding bilingualism in the familial context. *Family Relations* 55 (July): 292–305.

BLAKE, J. 1989. *Family size and achievement.* Berkeley: University of California Press.

BLAKE, S. M., R. LENSKY, C. GOODENOW, R. SAWYER, D. LOHRMANN, AND R. WINDSOR. 2003. Condom availability programs in Massachusetts high schools: Relationships with condom use and sexual behavior. *American Journal of Public Health* 93 (June): 955–62.

BLANCHARD, K. 1999–2000. Guy anxiety: What he's really nervous about. *Parents Expecting* 33 (Winter): 20–21.

BLANKENHORN, D. 1995. *Fatherless America: Confronting our most urgent social problem.* New York: HarperPerennial.

BLUESTEIN, G. 2005. 78-year-old accused of killing ex-flame. *Washington Post,* June 25, A2.

BLUESTONE, C., AND C. S. TAMIS-LeMONDA. 1999. Correlates of parenting styles in predominantly working- and middle-class African American mothers. *Journal of Marriage and the Family* 61 (Nov.): 881–93.

BLUMBERG, D. L. 2005. Hispanic kids go "home" for summer. *Christian Science Monitor,* July 28, 12–15.

BOBO, L. D., M. C. DAWSON, AND D. JOHNSON. 2001. Enduring two-ness. *Public Perspective* 12 (May/June): 12–16.

BODMAN, D. A., AND G. W. PETERSON. 1995. Parenting processes. In *Research and theory in family science,* eds. R. D. Day, K. R. Gilbert, B. H. Settles, and W. R. Burr, 205–25. Pacific Grove, CA: Brooks/Cole.

BOGART, T. 2006. African American women and family planning services: Perceptions of discrimination. *Women and Health* 42 (Jan.): 23–28.

BOGENSCHNEIDER, K. 1996. An ecological risk/protective theory for building prevention programs, policies, and community capacity to support youth. *Family Relations* 45 (Apr.): 127–38.

BOGENSCHNEIDER, K. 1997. Parental involvement in adolescent schooling: A proximal process with transcontextual validity. *Journal of Marriage and the Family* 59 (Aug.): 718–33.

BOLDUC, V. 2005. Gender gaps, old and new. Burlington Free Press online, November 25 (accessed November 28, 2005).

BOLLAG, B. 2002a. Incident raises issue of harassment of women in Swedish universities. *Chronicle of Higher Education,* Sep. 20, A41.

BOLLAG, B. 2002b. Wanted in Sweden: Female professors. *Chronicle of Higher Education,* Sep. 20, A40–A42.

BOND, J. T., ELLEN G., STACY S. KIM, AND E. BROWN-FIELD. 2005. *2005 National study of employers.* Families and Work Institute, http://familiesandwork.org (accessed May 12, 2006).

BONNER, R. 2003. A challenge in India snarls foreign adoptions. *New York Times,* June 23, A3.

BONNETTE, R. 1995a. Housing of American Indians on reservations: Equipment and fuels. *Statistical Brief SB/95–11.* U.S. Census Bureau. Washington, DC: U.S. Government Printing Office.

BONNETTE, R. 1995b. Housing of American Indians on reservations: Plumbing. *Statistical Brief SB/95–9.* U.S. Census Bureau. Washington, DC: U.S. Government Printing Office.

BONNIE, R. J., AND R. B. WALLACE, EDS. 2003. *Elder mistreatment: Abuse, neglect, and exploitation in an aging America.* Washington, DC: The National Academies Press.

BOODMAN, S. G. 1992. Questions about a popular prenatal test. *Washington Post Health Supplement,* Nov. 3, 10–13.

BOODMAN, S. G. 1995. The only child: Lonely or lucky? *Washington Post Health Supplement,* Oct. 24, 10–13.

BOODMAN, S. G. 2004. For more teenage girls, adult plastic surgery. *Washington Post,* Oct. 26, A1.

BOONSTRA, H. D., R. B. GOLD, C. L. RICHARDS, AND L. B. FINER. 2006. Abortion in women's lives. Guttmacher Institute, www.guttmacher.org (accessed September 21, 2006).

BOOTH, A., AND D. R. JOHNSON. 1994. Declining health and marital quality. *Journal of Marriage and the Family* 56 (Feb.): 218–23.

BOOTH, A., AND J. N. EDWARDS. 1985. Age at marriage and marital instability. *Journal of Marriage and the Family* 47 (Feb.): 67–75.

BOOTH, A., AND J. N. EDWARDS. 1992. Starting over: Why remarriages are more unstable. *Journal of Family Issues* 13 (June): 179–94.

BOOTH, S. 2005. Very personal personals: Dating with an STD. *Washington Post,* May 10, C9.

BORDERS, L. D., L. K. BLACK, AND B. K. PASLEY. 1998. Are adopted children and their parents at greater risk for negative outcomes? *Family Relations* 47 (July): 237–41.

BORLAND, D. M. 1975. An alternative model of the wheel theory. *Family Coordinator* 24 (July): 289–92.

BORNSTEIN, M. H. 2002. Parenting infants. In *Handbook of parenting,* 2nd ed., Vol. 1: *Children and parenting,* ed. M. H. Bornstein, 3–43. Mahwah, NJ: Erlbaum.

BORST, J. 1996. Relatively speaking. *Newsweek,* July 29, 16.

BORZEKOWSKI, D. L. G., AND T. N. ROBINSON. 2005. The remote, the mouse, and the no. 2 pencil. *Archives of Pediatrics & Adolescent Medicine* 159 (July): 607–13.

BOSMAN, J. 2005. WPP executive resigns over remarks on women. *New York Times,* Oct. 21, C1, C5.

BOSTIC, J. Q., AND M. C. MILLER. 2005. When should you worry? *Newsweek,* April 25, 60.

BOWLBY, J. 1969. *Attachment and loss,* Vol. 1: *Attachment.* New York: Basic Books.

BOWLBY, J. 1984. *Attachment and loss,* Vol. 1, 2nd ed. Harmondsworth, UK: Penguin.

Boys to men: Entertainment media, messages about masculinity. 1999. Children Now. www.childrennow.org (accessed Aug. 24, 2000).

BRADBURY, T. N., AND B. R. KARNEY. 2004. Understanding and altering the longitudinal course of marriage. *Journal of Marriage and Family* 66 (November): 862–79.

BRADBURY, T., J. R. ROGGE, AND E. LAWRENCE. 2001. Reconsidering the role of conflict in marriage. In *Couples in conflict,* eds. A. Booth, A. C. Crouter, and M. Clements, 59–81. Mahwah, NJ: Erlbaum.

BRADLEY-DOPPES, P. 2002. Men still have more opportunities. *Chronicle of Higher Education,* Dec. 6, B8.

BRADY, J. 1990. Why I still want a wife. *Ms.* (July/Aug.): 17.

BRAITHWAITE, D. O., P. SCHRODT, AND L. A. BAXTER. 2006. Understudied and misunderstood: Communication in stepfamily relationships. In *Widening the family circle: New research on family communication,* eds. K. Floyd and M. T. Moorman, 153–170. Thousand Oaks, CA: Sage.

BRAMLETT, M. D., AND W. D. MOSHER. 2002. Cohabitation, marriage, divorce, and remarriage in the United States. Centers for Disease Control and Prevention, Vital and Health Statistics. www.cdc.gov (accessed July 3, 2003).

BRANDER, B. 2004. *Love that works: The art and science of giving.* West Conshohocken, PA: Templeton Foundation Press.

BRANDON, J. 2005. Britain grapples with "honor killing" practice. *Christian Science Monitor,* Oct. 19, 4.

BRASSARD, M. R., AND D. B. HARDY. 1997. Psychological maltreatment. In *The battered child,* 5th ed., eds. M. E. Helfer, R. S. Kempe, and R. D. Krugman, 392–412. Chicago: University of Chicago Press.

BRAUND, K. E. H. 1990. Guardians of tradition and handmaidens to change: Women's roles in Creek economic and social life during the eighteenth century. *American Indian Quarterly* 14 (Summer): 239–58.

BRAVERMAN, L. 1989. Beyond the myth of motherhood. In *Women in families: A framework for family therapy,* eds. M. McGoldrick and C. Anderson, 227–243. New York: W. W. Norton.

BRAY, J. H., AND J. KELLY. 1998. *Stepfamilies: Love, marriage, and parenting in the first decade.* New York: Broadway.

BRAY, J. H., AND S. H. BERGER. 1990. Noncustodial father and paternal grandparent relationships in stepfamilies. *Family Relations* 39 (Oct.): 414–19.

BRAY, J. M. 1999. From marriage to remarriage and beyond: Findings from the developmental issues in Stepfamilies Research Project. In *Coping with divorce, single parenting, and remarriage: A risk and resiliency perspective,* ed. E. M. Hetherington, 253–71. Mahwah, NJ: Erlbaum.

Breast implants. 2002. U.S. Food and Drug Administration. www.fda.gov (accessed May 15, 2003).

BREHM, S. S. 1992. *Intimate relationships,* 2nd ed. New York: McGraw-Hill.

BREHM, S. S., R. S. MILLER, D. PERLMAN, AND S. M. CAMPBELL. 2002. *Intimate relationships,* 3rd ed. Boston, MA: McGraw-Hill.

BREINES, W. 1992. *Young, white, and miserable: Growing up female in the fifties.* Boston: Beacon.

BREMER, J. 2005. The Internet and children: Advantages and disadvantages. *Child and Adolescent Psychiatric Clinics of North America* 14 (3): 405–28.

BRENDGEN, M., ET AL. 2005. Examining genetic and environmental effect on social aggression: A study of 6-year-old twins. *Child Development* 76 (July/August): 930–46.

BRENNAN, R. T., R. C. BARNETT, AND K. C. GAREIS. 2001. When she earns more than he does: A longitudinal study of dual-earner couples. *Journal of Marriage and Family* 63 (Feb.): 168–82.

BRENNEMAN, G. R., A. O. HANDLER, S. F. KAUFMAN, AND E. R. RHOADES. 2000. Health status and clinical indicators. In *American Indian health: Innovations in health care, promotion, and policy,* ed. E. R. Rhoades, 103–21. Baltimore: Johns Hopkins University Press.

BRESLAU, K. 2001. Hate crime: He wasn't afraid. *Newsweek,* Oct. 15, 8.

BRETSCHNEIDER, J. G., AND N. L. McCOY. 1988. Sexual interest and behavior in healthy 80- to 102-year olds. *Archives of Sexual Behavior* 17 (2): 109–29.

BRIERE, J. N. 1992. *Child abuse trauma: Theory and treatment of the lasting effects.* Thousand Oaks, CA: Sage.

Bringing up baby. 1999. *Public Perspective* 10 (Oct./Nov.): 19.

BRINIG, M. F., AND D. A. ALLEN. 2000. "These boots are made for walking": Why most divorce filers are women. *American Law and Economic Review* 2 (1): 126–69.

BRINK, S. 1994. Too sick to be adopted? *U.S. News & World Report,* May 2, 66–69.

BROCK, L. J., AND G. H. JENNINGS. 1993. Sexuality education: What daughters in their 30s wish their mothers had told them. *Family Relations* 42 (Jan.): 61–65.

BRODERICK, C. B. 1988. To arrive where we started: The field of family studies in the 1930s. *Journal of Marriage and the Family* 50 (Aug.): 569–84.

BRODERICK, C. B. 1993. *Understanding family process: Basics of family systems theory.* Thousand Oaks, CA: Sage.

BRODEY, D. 2005. Blacks join the eating-disorder mainstream. *New York Times,* September 20, 1, 8.

BRODIE, M., A. STEFFENSON, J. VALDEZ, AND R. LEVIN. 2002. 2002 national survey of Latinos. Pew Hispanic Center/The Henry Kaiser Family Foundation. www.pewhispanic.org (accessed Apr. 16, 2003).

BRODY, G. H., S. DORSEY, R. FOREHAND, and L. ARMISTEAD. 2002. Unique and protective contributions of parenting and classroom processes to the adjustment of African American children living in single-parent families. *Child Development* 63 (January–February): 274–86.

BROMAN, C. L., V. L. HAMILTON, AND W. S. HOFFMAN. 2001. *Stress and distress among the unemployed: Hard times and vulnerable people.* New York: Kluwer Academic/Plenum.

BRONFENBRENNER, U. 1979. *The ecology of human development: Experiments by nature and design.* Cambridge, MA: Harvard University Press.

BRONFENBRENNER, U. 1986. Ecology of the family as a context for human development: Research perspectives. *Developmental Psychology* 22: 723–42.

BROOK, J. S., C. M. CONNELL, C. M. MITCHELL, AND S. M. MASON. 2002. Drug use and neurobehavioral, respiratory, and cognitive problems: Precursors and mediators. *Journal of Adolescent Health* 30 (June): 433–41.

BROOKS, A. 1994. Sexism's bitterest trick. *New Scientist,* Mar. 12, 48–49.

BROOKS, D. 2000. *Bobos in paradise: The new upper class and how they got there.* New York: Simon & Schuster.

BROOKS, D. 2003. Love, Internet style. *New York Times,* November 8, A15.

BROOKS, G. R. 1995. *The centerfold syndrome: How men can overcome objectification and achieve intimacy with women.* San Francisco: Jossey-Bass.

BROOKS-GUNN, J., P. K. KLEBANOV, AND G. J. DUNCAN. 1996. Ethnic differences in children's intelligence test scores: Role of economic deprivation, home environment, and material characteristics. *Child Development* 67 (Apr.): 396–408.

BROTHERSON, S. E., and W. C. DUNCAN. 2004. Rebinding the ties that bind: Government efforts to preserve and promote marriage. *Family Relations* 53 (October): 459–68.

BROWN, B. V., E. A. MICHELSEN, T. G. HALLE, AND K. A. MOORE. 2001. Fathers' activities with their kids. Washington, DC: Child Trends. www.childtrends.org (accessed Aug. 23, 2003).

BROWN, J. D., J. R. STEELE, AND K. WALSH-CHILDERS, eds. 2002. *Sexual teens, sexual media: Investigating media's influence on adolescent sexuality.* Mahwah, NJ: Lawrence Erlbaum.

BROWN, J. K. 1992. Lives of middle-aged women. In *In her prime: New views of middle-aged women,* 2nd ed., eds. V. Kerns and J. K. Brown, 17–30. Urbana: University of Illinois Press.

BROWN, N. M., AND E. S. AMATEA. 2000. *Love and intimate relationships: Journeys of the heart.* Philadelphia: Brunner/Mazel.

BROWN, P. M. 1995. *The death of intimacy: Barriers to meaningful interpersonal relationships.* New York: Haworth.

BROWN, S. 2002. Child well-being in cohabiting families. In *Just living together: Implications of cohabitation on families, children, and social policy,* eds. A. Booth and A. C. Crouter, 173–88. Mahwah, NJ: Erlbaum.

BROWN, S. I. 2005. How cohabitation is reshaping American families. *Contexts* 4 (Summer): 33–37.

BROWN, S. L. 2004. Family structure and child well-being: The significance of parental cohabitation. *Journal of Marriage and Family* 66 (May): 351–67.

BROWNE, A. 1993. Family violence and homelessness: The relevance of trauma histories in the lives of homeless women. *American Journal of Orthopsychiatry* 63 (July): 370–84.

BROWNING, S. W. 1994. Treating stepfamilies: Alternatives of traditional family therapy. In *Stepparenting: Issues in theory, research, and practice,* eds. K. Pasley and M. Ihinger-Tallman, 175–198. Westport, CT: Greenwood.

BRÜCKNER, H., AND P. BEARMAN. 2005. After the promise: The STD consequences of adolescent virginity pledges. *Journal of Adolescent Health* 36 (April): 271–78.

BRÜCKNER, H. A. M., AND P. S. BEARMAN. 2004. Ambivalence and pregnancy: Adolescents' attitudes, contraceptive use and pregnancy. *Perspectives on Sexual and Reproductive Health.* 36 (Nov./Dec.): 248–57.

BRULLIARD, K. 2006. Last rites, tailored to immigrant customs. *Washington Post,* April 24, A1.

BRUNI, F. 2002. Persistent drop in fertility reshapes Europe's future. *New York Times,* Dec. 26, A1.

BRYANT, C. M., R. D. CONGER, AND J. M. MEEHAN. 2001. The influence of in-laws on change in marital success. *Journal of Marriage and Family* 63 (Aug.): 614–26.

BRYNES, G. 2001. Dealing with dementia. Northern County Psychiatric Associates, Baltimore. www.ncpamd.com/dementia.htm (accessed Oct. 9, 2003).

BUCHANAN, C. M., E. E. MACCOBY, AND S. M. DORNBUSCH. 1996. *Adolescents after divorce.* Cambridge, MA: Harvard University Press.

BUCKS, B. K., A. B. KENNICKELL, AND K. B. MOORE. 2006. Recent changes in U.S. family finances: Evidence from the 2001 and 2004 survey of consumer finances. *Federal Reserve Bulletin,* www.federalreserve.gov/ (accessed May 2, 2006).

BUETTNER, D. 2005. The secrets of long life. *National Geographic,* November, 2–26.

BULCROFT, K., L. SMEINS, AND R. BULCROFT. 1999. *Romancing the honeymoon: Consummating marriage in modern society.* Thousand Oaks, CA: Sage.

BULCROFT, R. A., AND K. A. BULCROFT. 1993. Race differences in attitudinal and motivational factors in the decision to marry. *Journal of Marriage and the Family* 55 (May): 338–55.

BULCROFT, R., AND J. TEACHMAN. 2004. Ambiguous constructions: Development of a childless or child-free life course. In *Handbook of contemporary families: Considering the past, contemplating the future,* eds. M. Coleman and L. H. Ganong, 116–35. Thousand Oaks, CA: Sage.

BULIK, C. M., AND ET AL. 2006. Prevalence, heritability, and prospective risk factors for anorexia nervosa. *Archive of General Psychiatry* 63 (Mar.): 305–12.

BULLOCK, K. 2005. Grandfathers and the impact of raising grandchildren. *Journal of Sociology and Social Welfare* 32 (March): 43–59.

BUMPASS, L., AND H.-H. LU. 2000. Trends in cohabitation and implications for children's family contexts in the United States. *Population Studies* 54 (Mar.): 29–41.

BUMPASS, L. L., J. SWEET, AND T. C. MARTIN. 1990. Changing patterns of remarriage. *Journal of Marriage and the Family* 52 (Aug.): 747–756.

BUMPASS, L. L., R. K. RALEY, AND J. A. SWEET. 1995. The changing character of stepfamilies: Implications of cohabitation and nonmarital childbearing. *Demography* 32 (Aug.): 425–36.

BURGESS, E. W., H. J. LOCKE, AND M. M. THOMES. 1963. *The family from institution to companionship.* New York: American Book Co.

BURLESON, B. R., AND W. H. DENTON. 1997. The relationships between communication skill and marital satisfaction: Some moderating effects. *Journal of Marriage and the Family* 59 (Nov.): 884–902.

BURR, C. 1996. *A separate creation: The search for the biological origins of sexual orientation.* New York: Hyperion.

BURR, W. R. 1995. Using theories in family science. In *Research and theory in family science,* eds. R. D. Day, K. R. Gilbert, B. H. Settles, and W. R. Burr, 73–90. Pacific Grove, CA: Brooks/Cole.

BURT, M. R., L. Y. ARON, T. DOUGLAS, J. VALENTE, E. LEE, AND B. IWEN. 1999. Homelessness: Programs and the people they serve. Urban Institute, Washington, DC. www.urban.org (accessed Oct. 11, 2000).

BURTON, L. M., AND C. B. STACK. 1993. Conscripting kin: Reflections on family, generation, and culture. In *Family, self, and society: Toward a new agenda for family research,* eds. P. A. Cowan, D. Field, D. A. Hansen, A. Skolnick, and G. E. Swanson, 115–42. Hillsdale, NJ: Erlbaum.

BUSBY, D., M. BRANDT, C. GARDNER, AND N. TANIGUCHI. 2005. The family of origin parachute model: Landing safely in adult romantic relationships. *Family Relations* 54 (April): 254–64.

BUSHMAN, B. J., A. M. BONACCI, M. VAN DIJK, AND R. F. BAUMEISTER. 2003. Narcissism, sexual refusal, and aggression: Testing a narcissistic reactance model of sexual coercion. *Journal of Personality and Social Psychology* 84 (May): 1027–40.

BUSS, D. M. 2000. *The dangerous passion: Why jealousy is as necessary as love and sex.* New York: Free Press.

BUSS, D. M., AND D. P. SCHMITT. 1993. Sexual strategies theory: An evolutionary perspective on human mating. *Psychological Review* 100 (April): 204–232.

BUSS, D. M., R. J. LARSEN, AND D. WESTEN. 1996. Commentary: Sex differences in jealousy: Not gone, not forgotten, and not explained by alternative hypotheses. *Psychological Science* 7 (Nov.): 373–75.

BUSS, D. M., T. K. SHACKELFORD, L. A. KIRKPATRICK, and R. J. LARSEN. 2001. A half century of mate preferences: The cultural evolution of values. *Journal of Marriage and Family* 63 (May): 491–503.

BUSSEY, K., AND A. BANDURA. 1992. Self-regulatory mechanisms governing gender development. *Child Development* 63 (Oct.): 1236–50.

BUTLER, J. 2003. XXY marks the spot "X." FTM Australia, Jan. 21. www.ftmaustralia.org (accessed June 11, 2003).

BUTLER, R. N. 1975. *Why survive? Being old in America.* New York: Harper & Row.

BUTLER, R. N., AND M. I. LEWIS. 1993. *Love and sex after 60.* New York: Ballantine.

BUTRICA, B. A., S. G. SCHANER., AND S. R. ZEDLEWSKI. 2006. Enjoying the golden work years. The Urban Institute, May, www.urban.org (accessed August 3, 2006).

BYGREN, M., AND A.-Z. DUVANDER. 2006. Parent's workplace situation and fathers' parental leave use. *Journal of Marriage and Family* 68 (May): 363–72.

CACIOPPO, J. T., ET AL. 2002. Loneliness and health: Potential mechanisms. *Psychosomatic Medicine* 64 (May/June): 407–17.

CAFFARO, J. V., AND A. CONN-CAFFARO. 1998. *Sibling abuse trauma: Assessment and intervention strategies for children, families, and adults.* New York: Haworth.

CALDWELL, M. A., AND L. A. PEPLAU. 1990. The balance of power in lesbian relationships. In *Perspectives on the family: History, class, and feminism,* ed., C. Carlton, 204–15. Belmont, CA: Wadsworth.

CALL, V., S. SPRECHER, AND P. SCHWARTZ. 1995. The incidence and frequency of marital sex in a national sample. *Journal of Marriage and the Family* 57: 639–50.

CALVERT, S. 2003. Ruling on gays stirs up emotions. *Baltimore Sun*, June 28, 1A, 5A.

CALVERT, S. 2006. South Africans defend the price of tying the knot. *Baltimore Sun*, July 24, 1A, 10A.

CAMARILLO, A. 1979. *Chicanos in a changing society: From Mexican pueblos to American barrios in Santa Barbara and southern California, 1848–1930.* Cambridge, MA: Harvard University Press.

CAMPBELL, F., AND C. RAMEY. 1999. *The Carolina abecedarian project.* www.fpg.unc.edu/~abc (accessed Sep. 24, 2000).

CAMPBELL, K. 2001. A "woman shortage"? Reports shift men's views on dating. *Christian Science Monitor*, Dec. 27, 3.

CAMPBELL, K. 2002. Today's courtship: White teeth, root beer, and e-mail? *Christian Science Monitor*, Feb. 14, 1, 4.

CAMPBELL, K. 2005. Goodbye, computer dating. Hello, matchmakers! *Christian Science Monitor* (April 20): 11–13.

CAMPBELL, P. W. 1999. Researcher found guilty of misconduct. *Chronicle of Higher Education*, Jan. 15, A34.

CAMPBELL, W. K., C. A. FOSTER, AND E. J. FINKEL. 2002. Does self-love lead to love for others? A study of narcissistic game playing. *Journal of Personality and Social Psychology* 83 (Aug.): 340–54.

CANARY, D. J., W. R. CUPACH, AND S. J. MESSMAN. 1995. *Relationship conflict: Conflict in parent–child, friendship, and romantic relationships.* Thousand Oaks, CA: Sage.

CANCIAN, F. M. 1990. The feminization of love. In *Perspectives on the family: History, class, and feminism*, ed. C. Carlson, 171–85. Belmont, CA: Wadsworth.

CANEDY, D. 2002. Hospitals feeling strain from illegal immigrants. *New York Times*, Aug. 25. www.nytimes.com (accessed Aug. 25, 2002).

CANTWELL, H. B. 1997. The neglect of child neglect. In *The battered child*, 5th ed., eds. M. E. Helfer, R. S. Kempe, and R. D. Krugman, 347–73. Chicago: University of Chicago Press.

CAPIZZANO, J., AND G. ADAMS. 2000. The number of child care arrangements used by children under five: Variation across states. Urban Institute. newfederalism.urban.org (accessed Sep. 27, 2000).

CAPIZZANO, J., G. ADAMS, AND J. OST. 2006. The child care patterns of white, black and Hispanic children. The Urban Institute, www.urban.org (accessed May 10, 2006).

CAPLAN, J. 2005. Metrosexual matrimony. *Time*, Oct. 3, 67.

CAPPS, R., AND M. FIX. 2005. Undocumented immigrants: Myths and reality. Urban Institute, October 25, www.urban.org (accessed November 19, 2005).

CAPPS, R., M. E. FIX, J. OST, J. REARDON-ANDERSON, AND J. S. PASSEL. 2005. The health and well-being of young children of immigrants. The Urban Institute, www.urban.org (accessed May 10, 2006).

CARCAN, L., AND M. MELKO. 1982. *Singles: Myths and realities.* Beverly Hills, CA: Sage.

CAREY, B. 2005. Experts dispute Bush on gay-adoption issue. *New York Times*, January 29, A16.

CARLSON, D. K. 2001. Over half of Americans believe in love at first sight. Gallup News Service, Feb. 14. www.gallup.com (accessed May 19, 2003).

CARLSON, L. H., AND G. A. COLBURN, EDS. 1972. In *their place: White America defines her minorities, 1850–1950.* New York: Wiley.

CARLSON, M. J. 2006. Family structure, father involvement, and adolescent behavioral outcomes. *Journal of Marriage and Family* 68 (February): 137–54.

CARLSON, M., S. McLANAHAN, AND P. ENGLAND. 2004. Union formation in fragile families. *Demography* 41 (May): 237–261.

CARNOY, M., AND D. CARNOY. 1997. *Fathers of a certain age: The joys and problems of middle-aged fatherhood.* Minneapolis, MN: Fairview Press.

CARP, F. M. 2000. *Elder abuse in the family: An interdisciplinary model for research.* New York: Springer.

CARR, D. 2004. The desire to date and remarry among older widows and widowers. *Journal of Marriage and Family* 66 (Nov.): 1051–1068.

CARR, D., AND C. L. HAYS. 2003. 3 racy men's magazines banned by Wal-Mart. *New York Times*, May 5. www.nytimes.com (accessed May 6, 2003).

CARR, D., C. B. WORTMAN, AND K. WOLFF. 2006. How older Americans die today: Implications for surviving spouses. In *Spousal bereavement in late life*, eds. D. Carr, R. M. Nesse, and C. B. Wortman, 49–78. New York: Springer.

CARRASQUILLO, H. 2002. The Puerto Rican family. In *Minority families in the United States: A multicultural perspective*, 3rd ed., ed. R. L. Taylor, 101–13. Upper Saddle River, NJ: Prentice Hall.

CARRIER, J. M., AND S. O. MURRAY. 1998. Woman-woman marriage in Africa. In *Boy-wives and female husbands: Studies of African homosexualities*, eds. S. O. Murray and W. Roscoe, 255–66. New York: St. Martin's.

CARROLL, B. T. 2003. Salvaging a career. *Chronicle of Higher Education*, May 16, C4.

CARROLL, J. 2006. Drugs, smoking, alcohol most important problem facing teens. Gallup Organization, February 17, www.gallup.com (accessed May 27, 2006).

CARROLL, J. 2006. Whites, minorities differ in views of economic opportunities in U.S. Gallup Organization, July 10, www.gallup.com (accessed July 18, 2006).

CARROLL, J. 2006. Women more likely than men to say they've been divorced. Gallup News Service, April 5, www.gallup.com (accessed April 8, 2006).

CARROLL, J. S., AND W. J. DOHERTY. 2003. Evaluating the effectiveness of premarital prevention programs: A Meta-analytic review of outcome research. *Family Relations* 52 (April): 105–18.

CARTER, L. D. 2003. Trusted adults prevent HIV. *Democrat and Chronicle*, June 18. www.democratandchronicle.com (accessed June 20, 2003).

CARTER, S., AND J. SOKOL. 1993. *He's scared, she's scared: Understanding the hidden fears that sabotage your relationships*, New York: Delacorte.

CASEY, T. 1998. *Pride and joy: The lives and passions of women without children.* Hillboro, OR: Beyond Words.

CASLER, L. 1974. *Is marriage necessary?* New York: Human Sciences Press.

CASPI, A., ET AL. 2003. Influence of life stress on depression: Moderation by a polymorphism in the 5-HTT gene. *Science* 301 (July 18): 386–89.

CASSIDY, J., AND S. R. ASHER. 1992. Loneliness and peer relations in young children. *Child Development* 63 (Apr.): 350–65.

CASSIDY, M. L., AND G. R. LEE. 1989. The study of polyandry: A critique and synthesis. *Journal of Comparative Family Studies* 20 (Spring): 1–11.

CASSIDY, S. 1993. A single woman: The fabric of my life. In *Single women: Affirming our spiritual journeys*, eds. M. O'Brien and C. Christie, 35–48. Westport, CT: Bergin & Garvey.

CATALANO, S. M. 2004. *Criminal victimization, 2003.* Washington, DC: U.S. Department of Justice, Bureau of Justice Statistics.

CATE, R. M., AND S. A. LLOYD. 1992. *Courtship.* Thousand Oaks, CA: Sage.

CAUTHEN, N. K., AND H.-H. LU. 2003. Living at the edge. National Center for Children in Poverty. www.nccp.org (accessed Sept. 16, 2003).

CAVAN, R. S., AND K. H. RANCK. 1938. *The family and the Depression: A study of one hundred Chicago families.* Chicago: University of Chicago Press.

CAWLEY, J. 2001. Body weight and the dating and sexual behaviors of young adolescents. In *Social awakening: Adolescent behavior as adulthood approaches*, ed. R. T. Michael, 174–98. New York: Russell Sage Foundation.

CEBALLO, R., T. A. DAHL, M. T. ARETAKIS, AND C. RAMIREZ. 2001. Inner-city children's exposure to community violence: How much do parents know? *Journal of Marriage and the Family* 63 (Nov.): 927–40.

CEJKA, M. A. 1993. A demon with no name: Prejudice against single women. In *Single women: Affirm-*

ing our spiritual journeys, eds. M. O'Brien and C. Christie, 3–11. Westport, CT: Bergin & Garvey.

CENTER FOR THE ADVANCEMENT OF WOMEN. 2003. *Progress and perils: New agenda for women.* www.advancewomen.org (accessed Aug. 21, 2003).

CENTER FOR AMERICAN WOMEN AND POLITICS. 2005. Facts and findings: Women in statewide elective executive office. www.cawp.rutgers.edu (accessed November 30, 2005).

CENTER FOR LAW AND SOCIAL POLICY. 2004. Child support dramatically increases economic well-being of low- and moderate-income families. www.clasp.org (accessed July 3, 2006).

CENTERS FOR DISEASE CONTROL AND PREVENTION. 2003. First reports evaluating the effectiveness of strategies for preventing violence: Early childhood home visitation and firearms laws. Findings from the Task Force on Community Preventive Services. *Morbidity and Mortality Weekly Report* 52 (No. RR-14): 1–23.

CENTERS FOR DISEASE CONTROL AND PREVENTION. 2003. HIV/AIDS Surveillance Report, 2002, 14: 1–48. www.cdc.gov (accessed November 26, 2003).

CENTERS FOR DISEASE CONTROL AND PREVENTION. 2004. Diagnoses of HIV/AIDS—32 states, 2000–2003. *MMWR* 53 (December 3): 1106–10.

CENTERS FOR DISEASE CONTROL AND PREVENTION. 2005a. *HIV/AIDS Surveillance Report, 2004.* Atlanta, GA: U.S. Department of Health and Human Services.

CENTERS FOR DISEASE CONTROL AND PREVENTION. 2005b. *Sexually transmitted disease surveillance, 2004.* Atlanta, GA: U.S. Department of Health and Human Services.

CHADDOCK, G. R. 2003. For Hispanics, cultural shift and new tensions. *Christian Science Monitor*, Jan. 23, 1, 3.

CHADVIN, L. 2002. Catholic U. in Peru angers students by handing out pamphlet calling homosexuality an illness. *Chronicle of Higher Education*, Sep. 19. http://chronicle.com/ (accessed Sept. 20, 2002).

CHAFE, W. H. 1972. *The American woman: Her changing social, economic, and political roles, 1920–1970.* New York: Oxford University Press.

CHAMBERS, V. 2003. *Having it all? Black women and success.* New York: Doubleday.

CHAN, S. 1997. Families with Asian roots. In *Developing cross-cultural competence: A guide for working with children and families*, 2nd ed., eds. E. W. Lynch and M. J. Hanson, 251–353. Baltimore: Paul H. Brookes.

CHAN, S. 1999. Families with Asian roots. In *Developing cross-cultural competence: A guide for working with children and their families*, 2nd ed., eds. E. W. Lynch and M. J. Hanson, 251–344. Baltimore: Paul H. Brookes.

CHANCE, P. 1988. The trouble with love. *Psychology Today* (Feb.): 22–23.

CHANDRA, A., G. A. MARTINEZ, W. D. MOSHER, J.C. ABMA, AND J. JONES. 2005. Fertility, family planning, and reproductive health of U.S. women: Data from the 2002 national survey of family growth. *Vital and Health Statistics* (Series 23, No. 25). Hyattsville, MD: National Center for Health Statistics.

CHANG, G. 2000. *Disposable domestics: Immigrant women workers in the global economy.* Cambridge, MA: South End.

CHANG, J., AND A. MOON. 1997. Korean American elderly's knowledge and perceptions of elder abuse: A qualitative analysis of cultural factors. *Journal of Multicultural Social Work* 6 (1/2): 139–54.

CHANG, J., C. J. BERG, L. E. SALTZMAN, AND J. HERNDON. 2005. Homicide: A leading cause of injury deaths among pregnant and postpartum women in the United States, 1991–1999. *American Journal of Public Health* 95 (March): 471–77.

CHANG, J., L. D. ELAM-EVANS, C. J. BERG, J. HERNDON, L. FLOWERS, K. A. SEED, AND C. J. SYVERSON. 2003. Pregnancy-related mortality surveillance: United States, 1991–1999. *Morbidity and Mortality Weekly Report* 52 (Feb. 21): 1–8. www.cdc.gov (accessed Aug. 2, 2003).

CHAO, R., AND V. TSENG. 2002. Parenting of Asians. In *Handbook of parenting*, 2nd ed., Vol. 4: *Social conditions and applied parenting*, ed. M. H. Bornstein, 59–93. Mahwah, NJ: Erlbaum.

CHARLES, S. T., AND L. L. CARSTENSEN. 2002. Marriage in old age. In *Inside the American couple: New thinking/new challenges*, eds. M. Yalom and L. L. Carstensen, 236–54. Berkeley: University of California Press.

CHARLES, S. T., M. MATHER, AND L. L. CARSTENSEN. 2003. Aging and emotional memory: The forgettable nature of negative images for older adults. *Journal of Experimental Psychology* 132 (June): 310–24.

CHARLESWORTH, A., AND S. A. GLANTZ. 2005. Smoking in the movies increases adolescent smoking: A review. *Pediatrics* 116 (Dec.): 1516–28.

CHASE-LANSDALE, P. L., A. J. CHERLIN, AND K. E. KIERNAN. 1995. The long-term effects of parental divorce on the mental health of young adults: A developmental perspective. *Child Development* 66 (Dec.): 1614–34.

CHATTERS, L. M., AND R. J. TAYLOR. 2005. Religion and families. In *Sourcebook of family theory & research*, eds. V. L. Bengston, A. C. Acock, K. R. Allen, P. Dilworth-Anderson, and D. M. Klein, 517–30. Thousand Oaks, CA: Sage.

CHAUDRY, A. 2004. *Putting children first: How low-wage working mothers manage child care*. New York: Russell Sage Foundation.

CHAUVIN, 2002. Catholic U. in Peru angers students by handing out pamphlets calling homosexuality an illness. *Chronicle if Higher Education*, Sept. 19. http://chronicle.com (accessed Sept. 20, 2002.)

CHEKKI, D. A. 1996. Family values and family change. *Journal of Comparative Family Studies* 27 (Summer): 409–13.

CHELALA, C. 2002. World violence against women a great unspoken pandemic. *Philadelphia Inquirer*, Nov. 4. www.commondreams.org (accessed Nov. 7, 2002).

CHEN, A. S. 1999. Lives at the center of the periphery, lives at the periphery of the center: Chinese American masculinities and bargaining with hegemony. *Gender & Society* 13 (Oct.): 584–607.

CHEN, Z.-Y., AND H. B. KAPLAN. 2001. Intergenerational transmission of constructive parenting. *Journal of Marriage and Family* 63 (Feb.): 17–31.

CHERLIN, A. J., AND F. F. FURSTENBERG, JR. 1994. Stepfamilies in the United States: A reconsideration. *Annual Review of Sociology* 20: 359–81.

CHESHIRE, T. C. 2001. Cultural transmission in urban American Indian families. *American Behavioral Scientist* 44 (May): 1528–35.

CHESLER, P. 2002. *Woman's inhumanity to woman*. New York: Thunder's Mouth/Nation.

CHESNEY-LIND, M., AND L. PASKO. 2004. *The female offender: Girls, women, and crime*, 2nd ed. Thousand Oaks, CA: Sage.

CHEVAN, A. 1996. As cheaply as one: Cohabitation in the older population. *Journal of Marriage and the Family* 58 (Aug.): 656–67.

Child fatalities fact sheet. 2000. National Clearinghouse on Child Abuse and Neglect Information, Washington, DC. www.calib.com/ (accessed Oct. 18, 2000).

CHILDREN'S DEFENSE FUND. 2002. *The state of children in America's union*. www.childrensdefense.org (accessed Aug. 25, 2003).

CHILDREN'S DEFENSE FUND. 2005. *State of America's Children 2005*. Washington, DC: Children's Defense Fund.

CHILDREN'S DEFENSE FUND ACTION COUNCIL. 2005. Stand up for children *now*! State of America's children's action guide, www.cdfactioncouncil.org (accessed May 14, 2006).

CHILDTRENDS DATA BANK. Dating. 2005. www.childtrendsdatabank.org/pdf/73_PDF.pdf (accessed February 24, 2006).

Child welfare and chemical dependency fact sheet. 2001. Child Welfare League of America. www.cwla.org/ (accessed Sept. 19, 2003).

Child welfare outcomes: 1998 annual report. 2000. Washington, DC: Department of Health and Human Services.

CHIN, E. 2001. *Purchasing power: Black kids and American consumer culture*. Minneapolis: University of Minnesota Press.

China: Drug bid to beat child ban. 2006. CNN News, www.cnn.com, February 13 (accessed February 16, 2006).

CHION-KENNEY, L. 1991. Parents of divorce. *Washington Post*, May 6, B5.

CHIVERS, C. J. 2004. Russian gal seeking comrade? No, it's an Internet scam. *New York Time*, Nov. 3, A3.

CHLEBOWSKI, R. T. et al. 2004. Estrogen plus progestin and colorectal cancer in postmenopausal women. *New England Journal of Medicine* 350 (March 4): 991–1004.

CHO, D. 2003. For Koreans, changes in store; N. Va. grocery, churches reflect shifts in community. *Washington Post*, Jan. 13, A1. www.washingtonpost.com (accessed Jan. 13, 2003).

CHO, W., AND S. E. CROSS. 1995. Taiwanese love styles and their association with self-esteem and relationship quality. *Genetic, Social, and General Psychology Monographs* 121: 283–309.

CHOICE, P., AND L. K. LAMKE. 1997. A conceptual approach to understanding abused women's stay/leave decisions. *Journal of Family Issues* 18 (May): 290–314.

'Choose life' license plates. 2006. State Policies in Brief, The Alan Guttmacher Institute, www.guttmacher.org (accessed May 3, 2006).

CHOPRA, A. 2006. Childless couples look to India for surrogate mothers. *Christian Science Monitor*, April 3, 1, 11.

CHRISTAKIS, N. A., AND P. D. ALLISON. 2006. Mortality after the hospitalization of a spouse. *New England Journal of Medicine* 354 (February 16): 719–730.

CHRISTENSON, E. 2003. What women want. *Newsweek*, Feb. 17, 11.

CHRISTOPHER, F. S. 2001. *To dance the dance: A symbolic interactional exploration of premarital sexuality*. Mahwah, NJ: Erlbaum.

CHRISTOPHER, F. S., AND T. S. KISLER. 2004. Sexual aggression in romantic relationships. In *The handbook of sexuality in close relationships*, eds. J. Harvey, A. Wenzel, and S. Sprecher, 287–409. Mahwah, NJ: Lawrence Erlbaum.

Chronicle of Higher Education. 2006. Attitudes and characteristics of freshmen at 4-year colleges, Fall 2005. Almanac Issue 2006–7. 53 (August): 19.

CHU, H. 2001. Chinese psychiatrists decide homosexuality isn't abnormal: New guidelines are hailed as a "leap forward" bringing nation more in line with the West. *Los Angeles Times*, Mar. 6, A1.

CHU, H. 2006. Wombs for rent, cheap. *Los Angeles Times*, April 19, A1.

CHUN, H., AND I. LEE. 2001. Why do married men earn more? Productivity or marriage selection? *Economic Inquiry* 39 (Apr.): 307–19.

CIABATTARI, T. 2004. Cohabitation and housework: The effects of marital intentions. *Journal of Marriage and Family* 66 (February): 118–25.

CLARK, C. L., P. R. SHAVER, AND M. F. ABRAHAMS. 1999. Strategic behaviors in romantic relationship initiation. *Personality and Social Psychology Bulletin* 25: 707–20.

CLARK, J. M. 1999. *Doing the work of love: Men & commitment in same-sex couples*. Harriman, TN: Men's Studies Press.

CLARK-IBÁÑEZ, M., AND D. FELMLEE. 2004. Interethnic relationships: The role of social network diversity. *Journal of Marriage and Family* 66 (May): 292–305.

CLARKE, S. C. 1995. Advance report of final divorce statistics, 1989 and 1990. *Monthly Vital Statistics Report* 43 (9(S)), Mar. 22. Centers for Disease Control and Prevention.

CLARKE, S. C., AND B. F. WILSON. 1994. The relative stability of remarriages: A cohort approach using vital statistics. *Family Relations* 43 (July): 305–10.

CLARKSON, F. 2002. Priest group launches antisex-ed campaign. *Women's E-News*, Nov. 14, www.womensnews.org (accessed Nov. 15, 2002).

CLAYTON, M. 2001. The gender equation. *Christian Science Monitor*, May 22, 11–18.

CLAYTON, M. 2002. Has equality in sports gone too far? *Christian Science Monitor*, Dec. 27, 1, 4.

CLEARFIELD, M. W., AND N. M. NELSON. 2006. Sex differences in mothers' speech and play behavior with 6-, 9-, and 14-month-old infants. *Sex Roles* 54 (January): 127–37.

CLEMENTS, M. L., S. M. STANLEY, AND H. J. MARKMAN. 2004. Before they said "I do": Discriminating among marital outcomes over 13 years. *Journal of Marriage and Family* 66 (August): 613–626.

CLEMETSON, L. 2006. Adopted in China, seeking identity in America. *New York Times*, March 23, A1, A18.

CLEMETSON, L., AND F. MCROBERTS. 2001. A confession from Jesse. *Newsweek*, January 29, 38.

CLOUD, J. 2005. The battle over gay teens. *Time*, October 10, 43–51.

CLUNIS, D. M., AND G. D. GREEN. 2000. *Lesbian couples: A guide to creating healthy relationships*. Seattle: Seal.

COHAN, C. I., AND S. KLEINBAUM. 2002. Toward a greater understanding of the cohabitation effect: Premarital cohabitation and marital communication. *Journal of Marriage and Family* 64 (Feb.): 180–92.

COHEN, C. E. 1994. The trailing-spouse dilemma. *Working Woman* (Mar.): 69–70.

COHEN, D. 2000. The myth of the midlife crisis. *Newsweek*, January 16, 82–87.

COHN, D. 2000. Census complaints [in] home. *Washington Post*, May 4, A9.

COHN, L. 2003. One child, four parents. *Christian Science Monitor*, Feb. 19, 11–13.

COHN, L. 2005. Remarriage after retirement. *Christian Science Monitor*, June 8, 11–12.

COLAPINTO, J. 1997. The true story of John/Joan. *Rolling Stone*, Dec. 11, 54–73, 92–97.

COLE, A. 1996. Yours, mine and ours. *Modern Maturity* (Sep./Oct.): 12, 14–15.

COLE, M. G., AND N. DENDUKURI. 2003. Risk factors for depression among elderly community subjects: A systematic review and meta-analysis. *American Journal of Psychiatry* 160 (June): 1147–56.

COLEMAN, M., L. H. GANONG, AND S. WEAVER. 2001. Relationship maintenance and enhancement in remarried families. In *Close romantic relationships: Maintenance and enhancement*, eds. J. H. Harvey and A. Wenzel, 255–76. Mahwah, NJ: Erlbaum.

COLEMAN, M., L. H. GANONO, AND M. FINE. 2002. Reinvestigating remarriage: Another decade of progress. In *Understanding families into the new millennium: A decade in review*, ed. R. M. Milardo, 507–26. Minneapolis: National Council on Family Relations.

COLEY, R. L. 2002. What mothers teach, what daughters learn: Gender mistrust and self-sufficiency among low-income women. In *Just living together: Implications of cohabitation on families, children, and social policy*, eds. A. Booth and A. C. Crouter, 97–106. Mahwah, NJ: Erlbaum.

COLLIER, J. 1947. *The Indians of the Americas*. New York: Norton.

COLLINS, C. 2005. N.H. adoptees gain access to records. *Christian Science Monitor*, Jan 13, 11-12.

COLLINS, R. L. 2005. Sex on television and its impact on American youth: Background and results from the RAND television and adolescent sexuality study. *Child and Adolescent Psychiatric Clinics of North America* 14 (July): 371–85.

COLLINS, R. L., P. L. ELLICKSON, D. F. MCCAFFREY, AND K. HAMBARSOOMIANS. 2005. Saturated in beer: Awareness of beer advertising in late childhood and adolescences. *Journal of Adolescent Health* 37 (July): 29–36.

COLLISON, M. N.-K. 1993. A sure-fire winner is to tell her you love her; women fall for it all the time. In *Women's studies: Thinking women*, eds. J. Wetzel, M. L. Espenlaub, M. A. Hagen, A. B. McElhiney, and C. B. Williams, 228–30. Dubuque, IA: Kendall/Hunt.

COLTRANE, S. 1996. *Family man: Fatherhood, housework, and gender equality*. New York: Oxford University Press.

COLTRANE, S. 2000. Research on household labor: Modeling and measuring the social embeddedness of routine family work. *Journal of Marriage and the Family* 62 (Nov.): 1208–33.

COLTRANE, S., R. D. PARKE, AND M. ADAMS. 2004. Complexity of father involvement in low-income Mexican American families. *Family Relations* 53 (March): 179–89.

Come here often? 2002. *Public Perspective* 13 (Sep./Oct.): 52.

COMERFORD, L. 2005. Co-custody may have unintended results. *National Council on Family Relations Report* 50 (June): F28–F29.

COMIJS, H. C., A. M. POT, H. H. SMIT, AND C. JONKER. 1998. Elder abuse in the community: Prevalence and consequences. *Journal of American Geriatrics Society* 46 (7): 885–88.

CONDE-AGUDELO, A., A., ROSAS-BERMÚDEZ, AND A. C. KAFURY-GOETA. 2006. Birth spacing and risk of adverse perinatal outcomes: A meta-analysis. *JAMA* 295 (April 19): 1809–23.

CONGER, R. D., AND K. J. CONGER. 2002. Resilience in Midwestern families: Selected findings from the first decade of a prospective, longitudinal study. *Journal of Marriage and the Family* 64 (May): 361–73.

CONLEY, D. 2004. *The pecking order: Which siblings succeed and why.* New York: Pantheon.

CONLIN, M. 2001. Taking precautions—or harassing workers? *Business Week,* Dec. 3, 84.

CONLIN, M. 2002. The big squeeze on workers. *Business Week,* May 13, 96–97.

CONLIN, M. 2003. The new gender gap. *Business Week,* May 26, 75–78.

CONLIN, M., J. MERRITT. AND L. HIMELSTEIN. 2002. Mommy is really home from work. *Business Week,* Nov. 25, 101–3.

CONNELLY, J. 1989. The CEO's second wife. *Fortune,* Aug. 28, 53–62.

CONNOLLY, C. 2003. Texas teaches abstinence, with mixed grades. *Washington Post,* Jan. 21, A1.

COOK, A. 2005. Teen guilty of fetal murder. *LufkinDailyNews.com,* June 7 (accessed May 2, 2006).

COOK, C. D. 2002. Street corner, incorporated. *Mother Jones* (Mar./Apr.): 65–69.

COOLIDGE, S. D. 1998. Harassment hits higher profile. *Christian Science Monitor,* Mar. 2, B4–B5.

COONTZ, S. 1992. *The way we never were: American families and the nostalgia trap.* New York: Basic Books.

COONTZ, S. 2005. *Marriage, a history: How love conquered marriage.* New York: Penguin.

COONTZ, S. 2006. A pop quiz on marriage. *New York Times,* February 19, 12.

CORDES, H. 2003. Doping kids. *Mother Jones,* Sep./Oct., 17–18.

CORNELIUS, M. D., AND N. L. DAY. 2000. The effects of tobacco use during and after pregnancy on exposed children: Relevance of findings for alcohol research. *Alcohol Research & Health* 24 (4): 242–49.

COSE, E. 1995. Black men & black women. *Newsweek,* June 5, 66–69.

COSE, E. 1999. Deciphering the code of the street. *Newsweek,* Aug. 30, 33.

COSE, E. 2003. The black gender gap. *Newsweek,* Mar. 3, 46–51.

COSE, E. 2005. Does Cosby help? *Newsweek,* Jan. 3, 66–69.

COSTIGAN, C. L., D. P. DORIS, AND T. F. SU. 2004. Marital relationships among immigrant Chinese couples. In *Vision 2004: What is the future of marriage?* eds. P. Amato and N. Gonzalez, 41–44. Minneapolis, MN: National Council on Family Relations.

COTÉ, J. E. 2000. *Arrested adulthood: The changing nature of maturity and identity.* New York: New York University Press.

COTT, N. F. 1976. Eighteenth century family and social life revealed in Massachusetts divorce records. *Journal of Social History* 10 (Fall): 20–43.

COTT, N. F. 1977. *The bonds of womanhood.* New Haven, CT: Yale University Press.

COTT, N. F., AND E. H. PLECK, EDS. 1979. *A heritage of her own: Toward a new social history of American women.* New York: Simon & Schuster.

COTTEN, S. R. 1999. Marital status and mental health revisited: Examining the importance of risk factors and resources. *Family Relations* 48 (July): 225–33.

COVEL, S. 2003. Cheating hearts. *American Demographics* 25 (June): 16.

COVEL, S. 2003. The heart never forgets. *American Demographics* 25 (July/Aug.): 15.

COWAN, C. P., AND P. A. COWAN. 2000. *When partners become parents: The big life change for couples.* Mahwah, NJ: Erlbaum.

COWDERY, R. S., AND C. KNUDSON-MARTIN. 2005. The construction of motherhood: Tasks, relational connection, and gender equality. *Family Relations* 54 (July): 335–45.

COWLEY, G., AND K. SPRINGEN. 1997. Multiplying the risks. *Newsweek,* Dec. 1, 66.

COX, C. B., ED. 2000. *To grandmother's house we go and stay: Perspectives on custodial grandparents.* New York: Springer.

COY, P., AND L. COHN. 2003. Stats: Now you see 'em. . . *Business Week,* Feb. 10, 10.

CRABB, P. B., AND D. BIELAWSKI. 1994. The social representation of material culture and gender in children's books. *Sex Roles* 30 (1/2): 69–79.

CRAIG-HENDERSON, K. M. 2006. *Black men in interracial relationships: What's love got to do with it?* New Brunswick, NJ: Transaction.

CRANDELL, S. 2005. Oh, baby. *AARP Magazine,* September/October, 108–18.

CRAWFORD, D. W., R. M. HOUTS, T. L. HUSTON, AND L. J. GEORGE. 2002. Compatibility, leisure, and satisfaction in marital relationships. *Journal of Marriage and Family* 64 (May): 433–49.

CRENSHAW, A. R. 1992. Assessing the political power of seniors. *Washington Post Family and Retirement Supplement,* Apr. 29, 4–7.

CRISPELL, D. 1992. Myths of the 1950s. *American Demographics* (Aug.): 38–43.

CRISPELL, D. 1993. Planning no family, now or ever. *American Demographics,* 6 (Oct.): 23–24.

CRITTENDEN, A. 2001. *The price of motherhood: Why the most important job in the world is still the least valued.* New York: Metropolitan.

CRITTENDEN, D. 1999. *What our mothers didn't tell us: Why happiness eludes the modern woman.* New York: Simon & Schuster.

CRNIC, K., AND C. LOW. 2002. Everyday stresses and parenting. In *Handbook of parenting,* 2nd ed., Vol. 5: *Practical issues in parenting,* ed. M. H. Bornstein, 243–68. Mahwah, NJ: Erlbaum.

CROHAN, S. E. 1996. Marital quality and conflict across the transition to parenthood in African American and white couples. *Journal of Marriage and the Family* 58 (Nov.): 933–44.

CROSBIE-BURNETT, M., AND E. A. LEWIS. 1993. Use of African-American family structures and functioning to address the challenges of European-American postdivorce families. *Family Relations* 42 (July): 243–48.

CROSBIE-BURNETT, M., AND J. GILES-SIMS. 1994. Adolescent adjustment and stepparenting styles. *Family Relations* 43 (Oct.): 394–99.

CROSBIE-BURNETT, M., AND K. M. MCCLINTIC. 2000. Remarriage and recoupling: A stress perspective. In *Families & change: Coping with stressful events and transitions,* 2nd ed., eds. P. C. McKenry and S. J. Price, 303–32. Thousand Oaks, CA: Sage.

CROSBY, F. J. 1991a. *Illusion and disillusion: The self in love and marriage,* 5th ed. Belmont, CA: Wadsworth.

CROSBY, F. J. 1991b. *Juggling: The unexpected advantages of balancing career and home for women and their families.* New York: Free Press.

CROSNOE, R., AND G. H. ELDER. 2002. Adolescent twins and emotional distress: The interrelated influence of nonshared environment and social structure. *Child Development* 73 (Nov./Dec.): 1761–74.

CROSS, T. L. 1998. Understanding family resiliency from a relational world view. In *Resiliency in Native American and immigrant families,* eds. H. I. McCubbin, E. A. Thompson, A. I. Thompson, and J. E. Fromer, 143–57. Thousand Oaks, CA: Sage.

CROSSEN, C. 1994. *Tainted truth: The manipulation of fact in America.* New York: Simon & Schuster.

CROUTER, A. C., M. F. BUMPUS, M. R. HEAD, AND S. M. MCHALE. 2001. Implications of overwork and overload for the quality of men's family relationships. *Journal of Marriage and Family* 63 (May): 404–16.

CROWELL, J. A., AND E. WATERS. 1994. Bowlby's theory grown up: The role of attachment in adult love relationships. *Psychological Inquiry* 5 (1): 31–34.

CROWLEY, K., M. A. CALLANAN, H. R. TENENBAUM, AND E. ALLEN. 2001. Parents explain more often to boys than to girls during shared scientific thinking. *Psychological Science* 49 (May): 258–61.

CRUIKSBANK, M. 2003. *Learning to be old: Gender, culture, and aging.* Lanham, MD: Rowman & Littlefield.

CRUZ, S. 2003. Home health care exec hit with $1 million verdict in sex discrimination case. *Star Tribune,* Mar. 12. www.startribune.com (accessed Mar. 13, 2003).

CUBER, J., AND P. HAROFF. 1965. *Sex and the significant Americans.* Baltimore: Penguin.

CULLEN, T. T. 2005. A woman's approach to ending perilous rite of passage. *Christian Science Monitor,* June 8, 15, 17.

CUMMINGS, E. M., A. C. SCHERMERHORN, P. T. DAVIES, M. C. GOEKE-MOREY, AND J. S. CUMMINGS. 2006. Interparental discord and child adjustment: Prospective investigations of emotional security as an explanatory mechanism. *Child Development* 77 (Jan./Feb.): 132–52.

CUNNINGHAM, J. D., AND J. K. ANTILL. 1995. Current trends in nonmarital cohabitation: In search of the POSSLQ. In *Under-studied relationships: Off the beaten track,* eds. J. T. Wood and S. Duck, 148–72. Thousand Oaks, CA: Sage.

CUNNINGHAM, M., AND A. THORNTON. 2005. The influence of union transitions on white adults' attitudes toward cohabitation. *Journal of Marriage and Family* 67 (Aug.): 710–20.

CURRIE, J., AND E. TEKIN. 2006. Does child abuse cause crime? Cambridge, MA: National Bureau of Economic Research, Working Paper 12171, http://papers.nber.org/ (accessed June 12, 2006).

CURTIS, J. W. 2005. *Inequities persist for women and non-tenure-track faculty: The annual report on the economic status of the profession, 2004–05.* Washington, DC: American Association of University Professors (AAUP).

CUTRONA, C. E. 1996. *Social support in couples: Marriage as a resource in times of stress.* Thousand Oaks. CA: Sage.

D'AUGELLI, A. R., A. H. GROSSMAN, AND M. T. STARKS. 2005. Parents' awareness of lesbian, gay, and bisexual youths' sexual orientation. *Journal of Marriage and Family* 67 (May): 474–82.

Daily reproductive health report. 2002. The Henry Kaiser Family Foundation. www.kaisernetwork .org (accessed Mar. 16, 2003).

DALLA, R. L., AND W. C. GAMBLE. 1997. Exploring factors related to parenting competence among Navajo teenage mothers: Dual techniques of inquiry. *Family Relations* 46 (Apr.): 113–21.

DALY, K. J. 1999. Crisis of genealogy: Facing the challenges of infertility. In *The dynamics of resilient families,* eds. H. I. McCubbin, E. A. Thompson, A. I. Thompson, and J. A. Futrell, 1–40. Thousand Oaks, CA: Sage.

DANESI, M. 2003. *My son is an alien: A cultural portrait of today's youth.* Lanham, MD: Rowman & Littlefield.

DANIEL, J. L., AND J. E. DANIEL. 1999. African-American childrearing: The context of a hot stove. In *Communication, race, and family: Exploring communication in black, white, and biracial families,* eds. T. J. Socha and R. C. Diggs, 25–43. Mahwah, NJ: Erlbaum.

DANZIGER, S. K., AND S. DANZIGER. 1993. Child poverty and public policy: Toward a comprehensive antipoverty agenda. *Daedalus* 122 (Winter): 57–84.

2006 Dating Trends Survey. 2006. He says/she says: The real scoop on dating, America Online, http://personals.aol.com/sexsurvey (accessed March 13, 2006).

Dating violence. 2000. Centers for Disease Control and Prevention. www.cdc.gov (accessed July 3, 2003).

DAUER, S. 2002. Pakistan: Violence against women continues. *Interact* (Summer): 1, 5.

DAVEY, M., AND D. LEONHARDT. 2003. Jobless and hopeless, many quit the labor force. *New York Times,* Apr. 27.

DAVIES, C., AND D. WILLIAMS. 2002. *The grandparent study 2002 report.* AARP. http://research.aarp.org/ general/gp_2002.pdf (accessed Oct. 10, 2003).

DAVIES, P. T., M. L. STURGE-APPLE, M. A. WINTER, E. M. CUMMINGS, AND D. FARRELL. 2006. Child adaptational development in contexts of interparental conflict. *Child Development* 77 (Jan./Feb.): 218–23.

DAVIES, S. L., ET AL. 2004. Relationship characteristics and sexual practices of African American adolescent girls who desire pregnancy. *Health Education & Behavior* 31 (Aug.): 85S-96S.

DAVIS, E. C., AND L. V. FRIEL. 2001. Adolescent sexuality: Disentangling the effects of family structure and family context. *Journal of Marriage and Family* 63 (Aug.): 669–81.

DAVIS, K. E. 1985. Near and dear: Friendship and love compared. *Psychology Today* 19: 22–30.

DAVIS, L. E. J. H. WILLIAMS, S. EMERSON, AND M. HOURD-BRYANT. 2000. Factors contributing to partner commitment among unmarried African Americans. *Social Work Research* 24 (Mar.): 4–15.

DAVIS, M. 2002. Champion lovers share 83 years of marriage. *Lexington Herald-Leader*, Apr. 9. www.kri.com/ (accessed July 23, 2003).

DAVIS, P. W. 1996. Threats of corporal punishment as verbal aggression: A naturalistic study. *Child Abuse & Neglect* 20 (4): 289–304.

DAVIS, S., M., AND T. N. GREENSTEIN. 2004. Cross-national variations in the division of household labor. *Journal of Marriage and Family* 66 (Dec.): 1260–71.

DAVIS-PACKARD, R. 2000. Why the number of teen mothers is falling. *Christian Science Monitor*, Aug. 15, 1, 11.

DAWSEY, D. 1996. *Living to tell about it: Young black men in America speak their piece.* New York: Anchor.

DAWSON, G., AND R. GLAUBMAN. 2000. *Life is so good.* New York: Random House.

DAWSON, J. M., AND P. A. LANGAN. 1994. *Murder in families.* Washington, DC: Bureau of Justice Statistics.

DAY, R. D. 1995. Family-systems theory. In *Research and theory in family science*, eds. R. D. Day, K. R. Gilbert, B. H. Settles, and W. R. Burr, 91–101. Pacific Grove, CA: Brooks/Cole.

DAY, R. D. 2002. *Introduction to family processes.* Mahwah, NJ: Erlbaum.

DAY, R. D., G. W. PETERSON, AND C. MCCRACKEN. 1998. Predicting spanking of younger and older children by mothers and fathers. *Journal of Marriage and the Family* 60 (Feb.): 79–94.

DAY, S. 2003. Prosecutors call Tyson smuggling trial a case of "corporate greed." *New York Times*, Feb. 6. www.nytimes.com (accessed Feb. 6, 2003).

DEAL, J. E., M. STANLEY-HAGAN, AND J. C. ANDERSON. 1992. The marital relationships in remarried families. *Monographs of the Society for Research in Child Development* 57: 2–3, serial no. 227.

Dear Ann. 2001. *Washington Post*, Apr. 13, C7.

DE ANGELIS, C. D. 2000. Women in academic medicine: New insights, same sad news. *New England Journal of Medicine* 342 (Feb. 10): 426–27.

DE LA CANCELA, V. 1994. "Coolin": The psychosocial communication of African and Latino men. In *African American males: A critical link in the African American family*, ed. D. J. Jones, 33–44. New Brunswick, NJ: Transaction.

DE LA CHICA, R. A., ISABEL R., JESUS G., AND J. EGOZCUE. 2005. Chromosomal instability in amniocytes from fetuses of mothers who smoke. *Journal of the American Medical Association.* 293 (March 9): 1212–22.

DE MUNCK, V. C. 1998. Lust, love, and arranged marriages in Sri Lanka. In *Romantic love and sexual behavior: Perspectives from the social sciences*, ed. V. C. de Munck, 295–300. Westport, CT: Praeger.

DEBIAGGI, S. D. 2002. *Changing gender roles: Brazilian immigrant families in the U.S.* New York: LFB Scholarly Publishing.

DECALMER, P., AND F. GLENDENNING, EDS. 1993. *The mistreatment of elderly people.* Thousand Oaks, CA: Sage.

DEGLER, C. 1981. *At odds: Women and the family in America from the Revolution to the present.* New York: Oxford University Press.

DEGLER, C. N. 1983. The emergence of the modern American family. In *The American family in social-historical perspective*, 3rd ed., ed. M. Gordon, 61–79. New York: St. Martin's.

DEGARMO, D. S., AND C. R. MARTINEZ JR. 2006. A culturally informed model of academic well-being for Latino youth: The importance of discriminatory experiences and social support. *Family Relations* 55 (July): 267–78.

DEL CASTILLO, R. G. 1984. *La familia: Chicano families in the urban Southwest, 1848 to the present.* Notre Dame, IN: University of Notre Dame Press.

DELEIRE, T., AND A. KALIL. 2002. *How do cohabiting couples with children spend their money?* University of Chicago, Harris Graduate School of Public Policy Studies. http://harrisschool.uchicago .edu/ (accessed July 14, 2003).

DELEIRE, T., AND A. KALIL. 2002. Good things come in threes: Single-parent multigenerational family structure and adolescent adjustment. *Demography* 39 (May): 393–413.

DELEIRE, T., AND A. KALIL. 2005. How do cohabiting couples with children spend their money? *Journal of Marriage and Family* 67 (May): 286–95.

DELISLE, S. 1997. Preserving reproductive choice: Preventing STD-related infertility in women. *Siecus Report* 25 (Mar.): 18–21.

DEMARIS, A. 2001. The influence of intimate violence on transitions out of cohabitation. *Journal of Marriage and Family* 63 (Feb.): 235–46.

DEMARIS, A., AND W. MACDONALD. 1993. Premarital cohabitation and marital instability: A test of the unconventionality hypothesis. *Journal of Marriage and the Family* 55 (May): 399–407.

DEMARIS, A., M. L. BENSON, G. L. FOX, T. HILL, AND J. VAN WYK. 2003. Distal and proximal factors in domestic violence: A test of an integrated model. *Journal of Marriage and Family* 65 (Aug.): 652–67.

DEMO, D. H., AND A. C. ACOCK. 1996. Singlehood, marriage, and remarriage. *Journal of Family Issues* 17 (May): 388–407.

DEMOS, J. 1970. *A little commonwealth: Family life in Plymouth colony.* New York: Oxford University Press.

DEMOS, J. 1986. *Past, present, and personal: The family and the life course in American history.* New York: Oxford University Press.

DENAVAS-WALT, C., B. D. PROCTOR, AND C. H. LEE. 2006. *Income, poverty, and health insurance coverage in the United States: 2005.* Washington, DC: U.S. Government Printing Office.

DENIZET-LEWIS, B. 2004. Friends, friends with benefits and the benefits of the local mall. *New York Times*, May 30, F30.

DESPELDER, L. A., AND A. L. STRICKLAND. 2005. *The last dance: Encountering death and dying*, 7th ed. New York: Mc-Graw Hill.

DESTENO, D., M. Y. BARTLETT, J. BRAVERMAN, AND P. SALOVEY. 2002. Sex differences in jealousy: Evolutionary mechanism or artifact of measurement? *Journal of Personality and Social Psychology* 83 (Nov.): 1103–16.

DERLEGA, V. J., S. METTS, S. PETRONIO, AND S. T. MARGULIS. 1993. *Self-disclosure.* Thousand Oaks, CA: Sage.

DEVENY, K. 2003. We're not in the mood. *Newsweek*, June 30, 41–46.

DEVOR, H. 1997. *FTM: Female-to-male transsexuals in society.* Bloomington: Indiana University Press.

DIAMOND, M., AND K. SIGMUNDSON. 1997. Sex reassignment at birth: Long-term review and clinical implications. *Archives of Pediatrics & Adolescent Medicine* 15 (Mar.): 298–304.

DICKEY, C., AND D. MCGINN. 2001. Meet the bin Ladens. *Newsweek*, Oct. 15, 55–56.

DIENER, M. L., S. C. MANGELSDORG, J. L. MCHALE, AND C. A. FROSCH. 2002. Infants' behavioral strategies for emotion regulation with fathers and mothers: Associations with emotional expressions and attachment quality. *Infancy* 3 (May): 153–74.

DIGGS, N. B. 1998. *Steel butterflies: Japanese women and the American experience.* Albany: State University of New York Press.

DILLER, L. H. 1998. *Running on Ritalin: A physician reflects on children, society, and performance in a pill.* New York: Bantam.

DILMAN, I. 1998. *Love: Its forms, dimensions, and paradoxes.* New York: St. Martin's.

DILWORTH-ANDERSON, P., L. M. BURTON, AND W. L. TURNER. 1993. The importance of values in the study of culturally diverse families. *Family Relations* 42 (July): 238–42.

DILWORTH-ANDERSON, P., S. W. WILLIAMS, AND T. COOPER. 1999. The contexts of experiencing emotional distress among family caregivers to elderly African Americans. *Family Relations* 48 (Oct.): 391–96.

DION, M. R., S. L. BRAVER, S. A. WOLCHIK, AND I. N. SANDLER. 1997. Alcohol abuse and psychopathic deviance in noncustodial parents as predictors of child-support payment and visitation. *American Journal of Orthopsychiatry* 67 (Jan.): 70–79.

DITTMAR, H., E. HALLIWELL, AND S. IVE. 2006. Does Barbie make girls want to be thin? The effect of experimental exposure to images of dolls on the body image of 5-to 8-year old girls. *Developmental Psychology* 42 (March): 282–92.

DIVOKY, D. 2002. Utah women to highlight hazards of polygamy. *Women's E-News.* www .womensenews.org (accessed Jan. 8, 2002).

DIXON, N. 1996. Nike: How cool is exploitation? *Green Left Weekly.* www.greenleft.org (accessed Sept. 14, 2003).

DO, D. D. 1999. *The Vietnamese Americans.* Westport, CT: Greenwood.

DODSON, L., AND L. SCHMALZBAUER. 2005. Poor mothers and habits of hiding: Participatory methods in poverty research. *Journal of Marriage and Family* 67 (November): 949–59.

DOGRA, C. S. 2006. Death becomes her. *Outlook India*, Feb 27, www.outlookindia.com (accessed February 28, 2006).

DOHERTY, R. W., E. HATFIELD, K. THOMPSON, AND P. CHOO. 1994. Cultural and ethnic influences on love and attachment. *Personal Relationships* 1: 391–98.

DOHERTY, W. J. 1999. How therapy can be hazardous to your marital health. Paper presented at the annual conference of the Coalition for Marriage, Family, and Couples Education, July 3, www .smartmarriages.org (accessed July 14, 2006).

DOHERTY, W. J. 2001. *Take back your marriage: Sticking together in a world that pulls us apart.* New York: Guilford.

DOHERTY, W. J. 2002. How therapists harm marriages and what we can do about it. *Journal of Couple and Relationship Therapy* 1 (February): 1–17.

DOKA, K. J., AND M. E. MERTZ. 1988. The meaning and significance of great-grandparenthood. *The Gerontologist* 28 (2): 192–96.

DOLAN, M. 2005. Affairs at work subject to suits. *Los Angeles Times*, July 19, A1.

Domestic violence against women and girls. 2000. United Nations Children's Fund. www.uniceficdc .org/ (accessed Sep. 22, 2000).

DONNELLY, M. 2003. EEOC files suit against LI eatery. *Newsday*, Aug. 6. www.newsday.com (accessed Aug. 18, 2003).

DORIUS, C. J., S. J. BAHR, J. P. HOFFMAN, AND E. L. HARMON. 2004. Parenting practices as moderators of the relationship between peers and adolescent marijuana use. *Journal of Marriage and Family* 66 (May): 163–78.

DORRINGTON, C. 1995. Central American refugees in Los Angeles: Adjustment of children and families. In *Understanding Latino families: Scholarship, policy, and practice*, ed. R. E. Zambrana, 107–29. Thousand Oaks, CA: Sage.

DORTCH, S. 1997. Chinese Yellow Pages. *American Demographics* 19 (Oct.): 39.

DOTINGA, R. 2005. Online dating sites aren't holding people's hearts. *Christian Science Monitor*, Jan. 27, 11.

DOUGLAS, J. D., AND F. C. ATWELL. 1988. *Love, intimacy, and sex.* Beverly Hills, CA: Sage.

DOUGLAS, S. J., AND M. W. MICHAELS. 2004. *The mommy myth: The idealization of motherhood and how it has undermined women.* New York: Free Press.

DOWD, M. 2002. Men. Listen up. This one's for you. *New York Times*, Apr. 17. www.nytimes.com (accessed Apr. 18, 2002).

DOWNEY, D. B., AND D. J. CONDRON. 2004. Playing well with others in kindergarten: The benefit of siblings at home. *Journal of Marriage and Family* 66 (May): 333–50.

DOWNEY, D. B., J. W. AINSWORTH-DARNELL, AND M. J. DUFUR. 1998. Sex of parent and children's well-being in single-parent households. *Journal of Marriage and the Family* 60 (Nov.): 878–93.

DOYLE, L. 2001. *The surrendered wife*. New York: Fireside.

DUCK, S. 1998. *Human relationships,* 3rd ed. Thousand Oaks, CA: Sage.

DUNBAR, R. 1995. Are you lonesome tonight? *New Scientist* 145, Feb. 11, 26–31.

DUSH, C., M. KAMP, AND P. R. AMATO. 2005. Consequences of relationship status and quality for subjective well-being. *Journal of Social and Personal Relationships* 22 (Oct.): 607–27.

DUSH, K., C. COHAN, AND P. AMATO. 2003. The relationship between cohabitation and marital quality and stability: Change across cohorts? *Journal of Marriage and Family* (Aug.): 539–49.

DUVALL, E. M. 1957. *Family development*. Philadelphia: Lippincott.

DYE, J. L. 2005. Fertility of American women: June 2004. U.S. Census Bureau, Current Population Reports, P20-555, www.census.gov (accessed April 16, 2006).

DYL, J., J. KITTLER, K. A. PHILLIPS, AND J. I. HUNT. 2006. Body dysmorphic disorder and other clinically significant body image concerns in adolescent psychiatric inpatients: Prevalence and clinical characteristics. *Child Psychiatry & Human Development,* June, Online First, www.springerlink .com (accessed June 25, 2006).

DYSON, M. E. 2005. *Is Bill Cosby right? Or has the middle class lost its mind?* New York: Basic Civitas Books.

EARLE, A. M. 1899. *Child life in colonial days*. New York: Macmillan.

EASTMAN, K. L., R. CORONOA, G. W. RYAN, A. L. WARSOFSKY, AND M. A. SCHUSTER. 2005. Work-site-based parenting programs to promote healthy adolescent sexual development: A qualitative study of feasibility and potential content. *Perspectives on Sexual and Reproductive Health* 37 (June): 62–69.

EATON, D. K., ET AL. 2006. Youth risk behavior surveillance—United States, 2005. *Morbidity and Mortality Weekly Report 55* (June 9, No. SS-5): 1–112.

EATON, D. K., R. LOWRY, N. D. BRENER, D. A. GALUSKA, AND A. E. CROSBY. 2005. Associations of body mass index and perceived weight with suicide ideation and suicide attempts among U.S. high school students. *Archives of Pediatrics & Adolescent Medicine* 159 (June): 513–19.

EBERSTADT, M. 2004. *Home-alone America: The hidden toll of day care, behavioral drugs, and other parent substitutes*. New York: Penguin.

EBERSTADT, N. 2004. Power and population in Asia. *Policy Review* (February–March): 1–17.

EBLING, R., AND R. W. LEVENSON. 2003. Who are the marital experts? *Journal of Marriage and Family* 65 (Feb.): 130–42.

ECCLES, J. S., C. FREEDMAN-DOAN, P. FROME, J. JACOBS, and K. S. YOON. 2000. Gender-role socialization in the family: A longitudinal approach. In *The developmental social psychology of gender,* eds. T. Eckes and H. M. Trautner, 333–60. Mahwah, NJ: Erlbaum.

ECKLAND, B. K. 1968. Theories of mate selection. *Eugenics Quarterly* 15 (1): 71–84.

ECONOMIC POLICY INSTITUTE. 2003. Living wage: Frequently asked questions. www.epinet.org (accessed Sep. 9, 2003).

EDIN, K., AND L. LEIN. 1997. *Making ends meet: How single mothers survive welfare and low-wage work.* New York: Russell Sage Foundation.

EDIN, K., AND M. KEFALAS. 2005. Unmarried with children. *Contexts* 4 (Spring): 16–22.

EDMONSTON, B. 1999. The 2000 census challenge. *Population Reference Bureau* 1 (Feb.): 1.

EDMONSTON, B., S. M. LEE, AND J. S. PASSEL. 2002. Recent trends in intermarriage and immigration and their effects on the future racial composition of the U.S. population. In *The new race question: How the census counts multiracial individuals,* eds. J. Perlmann and M. Waters, 227–55. New York: Russell Sage Foundation.

EDWARDS, J. N., AND A. BOOTH. 1994. Sexuality, marriage, and well-being: The middle years. In *Sexuality across the life course,* ed. A. S. Rossi, 233–59. Chicago: University of Chicago Press.

EDWARDS, T. M. 2000. Flying solo. *Time,* Aug. 28, 47–51.

EGAN, T. 2002. Body-conscious boys adopt athletes taste for steroids. *New York Times,* Nov. 22, A1, A22.

EGAN, T. 2005. Polygamous settlement defies state crackdown. *New York Times,* Oct. 25, A16.

EGAN, T. 2006. The rise of shrinking-vacation syndrome. *New York Times,* Aug. 20, 18.

EGGEBEEN, D. J. 2005. Cohabitation and exchanges of support. *Social Forces* 83 (May): 1097–1110.

"Egypt: Abused women reluctant to come forward." 2006. Integrated Regional Information Networks (IRIN), February 16, www.irinnews.org (accessed February 18, 2006).

EHRENBERG, M. F., M. GEARING-SMALL, M. A. HUNTER, AND B. J. SMALL. 2001. Childcare task division and shared parenting attitudes in dual-earner families with young children. *Family Relations* 50 (Apr.): 143–53.

EHRENSAFT, M. K., ET AL. 2003. Intergenerational transmission of partner violence: A 20-year prospective study. *Journal of Consulting and Clinical Psychology* 71 (Aug.): 741–53.

EHRHARDT, A. A. 1996. Editorial: Our view of adolescent sexuality—a focus on risk behavior without the developmental context. *American Journal of Public Health* 86 (Nov.): 1523–25.

EHRLICH, A. S. 2000. Power, control, and the mother-in-law problem: Face-offs in the American nuclear family. In *New directions in anthropological kinship,* ed. L. Stone, 175–84. Lanham, MD: Rowman & Littlefield.

EISENBERG, D. 2002. "Ignorant & poor?" *Time,* Feb. 11, 37–39.

EISENBERG, M. E., L. H. BEARINGER, R. E. SIEVING, C. SWAIN, AND M. D. RESNICK. 2004. Parents' beliefs about condoms and oral contraceptives: Are they medically accurate? *Perspectives on Sexual and Reproductive Health* 36 (March/April): 50–57.

EISENBERG, N., ET AL., 2005. Relations among positive parenting, children's effortful control, and externalizing problems: A three-wave longitudinal study. *Child Development* 76 (Sept./Oct.): 1055–71.

EL-SHEIKH, M., J. A. BUCKHALT, J. MIZE, AND C. ACEBO. 2006. Marital conflict and disruption of children's sleep. *Child Development* 77 (Jan./Feb.): 31–43.

ELBOW, M., AND J. MAYFIELD. 1991. Mothers of incest victims: Villains, victims, or protectors? *Families in Society* 72 (Feb.): 78–86.

ELKIND, D. 2002. Empty parenthood: The loss of parental authority in the postmodern family. In *Taking parenting public: The case for a new social movement,* eds. S. A. Hewlett, N. Rankin, and C. West, 29–44. Lanham, MD: Rowman & Littlefield.

ELLICKSON, P. L., R. L. COLLINS, K. HAMBARSOOMIANS, AND D. F. McCAFFREY. 2005. Does alcohol advertising promote adolescent drinking? Results from a longitudinal assessment. *Addiction* 100 (2): 235–46.

ELLIS, A. 1963. *The origins and the development of the incest taboo*. New York: Lyle Stuart.

ELLIS, L., P. E. GAY, AND E. PAIGE. 2001. Daily hassles and pleasures across the lifespan. Paper presented at the Annual American Psychological Association meetings, San Francisco.

ELLISON, C., AND J. P. BARTKOWSKI. 2002. Conservative Protestantism and the division of household labor among married couples. *Journal of Family Issues* 23 (Nov.): 950–985.

ELMORE, C. 2005. Child-support collection cutbacks are shameful. Women's e-news, November 27, www.womensenews.org (accessed November 29, 2005).

ELSHTAIN, J. B. 1988. What's the matter with sex today? *Tikkun: A Bimonthly Jewish Critique of Politics, Culture and Society* 3 (3): 42–43.

ELSHTAIN, J. B., E. AIRD, A. ETZIONI, W. GALSTON, M. GLENDON, M. MINOW, AND A. ROSSI. 1993. *A communitarian position paper on the family*. Washington, DC: Communitarian Network.

ELSON, D., AND H. KEKLIK. 2002. Progress of the world's women: 2002. www.undp.org (accessed May 28, 2003).

ELSTER, N., ET AL. 2000. Less is more: The risks of multiple births. *Fertility and Sterility* 74: 617–23.

Employee compensation. 2006. U.S. Government Accountability Office, February, GAO-06-285, www.gao.gov (accessed May 15, 2006).

ENGEL, M. 2000. Stepfamilies are not blended. Stepfamily Association of America. www.saafamilies .org/faqs/faqs.htm (accessed Sept. 29, 2003).

ENGLANDER, E. K. 1997. *Understanding violence*. Hillsdale, NJ: Erlbaum.

EPSTEIN, G. A. 2005. Matchmaking is just a walk in park. *Baltimore Sun* (August 3): 1A, 11A.

ERICKSON, M. T. 1993. Rethinking Oedipus: An evolutionary perspective on incest avoidance. *American Journal of Psychiatry* 150 (Mar.): 411–16.

ERICKSON, R. J. 1993. Reconceptualizing family work: The effect of emotion work on perceptions of marital quality. *Journal of Marriage and the Family* 55 (Nov.): 888–900.

ERICKSON, R. J. 2005. Why emotion work matters: Sex, gender, and the division of household labor. *Journal of Marriage and Family* 67 (May): 337–51.

ERIKSON, E. 1963. *Childhood and society*. New York: Norton.

ESLER, A. 1994. *The Western world: Prehistory to the present,* 3rd ed. Upper Saddle River, NJ: Prentice Hall.

ESPELAGE, D. L., M. K. HOLT, AND R. R. HENKEL. 2003. Examination of peer-group contextual effects on aggression during early adolescence. *Child Development* 74 (Feb.): 205–20.

ESPINO, R., AND M. M. FRANZ. 2002. Latino phenotypic discrimination revisited: The impact of skin color on occupational status. *Social Science Quarterly* 83 (June): 612–23.

ESPIRITU, Y. L. 1995. *Filipino American lives*. Philadelphia: Temple University Press.

ESTES, R. J., AND N. A. WEINER. 2002. The commercial sexual exploitation of children in the U.S., Canada, and Mexico. University of Pennsylvania, School of Social Work. http://caster.ssw.upenn.edu (accessed Sep. 17, 2003).

ESTESS, P. S. 1994. When kids don't leave. *Modern Maturity* (Nov./Dec.): 56, 58, 90.

ETAUGH, C. E., AND M. B. LISS. 1992. Home, school, and playroom: Training grounds for adult gender roles. *Sex Roles* 26 (3/4): 129–47.

EVANS, S. 2000. The children of divorce. *Washington Post,* May 9, C4.

EVERETT, C., AND S. V. EVERETT. 1994. *Healthy divorce*. San Francisco: Jossey-Bass.

EVERTSSON, M., AND M. NERMO. 2004. Dependence within families and the division of labor: Comparing Sweden and the United States. *Journal of Marriage and Family* 66 (December): 1272–86.

Expanding resources for children: Is adoption by gays and lesbians part of the answer for boys and girls who need homes? 2005. Evan B. Donaldson Adoption Institute, March, www.adoption institute.org (accessed April 20, 2006).

FABRICIUS, W. V. 2003. Listening to children of divorce: New findings that diverge from Wallerstein, Lewis, and Blakeslee. *Family Relations* 52 (October): 385–396.

Facts about eating disorders. 2000. Harvard Eating Disorders Center. www.hedc.org (accessed Oct. 20, 2000).

FAIOLA, A. 2005. Sick of their husbands in graying Japan. *Washington Post,* October 17, A1.

FALLER, K. C. 1990. *Understanding child sexual maltreatment*. Beverly Hills, CA: Sage.

FALLIK, D. 2001. Women booking rooms of their own—and more. *Women's E-News,* Aug. 28. www.womensenews.org (accessed Aug. 31, 2001).

FAMILY VIOLENCE PREVENTION FUND. 2006. The facts on immigrant women and domestic violence. www.endabuse.org (accessed June 29, 2006).

FARAGHER, J. M. 1986. *Sugar Creek: Life on the Illinois prairie*. New Haven, CT: Yale University Press.

FARBER, B. 1972. *Guardians of virtue: Salem families in 1800*. New York: Basic Books.

FARLEY, J. 2002. Just a Hollywood ending. *Time,* Apr. 8, 90.

FARLEY, M. 2001. "Prostitution: The Business of Sexual Exploitation." *Encyclopedia of Women and Gender,* Vol. 2, pp. 879–91. New York: Academic Press.

FARLEY, N. 1996. A survey of factors contributing to gay and lesbian domestic violence. In *Violence in gay and lesbian domestic partnerships,* eds. C. M. Renzetti and C. H. Miley, 35–42. New York: Harrington Park Press.

FARLEY, R. 2002. Racial identities in 2000: The response to the multiple-race response option. In

The new race question: How the census counts multiracial individuals, eds. J. Perlmann and M. C. Waters, 33–61. New York: Russell Sage.

FARRAR, E. (Mrs. J.). 1837. *The young lady's friend.* Boston: American Stationers' Company.

FARRELL, D. M. 1997. Jealousy and desire. In *Love analyzed,* ed. Roger E. Lamb, 165–88. Boulder, CO: Westview.

FASS, A. 2004. The dating game. *Forbes* (July 5): 137, 139.

FASSEL, D. 1991. *Growing up divorced: A road to healing for adult children of divorce.* New York: Pocket Books.

FAVREAULT, M. M. 2005. Women and Social Security. The Urban Institute, December, www.urban.org (accessed August 12, 2006).

FEARS, D. 2001. Mixed-race question defies easy answers. *Washington Post,* Apr. 16, A1, A8.

FEARS, D., AND C. DEANE. 2001. Biracial couples report tolerance. *Washington Post,* July 5, A1, A4.

FEDERAL BUREAU OF INVESTIGATION. 2004. *Crime in the United States: 2004. Uniform Crime Reports.* Washington, DC: U.S. Department of Justice.

FEDERAL BUREAU OF INVESTIGATION. 2005. *Hate crime statistics 2004.* Washington, DC, www.fbi.gov (accessed January 2, 2006).

Federal Interagency Forum on Aging-Related Statistics. 2006. *Older Americans update 2006: Key indicators of well-being.* Washington, DC: U.S. Government Printing Office.

Federal Interagency Forum on Child and Family Statistics. *America's children: Key national indicators of well-being, 2005.* Washington, DC: Government Printing Office.

Federal Interagency Forum on Child and Family Studies. 2003. *America's children: Key national indicators of well-being: 2003.* Washington, DC. www.childstats.gov (accessed Aug. 15, 2003).

FEENEY, J. A., AND P. NOLLER. 2002. Allocation and performance of household tasks: A comparison of new parents and childless couples. In *Understanding marriage: Development in the study of couple interaction,* eds. P. Noller and J. A. Feeney, 411–36. New York: Cambridge University Press.

FEENEY, J., AND P. NOLLER. 1996. *Adult attachment.* Thousand Oaks, CA: Sage.

FEHR, B. 1993. How do I love thee? Let me consult my prototype. In *Individuals in relationships,* ed. S. Duck, 87–120. Thousand Oaks, CA: Sage.

FEHR, B. 1999. Laypeople's conceptions of commitment. *Journal of Personality and Social Psychology* 76 (Jan.): 90–103.

FEIN, E., AND S. SCHNEIDER. 1996. *The rules: Time tested secrets for capturing the heart of Mr. Right.* New York: Warner.

FEINBERG, L. F., K. Wolkwitz, AND C. GOLDSTEIN. 2006. *Ahead of the curve: Emerging trends and practices in family caregiver support.* AARP Public Policy Institute, March, http://assets.aarp.org (accessed August 5, 2006).

FEINGOLD, A. 1988. Matching for attractiveness in romantic partners and same-sex friends: A meta-analysis and theoretical critique. *Psychological Bulletin* 104 (Sept.): 226–35.

FELDMAN, H. 1931. *Racial factors in American industry.* New York: Harper & Row.

FELDMAN, S. S., E. CAUFFMAN, AND J. J. ARNETT. 2000. The (un)acceptability of betrayal: A study of college students' evaluations of sexual betrayal by a romantic partner and betrayal of a friend's confidence. *Journal of Youth and Adolescence* 29 (Aug.): 499–523.

FELDMANN, L., AND G. GOODALE. 1995. Custody cases test attitudes of judges. *Christian Science Monitor,* Mar. 3, 1, 18.

FELSON, R. B., AND A. C. CARES. 2005. Gender and the seriousness of assaults on intimate partners and other victims. *Journal of Marriage and Family* 67 (Dec.): 1182–95.

FELSON, R. B., AND P.-P. PARÉ. 2005. The reporting of domestic violence and sexual assault by non-strangers to the police. *Journal of Marriage and Family* 67 (Aug.): 597–610.

FERNANDEZ, S. 2005. Getting to know you. *Washington Post* (May 30): C1.

FESTINOER, T. 2002. After adoption: Dissolution or permanence. *Child Welfare* 81: 515–33.

Fetal alcohol syndrome. 2000. Centers for Disease Control and Prevention. www.cdc.gov (accessed Sept. 22, 2000).

FETTO, J. 2001. Gather 'round. *American Demographics* 23 (June): 11–12.

FETTO, J. 2002. "Till Death . . . Do Us Part." *American Demographics* 24 (September): 8–9.

FETTO, J. 2002a. Bringing up baby. *American Demographics* 24 (Oct.): 15.

FETTO, J. 2002b. "Woof, woof" means "I love you." *American Demographics,* 24 (Feb.): 11.

FETTO, J. 2002c. Guys who shop. *American Demographics* 24 (Nov.): 16.

FETTO, J. 2003. Love stinks. *American Demographics* 25 (Feb.): 10–11.

FETTO, J. 2003a. Don't forget your rubbers. *American Demographics* 25 (Mar.): 16.

FETTO, J. 2003c. Moms make the grade. *American Demographics* 25 (May): 12–13.

FEW, A. L., AND K. H. ROSEN. 2005. Victims of chronic dating violence: How women's vulnerabilities link to their decisions to stay. *Family Relations* 54 (April): 265–79.

FICHTER, M. M., N. QUADFLIEG, AND S. HEDLUND. 2006. Twelve-year course and outcome predictors of anorexia nervosa. *International Journal of Eating Disorders* 39 (March): 87–100.

FIELD, A. E., ET AL. 2005. Exposure to the mass media, body shape concerns, and use of supplements to improve weight and shape among male and female adolescents. *Pediatrics* 116 (August): 214–20.

FIELDS, J. 2001. Living arrangements of children: 1996. U.S. Census Bureau, Current Population Reports, p70–74. www.census.gov (accessed Feb. 15, 2003).

FIELDS, J. 2003. *Children's living arrangements and characteristics: March 2002.* Current Population Reports, P20–547. Washington, DC: U.S. Census Bureau.

FIELDS, J. 2004. *America's families and living arrangements: 2003.* Current Population Reports, P20–553. Washington, DC: U.S. Census Bureau.

FIELDS, J., AND L. M. CASPER. 2001. *America's families and living arrangements: 2000.* U.S. Census Bureau, Current Population Reports, P20–537. www.census.gov (accessed Feb. 25, 2003).

FIELDS, J., K. SMITH, L. E. BASS, AND T. LUGAILA. 2001. *A child's day: Home, school, and play (selected indicators of child well-being): 1994.* Current Population Reports, P70–68. U.S. Census Bureau. www.census.gov (accessed Aug. 24, 2003).

FIESE, B. H., ET AL. 2002. A review of 50 years of research on naturally occurring family routines and rituals: Cause for celebration? *Journal of Family Psychology* 16 (Dec.): 381–90.

FIESTER, L. 1993. Teen survey sparks concern. *Washington Post,* Feb. 2, 1, 3.

"Financial experience & behaviors among women." 2006. Prudential financial, www.prudential.com (accessed August 9, 2006).

FINCHAM, F. D., AND T. N. BRADBURY. 1987. The assessment of marital quality: A reevaluation. *Journal of Marriage and the Family* 49 (Nov.): 797–809.

FINE, G. A. 1993. Ten lies of ethnography: Moral dilemmas of field research. *Journal of Contemporary Ethnography* 22 (Oct.): 267–94.

FINER, L. B., AND S. K. HENSHAW. 2003. Abortion incidence and services in the United States in 2000. *Perspectives on Sexual and Reproductive Health* 35 (Jan./Feb.): 6–15.

FINER, L. B., L. F. FROHWIRTH, L. A. DAUPHINEE, S. SINGH, AND A. M. MOORE. 2005. Reasons U.S. women have abortions: Quantitative and qualitative perspectives. *Perspectives on Sexual and Reproductive Health* 37 (Sept.): 110–18.

FINER, L. B., S. K. HENSHAW, AND R. K. JONES. 2003. An overview of abortion in the United States. Physicians for Reproductive Choice and Health and the Alan Guttmacher Institute. www.agi-usa.org (accessed Aug. 5, 2003).

FINK, D. 1992. *Agrarian women: Wives and mothers in rural Nebraska, 1880–1940.* Chapel Hill: University of North Carolina Press.

FINKE, N. 1994. Trophy husbands. *Working Woman* (Apr.): 37, 39, 41, 88, 90, 91.

FINKELHOR, D., AND R. ORMROD. 2000. *Characteristics of crimes against juveniles.* Washington, DC: U.S. Department of Justice, Office of Juvenile Justice and Delinquency Prevention.

FINKELHOR, D., R. ORMROD, H. TURNER, AND S. L. HAMBY. 2005. The victimization of children and youth: A comprehensive, national survey. *Child Maltreatment* 10 (February): 5–25.

FINN, P. 2005. Russian adoptions orphaned by state. *Washington Post,* June 19, A1.

FISHER, H. 1999. *The first sex: The natural talents of women and how they are changing the world.* New York: Ballantine.

FISHER, H. 2004. *Why we love: The nature and chemistry of romantic love.* New York: Henry Holt.

FISHER, L. 2005. New gloss on motherhood, but few changes. Women's e-news, February 18, www.womensenews.org (accessed Feb. 20, 2005).

FISHMAN, B., AND B. HAMEL. 1981. From nuclear to stepfamily ideology: A stressful change. *Alternative Lifestyles* 4: 181–204.

FITZPATRICK, M. A., AND A. MULAC. 1995. Relating to spouse and stranger: Gender-preferential language use. In *Gender, power, and communication in human relationships,* eds. P. J. Kalbfleisch and M. J. Cody, 213–31. Hillsdale, NJ: Erlbaum.

FIXICO, D. L. 2001. Myths and realities of Indian gaming. *Journal of the West* 40 (Spring): 2–3.

FLECK, C. 2006. Double bind. *AARP Bulletin,* May, 18–19.

FLEESON, L. 2003. Leaving Laredo. *Mother Jones,* Sep./Oct., 24–27.

FLETCHER, G. 2002. *The new science of intimate relationships.* Malden, MA: Blackwell.

FLETCHER, M. A. 1997. Latinos see signs of hope as middle class expands. *Washington Post,* July 22, A8.

FLORES, C. 2002. Wrestling coaches sue education department over Title IX enforcement. *Chronicle of Higher Education,* Feb. 1, A39.

FLORES, G., AND J. BROTANEK. 2005. The healthy immigrant effect: A greater understanding might help us improve the health of all children. *Archives of Pediatrics & Adolescent Medicine* 159 (3): 295–97.

FLORES, G., ET AL. 2002. The health of Latino children. *Journal of the American Medical Association* 288 (July 3): 82–90.

Florida couple accused of starving 7-year-old girl. 2002. *Baltimore Sun,* Sep. 23, 2A.

FLOURI, E., AND A. BUCHANAN. 2003. The role of father involvement and mother involvement in adolescents' psychological well-being. *British Journal of Social Work* 33 (Apr.): 399–406.

FOGEL, C. I., AND N. F. WOODS. 1995. Midlife women's health. In *Women's health care: A comprehensive handbook,* eds. C. I. Fogel and N. F. Woods, 79–100. Thousand Oaks, CA: Sage.

FOGG, P. 2003. The gap that won't go away. *Chronicle of Higher Education,* Apr. 18, A12–A15.

FOGLE, J. J. 2006. *Preparing for divorce while happily married: Tips from a divorce lawyer.* Andover, MN: Expert Publishing.

FOLBRE, N. 1994. *Who pays for the kids? Gender and the structures of constraint.* New York: Routledge.

FOLK, K. F., J. W. GRAHAM, AND A. H. BELLER. 1992. Child support and remarriage: Implications for the economic well-being of children. *Journal of Family Issues* 13, 142–57.

FOLKES, V. S. 1982. Forming relationships and the matching hypothesis. *Personality and Social Psychology Bulletin* 8 (Dec.): 631–36.

FONG, T. P. 2002. *The contemporary Asian American experience: Beyond the model minority,* 2nd ed. Upper Saddle River, NJ: Prentice Hall.

FOO, L. J. 2002. *Asian American women: Issues, concerns, and responsive human and civil rights advocacy.* New York: Ford Foundation.

FORD, C., AND E. BEACH. 1972. *Patterns of sexual behavior.* New York: Harper & Row. (Originally published 1951.)

FOREMAN, J. 2005. Medical info on the Web. *Baltimore Sun,* February 12, 3D.

"For richer or poorer." 2005. *Mother Jones* 30 (January/February): 24–25.

FORRY, N. D., AND S. K. WALKER. 2006. Public policy, child care, and families in the United States. National Council on Family Relations, Family Focus on Families and Public Policy, March, F5–F6.

FORTENBERRY, D. J. 2005. The limits of abstinence-only in preventing sexually transmitted infections. *Journal of Adolescent Health* 36 (April): 269–70.

FORWARD, S. 1990. *Toxic parents: Overcoming their hurtful legacy and reclaiming your life.* New York: Bantam.

FORWARD, S. 2002. *Obsessive love: When it hurts too much to let go.* New York: Bantam.

FOSHEE, V. A., K. E. BAUMAN, AND G. F. LINDER. 1999. Family violence and the perpetuation of adolescent dating violence: Examining social learning and social control processes. *Journal of Marriage and the Family* 61 (May): 331–42.

FOST, D. 1996. Child-free with an attitude. *American Demographics* 18 (Apr.): 15–16.

FOX, G. L., AND V. M. MURRY. 2001. Gender and families: Feminist perspectives and family research. In *Understanding families into the new millennium: A decade of review,* ed. R. M. Milardo, 379–91. Lawrence, KS: National Council on Family Relations.

FOX, G. L., M. L. BENSON, A. A. DEMARIS, AND J. VAN WYK. 2002. Economic distress and intimate violence: Testing family stress and resources theories. *Journal of Marriage and Family* 64 (Aug.): 793–807.

FOX, J. A., AND M. W. ZAWITZ. 2003. *Homicide trends in the United States: 2000 update.* Washington, DC: U.S. Department of Justice.

"Fox tops list of family-unfriendly TV." 2005. *Baltimore Sun,* Oct. 20, 6C.

FRAME, M. W., AND C. L. SHEHAN. 1994. Work and well-being in the two-person career: Relocation stress and coping among clergy husbands and wives. *Family Relations* 43 (Apr.): 196–205.

FRANCE, D. 2006. "And then he hit me." *AARP Magazine,* Jan./Feb. 81–85, 112–13, 118.

FRANCIS, D. R. 2000. The unsolved mystery of the gilded economy. *Christian Science Monitor,* June 30, 1, 9.

FRANCIS, D. R. 2003a. Grass looks greener, but welcome cools. *Christian Science Monitor,* Mar. 20, 13, 16.

FRANCIS, D. R. 2003b. Moves afoot to curb CEO salaries. *Christian Science Monitor,* July 8, 2, 4.

FRANK, G. K., ET AL. 2005. Increased dopamine D2/D3 receptor binding after recovery from anorexia nervosa measured by positron emission tomography and [¹¹C]raclopride. *Biological Psychiatry* 58 (December): 908–12.

FRANK, M., AND E. F. ZIGLER. 1996. Family leave: A developmental perspective. In *Children, families, and government: Preparing for the twenty-first century,* eds. E. F. Zigler, S. L. Kagan, and N. W. Hall, 117–31. New York: Cambridge University Press.

FRAZIER, E. F. 1937. The impact of urban civilization upon Negro family life. *American Sociological Review* 2 (Oct.): 609–18.

FRAZIER, E. F. 1939. *The Negro family in the United States.* Chicago: University of Chicago Press.

FREEMAN, D. 1983. *Margaret Mead and Samoa: The making and unmaking of an anthropological myth.* Cambridge, MA: Harvard University Press.

FRENCH, H. W. 2006. In a richer China, billionaires put money on marriage. *New York Times,* January 26, A4.

FRIAS, S. M., AND R. J. ANGEL. 2005. The risk of partner violence among low-income Hispanic subgroups. *Journal of Marriage and Family* 67 (Aug.): 552–64.

FRIEDAN, B. 1993. *The fountain of age.* New York: Simon & Schuster.

FRISCO, M. L. 2005. Parental involvement and young women's contraceptive use. *Journal of Marriage and Family* 67 (Feb.): 110–21.

FROMM, E. 1956. *The art of loving.* New York: Bantam.

FROMM, S. 2001. Total estimated cost of child abuse and neglect in the United States: Statistical evidence. Prevent Child Abuse America. www.preventchildabuse.org (accessed Sep. 20, 2003).

FU, V. K. 2001. Racial intermarriage pairings. *Demography* 38 (May): 147–59.

FUCHS, D. 2003. In Spain's lonely country side, a Cupid crusade. *Christian Science Monitor,* June 10, 1, 14.

FUKUZAWA, R. E., AND G. K. LETENDRE. 2001. *Intense years: How Japanese adolescents balance school, family, and friends.* New York: RoutledgeFalmer.

FULIGNI, A. J., AND H. YOSHIKAWA. 2003. Socioeconomic resources, parenting, and child development among immigrant families. In *Socioeconomic status, parenting, and child development,* eds. M. H. Bornstein and R. H. Bradley, 107–24. Mahwah, NJ: Lawrence Erlbaum.

FULIGNI, A. J., V. TSENG, AND M. LAM. 1999. Attitudes towards family obligations among American adolescents with Asian, Latin American, and European backgrounds. *Child Development* 70: 1030–44.

FULTZ, O. 1991. *Roid rage. American Health,* May, 60–64.

FURGATCH, V. 1995. It's time to remove all barriers to adoption across racial lines. *Christian Science Monitor,* Sep. 12, 19.

FURSTENBERG, F. F., AND K. E. KIERNAN. 2001. Delayed parental divorce: How much do children benefit? *Journal of Marriage and Family* 63 (May): 446–57.

FURSTENBERG, F. F., JR., AND J. O. TEITLER. 1994. Reconsidering the effects of marital disruption: What happens to children of divorce in early adulthood? *Journal of Family Issues* 15 (June): 173–90.

GABRIEL, T. 1997. Pack dating: For a good time, call a crowd. *New York Times,* Jan. 5, 22.

GAGER, C. T., AND L. SANCHEZ. 2003. Two as one?: Couples' perceptions of time spent together, marital quality, and the risk of divorce. *Journal of Family Issues* 24 (Jan.): 21–50.

GAITER, L. 1994. The revolt of the black bourgeoisie. *New York Times Magazine,* June 26, 42–43.

GALAMBOS, N. L., E. T. BARKER, AND H. J. KRAHN. 2006. Depression, self-esteem, and anger in emerging adulthood: Seven-year trajectories. *Developmental Psychology* 42 (March): 350–65.

GALINSKY, E. 1999. *Ask the children: What American children really think about working parents.* New York: Morrow.

GALLAGHER, M. 1996. *The abolition of marriage: How we destroy lasting love.* Washington, DC: Regnery.

GALLAGHER, S. K. 2003. *Evangelical identity and gendered family life.* New Brunswick, NJ: Rutgers University Press.

GALLUP, G., JR., AND T. NEWPORT. 1990. Virtually all adults want children, but many of the reasons are intangible. *Gallup Poll Monthly* (June): 8–22.

GALVIN, K. M., AND B. J. BROMMEL. 2000. *Family communication: Cohesion and change,* 5th ed. New York: Addison-Wesley-Longman.

GAMACHE, D. 1990. Domination and control: The social context of dating violence. In *Dating Violence: Young women in danger,* ed. B. Levy, 69–118. Seattle: Seal.

GAMACHE, S. J. 1997. Confronting nuclear family bias in stepfamily research. *Marriage & Family Review* 26 (1/2): 41–69.

GAMERMAN, E. 2006. Dating Web sites now trying to prevent divorce. *Wall Street Journal,* April 3, (accessed April 5, 2006).

GANONG, L. H., AND M. COLEMAN. 1994. *Remarried family relationships.* Thousand Oaks, CA: Sage.

GANONG, L. H., AND M. COLEMAN. 1997. How society views stepfamilies. *Marriage & Family Review* 26 (1/2): 85–106.

GANONG, L. H., AND M. COLEMAN. 1999. *Changing families, changing responsibilities: Family obligations following divorce and remarriage.* Mahwah, NJ: Erlbaum.

GANONG, L. H., AND M. COLEMAN. 2004. *Stepfamily relationships: Development, dynamics, and interventions.* New York: Kluwer Academic/Plenum Publishers.

GANONG, L., M. COLEMAN, AND J. HANS. 2006. Divorce as prelude to stepfamily living and the consequences of redivorce. In *Handbook of divorce and relationship dissolution,* eds. M. A. Fine and J. H. Harvey, 409–434. Mahwah, NJ: Lawrence Erlbaum.

GANONG, L., M. COLEMAN, AND M. FINE. 1995. Remarriage and stepfamilies. In *Research and theory in family science,* eds. R. D. Day, K. R. Gilbert, B. H. Settles, and W. R. Burr, 287–303. Pacific Grove, CA: Brooks/Cole.

GANS, H. J. 1971. The uses of poverty: The poor pay all. *Social Policy* (July/Aug.): 78–81.

GANS, H. J. 1979. *Deciding what's news: A study of CBS Evening News, NBC Nightly News, Newsweek and Time.* New York: Pantheon.

GARBARINO, J. 1999. *Lost boys: Why our sons turn violent and how we can save them.* New York: Free Press.

GARBARINO, J. 2006. *See Jane hit: Why girls are growing more violent and what can be done about it.* New York: Penguin.

GARCIA, A. M. 2002. *The Mexican Americans.* Westport, CT: Greenwood Press.

GARCIA, C. Y. 1998. Temporal course of the basic components of love throughout relationships. *Psychology in Spain* 2 (1): 76–86. www.psychologyinspain.com (accessed Mar. 30, 2003).

GARCIA, M. T. 1980. *La familia:* The Mexican immigrant family, 1900–1930. In *Work, family, sex roles, language,* eds. M. Barrera, A. Camarillo, and F. Hernandez, 117–40. Berkeley, CA: Tonatiua-Quinto Sol International.

GARDNER, M. 2002. Grandmothers weigh in on providing child care. *Christian Science Monitor,* Aug. 14, 16.

GARDNER, M. 2003. Small towns confront an urban problem: A rise in homelessness. *Christian Science Monitor,* Mar. 7, 1, 4.

GARDNER, M. 2004. Is it cyber-flirting or cyber-betrayal? *Christian Science Monitor,* Aug. 19, 12, 14.

GARDNER, M. 2004. When equal custody is law, who gains? *Christian Science Monitor,* June 24, 11–12.

GARDNER, M. 2004. Will "I dos" end the gay-marriage debate? *Christian Science Monitor.* May 20, 12–13.

GARDNER, M. 2005. "Blondie" at 75. *Christian Science Monitor,* August 31, 13, 16.

GARDYN, R. 2001. A league of their own. *American Demographics* 23 (Mar.): 12–13.

GARDYN, R. 2002. The mating game. *American Demographics* 24 (July/Aug.): 33–37.

GARFINKEL, I., S. S. MCLANAHAN, AND P. K. ROBINS, EDS. 1994. *Child support and child well-being.* Washington, DC: Urban Institute.

GARLAND, E. 1999. An anthropologist learns the value of fear. *Chronicle of Higher Education,* May 7, B4–B5.

GARRISON, M. M., AND D. A. CHRISTAKIS. 2005. A teacher in the living room? Educational media for babies, toddlers and preschoolers. Kaiser Family Foundation, December. www.kff.org (accessed May 20, 2006).

GARROD, A., AND C. LARIMORE, EDS. 1997. *First person, first peoples: Native American college graduates tell their life stories.* Ithaca, NY: Cornell University Press.

GATES, G. J., AND J. OST. 2004. *The gay & lesbian atlas.* Washington, DC: The Urban Institute Press.

GATTAI, F. B., AND T. MUSATTI. 1999. Grandmothers' involvement in grandchildren's care: Attitudes, feelings, and emotions. *Family Relations* 48 (Jan.): 35–42.

GAUDIN, J. M., JR., N. A. POLANSKY, A. C. KILPATRICK, AND P. SHILTON. 1996. Family functioning in neglectful families. *Child Abuse & Neglect* 20 (Apr.): 363–77.

GAYLIN, W. 1992. *The male ego.* New York: Viking.

GEARON, C. J. 2003. Visiting the "kids" gets harder. *AARP Bulletin,* Feb., 6–7.

GECAS, V., AND M. A. SEFF. 1991. Families and adolescents: A review of the 1980s. In *Contemporary families: Looking forward, looking back,* ed. A. Booth, 208–25. Minneapolis: National Council on Family Relations.

GEER, J. H., AND G. M. MANGUNO-MIRE. 1996. Gender differences in cognitive processes in sexuality. *Annual Review of Sex Research* 7: 90–124.

GELLES, R. J. 1995. *Contemporary families: A sociological view.* Thousand Oaks, CA: Sage.

GELLES, R. J. 1997. *Intimate violence in families,* 3rd ed. Thousand Oaks, CA: Sage.

GELLES, R. J., AND C. P. CORNELL. 1990. *Intimate violence in families,* 2nd ed. Thousand Oaks, CA: Sage.

GELLES, R. J., AND M. A. STRAUS. 1988. *Intimate violence.* New York: Simon & Schuster.

GENDELL, M. 2006. Full-time work rises among U.S. elderly. Population Reference Bureau, www.prb.org (accessed August 15, 2006).

GENDER EQUALITY BUREAU. 2000. www.gender.go.jp (accessed Aug. 3, 2000).

GENERAL ACCOUNTING OFFICE. 1997. Defense of Marriage Act. GAO/OGC-97-16, www.gao.gov (accessed March 21, 2006).

General Social Survey. 2004: SDA codebook page for 'relig' (R's religious preference), http://sda.berkeley.edu (accessed August 30, 2005).

GENOVESE, E. D. 1981. Husbands and fathers, wives and mothers, during slavery. In *Family life in America: 1620–2000*, eds. M. Albin and D. Cavallo, 237–51. St. James, NY: Revisionary Press.

GENTLEMAN, A. 2006. Doctor in India jailed for telling sex of a fetus. *New York Times*, March 30, A13.

GERBER, R. 2002. Girls need not apply. *Christian Science Monitor*, June 24, 11.

GERDES, K., M. NAPOLI, C. PATTEA, AND E. SEGAL. 1998. The impact of Indian gaming on economic development. *Journal of Poverty* 4 (2): 17–30.

GERSHOFF, E. T. 2002. Corporal punishment by parents and associated child behaviors and experiences: A meta-analytic and theoretical review. *Psychological Bulletin* 128 (July): 539–79.

GERSHUNY, J., M. BITTMAN, AND J. BRUCE. 2005. Exit, voice, and suffering: Do couples adapt to changing employment patterns? *Journal of Marriage and Family* 67 (August): 656–66.

GERSON, K. 1997. The social construction of fatherhood. In *Contemporary parenting: Challenges and issues*, ed. T. Arendell, 119–53. Thousand Oaks, CA: Sage.

GERSON, K. 2003. Work without worry. *New York Times*, May 11 D13.

GETLIN, J. 2005. Pregnant and unwed, teacher fights church. *Los Angeles Times* November 26, A12.

GIBBS, N. 2002. Making time for a baby. *Time*, Apr. 15, 48–53.

GIBBS, N., J. JOHNSON, M. LUDTKE, AND M. RILEY. 1990. Shameful bequests to the next generation. *Time*, Oct. 8, 42–46.

GIBSON, J. T. 1991. Disciplining toddlers. *Parents* (May): 190.

GIBSON, P. A. 2005. Intergenerational parenting from the perspective of African American grandmothers. *Family Relations* 54 (April): 280–297.

GIBSON-DAVIS, C. M., K. EDIN, AND S. MCLANAHAN. 2005. High hopes but even higher expectations: The retreat from marriage among low-income couples. *Journal of Marriage and Family* 67 (Dec.): 1301–1312.

GIBSON-DAVIS, C. M., K. MAGNUSON, L. A. GENNETIAN, AND G. J. DUNCAN. 2005. Employment and the risk of domestic abuse among low-income women. *Journal of Marriage and Family* 67 (December): 1149–68.

GILBERT, S. 2005. Married with problems? Therapy may not help. *New York Times*, April 19, F1.

GILES-SIMS, J., M. A. STRAUS, AND D. B. SUGARMAN. 1995. Child, maternal, and family characteristics associated with spanking. *Family Relations* 44 (Apr.): 170–76.

GILGOFF, D. 2004. The rise of the gay family. *U.S. News & World Report*, May 24, 40–45.

GILLIS, J. R. 1996. *A world of their own making: Myth, ritual, and the quest for family values*. New York: Basic Books.

GILLIS, J. R. 2004. Marriages of the mind. *Journal of Marriage and Family* 66 (Nov.): 988–91.

GILLMORE, M. R. ET AL. 2002. Teen sexual behavior: Applicability of the theory of reasoned action. *Journal of Marriage and Family* 64 (Nov.): 885–97.

GLADSTONE, J. W. 1989. Perceived changes in grandmother–grandchild relations following a child's separation or divorce. *The Gerontologist* 28 (1): 66–72.

GLASS, S. 2002. *Not "just friends": Protect your relationship from infidelity and heal the trauma of betrayal*. New York: Free Press.

GLAUBKE, R., AND K. E. HEINTZ-SWENSON. 2004. Fall colors: 2003–04 prime time diversity report. Children Now, http://publications.childrennow.org (accessed December 4, 2005).

GLENN, E. N., AND S. G. H. YAP. 2002. Chinese American families. In *Minority families in the United States: A multicultural perspective*, 3rd ed., ed. R. L. Taylor, 134–63. Upper Saddle River, NJ: Prentice Hall.

GLENN, N. 2005. With this ring . . .: A national survey on marriage in America. National Fatherhood Initiative, www.fatherhood.org/doclibrary/nms.pdf (accessed April 2, 2006).

GLENN, N. D. 1991. Quantitative research on marital quality in the 1980s. In *Contemporary families: Looking forward, looking back*, ed. A. Booth, 28–41. Minneapolis: National Council on Family Relations.

GLENN, N. D. 1996. Values, attitudes, and the state of American marriage. In *Promises to keep: Decline and renewal of marriage in America*, eds. D. Popenoe, J. B. Elshtain, and D. Blankenhorn, 15–33. Lanham, MD: Rowman & Littlefield.

GLENN, N. D. 1997. A reconsideration of the effect of no-fault divorce on divorce rates. *Journal of Marriage and Family* 39 (Nov.): 1023–30.

GLENN, N. D. 2002. A plea for greater concern about the quality of marital matching. In *Revitalizing the institution of marriage in the twenty-first century*, eds. L. D. Wardle and D. O. Coolidge, 45–58. Westport, CT: Praeger.

GLENN, N., AND E. MARQUARDT. 2001. *Hooking up, hanging out, and hoping for Mr. Right: College women on dating and mating today*. Institute for American Values. www.americanvalues.org (accessed July 5, 2003).

GLENN, N., AND T. SYLVESTER. 2006. The denial: Downplaying the consequences of family structure for children. Institute for American Values, www.familyscholarslibrary.org (accessed July 11, 2006).

Glenn's health in space in line with colleagues. 2000. *Baltimore Sun*, Jan. 29, 3A.

GLYNN, L. M., N. CHRISTENFELD, AND W. GERIN 2002. The role of rumination in recovery from reactivity: Cardiovascular consequences of emotional states. *Psychosomatic Medicine* 64 (Sep./Oct.): 714–26.

GODDARD, H. W. 1994. *Principles of parenting*. Auburn, AL: Auburn University, Department of Family and Child Development.

GODFREY, S., C. L. RICHMAN, AND T. N. WITHERS. 2000. Reliability and validity of a new scale to measure prejudice: The GRISMS. *Current Psychology* 19 (March): 1046–1310.

GOETTING, A. 1982. The six stations of remarriage: Developmental tasks of remarriage after divorce. *Family Relations* 31 (Apr.): 231–22.

GOETTING, A. 1999. *Getting out: Life stories of women who left abusive men*. New York: Columbia University Press.

GOFFMAN, E. 1963. *Stigma: Notes on the management of spoiled identity*. Upper Saddle River, NJ: Prentice Hall.

GOLBY, B. J., AND I. BRETHERTON. 1998. Resilience in postdivorce mother–child relationships. In *The dynamics of resilient families*, eds. H. I. McCubbin, E. A. Thompson, A. I. Thompson, and J. A. Futrell, 237–65. Thousand Oaks, CA: Sage.

GOLD, D. T. 1989. Sibling relationships in old age: A typology. *International Journal on Aging and Human Development* 28 (1): 37–51.

GOLD, D. T. 1990. Late-life sibling relationships: Does race affect typological distribution? *The Gerontologist* 30 (December): 741–48.

GOLD, L. 1992. *Between love and hate: A guide to civilized divorce*. New York: Plenum.

GOLDBERG, A. E., AND A. SAYER. 2006. Lesbian couples' relationship quality across the transition to parenthood. *Journal of Marriage and Family* 68 (February): 87–100.

GOLDEN, O., P. LOPREST, AND S. ZEDLEWSKI. 2006. Parents and children facing a world of risk: "Next steps toward a working families' agenda" roundtable report. The Urban Institute, March 10, www.urban.org (accessed May 4, 2006).

GOLDSCHEIDER, F. K., AND C. GOLDSCHEIDER. 1993. *Leaving home before marriage: Ethnicity, familism, and generational relationships*. Madison: University of Wisconsin Press.

GOLDSCHEIDER, F., AND S. SASSLER. 2006. Creating stepfamilies: Integrating children into the study of union formation. *Journal of Marriage and Family* 68 (May): 275–291.

GOLOMBOK, S., AND F. TASKER. 1996. Do parents influence the sexual orientation of their children? Findings from a longitudinal study of lesbian families. *Developmental Psychology* 32 (1): 3–11.

GONNERMAN, J. 2005. The unforgiven. *Mother Jones*, July/August, 38–43.

GONZÁLEZ, R. 1996. *Muy macho: Latino men confront their manhood*. New York: Anchor.

GONZÁLEZ-LÓPEZ, G. 2004. Fathering Latina sexualities: Mexican men and the virginity of their daughters. *Journal of Marriage and Family* 66 (Dec.): 1118–30.

GOODE, E. 1990. *Deviant behavior*, 3rd ed. Upper Saddle River, NJ: Prentice Hall.

GOODE, E., ET AL. 1994. Till death do them part? *U.S. News & World Report*, July 4, 24–28.

GOODE, W. J. 1963. *World revolution and family patterns*. New York: Free Press.

GOODMAN, E. 2003. Here's a marriage proposal we should reject. *Baltimore Sun*, Feb. 24, 11A.

GOODMAN, P. S. 2006. Stealing babies for adoption. *Washington Post*, March 12, A1.

GOODSMITH, L. 2000. Taliban's yoke crushes women. *Baltimore Sun*, June 11, 1C, 4C.

GOODWIN, R., AND C. FINDLAY. 1997. "We were just fated together." Chinese love and the concept of *yuan* in England and Hong Kong. *Personal Relationships* 4: 85–92.

GORDON, L. H. 1993. Intimacy: The art of working out your relationships. *Psychology Today* 26 (Sep./Oct.): 40–43, 79–82.

GORMAN, C. 1995. Trapped in the body of a man? *Time*, Nov. 13, 94–95.

GORMAN, E. H. 2000. Marriage and money. *Work & Occupations* 27 (Feb.): 64–88.

GORMAN, J. C. 1998. Parenting attitudes and practices of immigrant Chinese mothers of adolescents. *Family Relations* 47 (Jan.): 73–80.

GOSE, B. 1994. Spending time on the reservation. *Chronicle of Higher Education*, Aug. 10, A30–A31.

GOSTIN, N. 2006. Spike Lee. *Newsweek*, April 3, 70.

GOTTMAN, J. M. 1982. Emotional responsiveness in marital conversations. *Journal of Communication* 32, 108–20.

GOTTMAN, J. M. 1994. *What predicts divorce? The relationships between marital processes and marital outcome*. Hillsdale, NJ: Erlbaum.

GOTTMAN, J. M., AND J. DECLAIRE. 2001. *The relationship cure: A five-step guide for building better connections with family, friends, and lovers*. New York: Crown.

GOTTMAN, J. M., AND N. SILVER. 1999. *The seven principles for making marriage work*. New York: Crown.

GOTTSCHALCK, A. O. 2006. Dynamics of economic well-being: Spells of unemployment 2001–2003. U.S. Census Bureau, Current Population Reports, P70–105, March, www.census.gov (accessed May 12, 2006).

GOULD, D. C., R. PETTY, AND H. S. JACOBS. 2000. For and against: The male menopause—does it exist? *British Medical Journal* 320 (Mar): 858–60.

GOYETTE, K., AND Y. XIE. 1999. The intersection of immigration and gender: Labor force outcomes of immigrant women scientists. *Social Science Quarterly* 80 (June): 395–408.

GRACIA, E., AND J. HERRERO. 2006. Public attitudes toward reporting partner violence against women and reporting behavior. *Journal of Marriage and Family* 68 (August): 759–68.

GRAHAM, E. 1996. Craving closer ties, strangers come together as family. *Wall Street Journal*, Mar. 4, B1, B5.

GRAHAM, L. O. 1996. *Member of the club: Reflections on life in a racially polarized world*. New York: HarperCollins.

GRALL, T. 2002. *Custodial mothers and fathers and their child support: 1999*. U.S. Census Bureau, Current Population Reports, P60–217. Washington, DC: U.S. Government Printing Office.

GRALL, T. S. 2003. Custodial mothers and fathers and their child support: 2001. U.S. Census Bureau, Current Population Reports, P60–225, www .census.gov (accessed July 4, 2006).

GRALL, T. S. 2005. Support providers: 2002. U.S. Census Bureau, Current Population Reports, P70–99, www.census.gov (accessed July 9, 2006).

"Grandparents Day 2006: Sept. 10." 2006, U.S. Census Bureau, *Facts for Features*, BB06-FF.13 (accessed July 28, 2006).

GRAVES, J. L., Jr. 2001. *The emperor's new clothes: Biological theories of race at the millennium*. New Brunswick, NJ: Rutgers University Press.

GRAY, H. M., AND V. FOSHEE. 1997. Adolescent dating violence: Differences between one-sided and mutually violent profiles. *Journal of Interpersonal Violence* 12 (Feb.): 126–41.

GRAY, M. R., AND L. STEINBERG. 1999. Unpacking authoritative parenting: Reassessing a multidimensional construct. *Journal of Marriage and the Family* 61 (Aug.): 574–87.

GREENBERG, J., AND M. RUHLEN. 1992. Linguistic origins of Native Americans. *Scientific American* 267:94.

GREENBLATT, C. S. 1983. The salience of sexuality in the early years of marriage. *Journal of Marriage and the Family* 45 (May): 289–99.

GREENFELD, L. A., AND S. K. SMITH. 1999. *American Indians and crime.* Washington, DC: U.S. Department of Justice, Office of Justice Programs.

GREENFELD, L. A., AND T. L. SNELL. 1999. *Women offenders.* Washington, DC: U.S. Department of Justice, Office of Justice Programs.

GREENFIELD, D. 1999. *Virtual addiction.* Oakland, CA: New Harbinger Publications.

GREENHOUSE, S. 2006. Hotel rooms get plushier, adding to maids' injuries. *New York Times,* April 21, A16.

GREENHOUSE, S., AND M. BARBARO. 2005. Wal-Mart suggests ways to cut employee benefit costs. *New York Times,* October 26, C1–C2.

GREENSTEIN, T. N. 2000. Economic dependence, gender, and the division of labor in the home: A replication and extension. *Journal of Marriage and the Family* 62 (May): 322–35.

GREENSTEIN, T. N. 2001. *Methods of family research,* Thousand Oaks, CA: Sage.

GREENSTEIN, T. N. 2006. *Methods of family research,* 2nd ed. Thousand Oaks, CA: Sage.

GREER, G. 1999. *The whole woman.* New York: Knopf.

GREIDER, L. 2000. How not to be a monster-in-law. *Modern Maturity* (Mar./Apr.): 57–59.

GREIDER, L. 2003. "The old skills kick in." *AARP Bulletin,* May, 12.

GREIDER, L. 2004. Unmarried together. *AARP Bulletin,* October, 14–16.

GRIMES, B. F., ed. 2000. *Ethnologue: Languages of the world,* 14th ed. Dallas, TX: SIL International. Online edition: www.ethnologue.com (accessed on Nov. 3, 2005).

GRIMSLEY, K. D. 2000. Panel asks why women still earn less. *Washington Post,* June 9, E3.

GRIMSLEY, K. D. 2001. More Arabs, Muslims allege bias on the job. *Washington Post,* Dec. 12, E1, E4.

GRISWOLD, R. L. 1993. *Fatherhood in America: A history.* New York: Basic Books.

GRITZ, E. R., ET AL. 2003. Predictors of susceptibility to smoking and ever smoking: A longitudinal study in a triethnic sample of adolescents. *Nicotine & Tobacco Research* 5 (July): 493–506.

GROSSMAN, L. 2005. Grow up? Not so fast. *Time,* January 24, 42–54.

GROTEVANT, H. D. 2001. Adoptive families: Longitudinal outcomes for adolescents. Report to the William T. Grant Foundation. http://fsos .che.umn.edu (accessed Aug. 17, 2003).

GROVES, E. R. 1928. *The marriage crisis.* New York: Longmans, Green.

GRUNBAUM, J. A., ET AL. 2004. Youth risk behavior surveillance—United States, 2003. *Morbidity and Mortality Weekly Report* 53 (May 21): 1–100.

GRUNBAUM, J. A., ET AL. 2002. Youth risk behavior surveillance: United States, 2001. *Morbidity and Mortality Weekly Report,* June 28. wwwcdc.gov/ (accessed June 13, 2003).

GRYCH, J. H. 2002. Marital relationships and parenting. In *Handbook of parenting,* 2nd ed., Vol. 4: *Social conditions and applied parenting,* ed. M. H. Bornstein, 203–25. Mahwah, NJ: Erlbaum.

GRZYWACZ, J. G., D. M. ALMEIDA, AND D. A. MCDONALD. 2002. Work-family spillover and daily reports of work and family stress in the adult labor force. *Family Relations* 51 (Jan.): 28–36.

GUBERMAN, N., P. MAHEU, AND C. MAILLE. 1992. Women as family caregivers: Why do they care? *The Gerontologist* 32 (5): 607–17.

GUEST, J. 1988. *The mythic family.* Minneapolis: Milkweed.

GUPTA, G. R. 1979. Love, arranged marriage and the Indian social structure. In *Cross-cultural perspectives of mate-selection and marriage,* ed. G. Kurian, 169–79. Westport, CT: Greenwood.

GURIAN, M. 2002. *The wonder girls: Understanding the hidden nature of our daughters.* New York: Pocket Books.

GUTMAN, H. 1976. *The black family in slavery and freedom,* 1750–1925. New York: Pantheon.

GUTMAN, H. G. 1983. Persistent myths about the Afro-American family. In *The American family in socio-historical perspective,* 3rd ed., ed. M. Gordon, 459–81. New York: St. Martin's.

GUTNER, T. 2000. Getting your fair share in a divorce. *Business Week,* May 29, 250.

GUTNER, T. 2001. Househusbands unite! *Business Week,* Jan. 22, 106.

GUTTMACHER INSTITUTE. 2005a. Induced abortion in the United States. 2005. Facts in Brief, The Alan Guttmacher Institute, www.guttmacher.org (accessed May 1, 2006).

GUTTMACHER INSTITUTE. 2005b. An overview of abortion in the United States. 2005. Physicians for Reproductive Choice and Health and the Guttmacher Institute, June, www.guttmacher.org (accessed April 28, 2006).

HAAG, P. S. 1999. *Voices of a generation: Teenage girls on sex, school, and self.* Washington, DC: American Association of University Women.

HACKER, A. 2003. *Mismatch: The growing gulf between women and men.* New York: Scribner.

HAFFNER, D. W. 1999. Facing facts: Sexual health for American adolescents. *Human Development & Family Life Bulletin* 4 (Winter): 1–3.

HAHN, R. A., AND D. M. KLEIST. 2000. Divorce mediation: Research and implications for family and couples counseling. *Family Journal* 8 (Apr.): 165–71.

HAIDER, S. J., A. JACKNOWITZ, AND R. F. SCHOENI. 2003. The economic status of elderly divorced women. Michigan Retirement Research Center, www.mrrc.isr.umich.edu (accessed July 10, 2006).

HALES, D. 2002. When *she* earns more. *Parade,* Mar. 17, 6.

HALEY, A. 1976. *Roots: The saga of an American family.* Garden City, NY: Doubleday.

Half of older Americans report they are sexually active; 4 in 10 want more sex, says new survey. 1998. National Council on Aging. www.ncoa.org (accessed Aug. 30, 2000).

HALFORD, W. K., K. L. WILSON, A. LIZZIO, AND E. MOORE. 2002. Does working at a relationship work? Relationship self-regulation and relationship outcomes. In *Understanding marriage: Development in the study of couple interaction,* eds. P. Noller and J. A. Feeney, 493–517. New York: Cambridge University Press.

HALL, C. C. I., AND M. J. CRUM. 1994. Women and "body-isms" in television beer commercials. *Sex Roles* 31 (Sep.): 329–37.

HALPERN, C. T., K. JOYNER, AND C. SUCHINDRAN. 2000. Smart teens don't have sex (or kiss much either). *Journal of Adolescent Health* 26 (Mar.): 213–25.

HALPERN-FELSHER, B. L., J. L. CORNELL, R. Y. KROPP, AND J. M. TSCHANN. 2005. Oral versus vaginal sex among adolescents: Perceptions, attitudes, and behavior. *Pediatrics* 115 (April): 845–851.

HAMER, D. H., S. HU, V. MAGNUSON, N. HU, AND A. M. L. PATTATUCCI. 1993. A linkage between DNA markers on the X chromosome and male sexual orientation. *Science,* July 16, 321–27.

HAMER, J., AND K. MARCHIORO. 2002. Becoming custodial dads: Exploring parenting among low-income and working-class African American fathers. *Journal of Marriage and Family* 64 (Feb.): 115–29.

HAMILTON, A. 2002. Sex, drinks and videotape. *Time,* Mar. 25, 8.

HAMILTON, B. E., J. A. MARTIN, S. J. VENTURA, P. D. SUTTON, AND F. MENACKER. 2005. Births: Preliminary data for 2004. *National Vital Statistics Reports* 54 (December). Hyattsville, MD: National Center for Health Statistics.

HAMILTON, B. E., P. D. SUTTON, AND S. J. VENTURA. 2003. Revised birth and fertility rates for the 1990s and new rates for Hispanic populations, 2000 and 2001: United States. *National Vital Statistics Reports,* 51, Aug. 4. www.cdc.gov (accessed Aug. 25, 2003).

HAMILTON, T. F. 2002. Caitlin's families: Two families overcome their differences for the sake of a 12-year-old girl. *Grand Rapids Press,* Sep. 15, J1.

HAMMER, H., D. FINKELHOR, AND A. J. SEDLAK. 2002. *Children abducted by family members: National estimates and characteristics.* Washington, DC: U.S. Department of Justice.

HAMMOND, R. J., AND B. Bearnson. 2003. *The marriages and families activities workbook.* Belmont, CA: Wadsworth.

HANCOCK, J. 1999a. A business bonanza paid by taxpayers. *Baltimore Sun,* Oct. 10, 1A, 16A–17A.

HANCOCK, J. 1999b. S.C. pays dearly for added jobs. *Baltimore Sun,* Oct. 12, 1A, 8A–9A.

HANCOX, R. J., B. J. MINE, AND R. POULTON. 2005. Association of television viewing during childhood with poor educational achievement. *Archives of Pediatrics & Adolescent Medicine* 159 (July): 614–18.

HANES, S. 2004. Mail-order bride wins damage award. *Baltimore Sun* (November 19): 1A, 4a.

HANNA, S. L. 2003. *Person to person: Positive relationships don't just happen,* 4th ed. Upper Saddle River, NJ: Prentice Hall.

HANS, J. D. 2002. Stepparenting after divorce: Stepparents' legal position regarding custody, access, and support. *Family Relations* 51 (Oct.): 301–7.

HANSON, R. K., R. GIZZARELLI, AND H. SCOTT, 1994. The attitudes of incest offenders: Sexual entitlement and acceptance of sex with children. *Criminal Justice and Behavior* 21 (June):187–202.

HARARI, S. E., AND M. A. VINOVSKIS. 1993. Adolescent sexuality, pregnancy, and childbearing in the past. In *The politics of pregnancy: Adolescent sexuality and public policy,* eds. A. Lawson and D. I. Rhode, 23–45. New Haven, CT: Yale University Press.

HAREVEN, T. K. 1984. Themes in the historical development of the family. In *Review of child development research,* Vol. 7: *The family,* ed. R. D. Parke, 137–78. Chicago: University of Chicago Press.

HARLEY, W. F. JR. 2002. *Buyers, renters & freeloaders: Turning revolving-door romance into lasting love.* Grand Rapids, MI: Fleming H. Revell.

HARMAN, D. 2005. Outsourcing moves closer to home. *Christian Science Monitor,* November 28, 13, 16.

HARMON, A. 2003. Lost? Hiding? Your cellphone is keeping tabs. *New York Times,* December 21, A1.

Harassment in the supermarket. 2002. ABC News. www.abcnews.go.com (accessed June 25, 2002).

HARRELL, W. A. 2005. Are prettier kids protected better? A field observational study of child safety in grocery carts. Population Research Laboratory, University of Alberta. Unpublished manuscript.

HARRELL, W. A. 2006. Are ugly children at risk in grocery stores? The impact of imputed marital status and adult attractiveness. Paper presented at the 17th annual Warren E. Kalbach Conference in Demography, University of Alberta, Canada, March 31.

HARRIS, D. 1995. Salary survey: 1995. *Working Woman* (Jan.): 25–34.

HARRIS, L. 1996. The hidden world of dating violence. *Parade Magazine,* Sep. 22, 4.

HARRIS, M. 1994. *Down from the pedestal: Moving beyond idealized images of womanhood.* New York: Doubleday.

HARRIS, M. 1996. Aggressive experiences and aggressiveness: Relationship to ethnicity, gender, and age. *Journal of Applied Social Psychology* 26: 843–70.

HARRIS, P. 2006. America's model housewife turns feminist as husband abandons her. *New York Observer,* January 8, www.observer.com (accessed January 10, 2006).

HARRIS, T. 2003. Mind work: How a Ph.D. affects black women. *Chronicle of Higher Education,* Apr. 11, B14–B15.

HARRISON, P. M., AND J. C. KARBERG. 2003. *Prison and jail inmates at midyear 2002.* Washington, DC: U.S. Department of Justice.

HARRYKISSOON, S. D., V. I. RICKERT, AND C. M. WIEMAN. 2002. Prevalence and patterns of intimate partner violence during the postpartum period. *Archives of Pediatrics & Adolescent Medicine* 156 (Apr.): 325–30.

HART, S. N., M. R. BRASSARD, N. J. BINGGELI, AND H. A. DAVIDSON. 2003. Psychological maltreatment. In *International encyclopedia of marriage and family,* 2nd ed., Vol. 1, ed. J. J. Ponzetti, Jr., 221–27. New York: Macmillan.

HARTILI, L. 2001. Vow or never. *Christian Science Monitor,* July 18, 15–17.

HARTSOE, S. 2005. ACLU challenges N.C. cohabitation law. *Washington Post,* May 10, A6.

HARVEY, J. H., AND A. L. WEBER, 2002. *Odyssey of the heart: Close relationships in the 21st century,* 2nd ed. Mahwah, NJ: Erlbaum.

HARVEY, J. H., AND M. A. FINE. 2004. *Children of divorce: Stories of loss and growth.* Mahwah, NJ: Lawrence Erlbaum.

HARWOOD, R., B. LEYENDECKER, V. CARLSON, M. ASENCIO, AND A. MILLER. 2002. Parenting among Latino Families in the U.S. In *Handbook of parenting,* 2nd ed., Vol. 4: *Social conditions and applied parenting,* ed. M. H. Bornstein, 21–46. Mahwah, NJ: Erlbaum.

HASS, A. 1979. *Teenage sexuality: A survey of teenage sexual behavior.* New York: Macmillan.

HASTINGS, D. 1994. Battered men continue to have no place to go. *Baltimore Sun,* Aug. 1, 1D, 5D.

HATCHETT, S., J. VEROFF, AND E. DOUVAN. 1995. Marital instability among black and white couples in early marriage. In *The decline in marriage among African Americans,* eds. M. B. Tucker and C. Mitchell-Kernan, 177–218. New York: Russell Sage Foundation.

HATFIELD, E. 1983. What do women and men want from love and sex? In *Changing boundaries: Gender roles and sexual behavior,* eds. E. R. Allgeier and N. B. McCormick, 106–34. Mountain View, CA: Mayfield.

HATFIELD, E., AND R. L. RAPSON. 1996. *Love and sex: Cross-cultural perspectives.* Boston: Allyn & Bacon.

HAUB, C. 2005. 2005. *World population data sheet.* Washington, DC: Population Reference Bureau.

HAWKE, D. F. 1988. *Everyday life in early America.* New York: Harper & Row.

HAYANI, I. 1999. Arabs in Canada: Assimilation or integration? In *Arabs in America: Building a new future,* ed. M. W. Suleiman, 284–303. Philadelphia: Temple University Press.

HAYASHI, G. M., AND B. R. STRICKLAND. 1998. Longterm effects of parental divorce on love relationships: Divorce as attachment disruption. *Journal of Social & Personal Relationships* 15 (Feb.): 23–38.

HAYS, S. 1998. The fallacious assumptions and unrealistic prescriptions of attachment theory: A comment on parents' socioemotional investment in children. *Journal of Marriage and the Family* 60 (Aug.): 782–95.

HAZAN, C., AND P. R. SHAVER. 1987. Conceptualizing romantic love as an attachment process. *Journal of Personality and Social Psychology* 52: 511–24.

HE, W., M. Sengupia, V. A. Velkoff, AND K. A. DeBarros. 2005. *65+ in the United States: 2005.* U.S. Census Bureau, Current Population Reports, P23–209. Washington, DC: U.S. Government Printing Office.

HEADDEN, S. 1997. The Hispanic dropout mystery. *U.S. News & World Report,* Oct. 20, 64–65.

Health, United States, 2004, with Chartbook on Trends in the Health of Americans. 2004. National Center for Health Statistics, www.cdc.gov/nchs/data/hus/hus04.pdf (accessed July 15, 2005).

HEALY, B. 2004. So what to do now, ladies? *U.S. News & World Report,* March 15, 68.

HEALY, M. 2003. Fertility's new frontier. *Los Angeles Times,* July 21, F1.

HEATON, T. B. 1990. Marital stability throughout the child-rearing years. *Demography* 27 (Feb.): 55–63.

HEBERT, L. E., P. A. SCHERR, J. L. BIENIAS, D. A. BENNETT, AND D. A. EVANS. 2003. Alzheimer disease in the US population. *Archives of Neurology* 60 (Aug.):1119–22.

HECHT, M. L., P. J. MARSTON, AND L. K. LARKEY. 1994. Love ways and relationship quality in heterosexual relationships. *Journal of Social and Personal Relationships* 11 (1): 25–43.

HEKKER, T. 1979. *Ever since Adam and Eve: The satisfactions of housewifery and motherhood in the age of do-your-own-thing.* New York: William Morrow.

HELLERSTEDT, W. 2002. Health and environmental risks associated with early childbearing. *Healthy Generations* 3 (May): 1–5.

HELMS-ERIKSON, H. 2001. Marital quality ten years after the transition to parenthood: Implications of the timing of parenthood and the division of housework. *Journal of Marriage and Family* 63 (Nov.): 1099–1110.

HENDRICK, C., AND S. HENDRICK. 1992a. *Liking, loving, and relating,* 2nd ed. Monterey, CA: Brooks/Cole.

HENDRICK, C., AND S. S. HENDRICK. 2003. Love. In *International encyclopedia of marriage and family,* 2nd ed., Vol. 3, ed. J. J. Ponzetti, Jr., 1059–65. New York: Macmillan.

HENDRICK, S. S., AND C. HENDRICK. 2002. Linking romantic love with sex: Development of the perceptions of love and sex scale. *Journal of Social and Personal Relationships* 19 (June): 361–78.

HENDRICK, S., AND C. HENDRICK. 1992b. *Romantic love.* Thousand Oaks, CA: Sage.

HENDRIX, H. 1988. *Getting the love you want: A guide for couples.* New York: Henry Holt.

HENNINGSSON, S., ET AL. 2005. Sex steroid-related genes and male-to-female transsexualism. *Psychoneuroendocrinology* 30 (August): 657–64.

HENRY, K. 1999. Chapter 11 for London Fog. *Baltimore Sun,* Sep. 28, 1A, 7A.

HERBERT, B. 2003. A crush of applicants. *New York Times,* Feb. 10, A23.

HERDT, G. 1997. *Same sex, different cultures.* Boulder, CO: Westview.

HERMAN-GIDDENS, M., G. BROWN, S. VERBIEST, P. J. CARLSON, E. G. HOOTEN, E. HOWELL, AND J. D. BUTTS. 1999. Underascertainment of child abuse mortality in the United States. *Journal of the American Medical Association* 282 (Aug.): 463–67.

HERN, W. M. 1992. Shipibo polygyny and patrilocality. *American Ethnologist* 19 (Aug.): 501–22.

HERRMANN, A. 2003. Children of divorce in no rush to repeat error. *Chicago Sun Times,* June 10. www.suntimes.com (accessed June 12, 2003).

HERRSCHAFT, D. 2005. *The state of the workplace for lesbian, gay, bisexual and transgender Americans 2004.* Human Rights Campaign Foundation, www.hcr.org (accessed March 15, 2006).

HERRSTROM, S. 1990. Sweden: Pro-choice on child care. *New Perspectives Quarterly* 7 (Winter): 27–30.

HESLAM, J. 2006. Happy New Year! I want a divorce. *Boston Globe,* January 1, www.boston.com (accessed January 4, 2006).

HETHERINGTON, E. M. 2003. Intimate pathways: Changing patterns in close personal relationships across time. *Family Relations* 52 (October): 318–331.

HETHERINGTON, E. M., AND J. KELLY. 2002. *For better or for worse: Divorce reconsidered.* New York: W. W. Norton.

HETHERINGTON, E. M., AND M. M. STANLEY-HAGAN. 1997. The effects of divorce on fathers and their children. In *The role of the father in child development,* ed. M. E. Lamb, 191–211. New York: Wiley.

HETHERINGTON, E. M., AND M. M. STANLEY-HAGAN. 2000. Diversity among stepfamilies. In *Handbook of family diversity,* eds. D. H. Demo, K. R. Allen, and M. A. Fine, 173–96. New York: Oxford University Press.

HETHERINGTON, E. M., AND M. M. STANLEY-HAGAN. 2002. Parenting in divorced and remarried families. In *Handbook of parenting,* 2nd ed., Vol. 3: *Being and becoming a parent,* ed. M. H. Bornstein, 287–315. Mahwah, NJ: Erlbaum.

HETHERINGTON, E. M., AND W. G. CLINGEMPEEL. 1992. Coping with marital transitions: A family systems perspective. *Monographs of the Society for Research in Child Development* 57, 2–3, serial no. 227.

HETHERINGTON, E. M., R. D. PARKE, AND V. O. LOCKE. 2006. *Child Psychology: A Contemporary Viewpoint,* 6th ed. Boston: McGraw-Hill.

HETRICK, R. 1994. London Fog workers swallow pride, cuts. *Baltimore Sun,* Sep. 27, A1, A14.

HEUBECK, E. 2005. Pressure grows to telecommute. *Baltimore Sun,* October 26, K1–K2.

HEUVELINE, P., AND J. M. TIMBERLAKE. 2004. The role of cohabitation in family formation: The United States in comparative perspective. *Journal of Marriage and Family* 66 (December): 1214–1230.

HEWLETT, S. A. 2002. *Creating a life: Professional women and the quest for children.* New York: Miramax.

HEYMANN, J. 2002. Can working families ever win? *Boston Review* 27 (Feb./Mar.): 4–13.

HEYN, D. 1997. *Marriage shock: The transformation of women into wives.* New York: Villard.

HICKMAN, J. 2002. America's 50 best companies for minorities. *Fortune,* July 8, 10–18.

"High-tech gadgets help parents keep track of what their kids are doing," 2005. *Baltimore Sun,* September 5, B2.

HILL, K. G., J. D. HAWKINS, R. F. CATALANO, R. D. ABBOTT, AND J. GUO. 2005. Family influences on the risk of daily smoking initiation. *Journal of Adolescent Health* 37 (September): 202–10.

HILL, R. B. 2003. *The strengths of black families,* 2nd ed. Lanham, MD: University Press of America.

HILL, R. B. 1993. *Research on the African American family: A holistic perspective.* Westport, CT: Auburn House.

HILL, S. A. 2005. *Black intimacies: A gender perspective on families and relationships.* Walnut Creek, CA: AltaMira Press.

HIMES, C. L. 2001. *Elderly Americans. Population Bulletin* 56 (Dec.): 1–40. Washington, DC: Population Reference Bureau.

HINES, D. A., AND K. MALLEY-MORRISON. 2005. *Family violence in the United States: Defining, understanding, and combating abuse.* Thousand Oaks, CA: Sage.

HINSCH, B. 1990. *Passions of the cut sleeve: The male homosexual tradition in China.* Berkeley: University of California Press.

HITT, J. 2006. Pro-life nation. *New York Times Magazine,* April 9, 40-50.

HITT, R. B., ET AL. 1993. *Research on the African-American family: A holistic perspective.* Westport, CT: Auburn House.

HOBBS, F. 2005. *Examining American household composition: 1990 and 2000.* U.S. Census Bureau, Special Reports, CENSR-24. Washington, DC: U.S. Government Printing Office.

HOBBS, F., AND N. STOOPS 2002. *Demographic trends in the 20th century.* U.S. Census Bureau, 2000 Special Reports, Series CENSR-4. www.census.gov (accessed May 25, 2003).

HOBSON, K. 2004. The biological clock on ice. *U.S. News & World Report,* Sept. 27, 62-63.

HOCHSCHILD, A., WITH A. MACHUNG. 1989. *The second shift: Working parents and the revolution at home.* New York: Penguin.

HOERLYCK, A. 2003. Racial disparity suit haunts housing market. *Baltimore Sun,* July 3, 21A.

HOFFERTH, S. L. 2005. Secondary data analysis in family research. *Journal of Marriage and Family* 67 (November): 891–907.

HOFFMAN, B. A. 2003. Gay rights as source of strength. *Baltimore Sun,* July 5, 11A.

HOJAT, M., R. SHAPURIAN, D. FOROUGHI, H. NAYERAHMADI, M. FARZANEH, M. SHAFIEYAN, AND M. PARSI. 2000. Gender differences in traditional attitudes toward marriage and the family: An empirical study of Iranian immigrants in the United States. *Journal of Family Issues* 21 (May): 419–34.

HOLDEN, C. 2001. General contentment masks gender gap in first AAAS salary and job survey. American Association for the Advancement of Science. http://recruit.sciencemag.org/ (accessed Oct. 15, 2001).

HOLDEN, G. W., P. C. MILLER, AND S. D. HARRIS. 1999. The instrumental side of corporal punishment: Parents' reported practices and outcome expectancies. *Journal of Marriage and the Family* 61 (Nov.): 908–19.

HOLLEY, H. 2006. *Retirement planning survey among U.S. adults age 40 and older.* Washington, DC: AARP.

HOLLINGSWORTH, L. D. 2003. When an adoption disrupts: A study of public attitudes. *Family Relations* 52 (Apr.): 161–66.

HOLLIST, C. S., AND R. B. MILLER. 2005. Perceptions of attachment style and marital quality in midlife marriage. *Family Relations* 54 (January): 46–57.

HOLM-DENOMA, J. M., ET AL. 2005. Parents' reports of the body shape and feeding habits of 36-month-old children: An investigation of gender differences. *International Journal of Eating Disorders* 38 (Nov.): 228–35.

HOLMAN, T. B., AND W. R. BURR. 1980. Beyond the beyond: The growth of family theories in the 1970s. *Journal of Marriage and the Family* 42 (Nov.): 729–41.

HOLMAN, T. B., J. H. LARSON, AND S. L. HARMER. 1994. The development and predictive validity of a new premarital assessment instrument: The preparation for marriage questionnaire. *Family Relations* 43 (Jan.): 46–52.

HOLT, T., L. GREENE, AND J. DAVIS. 2003. *National survey of adolescents and young adults: Sexual health knowledge, attitudes and experiences.* The Henry Kaiser Family Foundation. www.kff.org (accessed June 12, 2003).

HOLTZMAN, M. 2005. The family definitions continuum. *National Council on Family Relations Report 50* (June): F1, F3.

HONEY, M. 1984. *Creating Rosie the Riveter: Class, gender, and propaganda.* Amherst: University of Massachusetts Press.

HONG, P. 2005. The rich get smarter. *Los Angeles Times,* Oct. 23, M6.

HONG, P. Y. 2004. Colleges court a new minority: Boys. *Baltimore Sun* (December 2): 6A.

HOOYMAN, N. R., AND H. A. KIYAK. 2002. *Social gerontology: A multidisciplinary perspective,* 6th ed. Boston, MA: Allyn & Bacon.

HOPE, T. L., AND C. K. JACOBSON. 1995. Japanese American families: Assimilation over time. In *American families: Issues in race and ethnicity,* ed. C. K. Jacobson, 145–75. New York: Garland.

HOPPER, J. 2001. The symbolic origins of conflict in divorce. *Journal of Marriage and Family 63* (May): 430–45.

HORN, B., Ed. 2006. *Progressive agenda for the states 2006: State policy leading America.* Center for Policy Alternatives, www.stateaction.org (accessed May 2, 2006).

HORWITZ, A. V., H. R. WHITE, AND S. HOWELL-WHITE. 1996. Becoming married and mental health: A longitudinal study of a cohort of young adults. *Journal of Marriage and the Family 58* (Nov.): 895–907.

HOSLEY, C. A., AND R. MONTEMAYOR. 1997. Fathers and adolescents. In *The role of the father in child development,* ed. M. E. Lamb, 162–78. New York: Wiley.

HOSSAIN, Z. 2001. Division of household labor and family functioning in off-reservation Navajo Indian families. *Family Relations.* 50 (July), 255–61.

HOUSEKNECHT, S. K., AND S. K. LEWIS. 2005. Explaining teen childbearing and cohabitation: Community embeddedness and primary ties. *Family Relations 54* (December): 607–20.

HOWARD, J. A., AND J. A. HOLLANDER. 1997. *Gendered situations, gendered selves: A gender lens on social psychology.* Thousand Oaks, CA: Sage.

How late is too late? 2001. Letter to the editor. *Newsweek,* Sep. 3, 14.

HOWE, N., W. STRAUSS, and R. J. MATSON. 2000. *Millennials rising: The next great generation.* New York: Vintage.

HOYERT, D. L., M. P. HERON, S. L. MURPHY, AND H.-C. KUNG. 2006. Deaths: Final data for 2003. *National Vital Statistics Reports 54* (April). Hyatsville, MD: National Center for Health Statistics.

HUANG, C.-C., AND H. POUNCY. 2005. Why doesn't she have a child support order?: Personal choice or objective constraint. *Family Relations 54* (Oct.): 547–557.

HUBNER, K., ET AL. 2003. Derivation of oocytes from mouse embryonic stem cells. *Science 300* (May): 1251–56.

HUDAK, M. A. 1993. Gender schema theory revisited: Men's stereotypes of American women. *Sex Roles 28* (5/6): 279–92.

HUDSON, J. W., AND L. F. HENZE. 1969. Campus values in mate selection: A replication. *Journal of Marriage and the Family 31* (Nov.): 772–75.

HUDSON, V. M., AND A. M. DEN BOER. 2004. *Bare branches: Security implications of Asia's surplus male population.* Cambridge, MA: MIT Press.

HUMAN RIGHTS WATCH. 2003. World report 2003: South Africa. www.hrw.org (accessed May 15, 2003).

HUMAN RIGHTS WATCH. 2005. *World report.* http://hrw.org (accessed May 1, 2006).

HUNT, G., CAROL L., AND L. NAIDITCH. 2005. *Young caregivers in the U.S.: Findings from a national survey.* National Alliance for Caregiving and United Hospital Fund, September, www.caregiving.org (accessed August 2, 2006).

HUNT, J. 1991. Ten reasons not to hit your kids. In *Breaking down the wall of silence: The liberating experience of facing painful trust,* ed. A. Miller, 168–71. Meridian, NY: Dutton.

HUNTLEY, T., ED. 1991. *Helping children grieve: When someone they love dies.* Minneapolis: Augsburg.

HUPKA, R. B. 1991. The motive for the arousal of romantic jealousy: Its cultural origin. In *The psychology of jealousy and envy,* ed. P. Salovey, 252–70. New York: Guilford.

HURH, W. M. 1998. *The Korean Americans.* Westport, CT: Greenwood.

HURTADO, A. 1995. Variations, combinations, and evolutions: Latino families in the United States. In *Understanding Latino families: Scholarship, policy, and practice,* ed. R. E. Zambrana, 40–61. Thousand Oaks, CA: Sage.

HUSTON, M., AND P. SCHWARTZ. 1995. The relationships of lesbians and of gay men. In *Understudied relationships: Off the beaten track,* eds. J. T. Wood and S. Duck, 89–121. Thousand Oaks, CA: Sage.

HUSTON, T. L., AND E. K. HOLMES. 2004. Becoming parents. In *Handbook of family communication,* ed. Anita L. Vangelisti, 105–33. Mahwah, NJ: Lawrence Erlbaum.

HUTCHINSON, E. O. 1994. *Black fatherhood. II: Black women talk about their men.* Los Angeles: Middle Passage.

HUTCHINSON, M. K. 2002. The influence of sexual risk communication between parents and daughters on sexual risk behaviors. *Family Relations 51* (July): 238–47.

HUTCHISON, I. W. 1999. The effect of children's presence on alcohol use by spouse abusers and their victims. *Family Relations 48* (Jan.): 57–65.

HUTTENLOCHER, J., M. VASILYEVA, E. CYMERMAN, AND S. LEVINE. 2002. Language input and child syntax. *Cognitive Psychology 45* (Nov.): 337–74.

HUTTER, M. 1998. *The changing family,* 3rd ed. Boston: Allyn & Bacon.

HWANG, A. C., A. KOYAMA, D. TAYLOR, J. T. HENDERSON, AND S. MILLER. 2005. Advanced practice clinicians' interest in providing medical abortion: Results of a California survey. *Perspectives on Sexual and Reproductive Health 37* (June): 92–97.

HWANG, S.-S., R. SAENZ, AND B. F. AGUIRRE. 1994. Structural and individual determinants of outmarriage among Chinese-, Filipino-, and Japanese-Americans in California. *Sociological Inquiry 64* (Nov.): 396–414.

IHINGER-TALLMAN, M., AND K. PASLEY. 1987. *Remarriage,* Beverly Hills, CA: Sage.

IKONOMIDOU, C., P. ET AL., 2000. Ethanol-induced apoptotic neurodegeneration and fetal alcohol syndrome. *Science 287,* Feb. 11, 1056–60.

IMBER-BLACK, E., AND J. ROBERTS. 1993. Family change: Don't cancel holidays! *Psychology Today 26* (Mar./Apr.): 62, 64, 92–93.

"Immigration." 2006. Gallup Organization, May, http://poll.gallup.com (accessed August 2, 2006).

Infant homicide. 2003. Child Trends Data Bank. www.cdc.gov (accessed Sep. 20, 2003).

INGERSOLL-DAYTON, B., M. B. NEAL, AND L. B. HAMMER. 2001. Aging parents helping adult children: The experience of the sandwiched generation. *Family Relations 50* (July): 262–71.

INGERSOLL-DAYTON, B., M. B. NEAL, J.-H. HA, AND L. B. HAMMER. 2003. Redressing inequity in parent care among siblings. *Journal of Marriage and Family 65* (Feb.): 201–12.

INGRASSIA, M., AND M. BECK. 1994. Patterns of abuse. *Newsweek,* July 4, 26–33.

Inside-OUT: A report on the experiences of lesbians, gays and bisexuals in American and the public's views on issues and policies related to sexual orientation. The Henry Kaiser Family Foundation. www.kff.org (accessed June 18, 2003).

INTERNATIONAL LONGEVITY CENTER. 2006. *Ageism in America.* Open Society Institute, www.ilcusa.org (accessed July 28, 2006).

Interracial marriages rising, study of census data says. 1997. *Baltimore Sun,* Mar. 26, 3A.

Interracial wedding barred in Ohio. 2000. *Baltimore Sun,* July 11, 3A.

Iranian arbitrating body approves marriage age increase. 2002. Yahoo News, June 23. http://story.news .yahoo.com (accessed June 24, 2002).

ISHII-KUNTZ, M. 1993. Japanese fathers: Work demands and family roles. In *Men, work and family,* ed. J. C. Hood, 45–67. Thousand Oaks, CA: Sage.

ISHII-KUNTZ, M., 2004. Asian American families: Diverse history, contemporary trends, and the future. In *Handbook of contemporary families: Considering the past, contemplating the future,* eds. M. Coleman and L. H. Ganong, 369–84. Thousand Oaks, CA: Sage.

Issues and answers: Fact sheet on sexuality education. 2001. *SIECUS Report 29* (Aug./Sep.). www.siecus .org (accessed June 12, 2003).

ITANO, N. 2002a. Fighting tradition, girls yearn to learn. *Christian Science Monitor,* Mar. 18, 12.

ITANO, N. 2002b. How Rwanda's genocide lingers on for women. *Christian Science Monitor,* Nov. 27, 8.

It's just lunch. 2006. January 5, www.consumeraffairs.com (accessed January 10, 2006).

JACKSON, A. P., P. GYAMFI, J. BROOKS-GUNN, AND M. BLAKE. 1998. Employment status, psychological well-being, social support, and physical discipline practices of single black mothers. *Journal of Marriage and the Family 60* (Nov.): 894–902.

JACKSON, A. P., R. P. BROWN, AND K. E. PATTERSON-STEWART. 2000. African Americans in dual-career commuter marriages: An investigation of their experiences. *Family Journal: Counseling and Therapy for Couples and Families 8* (Jan.): 22–36.

JACKSON, S. 2003. Analyzing the studies. In *Batterer intervention programs: Where do we go from here?* ed. S. Jackson et al., 23–29. Washington, DC: U.S. Department of Justice.

JACKSON, S. A. 1998. "Something about the word": African American women and feminism. In *No middle ground: Women and radical protest,* ed. K. M. Blee, 38–50. New York: New York University Press.

JACKSON, S., L. FEDER, D. R. FORDE, R. C. DAVIS, C. D. MAXWELL, AND B. G. TAYLOR. 2003. *Batterer intervention programs: Where do we go from here?* Washington, DC: U.S. Department of Justice.

JACOBS, J. A., AND R. GERSON. 1998. Who are the overworked Americans? *Review of Social Economy 56* (Winter): 442–59.

JACOBS, J. L. 1990. Reassessing mother blame in incest. *Signs 15* (Spring): 500–14.

JACOBY, S. 1999. Great sex. *Modern Maturity* (Sep./Oct.): 41–45, 91.

JACOBY, S. 2005. Sex in America. *AARP* (July/Aug.): 57–62, 114.

JAFFEE, S. R., T. E. MOFFITT, A. CASPI, AND A. TAYLOR. 2003. Life with (or without) father: The benefits of living with two biological parents depend on the father's antisocial behavior. *Child Development 74* (Jan./Feb.): 109–26.

JAGSI, R., ET AL. 2006. The "gender gap" in authorship of academic medical literature—a 35-year perspective. *New England Journal of Medicine 355* (July 20): 281–87.

JAIMES, M. A., WITH T. HALSEY. 1992. American Indian women: At the center of indigenous resistance in contemporary North America. In *The state of Native America: Genocide, colonization, and resistance,* ed. M. A. Jaimes, 311–44. Boston: South End.

JAKUBOWSKI, S. F., E. P. MILNE, H. BRUNNER, AND R. B. MILLER. 2004. A review of empirically supported marital enrichment programs. *Family Relations 53* (October): 528–36.

JALALI, B. 1996. Iranian families. In *Ethnicity and family therapy,* 2nd ed., eds. M. McGoldrick, J. Giordano, and J. K. Pearce, 347–63. New York: Guilford.

JAMBUNATHAN, S., D. C. BURTS, AND S. PIERCE. 2000. Comparisons of parenting attitudes among five ethnic groups in the United States. *Journal of Comparative Family Studies 31* (Autumn): 395–406.

JANKOWIAK, W. R., AND E. P. FISCHER. 1992. A cross-cultural perspective on romantic love. *Ethnology 31* (Apt.): 149–55.

JANSON, L. 2005. The many faces of Victoria's Secret. *Proteus 52* (December): 27–30.

JARRETT, R. L. 1994. Living poor: Family life among single parent, African-American women. *Social Problems 41* (Feb.): 30–49.

JAYAKODY, R., AND A. KALIL. 2002. Social fathering in low-income, African American families with preschool children. *Journal of Marriage and Family 64* (May): 504–16.

JAYAKODY, R., AND N. CABRERA. 2002. What are the choices for low-income families? Cohabitation, marriage, and remaining single. In *Just living to-*

gether: Implications of cohabitation on families, children, and social policy, eds. A. Booth and A. C. Crouter, 85–96. Mahwah, NJ: Erlbaum.

JAYSON, S. 2005. Hearts divide over marital therapy. *USA Today*, July 22, D1.

JEFFERY, C. 2006. The perks of privilege. *Mother Jones* 31(May/June): 23, 25.

JELIN, E. 2005. The family in Argentina: Modernity, economic crisis, and politics. In *Handbook of world families*, eds. B. N. Adams and J. Trost, 391–413. Thousand Oaks, CA: Sage.

JENDREK, M. P. 1994. Grandparents who parent their grandchildren: Circumstances and decisions. *The Gerontologist* 34 (2): 206–16.

JENNY, C., K. P. HYMEL, A. RITZEN, S. E. REINERT, AND T. C. HAY. 1999. Analysis of missed cases of abusive head trauma. *Journal of the American Medical Association* 281 (Feb.): 621–26.

JERVEY, G. 2005. She makes more than he does. *Money*, May, 41–44.

JEUNE, B., AND J. W. VAUPEL, EDS. 1995. *Exceptional longevity: From prehistory to the present*. Odense, Denmark: Odense University Press.

JO, M. H. 1999. *Korean immigrants and the challenge of adjustment*. Westport, CT: Greenwood.

JOHN, D., AND B. A. SHELTON. 1997. The production of gender among black and white women and men: The case of household labor. *Sex Roles* 36 (Feb.): 171–93.

JOHN, R. 1988. The Native American family. In *Ethnic families in America: Patterns and variations*, 3rd ed., eds. C. H. Mindel, R. W. Habenstein, and R. Wright, Jr., 325–66. New York: Elsevier.

JOHNSON, B. K. 1996. Older adults and sexuality: A multidimensional perspective. *Journal of Gerontological Nursing* 22 (Feb.): 6–15.

JOHNSON, B. T., M. P. CAREY, K. L. MARCH, K. D. LEVIN, AND L. A. J. SCOTT-SHELDON. 2003. Interventions to reduce sexual risk for the human immunodeficiency virus in adolescents, 1985–2000. *Archives of Pediatrics and Adolescent Medicine* 157 (Apr.): 381–88.

JOHNSON, D. R., AND J. WU. 2002. An empirical test of crisis, social selection, and role explanations of the relationship between marital disruption and psychological distress: A pooled time-series analysis of four-wave panel data. *Journal of Marriage and Family* 64 (February): 211–224.

JOHNSON, E. M., AND T. L. HUSTON. 1998. The perils of love, or why wives adapt to husbands during the transition to parenthood. *Journal of Marriage and the Family* 60 (Feb.): 195–204.

JOHNSON, M. P. 2005. Domestic violence: It's not about gender—or is it? *Journal of Marriage and Family* 67 (December): 1126–30.

JOHNSON, R. 1985. Stirring the oatmeal. In *Challenge of the heart: Love, sex, and intimacy in changing times*, ed. J. Welwood. Boston: Shambhala.

JOHNSON, R. W. AND J. M. WIENER. 2006. *A profile of frail older Americans and their caregivers*. The Urban Institute, February, www.urban.org (accessed August 3, 2006).

JOHNSON, R. W., AND M. M. FAVREAULT. 2001. Retiring together or working alone: The impact of spousal employment and disability on retirement decisions. Center for Retirement Research at Boston College, Mar. www.bc.edu (accessed Oct. 9, 2003).

JOHNSON, R. W., G. B. T. MERMIN, AND C. E. UCCELLO. 2006. When the nest egg cracks: Financial consequences of health problems, marital status changes, and job layoffs at older ages. The Urban Institute, January, www.urban.org (accessed August 16, 2006).

JOHNSTON, J. 2005. Online dating finds some gray. *USA Today* August 30, www.usatoday.com (accessed September 3, 2005).

JOHNSTON, L. D., P. M. O'MALLEY, J. G. BACHMAN, AND J. E. SCHULENBERG. 2006. *Monitoring the Future: National results on adolescent drug use: overview of key findings, 2005*. Bethesda, MD: National Institute on Drug Abuse.

JONES, A. 1994. *Next time, she'll be dead: Battering and how to stop it*. Boston: Beacon.

JONES, A., AND S. SCHECHTER. 1992. *When love goes wrong: What to do when you can't do anything right*. New York: HarperCollins.

JONES, C. 1994. Living single. *Essence*. (May): 138–40.

JONES, J. 1985. *Labor of love, labor of sorrow: Black women, work and the family from slavery to the present*. New York: Basic Books.

JONES, J. M. 2002a. Parents of young children are most stressed Americans. Gallup News Service, Nov. 8. www.gallup.com (accessed Nov. 10, 2002).

JONES, J. M. 2002b. Public divided on benefits of living together before marriage. Gallup News Service, Aug. 16. www.gallup.com (accessed Aug. 18, 2002).

JONES, J. M. 2006a. Americans more worried about meeting basic financial needs. Gallup Organization, April 25, http://poll.gallup.com (accessed May 31, 2006).

JONES, J. M. 2006b. One in three U.S. workers have "telecommuted" to work. Gallup Organization, August 16, www.galluppoll.com (accessed September 28, 2006).

JONES, M. 2003. The mystery of my eggs. *New York Times*, Mar. 16, 44.

JONES, M. 2004. "The New Yankees." *Mother Jones* 29 (March/April): 65–69.

JONES, N. A., AND A. S. SMITH. 2001. *The two or more races population: 2000*. U.S. Census. www.census .gov (accessed Apr. 16, 2003).

JONES, R. K. 1993. Female victim perceptions of the causes of male spouse abuse. *Sociological Inquiry* 63 (Aug.): 351–61.

JONES, R. K., S. SINGH, AND A. PURCESS. 2005. Parent–child relations among minor females attending U.S. family planning clinics. *Perspectives on Sexual and Reproductive Health* 37 (December): 192–201.

JONES, W. H., AND M. P. BURDETTE. 1994. Betrayal in relationships. In *Perspectives on close relationships*, eds. A. L. Weber and J. H. Harvey, 243–62. Boston: Allyn & Bacon.

JOSEPH, S. ED. 1999. *Intimate selving in Arab families: Gender, self, and identity*. New York: Syracuse University Press.

JOSSELSON, R. 1992. *The space between us: Exploring the dimensions of human relationships*. San Francisco: Jossey-Bass.

JOYCE, A. 2004. Lawsuits shed new light on sexual harassment of teens. *Washington Post*, December 2, A1.

JOYCE, A. 2005. Office stereotyping and how it stifles. *Washington Post*, Oct. 20, F1.

JOYCE, A. 2006. Now it's time for women to get even. *Washington Post*, April 23, F1.

JOYCE, B. 2005. Rapist's prison sentence triggers outrage. 2005. XCAX-TV News, January 4, www .wcax.com (accessed January 6, 2005).

JUAREZ, V. 2006. www.findlovehere.com. *Newsweek* (February 20): 60.

JUBY, H., C. L. BOURDAIS, AND N. MARCIL-GRATTON. 2005. Sharing roles, sharing custody? Couples' characteristics and children's living arrangements at separation. *Journal of Marriage and Family* 66 (February): 157–172.

JUDGE, S. 2003. Determinants of parental stress in families adopting children from Eastern Europe. *Family Relations* 52 (July): 241–48.

JUSTICE, G. 1999. We're happily married and living apart. *Newsweek*, Oct. 18, 12.

KACAPYR, E. 1998. How hard are hard times? *American Demographics* 20 (Feb.): 30–32.

KADLEC, D. 2003. Where did my raise go? *Time*, May 26, 44–54.

KAKUCHI, S. 2003. Japan's battlers of sex abuse confront culture, law. *Women's E-News*, Apr. 21. www.womensenews.org (accessed Apr. 23, 2003).

KAKUCHI, S. 2004. Japan's fertility-treatment boom pressures women. Women's E-News, January 19, www.womensenews.org (accessed January 23, 2004).

KALB, C., AND V. JUAREZ. 2005. Small is beautiful. *Newsweek*, August 1, 46–47.

KALICK, S. M., AND T. E. HAMILTON. 1986. The matching hypothesis reexamined. *Journal of Personality and Social Psychology* 51 (October): 673–82.

KALIL, A. 2002. Cohabitation and child development. In *Just living together: Implications of cohabitation on families, children, and social policy*, eds. A. Booth and A. C. Crouter, 153–60. Mahwah, NJ: Erlbaum.

KALMIJN, M. 1993. Trends in black/white intermarriage. *Social Forces* 72 (Sep.): 119–46.

KALMIJN, M. 1998. Intermarriage and homogamy: Causes, patterns, trends. *Annual Review of Sociology* 24: 395–421.

KAMEN, P. 2002. *Her way: Women remake the sexual revolution*. New York: Broadway.

KAMERMAN, S. B. 1996. Child and family policies: An international overview. In *Children, families, and government: Preparing for the twenty-first century*, eds. E. F. Zigler, S. L. Kagan, and N. W. Hall, 31–48. New York: Cambridge University Press.

KAMO, Y. 1998. Asian grandparents. In *Handbook on grandparenthood*, ed. M. E. Szinovacz, 97–112. Westport, CT: Greenwood.

KAMO, Y., AND E. L. COHEN. 1998. Division of household work between partners: A comparison of black and white couples. *Journal of Comparative Family Studies* 29 (Spring): 131–45.

KANALEY, R. 2000. Women closing gap in Net use, report finds. *Baltimore Sun*, May 15, 1C–2C.

KANE, G. 2006. Changing a culture through marriage. *Baltimore Sun*, Feb. 18, 1B, 7B.

KANTOR, R. M. 1970. Communes. *Psychology Today* (July): 53–57, 78.

KANTROWITZ, B. 2006. Sex & love: The new world. *Newsweek* (February 20): 51–59.

KANTROWITZ, B., AND P. WINGERT. 1999. The science of a good marriage. *Newsweek*, Apr. 19, 52–57.

KANTROWITZ, B., AND P. WINGERT. 2001. Unmarried with children. *Newsweek*, May 28, 46–54.

KAO, L. C., ET AL. 2003. Expression profiling of endometrium from women with endometriosis reveals candidate genes for disease-based implantation failure and infertility. *Endocrinology* 144 (Apr. 10): 2870–81.

KAPLAN, J. 2004. *Interfaith families: Personal Stories of Jewish-Christian intermarriage*. Westport, CT: Praeger.

KARANJA, W. W. 1987. "Outside wives" and "inside wives" in Nigeria: A study of changing perceptions of marriage. In *Transformations of African marriage*, eds. D. Parkin and D. Nyamwaya, 247–61. Manchester, UK: Manchester University Press.

KARASIK, S. 2000. More latchkey kids means more trouble: High-risk behavior increases when parents are gone. www.apbnews.com (accessed Sep. 28, 2000).

KARJANE, H. M., BONNIE S. F., AND F. T. CULLEN. 2005. Sexual assault on campus: What colleges and universities are doing about it. National Institute of Justice, December, www.ncjrs.gov (accessed March 10, 2006).

KASHEF, Z. 2003. The fetal position. *Mother Jones* (Jan./Feb.): 18–19.

KASS, L. R. 1997. The end of courtship. *The Public Interest* 126 (Winter): 39–63.

KATZ, R., AND Y. LAVEE. 2005. Families in Israel. In *Handbook of world families*, eds. B. N. Adams and J. Trost, 486–506. Thousand Oaks, CA: Sage.

KAUFMAN, M. 1993. *Cracking the armour: Power, pain and the lives of men*. New York: Viking/Penguin.

KAUFMAN, M. 2002. Popularity of breast implants rising. *Washington Post*, Sep. 22, A1.

KAUFMAN, M. 2006. Pregnancy centers found to give false information on abortion. *Washington Post*, July 18, A8.

KAUKINEN, C. 2004. Status compatibility, physical violence, and emotional abuse in intimate relationships. *Journal of Marriage and Family* 66 (May): 452–71.

KAWAMOTO, W. T. 2001. Introduction. *American Behavioral Scientist* 44 (May): 1445–46.

KAWAMOTO, W. T., AND T. C. CHESHIRE. 1997. American Indian families. In *Families in cultural context: Strengths and challenges in diversity*, ed. M. K. DeGenova, 15–34. Mountain View, CA: Mayfield.

KAYSER, K. 1993. *When love dies: The process of marital disaffection*. New York: Guilford.

KELLEY, P. 1992. Healthy stepfamily functioning. *Families in Society: The Journal of Contemporary Human Services* 73 (Dec.): 579–87.

KELLEY, P. 1996. Family-centered practice with stepfamilies. *Families in Society: The Journal of Contemporary Human Services* 77 (Nov.): 535–44.

KELLY, D. 2005. Lost to the only life they knew. *Los Angeles Times*, June 13, A1.

KELLY, D., AND G. COHN. 2006. Blind eye to culture of abuse. *Los Angeles Times,* May 12, www.latimes.com (accessed May 13, 2006)

KELLY, G. F. 1994. *Sexuality today: The human perspective,* 4th ed. Guilford, CT: Dushkin.

KELLY, J. B., AND R. E. EMERY. 2003. Children's adjustment following divorce: Risk and resilience perspectives. *Family Relations* 52 (October): 352–362.

KELLY, J., AND S. L. SMITH. 2006. G movies give boys a D: Portraying males as dominant, disconnected and dangerous. Dads & Daughters Organization, www.seejane.org (accessed August 8, 2006).

KELLY, K. 2005. Just do it! *U.S. News & World Report* (October 17): 42–51.

KENDALL, D. 2002. *The power of good deeds: Privileged women and the social reproduction of the upper class.* Lanham, MD. Rowman & Littlefield.

KENEN, R. H. 1993. *Reproductive hazards in the workplace: Mending jobs, managing pregnancies,* New York: Haworth.

KENNEDY, M. 2005. *Without a net: Middle class and homeless (with kids) in America.* New York: Penguin Books.

KENNEDY, R. 2002. *Nigger: The strange career of a troublesome word.* New York: Pantheon.

KENNICKELL, A. B. 2003. A rolling tide: Changes in the distribution of wealth in the U.S., 1989–2001. *Federal Reserve Bulletin,* June. www.federalreserve.gov (accessed Sep. 14, 2003).

KENRICK, D. T., G. E. GROTH, M. R. TROST, AND E. K. SADALLA. 1993. Integrating evolutionary and social exchange perspectives on relationships: Effects of gender, self-appraisal, and involvement level on mate selection criteria. *Journal of Personality and Social Psychology* 64 (6): 951–69.

KENT, M. M., AND C. HAUB. 2005. Global demographic divide. *Population Bulletin,* 60, December. Washington, DC: Population Reference Bureau.

KENT, M. M., AND M. MATHER. 2002. What drives U.S. population growth? *Population Bulletin 57* (Dec.): 1–40. Washington, DC: Population Reference Bureau.

KENT, M. M., K. M. POLLARD, J. HAAGA, AND M. MATHER. 2001. First glimpses from the 2000 U.S. Census. *Population Bulletin 56* (June). Washington, DC: Population Reference Bureau.

Kenyan girls flee mutilation. 2003. BBC. http://news.bbc.co.uk (accessed Feb. 8, 2003).

KERCKHOFF, A. C., AND K. E. DAVIS. 1962. Value consensus and need complementarity in mate selection. *American Sociological Review* 27 (June): 295–303.

KERN, S. 1992. *The culture of love: Victorians to moderns.* Cambridge, MA: Harvard University Press.

KERNIC, M. A., ET AL. 2002. Academic and school health issues among children exposed to maternal intimate partner abuse. *Archives of Pediatrics & Adolescent Medicine* 156 (June): 549–55.

KERNIC, M. A., D. J. MONARY-ERNSDORFF, J. K. KOEPSELL, AND V. L. HOLT. 2005. Children in the crossfire: Child custody determinations among couples with a history of intimate partner violence. *Violence Against Women* 11 (August): 991–1021.

KERSHAW, S. 2003. Saudi Arabia awakes to the perils of inbreeding. *New York Times,* May 1. A3.

KERSTEN, K. K. 1990. The process of marital disaffection: Interventions at various stages. *Family Relations* 39 (July): 257–65.

KETTNER, P. M., R. M. MORONEY, AND L. L. MARTIN. 1999. *Designing and managing programs: An effectiveness-based approach,* 2nd ed. Thousand Oaks, CA: Sage.

KHESHGI-GENOVESE, Z., AND T. A. GENOVESE. 1997. Developing the spousal relationship within stepfamilies. *Families in Society: The Journal of Contemporary Human Services* 78 (May/June): 255–64.

KIBRIA, N. 1994. Vietnamese families in the United States. In *Minority families in the United States: A multicultural perspective,* ed. R. L. Taylor, 164–76. Upper Saddle River, NJ: Prentice Hall.

KIBRIA, N. 1997. The construction of "Asian American": Reflections on intermarriage and ethnic identity among second-generation Chinese and Korean Americans. *Ethnic and Racial Studies* 20 (July): 523–44.

KIBRIA, N. 2002. Vietnamese American families. In *Minority families in the United States: A multicultural perspective,* 3rd ed., ed. R. L. Taylor, 181–92. Upper Saddle River NJ: Prentice Hall.

KIECOLT-GLASER, J. K., AND T. L. NEWTON. 2001. Marriage and health: His and hers. *Psychological Bulletin* 127 (July): 472–503.

KIEFER, H. M. 2005. U.S. weddings: "Something borrowed" usually money. Gallup Organization, June 28, http://poll.gallup.com (accessed June 29, 2006).

KIEHL, S. 2005. Illicitly yours. *Baltimore Sun,* July 6, 1C, 3C.

KIERNAN, K. 2002. Cohabitation in Western Europe: Trends, issues, and implications. In *Just living together: Implications of cohabitation on families, children, and social policy,* eds. A. Booth and A. C. Crouter, 3–32. Mahwah, NJ: Erlbaum.

KIERNAN, K. 2004. Redrawing the boundaries of marriage. *Journal of Marriage and Family* 66 (Nov.): 980–87.

KIERNAN, K. E. 1992. The impact of family disruption in childhood on transitions made in young adult life. *Population Studies* 46: 213–34.

KIERNAN, V. 2002. Boston U. chancellor orders gay support group at university's prep school to disband. *Chronicle of Higher Education.* http://chronicle.com (accessed Sep. 10, 2002).

KILBOURNE, J. 1994. Still killing us softly: Advertising and the obsession with thinness. In *Feminist perspectives on eating disorders,* eds. P. Fallon, M. A. Katzman, and S. C. Wooley, 395–418. New York: Guilford.

KILBOURNE, J. 1999. *Deadly persuasion: Why women and girls must fight the addictive power of advertising.* New York: Free Press.

KILBURN, J. C., JR. 1996. Network effects in care-recipient violence: A study of care-givers to those diagnosed with Alzheimer's disease. *Journal of Elder Abuse & Neglect* 8 (1): 69–80.

KILPATRICK, D. G., B. E. SAUNDERS, AND D. W. SMITH. 2003. *Youth victimization: Prevalence and implications.* Washington, DC: U.S. Department of Justice.

KIM, E. 1999. Sexual division of labor in the Korean American family. Paper presented at the annual National Council on Family Relations meetings, Washington, DC.

KIM, J. E., E. M. HETHERINGTON, AND D. ROSS. 1999. Associations among family relationships, antisocial peers, and adolescents' externalizing behaviors. *Child Development* 70 (Sep./Oct.): 1209–30.

KIM, K. C., AND S. KIM. 1998. Family and work roles of Korean immigrants in the United States. In *Resiliency in Native American and immigrant families,* eds. H. I. McCubbin, E. A. Thompson, A. I. Thompson, and J. E. Fromer, 225–42. Thousand Oaks, CA: Sage.

KINDLON, D. J., WITH T. BARKER AND M. THOMPSON. 1999. *Raising Cain: Protecting the emotional life of boys.* New York: Random House.

KING, B. 2002. *Human sexuality today,* 4th ed. Upper Saddle River, NJ: Prentice Hall.

KING, J. E. 2003. Gender equity in higher education: Are male students at a disadvantage? American Council on Education, (accessed December 4, 2005).

KING, J. L. 2004. *On the down low: A journey into the lives of "straight" black men who sleep with men.* New York: Broadway Books.

KING, M., AND A. BARTLETT. 2006. What same sex civil partnerships may mean for health. *Journal of Epidemiol Community Health* 60 (March): 188–91.

KING, V. 1994. Variation in the consequences of nonresident father involvement for children's wellbeing. *Journal of Marriage and the Family* 56 (November): 953–972.

KING, V. 2002. Parental divorce and interpersonal trust in adult offspring. *Journal of Marriage and Family* 64 (Aug.): 642–56.

KING, V. 2003. The legacy of a grandparent's divorce: Consequences for ties between grandparents and grandchildren. *Journal of Marriage and Family* 65 (Feb.): 170–83.

KING, V., AND M. E. SCOTT. 2005. A comparison of cohabiting relationships among older and younger adults. *Journal of Marriage and Family* 67 (May): 271–85.

KING, W. 1996. "Suffer with them till death": Slave women and their children in nineteenth-century America. In *More than chattel: Black women and slavery in the Americas,* eds. D. B. Caspar and D. C. Hine, 147–68. Bloomington: Indiana University Press.

KINGTON, R. S., AND H. W. NICKENS. 2001. Racial and ethnic differences in health: Recent trends, current patterns, future directions. In *America becoming: Racial trends and their consequences,* Vol. 2, eds. N. J. Smelser, W. J. Wilson, and F. Mitchell, 253–310. Washington, DC: National Academy Press.

KINSELLA, K., AND V. A. VELKOFF. 2001. An aging world: 2001. U.S. Department of Health and Human Services, National Institute on Aging. www.census.gov (accessed Mar. 5, 2003).

KINSEY, A. C., W. B. POMEROY, AND C. E. MARTIN. 1948. *Sexual behavior in the human male.* Philadelphia: Saunders.

KINSEY, A. C., W. B. POMEROY, C. E. MARTIN, AND P. H. GEBHARD. 1953. *Sexual behavior in the human female.* Philadelphia: Saunders.

KIRBY, D. 2001. Understanding what works and what doesn't in reducing adolescent sexual risk-taking. *Family Planning Perspectives* 33 (Nov./Dec.): 276–81.

KIRBY, D. 2002. Effective approaches to reducing adolescent unprotected sex, pregnancy, and childbearing. *Journal of Sex Research* 39 (Feb.): 51–57.

KIRBY, D., ET AL. 1994. School-based programs to reduce sexual risk behaviors: A review of effectiveness. *Public Health Reports* 109 (May/June): 339–60.

KIRCHHEIMER, S. 2005. Anti-aging snake oil. *AARP Bulletin,* November, 36.

KIRKPATRICK, L. A., AND C. HAZAN. 1994. Attachment styles and close relationships: A four-year prospective study. *Personal Relationships* 1 (June): 123–42.

KIRSH, S. J. 2005. *Children, adolescents, and media violence: A critical look at the research.* Thousand Oaks, CA: Sage.

KISSMAN, K., AND J. A. ALLEN. 1993. *Single-parent families.* Beverly Hills, CA: Sage.

KITZINGER, S. 1989. *The crying baby.* New York: Penguin.

KIVISTO, P., and W. Ng. 2004. *Americans all: Race and ethnic relations in historical, structural, and comparative perspectives,* 2nd ed. Los Angeles, CA: Roxbury.

KLADKO, B. 2002. At computer camp, the gender gap is obvious. www.bergen.com (accessed July 29, 2002).

KLAUS, P. A. 2000. *Crimes against persons age 65 or older, 1992–97.* Washington, DC: U.S. Department of Justice, Office of Justice Programs.

KLAUS, P. 2004. "Carjacking, 1993–2002." Washington, DC: U.S. Department of Justice, Bureau of Justice Statistics.

KLEIMAN, C. 1993. Comparable pay could create jobs. *Orlando Sentinel,* Oct. 13, C5.

KLEIMAN, C. 2005. Women in the workplace contend with "mommy wage gap." *Baltimore Sun,* August 24, 3K.

KLEIN, K. 2006. Parents, wake up! Your kid is annoying. *Los Angeles Times,* January 3, B11.

KLEIN, R. 1993. Personal correspondence.

KLINKENBERG, D., AND S. ROSE. 1994. Dating scripts of gay men and lesbians. *Journal of Homosexuality* 26(4): 23–35.

KNAPP, M. L., AND J. A. HALL. 1992. *Nonverbal communication in human interaction,* 3rd ed. New York: Holt, Rinchard & Winston.

KNICKERBOCKER, B. 2000. Forget crime—but please fix the traffic. *Christian Science Monitor,* Feb. 16, 3.

KNICKERBOCKER, B. 2006. Crackdown on polygamy group. *Christian Science Monitor,* May 9, 2, 4.

KNOX, D., WITH K. LEGGETT. 1998. *The divorced dad's survival book: How to stay connected with your kids.* New York: Insight.

KOENIG, L. J., D. J. WHITAKER, R. A. ROYCE, T. E. WILSON, K. ETHIER, AND M. I. FERNANDEZ. 2006. Physical and sexual violence during pregnancy and after delivery: A prospective multistate study of women with or at risk for HIV infection. *American Journal of Public Health* 96 (June): 1052–59.

KOENIG, M., AND S. MULPURU. 2003. *Income of the aged chartbook, 2001.* Social Security Administration. www.ssa.gov (accessed Oct. 10, 2003).

KOHLBERG, L. 1969. Stage and sequence: The cognitive-developmental approach to socialization. In *Handbook of socialization theory and research,* ed. D. A. Goslin, 347–480. Chicago: Rand McNally.

KONO, T., ET AL., 2004. Birth of parthenogenetic mice that can develop to adulthood. *Nature* 428 (April 22): 860–64.

KOOP, C. 1989. *Letter to President Ronald Reagan concerning the health effects of abortion: Medical and psychological impact of abortion.* Washington, DC: U.S. Government Printing Office.

KOWAL, A. K., AND L. BLINN-PIKE. 2004. Sibling influences on adolescents' attitudes toward safe sex practices. *Family Relations* 53 (July): 377–84.

KRAFFT, S. 1994. Why wives earn less than husbands. *American Demographics* 16 (Jan.): 16–17.

KRATCHICK, J. L., T. S. ZIMMERMAN, S. A. HADDOCK, AND J. H. BANNING. 2005. Best-selling books advising parents about gender: A feminist analysis. *Family Relations* 54 (January): 84–100.

KRAUSS, C. 2003. Long lines mar Canada's low-cost health care. *New York Times,* Feb. 13, C1.

KREEGER, K. Y. 2002a. Sex-based differences continue to mount. *The Scientist* 16 (Feb. 18). www.the-scientist.com (accessed July 14, 2002).

KREEGER, K. Y. 2002b. X and Y chromosomes concern more than reproduction. *The Scientist* 16 (Feb. 4). www.the-scientist.com (accessed July 14, 2002).

KREIDER, R. M. 2003. *Adopted children and stepchildren: 2000.* U.S. Census Bureau, Census 2000 Special Reports. www.census.gov (accessed Sep. 3, 2003).

KREIDER, R. M. 2005. *Number, timing, and duration of marriages and divorces: 2001.* U.S. Census Bureau, Current Population Reports, P70–97, www.census.gov (accessed July 4, 2006).

KREIDER, R. M., AND J. M. FIELDS. 2002. *Number, timing, and duration of marriages and divorces: 1996.* U.S. Census Bureau, Current Population Reports, p70–80. www.census.gov (accessed Mar. 1, 2003).

KREIMER, S. 2004. Teens getting breast implants for graduation. Women's e-news, June 13, www.womensenews.org (accessed December 1, 2005).

KRISTOF, K. M. 2006. Will dating sites offer credit reports? *Los Angeles Times* (February 14): C1.

KROKOFF, L. J. 1987. The correlates of negative affect in marriage: An exploratory study of gender differences. *Journal of Family Issues* 8 (Mar.): 111–35.

KRUEGER, R. A. 1994. *Focus groups: A practical guide for applied research,* 2nd ed. Thousand Oaks, CA: Sage.

KRUG, E. G., L. L. DAHLBERG, J. A. MERCY, A. B. ZWI, AND R. LOZANO, EDS. 2002. *World report on violence and health.* World Health Organization. www5.who.int/violence_injury_prevention/downl oad.cfm?id=0000000582 (accessed May 15, 2003).

KÜBLER-ROSS, E. 1969. *On death and dying.* New York: Macmillan.

KUCZYNSKI, A. 2001. Men's magazines: How much substance behind the covers? *New York Times,* June 24, C1.

KULCZYCKI, A., AND A. P. LOBO. 2001. Deepening the melting pot: Arab-Americans at the turn of the century. *Middle East Journal* 3 (Summer): 459–73.

KULCZYCKI, A., AND A. P. LOBO. 2002. Patterns, determinants, and implications of intermarriage among Arab Americans. *Journal of Marriage and Family* 64 (Feb.): 202–10.

KUNJUFU, J. 1987. *Lessons from history: A celebration in blackness.* Chicago: African American Images.

KUNKEL, D., E. BIELY, K. EYAL, K. COPE-FERRAR, E. DONNERSTEIN, AND R. FANDRICH. 2003. Sex on TV3. Kaiser Family Foundation. www.kff.org (accessed June 15, 2003).

KUNKEL, D., K. EYAL, K. FINNERTY, E. BIELY, AND E. DONNERSTEIN. 2005. Sex on TV. Kaiser Family Foundation. www.kff.org (accessed January 6, 2006).

KURDEK, L. A. 1993. Predicting marital dissolution: A 5-year prospective longitudinal study of new-lywed couples. *Journal of Personality and Social Psychology* 64 (2): 221–42.

KURDEK, L. A. 1994. Areas of conflict for gay, lesbian, and heterosexual couples: What couples argue about influences relationship satisfaction. *Journal of Marriage and the Family* 56 (Nov.): 923–24.

KURDEK, L. A. 1998. Relationship outcomes and their predictors: Longitudinal evidence from heterosexual married, gay cohabiting, and lesbian cohabiting couples. *Journal of Marriage and the Family* 60 (Aug.): 553–68.

KURDEK, L. A. 2004. Gay men and lesbians: The family context. In *Handbook of contemporary families: Considering the past, contemplating the future,* eds. M. Coleman and L. H. Ganong, 96–115. Thousand Oaks, CA: Sage.

KURDEK, L. A., AND M. A. FINE. 1993. The relation between family structure and young adolescents' appraisals of family climate and parenting behavior. *Journal of Family Issues* 14: 279–90.

KURLAND, S. P. 2004. *Everlasting Love.* Baltimore, MD: Noble House.

KURZ, D. 1993. Physical assaults by husbands: A major social problem. In *Current controversies on family violence,* eds. R. J. Gelles and D. R. Loseke, 88–103. Thousand Oaks, CA: Sage.

KWONG SEE, S. T., AND C. RASMUSSEN. 2003. An early start to age stereotyping: Children's beliefs about an older experimenter. *University of Alberta News.* www.expressnews.ualberta.ca (accessed Dec. 3, 2003).

LACEY, M. 2003. African women gather to denounce genital cutting. *New York Times.* Feb. 6, A3.

LAFRANCE, M., M. A. HECHT, AND E. L. PALUCK. 2003. The contingent smile: A meta analysis of sex differences in smiling. *Psychological Bulletin* 129 (Mar.): 305–35.

LAFRANIERE, S. 2005. Forced to marry before puberty, African girls pay lasting price. *New York Times,* Nov 27, 1A.

LAGNADO, L. 2006. Staying put at 96. *Wall Street Journal,* May 6–7, A1, A5.

LAIRD, J. 1993. Lesbian and gay families. In *Normal family processes,* 2nd ed., ed. F. Walsh, 282–330. New York: Guilford.

LAKOFF, R. T. 1990. *Talking power: The politics of language.* New York: Basic Books.

LAKSHMANAN, I. A. R. 1997. Marriage? Think logic, not love. *Baltimore Sun,* Sep. 22, 2A.

LAMISON-WHITE, L. 1997. *Poverty in the United States: 1996.* U.S. Census Bureau, Current Population Reports, Series P60–198. Washington, DC: U.S. Government Printing Office.

LAMPMAN, J. 2001. Rev Moon raising his profile. *Christian Science Monitor,* Apr. 19, 18–19.

LAMPMAN, J. 2001. The new American dream. *Christian Science Monitor,* Sep. 24, 13–15.

LANCASTER, J. 2004. Women on the rise in India feel the riptide of tradition. *Washington Post* (November 8): A16.

LANDALE, N. S., AND S. E. TOLNAY. 1991. Group differences in economic opportunity and the timing of marriage. *American Sociological Review* 56 (Feb.): 33–45.

LANDERS, A. 2001. Husband shows his love in small ways every day. *Baltimore Sun,* June 16, 3D.

LANGELAN, M. J. 1993. *Back off! How to confront and stop sexual harassment and harassers.* New York: Simon & Schuster.

LANGER, G., C. ARNEDT, AND D. SUSSMAN. 2004. Primetime Live poll: American sex survey. ABC News,: http://abcnews.go.com (accessed January 16, 2006).

LANSFORD, J. E., ET AL. 2005. Physical discipline and children's adjustment: Cultural normativeness as a moderator. *Child Development* 76 (November/December): 1234–46.

LANTZ, H. R. 1976. *Marital incompatibility and social change in early America.* Beverly Hills, CA: Sage.

LAPCHICK, R. 2003. Racial and gender report card. University of Central Florida. www.bus.ucf.edu (accessed May 15, 2003).

LAREAU, A. 2003. *Unequal childhoods: Class, race, and family life.* Berkeley: University of California Press.

LARGE, E. 2002. Homeward bound. *Baltimore Sun,* June 9, 1N, 4N.

LARGE, E. 2006. Long-distance love. *Baltimore Sun,* February 12, 1N, 8N.

LARIMER, M. E., A. R. LYDUM, AND A. P. TURNER. 1999. Male and female recipients of unwanted sexual contact in a college student sample: Prevalence rates, alcohol use, and depression symptoms. *Sex Roles* 40 (Feb.): 295–308.

LAROSSA, R. 1986. *Becoming a parent.* Thousand Oaks, CA: Sage.

LAROSSA, R. ED. 1984. *Family case studies: A sociological perspective.* New York: Free Press.

LAROSSA, R., AND D. C. RETIZES. 1993. Symbolic interactionism and family studies. In *Sourcebook of family theories and methods: A contextual approach,* eds. P. G. Boss, W. J. Doherty, R. LaRossa, W. R. Schumm, and S. K. Steinmetz, 135–63. New York: Plenum.

LARZELERE, R. E. 2000. Child outcomes of nonabusive and customary physical punishment by parents: An updated literature review. Unpublished manuscript, University of Nebraska Medical Center, Omaha, and Father Flanagan's Boys' Home, Boys' Town, NE.

LARZELERE, R. E., P. R. SATHER, W. N. SCHNEIDER, D. B. LARSON, AND P. L. PIKE. 1998. Punishment enhances reasoning's effectiveness as a disciplinary response to toddlers. *Journal of Marriage and the Family* 60 (May): 388–403.

LASCH, C. 1977. *Haven in a heartless world: The family besieged.* New York: Basic Books.

LASLETT, P. 1971. *The world we have lost,* 2nd ed. Reading, MA: Addison-Wesley.

LASSWELL, T. E., AND M. E. LASSWELL. 1976. I love you but I'm not in love with you. *Journal of Marriage and Family Counseling* 2 (July): 211–24.

LASZLOFFY, T. A. 2002. Rethinking family development theory: Teaching with the systemic family development (SFD) model. *Family Relations* 51 (July): 206–14.

LATESSA, D. 2005. From financial aid to fatherhood. *Chronicle of Higher Education,* October 21, C3.

LAUER, J., AND R. LAUER. 1985. Marriages made to last. *Psychology Today* (June): 22–26.

LAUMANN, E. O., A. PAIK, AND R. C. ROSEN. 2001. Sexual dysfunction in the United States: Prevalence and predictions. In *Sex, love, and health in America,* eds. E. O. Laumann and R. T. Michael, 352–76. Chicago: University of Chicago Press.

LAUMANN, E. O., J. H. GAGNON, R. T. MICHAEL, AND S. MICHAELS. 1994. *The social organization of sexuality: Sexual practices in the United States.* Chicago: University of Chicago Press.

LAUMANN, E. O., STEPHEN E., JENNA M., AND A. PAIK. 2004. *The sexual organization of the city.* Chicago: University of Chicago Press.

LAWRANCE, K., AND E. S. BYERS. 1995. Sexual satisfaction in long-term heterosexual relationships: The interpersonal exchange model of social satisfaction. *Personal Relationships* 2: 267–85.

LAWSON, E. J., AND A. THOMPSON. 1999. *Black men and divorce.* Thousand Oaks, CA: Sage.

LAWTON, L., M. SILVERSTEIN, AND V. BENGSTON. 1994. Affection, social contact, and geographic distance between adult children and their parents. *Journal of Marriage and the Family* 56 (Feb.): 57–68.

LA VALLE, I., A. S. MILLWARD, C. SCOTT, AND M. CLAYDEN. 2002. *Happy families? Atypical work and its influence on family life.* Bristol, U.K.: Policy Press.

LEACH, P. 1994. *Children first: What our society must do—and is not doing—for our children today.* New York: Knopf.

LEAPER, C. 2002. Parenting girls and boys. In *Handbook of parenting,* 2nd ed., Vol. 1, ed. M. H. Bornstein, 189–215. Mahwah, NJ: Erlbaum.

LEARNER, N. 2002. A not-so-simple plan. *Christian Science Monitor,* Sep. 30, 11, 14–16.

LEBEY, B. 2004. *Remarried with children: Ten secrets for successfully blending and extending your family.* New York: Bantam Books.

LE BOURDAIS, C., AND E. LAPIERRE-ADAMCYK. 2004. Changes in conjugal life in Canada: Is cohabitation progressively replacing marriage? *Journal of Marriage and Family* 66 (November): 929–42.

LEDERER, W. J., AND D. D. JACKSON. 1968. *The mirages of marriage.* New York: Norton.

LEE, E., G. SPITZE, AND J. R. LOGAN. 2003. Social support to parents-in-law: The interplay of gender and kin hierarchies. *Journal of Marriage and Family* 65 (May): 396–403.

LEE, J. A. 1973. *The colors of love.* Upper Saddle River, NJ: Prentice Hall.

LEE, J. A. 1974. The styles of loving. *Psychology Today* (Oct.): 46–51.

LEE, M.-Y. 2002. A model of children's postdivorce behavioral adjustment in maternal- and dual-residence arrangements. *Journal of Family Issues* 23 (July): 672–730.

LEE, S. M., AND B. EDMONSTON. 2005. New marriages, new families: U.S. racial and Hispanic intermarriage. *Population Bulletin* 60 (June): 1–40.

LEE, Y.-S., AND L. J. WAITE. 2005. Husbands' and wives' time spent on housework: A comparison of measures. *Journal of Marriage and Family* 67 (May): 328–36.

LEHRMAN, F. 1996. Factoring domestic violence into custody cases. *Trial* 32 (Feb.): 32–39.

LEINWAND, D. 2006. Prescription drugs find place in teen culture. *USA Today,* June 13, www.usatoday.com (accessed June 14, 2006).

LEITE, R., AND P. C. MCKENRY. 1996. Putting non-residential fathers back into the family portrait. *Human Development and Family Life Bulletin* 2 (Autumn). www.hec.ohio-state.edu (accessed Feb. 3, 1998).

LEITENBERG, H., M. J. DETZER, AND D. SREBNIK. 1993. Gender differences in masturbation and the relation of masturbation experience in preadolescence and/or early adolescence to sexual behavior and sexual adjustment in young adulthood. *Journal of Social Behavior* 22 (Apr.): 87–98.

LEMIEUX, R., AND J. L. HALE. 2002. Cross-sectional analysis of intimacy, passion, and commitment: Testing the assumptions of the triangular theory of love. *Psychological Reports* 90 (June): 1009–14.

LENHART, A., M. MADDEN, AND P. HITLIN. 2005. Teens and technology. Pew Internet & American Life Project, July 27, www.pewinternet.org (accessed May 10, 2006).

LEON, J. J., J. L. PHILBRICK, F. PARRA, E. ESCOBEDO, AND F. MALGESINI. 1994. Love-styles among university students in Mexico. *Psychological Reports* 74: 307–10.

LEON, K. 2003. Risk and protective factors in young children's adjustment to parental divorce: A review of the research. *Family Relations* 52 (July): 258–70.

LEONARD, K. I. 1997. *The South Asian Americans.* Westport, CT: Greenwood.

LEONG, F., AND P. J. HARTUNG. 2001. Appraising birth order in career assessment: Linkages to Holland's and Super's models. *Journal of Career Assessment* 9 (Winter): 25–39.

LESLIE, L. A., AND G. MORTON. 2004. Family therapy's response to family diversity: Looking back, looking forward. In *Handbook of contemporary families: Considering the past, contemplating the future,* eds. M. Coleman and L. H. Ganong, 523–537. Thousand Oaks, CA: Sage.

LEVAY, S. 1993. *The sexual brain.* La Jolla, CA: MIP.

LEVENTHAL, B., AND S. E. LUNDY, EDS. 1999. *Same-sex domestic violence: Strategies for change.* Thousand Oaks, CA: Sage.

LEVESQUE, R. J. R. 1993. The romantic experience of adolescents in satisfying love relationships. *Journal of Youth and Adolescence* 11 (3): 219–50.

LEVIN, M. L., X. XU, AND J. P. BARTKOWSKI. 2002. Seasonality of sexual debut. *Journal of Marriage and Family* 64 (Nov.): 871–84.

LEVINE, M. V. 1994. A nation of hamburger flippers? *Baltimore Sun,* July 31, 1E, 4E.

LEVY, J. A. 1994. Sex and sexuality in later life stages. In *Sexuality across the life course,* ed. A. S. Rossi, 287–309. Chicago: University of Chicago Press.

LEWIN, E. 2004. Does marriage have a future? *Journal of Marriage and Family* 66 (November): 1000–06.

LEWIS, M. 1997. *Altering fate: Why the past does not predict the future.* New York: Guilford.

LEWIS, M., C. FEIRING, AND S. ROSENTHAL. 2000. Attachment over time. *Child Development* 71 (May/June): 707–20.

LIBBON, R. P. 2000. MediaChannels. *American Demographics* 21 (Feb.): 29.

LICHT, J. 1995. Marriages that endure. *Washington Post Health Supplement,* Oct. 31, 18–20.

LICHTENSTEIN, J., J. GIST, AND L. SOUTHWORTH. 2006. *The State of 50+ in America: 2006.* AARP, April, http://assets.aarp.org/ (accessed August 5, 2006).

LICHTER, D. T., AND D. R. GRAEFE. 2001. Finding a mate? The marital and cohabitation histories of unwed mothers. In *Out of wedlock: Causes and consequences of nonmarital fertility,* eds. L. L. Wu and B. Wolfe, 317–43. New York: Russell Sage Foundation.

LICHTER, D. T., AND M. L. CROWLEY. 2002. Poverty in America: Beyond welfare reform. *Population Bulletin* 57 (June). Washington, DC: Population Reference Bureau.

LICHTER, D. T., D. R. GRAEFE, AND J. B. BROWN. 2003. Is marriage a panacea? Union formation among economically disadvantaged unwed mothers. *Social Problems* 50 (February): 60–86.

LICHTER, D. T., Z. QIAN, AND L. M. MELLOTT. 2006. Marriage or dissolution? Union transitions among poor cohabiting women. *Demography* 43 (May): 223–40.

LIEBOWITZ, S. W., D. C. CASTELLANO, AND I. CUELLAR. 1999. Factors that predict sexual behavior among young Mexican American adolescents: An exploratory study. *Hispanic Journal of Behavioral Sciences* 21 (Nov.): 470–79.

LIEF, L. 1997. Kids at risk. *U.S. News & World Report,* Apr. 28, 66–70.

LIGHT, P. C. 1988. *Baby boomers.* New York: Norton.

Like a virgin? 2006. Today Online, January 11, www.todayonline.com/articles (accessed January 15, 2006).

LILLESTON, R. 2004. Survey: Gap between safe-sex claims, practices. *USA Today,* April 6, www.usatoday.com (accessed April 7, 2004).

LIN, G., AND P. A. ROGERSON. 1995. Elderly parents and the geographic availability of their adult children. *Research on Aging* 17 (Sep.): 303–09.

LIN, M. H., V. S. Y. KWAN, A. CHEUNG, AND S. T. FISKE. 2005. Stereotype content model explains prejudice for an envied outgroup: Scale of anti-Asian American stereotypes. *Personality and Social Psychology Bulletin* 31 (January): 34–47.

LINCOLN, K. D., L. M. CHATTERS, AND R. J. TAYLOR. 2005. Social support, traumatic events, and depressive symptoms among African Americans. *Journal of Marriage and Family* 67 (August): 754–66.

LINDBERG, L. D., S. BOGGESS, L. PORTER, AND S. WILLIAMS. 2000. *Teen risk-taking: A statistical portrait.* Washington, DC: Urban Institute. www.urban.org (accessed Sep. 4, 2000).

LINDSEY, L. L. 1997. *Gender roles: A sociological perspective,* 3rd ed. Upper Saddle River, NJ: Prentice Hall.

LINO, M. 2006. *Expenditures on children by families, 2005.* U.S. Department of Agriculture, Center for Nutrition Policy and Promotion.

LIPPA, R. A. 2002. *Gender, nature, and nurture.* Mahwah, NJ: Erlbaum.

LIPTON, E. 2005. Report finds U.S. failing on overstays of visas. *New York Times,* Oct. 22, A13.

LISSAU, I., ET AL. 2004. Body mass index and overweight in adolescents in 13 European countries and the United States. *Archives of Pediatrics & Adolescent Medicine* 158 (January): 27–33.

LITE, J. 2002. Report indicates gender-related violence is global. *Women's E-News,* Oct. 4. www.womensnews.org (accessed Oct. 6, 2002).

LIU, J., A. RAINE, P. H. VENABLES, AND S. A. MEDNICK. 2004. Malnutrition at age 3 years and externalizing behavior problems at ages 8, 11, and 17 years. *American Journal of Psychiatry* 161 (November): 2005–13.

LIU, P., AND C. S. CHAN. 1996. Lesbian, gay, and bisexual Asian Americans and their families. In *Lesbians and gays in couples and families: A handbook for therapists,* eds. J. Laird and R.-J. Green, 137–54. San Francisco: Jossey-Bass.

LIU, W. M. 2002. The social class–related experiences of men: Integrating theory and practice. *Professional Psychology: Research & Practice* (Aug.): 355–60.

LI, Y. -F., B. LANGHOLZ, M. T. SALAM, AND F. D. GILLILAND. 2005. Maternal and grandmaternal smoking patterns are associated with early childhood asthma. *Chest* 127 (April): 1232–41.

Living humbled, unhappy lives. 1996. *Baltimore Sun,* May 23, 2A.

LLANA, S. M. 2005. These Shakers won't be movers. *Christian Science Monitor.* December 20, 20.

LLOYD, E. A. 2005. *The case of the female orgasm: Bias in the science of evolution.* Cambridge, MA: Harvard University Press.

LLOYD, J. 2002. *Gamma hydroxybutyrate (GHB).* Washington, DC: Office of National Drug Control Policy.

LLOYD, S. A. 1991. The dark side of courtship: Violence and sexual exploitation. *Family Relations* 40 (Jan.): 14–20.

LLOYD, S. A., AND B. C. EMERY. 2000. *The dark side of courtship: Physical and sexual aggression.* Thousand Oaks, CA: Sage.

LOEB, S., M. BRIDGE, D. BASSOK, B. FULLER, AND R. RUMBERGER. 2005. How much is too much? The influence of preschool centers on children's social and cognitive development. December, NBER Working paper No. W11812, www.nber.org (accessed May 20, 2006).

LONKHUYZEN, L. V. 1994. Female gymnasts prone to eating disorders. *Baltimore Sun,* July 29, C1, C3.

LOPEZ-CLAROS, A., AND S. ZAHIDI. 2005. Women's empowerment: Measuring the global gender gap. World Economic Forum, www.weforum.org (accessed May 4, 2006).

LÓPEZ, R. A. 1999. *Las comadres* as a social support system. *Affilia* 14 (Spring): 24–41.

LORBER, J. 2005. *Gender inequality: Feminist theories and politics,* 3rd ed. Los Angeles, CA: Roxbury.

LOWELL, B. L. 2002. Recession pounds U.S. Hispanics. *Population Today* 30 (Apr.): 1, 4.

LUCAS, R. E. 2005. Time does not heal all wounds: A longitudinal study of reaction and adaptation to divorce. *Psychological Science* 16 (December): 945–950.

LUCAS, R. E., A. E. CLARK, Y. GEORGELLIS, AND E. DIENER. 2003. Reexamining adaptation and the set point model of happiness: Reactions to changes in marital status. *Journal of Personality and Social Psychology* 84 (Mar.): 527–39.

LUGAILA, T. A. 1998. *Marital status and living arrangements: March 1998 (update).* Current Population Reports, P20–514, U.S. Census Bureau. www.census.gov (accessed Aug. 8, 2000).

LUGAILA, T. A. 2003. *A child's day: 2000 (selected indicators of child well-being).* Current Population Reports, P70–89. Washington, DC: U.S. Census Bureau. www.census.gov (accessed Aug. 24, 2003).

LUKEMEYER, A., M. K. MEYERS, AND T. SMEEDING. 2000. Expensive children in poor families: Out-of-pocket expenditures for the care of disabled and chronically ill children in welfare families. *Journal of Marriage and the Family* 62 (May): 399–415.

LUND, E. 2005. Still single, in the city. *Christian Science Monitor,* Feb. 9, 13–14.

LUO, S., AND E. C. KLOHNEN. 2005. Assortative mating and marital quality in newlyweds: A couple-centered approach. *Journal of Personality and Social Psychology* 88 (February): 304–26.

LUPTON, D., AND L. BARCLAY. 1997. *Constructing fatherhood: Discourses and experiences.* Thousand Oaks, CA: Sage.

LYNN, D. B. 1969. *Parental and sex role identification: A theoretical formulation.* Berkeley, CA: McCutchen.

LYNN, M., AND M. TODOROFF. 1995. Women's work and family lives. In *Feminist issues: Race, class, and sexuality,* ed. N. Mandell, 244–71. Scarborough, Ont.: Prentice Hall Canada.

LYNSKEY, M. T., ET AL. 2003. Escalation of drug use in early-onset cannabis users vs. co-twin controls. *Journal of the American Medical Association* 289 (Jan. 22): 427–33.

LYONS, L. 2004. How many teens are cool with cohabitation? The Gallup Organization, April 13, http://poll.gallup.com (accessed April 20, 2004).

LYONS, L. 2004. The Gallup brain: Teens misbehavin'. Gallup Organization, February 24, www.gallup.com (accessed May 27, 2006).

LYTTON, H., AND L. GALLAGHER. 2002. Parenting twins and the genetics of parenting. In *Handbook of parenting,* 2nd ed., Vol. 1: *Children and parenting,* ed. M. H. Bornstein, 227–53. Mahwah, NJ: Erlbaum.

MACADAM, M. 2003. Sweatshop struggle strengthens solidarity: Campaign against exploitation of foreign workers unites activists. Policy Alternatives.

www.policyalternatives.ca (accessed Sep. 13, 2003).

MacDonald, G. J. 2003. Smarter toys, smarter tots? *Christian Science Monitor*, Aug. 20, 12–13.

MacDonald, W. L., and A. Demaris. 1996. The effects of stepparents' gender and new biological children. *Journal of Family Issues* 17 (1): 5–25.

MacDorman, M. F., J. A. Martin, T. J. Mathews, D. L. Hoyert, and S. J. Ventura. 2005. Explaining the 2001-02 infant mortality increase: Data from the linked birth/infant death data set. *National Vital Statistics Reports* 54 (January). Hyatsville, MD: National Center for Health Statistics.

MacKenzie, J. 2002. Britain toughens immigration stance. *Christian Science Monitor*, Aug. 16, 7, 9.

MacMillan, R., and R. Gartner. 1999. When she brings home the bacon: Labor-force participation and the risk of spousal violence against women. *Journal of Marriage and the Family* 61 (Nov.): 947–58.

MacPhee, D., J. Fritz, and J. Miller-Heyl. 1996. Ethnic variations in personal social networks and parenting. *Child Development* 67 (6): 3278–95.

Maccoby, E. E. 1990. Gender and relationships: A developmental account. *American Psychologist* 45 (4): 513–20.

Machamer, A. M., and E. Gruber. 1998. Secondary school, family, and educational risk: Comparing American Indian adolescents and their peers. *Journal of Educational Research* 91 (July/Aug.): 357–69.

Macomber, J. 2006. An overview of selected data on children in vulnerable families. Urban Institute and Child Trends, August 10, www.urban.org (accessed October 1, 2006).

Macunovich, D. J. 2002. Using economics to explain U.S. fertility trends. *Population Bulletin* 57 (Dec.): 8–9. Washington, DC: Population Reference Bureau.

Madden, M., and A. Lenhart. 2006. Online dating. PEW Internet & America Life Project, March 5, www.pewinternet.org (accessed March 9, 2006).

Madigan, N. 2003. Suspect's wife is said to cite polygamy plan. *New York Times*. www.nytimes.com (accessed Mar. 16, 2003).

Magnier, M. 2006. Sri Lanka still wed to system. *Los Angeles Times* (January 23): A1.

Mahay, J., E. O. Laumann, and S. Michaels. 2001. Race, gender, and class in sexual scripts. In *Sex, love, and health in America*, eds. E. O. Laumann and R. T. Michael, 197–238. Chicago: University of Chicago Press.

Mahoney, M. 2002. The economic rights and responsibilities of unmarried cohabitants. In *Just living together: Implications of cohabitation on families, children, and social policy*, eds. A. Booth and A. C. Crouter, 247–54. Mahwah, NJ: Erlbaum.

Mahoney, S. 2003. Seeking love. *AARP Magazine*, Nov./Dec.. www.aarpmagazine.org (accessed Sep. 28, 2003).

Mahoney, S. 2004. Hello, old love. *AARP Magazine* (September-October): 62–68, 122.

Maier, T. 1998. *Dr. Spock: An American life.* New York: Harcourt Brace.

Male latex condoms and sexually transmitted diseases. 2002. Centers for Disease Control and Prevention. www.cdc.gov (accessed Mar. 16, 2003).

Malley-Morrison, K., and D. A. Hines. 2004. *Family violence in a cultural perspective: Defining, understanding, and combating abuse.* Thousand Oaks, CA: Sage.

Malm, K., J. Murray, and R. Green. 2006. *What about the dads? Child welfare agencies' efforts to identify, locate, and involve nonresident fathers.* Washington, DC: U.S. Department of Health and Human Services.

Man who raped child retains visitation rights. 2002. *Women's E-News*, Apr. 22. www.womensnews.org (accessed Apr. 24, 2002).

Mancini, A. D., D. L. Pressman, and G. A. Bonanno. 2006. Clinical interventions with the bereaved: What clinicians and counselors can learn from the changing lives of older couples study. In *Spousal bereavement in late life*, eds. D. Carr, R. M. Nesse, and C. B. Wortman, 255–278. New York: Springer.

Manini, T. M., et al. 2006. Daily activity energy expenditure and mortality among older adults.

Journal of the American Medical Association 296 (July 12): 171–179.

Manning, C. 1970. *The immigrant woman and her job.* New York: Ayer.

Manning, W. D. 2002. The implications of cohabitation for children's well-being. In *Just living together: Implications of cohabitation on families, children, and social policy*, eds. A. Booth and A. C. Crouter, 121–52. Mahwah, NJ: Erlbaum.

Manning, W. D., and K. A. Lamb. 2003. Adolescent well-being in cohabiting, married, and single-parent families. *Journal of Marriage and Family* 65 (December): 876–93.

Manning, W. D., and P. J. Smock. 2005. Measuring and modeling cohabitation: New perspectives from qualitative data. *Journal of Marriage and Family* 67 (November): 989–1002.

Manning, W. D., S. D. Stewart, and P. J. Smock. 2003. The complexity of fathers' parenting responsibilities and involvement with nonresident children. *Journal of Family Issues* 24 (July): 645–67.

Mansfield, H. C. 2004. On the consensual campus. *Doublethink* (Winter): 24.

Mansnerus, L. 2003. Great haven for families, but don't bring children. *New York Times*, August 13, A1.

Marcus, A. D. 2003. Guys, your clock is ticking, too: doctors now say male fertility falls as early as age 35; the case for banking your sperm. *Wall Street Journal*, Apr. 1, D1.

Marcus, S. M., H. A. Flynn, F. C. Blow, and K. L. Barry. 2003. Depressive symptoms among pregnant women screened in obstetrics settings. *Journal of Women's Health* 12 (May): 373–80.

Marder, D. 2002. For $9,600, women taught how to find a mate. Knight Ridder News Service, Jan. 13. archives.his.com/smartmarriages (accessed Jan. 15, 2002).

Margolis, J., and A. Fisher. 2002. *Unlocking the clubhouse: Women in computing.* Cambridge, MA: MIT Press.

Markides, K. S., J. Roberts-Jolly, L. A. Ray, S. K. Hoppe, and L. Rudkin. 1999. Changes in marital satisfaction in three generations of Mexican Americans. *Research on Aging* 21 (Jan.): 36–45.

Marklein, M. B. 2005. College gender gap widens. *USA Today*, October 19, A1.

Markowitz, S., R. Kaestner, and M. Grossman. 2005. An investigation of the effects of alcohol consumption and alcohol policies on youth risky sexual behaviors. *American Economic Review* 95 (May): 263–66.

Marks, A. 2002. As teens' prospects rise, pregnancies fall. *Christian Science Monitor*, Oct. 22, 3.

Marks, A. 2005. Just say . . . nothing? The parental "drug talk" fades. *Christian Science Monitor*, March 7, 1, 4.

Markstrom-Adams, C. 1991. Attitudes on dating, courtship, and marriage: Perspectives on in-group relationships by religious minority and majority adolescents. *Family Relations* 40 (Jan.): 91–98.

Marquardt, E. 2005. *Between two worlds: The inner lives of children of divorce.* New York: Crown.

Marriage between blacks and whites. 2002. Gallup Poll Vault. www.gallup.com/poll (accessed Dec. 15, 2002).

Marshall, M. J. 2002. *Why spanking doesn't work: Stopping this bad habit and getting the upper hand on effective discipline.* Springville, Utah: Bonneville Books.

Marsiglio, W., and R. A. Greer. 1994. A gender analysis of older men's sexuality. In *Older men's lives*, ed. E. H. Thompson, 122–40. Thousand Oaks, CA: Sage.

Marsiglio, W., and R. Hinojosa. 2006. Stepfathers and the family dance. In *Couples, kids, and family life*, eds. J. F. Gubrium and J. A. Holstein, 178–196. New York: Oxford University Press.

Martin, A. 1993. *The lesbian and gay parenting handbook: Creating and raising our families.* New York: HarperPerennial.

Martin, C. E. 2006. Saying "I don't" to expensive weddings. *Christian Science Monitor*, June 15, 9.

Martin, C. L. 1990. Attitudes and expectations about children with nontraditional and traditional gender roles. *Sex Roles* 22 (Feb.): 151–65.

Martin, C. L., and R. A. Fabes. 2001. The stability and consequences of young children's same-sex

peer interactions. *Developmental Psychology* 37 (May): 431–66.

Martin, J. A., et al. 2005. Births: Final data for 2003. *National Vital Statistics Reports* 54 (September). Hyatsville, MD: National Center for Health Statistics.

Martin, K. A. 1998. Becoming a gendered body: Practices of preschools. *American Sociological Review* 63 (Aug.): 494–511.

Martin, L. R., H. S. Friedman, K. M. Clark, and J. S. Tucker. 2005. Longevity following the experience of parental divorce. *Social Science & Medicine* 61 (November): 2177–2189.

Martin, P. Y., and R. A. Hummer. 1993. Fraternities and rape on campus. In *Violence against women*, eds. P. B. Bart and E. G. Moran, 114–31. Thousand Oaks, CA: Sage.

Martin, P., and E. Midgley. 2003. Immigration: Shaping and reshaping America. *Population Bulletin* 58 (June). Washington, DC: Population Reference Bureau.

Martin, S. P., and S. Parashar. 2006. Women's changing attitudes toward divorce, 1974–2002: Evidence for an educational crossover. *Journal of Marriage and Family* 68 (February): 29–40.

Martin, T. C., and L. L. Bumpass. 1989. Recent trends in marital disruption. *Demography* 26 (Feb.): 37–51.

Martinez, E. A. 2001. Death: A family event for Mexican Americans. *Family Focus*, National Council on Family Relations, Dec., F4.

Martire, L. M., M. P. Stephens, and M. M. Franks. 1997. Multiple roles of women caregivers: Feelings of mastery and self-esteem as predictors of psychosocial well-being. *Journal of Women & Aging* 9 (1/2): 117–31.

Marvasti, A., and K. D. McKinney. 2004. *Middle Eastern lives in America.* New York: Rowman & Littlefield.

Maryland Special Joint Committee. 1989. *Gender bias in the courts.* Annapolis, MD: Administrative Office of the Courts.

Marzollo, J. 1993. *Fathers & babies: How babies grow and what they need from you from birth to 18 months.* New York: HarperCollins.

Mastekaasa, A. 1997. Marital dissolution as a stressor: Some evidence on psychological, physical, and behavioral changes during the preseparation period. *Journal of Divorce and Remarriage* 26: 155–83.

Masters, W. H., V. E. Johnson, and R. C. Kolodny. 1992. *Human sexuality,* 4th ed. New York: HarperCollins.

Mathes, V. S. 1981. A new look at the role of women in Indian society. In *The American Indian: Past and present,* 2nd ed., ed. R. L. Nichols, 27–33. New York: Wiley.

Mathews, T. J., F. MacDorman, and F. Menacker. 2002. Infant mortality statistics from the 1999 period linked birth/infant death data set. Centers for Disease Control and Prevention, *National Vital Statistics Reports* 50 (Jan. 30). www.cdc.gov (accessed May 10, 2003).

Mathews, T. J., F. Menacker, and M. F. MacDorman. 2004. "Infant Mortality Statistics from the 2002 Period Linked Birth/Infant Death Data Set. *National Vital Statistics Reports* 53 (November 24): 1–30.

Mathias, B. 1992. Yes, Va. (Md. & D.C.), there are happy marriages. *Washington Post*, Sep. 22, B5.

Matta, D. S., and C. Knudson-Martin. 2006. Father responsivity: Couple processes and the co-construction of fatherhood. *Family Process* 45 (March): 19–37.

Mattes, J. 1994. *Single mothers by choice.* New York: Times Books.

Matthaei, J. A. 1982. *An economic history of women in America: Women's work, the sexual division of labor, and the development of capitalism.* New York: Schocken.

Matthews, S. H., and T. T. Rosner. 1988. Shared filial responsibility: The family as the primary caregiver. *Journal of Marriage and the Family* 50 (Feb.): 185–95.

Matthias, R. E., J. E. Lubben, K. A. Atchison, and S. O. Schweitzer. 1997. Sexual activity and satisfaction among very old adults: Results from a community-dwelling Medicare population survey. *The Gerontologist* 17 (1): 6–14.

MATTINGLY, M. J., AND L. C. SAYER. 2006. Under pressure: Gender differences in the relationship between free time and rushed time. *Journal of Marriage and Family* 68 (February): 205–21.

MAULDON, J. 2003. Families started by teenagers. In *All our families: New policies for a new century*, 2nd ed., eds. M. A. Mason, A. Skolnick, and S. D. Sugarman, 40–65. New York: Oxford University Press.

MAUSHART, S. 2002. *Wifework: What marriage really means for women*. New York: Bloomsbury.

MAY, E. T. 1995. *Barren in the promised land: Childless Americans and the pursuit of happiness*. New York: Basic Books.

MAY, P. A. 1999. The epidemiology of alcohol abuse among American Indians: The mythical and real properties. In *Contemporary Native American cultural issues*, ed. D. Champagne, 227–44. Walnut Creek, CA: AltaMira.

MAYER, C. E. 1999. For a generation in denial, a fountain of youth products. *Washington Post*, May 6, A1, A16.

MAYNARD, M. 1994. Methods, practice and epistemology: The debate about feminism and research. In *Researching women's lives from a feminist perspective*, eds. M. Maynard and J. Purvis, 10–26. London: Taylor & Francis.

MAYNARD, R. A., ED. 1997. *Kids having kids: Economic costs and social consequences of teen pregnancy*. Washington, DC: Urban Institute.

MAYO, Y. 1997. Machismo, fatherhood, and the Latino family: Understanding the concept. *Journal of Multicultural Social Work* 5 (1/2): 49–61.

MAYS, V. M., L. M. CHATTERS, AND S. D. COCHRAN. 1998. African American families in diversity: Gay men and lesbians in family networks. *Journal of Comparative Family Studies* 29 (Spring): 73–88.

MAZZUCA, J. 2004. Teens plan to treat their *own* children differently. Gallup News Service, November 23, http://poll.gallup.com (accessed May 10, 2006).

MBURUGU, E. K., AND B. N. ADAMS. 2005. Families in Kenya. In *Handbook of world families*, eds. B. N. Adams and J. Trost, 3–24. Thousand Oaks, CA: Sage.

MCADOO, H. P. 2002. African American parenting. In *Handbook of parenting*, 2nd ed., Vol. 4: *Social conditions and applied parenting*, ed. M. H. Bornstein, 47–58. Mahwah, NJ: Erlbaum.

MCADOO, J. L. 1986. Black fathers' relationships with their preschool children and the children's development of ethnic identity. In *Men in families*, eds. R. A. Lewis and R. E. Salt, 159–68. Thousand Oaks, CA: Sage.

MCBRIDE, B. A., G. L. BROWN, K. K. BOST, N. SHIN, B. VAUGHN, AND B. KORTH. 2005. Paternal identity, maternal gatekeeping, and father involvement. *Family Relations* 54 (July): 360–72.

MCCARROLL, C. 2002. Coed sleepovers: Platonic or premature? *Christian Science Monitor*, Dec. 4, 1, 4.

MCCLAIN, C. 2005. Local gay men taking more risks, study says. *Arizona Daily Star*, July 18, www.azstarnet.com (accessed July 25, 2005).

MCCOY, E. 1986. Your one and only. *Parents*, Oct., 118–21, 236.

MCDANIEL, D. H. 2006. Anti-aging: dreams fulfilled. . . or empty promises? *Cosmetic Surgery Times* 9 (July): 4.

MCDONALD, K. A. 1999. Studies of women's health produce a wealth of knowledge on the biology of gender differences. *Chronicle of Higher Education*, June 25, A19, A22.

MCDONALD, M. 2000. A start-up of her own. *U.S. News & World Report*, May 15, 34–42.

MCDONALD, R., E. N. JOURILES, S. RAMISETTY-MIKLER, R. CAETANO, and C. E. GREEN. 2006. Estimating the number of American children living in partner-violent families. *Journal of Family Psychology* 20 (March): 137–42.

MCELVAINE, R. S. 1993. *The great depression: America, 1929–1941*. New York: Times Books.

MCFADYEN, J. M., J. L. KERPELMAN, AND F. ADLER-BAEDER. 2005. Examining the impact of workplace supports: Work-family fit and satisfaction in the U.S. military. *Family Relations* 54 (January): 131–44.

MCFARLANE, M., S. S. BULL, AND C. A. RIETMEIJER. 2000. The Internet as a newly emerging risk environment for sexually transmitted diseases. *Journal of the American Medical Association* 284 (July 26): 443–46.

MCGINN, D. 2004. Mating behavior 101. *Newsweek* (October 4): 44–45.

MCGINNIS, T. 1981. *More than just a friend: The joys and disappointments of extramarital affairs*. Upper Saddle River, NJ: Prentice Hall.

MCGOLDRICK, M., M. HEIMAN, AND B. CARTER. 1993. The changing family life cycle: A perspective on normalcy. In *Normal family processes*, 2nd ed., ed. F. Walsh, 405–43. New York: Guilford.

MCGONAGLE, K. A., R. C. KESSLER, AND I. H. GOTLIB. 1993. The effects of marital disagreement style, frequency, and outcome on marital disruption. *Journal of Social and Personal Relationships, 10* (Aug.): 385–404.

MCGRATH, D. 2003. Magazines still promote domestic chores as women's work. *Women's E-News*. www.womensenews.org Apr. 5 (accessed Apr. 7, 2003).

MCGUINESS, T., AND L. PALLANSCH. 2000. Competence of children adopted from the former Soviet Union. *Family Relations* 49 (Oct.): 457–64.

MCGUIRE, M. 1996. Growing up with two moms. *Newsweek*, Nov. 4, 53.

MCINTOSH, P. 1995. White Privilege and Male Privilege: A Personal Account of Coming to See Correspondences through Work in Women's Studies. In M. L. Andersen and P. H. Collins (eds.), *Race, Class, and Gender: An Anthology*, second edition. Belmont, CA: Wadsworth, pp. 76–87.

MCKAY, M. M. 1994. The link between domestic violence and child abuse: Assessment and treatment considerations. *Child Welfare* 73 (Jan./Feb.): 29–39.

MCKERNAN, S.-M., AND C. RADCLIFFE. 2006. The effect of specific welfare policies on poverty. The Urban Institute, April, www.urban.org (accessed June 15, 2006).

MCKINLAY, J. B., AND H. A. FELDMAN. 1994. Age-related variation in sexual activity and interest in normal men: Results from the Massachusetts male aging study. In *Sexuality across the life course*, ed. A. S. Rossi, 261–85. Chicago: University of Chicago Press.

MCLANAHAN, S., AND G. SANDEFUR. 1994. *Growing up with a single parent: What hurts, what helps*. Cambridge, MA: Harvard University Press.

MCLOYD, V. C., AND J. SMITH. 2002. Physical discipline and behavior problems in African American, European American, and Hispanic children: Emotional support as a moderator. *Journal of Marriage and Family* 64 (Feb.): 40–53.

MCLOYD, V. C., A. M. CAUCE, D. TAKEUCHI, AND L. WILSON. 2001. Marital processes and parental socialization in families of color: A decade review of research. In *Understanding families into the new millennium: A decade in review*, ed. R. M. Milardo, 289–312. Minneapolis: National Council on Family Relations.

MCNAMARA, R. P., M. TEMPENIS, AND B. WALTON. 1999. *Crossing the line: Interracial couples in the South*. Westport, CT: Greenwood.

MCNEELY, C., ET AL. 2002. Mothers' influence on the timing of first sex among 14- and 15-year olds. *Journal of Adolescent Health* 31 (Sep.): 256–65.

MCNICHOL, L., AND J. SPRINGER. 2004. State policies to assist working-poor families. Center on Budget and Policy Priorities, December 10, www.cbpp.org (accessed June 5, 2006).

MCPHARLIN, P. 1946. *Love and courtship in America*. New York: Hastings House.

MCQUILLAN, J. A. L. GREIL, L. WHITE, and M. CASEY JACOB. 2003. Frustrated fertility: Infertility and psychological distress among women. *Journal of Marriage and Family* 65 (November): 1007–18.

MCRAE, S. 1999. Cohabitation or marriage? Cohabitation. In *The sociology of the family*, ed. G. Allan, 172–90. Malden, MA: Blackwell.

MEAD, G. H. 1934. *Mind, self, and society*. Chicago: University of Chicago Press.

MEAD, G. H. 1938. *The philosophy of the act*. Chicago: University of Chicago Press.

MEAD, G. H. 1964. *On social psychology*. Chicago: University of Chicago Press.

MEAD, L. M. 1996. Work requirements can transform the system. *Chronicle of Higher Education*, Oct. 4, B6.

MEAD, M. 1935. *Sex and temperament in three primitive societies*. New York: Morrow.

MEAD, S. 2006. *The truth about boys and girls: The evidence suggests otherwise*. Education Sector, June, www.educationsector.org (accessed August 8, 2006).

"Median income barely grows." 2006. *Baltimore Sun*, February 24, E1, E3.

"Medical memo: Marital stress and the heart." 2004. *Harvard Men's Health Watch* (May): 7.

MEIER, A. M. 2003. Adolescents' transition to first intercourse, religiosity, and attitudes about sex. *Social Forces* 81 (Mar.): 1031–52.

MEKOS, D., E. M. HETHERINGTON, AND D. REISS. 1996. Sibling differences in problem behavior and parental treatment in nondivorced and remarried families. *Child Development* 67 (Oct.): 2148–65.

MELLOTT, L. M., Z. QIAN, AND D. T. LICHTER. 2005. Like mother, like daughter? The international transmission of union formation patterns. Paper presented at the annual meeting of the American Sociological Association, Philadelphia, August.

MELOSH, B. 2002. *Strangers and kin: The American way of adoption*. Cambridge, MA: Harvard University Press.

MELTZER, N., ED. 1964. *In their own words: A history of the American Negro, 1619–1865*. New York: Crowell.

MELZER, S. A. 2002. Gender, work, and intimate violence: Men's occupational violence spillover and compensatory violence. *Journal of Marriage and Family* 64 (Nov.): 820–32.

MENARD, S. 2002. *Short- and long-term consequences of adolescent victimization*. Washington, DC: U.S. Department of Justice.

MENDELSOHN, K. D., L. Z. NIEMAN, K. TSAACS, S. LEE, AND S. P. LEVISON. 1994. Sex and gender bias in anatomy and physical diagnosis text illustrations. *Journal of the American Medical Association*, Oct. 26, 1267–70.

MERGENBAGEN, P. 1996. The reunion market. *American Demographics* 18 (Apr.): 30–34, 52.

MERTEN, D. E. 1996. Going-with: The role of a social form in early romance. *Journal of Contemporary Ethnography* 24 (Jan.): 462–84.

MESTEL, R. 2003. Birth by test tube turns 25. *Los Angeles Times*, July 24, A1.

MetLife Mature Market Institute. 2006. The MetLife caregiving cost study: Productivity losses to U.S. business. July, www.caregiving.org (accessed August 4, 2006).

METTS, S. 1994. Relational transgressions. In *The dark side of interpersonal communication*, eds. W. R. Cupach and B. H. Spitzberg, 217–39 Hillsdale, NJ: Erlbaum.

MEYER, C. L., AND M. OBERMAN. 2001. *Mothers who kill their children: Understanding the acts of moms from Susan Smith to the "prom mom."* New York: New York University Press.

MIALL, C. 1986. The stigma of involuntary childlessness. *Social Problems* 33 (Apr.): 268–82.

MICHAEL, R. T., AND C. BICKERT. 2001. Exploring determinants of adolescents' early sexual behavior. In *Social awakening: Adolescent behavior as adulthood approaches*, ed. R. T. Michael, 137–73. New York: Russell Sage Foundation.

MICHAEL, R. T., J. H. GAGNON, E. O. LAUMANN, AND G. KOLATA. 1994. *Sex in America: A definitive study*. Boston: Little, Brown.

MIDDLEMISS, W., AND W. MCGUIGAN. 2005. Ethnicity and adolescent mothers' benefit from participation in home-visitation services. *Family Relations* 54 (April): 212–24.

MIELL, D., AND R. CROGHAN. 1996. Examining the wider context of social relationships. In *Social interaction and personal relationships*, eds. D. Miell and R. Dallos, 267–318. Thousand Oaks, CA: Sage.

MIKA, S. 2005. Parental advisory labels don't stick with teens. Gallup Poll News Service, August 2, http://poll.gallup.com (accessed May 23, 2006).

MILBOURN, T. 2006. Taking refuge. January 2, www.sacbee.com (accessed January 4, 2006).

MILES, B. W., AND P. J. FOWLER. 2006. Changing the face of homelessness: Welfare reform's impact on homeless families. In *The promise of welfare reform: Political rhetoric and the reality of poverty in the twenty-first century*, eds. K. M. Kilty, and E. A. Segal, 143–52. New York: Haworth Press.

MILKIE, M. A., M. J. MATTINGLY, K. M. NOMAGUCHI, S. M. BIANCHI, AND J. P. ROBINSON. 2004. The time squeeze: Parental statuses and feelings about time with children. *Journal of Marriage and Family* 66 (August): 739–61.

MILKMAN, R. 1976. Women's work and the economic crisis: Some lessons from the Great Depression. *Review of Radical Political Economics* 8 (Spring): 73–97.

MILLER, B. 1995. Household futures. *American Demographics* 17 (Mar.): 4, 6.

MILLER, B. C. 1986. *Family research methods.* Beverly Hills, CA: Sage.

MILLER, B. C. 2002. Family influences on adolescent sexual and contraceptive behavior. *Journal of Sex Research* 39 (Feb.): 22–26.

MILLER, J., AND M. MILLER. 2005. Get a life! *Fortune,* November 28, 109–23.

MILLER, W. C., ET AL. 2004. Prevalence of chlamydial and gonococcal infections among young adults in the United States. *JAMA* 291 (May 12): 2229–36.

MILLER, W. L., AND B. F. CRABTREE. 1994. Clinical research. In *Handbook of qualitative research,* eds. N. K. Denzin and Y. S. Lincoln, 340–52. Thousand Oaks, CA: Sage.

MILLNER, D., AND N. CHILES. 1999. *What brothers think, what sistahs know: The real deal on love and relationships.* New York: Morrow.

MIN, P. G. 2002. Korean American families. In *Minority families in the United States: A multicultural perspective,* 3rd ed., ed. R. L. Taylor, 193–211. Upper Saddle River, NJ: Prentice Hall.

MINTZ, S., AND S. KELLOGG. 1988. *Domestic revolution: A social history of American family life.* New York: Free Press.

MIRANDA, C. A. 2004. Fifteen candles. *Time,* July 19, 6.

MIRANDE, A. 1985. *The Chicano experience: An alternative perspective.* Notre Dame, IN: University of Notre Dame Press.

MIROWSKY, J. 2005. Age at first birth, health, and mortality. *Journal of Health and Social Behavior* 46 (March): 32–50.

MISHEL, L., J. BERNSTEIN, AND S. ALLEGRETTO. 2006. *The state of working America 2006/2007.* Ithaca, NY: Cornell University Press.

MISRA, D., ED. 2001. *Women's health data book: A profile of women's health in the United States,* 3rd ed. Washington, DC: Jacobs Institute of Women's Health and The Henry J. Kaiser Family Foundation.

MITCHELL, B. A., AND E. M. GEE. 1996. "Boomerang kids" and midlife parental marital satisfaction. *Family Relations* 45 (Oct.): 442–48.

MITCHELL, A. A. 2002. Infertility treatment: More risks and challenges. *New England Journal of Medicine* 346 (Mar. 7): 769–70.

MOCK, M. S. 2005. Confined by the stained-glass window. *Chronicle of Higher Education,* November 4, B24.

MODO, I. V. OGO. 2005. Nigerian families. In *Handbook of world families,* eds. B. N. Adams and J. Trost, 25–46. Thousand Oaks, CA: Sage.

MODO, V. O. 2005. Nigerian families. In *Handbook of world families,* eds. B. N. Adams and J. Trost, 25–46. Thousand Oaks, CA: Sage.

MODO, V. O. 2005. Nigerian families. In *Handbook of world families,* eds. B. N. Adams and J. Trost, 25–46. Thousand Oaks, CA: Sage.

MOEN, P. 1992. *Women's two roles: A contemporary dilemma.* Westport, CT: Auburn House.

MOHR, J. 1981. The great upsurge of abortion, 1840–1880. In *Family life in America: 1620–2000,* eds. M. Albin and D. Cavallo, 119–30. St. James, NY: Revisionary Press.

MONEY, J., AND A. A. EHRHARDT. 1972. *Man & woman, boy & girl.* Baltimore: Johns Hopkins University Press.

MONTENEGRO, X. P. 2004. *Divorce experience: A study of divorce at midlife and beyond.* Washington, DC: AARP.

MONTGOMERY, M. J., AND G. T. SORELL. 1997. Differences in love attitudes across family life stages. *Family Relations* 46 (Jan.): 55–61.

MONTLAKE, S. 2006. A town of foreign marriages. *Christian Science Monitor,* July 20: 20.

MOORE, D. W. 2003. Poll analysis: Family, health most important aspects of life. Gallup News Service, Jan. 3.www.gallup.com (accessed Jan. 5, 2003).

MOORE, F. R., C. CASSIDY, M. HANE L. SMITH, AND D. I. PERRETT. 2006. The effects of female control of resources on sex-differentiated mate preferences. *Evolution and Human Behavior* 27 (May): 193–205.

MOORE, J., AND H. PACHON. 1985. *Hispanics in the United States.* Upper Saddle River, NJ: Prentice Hall.

MOORE, K. A., ET AL. 2006. Depression among moms: Prevalence, predictors, and acting out among third grade children. Child Trends Research Brief, March, www.childtrends.org (accessed September 22, 2006).

MOORE, M. R., AND P. L. CHASE-LANSDALE. 2001. Sexual intercourse and pregnancy among African American girls in high-poverty neighborhoods: The role of family and perceived community environment. *Journal of Marriage and Family* 63 (Nov.): 1146–57.

MOORE, M. T. 2006. Parents, kids not necessary "family" everywhere. *USA Today,* May 15, www.usatoday.com (accessed May 17, 2006).

MOORE, P., WITH C. P. CONN. 1985. *Disguised.* Waco, TX: Word Books.

MOORE, R. L. 1998. Love and limerence with Chinese characteristics: Student romance in the PRC. In *Romantic love and sexual behavior: Perspectives from the social sciences,* ed. V. C. deMunck. 251–88. Westport, CT: Praeger.

MORALES, E. 1996. Gender roles among Latino gay and bisexual men: Implications for family and couple relationships. In *Lesbians and gays in couples and families: A handbook for therapists,* eds. J. Laird and R.-J. Green, 272–97. San Francisco: Jossey-Bass.

MORELL, C. M. 1994. *Unwomanly conduct: The challenges of intentional childlessness.* New York: Routledge.

MORGAN, D. I., ED. 1993. *Successful focus groups: Advancing the state of the art.* Thousand Oaks, CA: Sage.

MORGAN, P. D. 1998. *Slave counterpoint: Black culture in the eighteenth-century Chesapeake & lowcountry.* Chapel Hill: University of North Carolina Press.

MORGAN, R. 2002a. The men in the mirror. *Chronicle of Higher Education,* Sep. 27, A53–A54.

MORGAN, R. 2002b. States split on asking divorced parents to pay for children's tuition. *Chronicle of Higher Education,* Aug. 16, A28.

MORGAN, W. L. 1939. *The family meets the depression: A study of a group of highly selected families.* Westport, CT: Greenwood.

MORGENTHAU, T. 1997. The face of the future. *Newsweek,* Jan. 27, 58–60.

MORIN, R. 1994. How to lie with statistics: Adultery. *Washington Post,* Mar. 6, C5.

MORRIS, M. 2003. Love in a hurry. *Baltimore Sun,* Jan. 12, 1N, 4N.

MORRIS, N. 2005. Violence against women at crisis level in Britain. *The Independent,* November 24, http://news.independent.co.uk (accessed November 25, 2005).

MOSHER, W. D., AND W. F. PRATT. 1991. Fecundity and infertility in the United States: Incidence and trends. *Fertility and Sterility* 56 (Aug.): 192–93.

MOSHER, W. D., A. CHANDRA, AND J. JONES. 2005. Sexual behavior and selected health measures: Men and women 15–44 years of age, United States, 2002. National Center for Health Statistics, *Vital and Health Statistics,* September 15, www.cdc.gov (accessed January 10, 2006).

"Motherhood today: A tougher job, less ably done." 1997. Pew Research Center for the People & the Press. www.people-press.org (accessed Oct. 5, 1997).

MOTT, F. L., L. KOWALESKI-JONES, AND E. G. MENAGHAN. 1997. Paternal absence and child behavior: Does a child's gender make a difference? *Journal of Marriage and the Family* 59 (Feb.): 103–18.

MOWRER, E. R. 1972. War and family solidarity and stability. In *The American family in World War II,* ed. R. A. Abrams, 100–106. New York: Arno and New York Times.

MOYNIHAN, D. P., ED. 1970. *Toward a national urban policy.* New York: Basic Books.

MUELLER, M. M., AND G. H. ELDER, JR. 2003. Family contingencies across the generations: Grandparent–grandchild relationships in holistic perspective. *Journal of Marriage and Family* 65 (May): 404–19.

MULSON, M., Y. M. CALDERA, M. PURSLEY, A. REIFMAN, AND A. C. HUSTON. 2002. Multilevel factors influencing maternal stress during the first three years. *Journal of Marriage and Family* 64 (Nov.): 944–56.

MUMME, D. L., AND A. FERNAND. 2003. The infant as onlooker: Learning from emotional reactions observed in a television scenario. *Child Development* 74 (Jan./Feb.): 221–37.

MUNCY, R. L. 1988. Sex and marriage in utopia. *Society* 25 (Jan./Feb.): 46–48.

MUNDELL, E. J. 2002. Bye, bye love: How men, women dish out rejection. ABC News, Feb. 5. http://abcnews.go.com (accessed Feb. 6, 2002).

MUNDELL, E. J. 2003. No sex until marriage? Don't bet on it, study finds. Reuters Health, June 23. www.reutershealth.com (accessed Aug. 3, 2003).

MUNSON, M. L., AND P. D. SUTTON. 2004. Births, marriages, divorces, and deaths: Provisional data for 2003. *National Vital Statistics Reports* 52 (June 10): 1–7.

MUNSON, M. L., AND P. D. SUTTON. 2006. Births, marriages, divorces, and deaths: Provisional data for November 2005. *National Vital Statistics Reports* 54 (June): 1–7.

MUNTER, C. 1984. Fat and the fantasy of perfection. In *Pleasure and danger: Exploring female sexuality,* ed. C. Vance, 225–31. Boston: Routledge & Kegan Paul.

MURDOCK, G. P. 1967. Ethnographic atlas: A summary. *Ethnology* 6, 109–236.

MURPHY, D. 2002. Need a mate? In Singapore, ask the government. *Christian Science Monitor,* July 16, 1, 10.

MURPHY, E., AND E. J. GRAFF. 2005. *Getting even: Why women don't get paid like men—and what to do about it.* New York: Simon & Schuster.

MURRAY, C. I. 2000. Coping with death, dying, and grief in families. In *Families & change: Coping with stressful events and transitions,* 2nd ed., eds. P. C. McKenry and S. J. Price, 120–53. Thousand Oaks, CA: Sage.

MURRAY, J. E. 2000. Marital protection and marital selection: Evidence from a historical-prospective sample of American men. *Demography* 37 (Nov.): 511–21.

MURRY, V. M., A. P. SMITH, AND N. E. HILL. 2001. Race, ethnicity, and culture in studies of families in context. *Journal of Marriage and the Family* 63 (Nov.): 911–14.

MURSTEIN, B. I. 1974. *Love, sex, and marriage through the ages.* New York: Springer.

MUSGROVE, M., AND F. AHRENS. 2005. Online dating losing steam, but not for Valentine's day. *Washington Post* (February 12): E1.

MUSICK, K. 2002. Planned and unplanned childbearing among unmarried women. *Journal of Marriage and Family* 64 (Nov.): 915–29.

MYERS, S. M., AND A. BOOTH. 1999. Marital strains and marital quality: The role of high and low locus of control. *Journal of Marriage and the Family* 61 (May): 423–36.

NAGOURNEY, E. 2005. Nicotine changes sperm, and not for the better. *New York Times,* Oct. 25, D6.

NAJIB, A., J. P. LORBERBAUM, S. KOSE, D. E. BOHNING, AND M. S. GEORGE. 2004. Regional brain activity in women grieving a romantic relationship breakup. *American Journal of Psychiatry* 161 (December): 2245–56.

NAKONEZNY, P. A., R. D. SHULL, AND J. L. RODGERS. 1995. The effect of no-fault divorce law on the divorce rate across the 50 states and its relation to income, education, and religiosity. *Journal of Marriage and the Family,* 57 (May): 477–88.

NANCE-NASH, S. 2005. African American women gaining in biz starts. Women's e-news, February 18, www.womensenews.org (accessed February 20, 2005).

NASS, G. D., R. W. LIBBY, AND M. P. FISHER. 1981. *Sexual choices: An introduction to human sexuality.* Belmont, CA: Wadsworth.

NATIONAL ABORTION FEDERATION. 2006. Crisis pregnancy centers: An affront to choice. Washington, DC, www.prochoice.org (accessed September 19, 2006).

National adoption attitudes survey: Research report. 2002. Dave Thomas Foundation for Adoption. www.cdc.gov/df (accessed Aug. 17, 2003).

NATIONAL ADOPTION INFORMATION CLEARINGHOUSE. 2002. Pros and cons of each type of adoption for the involved parties. U.S. Department of Health

& Human Services. www.calib.com (accessed Aug. 17, 2003).

NATIONAL ADOPTION INFORMATION CLEARINGHOUSE. 2006. Openness in adoption: A bulletin for professionals. U.S. Department of Health and Human Services, http://naic.acf.hhs.gov (accessed April 27, 2006).

NATIONAL ALLIANCE FOR CAREGIVING AND AARP. 2004. *Caregiving in the U.S.* April, www .caregiving.org (accessed August 4, 2006).

National Cancer Institute posts on Web site "revised" online fact sheet on abortion, breast cancer. 2003. The Henry J. Kaiser Family Foundation, Mar. 25. www.kaisernetwork.org (accessed Mar. 28, 2003).

NATIONAL CENTER FOR HEALTH STATISTICS. 2005. *Health, United States, 2005 with chartbook on trends in the health of Americans.* Hyatsville, MD.

NATIONAL CENTER ON ADDICTION AND SUBSTANCE ABUSE. 2003. *National survey of American attitudes on substance abuse VIII: Teens and parents.* Columbia University. www.casacolumbia.org (accessed Aug. 25, 2003).

NATIONAL CENTER ON ELDER ABUSE. 2005. Fact sheet: Elder abuse prevalence and incidence. Washington, DC: National Center on Elder Abuse.

NATIONAL COALITION FOR THE HOMELESS. 2005a. Who is homeless? NCH Fact Sheet #3, www.nationalhomeless.org (accessed June 3, 2006).

NATIONAL COALITION FOR THE HOMELESS. 2005b. Why are people homeless? NCH Fact Sheet #1, www.nationalhomeless.org (accessed June 3, 2006).

NATIONAL COMMISSION ON CHILDREN. 1991. *Beyond rhetoric: A new agenda for children and families.* Washington, DC: U.S. Government Printing Office.

NATIONAL EMPLOYMENT LAW PROJECT. 2003. Unemployment insurance: Specific worker initiatives. www.nelp.org (Sep. 11, 2003).

NATIONAL INDIAN GAMING COMMISSION. 2006. National Indian Gaming Commission announces Indian gaming revenue for 2005. July, www.nigc .gov (accessed August 3, 2006).

NATIONAL LOW INCOME HOUSING COALITION. 2005. Out of reach 2005. www.nlich.org (accessed June 5, 2006).

NATIONAL MENTAL HEALTH ASSOCIATION. 2006. Eating disorders. www.nmha.org (accessed June 26, 2006).

NATIONAL RESEARCH COUNCIL. 1998. *Violence in families: Assessing prevention and treatment programs.* Washington, DC: National Academy Press.

National sexual health survey shows many women avoid discussing HIV/AIDS, STDs with partners, health providers. 2003. Kaiser Family Foundation. www.kaisernetwork.org (accessed June 20, 2003).

NATIONAL SLEEP FOUNDATION. 2005. 2005 sleep in America poll. Washington, DC, www.sleepfoundation.org (accessed January 15, 2006).

NAUCK, B., AND D. KLAUS. 2005. Families in Turkey. In *Handbook of world families,* eds. B. N. Adams AND J. TROST, 364–388. Thousand Oaks, CA: Sage.

NEFT, N., AND A. D. LEVINE. 1997. *Where women stand: An international report on the status of women in over 140 countries, 1997–1998.* New York: Random House.

NELSON, G. 1994. Emotional well-being of separated and married women: Long-term follow-up study. *American Journal of Orthopsychiatry* 64 (Jan.): 150–60.

NEUGARTEN, B. L., AND K. K. WEINSTEIN. 1964. The changing American grandparents. *Journal of Marriage and the Family* 26 (May): 199–204.

NEWACHECK, P. W., R. E. K. STEIN, L. BAUMAN, AND Y.-Y. HUNG. 2003. Disparities in the prevalence of disability between black and white children. *Archives of Pediatrics & Adolescent Medicine* 157 (Mar.): 244–48.

New Alzheimer projections add urgency to search for prevention, cure. 2003. Alzheimer's Association, Aug. 18. www.alz.org (accessed Oct. 8, 2003).

NEWPORT, F. 2001. Americans see women as emotional and affectionate, men as more aggressive. *Gallup Poll Monthly* 425 (Feb. 2001): 34–38.

NEWPORT, F. 2006. American teenagers split on gay marriage. Gallup Organization, March 9, http://poll.gallup.com (accessed March 12, 2006).

NEWPORT, F., AND J. CARROLL. 2004. Retirement continues to be major financial concern for Americans. Gallup Organization, April 29, www .gallup.com (accessed May 5, 2004).

NEWPORT, F., AND J. CARROLL. 2006. Different worlds: Financial problems across income groups. Gallup Organization, March 31, http://poll.gallup.com (accessed May 31, 2006).

NEWPORT, F., and L. SAAD. 2006. Religion, politics inform Americans' views on abortion. Gallup Organization, April 3, www.galluppoll .com (accessed April 5, 2006).

Newspaper content: What makes readers more satisfied. 2001. Readership Institute: Media Management Center at Northwestern University. www.readership.org (accessed May 23, 2003).

NG, F. 1998. *The Taiwanese Americans.* Westport, CT: Greenwood.

NICHD EARLY CHILD CARE RESEARCH NETWORK. 2003. Does amount of time in child care predict socioemotional adjustment? *Child Development* 74 (July/Aug.): 976–1005.

NICOLOSI, A., ET AL. 1994. The efficiency of male-to-female and female-to-male sexual transmission of the human immunodeficiency virus: A study of 730 stable couples. *Epidemiology* 5 (Nov.): 570–75.

NIE, N. H., AND L. ERBRING. 2000. Internet and society: A preliminary report. www.stanford.edu.

NIEVES, E. 2006. S.D. abortion bill takes aim at "Roe." *Washington Post,* Feb. 23, A1.

Night shift puts serious dent in family life. 1996. Ann Landers column. *Baltimore Sun,* Dec. 9, 3D.

NIKKAH, J., AND L. FURMAN. 2000. *Our boys speak: Adolescent boys write about their inner lives.* New York: St. Martin's.

NISSINEN, S. 2000. *The conscious bride: Women unveil their true feelings about getting hitched.* Oakland, CA: New Harbinger.

NOCK, S. L. 1998. *Marriage in men's lives.* New York: Oxford University Press.

NOGUCHI, Y. 2005. Life and romance in 160 characters or less. *Washington Post* (December 29): A1.

NOLAND, V. J., K. D. LILLER, R. J. MCDERMOTT, M. L. COULTER, AND A. E. SERAPHINE. 2004. Is adolescent sibling violence a precursor to college dating violence? *American Journal of Health Behavior* 28 (April): S13–S23.

NOLEN-HOEKSEMA, S., AND J. LARSON. 1999. *Coping with loss.* Mahwah, NJ: Erlbaum.

NOLEN-HOEKSEMA, S., J. LARSON, AND C. GRAYSON. 1999. Explaining the gender difference in depressive symptoms. *Journal of Personality and Social Psychology* 77 (Nov.): 1061–72.

NOLLER, P. 1984. *Nonverbal communication and marital interaction.* New York: Pergamon.

NOLLER, P., AND M. A. FITZPATRICK. 1993. *Communication in family relationships.* Upper Saddle River, NJ: Prentice Hall.

NONNEMAKER, L. 2000. Women physicians in academic medicine: New insights from cohort studies. *New England Journal of Medicine* 342 (Feb, 10): 399–405.

NORTHRUP, C. 2001. *The wisdom of menopause: Creating physical and emotional health and healing during the change.* New York: Bantam.

NORTON, A. J., AND L. F. MILLER. 1992. *Marriage, divorce, and remarriage in the 1990s.* U.S. Census Bureau, Current Population Reports, P23–180. Washington, DC: U.S. Government Printing Office.

NOWINSKI, J. 1993. *Hungry hearts: On men, intimacy, self-esteem, and addiction.* New York: Lexington.

NURIUS, P. S., J. NORRIS, L. A. DIMEFF, AND T. L. GRAHAM. 1996. Expectations regarding acquaintance sexual aggression among sorority and fraternity members. *Sex Roles* 35 (7/8): 427–44.

NUTA, V. R. 1986. Emotional aspects of child support enforcement. *Family Relations* 35 (Jan.): 177–82.

NYE, F. I., AND F. M. BERARDO, EDS. 1981. *Emerging conceptual frameworks in family analysis.* New York: Praeger.

OATES, R. K., AND R. S. KEMPE. 1997. Growth failure in infants. In *The battered child,* 5th ed., eds. M. E. Helfer, R. S. Kempe, and R. D. Krugman, 374–91. Chicago: University of Chicago Press.

O'DONNELL, P., S. STEVENSON, V. S. STEFANAKOS, AND K. PERAINO. 1999. Click and split. *Newsweek,* Nov. 22, 8.

OFFICE OF NATIONAL DRUG CONTROL POLICY. 2006. *Girls and Drugs.* February 9, www .mediacampaign.org (accessed June 10, 2006).

Officer accused of threat on wife. 2005. *New York Times,* November 23, B2.

OGUNWOLE, S. U. 2002. *The American Indian and Alaska Native population: 2000.* U.S. Census Bureau. www.census.gov (accessed Apr. 13, 2003).

OGUNWOLE, S. U. 2006. *We the people: American Indians and Alaska Natives in the United States.* U.S. Census Bureau, Census 2000 Special Reports, CENSR-28, www.census.gov (accessed August 2, 2006).

OLDENBURG, DON. 2006. Experts rip "Sesame" TV aimed at tiniest tots. *Washington Post,* March 21, C1.

Older Americans 2000: Key indicators of well-being. 2000. Federal Interagency Forum on Aging-Related Statistics. www.agingstats.gov (accessed Oct. 28, 2000).

Older women workers, ages 55 and over. 2006. U.S. Department of Labor, Women's Bureau. August 24, www.dol.gov/wb (accessed August 2, 2006).

OLECK, J. 2000. The kids are not all right. *Business Week,* Feb. 14, 74, 78.

OLFSON, M., C. BLANCO, L. LIU, C. MORENO, AND G. LAJE. 2006. *Archives of General Psychiatry* 63 (June): 679–85.

OLIVER, M. L., AND T. M. SHAPIRO. 2001. Wealth and racial stratification. In *America becoming: Racial trends and their consequences,* Vol. 2, eds. N. J. Smelser, W. J. Wilson, and F. Mitchell, 222–51. Washington, DC: National Academy Press.

OLSHANSKY, S. J., L. HAYFLICK, AND T. T. PERLS. 2004a. Anti-aging medicine: the hype and the reality—part I. *Journal of Gerontology: Biological Sciences* 59A (6): 513–514.

OLSHANSKY, S. J., L. HAYFLICK, AND T. T. PERLS. 2004b. Anti-aging medicine: the hype and the reality—part II. *Journal of Gerontology: Biological Sciences* 59A (7): 649–651.

OLSON, D. H., AND A. K. OLSON. 2000. *Empowering couples: Building on your strengths.* Minneapolis: Life Innovations.

OLSON, D. H., AND A. OLSON-SIGG. 2002. Overview of cohabitation research: For use with PRE-PARECC. Life Innovations. www.lifeinnovation .com (accessed July 15, 2003).

OLSON, I. R., AND C. MARSHUETZ. 2005. Facial attractiveness is appraised in a glance. *Emotion* 5 (December): 498–502.

O'MARA, R. 1997. Who am I? *Baltimore Sun,* June 29, 1J, 4J.

OOMS, T. 2002. Strengthening couples and marriage in low-income communities. In *Revitalizing the institution of marriage for the twenty-first century,* eds. A. J. Hawkins, L. D. Wardle, and D. O. Coolidge, 79–100. Westport, CT: Praeger.

OOMS, T. 2005. The new kid on the block: What is marriage education and does it work? Center for Law and Social Policy, July, www.clasp.org (accessed April 14, 2006).

OOMS, T., S. BOUCHET, AND M. PARKE. 2004. *Beyond marriage licenses: Efforts in states to strengthen marriage and two-parent families.* Center for Law and Social Policy, www.clasp.org/publications/beyond_marr.pdf (accessed Nov. 2, 2005).

ORCHARD, A. L., AND K. B. SOLBERG. 1999. Expectations of the stepmother's role. *Journal of Divorce & Remarriage* 31 (1/2): 107–23.

ORENSTEIN, P. 1994. *Schoolgirls: Young women, self-esteem, and the confidence gap.* New York: Doubleday.

ORENSTEIN, P. 1995. Looking for a donor to call dad *New York Times Magazine,* June 16, 26–35, 42–58.

ORENSTEIN, P. 2000. *Flux: Women on sex, work, kids, love, and life in a half-changed world.* New York: Doubleday.

ORNISH, D. 2005. Love is real medicine. *Newsweek,* Oct. 3, 56.

ORNSTEIN, C. 2005. Meth use by HIV-positive men rising. *Los Angeles Times,* June 16, B1.

OROPESA, R. S., AND N. S. LANDALE. 2004. The future of marriage and Hispanics. *Journal of Marriage and Family* 66 (November): 901–20.

ORTHNER, D. K., H. JONES-SAMPEI, AND S. WILLIAMSON. 2004. The resilience and strengths of low-income families. *Family Relations* 53 (March): 159–67.

OSHERSON, S. 1992. *Wrestling with love: How men struggle with intimacy with women, children, parents and each other.* New York: Fawcett Columbine.

OSTROWIAK, N. 2001. *Motherhood is not a rehearsal: Bottom-line mentoring for parents.* Hampton, GA: Southern Charm.

O'SULLIVAN, L. F., AND E. S. BYERS. 1993. Eroding stereotypes: College women's attempts to influence reluctant male sexual partners. *Journal of Sex Research* 30 (Aug.): 270–82.

OSWALD, R. F. 2002. Resilience within the family networks of lesbians and gay men: Intentionality and redefinition. *Journal of Marriage and Family* 64 (May): 374–83.

OUTCALT, T. 1998. *Before you say "I do:" Important questions for couples to ask before marriage.* New York: Perigee.

OVERTURF JOHNSON, J. 2005. *Who's minding the kids? Child care arrangements: Winter 2002.* Current Population Reports, P70–101. Washington, DC: U.S. Census Bureau.

OVERTURF JOHNSON, J., AND B. DOWNS. 2005. *Maternity leave and employment patterns: 1961–2000.* Current Population Report, P70–103. Washington, DC: U.S. Census Bureau.

PAASCH, K. M., AND J. D. TEACHMAN. 1991. Gender of children and receipt of assistance from absent fathers. *Journal of Family Issues* 12 (Dec.): 450–66.

PAGE, M. E., AND A. H. STEVENS. 2005. Understanding racial differences in the economic costs of growing up in a single-parent family. *Demography* 42 (February): 75–90.

Pakistani girl describes punitive gang-rape. 2002. *Baltimore Sun,* July 4, 13A.

PALMORE, E. B. 1999. *Ageism: Negative and positive.* New York: Springer.

PAPERNOW, P. L. 1993. *Becoming a step family: Patterns of development in remarried families.* San Francisco: Jossey-Bass.

PARAMESWARAN, L. 2003. Battered wives often recant or assume blame. *Women's E-News,* Aug. 2. www.womensenews.org (accessed Aug. 4, 2003).

PARCEL, T. L., AND E. G. MENAGHAN. 1994. *Parents' jobs and children's lives.* New York: Aldine de Gruyter.

PARIS, R., AND N. DUBUS. 2005. Staying connected while nurturing an infant: A challenge of new motherhood. *Family Relations* 54 (January): 72–83.

PARK, R. L. 2003. The seven warning signs of bogus science. *Chronicle of Higher Education,* Jan. 31, B20.

PARKE, R. D. 1996. *Fatherhood.* Cambridge, MA: Harvard University Press.

PARKE, R. D., ET AL. 2003. Managing the external environment: The parent and child as active agents in the system. In *Handbook of dynamics in parent–child relations,* ed. Leon Kuczynski, 247–69. Thousand Oaks, CA: Sage.

PARKER, R., AND C. CACERES. 1999. Alternative sexualities and changing sexual cultures among Latin American men. *Culture, Health, & Sexuality* 1: 201–6.

PARKER, S. 1996. Full brother-sister marriage in Roman Egypt: Another look. *Cultural Anthropology* 11 (Aug.): 362–76.

PARKS, K. A., AND D. M. SCHEIDT. 2000. Male bar drinkers' perspective on female bar drinkers. *Sex Roles* 43 (December): 927–941.

PARMELEE, L. F. 2002. Among us always. *Public Perspective* 13 (Mar./Apr.): 17–18.

PARNELL, T. F., AND D. O. DAY, EDS. 1998. *Munchausen by proxy syndrome.* Thousand Oaks, CA: Sage.

PARSONS, T., AND R. F. BALES. 1955. *Family, socialization and interaction process.* Glencoe, IL: Free Press.

PARTNERSHIP FOR A DRUG-FREE AMERICA. 2004. Partnership attitude tracking study: Parents with children 18 and younger. www.drugfree.org (accessed May 14, 2006).

PARTNERSHIP FOR A DRUG-FREE AMERICA. 2006. Partnership attitude tracking study (PATS): Teens in grades 7 through 12, 2005. www.drugfree.org (accessed May 14, 2006).

PASLEY, K., AND B. S. MOOREFIELD. 2004. Stepfamilies: Changes and challenges. In *Handbook of contemporary families: Considering the past, contemplating the future,* eds. M. Coleman and L. H. Ganong, 317–330. Thousand Oaks, CA: Sage.

PASSEL, J. S., R. CAPPS, AND M. E. FIX. 2004. Undocumented immigrants: Facts and figures. Urban Institute, January 12, www.urban.org/url.cfm?ID=1000587 (accessed November 15, 2005).

PASUPATHI, M. 2002. Arranged marriages: What's love got to do with it? In *Inside the American couple: New thinking/new challenges,* eds. M. Yalom and L. L. Carstensen, 211–35. Berkeley: University of California Press.

PATNER, M. M. 1990. Between mothers and daughters: Pain and difficulty go with the territory. *Washington Post,* Nov. 8, C5.

PATTERSON, C. J. 2001. Family relationships of lesbians and gay men. In *Understanding families into the new millennium: A decade in review,* ed. R. M. Milardo, 271–88. Minneapolis: National Council on Family Relations.

PATTERSON, C. J. 2002. Lesbian and gay parenthood. In *Handbook of parenting,* 2nd ed., Vol. 3: *Being and becoming a parent,* ed. M. H. Bornstein, 317–38. Mahwah, NJ: Erlbaum.

PATTERSON, J. M. 2002. Integrating family resilience and family stress theory. *Journal of Marriage and Family* 64 (May): 349–60.

PATTERSON, J., AND P. KIM. 1991. *The day America told the truth: What people really believe about everything that really matters.* Upper Saddle River, NJ: Prentice Hall.

PATZ, A. 2000. Will your marriage last? *Psychology Today* 33 (Jan./Feb.): 58–63.

PAUL, P. 2001. Childless by choice. *American Demographics* 23 (Nov.): 45–50.

PAUL, P. 2002. Make room for granddaddy. *American Demographics* 24 (Apr.): 41–45.

PAUL, P. 2003. The permaparent trap. *Psychology Today* 36 (September/October): 40–53.

PAULOZZI, L., AND M. SELLS. 2002. Variation in homicide risk during infancy: United States, 1989–1998. *Morbidity and Mortality Weekly Report* 51 (Mar. 8): 187–89.

PAULOZZI, L. J., L. E. SALTMAN, M. P. THOMPSON, AND P. HOLMGREEN. 2001. *Surveillance for homicide among intimate partners: United States, 1981–1998.* Centers for Disease Control and Prevention. www.cdc.gov (accessed Sep. 18, 2003).

PAULSON, A. 2006. Several states weigh ban on gay adoptions. *Christian Science Monitor,* March 15, 2.

PAULSON, A., AND D. B. WOOD. 2005. California court affirms gay parenting. *Christian Science Monitor,* August 25, 2–3.

PAULSON, R. J., ET AL. 2002. Pregnancy in the sixth decade of life: Obstetric outcomes in women of advanced reproductive age. *Journal of the American Medical Association* 288 (Nov. 13): 2320–23.

PAYNE, B. K. 2000. *Crime and elder abuse: An integrated perspective.* Springfield, IL: Charles C. Thomas.

PEARCE, D. 1978. The feminization of poverty: Women, work, and welfare. *Urban and Social Change Review* 11: 28–36.

PEARSON, J. C. 1985. *Gender and communication.* Dubuque, IA: Wm. C. Brown.

PEAVY, L., AND U. SMITH. 1994. *Women in waiting in the westward movement: Life on the home frontier.* Norman: University of Oklahoma Press.

PEDDLE, N., C.-T. WANG, J. DIAZ, AND R. REID. 2002. Current trends in child abuse prevention and fatalities: The 2000 fifty state survey. Prevent Child Abuse America. www.cdc.gov (accessed Sep. 15, 2003).

PEELE, S., WITH A. BRODSKY. 1976. *Love and addiction.* New York: New American Library.

PELCZARSKI, Y., AND S. P. KEMP. 2006. Patterns of child maltreatment referrals among Asian and Pacific Islander families. *Child Welfare* 85 (January/February): 5–31.

PELLERIN, L. A. 2005. Applying Baumrind's parenting typology to high schools: Toward a middle-range theory of authoritative socialization. *Social Science Research* 34 (June): 282–303.

PENHA-LOPES, V. 1995. "Make room for daddy": Patterns of family involvement among contemporary African American men. In *American families: Is-*

sues in race and ethnicity, ed. C. K. Jacobson, 179–99. New York: Garland.

PENHA-LOPES, V. 2006. "To cook, sew, to be a man": The socialization for competence and black men's involvement in housework. *Sex Roles* 54 (February): 261–74.

PEPLAU, L. A., R. C. VENIEGAS, AND S. M. CAMPBELL. 1996. Gay and lesbian relationships. In *The lives of lesbians, gays, and bisexuals: Children to adults,* eds. R. C. Savin-Williams and K. M. Cohen, 250–73. New York: Harcourt Brace.

PÉREZ, L. 1992. Cuban Miami. In *Miami now! Immigration, ethnicity, and social change,* eds. G. J. Grenier and A. Stepick III, 83–108. Gainesville: University Press of Florida.

PÉREZ, L. 2002. Cuban American families. In *Minority families in the United States: A multicultural perspective,* 3rd ed., ed. R. L. Taylor, 114–30. Upper Saddle River, NJ: Prentice Hall.

PERITZ, I. 2003. Miracle birth signals male moms? *Toronto Globe and Mail,* Aug. 15, A14.

PERLS, T. T. 2004. Anti-aging quackery: Human growth hormone and tricks of the trade—more dangerous than ever. *Journals of Gerontology: Biological and Medical Sciences* 59 (July): B682–B691.

PERLSTEIN, L. 2005. A user's guide to middle school romance. *Washington Post Magazine,* February 13, 20–23, 33.

PERRIN, E. C. 2002. Technical report: Coparent or second-parent adoption by same-sex parents. *Pediatrics* 109 (Feb.): 341–44.

PERRY, T., C. STEELE, AND A. HILLIARD III. 2003. *Young, gifted and black: Promoting high achievement among African-American students.* New York: Beacon.

PERRY-JENKINS, M., AND K. FOLK. 1994. Class, couples, and conflict: Effects of the division of labor on assessments of marriage in dual-earner families. *Journal of Marriage and the Family* 56 (Feb.): 165–80.

PERRY-JENKINS, M., C. P. PIERCE, AND A. E. GOLDBERG. 2004. Discourses on diapers and dirty laundry: Family communication about child care and housework. In *Handbook of family communication,* ed. Anita L. Vangelisti, 541–61. Mahwah, NJ: Lawrence Erlbaum.

PERTMAN, A. 2005. Improve press coverage of bad adoptions. *Christian Science Monitor,* Nov. 30, 9.

PESSAR, P. R. 1995. *A visa for a dream: Dominicans in the United States.* Boston: Allyn & Bacon.

PETERSEN, W. 1966. Success story, Japanese American style. *New York Times Magazine,* Jan. 6, 20ff.

PETERSON, B. D., C. R. NEWTON, K. H. ROSEN, AND R. S. SCHULMAN. 2006. Coping processes of couples experiencing infertility. *Family Relations* 55 (April): 227–39.

PETERSON, J. 2006. Many forced to retire early. *Los Angeles Times,* May 15, A8.

PETERSON, J. L., J. J. CARD, M. B. EISEN, AND B. SHERMAN-WILLIAMS. 1994. Evaluating teenage pregnancy prevention and other social programs: Ten stages of program assessment. *Family Planning Perspectives* 26 (May): 116–20, 131.

PETERSON, K. S. 2002. Having it all, except children. *USA Today,* Apr. 7, 2D.

PETERSON, K. S. 2003. Search for a soul mate, or love the one you're with? *USA Today,* May 28. www.usatoday.com (accessed May 29, 2003).

PETERSON, S. 2002. Gender meanings in grade eight students' talks about classroom writing. *Gender and Education* 14 (Dec.): 351–66.

PETRUNO, T. 2005. As profits surge, workers still wait. *Los Angeles Times,* Nov. 27, www.latimes.com (accessed November 28, 2005).

PEWEWARDY, C. 1998. Fluff and feathers: Treatment of American Indians in the literature and the classroom. *Equity & Excellence in Education* 31 (Apr.): 69–76.

PHILLIPS, J. A., AND M. M. SWEENEY. 2005. Premarital cohabitation and marital disruption among white, black, and Mexican American women. *Journal of Marriage and Family* 67 (May): 296–314.

PHILLIPS, K. A., AND W. MENARD. 2006. Suicidality in body dysmorphic disorder: A prospective study. *American Journal of Psychiatry* 163 (July): 1280–82.

PHILLIPS, K. R. 2004. Getting time off: Access to leave among working parents. The Urban Institute, April 22, www.urban.org (accessed May 3, 2006).

PHINNEY, J. S. 1996. Understanding ethnic diversity. *American Behavioral Scientist* 40 (Nov./Dec.) 143–52.

PHINNEY, J. S., B. HORENCZYK, K. LIEBKIND, AND P. VEDDER. 2001. Ethnic identity, immigration, and well-being: An interactional perspective. *Journal of Social Issues* 57: 493–510.

PIAGET, J. 1932. *The moral judgment of the child.* New York: Harcourt, Brace.

PIAGET, J. 1954. *The construction of reality in the child.* New York: Basic Books.

PIAGET, J. 1960. *The child's conception of the world.* London: Routledge.

PIENTA, A. M., AND M. M. FRANKS. 2006. A closer look at health and widowhood: Do health behaviors change after loss of a spouse? In *Spousal bereavement in late life,* eds. D. Carr, R. M. Nesse, and C. B. Wortman, 117–142. New York: Springer.

PIERRE, R. E. 2003. Northwest tribe struggles to revive its language project: A challenge for Klallam, others as native speakers age. *Washington Post,* Mar. 31, A3.

PILL, C. J. 1990. Stepfamilies: Redefining the family. *Family Relations* 39 (Apr.): 186–92.

PILLEMER, K., AND J. J. SUTTOR. 1991. Will I ever escape my child's problems? Effects of adult children's problems on elderly parents. *Journal of Marriage and the Family* 53 (Aug.): 585–94.

PIÑA, D. L., AND V. L. BENGSTON. 1993. The division of household labor and wives' happiness: Ideology, employment, and perceptions of support. *Journal of Marriage and the Family* 55 (Nov.): 901–12.

PINKER, S. 2005. Sniffing out the gay gene. *New York Times,* May 17, A21.

PIOKOWSKI, C. S., AND D. HUGHES. 1993. Dual-earner families in context: Managing family and work systems. In *Normal family processes,* 2nd ed., ed. F. Walsh, 185–207. New York: Guilford.

PIORKOWSKI, G. K. 1994. *Too close for comfort: Exploring the risks of intimacy.* New York: Plenum.

PITTMAN, F. 1990. *Private lies: Infidelity and the betrayal of intimacy.* New York: W.W. Norton.

PITTMAN, F. 1999. *Grow up! How taking responsibility can make you a happy adult.* New York: Golden Books.

PLATERIS, A. A. 1973. *100 years of marriage and divorce statistics: 1867–1967.* Rockville, MD: National Center for Health Statistics.

PLOTNICK, R. D., I. GARFINKEL, S. S. McLANAHAN, AND I. KU. 2004. Better child support enforcement. *Journal of Family Issues.* 25 (July): 634–57.

POGREBIN, R. 2006. Full tanks put squeeze on working class. *New York Times,* May 12, A1.

Police in Iran crack down on vice: Valentine's Day. 2003. *Baltimore Sun,* Feb. 13, 12A.

POLIT, D. F., AND T. FALBO. 1987. Only children and personality development: A quantitative review. *Journal of Marriage and the Family* 49 (May): 309–25.

POLLACK, W. 1998. *Real boys: Rescuing our sons from the myths of boyhood.* New York: Henry Holt.

POLLARD, K. M., AND W. P. O'HARE. 1999. America's racial and ethnic minorities. *Population Bulletin* 54 (Sep.): 1–48.

POMFRET, J. 2001. In China's countryside, "it's a boy!" too often. *Washington Post,* May 29, A1.

PONG, S.-L. 1997. Family structure, school context, and eighth grade math and reading achievement. *Journal of Marriage and the Family* 59 (Aug.): 734–46.

PONG, S. -L. HAO, AND E. GARDNER. 2005. The roles of parenting styles and social capital in the school performance of immigrant Asian and Hispanic adolescents. *Social Science Quarterly* 86 (December): 928–50.

PONIEWOZIK, J. 2002. The cost of starting families. *Time,* Apr. 15, 56–57.

POPE, J. R., H. G. R. OLIVARDIA, AND J. BOROWIECKI. 1999. Evolving ideals of male body image as seen through action toys. *International Journal of Eating Disorders* 26 (July): 65–72.

POPENOE, D. 1996. *Life without father: Compelling new evidence that fatherhood and marriage are indispensable for the good of children and society,* New York: Free Press.

POPENOE, D. 2002. The top ten myths of marriage. The National Marriage Project, March,

http://marriage.rutgers.edu (accessed April 6, 2006).

POPENOE, D., AND B. D. WHITEHEAD. 2002. *Should we live together? What young adults need to know about cohabitation before marriage: A comprehensive review of recent research,* 2nd ed. New Brunswick, NJ: The National Marriage Project, Rutgers University. http://marriage.rutgers .edu (accessed July 12, 2003).

POPENOE, D., AND B. D. WHITEHEAD. 2003. *The state of our unions, 2003: The social health of marriage in America.* The National Marriage Project, Rutgers University. http://marriage.rutgers.edu (accessed July 4, 2003).

POPENOE, D., AND B. D. WHITEHEAD. 2006. The state of our unions 2006: The social health of marriage in America. The National Marriage Project, http://marriage.rutgers.edu (accessed September 7, 2006).

POPULATION REFERENCE BUREAU. 1990. *America in the 21st century: Social and economic support systems.* Washington, DC.

POTTHOFF, S. J., L. H. BEARINGER, C. L. SHAY, N. CASSUTO, R. W. BLUM, AND M. D. RESNICK. 1998. Dimensions of risk behaviors among American Indian youth. *Archives of Pediatrics & Adolescent Medicine* 152 (Feb.): 157–63.

POTTS, L. 2003. PBS looks at how oral contraceptives changed women's lives. www.abqjournal.com (accessed Feb. 23, 2003).

POWELL, E. 1991. *Talking back to sexual pressure.* Minneapolis: CompCare.

Pregnancy discrimination charges. 2006. Equal Employment Opportunity Commission, www.eeoc .gov/stats/pregnanc.html (accessed May 12, 2006).

PRESS, J. E., J. FAGAN, AND L. LAUGHLIN. 2006. Taking pressure off families: Child-care subsidies lessen mothers' work-hour problems. *Journal of Marriage and Family* 68 (February): 155–71.

PRESSER, H. B. 2000. Nonstandard work schedules and marital instability. *Journal of Marriage and the Family* 62 (Feb.): 93–110.

PRESSER, H., AND A. COX. 1997. The work schedules of low-educated American women and welfare reform. *Monthly Labor Review* 120 (Apr.): 25–35.

PREUSS, U. W., ET AL. 2003. Predictors and correlates of suicide attempts over 5 years in 1,237 alcohol-dependent men and women. *American Journal of Psychiatry* 160 (Jan.): 56–63.

PREVITI, D., AND P. R. AMATO. 2003. Why stay married? Rewards, barriers, and marital stability. *Journal of Marriage and Family* 65 (Aug.): 561–73.

PRICE, J. 2001. Court bans man from having more kids. *Washington Post,* Nov. 23. www.washingtonpost.com (accessed Nov. 24, 2001).

PRICE, J. A. 1981. North American Indian families. In *Ethnic families in America: Patterns and variations,* 2nd ed., eds. C. H. Mindel and R. W. Habenstein, 245–68. New York: Elsevier.

PRICE, R. H., J. N. CHOI, AND A. D. VINOKUR. 2002. Links in the chain of adversity following job loss: How financial strain and loss of personal control lead to depression, impaired functioning, and poor health. *Journal of Occupational Health Psychology* 7 (4): 302–12.

PRIDONOFF, J. A. 1994. Is the right-to-die movement a danger? *Washington Post Health Supplement,* Oct. 18, 19.

PROCTOR, B. D., AND J. DALAKER. 2002. *Poverty in the United States: 2001.* U.S. Census Bureau, Current Population Reports, P60-219. www .census.gov (accessed Apr. 14, 2003).

PROCTOR, B. D., AND J. DALAKER. 2003. *Poverty in the United States: 2002.* U.S. Census Bureau, Current Population Reports, P60–222. www.census .gov (accessed Oct. 5, 2003).

Projections of the resident population by age, sex, race, and Hispanic origin: 1999 to 2100. 2000. U.S. Census Bureau, Population Division. www.census.gov (accessed Oct. 11, 2003).

PROTHROW-STITH, D., AND H. R. SPIVAK. 2005. *Sugar and spice and no longer nice: How can we stop girls' violence*? San Francisco, CA: Jossey-Bass.

PRUETT, K. D. 1987. *The nurturing father: Journey toward the complete man.* New York: Warner.

PRUSHER, I. R. 2000. Housemaids' woes spur Kuwait to review labor law. *Christian Science Monitor,* May 30, 1, 9.

PRUSHER, I. R. 2001. South Korea: Gay confession ignites debate. *Christian Science Monitor,* Jan. 17, 7.

PTACEK, J. 1999. *Battered women in the courtroom: The power of judicial response.* Boston: Northeastern University Press.

PULTE H. 2005. *Baby boomer study: Full report.* Harris Interactive Market Research, May, www.harrisinteractive.com (accessed August 1, 2006).

PURKAYASTHA, B. 2002. Rules, roles, and realities: Indo-American families in the United States. In *Minority families in the United States: A multicultural perspective,* 3rd ed., ed. R. L. Taylor, 212–24 Upper Saddle River, NJ: Prentice Hall.

PUTNAM, F. W. 2006. The impact of trauma on child development. *Juvenile and Family Court Journal* 57 (Winter): 1–11.

PUZONE, C. A. 2000. National trends in intimate partner homicide: United States, 1976–1995. *Violence against Women* 6 (Apr.): 409–26.

PYKE, K. D. 1994. Women's employment as a gift or burden? Marital power across marriage, divorce, and remarriage. *Gender and Society* 8 (Mar.): 73–91.

PYKE, K., AND S. COLTRANE. 1996. Entitlement, obligation, and gratitude in family work. *Journal of Family Issues* 17 (Jan.): 60–82.

PYLE, S. A., C. KEITH HADDOCK, N. HYMOWITZ, J. SCHWAB, AND S. MESHBERG. 2005. Family rules about exposure to environmental tobacco smoke. *Family Systems & Health* 23 (Spring): 8–16.

QIAN, Z., D. T. LICHTER, L. M. MELLOTT. 2005. Out-of-wedlock childbearing, marital prospects and mate selection. *Social Forces* 84 (September): 473–91.

QU, L., AND R. WESTON. 2001. Starting out together through cohabitation or marriage. *Family Matters* 60 (Spring/Summer, 2001): 76–79. Australian Institute of Family Studies. www.aifs.org.au (accessed July 10, 2003).

QUADAGNO, J. 2002. *Aging and the life course: An introduction to social gerontology,* 2nd ed. New York: McGraw-Hill.

QUEEN, S. A., R. W. HABENSTEIN, AND J. S. QUADAGNO. 1985. *The family in various cultures,* 5th ed. New York: Harper & Row.

QUICK, B. 1992. Tales from the self-help mill. *Newsweek,* Aug. 31, 14.

QUICK, D. S., P. C. McKENRY, AND B. M. NEWMAN. 1994. Stepmothers and their adolescent children: Adjustment to new family roles. In *Stepparenting: Issues in theory, research, and practice,* eds. K. Pasley and M. Ihinger-Tallman, 119–25. Westport, CT: Greenwood.

QUINTANA, S. M., AND V. M. VERA. 1999. Mexican American children's ethnic identity, understanding of ethnic prejudice, and parental ethnic socialization. *Hispanic Journal of Behavioral Sciences* 21 (Nov.): 387–404.

Race and ethnicity in 2001: Attitudes, perceptions, and experiences. 2001. The Henry J. Kaiser Family Foundation. www.kff.org (accessed Apr. 3, 2003).

RAFFAELLI, M., AND S. GREEN. 2003. Parent-adolescent communication about sex: Retrospective reports by Latino college students. *Journal of Marriage and Family* 65 (May): 474–81.

RAINE, A., C. REYNOLDS, P. H. VENABLES, AND S. A. MEDNICK. 2002. Stimulation seeking and intelligence: A prospective longitudinal study. *Journal of Personality and Social Psychology* 82 (Apr.): 663–74.

RAINIE, L., AND M. MADDEN. 2006. Not looking for love: Romance in America. Pew Research Center, February 13, http://pewresearch.org (accessed March 12, 2006).

RAINWATER, L., AND T. M. SMEEDING. 2003. *Poor kids in a rich country: America's children in comparative perspective.* New York: Russell Sage Foundation.

RAJ, A., AND J. G. SILVERMAN. 2002. Intimate partner violence against South Asian women in greater Boston. *Journal of the American Medical Women's Association* 57 (Apr.): 111–14.

RALEY, R. K., AND E. WILDSMITH. 2004. Cohabitation and children's family instability. *Journal of Marriage and Family* 66 (February): 210–19.

RAMACHANDRAN, N. 2005. The parent trap: Boomerang kids. *U.S. News & World Report,* December 12, 64.

RAMOS, V. M. 2005. HIV rate among local Hispanics alarms experts. *Orlando Sentinel,* Sep. 14, A1.

RANK, M. R. 1987. The formation and dissolution of marriages in the welfare population. *Journal of Marriage and the Family* 49 (Feb.): 15–20.

RANKIN, S. R. 2003. *Campus climate for gay, lesbian, bisexual, and transgender people: A national perspective.* National Gay and Lesbian Task Force Policy Institute. www.kff.org (accessed June 10, 2003).

RAPAPORT, J. 2000. Good life goals. *Christian Science Monitor,* July 6, 14.

RASCHICK, M., AND B. INGERSOLL-DAYTON. 2004. The costs and rewards of caregiving among aging spouses and adult children. *Family Relations* 53 (April): 317–325.

RATHUS, J. H., AND K. D. O'LEARY. 1997. Spouse-specific dependency scale: Scale development. *Journal of Family Violence* 12 (June): 159–68.

RAYBECK, D., S. DORENBOSCH, M. SARAPATA, AND D. HERRMAN. 2000. The quest for love and meaning in the personals. Unpublished paper.

READ, J. G. 2004. Family, religion, and work among Arab American women. *Journal of Marriage and Family* 66 (November): 1042–50.

READING, R. 2006. Child deaths resulting from inflicted injuries: Household risk factors and perpetrator characteristics. *Child: Care, Health & Development* 32 (March): 253.

REARDON, D. C., J. R. COUGLE, V. M. RUE, M. W. SHUPING, P. K. COLEMAN, AND P. G. NEY. 2003. Psychiatric admissions of low-income women following abortion and childbirth. *Canadian Medical Association Journal* 168 (May 13): 1253–56.

REARDON-ANDERSON, J., M. STAGNER, J. E. Macomber, and J. Murray. 2005. Systematic review of the impact of marriage and relationship programs. Urban Institute, February 11, www .urban.org (accessed November 1, 2005).

REARDON-ANDERSON, J., M. STAGNER, J. E. MACOMBER, AND J. MURRAY. 2005. Systematic review of the impact of marriage and relationship programs. The Urban Institute, February 11, www.urban.org/ (accessed April 14, 2006).

REARDON-ANDERSON, J., R. CAPPS, AND M. E. FIX. 2002. The health and well-being of children in immigrant families. Urban Institute. www .urban.org (accessed Apr. 4, 2003).

REAY, A. M., AND K. D. BROWNE. 2001. Risk factors for caregivers who physically abuse or neglect their elderly dependents. *Aging and Mental Health* 5 (1): 56–62.

RECTANUS, L., AND M. GOMEZ. 2002. Worker protection: Labor's efforts to enforce protections for day laborers could benefit from better data and guidance. United States General Accounting Office. www.gao.gov (accessed Apr. 13, 2003).

REDFEARN, S. 2005. Joy . . . or pain? *Washington Post,* August 2, HE1.

REEVES, S. 2005. Living together makes more sense than marriage. *Forbes* (August 3), www .forbes.com (accessed March 3, 2006).

REGAN, P. 2003. *The mating game: A primer on love, sex, and marriage.* Thousand Oaks, CA: Sage.

REGAN, P. C., AND E. BERSCHEID. 1999. *Lust; What we know about human sexual desire.* Thousand Oaks, CA: Sage.

REGIS, H. 1995. The madness of excess. In *Romantic passion: A universal experience?* ed. W. Jankowiak, 141–51. New York: Columbia University Press.

REGNIER, P., AND A. GENGLER. 2006. Men, women, and money. *Money,* March 14, http://magazines .ivillage.com (accessed April 14, 2006).

REID, J. 1993. Those fabulous '50s. *Utne Reader* 55 (Jan.): 18–19.

REILLY, P. R. 2000. *Abraham Lincoln's DNA and other adventures in genetics.* New York: Cold Spring Harbor Laboratory.

REIMER, S. 1999. Sex questions show how little our kids know. *Baltimore Sun,* Sep. 9, 1e, 4e.

REINER, W. G., AND J. P. GEARHART. 2004. Discordant sexual identity in some genetic males with cloacal exstrophy assigned to female sex at birth. *New England Journal of Medicine* 350 (January 22): 333–41.

REINISCH, J. M., WITH R. BEASLEY. 1990. *The Kinsey Institute new report on sex: What you must know to be sexually literate.* New York: St. Martin's.

REISBERG, L. 2000. 10% of students may spend too much time online. *Chronicle of Higher Education,* June 16, A43.

REISS, I. 1960. Toward a sociology of the heterosexual love relationship. *Marriage and Family Living* 22 (May): 139–45.

REISS, I. L. 1971. *The family system in America.* New York: Holt, Rinehart & Winston.

REISS, I. L., AND G. R. LEE. 1988. *Family systems in America,* 4th ed. New York: Holt, Rinehart & Winston.

REITMAN, V. 2002. Self-immolations on rise in Afghanistan. *Los Angeles Times,* Nov. 17, A5.

RENN, J. A., AND S. L. CALVERT. 1993. The relation between gender schemas and adults' recall of stereotyped and counterstereotyped televised information. *Sex Roles* 28 (7/8): 449–59.

RENNISON, C. M. 2001. *Intimate partner violence and age of victim, 1993–99.* Washington, DC: U.S. Department of Justice.

RENNISON, C. M. 2003. *Intimate partner violence, 1993–2001.* Washington, DC: U.S. Department of Justice.

RENNISON, C. M., AND S. WELCHANS. 2000. *Intimate partner violence.* Washington, DC: U.S. Department of Justice.

RENOUT, F. 2005. Immigrants' second wives find few rights. *Christian Science Monitor,* May 25, 17.

RENZETTI, C. M. 1992. *Violent betrayal: Partner abuse in lesbian relationships.* Thousand Oaks, CA: Sage.

REPAK, T. A. 1995. *Waiting on Washington: Central American workers in the nation's capital.* Philadelphia: Temple University Press.

Report cards for parents proposed in Lebanon, Pa. 2003. *Baltimore Sun,* Feb. 7, 3A.

Report of the defense task force on sexual harassment & violence at the military service academies. 2005. www.defenselink.mil (accessed December 1, 2005).

RESTAK, R. 2002. All in your head. *Modern Maturity,* Jan./Feb., 60–66.

RETSINAS, G. 2003. Hospital to pay $5.4 million in sex harassment lawsuit. *New York Times,* Apr. 10, A21.

RETSINAS, J. 1988. A theoretical reassessment of the applicability of Kübler-Ross's stages of dying. *Death Studies* 12 (3): 207–16.

Reuters highlights a Chinese periodical targeting gay men that discusses "taboo" subjects of homosexuality and HIV/AIDS. 2002. The Henry Kaiser Family Foundation, Oct. 1. www.kaisernetwork .org (accessed June 12, 2003).

REVELL, J. 2003. Bye-bye pension. *Fortune,* Mar. 17, 65–74.

REYNOLDS, A. J., AND D. ROBERTSON. 2003. School-based early intervention and later child maltreatment in the Chicago longitudinal study. *Child Development* 74 (Jan./Feb.): 3–26.

REYNOLDS, A. J., J. A. TEMPLE, D. L. ROBERTSON, AND E. A. MANN. 2001. Long-term effects of an early childhood intervention on educational achievement and juvenile arrest: A 15-year follow-up of low-income children in public schools. *Journal of the American Medical Association* 285 (May 19): 2339–46.

RHEE, K. E., J. C. LUMENG, D. P. APPUGLIESE, N. KACIROTI, AND R. H. BRADLEY. 2006. Parenting styles and overweight status in first grade. *Pediatrics* 117 (June): 2047–54.

RHEINGOLD, H. L. 1969. The social and socializing infant. In *Handbook of socialization theory and research,* ed. D. A. Goslin, 779–90. Chicago: Rand McNally.

RICCARDI, N. 2004. The new matchmakers in Pakistan: the Web and TV. *Los Angeles Times,* July 7.

RICE, G., C. ANDERSON, N. RISCH, AND G. EBERS. 1999. Male homosexuality: Absence of linkage to microsatellite markers at Xq28. *Science* 284 (Apr. 23): 665–67.

RICH, M. 2005. Living in a retirement village, back home with mom and dad. *New York Times,* May 22, A1.

RICHARDSON, B. 2004. What Japanese women want: A western husband. *Christian Science Monitor* (December 6): 1, 10.

RICHARDSON, C. R., P. J. RESNICK, D. L. HANSEN, H. A. DERRY, AND V. J. RIDEOUT. 2002. Does pornography-blocking software block access to

health information in the Internet? *Journal of the American Medical Association* 288 (Dec. 11): 2887–94.

RICHARDSON, R. A. 2004. Early adolescence talking points: Questions that middle school students want to ask their parents. *Family Relations* 53 (January): 87–94.

RICHARDSON-BOUIE, D. 2003. Ethnic variation/ethnicity. In *International encyclopedia of marriage and family,* 2nd ed., Vol. 2, ed. J. J. Ponzetti, Jr., 525–30. New York: Macmillan.

RICHEY, W. 1997. Girls, boys, sports, and fairness. *Christian Science Monitor,* Oct. 3, 1, 4.

RIDEOUT, V., AND E. HAMEL. 2006. The media family: Electronic media in the lives of infants, toddlers, preschoolers and their parents. Kaiser Family Foundation, May, www.kff.org (accessed September 22, 2006).

RIDEOUT, V., C. RICHARDSON, AND P. RESNIK. 2002. See no evil: How Internet filters affect the search for online health information. The Henry Kaiser Family Foundation. www.kff.org (accessed June 10, 2003).

RIDEOUT, V., D. F. ROBERTS, AND U. G. FOEHR. 2005. *Generation M: Media in the lives of 8–18 year-olds.* Menlo Park, CA: Kaiser Family Foundation.

RIEGER, G., M. CHIVERS, AND M. J. BAILEY. 2005. Sexual arousal patterns of bisexual men. *Psychological Science* 16 (August): 579–84.

RILEY, N. S. 2005. *God on the quad: How religious colleges and the missionary generation are changing America.* New York: St. Martin's Press.

RIMER, S. 2002. Sex advice enlivens newspapers on campus. *New York Times,* Oct. 14, A25.

RINGLE, K. 1999. Unamicable partners. *Washington Post,* Mar. 15, C1, C7.

RISMAN, B., AND P. SCHWARTZ. 2002. After the sexual revolution: Gender politics in teen dating. *Contexts* 1 (Spring): 16–24.

RIVERS, C. 2001. Study: Young people seeking soul mates to marry. *Women's E-News,* June 20. www.womensnews.org (accessed July 15, 2003).

RIVERS, C. 2002. Pop science book claims girls hardwired for love. *Women's E-News,* June 28. www.womensenews.org (accessed June 29, 2002).

RIVERS, C., AND R. C. BARNETT. 2005. Holiday toys sell girls on primping and passivity. Women's e-news, Nov. 27, http://womensenews.org (accessed November 28, 2005).

ROAN, S. 2003. The mind's role comes into focus: Knowledge of the profound connection between emotions and physical well-being is increasingly put to practice. *Los Angeles Times,* Jan. 20. www.latimes.com (accessed Jan. 22, 2003).

ROAN, S. 2005. Breasts, redefined. *Los Angeles Times,* June 13, F1.

ROBERTS, C. M. 2001. The view from 90. *Washington Post Health Supplement,* Jan. 23, 15–16.

ROBERTS, D. F., U. G. FOEHR, V. J. RIDEOUT, AND M. BRODIE. 1999. *Kids & media @ the new millennium.* Washington, DC: The Henry Kaiser Family Foundation.

ROBERTS, L. J. 2000. Fire and ice in marital communication: Hostile and distancing behaviors as predictors of marital distress. *Journal of Marriage and the Family* 62 (Aug.): 693–707.

ROBIN, R. W., B. CHESTER, J. K. RASMUSSEN, J. M. JARANSON, AND D. GOLDMAN, 1997. Prevalence, characteristics, and impact of childhood sexual abuse in a southwestern American Indian tribe. *Child Abuse & Neglect* 21 (Aug.): 769–87.

ROBINSON, J. P., AND G. GODBEY. 1999. *Time for life: The surprising ways Americans use their time,* 2nd ed. University Park: Pennsylvania State University Press.

ROCHE, T. 2002. The Yates odyssey. *Time,* Jan. 28, 40–50.

ROCK, E. M., M. IRELAND, M. D. RESNICK, AND C. A. McNEELY. 2005. A rose by any other name? Objective knowledge, perceived knowledge, and adolescent male condom use. *Pediatrics* 115 (March): 667–72.

ROCKOFF, J. D. 2005. FDA's acts on Plan B faulted. *Baltimore Sun,* Nov. 15, 1A, 6A.

RODBERG, G. 1999. Woman and man at Yale. www.culturefront.org (accessed Aug. 29, 2000).

RODGERS, A. Y., AND R. L. JONES. 1999. Grandmothers who are caregivers: An overlooked population.

Child and Adolescent Social Work Journal 16 (Dec.): 455–66.

RODGERS, J. L., P. A. NAKONEZNY, AND R. D. SHULL. 1997. The effect of no-fault divorce legislation on divorce rates: A response to a reconsideration. *Journal of Marriage and the Family* 59 (Nov.): 1026–30.

RODGERS, K. A. 1999. Parenting processes related to sexual risk-taking: Behaviors of adolescent males and females. *Journal of Marriage and the Family* 61 (Feb.): 99–109.

RODGERS, K. B., AND H. A. ROSE. 2002. Risk and resiliency factors among adolescents who experience marital transitions. *Journal of Marriage and Family* 64 (Nov.): 1024–37.

ROGERS, M. F. 1999. *Barbie culture.* Thousand Oaks, CA: Sage.

ROGERS, S. J. 1999. Wives' income and marital quality: Are there reciprocal effects? *Journal of Marriage and the Family* 61 (Feb.): 123–32.

ROGERS, S. J. 2004. Dollars, dependency, and divorce: Four perspectives on the roles of wives' income. *Journal of Marriage and Family* 66 (February): 59–74.

ROGERS, S. J., AND D. C. MAY. 2003. Spillover between marital quality and job satisfaction: Longterm patterns and gender differences. *Journal of Marriage and Family* 65 (May): 482–95.

ROGERS, S. J., AND D. D. DEBOER. 2001. Changes in wives' income: Effects on marital happiness, psychological well-being, and the risk of divorce. *Journal of Marriage and Family* 63 (May): 458–72.

ROHNER, R. P., AND R. A. VENEZIANO. 2001. The importance of father love: History and contemporary evidence. *Review of General Psychology* 5 (4): 382–405.

ROHYPNOL. 2003. Office of National Drug Control Policy, www.whitehousedrugpolicy.gov (accessed March 10, 2006).

Romance on the Web. 2003. *Newsweek,* May 12, E20.

ROMANO, L. 2006. Multiple single moms, one nameless donor. *Washington Post,* Feb. 27, A2.

ROMERO, G. J., AND G. E. WYATT. 1999. The prevalence and circumstances of child sexual abuse among Latina women. *Hispanic Journal of Behavioral Sciences* 21 (Aug.): 351–67.

ROSCHELLE, A. R., M. I. TORO-MORN, AND E. FACIO. 2005. Families in Cuba: From colonialism to revolution. In *Handbook of world families,* eds. B. N. Adams and J. Trost, 414–439. Thousand Oaks, CA: Sage.

ROSE, S., AND I. H. FRIEZE. 1993. Young singles' contemporary dating scripts. *Sex Roles* 28 (May): 499–509.

ROSEMOND, J. 2000. *Raising a nonviolent child.* Kansas City, Missouri: Andrews McMeel Publishing.

ROSEN, B. C. 1982. *The industrial connection: Achievement and the family in developing societies.* New York: Aldine.

ROSEN, K. H., AND S. M. STITH. 1993. Intervention strategies for treating women in violent dating relationships. *Family Relations* 42 (Oct.): 427–33.

ROSEN, R. 2003. Sentenced to stoning. *San Francisco Chronicle.* http://sfgate.com (accessed Mar. 31, 2003).

ROSENBAUM, J. E. 2006. Reborn a virgin: Adolescents' retracting of virginity pledges and sexual histories. *American Journal of Public Health* 96 (June): 1098–1103.

ROSENBERG, D. A. 1997. Unusual forms of child abuse. In *The battered child,* 5th ed., eds. M. E. Helfer, R. S. Kempe, and R. D. Krugman, 413–30. Chicago: University of Chicago Press.

ROSENBERG, J. 1993. Just the two of us. In *Reinventing love: Six women talk about lust, sex, and romance,* eds. L. Abraham, L. Green, M. Krance, J. Rosenberg, J. Somerville, and C. Stoner, 301–7. New York: Plume.

ROSENBLATT, P. C. 1994. *Metaphors of family systems theory: Toward new constructions.* New York: Guilford.

ROSENBLATT, P. C., AND R. A. PHILLIPS, JR. 1975. Family articles in popular magazines: Advice to writers, editors, and teachers of consumers. *Family Coordinator* 24 (July): 267–71.

ROSENFELD, M. J. 2002. Measures of assimilation in the marriage market: Mexican Americans 1970–1990. *Journal of Marriage and Family* 64 (Feb.): 152–62.

ROSENTHAL, C. J. 1985. Kinkeeping in the familial division of labor. *Journal of Marriage and the Family* 47 (Nov.): 965–74.

ROSENZWEIG, P. M. 1992. *Married and alone: The way back.* New York: Plenum.

ROSS, C. E., AND J. MIROWSKY. 1999. Parental divorce, life-course disruption, and adult depression. *Journal of Marriage and the Family* 61 (Nov.): 1034–45.

ROTHMAN, B. K. 1984. *Hands and hearts: A history of courtship in America.* New York: Basic Books.

ROTHMAN, E. K. 1983. Sex and self-control: Middle-class courtship in America, 1770–1870. In *The American family in social-historical perspective,* 3rd ed., ed. M. Gordon, 393–410. New York: St. Martin's.

ROTHMAN, S. M. 1978. *Women's proper place: A history of changing ideals and practices, 1870 to the present.* New York: Basic Books.

ROUG, L. 2005. The time seems ripe to tie the knot in Iraq. *Los Angeles Times,* June 12, A1.

ROUSE, L. 2002. *Marital and sexual lifestyles in the United States: Attitudes, behaviors, and relationships in social context.* New York: Haworth.

ROWE, J., AND R. KAHN. 1997. *Successful aging.* New York: Pantheon.

ROWLAND, M. 1994. Love and money the second time around. *Working Woman* (Aug.): 22, 24.

RUBIN, L. B. 1985. *Just friends: The role of friendship in our lives.* New York: Harper & Row.

RUBIN, L. B. 1994. *Families on the fault line: America's working class speaks about the family, the economy, race, and ethnicity.* New York: HarperCollins.

RUHM, C. J., AND J. L. TEAGUE. 1997. Parental leave policies in Europe and North America. In *Gender and family issues in the workplace,* eds. F. D. Blau and R. G. Ehrenberg, 133–56. New York: Russell Sage Foundation.

RUSSO, F. 2002. That old feeling. *Time,* Feb. 13, G1–G3.

RUSSO, F. 2005. Who cares more for mom? *Time,* June 20, F7–F10.

RUST, B. 2000. Walking the plain talk. *Advocasey* (Spring/Summer): 1–11.

RUTTER, V. 1994. Lessons from stepfamilies. *Psychology Today* (May): 30–33, 60ff.

RYAN, M. P. 1983. *Womanhood in America: From colonial times to the present,* 3rd ed. New York: Franklin Watts.

RYAN, S., J. MANLOVE, AND K. FRANZETTA. 2003. *The first time: Characteristics of teens' first sexual relationships.* Washington, DC: Child Trends.

SAAD, L. 2003. *Roe v. Wade* has positive public image. Gallup News Service, Jan. 20. www.gallup.com (accessed Jan. 21, 2003).

SAAD, L. 2004. Romance to break out nationwide this weekend. Gallup Organization, February 13, http://poll.gallup.com (accessed February 17, 2004).

SAAD, L. 2005. Gay rights attitudes a mixed bag. Gallup Organization, May 20, www.gallup.com (accessed May 28, 2005).

SAAD, L. 2006. Americans have complex relationship with marriage. Gallup Organization, May 30, www.gallup.com (accessed May 31, 2006).

SAAD, L. 2006. Americans still oppose gay marriage. Gallup Organization, May 22, www.gallup.com (accessed September 16, 2006).

SABATELLI, R. M., AND S. BARTLE-HARING. 2003. Family of origin experiences and adjustment in married couples. *Journal of Marriage and Family* 65 (Feb.): 159–69.

SADKER, M., AND D. SADKER. 1994. *Failing at fairness: How America's schools cheat girls.* New York: Scribner's.

SAFER, J. 1996. *Beyond motherhood: Choosing a life without children.* New York: Pocket Books.

SAFILIOS-ROTHSCHILD, C. 1977. *Love, sex, and sex roles.* Upper Saddle River, NJ: Prentice Hall.

SAGIRI, Y. 2001. *United National Indian Tribal Youth, Inc.* Washington, DC: U.S. Department of Justice.

SAILLANT, C. 2004. Internet dating goes gray. *Los Angeles Times,* May 19, A1.

SAITO, L. T. 2002. *Ethnic identity and motivation: Socio-cultural factors in the educational achievement of Vietnamese American students.* New York: LFB Scholarly Publishing.

SALDANA, D. H., AND A. M. DASSORI. 1999. When is caregiving a burden? Listening to Mexican American women. *Hispanic Journal of Behavioral Sciences* 21 (Aug.): 283–301.

SALTZMAN, A. 1993. Family friendliness. *U.S. News & World Report,* Feb. 22, 59–66.

SALTZMAN, A. 1999. From diapers to high heels. *U.S. News & World Report,* July 26, 57–58.

SALUJA, G., R. IACHAN, P. C. SCHEIDT, M. D. OVERPECK, W. SUN, AND J. N. GIEDD. 2004. Prevalence of and risk factors for depressive symptoms among young adolescents. *Archives of Pediatrics and Adolescent Medicine* 158 (August): 760–765.

SALUTER, A. F. 1994. *Marital status and living arrangements: March 1993.* U.S. Census Bureau, Current Population Reports, Series P20–478. Washington, DC: U.S. Government Printing Office.

SALUTER, A. F. 1996. Marital status and living arrangements: March 1995 (Update). U.S. Census Bureau, Department of Commerce, Economics and Statistics Administration.

SAMPSON, R. 2002. Acquaintance rape of college students. U.S. Department of Justice, Office of Community Oriented Policing Services, Guide No. 17, www.cops.usdoj.gov (accessed March 5, 2006).

SANCHEZ, M. 2003. Fast-food industry introduces some young women to sexual harassment. www.kansascity.comMay 6, A1.

SANCHEZ-WAY, R., AND S. JOHNSON. 2000. Cultural practices in American Indian prevention programs. *Juvenile Justice* 7 (Dec.): 20–30.

SANDBERG, J. F., AND S. L. HOFFERTH. 2001. Changes in children's time with parents, U.S. 1981–1997. *Demography* 38(3): 423–36.

SANDBERG, J. G., R. B. MILLER, AND J. M. HARPER. 2002. A qualitative study of marital process and depression in older couples. *Family Relations* 51 (July): 256–64.

SANDLER, L. 2003. Veiled and worried in Baghdad. *New York Times,* Sep. 16, A23.

SANTROCK, J. W., K. A. SITTERLE, AND R. A. WARSHAK. 1988. Parent–child relationships in stepfather families. In *Fatherhood today: Men's changing role in the family,* eds. S. P. Bronstein and C. P. Cowan, 144–65. New York: Wiley.

SAPOLSKY, R. 2000. It's not "all in the genes." *Newsweek,* Apr. 10, 68.

SARCH, A. 1993. Making the connection: Single women's use of the telephone in dating relationships with men. *Journal of Communications* 43 (Spring): 128–44.

SARGENT, J. D., ET AL. 2005. Exposure to movie smoking: Its relation to smoking initiation among US adolescents. *Pediatrics* 116 (November): 1183–91.

SARKISIAN, N., AND N. GERSTEL. 2004. Explaining the gender gap in help to parents: The importance of employment. *Journal of Marriage and Family* 66 (May): 431–451.

SARMIENTO, S. T. 2002. *Making ends meet: Income-generating strategies among Mexican immigrants.* New York: LFB Scholarly Publishing.

SARWAR, B. 2002. Brutality cloaked as tradition. *New York Times,* Aug. 6, A15.

SASSLER, S. 2004. The process of entering into cohabiting unions. *Journal of Marriage and Family* 66 (May): 491–505.

SAVIN-WILLIAMS, R. C., AND E. M. DUBÉ. 1998. Parental reactions to their child's disclosure of a gay/lesbian identity. *Family Relations* 47 (Jan.): 7–13.

SAYER, L. C. 2006. Economic aspects of divorce and relationship dissolution. In *Handbook of divorce and relationship dissolution,* eds. M. A. Fine and J. H. Harvey, 385–406. Mahwah, NJ: Lawrence Erlbaum.

SCHECTER, S., AND A. GANELY. 1995. *Domestic violence: A national curriculum for family preservation practitioners.* San Francisco: Family Violence Prevention Fund.

SCHEMO, J. 2002. Women who lead colleges see slower growth in ranks. *New York Times,* Dec. 8, A18.

SCHERER, R. 2003. Relaxing can wait, as retirees flood job market. *Christian Science Monitor,* Aug. 21, 1–2.

SCHMEECKLE, M., R. GIARRUSSO, D. FENG, AND V. L. BENGSTON. 2006. What makes someone family? Adult children's perceptions of current and former stepparents. *Journal of Marriage and Family* 68 (August): 595–610.

SCHMIDLEY, D. A. 2001. *Profile of the foreign-born population in the United States: 2000.* U.S. Census Bureau, Current Population Reports, Series P23–206. www.census.gov (accessed Mar. 1, 2003).

SCHMIEGE, C., L. RICHARDS, AND A. ZVONKOVIC. 2001. Remarriage: For love or money? *Journal of Divorce and Remarriage* 36 (Jan./Feb.): 123–140.

SCHMIEGE, S., AND N. F. RUSSO. 2005. Depression and unwanted first pregnancy: Longitudinal cohort study. *British Medical Journal* 331 (December): 1303–1305.

SCHMITT, D. P., AND D. M. BUSS. 2001. Interpersonal relations and group processes: Human mate poaching—tactics and temptations for infiltrating existing mateships. *Journal of Personality and Social Psychology* 80 (June): 894–917.

SCHNEIDER, J. 2002. 100 and counting. *U.S. News & World Report,* June 3, 86.

SCHOEN, R., AND P. TUFIS. 2003. Precursors of nonmarital fertility in the United States. *Journal of Marriage and Family* 65 (November): 1030–40.

SCHOEN, R., AND V. CANUDAS-ROMO. 2006. Timing effects on divorce: 20th century experience in the United States. *Journal of Marriage and Family* 68 (August): 749–758.

SCHOEN, R., AND Y.-H. A. CHENG. 2006. Partner choice and the differential retreat from marriage. *Journal of Marriage and Family* 68 (February): 1–10.

SCHOEN, R., N. M. ASTONE, K. ROTHERT, N. J. STANDISH, AND Y. J. KIM. 2002. Women's employment, marital happiness, and divorce. *Social Forces* 81 (December): 643–662.

SCHOENBORN, C. A. 2004. *Marital status and health: United States, 1999–2002. Advance data from vital and health Statistics.* Hyatsville, MD: National Center for Health Statistics.

SCHOLES, R. J., AND A. PHATARALAOHA. 1999. The "mail-order bride" industry and its impact on U.S. immigration. U.S. Citizenship and Immigration Services, Appendix A, http://uscis.gov (accessed March 3, 2006).

SCHOPPE-SULLIVAN, S. J., S. C. MANGELSDORF, C. A. FROSCH, AND J. L. MCHALE. 2004. Association between coparenting and marital behavior from infancy to the preschool years. *Journal of Family Psychology* 18 (March): 194–207.

SCHOR, J. B. 2002. Time crunch among American parents. In *Taking parenting public: The case for a new social movement,* eds. S. A. Hewlett, N. Rankin, and C. West, 83–102. Lanham, MD: Rowman & Littlefield.

SCHORR, M. 2001. Gay and lesbian couples do well at parenting. Excite News, Aug. 28. news excite.com (accessed Aug. 29, 2001).

SCHRADER, S. M. 2005. Research on bicycle saddles and sexual health comes of age. *The Journal of Sexual Medicine* 2 (September): 594–95.

SCHROF, J. M. 1999. Who's guilty? *U.S. News & World Report,* May 17, 60–62.

SCHULTZ, S. 2000. Talk to kids about drugs? Parents just don't do it. *U.S. News & World Report,* Feb. 7, 56–57.

SCHVANEVELDT, P. L., B. C. MILLER, E. H. BERRY, AND T. R. LEE. 2001. Academic goals, achievement, and age at first sexual intercourse: Longitudinal, bidirectional influences. *Adolescence* 36 (Winter): 767–87.

SCHWARTZ, D. J., V. PHARES, S. TANTLEFF-DUNN, AND J. K. THOMPSON. 1999. Devin body image, psychological functioning, and parental feedback regarding physical appearance. *International Journal of Eating Disorders* 25: 339–43.

SCHWARTZ, F. N. 1989. Management women and the new facts of life. *Harvard Business Review* 89 (Jan./Feb.): 65–76.

SCHWARTZ, M. J. 2000. *Born in bondage: Growing up enslaved in the antebellum South.* Cambridge, MA: Harvard University Press.

SCHWARTZ, P. 2006. *Finding your perfect match.* New York: Penguin.

SCHWEIGER, W. K., AND M. O'BRIEN. 2005. Special needs adoption: An ecological systems approach. *Family Relations* 54 (October): 512–22.

SCHWETTZER, M. M., ED. 1999. *American Indian grandmothers: Traditions and transitions.* Albuquerque: University of New Mexico Press.

SCOMMEGNA, P. 2002. Increased cohabitation changing children's family settings. *Population Today* 30 (Oct.): 3, 6.

SCOTT, D., AND B. WISHY, EDS. 1982. *America's families: A documentary history.* New York: Harper & Row.

SEAGER, J. 2003. *The Penguin atlas of women in the world.* New York: Penguin.

SECCOMBE, K. 2002. "Beating the odds" versus "changing the odds": Poverty, resilience, and family policy. *Journal of Marriage and Family* 64 (May): 384–94.

"Secret to wedded bliss." 2005. www.msnbc.com, June 1 (accessed June 3, 2006).

SEDLAK, A. J., D. Finkelhor, AND H. HAMMER. 2005. National estimates of children missing involuntarily or for benign reasons. U.S. Department of Justice, July, www.ncjrs.gov (accessed July 10, 2006).

SEDLAK, A. J., D. FINKELHOR, H. HAMMER, AND D. J. SCHULTZ. 2002. *National estimates of missing children: An overview.* Washington, DC: U.S. Department of Justice.

SEEMAN, T. E., B. H. SINGER, C. D. RYFF, G. D. LOVE, AND L. LEVY-STORMS. 2002. Social relationships, gender, and allostatic load across two age cohorts. *Psychosomatic Medicine* 64 (May/June) 395–406.

SEGAL, E. A. 2006. Welfare as we *should* know it: Social empathy and welfare reform. In *The promise of welfare reform: Political rhetoric and the reality of poverty in the twenty-first century,* eds. K. M. Kilty, and E. A. Segal, 265–74. New York: Haworth Press.

SEGAL, J. 1989. 10 myths about child development. *Parents* (July): 81–84, 87.

SEGAL, M. W. , AND J. J. HARRIS. 1993. *What we know about army families* (Special Report 21). Alexandria, VA: U.S. Army Research Institute for the Behavioral and Social Sciences.

SEGURA, D. A. 1994. Working at motherhood: Chicana and Mexican immigrant mothers and employment. In *Mothering: Ideology, experience, and agency,* eds. E. N. Glenn, G. Chang, and L. R. Forcey, 211–33. New York: Routledge.

SEIGEL, J. 2005. Fat chance. *New York Times,* May 15, A17.

SELTZER, J. A. 2004a. Cohabitation and family change. In *Handbook of contemporary families: Considering the past contemplating the future,* eds. M. Coleman and L. H. Ganong, 57–78. Thousand Oaks, CA: Sage.

SELTZER, J. A. 2004b. Cohabitation in the United States and Britain: Demography, kinship, and the future. *Journal of Marriage and Family* 66 (November): 921–28.

SHACKELFORD, T. K., A. T. GOETZ, D. M. BUSS, H. A. EULER, AND S. HOIER. 2005. When we hurt the ones we love: Predicting violence against women from men's mate retention. *Personal Relationships* 12 (December): 447–63.

SHADISH, W. R., AND S. A. BALDWIN. 2005. Effects of behavioral marital therapy: A meta-analysis of randomized controlled trials. *Journal of Consulting and Clinical Psychology* 73 (February): 6–14.

SHAKIR, E. 1997. *Bint Arab: Arab and Arab American women in the United States.* Westport, CT: Praeger.

SHANKMAN, P. 1996. The history of Samoan sexual conduct and the Mead-Freeman controversy. *American Anthropologist* 98 (3): 555–67.

SHAPIRO, B. J. 2004. The national Jewish population survey 2000–2001: Strength, challenge and diversity in the American Jewish population. United Jewish Communities, www.ujc.org (accessed September 11, 2006).

SHAPIRO, C. H. 2005. The infertile couple as an evolving family. *National Council on Family Relations Report* 50 (June): F15–16.

SHAPIRO, L. 1990. Guns and dolls. *Newsweek,* May 28, 57–65.

SHARIFZADEH, V.-S. 1997. Families with Middle Eastern roots. In *Developing cross-cultural competence: A guide for working with children and families,* eds. E. W. Lynch and M. J. Hanson, 441–82. Baltimore: Paul H. Brookes.

SHARMA, O. P. 2001. 2001 census results mixed for India's women and girls. *Population Today* 29 (May/June): 1–3.

SHATZKIN, K. 1996. Battered wife wants husband to keep job. *Baltimore Sun,* Dec. 7, A1, A4.

SHATZKIN, K. 2000. Perdue violated wage statute. *Baltimore Sun,* Feb. 29, C1.

SHATZKIN, K. 2004. Meeting of the minds. *Baltimore Sun,* June 6, 1N, 4N.

SHATZKIN, K. 2005. A twist in healthful benefits of marriage. *Baltimore Sun,* Nov 4, 1D-2D.

SHAVER, P., C. HAZAN, AND D. BRADSHAW. 1988. Love as attachment. In *The psychology of love,* eds. R. J. Sternberg and M. L. Barnes, 68–99. New Haven, CT: Yale University Press.

SHEA, J. A., AND G. R. ADAMS. 1984. Correlates of romantic attachment: A path analysis study. *Journal of Youth and Adolescence* 13 (1): 27–44.

SHELDON, K. M., A. J. ELLIOT, Y. KIM, AND T. KASSER. 2001. What is satisfying about satisfying events? Testing 10 candidate psychological needs. *Journal of Personality and Social Psychology* 80 (Feb.): 325–29.

SHENG, X. 2005. Chinese families. In *Handbook of world families,* eds. B. N. Adams and Jan Trost, 99–128. Thousand Oaks, CA: Sage.

SHENG, X. 2005. Chinese families. In *Handbook of world families,* eds. B. N. Adams and Jan Trost, 99–128. Thousand Oaks, CA: Sage.

SHERMAN, L. 1992. *Policing domestic violence: Experiment and dilemmas.* New York: Free Press.

SHEVELL, T., ET AL., 2005. Assisted reproductive technology and pregnancy outcome. *Obstetrics & Gynecology* 106 (November): 1039–45.

SHIMOMURA, M. 1990. Japan: Too much mommy-san. *New Perspectives Quarterly* 7 (Winter): 24–27.

SHIN, H. B., AND R. Bruno. 2003. Language use and English-speaking ability: 2000. U.S. Census Bureau, C2KBR, October, www.census.gov (accessed July 18, 2006).

SHINAGAWA, L. H., AND G. Y. PANG. 1996. Asian American panethnicity and intermarriage. *Amerasia Journal* 22 (Spring): 127–52.

SHIPLER, D. K. 2004. *The working poor: Invisible in America.* New York: Alfred A. Knopf.

SIDEL, R. 1998. *Keeping women and children last: America's war on the poor.* New York: Penguin.

SIEGEL, D. 2004. The new trophy wife. *Psychology Today* 37 (January/February): 52–58.

SIEGEL, S. 2005. Love notes for that "other" special someone. Gazette.net, May 18 (accessed May 20, 2006).

SIFAKIS, F., ET AL. 2005. HIV prevalence, unrecognized infection, and HIV testing among men who have sex with men—five U.S. cities, June 2004–April 2005. *JAMA* 294 (August 10): 674–76.

SILLIMAN, B., AND W. R. SCHUMM. 2000. Marriage preparation programs: A literature review. *The Family Journal: Counseling and Therapy for Couples and Families* 8 (Apr.): 133–42.

SILVER-GREENBERG, J. 2005. The color of "Charlie." *Newsweek,* Aug. 1, 12.

SILVERMAN, I. 2006. *I married my mother-in-law.* New York: Riverland.

SILVERMAN, J. G., A. RAJ, L. A. MUCCI, AND J. E. HATHAWAY. 2001. Dating violence against adolescent girls and associated substance use, unhealthy weight control, sexual risk behavior, pregnancy, and suicidality. *Journal of the American Medical Association* 286 (Aug. 1): 572–79.

SILVERMAN, P. R. 2000. *Never too young to know: Death in children's lives.* New York: Oxford University Press.

SILVERMAN, R. E. 2003. Provisions boost rights of couples living together. *Wall Street Journal,* Mar. 5, D1.

SILVERSTEIN, M., AND V. L. BENGSTON. 2001. Intergenerational solidarity and the structure of adult child-parent relationships in American families. In *Families in later life: Connections and transitions,* eds. A. J. Walker, M. Manoogian-O'Dell, L. A. McGraw, and D. L. G. White, 53–61. Thousand Oaks, CA: Pine Forge.

SIMMONS, A. M. 1998. Here beauty is measured in pounds. *Baltimore Sun,* Oct. 24, 2a.

SIMMONS, R. 2002. *Odd girl out: The hidden culture of aggression in girls.* New York: Harcourt.

SIMMONS, T. AND M. O'CONNELL. 2003. *Married-couple and unmarried-partner households: 2000.* Census 2000 Special Reports, CENSR-5. Washington, DC: U.S. Census Bureau.

SIMON, G. E., ET AL. 2006. Association between obesity and psychiatric disorders in the U.S. adult population. *Archives of General Psychiatry* 63 (July): 824–830.

SIMON, J. P. 1996. Lebanese families. In *Ethnicity and family therapy,* 2nd ed., eds. M. McGoldrick, J. Giordano, and J. K. Pearce, 364–75. New York: Guilford.

SIMON, R. J. 1993. *The case for transracial adoption.* Washington, DC: American University Press.

SIMON, R. J., AND H. ALTSTEIN. 2000. *Adoption across borders: Serving the children in transracial and intercountry adoptions.* Lanham, MD: Rowman & Littlefield.

SIMON, R. W. 2002. Revisiting the relationships among gender, marital status, and mental health. *American Journal of Sociology* 107 (January): 1065–1096.

SIMON, S. 2005. Parents cast fight as sexual vs. religious tolerance. *Los Angeles Times,* October 20, A14.

SIMONELLI, C. J., T. MULLIS, A. N. ELLIOTT, AND T. W. PIERCE. 2002. Abuse by siblings and subsequent experiences of violence within the dating relationship. *Journal of Interpersonal Violence* 17 (Feb.): 103–21.

SIMONS, R. L., C. JOHNSON, AND R. D. CONGER. 1994. Harsh corporal punishment versus quality of parental involvement as an explanation of adolescent maladjustment. *Journal of Marriage and the Family* 56 (Aug.): 591–607.

SIMPSON, S. 2006. Divorce can mean loss of job at university. *The Oklahoman,* January 11, www.newsok.com (accessed January 20, 2006).

SINGER, L. T., ET AL. 2002. Cognitive and motor outcomes of cocaine-exposed infants. *Journal of the American Medical Association* 287 (Apr. 17): 1952–60.

SINGH, J. P. 2005. The contemporary Indian family. In *Handbook of world families,* eds. B. N. Adams and J. Trost, 129–166. Thousand Oaks, CA: Sage.

SINGLETARY, M. 2005. Financial infidelity? *Washington Post,* Oct. 23, F1.

SINHA, G. 2004. The identity dance. *Psychology Today* 37 (March/April): 52–95.

SIWOLOP, S. 2002. In Web's divorce industry, bad (and good) advice. *New York Times.*

SKINNER, D. A., AND J. K. KOHLER. 2002. Parental rights in diverse family contexts: Current legal developments. *Family Relations* 51 (Oct.): 293–300.

SKOLNICK, A. 1991. *Embattled paradise: The American family in an age of uncertainty.* New York: Basic Books.

SMALL, S. A., AND D. KERNS. 1993. Unwanted sexual activity among peers during early and middle adolescence: Incidence and risk factors. *Journal of Marriage and the Family* 55 (Nov.): 941–52.

SMALLEY, S., AND B. BRAIKER. 2003. Suffer the children. *Newsweek,* Jan. 20, 32–33.

SMITH, C. A. 2005. Abduction, often violent, a Kyrgyz wedding rite. *New York Times* (April 30): A1.

SMITH, C. D. 1991. *The absentee American: Repatriates' perspectives on America and its place in the contemporary world.* Westport, CT: Praeger.

SMITH, C. S. 2002. Kandahar journal. Shh, it's an open secret: Warlords and pedophilia. *New York Times,* Feb. 21, A4.

SMITH, D. 2003. The older population in the United States: March 2002. U.S. Census Bureau, Current Population Reports, P20–546. www.census.gov (accessed Oct. 11, 2001).

SMITH, D. 2004. Black women ignore many of media's beauty ideals. Women's e-news, June 10, www.womensenews.org/article.cfm/dyn/aid/1865 (accessed December 1, 2005).

SMITH, D. M., AND G. GATES. 2001. Gay and lesbian families in the United States. The Urban Institute, August 22, www.urban.org/ (accessed March 4, 2006).

SMITH, K. 2000. Who's minding the kids: Child care arrangements: Fall 1995, Current Population Reports, P70–70. Washington, DC: U.S. Census Bureau.

SMITH, K., B. DOWNS, AND M. O'CONNELL. 2001. Maternity leave and employment patterns: 1961–1995. U.S. Census Bureau, Current Population Reports, P70–79. www.census.gov (accessed Sep. 10, 2003).

SMITH, M. C., L. R. VARTANIAN, N. DEFRATES-DENSCH, P. C. VAN LOON, AND S. LOCKE. 2003. Self-help books for parents of adolescents, 1980–1993. *Family Relations* 52 (Apr.): 174–79.

SMITH, P. K., AND L. M. DREW. 2002. Grandparenthood. In *Handbook of parenting,* 2nd ed., Vol. 3: *Being and becoming a parent,* ed. M. H. Bornstein, 141–72. Mahwah, NJ: Erlbaum.

SMITH, S. 2002. How the balancing act disadvantages women in the workplace. *Sociologists for Women in Society* 19 (Fall): 19–20.

SMITH, T. W. 1994. Can money buy you love? *Public Perspective* 5 (Jan./Feb.): 33–34.

SMITH, T. W. 1999. The emerging 21st century American family. www.norc.uchicago.edu (accessed Aug. 12, 2000).

SMITH, T. W. 2001. Ties that bind: The emerging 21st century American family. *Public Perspective* 12 (Jan./Feb.): 34–37.

SMITH, W. L. 1999. *Families and communes: An examination of nontraditional lifestyles.* Thousand Oaks, CA: Sage.

SMOCK, P. J. 2004. The wax and wane of marriage: Prospects for marriage in the 21st century. *Journal of Marriage and Family* 66 (November): 966–73.

SMOCK, P. J., W. D. MANNING, AND M. PORTER. 2005. "Everything's there except money": How money shapes decisions to marry among cohabitors. *Journal of Marriage and Family* 67 (August): 680–96.

SMOLAK, L., M. P. LEVINE, AND F SCHERMER. 1999. Parental input and weight concerns among elementary school children. *International Journal of Eating Disorders* 25: 263–71.

SNIPP, C. M. 2002. American Indians: Clues to the future of other racial groups. In *The new race question: How the census counts multiracial individuals,* eds. J. Perlmann and M. C. Waters, 189–214. New York: Russell Sage Foundation.

SNOWDON, D. 2001. *Aging with grace: What the nun study teaches us about leading longer, healthier, and more meaningful lives.* New York: Bantam.

SOARES, C. 2006. Women rethink a big size that is beautiful but brutal. *Christian Science Monitor,* July 11, 4.

SOCIAL SECURITY ADMINISTRATION. 2006. *Annual statistical supplement to the Social Security bulletin, 2005.* Washington, DC: U.S. Government Printing Office.

SOCIETY FOR ADOLESCENT MEDICINE. 2004. College students engage in "risky business," exposing themselves to the dangers of sexually transmitted diseases. Unpublished material provided by April Starling, Cohn & Wolfe, February 1, 2006.

SOLOMON, R. C. 2002. Reasons for love. *Journal for the Theory of Social Behaviour* 32 (Mar.): 1–28.

SOLOT, D., AND M. MILLER. 2002. *Unmarried to each other: The essential guide to living together as an unmarried couple.* New York: Marlowe & Company.

SOLTERO, J. M. 1996. *Inequality in the workplace: Underemployment among Mexicans, African Americans, and whites.* New York: Garland.

SOMERS, M. D. 1993. A comparison of voluntarily childfree adults and parents. *Journal of Marriage and the Family.* 55 (Aug.): 643–50.

SOMMERS, C. H. 2000. *The war against boys: How misguided feminism is harming our young men.* New York: Simon & Schuster.

SONFIELD, A. 2004. New refusal clauses shatter balance between provider "conscience," patient needs. The Guttmacher Report on Public Policy, August, www.guttmacher.org (accessed May 1, 2006).

SONG, J. 2003. Lavish ceremony escorts a Latina into womanhood. *Baltimore Sun* (July 18): 1A, 8A.

SONTAG, D. 2002. Fierce entanglements. *New York Times Magazine,* Nov. 17, 52.

SORENSEN, E., AND C. ZIBMAN. 2000. Child support offers some protection against poverty. Washington, DC: Urban Institute. newfederalism .urban.org (accessed Oct. 21, 2000).

SORIANO, C. G. 2006. "Bored" by her kids, she's getting it full-bore. *USA Today,* July 31, www.usatoday.com (accessed August 3, 2006).

SOUKUP, E. 2005. Happy-V-Day! (Just not in Pittsburgh.) *Newsweek,* February 14, 11.

SOUTH, S. J., K. D. CROWDER, AND K. TRENT. 1998. Children's residential mobility and neighborhood environment following parental divorce and remarriage. *Social Forces* 77: 667–93.

SPAKE, A. 1998. Adoption gridlock. *U.S. News & World Report,* June 22, 30–37.

SPEARS, G. 1994. Estate-planning musts for blended families. *Kiplinger's Personal Finance Magazine* 48 (Dec.): 91–96.

SPENCER, R. F., AND J. D. JENNINGS. 1977. *The Native Americans: Ethnology and backgrounds of the North American Indians.* New York: Harper & Row.

SPIEKER, S. J., N. C. LARSON, AND L. GILCHRIST. 1999. Developmental trajectories of disruptive behavior problems in preschool children of adolescent mothers. *Child Development* 70 (Mar.): 443–58.

SPITZE, G., J. R. LOGAN, G. DEANE, AND S. ZERGER. 1994. Adult children's divorce and intergenerational relationships. *Journal of Marriage and the Family* 56 (May): 279–93.

SPRECHER, S. 1999. "I love you more today than yesterday": Romantic partners' perceptions of changes in love and related affect over time. *Journal of Personality and Social Psychology* 76 (Jan.): 46–53.

SPRECHER, S. 2001. Equity and social exchange in dating couples: Associations with satisfaction, commitment, and stability. *Journal of Marriage and Family* 63 (Aug.): 509–613.

SPRECHER, S., AND K. MCKINNEY. 1993. *Sexuality.* Thousand Oaks, CA: Sage.

SQUIER, D. A., AND J. S. QUADAGNO. 1988. The Italian American family. In *Ethnic families in America: Patterns and variations,* 3rd ed., eds. C. J. Mindel, R. W. Habenstein, and R. Wright, Jr., 109–37. New York: Elsevier.

SRINIVASAN, P., AND G. R. LEE. 2004. The dowry system in northern India: Women's attitudes and social change. *Journal of Marriage and Family* 66 (December): 1108–17.

SRIVASTAVA, S., O. P. JOHN, S. D. GOSLING, AND J. POTTER. 2003. Development of personality in early and middle adulthood: Set like plaster or persistent change? *Journal of Personality and Social Psychology* 84 (May): 1041–53.

ST. JEAN, Y., AND J. R. FEAGIN. 1998. *Double burden: Black women and everyday racism.* Armonk, NY: M.E. Sharpe.

STACEY, J. 2003. Gay and lesbian families: Queer like us. In *All our families: New policies for a new century,* 2nd ed., eds. M. A. Mason, A. Skolnick, and S. D. Sugarman, 144–69. New York: Oxford University Press.

STACEY, J., AND T. J. BIBLARZ. 2001. (How) does the sexual orientation of parents matter? *American Sociological Review* 66 (Apr.): 159–83.

STALKING. 2005. National Crime Victims' Rights Week, April 10–16, www.ojp.gov (accessed January 9, 2006).

STANLEY, S. M., AND G. SMALLEY. 2005. *The power of commitment: A guide to active, lifelong love.* San Francisco, CA: Jossey-Bass.

STANLEY, S. M., H. J. MARKMAN, AND S. W. WHITTON. 2002. Communication, conflict, and commitment: Insights on the foundations of relationship success from a national survey. *Family Process* 41 (Winter): 659–75.

STANNARD, D. E. 1979. Changes in the American family: Fiction and reality. In *Changing images of the family,* eds. V. Tufte and B. Myerhoff, 83–98. New Haven, CT: Yale University Press.

STAPLES, R. 1988. The black American family. In *Ethnic families in America: Patterns and variations,* 3rd ed., eds. C. H. Mindel, R. W. Habenstein, and R. Wright, Jr., 303–24. New York: Elsevier.

STARK, M. 1998. *What no one tells the bride.* New York: Hyperion.

STARR, A. 2001. Shotgun weddings by Uncle Sam? *Business Week,* June 4, 68.

State of the world's mothers 2003: Protecting women and children in war and conflict. 2003. Save the Children. www.savethechildren.org (accessed May 25, 2003).

"Stats & facts: Love and money." 2005. *Redbook,* November, http://lawyers.com/lawyers/ (accessed April 14, 2006).

STAUSS, J. H. 1995. Reframing and refocusing American Indian family strengths. In *American families: Issues in race and ethnicity,* ed. C. K. Jacobson, 105–18. New York: Garland.

STEIL, J. M. 1997. *Marital equality: Its relationship to the well-being of husbands and wives.* Thousand Oaks, CA: Sage.

STEIN, P. J., ED. 1981. *Single life: Unmarried adults in social context.* New York: St. Martin's.

STEIN, R. 2003. More parents bring baby to bed. *Washington Post,* Jan. 14, A11.

STEINBERG, L., AND J. S. SILK. 2002. Parenting adolescents. In *Handbook of parenting,* 2nd ed., Vol. 1: *Children and parenting,* ed. M. H. Bornstein, 103–33. Mahwah, NJ: Erlbaum.

STEINBERG, L., AND R. M. LERNER. 2004. The scientific study of adolescence: A brief history. *Journal of Early Adolescence* 24 (February): 45–54.

STEINDORF, S. 2002. Women make the team, but less often coach it. *Christian Science Monitor,* Mar. 12, 13, 16.

STEINMETZ, S. 1978. The battered husband syndrome. *Victimology* 2 (3/4): 499–509.

STENSON, J. 2002. Morning-after pill not offered in many U.S. rape cases. Yahoo! News, May 6. http:/ /story.news.yahoo.com (accessed June 12, 2003).

STEPP, L. S. 2003. Sex in high school and college: What's love got to do with it? *Washington Post,* Jan. 19, F1.

STERK-ELIFSON, C. 1994. Sexuality among African-American women. In *Sexuality across the life course,* ed. A. S. Rossi, 99–126. Chicago: University of Chicago Press.

STERNBERG, R. J. 1986. A triangular theory of love. *Psychological Review* 93 (2): 119–35.

STERNBERG, R. J. 1988. *The triangle of love.* New York: Basic Books.

STERNBERG, S. 2005. HIV striking more women in South. *USA Today,* June 14, www.usatoday.com (accessed June 15, 2005).

STEVENS, D., G. KIGER, AND P. J. RILEY. 2001. Working hard and hardly working: Domestic labor and marital satisfaction among dual-earner couples. *Journal of Marriage and Family* 63 (May): 514–26.

STEWART, S. D. 1999. Nonresident mothers' and fathers' social contact with children. *Journal of Marriage and the Family* 61 (Nov.): 894–907.

STEWART, S. D. 2003. Nonresident parenting and adolescent adjustment. *Journal of Family Issues* 24 (Mar.): 217–44.

STEWART, S. D. 2005. How the birth of a child affects involvement with stepchildren. *Journal of Marriage and Family* 67 (May): 461–473.

STIEHM, J. 1997. Marriage long-distance style. *Baltimore Sun,* July 7, 1A, 6A.

STILLARS, A. L. 1991. Behavioral observation. In *Studying interpersonal interaction,* eds. B. M. Montgomery and S. Duck, 197–218. New York: Guilford.

STINNETT, N., AND J. DEFRAIN. 1985. *Secrets of strong families.* Boston: Little, Brown.

STOCKEL, H. H. 1991. *Women of the Apache nation.* Reno: University of Nevada Press.

STOLZENBERG, R. M. 2001. It's about time and gender: Spousal employment and health. *American Journal of Sociology* 107 (July): 61–100.

STONE, L., AND N. P. MCKEE. 2002. *Gender and culture in America,* 2nd ed. Upper Saddle River, NJ: Prentice Hall.

STOOPS, N. 2004. "Educational attainment in the United States: 2003." U.S. Census Bureau, Current Population Reports, P20-550, www.census .gov (accessed December 7, 2004).

STOUT, H. 2005. Family matters: Singles therapy. *Wall Street Journal* (April 28): D1.

STRAIT, S. C. 1999. Drug use among Hispanic youth: Examining common and unique contributing factors. *Hispanic Journal of Behavioral Sciences* 21 (Feb.): 89–103.

STRASBURGER, V. C. AND B. J. WILSON. 2002. *Children, adolescents, & the media.* Thousand Oaks, CA: Sage.

STRASSER, J. 2004. *Black eye: Escaping a marriage, writing a life.* Madison: University of Wisconsin Press.

STRATTON, J. L. 1981. *Pioneer women: Voices from the Kansas frontier.* New York: Simon & Schuster.

STRAUCH, B. 2003. *The primal teen: What the new discoveries about the teenage brain tell us about our kids.* New York: Doubleday.

STRAUS, M. A. 2006. Dominance and symmetry in partner violence by male and female university students in 32 nations. Paper presented at conference on Trends in Intimate Violence Intervention, New York University, May 23.

STRAUS, M. A., AND C. J. FIELD. 2003. Psychological aggression by American parents: National data on prevalence, chronicity, and severity. *Journal of Marriage and Family* 65 (November): 795–808.

STRAUS, M. A., AND C. L. YODANIS. 1996. Corporal punishment in adolescence and physical assaults on spouses in later life: What accounts for the link? *Journal of Marriage and the Family* 58 (Nov.): 825–41.

STRAUS, M. A., AND J. H. STEWART. 1999. Corporal punishment by American parents: National data on prevalence, chronicity, severity, and duration, in relation to child and family characteristics. *Clinical Child and Family Psychology Review* 2 (June): 55–70.

STRAUS, M. A., ED. 2001. *Beating the devil out of them: Corporal punishment in American families and its effects on children,* 2nd ed. Somerset, NJ: Transaction Publishers.

STRAZDINS, L., M. S. CLEMENTS, R. J. KORDA, D. H. BROOM, AND R. M. D'SOUZA. 2006. Unsociable work? Nonstandard work schedules, family relationships, and children's well-being. *Journal of Marriage and Family* 68 (May): 393–410.

STREISAND, B. 2006. Who's your daddy? *U.S. News & World Report,* Feb. 13, 53–56.

STRIEGEL-MOORE, R. H., ET AL. 2003. Eating disorders in white and black women. *American Journal of Psychiatry* 160 (July): 1326–31.

"Striving to keep up appearances." 2006. *Baltimore Sun,* March 2, 11A.

STROCK, M. 2002. Depression. National Institutes of Mental Health. www.nimh.nih.gov (accessed Oct. 9, 2003).

STROHSCHEIN, L. 2005. Parental divorce and child mental health trajectories. *Journal of Marriage and Family* 67 (December): 1286–1300.

STRUPP, J. 2002. Study: Fewer women hold top editor jobs. Associated Press, Sep. 18. www.editorandpublisher.com (accessed Sep. 20, 2002).

"Students." 2005. Almanac issue 2005–6. *Chronicle of Higher Education* 52 (August): 18.

"Students." 2006. *Chronicle of Higher Education, Almanac Issue 2006-7* 53 (August 25): 19.

Substance Abuse and Mental Health Services Administration. 2005. *Results from the 2004 National Survey on Drug Use and Health: National Findings.* Rockville, MD: Office of Applied Studies.

Substance use during pregnancy: 2002 and 2003 update. 2005. Office of Applied Studies, Substance Abuse and Mental Health Services Administration, http://oas.samhsa.gov (accessed May 1, 2006).

SUGG, D. K. 2000. Subtle signs of heart disease in women are often missed. *Baltimore Sun,* Jan. 25, 1A, 13A.

SUGGS, W. 2001. Top jobs in college sports still go largely to white men, study finds. *Chronicle of Higher Education,* Aug. 3, A42.

Suicide and suicidal behavior. 2000. National Center for Injury Prevention and Control. www.cdc.gov (accessed Oct. 19, 2003).

"Suicide: Fact Sheet." 2006. Centers for Disease Control and Prevention, www.cdc.gov (accessed June 25, 2006).

SULLIVAN, J. 2006. The *Cupid index. Christian Science Monitor* (February 14): 20.

SUM, A., N. FOGG, AND P. HARRINGTON. 2002. Immigrant workers and the great American job machine: The contributions of new foreign immigration to national and regional labor force growth in the 1990s. Prepared for National Business Roundtable, Washington, DC. www .nupr.neu.edu/ (accessed Apr. 12, 2003).

Summary of recent studies on the wage gap between men and women professors. 2000. American Association of University Professors, Washington, DC. www.aaup.org (accessed Oct. 15, 2000).

SUN, Y. 2001. Family environment and adolescents' well-being before and after parents' marital disruption: A longitudinal analysis. *Journal of Marriage and Family* 63 (Aug.): 697–713.

SUN, Y., AND Y. LI. 2002. Children's well-being during parents' marital disruption process: A pooled time-series analysis. *Journal of Marriage and Family* 64 (May): 472–88.

SURO, R. 1998. *Strangers among us: How Latino immigration is transforming America.* New York: Knopf.

SUTTON, C. T., AND M. A. BROKEN NOSE. 1996. American Indian families: An overview. In *Ethnicity and family therapy,* 2nd ed., eds. M. McGoldrick, J. Giordano, and J. K. Pearce, 31–54. New York: Guilford.

SWAN, S. H., E. P. ELKIN, AND L. FENSTER. 1997. Have sperm densities declined? A reanalysis of global trend data. *Environmental Health Perspectives* 105 (Nov.): 1228–33.

SWANBERG, J. E. 2005. Job-family role strain among low-wage workers. *Journal of Family and Economic Issues* 26 (Spring): 143–58.

SWANBERG, J. E., AND T. K. LOGAN. 2003. Intimate partner violence and employment: A qualitative study of rural and urban women. *Family Focus* (Mar.): F8–F9.

SWEENEY, M. M., AND J. A. PHILLIPS. 2004. Understanding racial differences in marital disruption: Recent trends and explanations. *Journal of Marriage and Family* 66 (August): 639–650.

SWIFT, E. K., ED. 2002. *Mental health: Culture, race, and ethnicity. A supplement to mental health: A report of the surgeon general.* Rockville, MD: U.S. Department of Health and Human Services.

SWINFORD, S. P., A. DEMARIS, S. A. CERNKOVICH, AND P. G. GIORDANO. 2000. Harsh physical discipline in childhood and violence in later romantic involvements: The mediating role of problem behaviors. *Journal of Marriage and the Family* 62 (May): 508–19.

SYMONDS, W. C., AND J. HEMPEL. 2004. The gay marriage dividend. *Business Week,* May 24, 50.

SZEGEDY-MASZAK, M. 1993. Dating passages. *New Woman* 23 (Mar.): 85–88.

SZINOVACZ, M. E., AND A. DAVEY. 2005. Retirement and marital decision making effects on retirement satisfaction. *Journal of Marriage and Family* 67 (May): 387–398.

SZINOVACZ, M. E., ED. 1998. *Handbook on grandparenthood.* Westport, CT: Greenwood.

SZYMANSKI, L. A., A. S. DEVLIN, J. C. CHRISLER, AND S. A. VYSE. 1993. Gender role and attitudes toward rape in male and female college students. *Sex Roles* 29 (1/2): 37–57.

TAKAGI, D. Y. 2002. Japanese American families. In *Minority families in the United States: A multicultural perspective,* 3rd ed., ed. R. L. Taylor, 164–80. Upper Saddle River, NJ: Prentice Hall.

TALVI, S. J. A. 2002. "Deadbeat" dads—or just "dead broke"? *Christian Science Monitor,* Feb. 4, 20.

TAM, V. C.-W., AND D. F. DETZNER. 1998. Grandparents as a family resource in Chinese-American families: Perceptions of the middle generation. In *Resiliency in Native American and immigrant families,* eds. H. I. McCubbin, E. A. Thompson, A. I. Thompson, and J. E. Fromer, 243–64. Thousand Oaks, CA: Sage.

TAMARACK, L. I. 1986. Fifty myths and facts about incest. In *Sexual abuse of children in the 1980s: Ten essays and an annotated bibliography,* ed. B. Schlesinger. Buffalo, NY: University of Toronto Press.

TAN, A. L. 2004. *Chinese American children & families: A guide for educators & service providers.* Olney, MD: Association for Childhood Education International.

TANNEN, D. 1990. *You just don't understand: Women and men in conversation.* New York: Ballantine.

TANNEN, D. 1994. *Talking 9 to 5: Women and men at work.* New York: Quill.

TANUR, J. M. 1994. The trustworthiness of survey research. *Chronicle of Higher Education,* May 25, B1–B3.

TATARA, T. 1998. *The national elder abuse incidence study.* The National Center on Elder Abuse and the American Public Humane Services Association. www.aoa.gov (accessed Oct. 19, 2000).

TAVRIS, C. 1992. *The mismeasure of woman.* New York: Simon & Schuster.

TAVRIS, C. 2002. Are girls really as mean as books say they are? *Chronicle of Higher Education,* July 5, B7–B9.

TAVRIS, C. 2003. Mind games: Psychological warfare between therapists and scientists. *Chronicle of Higher Education,* Feb. 28, B7–B9.

TAYLOR, P., C. FUNK, AND P. CRAIGHILL. 2006a. Are we happy yet? Pew Research Center, February 13, http://pewresearch.org (accessed June 14, 2006).

TAYLOR, P., C. FUNK, AND P. CRAIGHILL. 2006b. Once again, the future ain't what it used to be. Pew Research Center May 2, http:pewresearch.org (accessed May 10, 2006).

TAYLOR, R. L. 2002. Minority families and social change. In *Minority families in the United States: A multicultural perspective,* 3rd ed., ed. R. L. Taylor, 252–300. Upper Saddle River, NJ: Prentice Hall.

TAZ, V. 2005. Not dead yet. *Chronicle of Higher Education,* October 28, C1, C4.

TEACHMAN, J. D. 2002. Childhood living arrangements and the intergenerational transmission of divorce. *Journal of Marriage and Family* 64 (Aug.): 717–29.

TEACHMAN, J. D. 2003. Premarital sex, premarital cohabitation, and the risk of subsequent marital dissolution among women. *Journal of Marriage and Family* 65 (May): 444–55.

TEACHMAN, J. D., K. PAASCH, AND K. CARVER. 1996. Social capital and dropping out of school early. *Journal of Marriage and the Family* 58 (Aug.): 773–83.

TEASTER, P. B. ET AL. 2006. The 2004 survey of state adult protective services: Abuse of adults 60 years of age and older. National Center on Elder Abuse, February, www.elderabusecenter.org (accessed June 6, 2006).

TELLEEN, S., S. MAHER, and R. C. PESCE. 2003. Building community connections for youth to reduce violence. *Psychology in the Schools* 40 (September): 549–63.

TENENBAUM, H. R., AND C. LEAPER. 2003. Parent-child conversations about science: The socialization of gender inequities? *Developmental Psychology* 39 (Jan.): 34–47.

TERESI, D. 1994. How to get a man pregnant. *New York Times Magazine,* Nov. 27, 54–55.

TERGESEN, A. 2001. Cutting the knot—but not the benefits. *Business Week,* July 16, 87–88.

TERGESEN, A. 2003. Take the boys. *Business Week,* Apr. 23, 105.

TERZIEFF, J. 2002. Pakistan's fiery shame: Women die in stove deaths. *Women's E-News,* Nov. 1. www.womensenews.org (accessed Nov. 3, 2002).

TERZIEFF, J. 2006. New law puts brakes on international bride brokers. Women's e-news, March 8, www.womensenews.com (accessed March 12, 2006).

TESORIERO, H. W. 2002. "Without this ring. . . ." *Time,* Mar. 16, F9–F10.

TESSIER, M. 2003. Sexual assault pervasive in military, experts say. *Women's E-News.* www .womensenews.org (accessed Apr. 6, 2003).

THERNSTROM, M. 2005. The new arranged marriage. *New York Times Magazine,* Feb. 13, 35–41, 72–78.

THOMAS, A. J., AND S. L. SPEIGHT, 1999. Racial identity and racial socialization attitudes of African American parents. *Journal of Black Psychology* 25 (May): 152–70.

THOMAS, W. I., AND F. ZNANIECKI. 1927. *The Polish peasant in Europe and America,* vol. 2. New York: Knopf. (Originally published 1918 by the University of Chicago Press.)

THOMAS-LESTER, A. 1994. Carrying on: A joyless time for the grieving. *Washington Post,* Dec. 15, D5.

THOMPSON, K. M., AND F. YOKOTA. 2004. Violence, sex, and profanity in films: Correlation of movie ratings with content. *Medscape General Medicine* 6 (3): 1–19.

THOMPSON, L., AND A. J. WALKER. 1991. Gender in families. In *Contemporary families: Looking forward, looking back,* ed. A. Booth, 76–102. Minneapolis: National Council on Family Relations.

THOMPSON, P. M., ET AL. 2003. Dynamics of gray matter loss in Alzheimer's disease. *Journal of Neuroscience* 23 (Feb. 1): 994–1005.

THOMPSON, P., ET AL. 2005. Thinning of the cerebral cortex visualized in HIV/AIDS reflects CD4+T lymphocyte decline. *Proceeding of the National Academy of Sciences* 102 (October 25): 15647–52.

THOMPSON, R. S., ET AL. 2006. Intimate partner violence: Prevalence, types, and chronicity in adult women. *American Journal of Preventive Medicine* 30 (June): 447–57.

THOMSON, E. 1997. Couple childbearing desires, intentions, and births. *Demography* 34 (Aug.): 343–54.

THORNBERRY, T. P., C. A. SMITH, C. RIVERA, D. HUIZINGA, AND M. STOUTHAMER-LOEBER. 1999. *Family disruption and delinquency.* Washington, DC: U.S. Department of Justice, Office of Justice Programs, Office of Juvenile Justice and Delinquency Prevention.

THORNTON, A. 2001. The developmental paradigm, reading history sideways, and family change *Demography* 38 (Nov.): 449–65.

THORNTON, A., AND L. YOUNG-DEMARCO. 2001. Four decades in attitudes toward family issues in the United States: The 1960s through the 1990s. *Journal of Marriage and the Family* 63 (Nov.): 1009–37.

THORNTON, E. 1994. Video dating in Japan. *Fortune,* Jan. 24, 12.

TICHENOR, V. J. 2005. *Earning more and getting less: Why successful wives can't buy equality.* New Brunswick, NJ: Rutgers University Press.

TIMBERLAKE, C. A., AND W. D. CARPENTER. 1990. Sexuality attitudes of black adults. *Family Relations* 39 (January): 87–91.

TIMMER, S. G., AND T. L. ORBUCH. 2001. The links between premarital parenthood, meanings of marriage, and marital outcomes. *Family Relations* 50 (Apr.): 178–85.

TJADEN, P., AND N. THOENNES. 2000. *Extent, nature, and consequences of intimate partner violence: Findings from the National Violence against Women Survey.* Washington, DC: U.S. Department of Justice, Office of Justice Programs.

TJADEN, P., AND N. THOENNES. 2006. *Extent, nature, and consequences of rape victimization: Findings from the national violence against women survey.* Washington, DC: U.S. Department of Justice, Office of Justice Programs.

TODER, E. J. 2004. What will happen to poverty rates among older Americans in the future and why? The Urban Institute, November, www.urban.org (accessed August 16, 2006).

TOHID, O. 2003. Pakistanis abroad trick daughters into marriage. *Christian Science Monitor,* May 15, 1, 7.

TOLIVER, S. D. 1998. *Black families in corporate America.* Thousand Oaks, CA: Sage.

TOOSSI, M. 2005. Labor force projections to 2014: Retiring boomers. *Monthly Labor Review* 128 (November): 25–44.

TORO-MORN, M. I. 1998. The family and work experiences of Puerto Rican women migrants in Chicago. In *Resiliency in Native American and immigrant families,* eds. H. I. McCubbin, E. A. Thompson, A. I. Thompson, and J. E. Fromer, 277–94. Thousand Oaks, CA: Sage.

TORRES, B. 2005. Affairs are bad business. *Baltimore Sun* (March 8): 5A.

TOTH, J. F., AND X. XU. 1999. Ethnic and cultural diversity in fathers' involvement: A racial/ethnic comparison of African American, Hispanic, and white fathers. *Youth & Society* 31 (Sep.): 76–99.

TOTH, J. F., AND X. XU. 2002, Fathers' child-rearing involvement in African American, Latino, and white families. In *Contemporary ethnic families in the United States: Characteristics, variations, and dynamics,* ed. N. V. Benokraitis, 130–40. Upper Saddle River, NJ: Prentice Hall.

TOWER, R. B., S. V. KASL, AND A. S. DAREFSKY. 2002. Types of marital closeness and mortality risk in older couples. *Psychosomatic Medicine* 64: 644–59.

TRAFFORD, A. 2005. Grandparents help define family values. *Washington Post,* March 1, HE6.

TRAVIS, R., AND V. KOHLI. 1995. The birth order factor: Ordinal position, social strata, and educational achievement. *Journal of Social Psychology* 135 (Aug.): 499–508.

TREAS, J. 2004. Sex and family: Changes and challenges. In *The Blackwell companion to the sociology of the family,* eds. J. Scott, J. Treas, and M. Richards, 397–415. Malden, MA: Blackwell.

TREAS, J., AND D. GIESEN. 2000. Sexual infidelity among married and cohabiting Americans. *Journal of Marriage and the Family* 62 (Feb.): 48–60.

TRIMBLE, J. E., AND B. MEDICINE. 1993. Diversification of American Indians: Forming an indigenous perspective. In *Indigenous psychologies,* eds. U. Kim and J. W. Berry, 133–51. Newbury Park, CA: Sage.

TROST, J., AND I. LEVIN. 2005. Scandinavian families. In *Handbook of world families,* eds. Bert N. Adams and Jan Trost, 347–363. Thousand Oaks, CA: Sage.

TROTTER, R. J. 1986. Failing to find the father-infant bond. *Psychology Today* (Feb.): 18.

TROUNSON, R., AND N. WRIDE. 2005. USC student charged in infant's death. *Los Angeles Times,* October 14, www.latimes.com (accessed October 15, 2005).

TRUMBULL, D. A., AND D. RAVENEL. 1999. Spare the rod? New research challenges spanking critic. *Family Policy,* Family Research Council, Jan. 22.

TRUMBULL, M. 1995. Demographics, computers multiply Asian-language media in the U.S. *Christian Science Monitor,* July 24, 13.

TRUMBULL, M. 2005. Waning era of the middle-class factory job. *Christian Science Monitor,* December 8, 1, 4.

TSAI, G., AND J. GRAY. 2000. The eating disorders inventory among Asian American college women. *Journal of Social Psychology* 140 (Aug.): 527–29.

TSAI, J. L., D. E. PRZYMUS, AND J. L. BEST. 2002. Toward an understanding of Asian American interracial marriage and dating. In *Inside the American couple: New thinking/new challenges,* eds. M. Yalom and L. L. Carstensen, 189–210. Berkeley: University of California Press.

TUCKER, K. L., J. HALLFRISCH, N. QIAO, D. MULLER, R. ANDRES, AND J. L. FLEG. 2005. The combination of high fruit and vegetable and low saturated fat intakes is more protective against mortality in aging men than is either alone: The Baltimore longitudinal study of aging. *Journal of Nutrition* 135 (March): 556–61.

TUCKER, R. K. 1992. Men's and women's ranking of thirteen acts of romance. *Psychological Reports* 71: 640–42.

TURETSKY, V. 2005. The child support program: An investment that works. Center for Law and Social Policy, July, www.clasp.org (accessed July 8, 2006).

TURETSKY, V. 2006. Families will lose at least $8.4 billion in uncollected child support if Congress cuts funds—and could lose billions more. Center for Law and Social Policy, January 18, www.clasp.org/ (accessed July 10, 2006).

TURNBULL, S. K., AND J. M. TURNBULL. 1983. To dream the impossible dream: An agenda for discussion with stepparents. *Family Relations* 32: 227–30.

TUROW, J., AND L. NIR. 2000. *The Internet and the family 2000: The view from parents, the view from kids.* Annenberg Public Policy Center, University of Pennsylvania. http://appcpenn.org (accessed Aug. 13, 2000).

TURRISI, R., J. JACCARD, R. TAKI, H. DUNNAM, AND J. GRIMES. 2001. Examination of the short-term efficacy of a parent intervention to reduce college students' drinking tendencies. *Psychology of Addictive Behaviors* 15 (December): 366–72.

TUTTLE, W. M., JR. 1993. *Daddy's gone to war: The Second World War in the lives of America's children.* New York: Oxford University Press.

TWENGE, J. M., W. K. CAMPBELL, AND C. A. FOSTER. 2003. Parenthood and marital satisfaction: A meta-analytic review. *Journal of Marriage and Family* 65 (Aug.): 574–83.

TWENGE, J., AND W. CAMPBELL. 2003. "Isn't it fun to get the respect that we're going to deserve?" Narcissism, social rejection, and aggression. *Personality and Social Psychology Bulletin* 29 (2): 261–72.

TYRE, P., AND D. McGINN. 2003. She works, he doesn't. *Newsweek,* May 12, 45–52.

TYRE, P., J. SCELFO, AND B. KANTROWITZ. 2004. The power of no. *Newsweek,* September 13, 41–51.

TYSZKOWA, M. 1993. Adolescents' relationships with grandparents: Characteristics and developmental transformations. In *Adolescence and its social worlds,* eds. S. Jackson and H. Rodriguez-Tomé, 121–43. East Sussex, UK: Erlbaum.

TZENG, O. C. S. 1993. *Measurement of love and intimate relations: Theories, scales, and applications for love development, maintenance, and dissolution.* Westport, CT: Praeger.

"The big picture." 2000. *Business Week,* Mar. 20, 10.

"The content of federally funded abstinence-only education programs." 2004. United States House of Representatives. Committee on Government Reform—Minority staff, December, www.democrats .reform.house.gov (accessed January 20, 2006).

"The ties that bind." 2000. *Public Perspective* 11 (May/June): 10.

TUMULTY, K. 2006. Where the real action is. . . *Time,* Jan. 30, 50–53.

TYRE, P. 2005. Seek and you may find. *Newsweek,* Aug. 1, 49.

U.S. BUREAU OF LABOR STATISTICS. 2005a. Employed and unemployed full- and part-time workers by age, sex, race, and Hispanic or Latino ethnicity. *Employment and Earnings,* Table 8, www.bls.gov (accessed May 10, 2006).

U.S. BUREAU OF LABOR STATISTICS. 2005b. *Women in the labor force: A databook.* www.bls.gov (accessed June 1, 2006).

U.S. BUREAU OF LABOR STATISTICS. 2005c. Workers on flexible and shift schedules in May 2004. July 1, www.bls.gov (accessed June 2, 2006).

U.S. CENSUS BUREAU. 2001. Households by type and size. Current Population Survey. www.census.gov (accessed Apr. 22, 2003).

U.S. CENSUS BUREAU. 2002. *Statistical abstract of the United States: 2002.* Washington, DC: U.S. Government Printing Office.

U.S. CENSUS BUREAU. 2003. Detailed list of languages spoken at home for the population 5 years and over by state: 2000. www.census.gov (accessed Apr. 22, 2003).

U.S. CENSUS BUREAU. 2005. Current Population Survey, Annual Social and Economic Supplement, detailed tables. http://pubdb3.census.gov (accessed August 2, 2006).

U.S. CENSUS BUREAU. 2005. Historical income tables. www.census.gov (accessed June 7, 2006).

U.S. CENSUS BUREAU. 2005A. Unmarried and single Americans week. Facts for Features, www.census .gov/Press-Release/ (accessed May 1, 2006).

U.S. CENSUS BUREAU. 2006. *Parents and children in stay-at-home parent family groups:* 1994 to present. Current Population Survey, May 25, Table SHP-1, www.census.gov (accessed May 14, 2006).

U.S. CENSUS BUREAU. 2006. *Statistical abstract of the United States: 2006* (125th edition). Washington, DC: U.S. Government Printing Office.

U.S. CENSUS BUREAU. 2006. *Women-owned firms: 2002.* Washington, DC: U. S. Government Printing Office.

U.S. CENSUS BUREAU NEWS. 2006. Older Americans month: May 2006. www.census.gov (accessed July 10, 2006).

U.S. DEPARTMENT OF COMMERCE. 1993. *We the American foreign born.* U.S. Bureau of the Census. Washington, DC: U.S. Government Printing Office.

U.S. COMMISSION ON CIVIL RIGHTS. 1984. *Comparable worth: Issues for the '80s,* Vol. 1. Washington, DC: U.S. Government Printing Office.

U.S. CONSUMER PRODUCT SAFETY COMMISSION. 2001. *Home playground equipment-related deaths and injuries.* Washington, DC. www.cpsc.gov (accessed Aug. 27, 2003).

U.S. DEPARTMENT OF DEFENSE. 2005. *Report of the defense task force on sexual harassment and violence at the military service academies.* Washington, DC: U.S. Government Printing Office.

U.S. DEPARTMENT OF EDUCATION. 2004. "Degrees and other formal awards conferred" surveys. National Center for Education Statistics, http://nces.ed.gov (accessed December 4, 2005).

U.S. DEPARTMENT OF EDUCATION. 2005. *Digest of Education Statistics,* National Center for Education Statistics, http://nces.ed.gov (accessed August 8, 2006).

U.S. DEPARTMENT OF HEALTH AND HUMAN SERVICES. 1996. *National Center on Child Abuse and Neglect. Third national incidence study of child abuse and neglect: Final report* (NIS-3). Washington, DC: U.S. Government Printing Office.

U.S. DEPARTMENT OF HEALTH AND HUMAN SERVICES. 2004. *Child health USA 2004.* Rockville, MD: U.S. Department of Health and Human Services.

U.S. DEPARTMENT OF HEALTH AND HUMAN SERVICES. 2006. Teen chat: A guide to discussing healthy relationships. http://4Parents.gov (accessed September 22, 2006).

U.S. DEPARTMENT OF HEALTH AND HUMAN SERVICES, ADMINISTRATION ON CHILDREN, YOUTH AND FAMILIES. 2006. *Child maltreatment 2004.* Washington, DC: U.S. Government Printing Office.

U.S. DEPARTMENT OF HOMELAND SECURITY, OFFICE OF IMMIGRATION STATISTICS. *2005 Yearbook of Immigration Statistics.* www.uscis.gov (accessed August 3, 2006).

U.S. DEPARTMENT OF JUSTICE. 2001. *Stalking and domestic violence: Report to Congress.* Washington, DC: Government Printing Office.

U.S. DEPARTMENT OF LABOR. 2005. Characteristics of minimum wage workers: 2005. www.bls.gov (accessed May 31, 2006).

U.S. DEPARTMENT OF STATE. 2005. Immigrant visas issued to orphans coming to the U.S. www.travel .state.gov/ (accessed May 1, 2006).

U.S. SENATE SPECIAL COMMITTEE ON AGING, AMERICAN ASSOCIATION OF RETIRED PERSONS, FEDERAL COUNCIL ON THE AGING, AND U.S. ADMINISTRATION ON AGING. 1991. *Aging America: Trends and projections, 1991.* Washington, DC: Department of Health and Human Services.

UDRY, J. R. 1993. The politics of sex research. *Journal of Sex Research* 30 (May): 103–10.

UMAÑA-TAYLOR, A. J., AND M. A. FINE. 2003. Predicting commitment to wed among Hispanic and Anglo partners. *Journal of Marriage and Family* 65 (Feb.): 117–39.

UMAÑA-TAYLOR, A. J., AND M. Y. BÁMACA. 2004. Conducting focus groups with Latino populations: Lessons from the field. *Family Relations* 53 (April): 261–72.

UMBERSON, D. 2003. *Death of a parent: Transition to a new adult identity.* New York: Cambridge University Press.

UMBERSON, D., K. WILLIAMS, D. A. POWERS, H. LIU, AND B. NEEDHAM. 2005. Stress in childhood and adulthood: Effects on marital quality over time. *Journal of Marriage and Family* 67 (December): 1332–47.

UNAIDS/WHO. 2005. *AIDS epidemic update: December 2005.* www.who.int (accessed February 2, 2006).

Underage drinkers at higher risk of brain damage than adults, "American Medical Association report reveals." 2002. American Medical Association. www.alcoholpolicysolutions.net (accessed Sep. 17, 2003).

UNDERWOOD, R. C., AND P. C. PATCH. 1999. Siblicide: A descriptive analysis of sibling homicide. *Homicide Studies* 3 (Nov.): 333–48.

UNICEF. 2005. *Gender achievements and prospects in education: The gap report, part one.* www.ungei.org (accessed December 7, 2005).

UNICEF. 2005. *Child poverty in rich countries, 2005: Innocent Report Card* No. 6. Florence: UNICEF Innocenti Research Centre, www.unicef-icdc.org (accessed May 28, 2006).

UNITED NATIONS. 2002. *International migration report 2002.* www.un.org (accessed Apr. 15, 2003).

UNITED NATIONS CHILDREN'S FUND. 2005. *Changing a harmful social convention: Female genital mutilation/cutting.* New York, www.unicef-icdc.org (accessed January 5, 2006).

UNITED NATIONS ECONOMIC COMMISSION FOR EUROPE. 2005. Trends in Europe and North America: Divorces. www.unece.org (accessed July 11, 2006).

UNITED STATES HOUSE OF REPRESENTATIVES. 2006. False and misleading health information provided by federally funded pregnancy resource centers. Committee on Government Reform—Minority Staff, Special Investigations Division, July, http://reform.democrats.house.gov (accessed September 19, 2006).

UPCHURCH, D. M., L. A. LILLARD, AND C. W. A. PANIS. 2001. The impact of nonmarital childbearing on subsequent marital formation and dissolution. In *Out of wedlock: Causes and consequences of nonmarital fertility,* eds. L. L. Wu and B. Wolfe, 344–80. New York: Russell Sage Foundation.

UPDEGRAFF, K. A., S. M. THAYER, S. D. WHITEMAN, D. J. DENNING, AND S. M. MCHALE. 2005. Relational aggression in adolescents' sibling relationships: Links to sibling and parent–adolescent relationship quality. *Family Relations* 54 (July): 373–85.

UTZ, R. L. 2006. Economic and practical adjustments to late life spousal loss. In *Spousal bereavement in late life,* eds. D. Carr, R. M. Nesse, and C. B. Wortman, 167–192. New York: Springer.

VACCARINO, V., ET AL. 2002. Sex differences in hospital mortality after coronary artery bypass surgery: Evidence for a higher mortality in younger women. *Circulation* 105 (Feb. 18): 1176–81.

VAKILI, B., ET AL. 2002. Sex-based differences in early mortality of patients undergoing angioplasty for first acute myocardial infarction. *Circulation* 104 (Dec. 18): 3034–38.

VALADEZ-MELTZER, A., T. J. SILBER, A. A. MELTZER, AND L. J. D'ANGELO. 2005. Will I be alive in 2005? Adolescent level of involvement in risk behaviors and belief in near-future death. *Pediatrics* 116 (July): 24–31.

VALDEZ, E. O., AND S. COLTRANE. 1993. Work, family, and the Chicana: Power, perception, and equity. In *The employed mother and the family context,* ed. J. Frankel, 153–79. New York: Springer.

VALENZUELA, A., JR. 2000. Working on the margins: Immigrant day labor characteristics and prospects of employment, www.weingart.org (accessed Apr. 20, 2003).

VAN AUSDALE, D., AND J. R. FEAGIN. 2001. *The first R: How children learn race and racism.* Lanham, MD: Rowman & Littlefield.

VAN BAARSEN, B., AND M.I.B VAN GROENOU. 2001. Partner loss in later life: Gender differences in coping shortly after bereavement. *Journal of Loss and Trauma* 6: 243-62

VAN DER WERF, M. 2001. How much should colleges pay their janitors? *Chronicle of Higher Education,* Aug. 3, A27–A28.

VAN DULMEN, M. H. M. 2003. The development of intimate relationships in the Netherlands. In *Mate selection across cultures,* eds. R. R. Hamon and B. B. Ingoldsby, 191–206. Thousand Oaks, CA: Sage.

VAN DYK, D. 2005. *Parlez-vous* twixter? *Time,* January 24, 49.

VAN HOOF, H. B., and M. J. VERBEETEN. 2005. Wine is for drinking, water is for washing: Student opinions about international exchange programs. *Journal of Studies in International Education* 9 (Spring): 42–61.

VAN RIPER, K. K., AND W. L. HELLERSTEDT. 2005. Emergency contraceptive pills: Dispensing practices, knowledge and attitudes of South Dakota pharmacists. *Perspectives on Sexual and Reproductive Health* 37 (March): 19–24.

VANDELL, D. L., K. MCCARTNEY, M. T. OWEN, C. BOOTH, AND A. CLARKE-STEWART. 2003. Variations in child care by grandparents during the first three years. *Journal of Marriage and Family* 65 (May): 375–81.

VANDELLO, J. A., AND D. COHEN. 2003. Male honor and female fidelity: Implicit cultural scripts that perpetuate domestic violence. *Journal of Personality and Social Psychology* 84 (May): 997–1010.

VANDERPOOL, T. 2002. Tribes move beyond casinos to malls and concert halls. *Christian Science Monitor,* Oct. 22, 2–3.

VANDERPOOL, T. 2004. Arizona at forefront of foster-home shortage. *Christian Science Monitor,* November 25–26, 3.

VANDEWATER, E. A., D. S. BICKHAM, J. H. LEE, H. M. CUMMINGS, E. A. WARTELLA, AND V. J. RIDEOUT. 2005. When the television is always on: Heavy television exposure and young children's development. *American Behavioral Scientist* 48 (January): 562–77.

VANDIVERE, S., K. TOUT, J. CAPIZZANO, AND M. ZASLOW. 2003. *Left unsupervised: A look at the most vulnerable children.* Washington, DC: Child Trends. www.childtrends.org (accessed Aug. 23, 2003).

VANLANINGHAM, J., D. R. JOHNSON, AND P. AMATO. 2001. Marital happiness, marital duration, and the U-shaped curve: Evidence from a five-wave panel study. *Social Forces* 78 (June): 1313–1341.

VARGAS, J. A. 2004. Married men with another life to live. *Washington Post* (August 14): C1.

VEATCH, R. M. 1995. Death and dying. In *Ethics applied,* ed. M. L. Richardson and K. K. White, 215–43. New York: McGraw-Hill.

VEEVERS, J. 1980. *Childless by choice.* Toronto: Butterworth.

VEGA, W. A. 1995. The study of Latino families: A point of departure. In *Understanding Latino families: Scholarship, policy, and practice,* ed. R. E. Zambrana, 3–17. Thousand Oaks, CA: Sage.

VEMER, E., M. COLEMAN, L. H. GANONG, AND H. COOPER. 1989. Marital satisfaction in remarriage: A meta-analysis. *Journal of Marriage and the Family* 51 (Aug.): 713–25.

VENEMA, S. 2003. Gay wedding announcements a growing trend. *Women's E-News,* Jan. 5. www.womensnews.org (accessed Jan. 11, 2003).

VENTURA, S. J., C. A. BACHRACH, L. HILL, K. KAYE, P. HOLCOMB, AND E. KOFF. 1995. The demography of out-of-wedlock childbearing. In *Report to Congress on out-of-wedlock childbearing.* Hyattsville, MD: Centers for Disease Control and Prevention, National Center for Health Statistics.

VENTURA, S. J., J. A. MARTIN, S. C. CURTIN, T. J. MATHEWS, AND M. M. PARK. 2000. Births: final data for 1998. *National Vital Statistics Reports* 48, Mar. 28, Centers for Disease Control and Prevention. www.cdc.gov (accessed Sep. 22, 2000).

VENTURA, S. J., S. C. CURTIN, AND T. J. MATHEWS. 2000. Variations in teenage birth rates, 1991–98: National and state trends. *National Vital Statistical Reports* 48, Apr. 24, Centers for Disease Control and Prevention. www.cdc.gov (accessed Sep. 22, 2000).

VESELY, R. 2005. Hospital program identifies more domestic violence. Women's e-news, June 13, www.womensnews.org (accessed June 15, 2005).

VICK, K. 1998. Letter from Lagos: Abiola: A man of many parts and many wives, *Washington Post,* July 14, A9, A11.

VIDEON, T.M. 2002. The effects of parent-adolescent relationships and parental separation on adolescent well-being. *Journal of Marriage and Family* 64 (May): 489–503.

VINICK, B. H. 1997. Stepfamilies in later life: What happens to intergenerational relationship? Paper presented at the American Sociological Association Annual Meeting, Toronto.

VINICK, B. H. 2000. Sexuality among older couples: Perceptions of spouse and self. In *With this ring: Divorce, intimacy, and cohabitation from a multicultural perspective,* eds. R. R. Miller and S. L. Browning, 111–26. Stamford, CT: JAI.

VIORST, J. 2003. *Grown-up marriage.* New York: Free Press.

VISHER, E. B., AND J. S. VISHER. 1988. *Old loyalties, new ties: Therapeutic strategies with stepfamilies.* New York: Brunner/Mazel.

VISHER, E. B., AND J. S. VISHER. 1993. Remarriage families and stepparenting. In *Normal family processes,* 2nd ed., ed. F. Walsh, 235–53. New York: Guilford.

VISHER, E. B., AND J. VISHER. 1982. *How to win as a stepfamily.* New York: Dembner.

VISHER, E. B., AND J. S. VISHER. 1996. *Therapy with stepfamilies.* New York: Brunner/Mazel.

VISSING, Y. 2002. *Women without children: Nurturing lives.* New Brunswick, NJ: Rutgers University Press.

VOGLER, C., AND J. PAHL. 1994. Money, power and inequality within marriage. *Sociological Review* 42 (May): 263–88.

VOSS, K. W. 2003. New anti-violence campaigns aim at boys, young men. *Women's E-News,* Feb. 28. www.womensenews.org (accessed Mar. 3, 2003).

VOTRUBA-DRZAL, E. 2003. Income changes and cognitive stimulation in young children's home learning environments. *Journal of Marriage and Family* 65 (May): 341–55.

VUCHINICH, S. 1987. Starting and stopping spontaneous family conflicts. *Journal of Marriage and the Family* 49 (Aug.): 591–601.

VUCHINICH, S., E. M. HETHERINGTON, R. A. VUCHINICH, AND W. G. CLINGEMPEEL. 1991. Parent-child interaction and gender differences in early adolescents' adaptation to stepfamilies. *Developmental Psychology* 27 (4): 618–26.

WACHTER, K. W. 1997. Kinship resources for the elderly. *Philosophical Transactions: Biological Sciences* 352 (Dec. 29): 1811–17.

WADE, C., AND S. CIRESE. 1991. *Human sexuality,* 2nd ed. New York: Harcourt Brace Jovanovich.

WAGE. 2006. "Occupational segregation." WAGE: Women are Getting Even, www.wageproject.org (accessed May 9, 2006).

WAHLBERG, D. 2005. Secret sex, drug use fuel rise in AIDS. *The Atlanta Journal-Constitution,* June 16, 4E.

WAINRIGHT, J. L., S. T. RUSSELL, AND C. J. PATTERSON. 2004. Psychosocial adjustment, school outcomes, and romantic relationships of adolescents with same-sex partners. *Child Development* 75 (November/December): 1886–98.

WAITE, E. J., AND M. GALLAGHER. 2000. *The case for marriage: Why married people are happier healthier, and better off financially.* New York: Broadway.

WAITE, L. J., AND K. JOYNER. 2001. Emotional satisfaction and physical pleasure in sexual unions: Time horizon, sexual behavior, and sexual exclusivity. *Journal of Marriage and Family* 63 (Feb.): 247–64.

WAITE, L. J., AND L. A. LILLARD. 1991. Children and marital disruption. *American Journal of Sociology* 96 (Jan.): 930–53.

WAITE, L. J., ED. 2000. *The ties that bind: Perspectives on marriage and cohabitation.* New York: Aldine de Gruyter.

WAITE, L. J., D. BROWNING, W. J. DOHERTY, M. GALLAGHER, Y. LUO, AND S. M. STANLEY. 2002. *Does divorce make people happy?* Findings from a study of unhappy marriages. Institute for American Values. www.americanvalues.org (accessed Sep. 24, 2003).

WAKSCHLAG, L. S., B. L. LEVENTHAL, D. S. PINE, K. E. PICKETT, AND A. S. CARTER. 2006. Elucidating early mechanisms of developmental psychopathology: The case of prenatal smoking and disruptive behavior. *Child Development* 77 (July/Aug.): 893–906.

WALCZAK, L., ET AL. 2000. The politics of prosperity. *Business Week,* Aug. 7, 96–108.

WALKER, L. 1978. Treatment alternatives for battered women. In *The victimization of women,* eds. J. R. Chapman and M. Gates, 143–74. Beverly Hills, CA: Sage.

WALKER, L. 2003. College classes on human sexuality face heightened scrutiny. *Christian Science Monitor,* July 22, 17.

WALKER, L. E. A. 2000. *The battered woman syndrome,* 2nd ed. New York: Springer.

WALLER, G. 2001. Family court system hurts mothers. *Women's E-News,* Sep. 7. www.womensnews.org (accessed Sep. 9, 2001).

WALLER, M. R. 2002. *My baby's father: Unmarried parents and paternal responsibility.* Ithaca, NY: Cornell University Press.

WALLER, W. 1937. The rating and dating complex. *American Sociological Review* 2 (Oct.): 727–34.

WALLERSTEIN, J. S. 2003. Children of divorce: A society in search of policy. In *All our families: New policies for a new century,* 2nd ed., eds. M. A. Mason, A. Skolnick, and S. D. Sugarman, 66–95. New York: Oxford University Press.

WALLERSTEIN, J. S., J. M. LEWIS, AND S. BLAKESLEE. 2000. *The unexpected legacy of divorce: A 25 year landmark study.* New York: Hyperion.

WALSH, A. 1991. *The science of love: Understanding love and its effects on mind and body.* Buffalo, NY: Prometheus.

WALSH, D., D. Gentile, J. GIESKE, M. WALSH, AND E. CHASCO. 2004. Video game report card. National Institute on Media and the family, www .mediafamily.org (accessed November 30, 2005).

WALSH, F., ED. 1993. *Normal family processes,* 2nd ed. New York: Guilford.

WALSH, W. 2002. Spankers and nonspankers: Where they get information on spanking. *Family Relations* 51 (Jan.): 81–88.

WALSTER, E., E. BERSCHEID, AND G. W. WALSTER. 1973. New directions in equity research. *Journal of Personality and Social Psychology* 25 (2): 151–76.

WALTHER, A. N. 1991. *Divorce hangover.* New York: Pocket Books.

WALZER, S. 1998. *Thinking about the baby: Gender and transitions into parenthood.* Philadelphia: Temple University Press.

WANG, L., E. B. LARSON, J. D. BOWEN, AND G. VAN BELLE. 2006. Performance-based physical function and future dementia in older people. *Archives of Internal Medicine* 166 (May 22): 1115–1120.

"Want ad proves a woman's worth is never done." 1997. Ann Landers column. *Baltimore Sun,* Sep. 20, 3D.

WARD, M. L., AND K. FRIEDMAN. 2006. Using TV as a guide: Associations between television viewing and adolescents' sexual attitudes and behavior. *Journal of Research on Adolescence* 16 (March): 133–56.

WARNER, J. 2005. *Perfect madness: Motherhood in the age of anxiety.* New York: Riverhead Books.

WARNER, W., AND P. S. LUNT. 1941. *The social life of a modern community.* New Haven, CT: Yale University Press.

WARREN, E., AND A. W. TYAGI. 2003. *The two income trap: Why middle-class mothers & fathers are going broke.* New York: Basic Books.

WARSHAK, R. A. 2003. Payoffs and pitfalls of listening to children. *Family Relations* 52 (October): 373–384.

WARTIK, N. 2005. The perils of playing house. *Psychology Today* (July/August): 42–52.

WASSERMAN, G. A., ET AL. 2003. *Risk and protective factors of child delinquency.* Washington, DC: U.S. Department of Justice.

WATKINS, G. 2002. Inuit ingenuity finds a warm reception. *Christian Science Monitor,* Oct. 2, 14.

WATKINS, M. L., S. A. RASMUSSEN, M. A. HONEIN, L. D. BOTTO, AND C. A. MOORE. 2003. Maternal obesity and risk for birth defects. *Pediatrics* 111 (May): 1152–58.

WATKINS, T. H. 1993. *The great depression: America in the 1930s.* New York: Little, Brown.

WATTERS, E. 2003. *Urban tribes: A generation redefines friendship, family and commitment.* New York: Bloomsbury.

WAX, E. 2005. Namibia chips away at African taboos on homosexuality. *Washington Post,* October 24, A1.

WEATHERFORD, D. 1986. *Foreign and female: Immigrant women in America, 1840–1930.* New York: Schocken.

WEBER, L., T. HANCOCK, AND E. HIGGINBOTHAM. 1997. Women, power, and mental health. In *Women's health: Complexities and differences,* eds. S. B. Ruzek, V. L. Olesen, and A. E. Clarke, 380–96. Columbus: Ohio State University Press.

WEBSDALE, N. 1999. *Understanding domestic homicide.* Boston: Northeastern University Press.

WEBSTER, B. H., JR., AND A. BISHAW. 2006. *Income, earnings, and poverty data from the 2005 American Community Survey.* U.S. Census Bureau, American Community Survey Reports, ACS-02. Washington, DC: U.S. Government Printing Office.

WEIBEL-ORLANDO, J. 1990. Grandparenting styles: Native American perspectives. In *The cultural context of aging,* ed. J. Sokolovsky, 109–25. Westport, CT: Greenwood.

WEIL, E. 2006. Breeder reaction. *Mother Jones* 31, July/Aug, 33–37.

WEINER-DAVIS, M. 2003. *The sex-starved marriage: A couple's guide to boosting their marriage libido.* New York: Simon & Schuster.

WEIR, F. 2000. Adoptions stalled: Reform or red tape? *Christian Science Monitor,* June 16, 1, 8.

WEIR, F. 2002. East meets West on love's risky cyberhighway. *Christian Science Monitor,* June 11, 1, 7.

WEISS, C. H. 1998. *Evaluation research: Methods for assessing program effectiveness,* 2nd ed. Upper Saddle River, NJ: Prentice Hall.

WEISS, M. J. 2001. The new summer break. *American Demographics* 23 (Aug.): 49–55.

WEISSMAN, R. X. 1999. That magical night. *American Demographics* 21 (May): 80.

WELLNER, A. S. 2002. The female persuasion. *American Demographics* 24 (Feb.): 24–29.

WELLNER, A. S. 2003. The wealth effect. *American Demographics* 24 (Jan.): 35-47

WELLNER, A. S. 2003. Whither online focus groups? *American Demographics* 25 (Mar.): 31.

WELLNER, A. S. 2005. U.S. attitudes toward interracial dating are liberalizing. Population Reference Bureau, June, www.prb.org (accessed June 25, 2005).

WELTER, B. 1966. The cult of true womanhood: 1820–1860. *American Quarterly* 18 (2): 151–74.

WENDLER, D., et al. 2006. Are racial and ethnic minorities less willing to participate in health research? *PLOS Medicine* 3 (February): 202–10. www.plosmedicine.org (accessed July 31, 2006).

WENNERAS, C., AND A. WOLD. 1997. Nepotism and sexism in peer review. *Nature* 387 (May): 341–43.

WEST, C., AND D. H. ZIMMERMAN. 1987. Doing gender. *Gender and Society* 1 (June): 125–51.

WESTHOFF, C., L. PICARDO, AND E. MORROW. 2003. Quality of life following early medical or surgical abortion. *Contraception* 67 (1): 41–47.

WESTOFF, L. A. 1977. *The second time around: Remarriage in America.* New York: Viking.

"What's at stake? Help raise the minimum wage." 2006. Jobs with Justice, March 21, www.unionvoice.org (accessed June 5, 2006).

WHEELER, L. 1998. Excavation reveals slaves as entrepreneurs. *Washington Post*, Oct. 13, B3.

WHIPPLE, E. E., AND C. A. RICHEY. 1997. Crossing the line from physical discipline to child abuse: How much is too much? *Child Abuse & Neglect* 21 (May): 431–44.

WHITBERK, L. B., K. A. YODER, D. R. HOYT, AND R. D. CONGER. 1999. Early adolescent sexual activity. *Journal of Marriage and the Family* 61 (Nov.): 934–46.

WHITE, J. 2005. Four-star general relived of duty. *Washington Post*, (Aug. 10), A1.

WHITE, J. W., AND D. M. KLEIN. 2002. *Family theories*, 2nd ed. Thousand Oaks, CA: Sage.

WHITE, L. K. 1991. Determinants of divorce. In *Contemporary families: Looking forward, looking back*, ed. A. Booth, 150–61. Minneapolis: National Council on Family Relations.

WHITE, L., AND J. G. GILBRETH. 2001. When children have two fathers: Effects of relationships with stepfathers and noncustodial fathers on adolescent outcomes. *Journal of Marriage and Family* 63 (Feb.): 155–67.

WHITE, M. 2003. What's your favorite way to say "be mine": Card, candy, flowers? *Christian Science Monitor*, Feb. 12, 20.

WHITE, T. 2005. Back home again—with mom and dad. *Baltimore Sun*, November 20, 6N.

WHITEFORD, L. M., AND L. GONZALEZ. 1995. Stigma: The hidden burden of infertility. *Social Science and Medicine* 40 (Jan.): 27–36.

WHITEHEAD, B. D. 1996. The decline of marriage as the social basis of childrearing. In *Promises to keep: Decline and renewal of marriage in America*, eds. D. Popenoe, J. B. Elshtain, and D. Blankenhorn, 3–14. Lanham, MD: Rowman & Littlefield.

WHITEHEAD, B. D. 2002. *Why there are no good men left: The romantic plight of the new single woman*. New York: Broadway.

WHITEHEAD, B. D., AND D. POPENOE. 2001. *The state of our unions 2001: The social health of marriage in America*. The National Marriage Project, Rutgers University. http://marriage.rutgers.edu (accessed July 12, 2003).

WHITEMAN, S. D., S. M. MCHALE, AND A. C. CROUTER. 2003. What parents learn from experience: The first child as a first draft? *Journal of Marriage and Family* 65 (Aug.): 608–21.

WHITING, J. B., AND R. E. LEE III. 2003. Voices from the system: A qualitative study of foster children's stories. *Family Relations* 52 (July): 288–95.

WHITMER, R. A., ERICA P. GUNDERSON, E. BARRETT-CONNOR, C. P. QUESENBERRY, JR., AND K. YAFFE. 2005. Obesity in middle age and future risk of dementia: A 27 year longitudinal population based study. *British Medical Journal* 330 (June 11): 1360–1365.

WHITSETT, D., AND H. LAND, 1992. The development of a role strain index for stepparents. *Families in Society: The Journal of Contemporary Human Services* 73 (Jan.): 14–22.

"Who gets the most time off?" 2000. *Christian Science Monitor*, July 3, 12.

WHYTE, M. K. 1990. *Dating, mating, and marriage*. New York: Aldine de Gruyter.

WICHMAN, A. L., J. L. RODGERS, AND R. C. MACCALLUM. 2006. A multilevel approach to the relationships between birth order and intelligence. *Personality and Social Psychology Bulletin* 32 (January): 117–27.

WICKRAMA, K. A. S., F. O. LORENZ, R. D. CONGER, AND G. H. ELDER, JR. 1997. Marital quality and physical illness: A latent growth curve analysis. *Journal of Marriage and the Family* 59 (Feb.): 143–55.

WIDOM, C. S., AND M. G. MAXFIELD. 2001. *An update on the "cycle of violence."* Washington, DC: U.S. Department of Justice.

WIEHE, V. R. 1997. *Sibling abuse: Hidden physical, emotional, and sexual trauma*, 2nd ed. Thousand Oaks, CA: Sage.

WIEHE, V. R., WITH T. HERRING. 1991. *Perilous rivalry: When siblings become abusive*. Lexington, MA: Lexington.

WILCOX, S., ET AL. 2003. The effects of widowhood on physical and mental health, health behaviors, and health outcomes: The women's health initiative. *Health Psychology* 22 (5): 1–9.

WILCOX, W. B. 2002. Religion, convention, and paternal involvement. *Journal of Marriage and Family* 64 (August): 780–92.

WILCOX, W. B. 2002. Sacred vows, public purposes: Religion, the marriage movement and marriage policy. The Pew Forum on Religion and Public Life. http://pewforum.org (accessed Mar. 3, 2003).

WILCOX, W. B., AND S. L. NOCK. 2006. What's love got to do with it? Equality, equity, commitment and women's marital quality. *Social Forces* 84 (March): 1321–45.

WILD, R. 2005. Now you see it, now you don't. *AARP Bulletin*, November, 12–14.

WILGOREN, J. 2005. In Nebraska, rape charge follows legal marriage, in Kansas, to a 14-year-old. *New York Times*, Aug. 30, A10.

WILKINSON, D. 2005. True love: Finding a second act on the Internet. *New York Times*, April 12, www.nytimes.com (accessed April 13, 2005).

WILLIAMS, A. 2004. E-dating bubble springs leak. *New York Times*, December 12, I1.

WILLIAMS, L. 2002. Hispanic female athletes few and far between. *New York Times*, Nov. 6, D1.

WILLIAMS, N. 1990. *The Mexican American family: Tradition and change*. New York: General Hall.

WILLIAMS, W. M. 2001. Women in academe, and the men who derail them. *Chronicle of Higher Education*, July 20, B20.

WILLIE, C. V., AND R. J. REDDICK. 2003. *A new look at black families*, 5th ed. Walnut Creek, CA: AltaMira.

WILLING, R. 2005. Kids in legal gray area when gay couples split. *USA Today*, June 20, 3A.

WILLINGER, M., C. W. KO, H. J. HOFFMAN, R. C. KESSLER, AND M. J. CORWIN. 2003. Trends in infant bed sharing in the United States, 1993–2000. *Archives of Pediatrics & Adolescent Medicine* 157 (Jan.): 43–49.

WILLIS, S. L., AND J. D. REID, EDS. 1999. *Life in the middle: Psychological and social development in middle age*. San Diego, CA: Academic Press.

WILLIS, W. 1997. Families with African American roots. In *Developing cross-cultural competence: A guide for working with children and families*, eds. E. W. Lynch and M. J. Hanson, 165–202. Baltimore: Paul H. Brookes.

WILLSON, A. E., K. M. SHUEY, AND G. H. ELDER, JR. 2003. Ambivalence in the relationship of adult children to aging parents and in-laws. *Journal of Marriage and Family* 65 (November): 1055–1072.

WILSON, B. F., AND S. C. CLARKE. 1992. Remarriages: A demographic profile. *Journal of Family Issues* 13 (June): 123–41.

WILSON, C. 2001. Living single grows in USA. *USA Today*, Oct. 23, D1.

WILSON, J. Q. 2002. *The marriage problem: How our culture has weakened families*. New York: HarperCollins.

WILSON, R. 1999. An MIT professor's suspicion of bias leads to a new movement for academic women. *Chronicle of Higher Education*, Dec. 3, A16–A18.

WILSON, R. F. 2006. Sexually predatory parents and the children in their care: Remove the threat, not the child. In *Handbook on children, culture, and violence*, eds. N. E. Dowd, D. G. Singer, and R. F. Wilson, 39–58. Thousand Oaks, CA: Sage.

WILSON, S. 2002. The health capital of families: An investigation of the inter-spousal correlation in health status. *Social Science & Medicine* 55 (Oct.): 1157–72.

WILSON, S. M., L. W. NGIGE, AND L. J. TROLLINGER. 2003. Connecting generations: Kamba and Maasai paths to marriage in Kenya. In *Mate selection across cultures*, eds. R. R. Hamon and B. B. Ingoldsby, 95–118. Thousand Oaks, CA: Sage.

WILTENBURG, M. 2002. Minority. *Christian Science Monitor*, Jan. 31, 14.

WINCH, R. F. 1958. *Mate selection: A study of complementary needs*. New York: Harper & Row.

WINEBERG, H. 1991. Intermarital fertility and dissolution of the second marriage. *Social Science Quarterly* 75 (Jan.): 62–65.

WINEBERG, H. 1994. Marital reconciliation in the United States: Which couples are successful? *Journal of Marriage and the Family* 56 (Feb.): 80–88.

WINEBERG, H. 1996. The prevalence and characteristics of blacks having a successful marital reconciliation. *Journal of Divorce & Remarriage* 25 (1/2): 75–86.

WINEBERG, H., AND J. MCCARTHY. 1993. Separation and reconciliation in American marriages. *Journal of Divorce & Remarriage* 20: 21–42.

WINTON, C. A. 1995. *Frameworks for studying families*. Guilford, CT: Dushkin.

WISEMAN, P., AND N. NISHIWAKI. 2005. Japan struggles to cope with effects of divorce. *USA Today*, July 28, 12A.

WISEMAN, R. 2002. *Queen bees and wannabes: A parent's guide to helping your daughter survive cliques, gossip, boyfriends, and other realities of adolescence*. New York: Crown.

WISSOW, L. S. 2000. Suicide among American Indians and Alaska Natives. In *American Indian health: Innovations in health care, promotion, and policy*, ed. E. R. Rhoades, 260–80. Baltimore: Johns Hopkins University Press.

WITT, G. E. 1998. Vote early and often. *American Demographics* 20 (Dec.): 23.

WITTENBURG, M. 2003. Warehousing our children. *Christian Science Monitor*, June 19, 14–16.

WITTSTEIN, I. S. ET AL. 2005. Neurohumoral features of myocardial stunning due to sudden emotional stress. *New England Journal of Medicine* 352 (February 10): 539–48.

WIZEMANN, T. M., AND M. L. PARDUE, EDS. 2001. *Exploring the biological contributions to human health: Does sex matter?* Washington, DC: National Academy Press.

WOLANIN, T. R. 2005. Higher education opportunities for foster youth: A primer for policymakers. The Institute for Higher Education Policy, www.ihep.org (accessed May 10, 2006).

WOLCHIK, S. A., A. M. FENAUGHTY, AND S. L. BRAVER. 1996. Residential and nonresidential parents' perspectives on visitation problems. *Family Relations* 45 (Apr.): 230–37.

WOLCOTT, J. 2000. Finding Mrs. Right (and all the little Rights). *Christian Science Monitor*, Feb. 23, 15–17.

WOLCOTT, J. 2003. Single moms find roommates. *Christian Science Monitor*, Mar. 12, 11, 14.

WOLCOTT, J. 2004. Is dating dated on college campuses? *Christian Science Monitor* (March 2): 11, 14.

WOLF, D. L. 1997. Family secrets: Transnational struggles among children of Filipino immigrants. *Sociological Perspectives* 40 (3): 457–82.

WOLFE, L. 1981. *The Cosmo report*. New York: Arbor House.

WOLFINGER, N. 1999. Trends in the intergenerational transmission of divorce. *Demography* 36: 415–20.

WOLFINGER, N. 2000. Beyond the intergenerational transmission of divorce: Do people replicate the pattern of marital instability they grew up with? *Journal of Family Issues* 21: 1061–86.

WOLFRADT, J. J., S. HEMPEL, AND J. N. V. MILES. 2003. Perceived parenting styles, depersonalization, anxiety and coping behavior in adolescents. *Personality and Individual Differences* 34 (February): 521–32.

"Woman gives birth using her dead husband's sperm." 1999. *Baltimore Sun*, Mar. 27, 5A.

WONG, B. 1998. *Ethnicity and entrepreneurship: The new Chinese immigrants in the San Francisco Bay area*. Boston: Allyn & Bacon.

WOOD, H. M., B. J. TROCK, AND J. P. GEARHART. 2003. In vitro fertilization and the cloacal-bladder exstrophy-epispadias complex: Is there an association? *Journal of Urology* 169 (Apr.): 1512–15.

WOOD, J. T. 2002. *Gendered lives: Communication, gender, and culture*, 5th ed. Belmont, CA: Wadsworth.

WOODARD, E. H., IV, AND N. GRIDINA. 2000. *Media in the home: The fifth annual survey of parents and children, 2000*. Philadelphia: University of Pennsylvania, Annenberg Public Policy Center.

WOODS, R. D. 1996. Grandmother roles: A cross cultural view. *Journal of Instructional Psychology* 23 (Dec.): 286–92.

WOODWARD, K. L., AND K. SPRINGEN. 1992. Better than a gold watch. *Newsweek*, Aug. 24, 71.

"Work at home in 2004". 2005. U.S. Department of Labor, September, www.bls.gov (accessed June 14, 2006).

WORKING TO HALT ONLINE ABUSE. 2006. Online harassment/Cyberstalking statistics. www.haltabuse.org (accessed September 9, 2006).

WORLD HEALTH ORGANIZATION. 2005. *WHO multi-country study on women's health and domestic violence against women: Summary report of initial results on prevalence, health outcomes and women's responses.* Geneva: World Health Organization.

WOZNICKI, K. 2005. Pregnancy employment bias suits surge. Women's e-news, March 4. www.womensenews.org (accessed March 6, 2005).

WRIGHT, C. L., AND L. S. FISH. 1997. Feminist family therapy: The battle against subtle sexism. In *Subtle sexism: Current practices and prospects for change*, ed. N. V. Benokraitis, 201–15. Thousand Oaks, CA: Sage.

WRIGHT, J. 1997. Motherhood's gray area. *Washington Post*, July 29, E5.

WRIGHT, J. C., A. C. HUSTON, AND K. C. MURPHY. 2001. The relations of early television viewing to school readiness and vocabulary of children from low-income families: the Early Window Project. *Child Development* 72 (Sep./Oct.): 1347–66.

WRIGHT, J. M. 1998. *Lesbian step families: An ethnography of love.* New York: Haworth.

WRIGLEY, J., AND J. DREBY. 2005. Fatalities and the organization of child care in the United States, 1985–2003. *American Sociological Review* 70 (October): 729–57.

WTULICH, J. 1986. *Writing home: Immigrants in Brazil and the United States, 1890–1891.* Boulder, CO: East European Monographs.

WU, L. L. 1996. Effects of family instability, income, and income instability on the risk of a premarital birth. *American Sociological Review* 61 (June): 386–406.

WU, L. L., AND E. THOMSON. 2001. Race difference in family experience and early sexual initiation: Dynamic models of family structure and family change. *Journal of Marriage and Family* 63 (Aug.): 682–96.

WU, L. L., L. L. BUMPASS, AND K. MUSICK. 2001. Historical and life course trajectories of nonmarital childbearing. In *Out of wedlock: Causes and consequences of nonmarital fertility*, eds. L. L. Wu and B. Wolfe, 3–38. New York: Russell Sage Foundation.

WU, S. S., ET AL. 2004. Risk factors for infant maltreatment: A population-based study. *Child Abuse & Neglect* 28 (December): 1253–64.

WU, Z. 1994. Remarriage in Canada: A social exchange perspective. *Journal of Divorce & Remarriage* 21 (3/4): 191–224.

WU, Z., AND C. M. SCHIMMELE. 2005. Repartnering after first union disruption. *Journal of Marriage and Family* 67 (February): 27–36.

WU, Z., AND M. S. POLLARD. 2000. Economic circumstances and the stability of nonmarital cohabitation. *Journal of Family Issues* 21 (Apr.): 303–28.

WULFHORST, E. 2006. U.S. mothers deserve $134,121 in salary. May 3, http://today.reuters.com (accessed May 10, 2006).

XIE, Y., J. RAYMO, K. GOYETTE, AND A. THORNTON. 2003. Economic potential and entry into marriage and cohabitation. *Demography* 40 (May): 351–67.

XU, X., CLARK, D. HUDSPETH., AND J. P. BARTKOWSKI. 2006. The role of cohabitation in remarriage. *Journal of Marriage and Family* 68 (May): 261–274.

XU, X., C. D. HUDSPETH, AND S. ESTES. 1997. The effects of husbands' involvement in child rearing activities and participation in household labor on marital quality: A racial comparison. *Journal of Gender, Culture, and Health* 2(3): 171–93.

YANCEY, A. K., J. M. SIEGEL, AND K. L. MCDANIEL. 2002. Role models, ethnic identity, and health-risk behaviors in urban adolescents. *Archives of Pediatrics & Adolescent Medicine* 156 (Jan.): 55–61.

YARNALL, K. S. H., ET AL. 2003. Factors associated with condom use among at-risk women students and nonstudents seen in managed care. *Preventive Medicine* 37 (Aug.): 163–70.

YELLOWBIRD, M., AND C. M. SNIPP. 2002. American Indian families. In *Minority families in the United States: A multicultural perspective*, 3rd ed., ed. R. L. Taylor, 227–49. Upper Saddle River, NJ: Prentice Hall.

YEUNG, W. J., J. F. SANDBERG, P. E. DAVIS-KEAN, AND S. L. HOFFERTH. 2001. Children's time with fathers in intact families. *Journal of Marriage and Family* 63 (Feb.): 136–54.

YIN, S. 2002. Off the map: Looking for love. *American Demographics* 24 (Feb.): 48.

Yin, S. 2005. Abortion in the United States and the world. Population Reference Bureau, www.prb.org (accessed May 2, 2006).

YOON, I.-J. 1997. *On my own: Korean businesses and race relations in America.* Chicago: University of Chicago Press.

YOSHIHAMA, M., A. L. PAREKH, AND D. BOYINGTON. 1991. Dating violence in Asian/Pacific communities. In *Dating violence: Young women in danger*, ed. B. Levy, 184–95. Seattle: Seal.

YOUNG, K. 2001. *Tangled in the Web: Understanding cybersex from fantasy to addiction.* Bloomington, IN: 1st Books Library.

YU, Y. 1995. Patterns of work and family: An analysis of the Chinese American family since the 1920s. In *American families: Issues in race and ethnicity*, ed. C. K. Jacobson, 131–44. New York: Garland.

ZAFF, J. F., J. CALKINS, L. J. BRIDGES, AND N. G. MARGIE. 2002. *Promoting positive mental and emotional health in teens: Some lessons from research.* Washington, DC: Child Trends. www.childtrends.org (accessed Aug. 23, 2003).

ZAGORSKY, J. L. 2003. Husbands' and wives' view of the family finances. *Journal of Socio-Economics* 32 (May): 127–46.

ZAGORSKY, J. L. 2005. Marriage and divorce's impact on wealth. *Journal of Sociology* 41 (Dec.): 406–424.

ZAIDI, A. U., AND M. SHURAYDI. 2002. Perceptions of arranged marriages by young Pakistani Muslim women living in a Western society. *Journal of Comparative Family Studies* 33 (Autumn): 495–514.

ZAKARIA, F. 2005. First ladies, in the truest sense. *Newsweek*, Nov. 28, 39.

ZARIT, S. H., AND D. J. EGGEBEEN. 2002. Parent-child relationships in adulthood and later years. In *Handbook of parenting*, 2nd ed., Vol. 1: *Children and parenting*, ed. M. H. Bornstein, 135–61. Mahwah, NJ: Erlbaum.

ZASLOW, J. 2006. Mr. moms grow up: A new generation of granddads is helping raise the kids. *Wall Street Journal*, June 8, D1.

ZHANG, Z., AND M. D. HAYWARD. 2001. Childlessness and the psychological well-being of older persons. *Journal of Gerontology: Social Sciences* 56B: S311–20.

ZHOU, J.-N., M. A. HOFMAN, AND D. F. SWAAB. 1995. A sex difference in the human brain and its relation to transsexuality. *Nature* 378 (Nov. 2): 68–70.

ZHOU, M., AND C. L. BANKSTON III. 1998. *Growing up American: How Vietnamese children adapt to life in the United States.* New York: Russell Sage Foundation.

ZIELINSKI, D. S. 2005. Long-term socioeconomic impact of child abuse and neglect: Implications for public policy. Center for Child and Family Policy, www.pubpol.duke.edu (accessed June 25, 2006).

ZIMBALIST, K. 2005. Vanishing act. *Time Style & Design*, Fall, 80–84.

ZIMMERMAN, F. J., AND D. A. CHRISTAKIS. 2005. Children's television viewing and cognitive outcomes: A longitudinal analysis of national data. *Archives of Pediatrics & Adolescent Medicine* 159 (July): 619–25.

ZIMMERMAN, T. S., K. E. HOLM, AND S. A. HADDOCK. 2001. A decade of advice for women and men in the best-selling self-help literature. *Family Relations* 50 (Apr.): 122–33.

ZITO, J. M. ET AL. 2003. Psychotropic practice patterns for youth. *Archives of Pediatrics & Adolescent Medicine* 157 (Jan.): 17–25.

ZITO, J. M., D. J. SAFER, S. DOS REIS, J. F. GARDNER, M. BOLES, AND F. LYNCH. 2000. Trends in the prescribing of psychotropic medications to preschoolers. *Journal of the American Medical Association* 283 (Feb. 23): 105–1030.

ZOEPF, K. 2005. This doll has an accessory Barbie lacks: A prayer mat. *New York Times*, Sept. 22, A4.

ZOEPF, K. 2006. U.N. finds that 25% of married Syrian women have been beaten. *New York Times*, April 11, A5.

ZOROYA, G. 2005. Letters home from Iraq. *USA Today*, October 25, (www.usatoday.com accessed online October 26, 2006).

ZUCKERMAN, D. 2000. Child care staff: The low-down on salaries and stability. National Center for Policy Research for Women & Families. www.center4policy.org (accessed Aug. 28, 2003).

ZUCKERMAN, M. B. 2006. Hypocrisy on stilts. *U.S. News & World Report*, May 22, 60.

ZVONKOVIC, A. M., C. R. SOLOMON, A. M. HUMBLE, AND M. MANOOGIAN. 2005. Family work and relationships: Lessons from families of men whose jobs require travel. *Family Relations* 54 (July): 411–22.

ZWILLICH, T. 2005. HIV/AIDS Cases growing in U.S. adults over 50. WebMD Medical News, May 13, www.webmd.com (accessed January 18, 2006).

Photo Credits

Name Index

Subject Index